4TH EDITION

ORGANIZATIONAL
BEHAVIOUR & MANAGEMENT
JOHN MARTIN AND MARTIN FELLENZ

SOUTH-WESTERN
CENGAGE Learning™

Australia • Brazil • Japan • Korea • Mexico • Singapore • Spain • United Kingdom • United States

SOUTH-WESTERN
CENGAGE Learning™

**Organizational Behaviour &
Management, 4th Edition**
John Martin and Martin Fellenz

Publishing Director: Linden Harris

Publisher: Thomas Rennie

Development Editor: Anna Carter

Editorial Assistant: Charlotte Green

Content Project Editor: Adam Paddon

Senior Production Controller: Paul
Herbert

Marketing Manager: Amanda Cheung

Typesetter: MPS Limited, A Macmillan
Company

Cover design: Adam Renvoize

For product information and technology assistance,
contact **emea.info@cengage.com**.

For permission to use material from this text or product,
and for permission queries,
email **clsuk.permissions@cengage.com**

The Author has asserted the tight under the Copyright, Designs and
Patents Act 1988 to be identified as Author of this Work.

British Library Cataloguing-in-Publication Data
A catalogue record for this book is available from the
British Library.

ISBN: 978-1-4080-1812-5

Cengage Learning EMEA
Cheriton House, North Way, Andover, Hampshire,
SP10 5BE, United Kingdom

Cengage Learning products are represented in Canada by Nelson
Education Ltd.

For your lifelong learning solutions, visit **www.cengage.co.uk**

Purchase your next print book, e-book or e-chapter at
www.CengageBrain.com

Printed by Zrinski, Croatia
1 2 3 4 5 6 7 8 9 10 – 12 11 10

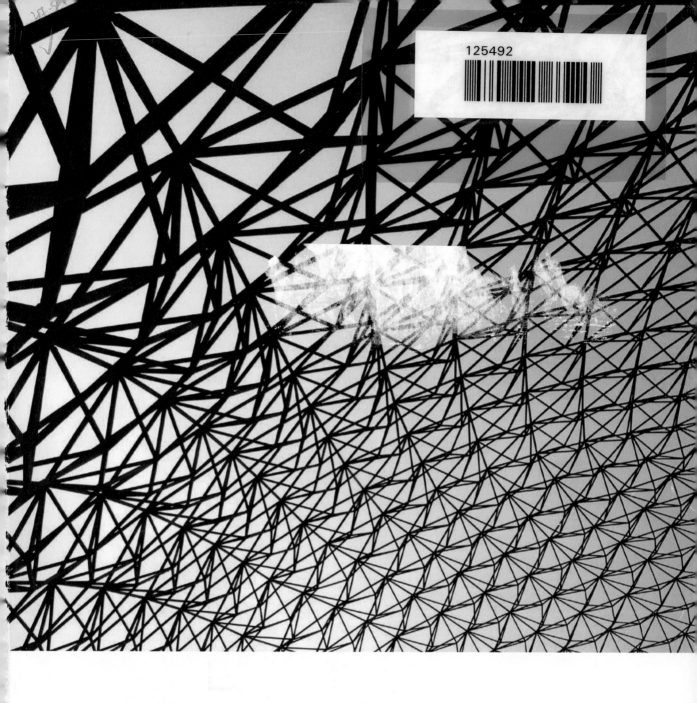

ORGANIZATIONAL
BEHAVIOUR & MANAGEMENT

"For Orla, Lily, Phoebe, Jake and Nathan - the new generation to join 'our organization'
For Louise, Sarah and Mark, who for better or worse have also decided to join
For Jeffrey, Richard and Shona, who had no choice but to join
And last but not least, for Valerie who helped to create 'our organization'."
John Martin

"With many thanks to my parents and to Mairead for all the help and support. I dedicate this book to
my favourite learners: Áine, Leah and Isabel."
Martin Fellenz

BRIEF CONTENTS

CONTENTS

5 MOTIVATION 151

PART THREE

INTERACTIONS
IN ORGANIZATIONS 187

6 LEADING AND MANAGING 189

7 GROUPS AND TEAMS 225

8 COMMUNICATION AND DECISION MAKING 259

9 CONFLICT AND NEGOTIATION 299

PART FOUR

FORMAL SYSTEMS AND ARRANGEMENTS IN ORGANIZATIONS 333

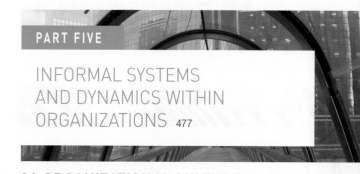

PART FIVE

INFORMAL SYSTEMS AND DYNAMICS WITHIN ORGANIZATIONS 477

LIST OF BOXED FEATURES

PREFACE

"Martin & Fellenz offers an extremely comprehensive overview of the main themes and issues within organizational behaviour. The authors cover recent developments in the field and their use of recent citations to offer critiques of long accepted theory will prove very valuable in developing students' critical acumen."

Louise Preget, Senior Lecturer, Bournemouth University Business School

"This is a brilliant new edition of 'Organizational Behaviour and Management' by Martin & Fellenz. Students and educators will enjoy the clear, concise way that it introduces and explores complex organisational concepts. It balances the theory and practical elements in a manner that brings ideas and concepts alive. It has superb and up-to-date coverage of all the important areas of organizational behaviour. The excellent range of learning features mark it out as a really student friendly text."

Roy Horn, Buckinghamshire New University

This preface introduces the major features of the fourth edition of this book, along with suggestions on how students and lecturers might make use of the content. Another important feature of this book available to both lecturers and students is the accompanying web site, which is also described in this preface.

This book is intended for those who are interested in gaining insight into people in organizations. More specifically, this book provides comprehensive input about the nature of individual and group behaviour in the context of work as well as other forms of organizations. It is intended to appeal to anyone who seeks to better understand these important aspects of human life. Major topics featured in the book include:

- Consideration of the nature of organizations and management.
- Consideration of what organizational behaviour (OB) is and the research that informs it.
- Reflection on four major management challenges of ethics, change, performance pressures and globalization in relation to every chapter topic.
- Consideration of those aspects of individuals and groups that form the human face of organizations.
- A review of processes such as communication, decision making and negotiation within an organizational context.
- Management and leadership of organizations.
- The structure and design of organizations, the jobs within them along with the impact of technology on work and the people aspects of organization.
- Organization culture.
- Power, control, conflict and organizational politics.
- Human Resource management and its relationship to OB.
- Issues associated with relationships, fairness and trust focusing on how people relate to each other and function within an organizational context.

CHANGES AND NEW FEATURES IN THE FOURTH EDITION

There have been a number of significant changes to this edition of this book, based on a comprehensive review of the strengths and weaknesses of the third edition by a number of anonymous reviewers, to whom a great debt of thanks is due. This edition also benefits greatly from the perspectives, academic strength and areas of expertise introduced through the contribution of Dr Martin Fellenz of Trinity College Dublin as co-writer. The significant changes introduced in this edition include:

- Restructuring of a number of the chapters to better reflect current OB teaching and practice in relation to people management practice within organizations.

- The introduction of a guiding model of management and OB that identifies and incorporates the wide range of core OB topics covered in the book. This model structures and clarifies the relationships between and among these topics and creates a unified model of the subject area.

- The introduction of new material and up-to-date research in each chapter to capture the important trends and developments in OB and people management issues within modern organizations.

- The development of part introductions intended to establish the reasons for inclusion of the material in that part in relation to the guiding model for the book.

- The inclusion of a separate and completely new chapter on relationships, fairness and trust as strongly emerging themes in OB research and practice.

- The introduction of a completely new feature of support boxes in each chapter relating the material from the chapter to each of the four management challenges of ethics, change, performance pressures and globalization as experienced in the real world of organizations and management. Each support box concludes with student tasks that help to reinforce the links with the academic content of the chapter.

- The introduction of at least two additional Stop and consider boxes in each chapter that provide additional opportunities for students to reflect more deeply on aspects of organizational behaviour theory and practice.

- The number of Management in Action and Employee Experience panels has been reduced to one each per chapter, but many have been updated or are new for this edition. Each has associated student tasks to better reinforce the links with the academic content of the chapter.

- The Glossary has been updated and designed to provide a reference point for the key terms used in the book.

- The inclusion of learning objectives specifically tied to the revised chapter content and structure at the start of each chapter along with an outline of the key learning points associated with each learning objective placed in the Conclusion for each chapter.

- An updated 'Further reading' section for each chapter.

- Discussion questions at the end of each chapter have been updated and extended.

- A considerable number of new and recent reference sources have added to the text in order to ensure that it is current in terms of research and practice in OB.

- The web site and lecturer support material has been completely updated to better reflect the needs of adopters and students.

THE AUDIENCE

There are many courses and degree programmes that contain aspects of organization, management or the people issues associated with running public or private sector businesses. These can include undergraduate degree programmes in management and business studies or those degrees with management as a minor component, as well as postgraduate degrees and other post-experience qualifications such as the Diploma of Management Studies, MA, M.Sc. and MBA programmes. There are also the many professional qualification programmes in management, accountancy, engineering and related disciplines that include behavioural, managerial and organizational modules, for whom this book provides important and highly useful contributions. Such courses are invariably offered on both a full- and part-time basis and many self-study or distance learning approaches to these routes to personal development also exist. This book, together with the available associated support material, is designed (based on the authors' considerable experience in teaching the subject to all of these groups and using each of the forms of delivery indicated) to be a valuable asset in the delivery of the subject.

Specifically, this book will appeal to a wide range of people including:

- *Undergraduate students* on a wide range of organizational behaviour, introduction to management or people management modules.
- *Practising managers* who seek to develop a more comprehensive and complete understanding of the topics through which to interpret their experience, perhaps as part of a diploma or degree programme.
- *Students that already have gained business or management experience* and are returning to higher education to further their development through an MBA or other post-experienced masters' programme.
- *Readers without formal management experience*, but perhaps with some employment experience, who are studying aspects of human behaviour and management within an organizational context, perhaps as part of a part-time degree programme.
- *Non-business graduates with science or social science qualifications* that have gained organizational experience and are engaged in further studies in the business, management or organizational studies through one of the many masters programmes intended to achieve this objective.
- *Individuals studying for the professional qualifications* offered by the professional associations and who inevitably include aspects of organization, management and behaviour within the syllabus.
- *Managers and employees participating in non-degree training and development programmes* that includes general management and leadership components, or those interested in the behavioural and organizational context of more specialized training on topics such as communication, conflict management, or negotiation.

The blend of theory, critical perspectives, management challenges and practical application is balanced throughout the book in an accessible and engaging writing style. This will appeal to the wide cross section of individuals indicated above, offering different challenges to each, without oversimplification or obfuscation, in each case seeking to further the understanding of the individual in this challenging and exciting field.

OBJECTIVES OF THE BOOK

It is human beings who design organizations and work within them. Human beings, therefore, determine both what is to be done and how it is to be achieved. Against this background the purpose of this book is to develop an understanding of the most important characteristics of this aspect of human experience, including:

- What defines organizations and management.
- Understanding how the management challenges of ethics, change, performance and globalization interact with, and inform, much of the OB theory and practice discussed in this book.
- The nature and impact of individuality on work activities.
- The ways in which groups form and interact as they carry out much of the work undertaken within organizations.
- The influence of technology on work organization.
- The nature of processes such as motivation and decision making on the functioning of organizations.
- The design and structural determinants of organizational form.
- Management issues such as leadership.
- The nature and impact of change on people and organizations.
- The power, political and control dimensions of organizational activity.
- The nature of HRM on people and organizations who employ them.

Specifically in relation to this purpose, the text sets out to achieve a number of objectives:

- *Provide a comprehensive introduction to organizational behaviour.* While offering an up-to-date and reflective perspective, the text does not seek to be of interest only to readers seeking to develop their existing knowledge in this area. It is intended to be of interest to those readers who need to develop the breadth and depth of their understanding of what makes an organization function. Such readers will find that the clearly presented theoretical material, supported by the applied illustrations, will effectively meet their development needs.

- *Include a critical perspective.* In addressing the first objective the text goes beyond the purely descriptive and introduces a critical perspective to the material, by seeking to recognize the embedded nature of much theory and the underlying power dimensions to management activity. A critical perspective suggests that knowledge, as well as organizations, is grounded in the social context that created them. Any understanding of relevant issues that claims to be real and comprehensive must therefore take such different viewpoints into account. This text comprehensively addresses such perspectives while balancing critical concerns with the managerial and pragmatic concerns reflected in many traditional approaches.

- *Demonstrate how OB informs theory and practice.* The book relates management and OB to relevant theory in relevant disciplines such as psychology, sociology, political science, neuroscience, anthropology, economics and other social sciences. Similarly, the text focuses on managerial and organizational practice and explores the relevance of theory for practicing managers, particularly in relation to the important challenges related to ethics, change, performance pressures and globalization.

- *Demonstrate a relevance for the broad range of organizational participants and their experiences.* To be of any value the study of organizational behaviour needs to retain a relevance to actual organizations and the experience of those within them. This is achieved in a number of ways, including the incorporation of applied research studies, the Management in Action panels, the Employee experience panels, Stop and consider boxes and the Case study at the end of each chapter.

- *Establish a basis for further study.* The referenced sources used as well as the indicated further readings are intended to provide a basis for readers to take their interest in particular topics further. This is an objective that can also be achieved through the use of additional web-based material and the links indicated in the web pages associated with this book.

- *Provide a student-centred and learning-oriented perspective.* There are a number of student-centred devices that have been used in the text as an aid to supporting and encouraging learning. These include the 'Part summaries' and 'Learning objectives' at the beginning (and Conclusion) of each chapter, frequent headings and the introduction of a Glossary to the text, the Management challenges panels (ethics, change, performance and globalization), Management in Action panels, Employee experience panels and the Discussion questions and Case studies at the end of each chapter. In addition, web based material that enables self-directed study to deepen knowledge in particular areas and coverage of selected research issues provide opportunities for developing further practical, theoretical and research related knowledge.

- *Comprehensive learning support.* The web site at http://www.cengage.co.uk/martinfellenz provides students and lecturers with extensive support material directly linked to topics in the text.

To cater for this breadth of audience, the material is presented as both academic and practical in nature. It is also presented in a way which encourages students to actively and reflectively interact with the material. For students studying alone, perhaps on a distance learning programme, the web site should be particularly useful in helping to offset the feeling of isolation that often accompanies such study patterns.

THE STRUCTURE OF THE BOOK

The new feature of the inclusion of a guiding model (see Figure 1) for the book clearly establishes that the topics and themes explored in each chapter are interconnected and provides a comprehensive framework that defines the theory and practice of OB. Each chapter is essentially self-contained but inevitably forms part of an integrated whole. For example, the groups that form part of every organization are made up of individuals, they are also part of the organizational hierarchy and there will be some degree of organizational politics displayed within them. However, for ease of research, study and book organization these issues have to be compartmentalized. Students should recognize that much of the richness and complexity of organizational behaviour arises from the linkages and interactions among the multiple elements present in any particular situation. This becomes increasingly evident as students work through the book, and is reinforced through the management challenges panels (ethics, change, performance and globalization), Management in Action panels, Employee experience panels, Stop and consider boxes and Case studies throughout the text.

Chapters 1 and 2 serve as an introduction to the study of management and organizations along with an overview of the evolutionary development of management thinking across history. Chapter 2 also introduces the four management challenges of ethics, change, performance and globalization that form a significant focus for understanding the real world application and the imperatives that all managers face in relation to the field of OB. This and the subsequent material provide the following framework:

- Part 1. Organizational Behaviour and the challenges facing management
- Part 2. Individuals in Organizations
- Part 3. Interactions in Organizations

Figure 1

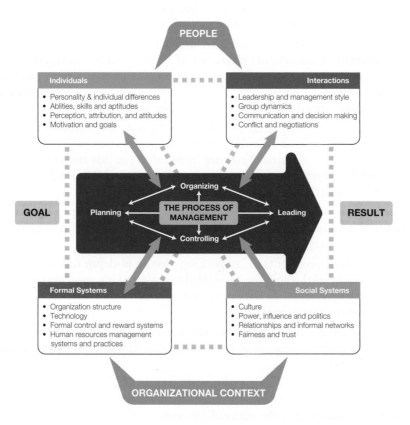

- Part 4. Formal systems and arrangements in organizations
- Part 5. Informal systems and dynamics within organizations

KEY FEATURES

- Part summary. Each part or group of chapters begins with a brief outline of the content which is intended to provide a clear indication how the material to be discussed fits into the guiding model of OB, of the range of material included and how it fits-in with the material that went before and the material that is to follow.

- Learning objectives. The Learning objectives for each chapter provide a clear statement of what students should expect to master by the end of their work on that material. The main points implied by each of the Learning objectives are summarised at the end of each chapter in the Conclusions. Progress in achieving the objectives can be assessed by individuals as they work through the Discussion questions; as well as the Stop and consider topics and Tasks associated with the management challenges panels (ethics, change, performance and globalization), Management in Action panels, Employee experiences and Case studies.

- Management challenges panels (ethics, change, performance and globalization). These reflect the major imperatives (pressures, requirements, obligations and demands) that face every manager and they seek to reflect aspects of the chapter content in relation to these imperatives as they would be experienced by managers and also seeking to explore how they might be dealt with and the OB significance of them. The associated Tasks are intended to provide students with the opportunity to reflect on the academic and theoretical OB perspectives as well as wrestle with the issues from a practical point of view.

- Management in Action panels. These are included to provide an indication of aspects of organizational behaviour as experienced by managers in a real organizational context. The associated Tasks are intended to provide students with the opportunity to reflect on the academic and theoretical OB perspectives as well as wrestle with the issues from a practical point of view.

- Employee experience panels are intended to specifically introduce this perspective to the understanding of what organizational behaviour means in practice. The associated Tasks are intended to provide students with the opportunity to reflect on the academic and theoretical OB perspectives as well as wrestle with the issues from a practical point of view.

- The Stop and Consider activities provides a means of reflecting upon the material in some depth and also identifying alternative perspectives and links with other concepts.

- The case study represents the opportunity for an in-depth review of the chapter material through the associated tasks, allowing students to explore the complex associations with organizational behaviour and also some of the realities of organizational life.

- Further reading. These suggestions provide students with a wide and diverse range of additional sources of material on aspects of the topics discussed within each chapter.

- Discussion questions. A range of questions that could be used as the basis of discussion, essays or exams is provided to allow students to test and further their understanding of the material covered.

- Glossary. The key terms used within the book are identified in the text the first time that they are used and occasionally on subsequent significant occasions. These terms are listed and defined in the Glossary at the end of the book.

- Web site. This represents an innovative feature for this book and provides extensive online support for lecturers and students.

HOW TO USE THE BOOK

Everyone has their own preferred way of studying. Most courses differ in the way in which they approach a topic and the emphasis given to particular perspectives. It is, therefore, not practical to offer precise advice on how to use this book and the available support material for every situation. There are, however, a number of general pointers that may be of use in seeking to gain maximum advantage from this book and your study of organizational behaviour. They include:

- Recognizing that this book is not attempting to provide you with a formula through which to manage other people or guarantee organizational success. That 'holy grail' does not exist; individuals and situations are too complex and dynamic for that type of simplistic approach to be credible.

- Evolution of knowledge is occurring all the time. New ideas, perspectives and interpretations are emerging almost every day. The study of organizational behaviour is not a fixed event. It is for that reason that monitoring appropriate sections of the business press and the management and academic journals and magazines pays dividends.

- Resources exist to be used in support of your study. This book is not a novel, but it does represent a major resource for your journey of discovery in organizational behaviour. The Part summaries and Learning objectives are intended to guide you in your travels. Also the Glossary, Discussion questions, support panel Tasks, Stop and Consider boxes and Further reading all act as pointers, maps and guides to help you gain the maximum benefit from the minimum effort en-route. They are there as a help, not a hindrance or a chore; do use them. During your course you will be examined or tested in some way. The resources provided through this book are attempting to prepare you for that process as well as ensure a fuller understanding of the subject. For example, the Discussion questions at the end of each chapter are designed to assist in your development of a breadth and depth of understanding of the theoretical material as well as the practical implications of it. Through discussion with other people of your collective views about these questions (along with the support panel tasks and Stop and Consider boxes) you will become better able to develop your understanding of them along with the ability to address any assignment or examination questions.

- Personal experience. Every student reader has had direct experience of organizational behaviour in some capacity. It may have been extensive through working in organizations as a paid employee or even a manager. It could have been a vacation job as a student. However, it may also have been through school, or membership of a sports or youth club. The important thing to keep in mind throughout your study of this book is that you will have seen many of the concepts in practice, whether you realize it or not. Consider for a moment a primary school and the way the total activity is organized (structure), the way teachers lead the learning process (leadership, management and control) and the interpersonal behaviour of the children (individuals, groups, power etc.). Reflect on your experience and its ability to enhance and illustrate this subject.

- Networking is an important aspect of any manager's experience. The same is true in your study of organizational behaviour. Every student will know many people who have been or are currently involved in organizations. Parents, grandparents, family members, friends, other students and lecturers are all likely to have had direct experience of a wide range of organizations across a considerable period of time. These are all valuable sources of material, examples and illustrations of organizational behaviour in practice.

- When studying each chapter consider the integrated nature of human behaviour. It is not possible to consider each chapter as an isolated 'chunk' of material than can be ignored once it is finished. Look for and consider the links between ideas and concepts as you work through the book.

SUPPORT MATERIAL

The supporting web site for the new edition of *Organizational Behaviour* is at http://www.cengage.co.uk/martinfellenz. This comprehensive resource provides open access learning materials to students of *Organizational Behaviour*. The lecturers' area of the site is password protected and the password is available to lecturers who recommend the book on their courses. Please register through the web site for your password.

ACKNOWLEDGEMENTS

Any organizational activity inevitably reflects the efforts of a great many people. Writing a book is no exception. It is not possible specifically to mention everyone who played a part in helping to create this text.

The following people were particularly generous with their time and talent in reviewing material and offering advice on the content of the first edition of this book.

- Professor Michael Brimm, Professor of Organizational Behaviour at INSEAD (Fontainebleau, France).
- Professor Gordon C Anderson, Principal of Caledonian College of Engineering, Sultanate of Oman and Visiting Professor of Business, The Philips College, Nicosia, Cyprus.
- Professor Derek Torrington, Emeritus Professor of Human Resource Management, UMIST.
- Professor Eugene McKenna, Professor Emeritus, University of East London, Chartered Psychologist and Director of Human Factors International Ltd.
- Professor Dave Tromp, Professor of Industrial Psychology and Chairperson of Industrial Psychology, University of Stellenbosch, South Africa.
- Dr Jim Barry, Reader in Organization Studies, University of East London.

The contribution of the above people played a significant part in making the first edition of the book the success it was which helped to create the opportunity to develop the second, third and now fourth editions. In addition, we offer our deepest thanks to the panel of reviewers who offered their time and talent in reviewing the third edition along with the proposals and chapters for the fourth edition. Their comments were both helpful and appropriate. The end result can only be described as a considerable improvement as a consequence of their efforts. We can but hope that they feel justified in devoting the time that they did when they inspect the finished fourth edition. The responsibility for any mistakes, errors and omissions remain, however, firmly our own.

- Cheryl Anne, London South Bank University
- Petru Curseu, Tilburg University
- Alison Davies, BPP Business School
- Roy Horn, Buckinghamshire New University
- Deborah Knowles, University of Westminster
- Sam Lynch, University of Kent
- Christian Poulsen, Copenhagen Business School
- Mia Pranoto, King's College London
- Louise Preget, Bournemouth University
- Susan Sayce, University of East Anglia
- Peter Wald, University of Applied Sciences Leipzig

At Cengage Learning a number of people have been supportive of the whole project and of invaluable help in attempting to steer the work in appropriate directions. Worthy of particular note in this context are Tom Rennie, James Clark, Anna Carter, Adam Paddon, Jen Seth and Charlotte Green. Without them this edition would never have happened.

There are many academics, managers, bosses, subordinates and colleagues with whom we have had the pleasure and sometimes pain of working over the course of our careers. Individually and collectively they have all played a considerable role in shaping our fascination with, and views on, organizational life and behaviour. The benefits and effects of their impact are in no small way reflected in the views and perspectives offered in this book.

Finally, and by no means least, JM would like to place on record the support and interest of my wife, family and friends, who tolerated the time spent on the project as well as continually showing interest in how it was progressing. MF would like to thank the friends and colleagues who provided valuable input in the form of discussions, suggestions and critiques. A particular thank you goes to Marion Fortin and Magdalena Cholakova for their valuable feedback on chapter drafts. Closer to home, the work on this book took a significant toll on family and friends – debts yet to be repaid!

We are also very grateful to the many contributors of material and examples for the support panels included in the text. Their generosity in giving their time and energy has hopefully been adequately reflected in the finished contributions. It is our hope that the many students who read their contributions will gain immeasurably from the breadth of relevant experience and understanding of management, employee and organizational perspectives, imperatives and practice that we could include in the book as a result.

We would also like to place on record our appreciation to the many copyright holders who have given permission to use material for which they hold the rights. Every effort has been made to identify and contact all copyright holders, but if any have been inadvertently omitted the publisher will be pleased to make the necessary arrangement at the earliest opportunity.

GUIDED TOUR

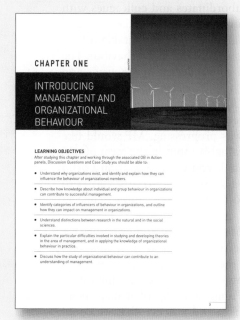

Learning Objectives – listed at the beginning of each chapter highlighting the core issues and perspectives that students would be expected to take away from their studies of the chapter content.

Glossary Terms – highlighted in the text where they first appear and defined in the margin. All terms are collated in a Glossary at the end of the text

Examining Ethics – explores ethical issues and pressures facing managers related to the chapter topic

Going Global – presents the chapter topic from an international perspective and highlight international dimensions and global dynamics relevant for managers

Managing Change – explores organizational change-related issues related to the chapter topic

Performance Demands – vignettes presenting performance-related issues from the chapter content

Management in Action – provides applied examples of aspects of OB as experienced by managers in a real organizational context

Employee Perspective – provides an insight into employee perspectives on aspects of the chapter content

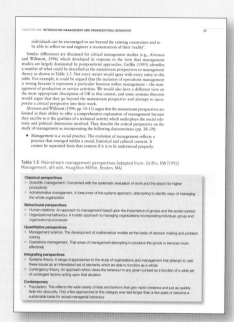

Stop and Consider – these encourage the reader to think and reflect on relevant OB issues. They also identify alternative perspectives and links with other concepts

Extend Your Learning – a margin icon denotes where additional material can be found on the student website

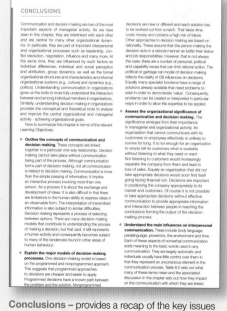

Conclusions – provides a recap of the key issues in each chapter and also a summary of the chapter content for each Learning Objectives

Discussion Questions – reinforces and tests knowledge and understanding of the chapter content and implications

CASE STUDY

Controlling the invisible?

This story describes events that occurred in a meat processing factory in the UK. The process involved the preparation of beef carcasses into joints, steaks and product suitable for curing as beef bacon (predominantly for export to Middle Eastern markets). James was the management accountant at the factory. He was responsible for the determination of product costing and he asked for a full breakdown of material and labour data for each process within the factory. The work study department were given the task of obtaining and collating the data needed for this cost exercise. A number of time studies were undertaken to determine the labour cost involved and the product weight was also checked at each stage of the process. The data collection phase of this exercise lasted for several weeks.

Among the findings from the studies was the rather surprising one that the total weight of meat reduced at each stage of the production process. Every beef carcass and joint was weighed before and after each stage in the butchery process (including the small trimmings, bones, etc.). There was always a slight difference between the total after-processed weight and the original weight. When this was first discovered it was thought to be due to careless weighing. Considerable effort was subsequently made to tighten the weighing process. As a result of this special initiative, everyone in the production and work study departments was satisfied that the weighing process was as comprehensive and accurate as it could be. The difference in weight

between production stages became known as the invisible loss and was on average about 4 per cent of the original weight. The food technologists and production specialists within the company concluded that it was probably due to moisture weeping out of the meat as it was cut. This 'conclusion' was included in the report presented to James as the management accountant.

James was not happy with the idea of having something that could not be properly accounted for and, even worse, with no physical evidence to see. This went against every aspect of his professional training and he refused to accept the report as the basis of product costing. For James, meat did not and could not simply become invisible. The fact that meat was a valuable commodity and the temptation for staff to 'divert' it for personal use was another factor in his thinking! He was being asked to price the company products on the basis that some 4 per cent of it was disappearing. Over a full year that represented a considerable volume of meat and monetary value. James argued strongly that the report must be wrong within the senior management team and demanded that more tests be done. He even refused to believe the evidence of his own eyes when he was present at a demonstration of the effect.

Clearly, there was a problem associated with the ability to control the processing of meat within the factory that needed to be addressed. It was at this stage that the politics and relative power of the key players began to influence events. James was not popular as an individual and was generally considered to be pedantic, rude, unhelpful and not well integrated with the rest of the senior management team. James's boss, the finance director, was a very quiet individual but was regarded by most of the senior managers as a 'safe and effective' director who tried to work with his colleagues. So the stage was set for a battle of who would win the argument about the invisible loss. The accountants had a natural advantage in that they determined the product costing upon which prices and profitability depended. But James was in a difficult personal and political position as he had alienated the key players from the operations functions and did not have strong support from his own superior.

After considerable behind-the-scenes discussion and lobbying by all concerned, together with

---

discussion with various other organizations in the meat industry, James was overruled and the invisible loss became a feature of the costing process.

TASKS

1. To what extent does this case demonstrate that control is a social process involving personalities, perception, shared frames of reference between all the parties involved and not just a process

involving procedures and numbers? Justify your answer.

2. What does the answer to the previous question imply about how control processes should be designed and implemented within an organization?

3. What should James learn from this experience and how might he regain his credibility in the situation?

FURTHER READING

Barling, J. (1994) Work and Family: In Search of More Effective Workplace Interventions. In Cooper, C.L. and Rousseau, D.M. (eds) Trends in Organizational Behaviour, Chichester: John Wiley. Considers the links between family and work roles and examines the assumptions surrounding the interrelationship between job design on family 'well-being'.

Hatch, M.J. and Cunliffe, A.L. (2006) Organization Theory: Modern, Symbolic and Postmodern Perspectives, Oxford: Oxford University Press. Useful discussion of many issues related to power throughout the book.

Jay, A. (1987) Management and Machiavelli, revised edn, London: Hutchinson Business. A humorous text which considers many aspects associated with power and authority in management. It does not take Machiavelli's work specifically as its basis, but his spirit is evident. A translation of Machiavelli's original work, which is very accessible and available as a 1981 Penguin book, is also well worth reading.

Jermier, J.M., Knights, D. and Nord, W.R. (eds) (1994) Resistance and Power in Organizations, London: Routledge. Provides a review of how attempts to use power as a basis of control inevitably leads to resistance in one form or another. It is grounded

in the labour process perspective and attempts to interpret the arguments from the perspectives implied by that model.

McMahon, P. (2002) Global Control: Information Technology and Globalization, Cheltenham: Edward Elgar. A solid review of information systems as the means of providing control in the cycles of capitalist reorganization and globalization.

Marchington, M., Grimshaw, D., Rubery, J. and Wilmott, H. (2004) Fragmenting Work: Blurring Organizational Boundaries and Disordering Hierarchies, Oxford: Oxford University Press. Considers the reality and complexity of modern organizations functioning and supply chain operations together with the structural and job-related issues that emerge from that reality.

Siddons, S. (2003) Remote Working: Linking people and organizations, Oxford: Elsevier. Considers the forms that remote working can take and what is necessary to support the people engaged in that form of employment.

Watson, T.J. (2006) Sociology, work and industry (5th edn), Routledge. Sociological treatment that characteristically focuses on power dynamics and structures throughout the book.

COMPANION WEBSITE

Online teaching and learning resources

Visit the companion website for Organizational Behaviour and Management 4th edition at: http://www .Cengagelearning.co.uk/martinfittelenz to find valuable further teaching and learning material. For full details, see 'About the website' at the start of the book.

Case Study – reflects how each chapter's main issues are applied in real-life business situations in different types of organizations. Each case is accompanied by questions to help test the reader and extend their understanding of the key issues

Further Reading – listed at the end of each chapter allowing the reader to explore the subject further

ABOUT THE WEBSITE

Visit the *Organizational Behavior & Management 4e* companion website at **http://www.cengage.co.uk/martinfellenz** or **www.cengage.co.uk** to find valuable teaching and learning material including:

STUDENT

- Extend your learning notes
- Study skills section
- Glossary
- PowerPoint slides
- Web links
- Case studies and commentaries with questions and activities
- MCQs/revision questions

LECTURERS

- Instructor's Manual with teaching notes
- Additional case studies
- PowerPoint slides

CENGAGENOW

Designed by lecturers for lecturers, CengageNOW for Martin & Fellenz mirrors the natural teaching workflow with an easy-to-use online suite of services and resources, all in one program. With this system, lecturers can easily plan their courses, manage student assignments, automatically grade, teach with dynamic technology, and assess student progress. CengageNOW operates seamlessly with Blackboard/WebCT, Moodle and other virtual learning environments. Ask your Cengage Learning sales representative for a demonstration of what CengageNOW for Martin & Fellenz can bring to your courses (http://edu.cengage.co.uk/contact_us.aspx).

PART ONE

ORGANIZATIONAL BEHAVIOUR AND THE CHALLENGES FACING MANAGERS

1   Introducing management and organizational behaviour
2   Organizational behaviour and current management challenges

Each of the five parts of this book will introduce and explore a particular aspect of organizational behaviour grounded in a comprehensive model introduced as a guiding framework in Chapter 1. This model, reminiscent of the open systems model, recognizes the goal-oriented nature of management and demonstrates the complex connections and interdependencies between and among the many facets of the topic in both academic and practical terms. The model prepares the ground for more thorough explorations of the major issues associated with the study of how human beings interact in and with organizations, and how their behaviour and experiences are impacted upon by the organizations that they work within.

The first chapter introduces issues such as the purpose and nature of organizations and management. It also considers what organizational behaviour is and why it is an important area of study for those interacting with and working in organizations. A central part of this chapter is the introduction of the guiding framework that informs the structure and approach adopted in the book in relation to what organizational behaviour is and how it relates to the complexity and interrelatedness of the specific issues discussed (see Figure 1). Chapter 1 also considers and briefly explores the nature of research in the social world in which organizations and the people who work in them exist.

This is followed in the second chapter by a brief review of how academic thought in relation to management has evolved over recent history. It will then focus on the contemporary management challenges faced by every manager and organization in the modern world. They are:

● Global interconnectedness and the resulting increase in linkages, scope and reach of many organizational activities.

● Ethical considerations and the demands for responsible action by organizations and by decision makers within them.

● The escalating levels of competition, growing scarcity in resource supply, and the resulting increase in productivity and performance pressures.

● The cumulative and interactive effects of the above factors and other environmental developments on necessary organizational change.

This first part thus introduces the main objects and topics that guide the treatment of management and organizational behaviour throughout the book. It sets the stage for considering the individual, interactions, formal and informal and social aspects of organizations in more detail in the following four parts.

Figure 1

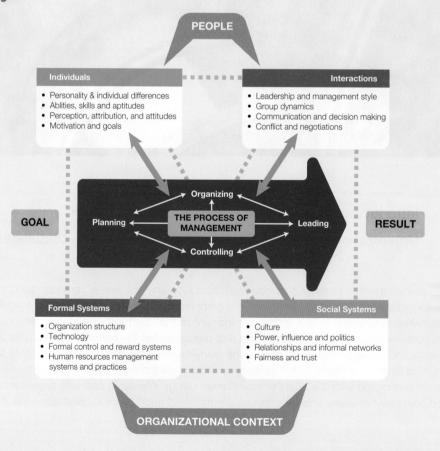

CHAPTER ONE

INTRODUCING MANAGEMENT AND ORGANIZATIONAL BEHAVIOUR

istock/VCNW

LEARNING OBJECTIVES

After studying this chapter and working through the associated OB in Action panels, Discussion Questions and Case Study you should be able to:

- Understand why organizations exist, and identify and explain how they can influence the behaviour of organizational members.

- Describe how knowledge about individual and group behaviour in organizations can contribute to successful management.

- Identify categories of influencers of behaviour in organizations, and outline how they can impact on management in organizations.

- Understand distinctions between research in the natural and in the social sciences.

- Explain the particular difficulties involved in studying and developing theories in the area of management, and in applying the knowledge of organizational behaviour in practice.

- Discuss how the study of organizational behaviour can contribute to an understanding of management.

INTRODUCTION

Organizations are an inescapable feature of modern social experience for all human beings. From the remotest village high in the Himalayan foothills to life in a large metropolis, organizations impact on all aspects of the human experience. Everyone

EXAMINING ETHICS

Misery of rag-trade slaves in the Pacific Rim

The capital of American Samoa, Pago Pago, is home to a number of high-volume garment factories, all with the right to claim that the goods are made in the USA. However, in 2003 a court heard from the then US attorney general that conditions in some factories were 'nothing less than modern-day slavery'. It was said that the 251 Chinese and Vietnamese workers at one factory each paid £126 per month for room and board, which consisted of a bunk in a 36 bed dormitory and three meagre meals each day. The pay for the workers was routinely withheld and when workers went on strike to recover lost earnings, the managers turned off the electricity, making the conditions in the living areas unbearable. During one such dispute a woman worker called Quyen Truong was dragged from her machine and had one eye gouged out with a plastic pipe. She has since had a partial eye transplant and now lives in Honolulu. She said she works at a job 'making sandwiches' and takes classes at a community college.

The clothes being made were for large name retail stores such as Sears and JC Penney as well as for the MV Sport and Spalding brands. Only JC Penney agreed to pay the workers the back pay owed to them. Workers are attracted to work at the factory by the higher wages available, more than could be earned in Vietnam. Sewing jobs paid $400 each month compared to the average in Vietnam of $30 per month. However, prosecutors said it was necessary for workers to pay anything up to $5000 to gain employment at the factory in the US territory. But once there, they were effectively enslaved. The parents of one worker had to remortgage their home in order to guarantee the fee. One worker earned only $672 during her 9 months' employment at the factory before it was closed down and could not pay off her debts unless she got more work in a similar factory.

Lou deBaca of the US Department of Justice said that Kil Soo Lee (the owner of the factory) had between March 1999 and November 2000 exploited over 200

Vietnamese and Chinese people in what amounted to nothing less than modern-day slavery. He faced sentences of up to 20 years for each of 11 counts of involuntary servitude and a maximum of 10 years for each of the other charges.

Charles Kernaghan, Director of the National Labour Committee in Washington said that the situation in American Samoa made it a perfect location for exploitation of labour. It was a US territory with an economy in desperate need of stimulation and it had no import tariffs in relation to mainland USA, looser immigration laws and tax incentives to encourage inward investment. Being eligible to display the 'Made in the USA' symbol on the labels of goods made there, it even implied that quality and labour practices were as they would be everywhere else in the USA, a distinct sales advantage. However, being more than 7000 miles from Washington it was in practice only lightly regulated, with government labour inspectors saying that they do not have a budget for travel to such remote locations in order to monitor working conditions.

TASKS

1 What does this example of the treatment of people at work suggest about the nature of management in a capitalist economy?

2 To what extent might similar conditions apply to people employed in a company in your own country?

3 How might an understanding of OB help to prevent such abuses (if at all)?

Sources:
Fickling, D. (2003) Misery of rag-trade slaves in America's Pacific outpost, *The Guardian*, Saturday 1 March, p. 20.
http://www.business-humanrights.org/Categories/Individualcompanies/J/JCPenney?&batch_start=41 (accessed 7 May 2009).
http://archives.starbulletin.com/2003/02/22/news/story2.html (accessed 7 May 2009).
http://news.bbc.co.uk/1/hi/world/americas/2789629.stm (accessed 7 May 2009).

experiences organizations in a number of different ways. We are the customers of organizations when we purchase goods or avail ourselves of services; we are members of organizations when we work, play and learn in them; we might even start an organization as an entrepreneur or as a founder of a club or voluntary organization!

Consequently, we are involved with and in organizations in almost all aspects of our lives. We certainly spend a great deal of our time interacting with them and belonging to them. It makes sense therefore to develop some understanding of the things that go on inside organizations, and in particular, how and why people in organizations behave the way they do. Consider for example the Examining Ethics feature 'Misery of rag-trade slaves in the Pacific Rim' for an example of exploitation and immoral organizational practice that still exist. This feature demonstrates the need for the understanding and implementation of good management practice and the support of law to ensure that bad practices are stamped out.

We begin that process by considering what organizations are, why they are so common and the role and nature of management in organizations is. We will then define what organizational behaviour (OB) is, and why – and how – to study it. Through exploring the linkages between management and organizations, this chapter then develops a framework for studying OB that will provide the structure for the rest of the book. We will also consider how knowledge about management and OB has been generated by research, and discuss characteristics of the main research approaches as well as critical and postmodern contributions.

WHAT ARE ORGANIZATIONS?

All of us interact with and are members of many social groupings such as families, friendship cliques, music bands, political parties, sport supporter groups, commercial organizations, sports clubs, churches, charities, and many more. But which ones of these are organizations? How can an organization be differentiated from other social groupings? There is no easy answer to these questions because there are no simple distinguishing criteria, as all forms of social grouping contain elements of similarity in terms of purpose, structure, people and systems.

Organizations are so common in our lives that we mostly take them for granted. Yet many of us are stumped when asked to define what an organization is. This is true, to a certain degree, also for scholars of organizations who have offered a range of definitions (see Table 1.1).

When considering these definitions it becomes clear that they contain some common elements that can help to define organizations. These are reflected in the definition we use in this book:

> Organizations are *social entities that are goal-directed, that are inextricably linked to their environment yet have nominal boundaries, and that employ deliberately designed and co-ordinated activities and approaches to achieving their objectives.*

These characteristics of organizations are so central for our understanding that we need to consider them in more detail.

Social entities Organizations always involve people, and they are characterized by their members *and* the relationships and interactions between and among them. This is true for other social entities such as families, interest groups, clans, or mobs. The difference between organizations and these other types of social entities become clearer when we consider the other characteristics of organizations.

Organizations
Social entities that are goal-directed, are inextricably linked to their environment yet with nominal boundaries, and that employ deliberately designed and co-ordinated activities and approaches to achieve their objectives.

Table 1.1 Definitions of organization

Definition of organization	Author
Organizations are a form of social system made up of people and a variety of resources and subsystems integrated to transform inputs into mission-appropriate outputs.	Bloisi *et al.* (2007)
Work organization is a deliberately formed social group in which people, technology and resources are deliberately co-ordinated through formalized roles and relationships to achieve a division of labour designed to attain a specific set of objectives efficiently.	Bratton *et al.* (2007)
Organizations are social entities that are goal-directed, are designed as deliberately structured and co-ordinated activity systems, and are linked to the external environment.	Daft (2007)
Organizations are social units (or human groupings) deliberately constructed and reconstructed to seek specific goals.	Etzioni (1964)
Organizations are collections of people who work together to achieve a wide variety of goals.	George and Jones (2005)
Organizations are social inventions for accomplishing goals through group effort.	Johns (1992)
Organizations are assemblages of interacting human beings and they are the largest assemblages in our society that have anything resembling a central co-ordinative system . . . the high specificity of structure and co-ordination within organizations . . . marks off the individual organization as a sociological unit comparable in significance to the individual organism in biology.	March and Simon (1958: p. 4)
Organizations have a number of important features including: ● organizations are artefacts ● goal directed ● social entities ● structured activities.	Rollison (2008)
Work organizations are social and technical arrangements and understandings in which a number of people come together in a formalized and contractual relationship where actions of some are directed by others towards the achievement of work tasks carried out in the organization's name.	Watson (2008)

Note: The above definitions are employing an *institutional* understanding of organizations or, in simpler terms, consider an organization to be a thing (i.e., 'an entity *is* an organization'). Other ways of thinking are also possible such as an *instrumental* conception of organization (i.e., 'an entity *has* an organization') or a *procedural* approach to organization (i.e., 'organization is a process') which views the entities we experience as the momentary outcomes of this process.

Objectives/goal orientation Organizations are created and used to achieve objectives. In fact, it is hard to conceive of an organization without identifying what it does and what it tries to achieve. Over time such objectives often change, and similarly we often find that organizations have espoused objectives that do not describe what they actually do or appear to be doing. Nevertheless, the notion of goals and objectives is crucial to our understanding of organizations and, as we will see later, central to the reason for why organizations exist.

Nominal boundary yet linked to environment Formal organizations typically have identifiable boundaries that set them apart. From a legal perspective, for example, it is quite clear who is a member of an organization and who is not, or what is part of the property of the organization. Other boundaries may be informal or even subjective, for example the feeling of belonging to an organization that individual members may have. The boundaries of organizations appear often quite flexible and even diffuse and shifting. This is due to the fact that organizations need continuous exchanges with their environment – in fact, they cannot exist without their environments. Not only do they draw their members from their environment, but also all the relevant tangible (e.g., people, material, energy) and intangible (e.g., information, legitimacy) resources they need to pursue their goals. To survive, organizations continuously interact and exchange such resources with their environment, and in changing environments these interactions also change over time. This is one of the reasons why organizations are often called open systems (see chapter 11).

Deliberately designed and co-ordinated activities and approaches Unlike some other social entities such as a friendship group or a mob, organizations have deliberately designed structures and co-ordination approaches. This is not to mean that all aspects of an organization are actively put in place. Nevertheless, organizations typically employ some form of division of labour which enables them to more effectively and efficiently achieve their objectives. In addition to the formal and deliberately designed structures, processes and rules that are put in place in organizations, norms and other informal structures, processes and interaction patterns emerge in organizations that also contribute to initiate, sustain, direct and co-ordinate individual and collective activities in organizations.

One central feature of organizations inherent in all the explicit parts of our definition needs some further clarification and attention. Like other social entities that we regularly experience as real (e.g., family, group, clique, neighbourhood, community), organizations are useful and convenient abstractions rather than real physical entities. When we talk about organizations as real we reify them, which is *treating as real what is merely a concept or abstract idea*. What we are reifying is the nominal organization (i.e., legal entity, name, brand) along with the observable patterns of repeated and often predictable behaviour of and interactions among individual members, and the artefacts (e.g., buildings, uniforms, logos, products) they create. We treat all this as the organization, and even though many of these aspects are real events and physical entities, the organization is not. To make matters worse, we often anthropomorphize organizations, which means that we *treat them as real actors with human features and abilities by assuming that they act, learn, compete, make decisions, and so forth*. While all this is often criticized as a fundamental fallacy (i.e., a logical mistake) of organizational studies, reification is the way we all conceive of, describe, and experience the world (in fact, families and other social phenomena often feel only too real!). Also, reification, unlike anthropomorphism (see Andersen, 2008), is an important analytical tool in many social sciences, and particularly in organizational studies and OB (see Koza and Thoenig, 2003).

Reify
To treat as real that which is merely a concept or an abstract idea.

Anthropomorphize organizations
Means that organizations are regarded as possessing the qualities of real actors with human features and abilities by assuming that they act, learn, compete, make decisions and generally function as if they were human.

STOP & CONSIDER

'Organizations are nothing more that collections of people brought together for a particular purpose. In that sense they are no different from any other social group and so attempting to theorize about an organization as an entity is pointless.' Does this statement have any value and if so what?

The study of organizations is conducted by social scientists from fields such as management, economics, sociology, political science, anthropology, and others. The interdisciplinary body of knowledge they contribute to is alternately called organization theory and design, macro-OB, and – particularly in Europe – organization studies or organizational analysis. This field focuses on the organization as the unit of analysis, and investigates phenomena that are relevant at the organizational level such as an organization's structure, culture and processes, as well as its relationship with the environment. Such an exclusive approach to studying organizations at a particular level of analysis is useful for researchers and theorists because it helps reduce the complexity inherent in their subject matter. However, as we will see throughout the book, it also introduces difficulties because it too often provides only partial insights into the complex and multi-faceted nature of organizations and the issues and dynamics within them.

The discussion of organizations in this section is for reasons of brevity and clarity deliberately selective and thus, of course, not complete. Many other, different views on organizations exist that can provide additional insights into this phenomenon. Scott (2003), for example, provides a thorough discussion of organizations based on contrasting three views of organizations as rational, natural and open systems. These three conceptions imply different types of goals, focused on formal objectives, survival, and environmental exchanges, respectively. Most views of organizations imply particular goal orientations, but it is useful to heed the warning that when we can assume or even identify overarching organizational objectives, multiple additional and often conflicting goals are typically pursued at the same time by individuals and collectives within these organizations (Watson, 2008). We will return to this important point in our consideration of such issues as leadership (Chapter 6), conflict (Chapter 9), structure (Chapter 10), control and job design (Chapter 11), culture (Chapter 14), power (Chapter 15), and others.

WHY DO ORGANIZATIONS EXIST?

The answer to this question is deceptively simple. Organizations exist because they enable us to do things we could not do without them, or could not do as well without them. Think of an everyday activity like making a cheese sandwich. You would go into a shop, buy the necessary ingredients, and then assemble the sandwich in your kitchen using the usual implements. But how would you go about doing this without organizations? There would be no large supermarket in which you could buy all necessary ingredients. In fact buying would be hard because without organizations you would not have money or another universally accepted currency. Even your kitchen and the furniture, plates and cutlery you use would probably not exist in the form you are used to because they too, have been produced by organizations.

Organizations are used to direct and co-ordinate the activities of their members (also called *hierarchical governance*, see Barney, 1999). Alternatives to this form of co-ordination include contractual and relationship-based approaches (e.g., networks and alliances; this is also called *intermediate governance*, see Barney, 1999) and markets (or *market governance*, see Barney, 1999). According to economic arguments, the boundaries of organizations are determined by what can be efficiently done by an organization. Thus, if a product (or service) can more easily and cheaply be bought elsewhere organizations would generally not produce it themselves (Coase, 1937; Barney, 1999). On the other hand, if a profit is to be made by engaging in a particular activity, organizations may try to capture the resulting economic benefits. They would be best placed to do this if the complexity and scope of the tasks involved, and the range of necessary resources (including people, capital, technology, knowledge and information, etc.) are so large that all relevant activities to provide the final product or service can most efficiently and effectively be directed and co-ordinated centrally. But note that some tasks are so large that individual organizations cannot successfully co-ordinate and conduct all relevant aspects. Hence we are noticing increasingly complex linkages and interactions among organizations within and across many areas, localities, countries and regions, a process also discussed as part of the phenomenon of globalization (e.g., Stiglitz, 2006; Friedman, 2005). Much has recently been written about the complex international linkages among financial service firms such as banks. Clearly, global finance is conducted and co-ordinated in ways that combine co-ordination mechanisms vested in organizations as well as networks and markets.

In addition to a purely economic explanation about the existence and the boundaries of organizations, however, other aspects may also feature in decisions to create and use organizations. They include the legitimacy of the goals and activities involved, the fit between organizational activities and the cultural and societal expectations about how they should be handled, non-economic factors (such as ideology or power) that may compel individuals or groups to support or oppose specific organizations, ethical and moral considerations, and others. Such factors can contribute to our understanding why in different circumstances some activities are predominantly handled by organizations, while elsewhere they are co-ordinated and conducted by markets, networks, or even individuals.

Following this logic, organizations exist only if they can contribute to more effective and efficient creation of value (which often is primarily economic but may also be cultural, social, political, moral, etc.), and their boundaries are mainly determined by what makes economic (or sometimes cultural, social, political or moral) sense. If you are looking for a friend who has not come back from a mountain walk (or if you are looking for a new job, or a review of a new MP3 player) you would probably not think about founding an organizations to help you achieve this objective. However, if hikers regularly went missing in your area (or if people often change jobs, or regularly search for product reviews) it may be more effective and efficient to have other people participate in these tasks. Their specialization in certain tasks (e.g., searching inaccessible areas for the missing hiker; checking with emergency services for sightings of the missing person; linking with local and regional media outlets to appeal for information; etc.) may make them more efficient and/or more effective at achieving these tasks. That is why we often find designated entities for such tasks: search-and-rescue organizations for missing people at sea or in mountains; job and employment agencies; and product-review organizations that publish magazines or review websites. For an example of an organization that was founded to efficiently and effectively address very specialized needs of a particular group of clients see the Management in action example on Acquired Brain Injury Ireland.

In summary, the reasons why organizations exist are that (a) they are more effective than the alternatives, i.e., organizations offer the opportunity to achieve objectives unachievable without them; and (b) they offer efficiencies compared to their alternatives, i.e., they help achieve these goals faster or with less economic, cultural, social, political or moral costs. The presented definition of organizations and the above explanation for their existence are in sociological terms *functionalist*, which means that they are adopting a perspective that focuses on purpose (goals) and utility (value). While functionalist approaches to understanding organizations can be criticized, we adopt them here because they provide the most general and comprehensive platform from which to learn about management and OB.

MANAGEMENT IN ACTION

Acquired Brain Injury Ireland

Established in 2000, Acquired Brain Injury Ireland formerly The Peter Bradley Foundation is a leading provider of flexible and tailor-made services for people with an acquired brain injury (ABI) in Ireland. Its mission is to enable people with an ABI to live an independent life within the community, by providing and maintaining a supportive living environment. Each person is an individual and each brain injury is particular so the services offered by the organization to each individual client have to provide a custom-made rehabilitation and care programme suitable to the specific individual needs that will help to maximize their abilities. Acquired Brain Injury Ireland is a value-driven organization. They pride themselves on the quality of services provided and they are the first organization in Ireland to receive internationally recognized CARF accreditation as a provider of quality services for people with ABI. Acquired Brain Injury Ireland is a strong advocate for the estimated 10 000 people per year who experience an ABI in Ireland today, and is constantly seeking improved support services for those with ABI and their families.

ABI can be defined as any brain injury that occurs with rapid onset during a person's life. It can be:

- Damage to brain tissue following traumatic injuries – resulting from road traffic accidents, falls, assaults, sports injuries.
- Damage to the brain following stroke (through haemorrhage or aneurysm), brain surgery or a brain tumour.
- Damage to brain tissue as a result of viral infection (e.g. following encephalitis, meningitis, syphilis).
- Damage to brain resulting from lack of oxygen (e.g. as a result of heart attacks, hypoxia or anoxia).

ABI has been described as a silent epidemic. People with ABI may often look fine but can have many problems which mean they cannot resume their previous lives or even return home.

All these affect a person's ability to take control of their lives and can lead to social isolation and depression. Financial and emotional strain on carers can be considerable.

Barbara O'Connell (Peter Bradley's sister) and her husband Maurice O'Connell, along with members of Peter's family, formed the Peter Bradley Foundation in direct response to Peter's particular situation. In partnership with the HSE East Coast, Peter's house was renovated and specially adapted for him and two other men with ABI. Peter Bradley suffered two major head injuries but was unable to access essential community support services following discharge from hospital – because they did not exist. So began the creation and development of the organization now known as Acquired Brain Injury Ireland - not only a leading ABI care provider in Ireland, but with a worldwide reputation for best practice in the care of and services for individuals and their families with ABI.

The organization has developed over the 9 years since its inception to one that is under the direction of a Board which provides strong support and direction to the management team responsible for the actual running of the organization and provision of services. The Board includes experienced healthcare professionals and business people, many of whom have personal experience of ABI. The management team is led by Barbara O'Connell, Chief Executive, who is supported by an experienced team of healthcare and business professionals committed to expanding the support services available to people living with ABI and their families.

Person centred planning by carers from Acquired Brain Injury Ireland ensures that the person served is fully involved in all decisions that affect his or her life. A personal profile is drawn up for each person that identifies their current abilities and their support needs. In partnership with the individual a personal rehabilitation programme is drawn up which is tailored to their needs and which enables them to realize personal goals which are meaningful to their lives. This approach, which is internationally recognized best practice, ensures that the services provided are never generic or based on assumptions of what is best for the individual. Acquired Brain Injury Ireland provides the following range of services throughout Ireland:

- assisted living service
- transitional living
- community rehabilitation service

- day resource service
- rehabilitation support team
- case management
- external awareness and education programme
- individual development.

The rehabilitation team involved with the care of each individual consists of clinical staff, local services managers, ABI case managers and rehabilitation assistants together with the person with ABI and family members/carers affected by ABI. The team is reflected in the following diagram:

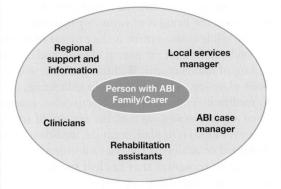

TASKS

1   Acquired Brain Injury Ireland is different in many ways to the commercial and 'for-profit' organizations that are the focus for much OB and management work. What differences (and similarities) might you expect to find between such organizations as a consequence, and why?

2   In response to your answer to Task 1, can you identify those differences and similarities in the material presented above (or from any of the material on the organization's website)? Explain and justify your conclusions to this task.

3   Reflecting on the creation and development of Acquired Brain Injury Ireland could suggest the following developmental process or stage model at work:

a   Stage 1. **Impetus**: identification of a gap in service availability through personal experience though a family member's situation.

b   Stage 2. **Idea**: finding the means to address the identified need.

c   Stage 3. **Response**: founding of the Peter Bradley Foundation with assistance from whatever public funding and (presumably) privately raised funds/resources can be accessed.

d   Stage 4. **Expansion**: development of the organization and extension of services offered as experience, funding and capability becomes available. Also as increased need for the service is identified. The aim being to provide support to more people and provide national coverage.

e   Stage 5. **Institutionalization** and **depersonalization**: Change in funding provision and scale; legitimization through international accreditation; depersonalization through name change; increasing professionalization of management and service provision structures, etc.

To what extent does this five-stage process reflect the process that Acquired Brain Injury Ireland has been through and to what extent would you expect that the same process could be applied to any organization in its formation and early years? What would you expect the next stage (stage 6) to be and why?

Source:
http://www.abiireland.ie/index.html, website of Acquired Brain Injury Ireland (accessed August 2009).

WHAT IS MANAGEMENT?

We use the terms 'management' and 'managing' everyday and employ it to describe a wide range of activities. You may talk about managing your time in preparing for exams, managing stress, managing to get a date with an attractive acquaintance. Similarly, you may use the terms to refer to processes as well, for example to the way airport security manages a large number of travellers arriving at the same time, or the way in which a store clerk manages to track down a particular piece of clothing in your size through the shop's stock control system. In everyday life as well as when applied to organizations, using these words (management and managing) invariably refers to actions and processes aimed at achieving particular goals.

This reflects both the dictionary definitions of the terms as well as common understanding, and is useful for considering the role of management in organizations. Formally, we define management as *a process that involves planning, organizing, leading (or deploying), and controlling resources in order to achieve goals* (see Figure 1.1). Note that the term 'controlling' here refers to assessing and responding to feedback rather than to simply exerting influence. This general definition of management closely reflects traditional views of management theorists (e.g., Fayol, 1947) which will be discussed in more detail in Chapter 6. Given the behavioural focus of OB, a shortened and more focused version of this definition may also be helpful. Thus, in this book we refer to people management as *the process of trying to achieve goals in organizations with and through people*.

The linkage between this discussion of management and the above considerations of organizations, their nature and their reason for being is obvious: organizations can be seen as *means* for achieving objectives, while management is the *process* of trying to achieve objectives. It is important to understand that the notion of goals and results is absolutely central to our understanding of management. Without goals there is no purpose that can guide decisions about planning, organizing, leading/directing, and about how to assess and respond to feedback. Thus, without objectives we cannot talk about management, and the task of anyone *managing* (i.e., the activity of trying to achieve a goal using resources of whatever kind) is to plan, organize, lead/direct and control in ways that maximize the likelihood of achieving the relevant objective.

For completeness' sake it is also useful to recognize that English speakers often talk about 'the management', a term that designates the group of people in an organization that is authorized to make decisions on behalf of the organization and direct the behaviour of other organizational members. This term is traditionally contrasted with 'labour', which designates those who are expected to follow the direction of 'the management'.

Anybody considering Figure 1.1 (The process of management) could be forgiven for thinking that management is easy. At face value, achieving objectives using the four major functions that are part of the definition of management appears unproblematic. If you decided to go out with a group of friends to celebrate your birthday it is not difficult to consider how to plan the event, get everyone invited and informed about the meeting place and time, lead them in the planned activities, and check if everything

Management
A process that involves the major functions of planning, organizing, leading (or deploying) and controlling resources in order to achieve goals. The jobs within an organization are charged with running the organization on behalf of the beneficial owner.

People management
The process of trying to achieve goals in organizations with and through people.

1.1 EXTEND
YOUR LEARNING

Figure 1.1 The process of management

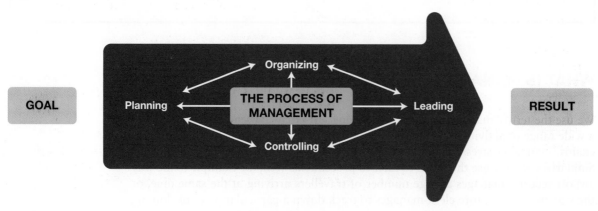

works out as planned. Yet anyone who has tried to achieve such a task has most likely quickly realized that this is considerably more challenging in reality than it appears in theory. Even apparently straightforward and relatively simple tasks quickly become very complex if other people and real environments come into play. This is because people and environmental factors introduce complexity (i.e., *a large number of potentially relevant factors that may have a bearing on the intended outcome*) as well as uncertainty (i.e., *the absence of sufficient information about the nature and likelihood of certain events that may have a bearing on the intended outcome*) to the process of management. Consider for example the following Change at Work example 'Sit in at the factory as it goes into administration' in relation to a company that is no longer financially viable and the difficulty faced by managers and administrators in persuading employees that they have done the best that they could on their behalf.

Complexity
Refers to the wide range of people and environmental factors that may have a bearing on the intended activity, functioning and outcome of an organization and management.

CHANGE AT WORK

Sit-in at the factory as it goes into administration

Visteon, a Belfast based factory that made car parts for Ford motors, was put into administration in early April 2009 by its American parent company with the loss of more than 200 jobs. As well as closing the Belfast site, Visteon UK is also axing another 360 jobs at its factories in Basildon and Enfield. Donald Stebbins, chairman and chief executive of the American parent company said: 'Despite extensive restructuring efforts the UK plants have continued to incur substantial losses. Regrettably, having exhausted all options, the Visteon UK board of directors had no alternative but to file for administration.' It was estimated that it currently owed more than £400m to creditors. Visteon UK has struggled since it separated from car giant Ford in 2000. There were redundancies at the Belfast factory in 2003 and again in 2006.

Devastated staff in Belfast staged an immediate sit-in at the factory and vowed to continue it until management agreed to talks that workers hoped would change the decision or improve the compensation to be paid for their dismissal. Workers are claiming they are entitled to Ford redundancy terms under an agreement that was reached when the plant was originally sold. John McGowan, shift leader at Visteon, said: 'I'm just dumbstruck. I feel it's totally unjust the way we're being treated by the company. They have had redundancies since 2000 due to the downturn in sales. Last year they were offering redundancy packages of

£30 000 minimum. Now they're telling me for my 30 years loyalty to this company I'm getting a redundancy package which is capped at just over £9 000. That's totally unjust and unfair.'

Davy McMurray, from the trade union Unite, said yesterday: 'It is a total shock; workers were only informed that the factory was closing at 1pm. We really need to get face-to-face talks with Ford and we really need our MLAs (local politicians) to use whatever influence they have to get Ford to the negotiating table. The redundancy that these workers are entitled to would go some way towards easing the blow.' Mr McMurray added: 'This news is a hammer blow for the economy of west Belfast where the highly skilled workforce is slowly being eroded.'

TASKS

1 Under the circumstance is it likely that the workers could change the management decision?

2 If you were a manager (or administrator) how would you react to a sit-in under such circumstances (and why)?

Sources:
http://www.belfasttelegraph.co.uk/news/local-national/devastated-visteon-staff-stage-sitin-as-200-jobs-go-in-factory-shutdown-14251293.html (accessed 1 April 2009).
http://news.scotsman.com/uk/Sitin-as-car-firm-axes.5127581.jp (accessed 1 April 2009).
http://news.sky.com/skynews/Home/Business/565-UK-Car-Jobs-Axed-As-Car-Parts-Maker-Visteon-Goes-Into-Administration/Article/200903415252624?f=rss (accessed 1 April 2009).

Uncertainty
Refers to the effect that the absence of sufficient information about the nature and likelihood of certain events may have on the intended activity, functioning and outcome of an organization and to the process of management.

This is particularly true in organizations. As we will see in the remainder of this chapter and throughout this book, the involvement of people and the particular characteristics of organizations provide an arena characterized by high levels of complexity and uncertainty. This provides an immensely challenging context for management, and is the reason why the study of OB is so important and valuable for everyone involved in managing in organizations! We will return to this point after considering what OB is, and why – and how – to study it.

WHAT IS ORGANIZATIONAL BEHAVIOUR?

We have defined and discussed organizations and management, and concluded that management is difficult, in large part because of the complexity and uncertainty introduced by people in the organization, and by the organizational context itself. Recognizing the variability of human behaviour and the important influence of the context in organizations appears obvious to most of us, but this was not always so. Early management theorists largely ignored the human element that contributes so much in terms of creativity, change and variability, and instead focused on structure, order, stability and predictability. Today, organizational behaviour (OB) provides one of the mainstream approaches to the study of management and organizations. OB is *concerned with the behaviour of individuals and groups in organizational contexts*. Its main sphere of interest includes anything relevant to the design, management and effectiveness of an organization, together with the dynamic and interactive relationships that exist within them. It draws some of its main inspiration from the human relations school of thought that emerged from the Hawthorne studies, which were directed by Elton Mayo during the late 1920s and early 1930s. These studies first highlighted the complexity of human behaviour in an organizational setting. This in turn led to recognition of the importance of the social context within which work occurred and of the ways in which groups become a significant influence on individual behaviour.

Organizational behaviour (OB)
That aspect of theory and practice concerned with the behaviour of individuals and groups in organizational contexts.

OB deals with individuals' thoughts (cognition), feelings (emotion, affect) and behaviours (actions) in response to or in the context of organizations; the interactions that ensue between individuals in organizations; the behaviour of groups of individuals in organizations; and the characteristics of the organizational context that contain and influence all of this. Given this enormously broad range of phenomena that OB deals with, the body of knowledge of OB is broad but often not very deep. Because of the complex and multi-faceted nature of its subject, the study of OB involves two distinct features:

1 *Interdisciplinary.* As a field of study, OB has developed out of a range of disciplines that have studied behavioural issues in organizations as well as organizations as the context for such behaviour. It continues to draw from research in psychology, sociology, political science, economics, anthropology, philosophy, ergonomics and many other disciplines particularly in the social sciences. As behavioural issues become more centre-stage in other academic specialties (e.g., finance, accounting, economics, computer science, engineering and operations management, among others), the theories, models, concepts, methodologies and approaches used in OB are applied to other areas. At the same time, the knowledge available from the study of behavioural and organizational issues in other areas feeds back into OB and enriches our understanding about individual and group behaviour and its interaction with organizational contexts. In addition to this wealth of base material OB also accommodates critical theory perspectives which seek to emancipate people from existing constraints and power relationships as

well as postmodern and poststructural approaches to understanding human behaviour in organizations that challenge the rationality underlying much of current organizational and management theory and practice.

2   *Explanatory.* OB sets out to explain the behaviour of individuals and groups in organizations. Because of the complexity of its subject matter, these explanations are not formulated in the form of general or natural laws that claim to be universal truths. Rather, they typically take the form of theories and models that describe the relationships between variables. These abstract models are not prescriptive by either indicating what people should do or by predicting what will inevitably happen. This would be impossible because when dealing with human behaviour at any level one is concerned with probability rather than certainty. In other words, no two people would react to a situation in exactly the same way, and even the same person might react differently on different occasions. As a result, OB does not provide general answers that always hold true. OB knowledge is mostly probabilistic rather than certain, and we derive value from it by informing our analysis and improving our insights, rather than by finding or creating ultimate answers that claim to be absolute truths.

WHY STUDY ORGANIZATIONAL BEHAVIOUR?

As lifelong, enthusiastic OB teachers, researchers, consultants and practitioners, our natural reaction to this question is: 'Why wouldn't anyone want to study OB?' But for anyone new to OB, it is of course a valid question.

People within an organization are trained to carry out their specific job responsibilities. This may be on the job, which is very realistic but often leaves little time for reflection and deeper learning, or off-the-job, which is often very specific but may not capture all important aspects of the job and new knowledge may not be fully transferred back to the real work setting. Moreover, many times the training that organizational members receive is focused on the practical and technical aspects of their particular work in sales, marketing, finance, operations, or other areas. But the technical aspects of any job represent only a small part of any work activity. Very few people work without direct contact with other people, and no one in any organization works without some form of interdependency with other members. People work in groups or teams, are members of specific departments, they have customers and suppliers (inside and outside of the organization), and they have superiors to report to and subordinates to direct and control. The resulting webs of relationships are both formal and informal in nature, but they all involve other people. Most jobs involve some degree of persuading people to co-operate with some priority, action, or request involving a degree of inconvenience to themselves. For employees, it is important to understand what the company expects of them in return for their pay, advancement opportunities, and continued employment. At the same time, it is important to understand how their colleagues and managers may think about work, management, leadership, collaboration and all the other important aspects of work life in organizations. For managers it is necessary to know how to deal with problem employees (not everyone co-operates all of the time), or with other managers who are seeking to advance their careers and are therefore in competition for more senior appointments. As we will discuss further in Chapter 2, it is also necessary for managers to almost continuously deal with changes originating inside and outside the organization, and to improve consistently the operational performance of their departments in a constant drive for higher productivity.

It should be apparent from this brief discussion that working successfully within an organization at any level involves a wide range of competencies beyond those

Team
Small groups whose members take individual and collective responsibility for their shared objectives and interactively co-ordinate their interdependent activities through roles and specific assignments.

required to carry out the technical aspects of a job. Therefore, the simple answer is that you should study OB in order to understand better the complexities of the world of work.

However, that is not the only reason to study it. It is not possible, as has already been suggested, for OB as a discipline to be prescriptive in setting out exactly what to do in every specific situation. Life in organizations is never that simple – and sadly, in OB there are no 'silver bullet' answers that can be used to address any and all problems. There are always too many different relevant variables active in any situation than could make that a realistic possibility. For this reason, the theories covered in this book are middle range theories, which are *theories that provide explanations of the generic features of a selected social phenomenon* (Merton, 1968; see also Bourgeois, 1979). Before they can be of practical value these theories need to be carefully applied to the specific situation by taking account of the particular and often unique circumstances that are found. Equally, as will become apparent the more that you study the subject, there are many different theoretical perspectives that can be usefully considered in trying to more fully understand a particular situation. One example of this indicated earlier was the range of separate academic disciplines that help to inform the mainstream perspective termed 'OB'. Studying OB helps you to understand and come to terms with the ambiguities that exist in the social world and to be more able to work with and around those uncertainties in whatever work experience you encounter. In short, rather than providing general answers, studying OB will help to equip you with the conceptual, theoretical and pragmatic tools that can enable you to find and create the answers that help to successfully address the questions that you come up against as a member, employee and manager of organizations.

Finally, people are the most fascinating – and often frustrating – aspect of organizational life. It is human beings who establish organizations and run them; it is human beings who work inside them and who are the customers and suppliers of these same organizations. We can neither escape organizations nor other people at any stage of our life – nor would we generally want to. Human nature and behaviour is for us an area worth studying for its own interest. As you will find when you engage with the material in this book, understanding other people will also help you understand yourself better. It is the knowledge about organizations and OB coupled with this increasing self-awareness that will help you understand better how you and others interface with organizations, and it will equip you to better survive the experience of doing so.

In summary, knowledge about OB can help us better understand the behaviour of individuals and groups in organizations – including our own behaviour. It provides the concepts and tools that can help you understand, predict and – within reason and limits – influence and even control individual and group behaviour in organizational contexts. Given the opportunities that all this offers to anyone working in or interacting with organizations, why wouldn't anyone want to know and learn more about OB? It can also be seen to influence management practice to the benefit of company, employees and customers as the High Performance example 'Working in Pret A Manger' implies.

Middle range theories, Theories that provide explanations of the generic features of a selected social phenomenon.

HOW TO STUDY ORGANIZATIONAL BEHAVIOUR

Get involved is the short answer!

OB is not a passive subject, but rather one that benefits from involvement and active participation. One of the mistakes many of those studying OB for the first

HIGH PERFORMANCE

Working in Pret A Manger

As part of the resourcing process, job candidates for 'team member' jobs in Pret A Manger sandwich shops are expected to work in a shop for part of the day. The team that they work with is then directly involved in the decision about whether or not the candidate should be offered work.

Getting the teams in the shops involved in the recruitment process resulted in existing staff feeling responsible for the new recruit and would subsequently help them become an effective part of the team more quickly. That in turn meant that the new recruit would be more likely to become an effective team member more quickly and stay with the company for a longer time. There exists a strong tradition of developing employees within the company, for example Collins Obamwanyi, a General Manager in one of the largest shops, began working as a team member in the first shop over 15 years ago; currently, 75 per cent of store managers began their Pret careers as team members.

Over the years, staff and managers have identified a range of behaviour traits that they believe makes a really successful employee – what they term a 'Pret Person'. They categorize these behaviours into three self-evident types – 'Don't Want To See', 'Want to see' and 'Pret Perfect!' Each is meant to reflect behaviours that are inappropriate, appropriate and ideal respectively. The 'standards cover three areas of the working environment, what the company term – 'Passion', 'Clear talking' and 'Team working'. Examples from each category of behaviour in relation to the areas from the working environment include:

Passion	Clear talking	Team working
(A) 'Don't want to see':		
Needs close management	Agrees blandly with others	Moody or bad tempered
Blames others	Over relies on e-mail	Annoys people
Does things only for show	Uses jargon inappropriately	Thinks only about their own needs

Passion	Clear talking	Team working
(B) 'Want to see':		
Has initiative	Listens	Creates a sense of fun
Takes ownership for their work	Admits when they don't understand or make a mistake	Is genuinely friendly
Works at pace	Uses an informal style	Helps others
(C) 'Pret perfect':		
Role model	Paints a clear picture	Anticipates others' needs
Never gives up	Constructively disagrees	Has presence
Goes the extra mile	Communicates upwards honestly	Goes out of their way to be helpful

TASKS

1 To what extent does this example reflect the adoption of sound OB principles to the management of people or simply the desire of management to achieve commercial success by getting the best value for money from employees in terms of performance and commitment?

2 Does that distinction matter and if so in what way?

Sources:
Human Resource Management International Digest (2002) *People: a key ingredient at Pret A Manger,* 10(6):6–8.
Nelson, P. (2002) Pret A Manger staff help choose the new recruits, *Personnel Today,* 23 April, p. 4.
http://www.pret.com/jobs/working_shop/ (accessed 5 May 2009).
http://www.pret.com/jobs/ (accessed 5 May 2009).
http://www.thejobsmine.co.uk/job/1313022/team-members-pret-a-manger-trafford-centre (accessed 5 May 2009).
http://www.sathnam.com/Columns/20/pret-a-manger (accessed 5 May 2009).

time make is to simply read the chapters and think that they 'know' all about it. The problem is that the theory of OB itself is not that difficult – it is the creation of value for yourself and others through the application of OB theories in real-life situations that is the challenge! Therefore, reading the chapters and testing yourself if you can recall the content accurately is only the first step in learning about OB. The next steps include reflecting on the content in the light of your own experience with and in organizations, and digging deeper into both your own experiences and the material by considering the complexity underneath the simple explanations. In fact, critically challenging your initial views, reactions, explanations and understandings of both the book content and your real-life experiences are necessary steps on the way to mastering OB. Also, by relating the book content to your own experiences you will discover what you already know about OB, and the implicit models about your own and others' behaviour in organizations that you use every day.

When reading and learning about OB think about the many organizations that you have encountered in your life (e.g., schools, colleges, shops, television and other media publishers, sports clubs, hospitals, voluntary organizations such as charities, etc.). You were probably a member or employee of many such organizations, and interacted as a customer, client, or in other ways with them. All of these experiences will have provided you with insights into how individuals and groups behave in organizations. You may have worked in organizations as an employee, or even as a manager in charge of directing other employees. You may have been a member of a sports team or a group at school trying to achieve a specific goal or task. Almost certainly you have had to work with and through others to achieve you own or collective goals. You may had to intervene in and manage conflicts between other members, to consider the use of power and influence to gain others' agreement, and to consider how best to organize, plan and structure the necessary tasks. In fact, you may not fully realize how much relevant organizational experience you actually have!

Consider the experience in and with organizations that you do have and bring it with you when you read and interact with the material in this book. For example, did you manage other people if you were a manager; or how were you managed if you were an employee? Was it simply a process of giving and following orders, or did it involve more subtlety than that? What about any experience as a student working part-time in a shop or other service organization? If you had several such jobs, was the style of management different across these organizations? If so, why and what difference did it make to how you worked and how effectively the customer was served? These experiences can all add to the material that is presented to you in this book, and additional material you find on the companion website or that will be introduced to you by the staff teaching your particular module. Also consider examples of management practice that you read about in magazines and the press.

A word of warning, however. A typical comment from those learning about OB for the first time is that much of OB is simply common sense. We have two answers to this. First, while it is correct to say that OB contains much that many of us already know and consider common sense, it is just as accurate to say that many times common sense about behavioural issues and dynamics in organizations will be wrong. The problem is that common sense is based on plausibility not accuracy. In other words, if we rely on common sense, any explanation that appears to make sense and that reflects some facts or beliefs we already hold will be accepted – unless we are prepared to dig deeper (some of the key dynamics related to this will be discussed further in Chapters 4 and 8). Thus, relying on common sense may seriously lead us astray unless we are willing and able to question and challenge our preconceived notions actively and regularly. Our second answer is that while common sense may sometimes be right, real value and understanding are often created by actively making *uncommon sense* – that is, by looking at familiar issues in new ways, by creating and considering different explanations, or by re-evaluating familiar elements and the relationships among them.

We invite and encourage you to use your natural curiosity – as well as your experience – when learning about OB. So many parts of your life involving both current and previous experience have prepared you to study OB. Actively bringing this prior knowledge and experience to your study of it will enable you to better understand the processes involved when people act and interact in organizations, and more effectively prepare you for your future career, in whatever form that might be. Learning about OB is an opportunity to create value for yourself now and into the future – and it can also be tremendous fun.

A FRAMEWORK FOR MANAGEMENT AND ORGANIZATIONAL BEHAVIOUR

So far in this chapter we have considered the nature of organizations and discussed what management and OB are. A traditional way of structuring the topics and issues that arise to manage in organizations is to consider the different levels of analysis that can be applied in studying these issues. Most commonly, these levels are called the individual, interpersonal/group, and organizational levels of analysis. Table 1.2 provides a comparison of similar hierarchical classifications often used to indicate this basic idea of ordering OB concepts, issues and areas according to different hierarchical levels, or different levels of aggregation.

In this section we will introduce a framework for management and OB that offers an overview of the book and, more importantly, that will provide a means of structuring and ultimately integrating the complex subject matter of OB. The framework we use in this book reflects these common orderings, but recognizes that the level of aggregation alone is insufficient to provide structure and order to the complex and interlinked issues and specific subject areas in OB.

As already discussed, management as a process of achieving goals through the use of any form of resources is not as simple a task as the core components of management might suggest. This is particularly true in organizations where both the people dimension and the specific circumstances of the organizational context introduce immense variety, complexity and uncertainty. Yet even though there is a lot of truth in it, the assertion that people and organizations are interfering with management (see Figure 1.2) is simplistic, or at least incomplete. It is true that they introduce

Table 1.2 Classifications of different levels of analysis in organizational behaviour

Individual	Micro	Individual	Individual
		Interpersonal	Interpersonal
Interpersonal/Group	Meso	Group	Group
		Organizational	Intergroup
Organizational	Macro	Environmental/ Societal	Organizational
			Interorganizational

Figure 1.2 The impact of people and organizations on management

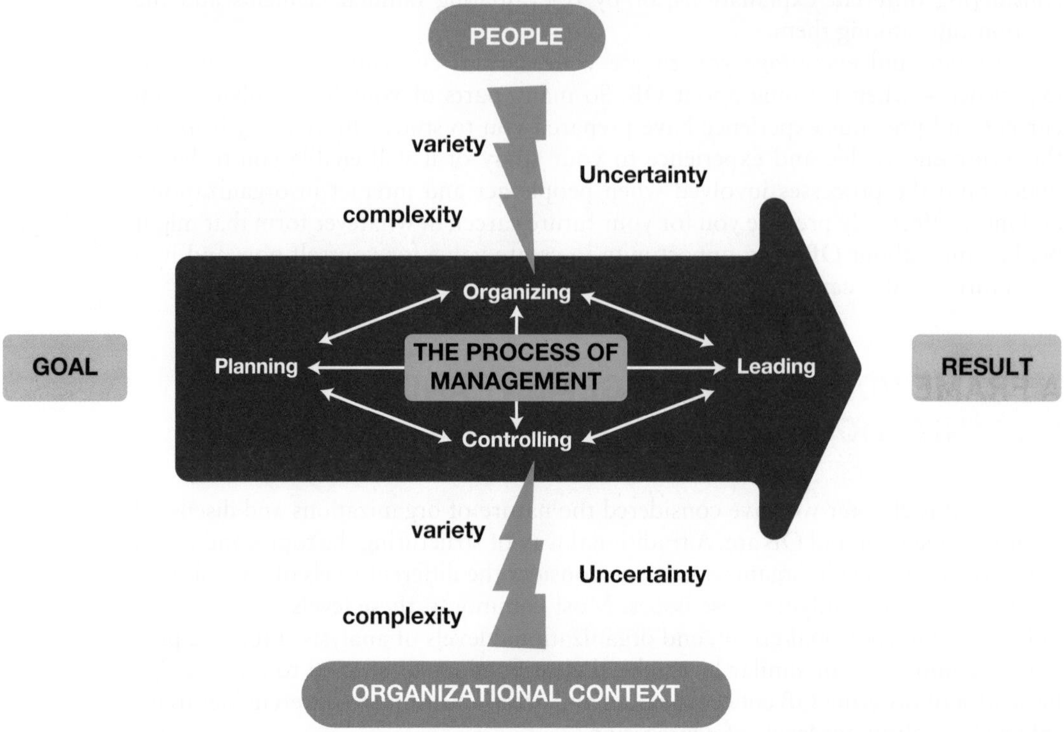

difficulties to the process of managing, yet people and organizations also provide the core resources that are used by managers to achieve their goals. It is important to remember that organizations are tools that are used to achieve goals that otherwise could not be achieved, or only at higher cost. Similarly, people are essential for achieving most organizational goals, and – more fundamentally – without them we simply would not have organizations!

A more complete model of the process of management in organizations is shown in Figure 1.3. In brief, it shows the reciprocal influence between management and people and organizations by identifying core issues and processes associated with (a) individual people, (b) interactions between and among individuals, (c) formal systems and (d) social systems in organizations. It is important to recognize the reciprocal nature of these influences because not only do these aspects impact on management, but the process of management in turn also affects them. In more detail, the first set of influences is related to individual members of organizations. It reflects the differences between individuals such as different personalities, different styles of thinking, and different levels of physical and cognitive abilities (e.g., intelligence). It also refers to the differences among individuals related to their particular ways of selecting and using information, of developing explanations about their world, and their particular goals and other factors that motivate them to behave in distinct ways.

The second set of influences is also related to people, but rather than focusing on particular individuals it reflects the impact of interactions between and among people in organizations. Aspects relevant here are leadership and management styles that can create very different experiences, and thus also results depending on the parties involved in such interactions. Similarly, it reflects the particular dynamics we can often observe in groups and teams. Some of these interpersonal issues are related to the exchange of information among people (communication) and the use of such

Figure 1.3 Reciprocal impact between management and aspects related to people and organizational context

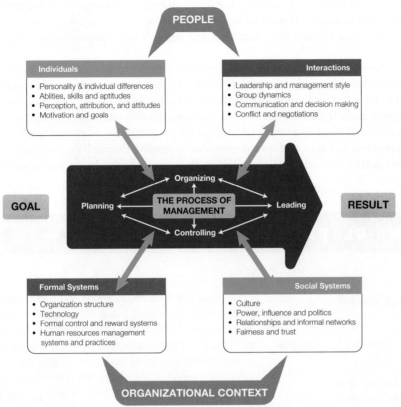

information for decision making. While individuals may well make decisions on their own, in organizations relevant decisions always affect other members as well, and joint decision making brings about distinct dynamics that need to be considered. Also, conflict and negotiation are ubiquitous in organizations that contain many different individuals who, while all having their own objectives and preferences, are also linked together through shared organizational goals and the need to collaborate to achieve them.

The third set of relevant aspects is related to the formal systems of the organization. Most fundamentally, this reflects the structure of the organization and its activities, which in part determines and is also in turn determined by the technologies deployed to achieve its objectives. It also includes formal systems for control of behaviour and activities, and evaluation and reward systems used to determine and administer formal rewards such as pay, bonuses or promotions. Similarly, it includes the formal processes and arrangements that reflect the human resource management systems and practices related to activities such as recruitment, placement, promotion, and training and development, among others.

Finally, the fourth set of influences is related to the social systems and dynamics in organizations, and reflects such fundamental issues as culture and the impact that shared norms and implicit social expectations can have on behaviour and cognition in organizations. Another aspect of the informal side of the organizational context is the use of power and influence both for achieving shared, organizational goals as well as for the pursuit of individual agendas. It also reflects the informal networks that arise out of social relationships between and among organizational members. Other relevant issues here also include fairness and trust as important aspects both of the social relationships among members, and as part of the organizational environment in terms of implicit expectations and subjective experiences. It is interesting to contemplate how factors change (or don't change) across time and locations. The Going Global example 'The art of war or is it management?' is taken from a military context in China some 2500 years ago and yet still has some relevance today – or has it?

As if these sets of variables and relationships were not complex enough, the framework would remain incomplete if it failed to recognize the myriad connections that exist between and among all of these variables. In fact, a fundamental source of complexity and uncertainty for anyone pursuing specific outcomes in organizations – be they official organizational objectives or personal agendas and goals – is the complex set of linkages and interdependencies among themselves, their actions, and all other actors and relevant variables in the organization. In organizations just as

GOING GLOBAL

Sun Tzu – The art of war or is it management?

The following extracts reflect the views of a Chinese military leader writing about 500 BC:

- The establishment of an effective military leadership depends upon five spheres:

  1 Leadership – causes people to follow their superiors willingly; therefore, following them in death and in life, the people will not betray the leader.

  2 Cyclical natural occurrences – include yin and yang, cold and heat and the seasons and lunar periods.

  3 Geographic factors – are the high and low, the wide and the narrow, the far and the near, the difficult and the easy, the lethal and the safe.

  4 Commandership – requires wisdom, credibility, benevolence, courage and discipline.

  5 Rules – are in regulations for mobilization, official duties and the management of material.

- All generals have to learn about these five spheres in their entirety. To know them is to be victorious, those who do not know them will fail.

- Each of the five spheres is evaluated through survey (research and planning).

- Military leaders who do not understand the five spheres and who do not heed the surveys will fail and should be dismissed.

It does not take much imagination to make the switch from the military leadership described above to the commercial practice of management. The need to understand and plan in relation to the market, customer needs, employee requirements and the use of rules and procedures to control the business are all as evident today as they were 2500 years ago. Equally, the need to train and evaluate leaders (managers) in relation to the role expected of them and to remove inefficient people are also described in graphic detail. It would appear from the translation used that Sun Tzu considers leadership and commandership to be related processes but consisting of different spheres. Perhaps similar to the distinctions between leadership and management as the terms would be used today.

TASKS

1 To what extent do you consider that the above ideas originating from a military context in China some 2500 years ago have any relevance to the practice of management in modern-day Europe?

Sources:
http://en.wikipedia.org/wiki/Sun_Tzu (accessed 7 May 2009).
http://www.chinapage.com/sunzi-e.html (accessed 7 May 2009).
Huang, J.H. (1993) *Sun Tzu: The New Translation. The Art of War*, New York: William Morrow and Company.
Sawyer, R.D. (1993) *The Seven Military Classics of Ancient China*, Boulder, Co: Westview Press.
Teck, F.C. and Grinyer, P.H. (1995) *Sun Tzu on Management: The Art of War in Contemporary Business Strategy*, Singapore: Butterworth-Heinemann.

in other complex social entities, deliberate actions or changes in any part can often have implications elsewhere or even throughout the whole system (Merton, 1936) – this is also known colloquially as the law of unintended consequences. Figure 1.4 indicates these interdependencies through the reciprocal arrows between management and the four sets of elements as well as through the dotted lines that connect all of these four sets of issues and processes to each other.

We will use this framework throughout the book to place the discussion of individual issues in context and to provide you with a 'roadmap' in your studies of management and OB. In more detail, in Chapter 2 we will outline the development of management thought and theory and identify some of the major challenges facing practising managers in the light of contemporary developments in business and organizations. This will complete the introduction to management and OB started in this chapter which provides the grounding for all further discussion of specific issues and topic areas. In Part 2 (Chapters 3 to 5) we will then consider 'Individuals in organizations', the first set of the issues identified in the framework above, in more detail. Chapter 3 focuses on personality and individual differences including such important issues as intelligence and emotional intelligence. Chapter 4 introduces the important concepts of perception, attribution and attitudes which are crucial for a fuller understanding of how individuals think and what contributed to their behaviour. The question of why people do what they do is central to the examination of motivation in Chapter 5. In Part 3 (Chapters 6 to 9), which focuses on 'Interactions in Organizations', we discuss leading and managing in more detail (Chapter 6). We move on to consider the nature of groups and teams and the typical dynamics within these social entities in Chapter 7. Chapter 8 focuses on the important processes of

Law of unintended consequences
Deliberate actions or changes in any part of an organization can often have implications elsewhere or even throughout the whole system that were not intended or anticipated.

Individual difference
See personality.

Figure 1.4 Comprehensive framework for organizational behaviour and management in organizations

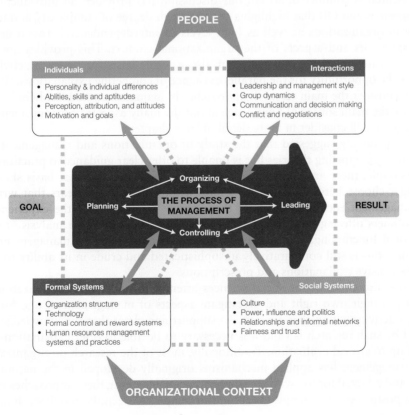

**1.2 EXTEND
YOUR LEARNING**

communication and decision making without which organizations could not exist. Chapter 9 concludes this part by examining the dynamics of conflict and conflict management, and by considering the important activity of negotiation in organizations. Part 4 (Chapters 10 to 13) addresses the 'Formal Systems and Arrangements in Organizations' in which we first focus on formal organization structures and structuring (Chapter 10). We then consider a particularly important determinant of structure, namely technology, in Chapter 11 which also explores the impact of modern information and communication technologies on management and OB. Chapter 12 examines specific formal arrangements used to control and reward behaviour in organizations, and discusses the way in which jobs are designed in organizations. Finally, we consider formal organizational practices for managing human resources in Chapter 13. We consider the next set of variables and processes, namely the 'Informal Systems and Dynamics in Organizations', in Part 5 (Chapters 14 to 16). We first consider the nature of culture in organizations in Chapter 14 and examine the role of power, influence and the use of political behaviour in Chapter 15. Chapter 16 then discusses relationships in organizations and focuses on fairness and trust, two particularly important aspects of such relationships and of OB in general.

PERSPECTIVES IN MANAGEMENT AND ORGANIZATIONAL BEHAVIOUR RESEARCH

To complete the introduction to management and OB we need to consider the kind of knowledge available about these subject areas as well as outline the ways in which such knowledge is developed through research. For this reason we will conclude this introductory chapter with a brief overview of how contemporary management and OB research is conducted. So far, our discussion has provided an introduction to management and OB that highlights the very high degree of complexity and uncertainty in organizations as well as high levels of interdependence between organizational actors and aspects of the organizational context. This provides not only challenges for practising managers but also a fertile basis for research activity as well as the opportunity for the parallel existence of competing explanations. We will briefly consider the main research approaches in management and OB here because they are the main source of knowledge about the many aspects of management and OB that we will consider in more detail in later chapters.

It is frequently suggested that the study of organizations and management provides many competing theories but is unable to offer clear guidance to practitioners. For example, there are many theories of motivation, but on what basis should a manager choose between them? It is only within the last 100 years that writings in management encompassed more than merely a reflection of the experience of practitioners offering their own recipes for success or an intuitive analysis of organizational functioning. It is hardly surprising that the study of management and organizations is still comparatively unsophisticated and crude in its ability to offer comprehensive explanations and prescriptions.

Many disciplines in the social sciences attempt to understand organizations as entities in their own right and investigate aspects of management as one form of human activity within that context. To support any claim that the knowledge generated by such research is valid it is necessary to be able to offer explanations that stand up to critical evaluation. Traditionally, most of the research on organizations and management has applied mechanisms originally developed in the natural sciences and adapted for use with social phenomena. However, these approaches which reflect postpositivist assumptions about how empirical scientific enquiries should be conducted, have not always been successful in trying to fully capture the complexity found in organizations, nor have they been able to deal with some of the philosophical challenges to the way they conceive of and describe the reality of organizations and the way that management operates.

In part this lack of success is due to the fact that the social phenomena under study are much more complex than the physical phenomena for which traditional scientific approaches were developed. The study of people and organizations is different from the study of the physical properties of metal or chemical reactions. Nevertheless, the principles of scientific enquiry can usefully be applied to research into some social areas. For example, many psychologists working at the micro level of human behaviour provide robust scientific explanations for aspects of it. Theories developed in this way are frequently based on laboratory studies in which much care is taken over the control of relevant variables and other conditions. The difficulty comes from the need to extrapolate adequately from laboratory conditions to the additional complexity and richness of human experience within real-life organizations.

Consider as an example a laboratory experiment in which decision-making strategies employed by managers are investigated. Variables such as the decision-making topic, characteristics of the individuals concerned, restrictions on extraneous factors and time limits can all be controlled and accounted for. Equally, the measurement of the process can successfully be achieved through a number of forms. For example, the actual decision made, time taken to reach a decision, individual interaction patterns and information used in the process can be assessed. However, it is difficult to be certain what such an experiment indicates about decision making by real managers in real organizations in real time and, perhaps more important, dealing with real problems with real outcomes. There are so many additional variables that can influence decision making in practice. Power, control, politics and the other complex social dynamics in organizational contexts cannot be totally accounted for in laboratory experiments. Thus, a key difficulty for applying traditional scientific approaches in organizational and management research is that it is not possible to isolate the key variables and replicate the complexity of real organizational functioning in well controlled laboratory and experimental conditions.

In a very simplified way, we can describe the empirical research on organizations and management along a continuum ranging from highly controlled but decontextualized on one side to loosely controlled yet very rich on the other. Figure 1.5 provides a simplified overview of these differences and key empirical research approaches in

Empirical research
Research that uses data on observable phenomena as the basis for generating knowledge.

Figure 1.5 Continuum of empirical research methodologies and selected specific approaches in management and organizational behaviour

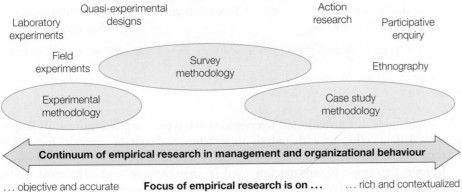

Laboratory experiments
Quasi-experimental designs
Action research
Participative enquiry
Field experiments
Survey methodology
Ethnography
Experimental methodology
Case study methodology

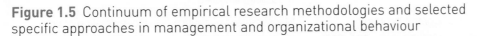

Continuum of empirical research in management and organizational behaviour

... objective and accurate description of causal relationships and control of alternative explanations

Focus of empirical research is on ...

... rich and contextualized understanding of social reality and subjective experiences

Table 1.3 Comparison of the three main social science research methodologies

	Experimental methodology	Survey methodology	Case study methodology
Main objective	Detect and confirm causal relationships	Investigate phenomenon of interest across a number of participants or units of analysis	Investigate phenomenon of interest in particular setting
Typical research designs	Experimental designs	Cross-sectional designs	Context-specific designs
Typical data collection methods	Experimental measurement	Questionnaires (often with standardized, closed question scales), interviews, occasionally observations	Interviews, observation, participant observation; occasionally supplemented by questionnaires (often with open rather than closed questions)
Typical data analysis methods	Multivariate statistics	Multivariate statistics, supplemented by appropriate qualitative data analysis (e.g., content analysis)	Appropriate qualitative data analysis, sometimes supplemented by multivariate statistical methods for quantitative data
Data type	Quantitative data	Quantitative data, sometimes supplemented by qualitative data	Qualitative data, sometimes supplemented by quantitative data
Opportunity for causal inferences from results	Strong causal inferences possible	Weak causal inferences if appropriate designs (e.g., longitudinal; quasi-experimental) or specific analytical methods (e.g., structural equations modelling) are used	Typically no causal claims, or only specific and not generalizable claims
Approach to control for unrecognized influences on results	Control through randomization and strict adherence to explicit experimental protocols	Measurement of control variables to statistically filter out their influence	Consideration of rich description of context to identify potential alternative influences

OB, while Table 1.3 provides an overview of the typical configurations of designs, data used, data collection and analysis approaches, and control strategies for the key methodologies used in OB.

Despite the range of approaches used in management and OB, most of the research on organizations reflects postpositivist thinking which is characterized by a focus on causal relationships and accurate measurement and description of an external, observable reality. Despite much internal debate in the organization studies communities about what to study and how to study it (e.g., Pfeffer, 1993; Cannella and Paetzold, 1994; Van Maanen, 1995; see also Burrell 1996; Weick, 1999), much of the mainstream organizational research that reflects psychological, sociological, political science, economic or other social science disciplines tends to adhere to such traditional approaches. One of the challenges for researchers from these fields investigating aspects of management and organizations is the ethical issue of carrying out research on human subjects. For example, Finch (1993) discusses the need to be sensitive to how any research output might be used in unintended ways (which might betray the implied trust between researcher and subject) when carrying out research grounded in the feminist tradition with other women. From another field, biochemists working in the field of new drug treatments inevitably reach a point at which they must be tested on human beings, which of course raises ethical issues.

There are research guidelines on how human beings should be studied and by which researchers must abide if they are to attract funding and recognition for their work (Kimmel, 2007). The primary difficulty presented by such requirements is that research subjects should knowingly participate and should not be subjected to risk, harm or damage in any way as a result of the process. The challenge for researchers under these conditions is to develop and test theory (or otherwise create understanding) in such a way that it is not affected by the subjects knowing that they are being studied, or at the very least that they give their informed consent to the process. Reason (1994: p. 1) even suggests that research should be carried out with people, not on them. The basic problem is how the behaviour of the subjects might have changed as a result of knowing that they were being studied. This however is only one of the problems in the research process. For example, how might the presence of the researcher influence the behaviour that they are seeking to record and understand? Again, to what extent does any response from a subject simply reflect what that person feels the researcher wishes to hear, rather than their true opinion?

STOP & CONSIDER

To what extent might it be true that any research into management or organizations has only one underlying purpose – to find out more about how and why people function and behave in such situations so that managers can more effectively exploit them in the search for greater efficiency and profit?

At the same time, organizational and management research is also home to many other approaches that take different views on the importance and role of traditional empirical methodologies and methods. Some more rationalistic research, particularly in areas such as decision making (see Keast and Towler, 2009, for an overview), extensively use modelling to develop normative and prescriptive models and to advance understanding about best practice. Another important area of research that departs from the traditional approaches discussed above is critical organizational and management studies which we will consider in more detail in turn.

Critical studies have been particularly influenced by sociological scholarship. In reviewing sociological research on organizations and management, Reed (1989) identifies three important sociological perspectives on management:

1 *Technical perspective.* A means-oriented approach to management in which it is regarded as a rationally designed 'tool' intended to achieve objectives through the co-ordination of social action.

2 *Political perspective.* Regards management as a social process intended to resolve conflict and difference between interest groups in order to allow the achievement of particular objectives.

3 *Critical perspective.* This approach regards management as a mechanism of control and domination. Managers are the representatives of the owners and as such intend to achieve results beneficial to that group. Management is therefore an instrument of the owners in pursuit of their interests.

The critical perspective in sociology reflects similar movements across the social sciences that challenge the traditional, natural-science-oriented mindset. Thompson and McHugh (1995) provide a means of defining what they term the mainstream and critical approaches to the development and interpretation of organizational theory. The main domain assumptions made in each tradition are identified in Table 1.4.

The assumptions of the mainstream approach to the study of organizations (see Table 1.4) emphasize a very rational view of the attribution of the qualities indicated. In short, they imply the application of the scientific method in the search for explanation and a science of organizations. The critical tradition, in contrast, requires approaches to the study of organizations to be:

- *Reflexive.* This implies that any approach to the study of organizations should attempt to ensure that the underlying values, practices, knowledge and expectations are not taken for granted.

- *Embedded.* This element insists that organizations need to be considered as part of a total environment. They are embedded in a context and that context needs to be understood and incorporated into any explanation.

- *Multi-dimensional.* The people dimension of an organization needs to be explained in terms of the multi-dimensional nature of human beings. Individual behaviour is formed in both a contextual and family setting, for example.

- *Dialectical and contradictory.* There are many inherently contradictory and inconsistent patterns of organizational functioning. For example, control of operational activity is a necessary aspect of managerial activity. However, this directly impacts on employee behaviour either in the form of work regulation or social control. In either case it is likely that employees will resist attempts to prescribe levels of control that they find unacceptable. This inevitably leads to attempts to increase the level of control and so a cycle of reciprocal behaviours is set up.

- *Socially transforming.* Critical theory seeks to empower all members of an organization. This notion, sometimes referred to as *praxis*, holds that

Table 1.4 Domain assumptions of the mainstream and critical approaches to the study of organizations

Domain assumptions of mainstream approaches	Domain assumptions of critical approaches
Organizations as goal-seekers	Reflexivity
Search for rational-efficiency-based order and hierarchy	The embeddedness of organizations
Managerialism	Multidimensionality
Search for organizational science	Dialectics and contradiction
	Social transformation

Source: Thompson, P. and McHugh, D. (1995), Work Organizations, London: Macmillan.

individuals can be encouraged to see beyond the existing constraints and to be able to reflect on and engineer a reconstruction of their 'reality'.

Similar differences are discussed for critical management studies (e.g., Alvesson & Willmott, 1996) which developed in response to the view that management studies are largely dominated by postpositivist approaches. Griffin (1993) grouped many of the relevant schools of thought he views as mainstream perspectives on management under headings that include *classical perspectives* (i.e., scientific management, administrative management), *behavioural perspectives* (i.e., human relations, OB), *quantitative perspectives* (i.e., management science, operations management), and *integrating perspectives* (i.e., systems theory, contingency theory). While many would see this classification as debatable, it provides a useful summary of the mainstream perspectives that have influenced the history of management thought, and that in many cases continue to influence today's research on management theory and practice.

Alvesson and Willmott (1996: pp. 10-11) argue that the mainstream perspectives are limited in their ability to offer a comprehensive explanation of management because they ascribe to it the qualities of a technical activity which underplays the social relations and political dimensions involved. They describe the critical perspective on the study of management as incorporating the following characteristics (pp. 38–39):

- *Management is a social practice.* The evolution of management reflects a practice that emerged within a social, historical and cultural context. It cannot be separated from that context if it is to be understood properly.

Table 1.5 Mainstream management perspectives

Classical perspectives
- Scientific management. Concerned with the systematic evaluation of work and the search for higher productivity
- Administrative management. A forerunner of the systems approach, attempting to identify ways of managing the whole organization

Behavioural perspectives
- Human relations. An approach to management based upon the importance of groups and the social context
- Organizational behaviour. A holistic approach to managing organizations incorporating individual, group and organizational processes

Quantitative perspectives
- Management science. The development of mathematical models as the basis of decision making and problem solving
- Operations management. That areas of management attempting to produce the goods or services more effectively

Integrating perspectives
- Systems theory. A range of approaches to the study of organizations and management that attempt to cast these issues as an interrelated set of elements which are able to function as a whole
- Contingency theory. An approach which views the behaviour in any given context as a function of a wide set of contingent factors acting upon that situation

Contemporary
- Popularism. This reflects the wide variety of fads and fashions that gain rapid credence and just as quickly fade into obscurity. Only a few approaches in this category ever last longer than a few years or become a sustainable basis for actual managerial behaviour

Source: Adapted from: Griffin, RW (1993) Management, 4th edn, Houghton Mifflin, Boston, MA.

EMPLOYEE PERSPECTIVE

What employees might think of their boss!

The following comments were made by employees about their experiences of their boss:

'I work in a sales support office and today I had a performance appraisal meeting with my boss. He told me that I was the best worker in the office and that productivity has improved since I started working in it about one year earlier. Then he said that because of the sales downturn as a result of the recession they were going to have to make someone redundant and because I had the shortest length of service it was going to be me.'

'I am a sales executive and was standing-in as sales manager for my boss while he was on his annual two week summer holiday. I am keen to develop my career and saw the temporary promotion as an opportunity to gain experience and demonstrate my abilities to my boss. During the time that I was acting as sales manager I did a good job, sales increased and I was able to instigate several new leads with strong conversion possibilities. When he came back to work I told him about what I had done, hoping for some acknowledgement of my good work or even praise. Instead all he could say was "You killed my plant!"'

TASKS

1   How would you react to these situations if you were the employees concerned? As an employee what would you 'learn' from these experiences about managers as people and as your superior? If you were a manager how could you avoid such situations?

- *Tensions exist in management practice.* The experienced reality of management as a political and social process is different from that postulated in the mainstream perspectives as a rational process seeking to apply impartial and scientific techniques to the problems of managing. This is evident in the Employee perspective example 'What employees might think of their boss!' in which managers might be 'managing as they see it', but that is not how the employees perceive it!

- *Critical studies are themselves embedded.* Although critical studies attempt to acknowledge the existence of the tensions inherent in management, they are themselves embedded in a particular context. Consequently, they need to incorporate a measure of reflexivity in them.

- *Critical studies seek to illuminate and transform power relations.* Critical studies attempt to transform the practice of management as well as illuminate it.

- *Critical theory contains an emancipatory intent.* One of the purposes of critical theory is to provide a basis for individuals within organizations to become free from the constrictions implicit in mainstream views.

- *Critical analysis is concerned with the critique of ideology.* It is implied that modern forms of control and domination are maintained through the theories and ideologies that underpin and inform the running of society and organizations. The questioning of received wisdom on how things should be provides a basis for liberation and emancipation.

- *Critical theory implies more than a reconstruction of mainstream perspectives.* Critical thinkers seek to achieve fundamental change in the essentially power-based nature of management.

In addition to the mainstream and critical perspectives discussed above, post-modernism as another approach is also enriching the landscape of organization and management studies. Thompson and McHugh (1995) discuss modernism and post-modernism as alternative formulations of social reality. Modernism refers to the representational aspects of a 'grand narrative, a coherent story about the development of the social and natural, revealed through the application of reason and science' (p. 378). Postmodernists, in contrast, reject that cohesion, arguing that reality is made up of a differing range of realities and that it is constructed by our ability to express (or formulate) it. It is a view that holds that the 'truth is a product of language games' (p. 379). In fact, postmodernism has roots going back to the 1920s in the arts and the 1940s in social commentary. In literature and social sciences, it has gained importance and influence in the 1960s. At its heart, postmodernism is based on a challenge to the comprehensive, cumulative, coherent and logic-based views of activities and developments brought forward in all areas of life, including work. A typical but not necessary style element of postmodernism is irony, which is often expressed through the overuse of distinctive elements of modern approaches and practices. In the sense that it often draws attention to conventions and shared assumptions it is similar to critical theory, although the shared intent, inherent in all critical theory approaches, of exposing and questioning existing power sources and structures itself would be challenged by postmodern commentaries.

In organization and management theory, postmodern approaches are valuable because they serve as a critical voice questioning the inevitability and totality of modern rationality as expressed in the ways in which organizations and jobs are structured and designed. Maybe more accurately, it is the way in which the resulting reality is named and presented as the central and only way to conceive of organizations that postmodernism most ferociously challenges. Chia (2003) for example describes the modernist approach of naming, classification and representation of organizational phenomena through language and managerial jargon as a reductionistic operation that subjugates the diverse lived experience of different organizational members, including both managers and employees, and instils as a result a misleading and false shared view and identity. Alternatively, the postmodern position would argue that 'the world is formless, fragmented and intertextual: there is no hidden order, what you see on the surface is all there is' (Hatch and Cunliffe, 2006). Further discussion of postmodern views can be found on the companion website.

1.3 EXTEND YOUR LEARNING

Modernism
An approach to management and organizational theory based on the existence of a 'grand narrative' – a coherent story about the development of the social and natural, revealed through the application of reason and science. See also postmodernism.

Postmodernism
An approach to management and organizational theory that rejects modernism, arguing that reality is made up of a differing range of realities and that it is constructed by our ability to express (or formulate) it through language. See also modernism.

CONCLUSIONS

This chapter has introduced organizations, management and OB and introduced the framework that provides both the outline for this book, and a means for integrating the many connected elements, issues, and theories relevant for OB. The purpose of this chapter has been to set the scene for much of the later work in the book. It also sets out to provide readers with some background to the research issues and approaches that are used to inform thinking in this and other areas of the study of management and organizations.

Now to summarize this chapter in terms of the relevant Learning Objectives:

- **Understand why organizations exist, and identify and explain how they can influence the behaviour of organizational members**.
Organizations are social entities that are goal-directed, that are inextricably linked to their environment yet have nominal boundaries, and that employ deliberately designed and co-ordinated activities and approaches to achieving their objectives. In summary, the reasons why organizations exist are that (a) they are more effective than the alternatives, i.e., organizations offer the opportunity to achieve objectives unachievable without them; and (b) they offer efficiencies compared to their alternatives, i.e., they help achieve these goals faster or with less economic, cultural, social, political or moral costs.

- **Describe how knowledge about individual and group behaviour in organizations can contribute to successful management**. People within an organization are trained to carry out their specific job responsibilities. This may be on the job, which is very realistic but often leaves little time for reflection and deeper learning, or off-the-job, which is often very specific but may not capture all important aspects of the job and new knowledge may not be fully transferred back to the real work setting. Moreover, many times the training that organizational members receive is focused on the practical and technical aspects of their work whether that be in sales, marketing, finance, operations, or whatever. But the technical aspects of any job represent only a small part of any work activity. Very few people work without direct contact with other people, and no one in any organization works without some form of interdependency with other members. People work in groups or teams, they are members of specific departments, they have customers and suppliers (inside and outside of the organization), and they have superiors and subordinates to report to and to direct and control. The resulting webs of relationships are both formal and informal in nature, but they all involve other people. Most jobs involve some degree of persuading people to co-operate with some priority, action, or request involving a degree of inconvenience to themselves. For employees, it is important to understand what the company expects of them in return for their pay, advancement opportunities and continued employment. At the same time, it is important to understand how their colleagues and managers may think about work, management, leadership, collaboration and all the other important aspects of work life in organizations. For managers it is necessary to know how to deal with problem employees (not everyone co-operates all of the time), or with other managers who are seeking to advance their careers and are therefore in competition for more senior appointments. In summary, knowledge about OB can help us better understand the behaviour of individuals and groups in organizations – including our own behaviour. It provides the concepts and tools that can help you understand, predict and – within reason and limits – influence and even control individual and group behaviour in organizational contexts.

- **Identify categories of influencers of behaviour in organizations, and outline how they can impact on management in organizations.** A comprehensive model of the process of management in organizations is shown in Figure 1.3. In brief, it shows the reciprocal influence between management and people and organizations by identifying core issues and processes associated with (a) individual people, (b) interactions between and among individuals, (c) formal systems and (d) social systems in organizations. Each of these is discussed in this and subsequent chapters.

- **Understand distinctions between research in the natural and in the social sciences.** This chapter has sought to introduce the distinction between natural and social science research. In the natural sciences, it is possible to utilize the scientific method of research and to seek to control closely each of the variables active in any situation in laboratory-based experiments. In the social world it is not often possible to provide such control and equally behaviour is an interactive, dynamic process occurring in real time and with many other variables influencing events. Consequently different research methods have to be employed to illuminate such events and equally it is rarely possible to offer definitive explanations of particular behaviours.

- **Explain the particular difficulties involved in studying and developing theories in the area of management, and in applying the knowledge of OB in practice.** The previous outline has provided a brief explanation of this objective. There are so many variables at work in even the simplest forms of human behaviour in an organizational context that it is very difficult to provide complete explanations or theories that might explain them. Therefore any theory is at best simply reflecting a probability that certain behaviours will occur in certain situations, given a range of other prerequisites. This is particularly true when considering management as a separate activity within organizations.

- **Discuss how the study of organizational behaviour can contribute to an understanding of management.** The study of OB is about understanding how people and organizations interact. As has already been suggested, this represents a complex relationship with many factors active in any situation. The purpose of studying OB is to begin to understand the variety of forces influencing behaviour within an organization, including the behaviour of other people, the design of organizations, the role of technology, political forces and stress. Management requires the achievement of objectives through other people at all levels both inside and outside an organization. Therefore OB seeks to illuminate the nature and responsibilities of management (among those of other stakeholders) in running organizations more effectively.

DISCUSSION QUESTIONS

1 'Management represents the combination of experience and practical skill, it cannot be taught. Therefore there is no point in studying management'. Discuss this statement and in so doing justify the study of OB.

2 'Management is a manipulative process.' Discuss the extent to which you agree or disagree with this statement and explain why.

3 'It is not possible to generate robust social science theories because there are so many variables at work. It requires the development of a totally new science.' To what extent would you agree with this statement and why?

4 'There is no such thing as a typical organization or management job therefore it is pointless attempting to theorize about them.' To what extent would you agree with this view? Justify your answer.

5 Table 1.3 and Figure 1.5 compare the major social science research methods. From that table and figure it is clear that the 'experimental' design has no real ability to contribute to an understanding of OB and management as it is not possible to control the variables at work in real organizations. Discuss this point of view.

6 'The anthropomorphic view of organizations held by many managers and writers is unhelpful to the theory and practice of management as it imbues qualities to an entity that does not have them.' Discus this statement.

7 'Because employees actually do the work of the organization they are in a stronger position than managers to know how to do things more effectively.' To what extent might this be taken to imply that if employees could be motivated more effectively, most management jobs could be eliminated?

8 What is an organization and why do you think that individual human beings seek jobs as managers in them?

9 'The study of OB enables managers to become more effective at their job.' Discuss this statement.

10 Figure 1.2 identifies that people bring variety, uncertainty and complexity to the organizational process. The major implication is that to achieve success every manager needs to have experience in managing people rather than an understanding of OB. Discuss this point of view.

CASE STUDY

The reality of management life!

The case study is based on a large multi-national service organization operating in the UK, although the parent group is based in the USA. The company makes and supplies office equipment and maintains existing equipment in client premises under service agreements. It also refurbishes equipment as clients need it updating or changing. The specific incidents reflected in the case study occurred in the refurbishment division of the company in the UK. The refurbishment division was headed by a manager (Mark) who had reporting to him seven field managers, each responsible for up to seven engineers who carried out any refurbishment and commissioning of

equipment on client premises. Each field manager was responsible for a refurbishment in a specific geographic location of the UK. In addition, the refurbishment manager had reporting to him seven sales managers, one in each geographic area as indicated for the field managers; and a number of other senior technical and administrative staff, including a planning manager, secretary and two administrative assistants. The refurbishment manager reported to the director of operations for the UK company.

The case study is based on a situation that developed involving one of the field managers. The individual concerned (James) was 63 years of age and had worked for the company for 35 years, beginning as a service engineer and working his way up to the position of field manager. He had always worked in the same geographic area of the country and was well known and respected by both clients and fellow engineers. He had held his present position for 3 years at the time of the incidents described. At the time that James was appointed to his current position the company had undertaken a major reorganization of its activities. He along with all of the other managers had to undergo a recruitment and selection process involving interviews, psychometric tests and assessment centres intended to select the best candidates for the reduced number of management jobs within the new organization structure. James met the appropriate criteria and was appointed to the position of field manager (refurbishment). This itself was a new department within the company as previously refurbishment had been undertaken as a service activity within the company.

As a consequence of the reorganization the refurbishment department was created from among existing employees brought together with the intention that a viable team and working unit would emerge over time. In some cases line managers within the company had engineered situations in which a number of their weaker employees were transferred over to the new department as a way of getting rid of low-performing individuals, those with less capability and those regarded as lazy or simply trouble-makers.

© Helen King/Corbis

Whilst there was no suggestion that James was one of these employees, some of his engineers fell into that category, as did some of the support staff moved into the department.

The refurbishment manager (Mark) was moved into the department from the position of area sales manager, having gone through the internal recruitment process and being identified as a high-flyer within the company. The brief that Mark was given was to generate increased sales of 10 per cent in the first year, to reduce customer complaints by 10 per cent over the same period and to create an effective refurbishment department across the entire UK operations. Not surprisingly there were many teething problems in the new department and Mark spent the first year firefighting in an attempt to limit the damage and achieve the objectives set whilst maintaining effective customer relations. He spent much of his time on the road visiting his managers, the worksites and customers. It quickly became apparent that the difficulties with the new department went further than a few underperforming employees. It was apparent that prior to the changeover to the new structure a number of managers had either deliberately or accidentally allowed jobs to become seriously delayed or badly planned. Also a number of unrealistic promises (and quotations) had been made to clients and potential customers. This situation increased the pressure on everyone in the refurbishment department, particularly the managers.

A broad sweep of measures was instigated by Mark to improve the effectiveness of the new department, including team meetings and team-building activities. This was on top of Mark spending a considerable amount of time with each team in order to monitor their work and ensure that they were working to the new procedures and requirements. It quickly became apparent to Mark that the department did not have enough people to undertake all of the work expected of them. The sales engineers were able to bring in enough orders, but the engineering side were unable to carry out the refurbishment work fast enough. This was partly due to the lack of engineers, partly due to the inexperience of some of the field managers, partly due to the quality of some of the staff (as implied earlier) and partly due to the need to improve team working across the new department. One particular area of difficulty was in the area under the leadership of James. He had considerable experience with the company, its products and the engineering processes involved, but there always seemed to be more problems in his area than in the others. Mark tried several ways to overcome the difficulties. He spent more time with James than with any of the other field managers to help James to plan his work and to deal with problem engineers. However, nothing seemed to work. One of the major problems was that James was finding it particularly difficult to use the new company computer-based systems. He did not like to use the e-mail system and was not comfortable with the inevitable politics that accompany management activity. For example, the sales engineers in his area were becoming so frustrated with the lack of completed work for their clients that they had taken to e-mailing James to complain on a frequent basis, at the same time circulating the e-mail to Mark and even his boss (the director) for information. This inevitably resulted in questions being asked of Mark and pressure being put on him to take action.

Mark eventually sat James down and had a frank discussion with him about what was going on. Eventually during the discussion, it emerged that James was very unhappy with the new job. It was completely different from his previous managerial task and required him to do jobs and tasks that he did not enjoy or feel competent to do. He even admitted that it was getting him down so much he was being physically sick most mornings before leaving home to go to work. He just felt so helpless and out of his depth in being able to do the job expected of him. Mark was taken aback by this revelation, not having suspected the personal nature of the situation. Thinking about the meeting afterwards, he decided to speak to his boss about a number of options. These included the possibility of re-assignment within the company or giving James an early retirement package to allow him to leave work with some dignity. In speaking to his boss, it quickly became apparent that these were not going to be options that would be allowed. Mark's boss said that James was not up to the job and should either be forced to resign or should be dismissed. It was not going to be possible to find James alternative

work within the company that would make use of his considerable experience and knowledge about the company, its products, processes and customers. No enhanced retirement or other package would be made available in his case. The management view was that the company should get tough with underperforming employees and that they should be made to perform by the threat that otherwise they would be dismissed without any compensation. The fact that James had very long service with the company and had always been a good employee was deemed to be irrelevant.

Mark was appalled by what he was told by his boss. It represented a completely different attitude by a senior manager to that common before the reorganization. Clearly, a new get tough approach was to be the new way of managing people within the company. Mark pushed as hard as he could within the company for a special case to be made for James, but to no avail. Mark was essentially told that if he did not deal with James he would be replaced as well. Mark arranged to see James, told him of the situation, and suggested that he would have good ground for legal action against the company if they dismissed him. James said that such an approach was not his style and that he was going to resign and walk away with his dignity intact. He handed Mark a letter of resignation and left the office. Mark felt so angry at how James had been dealt with that he also began to look around for another job and left the company about 3 months later.

TASK

1 What does this case suggest to you in relation to:
  (a) What management is?
  (b) What being an employee means?
  (c) How managers manage?
  (d) The signal that management's behaviour might send to other employees?
  (e) What an organization is and how they change over time?

FURTHER READING

Burrell, G. and Morgan, G. (1979) *Sociological Paradigms and Organizational Analysis: Elements of the Sociology of Corporate Life*. Aldershot. Ashgate. A classic review of different perspectives in organizational theorizing.

Clegg, S.R. and Palmer, G. (eds) (1996) *The Politics of Management Knowledge*, London: Sage. This text explores the relationship between management knowledge, power and practice within an increasingly global organizational environment.

de la Billière, General Sir P. (1994) *Looking For Trouble*, London: HarperCollins. An autobiography of a senior military officer, this book provides an insight into the nature of leadership as well as military organization.

Mills, A.J. and Murgatroyd, S.J. (1991) *Organizational Rules*, Milton Keynes: Open University Press. This text introduces the existence of the formal and informal rule frameworks that guide much of the human activity within organizations.

Morgan, G. (2006) *Images of organization* (new edn), Thousand Oaks, CA: Sage. A new edition of a classic – identifies and discusses stimulating and valuable perspectives on how organizations are and can be viewed.

Needle, D. (2010) *Business in Context: An Introduction to Business and its Environment.* Andover: Cengage Learning. Provides an introductory text on what business is and how it functions within its ever-changing environment.

Scott, W.R. (2003) *Organizations: Rational, natural and open systems* (5th edn), Prentice Hall. Useful updated version of the classic discussion on the nature of organizations.

Weick, K.E. (1979) The social psychology of organizing (2nd edn.), London: Sage. Well written, interesting, wide-ranging and thought-provoking classic contribution.

COMPANION WEBSITE

Online teaching and learning resources

Visit the companion website for Organizational Behaviour and Management 4th edition at: http://www.cengage.co.uk/martinfellenz to find valuable further teaching and learning material. For full details, see 'About the website' at the start of the book.

CHAPTER TWO

©ermingut/istock

ORGANIZATIONAL BEHAVIOUR AND CURRENT MANAGEMENT CHALLENGES

LEARNING OBJECTIVES

After studying this chapter and working through the associated OB in Action panels, Discussion Questions and Case Study you should be able to:

- Assess the significance of some of the ethical dilemmas facing managers.

- Explain why people and groups might be expected to resist change.

- Discuss the significance of the contemporary management challenges for the theory and practice of management and organizational behaviour.

- Outline the relative contribution to an understanding of management from the historical perspective and through each of the different schools and perspectives on management that have evolved across time.

- Understand the different approaches to ethics.

INTRODUCTION

Management theory has changed over time in response to historical changes in social, economic, cultural, technological, ecological and political arrangements and processes, as well as – obviously – the changing nature of management practice. In this chapter, we briefly review the development of modern management thinking to provide grounding for the study of current management and OB in this book. Moreover, we identify four central current management issues that characterize some of the most important challenges that managers and organizations face in the interlinked, networked and highly competitive world of today. We will discuss these four challenges in turn and use them throughout the book to explain, highlight and consider specific aspects of management and OB theory and practice.

THE DEVELOPMENT OF MODERN MANAGEMENT THINKING

Organizations have always existed in one form or another. When human beings began to develop collective activity as a means of improving their chances of survival and quality of life, the basis of the social organization was formed and management processes were employed. Some organizational principles and management practices used today have precursors going back thousands of years. The following Management in action panel identifies a number of management practices from ancient Babylon that are almost 4000-years-old that retain modern parallels. Many of the practices used during ancient and medieval times are still reflected in the way today's organizations are structured and managed, and many contemporary managers still take advice from some classic contributions such as Sun Tzu's *The Art of War* or Machiavelli's *The Prince*. The most obvious and well known origins of today's practices, however, have been developed during more recent times; especially during the first and second industrial revolution (see Table 2.1). The companion website provides further details on organizational and management practices in ancient and medieval times as well as more detailed discussions of the historical roots arising from the interactions among social, political, cultural, economic and religious factors that have given rise to modern organization and management practices.

2.1 EXTEND
YOUR LEARNING

Prior to the twentieth century the management literature tended to be based around the writings of individuals who tried to bring their own perspectives and experiences to the attention of a wider audience. For example, Charles Babbage (1832), a mathematician by training, attempted to offer ideas on how to improve the efficiency of operational activity. However, it was not until the beginning of the twentieth century that the study of management began to feature systematically as a major activity in its own right. This is also the time that business and management topics became formally part of university education. We have briefly alluded to the main perspectives on management research already in Chapter 1 and will provide additional insights into these perspectives and the way in which they contribute to contemporary management thinking in the next sections.

SCIENTIFIC AND ADMINISTRATIVE MANAGEMENT

Scientific management

The application of science to the running of organizations can be argued to have occurred even during ancient and medieval times. During the industrial revolutions in the eighteenth and nineteenth centuries, many individuals and firms

Table 2.1 Selected management concepts from the Industrial Revolution

Approximate year	Individual group	Contribution
1767	Sir James Stewart	Source of authority and impact of automation
1776	Adam Smith	*Wealth of Nations*, specialization, control
1799	Eli Witney	Scientific method, quality control, span of management
1800	James Watt	Standard operating procedures
	Matthew Boulton	Planning, work methods, incentive wages
1810	Robert Owen	Personnel management, training, workers' housing
1820	James Mill	Human movement at work
1832	Charles Babbage	Scientific approach to work organization
1835	Marshall Laughlin	Relative importance of management aspects of work

Source: George, CS. (1972) *The History of Management Thought* (2nd edn), Prentice Hall, Englewood Cliffs. Reproduced with permission.

in different countries employed highly structured and deliberate activities to improve work and management practices (see Currie, 1963; Jevons, 1888; Wren, 1994) However, it is F.W. Taylor (1911) who is probably best known for bringing together several strands of thinking into a single methodology for applying scientific principles to the design and organization of work. His approach, aptly named 'scientific management', advocates the use of work-study techniques in the systematic investigation of work and the subsequent matching of worker to job requirements (see also Chapter 12).

Taylor's approach to scientific management involved the systematic identification of what each job involved in terms of the demands made on the individual worker. The design of appropriate tools and equipment, the selection and training of appropriate employees capable of doing the job, the encouragement of high productivity through the use of incentive-based wage structures and the appropriate management of work all followed from that start. Taylor began to apply his ideas on work that was routine and repetitive. The example typically quoted is the loading of iron slabs that each weighed 92 pounds onto railroad trucks. This was carried out within the Bethlehem Iron Company, in which he had been employed to improve output. Through the systematic study of what was involved in the work, Taylor identified what he termed as the 'one best way' of performing the task. He then recruited men with the appropriate physical characteristics to undertake the heavy transportation task, taught them exactly what was required of them and paid them on a piecework basis. Piecework is an incentive wage system that pays a sum of money for each unit of output produced. The higher the output achieved, the higher the wage earned. By using this combination of factors, he was able to increase the daily output by a factor approaching 400 per cent.

Scientific management An approach to management based on the application of work study techniques to the design and organization of work in order to identify the 'one best way'; subsequently involves matching the worker to job requirements and motivating them to maximize output.

MANAGEMENT IN ACTION

Babylonian management practice

The following extracts from the Code of Hammurabi, originating from around 1800 BC, demonstrate that many of today's familiar management concepts were around and in practice at the time that the above code was written:

- *Minimum wage:*
  'If a man hires a field labourer, he shall pay him 8 gus of grain per year.'

- *Control:*
  'If a merchant gives to an agent grain, wool, oil or goods of any kind to trade, the agent shall write down the value and return the money to the merchant. The agent shall take a sealed receipt for the money, which he gives to the merchant. If the agent be careless and do not take a receipt for the money which he has given to his merchant the money not receipted for shall not be placed in his account.'

- *Responsibility:*
  'The mason who builds a house which falls down and kills the inmate shall be put to death.'
  'If a wine merchant allows riotous men to assemble in his house and does not expel them, he shall be killed.'
  'If a doctor operates on a wound with a copper lancet, and the patient dies, or on the eye of a gentleman who loses his eye in consequence, his hands shall be cut off.'

TASKS

1 To what extent do you consider that the concepts and practices described above are likely to be the same across the centuries, but that the social context within which they are carried out that changes?

2 What does your answer to the previous question imply about the understanding and practice of management today?

Source:
George, CS (1972) *The History of Management Thought*, 2nd edn, Prentice Hall, Englewood Cliffs. Reproduced with permission.

STOP & CONSIDER

If your boss proposed an incentive scheme to you that paid you extra money for producing more work, how much extra money would you want to achieve an increase in output of about 400 per cent? If you were the boss how much extra would you be prepared to pay a worker to produce 400 per cent more output (your objective is to maximize the profits of the company)? Can these two positions ever be reconciled? Why or why not? What does your work on this topic suggest about productivity as reflected in scientific management?

It was left to the people who followed Taylor to develop his ideas and approaches so that implementation could be achieved. Names such as Gantt and Gilbreth are among the most famous who developed aspects of his work and formed the basis of much modern industrial engineering practice. Wheatcroft (2000) for example, provides a brief overview of the trends in scientific management practice during the twentieth century. Taylor's ideas also found support in the fledgling Soviet Union as the country sought to develop the centralized approach to the mass production of goods and utilities with little by way of skilled labour to call on. The ideas inherent in scientific management will reappear again in several chapters of this book.

Administrative and classical management theory

Another stream of thinking emphasized the view that management as an activity involved the undertaking of tasks relative to the running of the organization as a whole. Individuals such as Weber, Fayol and Barnard would be considered to fall within this general category. Many terms have been used to classify this approach to management thinking and the one preferred here is administrative management. The other major term used in this area is classical management, both terms reflecting a view of what has been described as a traditional perspective on organizational functioning.

The ideas developed by these writers are discussed in more detail in Chapters 6 and 10 and will not be covered in depth here. Weber's ideas on bureaucracy were developed at a time when the size and complexity of organizations were increasing rapidly and there was no computer-based technology to assist with the routine processing of administrative work. The following Employee perspective illustrates one aspect of life in a large bureaucracy, the ability to 'play the system'. Fayol identified functions such as planning, organizing and controlling associated with the management process. He also indicated important principles of management that are still central to contemporary management approaches. Barnard was a practising manager (like Taylor, Fayol and many of his predecessors) and his contribution to management and organizational thinking was to describe an organization as a co-operative system. In this view, he was hinting at much of what was to follow in the human relations movement in which the people aspects of the organization feature more strongly. It is also an early recognition of the systems view of organizational thinking in which the integrated nature of many aspects of organization and environment are postulated to form an integrated, interactive and mutually dependent entity.

Administrative management
Considers management as those activities aimed at running the organization as a whole. See also classical management theory and bureaucracy.

Classical management theory
An approach to organizing emphasized issues such as the scalar chain, exception principle, unity of command, organizational specialization, span of control and the application of scientific management and not just structure. See also administrative management and bureaucracy.

EMPLOYEE PERSPECTIVE

Patricia's boss promoted his staff!

Patricia worked in a federal government department in the USA and she told the following story to one of the authors in a general conversation about working in the public sector.

Patricia worked for the Department of Agriculture in what was a large regional administrative headquarters located in Texas. Her department dealt with statistics in relation to crop yields, production and prices at a regional, national and international level. Consequently it involved considerable amounts of collecting data, computer analysis and modelling as well as the inevitable administrative 'paperwork'. Patricia's boss was very good at 'playing the system' and he recognized that the bigger his department became and the more highly qualified and skilled personnel that worked for him the higher his own grade and salary would become. Consequently, he was always looking to absorb new sections, jobs, work and people into his department. Also he was constantly encouraging his subordinates at all levels to ensure that their job descriptions were kept under review and if any changes in job content were justified he encouraged individuals to rewrite them and seek a re-evaluation of their jobs under the government job evaluation scheme.

He instinctively knew that the bigger his department became and the greater number of higher-graded people that worked for him the higher grade of job that he could claim to hold. With a higher grade his own salary and benefits package also grew. It was a 'game' that he played very successfully over a number of years until it became obvious that there was no more scope to gain promotion as the jobs above him were not capable of moving in parallel with his job changes. His next 'game-plan' was to seek early retirement, which it took him several years to achieve, but he eventually retired a happy man and was very satisfied with his career achievements in the public service.

TASKS

1 To what extent do you think that this example would be typical of how people approach work – they try to achieve their own objectives through the processes and procedures that the employer offers?

2 As a senior manager how could you judge if employees (at any level) were adopting such approaches to work?

3 Further to tasks 1 and 2, does it matter so long as the organization is successful?

4 How could you manage or control such self-serving behaviour?

Bureaucracy
An approach to organizing the activities within an organization which involves specialization of task, hierarchy of authority and decision making. See also classical management theory and administrative management.

Human relations movement
The school of management thinking that originated from the work of Elton Mayo in which the significance of social groups and social processes were emphasized.

Quantitative school
A mathematical approach to management that seeks to find ways of modelling relationships between variables so that causal relationships can be identified and predictions made.

2.2 EXTEND YOUR LEARNING

Appreciative enquiry
Deliberately focuses on investigating and strengthening what is already beneficial and successful in organizations rather than on adopting a problem or clinical approach that focuses on difficulties and failures.

THE HUMAN RELATIONS AND QUANTITATIVE SCHOOLS

There is a very strong emphasis on the task aspects of organizational functioning in much of the earlier work already discussed, particularly scientific management. In addition, there was the general unrest among workers and managers that followed from attempts to direct and control work activity. It is hardly surprising, therefore, to find a counter-trend emerging. This developed with the human relations approach to understanding behaviour within an organization. Equally, the emphasis on the soft issues associated with people and work relationships was followed in time by the emergence of a hard approach based on numbers and data – the quantitative school.

The human relations school

Early research on the human relations aspects of work activity revolved around the nature of groups and the interactive functioning of group effort. There were two broadly parallel initiatives underway, one in England, the other in America. In England towards the end of World War I a series of studies was set up by the Industrial Fatigue Research Board into aspects of working conditions. One report from that research programme, published in 1928, identified the existence of a slight benefit when operatives worked in groups (Huczynski and Buchanan, 2001). Similar work was also ongoing in the US, and the development of sociometry as a means for recording, analysing and determining group composition and interaction provided methodological support for research into social dynamics (Wren, 1994).

The Hawthorne studies are widely claimed to be the most significant forerunner of the human relations movement and of research on group activity within organizational settings. The studies are discussed in greater detail on the companion website. In short, they began in 1924 with the simple objective of discovering the effects of illumination on worker productivity and ended in 1933 with research output describing the importance of groups and group-based behaviour on activity at work. Gillespie (1991) provides an authoritative source on both the research itself and the organizational, social and academic conditions under which it was undertaken. From a reading of this work, it is quite clear that it is difficult, if not impossible, to separate research and the interpretation of its output, from the organizational, social, political and personal surroundings in which it takes place.

This is particularly true in a very active contemporary offspring of the human relations school called action research (also called action science). Action research focuses on combining an action or change orientation with collaborative problem solving that involves researchers (or managers) and members of the studied social system (e.g., group, organization) in often iterative, cyclical interactions (see e.g., Coghlan and Brannick, 2010). Much of action research draws from Kurt Lewin's work, and it typically reflects a strong humanistic value orientation but can take many different forms when applied in research or organization development and change. Reason and Bradbury describe it as 'a family of practices of living enquiry . . . [that] is not so much a methodology as an orientation to enquiry' (2008: p. 1; see also Cassell and Johnson, 2006). A particular form of such action research is appreciative enquiry (AE) which, as Cooperrider and Srivastva (1987) suggest, deliberately focuses on investigating and strengthening what is already beneficial and successful in organizations rather than on adopting a problem-oriented or clinical approach that focuses on difficulties and failures (see also Cooperrider and Whitney, 2005; Reed, 2007; Ludema and Fry, 2008). AE has become an important and useful approach to initiating and managing organizational change.

The quantitative school

The quantitative school (often also called Management Science) approach attempted to define management problems in numbers terms and sought to find ways of modelling relationships so that causal relationships could be identified and predictions made. World War II provided a significant impetus to the development of this approach with the creation of many operations research techniques in Britain which spread to America shortly after the war. The military need to move vast quantities of people, equipment, military supplies, food and clothing was a large-scale problem not encountered before. The development of mathematical models that allowed variables to be quantified and the relationships between them identified, helped to plan and execute these logistical necessities. The development of consulting practice as a means of adding to the problem-solving expertise and management capabilities of an organization became widespread during this period and the creation of operations research techniques further aided this development.

The techniques developed under the management science umbrella impacted significantly on issues such as quality through the introduction of statistical process control methods. This allowed the establishment of systematic methods of measuring process and product quality and of identifying acceptance and rejection criteria for product management. Production planning techniques also emerged during this period, as did forecasting methods and scenario planning. Scenario planning allowed the setting up of operational models that could have their parameters systematically varied in order to evaluate different decision options. Many of these issues are reflected in the principles of rational decision making discussed further in Chapter 8.

SYSTEMS APPROACHES TO MANAGEMENT

The systems approaches to management developed from early work in the biological sciences. Boulding (1956) and von Bertalanffy (1968) introduced the phrase 'general systems theory' as part of the view that there were common characteristics of the systems that were found across all disciplines and that these systems contained strong self-regulation tendencies (see Chapter 11 for further discussions of systems approaches). This perspective has been increasingly integrated into management thinking since the 1960s. Systems theorists often argue that earlier academic perspectives do not offer comprehensive explanations of management and organizational phenomena. These limitations can be described as follows:

Systems approaches to management
These developed from the biological sciences, are based on the view that 'systems' contain strong self-regulation tendencies and reflect something that can be separated from other systems and their environment by a boundary of some description.

- *Scientific management.* Concentrated on the tasks necessary in pursuit of the objectives to be achieved and on how to control employee activity within that process. As such it ignored the social and organizational factors associated with work and the people employed within it.

- *Administrative management.* Emphasized the structure and design of organizations together with the needs of the management process in running them. It generally ignored the worker, job and task aspects of organizational activity.

- *Human relations school.* This concentrated on the people aspects of work, the social conditions under which it was undertaken and the group dynamics involved. It paid scant attention to the organizational aspects relevant to work or the job design and environmental circumstances surrounding the work. It also ignored the technological and economic issues surrounding work and organizational functioning.

The systems approach led to a recognition of the existence of a continuum of complexity in systems development, from the very simple biological organisms through to complex social systems such as an organization. In the context of managing in organizations and groups, socio-technical systems theory has developed which is particularly concerned with the interactions and dynamics of both technical and social aspects of whole systems (e.g., Trist and Bamforth, 1951; Pasmore, 1988).

CONTEMPORARY MANAGEMENT CHALLENGES

The development of management thinking outlined in the previous section indicates an evolving set of perspectives, insights, tools and understandings that has emerged from the study of management, organizations and OB in a wide range of disciplines. The evolution of management theory also reflects historical changes in environmental conditions and in organizational and managerial practices. To provide value by assisting today's managers and organizations, theory in management and OB must actively recognize and address the particular conditions under which contemporary business and not-for-profit organizations operate. Therefore, we identify four related challenges that reflect many important factors and dynamics that influence people management in today's organizations. They include the challenges posed by

- global interconnectedness and the resulting increase in linkages, scope and reach of many organizational activities (these are explored in all chapters in feature boxes entitled "Going Global")
- ethical considerations and the demands for responsible action by organizations and by decision makers within them (see the "Examing Ethics" features)
- the escalating levels of competition, growing scarcity in resource supply, and the resulting increase in productivity and performance pressures (see the "High Performance" features)
- the cumulative and interactive effects of the above factors and other environmental developments on necessary organizational change (see the "Change at Work" features).

Just as managers in organizations cannot usually deal with individual issues and problems totally separately but need to consider the linkages between different aspects of the many tasks and responsibilities they face, the four management challenges we discuss in this chapter are not separate or even separable. In fact, there are many close and even reciprocal links between them. Globalization, for example, typically brings new competitors and increased competition (e.g., Sirkin *et al.*, 2008), while increasing competition in home markets often compels firms to consider expanding into new, international markets. Similarly, international diversification tends to improve corporate social responsibility (CSR) activities but is also associated with increased irresponsible corporate behaviour, partly due to the difficulties of managing subsidiary operations located in different countries (Strike *et al.*, 2006). The reason why we discuss these four related issues in separate sections is simply to highlight and analyse certain unique aspects of these challenges for managers. As we will show throughout the book, all of these challenges are relevant in the context of many different aspects of management and OB.

MANAGING IN THE GLOBAL CONTEXT: GLOBALIZATION AND CULTURAL DIVERSITY

Globalization
Reflects the growing tendency for individual businesses to become integrated into linkages and networks than span the whole globe.

Everyday life in most parts of the world, and business in particular, is increasingly integrated into linkages and networks that span the whole globe. This process called globalization is intensely debated (e.g., Bhagwati, 2004; Friedman, 2005; Stiglitz,

2006), but rather than arguing over its merits we treat it here simply as a fact (Dreher *et al.*, 2008) that may have origins, precursors, elements and examples going back to ancient times (Moore and Lewis, 2009).

As an example of the pervasive nature of globalization, consider that even the simplest task such as a child washing and vacuuming a neighbour's car has linkages to products and services (e.g., the detergent, brushes, vacuum cleaner, garbage bags, electricity, waste and waste water disposal) originating or ending up in many different countries (Fellenz and Brady, 2008: p. 41). Business organizations in particular are integrated into networks of such complex, international linkages. International trade in products and services, technology and innovation dispersion, as well as the global capital and investment flows provide – directly and indirectly - the life-blood for virtually all commercial businesses. Similarly, international agreements and multinational governance structures, the increasing migration of people and the international expansion of businesses make cross-cultural interaction even within organizations increasingly common.

All of this presents particular challenges for managers in all kinds of organizations for a number of reasons that include the rising number of potential and actual linkages and stakeholders, the growing complexity of external structures and processes, and the increasing internal complexity due to variety of task requirements and diversity of cultural backgrounds. In addition, organizations that respond to the challenges and opportunities that globalization offers with international expansion may operate in many fundamentally different business, legal, cultural, ecological and social environments. In short, the key managerial challenge arising from managing in organizations in a global and globalizing context is *matching the 'what' and 'how' with the 'where' and 'who'*.

Lahiri and colleagues argue that globalization introduces complexity that 'complicates top management's job of anticipating, recognizing, avoiding, neutralizing or adapting to the competitive landscape' (Lahiri *et al.*, 2008: p. 312), but the impact of globalization is actually felt throughout organizations. Organizational decision makers at all levels face increased uncertainty, variety and change that render their judgements more difficult and risky, and that complicate their decision making. Consider some of the implications of the following factors for managers:

- *Number and variety of external international linkages.* Globalization is often described as being fuelled by modern transportation and communication technologies. Having easy access – albeit electronically – to a large number of customers and suppliers as well as to colleagues across company sites in different countries can be highly beneficial. However, such linkages work both ways, and the easy access that this bestows on others can create intense pressure and stress through overload and multiple demands on managers' attention and time.

- *Number of external stakeholders.* International trade and finance can offer great opportunities for business organizations, just as international integration which can also aid social entrepreneurs and voluntary organizations in networking and collaboration which can improve their own and each other's effectiveness. However, many managers, especially in small and medium-sized enterprises (SMEs), find that they increasingly have to deal not only with local and national legislation but also with multinational regulations and directives (e.g., EU directives on health and safety or working time), and intense international competition within and across free trade areas that create single markets [as the EU, the Central American Common Market (CACM), or to a lesser extent the North American Free Trade Agreement (NAFTA)].

- *Complexity of the external environment.*   The number, diversity and variability of external linkages brought about by increasing internationalization and globalization, and the interactions between and among the many players involved in business as well as civic society has increased the degree of uncertainty that organizations and managers have to deal with (see also Chapter 10). This can create significant difficulties for managers at all levels because their ability to manage (i.e., to achieve objectives) is impeded by the uncertainty about current states and the unpredictability of future events.

- *Managing across different international sites.*   Operating in different national settings places demands on customizing and localizing products and services as well as management practices. Managerial behaviours that are socially and culturally acceptable and legal in one location may be unacceptable or illegal in others. Similarly, expatriates often need specific support and help to acculturate and become fully effective in novel cultural circumstances.

- *Variety of procedures and task requirements.*   The different external conditions and restrictions (e.g., local market preferences, local customs, legal requirements) can create the need to adapt the processes and tasks used to create and offer products and services. Especially in subsidiaries of multinational corporations (MNCs) this often leads to difficulties because formalized approaches prescribed by a (foreign) head office may not work as intended for cultural and social reasons. Examples may include Western-style egalitarian management approaches in cultures where high power distance exists between workers and managers, or formal performance evaluation and promotion systems in countries where *nepotism* (i.e., favouritism shown to family members or friends) is the norm and thus expected.

- *Cultural diversity within organizations.*   Staff with varied national and cultural backgrounds will have different expectations, different norms and different ways to interpret the world. This creates significant diversity, and challenges managers to educate themselves about cultural differences to increase their ability to constructively link with and co-ordinate the work of a diverse workforce. Chapter 14 in particular focuses on cultural dynamics in organizations.

Overall, international integration, globalization and cultural diversity create increasingly complex environments for organizations, which translate into new and more difficult challenges for those that manage people. Many tools and insights provided by OB can help deal with these challenges – yet managers often need to complement such theories and tools with their own understanding of the local context to adopt them for maximum relevance and thus for helping them find or create the most appropriate responses to the challenges they face. One organization's response to these challenges is outlined in the Global influences example.

ETHICS AND CORPORATE SOCIAL RESPONSIBILITY

Corporate governance
Defined by the Cadbury Committee as the systems through which companies are directed and controlled. It is about the ways in which ethics finds expression in business activities.

Business ethics
Takes as its focus of interest right, wrong, good and bad in relation to behaviour in an organizational context.

The business misdeeds of the last decade in the US (e.g., the Enron, Tyco and WorldCom accounting scandals; the fraudulent $65 billion Ponzi scheme run by Bernard Madoff) and Europe (e.g., the financial scandal involving Parmalat in Italy in 2003; the corruption scandal involving VW in Germany in 2005) and the far-reaching responses (e.g., the Sarbanes-Oxley Act in the US) have brought issues of corporate governance and business ethics to centre stage of public interest

GOING GLOBAL

Hall and Partners successfully expand into the USA with the help of Dramatic Resources

Hall and Partners, a successful advertising research agency expanding rapidly in America, needed its key personnel to develop the resilience and confidence to win and retain business with an important new client base involving companies across the USA. Terry Willie, the company's then CEO, recognized that their people needed to develop and maintain the skills and experience to handle the strenuous situations that arise when dealing with these clients. Looking for innovative approaches for training and developing people, Hall and Partners identified Arts-Based Initiatives as a way to speed up the process through which their people could become adept at handling difficult situations, difficult clients and negotiating.

To address these issues, Dramatic Resources was brought in to design a theatre-based programme, aimed at enabling employees to handle unexpected situations. Different scenarios were created and diverse roles were played in order to improve their improvisational skills, and equip them with the expertise to handle demanding situations. According to Terry Willie, 'There were some fantastic skills we could draw from in theatre – especially the ability to walk in other people's shoes and be able to read and understand roles, characters and plots. We also loved the idea that it was learning by doing, not just telling – and using acting/theatre approach got people to relax and try new things. It has proved to be just a lovely fresh perspective.'

Hall and Partners was voted as one of the top small businesses to work for by the *Sunday Times*.

This can be considered as a consequence, among other factors, of the adoption of innovative training approaches for people development, such as the theatre-based programme. Terry Willie stressed that

> We passionately believe the reason why the business has been successful is because we care so much about not just attracting the best and most creative talent, but keeping and developing them. And to that end we have developed an extensive 'curriculum' for training people at every level in the place. . . . [This] work is by far the most influential work we do – people universally came out of it raving about how much they got out of it; you could immediately see the change in their day-to-day work.

Richard Hahlo, Director Dramatic Resources
www.dramaticresources.co.uk

TASKS

1 What other innovative ways might you be able to identify that would have helped Hall and Partners achieve success in expanding into America?

2 If you were Richard Hahlo of Dramatic Resources how would you seek to develop your range of services to expand your ability to grow the business globally?

Source:
Taken from the Arts & Business Publication 'Mapping Arts-Based Initiatives: Assessing the organisational value of the arts' by Professor Giovanni Schiuma (2009) University of Basilicata (Italy), Visiting Research Fellow Cranfield School of Management (UK).

and discussion. In addition to such fraudulent and illegal corporate actions, issues of corporate and state responsibilities have also become prominent in public discourse in response to the global financial crisis that started in 2008. The mounting problems arising from the mismanagement of large companies, and especially banks, with disastrous implications for shareholders, employees and other stakeholders have resulted in many large-scale state interventions such as financial and liquidity assistance, state guarantees, conservatorship, or nationalization (e.g., Fortis in Belgium, The Netherlands and Luxemburg; Hypo Real/Depfa and

Commerzbank in Germany; Anglo Irish Bank, Bank of Ireland and Allied Irish Bank in Ireland; Banco Português de Negócios in Portugal; Royal Bank of Scotland, HBOS-Lloyds TSB, and Northern Rock in the UK; AIG, Fannie Mae and Freddie Mac in the US). Similarly, the role of sustainability and environmental protection ('green management', see Nidumolu *et al.*, 2009; Marcus and Fremeth, 2009; Siegel, 2009) has generated much academic argument as well as public activism. These issues have picked up on long-term debates regarding the role of large organizations and particular businesses in society (e.g., Friedman, 1962, 1972; Freeman, 1984; see Wartick and Cochran, 1985) especially with regard to their negative impact on people, communities, society and the natural environment. We will discuss the issue of CSR, which addresses many of these issues, below after first considering the fundamental issue of ethics and particularly business ethics in organizations.

Philosophy and ethics

Moral philosophy
A branch of philosophy that takes as its sphere of interest a philosophical enquiry about norms or values, about ideas of right and wrong, good or bad, what should and what should not be done.

Ethics is about doing the right thing. Moral philosophy is a branch of philosophy that takes as its sphere of interest 'philosophical enquiry about norms or values, about ideas of right and wrong, good or bad, what should and what should not be done' (Raphael, 1994: p. 8). Clearly, therefore, there are close associations between the study of ethics and that of moral philosophy. Moral philosophy seeks to tease out the underlying assumptions in ethical situations and critically evaluate them. Ethics takes as its focus of interest behaviour that contains rightness, goodness, correctness or appropriateness in a particular context. For example, recruiting of nurses from other countries has existed for many years, but recently there has been a vast upsurge in the recruitment of nurses from the developing world to work in developed countries, causing an imbalance in health provision in already impoverished locations. This clearly raises ethical issues for all countries that must be resolved (Singh *et al.*, 2003). Another way of considering the distinction is that ethics is related to aspects of interpersonal behaviour whereas moral philosophy covers a broader range of experiences in the human condition, including beauty and feelings. There are four different approaches to moral decision making that have emerged over the years, including:

- *Naturalism.* This view holds that morality can be judged on the basis of self-interest. What is right is in the best interests of the individual, therefore any particular morality will be situation-specific.
- *Rationalism.* This view suggests that there is an absolute truth which underpins ethical standards. The level of morality in any context is a reflection of the knowledge and understanding available at that time. As knowledge and understanding develop, so morality comes closer to the ultimate truth.
- *Utilitarianism.* This perspective proposes that doing what is right promotes happiness. However, happiness is a term that can have multiple meanings and selective impacts at the same time. For example, flogging individuals convicted of theft might create a feeling of happiness among victims, but at the same time create pain and unhappiness for the criminal and their family. A variation of this approach, referred to as intuitionism, proposed a number of values that stand the test of time and therefore reflect underlying and unchanging principles; Raphael (1994) identifies eight of these (see Table 2.2).

Table 2.2 Principles of intuitionism

Promoting the happiness of other people

Refraining from harm to other people

Treating people justly

Telling the truth

Keeping promises

Showing gratitude

Promoting one's own happiness

Maintaining and promoting one's own virtues

Source: Adapted from Raphael, DD (1994) Moral Philosophy, 2nd edn, Oxford University Press, Oxford. Reprinted with permission.

- *Formalism.* It was Kant who described a distinction between categorical and hypothetical imperatives in reaching moral decisions. The hypothetical imperative is based on the pragmatic approach to situations. It considers that actions should be designed to meet the self-interest of the decision maker. Kant argued that this approach did not explain all circumstances relating to moral decisions and that categorical imperatives reflected circumstances where the means-to-an-end perspective did not apply. For example, giving to charity can be seen in terms of goodness for its own sake and not just as a means of providing benefit to the giver. This provides a formalized approach to deciding between courses of action (self-interest or general) and requires the individual to apply three filters to the decision (see Table 2.3).

It should be apparent that the perspective adopted in Table 2.2 implies a democratic, consultative, or at least intersubjective approach to moral decision making. It can even be argued that this approach produces a basis for the regulation of society through legislative, political and procedural frameworks. Similar parallels have also been suggested to hold in organizations, for example through the development of rules that apply to all members equally, as in bureaucratic forms of organization.

One of the central debates regarding ethics and moral behaviour has been the issue of *moral relativism* which is particularly important in a globalizing world. The central issue here is the appropriateness of moral judgement of conduct taking place in a social and cultural context different from one's own. Extreme forms of moral relativism would preclude any such moral judgements, a view many find too

Table 2.3 A simplified form of Kantian ethics

1 Consider you are attempting to create a rule for every individual to follow

2 Consider that the human beings involved are ends in themselves and not a means to some personal gratification

3 Consider that everyone else in society has the same rights and freedoms to act as they see fit and that they should act on the basis of 1 and 2 above

Source: Adapted from Raphael, DD (1994) Moral Philosophy, 2nd edn, Oxford University Press, Oxford. Reprinted with permission.

extreme to countenance. At the other extreme, however, is the position of moral absolutism that is equally hard for many to accept. Sociologist Steven Lukes (2008) provides a comprehensive and compelling analysis of these matters and renounces moral absolutism by stating that 'there are multiple best ways for human beings to live' (p. 142). In reviewing the debate between moral absolutism and extreme moral relativism he concludes that making moral judgements can be combined with recognizing both the existence and authority of multiple moral standards. He suggests two approaches that can give grounding to such moral decision making. The first is rooted in the Kantian ethics described above which are based on an intersubjective or consultative approach to moral conduct. The second is based on expectations of minimal thresholds for the exercise of universal human capabilities informed by a basic respect for human nature and dignity (Nussbaum, 2006; Sen, 1999). Such capabilities include for example life; bodily health; imagination and thought; affiliation; and others (Nussbaum, 1999; 2006). Both of these approaches can guide individuals in making moral judgements about their own and others' conduct. This possibility of making moral judgements, however, does not take away from the difficulties inherent in making and ultimately adhering to them. We will explore some of the organizational and managerial implications of this in the next section.

Ethical perspectives in organizations

Ethical issues are about rightness, wrongness, good and bad. This is as much applicable within organizational activity as it is in the field of politics or society as a whole. Deciding the right thing to do in any particular context can be a demanding task. Consider for example the position of a subordinate who finds out that their manager is falsifying expenses claims. What would be the proper and right course of action for the subordinate to adopt? The choices include:

- Do nothing.
- Report the manager to a more senior manager.
- Let the manager know that they have been found out.
- Send an anonymous letter to the chief executive.
- Report the manager to the subordinates' trade union.
- Write a letter to the press.
- Write a letter to the largest shareholder.
- Report the manager to their professional association (if they belong to one).

Utilitarian approaches (to ethics)
Based on benevolence, these approaches require an evaluation of the options available on the basis of the future impact on those that are likely to be effected by the consequences. It comes in two forms – act utilitarianism and rule utilitarianism. See also contract approach to ethics.

Contract approaches (to ethics)
Based on fairness, these approaches to resolving ethical dilemmas are grounded in the notion that agreements, whether they be explicit or tacit, should be honoured. It comes in two variations, Restricted contractarianism and Libertarian contractarianism. See also utilitarian approaches to ethics.

Each of these options has a range of costs and benefits for the individuals involved in the situation. In identifying the most appropriate course of action the subordinate can adopt one of two approaches. First, they could take the decision based on their judgement of the rightness or wrongness of the act that they have encountered. In doing so they would be acting irrespective of any consequences for the manager involved, themselves or the organization. Second, they could form a judgement based on the possible consequences for the principal stakeholders. For example, if they had an extremely good working relationship with the manager and felt a high degree of personal loyalty towards them, an approach that ran counter to that would be likely to cause distress to the subordinate.

Cederblom and Dougherty (1990) use these ideas as the basis for deciding between alternative courses of action. They refer to the two approaches as utilitarianism and contractarianism. Utilitarian approaches are summarized as benevolence and contract approaches are about fairness. Within each model there are two versions, giving four different options which form the basis of choosing an appropriate course of action.

Utilitarian approach

This approach is grounded in the concept of utility or usefulness. In determining the right course of action in any given context a key feature should be the level of valued results produced. The approach to be adopted is one of benevolence towards the needs of others in determining one's own behaviour. This approach looks forward in assessing the ethical perspectives on any particular situation. It requires an evaluation of options on the basis of the future impact on those that are likely to be affected by the consequences.

ACT UTILITARIANISM

This version suggests that every dilemma should be regarded on its own merits. For example, telling a lie could be justified if it created happiness for the people involved. It would appear to run contrary to all the norms of society to be able to justify actions such as lying, cheating and even murder under some circumstances. For an interesting discussion on this area of ethics see Keep (2003).

RULE UTILITARIANISM

This approach takes the view that act utilitarianism might be a good thing to do in a specific instance, but still wrong if society is to operate in a consistent way. The rule approach to utilitarianism requires rule frameworks to be created which can allow individuals to identify appropriate courses of action in specific contexts.

Contract approach

This approach to resolving ethical dilemmas is grounded in the notion that agreements whether they be explicit or tacit should be honoured. Because of the social environment, co-operation between human beings is a necessity. As a consequence of the web of interaction, many mutual obligations (contracts) are created. In the execution of these contractual relationships, individuals are required to apply the general test of fairness to their behaviour. However, circumstances can create an inequality in the balance of power between individuals and so fairness is difficult to achieve. For example, inside knowledge of an impending takeover bid could allow certain individuals to buy shares cheaply before they rise sharply when the announcement is made. A contract view is one that looks backward at the obligations that have been entered into and assesses the implications of these for future behaviour.

RESTRICTED CONTRACTARIANISM

This approach takes the view that every agreement entered into should be assessed through the veil of ignorance (Rawls, 1971). This forces an individual to consider the rightness of any proposed action without knowing the outcome for themselves. Cutting a cake is frequently used to illustrate the need for fairness in this context. The person agreeing to cut the cake should be the last person to select a piece to eat. By so doing they cannot know which piece of cake will be left for them to eat, and so they will have an interest in cutting all pieces to the same size.

LIBERTARIAN CONTRACTARIANISM

This approach holds that the parties should be bound by any agreement voluntarily entered into as long as it does not conflict with the broader rules of a just society or cause harm to others. It is an approach that accepts the limitations on the concept of fairness in the dynamic nature of the social world. It implies that once a contract is entered into, individuals have an obligation to abide by the terms of that relationship and not to take action to terminate (or change) the contract. For example, an employee should fulfil their contractual obligations to their employer in following the instructions of management, unless they are being expected to break the law of the country in which they work, say to falsify the company accounts. That is because the 'contract' between each citizen and their country has a higher status than the contract with the employer. In the case described the employee would be acting ethically by upholding the rule of law. Of course this can lead to many difficulties in the area of whistleblowing in which the organization would argue that there was no conflict of 'contract' and that loyalty to the company should be upheld and the employee argues otherwise.

Considerable management and employee activity is associated with making choices or taking decisions. Ethical dimensions of such choices include the relative priority given to different stakeholders and their interests, the adherence to obligations, the resolution of conflicts that arise between different obligations, respect for the rights of others (e.g., right to privacy), and many others. Figure 2.1 shows a model that helps identify conflicts between different standards that often conflict with those at the opposite side of the diagram (Leys, 1962). However, this model does not provide a basis for identifying a course of action to resolve the moral dilemma facing the individual. Rather, it provides a useful starting point for thinking about the issues involved in a specific situation on the way to appropriate decisions and ethical conduct. The Examining Ethics example explores one area of ethical dilemma facing employees in difficult situations – that of taking the boss hostage.

Corporate governance and corporate social responsibility

Given the substantial impact that business organizations can have on society and the natural environment, the questions of how they are governed (corporate governance) and what obligations they have for outside stakeholders (CSR) are important and timely. In the UK, guidelines for *corporate governance* were developed by the Cadbury Committee in 1992 and updated and extended by a number of subsequent reports. The accumulated suggestions are reflected in the 'Combined Code on Corporate Governance' (Financial Reporting Council, 2008). Similar codes exist in

Figure 2.1 Conflicts between moral values

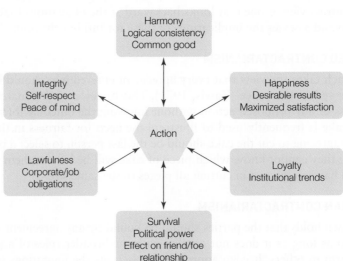

Source: Adapted from Leys, Wayne AR (1962) 'The Value Framework of Decision-Making,' in S Mailick and E Van Ness (eds.) Concepts and Issues in Administrative Behavior. Englewood Cliffs, NJ: Prentice-Hall. Reproduced with permission.

EXAMINING ETHICS

Taking the boss hostage as a protest!

The CEO of Sony in France Serge Foucher and the head of human resources Roland Bentz had travelled to the videotape factory at Pontonx-sur-l'Adour in south-western France for a final courtesy visit to more than 311 sacked workers before the plant closed on 17 April 2009. After the visit the two men were prevented from leaving the factory (by being locked in a meeting room) on Thursday night (12 March 2009) after dozens workers effectively took them hostage and barricaded the entrance to the factory with tree trunks. The workers were angry at the severance package that they were offered in comparison to other Sony workers in France and so decided to take the two senior executive hostage in order to force the company to concede more in severance payments. Trade union representatives said that the workers had been offered €3500 in payment if they agreed to relocate to other Sony factories whereas other Sony workers had been offered full relocation costs as well. 'We are all going to be fired. We want to be treated in a dignified manner,' said Patrick Achaguer, a representative of the CGT union. Chantal Omiciuolo, one of the workers, said that the detention of the two bosses was 'our last chance – we didn't have the choice'.

The two men were finally allowed to walk free from the factory on Friday morning (13 March) after local authorities persuaded both sides to go back to the negotiating table in the local town of Dax. 'I am happy to be free and to see the light of day again,' said an exhausted-looking Mr Foucher before boarding a minibus to drive to the negotiations under the auspices of the French authorities.

Taking the boss hostage is becoming an increasingly common form of protest in France. Last year, the English boss of a car-parts factory in eastern France was held in his office for 48, sleeping on a massage table and being provided with blankets and sandwiches. He said he felt like 'a prisoner in Alcatraz'. The country witnessed angry scenes earlier in March 2009 when the head of German tyre manufacturer Continental's plant in Clairoix, north of Paris, had raw eggs thrown at him after announcing that over 1000 workers were to lose their jobs. Continental's decision also angered President Sarkozy's government – which has given more than €12 billion in loans to protect France's auto sector – and it has complained to Germany Chancellor Angela Merkel.

In another incident last year, police stormed an ice-cream factory in Saint-Dizier to free a manager who had been held hostage by workers angry over job cuts. At least 14 staff were injured trying to stop police releasing him.

TASKS

1 To what extent can taking the boss hostage ever be justified as a legitimate tactic for employees trying to force management to concede more in negotiation situations?

2 Create an ethical analysis and justification to support both the 'for' and 'against' arguments in the above question.

3 What does your answer to task 2 suggest about the ability of ethical theory to interpret and guide behaviour at work?

Sources:
Chrisafis, A. (2009) Sacked French Sony workers release boss from captivity, The Guardian, 13 March.
Sage, A. (2009) Sony's French chief freed after protest at Factory. The Times. 14 March.
Samuel, H. (2009) French Sony Workers held company chief executive hostage overnight. The Telegraph, 13 March.

other countries as well such as Germany's 'Deutscher Corporate Governance Kodex' (Regierungskommission DCGK, 2009) which is updated yearly. These codes are backed up by laws and financial regulations that give them legal importance, particularly for publicly traded firms. These codes set out guidelines about governance that companies need to adhere to lest they provide explanations for any deviations. They also contain additional suggestions for best practice that are not binding.

2.3 EXTEND YOUR LEARNING

Such codes typically require high standards of integrity and ethical behaviour which leads many organizations to develop and adopt internal ethical guidelines and codes of practice to influence the behaviour of all members. Compliance with such external and internal codes is an important management responsibility. Unfortunately, many companies delegate specified control and compliance activities to middle managers and try to create buffers between top managers and lower-level managers who are made responsible for compliance with such codes. The difficulty for lower-level managers is that adherence to such requirements is not only difficult and time-consuming, but it also often creates immense pressure and stress because of the simultaneous operational and bottom-line responsibilities they have. Recent court decisions in the US have challenged such practices (see Dalton, 2009) but they are still widespread.

This issue is reflective of a fundamental challenge for managers in organizations. The authority they hold due to their position (see also Chapter 6) must be commensurate with their responsibilities and balanced by appropriate amounts of accountability regarding the ways in which they employ their authority and deal with their task and people management responsibilities. In simple terms, if managers' authority outweighs their accountability, the conditions for abuse of authority are given ('manager as monster'), while the opposite situation of managerial accountability for aspects that these managers have no authority over creates the conditions for the abuse of the respective managers ('manager as fool or marionette'). Both conditions are immensely unfair and counterproductive, and should be avoided at all costs in organizations.

Corporate social responsibility (CSR)
This refers to the rights and responsibilities of an organization relative to its social context.

This balance, albeit with an external focus, is also referred to in relation to corporate social responsibility (CSR). The *'iron law of responsibility'* was coined by Keith Davis, an early writer and researcher on CSR, which posits that 'the social responsibilities of businesspeople needed to be commensurate with their social power' (see Carroll, 2007). CSR refers to *the obligations that firms have to their wider stakeholders*. The Millennium Poll on Corporate Social Responsibility (Environics, n.d.) reflects the views of more than 1000 respondents on six continents which indicated that companies are broadly expected to:

- Demonstrate their commitment to society's values and their contribution to society's social, environmental and economic goals through actions.
- Fully insulate society from the negative impacts of company operations and its products and services.
- Share the benefits of company activities with key stakeholders as well as with shareholders.
- Demonstrate that the company can make more money by doing the right thing, in some cases by reinventing its business strategy.

However, expectations, attitudes and practices regarding CSR appear to differ (Williams and Aguilera, 2008) across individual managers (The Economist, 2005), industries (e.g., Strike *et al.*, 2006), countries (e.g., Habisch *et al.*, 2005) and cultures (e.g., Waldman *et al.*, 2006). Nevertheless, all indications point to generally increasing CSR expectations, which will require many organizations, especially business firms, to broaden their objectives beyond narrow profit maximization goals, particularly if they require legitimation through public attitudes, are closely regulated or otherwise heavily influenced by public bodies and institutions. Examples for issues that can arise here include the backlash against firms alleged to employ child labour (e.g., Nike, see Boggan, 2001) or to suppress union activity in developing countries (e.g., Coca-Cola, see Thomas, 2008). Environmental pollution, animal testing, exploitative work practices, and corruption are other common issues often taken up by activists and non-governmental organizations in this context.

Initial formal research on CSR, which began to emerge in the 1950s (Bowen, 1953), mostly focused on the role of business as seen from an aggregated perspective and considered macro-economic and societal level questions regarding the role and responsibilities of business in society. More recently, as Lee (2008) argues, CSR research started to focus on organization-level investigations that study the link between CSR and profitability. At the same time, the normative and ethics focused approach has been replaced by more implicit ethical considerations that are subsumed in managerially oriented concerns based on strategic considerations about how CSR can improve the competitive situation and ultimately the performance of firms (Lee, 2008; McWilliams *et al.*, 2006). More specifically, many researchers argue that active investment of resources to increase CSR can benefit the financial bottom line (Pfeffer, 2009) through favourable responses from stakeholders such as shareholders and capital markets (e.g., Mackey *et al.*, 2007; Neal and Cochran, 2008; Richardson *et al.*, 1999), customers (e.g., Kotler and Lee, 2005; Schuler and Cording, 2006), and potential high-quality employees (Laszlo, 2003; Turban and Greening, 1997).

For managers, the role of CSR in daily management introduces the challenge of balancing the *triple bottom line* of 'people, planet and profits' (Elkington, 1994). These goals may conflict with specified managerial goals, and resolving such conflicts with regard to internal issues (such as exploitative work practices) and external issues (such as environmental pollution) can often involve substantial difficulties for managers. At the heart of this matter is the inherent conflict between organizational goals and potentially conflicting expectations and interests of stakeholders. This is particularly difficult for managers in highly competitive environments, an issue we discuss in the next section.

2.4 EXTEND YOUR LEARNING

STOP & CONSIDER

'Business is about making money and anything lawful and within reason that achieves that objective is ethical.' To what extent and why do you agree (or disagree) with this statement?

TODAY'S PERFORMANCE IMPERATIVE

The global competitive landscape is changing substantially and swiftly. Economic production and purchasing power is shifting, with the BRIC countries (Brazil, Russia, India, China) expected to expand their global economic reach and power dramatically over the next decades (Hitt and He, 2008; Lehrer and Delaunay, 2009). Audretsch (2009) argues that the managed economy in the US, previously dominated by large corporate organizations, has been replaced by an 'entrepreneurial society' in which entrepreneurial activity has become a central focus for economic growth, job creation, and competitiveness in global markets. Together with globalization, rapid technological development, and ever accelerating and intensifying competition ('hypercompetition', see D'Aveni, 1994), the conditions under which commercial organizations operate are becoming increasingly characterized by uncertainty. 'Hypercompetition creates scarcity of critical resources like raw materials, human resources, distribution channels, business networks, and the like, which are needed to effectively and efficiently operate a business.' (Lahiri *et al.*, 2008: p. 314) In fact, esource scarcity as a result of competition and globalization is an important and increasingly unpredictable variable in many industries and markets (Beinhocker *et al.*, 2009; Friedman, 2005; Sirkin *et al.*, 2008). In addition, the pressures of social accountability, increasing regulation, more discerning customers, ever more assertive

Hypercompetition
Caused by globalization, rapid technological development, and ever accelerating and intensifying competition creates scarcity of critical resources including raw materials, human resources, distribution channels, business networks.

and even belligerent shareholders, and instant access through modern information and communication technology, have created immensely pressurized environments in which to manage. While there are critics that question if the intensity of competition has increased significantly compared to previous decades (e.g., McNamara *et al.*, 2003; Sorge and van Witteloostuijn, 2004), the above dynamics coupled with the global financial crisis and widespread recession that started in 2008 have undoubtedly introduced tremendous commercial and management challenges that directly and indirectly affect all businesses worldwide.

Therefore, in addition to the age-old challenge of how to achieve goals with and through others, many if not most of today's managers and organizations confront unprecedented trials regularly. The performance imperative of old where managers were expected to achieve their specified goals has been turbocharged: today's *performance imperative* requires managers and organizations to do and achieve ever more with ever fewer inputs and decreasing resources, and also to respond to environmental change and organizational requirements immediately. This 'doing more with less' and the resulting pressure to become and stay effective while always increasing efficiency places an enormous burden on all managers and employees as well as the formal systems and informal networks in organizations (see also Bates *et al.*, 2009). In such tough and challenging circumstances, managing cannot simply maintain 'business as usual'. Rather, specific responses are required to help managers and those they manage to stay successful. We will discuss three important challenges for managers, many of which increasingly also apply to non-managerial members of organizations: the challenge of managing themselves, leading others in difficult times, and the dual challenge of developing and improving organizational and environmental awareness.

2.5 EXTEND
YOUR LEARNING

Managers managing themselves

The picture we have painted of the performance imperative – the challenges and demands for ever improving effectiveness and efficiency - that managers face in today's organizations undoubtedly place many pressures on them. Humans tend to react to external pressure with either flight or fight responses, neither of which is usually particularly appropriate or helpful in organizations. In fact, in uncomfortable and threatening situations, people's ability to take in information reduces significantly, and people react in rigid ways (Staw *et al.*, 1981). Therefore, managing one's own stress, finding appropriate social support inside and outside the organization, staying open for input from others and for information from one's environment, and staying focused on the task at hand while considering the context of task accomplishment as well as future changes are important ingredients of managerial success. The book's companion website provides additional insights into stress and stress management, and many relevant issues and skills such as emotional intelligence, communication, team management, conflict resolution, negotiation, and building and maintaining relationships are discussed later in this book. It is important, however, for managers to recognize the role of self-awareness, and to make developing and increasing self-awareness a priority task (see e.g., Quinn *et al.*, 2003; Whetten and Cameron, 2007).

2.6 EXTEND
YOUR LEARNING

Managers supporting others

It is imperative that managers manage themselves and their needs in difficult times, but this cannot be allowed to take precedence over another crucial challenge: directing and supporting those that managers work with and through. The people management challenge is more intense, more difficult, but also more important during times of stress, crisis and turmoil. Employees experience such conditions as much as managers, but often feel more exposed because they have less control and less access to information than their superiors. Managers need to provide them with special support and care to enable them to cope with the difficult times, the stress of intensifying work, and the threat of layoffs or other negative changes. This is particularly difficult for managers to do because people in power 'tend to become more self-centered and less mindful of what others need, do and say' (Sutton, 2009: p. 44; see also Keltner *et al.*, 2003). Because of their perceived self-importance and their role in the organization, managers also tend to falsely overestimate their own awareness and understanding of what is going on in the organization (Sutton calls this the 'fallacy of centrality'). Moreover, in stressful times employees tend to scrutinize the verbal and non-verbal behaviours of their self-absorbed bosses more closely than usual. Sutton calls these two factors the *toxic tandem* and argues that the dynamic increases the challenges of providing appropriate support and leadership to employees in difficult times.

Sutton (2009) argues that in such circumstances, employees lack four ingredients that managers need to supply: predictability, understanding, control, and compassion. *Predictability* reduces people's perceived uncertainty and helps them manage their anxieties. Rather than worry about adverse events, employees who are provided with sufficient information, and who trust their managers to inform them of relevant changes, are likely to be less anxious and much more productive. *Understanding* helps people deal with difficult situations for a number of reasons. Like predictability, it increases perceived control, but it also helps them to feel treated fairly and to simply know what to do. Communications should be simple, clear and unambiguous, and may need to be repeated and also sent through different channels to increase understanding. Information overload can be a real concern if subordinates are stressed, preoccupied, or fearful. O'Toole and Bennis (2009) suggest that a culture of candor is an important asset for organizations in times of difficulties which can also help with providing understanding to employees. *Control* has already been alluded to with the first two ingredients, but it is important in its own right for helping to lower employees' anxieties and increase their feeling of self-worth, accomplishment, and satisfaction. Even if control cannot be achieved about outcomes controlled by outside forces (e.g., the economy, competitors, customers), there may be aspects that can be influenced (e.g., the timing of events, or aspects of response plans). Thus, control over the preparation of responses to uncontrollable events can already improve perceptions of control significantly. Finally, *compassion* is a crucial element that managers can bring to help their employees in tough times. Using empathy, providing appropriate explanations, showing interpersonal sensitivity, and generally communicating with authenticity can help express compassion. Avoiding anything that may demean or ridicule employees, including condescending behaviour or inappropriate language is important, as is behaviour that may negatively affect the managers' perceived integrity and trustworthiness. Many of these issues will be discussed in more detail throughout the book, especially in Chapters 8 (Communication and decision making) and 16 (Relationships, fairness and trust), but it is important from the start to recognize the central role of trust between and among organizational members: without trust, most of the benefits of managers' attempts to support their people will fail to deliver their intended results.

Managers developing and improving organizational and environmental awareness

In addition to managing themselves and supporting and leading their employees, managers also need to remain focused on their task objectives and the internal and external environment in which they are pursuing them. Lahiri *et al.* (2008) argue that managers need to be able to adopt and work with four different mindsets that enable them to deal successfully with the challenge of preventing organizational decline in ever more difficult external conditions (specifically, they identify the *global*, *innovation*, *virtual* and *collaboration mindsets* as important). Deploying their analytical abilities and making realistic judgements is of critical importance for this, but the uncertainty that comes with complexity, change and variety threatens to overwhelm managers. Deploying appropriate tools and using effective approaches to environmental scanning, analysis, planning and decision making is therefore critical, as are selecting and deploying appropriate support mechanisms that involve others in assuring decision quality and appropriate task execution. Using internal and external networks for information search and partnering with other managers that have complementary skills (Rigby *et al.*, 2009) can be effective ways of staying on top of – rather than being overwhelmed by – large amounts of information. Individual managers must also be discerning about which information they attend to, and manage how they can do this most effectively. Hemp (2009) suggests that both smart technology use and a different mindset that is proactive rather than reactive in dealing with incoming information can be helpful. Similarly, using up-to-date analytical approaches, tools and skills that help to make sense of the uncertain external environment (e.g., business cycle analysis, see Navarro, 2009, or big picture change metrics, see Hagel *et al.*, 2009), and reality testing them critically and from multiple internal (see also Chapter 8) and external perspectives (Coyne and Horn, 2009) is crucial. The lessons from the global crisis of 2008 is that many of the existing approaches and tools 'need to incorporate more-realistic visions of human behaviour' (Beinhocker *et al.*, 2009: p. 58) – in markets and inside organizations.

Whilst it is important to recognize that performance is an important aspect of modern organizations and management experience, it is worth spending a few moments to look backwards into history and reflect on what we can learn form the experience of previous generations. The High Performance example introduces an outline of one such example from the Middle Ages.

2.7 EXTEND YOUR LEARNING

HIGH PERFORMANCE

Performance is a modern management imperative, isn't it?

The traders of ancient Venice had a direct interest in protecting their trade routes and goods at an affordable price in the Middle Ages. Their management and working practices have been discovered in records that have survived from the Arsenal of Venice. This was effectively a government-owned shipyard, operational from around the early thirteenth century. Its purpose was to build naval ships in order to protect the Venetian merchant fleet. Its peak in terms of efficiency was in the sixteenth century when it employed around 16 000 people and could build about one ship each day. The ships were small by modern standards. They were about 106 feet long and approximately 20 feet wide. Each ship was divided into three sections: fighting platform at the front, space for the oars down the centre and a command centre at the stern. The purpose of the Arsenal was not just to build the ships but to make arms and other military equipment, to store such equipment and ships until needed and to refit ships as necessary.

The main features of the shipbuilding 'process' that made it such an efficient process included:

Management. The sheer size of the operation required a sophisticated form of management control. Three lords of the Arsenal who reported to the Commissioners – the link between the Arsenal as an operational unit and the Venetian Senate – officially headed the operation. Reporting to the lords of the Arsenal were the foremen – shipbuilders, book-keepers and pages – responsible for the financial aspects of the shipyard.

Warehousing. Components held in warehouses included rudders, benches, oars, pitch (for sealing joints) and masts. These were held in specified quantities in specific locations so that they could be found, used and replaced quickly. It took many years to introduce an equivalent system for raw material such as timber because of the vast quantity scattered throughout the shipyard and the difficulty in finding appropriate pieces.

Assembly. In order to be able to complete ships quickly an assembly-line-based system of production was used. The hull of a ship, once in the water, was towed along a canal past warehouses which would pass over the designated components (oars, masts, stores, weapons, etc.) until at the end it was ready for active service. It was not unknown for important visitors to be treated to a spectacular event in having a ship 'built before their very eyes'. For example, Henry III of France visited Venice in 1574 and during dinner one evening apparently saw a vessel built, finished and armed during the course of the meal.

People management. Recruitment was controlled in key crafts with admission tests being required before young people could become apprentice carpenters, for example. Wages and quality were also closely controlled in the manufacturing and assembly shops. Both piecework and day rates were used in appropriate situations. The making of oars was based on piecework with credit being given only for those finished pieces that were acceptable to the foreman. Each year a merit review of the master craftsmen was undertaken in order to evaluate performance and other contributions as the basis of wage determination and advancement. Starting and finishing times were also tightly managed as was the potential theft of timber etc. from the shipyard. Individual foremen were able to delegate some of their duties so that they could concentrate on the major issues such as volume, cost and quality. Employees were also entitled to a number of wine breaks (five or six) each day in order to allow some recovery of energy and to maintain productivity.

Standardization. The Venetians recognized that standardization was necessary and designed ships and components accordingly. Deck fittings, sails and rigging were standardized in order to allow uniformity and pre-manufacture.

Accounting. By 1370 the accounts comprised two journals and one ledger. The chief accountant kept a ledger from a journal produced by his deputy. At intervals the journal kept by the lord of the Arsenal responsible for cash transactions was reconciled against the ledger produced by the chief accountant. Every year the account books were balanced and sent to the treasurer's office for storage and audit.

Inventory control. There were a number of inventory control procedures implemented within the Arsenal. The quality and quantity of raw material and purchased components arriving at the Arsenal was checked by inspectors. Goods leaving the Arsenal were the responsibility of doorkeepers whose duties were to prevent anything leaving without proper authorization.

Cost control. It became apparent to the managers of the Arsenal that not all aspects of the operation were as tightly controlled as others. For example, the cost of finding an appropriate log was found to be three times as expensive as the log itself was worth. This formed the basis of a management initiative to improve the ability of the shipyard to store, retrieve and process wood.

TASKS

1 The assembly-line approach to building ships must have been an impressive sight. Why then do you suppose that it was approximately another 350 years before Henry Ford developed the idea into the factory approach as we would recognize it today?

2 To what extent does this historical example lead you to conclude that every generation has its own performance imperatives to deal with because the social, economic and other circumstances change?

3 What does this historical example suggest to you about performance as it might be relevant to today's managers?

Sources:
Lane, F.C. (1934) *Venetian Ships and Shipbuilders of the Renaissance*, Baltimore: Johns Hopkins Press.
George, C.S. (1972) The History of Management Thought, (2nd edn), Englewood Cliffs: Prentice Hall, pp. 37–38.

PERVASIVE ORGANIZATIONAL CHANGE

We have already remarked that the four challenges we identify and discuss in this chapter are interrelated. Nowhere is this more obvious than in the issues of organizational change because all the other issues require changes in organizations to successfully deal with them. In many ways, focusing on organizational change helps us to understand how the other three challenges as well as many other dynamics and factors external and internal to organizations become visible and are experienced in organizations. We will now consider the way in which change impacts on an organization, which is dependent on two factors, the scale of the change impact and the degree of planning for change involved. Figure 2.2 illustrates these as two axes in a matrix, which consequently generates four categories of change impact.

2.8 EXTEND YOUR LEARNING

Each of the four cells in Figure 2.2 reflects a different basis for particular response scenarios to the experienced situation. The two axes of the model will be discussed in the following subsections, but it is appropriate at this point to briefly consider each of the change impact cells in the matrix:

- *Surprise*. This reflects situations that are both unplanned and relatively minor in nature. For example, interest rates might unexpectedly change and require the finance managers of a company to adjust loan repayment schedules.

- *Incremental*. This could reflect situations which are anticipated and are relatively minor in nature. For example, the implementation of quality circle recommendations may require that small changes be made to the design of a particular component to make it easier to fit during the assembly operations. However, this will be only one of a series of changes planned by the circle to make the production process more effective.

- *Crisis*. This represents both the unexpected and the serious. An extreme example might be the destruction of a factory as the result of a gas explosion or terrorist attack. It contains the potential to destroy the organization unless the response is appropriate and effective.

- *Strategic*. This represents major planned events that attempt to position the organization more effectively in relationship to its environment. For example, a company making sensor technology decides to acquire a firm providing information management services to offer their customers more integrated solutions.

Adaptive change

The vertical axis of Figure 2.2 represents the relative impact of change. Changes categorized as adaptive are small in scale and scope and can be accommodated without major disruption or danger to the organization. They represent small adaptive

Figure 2.2 The change matrix

movements in absorbing and responding to day-to-day events, balancing and integrating operations with the environment within which they take place. However, such changes may still have a significant impact on individual employees, managers or workgroups.

Examples for *temporary* adaptive changes may include a sudden increase in sickness levels due to a flue epidemic which can be accommodated relatively easily but with some additional cost (e.g., employees at work could be asked to work overtime; temporary labour can be hired to cover for absent employees). Allowing production to fall behind schedule is another option. These represent the tactical levels of decisions that line managers engage in all the time in responding to the ever changing circumstances that they are exposed to.

Other adaptive changes may be more *permanent*. Examples here may include minor modifications to service provision procedures, or to product design which requires adjustments in the relevant production process. While these changes are important locally, they are relatively small in comparison to everything that the organization does.

Fracturing change

This scale of change impact in the change matrix (Figure 2.2) represents the major events that occur within the experience of all organizations. The scale of change represented by this category is very large and of such significance that it could seriously damage or destroy (hence 'fracture') the organization.

Products and services are all designed to meet particular needs among their consumers. There is always a danger that these needs can be met in different ways and thus eliminate the market for a particular product. Even companies that are well entrenched and may assume to have particular markets cornered may find sudden competitors emerging. An example of this is the US Air Force refuelling tanker contract that was won in February 2008 by a consortium including Northrup Grumman and the European Airbus parent, EADS. Few had expected that a foreign competitor could beat Boeing in such a big US defence contract, and in fact the contract was withdrawn in September 2008 after investigators questioned the selection process, but the challenge for Boeing remains (Brothers, 2009).

There is a scale of magnitude reflecting the level of real or potential threat to an organization. Equally, some issues which might be major in one context may be considered minor in another. For example, in a company with a poor industrial relations record frequent strikes may be the norm. Therefore, it may be part of the management planning process to build an allowance into their operations, schedules and costs to reduce the impact. Also, there are situations in which relatively minor events can slip out of control to threaten the survival of the organization if they are not handled effectively. Examples of such fracturing changes include natural disasters, industrial accidents, large-scale product recalls or public relations disasters such as a disgusting video made and posted by two Domino Pizza employees in North Carolina in April 2009 on YouTube (Clifford, 2009).

Planned change

The horizontal axis of Figure 2.2 reflects the degree of planning that can be brought to bear on change in organizations. Planned change is proactive rather than reactive, and represents those changes that managers either intend to occur or those for which they have prepared responses. There are many examples of planned change. Cost reduction measures in response to competitive threats represent planned responses, as do strategic moves made by organizations in order to reposition themselves to minimize the overall impact of declining markets or to realize the potential of market segment expansions. Examples include merger, acquisition and divestment strategies that many large organizations engage in as they search for higher returns, market dominance and growth. Similarly, many operational changes in organizations tend to be well planned, such as the introduction of total quality management (TQM) and lean production initiatives are attempts to capture and routinize the process of continuous improvement (Bates *et al.*, 2009) and bring with them subsequent and often ongoing small changes in operations. Planning for many small changes that occur every day is also an important part of normal managerial experience. The companion website presents a discussion of organization development, which refers to systematic approaches to initiate and manage planned change in organizations, as well as an overview of different approaches to organizational change including contingency models of change that can guide managers' attempts to design and lead such planned changes.

2.9 EXTEND
YOUR LEARNING

Unplanned change

This category within the change matrix (Figure 2.2) represents the unexpected events that arise and which can never be completely eliminated from an organization's environment. Earthquakes, hurricanes, tsunamis and other natural disasters are good examples of events that require responses but cannot be completely planned for. While measures can be taken to minimize the consequences through building design, backup systems and response plans, they can never prepare for all required reactions to keep organizational operations going in crisis situations. By definition, crises are events that organizations and managers are not prepared for, so responsiveness and decisiveness are key. It is one of the primary responsibilities of management to anticipate such adverse events, to minimize their likelihood and to develop appropriate emergency and recovery plans. Contingency planning approaches to change attempt to scan the internal and external environment and develop response scenarios for what might be expected to occur.

In the global recession many organizations have reduced employee numbers and rationalized operational activities. This is achieved in many ways including eliminating slack from the system or by deploying efficiency technology and process innovations (see Bates *et al.*, 2009). One of the potential dangers of such minimalist approaches is that they can reduce the capabilities needed for further adaptation, yet failure to respond actively to external change can also reduce such capabilities (Biedenbach and Söderholm, 2008). The inherent risk in this approach is that there is a higher potential to miss important signals from the environment, which in turn increases the likelihood of further reactive changes and ultimately crisis. Crisis is the least desirable and most dangerous cell in the matrix (Figure 2.2) and carries with it the greater threat to the survival of the organization.

The Change at Work example describes one form of change (outsourcing) that would be familiar in many Western companies as a means of achieving cost reduction and productivity improvement. However, it is discussed in relation to developing country applications and in particular Nigeria, which introduces a range of factors and influences that would not be expected in the normal course of events. It therefore forces a reappraisal of what change means in some organizational contexts.

Resistance to change

From a managerial perspective, and particularly in relation to planned change in organizations, the issue of resistance to change is of paramount importance. Cummings and Worley (2005) identify different forms of resistance to change including

CHANGE AT WORK

Outsourcing and change in Nigeria

The following material emerged in discussion with Richard Mack, who works as a consultant in many countries, including Nigeria.

Typically outsourcing has very negative connotations in Nigeria because it is seen primarily as the company getting rid of people to save money and suggests that the current workforce are not capable of doing their jobs the way the company expects them to be done within the allotted budget. When proposed, it causes a level of discontent among staff and an exodus of some of the best people who know they can get a job elsewhere without waiting to see what is going to happen to them. For reasons outlined in the Global influences example in Chapter 16, length of service and long-term career goals are not key motivators for employees in Nigeria. The lower-order needs forming Maslow's model of motivation (Chapter 5) are more significant to most employees.

What is outsourcing? In basic terms by adopting it organizations are looking for improved efficiency, productivity gains, increased capability, and to acquire skills they don't have. In doing so they are often seeking to make revolutionary step changes as opposed to evolutionary change in operational activity, efficiency and profitability. Richard suggested that in his experience the motivation for outsourcing was typically cost elimination and related factors. In Nigeria companies generally present themselves as being heavily involved in CSR; growing the organic capability of the country; improving education levels of the population; and growing the size of the middle classes (in turn creating more customers/consumers). So outsourcing presents an obvious dilemma for them, particularly when wages and inflation are running at such a high rate – approximately 10 per cent per year. In short, companies speak about being mandated to have a significant presence in Nigeria, doing business within Nigeria, developing Nigeria and its people and investing in Nigeria, but they also want the cost savings. Typically the savings from outsourcing come from the offshoring of back-office type jobs and development work to lower-cost countries; leveraging economies of scale around procurement and centralized services; supporting multiple clients, languages, technologies and countries from single dedicated centres (strategically placed based on low- cost areas, e.g. India, Brazil, Eastern Block countries, etc.). Achieving these off-shoring transformations is a direct contradiction with the previous statements and the rhetoric of CSR and the other intentions of companies in Nigeria. It is difficult to achieve a balance between the rhetoric and reality of operating under such conditions.

Richard explained that companies have to resolve this dilemma one way or another, in the process dealing with the internal and external political pressure that will be generated. He also thought that there was an outside possibility that the government would prevent or restrict data/information being taken offshore which would eliminate any benefits from outsourcing. It is very difficult for a company to plan for any year-on-year profit when an ongoing local presence is required, with all the necessary skills, capability, distribution channels and support infrastructure implied by that, if the business model is based on cost reduction. Under such arrangements it would not be possible to reduce the total headcount. Consequently, it may mean that outsourcing contracts may only be worthwhile if the company is looking to upgrade and expand their infrastructure and technology to grow and capture more market share - they have a pure investment and growth strategy and they recognize that they need to spend heavily to achieve it. The final decision will invariably be made by shareholders based on the potential return on their investment. Consequently capitalism and Taylorism may be alive and well in emerging markets such as Nigeria, with cultural tribal values regarded as a local problem and so long as money is made and the shareholders are happy. But the outcomes are not insignificant if developing countries are ever to change and develop. Or perhaps the outcome will be that the gulf between rich and poor will simply become wider.

Richard suggested that another option might involve some form of revenue share and joint reward contract with a reduction in percentage spend of the IT infrastructure over the life of the contract and as long as the company grows and reports increases in revenue year-on-year. Under such arrangements outsourcers should still be able to make money in the developing country with in-country resource through a focus on efficiencies such as consolidation, centralization, virtualization, productivity enhancement and shared 'on demand' infrastructures. Richard called these political positions which could define the requirements of the type of contracts and risk analysis for the potential markets in relation to achievable activities. Hence only a limited range of outsourcing possibilities may be offered to developing geographical markets, emphasizing growth and investment as opposed to cost saving and productivity improvement.

TASKS

1 To what extent does this example suggest that change is about finding ways of maximizing the returns to investors irrespective of social and cultural circumstances?

2 To what extent does this example demonstrate that change is a creative process that needs a wide range of variables and influences to be taken into account and is therefore a process that is not amenable to the application of any guiding model or theory?

Source:
Reproduced with grateful thanks to Richard Mack.

individual resistance (see also below and Chapter 4), *technical resistance* (due to habits of using established procedures or preferences; see also Chapter 11), *political resistance* (due to changes that threaten established power bases of individuals or groups, see Chapter 15), and *cultural resistance* (due to cultural inertia and established preferences for and internalization of informal values, norms and assumptions, see Chapter 14). In addition, *structural resistance* to change is based on the inertia that goes along with formal structures such as departmental groupings, established interaction processes, and communication linkages (see Chapter 10). Below we discuss the issue of resistance to change at the individual and the group and organizational levels of analysis.

The starting point for considering resistance to change is the image conjured up by the phrase itself. It implies that an individual or group hinders the implementation of a particular course of action. Kahn (1982) suggests that resistance behaviour during times of change is frequently indistinguishable from normal behaviour patterns. The difference is a function of the perspective of the person classifying the behaviour rather than the behaviour itself.

The following material has been compiled from a number of sources including Armstrong (1995), Hellriegel *et al.* (1989), Kanter (1983), Kotter and Schlesinger (1979), Moorhead and Griffin (1992), Mullins (1996) and Plant (1987).

Individual resistance to change

Individuals resist change for a number of reasons, including those indicated in Figure 2.3. Many of the reasons indicated in this figure are self-explanatory and easily understood. For example, fear of the unknown implies that the individual would prefer to remain with existing arrangements. Change can be a negative experience for many employees. Organizational experience soon indicates that managers do not always have the best interests of employees at heart, particularly when cutbacks are the norm! However, some of the reasons identified in Figure 2.3 need further explanation:

- *Symbolic meaning.* The entitlement to benefits such as a company car or the use of a private office rather than an area separated by partitions all provide symbols of status within the organization. Changes which impact on such visible signs can be fiercely resisted even if they are incidental.

Figure 2.3 Individual reasons for resisting change

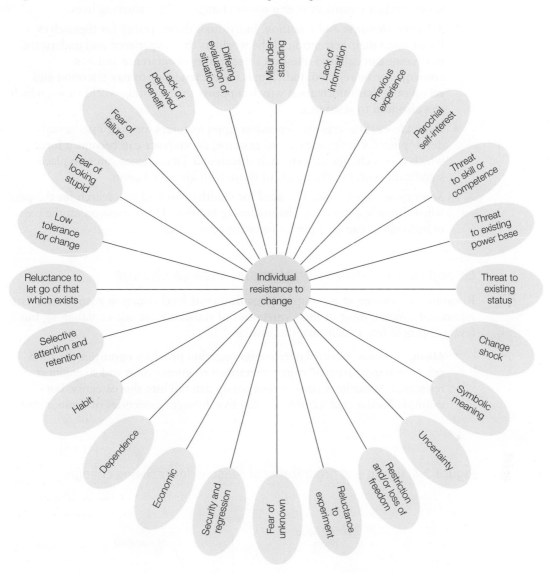

- *Change shock*. The previous routine will have been familiar and individuals will have known instinctively what they were supposed to do. Change can destroy that level of familiarity and create situations in which predictability is reduced, thus creating an experience of shock for the individual. It was widely reported in the press during May 2003, for example, that one company in the personal injury claims business (The Accident Group) dismissed all its 2500 workers by text message when it suddenly ceased trading. The personal injury claims industry is commonly referred to as 'ambulance chasing', as it seeks to obtain compensation for people who have suffered some form of accident. Its advertising slogan was, 'Where there's blame, there's a claim.' The text messages received by the staff told them that they would not be paid for the previous month's work and that their employment had ceased immediately. On hearing of this a number of staff went to local offices and either smashed or stole computers and other office equipment. This example demonstrates the reaction of angry employees in shock at their treatment over a major change in their working lives.

- *Selective attention and retention.* Individuals define reality for themselves based upon their perception of the world as they experience and understand it. Change can call into question these frames of reference and as a consequence be rejected. Individuals have a tendency to pay attention and retain only that information which supports their existing world views, which can also lead to resistance.

- *Dependence.* Students are dependent upon lecturers for their intellectual development. However, taken to extreme, dependence can become a force which resists change as security is threatened. Dependence can also place significant power in the hands of those who are relied upon.

- *Security and regression.* The need for security can lead to a search for the past when things appeared simpler and more familiar. This regression on the part of individuals can be a potent force for resisting change.

Group and organizational resistance to change

Resistance to change at a group or organizational level comes in many forms (see Figure 2.4). Again, most of these categories of resistance are self-explanatory, but a few will benefit from additional discussion:

- *Misinformation.* Control over communication provides opportunities for a group to impart particular interpretations to information and so engineer resistance. Sometimes rumour and gossip can fall into this category. For example Bordia *et al.* (2003) identify five different categories of rumour and

Figure 2.4 Group and organizational reasons for resisting change.

gossip. They also classified individual examples as either positive or negative depending on the content relative to the change. Not surprisingly, negative rumours were more prevalent during change than positive ones. The five categories of rumour identified were:

- Those about changes to jobs and working conditions
- Those about the nature of organizational change
- Those about poor change management
- Those about change and its consequences on organizational performance
- Interpersonal gossip about change and its impact.

- *Organization structure.* The bureaucratic form of organization was designed to deliver consistency and predictability of operations. Consequently, it is a structure that does not cope easily with change.

- *Previous agreements.* Arrangements entered into with another group or organization are designed to control events in the future. This restricts the ability to make changes in the interaction between these groups over the period of such agreements.

- *Fixed investments.* The investments that an organization makes in buildings, land and equipment place considerable restriction on what can be done in the future. In practice, they limit the ability to change because they represent assets that are not easy to liquidate in the short term.

- *Overdetermination.* The systems and procedures that organizations create to provide control can also restrict the ability to introduce change.

- *Narrow focus of change.* In considering change an organization very often takes the immediate zone of impact into account. It is possible for situations to arise in which groups not immediately affected by change resist involvement and so limit the benefits ultimately gained. For example, in addressing the production problems in one department, management may introduce team working and in the process replace supervisors with team leaders. Supervisors in other departments may see this as an attempt to erode their status and indeed job security. If they are not involved in the original exercise and supportive of the changes, then they may well resist any attempts to introduce change in the future.

Overall, to manage change and deal with resistance, it is important to understand the systemic linkages between the many aspects and dynamics related to people and the organizational context. Figure 2.5 refers back to the framework introduced in Chapter 1 and indicates how managers can conceptualize their options for initiating and leading organizational change. As indicated by the four change arrows in Figure 2.5, their change management activities must aim at generating changes in individuals, in the way they interact, in the formal organizational systems as well as in the informal social systems in the organization. Of course, given the systemic linkages between the four different sets of factors, any change in selected aspects can disturb or even destroy existing equilibriums and create unintended consequences. And as all of this is taking place in complex and changing environments, the capacity of managers to continuously adapt their organizations by creating appropriate change that matches external conditions and requirements is crucial (Biedenbach and Söderholm, 2008). Of all the challenges managers face, the deliberate and ongoing attempts to create constructive change in organizations may well be the most complex and most difficult, yet it is also the most important for achieving continued managerial and organizational success.

2.10 EXTEND
YOUR LEARNING

Figure 2.5 Managing organizational change in the comprehensive framework for OB and management in organizations

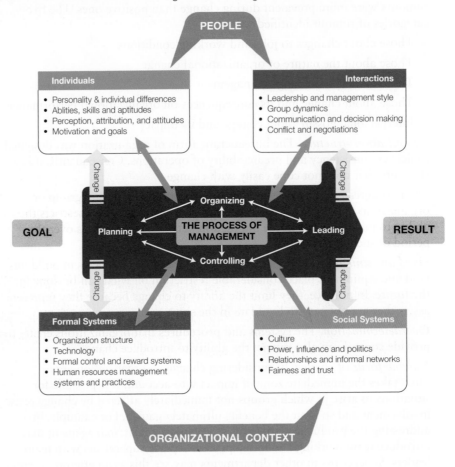

CONCLUSIONS

This chapter has considered the historical origins of management thinking and practice. It briefly reviewed some of the major perspectives that have emerged over many years. This included brief examples of management practice from many hundreds (and thousands) of years ago, and also academic approaches including scientific management, classical management theory, the human relations movement and systems approaches. This chapter also introduced topics that will be considered in much greater detail throughout this book to highlight the reality of management and OB in contemporary organizations.

Specifically, the four major contemporary management challenges that will be considered in each chapter of the book are:

- Managing in the global context: globalization and cultural diversity ('Going Global').
- Ethics and CSR ('Examining Ethics').

- Today's performance imperative ('High performance').
- Pervasive organizational change ('Change at Work').

Each of these challenges has a significant impact on management activity in every organization on a daily basis. For example, globalization impacts on even small organizations as the markets for goods, services and labour become ever more competitive and interlinked across borders. Ethics and CSR reflect ways of working and running organizations that take into account the impact on society and individuals of the actions and decisions that managers take. Performance is an ever present demand as all managers are expected to achieve more with fewer resources as a consequence of forces including globalization, CSR and change in markets, product offerings and competitor activity. Change is also another factor that impacts on managers as they seek to achieve their objectives in a constrained context and with political, economic, globalization, social and other forces acting on them all of the time.

Now to summarize this chapter in terms of the relevant Learning Objectives:

- **Assess the significance of some of the ethical dilemmas facing managers.** There are a wide range of possible ethical dilemmas facing managers, only some of which are represented in this chapter. How much value is actually provided to customers in return for doing business with the organization represents a fundamental ethical dilemma. Most companies seek the highest price for their products and services and the highest level of profit, and so there is a potential danger of seeking ways to 'cheat' the customer by providing inferior products and services at inflated prices. There are also areas associated with the management of people and how much they might be exploited in the search for lower cost and higher profit by the organization. Other ethical dilemmas include the area of CSR and the degree to which organizations should be expected to put effort into the communities of which they form part. It could be argued that this is achieved by the payment of wages and taxes in any location, but there is also a view suggesting that there should also be additional contributions to the community to cover the degree of interference in the local environment.

- **Explain why people and groups might be expected to resist change.** People resist change for a wide range of reasons and these are identified in Figure 2.3 and the associated discussion. These include being familiar with one way of doing things and not wanting to do anything differently; self-interest; threat to skill or competence; threat to status within the organization and the uncertainly associated with making change. In addition, there are group and organizational level factors which influence resistance to change and these are identified in Figure 2.4 and the associated discussion. For example; misinformation by one group or another can be used as a means of encouraging individuals or groups to resist; the existence of a low trust environment can also work against change being accepted. These figures and the associated text should be consulted for more detail on this objective.

- **Discuss the significance of the contemporary management challenges for the theory and practice of management and OB.** Each of the four contemporary management challenges are important areas of research and academic scholarship in their own right. They are also important forces on the day-to-day practice of management in that they impact on the normal functions of managers who are seeking to plan, forecast, organize, and so on the resources at their disposal in order to achieve the business objectives that they have been set. As such they drive (or impact on) just about every facet of management practice and therefore from an OB perspective they represent significant features that have relevance to every other aspect of OB. That is why they appear in each chapter in the form of discussion and support panels that illustrate and explore how they relate to management practice and each chapter theme.

- **Outline the relative contribution to an understanding of management from the historical perspective and through each of the different schools and perspectives on management that have evolved across time.** It should be apparent that management has existed in one form or another for many hundreds (if not thousands) of years and throughout that time the individuals 'doing' that job have had to try to achieve their objectives within the specific social, cultural and economic circumstances of the day. Some of these practices are still evident today, even though the surrounding circumstances are often very different. Each of the academic traditions reviewed in this chapter has a slightly different perspective to offer on the sphere of interest that they embrace. These perspectives are not mutually exclusive or capable of offering indisputable truth about a particular theme. The inherent difficulty in seeking to explain management and human behaviour in a complex and dynamic social environment is apparent from the material introduced in the first two chapters in this text. Each of the traditions reviewed offers some insight into the phenomena in focus and it is necessary to reflect on the positive and negative aspects of the various perspectives presented in order to formulate your own models and theories of what managing and working in an organizations means.

- **Understand the different approaches to ethics.** There are a number of different approaches to the study of ethics. In an organizational context, the model adopted in this chapter is based on the utilitarian and contract approaches. The utilitarian approach originates with the notion of usefulness and is split into act and rule subsets. Act utilitarianism is based on the idea that every dilemma should be regarded on its merits. For example, telling a lie could be justified in some circumstances. Rule utilitarianism suggests that taking each act separately might not be the best way to provide for the effective running of society as a whole and so a set of rules should be developed. The contract approach is based on the idea

that all social relationships are based on a contract (or agreement) of some description. All agreements should be honoured, it is argued. Restricted contractarianism suggests that every act should be viewed through a 'veil of ignorance' in terms of possible impact on the individual making the decision. Libertarian contractarianism argues that individuals should abide by the agreements entered into as long as they don't conflict with the broader rules of society or cause harm to others.

DISCUSSION QUESTIONS

1 The performance imperative of old where managers were expected to achieve their goals has been turbocharged: today's performance imperative requires managers to do more with ever decreasing resources, and also to respond to environmental change and organizational requirements immediately. That is termed hypercompetition. To what extent do you support that view, or does hypercompetition simply reflect the old performance imperatives in a different social context? Justify your views.

2 'Management is about managing the present, within the constraints imposed by the past, whilst seeking to prepare for an unknowable future. It is therefore an impossible task.' Discuss this statement.

3 'The only thing that people learn from history is that people learn nothing from history.' To what extent does this statement explain why some of the management and organizational issues identified in history still have relevance today?

4 Scientific management postulated that it was a management responsibility to identify the 'one best way' for workers to perform, and it was the employee's responsibility to follow the prescribed method of work. To what extent can

this approach ever identify the most effective means of meeting customer needs?

5 'Ethics has no part to play in managerial activities.' Discuss this statement.

6 'Human beings are their own worst enemy as they demand high-quality products and services at very low prices whilst at the same time demanding high-quality jobs and high wages. These demands are incompatible and change, which negatively impacts on jobs and people, is therefore inevitable.' Discuss this statement.

7 Provide a brief explanation for five of the individual reasons for resisting change.

8 Distinguish between planned and unplanned change, adaptive and fracturing change. What are the consequences of these distinctions?

9 Discuss the statement that globalization provides managers with more opportunities than problems.

10 'The true skill in management is to keep change happening so that everyone has to pay attention to what they are doing and they do not have any spare time to cause trouble for managers.' Discuss this statement.

CASE STUDY

To lie or not to lie, that is the question

This case is based on a discussion between one of the authors and the HR manager concerned. Only the names and incidental details have been changed.

The company employed about 800 people and was a large engineering manufacturer based in the North of England. The products made were precision automotive components, used in top of the range motor vehicles, predominantly bought as company cars for senior managers. There was an economic recession at the time of the case study and so the market for large, expensive company cars was rather depressed with orders from the car markers having reduced significantly. It was not anticipated that the market conditions would improve for some time and so the company decided that it needed to reduce its workforce by about 15 per cent.

©Jeff Greenberg /Photolibrary

The company had a good reputation as an employer in the area and was well respected for the quality of its training of shop-floor workers and the generosity of its pay levels. There were no other employers in the area that required the same high standard of engineering skill that those working at the company possessed. Neither were the rates of pay as generous in other organizations. Being a caring employer the company proposed a voluntary severance scheme to the trade union representing the engineering workforce on the factory floor. This would provide volunteers leaving with double the financial compensation that the company were required to pay to them under employment legislation. One of the scheme conditions was that if enough volunteers to leave were not found then compulsory termination of employment would be implemented with only the statutory compensation being paid. This was intended to encourage more people to volunteer to leave and so avoid the need to dismiss people who did not want to leave. Management retained the right to refuse to accept any particular person volunteering, and to select any people for compulsory termination if it were needed. Of course the trade union had the right to be consulted and to make representations to management on the selection criteria and in seeking alternatives to compulsory termination of employment.

The voluntary scheme was agreed by the trade union and notices were placed in the factory. These set out the basic terms of the scheme and asked people interested in applying to make informal enquires of the HR manager before deciding whether to apply formally for voluntary termination. A steady stream of people made appointments to talk to the HR manager about their circumstances, and to find out what the level of compensation would be in their particular situation. Behind the scenes line managers were making contingency plans to decide whom they would dismiss should enough volunteers not be forthcoming. However, this process had to be secret as by law any possible compulsory terminations through redundancy must be discussed with the trade union before selection rules were developed and before people were selected.

One of the longer-serving employees made enquires of the HR manager about their situation. However, they eventually decided that the money on offer was not enough to tempt them to apply for voluntary redundancy. The individual made the point to the HR manager that they were not certain to get another job at their age (56-years-old). Even if they could get another job, it would not provide the same level of income. Also with such long service at the company (40 years) they had only a few years to go until retirement and so would decline the offer and stay put. They also said that with such long service they would be very unlikely to be selected for compulsory termination within the present company. However, what the HR manager knew, and the employee did not, was that the selection criteria for compulsory termination was going to be based on a range of work-based factors such as productivity, timekeeping, attendance, range of skills, etc. Even though the precise nature of the compulsory selection criteria would not be known until discussions were held between the company and trade union, the management had decided that contribution to the business in one form or another would be the only acceptable way forward. Also what the employee was not aware of, was that if it became necessary to compulsorily select employees, then his overall performance was such that he was definitely going to be selected, irrespective of his length of service.

The HR manager explained that he felt very guilty about the position that this particular employee was in. In essence, the employee was turning down the offer to go voluntarily with a generous financial settlement, when it was certain that within a few weeks he would be compulsorily dismissed with about half of the financial compensation. The HR manager could not make the position clear to the individual because of the legislative requirements, but could only gently encourage serious consideration of the terms offered through the voluntary scheme. After several attempts to encourage the employee to volunteer, he refused, saying that he had always been happy at the company and the company would look after him in the future, until he retired. About 3 months later the employee was compulsorily made redundant and was personally devastated and left very bitter by the experience.

TASKS

1 Given that the example represents a real situation that occurred in the organization, how might it be interpreted through the ethical perspectives introduced in this chapter?

2 Is it acceptable for a manager to tell lies in this (or any) situation? Why or why not?

3 What would you have done had you been the HR manager faced with that situation?

4 How might an understanding of change management have helped the company manage this situation more effectively?

5 How might the study of OB help you deal with such situations if you were the personnel manager?

FURTHER READING

Burke, W.W. (2008) *Organization change: Theory and practice* (2nd edn), Thousand Oaks, CA: Sage. Useful discussion of organizational change management.

Coghlan, D. and Brannick, T. (2010) *Doing action research in your own organization* (3rd edn), London: Sage. Excellent source for anyone trying to understand how to learn about their own organizations while trying to change them. Highly recommended!

Cooperrider, D.L. and Whitney, D. (2005) *Appreciative inquiry: A positive revolution in change,* San Francisco: Berrett-Koehler. Useful source for those interested in learning about how to look for what works and making it better rather than simply 'trying to identify and stamp out suboptimal aspects of work and organizations'.

Cummings, T.G. and Worley, C.G. (2005) *Organization development and change* (8th edn), Thomson/Southwestern. Comprehensive overview of approaches to organizational change.

Friedman, T.L. (2005) *The world is flat*, Farrar, Straus and Giroux. Bestselling book on how globalization is changing the world.

Lukes, S. (2008) *Moral relativism*, London: Profile Books. Comprehensive treatment of the question of moral relativism. Not the easiest read but highly rewarding.

Rachels, J. and Rachels, S. (2009) *The elements of moral philosophy* (6th edn), McGraw-Hill. Readable and comprehensive introduction to moral philosophy. Highly useful for those interested in the relevant philosophical ideas.

Stiglitz, J.E. (2006) *Making Globalization Work,* London:
    Norton & Co. Together with Friedman, an important
    contribution to the debate on globalization from a
    Nobel prize winning economist.
Weisbord, M.R. (2004) *Productive Workplaces*
    (2nd edn), San Francisco: Jossey-Bass. New
edition of a classic book on changing organizations
collaboratively. Highly readable and excellent for
those looking for a comprehensive discussion of
how members of organizations can change their
organizations to create better workplaces.

COMPANION WEBSITE

Online teaching and learning resources

Visit the companion website for Organizational Behaviour and Management 4th edition at: http://www
.cengage.co.uk/martinfellenz to find valuable further teaching and learning material. For full details,
see 'About the website' at the start of the book.

PART TWO

INDIVIDUALS IN ORGANIZATIONS

3 Personality and individual difference

4 Perception, attribution and attitude formation

5 Motivation

After the introduction to organizational behaviour and the discussion of major contemporary management challenges, Part 2 starts the detailed exploration of organizational behaviour issues and dynamics. The chapters of Part 2 focus on the individual, their relevant characteristics, and their ways of experiencing organizations. Individuals are the basic building blocks of organizations, and are the source of any action and behaviour that occurs in organizations. Thus, understanding individuals in organizations is the starting point for much of what follows in this book on organizational behaviour.

Chapter 3 focuses on the individuality of people and introduces the notion of individual difference. People are obviously different in many ways, but not all are relevant to their connection with organizations. The study of personality seeks to explore just how people differ in important ways, how this may impact on their behaviour, their work and their interaction with others. Chapter 4 discusses perception, which is related to the way in which people experience and make sense of the world around them. It also considers the related dynamics of attribution and attitude formation. Finally, Chapter 5 considers internal and external determinants of motivation. This is important for understanding why people do what they do, and – particularly important in organizations – how this knowledge can be used by managers who seek to maximize the contribution from employees in pursuit of high performance and organizational objectives.

The themes introduced in Part 2 cover the important variables at work at the individual level of analysis. It is individuals that make up the teams and groups that work in the departments and sections that actually deliver the results achieved. Therefore, these themes, theories and variables will be used throughout the book in considering interactions between individuals, group behaviour and the role of individuals in the functioning of organizations.

Figure 1

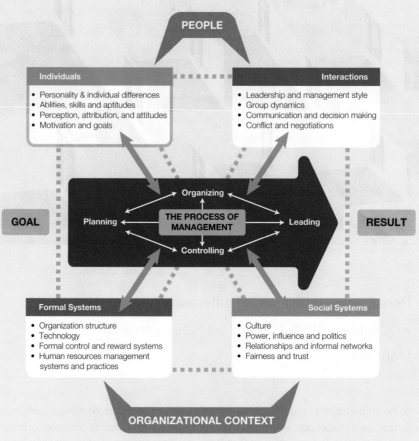

CHAPTER THREE

PERSONALITY AND INDIVIDUAL DIFFERENCE

LEARNING OBJECTIVES

After studying this chapter and working through the associated OB in Action panels, Discussion Questions and Case Study you should be able to:

- Outline the concept of individual difference.

- Describe the major theoretical approaches to the study of personality.

- Understand the strengths and weaknesses of each of the major theories of personality.

- Discuss the basic process involved in the development of psychometric tests.

- Explain the significance of individual difference as a basis for taking decisions relating to people within organizations.

INTRODUCTION

Human beings as individuals are unique – no two people think, feel or act the same way. This introduces enormous variety in organizations, especially for anyone trying to achieve goals with and through people. Understanding individual differences, and their implications for the thinking, feeling and behaviour of people in organizations, is therefore an important aspect of OB.

The concept of *individual difference* has a long tradition within psychology and can be traced back in philosophy to the early Greeks. For example, Theophrastus (a philosopher) was asking 2000 years ago why it was that with a common culture and education system people displayed different characteristics (Eysenck, 1982). We think about ourselves and others both in terms of similarities and differences, but ultimately we identify individuals by their specific and unique set of characteristics we can observe and infer. The psychological construct that has been used to embrace the features of individual difference is that of personality. Yet despite its central importance for both everyday thinking and the systematic psychological study of individuals, the notion of personality continues to elude precise and uniform definition. As far back as 1937, Allport identified about 50 different interpretations of the concept. Since then many writers have attempted to define personality and Hall and Lindzey (1970) suggest that the definition preferred by each writer reflects the theoretical perspective adopted by that person, rather than any underlying conceptual insight. In other words, the definition of personality used by a particular writer becomes

Personality
The relatively enduring individual characteristics that are inferred from observable, reasonably consistent patterns of an individual's behaviour over time.

HIGH PERFORMANCE

Organizations are zoos!

One motivational speaker (Nigel Risner) suggested that in the workplace individuals fall into one of four main categories of personality:

- *Lions*. Head straight for the end result doing almost anything to get the job done. They need achievement to measure success.

- *Monkeys*. Place high value on recognition and measure success through the amount of acknowledgement and praise received. They gravitate towards popularity, friendliness and prestige, whilst avoiding rejection, negativism and argument.

- *Dolphins*. These are steady, co-operative types placing a high value on sharing and trust. Routine and predictability make them feel safe, unplanned change makes them feel unhappy.

- *Elephants*. More concerned with content than congratulations. They need to know how things

work and this can lead to paralysis by analysis and following every rule in the book. Speed is never an issue with these types of people.

Risner goes on to make the point that good managers need to act like good zookeepers – understanding the animals in their zoo and communicating with them in appropriate ways to achieve effective team goals.

TASKS

1 As an employee would you be happy with this approach to classifying you? Why or why not?

2 As a manager would you be happy to use this approach to classifying your staff? Why or why not?

3 To what extent could this approach help to improve individual and/or team performance?

Sources:
Risner, N. (2003) *It's a Zoo Around Here*. London: Forest Oak Publications.
Risner, N. (2003) The human zoo, *People Management*, 9 January: p. 42.

apparent through the description and justification of a particular theory – see for example the High Performance example 'Organizations are zoos!' that are intended to carry a range of messages to clients of the developer. In this chapter we will consider personality, its origins and development, and discuss the different aspects that are particularly important in organizations.

THE STUDY OF INDIVIDUAL DIFFERENCE

Our everyday thinking about individuals is very much tied up to the notion of individual differences – so much so that the notion of personality is indispensable in our thinking about people. The problem of defining this term in part arises because personality (the construct that defines individual difference) cannot be directly observed. Thus, any stable, defining internal characteristics of a person can only ever be imperfectly known. Moreover, observable aspects that differentiate between people are not all linked to personality – examples here are height, gender or skin colour. Consider for a moment two people and how they differ from each other. Perhaps your description would include some of the following:

- *Physical description.* Height, weight, build, hair colour, dress.
- *Emotional description.* Gushing, withdrawn, nervous, aggressive.
- *Sociability description.* Friendly, responsive, giving, likeable, 'nice'.

These factors, along with many more, reflect ways in which people can be differentiated from each other. However, they are not all aspects of personality. Some characteristics reflect ability or physical qualities; others are probably a reflection of very transient emotional states or a function of the situation in which you observe them. And others with the same contact with these two people may form very different views of how they are. Thus, personality as a concept that describes individual differences is a social construction rather than simply reflecting the tangible aspect of others. This recognizes that our views of others' personalities are constructed rather than given – we are all lay-psychologists in that we infer people's personality from observing their behaviour. This is the reason why the definition we offer above suggests that personality is inferred on the basis of observable behaviour. This is not to say, however, that personality as it is commonly understood does not exist and cannot be represented.

Commonly, personality is seen as being visible in those aspects of behaviour that appear to be more stable across different situations and, to varying degrees, also over time. To complicate matters, some forms of behaviour may be more meaningful indicators of personality than others. People sitting quietly in church listening to a sermon may not all be reserved, quiet and introvert, while those shouting loudly as spectators at a sports match may not all be outgoing, excitable and extrovert. At the same time, we would expect that those that we view as quieter would tend to be quieter than others in church, at a sports match, and on other occasions. Yet some individuals are more influenced than others by their environment, and thus situational factors may have a greater impact on their behaviour. Moreover, some situations are commonly thought to have a strong influence on the thinking and behaviour of the majority of people and may overpower the influence of personality. As described in Table 3.1, such situations are called strong situations, while those thought to exert only a little influence and leave room for individual differences to manifest themselves in behaviour are called weak situations (Mischel, 1977; but see Cooper and Withey, 2009). Also consider the implications of the Employee perspective 'Personality or achievement?' in this context.

Strong situations (impacting on personality) Situations with a strong influence on the thinking and behaviour of the majority of people and which may consequently overpower the influence of personality.

Weak situations (impacting on personality) Situations exerting only limited influence on the thinking and behaviour of the majority of people and consequently leaving room for individual differences to manifest themselves.

Table 3.1 Strong and weak situational influences on the thinking and behaviour of people

Strong situations are ones that ...	Weak situations are ones that ...
lead everyone to construe the particular events the same way	include equivocality and therefore do not generate uniform interpretations
induce *uniform* expectancies regarding the most appropriate response pattern	do not generate uniform expectancies concerning desired behaviour
provide adequate incentives for the performance of that response pattern	do not offer sufficient incentives for its performance
require skills that everyone has to the same extent	fail to provide the learning conditions required for successful genesis of behaviour
have comparatively more precise if ... then contingencies.	have comparatively less clear-cut if ... then contingencies.

Source: Adapted from Mischel (1977); Shoda, Mischel & Wright (1989)

EMPLOYEE PERSPECTIVE

Personality or achievements?

Imagine you have been asked the following question by a friend:

I am a quiet person, yet I work hard and get good results. In a recent discussion about a possible promotion, I was told that to stand a chance of getting the post, I needed to be more 'lively' and 'outspoken'. I am perturbed that my work doesn't speak for itself, and convinced that my employers seem to want me to become a different person before I can move forward. Should I try to change my behaviour, or are they asking too much?

TASKS

1 The employee asking the question talks about 'changing their behaviour' and 'becoming a different person'. Does being asked to become more 'lively' and 'outspoken' refer to behaviour or personality and why?

2 How would you reply to your friend and why?

Now read the answer that was provided by Bullmore, J. (2002) What's your problem?, *Management Today*, December, p. 77 when he was asked that question. (summary answer on the companion web site).

As already mentioned, personality is typically considered to represent those personal characteristics that result in consistent patterns of behaviour (Burger, 1986). This general understanding leaves many important issues undecided. Consequently, psychologists have concentrated on part of the overall meaning of individual difference, namely the underlying psychological structures that bring about such consistent behaviour patterns. In addition to considering the nature of personality, these researchers have typically focused on some or all of these questions: What are the origins of personality? Does personality change over time? What differences and similarities can we find in the personality of different people? How can personality be measured? What are the implications of personality in organizations? We will consider all of these questions in the light of the theories and contributions we discuss in this chapter.

Nature versus nurture – on the origins of personality

What is the source of personality? Is personality something that each individual is born with, or does it develop over time through environmental influences and experience? This is the so-called nature–nurture controversy. Proponents of both sides have made strong arguments that personality is influenced by either genetic factors or by environmental influences. The answer that is emerging is that both appear to have an influence, and that it is often interactions between genetic and environmental influences that ultimately determine personality. The relationship between these variables is shown in Figure 3.1.

Genetic influences. Personality is influenced by the genetic inheritance of the individual. In common expression there are many examples of heredity being used to justify behaviour. For example: 'That [particular behaviour] is just like your father [or mother].' Increasing evidence has become available, much of it from the study of genetically identical yet separately raised twins, which indicates the often surprisingly high degree to which certain traits (including food preferences, clothing preferences and personal habits) are shared by twins despite fundamentally different upbringing and surroundings. Research in behavioural genetics on the correlation of major personality traits points to estimates of correlations of 0.5 (+/− 0.1) attributable to heritability (Bouchard and Loehlin, 2001).

Genetic influences (on personality)
The influence of the genetic inheritance of the individual on their personality.

It is becoming increasingly clear, however, that genetic influences on personality are not simple and straightforward. There is evidence to suggest that results indicating the heritability of personality arise both from direct genetic effects as well as from interactions between a person's genetic makeup and the environment (Rutter and Silberg 2002). This may mean that genetics determine the range of possible development for a particular characteristic, but that environmental influences determine the actual degree achieved (Pervin, 1984).

The interaction between genetic and environmental influences on personality and behaviour may be even more complex. Recent research from an emerging area called neuroplasticity, which deals with the way in which the human brain can change, indicates that many experiences, even living in a particular culture, can change both the physical properties and the functional structure of the brain (Doidge, 2007; Schwartz and Begley, 2002). The implications of these findings for personality psychology have yet to be fully explored and considered.

Figure 3.1 Relationship between the determinants of personality

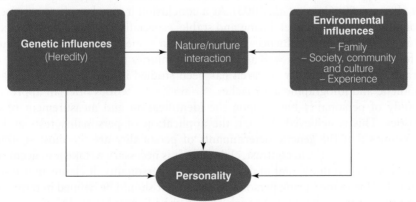

What has long been clearly established, however, is that a person's environment does affect personality development. Environmental influences typically believed to have such effects include:

Environmental influences (on personality)
The influence of the environment on the development of a person's personality.

- *Family.* When we are born we become part of a family. In our early years we are socialized into a family group and by that family into the wider society. Parents and siblings all have parts to play in introducing the individual to the behaviour patterns accepted within those cultures. Family in this context includes grandparents, aunts, cousins, and so on, as all have a part to play in establishing behaviour patterns in the child. There are many ways in which the family influences the development of the individual's personality. They include:

  - Parenting styles and family members' interaction with children which encourages particular behaviour patterns.
  - Older members serving as role models for the younger members to imitate.
  - The circumstances surrounding the family, including family size, family structure, birth order, economic status, religion and geographic location.

- *Society, community and culture.* The environment into which individual are born, and in which they grow up has a considerable influence on the behaviour norms to which they are exposed. This is true for relatively tangible differences in the environment like neighbourhoods and schools (Cleveland, 2003; Rose *et al.*, 2003), but also for society and culture (e.g., Heine and Buchtel, 2009). For example, Western cultures tend to emphasize individual characteristics while Asian cultures tend to emphasize collective values. Consequently, appropriate personality characteristics will be encouraged (through socialization) in individuals within each culture. However, there may be substantial variation of such culturally and socially consistent characteristics across different individuals within the same context.

- *Experience.* The friendship and other groups to which individuals belong, together with the general experiences of life, all have an effect on behaviour. For example, the experience of being bullied by other children in the school playground can have a significant influence on personality and self-esteem (Bradshaw, 1981).

Personality appears to be relatively stable in its rudimentary form already by age three. It continues to change but these changes are not as big during childhood and adolescence as could be expected given the often substantial environmental, developmental and identity changes typically associated with these stage of development (see Fraley and Roberts, 2005; Roberts and DelVecchio, 2000). Personality research reveals that personality change decreases until it reaches the highest plateau of stability after age 50 (Caspi *et al.*, 2005). As a conclusion it may be safe to assume that personality traits are quite enduring and stable, especially in adults, but that experience and environmental influences can bring about some change. This is particularly true for traumatic events as well as for physical injuries to the brain.

Traditionally, personality research has been studied in two major ways, namely nomothetic and idiographic approaches. Nomothetic theories offer an approach to the study of personality based upon the identification and measurement of characteristics. This is achieved through the application of personality tests and usually assumes that the genetic determinants of personality are the most significant. Idiographic approaches, in contrast, claim that it is necessary to take into account the uniqueness of each individual in describing their personality. It claims that tests are of limited value in measuring personality because it should be defined in terms of the self-concept of the individual. As such, within the idiographic tradition, personality

Nomothetic theories
These offer an approach based upon the identification and measurement of characteristics through psychometric tests.

Idiographic approaches
Are based upon the uniqueness of each individual and reject the use of psychometric tests.

is largely a function of the dynamic interaction between the individual and the environment in which they live.

As with many other areas of psychological research, this classification scheme does not account for all the theories that have been developed. There are approaches to personality that combine both idiographic and nomothetic elements. Such approaches are often individual contributions to the field that cannot easily be integrated into the above distinction. Below we will first consider some of the important nomothetic contributions to personality.

NOMOTHETIC PERSPECTIVES

The nomothetic approach reflects traditional positivist and post-positivist approaches to social science. It is characterized by the view that the social world consists of cause and effect relationships, just like the world of the natural sciences, and that the role of social science is to discover these causal connections (Kolakowski, 1993). Inevitably therefore, (post-) positivists tend to follow the experimental and scientific tradition in the search for underlying regularities or laws that create the social world. This is the approach taken by nomothetic personality research that concentrates on the identification and measurement of those dimensions that are generally considered to be the common characteristics of personality. This approach is based on the analysis of data obtained from research carried out on large numbers of individuals. In some ways, nomothetic researchers attempt to find the similarities among the individual differences in people to create models of personality that can be used to describe and compare people. There are many such approaches and measurement instruments, but the best known include those developed by Eysenck and Cattell. More recently, the 'Big Five' model of personality has received growing recognition as the most universally used approach to describe personality in psychology and OB. It is useful to remember that these nomothetic theories are descriptive of personality and do not in themselves explain issues such as origin of personality and so on, although some researchers have included such explanations as part of their theories.

Eysenck and the study of personality types

Hans Eysenck (1916–1997) was a German-born psychologist who focused during much of his prolific research career on the study of personality. Eysenck collected data, mostly from people in the UK, USA and Europe, and subjected the data to factor analysis in order to identify the underlying dimensions of personality. Factor analysis is a statistical technique that reduces the complexity inherent in data sets to identify the fundamental structure and properties of research results that cannot be observed directly. The outcome of his work was the identification of two dimensions along which personality could be said to vary:

- *Extroversion.* Measured on a scale running between the extremes of extroversion and introversion. The extrovert likes excitement, is sociable and lively. The introvert, by comparison, has a quiet and retiring aspect to their personality.

- *Neuroticism.* This implies a scale running from **neurotic** to stable in personality characteristics. The neurotic person tends to worry, is anxious, moody and unstable. The stable person tends to be calm, even-tempered, carefree and reliable.

Extroversion
The qualities of excitability, sociability and liveliness in an individual.

Introversion
An introvert has a shy, quiet and retiring aspect to their personality.

Neuroticism
Refers to a personality dimension characterized by anxiety, moodiness and lack of emotional balance and stability. Neuroticism is also called low emotional stability.

Eysenck used these two dimensions to construct a framework comprising four classical temperaments that had been referred to in classical sources as early as 1798 (Eysenck, 1965). The four temperaments can be described as follows: *Sanguine* refers to people who are carefree, hopeful, in the moment, easily fatigued and bored by work but constantly engaged in mere games, change-oriented and not known for persistence; *Phlegmatic* people display a lack of emotion, are steady, reasonable in interactions, and able to get their way through persistence while appearing to give way to others; *Melancholic* describes people as egotistic, anxious and pessimistic, insecure and suspicious in interactions; and *Choleric* people are seen as impulsive, impetuous, quick-tempered yet easily calmed down if opponents give in, frequently annoyed without lasting animosity, quick but not persistent, focused on image and externalities, and hurt if others do not subscribe to their pretensions.

The two personality dimensions identified by Eysenck and the relationship between these and the much older temperaments are reflected in the main axes and quadrants of Figure 3.2. This figure also indicates the main characteristics of each of the 'types' of personality in the words around the perimeter of the outer circle. For example, someone who was unstable would also score highly on tests measuring the concepts of touchy, moody, etc. These also reflect the concepts upon which the factor analysis indicated earlier was carried out. The angle between the basic characteristics (passing through the centre point of the circle) is a reflection of the relationship between them. For example, there are about 90 degrees between the characteristics of 'sober and rigid' and 'aggressive and excitable', implying that there is little or no correlation between them (in other words their presence in a person is largely independent of each other). Between the characteristics of 'sober and rigid' and 'lively and easygoing', however, there are 180 degrees, implying a negative correlation (i.e., more of one means less of the opposite).

Figure 3.2 Eysenck's model of personality

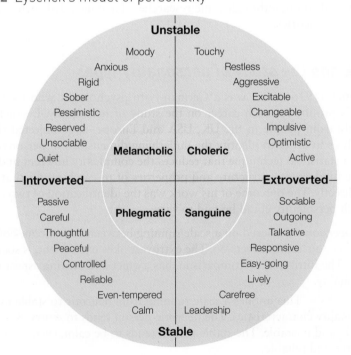

Source: Eysenck, H.J. (1965) *Fact and Fiction in Psychology*, Harmondsworth: Penguin.

ASSESSMENT OF THE THEORY

Eysenck claims that the two main personality dimensions are linked to physiological functioning in the human body. For example, he suggests that neuroticism is positively linked with those aspects of the autonomic nervous system that control body temperature, heartbeat, etc. As such his personality theory provides a very comprehensive attempt to causally explain the origins of and dynamics linked to personality. Yet many critics have taken issue with the role that his theory ascribes to nature and genetics in the development of personality. This criticism has been exacerbated by Eysenck's outspoken and often controversial views on issues such as intelligence and its link to race (e.g., Gottfredson, 1994). Others have criticized his personality theory on the grounds that two dimensions are overly simplistic when considering the complexity of human personality and behaviour. However, his work has been based on a considerable amount of detailed empirical research and so has strength. Eysenck himself does not claim that there are only two dimensions associated with personality, simply that they account for most of the published research and are, by implication, most significant in the description and understanding of personality and individual difference. In later work he also considered a third dimension (namely psychotism, which refers to a heightened vulnerability to psychoses).

Cattell and personality characteristics

Starting this research programme in the 1940s, British-born American psychologist Raymond B. Cattell (1965) used a data-driven approach to his model of personality which today is widely known as the 'Sixteen Personality Factor Questionnaire', or more commonly the '16PF'. The model emerged from his research that identified the hierarchical structure of the traits underlying a wide range of everyday behaviours thought to indicate individual differences. Just like Eysenck he employed multivariate statistics and data reduction techniques such as factor analysis to identify the structure of these underlying, relatively stable personality traits. In his decades-spanning research Cattell and his colleagues used different types of data (including observations, questionnaires and the evolving versions of the 16PF instrument) to refine the instrument and develop a comprehensive descriptive model of personality. A recent version of the 16 factors used in the 16PF questionnaire is shown in Figure 3.3.

Different formats of the 16PF questionnaire exist, but typically the 16PF test contains a number of questions appropriate for each of the factors. Responses to the 16PF are converted to scores from 1 to 10 for each factor which can be compared with published norms for the population to which the individual belongs. Figure 3.4 shows the 'average' profile of managing directors obtained by Cox and Cooper (1988) using an earlier version of the 16PF questionnaire than that shown as Figure 3.3. The test result for a specific managing director can be plotted on this chart to show a comparison with the average for that population. This can provide input for a development programme for that individual, or can be considered in assessing their suitability or readiness for holding such a position.

3.1 EXTEND
YOUR LEARNING

ASSESSMENT OF THE THEORY

The approach adopted by Cattell depends very much on the first step in his research process, which was to identify all the possible trait elements in the personality sphere. The statistical approach employed ensures that the results account for the variation in observed behaviour, but traits not included will not be considered. The initial trait selection is therefore crucial for the validity of this model and the test results. The premise of Cattell's approach is that because the behaviour exists and is meaningful to those acting or observing a particular behaviour, a verbal label is required to

Figure 3.3 Catell's 16PF® factors

Factor	Left meaning	Right meaning
Warmth	Reserved, impersonal, distant	Warm, outgoing, attentive to others
Reasoning	Concrete	Abstract
Emotional stability	Reactive, emotionally changeable	Emotionally stable, adaptive, mature
Dominance	Deferential, co-operative, avoids conflict	Dominant, forceful, assertive
Liveliness	Serious, restrained, careful	Lively, animated, spontaneous
Rule-consciousness	Expedient, nonconforming	Rule-conscious, dutiful
Social boldness	Shy, threat-sensitive, timid	Socially bold, venturesome, thick-skinned
Sensitivity	Utilitarian, objective, unsentimental	Sensitive, aesthetic, sentimental
Vigilance	Trusting, unsuspecting, accepting	Vigilant, suspicious, sceptical, wary
Abstractedness	Grounded, practical, solution-oriented	Abstracted, imaginative, idea-oriented
Privateness	Forthright, genuine, artless	Private, discreet, non-disclosing
Apprehension	Self-assured, unworried, complacent	Apprehensive, self-doubting, worried
Openness to change	Traditional, attached to familiar	Open to change, experimenting
Self-reliance	Group-oriented, affiliative	Self-reliant, solitary, individualistic
Perfectionism	Tolerates disorder, unexacting, flexible	Perfectionistic, organized, self-disciplined
Tension	Relaxed, placid, patient	Tense, high energy, impatient, driven

describe it. If no label exists then the behaviour is not relevant or meaningful. This, of course, raises many questions relating to behaviour, language and the way in which personality interacts with both. It also suggests that this model may be inherently culturally biased to the Western cultural setting (specifically the USA) in which it was conceived and developed.

Figure 3.4 16 PF profile of managing directors

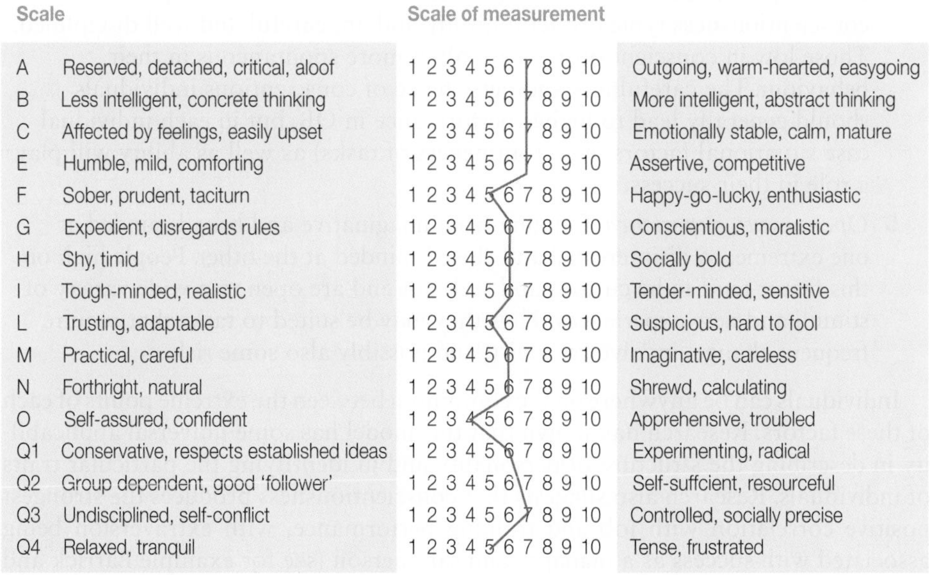

Scale		Scale of measurement	
A	Reserved, detached, critical, aloof	1 2 3 4 5 6 7 8 9 10	Outgoing, warm-hearted, easygoing
B	Less intelligent, concrete thinking	1 2 3 4 5 6 7 8 9 10	More intelligent, abstract thinking
C	Affected by feelings, easily upset	1 2 3 4 5 6 7 8 9 10	Emotionally stable, calm, mature
E	Humble, mild, comforting	1 2 3 4 5 6 7 8 9 10	Assertive, competitive
F	Sober, prudent, taciturn	1 2 3 4 5 6 7 8 9 10	Happy-go-lucky, enthusiastic
G	Expedient, disregards rules	1 2 3 4 5 6 7 8 9 10	Conscientious, moralistic
H	Shy, timid	1 2 3 4 5 6 7 8 9 10	Socially bold
I	Tough-minded, realistic	1 2 3 4 5 6 7 8 9 10	Tender-minded, sensitive
L	Trusting, adaptable	1 2 3 4 5 6 7 8 9 10	Suspicious, hard to fool
M	Practical, careful	1 2 3 4 5 6 7 8 9 10	Imaginative, careless
N	Forthright, natural	1 2 3 4 5 6 7 8 9 10	Shrewd, calculating
O	Self-assured, confident	1 2 3 4 5 6 7 8 9 10	Apprehensive, troubled
Q1	Conservative, respects established ideas	1 2 3 4 5 6 7 8 9 10	Experimenting, radical
Q2	Group dependent, good 'follower'	1 2 3 4 5 6 7 8 9 10	Self-sufficient, resourceful
Q3	Undisciplined, self-conflict	1 2 3 4 5 6 7 8 9 10	Controlled, socially precise
Q4	Relaxed, tranquil	1 2 3 4 5 6 7 8 9 10	Tense, frustrated

Source: After Cox, C.J. and Cooper, C.L. (1988) *High Flyers*, Oxford: Basil Blackwell, Oxford. Reprinted with permission.

Words are used to describe ideas and feelings as well as behaviour, needs and wants. Consequently, the words identified might not reflect individual difference characteristics alone. There is also a complex relationship between the observable behaviour of individuals and the underlying personality characteristics that help to shape that behaviour. The links between what is observable, the words used to describe it and the associated psychological structures are far from clear.

The 'Big Five' model

Research carried out on the structure of personality traits proposed by many of the nomothetic approaches, including those by Eysenck and Cattell, suggested that a five-factor structure is common to most of them (see for example McCrae and Costa, 1989; Digman, 1990). This approach has come to be known as the Five Factor Model ('FFM') or, more commonly, as the 'Big Five' personality factors. The Big Five are:

1 *Extraversion.* Ranging from outgoing and assertive at one extreme, to reserved and shy at the other. Individuals high in extraversion have a tendency to experience positive emotional states. They often do well in jobs that require extensive social contact such as service provision and sales positions.

2 *Neuroticism/Emotional stability.* Ranging from secure and self-assured at one extreme, to anxious and depressed at the other. People high in neuroticism (and low on emotional stability) are predisposed to negative emotional states and stress and generally to a more negative world-view. They are often quite critical of themselves, which can lead to higher performance in situations requiring active questioning and critical thinking.

3 *Agreeableness.* Ranging from co-operative and trusting at one extreme, to quarrelsome and hostile at the other. Individuals high in agreeableness tend to get along well with others, are compassionate and often good team players, and thus effective in positions that require the development and maintenance of good relationships. People low in agreeableness may be suitable to jobs that require more antagonistic behaviours.

4 *Conscientiousness*. Ranging from dependable and responsible at one extreme, to unreliable and disorganized at the other. Those high in conscientiousness typically act dutifully and are careful and well disciplined. Those low in conscientiousness are often more spontaneous in their behaviour. The carefulness and persistence of conscientious individuals should generally lead to higher performance in OB, but in each individual case situational factors (e.g., routineness of tasks) as well as ability will play a role in their success.

5 *Openness to experience*. Ranging from imaginative and broad-minded at one extreme, to disinterested and closed-minded at the other. People high on this factor tend to be curious and seek out and are open to a wide variety of stimuli and new experiences. Thus they may be suited to tasks that require frequent change, involve creativity, and possibly also some risk.

Individuals can be anywhere on the continuum between the extreme points of each of these factors. Research has shown that this model has some universal applicability in describing the structure of personality and in identifying the particular traits of individuals. Research also suggests that conscientiousness produces the strongest positive correlation with job and training performance, with extraversion being associated with success as a manager and salesperson (see for example Barrick and Mount, 1991; Hogan and Holland, 2003). Conscientiousness has also been shown to be a significant factor in predicting preclinical success in medical training (Ferguson *et al.*, 2003). However, it was also found to be related to worse performance in clinical assessment, perhaps as that involves a different type of learning together with strategic problem solving.

ASSESSMENT OF THE THEORY

The Big Five is a data-driven, descriptive model of personality. Despite its significant research support and its common acceptance across personality and social psychology, this model has been criticized on a number of grounds. Methodologically, the underlying analytical approach (factor analysis) has weaknesses in that it reduces relatively rich data sets to a small number of dimensions to create an explainable, simple structure – but the five factors of the model are only five of a range of possible solutions. The convergence to five factors found in many different data sets would support the Big Five but this is not conclusive. Also, the potential role of language used to construct the instruments for data collection may limit the application of the model to all populations (see Gill and Hodgkinson, 2007) and the transferability of the model to other cultures. Some recent measurement approaches have tried to provide useable, workplace-oriented instruments that address some of these concerns (Gill and Hodgkinson, 2007). Criticisms of the largely atheoretical nature of the model's development have also been voiced. In many critics' minds, a fully fledged personality model should be based on a complete and explicit underlying theory.

To summarize, the Big Five describes observations from personality research that remain to be fully explained, but it also represents the best validated and most universal descriptive model of individual differences available. Despite its general acceptance, it should not be used as a tool to identify ideal personality profiles. Rather, it can help describe personality differences that can help explain how personality and situational factors interact, and what that can tell us about the most appropriate ways in which individuals and organizations can go about achieving their objectives.

IDIOGRAPHIC PERSPECTIVES

Unlike nomothetic personality research that assumes a world consisting of cause and effect relationships that are independent of the researcher, the interpretivist tradition reflected in idiographic research holds that the social world is created (or given meaning and substance) within the minds of the people who live in it. Consequently, there will be differences in how individuals conceptualize the social world in which they live. Therefore, understanding the individual and their view of the social world is necessary in seeking to understand individual behaviour.

Thus, idiographic approaches emphasize the development of the self-concept aspects of personality rather than concentration on the identification and measurement of common characteristics. In the nomothetic approaches such as Eysenck's and Cattell's, the researchers' initial assumptions and choices have an enormous impact on the development of the ensuing instruments because the researcher's frame of reference guides data collection and analysis. In contrast, the idiographic approach focuses on the uniqueness of individuals and their personalities. Thus, idiographic theorists argue that in order to understand unique personality characteristics it is necessary to understand how the individual relates to the world in which they live and the individual qualities that make each person different from every other person. In short, unlike nomothetic approaches that attempt to find the similarities in the personalities of people to be able to describe and compare them in relation to external references (such as a model of personality or a measurement scale), idiographic approaches focus on the uniqueness and the differences of one individual compared to others.

Charles Cooley, an American sociologist, introduced the concept of the looking-glass self to the debate on personality. He draws attention to the interactive nature of much behaviour and the development of self-image as a result of this process. We begin to see ourselves as others see us through the responses that we generate from others. This is the looking-glass, or mirror, that reflects a perspective back to us. Through the interactions with the people around us we come to understand who we are and so learn to adapt our personality to accommodate our environment.

Charles Herbert Mead (1863–1931) added to this approach through the concept of the generalized other. This concept is intended to reflect the existence of two components in the 'self' (Mead, 1934). They are:

- *I.* The unique, spontaneous and conscious aspects of the individual.
- *Me.* The internalized norms and values learned through experience within society.

The generalized other refers to the understanding that the individual develops of the expectations that society has of them. It is in the 'me' element of the 'self' that this evaluation takes place. The 'I' component is the aspect of personality that attempts to ensure that the individual meets their own expectations, rather than becoming a creature totally of the 'me' component. It also allows the opportunity to provide for evolution in society through the adaptation of social norms to meet the needs of the individuals within it. Carl Rogers (1947) proposed that the main objective of personality development is the development of a self-concept which progresses from undifferentiated to fully differentiated. In many ways this reflects his humanistic orientation and the objective of humans to fully realize their potential. Like Mead, he also used the two components of 'I' and 'me' in describing the self-concept. His view of the linkages between 'I', 'me' and the 'self-concept' is illustrated in Figure 3.5.

One implication of this model of the self-concept is that the personality will be subject to change as the underlying personal self and social self change due to

Figure 3.5 Rogers' view of the 'I' and 'me'

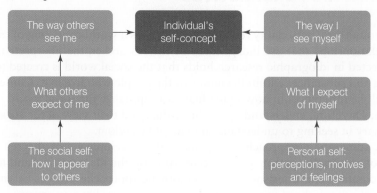

experience. This linkage is demonstrated in the model by the connections between the elements and the relationship implied by them. If this change did not occur, then a tension would be created which could lead to the emergence of personality disorders within the individual.

Erikson (1980) considered the personality to be continually developing throughout life. His view was that as the individual passed through the various life stages, tensions and conflicts arise which have to be dealt with. For example, Erikson's fifth life stage covers the years from 12 to 18 years of age when an individual experiences tensions between identity and role. In dealing with these conflicts the individual who successfully negotiates a resolution achieves healthy personality growth, whereas unresolved conflicts can lead to problems in later life. In this model there is a clear link between the concept of individual difference and the development of the 'self-concept' in a dynamic and ongoing relationship over time.

STOP & CONSIDER

To what extent is the idiographic approach to understanding personality nothing more than one person's view of another?

OTHER PERSPECTIVES ON INDIVIDUAL DIFFERENCE

Freud and psychoanalysis

Id

According to Freudian psychoanalysis the instinctual drives that remain largely unconscious in directing human behaviour.

Ego

According to Freudian psychoanalysis this is the conscious mind which serves as the locus of active decision making of the individual and mediates between wants [Id] and shoulds [Super-ego].

Austrian psychiatrist Sigmund Freud (1856–1939), one of the most influential intellectuals of the twentieth century, is possibly best known as the founding father of psychoanalytical approaches in psychology. While Freud's work is too large in scope to even appropriately summarize here in its entirety, there are some aspects that deserve attention because they provide value and insight into understanding personality and explaining human behaviour. In particular, his views on mental activities and how the mind is organized, and his work on defence mechanisms, can provide useful insights for students of OB.

Freud believed that personality is formed through early experiences and is the outcome of internal struggles occurring while people pass through predictable developmental stages. From this perspective adult behaviour can be a reflection of unconscious and subconscious memories that have been repressed but still exert tremendous, often distorted influence. According to Freud, the personality (or 'psyche') combines three aspects, named the Id (instinctual drives that remain largely unconscious), the Ego (the conscious mind which serves as the locus of active decision making of the individual and mediates between wants [Id] and shoulds [Super-ego]), and the Super-ego (which reflects an internal critical and moralizing authority that represents internalized cultural and social norms and codes of morality).

According to Freud, individual behaviour is a balance between these three components of the mind. A well adjusted individual will be controlled by their ego, a neurotic (driven by anxiety about the imposition of external control) through their super-ego, and the psychopath (driven by their own desires) through the id. It is through the id, ego and super-ego that adults manage their interaction with the world around them. Freud described a number of defence mechanisms adopted by the ego in order to maintain the balance between the id and super-ego and protect the individual from unresolved internal conflict. Knowledge about these defence mechanisms is useful in helping to understand many seemingly irrational actions and behaviour patterns in people. The main forms of ego defence mechanism include:

- *Sublimation.* This allows the desires emerging from the id to be expressed in an acceptable manner. For example, pottery making and painting can be described as sublimation for the anal drives to handle and smear faeces.

- *Repression.* This describes a process where the existence of something is deliberately kept hidden from the conscious thinking level because it might be too painful.

- *Denial.* This is a defence mechanism in which the ego alters the perception of a situation in order to maintain a balance in the mind.

- *Projection.* The transmission of feelings and motives to other people. A manager might seek to justify their own political activity on the basis that they interpret others' behaviour as blatantly self-serving and political.

- *Reaction formation.* This produces the opposite feelings and behaviour at the conscious level to those held at the unconscious level. So for example, unrequited love can become hate.

- *Regression.* The avoidance of problems between the id and super-ego through the adoption of patterns of behaviour that once produced satisfaction. For example, an older child may suck its thumb when being scolded by its parents.

- *Isolation.* This results in a separation of feelings and emotions from the experiences that normally produce them.

- *Undoing.* This attempts to 'undo' something from the past. The obsessional washing of hands, over and over again, could reflect a person attempting to cleanse themselves in a deeper way.

ASSESSMENT OF THE THEORY

Freud's approach to personality is not a single theory as such. It is a complex model, including aspects of intellectual and sexual development, training, education, mental structure, social process and the dynamics of interaction. As such it is difficult to offer specific criticisms and equally difficult to defend it against any that are raised. Among many others, Eysenck (1953) has identified a set of main criticisms that in part reflects the difference between the scientific method as applied in nomothetic approaches and the more introspective, interpretative and case-based development of Freud's contributions (see, for example, the discussion in Henwood and Pidgeon, 1993 on this type of debate). These criticisms include a lack of rigour in the collection and the multivariate analysis of the data; the nonrepresentative nature of the sample used to develop the theory (mostly female, middle-class, voluntary patients), a lack of conceptual clarity, and the format of the central tenets and propositions of Freud's theories which effectively makes them untestable.

Super-ego
According to Freudian psychoanalysis that part of the human mind which reflects an internal critical and moralising authority that represents internalized cultural and social norms and codes of morality.

3.2 EXTEND
YOUR LEARNING

Other arguments against Freud's work include that it offered circular arguments to support the ideas in it and that by emphasizing early childhood it produces a model that is deterministic and ignores the possibility of subsequent individual development (see, in contrast, the work of Erikson outlined earlier). However, Freud's model offers 'richness' in attempting to encompass the whole of personality in a grand theory. Parts of the theory have been subjected to a more rigorous form of testing with some success (Kline, 1972).

At a practical level Freud's work led to other research on the complexity of personality. Freud was interested in understanding the whole person and the part that early development played in the formation of the adult personality. The theory can be seen in some behaviour at work. For example, employees and managers often display 'temper tantrums' when things do not go according to plan, perhaps reflecting the ego defence mechanism of regression.

Jung and the cognitive approach

Carl Gustav Jung (1875–1961), a Swiss psychiatrist, was a close associate of Freud before they parted ways in 1913. Jung developed an approach to personality based on Freudian theory, but also incorporated aspects of the future goals held by an individual rather than simply emphasizing the past (Jung, 1968). It postulated three levels of personality:

1 *A conscious level.* This aspect of personality allowed for reality to be incorporated as a result of the everyday experience of the individual.

2 *An unconscious level.* This makes up the individuality of each person and is composed of the complexes and facets within individual difference.

3 *A collective unconscious.* This is the pool of inherited and socially derived universal experience that each person carries with them inside their personality.

Personality differences were reflected by a number of dimensions within Jungian theory, including the use of extroversion and introversion. Another dimension was that of cognitive style, reflecting four different approaches to information gathering and evaluation:

1 *Sensing.* People who prefer to deal with hard information in a structured context.

2 *Intuiting.* People who dislike routine activities, but who prefer to deal with possibilities rather than certainty.

3 *Thinking.* People who prefer the use of logic and rationality as the basis of problem solving, without the feelings of others entering into the process.

4 *Feeling.* People who prefer to have social harmony around them, get along with others and have sympathy for those around them.

From this description it might be apparent that there are two dimensions involved in this framework: sensing and intuiting are at opposing ends of a continuum as are thinking and feeling. This is reflected in Figure 3.6.

The main personality characteristics for each cell in the matrix shown in Figure 3.6 are described in Table 3.2. This indicates the application of Jung's theory in differentiating personality and in describing the consequences of that approach for job preferences. Further work using Jung's contributions on psychological types by mother and daughter team Katharine Cook Briggs and Isabel Briggs Myers, and later their collaborators, has led to the development of the Myers-Briggs Type Indicator (MBTI), one of the most widely used personality inventories in organizations.

Figure 3.6 Jung's cognitive styles

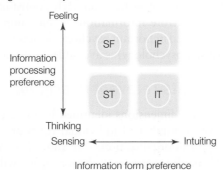

Table 3.2 Differences between Jung's cognitive styles

	Sensing/thinking (ST)	Intuiting/thinking (IT)	Sensing/feeling (SF)	Intuiting/feeling (IF)
Prefers	Facts	Possibilities	Facts	Possibilities
Personality	Pragmatic, down-to-earth	Logical, but ingenious	Sympathetic, sociable	Energetic, insightful
Work preferences	Technical skills	Theoretical problem solving	Providing help and services to others	Understanding and communicating with others
	Physician accountant, computer programmer	Scientist, corporate planner, mathematician	Salesperson, social worker, psychologist	Artist, writer entertainer

Source: *Adapted from* Vecchio, R.P. (1991) *Organizational Behaviour* (2nd edn), Hinsdale: Dryden Press.

The MBTI proposes four dichotomies (Extraversion ↔ Introversion; Sensing ↔ iNtuition; Thinking ↔ Feeling; and Judging ↔ Perceiving) and integrates additions to Jungian theory. It is important to note that the MBTI differs from many other psychological personality instruments in that it purports to indicate type rather than measure traits. This distinction is important in that the results of the MBTI (usually expressed by four-letter designators such as ENTP or ISFJ) reflect preferences, not traits or abilities. One important implication is that MBTI scores should not be used as predictors of job success.

ASSESSMENT OF THE THEORY

While some argue that Jung's psychological type theory lends itself more easily to testing than Freud's work, it was not developed by scientific methods. Rigorous research has generally provided only limited support for the theory, but MBTI scores have been found to align to a certain degree with other models of personality, especially the Big Five (see McCrae and Costa, 1989). Mixed support has been reported for the MBTI's psychometric qualities (Capraro and Capraro, 2002; Thompson and Borrello, 1986). However, the MBTI is widely and extensively used for occupational choice, and in organizations for leadership and management development. Many users praise the MBTI for the pragmatic value it brings, and some research support for such claims is available (e.g., Yen *et al.*, 2002).

**3.3 EXTEND
YOUR LEARNING**

Freud and Jung both contributed immensely to the development of personality theory, and many other important contributors have similarly contributed to our understanding of individual differences. More information on such important contributors as Henry A. Murray (who identified important psychogenic needs) and George Kelly (who developed personal construct psychology) is available on the companion website.

Other personality traits relevant in organizations

In addition to the personality dimensions identified by the theories discussed above (for example the Big Five) a number of individual traits are also often considered to be particularly important in organizations (see Table 3.3). We will consider these in more detail below. Throughout the book, however, we will identify and discuss additional personality traits that are particularly relevant for specific issues.

Locus of control
The degree to which an individual believes that they are subjected to outside control as opposed to having internal control over the forces influencing their behaviour.

Locus of control (Rotter, 1966) is a concept that describes the degree to which people believe that they themselves are in control of their destiny (and thus have an internal locus of control), and those who think that what happens to them is largely determined by forces outside their control (and thus have an external locus of control). People with an internal locus of control are more independent in the face of peer and group pressure or other influencing attempts (Renn and Vandenberg, 1991). They also tend to have higher-status jobs, receive higher incomes and experience faster career success (Andrisani and Nestel, 1976). Interestingly, the average locus of control as measured in US school and university students has become notably more external since the 1960s (Twenge *et al.*, 2004).

Individual also differ in the degree to which they seek to engage in and enjoy thinking about things. Such effortful cognitive activities, also called controlled, central-route or conscious processing, are one of the two main ways of processing information – the other is often called automatic, peripheral, or subconscious processing (this is discussed in more detail in Chapter 4). While many situational factors help account for differences in information processing, there are also individual differences

Table 3.3 Personality dimension particularly relevant in organizations

Big Five	Extraversion
	Neuroticism/Emotional stability
	Agreeableness
	Conscientiousness
	Openness to experience
	Locus of control
	Need for cognition
	Self-monitoring
	Proactive personality
	Need for achievement
	Need for power
	Need for affiliation

that predispose people to engage in one or the other approach. People high in need for cognition (Cacioppo and Petty, 1982) enjoy filling their time thinking – about anything! This characteristic is conceived as a stable but not unchangeable intrinsic motivation (Cacioppo *et al.*, 1996), and people high in need for cognition tend to focus on the quality not quantity of information in messages, actively seek out information and carefully consider it. People low in need for cognition act as cognitive misers, form attitudes using cues and heuristics, and spend less time seeking information and deliberating decisions. The organizational implications of need for cognition are obvious. People high in need for cognition tend to be more focused on thorough analysis, will seek out information more actively, and will come to more reasoned decisions. Yet people low in need for cognition may be suitable for situations in which quick decisive action is required, and tend to be more intuitive in their decision making.

Self-monitoring was posited by Mark Snyder (1974) as an individual difference which reflects individuals' tendencies to monitor their own behaviour and its fit with relevant social expectations. High self-monitors will be concerned with acting socially appropriately, try to adapt their behaviour to situational demands, and seek out social comparison information from others more actively. People low in self-monitoring should be more consistent in their behaviour across different situations and show less concern about the social appropriateness of their behaviour. Rather, they will respond more to inner feelings and attitudes rather than situational demands. In organizations, those with higher self-monitoring may be particularly suited to sales and service positions (Deeter-Schmelz and Sojka, 2007), especially if customer preferences and expectations vary widely, or if client contact does not take place in standardized situations. Low self-monitors may be appropriate in situations where situational demands can detract from their performance as in some conflict or negotiation situations.

Another important individual difference is a proactive personality, which describes the degree to which individuals actively initiate activities rather than reactively respond to environmental demands (Bateman and Crant, 1993). Proactive personality is linked to increased motivation to learn and engagement in development activities (Major *et al.*, 2006). People with proactive personalities are more likely to seek out change and offer solutions, demonstrate more political acumen in their organizations, and show more initiative in developing their own careers. (Seibert *et al.*, 2001a). Proactive personalities would suit particularly jobs in dynamic settings and decentralized organizational structures (Crant, 2000).

Another set of relevant individual differences was identified by David McClelland who was influenced by - and extended the work of – Henry Murray. His research investigated particular motivational orientations – or *needs* - in people. Unlike other contributions to personality theory, McClelland posited that these needs are at least in part socially acquired and thus these dimensions of personality may be substantially more open to environmental influence than other personality traits. He focused in particular on three important individual differences. Individuals high in need for achievement (nAch) are motivated to seek challenges and accomplish goals because they value the recognition of their achievements. They welcome independence and typically seek out tasks that are neither trivial (because the payoff would be negligible) nor prohibitively difficult (because of the low likelihood of success). Higher nAch scores are found at higher levels in organizations, and typically senior managers and entrepreneurs score highly. High levels of nAch are also associated with a predisposition to employ competitive strategies (Ward, 2006).

People high in need for power (nPow) value the ability to influence and control their environment, and particularly other people. Senior executives have very high nPow scores, and McClelland argued that this is very useful for organizations as long as these managers deploy this power in disciplined ways aligned with the goals of their organization (McClelland and Burnham, 1976). This form of power is also called socialized

Need for cognition
People with high levels of this aspect of individual difference enjoy filling their time thinking – about anything!

Self-monitoring
An aspect of individual difference which reflects individuals' tendencies to monitor their own behaviour and adapt it to fit with relevant social expectations.

Proactive personality
An aspect of individual difference which describes the degree to which individuals actively initiate activities rather than reactively responding to environmental demands.

Need for achievement (nAch)
People with high levels of this need are motivated to seek challenges and accomplish goals because they value the recognition of their achievements.

Need for power (nPow)
People with high levels of this value the ability to influence and control their environment, and particularly other people.

power. In contrast, individuals high in personalized power often act uninhibited and impulsively, and pursue power to increase their own status and payoffs (Yukl, 1989).

Another dimension is need for affiliation (nAff) which reflects a person's desire to have close, warm and meaningful relationships with others and belong to social groups. Being liked and accepted by others is important to them, as is regular contact with others. People with high nAff often are supportive team members, but can be less effective in leadership positions if their nAff outweighs their need for achievement.

Need for affiliation (nAff)
People with high levels of this desire to have close, warm and meaningful relationships with others and belong to social groups.

MEASURING PERSONALITY AND INDIVIDUAL DIFFERENCE

Many of the personality traits above can be measured with psychological measures (also called tests, instruments, inventories, or style indicators), some of which have already been introduced (e.g., 16PF, MBTI). A psychological test is usually defined as a set of tasks presented in a standard form and which produces a score as the output, allowing for comparison with population norms. The design, administration and interpretation of such mental measurement, an important part of both education and psychology, is called psychometrics. The development of such mental measures, which may focus on personality traits as well as aptitudes or abilities such as intelligence, is a complex and iterative process involving multiple steps and repeated modifications, refinements and tests. Figure 3.7 describes the steps typically employed when developing such measures.

Psychometrics
The process of mental measurement through the application of tests of personality or characteristics such as ability or aptitude.

The use of many psychological tests is regulated by either professional associations (in the UK for example, the British Psychological Society, the professional body representing psychologists, has developed and introduced a series of qualifications for those people seeking to use psychometric tests) or controlled by the publishers of the test themselves through certification programmes. This is done in response to a widespread concern that anyone could use (or misuse) these tests and in so doing inflict considerable damage on individuals, organizations and the psychology profession. There are two main reasons that psychometric tests are used. The first is to undertake scientific research into particular characteristics of people, for example to understand personality. The second is to enable decisions relating to people to be made, for example who to appoint to a particular job. In both of these examples there is a need for accurate information in relation to those aspects of people that are important to the purpose. There are many tests available that can offer insights into aspects of individual difference. They include tests of particular skills, abilities, intelligence, aptitudes, job preferences, psychological functioning and extroversion/introversion. Test batteries such as the 16PF introduced earlier seek to test a broad range of dimensions of individual difference within the one instrument.

There are three ways in which tests can measure individual difference:

1 *Comparison of performance against a standard* (e.g., measuring response times to undertake a particular task).
2 *Norm-referenced measurement* (e.g., comparing an individual's performance on a test with that of a peer group).
3 *Criterion-referenced measurement* (e.g., comparing performance on a test with an 'ideal' result).

The basis of a psychometric test is that the responses given by the person being tested can be interpreted as an indication of an underlying characteristic. Therefore, a test is claimed to be valid if it measures what it claims to measure (this is called *construct validity*). That does not mean, however, that there is a direct link between the test

Figure 3.7 Typical steps in developing psychological tests and scales

Example of psychometric test development	
Step 1: Specification of requirements and conceptual development	Step 1. The initial ideas for a test often emerge from a practical need, for example, assisting personnel managers to identify the most appropriate job applicants. Tests can also originate from a theoretical need to measure some characteristic of individual difference as part of research and theory development. This step involves a definition of the concept(s) to be measured.
Step 2: Development of instrument content: Item generation and instrument format design	Step 2. The development of appropriate test items is a creative process following inductive (theory driven – often involving expert panels) or deductive approaches (data driven – often employing grouping and judging of potential items by judging panels). It often takes a considerable amount of time and ingenuity to develop or identify an appropriate range of test items suitable for use. The general measurement approach is also decided on.
Step 3: Scale development *–design of development study (sample, sampling technique, administration format)* *–analysis based scale refinement (exploratory and confirmatory factor analysis) and initial validation support* *–design improvements to assure reliability and validity*	Step 3. Complete forms of the test are developed and appropriate test administration arrangements are designed. Sampling approaches are decided, and the data collection approach is finalized (including sampling, collection procedures, etc.). Data analysis supports scale refinement to assure clear dimensional structure, convergent and discriminant validity, and reliability and stability. Appropriate other data is collected to allow the above comparisons and analyses to be completed. For self report measures appropriate safeguards against 'faking' are designed (see Management in Action 4.2 for a historical input to 'cheating' on personality tests). If the scale does not perform adequately step 2 (or even step 1) needs to be revisited.
Step 4: Scale standardization and norming	Step 4. If the scale is intended to provide normed scores the relevant target popiulation(s) must be identified and appropriate samples must be identified and tested. These results can be used to calculate the standard scores or profiles against which a particular individual scores will be compared. For example, Figure 3.4 demonstrated the 16PF profile of managing directors against which an individual managing director could be compared.
Step 5: Use and periodic review	Step 5: At this stage, the test will be offered for use in research and in organizations. Typically, reliability and validity analyses are periodically repeated in order to establish and support the credibility and value of the test for the user markets. Theory development and/or changes in requirements may prompt scale reviews and further scale development.

question and the underlying characteristic. The question asked may bear no apparent relationship to the characteristic itself. It is, however, necessary that the question elicits responses that can discriminate between those people with the underlying characteristic and those without it. In addition a test needs to be reliable (i.e., *it needs to produce consistent results if the measured quality remains unchanged, or appropriately different ones if it has changed*) and valid (i.e., the scores obtained need to correspond to what they purport to represent). There are different forms of validity and reliability that concern psychometrics. Some of the most commonly considered include:

Reliable psychometric test
A test that produces consistent results if the measured quality remains unchanged, or appropriately different ones if it has changed.

Valid psychometric test
A test that produces results that correspond to what they purport to represent.

- *Construct validity.* This refers to the extent that a test can be related back to a theory.
- *Content validity:* This indicates the degree to which the instrument represents the kinds of material (or content areas) they are supposed to measure.
- *Face validity.* This refers to the degree to which a test appears as if it ought to measure what it sets out to measure.
- *Predictive validity.* This reflects the ability of tests to predict future events. A test would have predictive validity if high-scoring individuals were successful, while low-scoring individuals performed badly in the job for which the test was being used.
- *Test/retest reliability.* This reflects the ability of a test to produce the same score when it is administered on two different occasions and the measured quality remains unchanged.
- *Alternative form reliability.* Some tests are developed in two or more different forms. All the forms available should produce the same results when administered together.
- *Split half reliability.* This reflects the internal consistency within a particular test. Splitting the test up and comparing the results from the various combinations of questions or activities within it measures this form of reliability.

Most psychological tests are objective tests, which attempt to measure the psychological aspect of interest in a way independent of rater or respondent biases and analyse responses according to universal standards. The 16PF and MBTI are objective tests, as are the most common tests to assess the Big Five (e.g., the Revised NEO Personality Inventory [NEO PI-R] and the short NEO Five-Factor Inventory [NEO-FFI]). Other forms of assessing personality exist as well. They include projective tests which focus on a person's responses to ambiguous stimuli such as inkblots (e.g., Rohrschach test) that the participant describes, pictures (e.g., Thematic Apperception Test) that the person interprets, or half sentences (e.g., Rotter Incomplete Sentence Blank) that people are asked to complete. Other traditional forms of personality assessment that have fallen out of favour because of largely negative research findings about their accuracy and utility include graphology (the study of handwriting) and phrenology (the study of the shape of the skull).

Given modern developments in employment and equality laws, any psychological testing used for such decisions as hiring or promotion needs to be defensible. Particularly in the US a number of lawsuits have been won by plaintiffs claiming that the use of inappropriate psychological assessments by actual or prospective employers has discriminated against or even damaged them. However, that does not stop tests being used, or the interest of potential testees in learning how to do well in them. As far back as the 1950s, the following advice was given (only partly in fun) by one writer of the day – see the following Examining Ethics example 'How to cheat on personality tests'.

Projective tests

A process based on ambiguous images (such as inkblots) being presented to an individual who is then asked to interpret the image; thought to provide some insight into attitudes and personality characteristics.

ABILITY: INTELLIGENCE AND EMOTIONAL INTELLIGENCE

All the personality dimensions and traits discussed above help to distinguish people from each other because of their link to relatively stable patterns of observable behaviour. Another important set of individual differences is related to the general notion of ability, which refers to what people are able to do and achieve (rather than what they are likely to do or have done consistently). Individual ability is of immense importance

EXAMINING ETHICS

How to cheat on personality tests

As early as 1956 one author was offering the following advice on how to approach answering the questions in a personality test. The advice is premised on the view that while there are some tests in which a high score would be beneficial to the individual, many require the individual to demonstrate that they are broadly similar to many others. So, for example, if the test were intended to identify who would make a 'good chemist' then a high score in comparison with the population at large would be beneficial to the career prospects of the testee. By way of contrast, in a test of personality, it would be beneficial to produce results that indicate a 'normal' individual – one who displays characteristics in common with the bulk of the population.

To quote specifically from the advice offered by the author when taking personality tests:

By and large, however, your safety lies in getting a score somewhere between the 40th and 60th percentiles, which is to say, you should try to answer as if you were like everyone else is supposed to be. This is not always easy to figure out, of course […]. When in doubt, however, there are two general rules that you can follow: (1) when asked for word associations or comments about the world, give the most conventional, run-of-the-mill, pedestrian answer possible. (2) to settle on the most beneficial answer to any question, repeat to yourself:

(a) I loved my father and my mother, but my father a little bit more.

(b) I like things pretty well the way they are.

(c) I never worry much about anything.

(d) I don't care for books or music much.

(e) I love my wife and children.

(f) I don't let them get in the way of company work.

The rationale behind this advice is that psychometric tests are intended to identify the presence of those characteristics desired by organizations. The feeling emerging from the above quotation is that the individual so described would be a true organizational functionary - someone who would not think too much but would not easily be distracted from the task allocated. Such individuals would perform the tasks determined by management in a way which would not question them or pose a threat to their authority.

TASKS

1 To what extent do you think that it is possible to train yourself to answer psychometric tests in a way that would be more likely to match the profile sought by the test designer?

2 If your answer to question 1 was that it is not possible to do so to any significant extent, why is it that careers advisors and a number of websites (including those of test design companies) offer such practice?

3 Is it ethical to try to 'cheat' on tests as implied by the above quotation?

Source:
Whyte, W.H. (1960) *The Organization Man*, a Penguin special, Harmondsworth: Penguin.

for OB because it is closely linked to organizational performance or, in other words, to the capacity of individuals to contribute to and achieve organizational goals.

Human abilities exist in many forms. For OB, two types of ability are most relevant, namely physical and cognitive abilities. Physical abilities refer to *people's capacity to control and deploy their bodies and to manipulate their physical environment*. They are relevant to the degree that particular tasks require an individual to have strength, endurance, fine motor skills, hand-eye co-ordination, speed, reaction time, ambidexterity, or other physical attributes and capabilities. Physical abilities are, just like personality, determined by both genetic and environmental influences. Thus, many physical abilities can be enhanced through instruction and training, but the range of innate ability people start out with often

Physical abilities
These refer to people's capacity to control and deploy their bodies and to manipulate their physical environment.

differs markedly, as does the upper limit of individual achievement in these different categories of physical ability. Most people can improve their golf game or driving skills through coaching and practice, but only a minute minority would be able to compete with the likes of Tiger Woods or Michael Schumacher. In other words, very few individuals have the fine motor skills required to conduct successful neurosurgery, the strength and endurance to fly a modern fighter jet, or the stamina to work as a deep-sea diver.

Cognitive abilities
These refer to a broad range of mental capabilities.

Intelligence
This refers to the general mental ability to solve problems and successfully deal with environmental conditions and demands in varying situations.

Cognitive abilities refer to a broad range of mental capabilities. The most often general terms for these abilities is intelligence. Intelligence usually denotes mental abilities such as reasoning, abstract and conceptual thinking, planning, comprehension, language use and problem solving. For our purposes we will define intelligence as *the general mental ability to solve problems and successfully deal with environmental conditions and demands in varying situations.*

In psychology, the concept of intelligence has a long history characterized by active debate and many disagreements. Initially, intelligence was conceived of as a unitary ability that determines individual performance across a range of dimensions. Following the work of Charles Spearman, a British psychologist, psychologists often refer to this as 'g', for general intelligence (Spearman, 1904). The most common intelligence tests include the Stanford-Binet Intelligence Scale (currently in its fifth revised form) which grew out of groundbreaking research by a French research group under psychologist Alfred Binet, and the Wechsler Adult Intelligence Scale (WAIS; currently in its fourth revised form). Both of these tests measure intelligence and report an overall result, also called IQ (short for 'intelligence quotient'). However, both tests measure intelligence using multiple subscales and have been used by both proponents of intelligence as a unitary general ability, and by those who more recently posited that multiple different intelligences exist in humans.

These proponents of multiple intelligences, among them American psychologist Howard Gardner, argue that each individual has a particular cognitive profile made up of varying levels of different intelligences including linguistic, logic-mathematical, musical, spatial, bodily kinaesthetic, interpersonal and intrapersonal (Gardner, 1999). A central argument of these approaches is that rather than being high or low in ability across all levels of mental functioning, individuals differ in the particular areas in which they may excel.

Other approaches to multiple intelligences include the work of American J. P. Guilford (1967) who proposed a model of intelligence consisting of three dimensions (contents, products and operations). Each of these dimensions comprises a number of different abilities (four, six and five respectively). The model can be drawn as a cube with each of the three dimensions representing one of the three principal dimensions of the cube. Each of the individual intelligence abilities within the now three-dimensional model would intersect with the others, creating a total of 120 possibilities (later expanded to 180 – see Guilford, 1980) in intelligence variation (four, six, five). The three dimensions within the model are:

1 *Contents*. The four elements within this dimension reflect the base information on which subsequent actions are formed (e.g., the semantic and symbolic meaning of numbers).

2 *Products*. The six elements within this dimension reflect the form in which information is processed (e.g., the relationship between the weight and price of goods in a supermarket).

3 *Operations*. The five elements within this dimension reflect what the person actually does (e.g., solve a problem or evaluate alternative courses of action).

Sternberg (1985) proposed an information-processing-based theory of intelligence. In this model it was proposed that there exist three ways in which intelligent behaviour is evident:

1 *Components.* This aspect reflects the analytical abilities possessed by an individual.

2 *Experiences.* This aspect reflects the creative abilities that an individual has in being able to combine the things that they experience into novel patterns.

3 *Context.* This aspect reflects the ability of an individual to be aware of contextual circumstances and to exhibit an ability to utilize the environment to their own advantage.

Despite the debates and differences in conception, there is little doubt that intelligence is an immensely important individual difference in organizations. In fact, it is seen as the best general predictor of job performance (e.g., Ree and Earles, 1992), especially for those without prior experience for the job (Schmidt and Hunter, 1998). However, the effect of intelligence on performance will typically depend on the particular task, situational influences and the involvement of other people.

The last two decades have seen an increased focus on social and interpersonal abilities. John Mayer and Peter Salovey first developed a theory of emotional intelligence (EI) during the 1980s. They define EI as 'the ability to carry out accurate reasoning about emotions and the ability to use emotions and emotional knowledge to enhance thought' (Mayer *et al.*, 2008: p. 511). Their model of EI explicitly describes EI as an ability. Specifically, they claim that EI as an ability consists of four branches including the specific abilities to (a) manage emotions so as to attain specific goals; (b) understand emotions, emotional language and the signals conveyed by emotions; (c) use emotions to facilitate thinking; and (d) perceive emotions accurately in oneself and others. (Mayer and Salovey, 1997; Mayer *et al.*, 2008) This model was not directly intended to address the issue of success in an organizational context, as it originally emerged from an interest in how emotion and cognition could be used to influence individual thinking processes.

> **Emotional intelligence**
> Defined by the originators as 'the ability to carry out accurate reasoning about emotions and the ability to use emotions and emotional knowledge to enhance thought'.

It was Daniel Goleman (1995) who first popularized EQ (as EI has also become known) as an aid to organizational functioning. This has received immense attention by the popular business press, and a whole industry of EQ measurement, training and consultancy had grown up since the mid-1990s. Goleman's conception of EI revolves around individual competencies in emotional self-awareness, self-management, social awareness and relationship management. This approach has been in part reflected in research on a more trait-oriented conception of EI (e.g., Petrides *et al.*, 2007) which describes EI as related to individuals' behavioural dispositions and their professed abilities. This view of EI views it more as a personality trait than a mental ability (see Petrides and Furnham, 2001). Proponents of trait and ability conceptions of EI have been immensely critical of each other on a range of conceptual and methodological grounds (Mayer *et al.*, 2008; Petrides *et al.*, 2007), and this debate is likely to continue for the foreseeable future.

Other models of EI have taken a different view. Dulewicz and Higgs (Pickard, 1999) from the Henley Management College have developed a model consisting of three main components and a total of seven elements of EQ in relation to organizational success. Their model is as follows:

- *The drivers.* The two traits of motivation and decisiveness are responsible for energizing individuals to achieve their goals.

- *The constrainers.* The two traits of conscientiousness and integrity, and emotional resilience perform the function of modifying the potential of the drivers to push to excess or in the wrong direction.

- *The enablers.* The three traits of sensitivity, influence and self-awareness help to ensure that the other traits operate in the social context involving the individual and other people.

Dulewicz and Higgs (as described in Pickard, 1999) argue that for organizational success to be achieved it is also necessary for an individual to have what they describe as intellectual intelligence (creativity and external awareness, for example) and managerial intelligence (delegating and business sense, for example) in addition to EQ. Research on EI has shown that men and women have different EQ profiles, with women displaying stronger interpersonal skills, and men showing higher levels of independence and a sense of the self (Lucas, 2000).

A number of organizations have used the EQ concept to review individual difference profiles among work groups and claim to have had some success in changing behaviour patterns at work. It is, however, early days for this relatively new model in terms of its standing compared to conventional models of intelligence. Nevertheless, research is emerging that indicates the link between EI and important organizational dynamics and outcomes. For example, a range of studies indicates that individuals with higher EI are rated as more sociable by peers and supervisors and are seen as contributing more to a positive work environment (Lopes *et al.*, 2006). The ability to recognize others' emotions accurately appears to be positively related to workplace effectiveness (Elfenbein *et al.*, 2007), and such abilities are also correlated with ratings of productive working relationships and of personal drive and integrity (Rosete and Ciarroci, 2005). Mixed findings of links between such abilities and performance ratings have been reported, with correlations found by Elfenbein and Ambady (2002) but not by others (e.g., Rosete and Ciarroci, 2005). These inconsistent findings suggest that the role of EI for performance in organizations may be more complex that our brief discussion suggests. Côté and Miners (2006), for example, found that task performance and organizational citizenship ratings were more strongly predicted by EI for those university employees who had lower cognitive intelligence. Clearly, this indicates that more research is needed before we have clarity on how traditional cognitive intelligence and EI contribute, separately and interactively, to performance in organizations. It is possible that multiple intelligences exist and are of relevance in an organizational context as reflected in the Management in Action example 'Developing multiple intelligences'.

Finally, wisdom is another facet of human beings that is often aligned with intelligence. Wisdom has been defined as 'expert knowledge and judgement about important, difficult and uncertain questions associated with the meaning and conduct of life' (Baltes and Kunzmann, 2003). Wisdom in this sense is thought to be different from both intelligence and personality as it reflects the end point of a developmental process that can go on throughout life. It is, however, a relatively recent phenomenon in research terms and there is much more to learn about wisdom, what it is and how it develops.

ORGANIZATIONAL APPLICATIONS OF INDIVIDUAL DIFFERENCE

The study of personality has concentrated on providing mechanisms for describing characteristics that allow differentiation between individuals. However, the use of personality and personality measures in organizations is usually focused on the identification of individuals with characteristics acceptable or desirable to the organization. Below are a number of areas in which organizations employ personality concepts, theories and measures.

MANAGEMENT IN ACTION

Developing multiple intelligences

Based on the work of a number of writers, Lucas makes the case for there being 10 intelligences of relevance to workforce activity:

- *Linguistic.* The use of words and stories to express clearly and with style.
- *Mathematical.* The use of figures, with a preference for evidence, categories, systems and abstract problems.
- *Visual.* The use of pictures, shapes, diagrams and maps, with a good eye for colour.
- *Physical.* Preference for being active, expressive, quick to get on their feet, and enjoys new experiences.
- *Musical.* Preference for sound and rhythm, mood is affected by music.
- *Emotional.* Know how to manage emotions and their impact on others. Constantly seeking self-knowledge.
- *Social.* Preference for being with other people, showing empathy and helping them to solve problems.
- *Environmental.* Preference for the natural world, seeing patterns in nature that pass others by.
- *Spiritual.* Preference for dealing with the key questions in life and constantly explores the principles and values in life.
- *Practical.* Full of ideas and prefers to make things happen. Practical people enjoy finding workable solutions to everyday problems.

Lucas also suggests five ways to develop the fullest range of intelligences in the workplace:

1 *The environment (physical, musical and social).* Review of the environment and possible provision of a gym and use of music and encouragement of social interaction and knowledge sharing.

2 *People and learning (visual, spiritual and practical).* Recognize the feelings and values of employees. Build in good-quality training provision and action learning activities.

3 *Communication (visual, mathematical and social).* Review internal communications in terms of the range of intelligences present in the organization.

4 *Rewards (linguistic, emotional and practical).* Make sure reward systems acknowledge the full range of talent used. Reward more than the achievement of results, perhaps managing difficult situation with sensitivity. Reward means more than money, for example recognition and family-friendly policies.

5 *Management structures (visual, emotional and spiritual).* Make the structures apparent through a range of visual devices, not just a chart. Encourage the use of EI among managers.

TASKS

1 Are the intelligences indicated aspects of intelligence, or aspects of personality?

2 Why and to what extent should managers be concerned with the provision of facilities that might help to develop employee intelligences?

Source:
Lucas, B. (2002) Developing multiple intelligence, *People Management*, 26 December, pp. 40–41.

Recruitment and selection

The most obvious application of individual difference within an organization is recruitment and selection. In advertising a vacancy externally, the organization is seeking to encourage people not currently associated with it to come forward for consideration and selection. In such situations there is a need to find out as much as possible about applicants so that an appropriate decision can be made. Ultimately, this decision is based on the best fit between the person and the position to be filled.

CHANGE AT WORK

Shona's personality did not match

Shona graduated from a good university with a good first degree in history. She applied for several graduate training schemes and was interviewed for a few of them. For one job she was asked to take a personality test. The test lasted about one hour and Shona was told that she would be told the outcome in a few days. A few days later she was telephoned by the company and told that they would not be taking her application any further as the test result had indicated that she did not match the expected profile for graduate trainees. She was told that she had interviewed well and was clearly intelligent and quick to work through problems. But the test results indicated that she was not an assertive personality and did not have the group leadership qualities that they expected of high flyers. They apologized and wished her well for the future.

TASKS

1   If you were Shona, would you try to change yourself to become like the 'desired' profile (and how might you do this) or would you simply try to 'present' yourself more effectively?

2   Should organizations expect individuals to meet the profiles determined by managers as appropriate (as in this example), or are there any advantages to be gained from organizations learning how to adapt to capture the benefits of individual difference?

3   If your answer to question 2 was that organizations should learn to adapt more to accommodate individual difference, how might that be done?

A recent review and debate on this topic (Morgeson *et al.*, 2007) suggests a number of conclusions, including (a) that compared to ability or aptitude tests, faking in personality tests is possible and common; (b) such faking may not always be problematic as it can reflect socially adaptive personalities and may reflect useful abilities in applicants; (c) the ability to predict job performance based on standard personality measures appears quite limited; (d) when used for selection purposes personality tests should be combined with ability tests to improve their predictive power; and (e) personality tests used for selection should be chosen and/or customized to fit the particular job to be filled. The Managing change example 'Shona's personality did not fit' raises some interesting issues in relation to the implications of seeking to manage personality profiles to organizational advantage.

Development

Psychometric tests can also be used to provide a profile of individuals to determine their respective strengths and development needs. In organizations this can be used to provide a basis of control through access to promotion, development and related organizational 'rewards'. People with 'approved' characteristics, or prepared to develop or adopt them, will be the ones who find advancement within the organization. Thus management may be able to achieve its objectives more easily as employees align themselves with the managerially preferred behaviours. That is, always assuming that managers know which characteristics are the best – a major assumption!

Development programmes often include personality measures but typically also utilize ability measures and feedback from others in the organization. This is also called 360 degrees feedback to represent the fact that often subordinates peers, supervisors and externals (e.g., customers) contribute to provide as comprehensive a picture of the person. Note that these provide feedback on perceived behaviour, not necessarily on the underlying personality of the person. Development for specific careers or even positions often develops 'ideal' competency profiles and uses instruments to reflect an individual's current fit with such profiles. The British Psychological Society website (www.psychtesting.org.uk) also contains a comprehensive and accessible review of the issues.

Assessment centres were first used during World War II as a means of selecting officers for the military. Since then they have evolved to the point where many organizations use them for selection and development purposes. Assessment centres are events that are made up of a range of different activities, requiring individual and group performance. Individuals are observed by assessors and scored on their performance on each activity. At the end of the process the scorers pool all the information gained from the activities and decide on the outcome. The justification for this assessment is that the tasks can be designed to reflect real work activity. Performance is assessed in a live situation, multiple measures of personality and performance are obtained and the results are the combined effort of a number of trained assessors.

Assessment centre
Group-based recruitment or development device that typically includes tests, interviews, and group and individual exercises that are evaluated by a team of assessors.

Discrimination

Discrimination occurs in many forms. Women, ethnic minority groups, older people, younger people, religious groups, gay men and lesbians represent just some of the people who have found themselves discriminated against throughout history. Discrimination is associated with the attitudes (usually negative) of one group of people towards another. For example, women find it difficult to break through the 'glass ceiling' and obtain the highest positions within organizations. Studies of the influence of personality factors on negative attitude formation have a long history. For example, Adorno *et al.* (1953) demonstrated that people displaying the highest levels of prejudice towards other groups also had strongly authoritarian personalities.

Stress and bullying

Stress exists in many jobs and arises from a number of sources. One of the causes of susceptibility to stress in people is the nature of the individual. Traditional conceptions of different personality types are reflected in the Type A/Type B distinction (Rosenman *et al.*, 1964) which is summarized in Table 3.4. A well established research

Table 3.4 Type A and Type B personality characteristics

Type A personality characteristics	Type B personality characteristics
High need for achievement	Low need for achievement
Aggressive	Passive, doesn't lose temper
Competitive	Laid-back, enjoys leisure time
Restless	Easy-going, slow paced
Alert	Relaxed
Constantly feeling under pressure	Not usually feeling under pressure
Impatient	Patient

Core self-evaluation
A dispositional factor (i.e., a stable trait) that closely reflects locus of control, emotional stability (neuroticism) as well as self-esteem and generalized performance confidence. People with positive core self-evaluations view themselves positively across situations and see themselves as capable, in control and generally valuable.

finding is the association of Type A personalities and the tendency to experience heart disease (e.g., Friedman and Booth-Kewley, 1987). Type A people place a high emphasis on work at the expense of other aspects of their lives, frequently work at home and are less interested in exercise, for example. This approach to personality has also been used to explore managerial effectiveness and level of job in India – see the Going Global example below. People with positive core self-evaluation (which describes those individuals who consistently view themselves as capable and worthy individuals with the capacity to perform well across a wide range of situations) tend to be better able to cope with stress (Kammeyer-Mueller *et al.*, 2009).

Another aspect of stress at work arises through the phenomenon of bullying. Bullying has probably always existed, although there is a growing recognition that it is becoming more significant in its impact both on people and on organizations. Cooper (1999) reports a survey indicating that 18 per cent of respondents had been bullied during the previous year, while another 43 per cent had witnessed bullying over the same period. Adams (1992) draws attention to organizational bullying in all its forms. The case studies that she provides also give clear indications of the stressful impact of the experiences for the victims. Also included is a review of a number of the components of individual difference that contribute to the exercise of bullying (or victim) behaviour by individuals.

GOING GLOBAL

Western created personality profiles apply everywhere – don't they?

Vandana carried out a study into the effectiveness of a total of 80 top-level and first-line supervisors in both marketing and production departments of a number of private sector organizations in Uttar Pradesh, a state in the north central region of India. Uttar Pradesh has a population of about 16.6 million people and the capital city is Lucknow. It is a largely agricultural region with industry being primarily based on the processing of sugar and cotton.

Personality was assessed using the Type A-Type B self-test developed by Bortner (1985), and effectiveness through the Managerial Effectiveness Questionnaire (MEQ) developed by Gupta (1996).

The results of the study identified that both managerial level and personality type had a significant effect on the level of perceived effectiveness:

- In the production departments, both top level and first line supervisors having Type B personality were found to be more effective.

- In the marketing department top-level managers having Type A personality and first-line supervisors having Type B personality were found to be more effective in comparison to their counterparts.

TASKS

1 Given the results of this study, can you infer that the measures of personality used (and which were originally developed in the West) can be applied anywhere in the world?

2 Why or why not?

Sources:
Vandana, D. (2004) Managerial effectiveness: a function of personality type and organizational components, Singapore Management Review, 1 July. http://www.thefreelibrary.com/Managerial+effectiveness%3a+a+function+of+personality+type+and...-a0119370568
Bortner, R.W. (1985) A Short Rating Scale as a Potential Measure of Pattern in Behaviour, In Fred Luthans, *Organizational Behavior*, New York: McGraw-Hill.
Gupta, S. (1996) Managerial Effectiveness: Conceptual Framework and Scale Development, *Indian Journal of Industrial Relations*, 31(3):392-409.

The testing business

Another organizational effect of personality is the growth of an industry around the measurement of it. There are a considerable number of psychologists and consultancies that offer services to organizations based on the existence of personality and the measurement of it. Naturally, it is in the business interests of those practitioners to ensure that the opportunities for the application of personality are brought to management's attention. This includes the training of company staff to use and interpret particular instruments, the development of new tests and the application of the tests in organizational activity. The difficulties that can arise from poorly trained individuals applying psychometric tests has long been recognized and has led the British Psychological Society to introduce formal accreditation training. In addition the Institute of Personnel and Development has introduced a Code of Practice on Psychological Testing.

STOP & CONSIDER

'Individuals are just that, individual; therefore they cannot be understood through the application of standardized tests based on nomothetic perspectives on personality. The only 'use' for such approaches to understanding personality is that they are attractive to company managers in their search for greater levels of employee control. Therefore the 'purpose and value' of such tests is to provide lucrative business opportunities for psychologists and consultants.' Discuss this statement.

CONCLUSIONS

The concept of individual difference is a difficult one for managers to deal with. It operates at many different levels within the organization and has a number of different theoretical roots along with many different measurement mechanisms (over 5000 are available). At a common-sense level personality, which we define as the relatively enduring individual characteristics that are inferred from observable, reasonably consistent patterns of an individual's behaviour over time, is something that most people, including managers, would claim to recognize. It reflects how people get on with each other including features such as sociability and intelligence. It is only when an attempt is made to be more precise in the definition of individual difference and its measurement, followed by establishing specific links with work activities, that the real difficulties emerge. The links between personality and particular jobs are an area where managers might be expected to show interest, but there is little by way of agreement about the precise nature of that relationship.

Now to summarize this chapter in terms of the relevant Learning Objectives:

- **Outline the concept of individual difference.** There are many ways in which individuals differ from each other. Many are obvious such as gender or height and

of little value in organizational terms. However, the use of personality implies certain characteristics that reflect psychological processes and orientations which determine how people differ from one another in ways which could impact on the way that they work and the type of work for which they may be best fitted.

- **Describe the major theoretical approaches to the study of personality.** There are two major approaches to the study of personality. One approach, the nomothetic, is based on the existence of characteristics such as extroversion and neuroticism which can be measured using a variety of tests. Understanding personality therefore becomes a process of measuring the degree to which these characteristics exist in an individual person, creating a personality profile. The other approach, the idiographic, is based on seeking to understand the individual in terms of how they relate to the world in which they live. The argument is that the real world exists in the mind of the individual and it is they who construct the reality that they react to. Consequently, in seeking to understand the individual it is first necessary to understand how they relate to and construct the social world around them. In addition there are models which do not neatly fall into either of these two classifications.

- **Understand the strengths and weaknesses of each of the major theories of personality.** Each of the theoretical models discussed in this chapter contains strengths and weaknesses. To a significant extent the views about the relative strengths and weaknesses of each is determined by the epistemological views of the reader. Post-Positivists tend to the view that the laws of natural science can be applied to the social world, leading them to hold that the nomothetic models have more value than the ideographic. Interpretivists would tend to hold the opposite perspective, believing that in the social world each individual constructs reality for themselves within their minds and that consequently the normal rules of science cannot apply. Each of the models discussed in this chapter has a brief review of the theory attached to it. Without repeating that material here, it provides the essential answer to this objective.

- **Discuss the basic process involved in the development of psychometric tests.** Development tests go through a number of stages, as follows:

  Step 1. The identification of a practical or research-based need.

  Step 2. The development of appropriate test items.

  Step 3. The final forms of the test are developed and the administration arrangements designed.

  Step 4. The 'standardization' and 'norming' process.

  Step 5. Reliability and validity analyses.

- **Explain the significance of individual difference as a basis for taking decisions relating to people within organizations.** There are a number of ways in which personality is used within organizations, and in relation to the people who work in them. There are the marketing-related uses in terms of characterizing the customer (or potential customer). There are also the recruitment-related uses in which potential candidates are screened for the existence of desirable characteristics. There is also the opportunity to create work teams with a blend of particular characteristics and the identification of training and development needs based on the desire to encourage particular traits among employees. Such processes also signal the desired characteristics for those hopeful of promotion to more senior positions. There is a potential downside for these possibilities, that of socially engineering a particular type of workforce, which over time as conditions change cannot adapt to the new situation. There is also a question about the degree to which it is possible to socially engineer personality or workforce with any degree of success.

DISCUSSION QUESTIONS

1 'Psychometric tests make it easy to sell consultancy services to senior managers and that is the only value they have.' Discuss this statement.

2 To what extent does personality explain individual differences between people?

3 Describe the genetic and environmental origins of personality. Which do you consider the most important to the development of adult personality? Why?

4 Would it be desirable for all the employees within an organization to have similar personality characteristics? Why, or why not?

5 To what extent do you consider that it might be possible to use graphology (handwriting) to understand the personality characteristics of an individual?

6 'Emotional intelligence has no value in an organizational setting as emotion plays no part in business.' Discuss this statement.

7 Can personality be measured accurately by any form of psychometric test? Why or why not?

8 It has often been suggested that Freudian theory tells us more about Freud than it does about personality. Discuss.

9 To what extent is the 'Big Five' model of personality the best as it concentrates on the five most important dimensions of personality from an organizational perspective?

10 'Any organization needs "different" people within it in order to optimize performance and effectiveness through the unique contribution of each individual.' Discuss.

CASE STUDY

John and the sales administrator

John was the production manager in a medium-sized manufacturing company in the South East of England. The company produced black plastic rubbish sacks from recycled plastic waste. John was in his late thirties and had been recruited by the chief executive to be the production manager/director designate about one year earlier. His background was that of an industrial engineer and the brief given to him was to increase the productivity of the production unit through modernization, improved planning and control systems, together with better supervision and employee management.

The general atmosphere within the company was one of hostility between management and the workforce at all levels. No one trusted anyone else and disputes were common. Deliveries were invariably late; this was used as a pressure point by supervisors and employees as a way of getting overtime, as and when they wanted it. In return management did not respect the nonmanagement employees and would frequently threaten them with the sack or total closure of the company. When John was brought into the company it was hoped that his professional background and production experience would help to improve matters.

John began by spending most of his time in the factory 'walking the job' and speaking to employees and supervisors as often as possible. The poor performance of the factory was well known by all concerned and everyone would claim to have an interest in sorting it out, but nothing actually changed. A similar state of affairs existed in the administrative offices, where it was not uncommon to find staff saying to customers that it was 'Them in the factory' that were responsible for the late delivery and they were 'Just being awkward as usual'. The sales director was a remote individual and not a well integrated member of the senior management team, which also consisted of the chief executive, production manager (John) and the finance manager. The sales director had worked for the company the longest and spent most of his time away from the office visiting his favourite customers (current and potential) and supposedly helping to develop new products. His staff had to contact him by

phone most of the time if they needed him as he was only in the office about one day each week. Consequently, most of the sales activity was effectively controlled and managed by the sales office manager.

John was making slow progress in the factory. New planning methods and supervisor training had been introduced, as well as some of the human resource practices improved. For example, attendance control procedures had been tightened and employees having time off work for any reason were interviewed on their first day back at work. Discussions were underway with the trade union over changes to the terms and conditions of work, but this was only making very slow progress. Some impact was evident on delivery schedules, although not enough to deal with the major problem of delays being used to manufacture the need for overtime.

One of the key working relationships that existed was between John as the factory manager and Ann, the sales office manager as she was the most common point of contact between customers and the company. The working relationship between these two was particularly important when orders were delayed or changed for any reason. Unfortunately, Ann and John did not get on at either a personal or professional level. Ann considered that the customer was right every time irrespective of the effect on the factory and that the factory had a duty to accept that a customer might change their minds and quietly fit in with her 'demands' on behalf of the customer. These demands were inevitably passed on as instructions over the telephone, even though Ann was junior to John in the hierarchy. This was not John's preferred way of working and if there was a problem from his side of the company, he inevitably went to see Ann to explain what the situation was and to see if some form of compromise could be arranged. This approach was usually brushed aside with comments such as, 'It's your problem, what am I supposed to tell my customer? You have let me down again. You and your factory people are hopeless.' If pushed she would ring the customer to see if alternative delivery times could be agreed, but this was inevitably couched in terms of, 'The factory have let us down again by failing to produce when they should and they want you to compensate by changing delivery times.'

On one occasion, a customer had rung to change an order and Ann rang John to instruct him as to what he should do. John was in the middle of a production meeting and had all the supervisors and production planning staff in his office discussing the next week's activities when the phone rang. He picked it up and heard Ann begin to lay down the law as to what needed to be changed, which he realized would significantly change the plans so carefully worked out for the next week. So he simply said that he was in

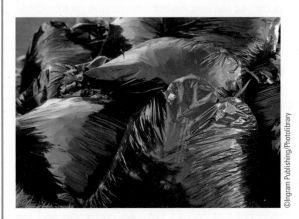

©Ingram Publishing/Photolibrary

a meeting and put the phone down. Well slammed it down might be a more accurate description!

Ann was shocked at this disrespect of her and her position as she saw it and immediately rang the sales director to tell him that John had been very rude to her etc. After speaking to him, she immediately went directly to see the chief executive and complained that she was too important to the company to be treated as she had been and that she expected the chief executive to immediately discipline John in order to put him in his place. John was subsequently asked to go and see the chief executive to provide his side of the story.

TASKS

1 In what ways and to what extent does this case study reflect issues of personality?
   How would you deal with this situation if you were the chief executive?

2 Could John have dealt with things differently and reduced the likelihood of this problem arising?

3 How might knowledge of personality theory have helped John to prevent the situation arising, or deal more effectively with the crisis?

FURTHER READING

Boyatzis, R., Goleman, D. and McKee, A. (2002) *Primal Leadership: Realizing the power of Emotional Intelligence*, Boston, MA: Harvard University Business Press. A review of leadership and its relationship with EI and personality generally.

Doidge, N. (2007) *The brain that changes itself*. Viking. Insightful overview of neuro-psychological issues based on recent advances in brain research.

Donnelly, J. (2003) Blot on the landscape, *The Psychologist,* May, 16(5): 246–269. This article reflects upon the current use of the Rorschach test.

James, L.R. and Mazerolle, M.D. (2002) *Personality in Work Organizations*, London: Sage. Reviews the literature on personality and its application to organizational practice and research.

Ridley, M. (2003) *Nature via Nurture: Genes, Experiences and What Makes Us Human*, London: Fourth Estate. Explains complex science in an accessible, anecdotal style. Shows how genes switch themselves on and off at different times throughout our development in response to outside stimuli and other genes. Takes a pure reductionist stance and is dismissive of interpretivist contributions.

Seligman, M.E.P. (2002) *Authentic happiness: Using the new positive psychology to realize your potential for lasting fulfilment*, New York: Free Press. Comprehensive and highly readable treatment of 'positive psychology'.

COMPANION WEBSITE

Online teaching and learning resources

Visit the companion website for Organizational Behaviour and Management 4th edition at: http://www.cengage.co.uk/martinfellenz to find valuable further teaching and learning material. For full details, see 'About the website' at the start of the book.

CHAPTER FOUR

©raduska-te/istock

PERCEPTION, ATTRIBUTION AND ATTITUDE FORMATION

LEARNING OBJECTIVES

After studying this chapter and working through the associated OB in Action panels, Discussion Questions and Case Study you should be able to:

- Describe the processes of perception and attitude formation.

- Explain the links between perception, attitude formation and impression management.

- Understand why employee perceptions and attitudes are difficult for managers to influence.

- Discuss the issues surrounding organizational attempts to shape the perceptions and attitudes of employees.

- Assess the significance of person perception in the behaviour of managers and employees.

- Recognize the role of attribution in organizations and differentiate the two modes of cognitive information processing in the Dual Process Model.

INTRODUCTION

Perception is one of the most important psychological processes for humans. Fundamentally, it is our link to the world around us – without perception we would not be able to link our inner world with the environment outside of ourselves! Perception involves a significant amount of simplification. A vast range of stimuli (sensations or pieces of information) impact upon the human senses all the time, even when we sleep. Because of the volume and range involved, it is not possible for anyone to pay attention to every stimulus and still be able to cope with the most simple of tasks. Imagine for example, trying to cross a busy street in the centre of a major city while listening intently to every sound, smelling every odour, feeling the

EXAMINING ETHICS

Women to work on submarines?

The following story was carried by several newspapers recently.

Within the UK it is the Ministry of Defence that is responsible for running the three armed forces (Royal Navy, Army and Royal Air Force). These days' women are allowed to serve in many branches of the military, including those offered by the Royal Navy. Women have served on board the surface ships of the Royal Navy for approximately 20 years but they remain banned from submarines. The reasons given for this are because they could be pregnant (but not aware of it) when they go to sea, potentially putting themselves and their unborn child in danger. There are also fears that chemicals on a submarine could be dangerous to a growing foetus. There could be a need for medical support and there is an ever present risk of complications developing – appropriate facilities are not available on a submarine. Consequently a commander could be forced to abandon a potentially important mission. Equally, submarines are cramped and it would not be possible to segregate crew areas for washing, sleeping, etc. - crew 'hot bed' - one shift gets out of a bed which then becomes available to a crew finishing theirs. The UK's nuclear missile submarines are typically on patrol for 4 months or more without surfacing, and the fleet of 'hunter-killer' submarines can also be submerged (intelligence gathering or monitoring ships) for several months.

However the Royal Navy is considering scrapping the ban on women serving in submarines and the next generation of Britain's nuclear submarines are being designed to carry female sailors. Ministry of Defence officials confirmed that the current rules barring the Royal Navy's 3700 female sailors from serving in submarines are 'under review', and indicated that design of a £20 billion new fleet of nuclear-missile submarines was taking into account 'the possibility of women serving on submarines in the future'. This review is taking place for several reasons. Partly because the Royal Navy is facing a shortage of suitably qualified engineers willing to serve for months at a time beneath the waves. Also officials believe that legal challenges based on gender equality laws could eventually require the current policy to be changed, forcing them to accept the need to cater for mixed gender crews.

TASK

1 To what extent is the basis for banning women serving in submarines ethical, or is it based on the perception that male and female colleagues should not be confined in such close proximity for such long periods of time? Justify your views.

Sources:
http://www.dailymail.co.uk/news/article-1083329/Women-set-serve-submarines-time-beat-manning-shortage.html, 5 November 2008, accessed 28 April 2009.
http://www.thisisplymouth.co.uk/news/Women-serve-navy-submarinesarticle-453808-details/article.html, 6 November 2008, accessed 28 April 2009.
http://www.express.co.uk/posts/view/69516/Navy-women-to-serve-on-submarines-, 5 November 2008, accessed 28 April 2009.

clothes worn press onto the body and watching every other person, and so on. A sure scenario for an accident! In addition to this volume-based need for simplification, human beings need to be able to classify the sensations that are experienced in order to make them meaningful. For example, the classification of a particular visual image as a fast-approaching car is necessary to be able to identify the benefits and hazards associated with it.

Important concepts related to perception are those of social cognition, attribution, sensemaking, attitudes and impression management. Human beings perceive themselves as well as other people, and the social world they inhabit and create; they explain what they experience and make sense of the world around them; they form attitudes about all manner of things. These processes are closely related, so much so that explanations and attitudes influenced by perception will in turn influence subsequent perceptions. This circular process between attitude and perception is evident in many aspects of human behaviour, not least discrimination against particular groups of people. (see for example the following Examining Ethics example).

THE SIGNIFICANCE OF PERCEPTION

To survive, humans must become aware of what is 'out there' – the vast range of 'things' that are external to themselves. They must then be able to decide which stimuli are significant (and why) in any particular context and give attention to the selected data. After processing this selected data to extract information, individuals can then determine how to respond to their environment. This is the basis of the process referred to as perception. Interestingly, much of this is happening without people being conscious of the psychological process of perception. They simply become aware of their environment (actually, of part of their environment because perception is so selective). The following list contains some of the main human senses representing the detection systems for external stimuli which impact on people and in which some form of perception occurs:

Perception
A psychological process involving individuals selecting stimuli from their environment and processing this data to develop awareness and understanding about their environment and determine responses.

- vision
- temperature
- sound
- taste/smell
- pain
- touch.

In addition there is another sense: an ability to be aware of spatial relationships. For example, a blindfolded individual could probably find their way around a familiar room without too much difficulty. A mental map of the room exists in the person's head which together with an awareness of distance, size and movement provides an indication of the relevant spatial relationships.

Perception links individuals to their environment, and thus to each other. It provides the basis for individuals making sense of their surroundings and understanding their world and each other. It provides the informational input on which people act and interact with others and the world around them. The significance of perception within organizations is that without it, individuals could simply not be members of an organization because they could not know about it, its goals and how they could contribute to achieving them. Perception enables all this, and moreover influences the ways in which people learn about and make sense of their world, other people and others' and their own place in it. Perception provides the inputs to people's conscious and unconscious decision making about their behaviour. Understanding the steps and processes involved in human perception, and the implications of perception for behaviour, is therefore of paramount importance for OB.

Perception is not simply a psychological phenomenon – it is also an intensely social process because the way we make sense of perceived data is strongly influenced by our previous understanding, which in turn is in large part socially influenced and constructed. This is one reason why there is no certainty that any two people (or groups of people) will perceive the same stimulus in exactly the same way. Similarly, as a result of learning about and experiencing their environment and interacting with others, individuals form attitudes about the world. Some attitudes

CHANGE AT WORK

Attitudes and perceptions in times of change

The organization in question (a small regional bank in the UK) was going through a significant period of change. As part of this, the HR department was expected to take an active lead in the process and a number of new appointments were made in order to increase its size and to strengthen its ability to do so. This involved the recruitment of a number of experienced HR specialists with significant change management experience: training and industrial relations being two examples.

The process also involved the reallocation of a number of the existing HR staff to new duties. One or two of the existing HR staff perceived that the newly appointed specialists were a threat to their standing within the organization and began to engage in hostile behaviour towards them. The situation became extremely political and resulted in many additional problems for the organization until the HR director was able to stabilize the situation.

Interpretation of this story from an attitudes and perception perspective suggests several things:

- The existing HR specialists perceived that the newly appointed people had skills that were more valued by the organization than theirs and this created negative attitudes towards them. They also perceived the increased number of staff as competition for any future career development opportunities. This resulted in attitudes and

behaviour that were openly hostile to the new people and anything suggested by them.

- The new HR specialists arrived with a set of attitudes that implied that the organization was not unique and that adopting their previously learned skills would enable it to achieve its objectives. Their attitude to existing staff was negative and patronizing - the new appointments were necessary to 'hide' a lack of existing capability. Resistance from the established HR specialists began as a minor irritation and was inevitable. However, continued hostility led the new HR specialists to interpret this as a deliberate attempt to undermine them.

- Effectively a 'doom loop' of deteriorating attitudes, fuelled by perceptions of other people's behaviour resulted. This led to appeals to higher authority to resolve the problem (usually by dismissing the 'other' people). Several conflict-resolving sessions were held and one or two of the new specialists left of their own accord. Some 3 years later the situation was not completely resolved and an uneasy truce emerged between the parties.

TASKS

1 Was the situation described inevitable as a result of the likely perception and attitudes of people in that situation?

2 Could the problems have been anticipated and how might the situation have been dealt with in order to avoid some if not all of them?

are deeply held and as a consequence probably difficult to change. Other attitudes are perhaps less entrenched and liable to change in line with experience. For example, attitudes towards fashion are notoriously fickle and liable to change quickly. There are obvious and strong links between perception and the attitudes that people hold. Attitudes are formed on the basis of perceived information. Perceptions are interpreted in the light of experience and attitudes as the Change at work example illustrates.

A MODEL OF PERCEPTION

Perception as a process can be described as a sequence of events from the receipt of a stimulus to the response to it (see Figure 4.1). The following sections of this chapter will consider each of the elements from this model in greater detail.

It is often assumed that as individuals we all perceive the reality of the world around us in the same way. However, a glance at a range of newspapers covering political or industrial relations events should provide adequate support for the view that there are always at least two points of view in any situation. This reflects something that has been acknowledged by psychologists for some considerable time. Look at Figure 4.2. What do you see?

Do you see a young woman or an old woman in the picture? Now ask one or two of your friends what they see? Does everyone you ask see the same? The raw material (the picture) is interpreted in the light of a range of internal and external influences. Neither of the two main interpretations of the same stimulus is 'right' or 'wrong' because they reflect a person's understanding of what is actually there. Given that perception represents a simplifying process intended to allow (among other things) individuals to identify significant issues, previous experience as well as the particular focus of the perceiver and the current situational and social context all influence the process of perception.

Virtually all aspects of the perceptual process outlined above can be handled either actively and consciously or automatically and subconsciously. In cognitive, social and neuro-psychology, distinguishing between these two different ways of selecting and processing information is also called the *Dual Process Model* (e.g., Feldman Barrett *et al.*, 2004). The two modes have been called by various names, but automatic vs. controlled processing, heuristic vs. systematic, peripheral vs. central route, or X-system vs C-system (for refleXive and refleCtive, respectively, see Satpute and Lieberman, 2006) are common and useful labels (see Table 4.1 for differences between the dual processes). This important distinction applies to virtually all cognitive processes in humans and has immense relevance for OB. We will discuss its significance for other topics throughout the book.

Figure 4.1 The perceptual process

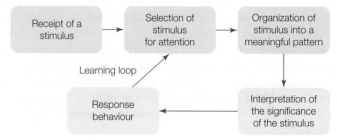

Figure 4.2 Ambiguous figure

Source: Originally published by Hill, W.E. (1915) *Punch*, 6 November.

In perception, distinguishing between automatic and controlled processing is important for a number of reasons. First, it helps to explain why we are aware of only some of the perceptual tasks we are continuously engaged in, and why it is impossible for us to deliberately do all perceptual tasks, or do some of them deliberately all the time. Second, it helps explain why we often commit errors, only some of which can be explained by faulty logic or inadequate decision making. Third, it provides insights into the differential nature of attitudes associated with the different processes.

Receipt of a stimulus

It is easier to illustrate the many aspects of the perceptual process using visual examples (see Figure 4.2). Readers should understand, however, that similar perceptual processes are at work in all the human senses. For example, Figure 4.3 illustrates an experiment in which a pair of coiled but separate tubes have cold and warm water running through them. Rather than averaging out this will lead to individuals holding these coils experiencing a hot, burning sensation because of the simultaneous stimulation of warm and cold sensation receptors in the skin. This illustrates that raw data (cold and warm coils close together) can stimulate subjective perceptions that are not accurate reflections of what is really happening.

The fact that our senses play tricks on us is even more apparent in the world of visual illusion. Indeed, magicians rely on just this phenomenon to amaze audiences during stage and television performances. Another aspect of this is demonstrated in the impossible figure, which at one and the same time exists and yet cannot exist (see Figure 4.4).

In this particular case, the difficulty lies with the ability of the eye to see two dimensions from the image presented and the perceptual system's ability to construct three dimensions from that data. Most of the time perceptual processes work consistently in creating meaning for the individual, but in this particular example the two systems provide contradictory messages and reality breaks down. In human terms, when such contradictions arise they force a switching from automatic to controlled processing while clarification is sought and the ambiguity resolved. This slows down reaction times, often significantly. While this might be acceptable in some situations, it could be dangerous if, say, the pilot of a passenger aircraft has to take valuable time to resolve conflicting images presented to them at a critical moment during a flight.

Table 4.1 Characteristics of the different modes of processing in the dual-process model

Name of processing mode	Automatic processing	Controlled processing
Other common labels for processing mode	• Heuristic processing • Peripheral route • X-system	• Systematic processing • Central route • C-system
Structure of information processing	Parallel processing	Serial processing
Speed of information processing	Fast operating	Slow operating
Speed of learning	Slow learning	Fast learning
Change resistance	Relatively resistant to change	Relatively open to change
Speed of potential change	Slow change	Fast change
Nature of memory linkages made during processing	Connections tend to be based on association drawing on automatic pattern-completion or similarity-based memory retrieval	Connections tend to be based on rules, reasoning and logic, drawing on deliberate matching connections and relevant cultural knowledge
Influence of past vs. present	Processing outcomes strongly determined by the past through use of pre-existing representations	Processing outcomes strongly determined by the present through use of newly created representations
Subliminal influences	Sensitive to subliminal influences	Insensitive to subliminal influences
Source of attention initiation	External, stimulus-driven, bottom-up, and reflexive attention initiation	Internal, goal-directed, top-down and reflective attention initiation
Agency for processing initiation	External and spontaneous processes	Internal and intentional processes
Nature of processing	Predominantly sensory	Predominantly linguistic, conceptual and symbolic
Impact of physiological arousal	Facilitated by physiological arousal	Impaired by physiological arousal
Impact of cognitive load	Cognitive load does not affect processing	Cognitive load does affect processing
Subjective experience	Lack of awareness of all the following: • processing attempts • self-direction (agency) • effort • control of competing efforts.	Awareness of all the following: • processing attempts • self-direction (agency) • effort • control of competing efforts.
Influence on attitudes	Contributes to generation of implicit attitudes that are slow changing and often remain subconscious	Contributes to generation of explicit attitudes that can change fast and are conscious

Source: Extended based on source material from Bargh, 1994; Bargh and Ferguson, 2000; Feldman Barrett *et al.*, 2004; Lieberman, 2007; Satpute and Lieberman, 2006; Smith and DeCoster, 2000.

Figure 4.3 Perception of 'hot' as a result of the simultaneous stimulation of warm and cold receptors

COLD WATER ⟶   ⟵ HOT WATER

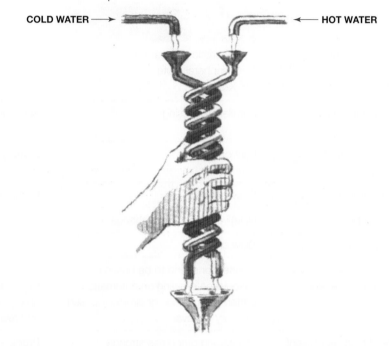

Source: Hilgard, E.R.,
Atkinson, R.C. and
Atkinson, R.L. (1971)
Introduction to Psychology
(5th edn), New York:
Harcourt Brace Jovanovich.

SELECTION OF STIMULI FOR ATTENTION

The selection of which of the many simultaneous stimuli impacting on the senses to pay attention to allows the individual to identify the most significant events. This could be either those that need to be attended to or those that are of most interest. If this decision is made automatically or in controlled mode is a function of characteristics of three main elements: the context, the target and the perceiver.

The context

Context and circumstances can have a direct impact on the selection of the stimuli to which attention will be directed. For example, senior managers of a company experiencing financial difficulties would pay more attention to every item of expenditure than when a healthy profit was being made. Also, people in expensive business suits walking around a factory floor can create a wide variety of rumours because they stand out as different from the people usually found in that context. By comparison

Figure 4.4 An impossible figure

Source: Hilgard, E.R.,
Atkinson, R.C. and
Atkinson, R.L. (1971)
Introduction to Psychology
(5th edn), New York:
Harcourt Brace Jovanovich.

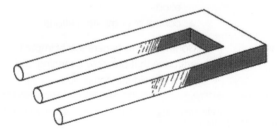

in a head office environment it would be people walking about in boiler suits who would attract attention.

Factors related to the target

There are a number of factors related to the target that can impact on its selection as a stimulus for attention. Certain features of a particular stimulus might increase its *salience*, which means that they *make it more likely to stand out from those around it* and therefore attract attention, including:

- *Repetition.* The more often something is repeated the more likely it is that the message gets through to the level of consciousness. Advertising and public relations often apply this principle to increase the awareness of a particular product or brand name. However, repetition can also lead to the senses turning off from the awareness of the presence of a stimulus. This is called habituation. This can create hazards in a working environment if individuals frequently ignore warning signs that are always present, for example.

- *Size.* It is perhaps obvious, but the larger a particular stimulus is, the more likely it is that it will attract attention.

- *Novelty and inconsistency with expectation.* The presence of the unusual (in a particular context) tends to attract attention. Marketing specialists in designing advertising campaigns also use this aspect of perception.

- *Intensity.* The brighter or louder a particular stimulus, the more likely it is to attract attention.

- *Motion.* Something which moves is more likely to attract attention than something which is stationary. Predatory animals use this feature when hunting their prey in moving very slowly to get close without being detected.

- *Familiarity.* For example, humans find it very easy to spot a familiar face among a crowd of strangers.

- *Contrast.* The relative size (and other features) of events placed near together can influence perception. For example, consider Figure 4.5.

Habituation
Constant repetition of a stimulus can lead to the senses turning off from the awareness of it.

Do you see:

A Two figures, one a large circle surrounded by small ones, and a small circle surrounded by large ones?

B Two figures, each with a same size of circle in the centre but surrounded by different sizes of circle?

Option B is a more accurate reflection of the two diagrams. However, many people report that option A is correct! The relative circle sizes influences the perception of the figures.

Figure 4.5 Contrast effect on perception

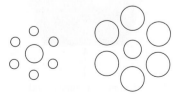

Source: Hilgard, E.R. *et al.* (1971) *Introduction to Psychology* (5th edn), New York: Harcourt Brace Jovanovich.

Factors related to the perceiver

There are a range of factors internal to the perceiver that influence which stimuli are likely to be attended to. Figure 4.6 shows the internal factors influencing stimulus selection which are discussed in turn below.

Schema
Cognitive structure stored in memory that represents some aspect of the world in an idealized and abstract way which can provide an interpretation frame for processing information.

Script
Cognitive structure build through experience and repeated practice that delineates the nature and sequence of behaviours.

SCHEMAS AND SCRIPTS

The processing of information in automatic mode is largely handled through schemas (or schemata) which are cognitive structures or models representing some aspect of the world. They are invoked automatically through key stimuli and determine the interpretation of settings and events. As an example, being approached in a hospital by a person wearing a white coat and stethoscope would compel most people to treat that person as a physician and interpret their behaviour according to this social role. Similarly, perception often invokes behavioural reactions that are somewhat automated. People often act according to predetermined scripts. As an example (you can easily try this out), in most Western cultures if you approach a stranger in a neutral setting while smiling and holding out your hand they almost invariably smile back and take your hand to shake it – without making a conscious decision to do so! Moreover, behavioural scripts often serve as schemas that we use to interpret others' behaviour (see the discussion on attribution later in the chapter). This process can also be seen at work in the Going Global example.

MOTIVATIONS AND OBJECTIVES

Both the physical and social needs that influence an individual at any point in time will influence which stimuli attract attention. This works in terms of direction (what is more likely to be perceived) and focus (the breadth of stimuli people will attend to). The more intense the motivation, the narrower the focus will be. For example, an employee paid a bonus based on the number of units of output is likely to pay much closer attention to events that impact on the volume of output. Similarly, people seek out those things and situations which are of value to them. For example, if you are interested in buying a particular car model you will notice similar cars and comments about them much more readily.

Figure 4.6 Internal factors Influencing stimulate selection

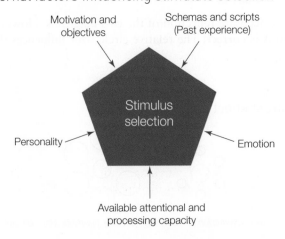

GOING GLOBAL

The Guards can't argue, but the family can!

The Spanish Civil Guard (Guardia Civil) was originally founded in 1844 is a police force that has both military and civilian functions. It undertakes peace-keeping missions overseas and holds military status, making it a federal paramilitary police force. As such, the Civil Guard is comparable to the French Gendarmerie, the Italian Carabinieri and the Dutch Royal Marechaussee. The Civil Guard uses as its motto 'El honor es mi divisa' (Honour is my emblem) stressing its esprit de corps and the importance of honour expected from members of the service. The Civil Guard precincts are called 'casa cuartel' (army house) and, like other military garrisons in Spain, they appear under the motto 'Todo por la patria' (All in the service of the country).

Given that the Civil Guard is a paramilitary police force, it follows a military structure and organization resulting in a strong hierarchical, top-down, culture. Also in the context of its paramilitary military responsibilities it would not be uncommon for officers to find themselves in confrontational, stressful or critical situations where a need for immediate, decisive action existed and so it would not be unexpected to find a dictatorial leadership style. There are a number of implications that might be expected to follow from such approaches to managing and organizing. For example, with a classically military culture combining discipline, honour, respect and obedience to senior officers, it would be unlikely that any junior or front-line officer would feel able to speak out about any perceived injustice, poor treatment or any of the many potential problems that 'normal' employees might expect to complain about. Such complaints would be unwelcome and discouraged by conventional ways of working and cultural norms.

However, that does not mean that problems that arise are not brought to the attention of senior officers. The question is how might that be done? The answer is that family members of the lower rank Civil Guards are the ones to bring into the open issues that need attention. In doing so their feelings become clear (and by implication those of their serving family members). For example, complaints about excessive working hours, long periods of overseas duty or lack of maintenance on camp housing might be issues difficult for a serving officer to raise, but about which family members could organize some form of protest. Such protests might involve demonstrations, petitions, talking to the press - all publicity intended to protect the serving officers, but achieve a solution to the problem by forcing senior officers, administrators and politicians to act.

TASKS

1 Imagine that you are a senior officer in the Civil Guard. How might you perceive the 'process' in which discipline is officially maintained, but conflict is expressed through the actions of family members?

2 As a lowest rank Civil Guard, what do you think your attitude to senior officers would be as a result of having to raise problems through the actions of family members rather than directly through the rank structure?

Sources:
Conversation with a Spanish colleague, Maria A Ortega Cerda.
http://hemeroteca.lavanguardia.es/preview/1989/12/30/pagina-11/33481342/pdf.html?search=mujeres%20de%20guardia%20civil%20manifestacion (accessed March 2009).
http://hemeroteca.lavanguardia.es/preview/1999/03/28/pagina-21/33021445/pdf.html?search=mujeres%20de%20policia (accessed March 2009).

PERSONALITY

The personality characteristics of individuals influence the way that they predispose themselves to seek information from the environment (Witkin *et al.*, 1954). There may also be individual differences in working memory capacity (Feldman Barrett *et al.*, 2004) that may make controlled selection of stimuli more likely.

ATTENTIONAL AND PROCESSING CAPACITY

Active and controlled selection of stimuli for perception is predicated on the availability of sufficient attentional capacity (Bargh, 1989). If people are very stressed, tired, in pain, or otherwise physiologically aroused or preoccupied with other mental tasks, they may not take in as many stimuli and rely more on salience cues rather than their own deliberate selection of stimuli.

EMOTIONAL STATE AND MOOD

Positive emotional states and good mood will increase the attention to positive aspects of a situation, while the opposite is true for negative emotions and moods (Isen and Baron, 1991; Thoresen *et al.*, 2003).

ORGANIZING STIMULI INTO MEANINGFUL PATTERNS

Infants are born with no direct experience of the world. Their understanding is based on the genetic material which they inherit from their parents and their experience while in the womb. Understanding, based upon the process of grouping stimuli from the environment into meaningful patterns, is one that develops in the child through early experience. The most important aspects of this process, studied by Gestalt (German for 'figure' or 'shape') psychology, include:

- *The figure-ground principle.* This principle is all about the process of perceiving a stimulus in a background context. Figure 4.7 illustrates the principle. Perceiving either a chalice or two faces in profile depends upon what you identify as background and what as foreground. Of course, social and cultural knowledge is important for perception because recognizing Figure 4.7 as a chalice is only meaningful in contexts where such drinking vessels are known.
- *The principle of continuity.* This relates to the tendency to detect continuous patterns in groups of individual stimuli. However, a row of numbers may be just that, they may not be related in a meaningful way. The daily sales returns from each of the outlets of a national retail company may not be related in any way, yet management frequently attempt to identify patterns from such data.
- *The principle of proximity.* Proximity refers to the perceptual process of creating association simply on the basis of nearness. For example, Figure 4.8 indicates how lines could be assumed to be associated, yet with a little more information a different relationship is suggested.

Figure 4.7 Reversible figure

Figure 4.8 The principle proximity

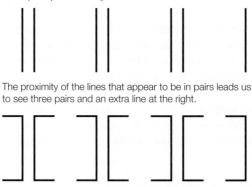

The proximity of the lines that appear to be in pairs leads us to see three pairs and an extra line at the right.

The same lines as above, but with extensions, lead to opposite pairing: three broken squares and an extra line at the left.

Source: Hilgard, E.R., Atkinson, R.C. and Anderson, R.L. (1971) *Introduction to Psychology* (5th edn), New York: Harcourt Brace Jovanovich.

- *The principle of closure.* The principle of closure is all about making a whole out of the parts available. Figure 4.9 is a series of dark shapes; what does it suggest to you? In an organization this could be reflected in the need to detect what marketing strategy a competitor is about to embark upon from only partial information available such as rumour and customer feedback. Perhaps Figure 4.9 appears to you to represent a dog? If it does, then it is doing so not because of the actual drawing, but because your perceptual system is seeking to draw together the available information and enclose it into a known and familiar image.

- *The principle of similarity.* This concept relates to the grouping together of stimuli based on similar characteristics. For example, 'all workers are lazy' might be the view of a particular manager. Consequently, such a manager seeing a worker standing around and not working might not recognize that the individual could be waiting for a machine to be repaired and therefore not able to work.

Figure 4.9 The closure principle

Source: Coon, D. (copyright © 1985, 1991) *Introduction to Psychology: Explorations and Applications*, West Publishing Company. By permission of Brooks/Cole Publishing Company, Pacific Grove, CA, a division of Thomson Publishing Inc.)

INTERPRETING THE SIGNIFICANCE OF A STIMULUS

The significance of a particular stimulus will be judged against a range of criteria. For example, it will depend upon the interpretation frame selected, together with the physical, mental and emotional state of the individual at the time. An individual feeling thirsty is likely to become more aware of stimuli that have a refreshment theme. This process within the perceptual model can be thought of as a filtering mechanism. It is a process that is subjective and goes beyond the information contained in the stimulus itself. The following paragraphs describe some of the major factors and processes involved in interpreting the significance of a stimulus.

Language and perception shaping

We make sense of the world based on our prior knowledge which we use as a frame of reference to interpret any new stimuli. In other words, anything we perceive we compare to what we already know so that we can classify it. Imagine a person living 2000 years ago (or even 200!) seeing an airplane or a car for the first time. Making sense of what they see would be immensely difficult because they would not be able to name this new stimulus – likely their attempts to interpret this would evolve around birds or animals. The creation of new understanding in any context is in large part based on the use of language.

Language is a shared symbolic system whose elements and conventions together convey meaning to others as well as ourselves. Our conscious thoughts are largely conceptual and linked to language. Making sense of perceived stimuli when we do not have concepts that can help us attach meaning to our perception of the world renders the process immensely more difficult. Thus, once we acquire a new concept it can help us select and interpret stimuli that otherwise would be less likely to attract our attention. Weick (1995) describes how the recognition, description and most importantly the formal naming of particular patterns of injuries to children as the 'Battered child syndrome' was necessary for physical abuse to be more readily recognized by health workers and addressed by lawmakers. Similarly, learning about OB in this book introduces you to many new concepts that, once understood and integrated into your memory and thinking, can help you select appropriate stimuli and make sense of your observations and experiences of behaviour in organizations.

Unlike laypeople who would not be able to make much sense of an X-ray picture or MRI image, a trained radiographer or medical doctor will be able to select and group stimuli to make a diagnosis. Similarly, a skilled rugby or basketball player may be able to 'read' the opposing team's next move from the way they are lining up for their next attack. Often experts are not able to explain exactly how they achieve such sensemaking, but the conceptual system of experts is considerably more complex and developed than that of novices, and they tend to quickly select the most appropriate stimuli and interpret them much faster and more accurately than novices.

Perceptual errors and biases

Perceptual errors reflect the mistakes that can occur during the process of taking in stimuli and making sense of this perceptual information. They can be mistakes of sensing, information processing, judgement or understanding. One form of perceptual 'error' has already been introduced in Figure 4.7 which can be interpreted in two distinct ways. Of course, the use of the term 'error' in this context is interesting in that it depends on the intention of the provider of the stimulus, not the perceiver.

Perceptual errors
The mistakes of judgement or understanding that can occur during the process of interpreting stimuli.

EMPLOYEE PERSPECTIVE

Dealing with the customer!

Call centres are used to dealing with a wide variety of order taking and customer service activities over the telephone. The employee is supposed to engage the customer in a seamless conversation, guided by the computer-generated script. However, things do not always go according to plan. Kathleen, a call centre employee based in Scotland, told of one incident, quite common it was suggested, in which a very short pause in the employee speaking occurred while they were typing a reply from the customer. The customer (also a woman) was distinctly heard to pass the following comment to someone else in the background. 'The bitch, she's gone and ******* well cut me off!'

Of course the employee had not done so and replied, 'I'm sorry, what did you say?'

The person on the other end of the phone then hung up.

TASKS

1 How would you have reacted to such a comment if you were Kathleen?

2 Does this experience suggest that the customer is 'king' in all circumstances?

3 To what extent should employees have to put up with bad or inappropriate behaviour from customers?

4 As the manager of a call centre, what would you want your staff to do in such circumstances, and why?

Therefore, if the provider of the drawing in Figure 4.7 intended a chalice to be seen then the 'error' would arise if the perceiver saw two faces. Perceptual biases are *systematic* errors such as perceptual distortions (in Figure 4.5 the contrast effect leads to biased assessment of the centre circles). In an organizational context, perceptual errors can lead to inappropriate reactions such as flawed decision making or insufficient error corrections. The Employee Perspective considers the reality of one aspect of customer contact for many employees working in the retail and service sectors.

Awareness of perceptual errors can be used deliberately. A simple example is the size of children's toy boxes which are designed to give children the impression of immensely 'big' presents. Of course this also applies to many products marketed to adults. There are a number of categories of perceptual error, such as evaluation biases like the harshness, leniency and central tendency effects that judges, raters and survey respondents (as well as college lecturers) often display. We will discuss a number of perceptual biases that are particularly important in organizations.

Perceptual biases
Systematic tendency to commit errors in perception that result in consistent and predictable inaccuracies.

Primacy and recency effects

Humans often make snap-judgements about people, things, events and other targets in the first few seconds of exposure, as Malcolm Gladwell discusses thoroughly in his book *Blink* (2005). The primacy effect describes the *biased perceptions that result from humans placing an inordinately high importance on the initial pieces of information about a target*. This can be a particular problem in organizations. In interviews, for example, the initial impression of a candidate (for example as well dressed, likable, punctual, courteous, and well spoken) may predispose the interviewer positively to that person so that bad interview performance later on is not taken into account. Thus, interviewers may hire lower-performing candidates based

Primacy effect
Describes the biased perceptions that result from humans placing an inordinately high importance on the initial pieces of information about a target.

Recency effect
The opposite of the primacy effect and describes the phenomenon that people tend to recall, and place disproportionate importance on, the most recent pieces of information about a target they have received.

on initial good impressions, or conversely may fail to hire high-quality applicants because of initially unfavourable impressions.

The recency effect is the opposite of the primacy effect and describes the *phenomenon that people tend to recall, and place disproportionate importance on, the most recent pieces of information about a target they have received*. Although the predictions for perception and recall from both primacy and recency effects are the exact opposite of each other, evidence exists for both of these effects (e.g., Frensch, 1994). It appears that the primacy effect influences the frame use for the selection and interpretation of later stimuli, while the recency effect influences memory and recall of information received.

Selective perception biases: confirmation, perceptual defence and automatic vigilance effects

Confirmation bias
(also known as confirmatory bias) A tendency to seek out information that is in line with expectations and existing knowledge.

Perceptual set
A temporary mental predisposition to perceive one thing and not another, or to perceive stimuli in a certain way.

Perceptual defence bias
Refers to the automatic discounting of disconfirming stimuli and is used to protect the individual against information, ideas or situations that are threatening to an existing perception or attitude.

Automatic vigilance
Suggests that negative social information, which has the potential to harm a person, is automatically and quickly attended to.

Prior expectations can significantly influence perception. Being told that a new boss is temperamental and a stickler for accuracy will lead to a different reaction and perception of their actions from being told that they are friendly with an informal style. The *tendency to seek out information that is in line with expectations and existing knowledge* is called confirmation bias (e.g., Watson, 1960). The confirmation bias, also known as confirmatory bias, is problematic in research as well as in organizations as in both environments initial expectations can overshadow the recognition and use of evidence that invalidates expectations and prior knowledge. Note that the confirmation bias contributes to the primacy effect by influencing how people select further stimuli after forming initial impressions of a target. The confirmation bias is a particular form of perceptual set, a notion that refers to *a temporary mental predisposition to perceive one thing and not another, or to perceive stimuli in a certain way*.

Like other biases, the confirmation bias also has an opposite which traditionally has been termed perceptual defence bias. This process refers to the *automatic discounting of disconfirming stimuli that protects the individual against information, ideas or situations that are threatening to an existing perception or attitude*. It is a process that encourages the perception of stimuli in terms of the known and familiar. For example, a manager having taken the decision to introduce a new product into the company is likely to avoid information that challenges the validity of the decision and to interpret information received in an overly favourable light. Information that is contradictory to the validity of the decision is likely to be seen as a challenge, requiring the decision to be proved correct rather than negating the decision itself. This partially reflects the view behind the often-heard statement that problems are opportunities in disguise. While overwhelming evidence exists for the confirmation bias, the methodologies employed in early research on perceptual defence bias has been severely criticized (Erdelyi, 1974; Voss *et al.*, 2008). However, evidence for a distinct yet related process of automatic vigilance exists (Pratto and John, 1991). This refers to the fact that *negative social information, which has the potential to harm a person, is automatically and quickly attended to*. The difference between perceptual defence and automatic vigilance is that the latter refers to information about others' negative views of oneself, not of information that is incompatible with one's views and attitudes.

Halo and horns effect

Halo effect
Positive bias introduced when attributing all of the characteristics of a person (or object) from a single positive attribute.

The halo effect is the bias introduced when *attributing all of the characteristics of a person (or object) in line with a single positive characteristic*. For example, a person who is a good timekeeper may be claimed to be a high-performing employee in all other respects. This has obvious dangers in forming judgements and deciding actions about other people. In seeking to reduce the number of employees, managers deciding who should stay only on the basis of (say) attendance records might result in the loss of more highly skilled and productive workers who have a less 'perfect' attendance record. The opposite of the halo effect is sometimes referred to as the horns effect. This takes the view that everything about a person is bad on the basis of a single negative attribute. It can be just as damaging to individuals and organizations as the halo effect.

Horns effect
The opposite of the halo effect and takes the view that everything about a person is bad on the basis of a single negative attribute.

Self-fulfilling prophecies and knowledge of predictor bias

A particularly important perceptual bias in organizations is the self-fulfilling prophecy. This effect describes the performance improvement of individuals and groups based on positive expectations about their capabilities by managers, teachers, or others working with them. In classic experiments random groups of students were introduced to teachers as either exceptionally bright, average, or far less capable than average. Subsequently, these groups performed exactly in line with these descriptions (Rosenthal and Jacobson, 1992). This effect has been shown across a range of settings (Snyder and Stukas, 1998), with the obvious implication for management and organizations that high expectations beget good performance. This may often be the case, but sometimes it may also be due to other factors such as attention (remember the Hawthorn effect discussed in Chapter 1) and the complex interactions between factors in an organizational setting. Another related effect is the well known *placebo effect* which describes the positive response of patients to an inert substance that they believe contains appropriate medication for their condition.

Self-fulfilling prophecy
Describes the performance (or behaviour) improvement (or reduction) of individuals and groups based on positive (or negative) expectations about their capabilities by other people.

If the positive expectation and subsequent differential treatment by managers or even co-workers is based on knowledge of valid performance indicators (for example, a new employee is known for her excellent performance in her previous employment) it is also called knowledge of predictor bias. This can work in both positive and negative ways depending on the particular knowledge others hold about a target person.

Knowledge of predictor bias
Refers to the positive expectation and subsequent differential treatment by managers or co-workers that is based on knowledge of valid performance indicators For example, a new employee is known to be an excellent performer from their previous employment.

RESPONSE BEHAVIOUR TO A STIMULUS

Individuals react to the perceptual world depending upon their needs at the time. In the usual course of events the stimuli that will gain attention at any point in time depends on a balance of forces active at that time. These include:

- pressure to achieve a particular objective
- interest in the task in hand
- distraction opportunity
- consequences of success or failure to achieve the end result
- physiological state.

The actual behavioural response to a perceived stimulus can fall into one of two main categories. They are:

1 *Internal behaviour shapers*. These response categories are not observable behaviours themselves. They are, however, the motivations, attitudes and feelings that help to determine much of the observable behaviour in people.

2 *Observable behaviour.* This refers to the actual behaviour that would be seen by other people. It is the tangible and physical expression of the underlying behaviour shapers. It is the reactions such as leaving a building when the fire alarm sounds, or work activity following job instruction from a supervisor.

THE LEARNING LOOP

The role of learning on the perceptual process itself is something that the model described in Figure 4.1 recognizes as feedback (the learning loop) which indicates that individuals learn from experience. The person involved will perceive the consequences of their behaviours and as a result adjust their subsequent perceptual frameworks and behaviour. The effect of learning on the perceptual process can be demonstrated through a number of illusions. Figure 4.10 is the Müller-Lyer visual illusion (named after the originators) which, it has been suggested, has a basis in the prior learning of individuals. Which of the two vertical lines is the longer? In practice, they are the same length, but most people perceive one as longer because based on prior learning they automatically associate the lines with rooms and buildings with corners.

PERSON PERCEPTION

Person perception is of particular interest in OB because of the significance of interpersonal interaction within work settings. Individuals' perceptions of managers, subordinates, fellow workers or customers can have a profound impact on the effectiveness of any organization. Much of the day-to-day activity in employee relations is concerned with the management of perceptions and subsequent attitudes relative to the work setting. Warr (1971) offers a detailed schematic model of person perception, which has been simplified as Figure 4.11.

The model comprises five sets of components, all interlinked in a complex array of information flow and decision making. They are:

1 *The person and context information base.* These provide the current and previously acquired information on the target person and the context within which the perception is set.

2 *Input selector.* This refers to the process by which the vast array of current and previously obtained information is to be sifted. The assumption is that it is not possible to process all available information and that a filtering device is needed to weed out unnecessary information.

3 *The perceiver's state.* This is intended to provide for the variable effect on perception of the perceiver. Their current physiological, psychological and

Figure 4.10 The Müller-Lyon illusion

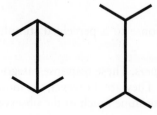

Figure 4.11 Model of person perception

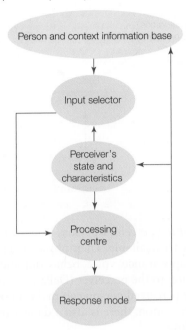

Source: Based on Warr (1971).

emotional state will influence their perceptions, as will their underlying personality characteristics.

4 *The processing centre.* This is a series of decision rules built up over time from the experience of interacting with people. It therefore allows output probability options to be identified from the available data. This is reminiscent of attribution theory, discussed later.

5 *The response mode.* Having developed a profile of the target person in terms of the attributes and expectations, the perceiver will develop an appropriate response. This will be not just in terms of actual behaviour, but will include attitudes such as liking, respect and interest, for example. These judgemental facets to person perception all feed back to the other levels, as the process is cumulative over time. The stored information is updated by current events and the entire process is interactive in real time.

In line with the discussion earlier in the chapter on how stimuli are selected generally in perception, a useful if simplified framework for person perception is to envisage it as a three-factor process, involving the characteristics of the perceiver, the target and the relevant situational variables. Figure 4.12 illustrates the main features of this framework of person perception.

The model of person perception reflected in Figure 4.12 also has strong links with attribution theory to be discussed later. Taking each determinant from the model in turn:

- *Perceiver characteristics.* This includes the internal aspects of an individual that influence perception about other people including personality, motivation, objectives, learning, past experience and the individual's value system. Working with someone from another culture is a useful way of experiencing the scope of a value system on person perception as new ways of thinking about people and their characteristics and traits emerge through the exposure.

Figure 4.12 Person perception: a simplified model

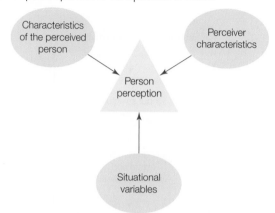

- *The characteristics of the perceived person.* When we meet someone, a wide variety of clues are available. Their physical appearance, skin colour, gender, age, general appearance, voice, behaviour and apparent personality all provide information to the perceiver (DePaulo *et al.*, 1987). Although the characteristics of the perceived person can make a positive contribution to the process of person perception, there is also a danger that it may lead to stereotyping (see below).

Stereotyping
The tendency to attribute everyone (or everything) in a particular category with the characteristics based on a single example.

- *Situational variables.* Meeting someone for the first time in the company of either a friend, or someone that you dislike, would be likely to influence the initial perception of the new individual. Social, business or other contexts with their differing degrees of formality and ritual are also likely to influence initial perceptions. The room in which a meeting takes place, its standard of decoration and the general atmosphere all produce stimuli, which influence perceptions about the people found there.

Table 4.2 provides an illustration of person perception in action. It reflects the perceptions of supervisors and subordinates about each other. The perception that was being examined related to the views that each group held about the other in terms of recognition for good performance.

Table 4.2 indicates a startling difference between the two groups, with supervisors perceiving that they provide more frequent positive responses to good performance than do their subordinates. This example highlights that managers need to be much more aware of all the signals that they give out, and how these are perceived, if they are to avoid misunderstandings. But, can the responses be relied upon as an accurate reflection of the true perceptions of the two groups? Might the supervisors indicate positive views compared to their actual behaviour because they feel they would be expected to be more supportive of employees than they actually are? Might employees undervalue what supervisor support is available in reaction to unrelated management actions?

Ample research evidence supports the view that perceptions of others and their behaviours are influenced by many factors unrelated to the actual picture as it may present itself to an objective outsider (if such a person even exists). Classic studies (e.g., Hastorf and Cantril, 1954) as well as personal experience bear this out – just consider your reactions to a referee's close-call decision compared to that of supporters of the opposing team! The influence and interactions among all the important elements of perception discussed above with the social context of perception typically leads to a range of simplifications and systematic errors and biases in person perception that will be discussed in more detail below.

Table 4.2 Person perception in the context of recognition behaviour

Table of recognition	Frequency with which supervisors say they give various types of recognition for good performance (per cent)	Frequency with which subordinates say supervisors give various types of recognition for good performance (per cent)
Gives privileges	52	14
Gives more responsibility	48	10
Gives more interesting work	82	13
Gives sincere and thorough praise	80	14
Trains for better jobs	64	9
Gives more interesting work	51	5

Source: Adapted from Likert, R (1961) *New Patterns in Management*, New York: McGraw-Hill.

Stereotyping and projection

A stereotype is a *preconceived notion that suggests that all members of a particular category share a set of characteristics* (e.g., 'union members are combative and anti-management'; 'accountants are detail-oriented and dull'; 'BMWs are fast and well built'). They can exist about people as well as inanimate objects, but our discussion here will focus on stereotypes about people. Fundamentally, stereotypes help individuals by simplifying sense-making about others. Perceivers can rely on stored knowledge about a category rather than having to attend to active information processing and sense-making about a person (Hilton and von Hippel, 1996). Stereotypical person perception is particularly common in situations of conflict and crises because of the diminished information processing capacity of individuals under stress.

In interpersonal and organizational settings, the mental shortcut offered by stereotypes can be beneficial but can also lead to problems. The benefits of stereotyping are associated with its ability to allow categorization of people into groups. It can significantly reduce the need for mental processing of people as individuals and therefore free mental capacity to deal with other relevant issues. However, in doing so there is a real danger of missing important aspects of individuality and differences among the people being stereotyped. Moreover, this simplifying process can only provide value as long as the basis for the stereotypes used are accurate. People often acquire stereotypes from others as part of socially and culturally shared views. Thus, it is very common for people to employ stereotypes even if they never directly interact with members of particular groups. As a result, members of many groups are

Stereotype
A preconceived notion that suggests that all members of a particular category share a set of characteristics.

treated based on often unfounded assumptions, which results in commonplace sex, race, disability and age discrimination in organizations.

Crisp (2002) suggests that increasing the complexity in the way that people categorize others might help to reduce negative reactions to them. This might imply that the more that managers and employees understand each other, the more the level of mistrust and number of problems will reduce. However, different perceptions can exist between managers and employees in relation to delegation of decision making which can lead to misunderstandings and conflict.

Not all information perceived could be expected to be either supportive or contradictory to a particular stereotype. For example, an employee might find that not all managers were seeking to exploit them. The employee must somehow deal with this apparently contradictory information. It has been suggested that information which supports a particular stereotype is processed more intensively than information which is inconsistent with it (Bodenhausen, 1988). This builds on an earlier study, which demonstrated that students presented with contradictory information in relation to a stereotype (Haire and Grunes, 1950) adopted various denial or protection devices. The purpose is to sustain the original stereotypical image, rather than accept the disconfirming evidence about the target.

Projection implies that others possess the same characteristics as ourselves. In other words, we tend to assume that everyone thinks and behaves in the same way that we do. This is a potentially dangerous assumption for managers to make in relation to their employees. Managers invariably express surprise when employees react in a way that was not anticipated or when they refuse to agree with management's point of view. However, there is no reason why employees should perceive the world the same way that managers do – that much should be obvious from the discussion in this chapter so far. Equally, managers who describe the behaviour of other managers as power- and politically motivated might actually be inclined to behave in such ways themselves and be seeking to protect themselves by projecting these characteristics onto other people.

Projection
A psychological process of projecting onto others characteristics that we see in ourselves.

Body language and perception

Body language is the third element of interpersonal communication which consists of verbal (spoken words), vocal (tone of voice) and visual (observable nonverbal behaviour) elements. It includes a wide range of features including posture, gestures and facial expression. All these observable aspects of communication provide signals that add to the content of verbal messages uttered by an individual. Thus, verbal and nonverbal signals are the basis on which others form their perceptions about what a person has actually said. It is possible for a person to lie, but it is very difficult for them to present the wide range of body language to make it consistent with their spoken words and thus to eliminate all nonverbal signals that would allow another person to become suspicious. In fact, classic research by Albert Mehrabian (1971) showed that in communications about likes and dislikes, the majority of meaning of a communication is drawn from nonverbal elements, especially if the actual attitudes and feelings of the speaker are not consistent with their spoken message.

Morris (1982: pp. 160–171) refers to inconsistent signals as nonverbal leakage, in other words, the means through which the individual's true feelings leak out into the observable domain. Some aspects of body language such as eye contact, smiling, frowning and other facial expressions may be partially controllable, but others (e.g., pupil dilation; sweating; blink rates) as well as some body posture, hand gestures and leg movements cannot be fully controlled.

A number of cultural aspects are associated with body language. Hand gestures can have significantly different meanings in different cultural contexts, including the thumbs-up sign, the OK ring and the V sign. For example the thumbs-up sign usually refers to an OK signal in English-speaking countries, but can be an obscene response in Greece (Pease, 1984). Similarly, personal space differs between cultures. As a rough guide, in European countries preferred personal space increases from Southern/Mediterranean countries to Northern-European.

Self-perception

Having introduced a number of features associated with the perception of other people, one further important aspect of perception is self-perception. In Figure 4.12 earlier, the perceiver's characteristics are suggested to impact on their perception of other people. However, these characteristics tend to be classified either in physical terms or as experience, motivation, personality, and so on. Just as important to the process of perceiving other people are the self-perceptions of the individual perceiver. Each person thinks of themselves in particular ways; they hold a perception of themselves that influences and is influenced by their self-identity. For example, an older person might consider that they are mature, successful, affluent, sociable, knowledgeable, worthy of respect, a pillar of the community, youthful and able to relate to young people. That defines their self-perception and it will to some extent impact on various aspects of that person's behaviour, including their perceptions of other people.

Self-perception is also an important issue for considering the linkages between perception and personality. Many researchers describe a dispositional factor (i.e., a stable trait) called core self-evaluation that closely reflects locus of control, emotional stability (neuroticism) as well as self-esteem and generalized performance confidence (e.g., Judge *et al.*, 2002). People with positive core self-evaluations *view themselves positively across situations and see themselves as capable, in control, and generally valuable.* Positive core self-evaluation is often associated with higher motivation, more effective work performance, and higher work and life satisfaction (e.g., Judge and Bono, 2001). Those with positive core self-evaluation appear to be better able to cope with stress (Kammeyer-Mueller *et al.*, 2009), in part because they tend to frame situations they encounter as positive rather than negative (Judge *et al.*, 1998). This example shows the complex and intricate relationships between perception, self-perceptions and personality traits.

> **Core self-evaluation**
> A dispositional factor (i.e., a stable trait) that closely reflects locus of control, emotional stability (neuroticism) as well as self-esteem and generalized performance confidence. People with positive core self-evaluations view themselves positively across situations and see themselves as capable, in control and generally valuable.

STOP & CONSIDER

Is the individual surrounded by, interacting with and living in the real world or does it exist in the mind of that individual? Does that distinction matter and if so, how?

ATTRIBUTION THEORY

Attribution is *the process by which we ascribe causes to events as well as to our own and others' behaviour.* It is of fundamental importance in organizations because it determines how people understand and behave towards their environment and particularly other people. As Malle (1999: p. 23) put it so eloquently, '*Explanations of behaviour guide people's perceptions, attitudes, and actions towards each other; they affect impressions, sway sympathies, and alter the path of relationships. By explaining behavior, people make sense of the social world, adapt to it, and shape it.*'

Attribution is part of the overall perceptual process, and like many other parts of perception it can happen in automatic or controlled mode. In either mode, people

> **Attribution**
> The process by which we ascribe causes to events as well as to our own and others' behaviour.

are sensitive to information that can give them an insight into the causes of what they observe. The most important principle of causal attribution is that of covariation (Kelley, 1967, 1973) which refers to *the degree to which two elements appear or change together*. Logically, covariation is necessary but not sufficient for a causal relationship to exist. For example, on a car assembly line good quality output is observed to occur when supervisors are walking the line; it is also noted that when they are absent from the line (say, at meetings) an increase in quality defects occurs. In this situation supervision and high quality covary, and it would be natural to suggest (attribute) that close supervision is the cause of good quality output. In reality this may be true, but there could also be other factors that determine good quality. Even if supervision is a cause of quality then this link would be mediated by the impact of supervision on worker behaviour which in turn would be a more immediate cause of high or low quality output. As this example shows, determining causal relationships is usually a very complex process.

As part of perception, however, humans do not usually try to find the most complete, comprehensive and accurate causal explanations. Human sensemaking is driven more by plausibility than by accuracy (Weick, 1995) and as 'satisficers' rather than 'optimisers' (e.g., Simon, 1957; March and Simon, 1958; see Chapter 8) humans accept as true the meaning of an observed behaviour if the explanation is good enough rather than perfect. Also, people use simple categories for explaining behaviour as either determined by the person or by the situation, named internal or external attributions, respectively (Heider, 1958). Thus, humans simplify and use cues that indicate the nature of explanations for the causes of what they observe and experience.

Harold Kelley's work on attributions (1967, 1973; Orvis *et al.*, 1975) identified that people use three fundamental attribution cues: Consensus, distinctiveness and consistency. These cues are based on perceived covariation and influence if causal explanations for people's behaviour will be internal or external. Table 4.3 describes the linkage of these cues to subsequent explanations).

- *Consensus (across different actors)*. If a situation or event produces the same effect on the behaviour of a range of people, then consensus is high. For example, if a manager who never praises worker performance suddenly raves about high performance, and many other people are also particularly complimentary, then consensus is high. This indicates that something common to both reactions exists – presumably the worker's performance.

- *Distinctiveness (distinctiveness to specific target or situation)*. If the particular event is not distinctive then it becomes pointless to imply a specific attribution as its cause. For example, if a manager considers it her

Covariation
This refers to the degree to which two elements appear or change together.

Internal attribution
Explanation for behaviour that is based on internal reasons for it such as intentions, personality, or other aspects of the person.

External attribution
Explanation for behaviour that focuses on external causes, such as situational demands and influences.

Table 4.3 Linkage between covariation clues and causal attributions about behaviour

Consensus (of actor's behaviour with other people's behaviour)	Distinctiveness (of actor's behaviour to target or situation)	Consistency (of actor's behaviour over time)	Likely type of attrtibution about causes of behaviour
Low	Low	High	Internal
High	High	Low	External

responsibility to improve the standard of English in all reports produced by her staff but never vetts reports prepared by a particular employee the behaviour is distinctive.

● *Consistency (over time)*. The sameness of reaction and behaviour over time and situations. If a manager is always rude and bad-tempered it would not seem to suggest anything unusual if they are abusive in a particular context. However, if the same manager were to praise, thank, or be pleasant on a particular occasion then it would become distinctive behaviour and worthy of further consideration.

Attribution is an important process because the subsequent responses depend upon how individuals interpret the original causes. In the instance described above, when the manager returned a report marked up for correction it did not cause offence or a problem. The reaction would be different where demands for reworked reports were the exception. Weiner (1975) developed a framework for determining a classification for different types of attribution and therefore appropriate or likely response behaviours (see Figure 4.13).

The diagram is designed assuming that the purpose is to identify the attributions of, and provide a response to, a subordinate's performance. Attributions about individual or group behaviour differ occasionally (e.g., O'Laughlin and Malle, 2002), an issue that will be discussed further in the chapters on groups and conflict. The model is built up from two axes, location and stability. Location can be determined from the perceived source of the behaviour:

● *Internal*. Based on the attributes of the individual in terms of ability, motivation, skill and effort for example.

● *External*. Based on the factors outside the individual, such as family circumstances, company policies and the attitudes of managers.

Stability is determined on the basis of the perceived degree of permanence of the attribute:

● *Permanent*. This reflects an enduring feature, something that is ongoing and which will remain a force in the future.

● *Temporary*. A transient feature, something that is likely to change over time. An example would be someone who is late for work one morning as a result of their car breaking down.

Each of the four cells in the matrix has been given a title that represents the underlying characteristics of behaviour that fall into that area. Consequently, the response to the attributions implied by those concepts will also differ:

Figure 4.13 Attributions and response determinants

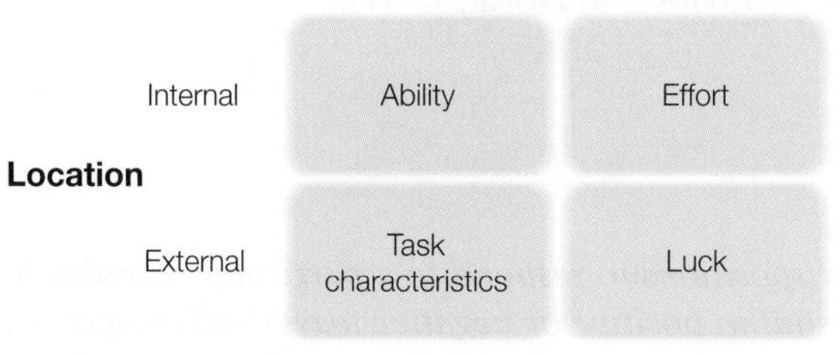

Stability

	Permanent	Temporary
Internal	Ability	Effort
External	Task characteristics	Luck

Location

Source: Weiner, W. (1975) *Achievement, Motivation and Attribution Theory*, Morristown, NJ: General Learning Press.

- *Ability.* This implies that the problem is the inability of the individual to do what is expected of them. If a subordinate were to produce a performance that implied this cell of the matrix, then retraining might be appropriate.
- *Effort.* This implies that the subordinate is capable of doing what is expected of them, but did not apply themselves adequately to the job. Under these circumstances, a telling off or some other punishment might be considered.
- *Task characteristics.* This implies that the subordinate had little direct control over what happened, therefore putting it right would also be beyond their control. Consequently, an appropriate response might be to seek ways of improving their ability to deal with the situation in future. This might include redesigning the work or procedures.
- *Luck.* There are occasions when things do not go according to plan. The subordinate in question may have experienced difficulties in obtaining information from another department because it was busy or short staffed.

Whatever the attribution, the appropriate approach will be to overcome the problem quickly. For the future, any lessons should be learned to prevent reoccurrence.

Malle (1999) distinguishes between explanations for intentional and unintentional behaviour that he calls 'reasons' and 'causes', respectively. Specific conditions determine when people typically judge behaviour to be intentional. They include (a) presence of a relevant goal; (b) belief about the behavior being useful to achieve the goal; (c) intention to perform the behaviour based on reasoning; (d) relevant skills to perform behaviour; and (e) awareness of intention when performing behaviour. In organizations, the presence or absence of such conditions can have fundamental effects on managerial judgement about intentionality, with potentially important consequences for both individuals and the organization. To further complicate matters with regard to attributions, a number of typical attribution errors and biases exist.

The fundamental attribution error (Ross, 1977; also called *correspondence bias*, Gilbert and Malone, 1995) refers to the tendency to overly rely on dispositional (i.e., personality-based) causal explanations, and to under-employ situational explanations, for the behaviour of others. Therefore, we typically assume that observed behaviour tells us what kinds of people others are, regardless of the situation in which these people act. At the same time, we tend to do the exact opposite when we create explanations for our own behaviour! This is called the actor-observer effect (Jones and Nisbett, 1972) which refers to the strong tendency to predominantly attribute one's own behaviour to situational factors. Recent research indicates that this may be particularly true if the observed behaviour is negative (Malle, 2006). This finding is also in line with the pervasive self-serving bias, an important systematic error that we will find again and again across many topics in OB (Gioia and Sims, 1985). This bias occurs when individuals make internal attribution for success but rely on external attribution for failures. Thus, gaining a promotion may be explained through an assessment of one's own excellent performance, while missing out on a promotion may be attributed to unfair selection criteria or other situational aspects. This bias also exists at group level and is called *group-serving bias* (Forsyth and Schlenker, 1977; Taylor and Doria, 1981).

Fundamental attribution error
Also called correspondence bias, refers to the tendency to overly rely on dispositional (i.e., personality-based) causal explanations, and to underemploy situational explanations, for the behaviour of others.

Actor-observer effect
Humans typically assume that observed behaviour tells us what kind of people others are, regardless of the situation. But humans tend to do the opposite and predominantly attribute their own behaviour to situational factors.

Self-serving bias
A bias that occurs when individuals make internal attribution for success but rely on external attributions for failures.

ATTITUDES

Attitudes
Predisposed feeling, thought or behavioural response to a particular stimulus.

Attitudes are *predispositions to respond to a particular stimulus (e.g., an object, setting, event or person) in positive or negative ways.* Such responses can be thoughts, feelings or actions. The term has entered everyday usage in that some people are described as having 'attitude'. At work, managers frequently look for a 'good attitude' in potential recruits. Moreover, attitudes are important factors in determining relevant behaviours as they are seen to influence people to act in particular ways.

Attitude structure and formation

Attitudes have three components: cognitive, affective (emotional) and behavioural. All people have attitudes towards things and people – school, university, parents, work, politics, sport, religion and other people. Some attitudes are deeply held and difficult to change, while others are more superficial and easy to drop or amend. One approach to the study of attitudes (Rosenberg, 1960) suggests that to change an attitude it is necessary to change either the underlying feelings or beliefs. This approach relies on a model of attitudes based on that shown in Figure 4.14.

Looking at each of the three components from Figure 4.14 in turn:

1 *Cognitive component.* This refers to the beliefs and values that the individual holds, perhaps in terms of support for a football club, say FC Barcelona. One belief related to support for the club might be that it is the best football club in Europe. A related value underlying support for the club would perhaps be that it has won an important competition that provides the individual with a source of pride. The key point of this example is that beliefs are evaluative in nature (the 'best' football team) while values reflect the judgemental criteria against which beliefs are measured (winning important competitions). Identification with the club may provide important meaning and value to the individual.

2 *Affective component.* The feelings and emotions that make up the affective component arise from an evaluation between the two elements within the cognitive component. A supporter of the football club just mentioned could be expected to develop feelings and attitudes according to the success of their team related to the underlying beliefs and values about it. The affective component of an attitude tends to be socially learned. We acquire the ability to express our reaction to the balance between the cognitive elements in ways that align with our social environment.

3 *Behavioural component.* This reflects the outcome of the process. It is the actual or intended behaviour. In the case of support for a football team that

Figure 4.14 Construction of an attitude

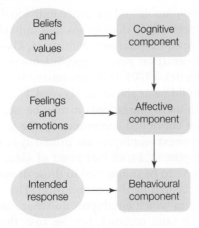

is not performing well, an individual could continue support and hope for better results in future, change their allegiance to another club, or give notice that if losses continue they will stop supporting them. The behaviour resulting from the affective component would also be influenced by the importance of the attitude for the individual (e.g., its centrality regarding the person's identity) and the degree of intensity with which it was held.

Attitudes develop as a result of experience, although some hereditary influences and links to personality exist (e.g., Tesser, 1993). Typical sources of attitudes include our own *experience* with an object or person (such that positive or negative experiences will influence our predispositions); *exposure* (people tend to develop more positive attitudes to familiar objects and people; Moreland and Zajonc, 1977), and *socialization and observational learning* (we adopt values and beliefs we find in our families, schools, peer groups, at work, etc.). In addition to these external sources, we may also develop ego-defensive and value-expressive attitudes (Katz, 1960). The former serves us by protecting our self-image from the implication of otherwise disturbing information. A telling example is the 'blame the victim' effect. This effect is common in people who hold strong beliefs that the world is a fair and just place. Thus, people that are high in 'belief in a just world' (Lerner, 1980) are more likely to find fault with the victim of a crime – else, how could they explain why in a just world something bad happens to an innocent person. Value-expressive attitudes serve to publicly express one's self-image and to 'mould that self-image closer to the heart's desire' (Katz, 1960: p. 170). Thus, such attitudes help define and express our aspirational selves. Not surprisingly, the advertising industry has focused in on the sources of attitudes and uses them to influence predispositions regarding the advertised products and services.

Some recent research into attitude formation suggests that people can develop dual attitudes named implicit and explicit (Rydell and McConnell, 2006; Wilson *et al.*, 2000). This once again reflects the dual process model discussed above in that implicit attitudes appear to be associated with unconscious processing and automatic cognitive, emotional and behavioural responses, while explicit attitudes reflect conscious, deliberate and reasoning-based processing (Rydell and McConnell, 2006). Consistent with these two modes, implicit attitudes are acquired and change slowly, often remain subconscious, and affect automatic responses. Explicit attitudes, on the other hand, can be quickly developed and changed through active reasoning, are conscious, and are linked to deliberate behavioural intentions. They are the attitudes that people are aware of and report when asked about. Sometimes people can hold different implicit and explicit attitudes about the same object, and unless the explicit attitude is consciously accessed reactions are guided by the implicit attitude. (Test differences between your implicit and explicit attitudes at http://www.project-implicit.net)

Implicit attitudes are very stable and influence individual thinking and behaviour almost like some of the personality dimensions and individual differences. Explicit attitudes are much more open to situational influences. These influences include sensory as well as social information people receive from others they are interacting with (e.g., Salancik and Pfeffer, 1977). In diagrammatic form, this process of attitude formation and change would be as shown in Figure 4.15.

In social contexts such as organizations, it may be necessary to suppress one's own feelings and values if continued acceptance by the group is to be maintained. For example, in a work context employees are primarily employed to undertake the tasks demanded by management. From that point of view, the personal beliefs and values of the individual have to be subjugated to those of management if the individual is to continue to be accepted by the organization. This is reflected in the instrumental approach to work in which employees do what management want because they need to keep the job (and income), not because they believe or agree with

Implicit Attitudes
Slowly acquired attitudes for which people have generally little awareness and which are activated by automatic processes.

Explicit attitudes
Reason-based attitudes that people can report and which they can actively control.

Instrumental approach to work
Based on a trading and value approach to work and the determination of contribution relative to benefits gained.

Figure 4.15 Situational construction of implicit and explicit attitudes

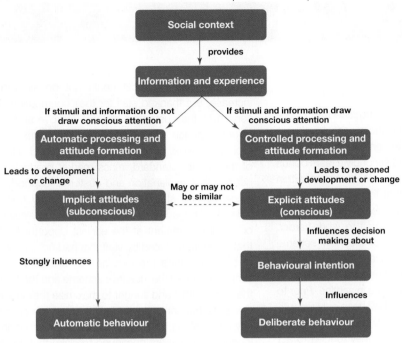

management's requirements. The High Performance example 'Chasing the targets' demonstrates that complex links exist between what workers perceive and what they actually do in earning their wages.

Attitudes and perception

There is a twofold relationship between attitudes and perception. First, individuals perceive the attitudes of other people. They do this through the receipt and interpretation of a range of clues (visual, speech, body language, dress, etc.). People then classify the people they perceive around them based on the clues detected. For example, a person may view a group of young males with shaven heads and covered with studs and chains as likely to be violent thugs. This perceiver is not experiencing the real attitudes of the group of young men but drawing stereotypical conclusions about attitudes and intentions from a number of stimuli which in turn will influence their own reactions.

Second, individuals seek to give out particular perceptions through the impression that they seek to create, perhaps by their dress code, attitudes or other signals. For example, a group of young people dressed as indicated above might be seeking to convey a particular image of themselves as a group or as followers of a particular fashion. Equally, it would not be expected that a bank manager would dress casually in jeans and sweater for an important business meeting, as to do so would give an unintended impression to clients.

Attitudes and behaviour

Attitudes have an influence on behaviour, but it is a complex relationship. One of the best known models in this area is Fishbein and Ajzen's (1975; Ajzen and Fishbein, 1980) *theory of reasoned action* which describes purposeful behaviour as a function of behavioural intentions which are in turn determined by attitudes

HIGH PERFORMANCE

Chasing the targets!

A large national retail company introduced an incentive scheme for its sales staff without consulting them first. The scheme had two elements in it; firstly sales achieved by individual staff and secondly a team bonus based on the sales achieved by each section within the store. Management felt that this would provide a good basis for encouraging teamwork as well as individual effort thereby motivating staff to work harder. Managers decided the targets of the new scheme without consulting employees. Over a period of a year staff became familiar with the scheme but some customers began to notice a difference in service. Prior to the new incentive scheme, staff had been only too willing to help customers by discussing products in relation to customer needs, but now they tended to act mechanically and were very reluctant to spend time with customers. Staff usually said that they were too busy to talk or that it was someone else's responsibility to deal with more general advice. A small number of customer complaints were received, but management took the view that things would settle down, and as sales had gone up this indicated that the scheme was working.

The following year staff were asked to help management review the targets used within the scheme in order to improve it. A couple of the staff did so, but their ideas were largely ignored as they sought to make the case for more staff and to make the targets more realistic. Management said that no concessions

could be made as cost could not be allowed to increase, but thanked staff for their contribution. The service to the customers did not improve and sales volumes began to decline slowly and sales of the more expensive, bespoke products declined in favour of the cheap, standard, mass market products that needed less explanation and customer support. The longer-serving staff and those with readily transferable skills began actively looking for jobs elsewhere or sought retirement at the earliest opportunity. Any that left were replaced by staff that had no experience of the company's previous service standards. They simply accepted the incentive scheme and the targets that went with it and sought to maximize their income. Generally they only stayed until a better job opportunity came along, or they could stand the situation no longer. Management continued to claim that the new incentive scheme was a great success in helping the company achieve its objectives.

TASKS

1 If you were an employee who had worked in this company for many years why do you think your attitudes would be as they are? What would you do and why?

2 Do you consider that the attitudes of the new staff are supportive of management's objectives in any real sense of the term? Why or why not?

3 Do you think that the management attitude that everything is fine can be supported? Why or why not?

Perceived behavioural control

The subjective assessment of the likelihood that particular behaviours can be performed.

and subjective norms. Ajzen (1985, 1991) later extended this model into the *theory of planned behaviour* which also includes perceived behavioural control (or *the subjective likelihood that the required behaviours can be performed*). In short, the theory argues that attitudes towards specific behaviours, subjective norms regarding the behaviours (which are internalized from the social environment), and perceived behavioural control determine intended behaviour which in turn predicts behaviour. Actual behavioral control (i.e., ability) as well as situational factors influence the linkages to behaviour. Figure 4.16 outlines these linkages between the central elements of the theory which has received significant research support (see Hale *et al.*, 2003; Sheppard *et al.*, 1988).

The theory of planned behaviour reflects a central characteristic of human attitudes, namely the consistency motive. This motive, which is the basis of a number of important behavioural theories (i.e., Heider's [1958] balance theory, Osgood and

Figure 4.16 Ajzen's theory of planned behaviour

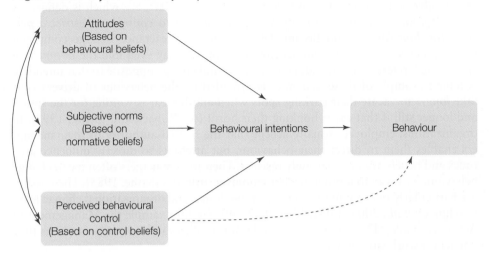

Tannenbaum's [1955] congruity principle, and Festinger's [1957] cognitive dissonance theory), describes the phenomenon that humans try to avoid holding contradictory beliefs and attitudes. Festinger (1957) developed the concept of cognitive dissonance to explain the dynamics in situations where conflicts exist between attitude components. Cognitive dissonance is *a cognitive state that motivates individuals to resolve perceived inconsistencies between attitudes, beliefs, values and behaviours.* The three ways in which this can be achieved is (a) change in at least one of the elements to restore consonance among the relevant elements; (b) acquisition of new information that increases consonance; and (c) re-evaluate the importance of the relevant elements and thus reduce the importance of the dissonance.

Essentially, Festinger describes a mechanism that seeks to provide consistency between perceptions, attitudes and actions. An employee may hold an opinion that they are a good worker and indispensable to the organization. The manager of that same individual may perceive that the person is a poor employee with barely acceptable performance. If the manager tells the employee of their opinion then the employee will be in possession of two sets of contradictory information. In order to deal with the dissonance created by that knowledge and to be able to rationalize the discrepancy, the individual may adopt a number of strategies. These could include working harder to meet the manager's expectations, suggesting that the manager does not have the knowledge to form a correct judgement, or implying that the manager's view is irrelevant.

Cognitive dissonance (and the consistency principle it reflects) is immensely important for OB because it describes a mechanism that can account for a number of different causal linkages between cognition and purposeful behaviour. Not only can behaviour be seen as the *outcome* of thoughts and emotions, but it can be the *origin* of attitude change. Specifically, when people behave in ways inconsistent with their attitudes they may experience cognitive dissonance. Instead of changing the behaviour to match the attitudes which would restore consonance among these elements, people may change their attitudes! Especially if the behaviour is an automatic response to environmental stimuli that is difficult to change because it has become habitual, or because environmental forces support the behaviour, this may be the only way for individuals to resolve dissonance. Extreme forms of influence such as coercive persuasion (e.g., brainwashing) often make use of behavioural control to ultimately influence deeply held beliefs, values and attitudes (e.g., Schein, 1961).

Cognitive dissonance
An aversive state that motivates individuals to resolve apparent conflict among attitudes, beliefs, values and behaviours.

Psychological reactance
Defined as anticonformity (a strong adverse reaction) in response to any perceived attempt to control or restrict a person's freedom.

Direct attempt to change attitudes, values, beliefs, and behaviour often result in strong adverse reactions. This is called psychological reactance which is defined as *anticonformity in response to any perceived attempt to control or restrict a person's freedom* (Brehm and Brehm, 1981). When the reactance is large compared to the persuasiveness of the influencing attempt, we may even find the *boomerang effect* which refers to an attitudinal or behavioural change opposite to that intended. A telling example of these dynamics is provided by the behaviour of drivers who take *longer* to vacate their parking spots when another car is waiting for the spot – and longer still if that car is honking their horn! (see Ruback and Juieng, 1997). In organizations, employees usually accept that the formal authority of their managers enables them to direct their behaviour, but attempts to directly influence attitudes and beliefs are often strongly resisted. Therefore, managers often try to change behaviour as a way to ultimately alter employee attitudes (Sathe, 1985). These issues are particularly relevant in the context of job design and organizational change (e.g., Laschinger *et al.*, 2004; Takeuchi *et al.*, 2009). See for example the Management in Action example, 'The new manager's tale' for an illustration of these issues as they impact on work situations.

MANAGEMENT IN ACTION

The new manager's tale

The manager (Jeffrey) had been in his post for about 3 months at the time of the interview. He was in his early twenties and it was his first managerial appointment. He had been employed by the organization for about 2 years prior to the interview and had been working in an administrative capacity during that time. Jeffrey had been promoted to the new position from within the team that he was to manage. The office was small with about six people working in it. The main activities within the office were the administration associated with sales planning and customer service on an international scale. As a result there was a considerable amount of information and paperwork flowing through the office at any one time. Customer records had to be kept up-to-date, as had the information flow to other departments and sections within the organization. A considerable proportion of the time was spent in liaison with customers and dealing with their queries. This process was made more difficult because of the different time zones involved.

It soon became clear to Jeffrey that the administrative systems were not of the highest quality, in terms of records, accuracy or information content. The department had grown very quickly and the previous manager had not been thorough in ensuring that the systems introduced were appropriate. In addition, staff

had been recruited without any previous experience in that type of work, neither had they been trained adequately in customer care or the work of the department. Consequently, a 'slack' attitude to work existed and the unit stumbled along rather than playing its full part in supporting the aims of the company. Jeffrey was judged capable by senior management of making the changes necessary to the operational processes within the department. Unfortunately, he was resented by the other staff, because they perceived him as a threat to their old, easy-going ways.

Senior management did not want Jeffrey to take a hard line with the staff, because they thought that the staff were capable of doing the job expected of them (if they were effectively led and procedures were improved). Consequently, pressure was put on Jeffrey to introduce change and make the situation work. Unfortunately, the staff became more entrenched in their views and openly hostile towards him – at one point saying to his face that he was the problem in the office and that they hated him. Repeated requests by Jeffrey to his boss for help produced little action. By this time, Jeffrey was of the view that even if the other staff were capable of doing the work, they were not acceptable to him. This inevitably made the situation even worse.

Jeffrey's boss would not take action against the other staff; neither would he do anything positive to support him. After a couple of months the staff went over the head of Jeffrey and his boss to the sales director and complained that the new manager was no good and that the more senior manager was showing favouritism by supporting Jeffrey. They claimed to have no confidence in either manager. When Jeffrey's boss found out that the staff had gone directly to the director he was furious. His view of the staff changed and they became less acceptable to remain within the department. What was previously the result of inadequate staff training and procedure design was now the fault of the staff themselves. He now attributed the behaviour of the staff to causes such as they did not want to co-operate with management and were trying to hide incompetence. Previously, he thought that they felt threatened by the situation and needed help to provide the expected service. He now expected Jeffrey to take decisive action against any member of staff that would not change their behaviour or attitudes.

TASK

1 To what extent does the situation described reflect perception in action or simply poor management? Justify your views.

Another area in which attitudes and behaviour are linked emerges through the spiritual side of human nature (see Giacalone and Jurkiewicz, 2003). Attitudes towards the role of spirituality within organizations vary tremendously. However, there is a developing awareness that it is not possible to keep driving for ever higher performance from each individual without some negative consequences. A feeling is growing that there is a role for organized religion, poetry, yoga and so on to offer opportunities for people to find peace within themselves, together with an improved balance between the various components of life, including work. Welch (1998) illustrates this through the example of a Benedictine monk offering residential weekends on meditation and discussions on spirituality as a way of helping individuals search for meaning in their lives. Another example refers to a firm of solicitors that recruited a poet in residence.

IMPRESSION MANAGEMENT

Perception is a process through which individuals make sense of others and their environment. This process can be influenced by individuals who try to present a particular image of themselves to the world around them and so encourage desired responses (Goffman, 1959). This process of self-presentation is also called impression management which is defined as *the processes used by individuals to influence and control the views others form about them*. Impression management can be conscious or subconscious, and usually serves instrumental and self-expressive functions. A whole range of specific impression management tactics exist (see e.g., McFarland *et al.*, 2005), and instrumental impression management typically involves *ingratiation* (e.g., projecting positive aspects to receive admiration), *supplication* (e.g., projecting need and vulnerability to receive attention and help), *defensiveness* (e.g., projecting innocence or powerlessness to avoid responsibility for past actions incompatible with preferred image) and *aggression* (e.g., projecting power and anger to get obedience). Self-expressive impression management is about communicating self-expressive attitudes as discussed above.

Impression management is common in organizations (Ferris and Judge, 1991) and is reflected in a range of different aspects:

- *Selection*: During selection candidates usually try to project an image the reflects what they believe their prospective employer is looking for. In fact

Impression management
The processes used by individuals to influence and control the views that others form about them.

the majority of undergraduate US students employed some form of 'faking' in employment interviews (Levashina and Campion, 2007). Most selection procedures are therefore designed to provide insights into prospective applicants that help selectors to see through such attempts (McFarland *et al.*, 2005).

- *Career strategies*. In order to enhance career prospects many employees try to create particular impressions among those able to deliver desired career outcomes. Giacalone (1989) identifies a number of what he describes as demotion-preventing and promotion-enhancing strategies including associations with the right people at the right time and providing plausible justifications for actions taken.

- *Organizational image*. Deliberate management of corporate identity symbols such as uniforms, badges and logos or more comprehensive design of company premises and staff dress codes can help companies portray a consistent house style (e.g., many fast food restaurants are instantly recognizable anywhere in the world). Rafaeli and Pratt (1993) present an approach for comparing organizations based on requirements for dress codes among employees. Other attempts at organizational image management aim at attracting employees from particular minority or underrepresented groups (Avery and McKay, 2006).

- *Managerial*. In industrial relations situations for example, it is necessary for the management team to present a unified front and to create an image of the organization that supports the public stance adopted during negotiations. Attempts to hold down pay increases by suggesting difficult financial conditions, while at the same time allowing managers to continue to spend heavily on entertainment, is unlikely to be accepted willingly by the workforce and leads to claims of double standards and the use of the 'fat cat' label. Rankine (2003) makes just this point in relation to pension provision of senior executives.

There is some evidence of a growing trend for impression management within organizations, including a management-imposed requirement for particular appearance characteristics. This is not a new phenomenon, for example a number of airlines have recruited only young attractive people to work as cabin staff for many years. However, this is now beginning to resurface in a number of ways that has led researchers at Strathclyde University to coin the term aesthetic labour to describe the management-determined mix of appearance, age, weight, class and accent characteristics. The researchers describe the trend using the example of a hotel seeking to project a total image concept, with the hotel building representing the hardware and the staff the software. Once recruited by such organizations, staff would experience pressure to mould themselves into the desired characteristics in order to provide the total experience sought by managers (Lamb, 1999). In the same article it is reported, by way of example, that three teenage girls were replaced with 'models' by a nightclub because they were described as too ugly.

Aesthetic labour
Describes the management-determined mix of employee characteristics including appearance, age, weight, class and accent and intended to create a specific impression or image of the organization.

PERCEPTION AND ATTITUDES WITHIN AN ORGANIZATIONAL CONTEXT

Perceptions and attitudes matter for formal and informal relationships and interactions in organizations. Individuals try to influence perceptions and attitudes of those around them for a number of reasons, and many organizations attempt to influence internal opinions and attitudes of employees. The success of such efforts depends much on the specific context, the design of formal messages, the perceived expertise and trustworthiness of the sender, the way in which the arguments are presented, the use of informal communication means and networks, and other factors (Aronson, 2004; Wray and Fellenz, 2007). By far the most central issue regarding perception and attitudes in organizations, however, is control. Whatever the nature of an organization, managers find themselves having to achieve objectives with and through other people. Therefore, managers need to shape the behaviour of other people in order to direct them towards the goals sought. In order to control behaviour within the organization, managers have to either:

- Order others to carry out management wishes, or
- Persuade individuals willingly to undertake what is required of them.

The first option implies force and coercion by managers while the second implies rationality, linked to the exercise of free will on the part of the employee. In practice, managers utilize a mixture of both approaches. The use of force and direct orders often brings about reactance and therefore rarely produces desired responses if it is used excessively. Neither is it likely to produce the necessary levels of engagement needed for high productivity in today's organizations. Perceptions and attitudes provide alternative means through which managers attempt to control the behaviour of employees. These issues will be discussed further throughout the book in the context of topics such as leadership, communication, conflict, control, culture, power and influence, and relationships.

4.1 EXTEND
YOUR LEARNING

STOP & CONSIDER

To what extent is the key skill for any manager the ability to 'manage' the perceptions of their subordinates - in order to disguise the inherent power, control and conflict in the employer–employee relationship - so that they develop management supportive attitudes?

CONCLUSIONS

The subjects of perception and attitude formation are key aspects of management. They raise issues of ethics as a result of the potential for managers to seek to influence others in an attempt to manipulate events. They are processes that involve every individual all the time. They are dynamic processes and are of value in helping to simplify the complexity of the world as it is experienced. Unfortunately, by so doing they also make people vulnerable to mistakes in classification by creating illusions and encouraging other errors. The challenge facing managers is to make positive use of these concepts while not becoming so cynical that individuals simply become pawns in the game of life, there to be manipulated at the whim of the master. Perception, attribution and attitude formation and change are fundamental cognitive processes with immense importance for the behaviour and the experience of individuals in organizations. Like other cognitive processes, they can operate deliberately controlled by individuals, or more or less automatic without conscious awareness and control. Teh Dual

Process Model distinguishes between these important and pervasive approaches to human information processing.

Now to summarize this chapter in terms of the relevant Learning Objectives:

- **Describe the processes of perception and attitude formation.** The perceptual process is described in basic terms in Figure 4.1. Attitudes reflect predispositions to behave in particular ways. So for example, a positive attitude demonstrated towards a company and a job opportunity, is often thought a necessary pre-requisite to being offered work. Figure 4.14 reflects the component parts of an attitude, although it has also been suggested that attitudes are socially constructed. In both possibilities, there are strong links between attitudes and perception as the means by which sensory information is captured and processed into meaningful information by the individual.

● **Explain the links between perception, attitude formation and impression management.** The relationship between these concepts is a complex and dynamic one. Perception is a process of making sense of the world around us and as such influences the attitudes that we hold. However, the attitudes that we hold also influence the perceptions that we make. For example, a customer will interpret the actions of an employee through the filter of their attitudes about the organization and its products and services. Impression management is a process that also links to attitude and perception in that it reflects the attempts of an individual to present a particular image to the world, which will in turn influence (or so it is intended) the perceptions of that person and the attitudes held about them.

● **Understand why employee perceptions and attitudes are difficult for managers to influence.** The processes are unobservable being inside the head of each individual. So managers cannot detect in absolute terms if employees have adopted the desired attitudes and perceptions, or if they are simply complying with the requirements for some private purpose. Public relations, internal marketing, reward systems, discipline systems, training, procedures, employee communications and involvement are all used to give out and reinforce the desired attitudes and perceptions that management seek. These processes all channel employee behaviour either directly or indirectly, and so allow managers to claim that the organization is unified in its pursuit of objectives. However, the degree to which that is actually the case is much more difficult to establish.

● **Discuss the issues surrounding organizational attempts to shape the perceptions and attitudes of employees.** There are many issues that impact on management's attempts to shape employee attitudes and perceptions. There is the ethical issue about how far it is right to go in seeking to create particular ways of interpreting and relating to the world in other people. There are the practical issues surrounding the degree to which it is possible to actually shape the attitudes and perceptions of others. There is also the problem of knowing which attitudes and perceptions are the most appropriate for employees to hold. For management to determine the preferred attitudes and perceptions reflects a 'top-down' perspective which ignores the potential benefits from 'bottom-up' or reciprocal influence. In addition, the attitudes held by employees can become so entrenched and strong that if the market moves on and they become outdated they can become a liability for the organization, but difficult to change.

● **Assess the significance of person perception in the behaviour of managers and employees.** The significance of person perception is that it provides the basis for the understanding and interpretation of other people. In an organizational context that is important because it determines the ways in which managers and employees relate to each other and it informs how each interprets the behaviours and intentions of the other. This is significant as it consequently forms the basis of the actions that each party takes in relation to the other which forms the dynamic and interactive behavioural patterns making up organizational experience. For example, an employee who perceives their manager to be exploitative and self-seeking will not be fully committed to supporting the manager. Equally, managers who perceive employees to be lazy and not interested in the long-term future of the organization will tend to adopt a more directive and authoritarian style.

● **Recognize the role of attribution in organizations and differentiate the two modes of cognitive information processing in the Dual Process Model.** Attribution is the process by which we ascribe causes to events as well as to our own and others' behaviour. It is of fundamental importance in organizations because it determines how people understand and behave towards their environment and particularly other people. The two modes in the Dual Process Model have been called by various names, but automatic vs. controlled processing, heuristic vs. systematic, peripheral vs. central route, or X-system vs C-system are common and useful labels (see Table 4.1 for differences between the dual processes). In perception, distinguishing between automatic and controlled processing is important for a number of reasons. First, it helps to explain why we are aware of only some of the perceptual tasks we are continuously engaged in, and why it is impossible for us to deliberately do all perceptual tasks, or do some of them deliberately all the time. Second, it helps explain why we are often committing errors, only some of which can be explained with faulty logic or inadequate decision-making. Third, it provides insights into the differential nature of attitudes associated with the different processes.

DISCUSSION QUESTIONS

1 Because perception is a process containing many elements and influences, one person can never fully understand another. To what extent does that imply that managers will never understand employees and vice versa – and what might that imply about organizational functioning?

2 Describe the perception process and explain the organizational significance of each stage in the process.

3 'Impression management is the key to being a successful manager. It is not what a manager actually does that matters, but how it is "sold" to others that is important.' To what extent would you agree with this statement and why?

4 To what extent are attitudes based on perception?

5 'The real world exists only in the mind of the individual.' To what extent do you agree with this statement and what implications does it hold for managers seeking to achieve maximum performance and contribution from employees?

6 Employees need the money that they earn through work and so managers can never be certain if employees simply comply with what is expected of them in order to maintain their income. Consequently talk of being an 'employer of choice' or of having a 'committed workforce' is irrelevant and only used to create a positive impression. To what extent is that view correct?

7 Why might different people interpret the same situation differently? Provide examples from your own experience.

8 To what extent can managers influence the attitudes and perceptions of their subordinates? How could they set about doing so?

9 'Management reflects the exercise of power and control, which is why employees tend to hold negative attitudes towards managers. Managers should therefore ignore the attitudes of subordinates and simply get on with the job of achieving their objectives.' Discuss this statement in the light of your experience and work on this chapter.

10 'Attribution theory reflects the application of perception and attitude processes to other people.' To what extent and why would you agree with this viewpoint?

CASE STUDY

Letters of complaint, or just PR?

The following is an extract from a letter of complaint sent by Oliver Beale, a disgruntled passenger on a Virgin Atlantic flight from Mumbai to London in December 2008. He was complaining about the food and entertainment on his flight. Mr Beale works for an advertising agency based in London. It was widely reported in the press and on the Internet at the time as being the perfect letter of complaint. It was said to be well crafted, hilarious and with supporting pictures. Virgin Atlantic revealed that Sir Richard himself had thanked Mr Beale for his 'constructive' letter. Paul Charles, director of communications for Virgin Atlantic, said:

We take customer complaints seriously and that is why Sir Richard rang the passenger personally to thank him for his constructive, if somewhat tongue-in-cheek, letter. We have also invited the passenger to our catering base to be part of the taster team that decides what food and drink should be on Virgin Atlantic flights.

Extracts from the letter:

Dear Mr Branson (technically Sir Richard Branson) I love the Virgin brand, I really do, which is why I continue to use it despite a series of unfortunate incidents over the last few years. This latest incident takes the biscuit.
Ironically, by the end of the flight I would have gladly paid over a thousand rupees for a single biscuit following the culinary journey from hell that I was subjected to at the hands of your corporation. Look at this Richard. Just look at it:

There then follows a picture of the meal. The following discussion refers to the picture and what it shows about the meal.

> *Just desserts . . . or is one the main (course)?*
> *I imagine the same questions are racing through your brilliant mind as were racing through mine on that fateful day.*
> *What is this? Why have I been given it? What have I done to deserve this? And which one is the starter, which one is the dessert?*
> *You don't get to a position like yours, Richard, with anything less than a generous sprinkling of observational power, so* **I KNOW** *you will have spotted the tomato next to the two yellow shafts of sponge on the left.*
> *Yes, it's next to the sponge shaft without the green paste. That's got to be the clue, hasn't it?*
> *No sane person would serve a dessert with a tomato, would they?*
> *Well, answer me this Richard: What sort of animal would serve a dessert with peas in?*

There then follows another picture of the meal. The following discussion refers to the picture and what it shows about the meal.

> *Being held in custardy . . . offensive food that looks like bhaji.*
> *I know it looks like a bhaji but it's in custard, Richard. Custard. It must be the pudding.*
> *Well, you'll be fascinated to hear that it wasn't custard. It was a sour gel with a clear oil on top.*
> *Its only redeeming feature was that it managed to be so alien to my palette that it took away the taste of the curry emanating from our miscellaneous central cuboid of beige matter.*
>
> *Anyway, this is all irrelevant at the moment.*
> *I was raised strictly but neatly by my parents, and if they knew I had started dessert before the main course, a sponge shaft would be the least of my worries.*
> *So let's peel back the tin-foil on the main dish and see what's on offer.*
> *I'll try to explain how this felt. Imagine being a 12-year-old boy, Richard.*
> *Now imagine it's Christmas morning and you're sitting there with your final present to open. It's a big one, and you know what it is.*
> *It's that Goodmans stereo you picked out from the catalogue and wrote to Santa about.*

> *Only you open the present and it's not in there.*
> *It's your hamster, Richard. It's your hamster in the box and it's not breathing. That's how I felt when I peeled back the foil and saw this:*

There then follows another picture of the meal. The following discussion refers to the picture and what it shows about the meal.

> *Now I know what you're thinking. You're thinking it's more of that bhaji custard.*
> *I admit I thought the same too, but no. It's mustard, Richard.* **MUSTARD**.
> *More mustard than any man could consume in a month.*
> *On the left we have a piece of broccoli and some peppers in a brown, glue-like oil, and on the right the chef had prepared some mashed potato.*
> *The potato masher had obviously broken and so it was decided the next best thing would be to pass the potatoes through the digestive tract of a bird.*
> *Once it was regurgitated, it was clearly then blended and mixed with a bit of mustard. Everybody likes a bit of mustard, Richard.*
> *By now, I was actually starting to feel a little hypoglycemic. I needed a sugar hit.*
> *Luckily, there was a small cookie provided. It had caught my eye earlier because of its baffling presentation:*

There then follows another picture of the biscuit in its packet. The following discussion refers to the picture and what it shows about the biscuit.

> *It appears to be in an evidence bag from the scene of a crime.* **A CRIME AGAINST BLOODY COOKING.**
> *Either that or some sort of backstreet, underground cookie, purchased off a gun-toting maniac high on his own supply of yeast.*
> *You certainly wouldn't want to be caught carrying one of these through Customs.*
> *Imagine biting into a piece of brass, Richard.*
> *That would be softer on the teeth than the specimen above.*
> *I was exhausted. All I wanted to do was relax. But obviously I had to sit with that mess in front of me for half an hour.*

There then follows a similar length of letter complaining about the entertainment and video screen.

The letter concludes with the following summary:

It reminded me of my first week at university. I had overheard that you could make a drink by mixing vodka and Refreshers.

I lied to my new friends and told them I'd done it loads of times.

When I attempted to make the drink in a big bowl it formed a cheese, Richard – a cheese. That cheese looked a lot like your bhaji mustard.

So that was that, Richard. I didn't eat a bloody thing.

My only question is: How can you live like this?

I can't imagine what dinner round your house is like. It must be like something out of a nature documentary.

As I said at the start, I love your brand. I really do. It's just a shame such a simple thing could

bring it crashing to its knees and begging for sustenance.

Yours sincerely,

Oliver Beale

Subsequently, Sir Richard Branson personally called Mr Beale back for a chat and to discuss his letter. The original letter somehow appeared in the press and on the Internet and Paul Charles the head of communications for Virgin Atlantic naturally found it necessary to comment about the situation. He pointed out that all complaints were taken seriously as the company tried to offer the highest standards of service to customers – Sir Richard calling back demonstrated just how seriously they took such issues, thereby sending out a clear message to staff, suppliers and customers alike.

TASKS

1   How might this story have appeared in the media in the first place? Would any company publish such material and if so, why?

2   It has been suggested in some quarters that it was published in order to create a good (positive) PR story. Using material from this chapter in relation to perception, attitudes and impression management, how might this story result in a positive outcome for Virgin Atlantic?

©Gary I Rothstein/epa/Corbis

Sources:
http://www.thesun.co.uk/sol/homepage/features/article2184622.ece (accessed 29 April 2009).
http://www.telegraph.co.uk/travel/travelnews/4344890/Virgin-the-worlds-best-passenger-complaint-letter.html (accessed 29 April 2009).
http://blog.mrandmrssmith.com/2009/01/oli-beale-branson-complaint-letter-virgin-atlantic-mumbai-heathrow/ (accessed 29 April 2009).

FURTHER READING

Aronson, E. (1995) *The Social Animal*, New York: Freeman. Highly readable, comprehensive introduction to social psychology.

Bromley, D.B. (1993) *Reputation, Image and Impression Management*, Chichester: John Wiley. A social psychological review of the subject of impression management in a variety of forms.

Cialdini, R.B. (1985) *Influence: Science and Practice*, London: HarperCollins. An interesting and readable text covering the psychology of influence and related behaviours. As such it covers many of the issues relevant to the behavioural consequences of attitudes and perception.

Fenton-O'Creevy, M., Nicholson, N., Stone, E. and Willman, P. (2003) Trading on illusions: Unrealistic perceptions of control and trading performance, *Journal of Occupational and Organizational Psychology*, 76:53–68. Reviews research on traders working in investment banks in the City of London in which the relationship between perception and performance was investigated.

Fiske, S. T. and Taylor, S. E. (2008) *Social cognition: From brains to culture*, McGraw-Hill. Useful overview from two of the most influential writers in the area of social cognition.

Gladwell, M. (2005) *Blink: The power of thinking without thinking*, Back Bay Books. Bestselling account of the dynamics and implications of snap-judgements.

Pease, A. (1981) *Body Language: How to Read Others' Thoughts by Their Gestures*. London: Sheldon Press. A practical guide on the interpretation of body language. Not an academic book but it does offer a wide-ranging review of areas that form a significant stimulus input to the perceptual system.

Segall, M.H., Dasen, P.R., Berry, J.W. and Poortinga, Y.H. (1990) *Human Behaviour in Global Perspective: An Introduction to Cross-cultural Psychology*. Needham Heights: Allyn & Bacon. Offers a broad review of the subject matter. There are a number of references to attitudes and perception, but Chapter 4 is of particular relevance.

Weick, K.E. (1995) *Sensemaking in organizations*, Thousand Oaks: Sage. Collection of Weick's work relevant to the important dynamics of sensemaking.

COMPANION WEBSITE

Online teaching and learning resources

Visit the companion website for Organizational Behaviour and Management 4th edition at: http://www .cengage.co.uk/martinfellenz to find valuable further teaching and learning material. For full details, see 'About the website' at the start of the book.

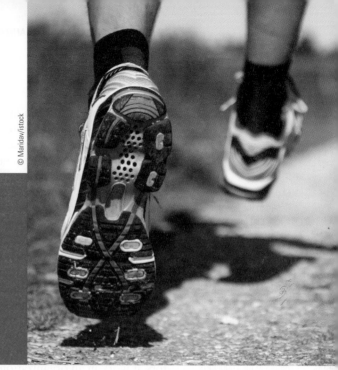

CHAPTER FIVE

MOTIVATION

LEARNING OBJECTIVES

After studying this chapter and working through the associated OB in Action panels, Discussion Questions and Case Study you should be able to:

- Describe the major motivation theories and the ways in which they can be classified.

- Explain the difference between content and process theories of motivation.

- Understand what makes the study of motivation difficult.

- Discuss the dilemmas and difficulties facing managers in applying motivation theory to a work setting.

- Assess the contribution of Bandura's social-cognitive theory to the understanding of motivation.

INTRODUCTION

The term (motivation) is a familiar one – we hear about motivation in the context of work as well as sports, learning and many other activities. In organizations motivation is of central importance because of its relation to performance – the achievement of organizational goals. The three central elements of performance that are - at least in part - under managerial control are motivation, ability and opportunity (Sprenger, 2002). Motivation refers to *the force that initiates, directs and sustains behaviour;* ability refers to *the capacity of individuals to achieve the tasks they are trying to accomplish* and opportunity refers to *the conditions under which motivation and ability are deployed.* If lack of performance is due to lack of ability or insufficient opportunity, any attempt to increase motivation is likely not only to fail, but to create even more serious problems (Sprenger, 2002). Thus, the consideration of motivation and the discussion of relevant theories, frameworks, approaches, tools and techniques in this chapter are a *part* of an overall approach to understanding, discussing, predicting and influencing performance that is dealt with throughout this book. However, high levels of motivation and performance achieved do not always guarantee success either for the organization or employee, as the High Performance example demonstrates. There are many other factors at work in an organization that can impact on the outcomes for both parties.

This chapter starts with a brief discussion and definition of motivation. It then identifies a number of central distinctions regarding motivation before considering traditional and more contemporary theories and approaches to understanding and explaining human motivation and behaviour in organizations.

Motivation
Refers to the set of internal forces that initiate, direct and sustain deliberate behaviour.

Ability
Refers to the capacity of individuals to achieve the tasks they are trying to accomplish.

Opportunity
Refers to the conditions under which motivation and ability are deployed.

MOTIVATION IN ORGANIZATIONS

**5.1 EXTEND
YOUR LEARNING**

Managers in organizations constantly seek ways to improve performance at every level of the business. Important drivers of organizational performance such as productivity,

HIGH PERFORMANCE

Motivated out of a job!

The following comments were overheard in a coffee shop recently. One individual (called Lily and aged in her mid-20s) was saying to her friend that recently (about 3 months previously) she and her co-workers had their annual performance appraisal meeting with their boss. They had been told that they were the best workers in the department, and that productivity had continually improved since they started working there. Lily was told that she was a good role model for other staff and that promotion would be possible with a little more experience. Lily's appraisal marking was the highest category possible and they would receive the highest pay rise in the department as a consequence. However a couple of days prior to Lily meeting her

friend in the coffee shop, she said that she had been called into the manager's office and told that the company was making redundancies and that because Lily had shorter service than anyone else in the department, she would be made redundant (as that was company policy) at the end of that month.

TASK

1 What effect would such a situation have on:

   A The individual's approach to motivation in their next job?

   B The level of motivation delivered by those employees who retained their jobs in the department?

cost, creativity and responsiveness are all directly and indirectly related to employee behaviour. Initiating, directing and sustaining such behaviour is therefore a central part of managers' jobs, and a core element of the process of management (see Chapter 1). In fact, the influence and control that managers try to exert in organizations can be traced back to their attempts to support the achievement of organizational goals (note that many critics would rightly point out that managers will typically also try to achieve their own personal goals and agendas – see Chapter 15). A central element of people management is therefore the application of practices aimed at motivating employees to engage in the desired behaviours to contribute to organizational success.

A central question in management and OB is 'Why do people in organizations do what they do?' Motivation is the concept used in any attempted answer to this crucial question. Despite the many different ways in which this term can and has been conceived (see Steers *et al.*, 2004; Latham, 2007; Pinder, 2008) we define motivation as *the set of internal forces that initiates, directs and sustains deliberate behaviour*. Our definition reflects the core elements of behavioural initiation, direction, and maintenance typically included in definition of work motivation (Steers *et al.*, 2004; Pinder, 2008). It also recognizes that there may be multiple forces at work that determine behaviour, some of them originating outside the individual. However, without some internal elements linking these external factors to internal dynamics, we would not talk about deliberate behaviour. Thus, the definition clearly identifies humans as the agents responsible for the considered actions. Our designation of deliberate behaviour also excludes some forms of human action (e.g., autonomous bodily functions such as digestion, and genetically determined actions such as reflexes and instinctual behaviour). This distinction is discussed further in the next section. Including multiple forces in our definition also indicates the view that human behaviour is over-determined, a perspective that recognizes the complexity of human nature and of the social context of behaviour. This complexity offers many more factors and dynamics than would be needed to explain any individual human action. Thus, our definition can accommodate the many different motivation frameworks and theories used in management and OB.

Psychologists have long recognized the distinction between drives and motives, reflecting the distinction between unconscious physiological reactions and the social process directing controllable behaviour in people. Drives reflect those behaviour forces that are based on the physiological/biological needs of the body. For example, if we are hungry, the smell of food will tend to push our behaviour in the direction of eating. A motive, on the other hand, reflects learned patterns of behaviour. For example, we actively seek out situations involving interaction with other people in an attempt to socialize with them rather than spend time on our own. The basic motivational process reflecting these distinctions is shown in Figure 5.1.

Drives and motives
These reflect the distinction between unconscious physiological reactions based on the physiological/biological needs of the body (drives) and the social process directing controllable behaviour in people (motives).

Figure 5.1 The basic motivational process

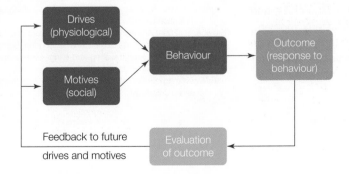

GOING GLOBAL

Motivated to engage in extreme sports

What are extreme sports? According to adverts extreme sports provide a reaction to the risk averse, safety-first, controlled and protected world surrounding most of life's experiences. They offer an individual the opportunity to follow their own path, take risks and find out where their limits are. They are about exhilaration, skill and danger. Usually involving individual activities (often undertaken in a collective setting), there are very few rules. Participants use their skill and experience to control the inherent risks that exist. The control of risk is what makes them extreme sports and not just dangerous, foolhardy behaviour.

When the term first emerged around 1990, it was used for adult sports such as skydiving, surfing, rock climbing, snow skiing, snowboarding, mountain biking, mountaineering, hang gliding and bungee jumping, which were undergoing a surge in popularity and media coverage at that time. The term has changed somewhat since then and is now usually applied to skateboarding, snowboarding, aggressive skating, FMX and BMX cycling type sports closely associated with the younger generation. Marketing and advertising associated with such sports has also shifted its focus towards that market. One recent example of extreme sport was reported as the attempt by a rider on a BMW R 1200 GS Adventure motorcycle to drive the treacherous Arctic Ice Road, Alaska, with temperatures of minus-60 degrees! It was however an advert for a new television programme on the attempt of motor cycle rider Jesse James to travel on a particularly dangerous road in dangerous conditions. The road is just snow and ice and is home to some of the world's most extreme conditions, including below-zero temperatures, piercing wind chills, and perilous ice itself that can open at any moment, swallowing a traveller instantly. With no traction on the unprepared ice and not a single gas station for miles for refuge or repairs, what motivates someone to engage in such pursuits?

However, not everyone is convinced that extreme sports are dangerous. For example, Nicholas Heyworth from Sports England suggests that many are less dangerous than traditional sports - the most dangerous sport statistically is horse riding. One cliff jumping website is covered with disclaimers and warnings not to drink and jump, or jump alone, etc. Heyworth also suggests that many extreme sportspeople have lots of safety equipment and a backup team. It has also been suggested that much of the 'danger' in extreme sports originates from marketing by the industries that surround it – sports equipment and clothing, TV programmes, and drinks for example. Advice is even available from the UK government on how to safely participate in an extreme sport holiday. Their advice includes think carefully before undertaking extreme sports:

- check which sports are covered by your insurance
- check that the airline will carry any specialist equipment
- ensure you are fit and healthy enough for strenuous activities
- tell the instructors about any pre-existing medical conditions or injuries
- be aware of the risks of altitude sickness when mountaineering and rock-climbing.

TASKS

1 How (if at all) could you motivate someone to take part in an extreme sport?

2 Explain the motivation to participate in an extreme sport using any of the theories included in this chapter.

Sources:
Appleton, J. (2005) What's so extreme about extreme sports? 30 August, http://www.spiked-online.com/Articles/0000000CAD26.htm (accessed July 2009).
Browne, D. (2004) *Amped: How Big Air, Big Dollars and a New Generation Took Sports to the Extreme*, London: Bloomsbury.
http://www.fco.gov.uk/en/travelling-and-living-overseas/ta-relevant-to-you/sports (accessed July 2009).
http://www.magxzine.com/modules.cfm?name=News&sid=314 (accessed July 2009).

Finally, the concept of motivation is used to explain three important aspects of deliberate behaviour. The first of these behavioural characteristics directly influenced by the degree of motivation is *direction*, which indicates *the type of activity chosen*. Often the direction of an activity is identified and described through a goal or objective (this is called a *teleological* explanation) which may vary in the degree of specificity. The second aspect is *effort*, which reflects *the amount of energy expended in relation to a particular activity*. Finally, the third behavioural characteristic is *persistence* which refers to *the duration of the behaviour in question, especially in light of difficulties or obstacles*. In general, the more effortful and persistent an observed behaviour is, the higher is the motivation assumed to be driving it. It is interesting in this context to reflect on one particular aspect of individual behaviour – the desire (and motivation) that many people have to engage in extreme sports. The Going Global example explores how this form of human behaviour might differ from other sporting activity and its implications for motivation.

THEORIES OF MOTIVATION

Few topics are as central and important to OB as motivation, which is reflected in the volume of research done in this area. Yet many of the theories found in typical OB textbooks date back to the 1960s and 1970s, and there are few new additions to this range of old favourites. However, relevant progress has clearly been made in research and theorizing on motivation, and we will review the traditional well known theories and models as well as some of the more important recent contributions.

5.2 EXTEND
YOUR LEARNING

There is no one theory of motivation that can be claimed to embrace the entire range of human behaviour. Here we therefore introduce some important distinctions about motivation and use them to clarify and justify the boundaries of the material covered in this book as well as prepare for the discussion of specific aspects of different contributions. First, many motivation theories apply to a broad range of settings and personal circumstances. We will focus specifically on organizational settings and the issue of *work motivation*, and this guides both the selection of appropriate material covered here and the thrust of our discussion.

'There is only one theory of motivation that works – grip employees warmly by the throat and squeeze gently until they do what management want.' How would you respond to a senior manager who gave you that advice early in your career?

Second, our discussion will not deal with the whole range of human behaviour. To simplify this issue, we distinguish between three general types of behaviours that differ in the form of their initiation and in the control humans exert over these actions. The first type of human behaviour ('*hardwired*') is instinctive, reflexive, or otherwise biologically hardwired behaviour. Typically, such behaviours are initiated by some form of external stimulus. In ethology, the science of animal behaviour, similar behaviours are also described as fixed action patterns (FAP) which refer to instinctual responses that, once started, are not usually stoppable. Examples for such biologically hardwired behaviours in humans include the grasping or sucking reflexes in newborns and the yawning or gagging reflexes in adults. People generally have only very limited control over such behaviours. The second type of human behaviour ('*automatic*') is based on automatic performance of well learned behaviour that requires little or no conscious control. This behaviour is controlled by behavioural scripts and cognitive schemas that reduce the need for active, conscious processing and control (see Chapter 4). Typical examples include well learned behaviours such as driving a car, riding a bicycle or brushing one's teeth. It is instructive to consider how difficult such behaviours are until they are well learned and can be performed more or less without active and conscious control. The third type of behaviour ('*deliberate*') is consciously controlled behaviour such as active problem solving (e.g., solving a riddle, or actively and consciously attending to diagnose a mistake). Such behaviour requires significant attention and cognitive resources. It is important to note that automatic behaviour can be based on active and conscious decisions that initiate it (e.g., 'I will brush my teeth now'), just as much deliberate behaviour may be prompted by behavioural responses that were initiated automatically (e.g., automatically responding to someone's questions and switching to a more engaged and conscious mode during the answer). The distinction between automatic and deliberate types of behaviour reflects common ways of distinguishing between actions in psychology where some behaviours may be classified as automatic responses while those based on conscious and deliberate choice are called purposive or volitional. In this chapter we will focus more on deliberate behaviour and behaviour based on conscious and deliberate choices. However, many motivational theories and frameworks also apply to a certain degree to automatic behaviours.

A related third distinction about motivation refers to cognitive as opposed to purely behavioural and environmental treatments of the origins of human behaviour. While some more contemporary frameworks tend to combine these aspects, many traditional contributions have typically fallen into one or the other of these camps. We include a section on classical and operant conditioning and classical behavioural learning theory in this chapter, although technically many relevant contributors would take issue with the inclusion of their work in a chapter on motivation.

An important fourth distinction addresses the origin of motivation and refers to the distinction between intrinsic and extrinsic motivation. Intrinsic motivation refers to *the impetus for behaviour originating in performing the action itself*, such as an enjoyable or otherwise satisfying task (in simpler term, the activity is done for its own sake). In contrast, extrinsic motivation describes the situation in which *the impetus for behaviour originates outside the person and the performed task* (i.e. it is done as a means to another end). An example for this may be pursuing a task for payment where the payment is the motivator for the task performed. While initially the distinction appears quite clear, tasks can be simultaneously intrinsically and extrinsically motivated. We will further discuss these matters when we consider self-determination theory (e.g., Deci and Ryan, 1985, 2000; Gagné and Deci, 2005) further below.

Finally, in this chapter we will use the convention of classifying theories into content or process theories wherever possible. Content theories concentrate on identifying the motives that produce behaviour – they address the question of *what* motivates human behaviour in organizations. Process theories, in contrast, emphasize those mechanisms and dynamics that encourage or discourage specific behaviour – they deal with the question of *how* human behaviour in organizations is motivated. It is also important to recognize that an ethical perspective exists in relation to motivation at work as the Examining Ethics example demonstrates.

CONTENT THEORIES

Content theories emphasize particular aspects of an individual's needs or the goals that they seek to achieve as the basis for motivated behaviour. The major theories falling into this classification include:

- Maslow's hierarchy of needs theory
- Alderfer's existence, relatedness and growth (ERG) theory
- Herzberg's two-factor theory.

Intrinsic motivation
This refers to the impetus for behaviour originating from performing the action itself, in simple terms the activity is done for its own sake. See also extrinsic motivation.

Extrinsic motivation
This describes the situation in which the impetus for behaviour originates outside the person and the performed task, in simple terms the activity is done in pursuit of another end. See also intrinsic motivation.

Kaizen
In Japanese, continuous improvement, and is based on employee 'voluntary' contributions to suggestion schemes or small-group activities geared to problem solving (quality or productivity circles).

Karoshi
Japanese term for sudden death from overwork.

EXAMINING ETHICS

Motivated to death!

How much work is it reasonable or acceptable for an employee to do in a day, week or year? This is an important question to ask and it is one that has plagued managers ever since the early days of collective effort. Today there is strong interest in high performance working and finding ways of achieving more output with the use of less resource. That is the basis of the performance imperative theme that runs throughout this book. One aspect of this pressure to achieve more with less is that employees and managers are expected to work longer hours and there is a real danger of individuals being required to do so much work that it becomes a threat to their health. The danger is of creating a vicious cycle of people working longer hours and then once that becomes the 'norm', being required to work even more in the drive to constantly increase productivity.

This can be described as an extreme (downside) of motivation. Normally motivation is regarded as an energizing force intended to achieve the best levels of contribution from employees. However, emerging from Japan has been the view that continuous improvement should be the normal approach to achieving productivity. The traditional view in Scientific Management was that the 'one best way' could be identified and when achieved produced the best possible level of productivity. Continuous improvement takes a view that the ultimate level of productivity is never achievable, and seeking it represents a never ending journey of constantly seeking ways of eliminating waste. Waste represents anything that does not directly add value. In Japanese, continuous improvement is called kaizen and it is based on employee 'voluntary' contributions to suggestion schemes and other group activities aimed at problem solving. The objective is to get workers directly involved in identifying 'waste' and the elimination of it and so directly support cost cutting, job reductions and to participate with management in changing work processes and practices. *Kaizen* encourages employees to treat each other as suppliers and customers or competitors rather than as co-workers. There is constant pressure on employees and managers to 'do' more as a way of retaining their jobs. Excessive work commitment, working ever longer hours, taking fewer holidays, working whilst on holiday can all be seen as

a way of demonstrating commitment, loyalty, support for management objectives and generally good corporate citizenship – leading to workaholism. If some colleagues are prepared to adopt such work habits then it is very difficult for an individual to stand against them in support of a better work–life balance.

This invariably creates stress for individuals and difficulties for organizations and society. For example in Japan there is now a cause of death known as karoshi - sudden death from overwork - that claims the lives of an estimated 10,000 people each year. The 1994 results of a survey in the UK revealed that 67 per cent of respondents claimed overwork, 55 per cent were fearful of being made redundant and 54 per cent claimed that they did not get enough support at work, all of which caused stress. The first case of karoshi was thought to have occurred in 1969 when a 29-year-old worker in a Japanese newspaper company died from a stroke. The major medical causes of karoshi-related deaths are heart attack and stroke. Most victims are claimed to have worked more than 3000 hours per year before their death - equating to 60 hours each week for 50 weeks each year. In Japan it is estimated that some 24 per cent of the workforce work in excess of these hours each year.

TASKS

1 To what extent do you consider that it would be possible to 'motivate an employee to death'?

2 What are the practical and ethical issues raised by the use of motivation theory by managers when some employees might react in an extreme manner?

3 How can any manager determine the 'right' amount of motivation to provide?

Sources:
Dawkins, W. (1993) More than the jobs worth, *Financial Times*, 16–17 October, p. 9.
Nishiyama, K. and Johnson, J.V. (1997) Karoshi-Death from overwork: Occupational health consequences of the Japanese production management. Accessed July 2009 at http://www.workhealth.org/whatsnew/lpkarosh.html.
http://www.iol.co.za/index.php?set_id=1&click_id=117&art_id=nw20070517081239240C435666 (accessed July 2009).
Economist (2007) Japan and Overwork, 19 December. Accessed July 2009 at http://www.economist.com/world/asia/displaystory.cfm?story_id=10329261.

Maslow's hierarchy of needs

Abraham Maslow, an American psychologist, produced the idea that humans have innate needs or wants which they seek to satisfy. He developed a hierarchical model of these needs to explain purposive behaviour (Maslow, 1943, 1987). According to Maslow, these innate needs have an in-built prioritizing system which underlies the hierarchical arrangement shown in Figure 5.2.

The five levels included in this hierarchy can be defined in the following way:

1 *Physiological needs.* These include the wide range of basic needs that every human requires in order to stay alive and function normally. Examples would include the need for food, air to breathe, water to drink and sleep. In an organizational context this would also include the need for wages.

2 *Safety needs.* This category incorporates needs that provide for the security of the individual in their normal environment. Examples would include the need to be free from harm and to have shelter from the elements. In an organizational context this would also include the need for job security.

3 *Social needs.* From this category individuals would look to draw on social support necessary to life. Examples would include friendship and a sense of belonging. In an organizational context this might include the need to work as part of a team.

4 *Esteem needs.* This would include individuals having self-respect. Also incorporated in this category are concepts of achievement, adequacy, recognition and reputation. In an organizational context this includes the formal recognition by management (e.g., employee of the month awards) as well as informal social recognition from peers and others.

5 *Self-actualization needs.* This category is related to the opportunity to realize one's full potential, that is, the ability to have a significant influence over one's own life. In an organizational context this could include the freedom to organize one's job to suit personal preferences and circumstances, or to be managed on the basis of ends, not means. Moral and ethical behaviour as well as creative tasks are also important sources of self-actualization for many people.

Figure 5.2 Maslow's hierarchy of needs

Maslow suggests that these elements in the hierarchy are not to be considered as a rigid framework, within which individuals move in a totally fixed and predictable way. He suggests that the hierarchy displays the following properties:

- *A need once satisfied is no longer a motivator.* For example, once employees become accustomed to being consulted by the employer on matters of company policy, it becomes the norm and therefore loses some of its motivational properties. In effect, the basis of comparison shifts to match the new circumstances.

- *A need cannot be effective as a motivator until those before it in the hierarchy have been satisfied.* For example, it would be of little value to offer employees who are currently very poorly paid the opportunity to work in teams in an attempt to increase productivity.

- *If deprived of the source of satisfaction from a lower-order need it will again become a motivator.* For example, if a self-actualizing employee is given notice of redundancy, their natural reaction would be to start looking for another job (reversion to a lower-level need for security). This reversing to focus on lower level needs (e.g., safety) if they become substantially unfulfilled is based on the concept of *prepotency*.

- *There is an innate desire to work up the hierarchy.* Employees working in a team may begin to plan and organize their work without management involvement.

- *Self-actualization is not like the other needs; the opportunities presented by it cannot be exhausted.* A marketing manager who has just enjoyed a successful sales campaign may also have a number of similar campaigns at earlier stages of development to form the basis of future motivation. However, Maclagan (2003) argues that self-actualization can only be properly understood as the realization of personal moral ideals. In other words, it is for the individual to decide for themselves (based on their moral values) what provides self-actualization opportunity. Consequently, attempts by management to impose participation schemes or particular job design can provide at best vicarious experiences of self-actualization (i.e., employees experience self-actualization in ways that managers would find motivating) that are likely to have only limited effects on employee motivation.

ASSESSMENT OF THE THEORY

Maslow did not specifically describe his theory as applicable to work situations, although that is where it has gained most exposure. In fact, it has become the best known and probably the most popular motivational theory among management researchers and practitioners (Miner, 1984) despite the fact that its applicability in work contexts is very limited. In part this may be because it is typically both misunderstood and oversimplified (Pinder, 2008), but even in its proper formulation there are a number of difficulties in applying this theory to humans in an organizational context, including:

- *Lack of domain specificity.* Not everyone is motivated only by things that go on inside the organization. There are many people who self-actualize outside the work setting, running youth groups, trade unions and participating in a wide variety of other leisure activities. Even the time of year can have an impact on the behaviour of a significant number of people. See for example, the Change at Work example which illustrates how one organization sought to respond to seasonal changes on employee behaviour and motivation.

- *Lack of developmental specificity.* People at different stages of their lives will be motivated by different things. For example, a young employee saving up to buy a car will be motivated by factors different from an employee 5 years away from retirement.

- *Lack of saturation specificity.* The amount of satisfaction needed at a specific level before a higher level need is activated is unknown.
- *Lack of explanation for untypical behaviour.* The theory cannot explain all behaviour. For example, how can it explain that many actors and artists are prepared to endure personal hardship in order to pursue their art?

CHANGE AT WORK

SAD syndrome assistance at Capital One

An estimated 5 per cent of the population - 2.5 million people – claim to suffer from Seasonal Affective Disorder (SAD). About 90 per cent of the population are said to experience subtle changes in mood, energy levels and sleeping patterns when the seasons change.

Catherine Hope, Human Resource Director in the UK for Capital One, reported that the company regularly surveyed their 2000 staff to find out how the working environment could be improved. Actions taken by management to ensure a positive working environment included:

- *Fun Budget.* A £50 per person per quarter budget to provide inside or outside work activities. Associates (employees) are encouraged to be creative in deciding how to spend it. Examples have included line dancing, hosting a medieval banquet and city breaks.
- *Listen to the staff.* Regular staff surveys on views about the work environment and how to improve it.
- *Appropriate use of colour.* Using colour co-ordination to blend internal and external themes with the style of the building keeps it fresh and energizing. Dark colours such as brown and dark green have been avoided as too depressing.
- *A view to the world outside.* Associates work in the offices next to the windows facing the outside of the building so that they always have a view of the surrounding environment. The windows are all floor to ceiling to allow maximum light into the building as well as allowing the outside into the workspace. Manager's offices are placed towards

the centre of the building to give Associates the best views.

- *Staff interaction.* The company provides lounge areas, meeting rooms, coffee shops and restaurants for informal meetings. This with the opportunity for staff to work in groups so that people can mix with each other provides a happier working atmosphere.

Hope argues that because people are the most important resource available to any organization it is important to keep them happy and motivated. The working environment is a key aspect of creating an enjoyable place of work.

TASKS

1   How would you feel as a manager knowing that your subordinates' motivational 'needs' were considered more important than yours in terms of working in an office with good light and views of the surrounding area?

2   How might you approach the issue of work environment design and motivation if you were a manager working in an old office block with old buildings or factories surrounding you?

3   As a senior manager would you be persuaded to accept lower levels of productivity in the autumn and winter months because of SAD? How might you seek to maximize motivation levels during those months?

Source:
Adapted from Newsdesk (2002) Capital one helps staff avoid 'SAD' syndrome, *Management Services*, December, p. 5.

- *Socio-historical and cultural boundedness.* The theory was conceived and developed in the USA during the 1940s, reflecting the values and culture of that time. The applicability to current circumstances and different cultures is questionable (but see Ronen, 1994).
- *Simultaneous need fulfilment.* Organizational events can impact on satisfaction at more than one level in the hierarchy. For example, money can be used to satisfy needs at several levels in the hierarchy. However, the use of money by employees is not under the control of managers, it is for the individual to determine the level of the hierarchy that is being met through the money given. This represents a very indirect motivational process.
- *Individual differences.* Individuals will place different values on each need. For example, some people prefer to work in relative security but with lower pay. It is just this issue that has over recent years been creating difficulties within public sector employment. Traditionally public sector employment has been very secure and some degree of advancement almost guaranteed. However, over recent years most countries have struggled with the desire to cut public spending and have as a consequence changed the basis of the psychological contract with employees. A not surprising reaction to that situation is that public sector employees now consider themselves to be just as vulnerable to high work demands and low security as those in the private sector and are demanding higher wages and better rewards in return.
- *Lack of empirical support.* While some research has provided partial support for Maslow's theory (e.g., Ronen, 1994), many of the results of empirical tests have been negative although especially earlier research may not have been methodologically best suited to that task (see Mitchell and Moudgill, 1976; Wicker *et al.*, 1993)

Having said all that, Maslow's theory has been very influential in assisting managers to prioritize elements in their attempts to motivate employees. It is an approach that encourages managers to 'get the basics right' before they attempt to undertake complex motivational initiatives. It can compel managers to examine motivation from the employee perspective and to consider the employees' perspective. It also provides a basis for managers to reinforce what they already provide through benefit and support programmes as part of the employee reward package (e.g., reminding employees of the existence and value of counselling services and pension schemes).

Overall, there are many potential advantages to managers seeking to apply the Maslow model to the design of motivation within the organization – which is why it has much popularity as a topic on management courses. However, that alone does not make it a good theory, and empirical support for the model has been limited. As a theory it must be seen in the context of the strong desire among managers for control of the process and outcome of work. It is in that context that, although originating outside the organizational context, it gains its significance (Townley, 1994).

Alderfer's ERG theory

Alderfer (1972) further developed Maslow's work and presented a simplified three-level hierarchy. The three needs included are:

1 *Existence needs.* This category is grounded in the survival, or continued existence, of the person. As such it would include many of the issues covered by the physiological and safety needs identified by Maslow.

2   *Relatedness needs*. This category is based on the need for people to live and function in a social environment. It would embrace the need to be part of a group and belong to a valued organization. It would incorporate many of the issues covered by the safety, belonging and esteem needs described by Maslow. Issues associated with this aspect of motivation (when things go wrong) are evident in the Employee Perspective titled 'The grey squirrels are taking over!'

3   *Growth needs*. This category is grounded in the need for people to develop their potential. As such it would cover self-actualization and many of the esteem needs described by Maslow.

Assessment of the theory

Despite its roots in Maslow's work, Alderfer did not merely simplify the original framework. For example, he suggests that individuals move from existence needs to relatedness needs to growth needs, as each becomes satisfied. However, he does make

EMPLOYEE PERSPECTIVE

The grey squirrels are taking over!

In one organization, management sought to dramatically increase the volume of work and how it was done by employees in a particular department. A new department manager was recruited to replace the previous manager who had been forced into early retirement. The new manager (Richard) obtained permission to recruit an additional 10 staff for the department on the understanding that the work produced would treble within 2 years. The job adverts were placed in the press and 10 new employees were recruited to the department, all from the company that Richard had previously worked for. They all knew each other and looked forward to leaving their present company as it was slowly losing its place in the market and its profitability.

When they arrived they all had an expectation that they would work as they had done in their previous organization, which was unlike the way that their new company operated. The department was now a total of twenty people, including the 10 new employees. Not surprisingly the newcomers mixed socially at work and outside; they also tried to change the way that work was done to match ways that were familiar to them - from their previous organization. The department manager

(Richard) supported the new staff in everything that they did and simply brushed aside the complaints of existing staff. The existing employees began to feel threatened and marginalized. One existing employee left the company which unsettled the others even more and so they also began to look around for other jobs, anywhere to get out of the department. One of the existing employees likened the situation in the department to that of a forest originally inhabited only by red squirrels. This forest had now been invaded by aggressive vermin called grey squirrels who were forcing the indigenous red squirrels into extinction by forcing them to abandon their natural home.

TASKS

1   Does it matter in the long run (and if so to whom) that so many of the existing employees became demotivated, unhappy and wanted to leave? Why or why not?

2   To what extent might this example suggest that new employees will naturally tend to have greater levels of motivation than existing employees and if so, why might that be and what does it imply for motivation practice within organizations?

more than Maslow of the variability inherent in all motivational situations. For example, he suggests that more than one need could be functioning at the same time, and that individuals may regress back down the hierarchy as the result of a frustration – regression mechanism – if they were prevented from meeting their needs at any level. In other words, if individuals find their attempts to meet their needs at one level frustrated, they may focus on needs fulfilment at a lower level.

Maslow's theory was not specifically work-related. Alderfer, by the same token, contains a more direct organizational basis in grouping together categories of need into a more usable framework (at least as might be perceived by managers). It is also a more robust theory than Maslow's. It postulates that managers should seek to motivate by addressing all three levels of need, but that if one (say growth) cannot be met then additional effort will need to be put into providing for the others as they will increase in significance for the individual. However, it largely suffers from the same criticisms as the Maslow theory in its evident cultural positioning, underlying assumptions and managerialist perspective.

Herzberg's two-factor theory

The original research carried out by Herzberg involved interviews with 203 accountants and engineers from organizations around Pittsburgh in the USA (Herzberg, 1974; Herzberg *et al.*, 1959). He used the critical incident technique and asked questions about what had made the individual feel good or bad about their work. The answers were then subjected to a content analysis which identified that those factors that led to satisfaction were fundamentally different from those issues that lead to dissatisfaction. This he labelled the two-factor theory of motivation and named the categories motivators and hygiene factors. The theory offers some insight into the relationship between motivation and job satisfaction, and is in many ways a theory about work-related attitudes as much as it is a theory about work motivation.

Critical incident technique
Data collection method that involves asking for the most relevant aspects of experiences. The collected answers can then be systematically analysed to shed light on a particular phenomenon.

The *hygiene factors* were those that, if absent, caused dissatisfaction. They are predominantly concerned with the context within which the job is carried out and other extrinsic issues. The presence of these factors will not motivate individuals as such, but their absence will serve to create dissatisfaction with the job and organization. They included:

- salary
- working conditions
- job security
- level and quality of supervision
- company policies and administrative procedures
- interpersonal relationships at work.

The *motivating factors* were those that could motivate the individual to improve their work performance. They were primarily concerned with the content of the work, together with the way in which it formed a meaningful whole (intrinsic factors). They included:

- recognition
- sense of achievement
- responsibility
- nature of the work itself
- growth
- advancement.

Figure 5.3 Comparison of the need theories

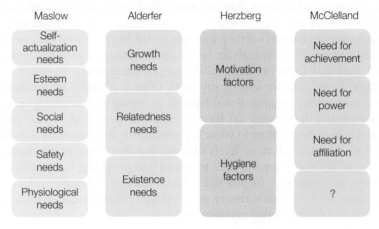

Although Herzberg did not claim a hierarchical relationship for the two factors, it is possible to compare this theory with those of Maslow, Alderfer and McClelland (see Chapter 3). This is most easily illustrated with a diagram, Figure 5.3.

The significance of Herzberg's model is that the two factors do not form opposite ends of a continuum. Lack of positive levels in the hygiene factors does not lead to demotivation, but to dissatisfaction. High levels in the hygiene factors do not lead to motivation, but to (maybe better termed contentment). High levels among the motivation factors will, however, lead to positive motivation. Conversely, low levels of motivating influences will reduce the overall level of motivation, but not create dissatisfaction; it would create feelings of nonsatisfaction. So in effect there is a nonoverlapping middle ground between these two factors, as shown in Figure 5.4.

The major implication of this theory for anyone seeking to make use of it in designing motivational practices is that they need to concentrate on two sets of factors at the same time if motivation and satisfaction are to be maintained.

ASSESSMENT OF THE THEORY

There have been a number of criticisms of Herzberg's work. They include:

- *The results obtained are research-method-dependent.* Studies which use the same research methodology as Herzberg tend to arrive at broadly similar conclusions. Research using different methods is less supportive of the conclusions.

- *The results obtained by Herzberg are capable of different interpretations.* This is the line developed by Vroom (1964). Also, the theory is not clearly set out, which has resulted in different interpretations when replicating his work (King, 1970).

Figure 5.4 Satisfaction and Herzberg's two factors

- *It does not provide for individual difference.* For example, close supervision may be resented by some yet welcomed by others.

- *In an organizational context the application of the principles implied by the model is often restricted to manual or unskilled workers.* This is surprising, given that it was developed from a research base drawn from accountants and engineers. It is often claimed that manual workers adopt an instrumental approach, concentrating on pay and security rather than the intrinsic aspects of the work. Work by Blackburn and Mann (1979), however, suggests that people in low-skilled jobs adopt a wide range of work approaches, not just economic factors.

- As with all content theories, the universal application of Herzberg's work has been criticized because of the underlying assumptions about people and work as well as the cultural basis of the work context.

These criticisms notwithstanding, the theory makes useful distinctions between different aspects of work environments and has provided important input to the development of theories and frameworks of work design (e.g., Hackman and Oldham, 1980). After the debates about the validity and usefulness of Herzberg's theory, recent reassessments of the two-factor theory indicate a surprising level of fit between the basic tenets of the theory and contemporary research in emotions and justice (e.g., Basch and Fisher, 2000) as well as in positive psychology and positive OB (Sachau, 2007). The latter areas consider issues such as well-being, happiness, and fulfilment, concerns that content theories such as Herzberg's clearly have something useful to add to.

In summary, content theories of motivation can be highly useful by providing frameworks for understanding humans, but not necessarily for providing useful predictive tools for specific behaviours. In other words, they help to explain human behaviour after the fact, but rarely allow for detailed predictions about specific human actions. Similarly, they are not usually very helpful as frameworks for developing managerial and organizational interventions aimed at influencing work motivation (see Ford, 1992). As such, we would suggest that they may serve managers and other organizational practitioners best as *part* of more comprehensive attempts to understand, predict and ultimately influence motivation at work.

5.3 EXTEND
YOUR LEARNING

PROCESS THEORIES

Process theories attempt to provide a model of the interactions between the variables involved in the motivation process. The major process theories include:

- expectancy theory
- equity theory
- goal-setting theory.

The Vroom/Porter and Lawler expectancy models

VROOM'S EXPECTANCY MODEL

The basis of expectancy models is that motivation is a function of the subjective desirability of the outcome of behaviour as well as of the perceived likelihood that behaviour will lead to such desired outcomes. Vroom (1964) first linked such subjective expectancies explicitly to work motivation in his expectancy theory (also known as VIE theory after the three key subjective components). Vroom's theory proposes that individual behaviour is based on choices people make among alternative courses of actions. These choices are determined by subjective perceptions of relative likelihoods regarding the achievement of relevant goals and the perceptions of the relevant available rewards on offer. For example, offered the opportunity to attend training courses leading to a professional qualification in return for higher performance, an employee seeking such an opportunity will be motivated. If, however, an employee was not interested in becoming professionally qualified, it would have no effect on their behaviour. Also, an offer of such training would not motivate the employee even if they were interested in becoming qualified, if they did not believe that the manager could or would deliver the opportunity.

At the heart of this theory are six elements: three observable aspects (effort, performance, outcomes), the linkages between them (expectancy, instrumentality) and the subjective value assessment of the ultimate outcomes for a person (valence). In one sentence, the theory posits that if individuals believe that behaving in a particular way will generate valued outcomes for them, they will be motivated to produce those behaviours (see Figure 5.5).

The six central elements of the theory are:

1 *Effort*. This element is the central behavioural component of the VIE model. It refers to *the actual effort people expect to have to expend to reach a specified goal or target* (which is called performance or first level outcome). In a work context this refers to the work tasks employees are charged to perform.

2 *First-level outcomes*. First-level outcomes *are the immediate results of the effort people expend*, and are thus those things that emerge directly from their behaviour and are related to the work itself. Examples include specific work outcomes such as a finished report for a business analyst, a changed break pad for a car mechanic, or a finished haircut for a hairdresser. In a work context first-level outcomes are typically what is required of workers by their supervisor or clients. While these results may well provide value for individuals, for example by providing intrinsic satisfaction, they are typically linked to some form of subsequent reward that is contingent on reaching these outcomes.

3 *Second-level outcomes*. These second-level outcomes are *the rewards that are provided to individuals depending on them performing at a satisfactory level in delivering first-level outcomes*. For example, higher levels of productivity (first-level outcome) may generate a financial bonus which is therefore a second-level outcome. The bonus is contingent on the

Figure 5.5 Vroom's expectancy model (VIE theory)

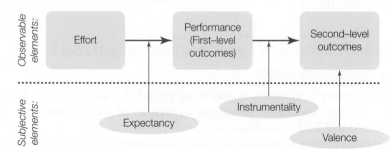

output produced, not on the original level of effort expended. For example, working harder may increase productivity (first-level outcome), but if the company did not have an incentive scheme then no financial bonus would be paid (no second-level outcome). Equally, in many organizational contexts individuals are rewarded for measured achievements rather than the amount of effort expended.

4 *Expectancy*. This refers to the *subjective assessment of the likelihood that a particular level of effort will lead to the specified performance (first-level outcomes)*. Machines and tools used in performing a particular task are liable to break down, parts may not arrive when required and other workers may not make their contributions. Also, individual ability and confidence will be taken into account. Thus, self-efficacy (see also the section on social learning theory below) is an important part of expectancy which also includes many other considerations. The result of variability and uncertainty inherent in such internal and situational factors is that the achievement of a first-level outcome may not be certain.

5 *Instrumentality*. This concept refers to the strength of the contingent link between first- and second-level outcomes. In other words, if achieving a specified first-level outcome will certainly lead to a specified second-level outcome (for example, if a sales person reaches their sales target they are assured to receive the specified commission) then instrumentality is said to be high.

6 *Valence*. This refers to *the subjective value individuals expect to receive from second-level outcomes*. Valence can be positive, negative or neutral. If positive, the individual wants to acquire or achieve the outcome, if negative the individual would wish to avoid the outcome. Neutral valence means that there are no motivational aspects attached to the particular outcome. Valance must be distinguished from value because it is based on subjective anticipation, while value reflects the actual satisfaction derived from the outcome. Thus, the motivational properties come from the anticipation of achieving the outcomes which may ultimately turn out to be inaccurate. In deciding whether to work overtime, an individual may take into account the family wish to go to the cinema that night. If the individual does not want to see the film, working late will allow them to achieve that objective (the valance). Subsequently, if the individual finds that the family could not get seats and so went to a restaurant instead, the value ultimately gained or lost through working overtime may be altered, but the valence (which was active earlier in motivating a choice and the relevant behaviour) has not changed.

The model can also formally be described in an equation which indicates the relationship among the relevant variables in determining the motivational force of a particular action alternative. A simplified formula that deals only with the positive valence is shown below (see for example Pinder, 2008, for a more complete formula). This simplified formula clarifies that the motivational force (M) of a particular action alternative (i) will be high if the relevant subjective probabilities (E, I) and value expectations (V) are relatively large. However, the multiplication also indicates that the motivational force will be negligible if any of these elements is zero. In practical terms, this means that if a salesperson does not think that she can deliver the required level of sales (i.e., expectancy = 0), and/or that the required sales performance will not lead to the expected bonus (i.e., instrumentality = 0), and/or that she does not value the expected bonus (i.e., valence = 0), she will not be motivated to try to reach the required sales level.

$$M_i = E_{ij} * I_{jk} * V_k$$

with	M_i = the motivational force associated with a particular action i i = Effort = specific action alternative i j = particular first level outcome of i E_{ij} = Expectancy = subjective probability of Effort (i) leading to result (j) I_{jk} = Instrumentality = subjective probability that 'j' will lead to second-level outcome 'k' Vk = Valence = the subjective value expected from second level outcome 'k'

THE PORTER AND LAWLER EXTENSION

Porter and Lawler (1968) developed Vroom's model further by attempting to link motivation, performance and satisfaction. It is important to note that Porter and Lawler's work focused particularly on pay rewards as outcomes and did not explicitly include any negative consequences. Their model specifies a number of additional relevant elements but retains the fundamental logic of Vroom's theory. Figure 5.6 gives a diagrammatic view of the extended model.

ASSESSMENT OF THE THEORY

Empirically, much research has used inappropriate designs that do not provide tests of the actual propositions advanced by Vroom's original theory. As an example, many researchers tested the theory across individuals rather than within individuals across different action alternatives, which was Vroom's original intention. More appropriate designs have been more supportive of the theory, but nevertheless the research support for the theory is mixed (see Pinder, 2008, for a comprehensive review). According to the expectancy model, individuals always seek to optimize the

Figure 5.6 Porter and Lawler expectancy model

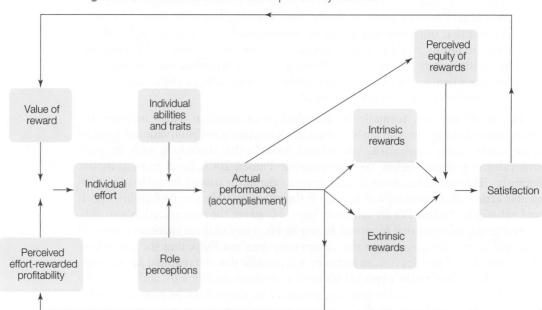

return on their effort investment. With this fundamental assumption and the theory's focus on choice it is more applicable to volitional behaviour rather than automatic behaviour.

In addition, in practice the model is difficult to apply for predicting employee motivation and behaviour because of the multitude of action alternatives. Also, human action may be motivated by long chains of means–ends relationships that are not fully captured in the two levels of outcomes specified in the model. For these reasons the analytical power of the theory may not fully capture the actual complexity of real-life situations. Nevertheless, as a basic model it can aid managerial analyses and decision making about motivational interventions by reducing otherwise prohibitively complex situations to a small number of key components. This may be one reason for the popularity of the model because it reduces complex decisions into its key components that can analysed and considered easier. Vroom (2005) himself indicates that the theory may best serve as a general heuristic for structuring managerial thinking and for developing analytical questions rather than a framework claiming accurate predictive power.

Another important aspect of VIE theory is its contribution to other areas in OB. For example, it is the basis for a theory of leadership, the *path-goal theory* (House, 1971; House and Mitchell, 1974), which is based on the leader's possible influence on followers' subjective beliefs about expectancy, instrumentality and valence through identifying a distinct path leading to particular goals. This is related to its implications for managers attempting to use it to guide their attempts to motivate employees. The key managerial use derived from expectancy theory is that managers must seek ways of strengthening the links between effort, performance and reward and the perceived value of relevant rewards. In order to apply this approach, managers need to be able to identify the employee calculus in order to be able to design appropriate arrangements. Because of the many and varied components in the equation, together with the changeable nature of it, this would become an almost impossible task to achieve with any accuracy. The complexity in attempting to apply the theory is reflected by Hollenback (1979) in which matrix algebra was needed to deal with the number and combination of variables.

Adams' equity theory

People develop strong feelings about the relative fairness of the treatment that they receive at work. When reaching a conclusion on fairness, individuals need a point of reference against which to judge what they actually experience. The main source of such comparisons are relevant other people. This formed the basis of the equity approach to motivation (Adams, 1965), based on social exchange theory (see Chapter 16). This model suggests that individuals consider and evaluate their social interactions by comparing them to standards which themselves are open to comparisons and other social influences.

Technically, equity theory argues that people compare the ratio of their own inputs (e.g., time, effort, talent, loyalty, contribution, etc.) and outcomes (e.g., pay, work conditions, benefits, learning and development opportunities, satisfaction, social recognition, fun, etc.) to that of referent others. The referent others are usually chosen based on perceived similarity and proximity. Typically, people automatically choose other employees performing the same job, the same job in other companies, friends, neighbours and professional colleagues. Industrial relations specialists are well aware of the issue of equity in pay comparisons.

If one's own exchange ratio (i.e., our input/outcome ratio) is larger than that of a chosen referent other (also called comparison other), which indicates that we provide relatively more inputs given the received outputs, we will experience *underpayment inequity*. Similarly, if our input/outcome ratio is smaller than the referent's and thus in our favour, we will experience *overpayment inequity*. The motivational aspect of equity theory lies in the proposition that *people who experience inequity will be motivated to restore feelings of equity*. This can be achieved in five fundamental ways:

1 Taking action to restore underpayment inequity through decreasing one's own exchange ratio (or decreasing the referent's). Examples may include asking for a rise in pay, requesting the referent to be assigned more demanding work, etc.

2 Restoring overpayment inequity through increasing one's own or decreasing the referent's exchange ratio. Examples may include more voluntary contribution in terms of role or extra role contributions; helping the referent directly by taking over part of the work they have to perform, etc.

3 Selecting a different referent with a comparable exchange ratio (this may also involve a change in one's preferred exchange ratio).

4 Leave the exchange relationship so the inequity is no longer relevant.

5 Cognitively re-evaluating the actual inputs and outcomes (own or referent's) to restore equity.

For Adams, the process of comparing can produce two possible outcomes, equity or inequity. Equity is achieved when a perceived balance between the individual and the comparison target is achieved. Inequity arises when the balance is disturbed in either a positive or negative direction. The individual would feel that an inequitable situation existed if, for example, they were paid more than the comparator, not just if they were paid less. Figure 5.7 reflects the operation of equity theory. Which option is chosen to restore equity will depend on a number of factors active in the situation and within the individual.

Figure 5.7 Adams' equity theory

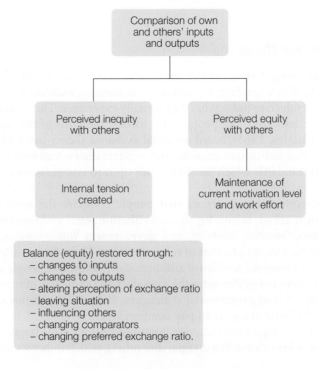

ASSESSMENT OF THE THEORY

Much of the research on equity theory has concentrated on its application to pay and rewards. Dornstein (1989) examined the basis of comparison in people's judgements about the fairness of received pay and found that it changed depending on a number of factors. Research in Hong Kong by Law and Wong (1998) suggests that the use of different methodologies to explore fairness produces differing results, further clouding the issue. Consequently, it is not clear how individuals apply the principles of equity theory; neither would managers find it easy to be sure that equity was being achieved for each individual. The problem for managers is that it is for each employee to undertake the evaluation of what 'equity' means for them because equity theory is purely based on subjective assessments of fairness. These issues will be further explored in Chapter 16.

Managers are not in a position to judge on behalf of employees what determines an equitable situation; they cannot know against what or whom the comparison is being made. However, some work in this area suggests that individuals use both instrumental and value-expressive standards when evaluating the fairness of pay procedures (Jones *et al.*, 1999), implying that not only does pay need to be allocated fairly, but that pay allocation procedures need to be perceived to be fair by those subject to them.

Working relationships are much less personal than those based on friendship and it is less likely that the same level of commitment to work-based relationships exists (Campbell and Pritchard, 1974). Consequently, it is argued that the perception of inequity will be reduced in a work context when overpayment is involved. It is more likely that in their own work context individuals will change the basis of their view of what forms an equitable payment (Locke, 1976).

Even with the limitations described, the model provides a useful mechanism for considering the significance of equity between employees along with the implications for motivation and performance of failing to achieve a perception of it. These points are particularly relevant to the subject of pay and other tangible outcomes of work (see Chapter 12). The theory implies that organizations should give close attention to the comparison process when designing pay structures, incentive schemes, merit awards and even promotion, to increase perceived equity for individuals. This may not be the same as actual ("objective") equity. The earlier chapter on perception (Chapter 3) provides enough basis for understanding the significance of it as a personal and largely subjective interpretation process rather than a simple registration of facts or reality.

Locke's goal-setting theory

Locke (1968) suggested that people's objectives play a significant part in formulating their behavioural patterns. In fact, the position that goals provide both direction and motivation for human behaviour is the basis for goal-setting theory. Goal-setting theory (e.g., Locke and Latham, 1990, 2002) posits that *goal difficulty*, *goal specificity* (e.g., target, time, achievement level and circumstances) and *commitment to the goal* will lead to higher task motivation and thus higher performance. In a work context, this can be used as a mechanism to motivate people to deliver desired behaviours. For the process to work it is necessary that organizations are able to ensure commitment to goals, for example through participative goal setting, alignment of individual and organizational goals, or through appropriate incentive schemes that make the achievement of organizational goals instrumental for individuals to achieve their own personal goals.

Goal setting is therefore used as the basis of performance appraisal systems which attempt to shape employee behaviour and achieve improved performance. The essence of such processes is that employees who meet the performance standards expected by management are likely to be rewarded with higher salary, career development opportunities or promotion. These are all objectives that most people value (the reason why that might be so represents an interesting question in its own right, but is beyond the scope of this discussion). Performance appraisal systems are a formal feedback mechanism to direct employee behaviour towards the achievement of management-determined objectives. A generalized model of goal theory is shown as Figure 5.8. Note 'goal deficiency' in the model refers to the level of desire in the individual to achieve the goal, which as mentioned above can be based on numerous different reasons.

In modern performance appraisal use these ideas have been refined into the so-called SMART objectives that form the basis of determining performance objectives. The acronym SMART stands for setting objectives that are specific, measurable, attainable, realistic and time bounded (Armstrong and Murliss, 1998: p. 247). SMART objectives are often used in a particular management approach called *management by objectives* (MBO) which focuses on achieving agreed goals in a system of recurring explicit and structured mutual goal setting and review.

SMART objectives
Refers to objectives that are Specific, Measurable, Attainable, Realistic and Time bounded.

ASSESSMENT OF THE THEORY

There have been a large number of studies of goal-setting approaches to motivation (for example, Early *et al.*, 1990; Erez *et al.*, 1985, Shalley *et al.*, 1987), and proponents of the theory claim that it is one of the empirically best supported theories in management and OB (e.g., Latham, 2007; Mitchell and Daniels, 2003). Generally the results have been very supportive of the approach, but raise questions that remain unanswered. For example, special circumstances (e.g., creativity goals, learning goals, unclear performance evaluation criteria, etc.) can introduce difficulties in determining the best way to apply goal-setting theory in particular situations. Also, issues such as subjective approaches to attribute and frame goals and goal-directed behaviour (Jain *et al.*, 2009), achievements (Koo and Fishbach, 2008) and performance (McCrea, 2008) provide interesting insights into micro-processes of goal-induced motivation. Much research addresses such specific issues, and the basic theory continues to be elaborated and extended based on sound research findings (see Latham, 2007; and Pinder, 2008, for detailed discussions).

Nevertheless, the current model does have limitations. In some work contexts it is difficult to specify goals, and increasingly turbulent operating environments require goals to be frequently adjusted and even changed mid-task. This makes it increasingly

Figure 5.8 Goal theory

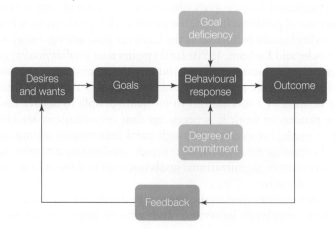

difficult for individuals to maintain performance targeted at specific goals over an extended period. Goal setting represents an individual level process, but most tasks within an organization require groups of people to co-operate in order to achieve them. This reality of organizational life means that it is frequently difficult to provide enough individual control over work activity to be certain that goal-setting theory is effectively motivating behaviour. Other critics argue that goal setting, if not used carefully and appropriately, can be associated with selective and thus incomplete performance, distorted risk preferences, increasing unethical behavior, inhibited learning, negative effects on organizational culture, and reduced intrinsic motivation (Ordóñez *et al.*, 2009a). These arguments are bitterly disputed between proponents and critics of the theory (Latham and Locke, 2009; Locke and Latham, 2009; Ordóñez *et al.*, 2009a, 2009b). Moreover, despite the research support for its key propositions, goal-setting theory as outlined by is proponents does not explain why and how goal setting actually motivates individual behaviour. Thus, its status as an explanatory theory remains questionable. However, in sales, production and stable service situations goal setting an clearly provide a highly appropriate and valuable framework for managerial action as long as potential detrimental effects are considered and actively managed.

5.4 EXTEND
YOUR LEARNING

BEHAVIOURIST THEORIES

Behaviourist approaches have a long and illustrious tradition in psychology. The basic argument of behaviourism is that behaviour is determined by its consequences. Thus, they focus on learning rather than motivation because they try to explain how an organism learns to behave in certain ways. This is the reason why these approaches are also called learning theories (the companion website provides material on other approaches to learning).

Fundamentally, behaviourism focuses only on observable behaviour and treats what happens inside the mind of people as a 'black box'. In practical terms, this means that such approaches do not deal with cognition at all, but rather restrict their investigations and theorizing to observable aspects of behaviour and do not directly engage with the concept of motivation. We are including them in this chapter, however, because they represent an important attempt to provide a comprehensive approach to explaining behaviour.

5.5 EXTEND
YOUR LEARNING

Pavlov and classical conditioning

Pavlov carried out his research in Russia and was concerned with how dogs learned their natural reflexes. Pavlov noticed that whenever his laboratory dogs were given food they salivated (1927). This was a natural reaction in the dogs, to which he gave the term 'unconditioned response'. This became the first step in the conditioning process. The second step was to link what Pavlov termed the unconditioned stimulus (food) with a conditioned stimulus (the ringing of a bell). This was done by ringing the bell on each occasion on which food was presented. Pavlov was trying to get the dogs to learn that the sound of the bell was associated with the appearance of food. After several repetitions, the dogs salivated automatically when the bell was rung. This was the third step in the conditioning process, the conditioned response. A direct link between the stimulus (bell sound) and the response (salivation) had been made - Figure 5.9. In the classical conditioning model, salivation was conditioned to occur because of the previously established association between bell and food.

The conditioned response is a relatively simple reaction when compared with human behaviour, particularly in a social setting. This theory was able to explain some of the simpler forms of learning but the conditioned response quickly extinguished if

Classical conditioning
An approach to learning developed by Pavlov in which he used dogs to demonstrate that when the conditioned stimulus (bell) was associated with an unconditioned stimulus (food) over several repetitions a conditioned response resulted (salivation to the sound of the bell). See also Operant conditioning.

Conditioned
The behaviour of an individual which results from the application of behaviourism techniques.

Figure 5.9 Pavlov's classical conditioning model

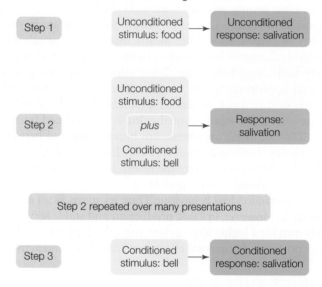

not frequently reinforced. This feature was referred to as an extinction response and makes it more difficult to explain how classical conditioning could build learning from the spontaneous, dynamic and random nature of much human interaction and experience. Pavlov was able to make his experimental dogs respond to a wide range of bell-related variables, so demonstrating a generalizable stimulus dimension which might explain some of the links with real experience.

Pavlov's work ran in parallel, although independently, with a number of American theorists. They included Watson, who coined the term 'behaviourism' to describe the emphasis on observable behaviour rather than the introspective approaches common in psychology at that time. Watson believed that learning in the environment was responsible for almost all development in the growing child. He introduced the concept of stimulus–response association (conditioning) as the basis of much routine behaviour (Watson, 1924). For example, a manager who sometimes shouts at employees to ensure that instructions are followed might discover after a while that employees do not respond to instructions that are not shouted.

Thorndike (1932) built on this stimulus–response model through his studies of cats trying to escape from puzzle boxes. From these observations he concluded that the cats could learn by trial and error (slow learning). Thorndike suggested that the process involved a slow strengthening of the stimulus–response connection through a number of repetitions of the cat being placed in the puzzle box, being allowed to escape and receiving a food reward immediately afterwards. The reinforcement offered by food made it more likely that the cat would repeat the same behaviour next time. Thorndike also coined the term 'law of effect' - *behaviour is a function of its consequences*. While this law has been criticized on both logical and empirical grounds, updated versions are still part of behaviourist theory today.

Law of effect
This states that behaviour is a function of its consequences.

Linked together, these early models and approaches provided the basis for applying behaviourist theory to more complex forms of learned behaviour. This basic stimulus–response model (S/R model) can explain simple cause and effect relationships evident in many activities. However, it cannot effectively explain the wide variety of more complex, purposeful behaviour. This classical model (as it became known) does not allow for choice in behaviour response options evident in most human interaction. The actual behavioural responses occurring will depend upon a wide variety of factors acting on the individuals in that situation.

Skinner and operant conditioning

B.F. Skinner, an American psychologist, is associated with operant conditioning (also called instrumental conditioning). Instrumental in this context refers to behaviour as 'instrumental' in producing an effect. For example, a hungry rat can be conditioned to press a lever by providing food for the delivery of the behaviour.

Skinner put forward a distinction between two types of behaviour, respondent and operant (1953). Respondent behaviour was said to be under the direct control of a stimulus (such as biologically hardwired responses). This was the stimulus–response relationship in classical conditioning, for example, salivation in response to food presentation. Operant behaviour, conversely, was seen in terms of spontaneity, with no direct or obvious cause. A stimulus controlling operant behaviour is referred to as a discriminative stimulus. An example would be the knocking on your front door, which tells you that someone is trying to see you for some purpose, but does not force you to answer the door. In this way the concept is synonymous with the term 'instrumental' in that the behaviour (answering the door) is instrumental in producing an effect (finding out why someone was knocking on it).

The best-known experiments in this area involve laboratory rats being placed in a Skinner box. A hungry rat is placed in the box and left to explore its new surroundings. As the rat approaches the lever in the box a pellet of food will be made available in the food tray. After a few repetitions of this, the rat may accidentally touch the lever and again food will be made available. Then only touching the lever produces food. Subsequently, this is also replaced with pressing the lever being required to release food. Lever pressing is reinforced by the presentation of food. There are an enormous range of variations that can be introduced to this basic process. Pigeons have been taught to play table tennis, whales and dolphins trained for wildlife shows and dolphins trained to hunt for underwater mines.

Operant conditioning works through the process of changing the likelihood or frequency of specific operant behaviours. A process called *reinforcement* is used to shape (i.e., to *create or encourage particular behaviour patterns through application of reinforcement*) the desired behaviour pattern (i.e., the target behaviour). In general, operant conditioning and the reinforcement process involves four different individual processes that are differentiated through their result (the increase or decrease in the likelihood of a target behaviour occurring) and through either the addition or removal of a contingent response. These four processes include positive (and negative) reinforcement which refer to *the process of administering (or removing) particular responses to increases the likelihood of the target behaviour occurring*. The other two related processes are punishment (i.e., *the administration of responses that reduces the likelihood of the target behaviour occurring*) and extinction. Extinction refers to *the removal of a response with the result that the likelihood of the target behaviour decreases*. Figure 5.10 provides an overview of the four processes used in operant conditioning as well as brief examples.

Once established, a target behaviour that has been shaped through reinforcement does not need to be reinforced every time to maintain it. There are four types of reinforcement schedules that can influence the level and rate of continued repetition of the target behaviour. They are:

1 *Fixed ratio*. Reinforcement occurs after a fixed number of repetitions of a particular activity. For example, one pellet of food every 20 lever presses. This tends to produce a consistently steady rate of response in order for the respondent to be able to maximize the reward.

2 *Variable ratio*. The reward (reinforcement) results from a randomly varied number of repetitions of the desired behaviour. This produces a consistently

Operant conditioning
An approach to learning based on the reinforcement of particular behaviours by a trainer, which consequently shapes it into the desired pattern. See also Classical conditioning.

Shape
To create or encourage particular behaviour patterns in another individual through the principles of reinforcement.

Reinforcement
The encouragement of particular behaviours through the application of positive and/or negative rewards, based on the application of four schedules: fixed ratio; variable ratio; fixed interval; variable interval.

Positive reinforcement
This refer to the process of administering particular responses to increase the likelihood of the target behaviour occurring. See also negative reinforcement, punishment and extinction.

Negative reinforcement
This refer to the process of removing particular responses to increase the likelihood of the target behaviour occurring. See also positive reinforcement, punishment and extinction.

Punishment
The administration of responses that reduces the likelihood of the target behaviour occurring. See also positive reinforcement, negative reinforcement and extinction.

Extinction
This refers to the removal of response with the result that the likelihood of the target behaviour decreases. See also positive reinforcement, negative reinforcement and punishment.

Figure 5.10 The four central processes used in operant conditioning

Administering or removing a consequence of behaviour?

	Administering consequence	Removing consequence
Increasing	**Positive reinforcement** Administering positive consequences for target behaviour. *Example:* Rat receives food for pulling a lever. *Result:* Rat increases lever pulling.	**Negative reinforcement** Removing negative consequences for target behaviour. *Example:* Loud noise is muted when rat steps on a button. *Result:* Rat increases stepping on the button.
Decreasing	**Punishment** Administering negative consequences for target behaviour. *Example:* Dog receives electric shock for crossing garden boundary. *Result:* Dog will stop crossing the garden boundary.	**Extinction** Removing whatever consequences currently reinforce target behaviour. *Example:* Dog is ignored when licking people's hands. *Result:* Dog will stop licking people's hands.

Increasing or decreasing likelihood of behaviour?

rapid rate of response as the respondent (rat in a Skinner box) has no way of predicting which response (lever press) will produce the pellet of food.

3 *Fixed interval.* This produces a reinforcement following the first appropriate behaviour after a set time interval. The behaviour pattern under this regime almost stops after a reward until the next time interval is due, when it starts again. This suggests that the animal is able to judge time and work out the schedule that it is being conditioned to.

4 *Variable interval.* The time interval at which food becomes available is randomly varied between upper and lower parameters. The animal responds with a consistently rapid rate of lever pressing. This would be expected as there is no way for the animal to know which lever press triggers food because it cannot predict the random variation in time. It must continually respond at a rapid rate in order to obtain food as it becomes available.

It is the partial reinforcement schedules described (2 and 4) that produce sustained and rapid response rates and are therefore the most effective in maintaining the desired behaviour. In one experiment a pigeon was 'reinforced' on average once every 5 minutes. That equated to 12 times every hour. Yet it sustained a pecking rate of approximately 6000 per hour! In human terms this form of reinforcement is used by gaming machines, lottery and other forms of gambling to 'hook' participants into continually spending their money - the next bet might produce the 'big' win!

Many experiments related to operant conditioning are based on animals, but they also work on humans. Stanley Kubrick's film *A Clockwork Orange* graphically depicts an example of such principles being used in a form of aversion therapy. In less extreme form the principles and processes of operant conditioning are used in many areas, including childrearing, education, health and mental health services, and in work organizations – see Organizational Behaviour Modification (OB Mod) which is discussed in Chapter 12.

The process of operant conditioning has a wider application than the classical approach. It provides for the shaping of behaviour into particular patterns. It has also been used to account for many of the beliefs and superstitions that pervade human life. Examples include blowing on the dice to make them lucky; putting on a particular item of clothing before an exam in order to guarantee success; and never watching a favourite football team live on television to improve their chance of winning. The difficulty arises in being able to explain how reinforcement operates in the everyday exposure to multiple and random experience. Despite its success in influencing many behaviours in a variety of settings, operant conditioning has limitations both in its application and in its ability to provide explanations and predictions. Individuals have objectives and purpose behind many of their behaviours which do not easily fit into a model based on the principles of operant conditioning.

RECENT CONTRIBUTIONS TO WORK MOTIVATION

Some additional motivational theories and frameworks have more recently generated significant interest and research attention and have become useful additions to the available frameworks that can be deployed to try to understand and influence work motivation. A number of recent contributions review and provide detail of current work on motivation theory (e.g., Kanfer *et al.*, 2008; Latham, 2007; Latham and Pinder, 2005; Locke and Latham, 2004; Pinder, 2008; Steers *et al.*, 2004). We will here focus on two of the most relevant approaches, and conclude with a brief discussion of current issues and future developments in motivation theory and research.

Bandura's social-cognitive theory

Social-cognitive theory (SCT) grew out of the behaviouristic approaches discussed above. In contrast to the purely behaviouristic approach, however, it includes cognitive elements (such as outcome expectancies, social influences, self-control, and others) in its consideration of the determinants of human behaviour. The main researcher associated with its development is Albert Bandura, an American psychologist long associated with Stanford University. His work in developing and specifying SCT (such as Bandura, 1977, 1986, 1997, 2001) has been one of the most influential individual contributions of the final quarter of the last century in both psychology and OB.

In short, SCT is based on the recognition that behaviour is determined by the *reciprocal determinism* among three elements, namely the person's cognition and other personal factors (e.g., thoughts, feelings, expectations, observations, etc.), the environment with the opportunities, limitations and consequences it provides, and the person's behaviour which produces changes and outcomes in both of the other elements. Important aspects of this theory that extend beyond its behaviouristic origins include (a) the notion of vicarious learning; (b) dynamics of self-control absent from behaviouristic views of behaviour; and (c) the important concept of self-efficacy.

Vicarious learning, which refers to *learning through observation of others*, is an important part of organizational life. Many newcomers learn how to behave by observing others. Similarly, people do not need to experience everything first-hand to change their behaviour subsequently. If an employee observes a co-worker failing to shut down a machine before conducting maintenance and subsequently getting injured she is likely to take note of this and change her own subsequent behaviour (i.e., she will more likely shut down the machine before repairing it). Vicarious learning works with positive as well as negative experiences of others (for example, observing which behaviours are rewarded or punished by managers). For vicarious learning to occur, conditions such as observability and accurate perception of other's behaviour, memory for the behaviour and/or the lesson learned, relevant ability and opportunity to apply the lesson learned, presence of relevant consequences, and

Vicarious learning
Refers to learning through
the observation of others.

appropriate attribution of the linkage between observed behaviour and such consequences, are necessary. Vicarious learning also highlights the role of social information and social influence in determining behaviour.

Self-control is a notion absent from behaviouristic explanations of behaviour. It refers to *the largely autonomous determination and adjustment of behaviour without simultaneous environmental influence*. Self-control is said to take place when individuals exert low-probability behaviours (i.e., behaviours not directly reinforced by their environment). Self-control requires the availability of self-reinforcers (i.e., consequences for own behaviour), and the presence of goals and application of self-reinforcement based on progress in goal achievement.

Self-efficacy is *the belief about one's ability to perform a particular behaviour successfully*. It is not a generalized orientation such as self-esteem, a general attitude based on assessments of one's own abilities such as self-confidence, or a reflection of one's own abilities such as a competence assessment. Instead, it is limited to a particular prospective behaviour in specific circumstances. As a belief, self-efficacy is open to social influence and other potential determinants. In fact, the four sources of self-efficacy include one's own experience with performing relevant tasks in the past, vicarious experiences of others, verbal persuasion or other social influence from others, and an assessment of one's own physiological (e.g., heartbeat, sweating) and emotional state (see also Bandura, 1997; Gist, 1987; Gist and Mitchell, 1992).

Self-efficacy is an important predictor of individual performance. Newer research has tried to assess if the aspect of task-specificity inherent in original conceptions of this concept can be relaxed, and if generalized self-efficacy, which refers to an *assessment of one's competence across different tasks and settings*, exists. Conceptual arguments and empirical evidence appear to support this notion (e.g., Chen *et al.*, 2001, 2004; deRue and Morgeson, 2007; Eden, 2001). Other extensions of this important motivational concept are the application to groups and other social entities as having collective self-efficacy (e.g., Gibson and Earley, 2007; Hardin *et al.*, 2007; Tasa *et al.*, 2007; Zaccaro *et al.*, 1995).

Self-determination theory (SDT)

Another theory that has grown out of substantial earlier research and debates is self-determination theory (SDT) (Deci and Ryan, 1985, 2000; Gagné and Deci, 2005; Ryan and Deci, 2000). The origins of this theory can be traced back to the distinction between intrinsic and extrinsic motivation discussed earlier in this chapter. Based on empirical research, Deci (1975) argued that extrinsic motivators can influence intrinsic motivation, such that payment for a voluntary activity can lead to different attributions about why the activity is undertaken (e.g., Deci, 1971). As an example, if a child helping to wash a car is paid for the work they do they may reappraise the reasons for participating and subsequently see car washing as work, not fun. This *overjustification* (or *undermining*) *effect* of extrinsic motivators on intrinsic motivation, central to cognitive evaluation theory (CET) which was developed by Deci and Ryan in the 1970s (Deci, 1975; Deci and Ryan, 1980), subsequently led to significant debates about the role of intrinsic and extrinsic motivators, the dynamics between these types of motivation, the nature of intrinsic and extrinsic motivation, and the role of choice for intrinsic motivation (see Gagné and Deci, 2005; Patall *et al.*, 2008; Pinder, 2008, for relevant recent reviews). Empirical support for the undermining effect is mixed, and CET in its original formulations has fallen somewhat out of favour.

Further work by Deci and colleages, however, led to the development of SDT. This theory distinguishes between *autonomous motivation* (where *behaviour is based*

Self-control
This a notion absent from behaviouristic explanations of behaviour. It refers to the largely autonomous determination and adjustment of behaviour without simultaneous environmental influence.

Self-efficacy
Belief about one's ability to perform a particular behaviour in specific circumstances successfully. See also generalized self-efficacy.

Generalized self-efficacy
This refers to an assessment of one's competence across different tasks and settings. See also self-efficacy.

Self-determination theory (SDT)
A theory that distinguishes between autonomous motivation (where behaviour is based on volition and active choice) and controlled motivation (where behaviour is based on external consequences determined by decisions or dynamics outside the person).

on volition and active choice) and *controlled motivation* (where *behaviour is based on external consequences determined by decisions or dynamics outside the person*). Autonomous motivation is based on internal needs (see below) and is associated with intrinsic motivation. In contrast, controlled motivation is based on *external regulation* (i.e., *the behaviour is 'initiated and maintained by contingencies external to the person'*, Gagné and Deci, 2005: p. 334) and is purely associated with extrinsic motivation.

SDT argues that three needs lie at the heart of human motivation: competence, autonomy, and relatedness. Also, SDT addresses shortcomings of the earlier CET by distinguishing between four different levels of extrinsic motivation depending on the degree to which behavioural regulation originates solely outside or is shared between external and internal control (see Ryan, 1995; Ryan and Deci, 2000). These four levels are called, in order of increasing autonomous control: external regulation, introjected regulation, identified regulation and integrated regulation (see Table 5.1 for an overview).

SDT provides a useful framework for considering the nature of motivation and the interaction between internal and external control of behaviour in many areas of human endeavour (Deci and Ryan, 2008). Furthermore, it offers an interesting direction for further research in applied areas, and Gagné and Deci (2005) have outlined many promising issues and avenues for further research into the role of intrinsic and extrinsic motivation for work motivation that should stimulate additional empirical studies and further theoretical development. Proponents of the theory have also argued that SDT is compatible with many of the other motivational theories used in OB (Gagné and Deci, 2005), and that it offers unique opportunities to investigate important questions about work motivation such as the role of pay and other rewards on motivation (Gagné and Forest, 2008). The mixed empirical support for earlier aspects of the theory notwithstanding, SDT appears promising. It is particularly valuable because of its focus on intrinsic motivation. This can help address the substantive criticism of the use of motivation theories as dehumanizing

Table 5.1 Continuum of self-determination according to SDT

Increasingly autonomous control of behaviour	Inherently autonomous regulation	Behaviour is intrinsically motivated by serving a person's needs for competence, autonomy and relatedness.
	Integrated regulation	Behaviour is autonomously controlled through complete integration (i.e., full internalization) of originally external motivation.
	Identified regulation	Behaviour is partially autonomously controlled through identification with external values, objectives, rules and expectations.
	Introjected regulation	Behaviour is mostly externally controlled but is administered in part internally through the partial internalization of external expectations injected into internal evaluation dynamics. Motivation is partially externally controlled.
	Controlled regulation	Behaviour is externally controlled through reward and punishment contingencies and their influence on controlled motivation.
	Lack of intentional regulation	No intentional behaviour and thus no intentional regulation of behaviour due to a lack of effective motivation (= '*amotivation*').

Source: Adapted from Deci and Ryan, 2000; Gagné and Deci, 2005; Gagné and Forest, 2008; Ryan, 1995.

MANAGEMENT IN ACTION

Motivation lessons from the 'Bear'

'Bear' (real name Rupert) Grylls was the youngest person to have climbed Mount Everest at the age of 23. Grylls nearly died twice on that climb, once when a massive sheet of ice over a ravine gave way and secondly when his oxygen ran out on the descent when he was still in the 'death zone' above 26 000 feet. Four people in his party of climbers died during that expedition. He is well used to danger and the role of motivation, having spent 3 years with the British Special Forces (SAS) during which he broke his back in three places when a parachute failed to open. He subsequently spent 18 months in rehabilitation and only his dogged determination and the support and encouragement of his family and friends meant that he walked again. One of his recent adventures was to sail round the Arctic Circle in an inflatable boat with four other people. To fund that adventure he had to raise £300 000 in sponsorship money, which he did in an amazing 9 months. Grylls believes that we live in a culture in which people are afraid to take risks in any area of life - but that taking risks brings the highest personal rewards.

Adventure implies a hazardous undertaking in which the outcome is uncertain. But today the level of tolerable hazard has been almost eliminated. For example, Grylls explained that on a visit to Nepal he had witnessed two young, highly intelligent trekkers express shock and anger that their Sherpa leader was not carrying a satellite phone to call for a helicopter when one of them became ill with altitude sickness. The concern was understandable, if ironic, as they had spent several thousand pounds to trek to Everest Base Camp. Yet they could not accept the same level of uncertainty, risk and adventure as the original 1953 pioneers. For example, Polar exploration in the early days involved:

- Taking a ship through treacherous ice and seas.
- The use of ponies or huskies as draft animals (until they had to be shot for food).
- The use of heavy wooden sledges.
- Clothes made from oilskins and to include woolly jumpers, longjohns and furs.
- The use of box camera, tripod, photographic plates to record journey.

- Food consisting of salted meat (ponies and husky).
- Navigation by compass and sextant.
- A record of the progress in a diary (often left in snow after death).

This can be compared with Polar exploration now, which involves:

- Travel by air taxi to the Antarctic.
- The use of a kite or sail attached to body harness.
- The use of a lightweight sled moulded from polyethylene.
- Clothing made from various synthetic materials and compounds including a polartech jacket, neoprene mask and polypropylene gloves.
- The use of a digital video camera, minidisc recorder to record journey.
- The consumption of vacuum-packed dried food.
- Navigation using a global positioning system and satellite tracking beacon linked to interactive Internet map.

In a talk to the Chartered Institute of Personnel and Development in October 2003, he said his key message about motivation and superior team performance in difficult conditions was:

- Look after each other.
- By giving a little extra you can turn the ordinary into the extraordinary.
- Give your whole heart to the project.
- Using your passion can create magic.

Grylls focuses his talks on those simple qualities that make the difference between life and death on a mountain: the intimacies and realities of teamwork, the honesty needed in intense environments and the courage that comes not from bravado but from something deep inside the individual. Bear's story focuses on that ability to find something special, deep inside, when it matters - not a transient, chest-beating form of motivation that fades when the going gets tough, but the discovery of a core drive, that sustains the individual through the most difficult times. They include:

- An instinct to achieve.
- A quiet strength.
- The realization that no-one is super-human and that we are all fragile.
- Understanding that as humans we are built to excel.
- It is about finding that little bit 'extra' – that vital word that makes the difference between the ordinary and the 'extraordinary'.

TASK

1 How might the ideas of the 'Bear' be turned into motivational practice by managers working in conventional organizations?

Sources:
Glover, C. (2003) A cold feat, *People Management*, 28 August, pp. 22–23.
Goodwin, Stephen (2003) Focus: Great Scott! Whatever Has Happened To Our Spirit Of Adventure? *Independent on Sunday*, Sunday, 5 January.
http://www.dailyecho.co.uk/heritage/hampshire100/100residents/1485263.Bear_Grylls/ (accessed July 2009).
http://www.beargrylls.com/talks.html (accessed July 2009).

and ultimately self-defeating managerial tools (e.g., Foucault, 1977; Sprenger, 2002; Townley, 1994). In this context it is worth considering the contribution to motivation from individuals who have achieved some measure of prominence though engaging in extremely challenging tasks, extreme sports, or undertaking other activities which place them voluntarily at considerable risk. One such individual is Rupert 'Bear' Grylls. Some of his contributions to motivational speaking are outlined in the Management in Action panel.

Other contemporary research directions into work motivation

A number of areas in current work motivation research promise useful insights for understanding and managing motivation in organizations. One important area is the research on organizational justice which in part is based on equity theory but has since far surpassed the propositions of Adams' (1965) work. Because of the fundamental impact that subjective fairness experiences have on employee experiences, attitudes, cognitions and emotions, this area is likely to contribute significantly to our insights into work motivation. We will review and discuss organizational justice in much more detail in Chapter 16.

Another area that promises insights into motivation, especially for peak performance (see also Fullagar and Mills, 2008), is the concept of flow (Csikszentmihalyi, 1990) which refers to *the complete involvement in an activity that enables all relevant task skills and emotional and cognitive resources to be employed in an experience that is intensely fulfilling and satisfying.* Such optimal experiences enable immense levels of performance – in sports players of talk about such experiences as being 'in the zone'. Clearly, the benefits for both organizations and individuals from finding ways to create *flow* promise to be immense. Similar ideas are addressed in research on passion at work. However, passion and other extreme forms of work motivation also harbour dangers of negative consequences for individuals and their families as well as for organizations (see also Linstead and Brewis, 2007). Particular negative aspects of extreme work-motivation are workaholism and other work-related addictions (see Burke, 2007; Burke and Fiksenbaum, 2009). See the Examining Ethics example introduced at the beginning of this chapter for a discussion of some of these issues.

Flow
This refers to the complete involvement in an activity that enables all relevant task skills and emotional and cognitive resources to be employed in an experience that is intensely fulfilling and satisfying.

Finally, an area of particular importance is the investigation of subconscious dynamics contributing to (or detracting from) work motivation. Similar to the distinction between conscious and subconscious aspects of personality (see Chapter 3) as well as the two modes in the dual process model of cognitions (e.g., Feldman Barrett *et al.*, 2004; Satpute and Lieberman, 2006) and the dynamics of explicit versus implicit attitudes (e.g., Rydell and McConnell, 2006; Wilson *et al.*, 2000) discussed in Chapter 4, implicit motives can interact with explicit, conscious motives and thus affect work motivation (Kehr, 2004). Implicit information processing can explain how complex motivational decision making, for example in expectancy models, can take place without overwhelming individuals (e.g., Lord *et al.*, 2003) and help account for higher information processing speed for more difficult goals (Wegge and Dibblett, 2000). In addition, subconsciously priming goals and activating implementation intentions along with conscious goals can have profound influence on task behaviour (e.g., Gollwitzer, 1999; Bargh *et al.*, 2001) by increasing persistence and effort. More generally, the complex roles of conscious and unconscious aspects of personality and their potential impact on work motivation deserve additional attention (Locke and Latham, 2004; Stewart and Roth, 2007).

5.6 EXTEND YOUR LEARNING

STOP & CONSIDER

Motivation is an individual level response. Yet organizations must operate in a collective environment – company policies, collective agreements, employment legislation and so on all expect people to be treated in broadly similar ways. To what extent does that imply that organizations cannot motivate all employees all the time; and what might the implications of that be?

CONCLUSIONS

Motivation is essentially an individual level response and yet managers must operate most of the time at a collective level. This reality of individual behaviour within a collective endeavour (organization) has many consequences. For example, how can managers ensure that every employee is fully motivated all of the time and yet retain internal consistency and fairness in the application of company policies and procedures? This dilemma, which exists (and must be constantly resolved) within an ever changing work and behavioural dynamic, places a heavy burden on most managers as they attempt to increase the levels of performance among their employees by adopting individual, collective and personalized collective methods intended to maximize motivation levels.

The general conclusion, therefore, seems to be that motivation is intuitively attractive in explanatory terms and offers opportunities for managers to enhance the nature and meaning of work for individuals. However, it

is not possible to offer a definitive explanation of motivation, how it relates to performance, or how it should be used in practice. It is a social and political concept as well as being psychological in nature and of practical significance. Its application represents another opportunity for creativity in the lives of managers as they seek to optimize corporate (and individual) performance by capitalizing on the potential available through that most valuable and adaptable of resources – the employee.

Now to summarize this chapter in terms of the relevant Learning Objectives:

● **Describe the major motivation theories and the ways in which they can be classified.** Motivation theories are usually split into two main groups - content and process. Content theories concentrate on identifying the motives that produce behaviour, whereas process theories emphasize mechanisms that encourage (or reward) behaviour in the dynamic context. There is a third category of motivation theory representing individual contributions to the field and do not fall neatly into either of the other two categories. The major content theories include contributions by Maslow, Alderfer and Herzberg. The major process theories include contributions by Vroom, Porter and Lawler, Adams and Locke. Among other approaches to motivation discussed are the behaviourist models of conditioning proposed by Pavlov, Watson and Skinner. Perspectives offered in more recent times proposed by Bandura (SCT); Deci (and others) – SDT; and flow based on Csikszentmihalyi's work.

● **Explain the difference between content and process theories of motivation.** Content theories emphasize particular aspects of an individual's needs or the goals that they seek to achieve as the basis for motivated behaviour. The major theories falling into this classification include:

   – Maslow's hierarchy of needs theory

   – Alderfer's existence, relatedness and growth (ERG) theory

   – Herzberg's two-factor theory.

Process theories attempt to provide a model of the interactions between the variables involved in the motivation process. The major process theories include:

   – expectancy theory

   – equity theory

   – goal-setting theory.

● **Understand what makes the study of motivation difficult**. The study of motivation is difficult because it is a cognitive process that cannot be observed directly so that inferences must be drawn from observable behaviour or answers to questions. Motivation is not something that can be physically taken apart and examined under a microscope in a laboratory. It is also subject to variation between individuals, groups, cultures and organizational experience. Because of the range of influences on how individuals relate to the work that they are expected to do and what it is that 'encourages' them to produce particular behaviours in that context it is very difficult to identify how these processes function for each individual. Consequently, different research approaches to the study of motivation can produce different models and explanations of how motivation might work.

● **Discuss the dilemmas and difficulties facing managers in applying motivation theory to a work setting**. One difficulty facing managers as they seek to motivate employees is that of trying to personalize the approach adopted to meet individual needs, whilst staying within the boundaries of collective consistency required by corporate policy and practice. Another difficulty for managers is to understand which theory of motivation they should follow. There are many different models of motivation available and each has something to offer in relation to understanding what it is and how it operates. Deciding which approach is most appropriate to the circumstances and individuals is no easy task. The manager's personal beliefs (and experience) play a significant part in their preference for which approach delivers high performance from employees. Some managers believe that money is the only way to motivate, others believe that such approaches only achieve compliance and will not deliver high levels of motivation consistently. There are ethical issues associated with seeking ever greater levels of performance from employees. Another difficulty is that performance often means different things for each stakeholder within the organization - begging the question 'what performance should be maximized?'

● **Assess the contribution of Bandura's social-cognitive theory to the understanding of motivation**. SCT grew out of the earlier behavioural approaches. In contrast to the purely behavioural approach, it actively includes cognitive elements (including outcome expectancies, social influences, etc.) in considering the determinants of behaviour. Bandura's work in developing SCT was a very influential individual contribution to both psychology and OB over the last 30 years. SCT recognizes that behaviour is determined by the reciprocal determinism among three elements. Firstly the person's cognition and other personal factors (e.g., thoughts, feelings, etc.). Secondly the environment with the opportunities, limitations and consequences it provides. Thirdly individual behaviour which produces changes and outcomes in both of the other two elements. Important aspects of this theory that extend beyond its behavioural origins include (a) vicarious learning; (b) dynamics of self-control absent from behaviourism; and (c) self-efficacy. Its value for motivation theory is its ability to integrate a broader range of variables into a complex set of relationships between variables which impact on individual motivation. It represents a 'richer' approach than many of the earlier formulaic or prescriptive approaches to the subject.

DISCUSSION QUESTIONS

1 Explain why people would become motivated to participate in extreme sports, using material discussed in this chapter to support your argument.

2 If you were a manager, would you prefer to have your team extrinsically or intrinsically motivated? Why?

3 Motivation is best achieved through offering employees a monetary reward for working harder. Discuss this statement in the light of the material presented in this chapter.

4 Briefly explain Bandura's SCT and compare its approach to motivation with that of Maslow. What conclusions about motivations at work do you draw from your answer?

5 Imagine that you are the manager of a call-centre selling car insurance and dealing with customer queries in relation to the same product range. How and to what extent could you build self-actualization into the jobs of your customer service staff?

6 What is motivation? Describe two theories of motivation and suggest in what organizational circumstances you think they might be most useful. Justify your answer.

7 To what extent would you support the view that motivation in an organizational context presents managers with techniques and processes that allow them to exercise more effective control over employee behaviour in support of managerially determined objectives? Justify your answer.

8 It is impossible for an organization to fully motivate all employees all the time. Discuss.

9 There are no ethical issues surrounding motivation, it simply represents the ways in which managers seek to encourage employees to contribute effectively. Critically evaluate this statement.

10 Motivation is an individual level response, yet managers must operate at a collective level in following company policies. Therefore because motivational practice cannot be personalized it is not possible to fully motivate every individual all of the time. Consequently it is not possible for organizations to achieve the highest levels of performance from all on a consistent basis. Discuss this statement.

CASE STUDY

Changes to the management of police services

The following is based upon the changes to how one divisional commander (Louise) sought to arrange policing in her area. The events described took place in a large semi rural police division based in Germany. Louise was in charge of all police activity within a specified geographic area. Her job invariably required her to work a normal day shift pattern of 9.00 till 5.00 Monday to Friday. In addition to these hours she would be called out to take charge of serious incidents as necessary. Louise's area included four medium-sized towns with populations of between

50 000 and 200 000 each. It also included large areas of agricultural land and about 65 small to medium villages, each with fewer than 10 000 inhabitants. It was a large area with the problems that might be associated with trying to provide effective police cover over such a diverse community with the relatively small number of police officers allocated to the division. Being semi-rural it was not seen as attractive in career terms by many promotion-minded officers, who preferred to be attached to the large cities and high-profile specialist crime squads that sought to deal with large-scale crime and major enquiries.

Staff within the division were allocated to one of four shifts, each under the control of a shift commander.

Each shift was in charge of all policing activity in the division for the duration of their shift. Within each shift team there were a number of subteams, each under the leadership of a sergeant. The divisional commander would be called-out if a significant event happened that needed a more senior officer to co-ordinate the police response, even if they were off duty at the time. This practice meant that the divisional commander had to be available 24 hours every day, 365 days each year, unless they appointed a deputy to cover for longer periods of absence, holidays or other reasons. This requirement was resented by Louise because she found it disruptive and often curtailed her private and social life. Consequently, she began to think how the system could be changed in order to maintain an effective policing service whilst reducing the demands on herself.

Eventually Louise identified what she thought was a workable staffing plan that would reduce the demands on herself and, she thought, improve the level of motivation among her subordinates. It would also, she thought, assist junior officers to gain more managerial and strategic policing experience and so assist their promotion chances. The plan was based around the four sub-divisional shift teams that already existed and involved no changes to the shift patterns or management structures that were in place. The change involved introducing a geographic split of the division into four subdivisions. Each of the four shift commanders was then given responsibility for primary policing within a specific geographic sub-division. The objective was to encourage each shift commander to develop a detailed knowledge of their allocated subdivision. This was a 24 hour, 365 day responsibility and in addition to their being in total charge of the division when their particular shift was on duty. The rules for

© Jochen Tack/Photolibrary

calling out a senior officer were also changed. Instead of the divisional commander (Louise) being called out when a serious problem arose, the shift commander was instructed to turn first to the particular shift commander responsible for that sub-division. That individual (which could be the shift commander if the incident occurred in their sub-division) then had a duty to deal with the incident using their expert knowledge of the area and its people. The incident was only to be 'escalated' upwards to Louise if the incident was of a very serious nature and needed interagency or departmental co-ordination – a murder or major traffic accident for example. The first question asked by Louise when she was called was, 'Why am I being called, what has the shift commander for that area done to deal with the incident?'

Louise thought that this approach would give the shift commanders some real responsibility and an opportunity to gain useful experience, thereby motivating them to enhance the performance of the entire division and enhance their career prospects. However, the practical effect was that the number of occasions on which the divisional commander was called out reduced, but the shift commanders now found that they would be called out at any hour of the day or night, in addition to having to work their normal rotating shift pattern. They found this very tiring and disruptive on top of an already disrupted work and private life. They resented this change and interpreted it as a cynical attempt by Louise as their boss to make her own life easier at the expense of the shift commanders.

In response to the changes implemented by Louise the shift commanders became de-motivated and began to grumble amongst themselves. After a period of time one of them developed an idea through which to make the changes more bearable. It was suggested that each shift commander should break down their geographic area into sub-units and make a sergeant responsible for each. This would mean that instead of the shift commander being called immediately a problem in their area was identified, it would be allocated to the appropriate sergeant to deal with. The shift commander with special responsibility for that area would only be called upon to become involved if the sergeant could not do so. The intention was to reduce the number of times that each shift commander would be called out, by requiring each sergeant to make themselves available at all times. Not surprisingly, this made the shift commanders feel better, but had the effect of demotivating the sergeants.

TASKS

1 Was Louise ever going to be able to motivate the shift commanders by making the changes that she did? Justify your answer.

2 How might Louise have been able to motivate her subordinates and still reduce the demands on herself? Justify your views in terms of the motivation theories and performance management material introduced in this chapter.

FURTHER READING

Bandura, A. (1997) *Self-efficacy: The exercise of control*, Stanford, CA: Freeman. Comprehensive account of a central concept in human behaviour with immense implications for motivation.

Csikszentmihalyi, M. (1990) *Flow: The Psychology of Optimal Experience*, New York: Harper and Row. Useful discussion of peak performances and what brings them about.

Kouzes, J. and Posner, B. (2003) *Encouraging the Heart: A Leaders Guide to Rewarding and Recognizing Others*, revised edition, Chichester: Wiley. This is an unusual book in that it focuses on an aspect of motivation and performance that is not directly addressed in this text, that of caring. The authors argue that people will aspire to achieve higher performance when they are genuinely appreciated for their dedication and publicly recognized for their achievements.

Latham, G.P. (2007) *Work motivation: History, theory, research & practice,* Thousand Oaks, CA: Sage. Useful discussion of contemporary motivation theory underpinned by interesting and often personal recollections of important historical aspects of the development of motivation theory and research.

Meyer, M.W. (2003) *Rethinking Performance Measurement: Beyond the Balanced Scorecard*, Cambridge: Cambridge University Press. Explores what performance management means in the light of the balanced business scorecard approach and the weaknesses that have been identified within it.

Pinder, C.C. (2008) *Work motivation in organizational behavior* (2nd edn), New York: Psychology Press. One-stop-shopping source for a cutting edge discussion of all dimensions of motivation. This is a clear, well written, and succinct yet comprehensive source-book on all things related to motivation in organizations. Outstanding!

Williams, R.S. (2002) *Managing Employee Performance: Design and Implementation in Organizations*, London: Thomson Learning. This text takes a practical approach to the design and implementation of the key mechanisms for performance management systems as used within organizations.

COMPANION WEBSITE

Online teaching and learning resources

Visit the companion website for Organizational Behaviour and Management 4th edition at: http://www.cengage.co.uk/martinfellenz to find valuable further teaching and learning material. For full details, see 'About the website' at the start of the book.

INTERACTIONS IN ORGANIZATIONS

The previous chapters introduced various aspects associated with individuals in an organizational context. Part 3 is also concerned with people but focuses on the wide range of interactions that take place between and among them (see Figure 1).

The important topics of management and leadership are addressed in Chapter 6. This chapter explores the nature and reality of management and leadership in organizations and the relationship between these two important topics. Understanding management and leadership is of vital importance because they are central processes in determining what should be done and how it should be done in groups and organizations. Chapter 7 addresses the topics of groups and teams in organizations. There are many different types of groups within organizations such as the board of directors, different departments, and work or project teams that create important outputs. In addition, organizations typically contain many forms of informal groups of people that simply exchange gossip or chat over lunch. Both formal and informal groups have a significant impact on the attitudes and opinions of employees and can exercising enormous influence over their behaviour and work activities.

Communications and decision making, discussed in Chapter 8, are other activities that directly (and sometimes indirectly) involve and affect other people. Without communication, which serves the purpose of making information available to the right people at the right time, organizations cannot survive. Similarly, it is inconceivable how organizations could function without choices being made about what is to be done, and how it should be achived. Therefore, both communication and decision making are the lifeblood of any organization, and understanding how these dynamics operate, and what difficulties and mistakes can occur, are important aspects of OB. Finally, Chapter 9 considers conflict which often arises among interacting parties. This is true in everyday life just as it is in organizations. Recognizing conflict, understanding its implications, and learning about different ways in which conflict can be prevented, managed and resolved is therefore important. A closely related topic is negotiation which can also be helpful in creating mutually beneficial interactions between different individuals and groups in organizations.

Figure 1

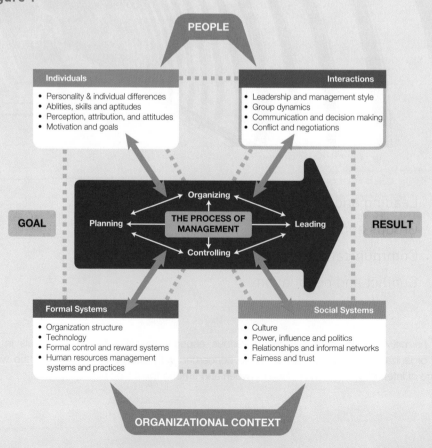

CHAPTER SIX

iStock/H-Gall

LEADING AND MANAGING

LEARNING OBJECTIVES

After studying this chapter and working through the associated OB in Action panels, Discussion Questions and Case Study you should be able to:

- Discuss the meaning of, and distinction between, leadership and management.

- Explain the contribution to understanding leadership of the various style approaches.

- Assess the contribution of the different theoretical approaches to the study of leadership.

- Understand the significance of the contingency approaches to the study of leadership.

- Outline the roles that managers perform and identify the significance of followership in allowing leadership to function effectively.

6.1 EXTEND
YOUR LEARNING

INTRODUCTION

We have already started to discuss the nature of management in organizations earlier in this book. In this chapter, we will focus again on some of the principles of management and consider in more detail the behavioural aspects of people management in organizations, including the skills and competencies necessary for successful management. We then consider the nature of management and leadership before we review in more detail the most relevant theories and models of leadership.

MANAGEMENT IN ORGANIZATIONS

Management
A process that involves the major functions of planning, organizing, leading (or deploying) and controlling resources in order to achieve goals. The jobs within an organization are charged with running the organization on behalf of the beneficial owner.

People management
The process of trying to achieve goals in organizations with and through people.

Primary functions of management
Fayol proposed that management had five primary function: planning and forecasting, organizing, commanding, co-ordinating and controlling.

In Chapter 1 we have already discussed and defined management as *a process that involves planning, organizing, leading (or deploying), and controlling resources in order to achieve goals*. We also referred to people management as *the process of trying to achieve goals in organizations with and through people*. The practice of management has a long history going back thousands of years (see Chapter 2 and the companion website). Many of the traditional approaches to achieve goals with and through people have been formalized by the classical management theorists such as Henri Fayol, F.W. Taylor, Mary Parker Follett, Oliver Sheldon, Lyndall Urwick and James Mooney. Their collective ideas, principles, and prescriptions reflect rational approaches to increase the efficiency and effectiveness of hierarchical organizations used to control and co-ordinate complex activities (see also Chapter 10).

The work of Fayol (1916), a French mining engineer and management theorist, offers one of the most influential definitions of management by proposing that management has five primary functions: (1) planning and forecasting, (2) organizing, (3) commanding, (4) co-ordinating and (5) controlling (Fayol, 1916, 1947). This definition of management (administrative functions in Fayol's words) is reflected in contemporary views and definitions of management including the one we use in this book. Like other classic management theorists, Fayol's conception describes management as an ordered process of achieving the objectives of the organization using well structured, well thought out principles. It assumes that formal authority can be bestowed on those who manage, and recognizes that both managers and those who follow their direction have individual interests and needs that may interfere with the efficient and effective running of the organization. Fayol wrote his views on how to run an organization for the benefit of other managers rather than as a theoretical model. He identified the following main functions of any organization.

- *Technical.* This function represents what would be clearly understood as manufacturing or operations in today's organizations.

- *Commercial.* This function represents what would be clearly understood as purchasing, sales and supply chain or logistics in today's organizations.

- *Financial.* This function represents what would be clearly understood as the provision of financial funds, capital budgeting, project management and risk assessment in today's organizations.

- *Security.* This function represents what would be clearly understood as protection of people, goods and property within the organization. Interestingly, Fayol would also incorporate human resource management activity in this category in the sense of avoiding strikes and so on.

- *Accounting.* This function represents what would be clearly understood as the management accounting function together with stocktaking, costing, and statistical analysis in today's organizations.

- *Administrative.* This function represents what would be clearly understood as the management responsibilities in today's organizations.

Fayol also proposed a set of 14 principles of management, which he argued would help to ensure that the process of management was successful (see Table 6.1). He pointed out that these principles should be used with some flexibility and adapted to the prevailing circumstances for the organization. Fayol's description of functions and his prescriptive principles are compatible with the scientific management approach of F.W Taylor (1911). However, his approach focused on the organization in general and the fundamental principles of managing, while Taylor's work was more targeted to managerial and organizational solutions to the challenges of specific tasks.

The classical and scientific management approaches have been further elaborated as well as challenged throughout the last century by the main modern schools of management (see Chapter 2). These elaborations and developments have all attempted to provide a body of knowledge that can help understand, predict and control how work can be achieved in organizations with and through people. Yet despite the

Principles of management
Fayol proposed a set of 14, which he argued would help to ensure that the process of management was successful (see Table 6.1).

Table 6.1 Fayol's 14 principles of management

1	**Authority and responsibility.** Authority cannot exist without responsibility. The exercise of authority ensures that the right things are done
2	**Unity of command.** Each worker should have only one boss
3	**Division of work.** Breaking the work down into small sets of tasks allows the worker to develop high levels of specialization and efficiency
4	**Discipline.** This is necessary for efficiency to exist. The manager must exercise appropriate discipline in maintaining order
5	**Subordination of individual interest to that of the organization.** The organization must be placed above personal or group interest if it is to succeed
6	**Equity.** Each person should be treated with equity as far as it is possible to do so
7	**Scalar chain.** There should be a proper hierarchy of grades and responsibilities from the bottom to the top of the organization
8	**Remuneration.** Payment methods should be fair and benefit both employer and employee
9	**Centralization.** The degree of centralization appropriate in any organization depends upon the circumstances
10	**Order.** Material and social order is necessary for the avoidance of loss in goods and people efficiency
11	**Esprit de corps.** Harmony and unity should be encouraged among the workforce to ensure that everyone works together in the interests of the organization
12	**Initiative.** This should be encouraged in all levels as a source of strength for the organization
13	**Stablility of tenure.** Where possible organizations should avoid the 'hire and fire' approach to managing people. With security of employment comes commitment and efficiency
14	**Unity of direction.** There should be one head and one plan controlling the overall direction of the organization

amount of work designated to investigate management, the question of what managers actually do is still valid and important – we will consider it in the next section.

THE PRACTICE OF MANAGEMENT

6.2 EXTEND YOUR LEARNING

Management roles
Mintzberg described 10 different roles that he grouped under three headings called interpersonal, informational and decisional.

What do managers actually do? This question has received much research attention over the years. Mintzberg's (1973) work on this matter is possibly best known. Mintzberg followed a range of senior managers and observed their activities. Based on the data he collected, he distinguished and described 10 different management roles that he grouped under three headings called interpersonal, informational and decisional (see Figure 6.1) .

1 *Interpersonal roles.* These roles reflect the form that the interaction with other people takes as a consequence of the status and type of managerial job held by a particular manager. For example, the industrial relations manager of a company would be expected to act as a figurehead in representing the company to the employees, the leader of the management–union negotiation body and a liaison between managers and the trade unions. This represents a different role pattern than might be expected to apply to the marketing manager in the same company.

2 *Informational roles.* These roles reflect the nature of the way that information is used in the job of the manager. These are heavily dependent on the dictates of the interpersonal roles of the position. For example, the industrial relations manager indicated above would find it necessary to disseminate particular types of information in particular ways to particular people as a result of their interpersonal roles.

3 *Decisional roles.* These roles reflect the nature of decision-making requirements within a particular managerial job. They are heavily dependent on the previous two categories of role indicated. For example, an industrial relations manager would be expected to play a leading role as a disturbance handler in the company as a consequence of their status and information networks.

Figure 6.1 Mintzberg's management roles

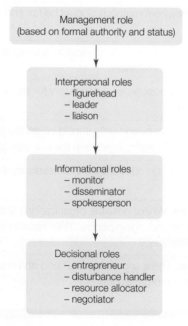

In reality, individual roles often overlap, and rather than describing management as an orderly, well structured activity, the picture of management that Mintzberg's work paints is one of fragmented, often interrupted activities that are determined as much by what is happening around them as it is by managers' choices and preferences. Other studies also highlight the complexity of managerial work (e.g., Kotter, 1982) where individual activities often address – and are influenced by - many different issues, agendas and dependencies. For example, rather than being able to determine their activities solely based on political and idiological preferences, the British Prime Minister, the French President or the German Chancellor have many of their priorities, time and activity dictated by the latest public opinion poll results and by stories that break in the media in relation to scandals, economic results, political pressure from opposition parties and military events which tend to arise with little or no pre-warning. The challenges arising from complexity, change and uncertainty in managers' work environment place sensemaking at the heart of managers' activities, and the interdependencies and interactions with others involve influence attempts in both directions. The following High Performance example illustrates one manager's attempt to reconcile the conflicting pressures from a number of the roles that he is expected to perform.

In order to successfully deal with the complex array of roles and responsibilities in complex and dynamic organizational environments, managers need to possess and apply a broad set of skills and competencies. One approach to the development of appropriate skills and competencies among managers using role theory is that based on the framework proposed by Pedler *et al.* (1994). This framework identifies 11 capabilities, grouped under three levels, which differentiate successful from unsuccessful managers. They are:

6.3 EXTEND
YOUR LEARNING

- *Basic knowledge* and information. This level includes those things necessary for taking decisions such as the possession of a relevant professional understanding, an awareness of events and a command of the basic facts.
- *Skills and attributes*. This level reflects the necessary ability to function as a manager in the specific context. It includes analytical and problem solving skills, social skills, emotional resilience and an ability to be proactive in situations.

HIGH PERFORMANCE

Should I keep my door open?

The following comment was made by a practising manager about his open door policy.

I have always kept an open door policy at work and encourage my direct reports to talk to me whenever they need to. Recently, the number of staff reporting directly to me has increased, and I'm finding it really difficult to get on with my own work with all the interruptions. Unfortunately, I've been told by my staff that what they like best about my management style is that I'm always available, unlike some of the other managers. How can I cut down on my 'availability time' without seeming to be letting them all down?

TASKS

1 Is an open door policy a good thing for both boss and subordinates? Why or why not?

2 What does this example suggest to you about the Mintzberg view of management roles?

3 What advice would you give to this manager and why? Compare your answers with that offered by Bullmore, J. What's your problem? *Management Today*, July 2003, p. 81 and reconcile the views expressed with yours (summary answer on the companion web site).

● *Meta qualities.* This level reflects the ability that some managers have to bring together the other skills and abilities in novel ways in dealing with situations. It includes such capabilities as being creative, displaying mental agility, having a balanced approach to learning and a sound self-knowledge.

Another influential managerial competency framework is shown in Figure 6.2 and Table 6.2. This framework (Quinn *et al.*, 2003) is based on the influential competing values approach developed by Quinn and his colleagues (Quinn, 1988; Quinn and Rohrbaugh, 1983). It identifies, along the dimension of internal/external focus and control/flexibility orientation, eight roles with the associated competencies and skills (see also Whetten and Cameron, 2007, for a similar framework based on the same underlying model).

Such managerial skills and competencies are applied across the range of managerial activities. Luthans (1995) describes four general types of management activity, along with the approximate proportion of time devoted to it, extracted from the 'Real Managers Study'. Although this model does not account for the range of different types and levels of management jobs, it provides a useful insight into the mix that occurs in the studies of what managers actually do:

1 *Traditional management.* Planning, decision making and controlling. This accounts for 32 per cent of management time.

2 *Routine communication.* Exchanging information and handling paperwork. This accounts for 29 per cent of management time.

3 *Networking.* Interacting with outsiders, socializing and politicking. This accounts for 19 per cent of management time.

4 *Human resource management.* Managing conflict, motivating, discipline, staffing and development. This accounts for 20 per cent of management time.

6.4 EXTEND
YOUR LEARNING

Figure 6.2 Managerial competency framework

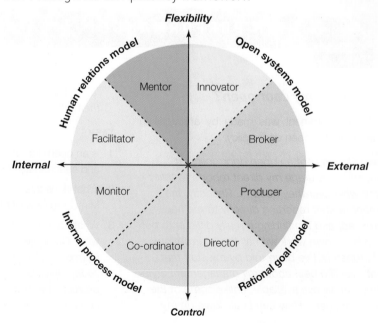

Source: Quinn *et al.*, (2003)
Becoming a Master Manager,
John Wiley & Sons, USA.
Reprinted with permission.

Table 6.2 Competencies in the managerial competency framework

Managerial role	Associated competencies
Facilitator	1 Building teams 2 Using participative decision making 3 Managing conflict
Mentor	1 Understanding self and others 2 Communicating effectively 3 Developing employees
Innovator	1 Living with change 2 Thinking creatively 3 Managing change
Broker	1 Building and maintaining power base 2 Negotiating agreement and commitment 3 Presenting ideas
Producer	1 Working productively 2 Fostering a productive work environment 3 Managing time and stress
Director	1 Developing and communicating a vision 2 Setting goals and objectives 3 Designing and organizing
Co-ordinator	1 Managing projects 2 Designing work 3 Managing across functions
Monitor	1 Monitoring individual performance 2 Managing collective performance and processes 3 Analysing information with critical thinking

Source: Quinn *et al.*, (2003) *Becoming a Master Manager*, John Wiley & Sons, USA. Reprinted with permission.

STOP & CONSIDER

All of the views expressed so far could be argued to focus on what managers should do. What managers actually do is determined by the level of pressure emanating from those above, customers, suppliers and those below. Therefore to what extent do these models fail to identify the things that managers actually do in their normal working day?

LEADERSHIP IN ORGANIZATIONS

Together with the topic of motivation, which we defined as the set of internal forces that initiates, directs and sustains deliberate behaviour (see Chapter 5), leadership is probably the most important and central topic in management and OB. Motivation is important because it helps us understand why people do what they do. Leadership, in comparison, helps us understand how we may influence others to do what we want them to do. Given the key role that people have in any attempt to achieve goals in and through organizations (see Chapter 1), the centrality of leadership for management and OB is understandable.

The importance of leadership also helps to explain why few other topics in OB have attracted as much research interest as leadership. As a result, there are many different and sometimes incompatible views and definitions of leadership. In this book, we adopt a broad definition that enables us to review the main streams of leadership theory and research and to link our discussion to many other aspects of OB and management in organizations. Leadership refers to '*The process of influencing others to understand and agree about what needs to be done and how to do it, and the process of facilitating individual and collective efforts to accomplishing shared objectives.*' (Yukl, 2010: p. 26) In short, leadership is a process of influencing others to get them to do what we want them to do. *Leadership effectiveness*, then, is about being successful in such influencing attempts.

Yet before we consider leadership research, theory and practice, we must clarify the relationship between leadership and management. While our definition of management as well as Mintzberg's (1973) managerial role model discussed above include leadership as part of management, there are also distinctions between the concepts we need to understand and consider.

COMPARING MANAGEMENT AND LEADERSHIP

The terms management and leadership are frequently used interchangeably, but are they the same? Is a manager automatically a leader and do leaders always manage? In most contexts, the terms management and leadership both imply the achievement of goals with and through people. It would be unusual, however, to describe a group of people as having a manager unless the group was in an organizational context, and more specifically, part of its formal structure. An informal, friendship or trade union group would not usually be described as having a manager, yet we would almost inevitably find a formal or informal leader of such groups.

In organizations, individuals become managers by being formally appointed. This appointment brings with it certain privileges (such as authority) and responsibilities (such as accountability for the use or nonuse of this authority). So what about leaders and leadership? What makes people leaders? Can leaders be appointed, and do managers always exert leadership?

Most people agree that leaders cannot be appointed. There is a vast literature on the emergence of leadership in social settings that identifies personal characteristics, situation factors and the nature of interactions among the influences that can help bring about leadership (e.g., Hogan *et al.*, 1994; Schneier and Goktepe, 1983; Zaccaro, 2007). However, there is no single factor that determines who becomes a leader, and the only observable factor that clearly and unequivocally indicates the presence of leadership is followers. Thus, leadership - unlike management - is not based on explicit appointments and formal roles or authority. Rather, it derives from social interaction and exists only if it is successful, that is, if potential followers understand and agree about what is to be done and pursue the intended goal. Thus, there is no leadership without followers. This fact is important to understand leadership, yet it is not sufficient to contrast the two concepts.

Kotter (1990) for example has made such a clear distinction between management and leadership. He described management as 'doing things right' and leadership as 'doing the right thing'. Along these lines he characterizes management as being about formal and often explicit activities such as planning and budgeting, organizing and staffing, creation and maintenance of formal processes and systems, and overall about the production of order and the achievement of specified goals. He describes leadership, in contrast, as creating and aligning people with a vision, producing imaginative ideas, motivating and inspiring followers, and overall producing change. Kotter argues that there can be problems if the proper balance between

Leadership
Refers to the process of influencing others to understand and agree about what needs to be done and how to do it, and the process of facilitating individual and collective efforts to accomplish shared objectives.

the two is not achieved. The moral overtones of the distinction between 'doing the right thing' and simply 'doing things right' does, however, not sit well with the many examples of historic and contemporary leaders who successfully lead others in highly questionable goals (e.g., Hitler, Stalin, Mao, ...). The sometimes complex relationship between 'leaders' and 'followers' in relation to 'doing the right thing' (and 'doing things right') is illustrated in the following Change at Work example.

Most researchers see management and leadership as distinct but not necessarily as mutually exclusive (see Bennis and Nanus, 1985, for an exception). Yukl argues that 'defining managing and leading as distinct roles, processes or relationships may obscure more than it reveals' (2010: p. 26) if this leads to overly simplistic conceptions. It may in fact not be crucial to create a final distinction between management and leadership. We also think that in organizations the two concepts are so intertwined that it may not even be possible to always fully distinguish between management and leadership. Nevertheless, there is a qualitative difference that we believe is important to recognize. Therefore, we view management as based on exercising formal authority in the pursuit of a goal. Leadership, in contrast, is rooted in the acceptance of influence by followers based on their explicit or implicit choice that reflects the legitimation of the leader by followers. In other words, we make an explicit link to motivation and legitimacy as explanation for followership, and view management in contrast to leadership as *the exercise of influence over others using extrinsic motivation and based on externally determined legitimacy*, while we consider leadership in contrast to management to be *the exercise of influence over others using their intrinsic motivation and reflecting subjective, follower-based legitimation*.

TRAIT THEORIES OF LEADERSHIP

For much of history it was assumed that leadership was a set of qualities or personal characteristics (i.e., traits) that someone was born with. The significance of this approach is that leaders cannot be trained and therefore must be selected. It also implies that successful leaders will be situation-specific. This view originated from the traditional and aptly named great man view of leadership (as at that time they were predominantly men) which suggested that in every situation, particularly in times of crisis, 'great men' would emerge to lead through the difficulties. As a natural extension of this view future successful leaders could be identified by seeking out people with the same characteristics as existing successful leaders. Handy (1993) suggests that by 1950 there had been over 100 studies attempting to identify appropriate traits. Unfortunately, little commonality was identified, with only about 5 per cent of the traits being common. Influential reviews by leading scholars (Mann, 1959; Stogdill, 1948) ended the wide acceptance of the trait-based view of leadership in the 1950s (Zaccaro, 2007). Since the 1980s, interest in the role of individual traits for leadership has revived (see Avolio *et al.*, 2009; Zaccaro *et al.*, 2004; Zaccaro, 2007), especially in response to interest in transformational and charismatic leadership which we will consider further below. In contrast to the earlier approaches, contemporary trait research in leadership focuses less on direct effects of individual traits and more on constellations of traits, interactions between traits and situational characteristics, and the implication of traits on skills and behaviours that affect leadership (e.g., Ng *et al.*, 2008; see Yukl, 2010; and Zaccaro, 2007, for discussion and assessment).

Those traits found to have some direct (*proximal*) or more remote (*distal*) association with successful leadership in large organizations include (e.g., Yukl, 2010; Zaccaro, 2007):

- General cognitive capacity and skills (e.g., intelligence, skills for solving abstract, complex problems)

6.5 EXTEND YOUR LEARNING

Management (in contrast to leadership)
The exercise of influence over others using extrinsic motivation and based on externally determined legitimacy. See also 'Leadership (in contrast to management)'.

Leadership (in contrast to management)
The exercise of influence over others using their intrinsic motivation and reflecting subjective, follower-based legitimacy. See also 'Management (in contrast to leadership)'.

Great man (view of leadership)
Originating at a time when the leaders were predominantly men, which suggests that in every situation, particularly in times of crisis, 'great men' would emerge to lead through the difficulties.

Traits (view of leadership)
Proposed the view that future successful leaders could be identified by seeking out people with the same characteristics as existing successful leaders.

CHANGE AT WORK

The supervisor was taking bribes

This example is based in a medium-sized manufacturing company based in the UK. The company made a wide range of screws, bolts and nuts for use in the engineering, construction and home improvement markets. They employed about 500 people on one site. The company was traditional in approach, having been owned by the same family for about 100 years. In charge of the factory was a production director who had managers in charge of production, planning, stores, warehouse and maintenance reporting to him. The production department was split into five production units, each responsible for making a particular type of product. Each unit employed around 75 people and was under the control of a production supervisor.

Each factory worker was paid a basic wage, plus a bonus directly related to the number of units produced over a week. Each product had a bonus price determined by the production director in discussion with worker representatives. Because each job had its own price, the supervisor and employees had to keep track of every job to ensure that the correct prices were being used and that no employee was over-claiming bonus. The bonus prices had been set over the years when jobs first arose and were not subsequently changed when production processes changed. Consequently, it was easy for employees to make high bonus from some – usually the older - jobs. There was keen competition among employees to work on the 'high bonus' jobs. This potentially gave the supervisors considerable power over employees through the ability to allocate work.

It became apparent to the production director that all was not well with the bonus scheme when the wages of particular individuals appeared as the top earners week after week. Enquiries confirmed that some individuals never (or rarely) earned high bonuses; whilst others worked only 3 or 4 days each week but earned the same as people working a full week.

The production director was worried because he trusted each of his supervisors and thought that they were respected as the leaders of their particular units. Matters came to a head when a shop floor employee resigned and in his exit interview suggested that the main reason for leaving was that he was never given the opportunity to earn high bonus because he would not pay the 'tax'. The personnel officer conducting the interview asked what he meant by the 'tax', but the employee would not explain. After the employee had left the company the production director was shown the interview notes and read the comment about the 'tax'. He too was perplexed and went to see the ex-employee in his home one evening. The employee was reluctant to discuss matters, but it eventually became apparent that one of the supervisors in the factory had invented a money making scam for himself based on the bonus prices. The production director could not believe his ears when he listened to the former employee's story. It was said that each morning the supervisor would auction each of the 'high bonus' jobs to be done that day. It started with the job likely to pay the highest bonus and each employee was given the chance to bid for it. The employee offering the most money to the supervisor was allocated that job. This was repeated until there was no realistic 'tax' potential in the jobs to be done that day. The remaining jobs were then allocated to other employees. The supervisor was essentially taking bribes from employees for the allocation of work. Employees called this 'paying the tax'.

TASKS

1 What does this example suggest to you about management and leadership in relation to 'doing the right thing' and 'doing things right'?

2 Could the supervisor concerned be a good leader under the circumstances of taking bribes from subordinates? Why or why not?

3 What would you have done if you were the production director to try and deal with the situation that had arisen?

4 Given that the employees who are the highest paid are unlikely to agree willingly to change, how could this situation be changed for the better?

Source:
Adapted from the personal experience of one of the authors.

- Internal locus of control
- Specific need structures (i.e., low need for affiliation, moderately high need for achievement, need for power if balanced by social awareness)
- Integrity
- Emotional stability and stress resilience
- Initiative and high energy levels
- Self-assurance and confidence
- Interpersonal abilities and skills
- Physical attributes (particularly height, but also perceived strength and attractiveness)
- High social status background.

The relative importance of these traits is determined by situational factors as well as by characteristics of followers. One way in which leadership traits operate is by affecting follower perception and attribution. Other conceptions of the role of leadership traits also exist. Zaccaro *et al.* (2004) proposed a model of leadership traits that distinguished between distal and proximal traits. Extending this model we can argue that distal traits such as individual differences in personality, general cognitive ability and motivational factors influence more proximal differences in specific cognitive and work-related skills and knowledge. These individual differences influence the behaviours and interaction in the leadership situation, which determines who is recognized as leader (i.e., who generates followership), the success and impact of leadership, and the subsequent selection/promotion and assignment of authority and other formal aspects supportive of exercising influence in organizations. These outcomes can be mutually reinforcing, such that increased leadership success and impact is likely to positively affect leader recognition and reward (and vice versa). Especially selection/promotion and assignment of authority will change the situation and create a potentially reinforcing cycle which can further amplify the leadership influence of a person (the extended model is shown in Figure 6.3). One aspect of the personal

Figure 6.3 Extended model of leader traits and leadership performance

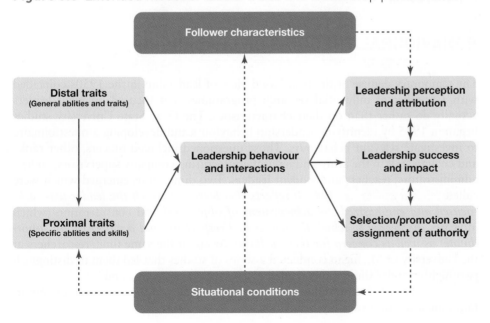

Source: Extended based on Zaccaro *et al.*, 2004.

EXAMINING ETHICS

Lose the accent if you want to succeed

Jake, a university graduate (from a well respected red-brick university) with good A' level grades as well as a very good first class law degree, applied for the Bar Vocational Course for Barrister training having already become a member of one of the Inns of Court. He was born in Sunderland, a fact obvious as soon as he spoke. He did very well in his Bar Vocational Course and was looking forward to completing his training with a Pupillage at a major barrister's chambers in London. In a discussion with his personal tutor on the Bar Vocational Course (having just been told that he had passed with high marks) Jake was told that he was very bright and that he had displayed qualities that could take him far in his chosen career. However, his tutor gave him one last piece of advice – his accent/speaking voice. The tutor said to Jake that the

best advice that he could give him, if he wanted to become a successful and significant figure in the legal profession, would be to make every effort to change his accent/speaking voice and cultivate a more appropriate one in relation to his chosen profession.

TASKS

1 What would you do in this situation if you were Jake?

2 Should accent make any difference to promotion in this (or any) situation? Explore both sides of the argument.

3 What might this example suggest about the traits approach to leadership?

4 What ethical issues about management does this example raise and how should they be dealt with?

Attribution of leadership
Suggests that leaders vary their reactions to subordinates based on observation of their behaviours.

Initiating structure
(in leadership style)
Originating from the Ohio State University studies which began in 1945 and reflects the degree to which the leader was task focused and emphasized the achievement of objectives. See also consideration.

Consideration
(in leadership style)
Originating from the Ohio State University studies which began in 1945 and reflects the degree to which the leader had respect and a rapport with subordinates as well as concern for their welfare. See also initiating structure.

characteristics of a potential leader is illustrated in the Examining Ethics example in the Examining Ethics example above. Follower characteristics are also likely to influence both leadership behaviour and interactions and the perception and attribution of leadership. Even though this extended model is quite intricate, the dynamics linked to leader traits in organizations are likely to be even more complex (see for example Ng *et al.*, 2008).

BEHAVIOURAL THEORIES OF LEADERSHIP

The temporary demise of the trait-based view of leadership in the 1950s coincided with a number of influential research programmes that focused on what leaders actually do rather than on their characteristics. The Ohio State University studies began in 1945 by identifying leadership behaviours and developing a questionnaire to investigate relevant behaviours. Those questioned included officers, other ranks and civilian staff in the army and navy, manufacturing company supervisors, college administrators, teachers and student leaders. Two dimensions emerged which were called initiating structure (*which reflects the degree to which the leader was task-focused and emphasized the achievement of objectives*) and consideration (which indicates *the degree to which the leader had respect for and a rapport with subordinates as well as concern for their welfare*). At about the same time, researchers at the University of Michigan conducted a series of studies that led them to distinguish two highly similar dimensions named task-oriented behaviour and people-oriented behaviour. The Michigan studies also identified participative behaviours as an important dimension of leadership behaviour.

These studies are important in establishing the task and people dimensions in the achievement of success. It has been argued that these studies do not necessarily identify actual leader behaviour but reflect the perceptions of those completing the form. For example, leaders could answer on the basis of how they think they behave (or would like to), rather than reflecting what they actually do. Equally a subordinate might complete the questions on the basis of personal feelings towards their boss rather than based on actual experience.

The importance of the two behavioural dimensions identified by these studies goes far beyond the topic of leadership. They are fundamental to many models and theories in OB (for example Goffee and Jones's (1996) cultural framework that reflects task and relationship dimensions, see Chapter 14). In the 1990s, a third general category, *change-oriented behaviour*, was identified in addition to the two traditional ones (see Yukl, 2010, for a review). Clearly, this third category adds an important and relevant behavioural dimension to considerations of leadership that is also recognized in approaches to transformational leadership discussed below.

In the area of leadership, the two classical leader behaviour dimensions provided the basis for the well known managerial grid model of leadership (Blake and Mouton, 1964). This approach emerged during the late 1960s and is based on the idea that differences in leadership approach are a function of two factors which they named concern for people and concern for production. Blake and Mouton offered a more comprehensive approach to identifying five generic leadership styles that represent combinations of the two behavioural leadership dimensions. They used a grid to represent these styles (see Figure 6.4). Looking at the five leadership styles indicated in the model:

1 *Impoverished management*. This style would be typified by a low concern for both people and production. Such a leader would be considered as remote from their subordinates and with little interest in achieving the business goals set for their department or section.

2 *Authority–compliance management*. This style would be typified through a very high concern for production but very low concern for people. Such a leader would rely on the application of standard procedures and policies to determine action rather than the possible contribution from staff. They would be considered to be drivers of staff in the search for the achievement of objectives.

3 *Country club management*. This style would be typified by a very high concern for people but with low levels of concern for production. Such a leader would be concerned with the need to create harmony and avoid conflict, thereby allowing subordinates to get on with the job. They would tend to be regarded as one of the workers by subordinates. They tend to seek a comfortable working environment in relationship terms, often in the belief that this ensures that production will follow automatically.

4 *Middle of the road management*. This style is typified through a medium level of concern for both people and production. Keeping everyone happy is a typical approach of such individuals. Unfortunately, because they are not strong on either index, they tend to underachieve on both, achieving neither good levels of production nor highly integrated work teams.

5 *Team management*. This style is typified by an equally very high concern for both people and production. Managers with this profile seek to create teams in which both the needs of individuals and the search for output become integrated.

Blake and Mouton found that managers tend to have one dominant style but that many have a back-up style if the first proves unsuccessful. They also found that many managers could vary their dominant style to some degree. The factors that influence the style adopted by an individual manager are shown in Figure 6.5. Overall, the managerial grid has had an important impact on the thinking about and the practice of leadership. However, its focus on leader behaviours too readily suggests the superiority of one style over others without considering relevant situational or other factors relevant in determining the most appropriate leadership approach.

Figure 6.4 The Leadership Grid®

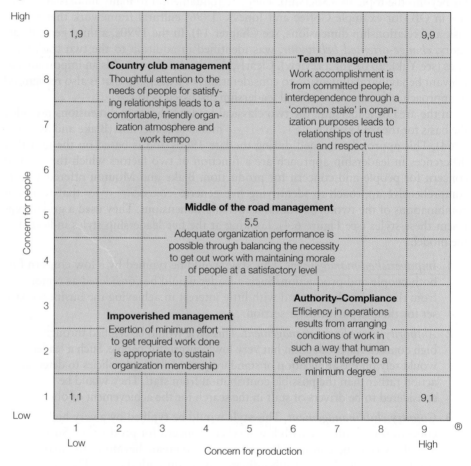

Figure 6.5 Management style determinants

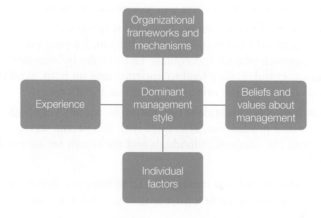

TOWARDS SITUATIONAL AND CONTINGENCY THEORIES OF LEADERSHIP

The behavioural research of the Ohio State and Michigan studies provided important input for the development of leadership models and theories that included additional leadership contingency factors. Among the best known leadership contingency models are some that explicitly include follower, situational and interaction aspects. We will present and discuss selected models below.

Contingency models (of leadership)
Takes the view that the best style of leadership depends upon the factors active in the specific situation.

Hersey and Blanchard's situation leadership theory

Hersey and Blanchard (1982) developed a leadership theory that specifies the amount of support, encouragement and two-way communication that the leader provides and engages in. Their approach is based on the two dimensions of leader behaviour already discussed: *task behaviour* and *relationship behaviour*. As an additional variable Hersey and Blanchard also include the degree of follower maturity (or readiness), which refers to *followers' ability and willingness to achieve a particular task*. Similar to the managerial grid, the two behavioural dimensions (task and relationship behaviour) are used in conjunction with follower maturity. The model prescribes the use of particular behaviour combinations (also called *styles*) depending on the maturity or readiness of followers (see Figure 6.6). Note that the amount of task behaviour decreases steadily with increasing follower maturity/readiness, while relationship behaviour starts low, then increases and finally decreases again. The four actual styles of leadership are:

Follower maturity (or readiness)
Hersey and Blanchard identified this dimension within their model which refers to followers' ability and willingness to achieve a particular task.

1 *Telling.* If the subordinates display a low level of readiness to be willing and able to achieve the task then the leader should adopt a task-oriented style by telling subordinates what is expected from them.

2 *Selling.* This style would be most appropriate where the subordinates display moderate levels of readiness towards the task to be achieved.

3 *Participating.* Where medium levels of subordinate readiness towards the task are found it is possible for the leader to lean towards the relationship aspects of the situation in terms of style.

Figure 6.6 Hersey and Blanchard's situational model of leadership

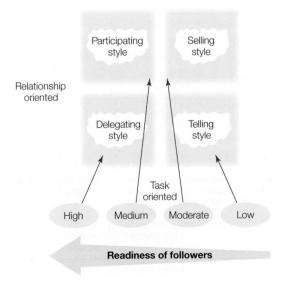

4 *Delegating*. With high levels of subordinate readiness there is an opportunity to delegate much of the responsibility for both task and relationship dimensions. The leadership role then becomes facilitation rather than managerial.

The model is intuitively appealing to many practicing managers and is extensively used in management and leadership development programmes. It emphasizes the important point of leaders' behavioural adjustment to follower characteristics and can also be used as a reminder for leaders to develop their followers' ability, motivation and task-related confidence. It has not sparked, however, many empirical investigations and there is little research to support the claim that adjusting leadership behaviours in line with the model's prescriptions and based on follower characteristics will increase leadership effectiveness.

The Tannenbaum and Schmidt continuum

One of the styles in the Hersey and Blanchard models is called participating. The degree to which followers participate in activities, especially decision making, is an important aspect of the leader-follower interactions that is at the heart of several leadership models (see the website for a discussion of Likert's four systems of management that reflect an autocratic-participative-democratic continuum). Tannenbaum and Schmidt (1973) for example utilize concepts of *boss-centred* and *subordinate-centred leadership* to represent a continuum of different leadership styles. In their model they express the power and influence of managers and subordinates as factors determining the level of managerial authority and freedom for subordinates in any given context. Figure 6.7 reflects this approach to leadership.

It should be noted that within the model, the use of authority or access to freedom never completely disappears. Even at the freedom for subordinates extreme of the continuum the boss still retains the power to say no and to require something to be done in a particular way. However, at the other extreme, employees also retain some freedom, even if it is only the opportunity to display token resistance. Although there are a number of different styles that can be identified within the model (Figure 6.7

6.6 EXTEND
YOUR LEARNING

Figure 6.7 Continuum of leadership behaviour

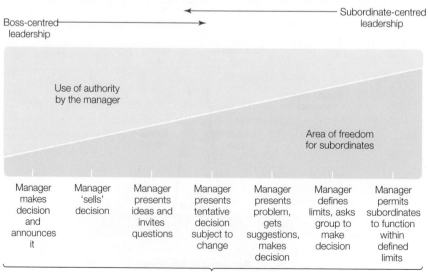

Source: Luthans, F (1995) *Organization Behaviour*, 7th edn, McGraw-Hill, New York. Copyright © The McGraw-Hill Companies, Inc. Reprinted with permission.

indicates seven of them) there are four main categories that are most frequently described:

- *Tells*. The leader identifies appropriate solutions to problems and the appropriate courses of action and thereafter tells the subordinates what they are supposed to do.
- *Sells*. The leader still decides upon the appropriate course of action in any given situation but attempts to overcome disagreement and resistance among the workforce by selling the decision to them. Often this involves justifying the decision (taken by the boss) as the best course of action in the circumstances.
- *Consults*. The leader allows time for subordinates to discuss the problem and present ideas and solutions to the boss. These are then used by the leader to make decisions which are then announced to, and actioned by, the subordinates.
- *Joins*. The leader defines the nature of the issue to be decided along with any constraints and presents these to the group. The leader then becomes part of the group in finding and implementing acceptable solutions.

The Vroom, Yetton and Jago model of participative leadership

The autocratic–democratic dimension underlying the Tannebaum and Schmidt framework is also reflected in the influential Vroom-Yetton decision-making model which structures the decision about how much participation a leader should use. This model was introduced in 1973 by Vroom and Yetton and expanded by Vroom and Jago (1988). Like other contingency models, it attempts to identify leadership approaches appropriate in particular situations (see Table 6.3 for an overview of these approaches). These approaches differ in the amount of process control (i.e., *opportunity to influence or even determine the process of decision making*) and decision control (i.e., *the authority to make the decision*) that is shared with or given to followers individually or in a group.

The model presupposes that leaders can vary their style of behaviour and that situational characteristics should be taken into account when deciding how much participation to employ. The model postulates the level of participation, which refers to *the degree of subordinate involvement in decision-making processes*, as an important aspect of leader behaviour. The model is managerial in orientation in that it attempts to offer ways to determine a high-quality decision in relation to the task itself, but at the same time ensure that subordinates will actively support the decision. In application this model uses decision trees as the basis of working through the variables involved in identifying the appropriate style for the circumstances. Decision trees are structured approaches that follow a set of questions, the answers to which determine the next questions. This sequence of questions and choices ultimately leads to a prescription of which approach suits the situation best.

There are four decision trees offered by the model, two for group problems and two for individual problems. Each pair contains a decision tree for emergency (or time-pressured) situations and one for less time-sensitive events. The latter variation also allows managers to develop subordinate decision making through their involvement in the process. The decision tree does not provide the answer to the problem itself, but offers a suggestion for a leader style that should generate the best decision in the circumstances, based on levels of subordinate involvement.

Process control (in leadership)
This was identified by Vroom and Yetton in their model of leadership and reflects the opportunity to influence or even determine the process of decision making. See also decision control.

Decision control (in leadership)
This was identified by Vroom and Yetton in their model of leadership and reflects the authority to make the decision. See also process control.

Participation
Refers to the degree of subordinate involvement in decision-making processes.

Table 6.3 The five Vroom and Yetton leadership approaches to follower participation

	Name	Process control	Decision control	Description
Autocratic	A I	Leader	Leader	Decision is made by leader alone without any involvement of followers.
	A II	Leader or shared (very limited)	Leader	Decision is made by leader after information input from followers has been received. Followers may or may not be informed why their input is requested.
Consultative	C I	Shared	Leader	Problem is shared with followers individually who are asked for their views and input. Decision is made by leader after individual consultations and may or may not reflect views of followers.
	C II	Shared	Leader	Problem is shared with followers as a group. Group members are asked for their views and input. Decision is made by leader after collective consultations and may or may not reflect views of followers.
Group	G II	Shared/ followers	Followers	Problem is shared with followers as a group. Group members share views and jointly consider issues. Decision is made by group and may or may not reflect the views of the leader.

There is a potential difficulty in this model for leaders in that changing style dependent on the situation could lead to them being thought inconsistent in their style by subordinates. Equally, for a leader to change style may create conflict, confusion or lower morale and productivity among subordinates. Subordinates may become accustomed to being involved in decision making or become unsure of the degree of involvement that they will enjoy at any given time. That said there is some research evidence that decisions consistent with the model are more effective than inconsistent ones.

Fiedler's contingency model

This model attempts to identify situational influences on leadership within a framework that also incorporates the notion of effectiveness in achieving success. Fiedler (1967) brought together three situational aspects that together determine the degree of *situational favourableness* which in turn indicates which leadership style is most effective in the particular situation. The three situational variables are:

- *Leader–member relationships*. It would be reflected in the degree of trust between the parties and a willingness to follow the leader's direction on the part of the subordinates.
- *Task structure*. Tasks are either structured or unstructured in the degree to which the task is capable of being achieved through standard procedures (see discussion of programmed and nonprogrammed decisions in Chapter 8).
- *Position power*. This construct reflects the degree of formal authority held by the leader.

The model contains two levels for each of these three constructs (i.e., position power is either high or low) which produces eight situational combinations indicating one of three levels of *situational favourableness*. Each of these three levels indicates that either task-oriented or person-oriented behaviour is the most effective leadership style. Figure 6.8 provides an overview of these linkages and shows that when the situation is either very favourable or very unfavourable to the leader then a task-oriented style would be most effective. When the situation is highly favourable to the leader then task orientation ensures that the objectives are achieved. In such situations it would be all too easy for a 'good time to be had by all' but for nothing to be achieved. When the situation is very unfavourable to the leader then a single-minded, driving approach is necessary in order to achieve the objectives against the balance of forces acting against the leader. When the situation is moderately favourable to the leader, a relationship style is necessary in order to gain maximum employee support for the achievement of the objectives.

Even though these two recommended leadership styles reflect the two behavioural dimensions identified in the traditional behavioural leadership frameworks, Fiedler's theory departs from the behavioural theories not only in explicitly including situational aspects as central contingency factors, but also by treating these different leadership styles not as behavioural choices, but rather as an expression of a leader's deep-seated personality preferences for either a task or relationship approach. As a consequence, leaders are not free to choose the most appropriate style, but are limited in their behavioural flexibility due to the ingrained preferences. The actual person- or task-orientation of a leader is measured with Fiedler's Least Preferred Co-worker (LPC) scale.

Fiedler's work reflects the view that success is a function of the interaction between the relationships in the workplace, the task to be achieved, the relative power balance between leader and followers, and the preferred style (a trait) of the leader. Fiedler suggests that in attempting to optimize effectiveness, organizations should allow managers to maximize the fit between their preferred style and the other variables. This could be achieved through action plans for improving relationships or perhaps by moving key individuals. This approach has attracted some criticism on the basis that they are not consistent with the original model (Jago and Ragan, 1986). There has also been criticism of the research studies that were used to support the development of the model. However, there has also been support for the methodology (Strube and Garcia, 1981). Fiedler subsequently developed his work into a *cognitive resource theory* (CRT) (Fiedler, 1986). This model attempts to identify the situational circumstances which interact with the cognitive characteristics of the leader and which impact on group performance. As with all research this approach has

Figure 6.8 Fiedler's contingency model of leadership

Leader/member relations	Good				Poor			
Task structure	Structured		Unstructured		Structured		Unstructured	
Position power	High	Low	High	Low	High	Low	High	Low
Situational favourableness	Very favourable				Moderately favourable		Very unfavourable	
Recommended leader behaviour	Task-oriented behaviour				Person-oriented behaviour		Task-oriented behaviour	

not been without its critics (Vecchio, 1992). However, it does offer value in identifying relevant situational factors that affect leadership effectiveness even though the degree of behavioural flexibility of leaders remains a debated aspect of this theory.

House's path–goal leadership theory

The path–goal model of leadership links leader behaviour with subordinate motivation, performance and satisfaction (House, 1971; House and Mitchell, 1974). This approach is closely linked to *expectancy theory* (see Chapter 5). It postulates that subordinate motivation will be improved if the expectation that positive rewards will be forthcoming is likely to be realized. House identified four styles of leader behaviour:

- *Directive leadership.* Under this style the leader is expected to provide precise instruction on what is required and how it is to be achieved.
- *Supportive leadership.* This reflects a style that adopts a friendly approach concerned with the needs and welfare of subordinates.
- *Participative leadership.* This reflects a style in which the leader tends to seek opinions and suggestions from subordinates before making a decision.
- *Achievement-oriented leadership.* This reflects a style in which the leader is task-oriented and sets challenging goals for subordinates.

This contingency approach is based on the notion that individual leaders are capable of changing their style to match the needs of the situation. The two situational factors are:

1 *Subordinate characteristics.* Leader acceptability depends to a significant extent on the degree to which subordinates perceive leader behaviour as a source of present or future satisfaction.

2 *Demands facing subordinates.* Leader behaviour would motivate performance in subordinates if the satisfaction of subordinate needs were dependent on their performance in the work itself and/or other aspects of the work environment.

The path–goal model reflects the influence of leader behaviour on subordinate activity within a directional flow of activity towards the goal to be achieved (see Figure 6.9).

Attempts to empirically substantiate the model have brought mixed results. A review of 48 studies demonstrated mixed levels of support for aspects of the model and suggested the continued testing of it (Indvik, 1986). Also, some suggest that the theory applies better to hierarchical than to peer-leadership situations (Bowditch *et al.*, 2008).

Figure 6.9 Path–goal model of leadership

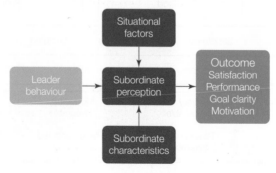

In summary, situational and other contingency models of leadership have broadened out the scope of leadership theory and research to include not just leader traits and behaviours, but also situational and follower characteristics. Sims and colleagues (2009) argue that leaders should develop their own specific situational leadership approach suited to the particular situations they lead in. In the next section we will consider additional leadership contributions that highlight specific aspects of leadership and consider leadership in particular contexts. The Going Global example provides the opportunity to reflect on two particular aspects of leadership.

OTHER APPROACHES TO LEADERSHIP

Leader-member exchange theory (LMX)

The leader-member exchange theory (LMX) approach to leadership, originally called the vertical dyad linkage (VDL) theory because it focused on dyadic relationships where one party has formal authority over the other, was developed by Dansereau, Graen and their colleagues (Dansereau *et al.*, 1975; Graen and Cashman, 1975). It suggests that leaders behave differently with different subordinates. Between the leader and each subordinate is an individual relationship, referred to as a vertical dyad. The model postulates that leaders create an in-group and an out-group around themselves and that these groups receive different treatments from the leader. The in-group is made up of a few special individuals, who are more trusted, and given more preferential treatment and special privileges than the out-group. Leadership in this model depends on leaders and followers being able to develop effective relationships that are the basis for mutual influence (Uhl-Bien, 2006). Figure 6.10 reflects the basis of the vertical dyad linkage model.

Research on LMX theory, however, has been plagued by different conceptions and definitions of central elements such as the specific nature of in-group and out-group relationships. Also, many different and at times incompatible measures have been used, making it all but impossible to directly compare and assess all relevant research. However, Ilies *et al.* (2007) recently reported that LMX is positively related to both performance on the job and to positive extra-role behaviours (called organizational citizenship behaviour or OCB). Also, there is little debate that differential relationships often develop between leaders and different followers. Recent work that more fully addresses the implications of such differential relationships on in-group and out-group members appears promising (e.g., Bolino and Turnley, 2009; Kacmar *et al.*, 2007), and longitudinal research addressing leader-member relationship development should offer valuable insights.

Leader–member exchange theory (LMX)
An approach to leadership, originally called the vertical dyad linkage (VDL) theory because it focused on dyadic relationships that included one party having formal authority over the other. It suggests that leaders behave differently with different subordinates.

Organizational Citizenship Behaviour
Voluntary behaviour that goes beyond the formal role of an employee; this behaviour generally contributes to organizational effectiveness but is not directly or explicitly recognized by the formal reward system.

Figure 6.10 The leader-member exchange model of leadership

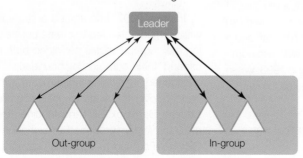

GOING GLOBAL

Interim management in France, the UK and Ireland

Interim management started in Holland during the 1980s as a means of circumventing the strict regulation of employment and labour. It is developing rapidly across Europe as a way of either tackling a specific issue or temporally filling a gap. It is, however, a grey area not yet well understood and is often confused with consulting or contracting. In the UK the market for such services has grown from about £75m in 1995 to around £268m in 2003. It should be seen as less reactive and more of a proactive, added value management approach, according to Richard Lambert, chairman of the Interim Management Association.

CEO Europe started in 2001 as a key facilitation company for temporary, interim and permanent senior executive appointments across Europe. They have many clients and interim managers based around the world and can react to a request for an interim appointment at short notice. One major assignment in January 2007 was for a company called Glowria, the French number one online video rental and video on demand (VoD) provider. Glowria was looking for a senior manager capable of quickly returning it to profitability. The gap between the business plan and what Glowria was actually achieving was widening, with a resulting loss of confidence in the existing management team among investors. Glowria's shareholders and directors decided to entrust the company to an interim manager with the clear brief of turning the company around or closing it.

Within 5 days of the request for assistance, CEO Europe presented Glowria with a short-list of candidates that matched the project profile. The successful candidate, Eric Caen started his mission on March 15th. Eric had the ideal profile to help Glowria. He founded the video games company Titus Interactive at the age of 19 in 1985 and by 2000 it was ranked 3rd in Europe and 7th worldwide with over 700 staff and a turnover of more than 175m Euros. He was also nominated entrepreneur of the year in France in 1998. When Eric arrived, the situation at Glowria was as follows:

- Turnover was stagnant at 5.8m Euros.
- Financial losses were high and cash-flow was a problem.

- The staff were demotivated and either defiant or even hostile towards his arrival and the purpose of his mission.
- Existing and potential commercial partners were worried about future business prospects, getting paid, etc.

Eric quickly developed a strategy to turn the company around that was based on:

- Structure – reorganize the business; convince – management and staff that success was possible; motivate – managers and staff to turn the business around.
- Getting back into positive growth.
- To make the best possible start by showing himself (and his senior managers) as organized, firm, decisive as well as clear in their direction and intention to succeed.
- Develop a relationship of trust with the staff. Based on keeping them informed and reassured – intended to find and build a consensus for the company, its activities, processes and future.
- Remotivate all the levels of employee and manager to regenerate a dynamic of achievement of immediate commercial results.

The company was managed out of the crisis within 7 months, the results being:

- The turnover increased by 20 per cent to reach 7m Euros.
- All employees were retained within the company.
- The company stopped its loss making activities in Germany (DVD Germany) and intensified its commercial efforts in France (DVD France and VoD as White Label products).

In June 2007, Eric agreed a strategic partnership with Netgem intended to create business leads. Uniting their competencies permitted both companies to expand their commercial boundaries. Glowria also succeeded in signing agreements with new major partners over that summer, including Fnac.com, Neuf Cegetel, Dartybox, SFR and Allocine. Towards the end of 2007, Netgem proposed an exchange of shares with Glowria. Eric had to convince Glowria's shareholders of the benefits of joining with Netgem - a company quoted on the stock exchange. The deal was finalized in December 2007 with the takeover of Glowria by Netgem, Glowria being valued at 18m Euros – a measure of the success of the project.

Alan Charlesworth is also an interim manager who spent 9 months on one assignment seeking to consolidate a business in order to make it profitable. This involved closing either the London or Dublin office. The job involved keeping everyone onside, dealing with people's natural concerns and sensitivities as well as maintaining operations during a period of dramatic change. The job involved split weeks between London and Dublin, living in hotel rooms for much of the

time and working long hours trying to overcome initial resistance and concerns.

TASKS

1 Which (if any) style of management would it be appropriate for interim managers such as Eric and Alan to adopt in these situations and why?

2 Could the contingency approach to leadership offer a better explanation of how to approach leadership in this situation? Why or why not?

Sources:
http://www.ceo-europe.com. Accessed August 2009. www .glowria.fr (accessed August 2009).
Mann, S (2003) Working away, *Professional Manager*, May, pp. 29-32.

In addition, the core idea of LMX theory has also been applied to relations between individuals and other members of workgroups (Seers, 1989). Such team-member exchange (TMX) has shown to predict commitment and job performance (Liden *et al.*, 2000) and is also associated with more positive emotions (Tse and Dasborough, 2008) and more within-group agreement (Ford and Seers, 2006).

Transactional and transformational leadership

An important distinction that focused attention on different leadership processes was introduced by Burns (1978) in the political arena. Bass (1985, 1996) and Kuhnert and Lewis (1987) further applied this distinction in management contexts. They suggested that there are two types of management activity, each demanding different skills. *Transactional activities* include the allocation of work, making routine decisions, monitoring performance and interacting with other functions within the organization. *Transformational activities*, in contrast, require the skills and personal qualities to be able to recognize the need for change and being able to identify appropriate courses of action to bring it about.

The difference between these two dimensions as distinctions of leadership approaches lies in the nature of the relationship between leaders and followers. Transactional leadership is based on an implicit and explicit calculation (such as 'economic cost-benefit assumptions', Bass, 1985: p. 5) of both parties that motivates followership through the exchange relationship between leaders and followers (hence 'transactional'). Bryman (1992) points out that most of the traditional behavioural, situational and contingency leadership theories are based on such a transactional logic.

Transformational leadership, in contrast, links followers' motivation to the role and the pursued outcomes. Bass (1985, 1996) argues that transformational leaders increase awareness of the value of these outcomes, transform follower's self-interest to include these larger objectives, and tap into higher-level needs of followers. While the relevant behaviours associated with transformational and transactional leadership are different, both approaches can be used by the same leader (Bass, 1985). Avolio and his colleagues (1999) argue that transformational leadership includes the subcomponents of charisma, intellectual stimulation and

Transactional leadership
This is based on an implicit and explicit calculation by both parties that motivates followership through the exchange relationship between leaders and followers (hence 'transactional'). See also transformational leadership.

Transformational leadership
This is based on linking followers' motivation directly to the pursued outcomes. Transformational leaders increase awareness of the value of these outcomes, transform follower's self-interest to include these larger objectives and tap into higher-level needs of followers. See also transactional leadership.

individualized consideration. Similarly, Bass (1990) identified the characteristics of both types of leader (see Table 6.4). He suggests that transactional leaders are a hindrance to change and foster a climate of mediocrity. Transformational leaders, by the same token, can produce improved performance in situations of uncertainty and change.

Tepper (1993) found that transformational leaders more frequently adopted legitimizing tactics than transactional leaders in explaining their decisions and selected courses of action. They were also able to achieve higher acceptance of objectives among subordinates than were transactional leaders. The major issue highlighted through this model is that most leaders are required to engage in both transactional and transformational leadership as part of their responsibilities. If leaders tend to one 'type' then it will be difficult for them to achieve an effective performance across the full range of their responsibilities.

Transformational leadership is particularly important in dynamic environments that require substantial change and quick responses. Despite the substantial evidence for the importance of transformational leadership (Judge and Piccolo, 2004; Zaccaro *et al.*, 2004), transformational leadership behaviours alone may not always be enough. In teams with innovation tasks, for example, transformational leadership was found to be necessary but not sufficient. It was found to only support team innovation when behavioural and cultural support for innovation was also present (Eisenbeiss *et al.*, 2008). Transformational leadership was also shown to be an important resource in achieving high performance in demographically diverse teams with less of an impact in more homogeneous teams (Kearney and Gebert, 2009).

Table 6.4 Characteristics of transactional and transformational leaders

Transactional leaders	
1	Contingent reward: Contracts exchange of rewards for effort, promises rewards for good performance, recognizes accomplishments
2	Management by exception (active): Watches and searches for deviations from rules and standards, takes corrective action
3	Management by exception (passive): Intervenes only if standards are not met
4	Laissez faire: Abdicates responsibilities, avoids making decisions

Transformational leaders	
1	Charisma: Provides vision and sense of mission, instils pride, gains respect and trust
2	Inspiration: Communicates high expectations, uses symbols to focus efforts, expresses important purposes in simple ways
3	Intellectual stimulation: Promotes intelligence, rationality and careful problem solving
4	Individual consideration: Gives personal attention, treats each employee individually, coaches, advises

Source: Bass, B.M. (1990) From transactional to transformational leadership: learning to share the vision, Organizational Dynamics, Winter.

Charismatic leadership

House (1977) characterized charismatic leaders as full of self-confidence, with a high level of confidence in subordinates and high expectations for results. They also have a clear vision of the goal to be achieved, are able to communicate this effectively and lead by example. Richard Branson is frequently held up as a significant (and very successful) example of a charismatic business leader. Charismatic leaders can, however, create problems for organizations. They may not fully understand the business or its environment and so may lead it in the wrong direction. Equally, if they do not make effective provision for succession to the leadership position when they wish to relinquish control the organization can flounder.

It has been argued that the emergence of charismatic leadership could be a function of both leader traits and situational variables (Conger and Kanungo, 1988). Personal traits that may produce a charismatic approach include self-confidence, skills in impression management and social sensitivity. Contextual variables that could encourage the emergence of a charismatic leader include crisis situations and high levels of subordinate dissatisfaction with the current leadership. Howell and Avolio (1992) introduce an ethical perspective to the discussion, pointing out that it is possible for charismatic individuals to abuse their capabilities in order to achieve an unquestioning following and hence a leadership position. Similarly, ethical behaviour by leaders affects the behaviour of employees. However, the trickle-down impact of senior managers' behaviour on lower-level employees is also dependent on the ethical leadership behaviour of direct supervisors. (Mayer *et al.*, 2009)

Conger (1999) suggests that many skills associated with charisma can be developed, including speaking skills as part of developing the ability to communicate effectively, and learning how to think critically about the status quo and what could be improved in it. It is also possible to use impression management tactics and to stage events that send powerful symbolic messages to other people (see Chapter 14). However, Conger suggests that passion is not learnable – it has to be discovered and developed at a personal level. Passion about what they are doing is a great driver of charismatic leaders and creates enthusiasm in the followers for achieving the vision. It also suggests that it takes courage to become unconventional and a risk taker, the other major skills of a charismatic leader.

Charismatic leadership
The ability to exercise leadership through the power of the leader's personality.

STOP & CONSIDER

'Charismatic leaders in the middle ranks of an organization would be a senior manager's worst nightmare as they are likely to undermine the authority of senior managers by creating an alternative power base and drawing the focus of employee attention away from senior figures.' Discuss this statement.

Value-based leadership

One of the important departures marked by work on transformational and charismatic leadership was the explicit consideration of values as a part of leadership. This is also reflected in a number of related concepts and leadership approaches that all share a concern for *leadership that is focused on expressing and promoting particular pro-social values* (our definition of value-based leadership). These include *stewardship* (Block, 1993; Caldwell *et al.*, 2008; Davis *et al.*, 1997; Hernandez, 2008; Zahra *et al.*, 2008), *servant leadership* (Greenleaf, 1991; Russell and Stone, 2002; Spears, 2004; Washington *et al.*, 2006), *ethical leadership* (Brown *et al.*, 2005; Brown and Treviño, 2006; Mayer *et al.*, 2009), *socialized charismatic leadership* (Brown and Treviño, 2009), and *authentic leadership* (e.g., Avolio and Gardner, 2005; Shamir and Eilam, 2005; Walumbwa *et al.*, 2008).

Value-based leadership
Leadership focused on expressing and promoting particular prosocial values. Specific approaches include stewardship, servant leadership, ethical leadership, socialized charismatic leadership and authentic leadership. See also these individual terms.

Stewardship
Refers to the attitudes and behaviours that place the long-term best interests of a group ahead of personal goals that serve an individual's self-interests. See also value-based leadership.

Servant leadership
Is defined as leadership that has service to others including followers as its main motivator. Trust, integrity, empathy, support, community building, empowerment and follower development are aspects particularly associated with such leadership. See also value-based leadership.

Ethical leadership
Leadership that is aligned with a moral code that provides consistency among the ends, means and consequences of the behaviour that leaders themselves exhibit and induce in followers. See also value-based leadership.

Socialized charismatic leadership
Can be defined as leadership that attempts to convey values-based messages and to bring about value congruence between leader and followers. See also value-based leadership.

Authentic leadership
This describes leaders that use balanced and reasoned information processing, have an internalized moral perspective, offer relational transparency and exhibit high levels of self-awareness. See also value-based leadership.

In more detail, stewardship refers to '*The attitudes and behaviours that place the long-term best interests of a group ahead of personal goals that serve an individual's self-interests.*' (Hernandez, 2008: p. 122) It is closely related to and can be seen as part of servant leadership (Spears, 2004). Servant leadership is defined as *leadership that has service to others including followers as its main motivator*. Trust, integrity, empathy, support, community building, empowerment and follower development are aspects particularly associated with such leadership (Joseph and Winston, 2005; Spears, 2004; Washington *et al.*, 2006). Definitions of ethical leadership are more contested (see Yukl, 2010) because the values expressed by particular ethics can differ fundamentally. We define ethical leadership as *leadership that is aligned with a moral code that provides consistency among the ends, means and consequences of the behaviour that leaders themselves exhibit and induce in followers.* Closely related to the concept of ethical leadership is socialized charismatic leadership which can be seen as *leadership that attempts to convey values-based messages and to bring about value congruence between leader and followers* (Brown and Treviño, 2009; see also Howell and Shamir, 2005). Finally, authentic leadership describes *leaders that use balanced and reasoned information processing, have an internalized moral perspective, offer relational transparency and exhibit high levels of self-awareness* (Avolio *et al.*, 2009; Walumbwa *et al.*, 2008).

These value-based leadership approaches are normative leadership theories, which means that they are prescriptive about how leaders should act, what kind of goals they should pursue and how they should relate to their followers. Unlike most other leadership theories we have discussed, they explicitly consider nonperformance-related consequences for followers and, to a lesser degree, for other stakeholders. Conceptually, they are less clearly and uniformly defined than other, more traditional approaches to leadership which reflects an earlier stage of theory and paradigm development in this area (Avolio and Gardner, 2005). This early stage in theory development also explains why these theories include many different types of variables and constructs (e.g., behaviours, values, cognitions, skills, etc.) which make them considerably harder to investigate and test empirically. Nevertheless, these value-based theories of leadership clearly address an important area. In light of current issues with corporate governance and organizational misbehaviour and increasingly demanding public expectations regarding both corporate social responsibility and corporate accountability, they offer important, timely and useful perspectives on leadership in organizations.

Followership

In addition to the focus on values and the reintroduction of leader traits to contemporary leadership research, the development of transformational and charismatic leadership theories also serve as a reminder of the interactive nature of leadership. As already discussed, leadership cannot exist without followership, and follower traits as well as the nature of leader–follower interactions and the ensuing relationship play a profound role in determining leadership effectiveness (e.g., Howell and Shamir, 2005). In fact, effective leadership depends on effective followership (Shamir, 2007), and we can consider followership as an enabler of leadership or even, especially in closely interacting teams, as a form of leadership. This view is closely linked to the idea of shared and distributed leadership which we will consider further below.

The impact of followers on leadership effectiveness is influenced by a number of factors including the way in which they (and relevant others) think about themselves (e.g., Carsten *et al.*, 2007; Collinson, 2006; Hollander, 1992; Lord and Brown, 2004). Chaleff (1995) argues that responsible and proactive followers who are able to challenge as well as support leaders can help overcome leader weaknesses and balance out leader biases in perceptions and decision making. This can best happen if the relationship between followers and leader is good. Shamir and Eilam (2005) introduce the construct of authentic followership, which is achieved by *those who freely choose to follow based on their realistic view and assessment of the consistency of the leader's values and behaviours, the congruence of these values with their own, and their own assessment of the leader's authenticity, honesty and integrity in leading them.*

Drawing form the work of Chaleff (1995), Kelley (1992) and Whetten and Cameron (1991), Yukl (2010: pp. 255-259) provides a set of guidelines for followers that summarize how *active followership* can support and enhance leadership effectiveness. These guidelines include:

- Find out what you are expected to do
- Take the initiative to deal with the problem
- Keep the boss informed about your decisions
- Verify the accuracy of the information you give the boss
- Encourage the boss to provide hones feedback to you
- Support leader efforts to make necessary changes
- Show appreciation and provide recognition when appropriate
- Challenge flawed plans and proposals made by leaders
- Resist inappropriate influence attempts by the boss
- Provide upward coaching and counseling when appropriate.

What is important to remember about the role of followership is that the individual differences of followers, for example their motivations, beliefs and preoccupations, can substantially impact on leadership effectiveness (e.g., De Cremer *et al.*, 2009; Dvir and Shamir, 2003; Howell and Shamir, 2005; Kark and Van Dijk, 2007; Van Kleef *et al.*, 2009; Zhu *et al.*, Note that this article has appeared in print: Zhu, W., Avolio, B.J., Walumbwa, F.O. (2009). Moderating role of follower characteristics with transformational leadership and follower work engagement.

Group & Organization Management, 34(5): 590-619. (2009). Similarly, perceptual and attributional processes strongly influence leader–follower interactions see Yukl, G (2010) *Leadership in Organizations. Prentice Hall*, Englewood Cliffs, for a comprehensive discussion), and the interpersonal and social dynamics of other hierarchical and nonhierarchical relationships (see Chapters 7, 8, 15 and 16) of course also apply to leader–follower relationships.

LEADERSHIP NEUTRALIZERS AND SUBSTITUTES

In organizations, a number of factors can affect effective leadership. Kerr and Jermier (1978) discuss such leadership neutralizers and leadership substitutes. Leadership neutralizers are those *factors that can reduce the opportunities for or effectiveness of leader influence*, while leadership substitutes are any *factors that can replace, or reduce the need for, leadership*.

Leadership neutralizers can pose problems for leaders because they can counter any efforts to exert leadership. They need to be taken into account both by leaders in their attempts to work with and through their followers, and in the deliberate structuring of tasks, jobs and organizations. Leadership neutralizers can be categorized as arising from one of three aspects of organizations (Kerr and Jermier, 1978):

- *Subordinate characteristics.* Situations where employees are professionally qualified, highly experienced and very able to undertake the duties expected of them do not need leadership in the conventional sense of the term. Also, where a subordinate is indifferent to the rewards that the leader can offer for co-operating and acceptance of their position there is little scope for the

Followership
This is often defined as an enabler of leadership or even, especially in closely interacting teams, as a form of leadership. This view is closely linked to the idea of shared and distributed leadership. See also authentic followership.

Authentic followership
which is achieved by those who freely choose to follow based on their realistic view and assessment of the consistency of the leader's values and behaviours, the congruence of these values with their own, and their own assessment of the leader's authenticity, honesty and integrity in leading them. See also followership.

6.7 EXTEND
YOUR LEARNING

Leadership neutralizers
Those factors that can reduce the opportunities for or effectiveness of leader influence.

Leadership substitutes
Any factors that can replace, or reduce the need for, leadership.

EMPLOYEE PERSPECTIVE

Managers are employees too!

Harry was a production manager with about 25 years experience working in a range of industrial textile sewing factories within the same group. He had a good reputation among senior managers and was also well liked by his subordinates. He was transferred to a new company bought by the group as it was felt that he had the best range of skills to assist with its integration into the group. Harry's predecessor had been dismissed after the takeover of the company, as he was regarded as ineffective in managing staff and incapable of running the factory.

The new company that Harry joined as production manager was based in the North of England and employed about 250 people, mostly females engaged in sewing webbing and camouflage products for military use. Unfortunately for Harry the workforce in the new factory was dominated by a small number of shop-floor workers who had very strong personalities and who could be very aggressive if they did not get what they wanted. They had a history of terrorizing their colleagues (and managers), always managing to get their own way one way or another. Harry regarded this as unreasonable and set out to change the

behaviour of the people concerned. It did not work. On one occasion two of the leading 'terrorists' in the factory kicked Harry's office door off its hinges as he had refused their demands to see them immediately.

Eventually the stress got to Harry and one day the managing director of the company found him in his office sitting in the corner sucking his thumb, having had a complete nervous breakdown. He was hospitalized and soon recovered, but was never again able to take up a senior managerial position within the group. His confidence had been shattered, as had his desire to do the job.

TASKS

1 Could Harry have prevented this happening to himself? How?

2 What if anything could the new owners have done to prevent this situation developing as it did?

3 What would you do now if you were Harry's replacement as production manager and why?

Source:
Personal experience of one of the authors as the production manager that replaced Harry in the company!

practice of leadership. The following Employee Perspective illustrates one aspect of this.

- *Task characteristics.* Where the work is highly routine and contains immediate feedback on performance and achievement there is little scope for the exercise of leadership. The employee is effectively controlled by the job that they undertake and feedback on performance is automatically and quickly received through the work itself. Leadership in such situations becomes restricted to ensuring that work is provided to the employee and that it is taken away when it is completed, and to supporting employees as required.

- *Organizational characteristics.* An organization that is highly routinized with little flexibility will have limited need for leader activity as it will almost run itself. Similarly, spatial distance or other structural arrangements that create distance or filters between leaders and followers can neutralize leadership efforts. Strong cultural values or group norms can also counter leader efforts to influence behaviour.

Many of the factors identified above as neutralizing leadership can also be used to substitute for the need to exert ongoing leadership. Thus, they can offer solutions in situations where it is difficult to provide continuous leader presence and involvement. Factors that can be used include self-management (Manz and Sims, 1980, 1991), which refers to *activities and strategies a person uses to influence, maintain or change their own behaviour*, as well as self-managed and autonomous work teams. Strong normative influences through organizational culture or group norms as well as socialized behaviour through organizational or professional socialization can also substitute for leadership.

Despite the high intuitive value of the original theory of leadership neutralizers and substitutes (Kerr and Jermier, 1978), research support for the theory has been limited (e.g., Dionne *et al.*, 2002; Dionne *et al.*, 2005; Keller, 2006). This may be due to measurement problems and to a lack of longitudinal and appropriately comprehensive research designs that investigate the complex set of factors that influences leadership effectiveness. However, as a reminder of important aspects to consider in work design and organizational structuring as well as a useful set of factors to consider for leaders it remains valuable. Further research that more clearly identifies the boundary conditions under which certain factors may neutralize or substitute for leadership would further enhance the contribution of this theory (Howell *et al.*, 2007).

Distributed, shared and virtual leadership

There are some groups that attempt to operate without a formal leader, for example, workers' co-operatives and autonomous work teams. A form of democracy or other decision-making procedures can exist in such groups, replacing the traditional leadership role. It is important, however, to recognize that even with this role and a particular person filling it, the function of leadership remains important. The often hierarchical implications of the leader role are replaced by a collective set of responsibilities and privileges that in more traditional settings is typically enjoyed by a leader. Therefore, such distributed or shared leadership refers to situations in which *the function of leadership is jointly exercised by a number of highly interdependent, intensely collaborating and closely interacting individuals*. This can be achieved through extensive delegation among members of such a group (Klein *et al.*, 2006), through patterns of intensive and extensive reciprocal influence among members that reinforce relationships and joint responsibilities among them (Carson *et al.*, 2007) and through the serial emergence of official and unofficial leaders (Pearce, 2004). The development and practice of shared leadership poses specific challenges that differ from other forms of leadership (Ross *et al.*, 2005).

Other perspectives on shared leadership recognize that the impact of single leaders in organizations is always dependent on the actions and contributions of many other members (Day *et al.*, 2004), and that shared leadership is always present when followers take an active role which, as discussed above, makes followership a form of leadership. A particular conception of leadership offered by Drath and Palus (1994) offers an interesting and useful perspective on this. They conceive of leadership as meaning-making in a community of practice (see also Chapter 11). Shared understanding and meanings are important ingredients of distributed and shared leadership. The Management in Action panel illustrates a partnership management arrangement that has some similarity with the shared leadership model identified above.

Finally, many international and global organizations increasingly use virtual work, particularly for teams (Kirkman *et al.*, 2002). Leadership interactions in such teams are largely mediated through technology, and leaders of virtual teams face particular challenges including questions about how to structure and conduct the interpersonal aspects of leadership such as motivational and relationship building activities and how to support sufficient collaboration and co-ordination in the team (e.g., Kirkman *et al.*, 2002; Zigurs, 2003). Interaction and communication styles among virtual team members are often less constructive and more defensive compared to face-to-face teams

Self-management
Refers to activities and strategies a person uses to influence, maintain or change their own behaviour.

Distributed or shared leadership
Refers to situations in which the function of leadership is jointly exercised by a number of highly interdependent, intensely collaborating and closely interacting individuals.

MANAGEMENT IN ACTION

Running a general practice

In the UK, family doctors are called general practitioners (GPs) and are self-employed under contract to the National Health Service (NHS). It is common for groups of GPs to band together and form partnerships that then bid to run general family medical practices in a specific geographic area. The partnership is then free to organize itself according to its size, services offered, location and the way in which the partners wish to manage the practice. The partners have two distinct roles to perform within their practice as an independent business. The first is to run the business as they are the owners of it. It is their capital that set it up and they must decide how it should function and what it should do in order to achieve a return on that investment. The second role that they have is to provide the medical expertise to the practice in their capacity as qualified GPs. In that role they are effectively the specialist, technically qualified employees forming the backbone of the partnership. Of course the partners may not be the only GPs (or medical specialists) employed within the practice. For example some GPs employed by the practice may not be partners and may hold the status of salaried employee; there may be physiotherapists, locum doctors, phlebotomists, travel clinic nurses, social workers and other specialist medical and support workers either employed directly (part- or full-time) or effectively renting rooms and facilities from the main practice.

It is usual for each practice to employ a Practice Manager who, although subordinate to the partners, is responsible for the day-to-day running of the practice. In practice that means that they are the business manager for the practice. That would involve staffing matters, administration, accounting processes, facilities management, patient involvement, statutory returns and fee and other income flows. They would also be responsible for helping to formulate business strategies on behalf of the partners and of ensuring that the business and medical strategies and priorities agreed by partners were implemented.

The partners, all being GPs, are trained doctors and traditionally received no training on how to run a practice during that process. Today all vocational training schemes for GPs include some insights into how to run a practice. In discussing these issues with David (a GP who was also a partner) he explained that in his view the necessary qualities of a doctor that were developed in general medical and specifically GP training were:

● to be patient-centred
● to be empathic
● to co-operate and assist in diagnosis/overcoming problems.

However, by comparison, his experience over the past 15 years of being a partner GP led him to suggest that the necessary drivers (qualities necessary for a partner) were:

● personal gain
● profitability
● competition
● efficiency.

TASKS

1 If you were a practice manager as described above, how would you seek to manage (or should it be direct?) doctors who are providing the basic services but who are also the owners of the business that you are 'responsible' for running?

2 As a doctor and partner in such a practice, how could you be expected to deal with staff issues (say, dealing with a patient complaint against a particular member of staff) when the employee might also be one of your patients?

3 Individuals such as David have two very different roles within general medical practices such as the one outlined in this example – they are partners (owners of the business) as well as a doctor providing medical care to patients. Identify some of the implications for David (and people in similar positions) of these two different and potentially conflicting roles.

4 How and in what ways might an understanding of the material in this chapter on leadership and management help doctors who are also partners (such as David) in running their business effectively?

Source:
Conversation with Dr David Lightwing, GP and partner based in the North of England.

(Balthazard *et al.*, 2008). In a study on real-life surgery teams, Xiao and colleagues (Xiao *et al.*, 2008) reported that under task urgency and time pressure (such as in crises situations) communication between leader and senior team members increased while leader communication with junior members was reduced. Often, virtual teams suffer from reduced individual and collective commitment to goals and lower cohesion (Balthazard *et al.*, 2008). This is in line with the finding that the richness of communication media used has a positive impact on the interaction styles and cohesion in teams (Hambley *et al.*, 2007) which provides challenges for virtual teams that typically use electronic media extensively. The challenge for leaders is to overcome this and other difficulties imposed by the lack of co-location such as geographic dispersion, time differences and resultant reduced contact availability, incompatibility of information and communication technology platforms as well as other task technology used, and differential local demands that place uneven pressures on team members (Weisband, 2008). These aspects of virtual teamwork create challenges that traditional leadership theories and models may not fully address (Zigurs, 2003). In this context Malhotra *et al.* (2007) identify six leadership practices of effective virtual team leaders (see also Rosen *et al.*, 2006, for general suggestions of how to support virtual teamwork):

1 Establish and maintain trust using communication technology.
2 Ensure that distributed diversity is understood and appreciated.
3 Manage virtual work-life cycle (meetings).
4 Monitor team progress using technology.
5 Enhance visibility of virtual members within the team and outside in the organization.
6 Enable individual members of the virtual team to benefit from the team.

6.8 EXTEND
YOUR LEARNING

CONCLUSIONS

This chapter has considered many of the variables associated with the practice of management and leadership. The chapter began by considering what management actually is and some of the theoretical models developed to explain its function. It also considered what it is that managers actually do, and the roles that managers adopt while performing their duties. The major theoretical approaches to the study of leadership have been introduced and critically evaluated. In addition, we have discussed a number of other approaches to the subject, such as the contingency models of leadership, and related these to features of management. We have considered alternative approaches to the subject of leadership including charismatic leadership, leader-member exchange theory and value perspectives on leadership. Also considered were the topics of leadership neutralizers and substitutes together with issues such as virtual, shared and distributed leadership.

Now to summarize this chapter in terms of the relevant Learning Objectives:

● **Discuss the meaning of, and distinction between, leadership and management.**
Management represents a formal role within an organization. In that sense it is a job which contains particular responsibilities for an area of organizational activity and probably a number of subordinate employees. It is an activity that involves planning, organizing, leading and controlling resources in order to achieve goals. Mintzberg described 10 different roles in management work that he grouped under three headings called interpersonal, informational and decisional. Leadership is defined as 'The process of influencing others to understand and agree about what needs to be done and how to do it, and the process of facilitating individual and collective efforts to accomplishing shared objectives.' Leadership is generally regarded as the activity or process by which a pewrson can get other people to follow. The terms management and leadership are frequently used interchangeably but there are differences. In organizations, managers are formally appointed. This brings with it certain privileges (authority) and responsibilities (accountability). Leadership however is not based on formal roles or authority but emerges from social interaction and exists only if it proves successful.

- **Explain the contribution to understanding leadership of the various behavioural approaches.** These offer an explanation of leadership based on the relative contribution of subordinates to the process of leading. The democratic end of the style spectrum involves leaders delegating some of their authority and power to subordinates through involvement. At the autocratic end of the spectrum leaders retain control of everything and simply requires an unquestioning following by subordinates. Between these two extremes variation in the degree of involvement and delegation are allowed by the leader. The democratic end of the spectrum produces (it is claimed) more effective working relationship between leader and led and hence higher productivity. The contingency models go further in suggesting that circumstances can impact on the style of leader behaviour likely to be successful in particular contexts. The behavioural approaches can also be contrasted with the trait and other approaches to leadership. For example, trait approaches emphasize personal characteristics of the leader. The availability of other approaches to leadership do not automatically rule out the importance of behavioural models. For example, charisma might influence the behavioural 'style' of the leader in subordinate interaction.

- **Assess the contribution of the different theoretical approaches to the study of leadership.** There are many theoretical perspectives on leadership. The trait model seeks to explain the personal characteristics of successful leaders. This proved difficult to sustain as so many variables have been identified and there are many exceptions to the rules found among successful leaders. The behavioural approaches reflect a continuum between autocratic and democratic 'styles' and usually claim the democratic 'style' leads to success. However in a crisis there may not be time to involve everyone and so an autocratic approach may be required. The contingency modules deal with this by suggesting that the most appropriate style depends on a range of contextual factors. However 'success' is difficult to define and hence a problem for all leadership models – over how long should it be displayed and what does it mean (share price, profit, happy employees)? The other approaches to leadership do not reflect a cohesive group in any meaningful sense - they reflect the perspectives of the writers in seeking to explain leadership. For example the charismatic approach suggests that successful leadership reflects personality characteristics and the ability to draw

follower responses that are largely unquestioning. The leader-member exchange theory model suggests that different leader behaviours towards different groups and individuals are relevant understanding leadership. The transactional and transformational leadership model describes two different aspects of leadership in ways that are not dissimilar to the style perspective. The value-based approaches to leadership introduce another range of leadership features that have significance. A grand theory of leadership has not yet been developed that can fully explain what it is, but the range of models and theories available can contribute to an improved understanding of it.

- **Understand the significance of the contingency approaches to the study of leadership.** Contingency models reflect approaches that seek to capture a broader range of factors that impact on the ways in which leaders can exercise their responsibilities. Inevitably they work thorough the factors that each model sees as important and then emerge with the suggestion that particular leader behaviours would be most appropriate to the circumstances identified. They are usually regarded as extensions of behavioural theories. What emerges from the contingency models, however, is that because of the variation in context, variation in leader behaviour is also necessary. That in turn implies that either a leader needs to be able to vary their behaviour, or that the leader should be changed when the circumstances change. This has major implications for the management of organizations. If leadership represents a set of characteristics, then leaders must be trained to vary their use of them according to the needs of the situation. If on the other hand leadership represents a set of personality characteristics then it may not be possible for the leader to vary their behaviour to a significant degree - the implication being that the leader should be changed. This has obvious implications for careers and training in the management area. Some of the models suggest that managers have dominant and backup behaviour repertoires and that the necessary qualities of leadership can be acquired through training.

- **Outline the roles that managers perform and identify the significance of followership in allowing leadership to function effectively.** Mintzberg described 10 different management roles that he grouped under three headings called interpersonal, informational and decisional:

1 *Interpersonal roles.* These roles reflect the form that the interaction with other people takes

as a consequence of the status and type of a managerial job.

2 *Informational roles.* These roles reflect the nature of the way that information is used in the job of the manager.

3 *Decisional roles.* These roles reflect the nature of decision-making requirements within a particular managerial job.

Individual roles often overlap, and rather than describing management as an orderly, well structured activity, the picture of management that Mintzberg's paints is one of fragmented, often interrupted activities that are determined as much by circumstances as it is by choice and preference. Leadership cannot happen without followership, and follower traits as well as the nature of leader–follower interactions and the ensuing relationship all play a profound role in determining leadership effectiveness. Authentic followership refers to those who freely choose to follow based on their assessment of the consistency of the leader's values and behaviours; the congruence of those values with their own; and their assessment of the leader's authenticity, honesty and integrity in leading them. Followership is significant because the individual differences of between them can substantially impact on leadership effectiveness.

DISCUSSION QUESTIONS

1 Compare and contrast the views on the management process as outlined by Fayol and Mintzberg's description of the 10 management roles.

2 'Successful management is about acquiring power and using it to ensure that you achieve your objectives.' Based on the material introduced in this chapter to what extent could this viewpoint be justified?

3 To what extent might the context play a significant part in determining what managers actually do?

4 Discuss what it is that managers spend their time doing, in the process making use of the material presented in this chapter.

5 'The top leaders in an organization are there simply to provide a symbolic focus for the world outside the organization. It is the management in the middle ranks of the organization that actually delivers the level of success achieved.' Discuss this statement.

6 Discuss the differences and similarities between the concepts of management and leadership.

7 'Come the hour, cometh the leader.' Discuss this statement in the light of the approaches to leadership discussed in this chapter.

8 'Leaders need to find the right group and context before they are able to exercise their leadership.' Discuss this statement.

9 To what extent is leadership simply a means of expressing management in a way that employees would find more acceptable and therefore work harder?

10 'Charismatic leaders are not appropriate in the middle ranks of managerial jobs because they could encourage an organization within an organization to develop.' Discuss this statement.

CASE STUDY

Micro management or working for a control freak!

Most workplaces have at least one-a boss who is a control freak. Micro managing by always looking over people's shoulders, monitoring their every move, checking every detail of their work, continually questioning their ability to do (to the desired standard) what is expected of them in the timescales set. There can be many reasons why a manager micro manages, including:

- Perhaps their boss treats them that way and expects everyone to be the same.
- Perhaps they've been let down by poor quality staff in the past.
- Perhaps the problem lies at the top with the chief executive micro managing their subordinates and it becomes part of the company culture, working down through the managerial levels.
- Managers promoted from technical jobs can struggle with the people aspects of a managerial role.
- Poor recruitment of managers can fail to identify warning signs.
- Poor training means that if managers don't fully understand their role (or have the capability to fulfil it) they will make it up, or fall back on what they do know.
- Perhaps they have such a strong ego that they actually believe that their subordinates cannot do the job unchecked.
- Perhaps they are frightened for their own job and don't trust their subordinates not to undermine them.
- Perhaps the organization has a blame culture which encourages people to act defensively to avoid punishment.

Whatever the cause, they have a 'compulsion' or 'disposition' to behave the way that they do (or the

© Tim Garacha/Corbis

company requires them to do so) which will continue unless they (or the organization) get help to change. Control freaks tend to be skilled manipulators, intimidating, rehearsed debaters, artful and clever at distorting reality in support of justifying their actions and approach to management. Among the many warning signs that such a manager exists include a high turnover of staff, low morale, low productivity, staff lacking in enthusiasm, creativity or innovation. The reason is simple; good employees won't tolerate micro management and they will either leave, or if they cannot, they will psychologically withdraw from engagement with the organization and its objectives. In coping they will adopt a self-preservation approach to complying with the management style and instructions.

Some coping strategies that have been identified to help subordinates deal with micro management or control freakery include:

1 **Stay calm, speak softly.** If you don't stay calm and speak softly you are engaging in a 'battle' on their terms.

2 **Pay attention to your reactions to them.** Understanding how you react to the pressure felt by being micro managed will give you clues as to how to deal with such situations and people more effectively.

3 **They might control the agenda, but try to control pace.** By staying calm and speaking slowly, you will tend to control the pace and tone of the conversation.

4 **Don't join in the 'game'.** Don't pass on the pressure or approach to management implied by micro management and control freakery. Retain your dignity and professionalism in your work. Don't take responsibility for actions pushed onto you by being able to separate your work from that 'forced' on you.

5 **Turn micro management back on the boss.** Ask them for clarification, specific instructions or for clear guidance. By asking something of them, you will be indicating that you are prepared to hold them to account, are willing to learn, and not intimidated or diminished by their behaviour.

6 **Be prepared to raise a grievance of harassment complaint.** It is always possible to take matters further and to raise a complaint based on unreasonable treatment, discrimination,

harassment, etc. as a way of forcing senior management to take the issue seriously – following company procedures of course.

Some of the strategies for helping managers and organizations avoid the problems associated with micro management include:

1 **Encourage managers to develop delegating skills.** Empowering subordinates and encouraging delegation increases a manager's opportunity to control as it allows more time for planning and strategy issues. Also stop taking ownership away from subordinates by answering every job-related question that they ask – start asking them what they think they should do? Identify projects, issues or challenges that could be delegated to a project team or empower an individual to solve the problem.

2 **Engender trust in your employees.** Employees should be capable of doing what is expected of them if the company resourcing and training processes are adequate. Consequently they should be trustworthy. If they cannot be trusted then something is going wrong and needs to be addressed rather than simply taking over their responsibilities.

3 **Identify the necessary competency and skills for every key employee.**

4 **Consider adopting employee feedback and similar survey/review processes.** That should help to identify issues associated with management style, micro management and culture that need addressing.

5 **Let subordinates make mistakes (but not too many)!** The hardest thing to do is to watch someone make a mistake – but people learn from the mistakes that they make. But the right approach is needed. For example, occupational psychologist Peter Honey stresses the need for a coaching approach when things go wrong, rather than pointing the finger and seeking to allocate blame.

6 **Learn from successes.** For example, Laura Parrish, a watch leader aboard the LG *Flatron* (the winning yacht in the BT Global Challenge round the world race a few years ago) explained that the crew had agreed to look only at the things that went right, not the things that went wrong. If a good sail change occurred, they considered what happened in great detail in order to be able to achieve the same performance every time.

7 **Provide a broad based employee development programme.** It should be based on developing skills for future roles as well as empowering employees to make tough decisions. Intern programmes are also an effective base for future development.

8 **Encourage results and initiative.** There are many ways to create success and achieve results. Slavish adherence to a traditional/single way of doing things may not produce the best results. Encourage subordinates to achieve the results expected, give them credit praise when it happens.

TASKS

1 How can a manager become tolerant of mistakes without encouraging carelessness?

2 To what extent does the advice to subordinates make sense in relation to helping to deal with a boss who micro manages?

3 Is micro management always the same as being a control freak? When might they be different and what might that imply about such individuals?

4 To what extent do the strategies identified above provide a means of minimizing the risk of micro management arising in an organization?

5 How might the material in this chapter help to minimize the risk of micro management arising or of dealing with it effectively if it is found to exist?

Sources:

BrainDeath by Micromanagement: The Zombie Function, http://headrush.typepad.com/creating_passionate_users/2005/12/braindeath_by_m.html (accessed August 2009).

Johnson, R. (2009) Avoid Micro Management, Wednesday, 11 February, http://www.4hoteliers.com/4hots_fshw.php?mwi=3761 (accessed August 2009).

Lucas, E (2003) Eye for Minutiae, *Professional Manager*, May, pp. 20–22.

Schumacher, T. J. (2002) *Dealing With Control Freaks.,* http://www.ec-online.net/knowledge/Articles/control.html (accessed August 2009).

FURTHER READING

Cranwell-Ward, J., Bacon, A. and Mackie, R. (2002) *Inspiring Leadership: Staying Afloat in Turbulent Times*, London: Thomson Learning. Based on the BT Global Challenge Round the World Yacht Race, the authors were given unrivalled behind the scenes access to crew and events. This book brings the lessons learned from such major sporting activity to the reader in the hope that they can learn from such events.

Deering, A., Kearney, A.T., Dilts, R. and Russell, J. (2002) *Alpha Leadership: Tools for Business Leaders Who Want More from Life*, Chichester: John Wiley. A focus on the application of the three concepts of anticipation, alignment and action as the main drivers of successful leadership, the writers provide the tools through which leaders can ensure an effective balance between career and personal success.

Fletcher, W. (2002) *Beating the 24/7:* How *Business Leaders Achieve a Successful Work-life Balance*, Chichester: John Wiley. A book in which several of today's most visible business leaders explain how they achieve both business and personal success through an effective work-life balance.

Hartley, R.F. (2002) *Management Mistakes and Successes*, 7th edn, Chichester: John Wiley. This text has been around for about 25 years now and this latest edition seeks to bring it up to date in terms of episodes introduced and the way that learning material is extracted from the examples.

Quinn, R.E., Faerman, S.R., Thompson, M.P. and McGrath, M. (2003), *Becoming a master manager: A competency framework* (3rd edn), New York: Wiley. Valuable resource for identifying and developing important leadership and management skills.

Watson, T.J. (2001) *In search of Management: Culture, Chaos and Control in Managerial Work*, London: Thomson Learning. A research based book based on the observation of real managers working in real organizations. Draws out a wide range of management issues and provides a real 'feel' for the life and work of managers as they struggle to deal with the dynamic environment around them.

Whetten, D.A. and Cameron, K.S. (2007) *Developing management skills* (7th edn), Pearson. Very useful book that provides valuable and structured input on many important aspects of leadership and management development.

Yukl, G. (2010) *Leadership in organizations* (7th edn), Upper Saddle River, NJ: Pearson. Encyclopaedic treatment of leadership theory and research – excellent and up-to-date sourcebook.

COMPANION WEBSITE

Online teaching and learning resources

Visit the companion website for Organizational Behaviour and Management 4th edition at: http://www.cengage.co.uk/martinfellenz to find valuable further teaching and learning material. For full details, see 'About the website' at the start of the book.

©iStock/mihau

CHAPTER SEVEN

GROUPS AND TEAMS

LEARNING OBJECTIVES

After studying this chapter and working through the associated OB in Action panels, Discussion Questions and Case Study you should be able to:

- Outline the concept of a group as distinct from a team or a collection of individuals.

- Understand the differences between formal and informal groups.

- Explain group development processes and how they might impact on group performance.

- Discuss the nature and value of role theory together with its relevance to the structure of groups and teams.

- Assess how control can be achieved within groups through such mechanisms as norms, rules and roles.

INTRODUCTION

Inside and outside of organizations, groups and teams form a significant part of the everyday experience of people. Inside of organizations, they have particular importance and play a variety of roles. They exists both as formal entities with explicit goals and functions in organizations, and as informal groupings that serve emerging social needs of their members. Groups and teams are so important for OB because they are at the same time an important tool for managers and organizations to achieve goals, and a social phenomenon with profound influence on individual and collective thinking, feeling, and behaviour.

In this chapter we will define groups and teams and discuss the significance of different forms of groups for organizations. We will consider how groups form and develop, how they are structured, and how they influence cognitions and behaviour of their members. We will also discuss the specific behavioural dynamics in groups and identify their implications for important other topics such as decision making and conflict in organizations.

FORMAL AND INFORMAL GROUPS

Generally, any number of people who share a characteristic can be seen as a group (e.g., all students in a lecture who have brown eyes; all people born on the same day; all passengers on Flight number 733); but such *aggregates* (which can include such groupings as an audience, crowd, extended family, household, mob, etc.) are not of central concern to us here in relation to management and OB. What we are interested in is the phenomenon of groups as a social entity that has an impact internally on its members (i.e., their thinking, feeling and behaviour), and externally on others affected by the (in)actions of the group, or even simply by its existence. This kind of group is also often called a psychological group.

A wide range of definitions for the term 'group' exists, but we are interested in what distinguishes psychological groups from mere aggregates. These concerns are reflected in definitions such as Shaw's (1981) who suggests that a group consists of two or more people who interact with each other in such a way that each influences and is influenced by the others. Many other definitions also include aspects such as a common goal or objective, active communication among all members, defined and differentiated roles for members, and others. As we will see in this chapter, all these aspects can be found in some types of groups, but the necessary (and sufficient) elements of groups are reflected in this definition that provides a useful way to think about groups in organizations: Groups are *social entities of two or more people who interact with each other, are psychologically aware of each other, and think of themselves as a group* (Schein, 1988).

In organizations we find both formal and informal groups. Formal groups are typically set up and sanctioned by the organization, and thus have specific objectives intended to contribute to achieving organizational goals. One important type of formal group usually set up by organizations is teams which we will discuss in more detail below. Formal groups may be established permanently, or for specific tasks or durations. They are designed and imposed by managers on the workforce as a way of achieving the desired objectives. They also represent an attempt to impose social control on the workforce in encouraging certain behaviours and discouraging others through adopted (or imposed) norms, without the need for formal control mechanisms. Some formal groups exist in and around organizations that are not established by the organizations, for example unions. In general, the grouping of members around differentiated tasks (called *departmentation*) is the source of the formal structure of an organization (see Chapter 10). Specific types of formal and informal groups in organizations are presented in Table 7.1.

Groups
Social entities of two or more people who interact with each other, are psychologically aware of each other, and think of themselves as a group.

Formal groups
Established by the organization to achieve particular objectives intended to contribute to achieving organizational goals.

Table 7.1 Different types of groups found in organizations

Type of group	Description
Group	Social entities of two or more people who interact with each other, are psychologically aware of each other, and think of themselves as a group.
Formal group	Established by the organization to achieve particular objectives intended to contribute to achieving organizational goals.
Natural work group	Groups that form around normal work processes.
Command group	Employees who report to the same manager.
Teams	Small groups whose members take individual and collective responsibility for their shared objectives and interactively co-ordinate their interdependent activities through roles and specific assignments.
Task-forces	Temporary groups set up to deal with a particular issue or objective. Typically staffed with individuals from different departments or even organizations.
Cross-functional teams	Teams set up with memberships that deliberately include different functions or groups. Usually temporary, but are sometimes used permanently to increase communication and integration between different functions.
Project teams	Teams set up to complete a particular task.
Committees	Groups that meet at regular intervals to consider issues of interest to different groupings or departments. Can be temporary or permanent.
Informal groups	Groups that arise through interactions among organizational members and serve their sociability, support and dependency needs without official recognition or sanction.
Friendship groups	Informal groups of members with friendship ties and positive attitudes towards each other.
Interest groups	Informal groups with shared objective(s) exerting active efforts *vis-à-vis* the organization to achieve the shared objective(s).
Minimal group	Groups without member interaction or goals but whose members act like they would if a real and meaningful group existed.

Researchers and practitioners alike often use the terms 'group' and 'team' interchangeably. However, it is useful to recognize that particular features identify teams as a particular type of group. Therefore, all teams are groups, but not all groups are teams. In practice it may often be difficult to distinguish if a particular group is a team or not. However, teams differ from other groups in that they are small, cohesive groups that work effectively as a single unit through being focused on a common task. What distinguishes them from other types of groups is that they are usually formally set up and have specific objectives that they pursue with co-ordinated, interdependent

Team
Small groups whose members take individual and collective responsibility for their shared objectives and interactively co-ordinate their interdependent activities through roles and specific assignments.

interactions (Cohen and Bailey, 1997). Their members are actively selected and team boundaries therefore tend to be clear (Belbin, 2000). In addition, teams usually employ some form of internal differentiation through roles and specific assignments (Humphrey *et al.*, 2009). Also, team members feel individually and collectively responsible for team performance (Cohen and Bailey, 1997), and one of the implications of this is that teams often employ some form of shared or distributed leadership (see Chapter 6). As all teams are by definition special types of groups we will not consistently distinguish between them in this chapter unless a clear distinction is of particular significance.

In their work on teams, Katzenbach and Smith (1993) draw many of the ideas about teams together by suggesting that the distinction between groups and teams can be reflected in the relative performance achieved. They propose that a positive correlation exists between the team-type and level of performance (see Table 7.2 for details). The concept of high-performance teams suggests teams that reflect values and mindsets fully aligned with the organization. Such teams encourage individuals to go beyond their contract in continually giving more than required, and reducing conflict and the need for close supervision. One aspect of this process over recent years is the attempt by many organizations to change the role and title of the traditional supervisor to that of team leader. The idea here is that a team leader would act in less hierarchical and more team-oriented ways to support team functioning and performance. However, if not handled effectively, the introduction of such changes can create more problems than they solve, as is evident from the following Employee Perspective example.

Informal groups
Social structures that arise through interactions among organizational members and serve their sociability, support and dependency needs.

Informal groups are groups that form through interactions among organizational members. They typically emerge naturally and over time (e.g., friendship groups) and resemble other naturally occurring social structures, but can also be formed

---

EMPLOYEE PERSPECTIVE

David was a team leader, or was he?

David was a production supervisor in a large engineering factory in the Birmingham area. He had served his apprenticeship as a toolmaker and had been promoted to supervisor some 5 years prior to the incidents described. He was paid slightly more than the employees he supervised but did not earn any production bonus. He was, however, paid overtime at the same rate as the other workers.

The company for which David worked undertook a restructuring exercise and among the changes made was the elimination of the supervisor job. This was replaced with a team leader job – intended to work closely with the work group and lead them rather than manage them. Among the other changes made were an increase in salary for the team leader, but they would not be paid for working overtime.

The changes were introduced without too many difficulties. However, the factory then received a large order and had to increase the amount of overtime worked in order to make the products. The workers were very keen to put in the additional hours, but the new team leaders were not, as they would not get any extra money. As David said, 'They created the new job of team leader which in practice is no different from the old supervisor's job, stop our overtime pay and then expect us to work all the hours available – for free. We have been conned.'

TASKS

1 What would you do if you were David?

2 What would you do if you were a manager in the same firm?

3 What might you expect the differences between a team leader and a supervisor to be?

Table 7.2 Types of groups and teams reflecting increasing performance potential

	Type of group/team	
Increasing performance potential →	Working group	A collection of individuals working collectively to a limited degree. Performance largely reflects the efforts of individual members.
	Pseudo-teams	A collection of individuals who could achieve higher performance if they worked in a more integrated and effective way.
	Potential teams	This category is essentially the same as pseudo-teams, but the individuals recognize that they could integrate more effectively and seek to do so.
	Real teams	This category of team is committed to the common purpose and has developed appropriate ways of working.
	High-performance teams	Real teams with the additional features of encouraging personal growth and going beyond performance expectations among members.

Source: Katzenbach, JR & Smith, DK (1993) *The Wisdom of Teams: Creating the High Performance Organization*, Harvard Business School Press, Boston. Reprinted with permission.

deliberately by organizational members (e.g., a company football team). Membership in informal groups is voluntary and the significance of their existence is frequently understated. In organizations, they often fulfil social roles but can also affect the organization's functioning in positive and negative ways (Bryan *et al.*, 2007; Cooper and Davidson, 1982; Cross *et al.*, 2009; Kratzer *et al.*, 2004). Hofstede (1984) for example draws attention to the concept of a marketplace bureaucracy which he suggests is more commonly found in Scandinavian countries, the UK and Ireland. The essence of this concept is that individuals depend more on personal relationships than formal reporting relationships to get things done. Facilitation in this form of bureaucracy is achieved through the trading of support for mutual advantage. It is based on the assumption of, 'You help me this time and I will help you in future', hence the term marketplace.

Friendship groups form on the basis of relationships within an organization. Cultural norms and specific local circumstances will determine how much they extend across hierarchical levels. The more that close social relationships such as friendships exist in organizations, the more informal influence is likely to take place, especially if the work is particularly demanding or even dangerous (e.g., Zohar and Tenne-Gazit, 2008). If friendship groups become strong they may attempt to deliberately influence events in their favour. It is at this point that friendship groups become interest groups.

Informal groups and networks can also contribute to discrimination and exclusion of women and minorities from management positions (Cooper and Davidson, 1982). Some writers on the subject refer to informal groups and networks as shadow organizations (Stacey 2000: p. 386) which reflects their uncontrolled and possibly uncontrollable nature. Others, however, argue that the power of such networks and groups can be used by organizations to increase performance (Bryan *et al.*, 2007). A particular case of informal groups are groups based on the minimal group paradigm (e.g., Tajfel, 1970). This paradigm states that simply assigning group membership to people (even if this is in fact randomly done) according to some meaningless category (researchers have for example used alleged preferences of different painters that even experts can hardly distinguish) to groups will start the typical individual reactions to group membership such as in-group bias and

Marketplace bureaucracy
The need to get things done within an organization requires the continuous trading of favours between colleagues outside formal procedures.

Shadow organizations
Informal groups can form a parallel organization within the host and become a threat to management's ability to control.

Minimal group paradigm
Social dynamic that makes individuals behave like group members simply based on their categorization as group members. This works even in the absence of any meaningful reason for group membership and without any contact and interaction with other members.

out-group stereotyping. For better or for worse, the emergence of informal groups in organizations is inevitable as a result of informal grouping and categorization as well as of social interactions in organizations. The Management in Action panel provides one example of teams that were created under the United Nations requirements to provide a police contingent to contribute to the rebuilding of the war-torn country of Kosovo. Despite having been trained in teams to perform their duties, the police officers needed to be highly self-reliant when working with colleagues drawn from many different nations.

GROUPS, TEAMS AND ORGANIZATIONS

The division of labour used to conduct organizational activities provides for many different groupings in all but the very smallest organizations. As organizations grow and evolve, the necessary structural elaboration groups members into appropriate units by function or based on other principles (see Chapter 10). This tends to focus the attention of members inwards on the tasks, needs and perspectives of their group rather than the overall objectives of the organization. In response to such differentiation it is necessary to also provide integration arrangements in order to ensure that the organization is able to function effectively.

There are many types of formal groupings in organizations. Some of the more obvious are based on *hierarchical differentiation* which represents the seniority and status-based organization of work. This results in the groupings of management (again divided into senior, middle and junior management levels), staff and manual worker categories which reflects the decision-making and responsibility scope of work activity commonly used as the basis of payment and reward within organizations. *Specialism groupings* are based on the collection of people into categories based on special skills (such as electricians within the maintenance department). Often this is done to enhance performance and concentrate expertise. *Activity groupings* such as project teams, committees or working parties often form in response to the limitations of the departmentation approach used in an organization. In functional structures for example, cross-functional groupings often help to counteract and break down the insularity of individual functions. Finally, *professional groupings* arise based on the particular skill set, work orientations and values associated with particular professions (such as medical doctors, accountants, engineers or lawyers). The Going Global example seeks to demonstrate how one company sought to create project teams of largely professional engineers and other specialists that would have to work together on complex projects across the world.

Likert (1961) developed the idea that organizations should be considered as a collection of groups, rather than individuals. In his view individuals would inevitably belong to more than one group and consequently the groups would overlap. This he described as a linking pin model (see Figure 7.1). Likert acknowledged the model's simplistic representation of the nature of groups within organizations, as the actual level of group activity within organizations is much more complex. Any individual belongs to many teams and groups at the same time. A university library assistant, for example, may belong to the issue desk team, the copyright monitoring team, the book repair team, the student debts working group as well as the service development working group. In addition they may have supervisory responsibilities for a number of other staff and be part of a number of friendship and social groupings.

The linking pin model largely ignores the instrumental value of groups to individual members. For example, Handy (1993) argues that individuals join and use groups for a number of purposes, including meeting social and affiliation needs and

Linking pin model
This model reflects the overlapping and connected nature of groups within an organization.

MANAGEMENT IN ACTION

Keeping the peace

The United Nations (UN) frequently finds itself in the difficult situation of trying to keep the peace and helping to rebuild communities following war or similar disasters. These can be very dangerous environments and it needs special skills to work in them. The UN seeks to second appropriately skilled and qualified personnel from member nations for this type of work. Individuals are volunteers and often serve for 1 year in the field. Over the past 10 years Britain provided a number of police officers from the Ministry of Defence Police Service (MDP) to the Kosovo region of the former Yugoslavia in seeking to restore order and some form of criminal justice system.

The MDP is a specialized civilian police service within Britain looking after Ministry of Defence (MOD) interests and policing. Their duties require them to work alongside the military and civilian police forces across Britain. When the war ended in 1999, Serbian authorities withdrew from Kosovo, leaving it with no civil government or police service and with badly damaged infrastructure. Water and power supplies were unreliable, refuse collection was nonexistent and roads were in an appalling state of repair. Crime was also rife within the country. The country was awash with guns, and had become the route into Europe for illegal drugs.

The UN sought to restore normality and order, hence the need for police teams. The MDP service was particularly well placed to help because of its close association with both military and civilian policing. A reconnaissance visit was made in order to assess the logistical and training needs for staff to be posted and advice was also sought from the Police Service of Northern Ireland who already had officers working in Kosovo. Volunteers from within the MDP were sought for the 1-year posting. A key requirement for individuals was that they needed to be self-reliant and able to sustain themselves physically and emotionally. This was because they would not be part of a dedicated MDP team, but would be part of a team made up of personnel drawn up from any of 32 countries contributing police officers. Selected officers undertook a four-week training course covering firearms tactics, personal security, UN rules of engagement, mine awareness, environmental hygiene and other organizations working in the area. Once in Kosovo, officers were given further training by local UN staff and then assigned to specific roles. For example, Station Commander (responsible for about 400 other officers); close protection for visiting dignitaries; traffic, communications and community relations roles.

MDP officers have gained considerably from the experience. According to the Chief Constable of the MDP, they brought back to their home force:

> *tremendously enhanced skills in areas like negotiation, investigation and management capability. It is a real eye-opening, life-enhancing opportunity which has also given them a greater tolerance of other people and communities.*

However,

> *Many of our staff have wanted to stay out there because of the extra responsibility – and when they come back to a less demanding job – ouch – that's been difficult. But we had to make a management decision that the maximum stay is 18 months, and when they come back they are not automatically promoted. They have to go through the same selection processes and meet the same requirements as everyone else.*

TASKS

1 The MDP process of selecting and training officers is likely to reinforce group identity among them. Yet they are reformed into groups with personnel from different countries once they are given their specific roles. To what extent can this process be effective?

2 To what extent would the teams created in the way described be useful for the social, psychological and emotional support of individuals working under such difficult conditions?

3 If you were a senior UN official in Kosovo how would you prepare the wide range of police officers for the roles expected of them?

Sources:
Lucas, E. (2002) Keeping the peace, *Professional Manager*, November, pp. 26–27.
https://www.cia.gov/library/publications/the-world-factbook/geos/ kv.html (accessed March 2009).
http://news.bbc.co.uk/hi/english/static/kosovo_fact_files/default.stm (accessed March 2009).

GOING GLOBAL

Construction on a united front

M.W. Kellogg Limited is an international project management and construction company. It is described by Stewart Watson, the Managing Director as 'A London-based full service contractor primarily serving the hydrocarbon market with the capability to execute worldscale international projects from conceptual feasibility studies through fixed price turnkey mega-projects.' The company has two shareholders, Kellogg Brown & Root (KBR) based in the USA and JGC Corporation of Japan, both major international process contractors in their own right and employing more than 100 000 people worldwide.

M.W. Kellogg Limited was established in the UK in the 1930s, and enjoys a strong worldwide reputation for technology-based engineering, procurement and construction services within the process plant industries. Process plants are typically found in the petrochemical, natural gas and polymer industries. Such large-scale multimillion-dollar projects can last from a few weeks to several years, each requiring a dedicated team brought together from a range of professions and disciplines. This can create difficulties as the project team have to learn how to work effectively together in another country (sometimes several in the same project) and at the same time manage local labour and subcontractors. This naturally involves the cultural, language and professional differences that might be expected to create significant difficulties.

Some years ago the company was looking for ways of encouraging the creation of effective cross-functional project teams in this context. Purpose-designed courses were introduced with the help of an outside training company. The process for each project group followed a similar pattern:

- Once the project group was selected, the training company visited each member in order to identify development issues.

- This information was collated (with the personnel department) and used to design a 3-day team development course.

- Each course had a common theme. The first 2 days were intended to break down barriers and to build team spirit. The third day focused on project-specific issues.

- Noncompany people who were to be part of the project team were also encouraged to attend.

- The courses used both indoor and outdoor training, depending upon the background and experience of the participants. Every member of the team was required to be a team leader for some activities as well as being a team member for others.

TASKS

1 To what extent do you think that development activity such as that outlined above (delivered in the UK) would help create an effective multi-disciplinary team that could operate in other countries?

2 If you were the Managing Director how would you ensure that project teams that change with every project and international location (with everything implied by that) were able to work effectively together?

Sources:
www.mwkl.co.uk/ (accessed March 2009).
Simons, C. (1992) Construction on a united front, *Personnel Today*, 30 June, pp. 33–34.

gaining support for their objectives. Groups in organizations are not just imposed on people from above – individuals create groups and vary their level of participation in groups and teams depending upon a range of personal and organizational factors. Nevertheless, the linking pin model provides a useful means of describing the overlapping memberships of individuals as part of the formal organization structure as well as the cascading levels of formal group membership and the communication chains that reflect these structures.

Traditional organizational hierarchies are focused on functional groupings and hierarchical management responsibility typified in the Likert model (Figure 7.1). However the customer experience of an organization is not hierarchical, it is horizontal. Consider shopping at a supermarket or purchasing new equipment for a company. In each transaction the customer will encounter the lower-level staff that process the order or sale. In meeting the needs of customers a cross-functional approach is inevitably needed. For example orders pass through sales, finance, warehouse and dispatch departments. The boundaries between the various functional groups involved can act as fences or friction points, preventing a seamless customer-focused experience. Also senior managers tend to become remote from the experience of customers as they spend more time 'managing the process' rather than 'managing customer activity' within the organization. To what extent does this suggest the existence of a **conflict model of customer experience and organizational functioning** (see Figure 7.2)? And to what extent does that model imply that for an organization to be effective in relation to customer needs the groups and teams within it need to be reorganized horizontally to better focus on customer needs? How could you create such groups in, say, a supermarket? How can (if at all) senior managers avoid losing touch with the customer experience?

Conflict model of customer experience and organizational functioning This reflects the difficulty of functional groups being able to meet customer needs in a hierarchical organization.

Figure 7.1 Likert's linking pin model of organizational groups

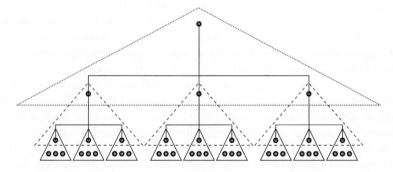

Source: Likert, R (1961) New Patterns of Management, McGraw-Hill, New York. Copyright © The McGraw-Hill Companies, Inc. Reprinted with permission.

Figure 7.2 The hierarchical/customer conflict

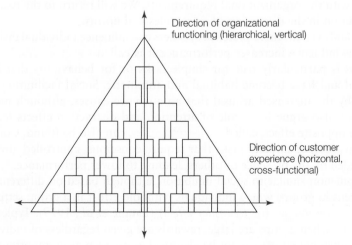

Direction of organizational functioning (hierarchical, vertical)

Direction of customer experience (horizontal, cross-functional)

WHY DO ORGANIZATIONS USE GROUPS?

There are a number of aspects that help answer this question. In brief, organizations use groups because they can provide value for the organization. Groups can often do this through (a) offering synergy effects; (b) providing additional means of control; (c) improving individual performance; (d) offering successful performance for particular tasks or goals that could not be achieved as effectively or efficiently by individuals; and (e) offering psychological and social benefits that counter negative impact of work on individuals. We will look at these reasons in turn below.

Group synergy
The increase in performance or value from groups compared to the outcomes that a number of individuals working on a task alone could achieve.

Groups have the potential to provide group synergy effects, which means that using groups can *enhance the outcomes that a number of individuals working on a task alone could achieve*. You may have heard synergy described as meaning that $2 + 2 = 5$. This is not correct – synergy is not about a wrong mathematical formula, it is about understanding that the same elements working together appropriately may create more value than their component parts could alone. Thus, it describes an interaction effect. A formula that describes synergy better would be the comparison between the sum of two elements (e.g., $3 + 3 = 6$) and the product of multiplying them (e.g., $3 \times 3 = 9$). The positive difference between the two ($9 - 6 = 3$) is called synergy – which is the degree of extra value derived from changing the way in which the same elements are combined. This logic can also hold true for groups as, under the right conditions, groups can provide synergy effects. What is important is that the way in which group members work together allows improved performance overall to be achieved. This idea is the basis for Katzenbach and Smith's (1993) claim about the increasing performance potential of teams (see Table 7.2).

Social control
Social mechanisms that influence behaviour in particular social settings.

Concertive control
Informal social control groups can exercise over their members.

Groups have many tangible and intangible effects on individuals, including a profound influence on individual thinking, feeling and behaviour. Therefore groups provide organizations with an effective means of influencing and even controlling individual behaviour. The informal social control that groups exercise (also called concertive control) can, if aligned with the formal social control through organizational rules, rewards and objectives (see Chapter 12), aid the organization in achieving its objectives without requiring the effort and expense of close managerial supervision. This control can direct individual attention and behaviour and so contribute to higher performance. Beyond ongoing informal social control, groups are also an important means of socializing individuals, which means that they convey informal norms and expectations to their members. A potential downside of groups' enormous influence on individuals is that they can also influence individuals in counterproductive ways for an organization if the informal social control they exert is not in line with the organizational requirements. We will return to the issue of social control later on in the discussion of roles, rules and norms.

Social facilitation
The phenomenon that the presence of others can increase performance.

Social inhibition
The phenomenon that the presence of others can decrease performance.

Groups and even the mere presence of others can influence individual task performance. If this influence increases performance it is called social facilitation (Zajonc, 1965). This is particularly true for simple tasks or for behaviours that have been overlearned and have become habitual and automatic. Social facilitation is usually explained by the increased arousal that an audience causes, although more recent explanations also argue for a role of attention and distraction effects (e.g., Baron, 1986). The opposite effect, called social inhibition, can also be found. Complex and novel behaviours, or difficult tasks that require conscious, controlled attention, are often impeded by the presence of others, leading to lower performance.

Social loafing
The tendency for individuals to exert less effort in groups compared to working individually.

A phenomenon similar to social inhibition, although based on different dynamic, often happens in groups where individuals withhold effort in a group setting. This is also called social loafing (or *free-rider effect*) (Latané *et al.*, 1979). Typically, social loafing occurs when groups are large, rewards are given regardless of individual contribution, individual efforts cannot be identified or are seen as unimportant, and task interdependence among group members is low (Kidwell and Bennett, 1993; Latané *et al.*, 1979; Harkins and Jackson, 1985). Other factors that increase the likelihood of social loafing include low preference for groupwork and low winning orientation (Stark *et al.*, 2007). Sometimes individuals deliberately withhold their effort because they believe other group members are or might be loafing. This is called the sucker effect because these individuals want to avoid being exploited (Veiga, 1991).

Organizations also use groups for tasks where individuals would not be able to achieve the relevant objective, or where groups are particularly suited to the task. Tasks where complex problems need to be solved, or where a variety of different forms of expertise is needed, are often more suited to groups than individuals. Groups can offer benefits of a very mundane yet important nature. For example, they can offer easy access to clarification of individual questions, provide a context for learning and sharing of experience, afford the opportunity to pass work on (or obtain it), or make several sources of help in undertaking something available. They also provide an opportunity for what in the animal kingdom would be recognized as the herd instinct. There is obvious safety in numbers for both managers and employees, just as there is for animals when predators are looking for easy prey (or perhaps productivity improvements and cost savings in the case of organizations). The High Performance example illustrates how complex it can be to identify just what is happening when numbers of employees are being reduced at the same time as increasing them.

Traditionally, considerations of task characteristics that matter for groups have focused on task structure. Distinctions have been drawn between additive, conjunctive and disjunctive tasks (Steiner, 1972) that all have particular implications for group performance. In *additive tasks*, group performance is simply the sum of

> **Sucker effect**
> The tendency for individuals to deliberately withhold effort within a group activity because they believe other group members might do the same because they want to avoid being exploited.

HIGH PERFORMANCE

Safety in numbers?

It was widely reported in March 2009 that the UK civil service had paid out approximately £882 million during the previous 4 years in voluntary and involuntary redundancy payments in order to reduce the total headcount by 15 000 staff. This was aimed, it was argued, at improving civil service efficiency and reducing cost. The Cabinet Office indicated that total efficiency saving over the 4 years was £26.5 billion.

However, figures also made available at the same time indicate that during the same 4-year period approximately 42 000 new permanent staff had been recruited. It was estimated by some commentators and politicians that the total wage bill for the new staff would be close to £1 billion. Also the above figures do not include 27 000 temporary staff and 11 000 agency staff employed by the civil service during the same period. The Department for Work and Pensions for example, made 8 479 staff redundant at a total cost

of £401 million, but recruited 16 544 new staff at a total wage cost of £413 million.

TASKS

1 In the above example apparently some £26.5 billion of savings were made by replacing 15 000 people with 42 000 – can this be possible and if so how?

2 How should the 27 000 temporary staff and 11 000 agency staff indicated above impact on the savings and cost aspects of performance?

3 What might the above example imply that 'performance' means?

Sources:
The *Sunday Times*, 8 March 2009, p.15.
www.civilservicenetwork.com/people/profile-article/newsarticle/civil-service-redundancy-bill-revealed/?no_cache=1 (accessed 9 March 2009).
www.guardian.co.uk/politics/2008/feb/12/whitehall (accessed 9 March 2009).

7.1 EXTEND
YOUR LEARNING

individual contributions (for example, workers filling a hole with shovels); in *conjunctive tasks*, group performance is determined by the performance of the weakest members (for example a group race where all members must pass the finishing line); and in *disjunctive tasks*, group performance is a function of the strongest individual performance (for example, in a language translation task). In theory, groups will outperform the same set of people working as individuals on disjunctive tasks, underperform on conjunctive tasks, and perform about equally on additive tasks. However, the particular structure of the group and the task, the ensuing group dynamics and processes, and the quality of task orientation and co-ordination can strongly influence group performance.

A related issue is that some tasks require particular safeguards and controls. Many organizations use the 'four-eyes principle' which refers to the need to have important tasks checked by more than one person (e.g., many firms require payments above a certain amount to be countersigned by a second person).

Other organizational reasons for using groups are based on the psychological and social benefits of group membership on individual members. These benefits include subjective (e.g., feelings of belonging, perceived social support) and objective aspects (e.g., increased regular social contact; opportunity to rotate particular tasks). Particularly in dangerous or otherwise adverse working conditions groups can thus provide important consequences for their members.

These psychological and social benefits of formal groups are also prominent among the reasons why informal groups form in organizations. While sometimes encouraged by organizations, the formation of such groups is the unavoidable result of proximity and social interaction among organizational members. Cultural and other environmental factors may influence the number and nature of informal groups in particular settings, but they invariably come into being for a number of reasons, including:

- *The need for human beings to function in a social environment and to form relationships of their own choosing.* Schein (1956) describes the manipulation of prisoners of war by the Chinese Communists during the Korean War. The use of rank was dispensed with and groups were reorganized when it became apparent that something approaching an effective structure was emerging.

- *The voluntary nature of many informal groups offsets the involuntary nature of many formal, organizational groups.*

- *The approach adopted by managers to the running of the organization will also influence the formation of informal groups.*

- *The need for individuals to exert influence and to achieve their formal and personal goals.* Organization structures and procedures are the mechanisms that determine what should be done where and when. However, procedures cannot cater for the interpersonal and dynamic nature of organizational activity. Organizational functioning depends to a significant extent on individuals co-operating in a reciprocal network of activity. Inevitably, in such situations self-help networks of mutual dependency (informal groups) form (e.g., Bryan *et al.*, 2007; Cross *et al.*, 2009).

The nature of social processes and the role of informal groups, and their respective impact on organizations and their performance, was first formally recognized and researched in the famous Hawthorne studies in the 1930s (for British research on similar issues see Wyatt *et al.*, 1928). Many trace the origins of OB back to this seminal work which also sparked the human relations movement, which had a profound impact on the study of OB as well as on managerial and organizational practices around the world (see Chapter 2).

GROUP FORMATION AND DEVELOPMENT

7.2 EXTEND
YOUR LEARNING

We have already seen the immense variety of groups that exist in and around organizations. Although not all groups are formally initiated, groups typically all go through similar developmental stages that start when groups are formally or informally established. A classic theory of group formation is Homans' (1950) work which is discussed on the companion website. The best-known model of group development – probably in part because its stages are so easy to remember – is Tuckman's stage model of group development. Tuckman initially posited four stages that groups pass through in their development towards becoming performing, entities (later extended to include the fifth stage, see Tuckman and Jensen, 1977). The stages of the model are called forming, storming, norming, performing and adjourning and are discussed below. Figure 7.3 provides an overview of the relevant interpersonal, leadership, task and group behavioural issues associated with the four stages of the original model.

Group development
Process of individuals coming together to form a group capable of achieving both task and member satisfaction.

Figure 7.3 Issues associated with Tuckman's first four stages of group development

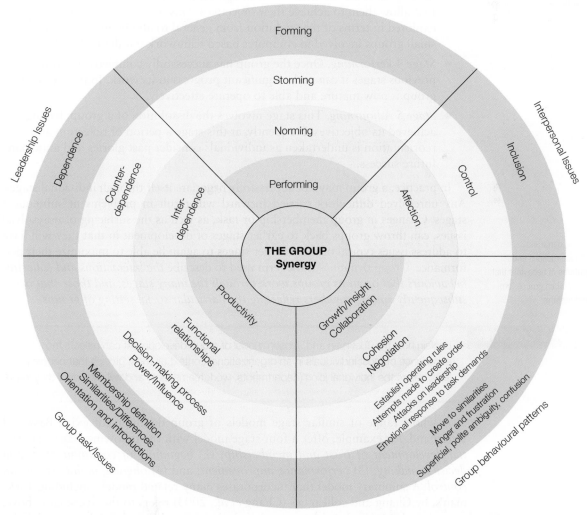

Source: Weber, RC (1982). The group: A cycle from birth to death. In L Porter & B Mohr (eds.), *NTL Training Book for Human Relations Training* (7th ed.), 68-71. NTL Institute.

Roles
Specific set of responsibilities and expected behaviours associated by an individual based on their particular position in group or organization.

Norms
Implicit standards that express the expected and acceptable (or shunned and unacceptable) behaviours in a particular social setting.

- *Stage 1 Forming.* This stage occurs when the individuals first come together. It involves each individual getting to know the others, their attitudes, personalities and backgrounds. Individuals use this stage to make a personal impact within the group. It is also likely that anxiety is felt by the individuals as they attempt to define their position within the group. This process also begins to define the hierarchy and roles that will exist within the group.

- *Stage 2 Storming.* As a formal structure begins to emerge and individuals begin to feel more confidence in their position within the group, conflict arises. Individuals begin to bring their own agendas to the group, and the ensuing conflict needs to be addressed and resolved. If successfully handled, this leads to clearer relationships between members which can facilitate later collaboration. Not all groups successfully negotiate their way through this stage and lingering problems can continue to inhibit development and task performance. In extreme cases groups can collapse at this stage.

- *Stage 3 Norming.* This stage reflects the process of establishing the norms to be operated within the group. This includes the behavioural standards among members, for example to allow (or prevent) jokes and other diversions. Also the procedural rules that provide the group with its operating framework are developed. Someone with a hidden agenda may also seek to introduce items that allow them to achieve their objectives. This process has recently been explored in terms of the evolution from general to an operational state in small groups involved in computer based teamwork (Graham, 2003).

- *Stage 4 Performing.* Once the group has successfully completed the three previous stages it can make significant progress in its work. In that sense the group is now mature and able to operate effectively.

- *Stage 5 Adjourning.* This stage involves the dissolution of a group, having achieved its objectives. Frequently, at this stage a period of reflection and reorientation is undertaken as individuals consider past glories and anticipate future success.

In practice, a group may not successfully negotiate itself through individual stages. Any unresolved difficulties carried forward will result in problems at subsequent stages. Changes in group membership or task, as well as the surfacing of unresolved issues, can throw groups back to earlier stages of development in that they will have to address issues typical of these earlier stages to again be able to maximize their performance. Group dynamics is the term used to describe *the interactions and collective behaviours that occur as groups work through the many stages, and those that occur subsequently among members reflecting the particular social setting of groups.*

Group dynamics
The interactions and patterns of behaviour that occur when groups form and perform.

STOP & CONSIDER

Explain how the Tuckman and Jensen model of group development can reflects the experience of most individuals in an organizational context as most groups that people join exist before the individual joins (departments, work teams, etc.) and will exist after they leave.

A whole range of similar stage models of group development exist. Bass and Ryterband, for example, offer a four-stage model with the following stages: (1) *Initial development of trust and membership*; (2) *beginning of communication and decision making*; (3) *performance improvement*; and (4) *ongoing maintenance and control*. A summary model that incorporates many related models, including Tuckman's, by Chang and colleagues (Chang *et al.*, 2003) refers to the five stages above, renaming them (1) dependency and inclusion; (2) counterdependency and fight; (3) trust and structure; (4) work; and (5) termination.

In contrast to these stage models of group development Connie Gersick introduced the notion of 'punctuated equilibrium' to group development (Gersick, 1991). Her research indicates that many temporary or project groups (such as student groups working on assignments) experience a fundamental transformation, often at about midpoint of their planned time together, at which they regroup to move into more productive, task-oriented mode (Gersick, 1988, 1989; Waller *et al.*, 2002).

Other more recent models of group development focus on particular group characteristics or dimensions. Important examples include an input-throughput-output model of team adaptation which describes how teams adjust their actions according to situational requirements (Burke *et al.*, 2006), and developmental models of group cognition that identify the phases of information *accumulation* (perception and storing of information); interaction (retrieving, exchanging and interactively structuring information); examination (meaning is socially negotiated and evaluated), and accommodation (members integrate information, make decisions and take action) (Gibson and Earley, 2007; Gibson *et al.*, 2009). An important example of such socially developed and shared group cognitions that fundamentally affect groups is group efficacy beliefs, which is an important predictor of group performance (Gibson and Earley, 2007).

7.3 EXTEND
YOUR LEARNING

Group efficacy beliefs
A group's shared belief in its ability to perform a particular task successfully.

GROUP STRUCTURE

The group development models discussed above attempt to describe how groups form and progress to a point where they can perform tasks effectively. There are other factors that are important in understanding what determines the effectiveness of groups. One of these factors is the structure of the group. In formal groups the structure of the group may be dictated by the organization. For example, a department (or project team) will be created, designed and the members designated by management. The individual members have often little direct say in who will be appointed to the team and what role they will perform. In other situations, particularly informal groups, the membership is self-selected and members have a greater influence on both structure and roles. Many groups within an organization are comprised of representatives of other groups or departments, perhaps even from outside the organization itself. Consequently, these representatives are subject to report-back requirements and direction from their sponsoring groups. This can sometimes create conflict between personal, professional and group loyalty for the individuals concerned.

Group structure can be described from a variety of perspectives which can focus on formal, communication, role-related and informal aspects of groups. Formal structure includes characteristics such as *membership*. In formal groups, membership is typically based on appointment by those setting up the group. In informal groups, it can be difficult to determine membership objectively because joining and leaving a group is an informal, often implicit process. In *homogeneous groups*, members are very similar to each other (for example, in age, experience, attitudes, values, personality, race, gender, aspiration level or similar variables), while *heterogeneous groups* are characterized by very dissimilar members. Typically, homogeneous groups progress faster through the developmental tasks of the forming, storming and norming phases of group development. Heterogeneous groups, on the other hand, often have a wider variety of skills, experiences and information available and therefore typically have an advantage in performing creative tasks. Harrison and Klein (2007) distinguish between different kinds of heterogeneity or diversity. Separation refers to differences in opinions, beliefs, values and attitudes, variety to differences in expertise, functional background and external connections, and disparity to differential status, authority and social power, and resource access. Another aspect of formal

Separation (in groups)
Refers to differences in opinions, beliefs, values and attitudes.

Variety (in groups)
Reflects differences in expertise, functional background and external connections among the members of a group.

Disparity (in groups)
Refers to differential status, authority and social power, and resource access.

structure is group *size*. The larger the number of participants, the broader the range of experience and other resources that can be brought to bear on the task. By the same token, the more people involved, the smaller the contribution any individual can make. Other considerations associated with size of a group include the increased need for co-ordination, the potential domination of a group by a subgroup, and the time to reach a decision, which also increases with size.

Formal structure also reflects *authority differences* in the group. A supervisor or manager of a formal group has authority instilled by the organization. Explicit delegation of authority by members with such formal authority, or their informal preferences for selected members, can create an 'inner circle' (called *in-group*). In-group members have easier access to the formal leader and develop higher status and more influential positions in groups. Other aspects of formal group structure are official *goals*, the explicit *rules* imposed on or developed by the group and the formal *roles* imposed on the group from outside or by the formal leader.

Communication structure in groups refers to *the patterns through which individuals within a group communicate with each other*. Figure 7.4 indicates typical structures that can be found in groups based on the work of a number of writers (e.g., Bavelas, 1948; Leavitt, 1978; Shaw, 1978). Each of these structures is determined by communication between group members and in turn has implications for subsequent interactions. Thus, communication structure can influence leadership styles as well as decision-making approaches and problem-solving capabilities of the group. The Wheel and Y structures, for example, have a focal person who connects other members with each other. The centrality in communication flows will give this person immense influence and power compared to more peripheral members of the group (see Chapter 15). As a general rule, the more complex a group's task is, and the higher the task interdependence between its members, the more complex the communication structure needs to be in order to support successful groupwork. These issues are discussed further, albeit targeted more at the organizational level, in Chapter 10 on structure. Communication structure in groups is of particular importance in virtual teams which are considered in more detail in Chapter 11 on technology.

A highly important dimension of group structure is reflected in the roles that are imposed on or are developed in the group. Belbin (1993) argues that nine team roles

Delegation of authority
An action by managers in which they give some of their authority for decision making to subordinates.

Team roles
Model consisting of nine roles that exist within a group including plant, resource investigator, implementer and completer.

Figure 7.4 Communication patterns in groups

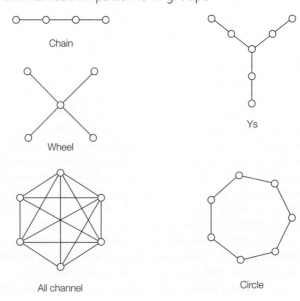

Chain

Wheel

Ys

All channel

Circle

Table 7.3 The nine Belbin team roles

Roles and descriptions – team role contribution	Allowable weaknesses
Plant. Creative, imaginative, unorthodox. Solves difficult problems	Ignores details. Too preoccupied to communicate effectively
Resource investigator. Extrovert, enthusiastic, communicative. Explores opportunities. Develops contacts	Over-optimistic. Loses interest once initial enthusiasm has passed
Co-ordinator. Mature, confident, a good chairperson. Clarifies goals, promotes decision making, delegates well	Can be seen as manipulative. Delegates personal work
Shaper. Challenging, dynamic, thrives on pressure. Has the drive and courage to overcome obstacles	Can provoke others. Hurts people's feelings
Monitor/evaluator. Sober, strategic and discerning. Sees all options. Judges accurately	Lacks drive and ability to inspire others. Overly critical
Teamworker. Co-operative, mild, perceptive and diplomatic. Listens, builds, averts friction, calms the waters	Indecisive in crunch situations. Can be easily influenced
Implementer. Disciplined, reliable, conservative and efficient. Turns ideas into practical actions	Somewhat inflexible. Slow to respond to new possibilities
Completer. Painstaking, conscientious, anxious. Searches out errors and omissions. Delivers on time	Inclined to worry unduly. Reluctant to delegate. Can be a nit-picker
Specialist. Single-minded, self-starting, dedicated. Provides knowledge and skills in rare supply	Contributes on only a narrow front. Dwells on technicalities. Overlooks the 'big picture'

Source: Belbin, M (1993) Team Roles at Work, Butterworth Heinemann, Copyright © Elsevier (1993) Reprinted with permission.

are particularly important for group performance. The roles, the contributions they can make and the weaknesses associated with them are presented in Table 7.3. Belbin argues that these roles cover the main requirements of groupwork. If appropriately deployed in groups they enable, according to Belbin, high group performance. Information about another model of role structure in groups by Margerison and McCann (1990), called the team management wheel, is available on the companion website. We will further consider roles and role structure in the section on group process and effectiveness.

The informal structure in groups reflects many of the dimensions of group development discussed above. Informal structures arise from the patterns of interactions between group members, for example based on personal liking and disliking, and the resulting differences in the level and nature of interpersonal interactions between group members. Moreno (1953) developed the sociogram, a graphical representation

7.4 EXTEND YOUR LEARNING

Team management wheel
A model of individual work preferences that relates to the roles that individual's play in a team.

Sociogram
A diagrammatic representation of individual preferences and interactions among group members.

of the informal relationship structure in a group. It is a useful tool to identify subgroups such as cliques in social groupings. Another approach to analysing informal group structure is based on Bales's (1958) work on interaction analysis which provides a categorization framework to help classify and analyse observable interactions among group members. Further information about interaction analysis and sociograms can be found on the companion website. Contemporary approaches to mapping informal structure called social network analysis are a central tool in sociological as well as organizational research and are used to study informal structures within, across and outside of groups.

GROUP PROCESS AND EFFECTIVENESS

Fundamentally, organizations use groups because of the benefits they offer. However, the actual performance of groups in organizations typically varies widely. There are many factors that can contribute to good – and bad – group performance. Managers and organizations are intensely interested in understanding and controlling the factors that determine group performance or group effectiveness, which refers to *the degree to which groups achieve their intended objectives*. This singular focus on achieving formal goals is common in organizations, although some researchers have defined group effectiveness in broader terms. Early research in the Hawthorne studies already indicated the interlinkage between task success and worker satisfaction. Similarly, McGregor (1960) argued in his classic contribution that 'unity of purpose' is important for some managerial groups to perform effectively. With this term he draws attention to the commitment of individuals to the group and to the achievement of objectives. He describes the features that differentiate effective from ineffective groups (see Table 7.4). Similarly, well known team expert J. Richard Hackman identifies criteria of team effectiveness in organizations that include but go beyond the focus on goal achievement. He argues that team effectiveness criteria include the degree to which a team satisfies external expectations (such as organizational goals), the degree to which the team and its members learn and develop, and the degree to which they would be able and willing to work together again (Hackman, 2002).

The understanding of what factors contribute to group effectiveness has evolved in OB over time (see Ilgen *et al.*, 2005 for a comprehensive review). Traditionally, group structure and individual member characteristics that determine their potential for contributions to the team (determined for example by personality, motivation, ability, or experience) were seen as key (Bell, 2007; Kozlowski and Bell, 2003; Stewart, 2006). Because of this view, and the relative ease with which these matters can be influenced from outside, managerial and organizational efforts to improve group performance focus often on selecting the right individuals and deliberately structuring groups and group tasks to enable high performance.

Available research lends support for these practices by indicating that some individual differences have a clear impact on team performance (Sonnentag and Vollmer, 2009). In general, enduring personality and ability differences appear to be more important than demographic differences (see Harrison *et al.*, 2002; Hollenbeck *et al.*, 2004). There is evidence that general mental ability of the team members is related to better goal achievement (Devine and Phillips, 2001; Stewart, 2006). Also, available research in actual organizational settings indicates that factors such as group member agreeableness, conscientiousness, openness to experience and members' preference for teamwork appear to be related to team performance (Bell, 2007).

While certainly relevant, treating individual characteristics of group members as the main internal driver of group performance negates the fact that unique

Table 7.4 Features of effective and ineffective groups

	Dimension	Effective group	Ineffective group
1	Atmosphere	Informal, comfortable, relaxed	Indifference, boredom, tension
2	Discussion	Participative, pertinent to task	Dominated by a few people, drifts off point
3	Objectives	Understood and accepted by all	Lack of clarity, not fully accepted by individuals
4	Active listening	Members listen to each other, contribution to debate and ideas	Pushing of own ideas, no evidence of building on others, talking for effect
5	Disagreement	Brought into the open and resolved or accepted	Not resolved, suppressed by leader, perhaps warfare domination is the aim
6	Decision making	By consensus	Premature decisions and actions before full examination. Simple majority voting
7	Criticism	Frank but not personal	Embarrassing, tension producing. Involves personal hostility, destructive approach
8	Feelings	Expressed on group activity as well as ideas. Few hidden agendas	Hidden, not thought appropriate to group activity
9	Action	Clear allocation and acceptance	Unclear in allocation, lack of commitment to achieve result
10	Leadership	Not chair dominated, 'experts' lead depending on circumstances, no power struggles	Chair dominated
11	Reviews	Self-consciousness about present operations, frequent reviews	No discussion of group maintenance issues

Source: Adapted from McGregor, D. (1960) *The human side of enterprise*, New York: McGraw-Hill.

group-level dynamics mediate all individual characteristics and their influences on the group. More specifically, relationships between individual member characteristics and performance appear to be influenced by the particular ways in which groups and teams work together. As an example, Edwards and colleagues showed how the general mental abilities of the team are related to higher performance in particular when teams have developed shared mental models (Edwards *et al.*, 2006). This points to the importance of the processes of collaboration through which member's abilities and individual differences are deployed for the benefit of group performance (see also Curşeu *et al.*, 2007). In fact, contemporary models of team performance and effectiveness increasingly focus on these team-level co-ordination processes and role structures (e.g., Fay *et al.*, 2006; Humphrey *et al.*, 2009; LePine *et al.*, 2008; Stewart *et al.*, 2005).

An important and influential framework in this area was proposed by Marks *et al.* (2001). These authors explicitly distinguish between taskwork and teamwork

Taskwork
Describes what a group or team does to achieve its objectives.

Teamwork processes
Describe how a group or team goes about its taskwork. Refers to members' interdependent acts that convert inputs to outcomes through cognitive, verbal and behavioral activities directed towards organizing taskworks to achieve collective goals.

processes. Taskwork describes *what* a team does and is defined as 'A team's interactions with tasks, tools, machines' and systems.' (Bowers *et al.*, 1997: p. 90) Teamwork processes, in contrast, are *how* a team goes about its taskwork, and are defined as '*Members' interdependent acts that convert inputs to outcomes through cognitive, verbal, and behavioural activities directed towards organizing taskwork to achieve collective goals.*' (Marks *et al.*, 2001: p. 357) The framework is based on the argument that different team processes are important at different phases of task execution (taskwork). These phases reflect the rhythm of teamwork, which consists of periods during which teams focus on a particular task (called action phases), and periods during which teams transition between tasks (called transition phases). Particular processes are associated with these tasks called action processes and transition processes. In addition, interpersonal processes continuously take place in teams, supporting the action and transition processes. Figure 7.5 provides an overview of their framework, and Table 7.5 provides more detail on the specific subprocesses that form part of their taxonomy.

The model and taxonomy of relevant team processes that Marks and her colleagues present show the complex nature of team processes. The distinction between structural and task characteristics of teams (often referred to as 'content') and the teamwork aspects (often called 'process') goes back to early contributions to research on small groups (e.g., Deutsch, 1949; Lewin, 1948). The skills of recognizing and understanding both content and process in groups is invaluable for group members as well as managers trying to deploy groups and teams for increased performance. Schein (1982) argues that most observers focus on content in an abstract, future- or past-oriented, and somewhat removed way ('there and then'). In contrast, understanding process

Figure 7.5 Manifestation of team processes in action and transition phases

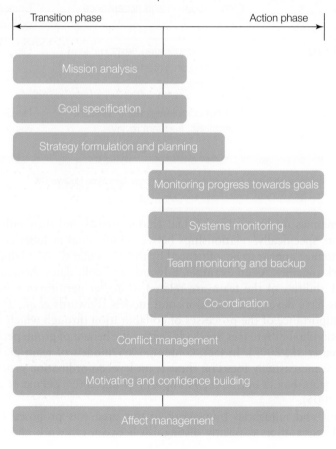

Source: Marks, MA, Mathieu, JE & Zaccaro, SJ (2001) *A temporally based framework and taxonomy of team processes*. Academy of Management Review, 26: 355-376.

Table 7.5 Group process dimensions

Name of processing mode	Transition processes
Mission analysis, formulation, and planning	Interpretation and evaluation of the team's mission, including identification of its main tasks as well as the operative environmental conditions and team resources available for mission execution
Goal specification	Identification and prioritization of goals and subgoals for mission accomplishment
Strategy formulation	Development of alternative courses of action for mission accomplishment
Action processes	
Monitoring progress towards goals	Tracking task and progress towards mission accomplishment, interpreting system information in terms of what needs to be accomplished for goal attainment and transmitting progress to team members
Systems monitoring	Tracking team resources and environmental conditions as they relate to mission accomplishment, which involves (1) internal systems monitoring (tracking team resources such as personnel, equipment and other information that is generated or contained within the team); and (2) environmental monitoring (tracking the environmental conditions relevant to the team)
Team monitoring and backup behaviour	Assisting team members to perform their tasks. Assistance may occur by (1) providing a team-mate verbal feedback or coaching; (2) helping a team-mate behaviourally in carrying out actions; or (3) assuming and completing a task for a team-mate
Co-ordination	Orchestrating the sequence and timing of interdependent actions
Interpersonal processes	
Conflict management	Pre-emptive conflict management involves establishing conditions to prevent, control, or guide team conflict before it occurs. Reactive conflict management involves working through task and interpersonal disagreements among team members
Motivation and confidence building	Generating and preserving a sense of collective confidence, motivation and task-based cohesion with regard to mission accomplishment
Affect management	Regulating member emotions during mission accomplishment, including (but not limited to) social cohesion, frustration and excitement

Source: Marks, MA, Mathieu, JE & Zaccaro, SJ (2001) *A temporally based framework and taxonomy of team processes*. Academy of Management Review, 26: 355–376. Reprinted with permission.

in real groups forces us to focus on the 'here and now', trying to understand how the group is operating at present. Skilled observes are able to understand groups and group dynamics in a situated way, taking into account the groups' and the individual members' past history and present motives, and how they affect the collective future of the team. The relevant skill-sets have long been recognized, and the well known work associated with the human relations movement, particularly at the Tavistock Institute in London and the National Training Laboratories in the US, has provided

7.6 EXTEND
YOUR LEARNING

important contributions to management theory and practice. Modern approaches to analysing individual and collective contributions to teamwork also employ statistics and other approaches to try to indentify how individuals can or do contribute (e.g., Boon and Sierksma (2003) propose an interesting model for identifying appropriate new soccer and volleyball players by evaluating their potential to contribute to team success – see also the case study at the end of this chapter).

Group and team processes are so important because they determine how individuals collaborate in their interdependent efforts to achieve collective goals. Such collaboration on interdependent tasks is the fundamental requirement for any benefit to accrue from groups and teams. In turn, co-ordination can only happen if individuals can be compelled to constructively participate in and contribute to co-ordinated collective tasks. Therefore, the ability of groups to influence and control individual behaviour is crucial. The most important formal and informal means of group control of individual behaviour include rules, norms and roles.

STOP & CONSIDER

A team met to design a race horse and the result was a camel! Discuss and evaluate the implications of this statement – namely that team processes invariably involve compromise therefore it is impossible for them to be efficient or arrive at the 'best' answer.

GROUP CONTROL AND ROLE THEORY

Rules
Explicit descriptions of acceptable and unacceptable behaviour that serve as standards to which actual behaviour is compared.

In brief, rules refer to explicit informal agreements or formal statements about acceptable and unacceptable behaviour. They serve as standards to which actual behaviour is compared, with informal (e.g., social pressure) or formal (e.g., disciplinary action) reactions to rule breaking. In organizations they are particularly important because their explicit nature makes them relatively easy to formulate, communicate and change. Formal rules are an important tool of managers and organizations, and they feature prominently in the arsenal of organization designers (see Chapter 10 on structure) and all those managing people in organizations (see Chapters 12 and 13).

Norms
Implicit standards that express the expected and acceptable (or shunned and unacceptable) behaviours in a particular social setting.

Norms, already briefly discussed in the section on group development, are implicit and informal expectations for behaviour within social entities. They provide a powerful group mechanism for exerting social control on group members. Behavioural norms become internalized by individuals and institutionalized in the accepted patterns of behaviour. Group membership in informal groups is often predicated on adherence to group norms. Norm violations in any group will usually result in negative responses (called sanctions) by other group members. High-status group members may have more leeway than new or low-status members with regard to violating norms. Feldman (1984) suggests that groups will adopt a satisficing approach to regulating individual behaviour, unless:

- Group survival is at risk. If the behaviour of an individual threatens the group, then they will be dealt with.
- Lack of clarity in the expected behaviour of group members is creating problems in group activity or performance.
- By taking action the group can avoid bringing into the open things that it would be embarrassing or difficult to resolve.
- The central values held by the group are being threatened. If by allowing something to continue the status of a group might be compromised then action would be taken.

Because of their implicit nature, norms are harder for managers and organizations to design and change than rules. The acquisition of norms will be discussed further in Chapter 14 on culture.

Just like rules and norms, roles exist in many social contexts, but are of particular importance in groups and teams. In fact, many researchers see roles and the particular role structure of a group or team as the key feature that determines group performance. Humphrey and colleagues, for example, argue that '*Team performance is the amalgamation of the performance of a system of interconnected roles.*' (2009: p. 49) We have introduced Belbin's well known model of team roles earlier in the chapter, but many other contemporary models and research efforts also focus on roles and their contribution to team processes and successful group and teamwork (e.g., Humphrey *et al.*, 2009; LePine *et al.*, 2008; Mumford *et al.*, 2006; Mumford *et al.*, 2008; Stewart, 2006; Stewart *et al.*, 2005). In general, Humphrey and colleagues argue that specific roles in a team are more important if they encounter more of the problems the team has to solve in their work, perform more of the team's work activities (i.e., have greater exposure to the team tasks), and are more central to the workflow among all team members. Important roles in a team are said to form the team's strategic core (Humphrey *et al.*, 2009), and investment into these roles increases team performance. For different performance dimensions, however, different roles may be part of the core. The ability of groups and teams to adapt to changing conditions (Burke *et al.*, 2006) and to create appropriate roles and role structures is crucial for continued group success.

Another way of looking at the notion of roles within an organizational context is to consider the implications in terms of the individual concerned. For most people their primary role within an organization is defined by the job description. This document sets out what tasks and responsibilities are expected from the postholder. The job description therefore defines the expected role for the individual, at least as far as the organization, customers, suppliers and other employees are concerned. For example, to know that someone holds a job with the title of personnel manager would immediately convey a range of expectations about what that person should do at work.

However, that is not the end of the matter, because individuals are not simply a function of other people's expectations. Each individual will interpret the expected role in terms of their personality characteristics and a range of other factors such as past experience, beliefs and intentions. In effect they must perceive the expected role and interpret it for themselves. This has been referred to as the perceived role in which the individual brings to the job their own understanding of it. Finally, there is the enacted role, which reflects what the individual actually does in carrying out the tasks for which they are responsible. It reflects their actual behaviour on the job.

According to Handy (1993) role theory consists of a number of components. They include:

- *Role set.* The role set reflects the people, or more accurately the other roles, surrounding the individual forming the basis of the analysis. For example, the role set for a university lecturer might contain the roles and people reflected in Figure 7.6.
- *Role definition.* The role definition is based on the role expectation discussed earlier and sets out what the role of the focal person should be. Job descriptions and common knowledge were introduced as the basis of role expectations but they are not the only signals used to define a particular role. Uniforms, badges of rank, office location, style and equipment are all signals of the expected role of the person occupying the role.
- *Role ambiguity.* This reflects the degree of uncertainty in the minds of the role set as to exactly what their respective roles should be at any point in time. For

Expected role
The specific role that an individual is to fulfil, frequently specified in a job description.

Perceived role
What the individual understands their role to be.

Enacted role
What the individual actually does in fulfilling their role responsibilities.

Role set
The roles around a focal role.

Role definition
The sum total of things that define a particular role, including job description, uniforms, badges of rank and office location.

Role ambiguity
The degree of uncertainty among individuals as to exactly what a particular role's responsibilities are at a given point of time.

Figure 7.6 Role set of a university lecturer

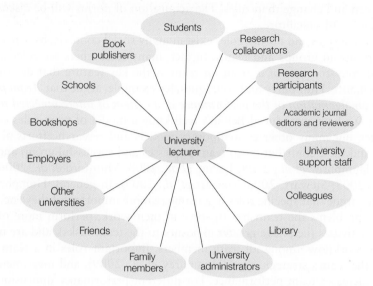

example, a subordinate going to a meeting with an unpredictable boss might not know their role until the boss makes clear what their respective roles should be on that particular occasion. On one occasion the subordinate might be expected to be humble, contrite and accept that the boss was not happy with something and be prepared to be told off without question. On other occasions they might be expected to be outgoing, jovial and prepared to join in the fun that the boss has decided to engage in. Clearly to engage in inappropriate role behaviour (the enacted role) would cause problems for both parties to the encounter.

- *Role incompatibility.* This reflects incompatible expectations between members of the role set about their respective roles. Role incompatibility reflects an aspect of the perceived role discussed earlier. A manager might expect subordinates to accept every instruction without question, whereas the subordinates might expect to have a much higher degree of freedom over their work activities. These two expectations are clearly incompatible and need to be resolved if conflict is to be avoided. The following Examining Ethics example reflects one female's story about being an executive and her treatment by male colleagues.

- *Role conflict.* This arises as a result of the conflicting role requirements acting on an individual at the same time. For example, a manager is expected to support and help subordinates as well as achieve objectives with a finite level of resources. Clearly, these two realities come into conflict on occasions – role conflict. A subordinate may be experiencing personal or medical problems and not be able to perform at full capacity during a prolonged period. However, the manager may not have the budget to allow additional staffing to maintain the output objectives and so needs to pressure the individual to do more work, which will conflict with their desire to help the person.

- *Role overload/underload.* These situations arise when an individual is either faced with too many roles, each competing for pre-eminence (role overload), or they do not have enough role-demand placed upon them for their existing capability (role underload). Many managers (particularly women) faced with the competing demands of work and home roles find that they cannot achieve a satisfactory balance between them and so they experience role stress and other problems. Similarly an individual who considers themselves to be underloaded becomes bored and frustrated because they feel underutilized and undervalued.

Role incompatibility
Incompatible expectations between members of the role set about their respective roles.

Role conflict
Arises as a result of a range of conflicting role requirements acting on an individual at the same time.

Role overload/underload
Arise when an individual has either too many roles, or not enough roles for their existing capability.

Can relationships in a team cause ethical problems?

The following quotation from a female executive is taken from Milwid (1987: p. 113).

> At one time or another, I've been propositioned by two of the six executives in this company, a couple of times by employees and managers who work for me, and more times than I can count by customers or field people. It's happened frequently enough now that it doesn't bother me.
>
> The first time it happened, it bothered me a lot because then I felt like they were discounting me. I thought that to them I wasn't a whole person anymore. I was just the person in the centrefold. I felt then that somehow their interest in me sexually meant that I wasn't powerful or that I wasn't being professional.
>
> Now, I just think it means they think I'm attractive. And I like that. I don't lead them on, because that's unfair. If I'm not interested in them,

I'm not interested. But being a sexually alive person doesn't mean you're not powerful, and it certainly doesn't mean you aren't capable.

A team that is to work well as a cohesive unit needs to develop close and effective working relationships. Close working relationships between the sexes, and also between those with a same-sex orientation, can sometimes spill over into inappropriate behaviour - evident from the above quotation. It is also a fact that many people meet their life partners at work.

TASK

1 How (and on what basis) can the boundaries of appropriate interpersonal behaviour between colleagues, team members and customers be determined and managed?

Source:
Milwid, B. (1987) *What You Get When You Go For It*, New York. Dodd, Mead and Company.

- *Role stress.* Each of the role concepts discussed can lead to role stress under certain circumstances. It is generally considered that a certain degree of stress is necessary if effective performance is to be achieved. There is an old saying in organizations that if you want something done give it to a busy person. The logic is that busy people have to be organized and that they develop a level of efficiency which a person who is not busy does not achieve. However, what is not clear is the desirable level of stress either for efficient working or to allow an individual to be able to cope without danger to themselves or others. What is clear, however, is that role stress can result in poor performance, health problems and a host of other difficulties for both individuals and organizations.

Role stress
The level of stress experienced by individuals as they act out the various roles allocated to them.

GROUP COHESION

According to Piper *et al.* (1983) group cohesion (also called *cohesiveness*) refers to the attractiveness of a group to its members, reflected in their motivation to be a part of it, and the degree of resistance to leaving it. In real terms cohesion represents the strength of the feelings of togetherness among the members of a group. This can apply to both formal and informal groups. It can be represented as a scale of measurement running from strong to weak.

A group with low cohesion is effectively a loose combination of people, each person having little or no commitment to the other members or the intended objectives

Group cohesion
Refers to the attractiveness of a group to its members and their motivation to remain members. It also reflects the strength of mutual bonds and positive attitudes among members.

of the group. Conversely, a group with a high level of cohesion is likely to display behaviour patterns that are tightly focused on the objectives to be achieved and support for each member of the group. Cohesive groups meet their objectives more frequently (Keller, 1986), especially when they are working in highly interdependent ways (Barrick *et al.*, 2007; Beal *et al.*, 2003). There are a range of factors which contribute to the level of cohesion developed within a group. They include (see Figure 7.7)

- *Environmental factors.* These can include perceived threats to the group and the desire to achieve available rewards.
- *Organizational factors.* These can include the nature of the task to be achieved, the perceived status of the group and the importance of the task to the organization.
- *Group factors.* These can include the size and composition of the group, the personality characteristics of the leader, frequency of interaction and the timescales for achieving the objectives of the group, and the difficulty experienced in becoming a member of the group.
- *Individual factors.* These can include the desire (or needs) of individual members to be part of a cohesive group, the level of commitment by individuals to group objectives, the perception of the other members' intentions, the degree to which the particular group helps fulfil any social or material needs (including identity needs) the individual has, and the perception of the other forces acting upon the situation.

From an organizational perspective it would be very useful for all formal groups within the organization to be highly cohesive, as long as they were supportive of the management-determined objectives. However, there is a real danger for managers from any strongly cohesive groups that are hostile to their intentions, such as group objectives or norms that are in direct opposition to organizational goals (see Figure 7.8). Such groups are likely to resist any official attempts to align their goals and behaviour with official goals. The Change at Work example illustrates that change, group cohesion and factionalism are forces and processes that can all interact. But such interaction does not automatically produce the intended results or even positive and effective outcomes for those involved.

Figure 7.7 Determinants of group cohesion

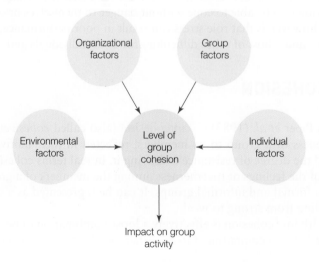

CHANGE AT WORK

Is change acceptable as long as it achieves the intended objective?

This story was told to one of the authors by the manager concerned (called Jake below) who preferred to remain anonymous.

Jake was recruited by his employer to run the computer department. Internal candidates had also been interviewed for the job, but Jake had gained significant managerial experience in his previous jobs. Most internal candidates for the manager's job accepted the situation and co-operated with Jake in running the department. However, one person thought that he should have been promoted and resented Jake for being appointed to 'his' job. He was uncooperative and tried to undermine Jake at every turn; but he was very clever (or so he thought) in how he sought to do this.

He was always polite and agreed with Jake when it was necessary to do so. He willingly co-operated with instructions and gave no cause for doubting his support. However, under the surface he was plotting his revenge. On several occasions he brought a 'problem' to Jake's attention and asked for advice. He would then follow the advice to the letter. Of course he had not given Jake the complete picture and the advice inevitably caused a bigger problem – to which his response was 'I was only following Jake's instructions!' The first couple of times this happened Jake accepted that it was a genuine mistake on the part of his subordinate. However, when it happened the fourth time in 3 months he became convinced that he was being 'set-up' in some way or another and paid closer attention to the behaviour of this particular subordinate. After another couple of 'incidents', Jake set about trying to deal with the situation. He consulted the HR department who said that with no specific evidence there was little chance of disciplinary action succeeding and that Jake should try to resolve matters through discussion with the individual concerned.

Jake went away to think about the situation and became convinced that serious action was necessary if his plans, job and prospects within the company were not to be put in jeopardy. He concluded that under the circumstances it was either going to be the subordinate or Jake who left the company, and decided that it was not going to be Jake! The only question was how

to achieve the end result? He also concluded that he would get little or no support from the HR department for any action that he might ultimately take.

Jake's brief was to introduce change in the computer department which gave him the 'right' to reorganize structure and the way that work was done. Consequently he engineered a reorganization that would result in a single redundancy among Jake's immediate subordinates. Then Jake had to 'define' the redundancy selection criteria to ensure that the 'problem' subordinate was selected. Jake used performance criteria to select – all subordinates were equal in that respect – leaving length of service as the next criteria to be used. Length of service could be interpreted as either with the company, or at the level of jobs facing redundancy. Strangely (or was it deliberately) both service-based criteria meant that either the subordinate in question or his wife (also a manager in the department, but who had not supported her husband's reaction to Jake) would be made redundant! He interviewed all of the people involved and offered the subordinate and his wife the option of deciding which 'service' definition should be applied. Naturally the subordinate realized that he was being set up and told Jake so, saying that he would fight his case at appeal and if necessary through the courts.

Jake made his subordinate redundant and introduced the reorganization. The employee appealed against the dismissal both internally and to an employment tribunal, but lost at each stage. Jake had been careful enough to do everything 'by the book' in his approach, meetings, record keeping, etc. Jake felt vindicated and smiled to himself every time that he thought about it. The other employees in the computer department also learned that Jake was not a manager to 'mess' with and so they were more willing than ever to support and work with him.

TASKS

1 Was the change a success and on what basis should this be determined?

2 Was the method of achieving the change acceptable or could/should it have been achieved in other ways and if so, how?

3 Was Jake 'right' to deal with this situation as he did? Justify your views.

7.7 EXTEND
YOUR LEARNING

Figure 7.8 Relationship between group cohesion and group performance on organizational goals

	Opposed	Fully aligned
High	**Very low performance on organizational goals** (group able to control individual behaviour in line with own objectives/norms)	**Very high performance on organizational goals** (group able to control individual behaviour in line with organizational goals)
Low	**Moderately low performance on organizational goals** (group able to control individual behaviour in line with own objectives/norms only to a limited degree)	**Moderately high performance on organizational goals** (group able to control individual behaviour in line with organizational goals only to a limited degree)

Group cohesion

Relationship of group objectives and norms with organizational goals

CONCLUSIONS

This chapter has discussed the nature and significance of groups along with the effects of group membership on organizational activity. We have considered how it is that groups set about structuring themselves and how they function. It is clear that groups, both formal and informal, are significant in terms of organizational activity, and employee and management functioning. By making effective use of the ideas contained within these chapters, management can attempt to enhance internal efficiency and effectiveness. Groups are also a means through which some of the social needs of individuals can be provided for within work settings.

The existence of groups within organizations is closely associated with the need for managers to exercise control over the processes for which they are responsible. Informal groups within organizations present a particular challenge for managers as they are essential, unavoidable and largely unmanageable. They represent the grease on the wheels of the formal organization as people help, support or hinder each other in practice yet they lie outside the formal organization framework.

In this chapter we have introduced some of the main issues surrounding the ways in which groups operate and achieve success. As managers seek to improve the performance of their organizations, the levels of effectiveness of the groups within them becomes a more critical factor.

Now to summarize this chapter in terms of the relevant Learning Objectives:

- **Outline the concept of a group as distinct from a team or a collection of individuals.** This chapter suggests that a group consists of two or more people who are psychologically aware of each other and interact in such a way that each influences and is influenced by the others. The notion of a team implies a small, cohesive group that works effectively as a single unit through being focused on a common task. Belbin also suggests that there are crucial differences between the two in how people are selected for membership and the nature of leadership. Katzenbach and Smith draw these ideas together by suggesting that a positive correlation exists between the type of team or group and the levels of performance achieved.

- **Understand the differences between formal and informal groups.** Formal groups within an organization are created specifically to achieve objectives as part of the need to integrate the skills and capabilities of a number of people and the need to compartmentalize activity. Informal groups emerge naturally as a result of interpersonal, social and common-purpose needs of individuals operating within a largely constrained and formal organizational framework. Informal groups sometimes emerge as a result of the need for individuals to achieve their job objectives by interacting with other employees outside of the formal arrangements provided, or in order to influence the priorities of other people. Management have little influence over the range and type of informal groups that emerge in an organization, yet such groups can be very influential in the way that the organization functions.

- **Explain group development processes and how they might impact on group performance.** Two basic possibilities are associated with group development. The first is when a completely new group is formed and must become a unified entity in order to achieve its objectives. The second and more common situation, is when a group already exists and a new member joins the pre-existing group. Other factors that can impact on the development process include the anticipated lifespan of the group, whether it is a formal or informal group, and the purpose for which the group has been formed. There are two models discussed in the chapter which relate to group development processes. One is the four-stage model offered by Bass and Ryterband, the other and better known model is that proposed by Tuckman and Jensen. This model has the stages of forming, storming, norming, performing and adjourning. These models provide for a process of individuals coming together and over time developing the mechanisms and relationships to be able to work effectively together in pursuit of the objectives to be achieved. The models recognize that there is no certainty in being able to negotiate the passage through each of the stages, and failure, or that the creation of an ineffective group is an ever present reality. It is also possible that the members may be able to achieve the objectives but gain no personal satisfaction from the process. The models do not specifically provide for the situation in which a new member joins an existing group. In such situations the degree to which the individual and/or the group adapts to the change in membership is not clear.

- **Discuss the nature and value of role theory together with its relevance to the structure of groups and teams.** There are different ways of thinking about the roles that people perform within a group. One considers role to equate with the formal designation of a job within a group, for example, treasurer or secretary. Another way to think about role is through the work of writers such as Belbin who consider groups in terms of process and take the view that a number of process-related roles exist based upon personal characteristics such as being a 'plant' or an 'implementer' for example. The value of role theory is that it allows issues to be considered about how groups set about the activities associated with their purpose and how the individuals taking part in that process are likely to interact and engage with each other and the objectives. This is important for understanding the implications of issues such as role conflict and incompatibility which are introduced in the chapter.

- **Assess how control can be achieved within groups through such mechanisms as norms, rules and roles.** The process of socialization involves individuals learning how things are done within a particular context. Control within groups can be achieved through this process as the norms of behaviour established by a group will be passed on formally and informally to new members. All members of a group are expected to adhere to the norms established for the group and sanctions will be applied by other members if these are not followed. This process in action was clearly demonstrated in aspects of the Hawthorne studies. Authority refers to the ability of a leading or significant figure within a group to directly influence the behaviour of the group.

DISCUSSION QUESTIONS

1 What is role theory and how might it offer an insight into how groups form and function within an organization?

2 Groups within organizations are different from groups in other contexts. To what extent and why might this statement be true? Do any differences that exist matter in an organizational context?

3 The use of 'team' rather than 'group' in an organizational context represents an attempt by managers to retain control whilst appearing to delegate power and authority to employees. Discuss this statement.

4 To what extent is the distinction between the concept of formal and informal groups a useful one in an organizational context?

5 What is 'social loafing'? How and to what extent can managers and/or fellow group members control or eliminate it?

6 Should management do everything it can to prevent informal groups from forming in the organization? Justify your answer.

7 Should individuals be trained in the theories of group formation and structure in order to ensure

that they can become effective contributors to group activities? Why or why not?

8 Tuckman and Jensen (1977) describe a model of group development which describes the process that a new group goes through. How might the process differ when a new member joins an existing group?

9 To what extent is the creation of formal groups within an organization an attempt to provide managers with the means of social control?

10 Individuals within an organization belong to so many formal and informal groups as part of their work that it is not possible for managers to control individuals with any degree of success. Discuss this statement.

CASE STUDY

Shane Battier – useless player or best team player in basketball?

Shane Battier is often described as a phenomenon among the professional basketball players in the USA. In one sense he is not a good team player. For him the worst part of any game day is the 11 minutes between the end of the pre-game warm-up and the introduction of team payers as they emerge into the arena. For most players that time is spent horsing around with team-mates, trying to maintain physical readiness whilst releasing nervous energy. In the process players make exaggerated gestures of affection towards one another, but they don't actually know one another that well or even want to. Instead of engaging in the pretence adopted by other professional basketball players – that they actually know and like each other – Battier slips away on his own to the locker room. Once the introductions are over comes the best part of his day. He is quoted as saying 'I hate being out on the floor wasting that time. I used to try to talk to people, but then I figured out no one actually liked me very much.'

Battier has routinely guarded the league's most dangerous offensive players – LeBron James, Chris Paul, Paul Pierce – and has usually managed to render them ineffectual, or a lot less effectual than normal. He does it so quietly that no one really notices how he does it. When asked, players say that he had prevented them from playing to their full potential, if Battier did something. They usually blame it on an 'off' night. Battier senses that some players look forward to being 'guarded' by him. The team coach confirmed as much: 'That's actually true. But for two reasons: (a) they don't think anyone can guard them; and (b) they really scoff at the notion Shane Battier could guard them. They all think his reputation exceeds his ability.'

Whilst still at school, one basketball magazine named Shane Battier the fourth-best seventh grade player in the USA. However, his professional career did not get off to a good start with the Memphis Grizzlies, a weak basketball team with the worst winning percentage in NBA history – and he was sold after about 3 years. The year after Battier joined the Grizzlies, the team's general manager was fired and the replacement immediately sought to sell him as one of his weakest players. However, during his time with the Grizzlies their performance improved and they made the NBA play-offs in each of his final three seasons with the team. Before the 2006-2007 season, Battier was sold to the Houston Rockets, who also improved their achievements when he was a team member – including one stretch of 22 wins in a row. The player who spent the most time actually on court playing for the Rockets during this winning streak was Battier. The team coach said, 'We have been a championship team with him and a bubble play-off team without him.'

Battier is a basketball mystery: a player who is widely regarded inside the NBA. as a replaceable cog in a machine driven by superstars. Yet every team he has played for has acquired some magical ability to win. Solving that mystery is Daryl Morey's job. In 2005, the Houston Rockets' owner, Leslie Alexander, decided to hire new management for his losing team and went looking specifically for someone willing to rethink the game. Alexander said

We now have all this data (on players etc.). And we have computers that can analyse that data. And I wanted to use that data in a progressive way. When I hired Daryl, it was because I wanted somebody that was doing more than just looking at players in the normal way. I mean, I'm not even sure we're playing the game the right way.

Basketball is a game grounded in player and team statistics to find new and better ways to value players and game strategies. The sport has now become one of success, coming from playing the odds. Like professional card players, team managers want to play the odds; but of course first they must know the odds. Hence the development and use of team and individual player statistics. There is a quest to acquire new data, and an intense interest in measuring the impact of every little thing a player does on his team's chances of winning. Daryl Morey was trying to find ways of rethinking how to use player data in basketball with some success and so he was hired by the Houston Rockets to help turn their fortunes around. When Morey joined the Rockets, a huge chunk of the team's allotted payroll – the NBA caps payrolls and taxes teams that exceed it – was committed to just two players, admittedly both superstars. But that did not leave much for other players already in the team and certainly not for the purchase of high-calibre new players. Consequently, Morey had to find ways to improve the Rockets results without spending money. He said:

We couldn't afford another superstar, so we went looking for nonsuperstars that we thought were undervalued and hence underpaid. That's a scarce resource in the NBA.

Sifting the population of mid-level NBA players, Morey came up with a list of 15 that were 'undervalued' using a new scoring model. Near the top of the list was Battier. This perplexed everyone including the man who hired Morey to improve the Rockets' performance. Morey had a tough time trying to persuade everyone that they should follow the implications of the new statistics model. It was far easier to spot what Battier didn't do than what he did. His conventional statistics were unremarkable: he didn't score many points, catch many rebounds, block many shots, steal many balls or dish out many assists. 'Battier can't create an offensive situation. He needs to be in relatively open space to shoot for the hoop.' Battier's weaknesses arise from his physical limitations. As Morey puts it, 'He can't dribble; he's slow and hasn't got much body control.'

Battier's game is a weird combination of obvious weaknesses and nearly invisible strengths. But when he is on the court, his team-mates get better, often a lot better, and his opponents get worse – often a lot worse. He may not grab huge numbers of rebounds, but he has an uncanny ability to improve his team-mates' rebounding. He doesn't shoot much, but when he does, he takes only the most efficient shots. He also has a knack for getting the ball to team-mates who are in a position to do the same, and he commits few turnovers. On defence, although he routinely guards the NBA's most prolific scorers, he significantly reduces their shooting percentages. At the same time he somehow improves the defensive efficiency of his team-mates – probably, Morey surmises, by helping them out in all sorts of subtle ways. Morey says:

I call him Lego. When he's on the court, all the pieces start to fit together. And everything that leads to winning that you can get to through intellect instead of innate ability, Shane excels in. I'll bet he's in the hundredth percentile of every category.

There is a tension, peculiar to basketball, between the interests of the team and the interests of the individual. The game continually tempts the people who play it to do things that are not in the interests of the group. Each player faces choices between maximizing his own perceived self-interest and contributing to the team efforts in seeking to maximize the chances of winning. The choices are complex and there is a fair chance that the individual player doesn't fully realize that they are making them. Blocked shots are an obvious example – they look great, but unless you secure the ball afterward, you haven't helped your team. Players love the spectacle of a ball being swatted into the spectators, but it becomes a matter of personal indifference that the other team gets the ball afterwards. For example, Dikembe Mutombo made his name by doing a finger wag – he grabs the ball, holds it against his hip and wags his finger at the opponent from whom he has just taken it as if to signal, 'naughty, naughty!' He loves the crowd reaction to his now famous finger wag routine. His team of course would be better off if he didn't hold onto the ball long enough to wag his finger.

Having watched Battier play for the past 2.5 years, Morey has come to think of him as an exception: the most abnormally unselfish basketball player he has ever seen. Or rather, the player who seems one step ahead of the analysts, helping the team in all sorts of subtle, hard-to-measure ways that appear to violate his own personal interests. When the Rockets played the San Antonio Spurs Battier was assigned to guard their most dangerous scorer, Manu Ginóbili. Ginóbili, however, did not play during the whole game and so he was less tired than Battier who was intended to be on court during the entire game. Battier privately went to the team coach and asked to bring him on only when Ginóbili entered the game. 'No-one in the NBA does that,' Morey says. 'No-one says put me on the bench so I can guard their best scorer all the time.'

Before the Rockets bought Battier, the analysts obviously studied his value. They knew all sorts of details about his efficiency and his ability to reduce

© The Columbian/Troy Wayrynen/NewSport/Corbis

the efficiency of his opponents. They knew, for example, that stars guarded by Battier suddenly lose their shooting touch. What they didn't know was why. Two hundred or so basketball games later, Morey's the world's expert on the subject. He pointed out that instead of grabbing uncertainly for a rebound ball, Battier would tip the ball to a team-mate. Battier would, when the ball was in the air, leave the player that he was guarding and block out the other team's best catcher. Morey says, 'You see that his whole approach is to stay in front of opposing players and try to block their vision when they shoot. We didn't even notice that was what he was doing until recently.'

TASKS

1 Teams in both sports and business are made up of individuals. To what extent can an individual be made or encouraged to behave in such a way that they put the interests of the team ahead of their own in either business or sport?

2 What can business learn about teamwork from sports, if anything? Justify your answer.

3 To what extent is it possible for a top-flight athlete (with no real business or management experience) to teach managers how to get the best out of work teams?

Source:
www.nytimes.com/2009/02/15/magazine/15Battier-t.html?_
r=3&ref=magazine&pagewanted=all New York Times March 1st
2009. Reprinted with permission of The New York Times.

FURTHER READING

Armstrong, P. (1984) Competition between the Organizational Professions and the Evolution of Management Control Strategies, in Thompson, K. (ed.) *Work, Employment and Unemployment*, Milton Keynes: Open University Press. This text considers how professional groups attempt to 'engineer' access to decision making through restrictions on the interpretation of information and what can be described as hostile strategies towards other groups.

Belbin, R.M. (2000) *Beyond the Team*, Oxford: Butterworth-Heinemann. Key text for understanding the Belbin model of groups.

Gillespie, R. (1991) *Manufacturing Knowledge: A History of the Hawthorne Experiments*, Cambridge: Cambridge University Press. As the title suggests, this work looks at the intellectual and political dynamics of this famous collection of research into work activity. In doing so it examines the way that scientific knowledge itself is produced.

Hackman, J.R. (2002) *Leading Teams: Setting the stage for great performances*, Boston, MA: Harvard Business School Press. Self-explanatory title outlines what this text is about and its relevance to this chapter.

LaFasto, F. and Larson, C. (2001) *When Teams Work Best: 6000 Team Members and Leaders Tell What it Takes to Succeed*, London: Sage. This text looks at theory and practice about what it takes to make teams work effectively in an organizational context.

Smith, K.K. and Berg, D.N. (1987) *Paradoxes of Group Life*, San Francisco, CA: Jossey-Bass. This text discusses the conflicts that exist for the individual as a result of group membership. Some cultures have a cultural orientation towards the group, others lean towards an emphasis on the individual. In either context, the individual must forgo certain freedoms once within the group. This text introduces the main issues surrounding this debate.

Thompson, L.L. (2008) *Making the Team: A Guide for Managers* (3rd edn), Pearson. A practical book aimed at explaining what a manager needs to do in a work context with regard to teams.

West, M., Tjosvold, D. and Smith, K. (2003) *International Handbook of Organizational Teamwork and Cooperative Working,* Chichester: Wiley. Explores the psychological and social processes that stimulate successful teamwork for modern competitive situations.

COMPANION WEBSITE

Online teaching and learning resources

Visit the companion website for Organizational Behaviour and Management 4th edition at: http://www.cengage.co.uk/martinfellenz to find valuable further teaching and learning material. For full details, see 'About the website' at the start of the book.

CHAPTER EIGHT

COMMUNICATION AND DECISION MAKING

©mflippo/istock

LEARNING OBJECTIVES

After studying this chapter and working through the associated OB in Action panels, Discussion Questions and Case Study you should be able to:

- Outline the concepts of communication and decision making.

- Explain the major models of decision-making processes.

- Assess the organizational significance of communication and decision making.

- Understand the main influences on interpersonal communication.

- Discuss the significance of groupthink in organizational decision making.

INTRODUCTION

Communication and decision making are fundamental aspects of everyday life for all employees and all organizations. Communication is a process involving interaction and information exchange. One definition states that communication in an organizational context 'is an evolutionary, culturally dependent process of sharing information and creating relationships in environments designed for manageable, goal-oriented behaviour' (Wilson *et al.*, 1986: p. 6). More generally, we refer to communication as *the process by which people convey and receive information to and from each other*. Decision making as a process represents a means of selecting a particular course of action from among the options available. Although it is closely relate to problem solving, and the terms are sometimes even used interchangeably, problem solving refers to the activity of generating a solution to a recognized problem. Thus, it can be part of decision making, but the two describe different activities in organizations.

Both communication and decision making processes are essential for organizations. Without communications, organizations as social entities cannot exist. And without decision making, organizations do not function. Moreover, the two processes are closely linked, as much of organizational communication is deliberate and therefore based on decision making, and decision making that has any relevance for organizations ultimately involves communication of decisions and actions to other organizational actors. A central link between communication and decision making on organizations appears obvious: both are about information – or more specifically, about sending, receiving and using it. However, not all communication and decision making in organizations is deliberate, and not all of these activities are in the service of organizations. In this chapter we will review forms of communication relevant for management and organizations and consider their implications for individuals, groups and the organizations as a whole. We will also consider different types of decisions as well as decision-making models and dynamics at the individual, group and organizational level, and the pragmatic implications of decision making for organizations, their functioning and their members.

HUMAN COMMUNICATION

So what exactly is communication? Communication is generally seen as the process of exchanging information between two entities that result in a message originating by the sender being received by the receiver. The Shannon-Weaver communication model is the best known and most widely used model for communication (see Figure 8.1). It was developed by mathematician Claude E. Shannon (1948) and popularized in a book by Shannon and his colleague Warren Weaver (1949). This model includes many of the relevant elements and processes of communication, but because it was developed as an abstract model of general communication it needs to be adapted to fully capture the nature of human communication.

The key elements of human communication include sender, message, encoding, transmission, noise, channel, receiver, decoding, decoded message and feedback. Table 8.1 defines and describes these elements in more detail and highlights the particular issues necessary to more fully describe formal communication between humans. This qualifier ('formal') is important because not all human communication is intentional, and unintentional communication (e.g., much of nonverbal communication talking place in human interaction) is not deliberately encoded and transmitted. For such instances and aspects of human communication the model still applies in principle but needs some further adaptations.

Communication
The process by which people convey and receive information to and from each other.

Decision making
A process through which a course of action or solution is identified and chosen from the options available.

Problem solving
The activity of generating a solution to a recognized problem.

Noise
The peripheral and background contamination surrounding a communication that interferes with the ability of the recipient receiving the complete message sent. For example, noise from a television playing in the background can prevent someone hearing every word spoken during a telephone conversation.

Figure 8.1 Schematic diagram of a general communication system

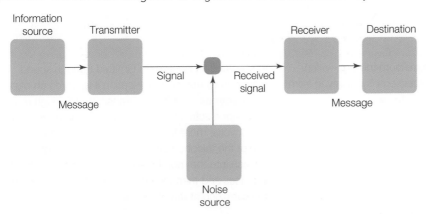

Source: Shannon and Weaver, 1949.

Table 8.1 Key elements and processes in human communication (focus on formal communication)

Elements and processes	Definition/ description	Special issues in human communication
Sender	Individual (or other entity) who originates a message.	Not only humans but other social entities (e.g., groups, organizations) are often perceived to be senders of communication. However, any human communication is based on individual behaviours, even though they may be planned and co-ordinated with others. Machines can also generate messages if programmed appropriately.
Message	Information that is to be transmitted by the sender.	For deliberate communication the message is deliberately selected by the sender, but typically many messages are not actively or consciously chosen by the sender (e.g., spontaneous verbal responses to fright or surprise or many nonverbal messages).
Encoding	Process of designing the message to be sent.	Many messages (e.g., nonverbal messages such as inadvertent facial expressions) are not deliberately encoded.
Transmission	Process of sending the message through the selected channel.	Messages such as spoken sentences or SMS texts are usually deliberately transmitted, but nonverbal communication is often sent without any deliberate or even conscious decisions.
Noise	Any interference or contamination that changes the signal through which the message is transmitted or leads to errors in its decoding.	Noise may be anything that affects the actual content of the message (such as background noise in a busy office that makes it difficult to hear a telephone conversation) or that biases the decoding of the message (such as the context in which the message is received which may invoke an interpretation frame that biases the decoding of the message). A particular form of noise is communication overload which may lead to individual messages being overlooked.

(Continued)

Table 8.1 (*Continued*)

Elements and processes	Definition/ description	Special issues in human communication
Channel	The medium through which the message is conveyed from sender to receiver.	In speaking it is words transmitted through sound waves, in written communication it is words on paper and electronically it is data transmitted through radio waves or electrical impulses. A message transmission may involve more than one conversion of form. The use of the telephone involves the transmission of speech into the mouthpiece, a conversion into electrical impulses and then the conversion into sound energy in the ear piece at the other end.
Receiver	Individual (or entity) who receives the transmitted message.	Intended and actual receiver may not be the same. Also, if messages are received by groups, involved members may decode the message collectively or individually which can lead to different results for different individuals.
Decoding	Process of taking in and interpreting the received message.	This involves the receipt of signals and the application of prior experience and knowledge to their interpretation. This can be an automatic process, as when speaking to someone in a language understood by both sender and receiver; or it can require interpretation, as with the need to refer to a phrase book if translation between languages is necessary or if the received message is equivocal or ambiguous.
Decoded message	Information that is received and can be attended to by the receiver.	The decoded message represents the meaning attached to the received signal by the receiver. This meaning may not be that intended by the sender.
Feedback	Any response to a received message transmitted to the sender of the message.	Refers to the deliberate or unintentional reactions communicated back to the sender of the received message. Typically, it may convey that a message has been received, and in efforts to reduce errors in the communication process to persist it can include a paraphrased version of the received message to enable the sender to compare this to the original message. Feedback closes the loop between the sender and receiver and makes the communication process a cyclical one. This is crucial for managers while attending to the function of controlling as discussed in Chapters 1 and 6.

The process of communication is a social activity involving two or more people across time. Figure 8.2 reflects the essential nature of this process and it should be noted that it is circular. The process involves the sender initiating a communication sequence with the receiver responding and providing feedback to the originator, thus beginning an iterative process.

An important aspect of this model of human communication is the notion of *error*, which refers to any distortion of the information as it is conveyed from sender

Figure 8.2 The communication loop

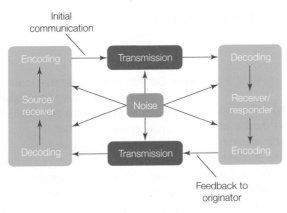

to receiver. At any of the steps described in the communication process model, error can be introduced or amplified. As examples, errors may include the sender selecting the wrong information for transmission (e.g., sales figures for the previous instead of the current month), senders encoding information wrongly (e.g., the wrong key pressed on the keyboards when typing an e-mail), selection of a transmission channel that is not appropriate (e.g., sending an e-mail from a computer not connected to the Internet), the destruction of part of the information through noise (e.g., parts of phone conversation drowned out by a 'call-waiting' beep), and receivers who screen out part of a message (e.g., a person who fails to recognize the sarcastic tone of a verbal message) or make other errors in decoding the message (e.g., misreading or misinterpreting a sentence). The same errors can happen during feedback communication. Generally, human as well as environmental (e.g., technological) factors can contribute to error in communication.

With regard to error in human communication, the steps of encoding and decoding are of particular importance. Encoding of deliberate communication typically includes the conversion of ideas into a form suitable for transmission. In sending a letter to customers, ideas must be encoded into words before they can be written on paper. In converting an idea into words (encoding or expressing the ideas in symbolic form) there is inevitably a loss of precision and richness from the original thought. Words also have shades of meaning and can convey different things to different people. This is particularly true when the sender and receiver come from different cultures and therefore have a different frame of reference against which to judge meaning. Spoken words also take on meaning from the context in which they are used and the nonverbal cues that accompany them (i.e., that are deliberately or inadvertently encoded as part of the message). For example, 'Can I help you?' said with a sneer conveys a totally different meaning from when it is said with a smile.

Similarly, decoding involves the receipt of signals and the application of prior experience and knowledge for their interpretation. The human perceptual system is the key mechanism of decoding in human communication. As discussed in Chapter 4, such perceptual processes can be automatic (e.g., listening to a message in a language understood by the receiver) or it can require substantial effort (e.g., the translation of ill-understood technical jargon into meaningful words with the help of technical manuals or dictionaries). Perceptual and cognitive biases and errors often contribute to errors during decoding. The meaning attached to a signal by the receiver may not be that intended by the sender as is apparent in the Employee Perspective panel.

EMPLOYEE PERSPECTIVE

Reading between the lines

John worked as a joiner in a factory making doors and windows for sale through DIY stores and directly to house-builders. The work was cyclical and employees could be laid off work for 2 or 3 months at a time when order levels reduced significantly. When the credit crunch began in 2008 workers expected layoffs to begin shortly afterwards. Management of the company were aware of the growing employee concerns about the future and in December 2008 sought to reassure staff by sending out a newsletter setting out the company situation and intentions for the coming few months. It was intended to reassure employees by indicating that although orders had begun to slow down and costs would have to be reduced, no job cuts were being planned – unless orders dropped even further over the following 4 months. John had worked in the company for 5 years and had not seen a newsletter of this type before.

The newsletter became the topic of many conversations between employees in canteen and coffee breaks. People were generally not sure how to interpret the message contained in the newsletter. Some said it was good news, providing a clear indication of management's intentions to keep everyone in jobs as long as possible. Others said that management were being devious and hiding their real intentions. They pointed out that in the past when orders had dropped no newsletter had been sent out, so what was different this time? This view held that something was going on behind the scenes which prompted management to send out the letter. Consequently, it was safe to assume that whatever 'it' was would not benefit employees. John did not know what to make of the two different interpretations of the newsletter.

Some managers became aware of the negative interpretation of the newsletter by some employees and so called a series of departmental meetings in which the production director of the company and appropriate departmental manager tried to make it clear that the company was not going bankrupt in the foreseeable future; that there was no hidden agenda behind the newsletter and that the company intended to preserve jobs for as long as possible. There was also opportunity for employees to ask the managers questions, but in responding to questions about long-term job security, they were unable to offer definite guarantees. Those employees who had formed a negative interpretation of the first newsletter were not persuaded or reassured by the meetings. Some employees who had initially been positive about the newsletter changed their views as a result of the vague assurances on long-term job security. Management did not know what to do next to convince employees that although there could be no guarantees, their intentions were genuine.

TASKS

1 What would you do next if you were the senior HR manager in that company?

2 Could the negative reaction to the first newsletter have been prevented and if so, how?

COMMUNICATION WITHIN ORGANIZATIONS

Without communication, organizations cannot exist. But why is communication so important and central? As communication is the only process by which people exchange information, it is a fundamental aspect of any interaction among individuals or groups. Without interactions, organizations would not and could not exist as *social* entities. Moreover, they would not exist and could not function without shared goals or without co-ordination among members, all of which can be achieved only through communication among organizational members.

In organizations, human communication takes place between many different partners and has many important roles. Some examples of such roles between selected partners are outlined in Figure 8.3. This figure includes external as well as internal communications within the model. This is because many people within an organization engage in a considerable degree of communication with other organizations and groups. For example, suppliers, government departments, customers, professional associations and competitors all have business-related communications links with an organization. In addition to the formal links implied in Figure 8.3, a wide range of other formal and informal communication networks exist both in and around any organization. For example, all employees communicate with family members and friends and some of this interaction will contain an organizational dimension or relevance. In one form, this could involve an employee describing their feelings about work to family or friends; in another, it could involve an employee selling company secrets to a competitor. More formal links could involve an employee filling in a tax return setting out their earnings. All of the communication links indicated may contain various degrees of association with organizations, both formal and informal.

From an organizational perspective it is possible to distinguish communication along a number of different dimensions. We may consider the degree of formality involved or the routes (or channels) chosen for exchanging information directly or indirectly, among many others. Using the two mentioned dimensions can help us create a framework for analysing different types of communication. Formal communication would be associated with highly structured commercial activities of the organization, and informal communication with more unstructured information exchange with external constituents (perhaps public relations in a very general sense). The second dimension relates to direct and indirect aspects of the purpose of the communication process. So, for example, the organization would be directly involved in communicating to its customers, but only indirectly involved with an individual's tax affairs. These two dimensions can be reflected as a diagram (Figure 8.4) along with an illustration of what form of communication might fall in each quadrant. Competitor intelligence (or, more dramatically, industrial espionage) is an interesting phenomenon in relation to organizational activity in that all organizations engage in it to some degree. It reflects the processes of seeking to understand the environment and competitor activity. Obtaining company accounts and other publicly available information represents one form of trying to understand what competitors are doing, as does *reverse engineering* (the purchase of competitor products and stripping them down to establish manufacturing methods, technologies used and costs involved). Recruiting key employees from competitors represents another way of seeking to gain understanding, albeit potentially restricted by contractual or legal requirements. There is, however, a much more covert level of espionage that it is possible to engage

Figure 8.3 Examples of organizational communications

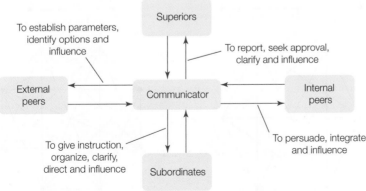

Figure 8.4 The two dimensions of communications

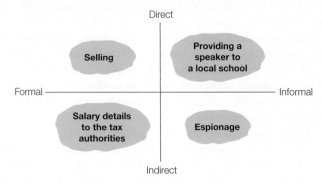

in and occasionally such practices as placing listening devices in offices or searching the refuse of executives for discarded documents have all been used by unscrupulous people in the search for greater knowledge about competitor (or even employee) activity. Clearly, these activities raise both ethical and legal issues.

Given the complexity involved in organizations, and particularly large ones, the co-ordinated management of organizational activities requires immensely complex communication linkages. Structurally, complexity in communication is an exponential function of the number of people involved (see Figure 8.5). There are six channels between the four people in the first group in Figure 8.5, reflecting the number of communication possibilities. Any particular episode could be initiated by either party, which increases the number of possible communication flows to 12. This number, which reflects the possible connections in internal organizational communication networks, increases dramatically to 20 with five members, 30 with six members,

Figure 8.5 Increasing number and complexity of communication linkages as a function of member number

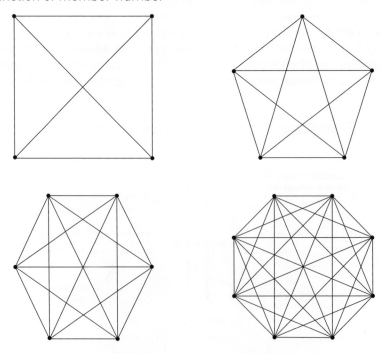

and 56 with eight members. Now consider the number of possible communication flows in a firm with 2000 employees - the actual number is 3 998 000. Of course, not every individual in large organizations needs or wants to communicate with every other member. At the same time, other entities within organizations (such as groups or departments) as well as individuals and groups outside of the organization will also have communication linkages to individuals within the organization.

Clearly, in large organizations the communication process needs to be managed carefully if total chaos is to be avoided. There are many ways in which organizations seek to achieve this in practice, including:

- *Limitation.* Not every employee would be expected to interact with every other member of the company. This is achieved through a number of organizational devices including hierarchical and departmental structures.

- *Procedure.* The development of appropriate procedural arrangements sets out to ensure that information is circulated only to those individuals needing it (or with a presumed right to access it).

- *Teamwork.* The use of teams and committees allows a degree of informality to facilitate communication between members; also the use of group representatives ensures that not every member is involved in communicating with every other group; group activity also concentrates communications on relevant issues at specific times.

- *Automation.* The use of electronic media should increase the opportunity for easier communications as individuals can access parts of the overall information available as necessary to their jobs and at a time appropriate to them. They can then process and transmit transformed data through the same media, allowing others flexibility in reacting to it.

- *Separation.* The identification of activities that require communication and those which can be designated as information flow. For example, employee communications are often separated into categories such as newsletters (one-way) and formal meetings between employee representatives and human resource managers (two-way).

- *Jargon.* The use of jargon, which refers to *specific terminology consisting of specialized words or common words with specialized meaning,* can help the speed and accuracy of communication among and sensemaking by members of organizations or specific units or groups. Similarly, common language and terms (e.g., specific abbreviations) serve similar functions.

Jargon
Refers to specific terminology consisting of specialized words or common words with specialized meaning which can help communication among, and sensemaking by, members of professions or specific communities of practice.

To what extent are all problems and conflict in an organization the result of poor communications?   **STOP & CONSIDER**

COMMUNICATION PROCESSES

Figure 8.6 reflects the main interaction networks that form the basis of communication for managers. In addition to the work-related internal and external network reflected in Figure 8.6, managers will (in common with other employees) be part of friendship and family-based communication networks.

Communication serves four general functions within an organization:

1 *Information processing.* Communication is more than the simple transmission of information. Data will be collected and turned into information that

Figure 8.6 The manager's communication network

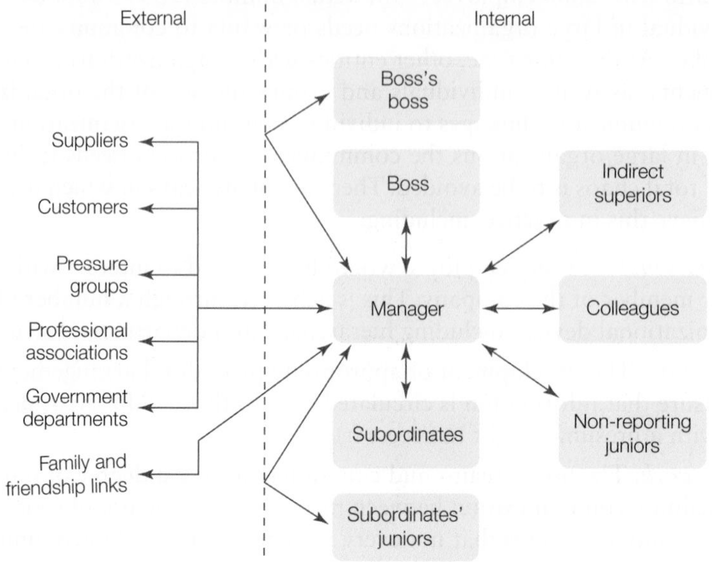

Source: Adapted from Hellriegel / Slocum / Woodman. *Organizational Behavior*, 5E. © 1989 South-Western, a part of Cengage Learning, Inc. Reproduced by permission. www.cengage.com/permissions.

has meaning and purpose. The ability of individuals to create and share information is what generates effective activity. It is on the basis of information that decisions and planning can be undertaken.

2 *Co-ordination.* Communication also allows the integration of activity within the organization. For example, if a sudden drop in sales is identified, all departments can be alerted to take action. This could include reducing expenditure, cutting output, product review, speaking to customers and bankers, and so on.

3 *Visioning.* Through the exchange of thoughts and ideas, communication is a process that can develop and convey the vision, mission and strategies to employees throughout the organization. It contributes to commitment and the shaping of organizational culture by creating shared understandings.

4 *Personal expression.* Everyone in an organization will have their own views and opinions about work and nonwork issues. These include opinions and attitudes about products and services offered, senior management, or how the company compares with other employers. Understanding these attitudes and feelings is an important aspect of management activity. Indeed attempts to shape employee attitudes and feelings form a significant focus for much internal company communications. This is the basis of the social partnership approach to engaging employees in a form of management-worker relationship supposedly based on mutual commitment, understanding and respect so much talked about today.

The methods of communication that occur within organizations include:

● *Written.* The use of memos, letters and reports are the chief means of communicating through this medium. In addition, there are the company procedures, the majority of which will be committed to writing.

● *Oral.* Individuals interact with each other in a variety of ways within organizations. Meetings to discuss important items involve considerable oral communication. Meetings can also be used to waste time (procrastination) and avoid decision making as the Change at Work example illustrates. Less

CHANGE AT WORK

Procrastination – the real alternative to decision making?

Procrastination is about putting off things that should be done. Meetings are a common way that groups of people can procrastinate. The following quotation was seen by one of the authors on an office wall:

Are you lonely? Work on your own? Hate making decisions? Hold a meeting! You can see other people, draw flowcharts, feel important and impress your colleagues. All in work time. **Meetings** *– the practical alternative to work.*

Some other quotations on procrastination:

1 Mark Twain: 'Never put off till tomorrow, what you can do the day after tomorrow.'

2 Douglas Adams: 'I love deadlines. I like the whooshing sound they make as they fly by.'

3 Ellen DeGeneres: 'Procrastinate now, don't put it off.'

4 Spanish singer Julio Iglesias was on British television when he used the word 'manyana'. Asked to explain, he said that the term means 'Maybe the job will be done tomorrow, maybe the next day, maybe the day after that. Perhaps next week, next month, next year. Who cares?' Irishman Shay Brennan (on the same show) was asked if there was an equivalent in Irish. 'No. In Ireland we don't have a word to describe that degree of urgency,' replied Brennan.

5 The fontayne website has a list of 27 tips for effective procrastination including:

  ← Check your voice mail for last-minute cancellation of the deadline. Again.

  ← Sharpen pencils. All of them. Even if you only use ink.

  ← Rearrange your desk and drawers. Relabel all files with newly-typed labels.

  ← Make lists. . . . To Do lists.

Piers Steel (University of Calgary) identifies the following Procrastinator's Creed:

1 I believe that if anything is worth doing, it would have been done already.

2 I shall never move quickly, except to avoid more work or find excuses.

3 I will never rush into a job without a lifetime of consideration.

4 I shall meet all of my deadlines directly in proportion to the amount of bodily injury I could expect to receive from missing them.

5 I firmly believe that tomorrow holds the possibility for new technologies, astounding discoveries and a reprieve from my obligations.

6 I truly believe that all deadlines are unreasonable regardless of the amount of time given.

7 I shall never forget that the probability of a miracle, though infinitesimally small, is not exactly zero.

8 If at first I don't succeed, there is always next year.

9 I shall always decide not to decide, unless of course I decide to change my mind.

10 I shall always begin, start, initiate, take the first step and/or write the first word, when I get around to it.

11 I obey the law of inverse excuses which demands that the greater the task to be done, the more insignificant the work that must be done prior to beginning the greater task.

12 I know that the work cycle is not plan/start/finish, but is wait/plan/plan.

13 I will never put off until tomorrow, what I can forget about forever.

14 I will become a member of the ancient Order of Two-Headed Turtles (the Procrastinator's Society) if they ever get it organized.

TASK

1 If procrastination is a common human trait how can effective decision making ever be achieved?

Sources:
Piers Steel: http://webapps2.ucalgary.ca/~steel/Procrastinus/
  funsites.php (accessed 16 April 2009).
http://www. fontayne.com/ink/putoff.html (accessed 16 April 2009).
http://www.quotationspage.com/quotes/ (accessed 16 April 2009).
http://haveachuckle.blogspot.com/2008/04/manana.html
  (accessed 16 April 2009).

Figure 8.7 Seating arrangements for effect

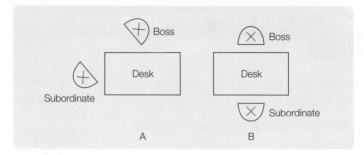

formal interactions also take place frequently. For example, an administration assistant may telephone the accounts department to query a particular entry in the weekly budget report.

- *Nonverbal.* There are a host of nonverbal communication signals that accompany interaction and which provide interpretative information between the individuals involved. Examples include tone of voice, body posture and spatial positioning. For example, the seating arrangements can set the tone for a meeting. Sitting across the corner of the desk (Figure 8.7A) provides a less distant, imposing or threatening layout than sitting across the desk (Figure 8.7B). The physical environment in which an individual works can also provide powerful clues to the status and authority of that particular person

- *Electronic.* With an increase in the availability and sophistication of electronic devices, the opportunity to communicate in new ways has emerged. The ability to use e-mail instead of written memos, teleconferencing in place of face-to-face meetings and the use of the fax machine to send written information have all changed the nature of organizational communication. The Internet and intranet facilities have also developed very rapidly and can provide employees, managers and other stakeholders access to large quantities of information at times chosen by recipients rather than at times dictated by the sender. It can also be easier to hold information necessary for reference purposes (reports, procedures and background information for example) in electronic form than as a paper copy in a filing cabinet. However, easy accessibility of information can contribute to information overload, which refers to the phenomenon when available information cannot be sorted, assimilated and used, leading to stress and negative cognitive, emotional and behavioural reactions (e.g., Hemp, 2009). For example, e-mail rage is emerging as a reaction in individuals who find themselves being overwhelmed, abused or threatened through the volume and nature of e-mails.

Information overload
Phenomenon that occurs when available information exceeds an individual's ability to filter, select, sort, assimilate and use it, resulting in stress and negative cognitive, emotional and behavioural reactions.

Interpersonal communication

At its most basic level, interpersonal communication involves two people in a dyadic interaction that involves the elements of the process described in Figure 8.2. Of the communication channels open to individuals, nonverbal signals are the least obvious and yet carry much information (see Chapter 4 – 'Body language and perception'). Table 8.2 provides a summary of the main nonverbal communication categories used to support other forms of communication. An emerging theme referred to as the theory of equivocation is beginning to offer explanations on how individuals such as politicians interact with interviewers and members of the public when direct answers to questions might prove embarrassing or involve loss of face (Bull, 2003). This invariably involves

Table 8.2 Nonverbal communications

Body language	Touching, eye contact, gestures, dress, etc.
Paralanguage	Voice tone, speed, pitch, etc.
Proxemics	Seating arrangements, personal distance, management of personal space, etc.
Environmental	Room design and facilities, etc.
Temporal	The use of time to create effect and influence

seeking to understand how question and answer types of interaction develop and how they are managed in the dynamic context in order to convey a particular message.

Taking each category in turn:

- *Body language.* An individual can stop speaking but their body keeps on sending signals through gesture, touch, posture, facial expression and eye contact for example. The following quote illustrates this process: 'In 20 minutes Mr Roosevelt's features had expressed amazement, curiosity, mock alarm, genuine interest, worry, rhetorical playing for suspense, sympathy, decision, playfulness, dignity and surpassing charm. Yet he said almost nothing.' (Gunther, 1950: p. 22) There are also cultural differences in the meaning of many of the signals given (Pease, 1984).

- *Paralanguage.* This aspect of verbal communication conveys a number of clues and can be split into four separate areas (Trager, 1958). Voice quality (pitch, range, resonance, etc.), vocal characteristics (whispering, groaning, coughing, etc.), vocal qualifiers (momentary variations in volume or pitch) and vocal segregates (pauses, interruptions such as 'ah', 'um', etc.).

- *Proxemics.* This refers to the spatial needs of people and their environment. This links together communication distance and the type of message. Seeing two people physically very close, heads almost touching, would tend to suggest that a secret was being shared, whereas the same individuals separated by several feet could be discussing the weather.

- *Environment.* The layout of a room can have a powerful effect on the communication process. A meeting between a boss and a subordinate over a pay rise will be more likely to take place in the boss's office (or territory), a home base to give support to the boss's views. The following describes the feelings of a lawyer summoned to appear before the US Justice Department to explain why criminal proceedings against a client should not be instituted:

  They were immediately shown to the criminal division's coldly utilitarian conference room. 'It's the most perfect government room you ever saw,' Trott says. 'It's nothing but a table, some chairs, a picture of the president and the attorney general on the walls.' 'It was,' he adds, 'an icebox, a meat locker.'

  (Carpenter and Feloni, 1989: p. 74)

- *Temporal.* The use of time to create an impression is well understood by most effective communicators. Calling all employees together for a meeting at a time which requires them to interrupt their normal work will give the message greater impact. A manager making someone wait outside their office a few minutes before a meeting creates pressure and can destabilize the person kept waiting. This is demonstrated in the case study at the end of this chapter (The power of time) and is a true story of how one manager used time to control an employee relations situation as well as illustrating other aspects of communications and decision making. In addition to the time pressure Sengupta *et al.* (2002) suggest that care is needed because the need to create a particular impression can lead to misrepresentation of the message itself.

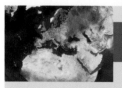

GOING GLOBAL

What were they trying to say?

Speaking at a conference on biofuels, the director for economics of agricultural markets at the European Commission's Directorate General for Agriculture and Rural Development asked whether the increased cultivation of biofuel crops compared to ordinary food crops was driving up food prices? He began by explaining that because biofuel crops were a very small part of overall crop production in Europe it had little impact on food prices. He then deviated from his script and is quoted as saying 'There is no danger, due to our wealth, of running out of food in the EU.'

Whilst that might be true, it was not welcomed or interpreted positively by people in developing countries where food is disproportionately expensive (and for whom it is difficult to achieve an adequate, balanced diet). Politically it could also be interpreted a hostile intention on the part of the European states towards developing countries. This demonstrates that technical experts need to understand the broader implications of what they say when speaking in public - particularly when they are trying to interpret the technical aspects of their brief. It is possible that the speaker's comments were mis-translated or quoted out of context, but on the international stage it is necessary to anticipate this possibility in relation to the intended message.

Business communication across cultures can become problematic because of the culturally deter-mined differences in practices, traditions, processing and meaning. Factors that affect cross-cultural communication include:

- *Language*. Good quality, accurate translation services are important. Even the use of a common language can hide differences in meaning.
- *Environment*. The level of development, size of population, type of geography, climate, business and organizational structures for example.
- *Technology*. The availability and use of different technologies predisposes individuals, suppliers and customers to different levels and types of international and cross-cultural influence that impact on communications.
- *Social organization and history*. The nature of society, its traditions and how it functions will also influence communication between participants.
- *Conceptions of authority*. The nature of authority, respect and deference also impacts on how people from different cultures respond and expect to interact with each other.
- *Nonverbal communication*. Body language and other 'signals' vary across the world and contribute to the message in other forms of communication. These can easily be misinterpreted in international contexts.

TASKS

1 Given language, culture and social differences between countries, to what extent can any communication be error free? What does this imply for any international business activity?

2 How can a business minimize the risks that this might create?

3 How might the environment influence cross-cultural communications?

Sources:
http://www.answers.com/topic/cross-cultural-international-communication (accessed 16 April 2009).
http://www.prconversations.com/?p=342#more-342 (accessed 16 April 2009).

Another form of interpersonal communication arises in international situations. Many businesses, not just large ones, operate internationally these days and so the need to communicate with people speaking different languages and with different cultures arises. It can be a difficult area to get right and the Going Global example seeks to illustrate aspects of this.

Effective interpersonal communication in organizations

Interpersonal communication is effective if it helps convey the relevant messages and helps maintain or improve the relationship between sender and receiver. A number of potential barriers to effective interpersonal communication exist. Such barriers have been described as 'something that keeps meanings from meeting' (Howe, 1963: p. 23). When such barriers go beyond the difficulties related to error discussed as part of the human communication model above, they are typically related to psychological reactions to communication. Such reactions include psychological reactance (see Chapter 4) which occurs when messages appear to try to influence or otherwise limit the freedom of receivers. Other reactions include defensiveness, especially in response to messages that appear to affect the receiver's self-image in negative ways, as well as aggressive or withdrawal behaviours. These communication barriers are induced by messages that appear to be judging, impose solutions on the receiver, or fail to address the receiver's concerns (Bolton, 1979).

In this context, Whetten and Cameron (2007) define communication as constructive if it helps overcome defensive behaviour in others and patronizing behaviour in ourselves. Defensive behaviour in organizations in response to communication happens frequently because many times the content is evaluative, or because it is construed as such. Hierarchical differences between sender (e.g., boss) and receiver (i.e., subordinate) as well as competitive environments (e.g., among work groups) can increase such effects. Similarly, patronizing behaviour and communication from managers can easily be perceived because of the status and authority differences. However, it is also common among peers and can even occur in communication from subordinates to their managers. Fundamentally, it is the reaction of any communication receiver who experiences feelings of incompetence, unworthiness or insignificance during or after communicating. The specific problem with such patronizing communications is that receivers will attempt to re-establish self-worth. Such efforts to portray self-importance take precedence over listening, and showing off, self-centred behaviour, withdrawal, and/or loss of motivation are common reactions (Whetten and Cameron, 2007).

A range of skills and strategies can help avoid these and other barriers to effective interpersonal communication, but despite their universal applicability and their often quite basic nature our experience as educators, consultants, and executive coaches has taught us that even senior managers often have gaps in these skill sets (or even appear to lack them altogether!). These skills include listening skills such as reflective listening (sometimes called active listening), paraphrasing, reading body language and supporting communication with consistent body language (see Table 8.3), empathy, as well as the more commonly found skills in logic, reasoning and content-oriented message design. These latter skills are typically part of the formal education and training employees and particularly managers receive in organizations. The link between communication and the development, maintenance and improvement of interpersonal relationships in organizations will be further discussed in Chapter 16.

Feedback

A particularly important type of communication is feedback, which goes beyond the use of the term as part of the general communication model discussed above. In

Table 8.3 Listening skill sets

Attending skills	A posture of involvement
	Appropriate body motion
	Eye contact
	Nondistracting environment
Following skills	Door openers
	Minimal encouragers
	Infrequent questions
	Attentive silence
Reflecting skills	Paraphrasing
	Reflecting feelings
	Reflecting meanings
	Summative reflections

Source: Bolton, 1979.

Performance feedback
Communication that conveys information about performance to maintain and enhance work performance.

Interpersonal feedback
Communication that conveys information about how a person's behaviour is perceived and experienced.

organizations, much of the feedback people receive is performance feedback which contains evaluative information focused on their performance (or lack of same). The purpose of performance feedback is to maintain and enhance work performance. As such, it has an *instructional function* (e.g., teaches new behaviours, clarifies roles) and a *motivational function* (e.g., by providing information about progress towards goals). To be effective, such performance feedback should generally be clear and unambiguous, be linked to relevant activities and goals, clearly indicate the actual performance achieved, be given during or immediately after task performance, be evaluative of the work done or not done rather than the person doing it, and be provided in a socially acceptable manner and setting.

In contrast to performance feedback, an important type of feedback in organizations, and indeed more generally in interpersonal relationships, is interpersonal feedback which conveys information about subjective experiences and reactions to others' behaviour. The purpose of interpersonal feedback is to build and maintain relationships, and to provide input to others on the impact and perceptions of their behaviour. Thus, interpersonal feedback has a *relationship function* (e.g., disclosure of emotional responses to others' behaviour) and a *developmental function* (e.g., provision of information that can raise others' awareness about how they are experienced). In organizations, provision of interpersonal feedback tends to depend on local norms as well as on the particular relationship between the people involved. In general, there are guidelines that can aid in providing effective interpersonal feedback. The main ones include that interpersonal feedback should never contain any evaluation, and must be given with considerable care and respect for the receiver. Tables 8.4 and 8.5 provide overviews of typical guidelines and suggestions that can help improve the success of such interpersonal feedback.

In general, receiving interpersonal feedback can be tremendously valuable for individuals' understanding about how their own behaviour affects others. In organizations, it is of particular importance in the development of relationships among group members. Also, the impact that managers and leaders have on others is an important aspect of their overall performance. Unfortunately, experience shows that

Table 8.4 Guidelines for giving interpersonal feedback

Be specific and direct
Own your message
Support your comments with evidence
Separate the issues from the person
Focus on behaviours that the person can do something about
Consider 'sandwiching' difficult messages between more positive ones
Treat feelings as real
Check for clarity, both of others' behaviour and of your feedback
Deliver feedback close to occurrence
Make sure that receiver is open for feedback – never force interpersonal feedback on others
Use an authentic manner of delivery
Show respect!

the higher up in the hierarchy individuals are, the less they receive direct and honest interpersonal feedback. This is not surprising as many employees find it difficult to let senior managers know how their behaviour is affecting them.

The value of interpersonal feedback and the self-awareness it helps develop is immense. Joseph Luft and Harry Ingham (1955) developed a graphic model of interpersonal awareness which they called the Johari Window (reflecting their first names) which is based on the premise that knowledge of self and others is an important aspect of interpersonal relations. The Johari Window reflects the notion that we ourselves and others are aware of some of our behaviour but not all, and that our

Table 8.5 Guidelines for receiving interpersonal feedback

Be open to the value that any feedback can provide
Prepare to be open for difficult feedback
Take notes of feedback and of your initial reactions
Be alert for and avoid defensiveness
Listen carefully
Do not start to argue – this is not the time and place for arguments and influencing attempts
Ask clarifying questions
Speak up if your limit for feedback is reached
Show appreciation for the gift of feedback (even – or especially – for messages that are difficult to accept)
Be respectful!

knowledge and that of others may differ. Combining these two dimensions creates a 2-by-2 matrix with four different combinations of self- and other-knowledge: the Arena (or Marketplace) which is an area where both self and others are aware of one's behaviour; the Secret Garden which reflects what we know about ourselves but do not show or share; the Blind Spot which indicates those aspects that others know but we do not see ourselves; and the Unknown area (we can think of this also as Potential) of our sub- or unconscious behaviour that neither we nor others are aware of. Figure 8.8 shows the original Johari Window as well as the dynamics that create increased awareness and can move the boundaries between the four quadrants for a particular person.

Electronic communication

In today's organization the use of computer-based technology to communicate is widespread and becoming increasingly commonplace. The fax machine is now a basic piece of 'old technology' equipment for sending messages and documents between locations, and intranets and e-mail systems are standard communication tools. Many companies are introducing more and novel information and communication technology (ICT) to support internal and external communication (Brady *et al.*, 2008). Such ICT allows information to be circulated more widely and rapidly than ever before. In manufacturing companies, the ability to design products on computer systems that produce parts lists and production schedules makes the task of ordering and invoicing that much easier. In service organizations the ability to call up a client file on computer allows the transaction to be more effectively tailored to client needs. The deployment of such ICT promises efficiency and effectiveness benefits, but oftentimes the managerial and organizational implications of technology deployment are not fully grasped, and unintended consequences can arise (see Chapter 11).

Organizations can design computer systems that allow designated individuals access to appropriate information from a database. For example, a computerized personnel system can hold information on each employee's career history, references, performance evaluations, pay progression, attendance record, disciplinary warnings and so forth. Access to the available information can be restricted in various ways. For example, job history, references and previous performance markings could be available to the department head but not the immediate supervisor of the person. The same principles can be applied to any of the company information systems including finance, budgets and marketing data.

Figure 8.8 The Johari Window and the processes for increasing awareness

As with all areas of management activity, the potential of electronic communication needs to be balanced with the other forms of communication available in order to produce an effective process at a cost that the organization can afford. This forms part of what is referred to as the knowledge management activities within an organization. For example, little would be gained from introducing teleconferencing between two locations only five miles apart when the usual communication between them is twice each year.

Communication and the law

It has long been realized within organizations that information is a source of power and that there is unequal access to it between managers and employees. Indeed, there also exists unequal access to information between levels of management and across functions. In an attempt to redress the balance between employers and employees, European employment legislation requires managers to communicate certain information to trade unions in specific industrial relations circumstances. This includes areas of collective bargaining and proposals to declare redundancies. Where trade unions have a need for particular types of information, they can reasonably expect employers to disclose these so that they can undertake their responsibilities for representing members more effectively. Recent research has shown support for the view that consultation does help to save jobs in such situations (Edwards and Hall, 1999).

Additionally, limited liability organizations with more than 250 employees have to include a statement in their annual reports identifying any actions taken over the year to introduce, maintain or develop communication with employees. Within the European Union (EU) there are expectations that employee participation will go further than simply being entitled to information and regular communication. The introduction of works councils is now built into employment legislation within the EU.

DECISION MAKING WITHIN ORGANIZATIONS

Just as communication, decision making is an essential process in management and organizations. Choosing goals and determining the ways to achieve them is an activity found at all levels of the organization and in all aspects of management. This is true for fundamental strategic choices (e.g., about strategic reorientations of a firm, or about large-scale investments in production facilities) as well as the most mundane everyday activity in organizations such as in which order to read incoming mail, or where to entertain a client. As these examples show, the decisions made in organizations can differ widely.

One of the central distinctions between decisions is related to their degree of risk, which is in turn related to the uncertainty involved in the decision as well as the importance of the decision and its implications for achieving organizational goals. Thus, decisions that involve a high degree of uncertainty and are also central for achieving critical organizational objectives are the most risky decisions made in organizations. Some of the important dimensions of decisions that influence risk and uncertainty include their structure and content, the specific decision context, and the characteristics of the decision makers.

Important distinctions in a decision's *structure* include differences in its complexity (i.e., the number of relevant aspects involved in the issue to be decided), its *analysability*, and the degree of *novelty or routine* involved. Another set of variables related to the decision *content* also distinguishes the nature of different decisions. Important aspects here include the decision *magnitude* (i.e., the range of different aspects of the organization affected by the decision), its *timeframe* (the duration during which the

Complexity
Refers to the wide range of people and environmental factors that may have a bearing on an issue.

decisions will have an impact on the organization), and its *centrality* for important organizational activities and objectives. This determines the importance of getting the decision right because of the adverse impact of a wrong choice, or because of the opportunity costs involved in making a wrong decision. Important distinctions can also be drawn between different decision *contexts* (for example, the degree to which there is time pressure, agreement among involved organizational actors about the actual problem necessitating a decision or about the appropriateness of different possible solutions), the presence of established and legitimized decision-making approaches for certain types of decisions, and the social and group dynamics that can affect decision making. In addition to decision structure, content and context, there are of course also the specific *characteristics of the decision maker* (for example, relevant knowledge and experience, analytical and cognitive abilities, individual preferences, biases and other cognitive limitations, and the possible interactions among them (e.g., Curşeu and Louwers, 2008) that influence the decision-making process and outcome (see Figure 8.9).

Yet even seemingly small decisions that according to the above dimensions would not warrant much attention can have a profound impact on organizations. The Management in Action demonstrates that anyone, and particularly senior managers, must carefully consider their comments in terms of the potential implications for themselves and their organizations. This is easier said than done for a number of reasons. As discussed earlier the particular nature of the decision may involve a high degree of uncertainty and unless the implications of all choices are known there is always risk involved. Moreover, many decisions in organizations are made without much consideration, attention and reflection. This often applies to programmed decisions (Simon, 1977) which are expected, routine decisions for which appropriate decision processes have been developed beforehand. Thus, much routine decision making is highly structured and prescribed through standard operating procedures, manuals, rules and other explicit means that guide the decision process. By implication, once these programmed decision processes are invoked, decision makers tend to follow their predetermined structure and logic and simply execute the decisions as laid out for them.

In contrast, nonprogrammed decisions are those that are novel, have not happened before, do not fit into established decision categories and therefore cannot be handled through previously determined decision-making processes. Rather, the

Programmed decisions
Routine, repeated, highly structured decisions that allow decision makers to follow clearly prescribed procedures.

Nonprogrammed decisions
Novel, unique, poorly structured decisions that require decision makers to define the issue and to actively develop an appropriate process to make the decision.

Figure 8.9 Factors influencing decision processes and outcomes in organizations

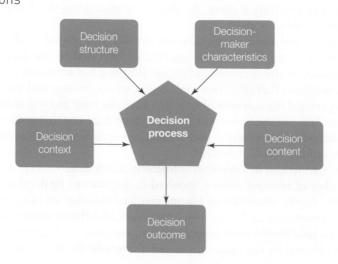

MANAGEMENT IN ACTION

Mouth in gear, brain in neutral

Gerald Ratner was the owner and chief executive of a jewellery chain in the UK and the USA which bore his family name. By 1989 it had a total of 2000 shops and could claim to be the largest jewellery chain in the world. It specialized in selling mass market value-for-money products and had a shop in most large towns. It was also a very profitable company. In April 1991 Mr Ratner was to give an after-dinner speech on why his company was so successful to members of the Institute of Directors in London.

During his speech he made two throw-away comments intended to be jokes. One was along the lines of, 'People often ask how we can sell a sherry decanter for less than £10. My reply is because it is total crap!' The second was that they sold a pair of earrings for less than the price of a prawn sandwich from Marks & Spencer – and that the prawn sandwich will probably last longer than the earnings! His after dinner speech went down well, diners laughed at the jokes and he received a standing ovation at the end of it. Unfortunately the press picked up on his comments and they made the headlines the next day – the line being that he had said his customers paid low prices for rubbish!

Mr Ratner had (according to his autobiography) consulted other people (including his wife and a fellow director) on the content of his speech and some thought the jokes were OK while others thought that they were inappropriate. He decided to leave them in!

At the time of the speech the UK was in the middle of recession and, not surprisingly, a public relations nightmare erupted with the press running the story for a couple of weeks. Customers deserted his shops and some demanded their money back. Sales and the share price slumped and the company had to make several changes in an attempt to survive. They included cutting back on Mr Ratner's pay and perks as well as appointing a new chairman. By October 1992, Mr Ratner was dismissed as CEO of the company that his grandfather had started. The company was eventually bought out, and merged into another retail jewellery chain.

TASKS

1 Should senior business leaders ever use humour in a speech as an aid to communication? Justify your answer.

2 Could he have made the same point in a way that did not provoke the negative reaction? How?

3 Could the situation have been salvaged once the storm had erupted and if so, how?

Sources:
Ratner, G. (2007) *The Rise and Fall…and Rise Again*, Chichester: John Wiley.
The Sunday Times, 21 October 2007. Accessed April 2009 at: http://entertainment.timesonline.co.uk/tol/arts_and_entertainment/books/book_extracts/article2701311.ece.
The Guardian, Saturday 7 March 2009, Hattenstone, S. Accessed April 2009 at: http://www.guardian.co.uk/business/2009/mar/07/gerald-ratner-interview.

relevant solution needs to be worked out in response to the decision opportunity arising. While even nonprogrammed decisions have common features and an enacted structure (Mintzberg *et al.*, 1976), they typically do not lend themselves to be handled in routine fashion and require deliberate consideration and attention instead. If managers do not have the capacity because they are overworked or distracted, such decision opportunities may not reach the threshold necessary to be recognized as unique and requiring active attention (e.g., Keil *et al.*, 2007). Thus, individual managers as well as groups or units may fall back on individual or collective standard routines and responses rather than active and reflective consideration. Norms and cultural factors can contribute to such individual and collective reactions.

It is clear that decision making is of fundamental importance for organizations. Below we will consider the classical approach to decision making and consider how individuals and groups often fail to live up to the standards of this abstract, rational model. We will then consider models of organizational decision making and conclude with a brief discussion on how decision making on organizations can be improved.

Classic decision theory – the rational decision model

The range and number of decisions taken in organizations is vast. They can be individual or collective decisions, they may refer to official organizational business or private and personal issues, they can be programmed or nonprogrammed, and they may turn out to be inconsequential or of huge importance for the organization and its members. Despite this variety, however, decision making is usually described, discussed and evaluated in relation to an abstract ideal – the *rational decision model*, also called the rational economic model because it reflects the traditional economic view of behaviour.

In short, the rational decision model posits that selecting the optimal choice is a rational process that involves three main steps of (1) identifying and defining the decision problem, (2) inventing and designing alternatives and (3) selecting the best course of action (Simon, 1960). According to this model, rational decision makers are *optimizers* (or *maximizers*), which means that they select the optimal alternative and thus maximize the value that can arise from their decision. However, this model is based on a number of assumptions including:

- That decision makers appropriately recognize and define the decision problem.
- That they have all needed information (including full knowledge of all possible options and their costs and benefits for all stakeholders).
- That they are perfectly rational and use the same objective criteria to evaluate all options consistently and without changing such evaluations.
- That they can successfully process all relevant information and make an unbiased choice.
- That they do not incur information acquisition and processing costs.

As the discussion in the previous section has already indicated, these assumptions do not typically apply to real organizational decision-making situations. Some specific decisions in organizations come close to the requirements for using the rational decision model. For example logistical decisions about optimal order sizes in procurement or operational decisions about optimal lot sizes in production may well be taken in situations where all the relevant information is available. Similarly, some financial decisions about investments appear to satisfy the requirements of the rational decision model. However, as recent events in the world of global finance have shown so dramatically, even assertions widely accepted to be facts may ultimately be undermined and not hold true.

In organizations, decision making can rarely be fully described by the normative rational decision model. Many aspects of the organizational context influence decision making, among them the facts that information search and processing takes time and costs money; some uncertainty always remains; and influencing attempts, group dynamics, politics as well as serendipity play significant parts in actual organizational decision making. From a behavioural perspective, however, it is the limitations of humans as decision makers that provide particularly obvious challenges to the rational decision model. Real decision makers, unlike homo economicus, the idealized rational decision maker of economic theory (see Thaler, 2000), are neither always rational, objective and unbiased, nor are they capable of processing (or even remembering) all relevant information for even relatively simple decision situations (Simon, 1983; see also the discussion on Rational Choice Theory, Chapter 16). Real people tend to be 'dumber, nicer, and weaker' than traditional economic perspectives suggest (Thaler, 2000).

Bounded rationality – a behavioural model of decision making

The limitations of classic decision theory were recognized by Herbert Simon (1957) who coined the phrase bounded rationality to describe the ways in which both internal and situational factors limit human decision makers' efforts to behave perfectly rationally. For his influential work on research into the decision-making process in economic organizations he received the Nobel Prize in Economics in 1978. Fundamentally, bounded rationality describes the ways in which humans make decisions when trying to be rational. but having to contend with distractions, biases, limited cognitive capacity, incomplete information, as well as with potential errors in information processing. As a result, bounded rational decision makers will not typically act as maximizers or optimizers, but rather will display *satisficing* in their decision making. This means that they will follow a process similar to that described by the rational decision model but evaluate each alternative as it becomes known and select the first alternative that satisfies their internal threshold for acceptance. According to the behavioural model of decision making, acting as a satisficer does not usually lead to the choice of the best alternative, but to the choice of the first acceptable one. Simon (1957) used the analogy of a haystack with needles in it. Rather than looking for the sharpest needle in the haystack (optimizer), a satisficing decision maker would look for the first needle that is good enough for the sewing job at hand.

> **Bounded rationality**
> Concept that describes the limits within which humans try to act as rational decision makers.

Given their cognitive limitations, decision makers in complex, real-life situations typically reduce the demands and the complexity of the decision-making process by employing heuristics. Heuristics refer to mental shortcuts or cognitive 'rules of thumb' such as considered guesses, rough estimates, intuitive preferences, simplifying assumptions, or common sense judgements. Like other cognitive structures (see Chapter 4), heuristics are based on past experience and, once developed and established, are invoked mostly automatically (Evans, 2006, 2008). Heuristics are often seen as problematic because while they can result in automatic and appropriate behaviour (e.g., a parent unreflectively taking a small child's hand when approaching a busy road), they often lead to a lack of reflective and critical thinking and can result in poor judgement and decision making (West *et al.*, 2008). In the next section we will consider specific heuristics and biases that limit the rationality of individual decision making in organizations.

> **Heuristics**
> Experience-based rule or mental shortcut used in making judgements or solving problems.

In comparison to the rational decision model, the behavioural model of decision making recognizes real limitations in human cognition as well as the influence of past experience and situational factors on decision making. Unlike the rational decision model it is not a normative model that attempts to guide or prescribe decision-making approaches. Rather, it is a descriptive model that tries to aid understanding of how decisions are made by individuals in organizations and can be used in understanding limitations and shortcomings to help identify remedies and strategies to improve real organizational decision making.

Judgemental heuristics, biases and errors

Heuristics in decision making are like a double-edged sword: they can work both for and against the decision maker. In some situations, general heuristics like the ones discussed below can be counterproductive, while specific heuristics developed on the basis of relevant experience and expertise can improve decision making (e.g., Curşeu and Louwers, 2008). On the positive side (see Gigerenzer and Todd, 1999), heuristics help to reduce complexity and simplify the situation to be considered; they help to quickly and easily deploy prior experience in considering problems and finding solutions; and they often lead quickly to correct or at least acceptable answers to the problems addressed. On the negative side, however, they can introduce systematic errors to judgements. To make matters worse, most people are not aware of the heuristics they use, or even that they are using them! It is important for decision makers as well as for students of OB to learn about heuristics, because only if we become aware of the heuristics typically used can we take action to eliminate or at least attempt to counteract these sources of bias and potential error in our own and others' decision making.

Much of the work on the nature and role of heuristics, which we can also think of as judgement strategies, has been done by Daniel Kahneman and Amos Tversky (1980; Tversky and Kahneman, 1981). They discuss the availability heuristic which relates to the ease with which a person can access a particular object or event through memory or imagination. The degree to which an event or object is particularly salient, evokes strong emotional responses, is easy to imagine, and is concrete and specific will influence its availability. A retail manager who considers the performance of employees will be more likely to give a particular salesperson a negative performance review if she has just been called to the shopfloor to address a customer's complaint about this salesperson because this event will be easily available in the manager's mind. The availability heuristic is useful because it focuses decision makers' minds on aspects that occur more frequently. All other things being equal, those aspects are likely to be more relevant for the decision at hand. However, as other factors can also affect the availability or ease of recall, the heuristic can also introduce bias and error to decisions.

Another potential source of bias and error is the representativeness heuristic which refers to the degree of similarity perceived between people or objects. If a person or object appears to be representative of a category we have experience with or simply preconceptions about, we are likely to assume in our decision making that that person or object possesses the central characteristics of their respective category. A financial manager who had good experiences with a particular investment will likely choose other investments that appear similar to this. This heuristic is very similar to stereotyping discussed in Chapter 4 – in fact, the mental shortcuts it represent are involved in stereotyping.

There are a range of other important heuristics and cognitive biases that contribute to skewed decision making. *Framing effects*, discussed by Tversky and Kahneman (1981) in their prospect theory, refer to the distinctly different choices people make depending on the way their alternative options are described. In short, if options are framed as potential savings or gains, then people tend to favour risk-avoiding choices. In contrast, if they are framed in terms of losses, then risk-seeking behaviour results. Prospect theory also indicates that people's negative response to a loss is more pronounced than their positive response to an equal gain (consider your reaction to losing compared to finding a £50 or €50 note). This is also related to the endowment effect, the phenomenon that people tend to value an item higher if it is in their possession compared to their valuation if it is not. Another decision-making dynamic discussed by prospect theory are anchoring and adjustment effects. These effects occur because after being exposed to a particularly positive or negative experience or after receiving reference information, however relevant and legitimate it appears, people do not adjust their expectation for future events accordingly. Anchoring effects are often deliberately used in negotiations and will be discussed further in Chapter 9. A different yet related bias is the status quo bias which describes the tendency of decision makers to favour stability over change in their choices. (Kahneman *et al.*, 1991).

Another decision-making bias is based on the illusion of control (Langer, 1975) which refers to the fact that people tend to overestimate the influence they can have on uncontrollable events such as lotteries. Much superstitious behaviour is based on the irrational illusion of control. A bias that makes learning from experience difficult is the hindsight bias which refers to the tendency of people to exaggerate

Availability heuristic
Relates to the ease with which a person can access a particular object or event through memory or imagination.

Representativeness heuristic
Refers to the degree of similarity perceived between people or objects.

Prospect theory
Refers to the distinctly different choices people make depending on the way their alternative options are described.

Endowment effect
People tend to value an item higher if it is in their possession compared to their valuation if it is not.

Anchoring and adjustment effects
After being exposed to a particularly positive or negative experience or after receiving reference information, however relevant and legitimate it appears, people do not adjust their expectation for future events accordingly.

Status quo bias
The tendency of decision makers to favour stability over change in their choices.

Illusion of control
Refers to the fact that people tend to overestimate the influence they can have on uncontrollable events such as lotteries.

Hindsight bias
Refers to the tendency of people to exaggerate the likelihood of events that they know have occurred.

the likelihood of events that they know have occurred. When the underdog wins in sports their triumph appears often much less surprising after the fact than before. This bias is closely related to the *confirmatory bias* (discussed in Chapter 4) as well as to the related and well documented *prior belief bias* which states that logical conclusions in line with prior beliefs are more likely to be accepted (e.g., West *et al.*, 2008). A functionally similar dynamic plays out in the implicit favourite bias which describes often subconscious tendencies of decision makers to evaluate information and make choices that lead to their preferred outcomes. The difference is that the implicit favourite bias is influenced by motivation (i.e., valued goals and preferences) while the confirmatory bias and belief bias are perceptual and cognitive biases, respectively. Clearly, many of the other perceptual biases discussed in Chapter 4 can also influence decision making.

Finally, a decision-making problem that frequently occurs in organizations is the nonrational escalation of commitment (Staw, 1981). This phenomenon occurs when people continue and even increase their commitment to a failing course of action despite strong feedback that shows the negative consequences of their decisions. Examples of continued commitment include people who invest in stocks or bonds and, after the value has dropped dramatically, decide to wait for them to recover their previous price levels before selling. More extreme examples of escalating commitments can be found, for example, among commercial lenders who, having made an initial loan to a small business, continue to 'throw good money after bad' by giving additional loans to help bail out the failing company. Commercial lenders and other decision makers are advised to ignore any previous commitments and judge any follow-on decision from a neutral vantage point. In practical terms, that means that the consideration of *sunk cost* (i.e., resources already committed to the course of action) must be excluded from the analysis in making decisions. While logical, this advice is often hard to follow. Bringing in outside advisers with no responsibility for previous decisions may help in such situations (Staw, 1981).

The nonrational escalation of commitment has several causes that can all contribute to its occurrence. They include perceptual biases (such as the confirmatory bias), motivational biases (such as ego-defensiveness which makes people try to appear consistent to themselves), judgemental biases and errors (for example framing effects, illusion of control, or the consideration of sunk costs), impression management (trying to save face, appearing consistent to others) and competitive irrationality. *Competitive irrationality* occurs when it appears that other people's (or organizations') actions benefit them to the detriment of oneself. Price wars are a typical example. They ensue if one competitor in an industry drops prices to 'corner the market'. However, in many situations (e.g., when goods or services are undifferentiated and when prices are highly transparent) price wars lead to lowered margins for all firms in an industry because each one feels that they have to match their competitors' prices. It is rational only for the first firm to drop prices – but only if others cannot easily follow this move. Price wars are often counterproductive for all competitors, although great for their customers! Staw also identified the *hero effect* (Staw and Ross, 1980) which refers to employees' favourable attributions regarding managers who have shown consistency in their decision making despite negative feedback – but only if they end up being successful.

Even though the phenomenon of irrational escalation of commitment appears extreme, the factors and dynamics that contribute to it are very common. In a classic contribution, Salancik (1977) identified the factors that contribute to the commitment people feel towards a belief or decision. According to Salancik, commitment occurs when there is *voluntary* choice, when the choice or aspects associated with it (such as sunk costs) are *irrevocable*, when it is made in *public*, and when it is or can be made *explicit*. Many or even all of these aspects are present in typical escalation

Implicit favourite bias
Describes often subconscious tendencies of decision makers to evaluate information and make choices that lead to their preferred outcomes.

Nonrational escalation of commitment
Occurs when people continue and even increase their commitment to a failing course of action despite strong feedback that shows the negative consequences of their decisions.

of commitment situations. In particular, the felt that responsibility associated with active choice appears to be important for commitment to escalate. While much traditional research has focused on this *responsibility effect* (Staw, 1976), recent work (Schulz-Hardt *et al.*, 2009) has identified that it may be preferences for the chosen course of action and not only perceived responsibility for the choice that contributes to enduring and potentially escalating commitment.

Group-level decision making

Many organizational decisions are made by groups, for example an investment committee that determines which internal project proposals will receive funding, or a new product development team that needs to decide which features to include in a new prototype. Group decision making tends to have both advantages and disadvantages compared to individual decision making. Based on logical assessment of collective decision making, French philosopher and mathematician Nicolas de Condorcet posed in 1785 the Concordet Jury Theorem which states that groups voting on decisions will improve their decision quality if they add members who on average are right in their votes more often than they are wrong. However, if new members are worse, adding members to decision-making groups will lower the quality of resultant decisions – appropriate staffing therefore matters! However, Concordet also showed that majority preferences can be *intransitive* – that means that in the same group a majority may prefer option A over B, another majority may prefer option B over C, and a third may prefer C over A. This is known as Concordet's Paradox and highlights potential problems with group decision making because the outcome of group decisions may depend on the order of options considered. Concordet's contributions show that structurally – not even considering group dynamics or the aggregation of individual level biases – group decision making has distinct characteristics that need to be actively managed to prevent bad decisions.

Contemporary research on group decision making in organizations indicates that groups are particularly effective in dealing with complex issues that require the deployment of varied knowledge and expertise. This performance advantage is due to the varied skills and knowledge that different members can bring to bear in the course of the decision process. However, this presupposes that the group has the appropriate kind and level of diversity, and that it can manage the differences among its members as well as the challenges of group development and collective task performance sufficiently (see Chapter 7). Other benefits typically associated with group decision making include a higher capacity to remember complex information (e.g., Johnson and Johnson, 1994) and the increased likelihood of decision acceptance based on participation in the development of the decision.

Unfortunately, group decision making is also associated with a number of potential problems including the difficulties arising from social loafing, or from group norms and objectives that may not be aligned with organizational goals (see Chapter 7). In addition, group decision making needs more time and co-ordination effort than individual decision making, especially if individual agendas interfere and when either the decision problem or relevant information is ambiguous. Some further specific problems that arise in group decision making are group polarization and groupthink.

Stoner (1961) suggested that groups take decisions that involved greater risk than an individual alone would be prepared to take. Originally known as the *risky shift phenomenon*, it is now generally called group polarization (Moscovici and Zavalloni, 1969) which refers to the tendency of groups to amplify shared individual attitudes. Under certain circumstances, it occurs in both riskier and more conservative dimensions. The two main determinants of this phenomenon are *social comparison* and *persuasive argumentation* processes in groups (Isenberg, 1986). Social comparison

Concordet Jury Theorem
States that groups voting on decisions will improve their decision quality if they add members who on average are right in their votes more often than they are wrong.

Concordet's Paradox
Highlights potential problems with group decision making because the outcome of group decisions may depend on the order of options considered.

Group polarization
Refers to the tendency of groups to amplify shared individual attitudes in their joint decision making.

processes are part of the social control mechanisms in groups (discussed in Chapter 7) and are based on the logic that individual members want to be seen in a positive light by other group members. Deviance from expected behaviour and expression of nonfavoured attitudes will likely result in negative social consequences for them in the group, so individuals will try to adhere to what they consider the appropriate responses, which explains why groups may overshoot the average of individual member's attitudes. Persuasive argument theory (PAT), in contrast, explains group polarization on the basis of the impact of the relative frequency and persuasiveness of arguments for or against a particular issue. Following the PAT logic a risky shift would occur if group members perceive a larger number of risk-favouring arguments in a group discussion, and also if they judge them to be more persuasive than counter-arguments. Isenberg (1986) concludes that both processes contribute to group polarization, although pervasive arguments appear to have a stronger effect. Interestingly, group polarization also occurs in groups that interact only electronically (Sia *et al.*, 2002), and the specific findings from this research appear to be more consistent with persuasive argumentation processes.

Another well known and potentially serious problem associated with group decision making named groupthink was first discussed by Irvin Janis in 1972. It refers to a particular pattern of dynamics that leads to seriously flawed decision-making processes – and ultimately faulty decisions – in cohesive groups. It occurs when group norms for compliance and consensus affect realistic option appraisal and reasoned decision making. Table 8.6 provides an overview of typical symptoms of groupthink. Groupthink is a phenomenon that has been linked to such tragic political decisions as the US invasion of North Korea, the Bay of Pigs fiasco and the escalation of the Vietnam war in the 1960s (Janis, 1982). In organizations, it has been linked to flawed decision making about aeronautic projects such as the Space Shuttle *Challenger*

Groupthink
Tendency of a strongly cohesive group to emphasize unity at the expense of critical evaluation of problems and options.

Table 8.6 Symptoms of groupthink in groups

Illusion of invulnerability	Group members become overly optimistic and convinced of the group's invulnerability.
Collective rationalization	Any evidence or suggestion contrary to the accepted thinking is conclusively countered irrespective of the relative merit of the challenging arguments.
Moral superiority beliefs	Shared belief in the moral correctness of any accepted group decision.
Stereotyping of others	Individuals or groups with opposing points of view are frequently stereotyped as weak, stupid or evil, and information from these sources is automatically disregarded as irrelevant, contaminated or insignificant.
Pressure on dissenters	Strong enforcement of compliance and consent through social control in ways that provide the appearance of free speech while preventing active consideration of the views expressed.
Self-censorship	Members of the group self-censor their contributions and increasingly their thoughts to hide doubts and protect group cohesion. Individuals may engage in this deliberately for image-management purposes.
Illusion of unanimity	Members mistake silence for agreement and overestimate actual agreement among members.
Emergence of mind-guards	Informal mindguards to filter information flows and to protect the group from adverse comment. Collective responsibility is invoked as justification for supporting a decision and to marginalize any dissent.

Source: Janis, 1982.

disaster (Moorhead *et al.*, 1991; Kray and Galinsky, 2003) and the Hubble telescope (Chisson, 1994) as well as failed strategic initiatives at Marks & Spencer and British Airways (Eaton, 2001). The dynamics leading to groupthink are serious threats to the quality of decision making and lead to self-reinforcing errors in the decision-making process used in cohesive groups. Groupthink can also be seen as closely related to the irrational escalation of commitment at the group level.

Janis also suggested a number of mechanisms through which groups could guard against groupthink, shown in Figure 8.10. They included encouragement for individuals to voice any doubts; the use of subgroups to broaden the search for ideas and to serve as a cross-check on ideas and analysis; encouraging self-criticism among the group; and ensuring that junior members are allowed to speak first.

The role of the devil's advocate in Figure 8.10 is based on the idea that someone should be specifically appointed within the group to explore an opposing point of view. It is suggested as a means of preventing a group from simply going along with the accepted case by being forced to consider alternative perspectives. All of the mechanisms suggested by Janis reflect the view that it is the senior members of a group, particularly in an organization, who hold formal power and influence over the careers, lives and development of subordinates. Senior people therefore naturally take the lead in groups and are expected to signal the direction of preferred solutions. This can work to the disadvantage of the group in seeking to deal with complex problems, as no one person can hold total understanding, and therefore they should hold back until others have contributed. They can then begin to summarize and bring together the divergent views and perspectives into a solution.

Another way to counter some of the dysfunctional effects of cohesion in decision-making groups is to prime group members with *counterfactual mind-sets*, which refers to mental orientations that encourage people to consider what could be (or could have been) instead of just what is (or was). Primed to consider such alternatives, groups were found to increase the search for disconfirming information and

Devil's advocate
A person specifically tasked with challenging the argument or opinion put forward by another person or group.

Figure 8.10 Preventing groupthink

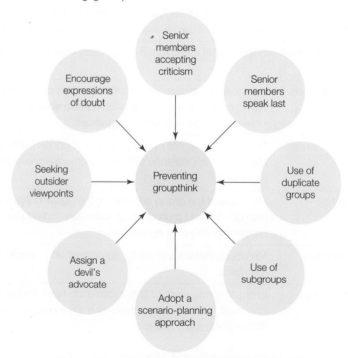

ultimately make better, more accurate decisions (Kray and Galinsky, 2003). Unfortunately, depending on the task, counterfactual mind-sets may also introduce additional bias to group deliberations (Galinsky and Moskowitz, 2000).

'A decision not to make a decision is a decision.' Is this statement true? Try to explain the statement in the light of the material on decision making presented in this chapter.

Improving decision making within groups and teams

Drawing from the normative models of classic decision theory but recognizing both the bounded nature of managers rationality (Simon, 1976) and the decision-making dynamics in groups, Janis (1982, 1989; Janis and Mann, 1977) suggests a vigilant decision-making approach that involves the following steps:

- Identifying decision objectives and the requirements that make the decision successful.
- Developing as complete a set of well defined options as possible.
- Searching out extensive information regarding the relative merit of different options.
- Engaging in critical and reflective assessment of the options.
- Reconsidering and re-examining all the pros and cons of the alternatives.
- Assessing and if possible improving the costs, benefits and risks associated with the preferred choice.
- Developing implementation plans, monitoring of progress and appropriate action of risk factors that interfere with decision implementation.

These steps should not be seen as a prescribed process, but rather as a checklist of activities that can all help to improve decision making in organizations. Interestingly, groups that have very high or very low self-efficacy regarding decision-making tasks (i.e., that are either very high or low in their confidence to do well) appear less likely to use these processes (Tasa and Whyte, 2005). This may be explained by the negative effect of prior group successes which may reduce the likelihood that groups try to use the most comprehensive and demanding decision-making processes (we may call this the '*swagger effect*'), and those groups with little collective confidence, possibly due to prior bad performance, who tend to fail to engage seriously with a decision making task (a '*shuffle effect*').

Other proposals for avoiding negative group dynamics influences on decision-making processes include the deliberate use of devil's advocacy, dialectical enquiry and reflexivity. The use of a devil's advocate in groups, which refers to the deliberate inclusion of a person or subgroup providing challenges and critiques at significant steps in the group's decision making, tends to be useful in improving decision quality in groups (e.g., Schweiger *et al.*, 1989), especially if initial group assumptions about the situation are false (Schwenk and Cosier, 1980). A related approach is dialectical enquiry (Schwenk and Cozier, 1980) which is an approach that uses subgroups that sequentially develop assumptions and decision options, with a second subgroup charged to deliberately develop assumptions that differ from and even challenge the first subgroups' work. In a later stage, the subgroups then debate the different assumptions until they agree on a jointly accepted version which will then be used in finalizing the decision. The core logic of this approach is that it helps to give expression to cognitive conflict during the early stages of group decision making. Reflexivity refers to the degree to which group members overtly reflect on the group

Dialectical enquiry
An approach that uses a subgroup to sequentially develop assumptions and decision options, with a second subgroup charged with deliberately developing assumptions that differ from and even challenge the first subgroups' work.

Reflexivity
Refers to the degree to which group members overtly reflect on the group decision process or content.

Production paradox
Refers to the fact that,
especially in complex
tasks, many groups would
benefit from planning
and the development of
an appropriate decision-
making strategy, instead
they show tendencies to act
immediately.

decision process or content (see West, 1996). Reflexivity helps to avoid the production paradox (Carroll and Rosson, 1987) which refers to the fact that groups, especially in complex tasks that would benefit from planning and the development of an
appropriate decision-making strategy, show particular tendencies to act immediately
instead of analysing and planning (Karau and Kelly, 1992). Reflexivity can help to
improve performance on group decision-making tasks, although success in group
decision making often depends on the fit between the decision-making approach
used and the specific group task (e.g., Gurtner et al., 2006). Also, under some conditions techniques such as dialectical enquiry, which provides for cognitive conflict to
be actively managed, increases group cohesion and decision acceptance (Priem et al.,
1995), while in other situations simple unstructured decision making using a consensus approach appears to be comparatively superior for increasing satisfaction and
decision acceptance among group members (Schweiger et al., 1986). Thus, no one
approach is always superior, and the particular objectives, task structure, situational
factors and group member characteristics need to be carefully considered.

Brainstorming
An approach to decision
making in which groups try
to generate as many ideas
as possible, avoid criticism
of any ideas and strive to
extend and build on others'
ideas.

In addition to the above approaches to avoiding negative impact of group dynamics on decision making, a number of structured decision-making models have also
been proposed. They include brainstorming, the nominal group technique, the Delphi
method, and the stepladder technique. Brainstorming was introduced in the 1950s
by advertising executive Alan Osborn (1957) who concluded that traditional group
decision-making processes inhibited the level of creativity displayed by members.
Brainstorming groups try to generate as many ideas as possible, to avoid criticism of
any ideas, and to strive to extend and build on others' ideas. Despite its wide usage,
a recent review of the empirical evidence indicates that brainstorming often does not
live up to its promise because of difficulties in providing appropriate contribution
opportunities for individuals in the group setting (also called production blocking),
members' evaluation apprehension, and processes, similar in effect to social loafing,
of convergence to low performance standards in brainstorming groups (Kerr and
Tindale, 2004). However, when appropriately supported by trained facilitators (e.g.,
Offner et al., 1996), specific rules (Paulus et al., 2006), or by appropriate ICT (e.g.,
Nijstad et al., 2003), brainstorming can help groups in the creative tasks of decision
making such as option generation (Kerr and Tindale, 2004; Paulus et al., 2006).
Edward de Bono developed the six hats approach to creative thinking and decision
making as a way of improving the process – see the High Performance example.

Production blocking
Empirical evidence
indicates that brainstorming
does not often live up to
its promise because of
difficulties in providing
appropriate contribution
opportunities for individuals
in the group, members'
evaluation apprehension
and processes similar in
effect to social loafing.

Nominal group technique
Closely modelled on the
brainstorming approach but
enables group members to
quietly develop and record
ideas for a period before
they are shared with the
group. All ideas are then
discussed and critiqued
by the group before
members privately rank the
alternatives. The highest
ranked alternative is then
chosen.

A technique designed to avoid production blocking is the nominal group technique. It is closely modelled on the brainstorming approach but enables group
members to quietly develop ideas and record them for a period before they are
shared with the group. All ideas are then discussed and critiqued, and members
privately rank order all alternatives in terms of their preferences. The highest-
ranked alternative is then chosen. The nominal group technique is designed to
counter some of the inhibiting social dynamics of group decision making. It can
be very effective for many decision situations, but is less suitable to complex decisions or to decisions where the commitment of all participants is crucial. Also, the
majority decision making, although based on private rankings, is open to political
and social influence dynamics, and the order of considering and voting on questions can also influence outcomes (so Concordet's Paradox).

Delphi technique
A decision-making process
that enables large numbers
of people to be involved
without them ever having to
meet in person.

Another technique that can help avoid production blocking and other social
inhibitors of decision making is the Delphi technique which enables large numbers of
people to be involved in decision making without them ever having to meet in person.
Often, the Delphi technique is used with experts scattered around the globe which
enables the highest level of individual expertise to be deployed to make a decision. In
short, this technique involves a facilitated process of soliciting input from potentially
large numbers of individuals. The leader or co-ordinator of the process describes the

HIGH PERFORMANCE

Put on your thinking caps

Edward De Bono developed the six thinking hats approach to creative thinking and effective decision making. He argues that approaches to thinking in the West are too rigid and lock creative processes into patterns that are not appropriate to today's fast-changing world. His six thinking hats approach links different coloured hats to particular thought processes. The colours are:

- *White*. This hat is used to denominate the information-gathering stage of thought.

- *Red*. This hat represents the feelings and emotions towards the thought object.

- *Black*. This hat represents the evaluation of risk, critical appraisal and the adoption of a cautious approach to the issue.

- *Yellow*. This hat requires the wearer to concentrate on issues associated with the feasibility of solutions and their benefits.

- *Green*. This hat emphasizes creativity, the development of new ideas, options and possibilities.

- *Blue*. This hat is the 'meta' one. It concentrates on the total process, ensuring that the end result takes the other hats into account.

In a meeting, everyone would wear the same coloured hat at the same time and would examine the problem from that perspective. The meeting would apply each of the hats in sequence, considering the problem from every angle. There are other ways in which the hats can be used to improve decision making. The approach has been used around the world by many large organizations in the public and private sectors. It is also used in schools to encourage children to become effective thinkers and decision makers.

De Bono argues that by adopting the six hats approach, chemical actions in the brain change compared to when an unstructured approach is used. The result is a more efficient thinking process because the individual concentrates on the hat colour perspective, thereby eliminating political and ego-based 'contaminants' that otherwise disrupt effective thought and decision making. He claims that meeting times can be reduced by approximately 50 per cent, saving some executives the equivalent of about one day each week.

TASKS

1 Could you envisage using the thinking hats approach in practical decision making? Why or why not?

2 How would you persuade other people to join a decision-making process based upon the thinking hats approach?

Sources:

De Bono, E. (2000) *Six Thinking Hats*, London: Penguin Books.
http://www.dystalk.com/talks/25-de-bonos-thinking-hats (accessed 16 April 2009) – a video discussing the use of the six hats approach in a school context.
http://www.valuebasedmanagement.net/methods_bono_six_thinking_hats.html (accessed 16 April 2009).
http://www.debonoonline.com/Six_Thinking_Hats.asp (accessed 16 April 2009).
http://www.independent.co.uk/news/education/schools/put-your-thinking-hat-on-how-edward-de-bonos-ideas-are-transforming-schools-1518507.html (accessed 16 April 2009).

situation or problem and solicits written input from members of the Delphi panel (often with questionnaires). After receiving the inputs, the co-ordinator summarizes the responses and feeds the summary, along with additional questions, to all participants. This is repeated until a consensus or clear majority view emerges. The benefit of this approach, which is often used in trend identification and in research, is the quality of experts that can be brought to the task without having to physically meet. However, this approach is very time-consuming, and the quality of the decisions made depends in large part on the quality of the facilitation and summarization used to combine the varied inputs from Delphi group members.

Stepladder technique
Initially only two people start discussing a particular issue. Other members then join the discussion one after the other, with each having a specified time to make their contribution to the existing subgroup which then collectively discusses the new input. Ultimately, all members of a group will have joined the subgroup and have contributed to the discussion. The reunited group then makes the final decision.

The stepladder technique (Rogelberg *et al.*, 1992) suggests that initially only two members of a group start discussing a particular issue. Other members join them, one after the other, and each has a specified time to bring their individual contributions to the existing subgroup which then collectively discusses the new input. Ultimately, all members of a group will have joined the subgroup and have contributed to the discussion. The reunited group then makes the final decision. This technique can be managed by the group members themselves (Rogelberg and O'Connor, 1998) or by an external facilitator who decides when new members are invited into the subgroup (Rogelberg *et al.*, 1992). This technique has also been suggested as an effective way to structure electronically mediated group discussions (Rogelberg *et al.*, 2002). While this technique can undoubtedly bring benefits such as structure and control in certain situations, recent research questions the benefits of this technique compared to using unstructured group decision making (Winquist and Franz, 2008).

Models of organizational decision making

In addition to theories and models concerned with individual and group decision making, other attempts to describe and explain decision making in organizations exist. These are important because they draw attention to the particular decision-making dynamics that arise in organizational contexts. Two of these models, the management science approach and the Carnegie model, are directly linked to classic decision theory and the bounded rationality model, respectively. In brief, the management science model consists of analysis-based decision-making processes under conditions of little uncertainty. Management science was developed during World War II when mathematical and statistical techniques were applied to large-scale military, production and logistics problems. With the development of computers and the ever advancing technological support for data collection, analysis, modelling and computation, this approach was quickly adopted in industry and is now standard in the management of industrial production, logistics and transport scheduling, manufacturing and service operations, across virtually all industries. It is a valid, appropriate and often highly valuable approach to decisions where the relevant problems can be fully understood, and information about all relevant variables is available.

Management science model
This consists of analysis-based decision-making processes under conditions of little uncertainty.

The Carnegie model is named after Carnegie-Mellon University which hosted the most influential researchers, Herbert Simon, James March and Richard Cyert, who contributed to its development. In addition to developing the bounded rationality model of individual decision making, they also contributed new insights to the ways in which decisions are made in organizations. In particular, they highlighted the role of political dynamics such as coalition formation and the use of power in decision making. Coalitions are groups of managers whose views of organizational goals and relative problem importance are aligned (Stevenson *et al.*, 1985). They arise because in organizations there is typically uncertainty which means that many different interpretations and evaluations of both problems and solutions are possible. Also, because it is often not possible to make decisions rationally or to follow programmed decision-making processes, individual interests and goals can often be pursued by those involved in organizational decisions. Creating an alliance with others under the guise of pursuing organizational goals can give individuals opportunities for such opportunistic behaviour.

Coalitions
Groups of managers or others whose views of organizational goals and relative problem importance are aligned at least temporarily. They emerge as a result of differing individual (and/or group) interests and because of the level of uncertainty present in an organization.

Related to the political nature of organizational decision making, the Carnegie model also considers the implications of bounded rationality at the level of organizational decision-making processes. Just like individual choices under bounded rationality, decision making in organizations typically aims at finding satisfactory rather than perfect solutions. Moreover, managers in organizations engage in problemistic search, which refers to the tendency to look in the immediate situation for a solution that will quickly address the problem or at least help manage the problem's symptoms. Clearly, this approach of choosing satisficing local solutions contrasts substantially with the comprehensively analysed, rational choice prescribed by the management science model. Another important difference between these approaches is the way in which the agreement necessary to get the support for important organizational decisions is developed. In the management science model, the analysis of valid data through sound logic and appropriate analytical methods would lead to agreement for action, while the Carnegie model describes a much more political process.

Another important perspective on organizational decision making is offered through the incremental decision-making model. Based on research on unprogrammed decision making in organizations, Henry Mintzberg and his colleagues (Mintzberg *et al.*, 1976) described the way in which such decision are made in incremental steps from problem recognition to solution. The research indicated three distinct phases of decision making (the *identification phase*, *option development phase*, and *option selection phase*) which all contain multiple small steps, many of which are repeated if progress is interrupted. In the identification phase such decision interrupts are often internal, such as when a new or different problem is recognized, or when a particular problem diagnosis is incompatible with new data or is challenged by other organizational members. In the option development and selection phases, the recognition or imposition of new options can force a recycling through steps already taken, while in the final steps of the option selection phase where authorization of the decision occurs, external interrupts (e.g., an important customer vetoing a particular decisions) would cause a recycling of some or even all steps of the process. In essence, the incremental decision making model describes organizational decision making as an incremental, often iterative process of many small steps that applies to unstructured problems. This reflects other perspectives on decision-making processes such as Lindblom's (1959) description of the science of muddling through. The incremental decision making model also reflects the continuous process of readjustment of actions in line with perceived deviation from a short-term objective that Cyert and March (1964) call *uncertainty absorption*.

Finally, the *garbage can model* (Cohen *et al.*, 1972) suggests a much less clear, rational, or structured process than that described by the other models of organizational decision making. The title of the model refers to the metaphor of a garbage can filled with all kinds of problems, decision makers, resources (such as time, access to executives, political influence, money), and solutions. A decision is made if and when the right combinations of these elements happen to come together. Of course, such an uncertain, unstructured and even anarchic model flies in the face of how most of us think about organizations and decision making. However, coincidence and serendipity do play important roles in an organization's life, and in highly uncertain conditions the organized anarchy described by Olsen and his colleagues offers a good approximation of the context and process of how decisions may occur. This is particularly true under conditions characterized by ambiguous goals and preferences, unclear and poorly understood cause–effect relationships, and a lack of accumulated relevant experience. Daft (2004) identifies four consequences of the garbage can model for organizational decision making:

1 Solutions are offered where no problems exist.

2 Decisions made may not solve any problems.

3 Problems may persist without ever being solved or even addressed.

4 Some problems are solved – even if the decision quality can vary.

Incremental decision-making model
Based on research on unprogrammed decision making in organizations reflecting the way in which such decisions are made in incremental steps from problem recognition to solution.

Decision interrupt
Events originating within or outside the decision-making process that force the recycling through steps already taken.

Science (The) of muddling through
A short-term approach to control, based on frequent reviews of performance against target, rather than a strategic approach based on the long-term achievement of goals.

EXAMINING ETHICS

Getting a better company car

This event was described by a manager in the company concerned and who preferred to remain anonymous. He thought it rather humorous and demonstrated how decisions were actually influenced and made involving communications.

The head of the pay and benefits section with the HR department of the company thought he deserved a bigger, more expensive company car than the existing company car policy allowed. So at the next review of pay and benefits he proposed (having first consulted sales managers) that it would be in the company's interest for sales staff to be given a more prestigious car. This (he argued) would enhance their perceived status with customers and motivate them to sell more. The cost of the bigger cars was justified financially on the basis of additional sales and reduction of labour turnover among sales staff. After discussion by the management team and the Board, the revised car policy was agreed and the new cars were provided. Stage one of the plan had been achieved!

Stage two involved the pay and benefits manager waiting a few months and then informally 'pointing out' to a number of head office managers that 'junior' sales staff now had bigger cars and to ask for their views. Naturally, most responded that the change in car policy had effectively reduced their perceived status. This 'planted the seed' of an idea among these managers that a 'problem' existed. Next, the pay and benefits manager 'raised' the issue with the company car fleet manager. This was where the greatest risk of failure existed as he had to pass the 'problem' over to another manager and allow them to deal with it. His approach was to raise the issue as a possible problem whilst implying (very gently) that senior managers (including the car fleet manager) might expect a car upgrade if the 'problem' were addressed. The car fleet manager was persuaded to carry out a survey among executive level company car drivers intended to assess levels of resentment towards the new car policy. Not surprisingly, resentment was found in the survey results (which also helped to raise the significance of the 'issue' through people talking openly about it) and the car fleet manager wrote a report to his manager and the head of HR to that effect.

The pay and benefits manager was asked to identify possible solutions that could be accommodated within the company's overall reward strategy. He carried out his own car policy and benefits survey and proposed that car upgrades could be provided to senior managers, the extra cost involved being covered by:

- Additional money could be made available because the company had enjoyed profit growth over recent years.

- The changes could be phased in over a number of years as new cars would only be allocated when existing cars were replaced.

- Pay increases could be marginally reduced over the whole company to help cover the cost.

- The proportion of money allocated to incentive payments could also be marginally reduced to help cover the cost.

- The lease agreement could be opened up for renegotiation and competitive tendering that would also help to minimize cost.

It was also argued that if the 'problem' were not addressed the reward package might become uncompetitive and so the turnover rate among key personnel might start to increase. The head of HR supported this proposal as the overall cost was marginal and it would avoid other problems. The fact that the head of HR (along with all other senior managers) would also get a bigger car was never mentioned or part of discussions or decision. The proposal was put to the board, who unanimously supported it! So the company car policy was changed and all managers (including the pay and benefits manager) got a bigger car!

TASKS

1 What ethical issues associated with decision making are present in this example?

2 To what extent does this example demonstrate that managers who act in their own best interests ultimately benefit the organization within a capitalist economic system?

3 Based on this example, to what extent do you think that any organizational decision can be taken on a purely rational, objective and nonpartisan basis?

Figure 8.11 Daft's contingency framework for using decision models

Source: Daft, RL (2004) *Organization Theory and Design,* International Edition, 8th ed. © 2004 South-Western, a part of Cengage Learning, Inc. Reprinted with permission.

The Examining Ethics example reflects aspects of the garbage can model in practice but also incorporates aspects of political behaviour and the manipulation of the perceptions and expectations of others.

Daft (2004) offers a useful contingency framework that combines the four organizational decision-making models discussed above and also links in with individual and group level behaviour and decision making. This model is presented in Figure 8.11. It describes the context in which these models and approaches to decision making may be particularly valuable when trying to describe, analyse and understand decision making in organizations. In essence, this framework distinguishes between high and low levels of technical knowledge about how a problem can be solved, and high and low levels of consensus on the goals to be achieved (see also Figure 8.12). Thus, high levels of technical knowledge will be more associated with deliberate decision-making models (management science, Carnegie models) while low levels are linked to the more iterative, trial and error and even anarchic models (incremental decision making, garbage can). At the same time, relatively higher levels of uncertainty about the actual problem to be solved and the goals to be achieved are associated with the models that focus more on political processes (Carnegie, garbage can) while higher clarity and unity regarding preferred outcomes is associated with those that do not focus much on politics and conflict (management science, incremental decision process).

8.1 EXTEND
YOUR LEARNING

Figure 8.12 Conditions regarding technical knowledge and goal consensus

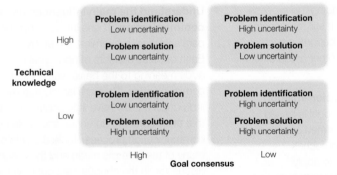

Source: Daft, RL (2004) *Organization Theory and Design,* International Edition, 8th ed. © 2004 South-Western, a part of Cengage Learning, Inc. Reprinted with permission.

CONCLUSIONS

Communication and decision making are two of the most important aspects of managerial activity. As we have seen in this chapter, they are interlinked with each other and are central for many other organizational dynamics. In particular, they are part of important interpersonal and organizational processes such as leadership, conflict resolution, negotiation, influence and many more. At the same time, they are influenced by such factors as individual differences, individual and social perception and attribution, group dynamics, as well as the formal organizational structures and characteristics and informal organizational systems (e.g., culture) and dynamics (e.g., politics). Understanding communication in organizations gives us the tools to more fully understand the interaction between and among individual members in organizations. Similarly, understanding decision making in organizations provides the conceptual and theoretical tools to analyse and improve the central organizational and managerial activity - achieving organizational goals.

Now to summarize this chapter in terms of the relevant Learning Objectives:

- **Outline the concepts of communication and decision making.** These concepts are linked together in a particular one-way relationship. Decision making cannot take place without communication being part of the process. Although communication forms part of decision making, not all communication is related to decision making. Communication is more than the simple passing of information; it implies an interactive process involving more than one person. As a process it is about the exchange and development of ideas. It is also difficult in that there are limitations in the human ability to express ideas in an observable form. The interpretation of transmitted information is also subject to similar difficulties. Decision making represents a process of selecting between options. There are many decision-making models that contribute to understanding the process of making a decision, but that said, it still represents a human activity and consequently becomes subject to many of the tendencies found in other areas of human behaviour.

- **Explain the major models of decision-making processes.** One decision-making model is based on the programmed and nonprogrammed approach. This suggests that programmed approaches to decisions are cheaper and easier to apply. Programmed decisions have a known path between the problem and the solution. Nonprogrammed

decisions are new or different and each solution has to be worked out from scratch. That takes time, costs money and contains a high risk of failure. Other approaches to decision making are based on rationality. These assume that the person making the decision acts in a rational manner as befits their status and job responsibilities. However, that is not always the case; there are a number of personal, political and capability issues that can limit rational action. The political or garbage can model of decision making reflects the reality of OB influences on decisions. Equally many specialist functions have a range of solutions already available that need problems to exist in order to demonstrate 'value'. Consequently, problems can be created or interpreted in particular ways in order to allow this expertise to be applied.

- **Assess the organizational significance of communication and decision making.** The significance emerges from their importance in managerial and organizational activity. An organization that cannot communicate with its customers or employees effectively is unlikely to survive for long. It is not enough for an organization to simply tell its customers what is available without listening to what they need or want. Not listening to customers would increasingly separate the company from them and lead to loss of sales. Equally an organization that did not take appropriate decisions would soon find itself going facing financial ruin. Decisions are important in positioning the company appropriately to its market and customers. Of course it is not possible to take appropriate decisions without effective communication to provide appropriate information and interaction between people in reaching the conclusions forming the output of the decision-making process.

- **Understand the main influences on interpersonal communication.** These include body language, paralanguage, proxemics, the environment and time. Each of these aspects of nonverbal communication adds meaning to the basic words used in any communication. They are largely automatic and individuals usually have little control over them in that they represent an unconscious element in the communication process. Table 8.2 sets out what many of these terms mean and the associated discussion in the chapter sets out how they impact on the communication with which they are linked.

- **Discuss the significance of groupthink in organizational decision making.** The term 'groupthink' was first discussed by Irvin Janis in 1972. It refers to a pattern of dynamics that lead to flawed decision-making processes in cohesive groups. It occurs when group norms of compliance and consensus affect realistic option appraisal and reasoned decision making. Table 8.6 provides an overview of typical symptoms of groupthink. Groupthink is a phenomenon that has been linked to tragic political decisions as the US invasion of Cuba (Bay of Pigs fiasco). In organizations, it has been linked to flawed decision making in the Space Shuttle *Challenger* disaster as well as failed strategic initiatives at Marks & Spencer and British Airways. Groupthink can also be seen as related to the irrational escalation of commitment at a group level. Janis suggested a number of mechanisms through which groups could guard against groupthink, shown in Figure 8.10. They included encouragement for individuals to voice any doubts; the use of subgroups to broaden the search for ideas and to serve as a cross-check on ideas and analysis; encouraging self-criticism among the group; and ensuring that junior members are allowed to speak first.

DISCUSSION QUESTIONS

1 Discuss the extent to which problem solving is the same as decision making in an organizational context.

2 Explain the differences between programmed and nonprogrammed decision making, providing examples of each. To what extent can all decisions within an organization be said to fall within this framework?

3 'Managers don't really communicate with employees as to do so implies that they should act upon what employees say and to do so might undermine management's authority.' Discuss this statement.

4 Describe how communication can be thought of as a perceptual process.

5 Is rationality the only basis on which decisions are taken? Illustrate your answer from your own experience.

6 Whetten and Cameron (2007) define communication as constructive if it helps overcome defensive behaviour in others and patronizing behaviour in ourselves. Explain the significance of this view in relation to communications in an organizational context.

7 What is interpersonal communication and why is it important for an organization?

8 Explain the purpose of heuristics in the decision-making process.

9 Outline the brainstorming approach to decision making and explain how it differs from the nominal group technique. How would you decide which of the two approaches to use in a particular situation?

10 'Communication and decision-making skills are so closely linked to the personality of the individuals that they cannot be learned.' Discuss this statement.

CASE STUDY

The power of time

The employee relations manager of a large privately owned manufacturing company based in the West Midlands told the following story, which he said had taken place just before he joined the company in 2005.

The employee relations climate within the company had always been difficult and confrontational in tone. From a management point of view everything was an uphill battle. For example, it was not uncommon for the senior shop stewards to refuse to allow workers to operate a new piece of equipment unless manning levels and machine speeds were agreed before it was commissioned. Frequently they used threats of strike action to force management into conceding higher manning levels and slower machine speeds than were possible.

In one instance, the shop stewards had threatened (on a Friday morning) that unless their demand for a specific manning level for a new machine was agreed immediately a strike would be called that day – irrespective of the requirement to ballot members first. The factory finished work at 12.30 lunch time each Friday and so any strike would mean an early finish then and probably the following Monday off work as well (effectively giving everyone a long weekend). This was a tactic that had been used many times over the years, especially in the summer months when the weather was sunny and warm! Any threat by the company to use legislation to go to court to prevent the strikes was greeted with threats of reprisal. The trade union officially distanced itself from this type of local action (partly to prevent it being sued by the company), but that did not prevent it being used. The managing director (who had decided to deal with the matter on this occasion) said to the shop stewards (at 9.45 on the Friday morning) that he had been called to a meeting with the group chief executive (the corporate headquarters was based at the same site), but that he would be back as soon as possible to meet with them and deal with the situation. The shop stewards were asked to wait in the managing director's office and they were given coffee.

The managing director had a short (45 minute) meeting with his boss and then sent for the HR manager to meet him in the head office complex. The HR

manager was instructed to tell the shop stewards that he too had been called to meet the two directors. The managing director and HR manager then had coffee, followed by a general discussion about HR issues and then lunch in the head office building. Protestations by the HR manager that a strike was imminent drew little reaction and a leisurely lunch resulted. During this time the factory employees went home at their normal finishing time (no strike having been called). The shop stewards still waited in the managing director's office. A strike could not be called as management had not refused a meeting, so all the shop stewards could do was wait. They became increasingly frustrated and made several attempts to contact the managing director to press for the meeting, as they could see their original advantage slipping away. Responses from the managing director were that the senior managers were still meeting and would be back in the factory as soon as possible.

After a very leisurely lunch, which lasted until about 3.30 in the afternoon, the managing director decided that it was time to return to the factory. Not surprisingly, the shop stewards had left by then (at about 2.30 according to the MD's secretary), refusing to wait any longer. The long wait was taking up their leisure time, even though under company rules they were still being paid for being at a meeting. Consequently, the two managers also went home for the weekend. First thing the following Monday morning the shop stewards stormed into the managing director's office to demand an explanation of the events of Friday. They were not used to having to face their union members – to whom they had promised a long weekend – and explain why they had failed to deliver it! The response of the managing director was calm and he asked if they would have preferred him not to have attended the meeting with the group chief executive when the long-term future of the factory was to be discussed. He said that he had the long-term interests of the factory and its employees at heart; even if they could not see beyond today. In any case, he had returned to his office as early as he could, only to find that the shop stewards had gone home. Clearly, the problem that they wished to discuss was not important enough to make them want to give up some of their free time to solve it. There was little response from the shop stewards and they left his office grumbling quietly.

©/Duncan Smith/Photolibrary

TASKS

1 Is the situation described an example of good or bad communication and decision making on the part of the company management? Justify your answer.

2 Does the situation described simply reflect a pragmatic reaction and approach to the use of power and control by the shop stewards? Justify your answer.

As the new employee relations manager in the company, how would you go about using communication and decision making to prevent such situations arising in the future and to generally improve employee relations?

FURTHER READING

Bazerman, M.X. and Moore, D.A. (2008) *Judgment in managerial decision making* (7th edn), New York: Wiley. Up-to-date overview of many areas related to making judgements in organizations. Highly readable and comprehensive treatment on issues such as decision-making biases.

Bolton, R. (1979) *People Skills,* New York: Simon & Schuster. Almost classic text on the basics of interpersonal relations and communication. Excellent material for fundamental skills such as listening.

Cialdini, R.B. (2008) *Influence: Science and Practice* (5th ed.), Boston: Pearson/Allyn and Bacon. A highly readable text on the general topic of persuasion in all its forms. It includes consideration of all three topics covered in this chapter, but from a different perspective.

Fisher, D (1993) *Communications in Organizations*, 2nd edn, St Paul, MN: West Publishing. This text considers communication from many perspectives relevant to material within the organizational behaviour field.

Hickson, D.J., Butler, R.J., Cray, D., Malory, G.R. and Wilson, D.C. (1986) *Top Decisions: Strategic Decision Making in Organizations*, Oxford: Basil Blackwell. This book describes the decision-making activities across organizations ranging in size from very small to very large. Among its strengths is that it shows how the political dimension of organizations manifests itself in the decision-making process.

Keast, S. and Towler, M. (2009) *Rational decision-making for managers: An introduction*, Chichester, England: Wiley. Good overview of how rational approaches can be applied in real-life organizations and managerial situations.

Rosenhead, J. and Mingers, J. (2001) *Rational Analysis for a Problematic World Revisited: Problem Structuring Methods for Complexity, Uncertainty and Conflict*, 2nd edn, Chichester, *wiley*. Explores a broad range of approaches to problem solving and uses a case study to demonstrate the application of each model.

Spitzer, Q. and Evans, R. (1999) *Heads You Win: How the Best Companies Think*, London: Touchstone Books. Based on a specific problem-solving approach the authors review the practical implementation issues around the model. It is intended as a practitioner text and is supported by the consultancy experience of the authors.

Sutherland, S. (2007) *Irrationality* (2nd rev. edn), London: Pinter & Martin. Popular account of psychological research that highlights the limits of human rationality.

COMPANION WEBSITE

Online teaching and learning resources

Visit the companion website for Organizational Behaviour and Management 4th edition at: http://www.cengage.co.uk/martinfellenz to find valuable further teaching and learning material. For full details, see 'About the website' at the start of the book.

CHAPTER NINE

CONFLICT AND NEGOTIATION

©Gannet77/istock

LEARNING OBJECTIVES

After studying this chapter and working through the associated OB in Action panels, Discussion Questions and Case Study you should be able to:

- Explain the major conflict handling strategies used within organizations.

- Understand the different perspectives on the concept of conflict.

- Outline the sources of conflict within an organization.

- Assess the organizational significance of negotiation.

- Discuss how principled negotiation is intended to achieve a satisfactory and consistent result for all parties.

INTRODUCTION

Conflict
Refers to situations in which the interests of different parties are not aligned. This frequently emerges when the differences between two or more groups or individuals become apparent.

Conflict is a natural occurrence in social situations. In its widest sense, conflict refers to circumstances in which the interests of different parties are not aligned. Of course, sometimes this can lead to open hostilities, while at other times the parties may remain completely unaware if this misalignment. Traditionally, conflict has been seen as negative and counterproductive, but the role of conflict – and of conflict management – has evolved drastically. In this chapter we will review a variety of perspectives on conflict and also consider the nature, sources, forms and consequences of conflict. We then discuss a general conflict management framework and specific strategies that can be employed to deal with conflict in organizations. There are inevitably ethical aspects to conflict and how it is dealt with by managers (and others) in an organizational context as is evident in the following Examining Ethics example.

Negotiation
A process of maximizing one's value through interpersonal decision making in situations where outcomes for each party are interdependent. It broadly reflects a process of difference reduction through the forming of agreements between individuals and groups who have mutually dependent needs and desires.

Just like conflict, negotiation (also often called *bargaining*) is commonplace in social and organizational settings. Negotiation is a process of maximizing one's value through interpersonal decision making in situations where outcomes for each party are interdependent. Of course, such situations occur nearly everywhere in everyday life and are particularly prevalent in organizations. Negotiation can help address conflict, and conflict frequently arises in negotiations. In this chapter, we will discuss both of these closely linked topics. With regard to negotiation, we will present different approaches that focus on the two central aspects of *value generation* and *value claiming*. We will discuss relevant tactics and identify areas in which virtually all negotiators can improve their outcomes.

PERSPECTIVES ON CONFLICT

There are a number of perspectives on the topic of conflict and organizations. We begin this chapter by reviewing traditional points of view, with a particular emphasis on the labour process theory perspective on conflict. The labour process debate, which originates with Braverman's (1974) writings, will be discussed further in later chapters in the context of the use of technology (Chapter 11), and managerial control (Chapter 12) and power (Chapter 15) in organizations. The traditional views on conflict were encapsulated by Fox (1966) who describes three major perspectives on organizations, each of which has a different underpinning based on the nature of conflict.

Labour process theory
Seeks to explain the use to which human labour is put in capitalist organizations and the part played by managers in the organization of that work for the benefit of capital owners. See also Unitarism, pluralism and the Marxist perspective.

Unitarist perspective

Unitarism
A perspective on conflict that regards organizations as collections of groups but within a cohesive whole. Conflict resolution is based on the pre-eminence of the management perspective. See also pluralism, the Marxist perspective and labour process theory.

Unitarism views the whole organization as the natural unit of consideration and suggests that within this unit, objectives are aligned. This view also reflects the classical management theory view of organizations as legitimate tools for achieving specified outcomes. Thus, organizations can be likened to a family where, despite the different branches and factions that might exist, the family is of central and paramount concern for all members. Conflict in this view is something that reflects a major breakdown in the normal and desirable state of affairs. Thus, this perspective suggests that conflict should be avoided if possible and eliminated if it arises. Conflict is viewed as emanating from members classed as deviant which should be dealt with severely as they endanger the overall harmony of the group. While still deeply engrained in some forms of managerial thinking, the unitarist perspective is relatively little used in contemporary management theory and research. It largely fails to recognize the roles of and the complex interactions among different stakeholders and their respective interests in today's increasingly dynamic, globalized and knowledge intensive organizations.

EXAMINING ETHICS

Sharing out the overtime!

Pam worked in the customer service department of a water utility company. The department was small, employing eight people. The department was the first point of contact for customers with queries over their bill, reporting some problem with the water supply etc. The office was staffed during normal office hours Monday to Friday. The management of the company wanted to extend the service beyond normal office hours, but wanted to do so without increasing the number of staff and at a minimal extra cost. To determine the most suitable additional opening times, management decided to experiment with different options over 6 months before deciding what to do in the longer term. Consequently, a schedule of additional department open hours was drawn up with the intention of using overtime to fill the available slots.

Terri (the manager of the customer service department) was presented with the plan for additional working and asked for her views and who would be the most appropriate people to work the overtime. The plan called for the office to be staffed every Saturday morning for the first 2 months of the experiment. Thereafter it involved extended opening hours on different days of the week. Terri thought that it would be useful to have the same person working the extra hours throughout the experiment as that would provide an in-depth review of the different options. She also recognized that each one of the employees in the department, including Pam, would jump at the chance to work overtime as they each needed extra money because of their personal circumstances. Management accepted the need to have the same person working each week and Terri was told to go

ahead and organize the overtime. However, as every employee would want the additional overtime this presented Terri with a problem.

Terri recognized that if she nominated the person to work the overtime, arguments and conflict would be very likely and she would become the focus for the negative reactions. So she tried to devise a way to overcome this 'problem'. Terri eventually identified what she thought was a good idea. She called Pam and her colleagues into a meeting and told them about the experiment and need for the office to be staffed by the same person each week for the 6 months. Terri went on to say that management had thought that the best (and fairest) approach would be for the employees to decide among themselves who should work the overtime. Management did not mind who it was. Terri then told the employees to discuss it among themselves and decide who would work the extra overtime. Once everyone agreed who it should be they should give the name to Terri who would then make arrangements to start the experiment the following week.

TASKS

1 If you were Pam, how would you react to this situation and on what basis would you seek to decide who worked the overtime?

2 What ethical issues does this approach to sharing out the overtime raise?

3 Is Terri's approach simply an attempt to avoid management responsibility for a difficult decision or is it an example of employee involvement? Justify your views.

Pluralist perspective

In contrast to unitarism, pluralism holds that an organization comprises a collection of groups each with their own objectives, aspirations and agenda to follow. This idea of coalitions is also central to the Carnegie model of organizational decision making (see Chapter 8) and of the behavioural theory of the firm (Cyert and March, 1963) that explicitly place individuals' and groups' different interests and agendas at the heart of their models. Coalitions *are groups of managers whose views of organizational goals and relative problem importance are aligned* (Stevenson et al., 1985), at

Pluralism
A perspective that regards organizations as collections of groups which have some objectives in common and some in competition. Conflict with results but can be usually resolved as all parties recognize the need to compromise in order to achieve some of their objectives. See also Unitarism, the Marxist perspective and labour process theory.

Coalitions
Groups of managers or others whose views of organizational goals and relative problem importance are aligned at least temporarily. They emerge as a result of differing individual and or group interests and because of the level of uncertainty present in an organization.

Marxist or radical perspective on conflict
This suggests that conflict is an inevitable function of the exploitation of employees within a capitalist system. See also Unitarism, pluralism and labour process theory.

least on a temporary basis. They arise because of differing individual interests and because of the level of uncertainty present in any organization. The more uncertainty that exists, the more different individual and group-level interpretations and evaluations of both problems and solutions will emerge. Fully rational and agreed-upon ways of making and implementing decisions usually do not exist in organizations (see Chapter 8), and individual interests and goals are often pursued by those involved. Creating alliances with others under the guise of pursuing organizational goals can give individuals opportunities for such opportunistic behaviour.

Inevitably, the interests of different groups will diverge in some areas but converge in others. Employees seek to maximize earnings and organizations seek the lowest labour costs. These different perspectives are irreconcilable and are therefore a basis for conflict between the groups involved. However, such differences do not automatically cause all collaboration in organizations to stop functioning. All of the groups recognize that compromise is essential if they are to stand any chance of partially achieving their objectives. For example, if the cost of labour becomes too expensive the company may become uncompetitive and close down, resulting in everyone losing their jobs. So the wage–work bargain becomes a major area of potential conflict in the search for balance between these conflicting interests.

In the pluralist model conflict provides an indication of the issues on which there are fundamental differences between the various stakeholders. In effect, it provides a relationship regulation mechanism, surfacing problems while preventing major fracture (through the recognition of the need to compromise) which would be to every group's disadvantage. This perspective is reflected in many psychological, behavioural and human resource management oriented approaches to management and OB.

Marxist and radical perspective

The Marxist or radical perspective as it is sometimes called suggests that conflict is an inevitable function of capitalism. Under this view, employees are fundamentally exploited by the controllers of the means of production (capitalist). One of the consequences of this is resistance to the will of management in the form of conflict. Not only is this inevitable, but it is desirable in the Marxist tradition as it assists the breakdown of capitalism in the revolutionary creation of socialism. From this perspective, the conflict between capitalists and worker classes is an inevitable but ultimately temporary characteristic of capitalist systems and of organizations organized according to exploitative principles. This perspective is at the heart of many sociological and critically oriented views of conflict. It is at the heart of the labour process debate that has been particularly influential in UK and European considerations of industrial relations, organizations and conflict. We will consider it in more detail below.

Labour process theory and conflict

The concept of the *labour process* developed out of the Marxist tradition and has been defined in the following terms:

> *The means by which raw materials are transformed by human labour, acting on the objects with tools and machinery: first into products for use and, under capitalism, into commodities to be exchanged on the market.*

> *(Thompson 1989: p. xv)*

As an area of study it began with Braverman, who in 1974 published *Labour and Monopoly Capital* which stimulated the rediscovery of the earlier Marxist material on the nature of labour. Labour process theory, therefore, seeks to explore the nature of work relations within a specific system of production. In most analyses this is reflected in the way in which capitalism acquires labour as a commodity and uses it to produce other commodities to the benefit of the capital owners. Within this analysis conflict between workers and managers (or more accurately capital owners represented by managers) is inevitable as more and more control is exercised in the search for increased efficiency in the value extracted from the labour process. Of course, the workers are not passive in this process and are well able to resist this search for ever more profitable use of their labour. For example, McKinlay (2002) demonstrates that the approach to enhancing the contribution of employees through knowledge management practices does not usually take account of organizational politics or the impact of such initiatives on the labour process. The effect of even passive resistance brought about by negative reactions among employees can significantly limit the success of such programmes. Thompson and McHugh (1995) indicate that the twin pressures on any capitalist organization of market competition and conflict within the employment relationship require managers to continually reappraise the production capabilities. This inevitably places more pressure in the system, resulting in ever greater levels of potential conflict. Even outside of traditional employment relationships, corporate involvement and attempts to extract economic value from free and voluntary labour can bring about resistance and conflict – Dafermos and Söderberg (2009), for example, argue that the hacker movement in relation to computer networks is a response to such exploitation.

In this context, a number of consequences that flow from the capitalist nature of the labour process (identified by Thompson and McHugh, 1995: pp. 373–374) are of particular relevance:

- Work organizations are distinct from other organizations and must be understood within a theory of capital accumulation and labour process.

- Organizations are structures of control, and management act as agents of capital owners and as the means of achieving control.

- Organizational structures and processes involve political issues, decisions and choices on such matters as job design, control systems, etc.

- Organizations do not embody a universal rationality, but rather a contested rationality arising from the antagonistic and conflictual relationships between capital and labour.

- Organizational change reflects the balance between control and resistance expressed in the daily dynamic of experience.

Five core elements to a theory of labour process (Thompson, 1989) are particularly relevant for understanding organizational conflict. They are closely linked to each other and include:

1 *Labour as a unique commodity*. Of the variety of resources necessary to create value and ultimately extract economic profits, labour is the one that differs because of human free will and self-determination. While such self-determination is used by capitalist organizations in the management ranks, among workers and front-line employees such human traits have traditionally been ignored and even suppressed (see the discussion of control in Chapter 12). Human labour in its many forms is essential for value creation in organizations, but it brings with it qualities and obligations that can make it problematic and even undesirable from a capitalist perspective.

2 *Labour as a special focus of attention*. Capitalist organizations employ labour as a means of value creation. However, means of production should

contribute more value than the cost their use brings. For human labour, this surplus is contested between employers (capitalist organizations) and employees (labour), a contest that brings with it a predisposition for conflict.

3 *Capitalism forces minimization.* Labour process theory considers the role of labour and the labour process within the framework of the drive for surplus generation (profit) in uncertain and volatile capitalist markets. Individual organizations are unable to control competitive market forces and therefore typically pursue profit maximization through exercising intraorganizational control. With regard to labour this is typically achieved through exploitative and exclusionary measures. In other words, because in capitalist organizations labour is primarily seen as a means to an end (profit), its cost is continuously queried and attempts are made to minimize labour and associated cost.

4 *Control as an imperative.* Given the competitive context of capitalist markets and the different interests of relevant stakeholders (e.g., capital owners, management as their agents, labour, competitors, suppliers, customers, etc.), profit maximization is a contested activity. Thus, the process of value creation, which is at the heart of profit generation, must be controlled. This also applies to the influence of other stakeholders that pursue their own interests within the organization which also needs to be controlled. Control, for example through the acquisition and use of power, is therefore a central issue in all interactions among the different stakeholders. Different types and levels of control and many different means of exercising it can be distinguished in organizations (see Chapter 12). Labour and industrial relations typically reflect such attempts to exercise power and gain control. Similarly, the principal-agent problem (i.e., *the fact that hired managers may have self-interest motives that conflict with capital owners' interests*) plays out quite publicly with the increasingly vocal and active shareholders particularly in publicly traded companies (Martin and Moldoveanu, 2003; see also Eisenhardt, 1989).

Principal-agent problem
The fact that hired managers may have self-interest motives that conflict with capital owners' interests

5 *Institutionalized conflict.* Because of the central place that the structural reasons for worker exploitation by capital owners has in labour process theory, the classic Marxist view of the class struggle is also part of the labour process. Employees are paid less in wages than the true value of their labour – this is the basis of the wage–work bargain. Managers permanently attempt to seek better value from the employee resource, and employees attempt to balance their contribution with the reward achieved. Thus, conflict between employees on one side and owners and managers on the other is inherent in the capitalist market system. Moreover, in addition to the principal-agent problem, most managers are also employees and are often exposed to changes and pressures in their work similar to front-line employees (McCann *et al.*, 2008) which also bring about immense potential for conflict. In short, 'Capitalist workplaces are arenas of contest especially around the question of skill, power and worker well-being.' (Lewis, 2007: p. 400)

Despite these differences in interest among these groups, they are also mutually dependent on each other, and capitalist organizations can only function and survive if ways to deal with these conflicts are found and institutionalized within organizations and across wider societal and economic systems. Legal frameworks and state actions are also relevant (e.g., Kalev *et al.*, 2008) in this context. Finally, the viability of the capitalist organizations depends on the presence of markets for the value they generate in products and services, and these markets are becoming ever more complex in the content in globalization, outsourcing, and many other contemporary developments. Employees are also dependent upon the owners of capital for the ability to earn money and acquire the necessities of life. This represents a low-trust conflictual approach to organizing.

As Thompson readily admits, there are many who would argue with the views put forward by labour process theorists. They include those who would see it as moving away from a traditional Marxist view of the common ownership and those who would prefer to see an emphasis on management study as a traditional social science. It does, however, provide a way of considering the nature of labour in capitalist organizations and perhaps placing conflict into a broader context. It is also an inescapable fact that not all organizations are capitalist, even in a predominantly capitalist society. Examples include public service, voluntary and charitable organizations. Most of these institutions make use of modern management techniques and would be indistinguishable from capitalist organizations apart from the profit motive. Nevertheless, we see conflicts between employers and employees play out in virtually identical ways even in not-for-profit organizations such as state-run health systems (e.g., Canada, France, Ireland, UK) as well as in public and civil service organiztions. Overall, perhaps the labour process approach is fundamentally limited as a means of being able to provide an all-embracing perspective on every type of organization. Nevertheless, it provides a useful perspective on conflict and helps identify sources of intraorganizational conflict. In the next section, we will further consider the nature of conflict and then consider sources of conflict beyond those identified by labour process theory.

9.1 EXTEND
YOUR LEARNING

NATURE AND SOURCES OF ORGANIZATIONAL CONFLICT

As already stated in the introduction to this chapter, conflict is a natural occurrence in any social situation and particularly in organizations. While conflict originates in situations where the interests of different parties are not aligned, such conditions do not always lead to open conflict. Therefore we distinguish between latent and open or explicit conflict. Latent conflict refers to the *condition where the relevant interests of interacting parties are not aligned.* Note that simply diverging interests are not sufficient to talk about latent conflict – it must be a divergence of interests that is in some way *relevant* to the nature of the interaction between two parties. Open or explicit conflict, which we will refer to simply as 'conflict' in this chapter, refers to *situations in which the goal-oriented behaviour of one party negatively affects the goal-oriented behaviour of another party which results in changes in the interactions between the parties.* According to this definition, open conflict exists only if the interests of different parties that are actively pursued are interfering with each other and the parties respond to this interference. Thus, what is sometimes called a 'conflict of opinion' is not a conflict but a divergence of opinions. It would be a latent conflict if the opinions are relevant for the interactions between the parties, and be considered an open conflict if the parties act on their opinions with actual implications for the relationship between the parties, no matter if and how the other party responds.

Sources of organizational conflict

Conflict can be considered as something that disrupts the often desirable states of stability and harmony within an organization. Under this definition it is something to be avoided and if possible eliminated from the operation. However, it is also possible to consider conflict as an inevitable feature of human interaction and perhaps something that, if managed constructively, can offer positive value in ensuring an effective performance within the organization. Moreover, conflict can have positive outcomes in organizations such as improved performance and facilitation of change. We will consider the consequences of conflict in a later section.

Latent conflict
Refers to the condition where the relevant interests of interacting parties are not aligned. Note that simply diverging interests are not sufficient to talk about latent conflict – it must be a divergence of interests that is in some way relevant to the nature of the interaction between two parties.

Open or explicit conflict
Refers to situations in which the goal-oriented behaviour of one party negatively affects the goal-oriented behaviour of another party, which results in changes in the interactions between the parties.

There are six major areas within an organization that can give rise to conflict (see Figure 9.1). Each of these sources of conflict will be discussed in the following subsections.

Intrapersonal

This represents the conflicts that arise within the individual. There are many forms in which this can arise, but essentially it stems from the multiplicity of objectives and values that individuals hold (see Chapters 3, 4 and 5), the choices or decisions that each individual must make in dealing with internal misalignments among them, and the challenges of resolving perceived external demands with internal interests and preferences. Examples for internal conflict include relatively mundane issues such as decisions to go to work or stay home when feeling unwell, more persistent problems such as role conflict between work and family roles, and profound issues such as ethical dilemmas.

Interpersonal

Whetten and Cameron (2007) identify four sources of interpersonal conflict. They are:

1 *Personal difference.* No two people are exactly alike. It is not possible to like everyone with whom one works and personalities frequently clash. However, Jensen-Campbell *et al.* (2003) suggest that agreeableness as a personality factor in individuals plays a large part in minimizing the risk of conflict and also facilitates its easy resolution in children.

2 *Role incompatibility.* The functional nature of work activity creates very real potential for interpersonal conflict. For example, a personnel manager may seek to organize training courses for employees. However, an operations manager with tight production schedules to meet and with no spare labour may resent the efforts of the personnel manager. There exists a high probability of conflict between the two managers in this type of situation.

3 *Information deficiency.* An individual with access to information is better able to perform more effectively. They also know more in Foucault's (1975) terms and

Figure 9.1 The major sources of conflict

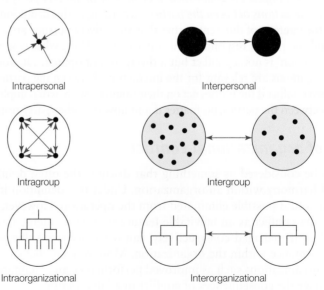

are therefore better able to exercise power over the situation and other people. Consequently, information (or at least the imbalance in access to it) can provoke conflictual relationships between individuals. At a less political level the quality of information provided to a computer system designer could easily become the subject of conflict if the system does not subsequently meet user expectations.

4 *Environmental stress.* Conflict can become more likely in times of severe competitive pressure. Most organizations have been going through significant periods of downsizing, re-engineering and change over the past decade. As a consequence individuals can find that their ability to retain a job and career is continually under threat. Because the individuals within such organizations feel under constant threat, the environmental conditions exist for fractious relationships and open conflict to emerge.

Intragroup

One particular context within which interpersonal conflict can be found occurs within a group. These conflicts are often related to group development dynamics in their efforts to become functioning entities (see Chapter 7) but can also reflect relationship difficulties among individual members. We will discuss these different types of conflict – task and relationship conflict – in more detail below. It is useful to note, however, that contradictory and complex links exist between task and relationship conflict within groups, and that they have effects on team performance and member satisfaction with the team process (DeDreu and Weingart, 2003). Moreover, the reward structure in organizational groups such as teams often contributes to conflict (e.g., Johnson *et al.*, 2006). Consideration of member roles can help address such difficulties (Beersma *et al.*, 2009). Nevertheless, group activity inevitably brings the differing characteristics, attitudes and opinions of individual members into focus. The interaction of these variables on the group decision making process and conflict are reflected in Figure 9.2.

Intergroup

Many different formal and informal groups exist within organizations and almost inevitably they experience differences and conflict at some point in time. Employees seek to earn as much money as possible, while employers want labour to be as cheap

Figure 9.2 Group decision making and conflict

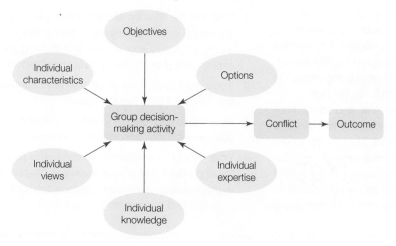

as possible. Marketing departments may press hard for a diversified product range with regular changes in order to compete in turbulent markets while production departments demand stability to be able to achieve economies of scale. There is an inherent basis for conflict in this situation. Structural differentiation (see Chapter 10 for a discussion of this *silo effect*), perceptual (see Chapter 4) and group dynamics (see Chapter 7) along with many other aspects of organizations contribute to conflict among groups. The following Change at Work example illustrates several aspects of how conflict can arise from even well intentioned management actions.

CHANGE AT WORK

To smoke or not to smoke, that is the question

Joanne worked in the London-based regional office of a large multinational bank. Her employer had been trying to encourage staff to give up smoking and had introduced a range of policies and support facilities to encourage this. For example, smokers had a rest room where they could go whenever they felt the desperate need to light-up. The occupational health department also provided a number of support services such as nicotine patches and gum, counselling sessions and regular heath checks.

Officially employees were allowed two 15-minute coffee breaks each day. Smokers inevitably took these breaks, along with Joanne and her nonsmoking colleagues; however, they also disappeared in-between these official breaks, usually saying as they left, 'I need a quick smoke, I won't be long.' Comments began to circulate about how these 'smoke breaks' happened when something urgent needed to be done or the office became busy. Joanne tackled Mike about this one day when he was going for his third smoke break in as many hours. Mike just laughed and said that she had no idea what it was like being a nicotine addict and she should have sympathy for him as he was not allowed to smoke at his desk. The company were punishing him enough for being a smoker and the privilege of being allowed to go for a smoke when he needed it was only fair.

Joanne, however, felt that she and other non-smokers were being taken advantage of and made to do more than their fair share of work, whilst the smokers such as Mike were taking advantage of the situation. Joanne and some of her colleagues spoke to their boss Lydia about this situation. Lydia was sympathetic as she herself had noticed the effects of the smoke breaks on department work. However, she said that there was little she could do as it was company policy to help smokers quit and to offer support in doing so. Joanne pointed out that Mike (as an example) showed no signs of wanting to give up smoking and it was unfair that the nonsmokers had to do more work as a result. Lydia promised to speak to the smokers about the situation. When she did so Mike and the other smokers just laughed and said that the company allowed them to take smoke breaks when they needed them and that they would continue to do so. Lydia's appeal to pull their weight in the department for the sake of fairness and harmony made no impact. Joanne was furious at this response from the smokers. She and some of her colleagues went to their staff association representative and demanded that management be formally made aware of the situation through the raising of a grievance. The only acceptable solution to Joanne was that nonsmokers be allowed additional breaks to compensate for the extra time away from work that smokers 'enjoyed'.

TASKS

1 Which of the sources of conflict (interpersonal, intragroup or intergroup) are evident in this example? Justify your answer and in doing so explain why (if at all) this classification matters.

2 If you were Lydia, how would you have handled the 'problem' that Joanne raised?

3 How would you react (and why) to this station if you were the staff association representative?

4 What would be the fairest solution to this problem for all parties? Justify your answer, in the process explaining how you would convince everyone to accept it and co-operate in its application.

Figure 9.3 Organization and the determinants of conflict

Intraorganizational

Individuals and groups play such a significant part in organizational activity that they inevitably account for much of the incidence of conflict. However, there are other features of organization that favour the emergence of conflict (Figure 9.3).

Formal organizational systems (e.g., structure, hierarchy, career development and reward systems, information flows and communication structures, etc.) compartmentalize and differentiate activity. This creates the need for co-operation, but resource limitations also induce competition. There is a very narrow line between competition and conflict. If one party considers that it has not been fairly treated in the competitive process or attempts to influence outcomes in its favour, then conflict can arise. There are also propensities to conflict in the nature of organizational ownership and the relative exclusion of employees (see the discussion of labour process theory above). The impact of technology on jobs linked to the concepts of power, control and politics are other endemic features of organizational functioning that allow conflict to emerge.

Interorganizational

Markets provide a scenario in which organizations are inevitably in conflict with each other. All of the competitors in a particular industry attempt to meet the needs of the customer in such ways as to maximize profit and market share for themselves. The unfair use of state subsidy can support otherwise uneconomic organizations to the disadvantage of organizations that do not have access to those funds. In a variation of interorganizational conflict there is considerable unease in some quarters at the potential for it to exist in relation to how the large accountancy practices function and interact with the large banks, all of which offer a wide range of services.

TYPES AND FORMS OF ORGANIZATIONAL CONFLICT

This section explores how conflict finds expression within an organizational setting. Disagreement that escalates to the level of conflict can become apparent in many forms including arguments and adversarial, antagonistic and hostile behaviour.

Task conflict
Sometimes referred to as cognitive conflict, it arises from 'disagreements among group members about the content of the tasks performed, including differences in viewpoints, ideas and opinions. See also relationship conflict and process conflict.

Relationship conflict
Sometimes called emotional or affective conflict, it refers to interpersonal incompatibilities among group members, which typically includes tension, animosity and annoyance among members within a group. See also task conflict and process conflict.

Process conflict
This arises from disagreements about aspects of how task accomplishment will proceed. See also task conflict and relationship conflict.

Sabotage
A deliberate attempt to interrupt operations or damage the interests of an organization (or another person or group) by an individual (or group) that wishes to do so, or considers that they have some reason to feel aggrieved.

Bullying
The act of intimidating or seeking to force someone to do something by subjecting them to persecution intended to undermine their confidence and self-esteem. A persistent, enduring form of abuse at work involving a power differential.

Whistleblowing
Individuals who publically allege real or perceived wrongdoing or that some misconduct (legal, financial, ethical, environmental) has been concealed by their employer.

An important distinction in organizations refers to the difference between task, relationship and process conflict. Task conflict (sometimes also referred to as *cognitive conflict*) arises from 'disagreements among group members about the content of the tasks performed, including differences in viewpoints, ideas and opinions' (Jehn, 1995: p. 258). Relationship conflict (also called *emotional* or *affective conflict*) refers to 'interpersonal incompatibilities among group members, which typically includes tension, animosity, and annoyance among members within a group' (Jehn, 1995: p. 258). Finally, process conflict arises from 'controversies about aspects of how task accomplishment will proceed' (Jehn and Mannix, 2001: p. 239). These types of conflict differentially impact on performance and other outcomes which have been extensively studied at the group level (DeDreu and Weingart, 2003). We will consider the implications of these forms of conflict further below. The Employee Perspective panel illustrates many aspects of process conflict in relation to productivity and control of the work process.

Conflict in organizations is expressed in many different forms. Because conflict can instigate a wide variety of individual and collective behaviours it can become visible in many different ways. Conflict behaviour can sometimes take the form of *clandestine individual actions* aimed at another party. Extreme forms of such behaviour can include other violent acts such as sabotage or vandalism. Such behaviours may also include the starting of malicious rumours about others, negative gossiping, or other uses of informal communication.

There are also many forms of more direct and *open individual action* against another party. Many forms of social incivility (see Andersson and Pearson, 1999; Pearson *et al.*, 2004) and more extreme interpersonal treatments such as sexual and ethnic harassment, verbal abuse, discrimination, bullying, and other victimization behaviours directed at other organizational members or customers can be indicators of conflict (Lee and Brotheridge, 2006; Neuman and Baron, 2005). Note that bullying (which refers to *a persistent, enduring form of abuse at work involving a power differential*, see Lutgen-Sandvik *et al.*, 2007) and harassment have many determinants and can be both a source and an indicator of conflict (e.g., Lee and Brotheridge, 2006). More extreme forms of individual actions against others may include physical violence against managers or co-workers. Some forms of individual behaviour against others have more positive connotations. Whistleblowing for example, while often violating organizational rules and norms, can well be the source of value for others (e.g., customers, the environment, etc.). Also, assertive behaviour that confronts perceived violators can indicate conflict in organizations.

Conflict can of course also motivate actions that are part of typical work behaviours. Managers may punish subordinates whom they are in conflict with by using their decision-making authority to assign unpleasant work, withhold rewards, and many other acts (see also Chapter 12 for a discussion of managers' informal means of exerting control). Similarly, subordinates may engage in passive aggressive behaviour that stays within the formal rules of the organizations (or at least cannot easily be shown to violate formal rules). Such behaviour may simply include reducing effort (e.g., by working slower), withholding effort (for example calling in sick on a day their presence is particularly important), and creating more work for managers and supervisors by asking for help or confirmation even when it is not needed.

Such behaviours, called work manipulation, can occur at individual and collective levels. It is not unknown for new work procedures to be followed to the letter by those onto whom they have been forced, even though they recognize that problems will occur. This can be motivated as an expression of dissatisfaction or even revenge. Thompson (1989: p. 137) quotes a telling example from Chrysler in which assembly line operators followed new assembly instructions. Part of these instructions was a specific sequence in which to hang car doors that did not work. The workers,

EMPLOYEE PERSPECTIVE

Time for a break?

This story was described by the factory industrial engineer. The particular factory in question was located in Germany and made fibreboard ceiling panels. These were approximately 3 metres by 2 metres in size, which were then cut down to smaller panels as dictated by specific customer orders. The order would specify which textured finish would be applied to the panels, which would then be finished by having several paint coatings applied. These panels would be used in offices, banks, retail outlets government buildings, etc. Given the nature of the production process, considerable quantities of dust were created by the cutting and sanding processes involved. Much of the dust was removed by extraction systems, but some still found its way into the factory environment.

The final painting and packing line was about 100 metres in length with a normal crew of 24. This allowed for the machine to run continuously during the production shift. There was a rota which allowed each employee to have regular 20 minute breaks, meaning that the machine only required 18 people to operate it at any point in time. The machine was loaded with ceiling panels and a final coat of paint was applied in a spray booth. The panels then went through a drying oven, followed by a final quality check and packing into boxes. The finished boxes were stacked on pallets and moved into the finished goods warehouse. The process was not technically complex, consisting of conveyor belts; a paint spray booth; gas heated drying oven; and a cooling section. The quality checks were done on a large flat conveyor belt and the boxes were manually packed by picking tiles off the conveyor belt.

The machine had a record of inconsistent production and had to be stopped several times each shift for corrections and adjustments to be made. For example, about twice each shift the safety trips on the motors driving the conveyor belts would operate and stop the motors from working. The electricians found that the motors were very hot, but once cooled down

they started and worked as expected. No electrical or mechanical fault could be found either on the equipment or as a result of the way in which operators were using it. Each time this occurred the machine was idle for about 30 minutes and the crew would go the canteen for a short 'extra' break.

The cause of the problem was a puzzle, until that is, one day purely by chance, the industrial engineer appeared by the machine and found the cause. A pile of dust had built up around one of the conveyor belt motors. An investigation followed. It transpired that the operators had been building piles of dust around the electric motors, effectively insulating them and allowing the heat to build up until the safety trip switched them off. When the electricians were called, the operators quickly disposed of the dust, leaving a very hot motor to be examined by the electricians.

The operators claimed that the jobs they did were so boring that 'playing this game' added a bit of interest to their daily routine and gave them more time in the mess room chatting to their friends and playing cards, etc. The management view was that this represented sabotage and formal disciplinary hearings were held. No employee was actually dismissed as a result, partly because it was not clear just how much the supervisors had known about this 'game'. However, it was made clear that if it happened again dismissal would result!

TASKS

1 Does this example demonstrate sabotage, or does it reflect alienation, frustration, resistance, boredom, bad job design or ineffective management? Justify your views.

2 It is suggested that the supervisors might have known what was happening. Why do you think that they may have known but chose to ignore it? Why or why not?

3 How might this situation reflect conflict within the employer/employee relationship?

---

dissatisfied with the changed forced upon them, followed the erroneous instructions exactly, which led to chaos. Managers begged the workers to go back to the ways of working that the workers themselves had developed. However, the workers initially

9.2 EXTEND
YOUR LEARNING

Work manipulation
Individual and/or collective behaviours that stay within the formal rules of the organizations (or at least cannot easily be shown to violate formal rules but have the effect of reducing effort, withholding effort or creating more work for managers and supervisors. See also work-to-rule and work restriction.

Work-to-rule
Refers to a situation when workers adhere strictly to prescribed approaches (policies, procedures and rules) on how work should be performed, refusing to deviate from any formal agreement, rule or standard procedure in the process. See also work manipulation and work restriction.

Work restriction
The collective withholding of effort as the result of a work group determining the level of effort that it is prepared to invest on the employer's behalf. See also work manipulation and work-to-rule.

Strike
The formal withdrawal of labour by employees. See also lock-out.

Lock-out
The prevention of work activity by management. See also strike.

refused and insisted on following the new instructions for the rest of the shift. Management then withdrew the new job instructions and allowed the workers some discretion over the process.

Work manipulation like the one described above is often part of workers' arsenal during industrial strife. Because workers' skill, knowledge and experience is important even in very structured and prescribed activities (see also the discussion of canonical and noncanonical practice in Chapter 11), such work-to-rule (i.e., *workers adhering strictly to agreed approaches to how work should be performed and refusing to deviate from any formal agreement, rule or standard procedure*) is an immensely powerful weapon. Similarly, collective withholding of effort through informal work restriction (i.e., *groups determining the level of effort that they are prepared to invest on the employer's behalf*) is a common occurrence already shown in the classic Hawthorn studies. A frustrated group of employees who feel some sense of grievance with an employer can find many ways to reduce their input.

Industrial conflict often includes strikes and lock-outs. The *formal withdrawal of labour by employees* (strike) or *the prevention of work activity by management* (lock-out) are two sides of the same coin. During a collective dispute between managers and trade unions, the final lever that either party holds is to restrict the activities of the other. If all employees go on strike they effectively prevent the business from operating. If managers lock out the workers they prevent them from working and from earning any wages. The intention of both courses of action is to force one side to concede to the demands of the other or at least to negotiate further to find an acceptable compromise.

THE CONSEQUENCES OF CONFLICT

The traditional, unitarist view of conflict views conflict as negative because it disrupts the organization's smooth working to achieve its goals. Interpreted as a negative force, it is therefore something to be driven out, or at least minimized. Conflict from this perspective is regarded as something that disrupts effective relationships or company operations. It follows, therefore, that if employees can be persuaded, or forced, to see things as managers do, then conflict would largely disappear because there would be only minor differences between them. Pluralist perspectives accept conflict in organizations as inevitable because of the complexity of organizations, the high degree of interdependence among differentiated subunits and the variety of interests of its members. Thus, they often focus on political dynamics and propose structural and behavioural approaches to dealing with conflict. Similarly, Marxist/radical perspectives also view conflict in organizations as inevitable because of the profit motive and capital owners' use of exploitative means to extract value from workers.

In a departure from these views, contemporary management and OB research on conflict in organizations generally applies a modified pluralist view that recognizes conflict as inevitable yet often manageable. More specifically, this approach (sometimes called an interactionist or contingency approach to organizational conflict, see for example Jehn and Bendersky, 2003; Rollison, 2008) tries to identify the positive and negative roles conflict can and does play in organizations, and the factors that influence the outcomes of conflict, and tries to determine the best way of managing conflict in any particular setting.

A premise of this approach is that often a particular level of conflict can be found that contributes best to organizational performance (see Figure 9.4). Too little conflict brings about complacency and inertia, while too much conflict can cause stress, burnout, and negatively affect co-ordination and collaboration. Essentially in this

Interactionist approach to organizational conflict
Sometimes called the contingency approach to organizational conflict, this represents a modified pluralist view that recognizes conflict as inevitable yet often manageable.

Figure 9.4 Conflict impact on performance

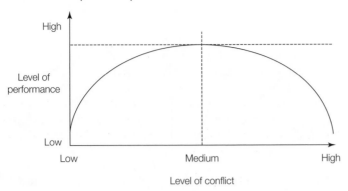

Source: *Adapted from* Ivancevich, J.M. and Matteson, M.T. (1993) *Organizational Behaviour and Management*, 3rd edn, Homewood, IL: Irwin.

view, conflict is being defined as a pressurizing force. Using the analogy of a domestic water pipe, too little pressure in the system and no water will come out of the tap. Too much pressure and the pipe is likely to burst. Just the right amount of pressure is needed in order to make the system function effectively as intended. Conflict in this model is regarded as a force that can be harnessed to ensure that slackness is kept out of the workings of the organization. For example, if management cannot take for granted the loyalty and commitment of employees, they will find it necessary to ensure that they keep in touch with the thinking and aspirations of the workers. In so doing, a continual reassessment of the working relationship will be undertaken and the potential for major conflict is minimized.

With no challenge, which is inherent in conflict, people and groups could begin to act as if they were operating on automatic pilot, simply going through the motions at work without thinking about them and taking everything and everyone else for granted. In this view such an organization would become slack and desensitized to the activities going on around it. Equally, at the other extreme, excessive conflict, for example a protracted labour stoppage, would bring the organization to a standstill and thereby reduce performance to zero. In practice there are a number of consequences of conflict within an organization that range from harmful to beneficial. Not all would be active in every situation. They include the items identified in Figure 9.5.

Most of the consequences identified in Figure 9.5 are self-explanatory, but some need further elaboration. Items such as stress, high labour turnover and difficult relationships can easily be understood as a direct consequence of conflict. However, items such as training and involvement will be better understood if they are considered further:

- *Learning, training and development.* Where conflict is a real possibility, joint learning and related activities can be effective means of exploring and resolving the difficulties. Thus, training and other developmental activities can be deployed to address perceived conflict. For example, socialization achieved through training and joint problem solving could help to integrate groups by developing a common framework and culture as the basis of the relationship. Equally, such joint problem solving can encourage conflicting groups to work together and find new ways of co-operating towards a common goal. Lukes' (2005) view of power (see also Chapter 15) would suggest that such activities align views and perceived interests of employees with those of management and thus reduce open conflict.

- *Autocratic leadership.* There is a view suggesting that conflict represents unwillingness to compromise and a direct challenge to authority. Therefore, one consequence could be to become more autocratic in management

Figure 9.5 Some consequences of conflict

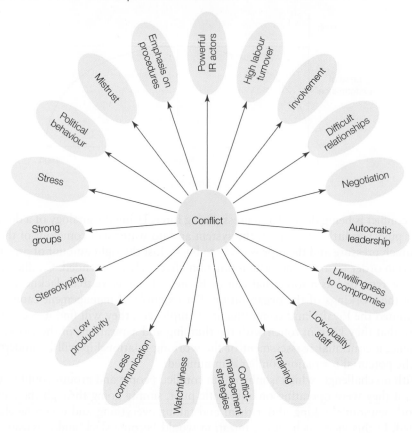

style, thereby eliminating the opportunity and desire to compromise. This view can be based on the assumption that conflict emerges as a result of perceived weakness and willingness to compromise under pressure. Making the leadership position strong and clear eliminates conflict as subordinates recognize that it is pointless. The counter-argument is that such approaches bottle up resentment which always finds expression at some point in time and in a form damaging to the organization.

● *Low-quality staff.* There are organizations with a reputation for autocratic management and conflictual working relationships. Consequently, in a local labour market potential employees tend to regard such employers as a last resort and only remain until something better comes along. High labour turnover, poor-quality products and services typify such organizations.

● *Less communication.* When people are in conflict the level and quality of communication drops. This can be seen in any industrial dispute, or even a family argument. There are also consequences such as the emergence of strong subgroups along with increased political behaviour among the groups and individuals concerned. As a consequence of this there is a tendency to attempt to institutionalize the procedures and processes by which conflict is resolved.

Many of the items incorporated into Figure 9.5 reflect the negative consequences of conflict. Some may argue that this implies that the interactionist or contingency view of conflict is invalid because such few positive consequences of conflict cannot be taken to support the value of conflict for performance. However, properly handled conflict that is kept at appropriate levels through strategies such as conflict prevention, conflict management and negotiation can make positive contributions in organizations. Offsetting the negative consequences of conflict should also improve performance through the removal of barriers to performance. Conflict resolution can also increase collaboration and unity within organizations which can help improve performance. One potential difficulty of this perspective is that the idea of increasing conflict to appropriate levels does not sit comfortably with many managers who may prefer to see performance achieved through more conventional mechanisms. Thus, managers' increased understanding of the role of conflict as well as the necessary skills in managing conflict are important for realizing the full value of conflict in organizations.

STOP & CONSIDER

Discuss the view that because conflict in organizations is inevitable it should be welcomed as it helps to keep in check the exploitation of workers by managers.

CONFLICT-HANDLING STRATEGIES

There are a number of conflict handling strategies that can be employed. They include conflict prevention, conflict management and conflict resolution. The most obvious one of them may be conflict prevention which refers to *any organizational or interpersonal arrangement or process that reduces the risk of open conflict*. Examples include increased communication among individuals, groups and subunits to create more mutual understanding and opportunities to integrate views and find joint solutions to emerging problems. Structural approaches to such social integration called integration mechanisms are discussed in Chapter 10. Social approaches can include rotating group memberships and increased social contact among members of different groups or subunits. However, despite the commonality with which such approaches are suggested and used, they can also create additional problems. The complex dynamics in intergroup relations can often create conditions under which well meaning interventions fail to work or even create counterproductive results. Vorauer and her colleagues (Vorauer and Turpie, 2004; Vorauer *et al.*, 2009) for example found that while supporting perspective-taking among group members with high prejudices had some positive effects, it increased problems with outgroup contacts among those with few prejudices. Also, increased contact with other groups appears to have less effect on minority group members than majority group members (Binder *et al.*, 2009), so the impact of managerial and organizational interventions needs to be carefully monitored.

Other examples of conflict prevention include a focus on shared aspects such as values and culture. Socialization (see Chapter 12) and strong cultures (see Chapter 14) can help align the thinking and behaviour of organizational members and prevent some conflicts from developing. Another approach is the focus on fair procedures that can help to offset the negative impact of outcomes that individuals and groups might otherwise actively object to (see Chapter 16). While the varied options of conflict prevention offer advantages, a central limitation of any prevention approach is that organizations by their very nature as deliberately structured and co-ordinated activity systems must exercise some form of control over their members. This invariably causes conflict that can never be fully prevented.

Given the inevitability of conflict in organizations, conflict management strategies are important and frequently employed in organizations. Conflict management is defined as *any activity or provision that aims at reducing, increasing, creating or solving conflict to achieve an appropriate level of conflict*. Despite this broad

Conflict prevention
Refers to any organizational or interpersonal arrangement or process that reduces the risk of open conflict. See also conflict management and conflict resolution.

9.3 EXTEND
YOUR LEARNING

Conflict management
Defined as any activity or provision that aims at reducing, increasing, creating or solving conflict to achieve the most appropriate level of conflict. See also conflict prevention and conflict resolution.

Conflict resolution
Refers to any attempt to lower the level of conflict by reducing the source or consequence of differences in interests between conflicting parties. See also conflict prevention, conflict management and conflict resolution efficacy.

definition that recognizes the need to sometimes create or increase conflict deliberately, our discussion in this section will mainly focus on those approaches that aim at reducing and solving conflict. These approaches are also called conflict resolution, which refers to *any attempt to lower the level of conflict by reducing the source or consequence of differences in interests between conflicting parties.* Sometimes conflict resolution is also defined as *the subjective perception of participants that a conflict is worked out and finished* (e.g., Jehn *et al.*, 2008).

Fundamentally, conflict arises in the context of a party pursuing their own interest in ways incompatible with the interests of another party. Thomas (1976) identified five well known generic conflict-handling styles based on combinations of two relevant dimensions: the degree to which a party tries to satisfy their own concerns (called self-assertion or concern for own outcomes), and the degree to which they try to address the concerns of the other party (called co-operation, or concern for another party's outcomes). Figure 9.6 shows the location of five different conflict management approaches in relation to these two dimensions. We will discuss these approaches in turn below.

The five conflict-handling styles identified in Figure 9.6 are:

- *Accommodation.* This approach reflects a style that would allow the other party to achieve what they desire from the situation. It is an attempt to maintain unity and harmony though subjugating one's own wishes to those of the other party. This could be as a consequence of indifference towards any personal needs in the situation. However, it could also reflect a fear of the consequences of not allowing the other party to have their way.

- *Avoidance.* This style reflects a minimalist approach and the avoidance of any open confrontation or hostility in the situation. It can constitute a desire to ignore the problem and hope that it will go away, or simply a lack of willingness to engage with the issue and the other party. Common responses include ignoring the problem, evading specific attempts to deal with it and prolonging the use of any procedural devices invoked to deal with it.

- *Integration.* This represents an approach to conflict resolution which seeks to maximize the possibility of all parties working effectively together in the search for a viable outcome. It reflects the win–win approach to negotiation and problem solving (Fisher and Ury, 1986). This style gives equal recognition to the need to resolve conflict through meeting the objectives and desires of both parties if a lasting settlement is to be achieved. Leaving one party disadvantaged is a recipe for future conflict.

Figure 9.6 Five conflict handling styles

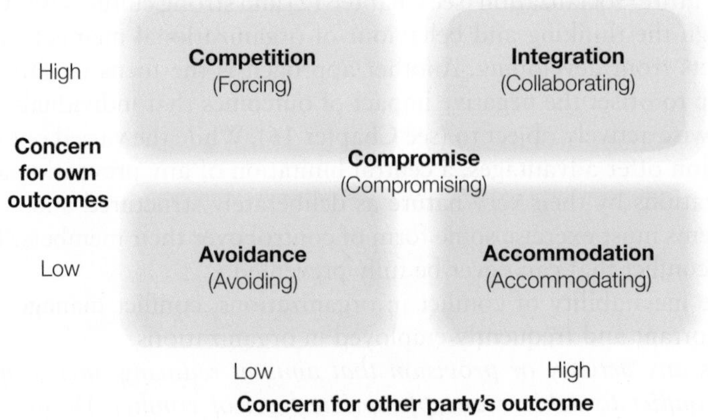

Source: Adapted from Thomas, 1976.

- *Competition.* This style reflects the win-at-all-costs approach to conflict resolution. It contains little or no consideration of the other parties' interests in the situation and simply concentrates on the desires of the 'self' in the process. In negotiation terms it represents the view that anything conceded is something lost.
- *Compromise.* This is the search for the acceptable. It represents the satisficing approach to conflict resolution. It is the search for the acceptable middle ground between two points of view so that no one completely wins or loses.

The style adopted in a particular conflict situation will be a reflection of a number of forces. For example, the preferences of the individuals will play a part. Prior experience will also create a tendency towards a particular style. For example, a trade union which encountered an aggressive style from managers during previous negotiations is more likely to begin meetings using the same style in future. Also, in emergency situations where little time is available to seek mutually acceptable solutions, directive/authoritarian styles are more likely to be used.

In organizations, conflicts are often handled in formalized ways. Official communications such as memos, newsletters, e-mail and intranets are used to keep all members informed about current operations and new developments. While this can help to create transparency, clarity and openness and thus avoid misunderstandings and conflict, such formal communication may not always be able to counteract informal gossip and rumours. Similarly, managers often try to avoid conflicts by creating official procedures for resource allocation. To the degree that such procedures are seen as fair (see Chapter 16), they can help avoid conflicts. For example, clear policies for the allocation of training opportunities or educational allowances to staff members can avoid conflict based on the perception of favouritism. Similarly to such policies, formal, institutionalized and fair-operating communication and consultation procedures as well as joint decision-making practices can help avoid and resolve conflict. Specific internal and external consultation and conflict resolution approaches such as grievance procedures or external industrial relations procedures are also examples of such organizational approaches to managing conflict. The High Performance example, however, illustrates an instance where conflict was not handled effectively, to the detriment of a number of people and the organization.

At a micro level, managers and other organizational members can help avoid and manage conflict through their own interpersonal behaviour and through selecting and using appropriate approaches to interacting and collaborating at work. For example, selecting the right approach to dealing with interpersonal conflict (e.g., Ren and Gray, 2009), or working to resolve process conflict in work groups early on is important to avoid increased task and interpersonal conflict later on (Greer *et al.*, 2008). Similarly, building conflict management skills at the individual level and increasing the perceived conflict resolution efficacy (i.e., *the belief that the conflict can be easily resolved*, see Jehn *et al.*, 2008) at the group level are important steps to maximize the constructive management of conflict in organizations. Another important activity that can help manage conflict is negotiation.

Conflict resolution efficacy
The belief that the conflict can be easily resolved. See also conflict resolution.

NEGOTIATION IN ORGANIZATIONS

Negotiation is an activity that takes place everywhere in and around organizations, for example as part of formal interactions taking place in exchange relationships with internal (e.g., employment contract with employee) and external (e.g., supplier contract with another firm) stakeholders, as well as in formal and informal interactions between managers and subordinates, and among co-workers and friends. The essence of negotiation is simple: it is about getting more of what you want when

HIGH PERFORMANCE

Getting rid of the boss!

This event was described by the personnel director of the organization concerned, only names and incidental details have been changed. A large manufacturing company contained one small department that dealt with sales and marketing for a single product in a niche market. Over the years it had gained the reputation for being a problem area, containing difficult staff and ineffective management. The standard of service was always poor with frequent mistakes and 'lost' orders being commonplace.

Eventually the manager was moved sideways and replaced by one of the staff who up to that point had enjoyed a good reputation for organization, customer relations and generally attempting to do things effectively.

Unfortunately, this created a number of additional and unforeseen problems. The previous boss resented being moved to another job and attempted to 'stir-up' the staff in his old department to make life difficult for his replacement. The staff themselves began to see that change was to be forced upon them and sought ways to undermine their new boss. The new manager had no management experience; neither did he receive any training. Senior managers made no attempt to ensure that staff took the situation seriously. The result was escalating resentment, frustration, a sense of grievance and unresolved conflict among everyone involved.

Negative rumours began to spread about the capability and personal life of the new boss and staff would not talk directly to him. Life became very difficult

for the new boss, but senior management would not take any direct action to change matters. Customer service, work quality and accuracy deteriorated further and the atmosphere in the department grew ever more hostile. Three anonymous letters were sent to senior managers purporting to show inappropriate behaviour and general lack of ability in the new manager. Investigations failed to reveal the source of these letters (or to support the claims) but the situation did not improve. Eventually, after 6 months, the new boss asked to be moved to another job and this was done – he left the company altogether after another 3 months.

A new boss was recruited from outside the organization but she was not given the necessary support to change the situation. Things did not deteriorate further but neither did they improve. The department was eventually closed down when the product line they supported was sold.

TASKS

1   Which (if any) of the conflict-handling strategies discussed in the chapter are evident in this example?

2   Imagine that you were the new boss in department described. Which conflict-handling strategies would you seek to apply in seeking to deal with the situation? Justify your answer and outline any contingency plans that you would develop?

3   Would recruiting a manager with previous experience have helped and if so, how?

Negotiation
A process of maximizing one's value through interpersonal decision making in situations where outcomes for each party are interdependent. It broadly reflects a process of difference reduction through the forming of agreements between individuals and groups who have mutually dependent needs and desires.

what you get depends – at least in part - on others. Therefore we define negotiation as the *process of maximizing one's value through interpersonal decision making in situations where outcomes for each party are interdependent.*

Like all the other topics we cover in this book, we can only offer an introduction to the full breadth and depth of the research-based knowledge about negotiation theory and practice. However, in our experience virtually everyone can benefit from learning about and applying even the basics of negotiation theory. In this section we will introduce two main approaches to negotiation as well as the key concepts associated with them. As part of this we will consider the central tasks of *value claiming* and *value creation*, and discuss relevant negotiation strategies and tactics. We also identify the two areas in which virtually all negotiators can improve their performance.

Distributive approaches to negotiation

A typical situation for negotiation involves deciding who is getting what – no matter if this is about distributing a bag of sweets, assigning tasks among group members jointly responsible for a project, or bargaining about the price and terms of a large company acquisition. Imagine it is about a bag of sweets and only you and another person are involved the situation; how do you go about making this decision? (By the way, you have just started to negotiate - because thinking about your approach is already part of preparing for negotiations which is an important element of negotiation.) There are many possible outcomes to this situation. You may get all the sweets while the other person gets nothing, or the other way around. Of course you may also equally share the sweets with each of you getting the same amount, or many other possible combinations. In short, whatever you are getting is not available to the other party and *vice versa*. This described a purely *distributive situation* (i.e., *the available value is fixed and can be distributed between the involved parties*). This is also often referred to as a *fixed pie* situation.

In this situation, your outcomes are directly dependent on the other party's outcomes in an inversely linear way (see Figure 9.7). In such situations, many people start to focus not only on their own outcomes, but automatically compare it to the other party's outcomes. More importantly, most people frame this situation as one of competition and conflict. While this may be technically correct, it creates particular dynamics that can often lead to counterproductive dynamics. These include negotiation goal drift, which refers to *the change in negotiators' objectives from gaining absolute value to competitive or even punitive goals*. By increasingly focusing on the interpersonal and competitive nature of the interaction instead of their initial goal (e.g., 'I want to get at least half of the chocolate bars and as many of the lollipops as possible', or 'I want to walk away with a price that assures me a profit of at least 15 per cent') they may suddenly start to focus on such goals as 'getting any deal' or 'extracting every last penny from the other party'. If the competitive and conflict aspect of the negotiation takes over in negotiators' minds, they may even focus solely on punitive goals as 'they must make more concessions than me' or even 'they must hurt more than me'. This is counterproductive because the reason for entering the negotiation in the first place was not to get into a fight, but to get more of what they want.

This overarching objective should guide negotiators at all times. The reason for entering negotiations in the first place can help keep them focused on the most

Distributive situation
Also called Fixed-pie Situation, this refers to an instance where the interests of negotiating parties are such that the value the parties can gain from negotiation is fixed and can only be distributed between them without any potential to generate added value through integrative approaches.

Negotiation goal drift
Refers to the change in negotiators' objectives from gaining absolute value to competitive or even punitive goals.

Figure 9.7 A purely distributive two-party negotiation situation with possible outcome options

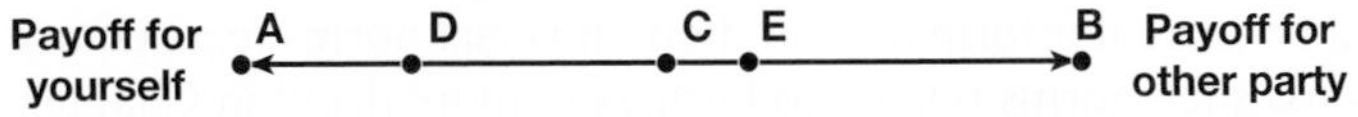

Possible outcome options in distribution of value

Options	Outcome for yourself (per cent)	Outcome for the other party (per cent)
A	100	0
B	0	100
C	50	50
D	80	20
E	40	60
...	100–X	X

BATNA
Stands for the Best Alternative To a Negotiated Agreement.

Reservation point
Sometimes also called the resistance point, it is determined by a party's BATNA and refers to the lowest value that makes an offer acceptable. See also aspirations and anchor.

Bargaining zone
The range of possible agreements in a negotiation that is determined by the respective reservation points of the parties involved. See also Reservation point, BATNA.

Aspirations
Sometimes called target points, these are a party's optimistic negotiation goals, i.e., what they hope to get out of a negotiation in the most favourable circumstances. See also anchor and reservation point.

Anchor
A comparison point for all further considerations of acceptability of an offer. See also aspirations and reservation point.

Concessions
Represent improvements in an offer made to the other party as part of the progress towards reaching a negotiated agreement.

constructive and productive negotiation behaviours. Therefore, probably the single most important concept in negotiations is BATNA which stands for *Best Alternative To a Negotiated Agreement* (Fisher and Ury, 1981). A negotiator's BATNA is a constant reminder of the focus of the negotiation (i.e., the reason for entering into it) and also clarifies the alternatives to be had outside the negotiation. The better one's BATNA, the more value a negotiated agreement needs to offer to be attractive. In this sense, one's BATNA determines one's power in a negotiation (Thompson, 2009). Any agreement that is not at least equal in value to one's BATNA should be rejected. Thus, the BATNA determines a party's reservation point (or *resistance point,* Lewicki *et al.,* 2003), which is *the lowest value that makes an offer acceptable.* The implication is that in negotiations we should always try to improve our own BATNA, and – if possible – determine and lower the value of the other party's BATNA.

In distributive negotiations, a small set of concepts and strategies can help in the important task of *claiming value.* We already discussed BATNA and reservation point, but some other concepts can also help to understand this task better. First, the respective reservation points of the parties involved determine the bargaining zone which indicates the range of possible agreements that offer improved outcomes compared to the parties' BATNAs. Aspirations or *target points* are optimistic negotiation goals, i.e., they *reflect what a party hopes to get out of a negotiation in the most favourable circumstances.* All other things being equal, high aspirations tend to lead to better negotiation outcomes (e.g., Thompson, 1995). In part this may be due to the *anchoring effect* of first offers which are often determined by aspirations. This effect works because the first offer, or even the first price mentioned, is used as an anchor, i.e., as *a comparison point for all further considerations.* Thus, despite the reluctance of almost all untrained (and many trained) negotiators to make the first move in negotiations it is always advisable to make the first offer, and make it based on high but realistic aspirations. Anchoring does not work and can create problems for further negotiation if the anchor is unrealistic or even outrageous. This is also called the *chilling effect.* Another dynamic is the *winner's curse* which refers to the feelings of remorse usually experienced when an initial offer is immediately accepted. This remorse is based on the perception that more value could have easily been obtained if only the first offer had been more ambitious.

Concessions are another important aspect of distributive negotiation. Concessions are *improvements in the offer made to the other party on the way to reaching negotiated agreements.* If initial offer and counteroffer have been made, concessions are often used to move the negotiation along. As a general rule concessions should not be made without some form of counter-concession, otherwise the negotiation is purely one-sided. Asking for or trading concessions is generally more productive that unilaterally offering concessions. Another important negotiation tactic is the use of arguments based on factual information and on universal norms (e.g., equity or equality). We will discuss such norms related to fairness in more detail in Chapter 16.

The tactics used in distributive negotiations are influenced by many factors (see Figure 9.8). Some tactics are used in distributive negotiation especially when they turn competitive or even conflictual. Many of these tactics are counterproductive because they create reactance (see Chapter 4) and often intense negative emotional reactions. Examples of some of these confrontational tactics are included in the list below (Scott, 1981):

- *Probing.* From the outset seeking information of value, without giving anything away that may help the other side.
- *Good guy/bad guy.* The 'reasonable' member follows the 'aggressive' and 'unreasonable' one and builds on the advantage gained by the threat of more to follow. This is a very familiar theme from many police movies.

Figure 9.8 Factors influencing negotiation tactics

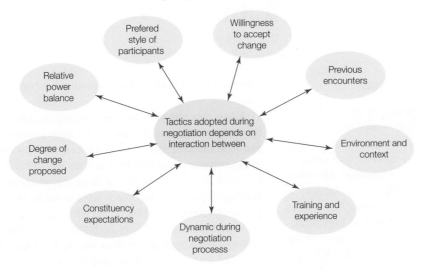

- *Poker face.* The ability to manage the body language and verbal cues allows the negotiator to cloak their feelings and intentions.
- *Managing minutes and agenda.* The person producing the minutes can often slant the official record. The careful choice of words and phrasing can be used to great effect, as can partisan management of the agenda.
- *Understanding, not agreement.* One side may signal understanding of the other's position throughout the negotiations, only to fail to accept any agreement offers that are developed. The contrast between understanding and the failure to accept any possible agreement can destabilize the other party and thus encourage further last-minute concessions.
- *Getting upstairs.* Going over the head of the negotiating team to the boss is a threat that can be used if the other party is not in line with behavioural, ethical, strategic or outcome expectations of their side.
- *Forcing.* There are various forms of force that can be used. Threats of withdrawing from the relationship (strikes or stopping of supplies) is one form, but bribes, blackmail and dirty tricks are other options that have been used. The following Management in Action panel is an example of how a particular form of 'force' was used to influence the negotiation process.

One problem with purely distributive bargaining is the sole focus on claiming value. While this is in line with our definition of negotiation – trying to maximize one's own outcomes – it is based on the assumption that there is a predetermined and limited amount of value that needs to be distributed. As we will see in the next section, in organizations such fixed pie assumptions are often not appropriate, and other approaches can help to maximize the value for all parties involved.

Distributive bargaining
Describes an approach to negotiation in which whatever one party gets is not available to the other party and vice versa. See also distributive situation, integrative bargaining.

Integrative approaches to negotiation

The distributive approaches to negotiation are based on the assumption that the total value to be gained by the negotiating parties is limited. In a two-party negotiation, this is indicated by the direct trade-off in outcomes for the parties indicated in Figure 9.7. Of course, we all have been in situations where not even this value has

MANAGEMENT IN ACTION

The boss who lost his temper

Valerie was the production manager in a medium-sized company employing 300 people making printed circuit boards used in motor cars. The company recognized a trade union and terms and conditions of employment were negotiated each year between the senior factory managers and trade union representatives.

The relationship between the parties had always been cordial and few real problems had been experienced over the years. The chief executive of the company, Bernard, had been in post for about 2 years and was keen to reduce unit labour cost as cheaper options were easily available from competitors in Asia. Consequently, Bernard and the other managers had decided that at the next annual negotiations new productivity schemes would have to be implemented in order to raise productivity and reduce cost.

A package of measures was designed by management which included minimal increases in basic pay, a new bonus scheme, profit share scheme and the following year's pay increase to be determined by the reduction in unit labour cost over the preceding 12 months. This represented a completely new way of deciding pay for the employees and when the document was presented to the trade union representatives they were shocked by the changes proposed. Management had expected such a reaction and were prepared to discuss the ideas in considerable depth and over an extended period of time.

The trade union was not sure how to react to the negotiation package offered and spent many hours during the negation meetings discussing the proposals. They wanted a rise in the basic wage which exceeded the increased cost of living, which was how things had been done in the past. Management kept repeating that this was no longer possible in the changing economic and trading conditions. Progress was very slow and at one meeting Valerie said that her boss Bernard, who was chairing the meeting, leaned across to her and whispered, 'Watch what happens next!'

A few seconds later Bernard jumped up, banged the table with his fists, shouted at the trade union side that they were not interested in the long-term survival of the company and that their attitude would inevitably result in the closure of the company as cheaper sources of printed circuit boards were available. During this tirade his face went bright red with anger; he was waving his arms around, shaking his fists and stabbing his finger at the trade union officer leading the employee side. The trade union side were shocked into silence, never having heard Bernard react so violently before. They then began to shout at him to sit down and to be calm or he was in danger of having a heart attack. Everyone began to talk at once and the meeting soon became chaotic mix of noise and confusion.

Bernard sat down, leaned across to Valerie and whispered to her, 'I enjoyed that, I was getting bored. Let's see what happens now!' Valerie was shocked. Bernard then just sat back and watched the people in the meeting shouting and arguing with each other. After a few minutes, the trade union officer leading the employee side began to restore order to the proceedings and suggested an adjournment until the next day for tempers to cool and to restore order to the process. This was agreed and the meeting ended. The next day a much more constructive atmosphere was evident in the meeting and the outline for a new deal was quickly identified and after another couple of meetings agreement was reached on a new pay deal.

TASKS

1 Is this an example of good or bad negotiating tactics? Justify your views.

2 How much of a risk was Bernard taking when he lost his temper and what might have happened?

3 Could the same end result have been achieved in a different way and if so, how?

been achieved. A fight between two boys arguing over a bag of sweets may see the sweets end up in the mud. Similarly, a negotiation of a company merger may see both parties walk away empty-handed even though their respective BATNAs offer only miniscule value to each. Such outcomes are not described in the one-dimensional

Figure 9.9 Integrative potential in two-party negotiations

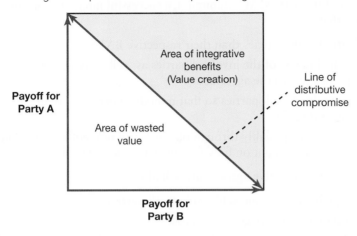

depiction in Figure 9.7, and neither are situations where both parties gain value in excess of the original identified opportunity. To make such outcomes visible, we need to distinguish between the outcomes of each party involved. For a two-party negotiation, we have come across such a framework already in Figure 9.6. When merging the two approaches (see Figure 9.9), the area above the line indicating distributive compromise indicates possibilities for value creation, while the area below this line indicates wasted value, in other words: the negotiators leave value on the table.

Just as value claiming is the key activity in distributive negotiation, value creation is the central task of integrative negotiation. In short, value creation is based on *increasing the total value available for claiming by the parties through the development of integrative solutions*. Integrative solutions are characterized by *combinations of outcomes for each party that exceed the total benefits available for claiming from purely distributive compromise*. Such additional value can be created by using differences in the respective interests of the negotiating parties. A manufacturing company may have agreed on a contract with one of its component suppliers for a given number of components per year. Its main interest may be the price of each component. However, for production planning purposes the supplier may benefit from advance warning of what number of components will be required when. Any arrangement that provides such advance warning would allow the supplier to save significant cost. Thus, if the interest of the customer in price and of supplier in advance warning are traded off against each other, both may increase the value they receive from a renegotiated deal that specifies delivery times or requires advance notice of specific delivery requests (= increased value to the supplier) at a lower unit price (= benefit for the customer).

The existence of differences of interests between parties is at the heart of value creation. *When value is created through trading differences in the value of particular aspects of an agreement for different partners* (as in the example above) this technique is also called logrolling. Such differences may be based on different needs and interests, different opportunities not open to – or dangers not affecting – all parties equally, different attitudes to risk, or different expectations about future developments.

Negotiations do not always offer the opportunity for creating additional value through integrative solutions, but a number of indicators of such potential exists. Integrative potential is typically high when negotiations are complex and include multiple issues or if additional issues can be brought into the negotiation; when parties differ in their preferences across different issues; and when parties have the expectation of future negotiations or an otherwise enduring relationship.

Integrative negotiation can be immensely successful. Success in this case is measured by looking at the outcomes for all negotiation parties and by considering the

Value creation
Based on increasing the total value available for claiming by the parties through the development of integrative solutions. See also integrative bargaining.

Integrative solutions
These are characterized by combinations of outcomes for each party that exceeds the total benefits available from purely distributive negotiating. See also integrative bargaining and value creation.

Logrolling
Describes situations when value is created through trading differences in the value of particular aspects of an agreement for different partners.

implications of agreements on the future of the relationship between the parties and the impact on third parties. At a minimum, a successful integrative negotiation leads to outcomes that:

- Are better for the parties than their respective BATNAs.
- Satisfy the interest of the involved parties as well as avoid problems with third parties due to the agreements.
- Are acceptable for all parties so that nobody experiences remorse or feels taken advantage of.
- Are enforceable, possibly through planned commitment keeping (such as legal contracts or agreement on how problems will be resolved).

Ideally, successful integrative agreements will also:

- Maximize the total value achievable to all parties.
- Be based on efficient negotiation processes.
- Contribute to a well maintained or even improved relationship among the parties.

The strategies and tactics that have proven to be valuable in integrative negotiation include:

- Actively sharing information about own interests
- Building trust within the context of the negotiation
- Asking diagnostic questions to determine the other parties' interests and any relevant differences
- Separating issues in the discussion
- Separating discussion and exploration of issues from decision making about issues
- Making decisions about packages that include all relevant aspects rather than dealing sequentially with different tissues
- Making multiple offers simultaneously to communicate options of equal value to one's own party
- Trade-off differences in interests, preferences, values and perceptions for mutual gain.

Integrative bargaining
Describes an approach to negotiation in which the focus is on creating value for all parties. It is not a fixed sum, or fixed pie situation. See also distributive bargaining and value creation.

Principled negotiations
An approach to integrative negotiation developed by Fisher and Ury and based on four elements: separate the people from the problem; focus on interests, not positions; invent options for mutual gain; and insist on objective criteria.

A central issue in integrative bargaining is the basis on which arguments can be made while maintaining an integrative process. In their classic contribution, Fisher and Ury (1986) called attention to what they term principled negotiations. This is an approach fully aligned with the integrative approach discussed above that requires negotiators to concentrate on four elements within a negotiation process:

1 *Separate the people from the problem.* It is the issues that are important, not the people discussing them. By forcing attention onto the issues, the people involved on all sides become focused on finding mutually acceptable solutions rather than the personalities of other negotiators.

2 *Focus on interests, not positions.* The purpose of a negotiation is to reach agreement. All parties have interests relative to the negotiation which may not be reflected in the position that they adopt at the start of the process. For example, a trade union may demand a 20 per cent pay rise (their position), but their interests may include having secure, well paid and interesting jobs with long holidays. Identifying and focusing on these places an emphasis on finding mutually acceptable real solutions of long-term benefit to all parties.

3 *Invent options for mutual gain.* This is the major difference from purely distributive negotiation. For example, in negotiations over price increases, the discussions need not be about profit, loss and cost alone. It is possible that an increase in price may be acceptable if conditions regarding guaranteed delivery, quality and packaging can be met. It is up to the negotiators to seek out ways by which they can both win from the process.

4 *Insist on objective criteria.* The means by which success and failure should be judged needs to be objective and sound in the circumstances. Often a negotiation can degenerate into a horse trading event in which issues are traded so that each party wins some and loses some. 'Objective criteria' means a decision basis that is independent of either side. This approach should ensure that it is the merits of the case that decide the outcome, not pressure or trading tactics.

Of course, not every negotiation that has integrative potential will lead to superior negotiation outcomes. Difficult negotiation partners, external pressures and many other factors threaten to derail integrative bargaining approaches. The two main areas in which virtually all negotiators we have worked with can improve their performance are preparation and managing emotions. Preparation for negotiation involves not only a comprehensive assessment of the relevant parties and their interests and dependencies (including one's own), issues, options and alternative (including the relevant BATNAs!), but also learning from past successes and failures. Fisher and Ertel (1995) argue that learning from experience, practising negotiation and using input from others in debriefing and preparing can increase negotiation success immensely. Thompson (2009) and Fisher and Ertel (1995) provide comprehensive frameworks for negotiation preparation that guide negotiators through steps aligned with the integrative negotiation approach discussed above.

9.4 EXTEND YOUR LEARNING

STOP & CONSIDER

To what extent would it be better for all stakeholders if managers sought ways of dealing with employees and trade unions that eliminated the need for negotiation (for example by making a justified 'final award' announcement on wage rises to employees and refusing to negotiate)?

The second area for improvement is the management of one's own and the other parties' emotions in the negotiation process. Understanding the negotiation approaches, strategies and tactics is not enough for good negotiation performance and outcomes. The best preparation and the most knowledgeable negotiator can be derailed if emotions and automatic responses take over from carefully planned and thought out courses of action. Fisher and Shapiro (2005) provide a useful framework for considering and executing strategies that help to make emotion a constructive part of the negotiation process. It is increasingly likely that many managers will experience international negotiations during their careers and it is worthwhile stopping to consider some of the issues that might arise in that context and which will be different from the more common domestic negotiations that most managers are familiar with – see for example the Going Global example for ideas on some of the differences that might be expected.

Finally, without going into detail it is important to identify the potential roles of third parties in negotiation as well as in conflict resolution. Third parties can provide useful external help and guidance to get negotiations back on track and to avoid 'leaving value on the table'. Key roles here include conciliators (i.e., *content experts who can provide advice on the negotiation content and suggest agreement options*), mediators (i.e., *third parties who act as facilitators to improve communication and other aspects*

Conciliators
Third parties who can provide advice on the negotiation content and suggest agreement options. See also arbitrators and mediators.

Mediators
Third parties who act as facilitators to improve communication and other aspects of the negotiation process (perhaps also making recommendations) to increase the chances of mutually acceptable agreements. See also arbitrators and conciliators.

GOING GLOBAL

Negotiating in international business

Businesses of all sizes and types are involved with both suppliers and customers from many different countries. International competition is also an ever present reality of commercial life. However, international opportunities can also present significant business development – assuming appropriate deals can be struck! For this to be successful managers need to approach the inevitable negotiations from a global business point of view - likely to be very different from the familiar domestic negotiations. International business dealings need to take into account:

1 The negotiating environment
2 Cultural and subcultural differences
3 Ideological differences
4 Foreign bureaucracy
5 Foreign laws and governments
6 Financial insecurity due to international monetary factors
7 Political instability and economic changes.

There are also a range of other factors to take into account when seeking to negotiate across cultures and countries, including for example:

- *The goal of negotiating.* The purpose of business negotiation may be a specific agreement (American approach) or the establishment of a long-lasting business relationship (Japanese approach).

- *Protocol.* These include dress codes, number and status of negotiators involved; the offer and type of entertainment provided for the visiting delegation; degree of formality in the meeting; the type and level of gift giving; process of meeting and greeting; presentation of business cards; and seating arrangements, table size and shape, room layout, etc.

- *Communications.* Verbal, nonverbal communication, body language and tone of voice are culturally based and significant in how the parties and individuals establish credibility and understanding.

- *Approach to risk.* Some cultures are more risk averse than others, meaning that a more limited range of innovative and creative options are likely to arise during negotiation. Hence the need to create a trust-based relationship before progress can be made.

- *View of time.* For example, in countries such as China or Japan, being late would be taken as disrespectful and insulting to the host. Also the time frame of the negotiations might be important – a one-deal relationship in some countries as compared to the basis of a long-term relationship in others.

- *Decision-making system.* When negotiating with a team from another country it is important to understand their team dynamics - who the leader is, how any decision will be made and by whom, the role of each team member in the negotiation process etc.

- *Role of agreement.* The role of the contract in resolving any problems that might arise with a 'deal' as compared to the role of relationships in resolving problems is important to understand, as not all cultures are the same in this regard.

- *Power distance.* Cultures with low power distance tend to focus more on 'earned' status than 'ascribed' status. Consequently negotiators from a high power distance culture would tend to have clear hierarchical structures and lines of authority in their negotiation teams.

- *Personal preferences.* These impact on communication style, friendliness, openness, etc. and can have an impact on how international negotiations will unfold. For example in America, a relaxed, informal style may help to create friendly relationships and accelerate problem solving; but in China, an informal approach is acceptable only if the working relationship has already achieved a high level of trust.

TASK

Imagine that you work for a large UK-based supermarket chain hoping to expand into China for the first time by opening a new store in Beijing. You have been appointed to the development team and your specific task is to prepare a briefing document for the senior managers on how the negotiations on the introduction of a UK style of supermarket into China and the specific location etc. should be conducted. What advice would you include in the briefing document and where would you find the information to include? Perhaps most importantly, how would you know that the advice that you offered was accurate?

Sources:

Zieba, M. (2009) Cross Cultural Negotiation. Accessed July 2009 at: http://www.calumcoburn.co.uk/articles/cross-cultural-negotiation/.

Numprasertchai, H.P. and Swierczek F.W. (2006) Dimensions of Success in International Business Negotiations: A Comparative Study of Thai and International Business Negotiators, *Journal of Intercultural Communication, issue 11. Accessed July 2009 at*: http://www.immi.se/intercultural/nr11/numprasertchai.htm.

Salacuse, J. (1991) Making Deals in Strange Places: A Beginner's Guide to International Business Negotiations, in Breslin, J.W. and Rubin, J.Z. (eds), *Negotiation Theory and Practice*, Cambridge, MA: Harvard Law School.

of the negotiation process to increase the chances of mutually acceptable agreements) and arbitrators (i.e., *independent third parties who can impose binding agreements on the parties involved*).

Arbitrators
Independent third parties who can impose binding agreements on the parties involved. See also conciliators and mediators.

CONCLUSIONS

The topics of conflict and negotiation have strong links with many of the other chapters in this book that are indicated in the text at appropriate points. Both conflict and negotiation can be argued to be endemic to organizational life - following the Marxist and labour process perspectives, and much common experience, they are ever present within the employment situation. Conflict and negotiation are also among the most significant aspects of managerial activity. They are interlinked in a way that makes them difficult to separate and consider in isolation. From the point of view of anyone connected with organizations they are all about the process of influencing others in some way or other. For example, conflict is frequently a reaction to some attempt at the exercise of control by one person (or group) over another. Negotiation represents an attempt to influence another individual or group to offer more than initially they proposed to offer in relation to something valued or sought. Negotiation is about persuading others to reach agreement (or agree an exchange) on a mutually acceptable basis.

Now to summarize this chapter in terms of the relevant Learning Objectives:

● **Explain the major conflict handling strategies used within organizations.** The main conflict handling strategies include the following. Clarity and openness in making sure that everyone knows what is going on within the organization and why. The signals and messages that managers send out to employees is another area that can significantly reduce the level

of potential conflict. Rewarding appropriate behaviour and not responding to threats and argument make clear what management value and how it operates. The use of training can help to reinforce management perspectives of what is valued. Training also assists socialization and encourages employees to deliver appropriate attitudes and behaviours in order to gain further development opportunity. Management style and structure can contribute to (or hinder) the likelihood of conflict. Procedures can contribute to the management of conflict by helping to institutionalize the means of dealing with it and minimizing the risk of its emergence. Figure 9.6 identifies a number of conflict handling styles which have relevance in this context.

● **Understand the different perspectives on the concept of conflict.** The major perspectives on conflict introduced in this chapter were pluralist, unitarist and Marxist. The pluralist perspective holds that different groups exist within an organization and their interests and objectives inevitably conflict on occasion. However, all parties recognize that compromise is necessary if their objectives have any chance of even partial achievement. The unitarist perspective holds that different groups exist but that an ultimate loyalty to the larger collective group to which they all belong takes precedence, and so it is that dominant group's perspective that determines the nature of any compromise or solution to the conflict. The Marxist tradition holds that conflict within an organization is an inevitable reaction to the nature of capitalism and the exploitation of labour that exists within that form of political economy. It also holds that such conflict is to be welcomed in the pursuit of the demise of capitalism and the emergence of socialism. Labour process theory also has relevance in this context.

- **Outline the sources of conflict within an organization.** Intrapersonal conflict involves the inevitable conflict that arises within each individual over matters such as how much work to do for their employer. Interpersonal conflict describes the conflict that arises between individuals, perhaps as a consequence of personality clashes. Intragroup conflict is a special form of interpersonal conflict that emerges between members of a group. Intergroup conflict reflects the conflict that can arise between groups. Intraorganizational conflict emerges within an organization and reflects situations in which the groups, departments and individuals are fighting each other in some way or another. Interorganizational conflict represents the expressions of conflict that can arise between organizations. In a free market economy, organizations are in competition with each other for sales and market share. This inevitably puts them in conflict with each other, but such activity is usually described as marketing. However, it can sometimes lead to other forms of conflict which can result in legal action or open hostility.

- **Assess the organizational significance of negotiation.** Negotiation is significant to every organization as various contracts will be needed right from its early days. For example, the rent charged for premises, the purchase and delivery arrangements with suppliers and contracts of employment for employees are all areas which involve negotiation. As organizations grow, the number and level of negotiations become more complex and many elements within the actual processes of negotiation

can influence the quality and value of the result achieved. Equally there are annual negotiations with employees over pay rises, and changes to the terms and conditions of employment that form part of the ongoing employment relationship and dynamic. Also at an informal level there are the daily 'negotiations' between boss and subordinate over work activities and priorities that form part of the daily work experience of everyone and which help to facilitate effective customer service without the need to constantly refer back to formal procedures, contracts of employment, rule books or authority.

- **Discuss how principled negotiation is intended to achieve a satisfactory and consistent result for all parties.** Principled negotiation contains four elements within it:

  - Separate the people from the problem. This is at the heart of negotiation – the issue, is important, not the people involved in the process. Concentrate on the issue, not the people.

  - Focus on interests, not positions. Negotiations often begin with all parties setting out their position. These positions are intended to indicate what is acceptable, however they bear little relationship to the underlying interests of the parties. Seek to identify the underlying interests of the parties.

  - Invent options for mutual gain. This is about seeking to create a win–win basis in finding solutions to the problem.

  - Insist on objective criteria. How is it possible for any party to a negotiation to know when a deal is a good deal? If the measures used to determine the value of a deal are objective and neutral to all parties then the result is likely to be more appropriate and acceptable to everyone.

Each of these elements is designed to achieve a particular benefit in a consistent manner for the all of the participants.

DISCUSSION QUESTIONS

1 Discuss the pluralist, unitarist and Marxist perspectives on conflict, using examples from organizations with which you are familiar to illustrate your answer.

2 Describe the various sources of conflict that exist within an organizational context. To what extent can any of them be eliminated?

3 Outline some of the consequences that might be expected to arise from the existence of conflict, illustrating them where appropriate with examples from your experience.

4 Identify and provide an analysis of the conflict-handling strategies that could be used within an organization.

5 'Conflict management represents the biggest challenge for every manager.' To what extent and why do you agree with this statement?

6 Outline labour process theory and explain how it could inform an understanding of the concept of conflict within an organizational context.

7 Describe some of the tactics used in negotiation. How do you think that you could counter some of the aggressive tactics described?

8 Can negotiation be seen as group dynamics in a particular situation? Justify your answer.

9 'Negotiation between managers and employees is nothing more than a power struggle between two unequal parties.' Discuss this statement.

10 'Because customers will only pay a certain price for any product or service and competitors are ways seeking to steal business, the only practical approach to negotiating within an organization is based on the distributive approach.' Discuss this statement.

CASE STUDY

Not paying the wages and conflict

Lowsling was a small company based in a market town in the North of England. It had been in existence for about 4 years and made one-trip bags for the transport of sand, gravel and fertilizer used in the construction, farming and DIY industries. Each bag was designed to hold 1000 kg of material and to be capable of being lifted by fork-lift truck. The design of the bag had been developed by the owners of the business who had then set up a small factory to make them. The business had been very successful and had grown rapidly. At the time of the case it employed 100 people in the factory and 12 people in the administrative, sales and management areas.

The company always had a difficult time in terms of cashflow. Also the quality of management was not high in terms of leadership or ability to control the business. Employees had little effective supervision or clear support from managers. The owners of the business were more interested in the technical aspects of the product, looking for new markets and increasing sales volume than in running the factory. The three production supervisors organized things as they thought appropriate, for example they scheduled work on the basis of the easy jobs first. The production manager was also in charge of maintenance and had very little idea of either activity, but being the brother-in-law of the chief executive his position was secure. The workforce was not highly paid, but the working atmosphere was generally good. People were not expected to work too hard and overtime was available on a regular basis.

The payment system included a bonus paid over and above the basic wage for each unit of production produced. The price for each job was negotiated between the workers' representatives and the production manager. Any job which did not have an agreed price paid bonus based on the average bonus earnings over the past 3 months. Not surprisingly, this system had been compromised over the time it had been in place and so although the total wages paid were not high, the amount of work done was also relatively low.

Orders were frequently late in being delivered and high levels of overtime became the norm. Attempts by the production manager to negotiate reasonable prices for jobs were met with strong resistance and threats of conflict. Similar reactions occurred when attempts were made to deal with the large number of jobs which attracted average earnings. People would try to find out what jobs were being planned in order to be able to keep their average pay high and then they sought average earnings jobs which they then took a long time to produce! Naturally in this environment the supervisors held considerable power and they took advantage of the situation to enhance their own position. Having said all of that, the factory was regarded as a happy place to work in and one which produced a reasonable wage for a reasonable amount of work. Labour turnover was low and absence levels average for the area. However, difficulties from the tight company cashflow caused significant problems.

Wages were paid in cash to shop floor workers every Friday for the previous week's work. Time sheets would be filled in every day and passed back to the wages office by the supervisors, who were supposed to check and authorize the information on them for each worker. On a Monday morning the task of collating all the previous weeks' wages information was undertaken and the wage bill worked out by Tuesday afternoon. This was a tight schedule as all queries had to be resolved by then for the wages to be paid correctly the following Friday. On the Wednesday morning a cheque would be made out for the total wages bill and this would be taken to the bank for collection. The cash would be brought back to the factory and the task of making up individual wages packets began. The individual wage packets would be collected by employees when they finished work on the Friday afternoon.

Within Lowsling cashflow was always a problem and there was often just enough money in the bank to be able to pay the wages. Employees were generally not aware of this problem, but occasionally they were made aware of it in the most direct manner. Occasionally they did not get paid on a Friday! This did not happen often, perhaps only once every 3 months, and when it did the chief executive always came down into the factory late on a Friday and told the workforce about it, apologizing and saying that it would all be sorted out on Monday. Invariably the employees were paid on the Tuesday, usually with a few extra pounds in the packet to 'compensate' them for the problem. However, this became such a regular occurrence that staff began to look out for which senior managers were at work on a Wednesday morning.

The banking arrangements for the company required that cheques be signed by two directors before they could be cashed. There were only two directors, the chief executive and the finance director. So if one of these people was absent then no cheques could be cashed. For most purposes this was not critical as invoices were cleared on set days each month when both people were always around, and if one or the other was going to be away arrangements could be made to sign the cheques early. However, this practice was not followed with regard to the wages cheque. If one or the other director was not at work then the cheque was not signed or cashed. Equally the directors would not sign the blank cheque early if they were going to be absent on the Wednesday because the sum of money was comparatively large and they argued that close control was needed.

Over time the directors realized that delaying wages payment could be a useful way of managing the cashflow more effectively and so the incidence of late payment began to rise. It did not rise significantly but became about once every 10 weeks rather than every 3 months. The chief executive also began to resent the abuse that he had to take every time that he went onto the shop floor to break the bad news and so he started to delegate the task to the production manager. Staff gave him an even harder time as they did not respect him as a manager and recognized that being the brother-in-law of the chief executive he kept his job because of it. Consequently, the production manager also tried to avoid telling the staff, which meant that it was the wages office that had to tell staff that no pay was available! This made matters even worse; complaints began to surface and morale and working atmosphere dropped significantly. That was when the workforce began to pay more attention to which directors were at work on a Wednesday morning. Working relationships began to deteriorate, quality began to suffer and orders were further delayed. People began to join a trade union to try to fight management over a range of problems that had become the focus of attention and labour turnover began to increase.

©Emmanuel LATTES/Alamy

TASKS

1 Analyse this case using the material included in this chapter on conflict and negotiation.

2 What are the key problems and how might they be tackled assuming that the position of the parties is as indicated at the conclusion of the case?

3 Given that the basic arrangements, personalities and financial position of the company cannot be changed, could conflict have been prevented, and if so, how?

FURTHER READING

Bazerman, M.H. (ed.) (2004) *Negotiation, Decision Making and Conflict Management*, Cheltenham: Edward Elgar. A three-volume set that explores themes from a number of significant publications covering these themes over the past 50 years.

Cialdini, R.B. (1988) *Influence: Science and Practice*, New York: HarperCollins. A highly readable text on the general topic of persuasion in all its forms. It includes consideration of relevant topics covered in this chapter, but from a slightly different perspective.

Cooper, C., Einarsen, S., Hoel, H. and Zapf, D. (eds) (2002) *Bullying and Emotional Abuse in the Workplace: International Perspectives in Research and Practice*, London: Taylor and Francis. This text looks at one aspect of conflict–that of bullying at work. The edited work considers the research approach in Europe which emphasizes the 'mobbing' approach and also 'emotional abuse' and 'mistreatment' perspectives.

Fisher, R. and Ury, W. (1986) *Getting to Yes: Negotiating Agreement Without Giving In*, New York: Penguin. The 'bible' of contemporary negotiation theory, research and practice. Extremely readable and full of gems. It was followed by a second text (*Getting Past No*, W. Ury, 1991, London: Business Books.) which outlines how to deal with difficult people in a negotiation.

Fisher, R. and Ertel, D. (1995) *Getting ready to negotiate: The getting to yes workbook*, New York: Penguin. Helpful source for structuring and preparing for negotiations.

Fisher, R. and Shapiro, D.L. (2005) *Beyond reason: Using emotions as you negotiate*, London: Random House. Provides a useful framework and discussion of the role of emotion in negotiations and how they can be managed constructively.

Fridl, D.D. (2009) Kosovo Negotiations: Revisiting the Role of Mediation, *International Negotiation*, 14 (2009) 71–93. Accessed at http://docserver.ingentaconnect. com/deliver/connect/mnp/1382340x/v14n1/s4.pdf?

expires=1249040763&id=51428640&titleid=5231& accname=Guest+User&checksum=8FFE64C893D5 C5F50E950CCC7E7A57B1, July 2009. This article reviews in great detail the processes, successes and failures in Kosovo negotiations involving Serbia and Albania, plus delegations from Europe and the United Nations in protracted mediation and negotiation over several years. It provides a fascinating insight into international negotiation processes not often open to public scrutiny.

Kennedy, G. (1999) *The New Negotiating Edge*, London: Nicholas Brealey. One of many texts on negotiation but it provides a good balance between theory and practice.

Kolb, D.M. and Bartunek, J.M. (eds) (1992) *Hidden Conflict in Organizations: Uncovering Behind-the-Scenes Disputes*, Newbury Park, CA: Sage. This book provides an insight into a wide range of dispute and conflict situations that are not at first glance formally part of organizational life. The book surfaces many otherwise hidden or cloaked features of conflict and its resolution.

Lewicki, R.J., Barry, B. and Saunders, D.M. (2006) *Essentials of negotiation* (4th edn), McGraw-Hill. Useful overview of contemporary negotiation theory and research.

Pascale, R.T. (1991) *Managing on the Edge: How Successful Companies Use Conflict to Stay Ahead*, London: Penguin. This book takes the view that conflict is an aspect of human behaviour which is to be welcomed within an organizational setting. It encourages a healthy tension between the individuals and functional groupings which can be used to the benefit of the business through the synergy generated.

Thompson, L.L. (2009), *The heart and mind of the negotiator* (4th edn), Upper Saddle River, NJ: Pearson Educational. Brilliant one-stop-shopping treatment of all aspects of negotiations. Fully up-to-date on cutting-edge research yet a joy to read.

COMPANION WEBSITE

Online teaching and learning resources

Visit the companion website for Organizational Behaviour and Management 4th edition at: http://www .cengage.co.uk/martinfellenz to find valuable further teaching and learning material. For full details, see 'About the website' at the start of the book.

PART FOUR

FORMAL SYSTEMS AND ARRANGEMENTS IN ORGANIZATIONS

While the previous sections looked at aspects of people and the nature of their interactions in organizational contexts, Part 4 focuses on the formal systems and arrangements in organizations that provide the context for the behavioural dynamics discussed previously in the sections on individuals and interactions in organizations (see Figure 1). Chapter 10 introduces organizational structure as the main framework that allows people, information, material, and other resources to be deployed and co-ordinated in pursuit of organizational goals. The differentiation and grouping of activities and the integration of these dispersed efforts determines to a significant extent the interaction patterns and processes that individuals and groups engage in as they carry out their work. Many different structural forms are available, each with different advantages and disadvantages, and the relative merits of different forms are investigated and considered.

Chapter 11 discusses organizational technology which includes both hardware and software as well as administrative and social technologies that also impact on the jobs that individuals do and the performance that they achieve. The control processes and design of the jobs that people do within the organization are discussed in Chapter 12. The different approaches used to control activities and design jobs substantially influence interactions and behaviour of individuals and groups and are a central determinant of performance. Similarly, individual and collective reactions to such structures and processes are also important for understanding the functioning – or otherwise – of particular arrangements and approaches. Control and job design are important considerations in all organizational settings where managers and employees pursue meaningful work and high productivity. The formal arrangements and processes used to manage the contributions of employees are discussed in more depth in Chapter 13 on Human Resource Management in organizations. In many ways many of the formal HRM approaches represent practical applications of management and OB theory discussed throughout the book.

The formal systems and arrangements that exist within organizations introduced in this section are part of the context in which individual and collective action takes place in organizations. The informal aspects of organizations will be further explored in Part 5.

Figure 1

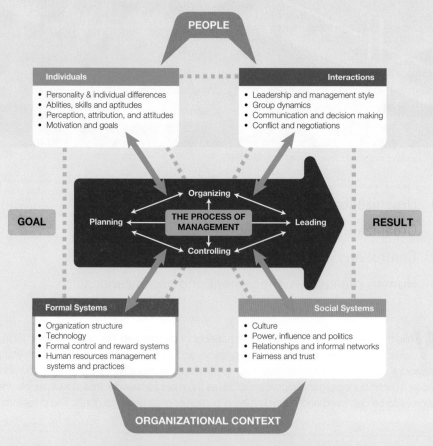

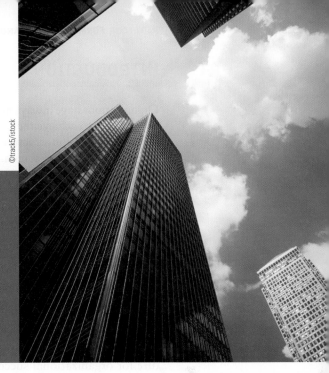

CHAPTER TEN

ORGANIZATION STRUCTURE

LEARNING OBJECTIVES

After studying this chapter and working through the associated OB in Action panels, Discussion Questions and Case Study you should be able to:

- Describe the main structural choices available to organizations.

- Understand how the need to differentiate and compartmentalize the work of an organization is at variance with the need to integrate activities.

- Assess the significance of the development of more recent perspectives on structure.

- Explain the life-cycle concept as it would be applied to an organization.

- Discuss the contingency model and its relationship to organizational structure.

INTRODUCTION

Organizations have always needed to arrange their resources and processes in ways that enable them to achieve their objectives, ideally in the most efficient way possible. Imagine the organization structure necessary to build the great pyramid of Cheops in Egypt. It covers an area of 13 acres and was constructed from approximately 2.5 million blocks of stone, each weighing an average of 2.5 tons. Construction is estimated to have lasted some 20 years involving a total labour force of 100 000 men (George, 1972: p. 4).

There are obviously many differences between the way work was organized in ancient Egypt and the way in which it is organized today, but there are also many organization design principles that were applied then that still apply now. Organization design choices are important strategic issues, yet often they are not considered as deliberately and carefully as many other strategic decisions (for example large acquisitions or new market entry decisions). This may have many reasons, such as that organization design is determined not only by organizational decision makers, that the structure of the organization may be seen as less important than other strategic deliberations, or that the relevant decision makers lack the insight and understanding necessary to consider the strategic role and importance of structure for organizational success. However, there is ample evidence that organization design and structure can have a profound impact on the performance of firms (e.g., Eddleston *et al.*, 2008; Payne, 2006; Short *et al.*, 2008; Wiklund and Shepherd, 2005). A recent study of the two largely parallel stock markets within India, the Bombay Stock Exchange (BSE) and the National Stock Exchange (NSE), highlights this issue. These organizations are involved in the same activities and trade essentially identical stocks, but are owned differently and have different organization structures. Using a standard industry measure of market quality, the NSE was found to provide a superior quality market compared to BSE (Krishnamurti *et al.*, 2003). Most organization designers are faced with adapting that which already exists – in many ways a more complex process than creating a new organization. Changing existing organization structures requires a major effort by all concerned, particularly if it is a large and complex entity, as is evident in the Change at Work example.

PERSPECTIVES ON ORGANIZATION STRUCTURE

Organization structure
The formal arrangement of task, communication and authority relationships that influence and control how people co-ordinate and conduct their work.

As discussed in Chapter 1, we find that organizations are used where they enable people to achieve objectives that cannot be reached – or not be reached as well – without them. These benefits are linked to the specific goals of the organization, and arise from the particular ways in which these goals are pursued. An important aspect of the goal achievement strategy of any organization is the particular way in which they are structured. Organization structure refers to *the formal arrangement of task, communication and authority relationships that influence and control how people co-ordinate and conduct their work*. Traditional approaches to organizing emphasize the task aspects of the work being undertaken in the structure of the organization. In essence, the resulting organizational structures typically reinforce hierarchical control and segmented responsibilities. This is reflected in the most typical way in which organizations are depicted – the organigram or organization chart which consists of boxes (representing groupings, positions or other structural units) and lines (depicting reporting relationships). The companion website provides a rich discussion of different approaches to charting and representing organizations.

In this chapter we will explore a number of the major views in relation to the determinants of structure from a range of sociological, managerial and organization

10.1 EXTEND
YOUR LEARNING

CHANGE AT WORK

Organizational change is a constant feature of modern working life

A 3-year study (commissioned by the CIPD and led by Richard Whittington of Oxford University) involved surveys of 1500 CEOs and other senior managers, into change, how it works, and where it fails. The study results show that 33 per cent of major reorganizations failed to achieve efficiency or effectiveness objectives, 40 per cent were not completed on budget, and 60 per cent were not completed on time. The study concluded that change was a constant feature of modern working life. It suggests that because reorganization in all organizations is constant, trying to identify the perfect organizational design is pointless. The best approach requires an ongoing effort to develop more fluid forms of organization. The research studied reorganizations taking place in organizations including:

- Cadbury-Schweppes
- Lever Faberge
- Ordnance Survey
- Lewisham Borough Council.

The report identifies a set of practical skills and capabilities required to undertake reorganizations and other change effectively – 'The Seven Steps to Successful Organizing'.

1 **Sustained top management support** – personal commitment and political support from top management was a crucial differentiator between reorganization success and failure.

2 **Coherent change** – reorganization initiatives should occur within the broader strategic agenda to ensure business objectives continue to be delivered.

3 **Substantive involvement** – successful reorganizations demonstrate that they involved and consulted staff (not just informed and explained) before and during the process.

4 **Communications** – multichannel internal and external communications are essential if employees, customers and other stakeholders are not to be adversely affected.

5 **HR involvement** – good people skills in a reorganization team differentiates between success and failure.

6 **Project management** – flexible project managing differentiates between success and failure.

7 **Skilled teams** – major change occurs about every 3 years and end-of-project reviews ensures that reorganization skills are incorporated into the organization.

Vanessa Robinson, from the CIPD said:'The pace of reorganizations is accelerating . . . organisations are unlikely to succeed by simply trying to pick the best organizational structure "off the shelf". . . . The truly successful organization is developing new capabilities to handle and absorb this kind of repeated change.'

Richard Whittington said: 'Organizational structures have shorter life cycles today than in the past. There needs to be a dynamic approach – leading to a shift from structure to structuring, and from organization to organizing. People issues are central to any such dynamic approach.'

TASKS

1 Is the planned process of change outlined in this example realistic in all situations? Why or why not?

2 How might the foregoing discussion help an organization reorganize?

Sources:
http://www.sbs.ox.ac.uk/news/media/Press+Releases/Organisation al+change+is+a+constant+feature+of+modern+working+life.htm (accessed June 2009).
http://www.cipd.co.uk/pressoffice/_articles/12092005131100. htm?IsSrchRes=1 (accessed June 2009).
CIPD (2005) HR's Role in Organising: Shaping Change. Research Report, London: CIPD.

theory perspectives. We then discuss the challenges of designing appropriate organizational structures along with the main principles employed for this task. We consider the most common organizational forms and configurations, and finally introduce different frameworks for the development of organization structures over time.

The determinants of structure

Managerial choice perspective
Holds that it is managers' decisions that determine how an organization is structured.

What is it that determines the structure of an organization? Most people would agree that managers' decisions play a central role. This approach to understanding the origins of organization structure is also called the managerial choice perspective. It argues that deliberate decisions about how to conduct the division of labour among organizational members, about the grouping of individuals and tasks, about formal authority, reporting relationships, and so on are at the heart of the particular structural arrangements found in an organization. Classical management theory (e.g., Fayol, 1916; Taylor, 1911) has

EXAMINING ETHICS

Corporate social responsibility in the TNT group

TNT is incorporated in The Netherlands and, through its Mail and Express divisions, transfers goods and documents around the world. The holding company has a Board of Management which is responsible for legislative and regulatory compliance, managing the risks associated with TNT's activities, finance and external communications. The Board of Management also provides the Supervisory Board with the information and support necessary for the proper performance of its duties. The Supervisory Board is charged with supervising the policies of the Board of Management in relation to the activities of the company (including structure and other control mechanisms), and providing advice. In performing its duties, the Supervisory Board is charged with acting in accordance with the interests of all of TNT's stakeholders. The company publishes a Corporate Responsibility (CR) Report each year which reviews its activities, achievements and forthcoming priorities. Its corporate responsibility strategy states that:

It is clear that, in the current economic environment, we will need to manage our financial performance more prudently than ever. And yet, it is our view that in the current age a responsible company cannot be led anymore by focusing on its financial performance alone. In order to perform well, to attract and motivate the people in our workforce, and retain our licence to operate, we need to broaden our focus on all company stakeholders.

For this reason, we have reviewed and updated our corporate responsibility strategy. Corporate responsibility for us combines sustainability, which focuses on the environment, and corporate social

responsibility, (CSR), which deals with our people, our customers, our investors and society as a whole.

Since (the first report was produced in 2004) we have been working hard on implementing management systems and standards throughout our operations. We are continuing our efforts to integrate our standards into our supply chain and we benchmark our corporate responsibility practices. For the past 2 years, we have led the Industrial Products and Services super sector in the Dow Jones Sustainability Index with the highest score of any company.

No matter how pleasing some of the recognition for our CR work is, there are also clear points for improvement, especially in aligning the priorities in our CR strategy with the areas where we make the biggest impact: our employees and the environment. Our review concluded that responsibility for health and safety and CO_2 management must be firmly embedded in the operational areas of the TNT organization. We will also prioritize the development of a framework that establishes the CR standards for our subcontractors.

TASK

This example clearly suggests that the company is CSR driven. Explore TNT's website and those of other organizations to identify how the CSR commitments influence organizational design.

Sources:
http://group.tnt.com/aboutus/ourbusiness/strategy/corporate responsibilitystrategy/index.aspx (accessed 16 June 2009).
http://group.tnt.com/Images/tnt-corporate-responsibility-report-2008_tcm177-427051.pdf (accessed 16 June 2009).
Reprinted with permission.

identified important principles related to control and co-ordination (such as task specialization, unity of command and span of control) that are typically used in managerial decisions about structure. Similarly, the adage that 'structure follows strategy' (see Chandler, 1962) refers to the need for structural arrangements to change if strategic directions and objectives change. Indeed, Porter (1985: p. 23) argues that 'Each generic [competitive] strategy implies different skills and requirements for success, which commonly translate into differences in organizational structure and culture.' Thus, managerial decisions on business strategy can be seen as a direct and indirect determinant of organization structure.

Other theoretical contributions such as institutional theory (e.g., DiMaggio and Powell, 1983; Meyer and Rowan, 1977; Powell and DiMaggio, 1991) and stakeholder theory (e.g., Donaldson and Preston, 1995; Freeman, 1984) have pointed out the influence of other considerations such as legitimacy and external expectations on managerial decisions such as those regarding structure. The topic of corporate social responsibility (CSR) (see Chapter 2) that has gained immense attention in the past decade is an example of such dynamics. One implication of these views is that managerial decisions are important determinants of structure, but that they may not always reflect the rational approach to structuring organizations for improved effectiveness and efficiency that the classical views focused on. Thus, managerial decision making plays an important role in determining structures (see for example the Examining Ethics example), but it may not be the only determinant of structure, and some would even argue that other factors are much more important.

One alternative view is based on Giddens' (1979, 1984) structuration theory (see also work on autopoiesis for different yet compatible explanations, e.g., Drazin and Sandelands, 1992; Morgan, 1986/2006). This sociological theory discusses the process of structuration as a way of reflecting the creation of social structure through repeated human interaction. In other words, the social structures we see as and in organizations – or other social entities such as families, neighbourhoods, communities and even society as a whole – arise from the repeated patterns of interaction among people which are influenced by many social and other factors. The constancy of these interaction patterns provides the basis for our perception of them as real structures, that is, as certain and enduring phenomena. This view again reveals the issue of reification, already discussed in Chapter 1, which refers to the phenomenon that we regularly experience social phenomena such as organizations as real even though they are merely useful and convenient abstractions rather than real physical entities. From a structuration perspective managerial decisions alone do not determine organization structure (or strategy, see Jarzabkowski, 2008), but rather provide one of the factors influencing the patterns of interactions among organizational members that form the process of structuration.

There is an in-built contradiction with this approach to organization structure that has been described as the duality of structure. This refers to the circular

Institutional theory and **stakeholder theory (of structure)** Point out the influence of other considerations such as legitimacy and external expectations on managerial decisions such as those regarding structure.

Corporate social responsibility (CSR) This refers to the rights and responsibilities of an organization relative to its social context.

Structuration theory Reflects the perceptual creation of social structure through repeated human interaction.

Figure 10.1 The duality of structure

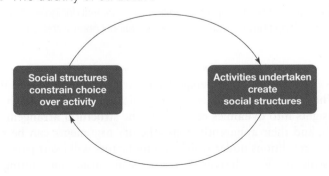

and interactive relationship between structure and behaviour (see Figure 10.1). Human behaviour creates social structure, but the structures created also constrain what humans do. 'Constrain' in this context is used not only in the sense of restrict, but also implies to channel and direct. From that perspective the social structures that exist within an organization both depend upon and create adaptations in the actual organization structure, and vice versa.

To provide a better insight into this view of structure as the result of structuration, consider the routine process of individuals in the production department passing information to other individuals in the finance department that creates an understanding of the 'compartments' and structure of the production and finance departments. Just as important in the establishing of social structure are the patterns of noninteraction. For example, if engineers hate designers then contact between them will be hostile and very limited. As a consequence that will contribute to the real meaning (and functioning) of the structure in that organization. Many attempts at business process re-engineering (BPR) or other major reorganizations have failed because senior managers have not been able to change the actual patterns of social interaction at the lower levels of the company, despite dramatic changes in job function and formal structure.

In contrast to the perspectives that place managerial choice or the bottom-up effects of repeated interaction patterns at the heart of explaining structure, deterministic views describe structure as a function of factors largely outside of human influence. Such factors usually refer to the technology employed in the organization, or to specific situational or environmental factors such as the size and age of the organization or the complexity and variability of relevant aspects of the environment (e.g., customer preferences, market circumstances, competition, supply of core resources, etc.). Some of the research contributing to such deterministic frameworks primarily aims at the level of industries and the population of organizations within them. Population ecology (Aldrich, 1979; Hannan and Freeman, 1977), for example, studies how the variation in organizations brought about by factors such as age, size and human action interacts with the specific environmental conditions to result in certain organizational forms being selected by the environment in evolutionary dynamics reminiscent of Darwin. Managerial decision making is relegated to a rather minor role within this perspective. Other deterministic frameworks focus on the impact of the technologies employed in the organization (these will be discussed in more detail in Chapter 11) and on the characteristics of the specific task environment an organization faces. For example, environments characterized by high levels of complexity, variety and change will compel organizational structures that are capable of dealing successfully with the resulting high levels of uncertainty. Similarly, environments characterized by scarce resources needed by an organization will determine structures that enable the organization to successfully acquire such resources (*Resource Dependence Theory*, Pfeffer and Salancik, 1978).

Business process re-engineering (BPR)
An approach to reorganization in which the key business processes are identified, followed by the elimination of other activity and the rapid transformation of the organization to the desired process orientation.

Deterministic views (of structure)
Describe structure as a function of factors largely outside of human and managerial influence.

Population ecology
Studies how the variation in organizations are brought about by factors such as age, size and human action and their interaction with specific environmental conditions in an evolutionary dynamic. A deterministic view of structure.

STOP & CONSIDER

To what extent could it be that approaches to organizational design evolve across history as a way of matching human capability to organizational need within a particular social context?

Ultimately, all these different perspectives have something to add to our understanding of the factors that co-determine organization structure. Each one provides particular insights into dynamics resulting in the structural arrangements found in organizations, and their apparently contradictory arguments can be reconciled by recognizing the conditions under which certain factors will exert particularly strong influence on structure. We will return to this issue in considering contingency theories of structure below. Figure 10.2 reflects a number of the environmental factors that impact on any organization and its structure. Managerial choice in the process is reflected in the ways in which these forces are interpreted and subsequently acted upon by managers. Below, we will consider some of the underlying challenges, principles and mechanisms of organization structure before we discuss contingency theory and particular organizational forms and configurations in more detail.

Principles and challenges of designing organization structure

Among the most important decision areas that can influence the structure of an organization are those that relate to the ways in which managers plan, organize, deploy resources, and control activities in their efforts to achieve goals with and through the work of others. Many of the central principles of such decisions have been formally specified by early management theorists such as Fayol (1916) and Taylor (1911). Fayol, for example, identified a number of such principles associated with the management process which he considered impacted on the structure of the organization (see Chapter 6). They included centralization and decentralization, the division of work into compartments and the unity of command, principles still important in today's organizations. The basic approach to organizing described by Fayol has been developed by a number of people over the years and has become known as classical management theory. Names such as Mary Parker Follett, Oliver Sheldon, Lyndall Urwick and James Mooney are all commonly linked to these ideas. That is not to suggest that they all worked together (or even in the same country), but their ideas were broadly similar and so common themes between them could be identified. Lussato (1976) described his views on what were the main principles associated with classical management theory (see Table 10.1). In a real sense, the classical approach to organizing went beyond purely administrative and control-oriented considerations and emphasized the need to consider the whole organization

Unity of command
Each employee should have only one boss.

Classical management theory
An approach to organizing emphasized issues such as the scalar chain, exception principle, unity of command, organizational specialization, span of control and the application of scientific management and not just structure. See also administrative management and bureaucracy.

Figure 10.2 Organizational environments

Table 10.1 Classic form of management

Scalar chain	Hierarchy of grades, seniority
Exception principle	Delegation of decision making to the lowest level possible
Unity of command	Each employee should have only one boss
Organizational specialization	Creation of appropriate departments and functions
Span of control	The achievement of an optimal number of subordinates for each boss
Application of scientific management	The application of FW Taylor's ideas in running organizations through the use of work study techniques and principles

Exception principle
Delegation of decision making to the lowest level possible.

in structural and process terms, with a particular focus on the actual tasks necessary to achieve organizational goals. The size of an organization and the complexity of operational activity create the need for the work to be compartmentalized in order to ensure that it can be done.

These classical contributions focus particularly on the structural aspects that enable managers to exert control by designing – and assigning – specific tasks to subgroups, by centralizing decision making and command through clear and hierarchical arrangements, and by creating clear prescriptions of how tasks are to be executed. Together with the bureaucratic focus on standardization that we will discuss in more detail below, they provide a blueprint of an organizational structure that is often compared to a machine: all the parts are clearly aligned to work together in prescribed, predetermined and stable ways. We will consider the strengths and weaknesses of mechanistic and other forms of organizations further below.

Mechanistic organizations
These provide a blueprint of an organizational structure that is often compared to a machine: all the parts are clearly aligned to work together in prescribed, predetermined and stable ways. See also organic organizations.

Mechanistic organizations are but one of many approaches that can be taken in designing organizations. Organization design is the *process by which managers select and manage aspects of an organization's structure and culture so that the organization can control the activities necessary to achieve organizational goals.* Culture and other informal aspect that can contribute (or detract) from an organization's effectiveness are discussed in Part 5 of the book.

The central challenges of organization design (see also Jones, 2004) can be summarized in three categories which include (a) appropriate horizontal and vertical division of labour through differentiating the tasks that various individuals and groups in specific subunits and at particular levels need to perform; (b) structurally integrating these differentiated actors and their activities and implementing mechanisms to enable constructive co-ordination and control; and (c) determining the locus of decision making (i.e., the degree of centralization or decentralization of decision-making authority) especially in relation to nonroutine decisions.

Organization design
The process by which managers select and manage aspects of an organization's structure and culture so that the organization can control the activities necessary to achieve organizational goals.

It is important to recognize that these challenges cannot be resolved comprehensively and completely for any long duration – rather, they stay constantly present, albeit in ever changing ways. Internal changes through the deployment of updated technologies, changes in skill levels, orientations or objectives of individuals, and growth and ageing of the organization and its members as well as external changes in the economic, legal, institutional, competitive and market environments (among many other factors) will affect the way the organization needs to structure its activities to become and remain effective. Thus, one of the central elements of organization design is the need to enable successful adaptation to the changing internal and external conditions. Change, learning and adaptation are crucial for continued organizational survival and success. This issue will be again considered below when we address the developmental aspects of organization structure and design.

There are many different approaches to dealing with these design challenges. Guidance for managers involved in organization design provided by prescriptive theories have traditionally taken one of three forms. Universalistic theories, such as scientific management and other classical management contributions, argue that individual aspects of structure should be handled in one particular way (the 'one best way approach') because they are, regardless of other considerations, always superior in achieving intended outcomes. As an example, classical management theorists would argue that the unity of command principle should never be violated. As we will see below, this advice is not always heeded, and other theories argue that the relationships between structural aspects and the intended outcomes is not stable and universal.

Contingency theories of organization reject as simplistic such universalist tenets and instead consider the impact that interactions between structural aspects and relevant environmental, situational, or organizational factors may have on the intended outcomes. 'Central to a structural contingency theory is the proposition that the structure and process of an organization must fit its context . . . to survive or be effective.' (Drazin and Van de Ven, 1985: p. 515) Typical variables considered by structural contingency theories include size, age, technology, strategy, environmental complexity, competition, or the degree of environmental uncertainty. For example, contingency theorists would argue that the appropriateness of specific efficiency-oriented structural arrangements such as high degrees of formalization, standardization, or centralization may depend on their ability to match the organization's information processing capacity with the levels of environmental uncertainty the organization has to deal with (see Chapter 8) to create a fit between environmental uncertainty and the capability of the organization to deal with this uncertainty successfully.

When broadened out to simultaneously include multiple variables, certain ideal types of structural arrangements will likely be more successful than others because they create a systemic fit (Drazin and Van de Ven, 1985) between the structural design and the specific circumstances. This is addressed by configurational theories that are more complex than contingency theories because they more holistically consider complex structural arrangements and patterns and their link to success or fit and because they assume that different patterns can be equally appropriate in specific environments by creating similar levels of fit in different ways (see also Delery and Doty, 1996). This latter point is also described by the concept of equifinality, which refers to the phenomenon that *different sets of factors and structural arrangements can lead to similar outcomes* (or, more colloquially, that many different ways can lead to the same destination).

We will consider both structural contingency theories and configurational approaches further after identifying and discussing the most important elements and principles of organizational structure and structuring. These include:

- *Horizontal differentiation.* This is the most important and fundamental aspect of structuring organizations. Almost all important functional (but not necessarily social) benefits arising from organizations are in some form based on the division of labour. Horizontal division of labour refers to the distinction between the different activities that contribute to achieving organizational goals.

- *Vertical differentiation.* Vertical differentiation refers to the division of labour across different levels of an organization. The term 'height' is often used to denote the relative number of levels used to establish a hierarchy of authority

Universalistic theories
Include scientific management and classical management theory and argue that structure (among other aspects of management) should be handled in one particular way (the 'one best way approach') because these are, regardless of other considerations, always superior in achieving intended outcomes.

Contingency theories (of organization)
Reject simplistic and universalist ideas and consider the impact that interactions between structural and relevant environmental, situational, or organizational factors may have on the intended outcomes.

Ideal type
A model which would be identifiable only to a greater or lesser extent in practice.

Configurational theories (of structure)
More complex than contingency theories because they integrate more variables into structural arrangements and because they assume that different structures can be equally appropriate in the same environment. See also equifinality.

Equifinality
Holds that different sets of factors and structural arrangements can lead to similar outcomes (or, more colloquially, that many different routes can lead to the same destination).

in an organization. This vertical differentiation, based on different degrees of authority to make decisions, is an important feature of most organizations. All other things equal, large number of levels will result in tall organizations and smaller spans of control, while few levels result in flat organizations with larger spans of control. This is frequently reflected in the height and width of the pyramid used to diagram most organizations (see Figure 10.3). See also the Management in Action panel for an example of a flat organization form.

- *Centralization and treatment of nonroutine decisions.* This issue reflects the degree to which an organization operates in a centralized or decentralized manner in terms of decision making, particularly of nonroutine decisions (i.e., unprogrammed decisions, see Chapter 8). Typically, they are either handled in a decentralized fashion which means that they are dealt with by decision makers at the level at which they arise, or in more centralized ways which involves the decisions being referred up the chain of command to be dealt with centrally by decision makers at higher levels. The delegation of decision-making authority for nonroutine decisions has a strong influence on the structural design of an organization.

- *Communication, co-ordination and integration.* The formal communication and co-ordination systems, linkages, mechanisms and procedures for ensuring that whatever form of segmentation is adopted, the various subunits are integrated in an effective way.

- *Formalization and standardization.* These concepts relate to the degree of prescription used in determining the activities and processes by which the organization undertakes its activities. Formalization refers to a high degree of codified activities (i.e., the use of written or otherwise specified processes), while standardization refers to the limitation of variety through imposed similarity of operations across actors, locations and situations.

- *Job design.* The way individual tasks are organized, structured and grouped to create specific roles, jobs and areas of responsibility. This dimension is discussed in more detail in Chapter 12.

The most fundamental of these principles of structuring organizations is horizontal differentiation. Because of its central importance we will consider the basic forms of horizontal differentiation in the next section in more detail.

Departmentation – basic forms of horizontal differentiation

There are a number of different approaches to horizontal differentiation. Almost all organizations use one or a combination of these approaches which provide the

Figure 10.3 Organizational height

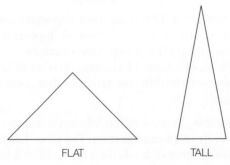

FLAT   TALL

basis for most deliberate attempts to structure organizations. The term 'departmentation' is often used to describe these approaches. Departmentation refers to the *grouping together of activities in organizational subunits*. It reflects the particular principle or principles based on which the horizontal division of labour and the differentiation of tasks occur in an organization. The most common form of resulting departmental grouping is the functional structure, which occurs when *individuals and groups are located together based on the function their tasks have for the more general objectives of the organization*. This means that all people in finance are grouped together, as are all those in sales, marketing, production, or in any other function (see Figure 10.4). These are also sometimes referred as line and staff functions (or departments) depending on their operational or support role in relation to the core activities of the organization. According to Duncan (1979), the functional structure has certain advantages which include a critical mass of functional activity that supports efficiency within a function as well as in-depth skill development which helps to sustain functional expertise. Also, this structure supports functional goal achievement. It is most appropriate if the organization offers only a limited range of products and services. Some of the weaknesses associated with this structure include relatively slow speed of response to environmental change, lower innovation and change readiness, frequent decision overload at the top of the function, and interfunctional communication and co-ordination problems due to different and even conflicting objectives and orientations (this is also called the silo effect).

Another common form of departmentation is the divisional structure, which is also sometimes called product, geographic or strategic business unit (SBU) structure (see Figure 10.5). The divisional structure results in *multiple subunits that are focused on different products, regions, and markets or market segments*. These subunits typically have a functional structure, but can also be structured according to other principles. Internal communication and co-ordination across functions within each division is improved compared to a single functional structure because each division serves a particular audience and has a clearly defined, narrower focus. Compared to a single functional structure, a divisional structure reflects subdivisions that are more suited to fast response to changing environmental conditions. Customer satisfaction is typically higher because customer-facing personnel is more in tune with the specific expectations and experiences of their customers. This is

Departmentation
Refers to the grouping together of activities in organizational subunits.

Functional structure
Occurs when individuals and groups are located together based on the function their tasks have within the organization.

Line and staff functions
Line functions deliver the main purposes of the organization – operations departments; staff functions are the support activities.

Silo effect (in functional structures)
The phenomenon found in many functional structures where inter-functional communication and co-ordination problems arise due to different and even conflicting objectives and orientations and the resulting social differences in identity and culture.

Divisional structure
Sometimes called product, geographic or strategic business unit (SBU) structure. The divisional structure results in multiple subunits that are focused on different products, regions and markets or market segments.

Figure 10.4 Functional organization structure

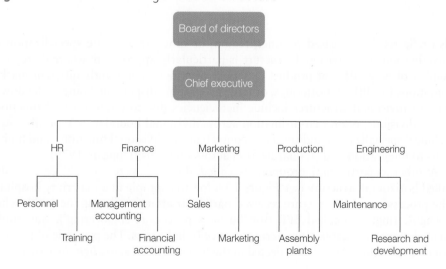

Figure 10.5 Product-based divisional structure

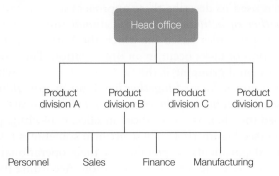

Figure 10.6 Process-oriented structure

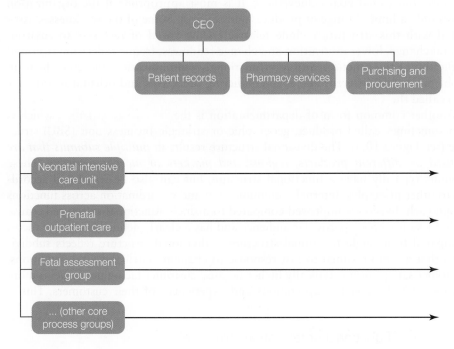

also reflected in increased product, region, or other appropriate specialization of each division. The divisional structure is particularly appropriate where there are a number of very different product or service offerings, significantly different market conditions for different offerings, or large geographic dispersion. Some of the downsides of divisional structures include inefficiencies due to duplication of functions across divisions; poorer co-ordination across divisional boundaries; typically lower technical specialization and specialist competence in divisional functions; and limitations to integration and standardization across divisions (Duncan, 1979).

Another departmental grouping is called the process-oriented structure, also called horizontal structure (see Figure 10.6 for an example in a maternity hospital). The process-oriented structure received particular attention during the 1990s when re-engineering, also called BPR (for 'business process re-engineering'), was implemented in many organizations across a range of industries. The principle of process-oriented structures (which is reflected in the focus of BPR) is to *align the structure of*

Process-oriented structure
Also called horizontal structure. The process-oriented structure seeks to align the structure of the organization with the workflows and core processes that aim at addressing and meeting customer needs.

the organization with the workflows and core processes that aim at addressing and meeting customer needs. Typical examples include customer service teams that combine many different specialists to enable quicker, more customer-oriented responses to received queries. We often find such teams in financial service firms such as insurance companies or in health care settings. Many hospitals have moved to interdisciplinary care teams that can comprehensively address patient needs without the immense co-ordination difficulties that are found in functionally structured hospitals. The recent focus on process-oriented structures is in large part a response to the available communication and co-ordination support arising from modern information and communication technology deployment in organizations, and particularly service firms (Fellenz and Brady, in press). Process-oriented structures can provide for flexible and responsive reactions to customer demands, as well as a good sense of the workflow and of the role of all internal and external participants among those involved in the work processes. They can help to identify and manage the boundaries between processes to 'minimize the disconnects in flows of information, materials or people' (Armistead and Rowland, 1996: p. 53). The high degree of participation and collaboration, as well as the delegated decision-making authority for those involved in these processes provide for very rich and potentially satisfying work environments. At the same time, it is often difficult to emphasize the horizontal processes while also accommodating the inevitable vertical dimension of work. Moreover, process-based restructuring is a challenging and resource intensive task, and the outcomes of large-scale BPR efforts have been mixed. In fact the concept of BPR is heavily criticized, even by its originators, as the level of failed applications is high, it can be too complex to apply easily, and the costs can outweigh the benefits.

Some structures do not fall squarely into one of the already introduced structures because they apply more than one of the departmentation principles simultaneously. They are referred to as hybrid structures, the best known of which is the matrix structure (see Figure 10.7). In essence, hybrid structures *combine key elements of different departmentation approaches.* A consulting company, for example, may apply

Hybrid structures
These apply to more than one of the departmentation principles simultaneously. The best known of which is the matrix structure.

Figure 10.7 Matrix structure

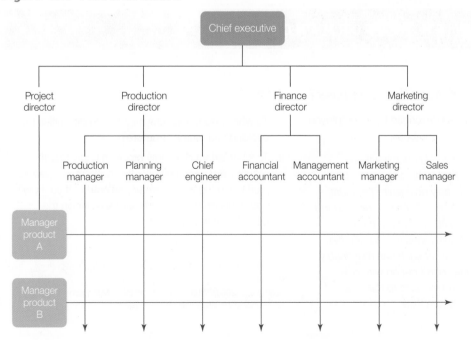

a project structure for client projects with a functional structure for its support functions. Another typical example is the brand management structure used by most fast-moving consumer goods (FMCG) companies such as Procter and Gamble, Unilever, L'Oreal and Nestlé. A particular brand is managed by a designated brand management group which liaises and co-ordinates across a range of functional departments such as research and development, production, finance, and logistics to bring their products to market. Hybrid structures often reflect a response to a particular set of demands. The matrix structure, for example, which reflects the brand management structure introduced above, is often credited with the ability to deliver dual customer demands for both low price and differentiation. It also allows for the sharing of key people and expertise across products, allows for the simultaneous development of functional and product-related expertise in the respective groupings, and facilitates the intense communication and co-ordination needs arising from the management of complex processes and decisions in fast-changing environments. It is often found in medium-size firms (or divisions). Along with this impressive list of advantages, however, hybrid structures such as the matrix structure also bring challenges and difficulties. Often, their complex arrangements are characterized by multiple reporting relationships which violates some of the classic management principles such as the scalar chain and unity of command principles, and obscures the effective span of control individual managers may have. For individual employees, they often create intense conflict because of competing and potentially incompatible expectations, demands and objectives (see for example the following High Performance example). Atkinson (2003) suggests that a matrix should be regarded as a process rather than a structure and as such it should evolve and self-renew based on feedback from the members and the environment. He also suggests that for success to be achieved, an appropriate and supportive culture needs to be in existence. It is useful to note that although divisional structures combine functional structures with the particular product, market, or geographical orientations, they are not generally seen as hybrid structures because they apply the different departmentation principles at different

Scalar chain
This reflects the strictly hierarchical nature of formal reporting relationships in organzations.

Span of control
Refers to the number of subordinates reporting to a single boss.

HIGH PERFORMANCE

How can I work for more than one boss?

The following situation was described by an employee who reported to more than one boss:

My job has expanded and I now have three bosses to report to rather than one. I have tried to point out that I can only do a limited amount for each boss, but they don't seem to understand the difficulties involved in reporting to three different masters. My initial idea was to get them all together to discuss what each can reasonably expect of me, but they don't get on with one another and have found excuses to miss the meetings. How can I tackle this?

TASKS

1 To what extent and how might such difficulties be avoided in a matrix structure?

2 To what extent does this problem imply that the matrix will only deliver effective outcomes if people working in them are carefully selected? If so, how could this be done? (summary answer on the companion web site).

Source:
Bullmore, J (2003) 'What's your problem?' in Management Today, December, p.75. Reprinted with permission.

levels (e.g., product principle to form division, functional principle for structure within the product divisions).

Finally, project and networked structures are rather fluid structural arrangements that are configured for particular purposes. Project structures (also called *internal network structures*, see Herber *et al.*, 2000) refer to *structural arrangements within organizations that are essentially designed anew for each project that is conducted*. More specifically, these structures reflect the particular way in which a specific project is approached and matched with internal resources (see Figure 10.8). These structures are typically changed or at least reconsidered after a particular project is completed and a new one is started. Project structures require experienced, skilled and willing participants, as well as distinct skills at designing and managing the activities carried out for the project. If the resources are not just predominantly internal it makes sense to talk about network structures (or *external network structures*, see Herber *et al.*, 2000), which are structures that extend beyond the nominal boundaries of the organization and draw together and deploy resources that can include individuals and groups that are contracted but do not become formally part of the organization. This also applies to other organizations in their entirety. Therefore they are also likened to *boundaryless organizations* (e.g., Francesco and Gold, 2005; Jones, 2004). Network structures are usually temporary. The necessary resources are aligned and co-ordinated for particular temporary objectives, and disbanded after the objective is reached. During that period, however, or if they are used in more permanent ways, they are deployed like other organizations. These temporary or enduring organizations are also called *virtual network structures* (Daft, 2007), *modular organizations* (Schilling and Steensma, 2001), or *cellular forms* (Miles *et al.*, 1997). Examples of such network structures include film project organizations, temporary political campaign organizations, or special event management organizations such as those behind the Live 8 (2005) and LiveEarth (2007) events. Similar principles are also applied in responses to emergencies and natural disasters. In the US, for example, emergency response units dealing with issues from small fires to cross-state natural catastrophes typically apply the Incident Command System (ICS), and for

Project structures
Also called internal network structures, refer to structural arrangements within organizations that are essentially designed anew for each project that is conducted, matching project needs with internal resources.

Network structures
Sometimes called external network structures or boundaryless organizations, which are structures that extend beyond the nominal boundaries of the organization and draw together and deploy resources that can include individuals, groups and/ or organizations that are contracted but do not become formally part of the organization. Network structures are usually temporary.

Figure 10.8 Project structure

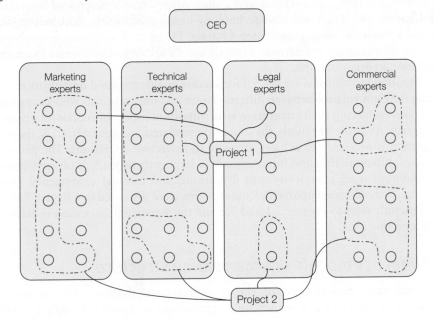

larger emergencies the National Incident Management System (NIMS), which reflect organizing principles found in many network organizations. Network structures can offer flexibility and cost benefits, but also provide co-ordination and control challenges. Particular issues in network structures are the danger of individuals or groups working for their own benefits, or defecting because the benefits they can gain elsewhere appear greater. Also, network structures face the challenges of retaining the necessary knowledge and skills if individuals or partners leave the network, as well as the difficulty of protecting proprietary information, skills and knowledge.

Mechanisms of integration

Horizontal differentiation needs to be balanced by effective integration to enable organizations to achieve their objectives. This is important both in terms of the different tasks to be achieved by individuals and groups separated through departmentation, but also in terms of the psychological and social differentiation that invariably follows such divisions (see Chapter 7). Specific subunit orientations develop that reflect the specific tasks, technology, time frames, social and interpersonal approaches, management and leadership styles, and other characteristics of specific units (e.g., Lawrence and Lorsch, 1967). Such subunit orientations can contribute to the *silo effect* and often contribute to conflict that poses problems in the co-ordination of effort across internal unit boundaries (see also Chapter 9).

To ensure effective information flow and constructive co-ordination between and among internal subunits, a number of integrating mechanisms can be used that differ in their speed and capacity to integrate complex and dynamic activities to which multiple units and actors contribute. They typically also differ in the resources they require, such that a trade-off is often required between speed and capacity on the one hand and resource intensity (e.g., cost, time, effort, management attention) on the other. Galbraith (1973) identified a range of integrating mechanisms that differ in their capacity to provide co-ordination and integration. Jones (2004) lists them in order of increasing complexity as hierarchy of authority, direct contact, liaison roles, task forces, teams, integrating roles and integrating departments (Table 10.2 provides further information on these mechanisms). In addition to these structural integrating mechanisms, organizational culture also plays an important role in helping communication, co-operation and collaboration across functional boundaries (see Chapter 14). There are also technology-based solutions to information sharing and knowledge management (see Chapter 11) as well as connections through informal relationships and networks (see Chapter 16) that can contribute to effective integration in organizations.

Integration mechanisms are crucial for success in differentiated organizations, and finding the right balance between differentiation and integration as well as appropriate ways of achieving such integration is an important aspect of successful organization design. As a rule of thumb, the more differentiated an organization is, the more integration is necessary to achieve efficient and effective operations. The necessary degree of differentiation and integration is in large part dependent on environmental conditions (e.g., complexity and dynamism) and internal contingency factors (e.g., size, technologies employed). Similar points were discussed in Chapter 7 so you could usefully refer to Figures 7.1 and 7.2 and the associated discussion in reflecting further on this issue.

Contingency models of organization structure

The *universalist* prescriptions of classic management theories such as scientific management produced a tendency for organizations to become broadly similar in

Table 10.2 Types of structural integrating mechanisms

Hierarchy of authority	Incumbents of hierarchical positions typically have the authority to make decisions regarding the resources under their command. Thus, if the integration of activities relies solely on the hierarchy of authority, any decision that involves activities and resources from different subunits is referred to a position that has authority over all involved subunits.
	As such decisions would quickly overwhelm those at the top of the hierarchy, most *routine* decisions regarding integrative matters are programmed and handled in prescribed ways without the need for hierarchical referral. For this reason formalization and standardization are extensively used in organizations that use hierarchical referral as a central means of integration (see section on bureaucracy).
Direct contact	Direct contact beween members of different subunits that need to integrate their activities is a means of achieving co-ordination through direct information exchange and joint decision making. Often, co-ordination problems that arise can be addressed through social influence processes and collective problem solving. Disputes or problems that cannot be solved can still be referred up the hierarchy for arbitration through a hierarchical superior to all parties.
Liaison roles	Selected members of a subunit may have responsibility to liaise with other subunits to co-ordinate joint activities. These liaisons will develop better insights and closer working relationships and can thus help avoid problems or solve any arising difficulties better. Their liaison tasks are part of their overall job responsibilities.
Task forces	A task force is a temporary group set up to address a specified problem or set of problems. As an integrating mechanism the task usually concentrates on solving co-ordination challenges through the development of specific solutions. Often, task forces also try to address recurring co-ordination needs through the development of structural or procedural solutions to the integration challenges.
Teams	If integration problems between subunits exists, task forces are replaced by more enduring teams that typically contain representatives from all involved subunits. These teams are charged with solving co-ordination and integration problems and serve as communication hubs for the involved units. Members are responsible for representing their subunits in the team, and for communicating back to their subunits.
Integrating roles	Individuals may be appointed as permanent integrators between subunits. Generally such full-time integrators are not members of the relevant units and have no other functional tasks. They are also not in charge of the units involved, otherwise this role would be an additional hierarchical position and the integration would be through the formal hierarchy. They may have a nominal advisory capacity but tend to have direct access to the superiors of the involved subunits so that hierarchical authority can be deployed if needed to help in integrating activities.
Integrating departments	The most resource-intensive structural solution to integrating existing subunits (short of a restructuring to find more profound and lasting solutions to the integration challenges such as matrix structures) is the creation and use of an integrating unit such as a department. Such departments are typically staffed with full-time members whose main responsibility is to co-ordinate and support collaboration among different subunits.

terms of the approach to structure and the tasks to be done. If there were one best way to be identified, then every organization would eventually discover and follow it. This approach underestimated the ability of individual employees to manage their own working environment together with the organizational value and benefits to be gained from so doing. It assumed a managerial superiority.

The human relations movement recognized the significance of people in organizations. In performing the tasks designated to them, individuals are still people, they are not machines that can and will follow precise instructions over and over again without error or variation. Human beings have free will and an ability to think. Based on the work of Elton Mayo and the Hawthorne studies, it began where scientific management stopped. Unfortunately, exclusive concentration on the people issues of an organization can easily lead to the insufficient consideration of technological or commercial constraint on organizational functioning, which results in a limited perspective on what creates an effective organization.

The contingency model arose out of a realization that the classical perspectives on structure were limited. A broad range of factors influences the structural arrangement of an organization – the design of an organization is said to be contingent upon the forces acting on the situation. The contingency approach links together circumstances and structure, but in a different way from the classical view. The traditional view seeks to impose a cause and effect relationship between circumstances and structure. The contingency model takes a more holistic view and suggests that structure is the result of a range of forces impacting upon the situation, management's interpretation of them and the identified business objectives. Figure 10.9 illustrates the contingency model.

Taking each element in the model illustrated in Figure 10.9 in turn:

- *External contingency factors.* A wide range of external factors can impact on the situation. For example, the activities of competitors, the industry and the markets in which the organization operates, and its location will all impact on the structural arrangements adopted. In their seminal work Burns and Stalker (1961) developed the concepts of *mechanistic* and *organic* (also called *organismic*) to describe the way in which organizations are organized relative to their environments. This influential distinction is further discussed in the next section. Similarly, the complexity and uncertainty of the environment will also influence the structural complexity inside the organization. Lawrence and Lorsch (1967) focused in particular on the structural

Figure 10.9 Contingency model of organization design

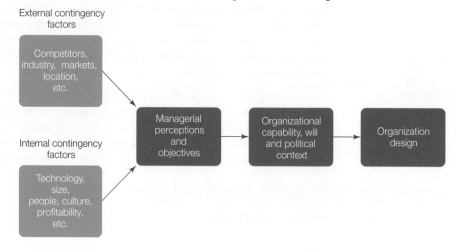

External contingency factors

Competitors, industry, markets, location, etc.

Internal contingency factors

Technology, size, people, culture, profitability, etc.

Managerial perceptions and objectives

Organizational capability, will and political context

Organization design

properties of differentiation and integration discussed above. They argue that in highly complex and uncertain environments, organizational structure will be much more elaborate to deal with the particular challenges arising for the organization. They concluded that in complex, uncertain environments high levels of both differentiation and integration were needed for success. In more stable environments, they found that relatively high levels of integration but considerably lower levels of differentiation could produce success.

- *Internal contingency factors.* A wide range of internal forces influence structure such as size, age, technology, resource availability culture, and other factors such as knowledge. Birkinshaw and colleagues (2002) demonstrate that the knowledge base within an organization is one of the variables that impacts on the structural arrangements adopted. Technology as an important determinant is discussed further in Chapter 11.

- *Managerial perceptions and objectives.* There are few situations where a manager is given the opportunity to create an organization from first principles; it usually involves changing an existing design. This can involve adapting to circumstances such as a new product introduction or competitive threat. Personal preference and preconceptions about how things should be organized influence how one responds to circumstances. Culturally determined perspectives and preferences also influence the way in which managers exercise their roles (Child and Kieser, 1979).

- *Organizational capability, will and politics.* The organization needs to have the capability to achieve its desired objectives. If an organization does not possess the expertise to do something or the will to make changes happen, then it is likely to fail to match the needs of its situation. To succeed in adapting or changing an organization, the political realities must be taken into account and appropriate strategies developed.

The contingency model is very useful for explaining the diversity in organization design that is found to exist. It provides for the forces external to the organization to be mixed with forces internal to the company. These forces, together with managerial choices based on their interpretations of the situation and all relevant factors, all influence the structural arrangements which will be specific to that organization at the particular point in time.

During the 1960s the Industrial Administration Research Unit emerged at Aston University as a leading multidisciplinary research group. They developed a research approach which examined three elements (Pugh and Hickson, 1989: pp. 9–15):

1 *Change and complexity.* Because of the degree of change to which organizations are subjected, it is necessary to develop theories that are incremental rather than discrete. The structure of an organization is the result of a number of forces acting and interacting in the situation.

2 *Institutional arrangements.* These include the control, hierarchical and work arrangements that exist. In many organizations these arrangements exist before employees join and will be there after they leave. Consequently, individuals are slightly detached from total ownership and control as they are in practice custodians of these features during their employment.

3 *Multiple perspectives.* In order to create a full understanding, it is necessary to consider more than one point of view. Different perceptions of an organization might exist among the different stakeholder groups. One way of illustrating this necessity is to consider the notion of perspective, illustrated in Figure 10.10.

Figure 10.10 Multiple perspectives of an object

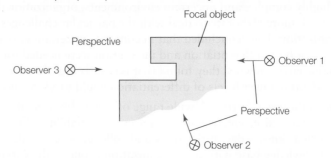

Each one of the individual observers sees only part of the shape and each view is different. Consequently, each can only be considered a partial reflection of the whole. For a realistic description of the object it would be necessary to integrate the three individual reports into a cohesive framework. The approach to identifying multiple perspectives is inevitably much more complex for social entities (that have not only a physical representation, but include social, psychological and other dimensions) such as organizations.

Structural contingency theory has been the subject of a number of criticisms. The assumed link between structural arrangements and organizational performance as a function of the fit with particular internal and external factors and characteristics has not consistently been supported by empirical research (Pfeffer, 1997). Legge (1978) suggests that the contingency model is intuitively attractive because it contains powerful normative connotations, and it appears to have a pro-managerial bias that some contemporary organization theories lack (Donaldson, 1995). Nevertheless, Pfeffer (1997) argues that many of the variables used (e.g., formalization, centralization, specialization) are highly abstract and do not reflect the characteristics managerial decisions address directly (see also Starbuck, 1981) and thus limit the pragmatic value of structural contingency theory. At the same time, the theory ignores the ability and performance of managers at a personal level as well as a range of other factors independent of structure. For example, an incompetent sales person is unlikely to win many orders irrespective of the structure of the sales department.

Overall, structural contingency theory encourages the view that effectiveness can be achieved if only the context could be interpreted properly, retaining the essence of a formulaic approach to success (Legge, 1978). The contingency model does not take account of the role of power or control in dynamic work relationships. In addition, technology, for example, is not a neutral force within an organization. Managers decide that they will utilize a particular form of technology and they decide upon its use and application in order to achieve particular objectives, including control over operational processes. They therefore determine to a significant extent how a range of factors will impact on the process of organizing.

Organizational forms and configurations

Organizational configurations
Also called organizational forms or archetypes. Refers to constellations of structural characteristics that tend to appear together, that can be found more frequently than others.

Given the numerous aspects and variables to be considered in structuring organizations, there is no limit to the range and number of possible different structures that organizations can adopt. In fact, there is immense variety in the way organizations are structured across and even within specific industries and sectors. Nevertheless, there are some organizational configurations, which refer to *constellations of structural characteristics that tend to appear together*, that can be found more frequently than others. The study of organizational configurations, also called *forms* or *archetypes*, has a long history in sociology and organization theory. Some configurations are more common in certain environments because they appear to 'fit better than others within any given context and thus are more successful' (Short *et al.*, 2008: p. 1054). This link between configurations and success has also attracted recent research attention from such areas as strategic management, human resource management, and entrepreneurship and new venture research (e.g., DeSarbo and Grewal, 2008; Eddleston *et al.*, 2008; Harms *et al.*, 2007; Korunka *et al.*, 2003; Payne, 2006; Steffens *et al.*, 2009; Toh *et al.*, 2008; Wiklund and Shepherd, 2005). In this section we introduce important contributions to the analysis of specific forms as well as selected frameworks and taxonomies of organizational configurations.

Weber and bureaucracy

An important contribution to the systematic study of the structure of large formal organizations was the comprehensive description of bureaucracy by the German sociologist Max Weber (1864–1920). He articulated the essence of bureaucracy with its hierarchy of control, rule frameworks and task specialization (1947). Weber developed his ideas in the early years of the twentieth century, a time when organizations were generally becoming much larger and more complex but did not have the benefits of modern information and communication technology to aid the process. The consequence was a need to deploy other means of efficiently administering large organizations and of effectively co-ordinating the varied activities within them: bureaucracy. He postulated three types of bureaucratic forms differentiated through the way in which authority was legitimized within them. He described these organizational forms as ideal types – not necessarily found in the precise form described. He also suggested that any combination, or even all three might exist within parts of the same organization. The three types of organization were:

Bureaucracy
An approach to organizing the activities within an organization which involves specialization of task, hierarchy of authority and decision making. See also classical management theory and administrative management.

1 *Charismatic.* In the charismatic form of organization authority is based around the personal qualities of the leader. Frequently found in religious or political movements, this type of organization might also be found among small owner-managed companies in the commercial world. However, as a result of the strong reliance on the charismatic qualities and authority of the leader, the issue of succession is invariably a problem that is not easy to resolve. If the succession process can be institutionalized, then the organization invariably transforms into one of the two remaining categories.

2 *Traditional.* The traditional form of organization relies on accepted precedent as the dominant form of authority. The leader in such an organization relies on tradition and accepted custom as the basis of being obeyed. It maintains the status quo by constantly referring back to precedent or position as the ultimate arbiter of the legitimacy of a rule or instruction. Many family-owned organizations rely on this form of organization as leadership and authority are restricted to family members, irrespective of ability or experience.

3 *Rational–legal.* The rational–legal notion of authority forms the basis of the bureaucratic form of organization according to Weber. This approach is termed rational because the organization is established to achieve specific (rational) objectives. It is also legal in the sense that it adopts a rule- and procedure-based approach to the exercise of authority. The exercise of authority is prescribed by the rule frameworks and is therefore independent of the individual postholder. Weber argued that this allowed precision, speed, continuity, unity, strict subordination and the minimization of labour cost, and so on. All of the resources of the organization are effectively directed towards the objectives being sought, without undue interference or whim.

The basis of a bureaucratic form of organization is reflected in Table 10.3, adapted from Scott (1992). The points included do not individually or collectively suggest a specific structural form in itself, but more an approach to the process of arranging the resources, including people. If these principles and guidelines are followed, whatever the framework adopted actually looks like, it will be bureaucratic in essence and approach. It reflects an attempt to provide a sound basis for a factory-based analogy to efficiency at a time when neither information and communication nor administrative technology was well developed. Weber also linked his ideas on bureaucracy to his views in relation to economic development and the emergence of Protestantism with its associated work ethic.

Gouldner (1954) introduced the idea of different types of bureaucracy. He suggested three types of bureaucracy:

Mock bureaucracy
Organizational rules and procedures are largely ignored by all inside, having been imposed by an outside agency.

Punishment bureaucracy
A variant on the mock bureaucracy in that rules are imposed on the workers by management.

Representative bureaucracy
The rules and procedures are generally supported within the organization having been developed by managers with employee involvement.

1 *Mock.* The rules and procedures in a mock bureaucracy are largely ignored by all inside the bureaucracy, having been imposed on them by an outside agency.

2 *Punishment.* In practice the punishment bureaucracy represents a variant on the mock bureaucracy in that the rules are imposed on the workers inside the organization. However, the difference is that in the punishment bureaucracy it is management alone that develops the rules and procedures and then imposes them on the other groups. Not surprisingly, Gouldner felt that this approach would not encourage the full commitment and support of the employees because they did not accept the legitimate basis of the authority implied under these circumstances. Some of the issues that arise in situations in which management seeks to impose control within a university are described in the Employee Perspective example.

3 *Representative.* In a representative bureaucracy the rules and procedures are generally supported by those inside the organization having been developed by managers with the involvement of the other worker and stakeholder groups.

Table 10.3 Characteristics of the bureaucratic form of organization

Fixed division of labour
Postholders selected on the basis of capability
Postholders appointed and not elected
Administrative basis for keeping files and records
Separation of business and private affairs
Postholders paid by salary paid in money
Work in the organization is primarily occupation of postholder
Promotion based on achievement or seniority
Rules govern work routines
Depersonalization of decision making
Disciplined approach to work required

EMPLOYEE PERSPECTIVE

Control through workload models

Sarah worked as a university lecturer. Teaching was done in large groups often involving six staff delivering a module to about 800 students. Management sought to minimize the cost of teaching by increasing class sizes and by requiring lecturers to follow standardized procedures.

A workload model was introduced which used work measurement to give a time value to each aspect of a lecturer's job. Lecturers had to 'earn' a given number of hours each year by fulfilling the designated tasks. Procedures for dealing with students were prescribed and forms introduced to record all contact and so on. Changes were introduced with no consultation with lecturers. The university moved away from a collegiate approach, with staff involved in all decisions, to a managerial approach, with decisions communicated to lecturers. Lecturing staff began to feel that they were not valued and were not being treated as the professionals they were supposed to be.

Over time resentment increased among Sarah and her colleagues. Inevitably staff began to cut corners (as management described it) seeking to retain some control over their work. Sarah dropped a range of tasks for which she was not allowed any time in her workload hours – for example she stopped attending meetings and she was only available for student consultation for the minimum time required by the workload model. Sarah always fulfilled the minimum requirements of her job but along with most colleagues resented the way that they were being managed. Over time the number and severity of student complaints began to increase. Also most lecturers constantly looked for other jobs to escape the pressure of working in that particular environment. The only staff to remain for any length of time were those close to retirement; those who could not get a job elsewhere; those who were trapped in that location for personal reasons; and those who, for whatever reason, aligned themselves to the management approach and appeared to support the changes made. Sarah concentrated on activities that supported her career plans irrespective of the workload requirements and moved to another university after 6 months.

TASKS

1. To what extent can professional staff such as lecturers be managed effectively through bureaucracy and top-down management practice?

2. How can professional services such as universities be organized to ensure the best result for all stakeholders within a cost-effective process?

3. This example suggests that some lecturers supported the general approach taken by managers of the university. Why might that be and what does it imply about organization design?

A number of criticisms have been levelled at bureaucracy, based on the negative impact on people as well as on the limitation of this approach to control and co-ordinate performance. Weber's analysis of bureaucracy and its description as an ideal type is often mistaken as an argument for the superiority of bureaucracy over other structures and approaches. However, Weber's argument simply states that bureaucracy and the appropriate use of its underlying principles promise 'reliable decision making, merit-based selection and promotion and the impersonal and, therefore, fair application of rules' (Hatch and Cunliffe, 2006: p. 103). Weber himself recognized the potential negative effect of boring, routine and monotonous jobs on the people who did them, but insisted that it was the only way to create efficient administrative and organizational structures. It is also the basis of work by Merton (1968) who describes the development of a bureaucratic personality as a result of being tied to the application of rules and fixed procedures. This is similar to the notion of the 'organization man phenomenon' described by Whyte (1956) in which he describes in graphic detail the implications of working and succeeding in a bureaucracy. Another view of bureaucracy is that the tight structures and procedures that are evident in the principles of it cannot eliminate political and interactive human behaviours. Crozier (1964) studied a number of bureaucracies and described them in terms of dynamic social systems. He identified individuals who sought ways to achieve their own goals and position in the overall scheme of things through capitalizing on areas of uncertainty or ambiguity in the rules, procedures and responsibilities of individuals and groups within the organization.

In recent years the concept of bureaucracy has become a term of derision. This is a result partly of the inability of bureaucracies to change with the times and partly of the frequently perceived unwillingness of staff in such organizations (at least from the customer or client perspective) to accommodate nonstandard events. Equally, the notion of a bureaucratic form of organization is not appropriate to all situations. For example, organizations that operate in an industry or market in which flexibility or adaptability represent key factors for success will not do well if they are bureaucratic in structure. Also, organizations that employ large numbers of professional employees (accountancy or legal practices being examples) would not get the best out of their staff if they relied on bureaucratic structuring. As Hatch and Cunliffe (2006) suggest, professionals are highly trained and socialized to adopt high standards of both work quality and performance, hence rules and procedures seeking closely to direct such employees are redundant and often perceived by them as inappropriate and offensive.

Mechanistic and organic organizational forms and other metaphors

Mechanistic organizations
These provide a blueprint of an organizational structure that is often compared to a machine: all the parts are clearly aligned to work together in prescribed, predetermined and stable ways. See also organic organizations.

A number of summary terms and descriptions of different organizational forms and configurations exist. Some of them are part of more general frameworks, while others exist because they are useful in describing recognizable forms. An important and influential distinction was developed by Burns and Stalker (1961) who distinguished mechanistic and organic organizations (see Table 10.4). Mechanistic refers to organizational forms that tend to emerge in stable and predictable conditions. In essence it reflects the application of clear hierarchical structures and specialization of tasks and has many similarities to the bureaucratic form of organization discussed above. Organic (sometimes also referred to as *organismic*) reflects an organizational form emerging in fluid and relatively unpredictable situations. It is typified by a high level of flexibility in job responsibilities, also incorporating high levels of technical expertise at the lower levels of the organization and recognition of the value of individual contribution.

Organic organizations
Sometimes referred to as organismic organizations. Reflects an organizational form emerging in fluid and relatively unpredictable situations. It is typified by a high level of flexibility in job responsibilities, also incorporating high levels of technical expertise at the lower levels of the organization and recognition of the value of individual contribution. See also mechanistic organizations.

Burns and Stalker's (1961) distinction between mechanistic and organic organizations focuses largely on structural properties but is highly compatible with cultural, environmental, strategic, procedural and systemic features of specific organizations. To show the linkages between these dimensions Johnson and his colleagues (Johnson *et al.*, 2005) discuss the concept of reinforcing cycles that support the consistency between such different elements. They argue that strategy, culture and configuration all are important elements that co-determine through their dynamic interaction if a particular organizational form leads to success in specific environmental conditions. A good fit between these elements and the particular environment supports success, and these reinforcing cycles preserve the status quo, which is helpful as long as good fit is maintained. Yet according to the logic of such reinforcing cycles, they can also lead to strategic drift and performance problems, particularly if only one of the elements is changed and thus proper fit and alignment is destroyed.

Table 10.4 Design differences between mechanistic and organic organizational forms

Overall organizational form	Mechanistic	Organic
Nature of tasks	Routine	Nonroutine
Degree of standardization	High	Low
Degree of formalization	High	Low
Co-ordination approach	Indirectly through plans, standardization and hierarchical referral	Directly through interaction and dynamic integration mechanisms
Differentiation and specialization	Low to medium	Medium to high
Hierarchy of authority	Tall with narrow span of control	Flat with large span of control
Decision making	Centralized	Decentralized
Location of specialist knowledge and expertise	Concentrated	Dispersed

The mechanistic form is typically found in stable environments where low-cost strategies frequently lead to success. Such strategies in turn require standardized processes which are enabled through tightly controlled (and controlling) systems. Such systems are consistent with a particular culture (in this case the Defender culture, see Chapter 14) which they argue leads to the firm seeking out stable environments – thus closing the loop. According to Johnson and his colleagues (2005) such reinforcing cycles also exist for organic structures that show many of the features of adhocracies (further discussed below). Organic structures are typically found in dynamic environments which often favour differentiation-based strategies. These in turn require flexible operating processes that can support variety and customization which are supported and enabled through flexible systems and control approaches which fit in with the prospector culture typical in such firms. Again, such cultures show preferences for dynamic environments full of opportunities, and this closes the reinforcing cycle for organic organizations. Figure 10.11 shows these two reinforcing cycles.

The terms 'mechanistic' and 'organic' are useful metaphors that provide summary descriptions of relevant structural and procedural aspects of organizations. Such metaphors are frequently used to denote different forms of organization. Morgan (1986/2006) provides an influential and useful account of such metaphors that shows many of their benefits and limitations. Metaphors are used 'whenever we attempt to understand one element of experience in terms of another' and take the form of 'implicit or explicit assertions that A *is* (or is like) B' (Morgan, 1986/2006: p. 4). In general, metaphorical thinking and the use of metaphors is immensely valuable because of the insights they can help generate. At the same time, metaphors always provide limiting and even distorting insights. As Gianfranco Poggi said, 'way of seeing is also a way of not seeing' (1965: p. 284), and looking at an organization as a machine or as an organism (i.e., describing types of organizations as mechanistic or organic) will highlight certain aspects but at the same time will simultaneously cover up other important characteristics. In the case of mechanistic and organic

Metaphor (organizational)
The explanation of something complex through reference to something simpler, but in a way which conveys additional meaning in the process.

Figure 10.11 Reinforcing cycle for mechanistic and organic configurations

Reinforcing cycle for mechanistic configurations:

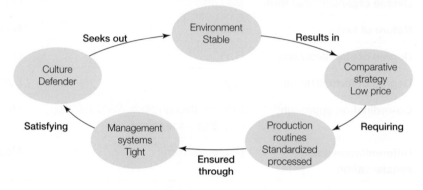

Reinforcing cycle for organic configurations:

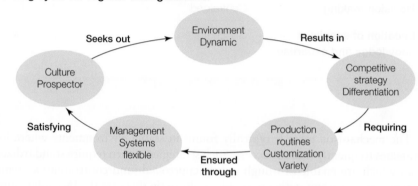

Source: Adapted from Johnson, G., Scholes, K. R. and Whittington, R. (2005). *Exploring Corporate Strategy* (7th edn), Prentice Hall/FT.

organizations, the discrepancy these particular metaphors highlight between these two types of organizations are helpful in distinguishing and understanding their differences by framing the nature of each in starkly different terms. It is important, however, to recognize that these organizational forms all also share significant elements and properties, and the highlighted and perceived differences (as well as similarities) can cloud the fuller understanding of their nature.

A closer look at the distinctions highlighted in Table 10.4 shows that these are generally differences of degree, which means they are relative rather than absolute. This is true for many if not most of the differences highlighted by the metaphors used to describe organizations, and reminds us that for all their value, metaphors of organizations provide at best only partial insights. Categorization based on relative differences always introduces a reduction of complexity that can leave out particularly important shared aspects and introduce overstated distinctions. Categorical as well as metaphorical thinking needs to be carefully considered to determine type and degree of the potential bias it introduces.

Nevertheless, both for research and applied purposes, metaphors are important and can provide immense value. Using organizational metaphors disguises difference and simplifies complexity arising from the wide variation among organizations. Metaphors aid human understanding, and the metaphors managers use relating to organizations determine how they subsequently think about, manage and structure them. Morgan identifies a number of metaphors that illustrate this point (see Table 10.5). Metaphor becomes the basis of belief about how organizations should function. The 'facts' encountered are 'fitted' into the metaphorical image. The importance of metaphor in

Table 10.5 Selected metaphors of organizations discussed by Morgan (1986)

Machine	A network of parts: functional departments . . . which are further specified as networks of precisely defined jobs (p. 27)
Organisms	Living systems, existing in a wider environment on which they depend for the satisfaction of various needs (p. 39)
Brains	Utilizes the concepts of intelligence, feedback and information processing to model organizational functioning
Culture	Directs attention to the symbolic or even 'magical' significance of even the most rational aspects of organizational life (p. 135)
Political	Managers frequently talk about authority, power and superior–subordinate relations . . . Organizations as systems of the government that vary according to the political principles employed (p. 142)

contingency thinking is that it provides a means through which humans understand organizations and how they function in a specific context. That understanding can provide a basis for deciding how the organization could be structured. Oliver (2002) uses biological and gene structure metaphors to demonstrate that survival in the long term is achieved by what he terms organic organizations using strategies that mimic biological, complex, self-regulating development rather than mechanistic strategy models. Similarly, Palmer and Dunford (2008) use different metaphors of organizational change management strategies and Caldwell and colleagues (Caldwell *et al.*, 2008) use the mechanical metaphor of a clutch in considering how task co-ordination can best be achieved in organizations. Another metaphor of organization structure suggests that it reflects a set design as might be used in the theatre. Bolman and Deal (2008) discuss this theatre metaphor in detail and show how it can add to purely rational approaches to and accounts of organization design and action, for example by focusing attention on the role of the audience – implying the customers/suppliers and other observers of particular activity within the organization. Even employees could be the 'audience' for some of the actions of managers.

Mintzberg's framework of organizational forms

Henry Mintzberg, an influential Canadian strategy and organization scholar, developed an approach to classifying different organizational forms based on the observation that while unlimited numbers of different configurations are possible, the structural arrangements actually used by different organizations tend to cluster around a number of ideal types (Mintzberg, 1979; 1991). In short, these forms are distinguished by the specific appearance of six distinct organizational parts and are a result of the interplay of particular ways of co-ordinating activities, the application of the principles of organizational structuring (also called 'design parameters') which in turn are determined by specific forces that express different objectives, values and preoccupations, and the internal and external contingency factors the organization faces. Figure 10.12 identifies in schematic form the six parts of organizations which include the strategic apex (which reflects the top echelon of the hierarchy such as the owner in small firms or the top management rank in larger companies), the middle line (i.e., intermediate levels of management), the operating core

Strategic apex
Reflects the top echelon of the hierarchy such as the owner in small firms or the top management rank in larger companies.

Middle line
Intermediate levels of management in the Mintzberg model of structure.

Operating core
All those involved in operational activity of the business such as factory based functions or service delivery staff in the Mintzberg model of structure.

Figure 10.12 Mintzberg's six elements of organizational forms

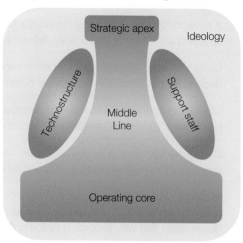

(i.e., all those involved in operations such as manufacturing or service delivery staff), the technostructure (specialist functions such as industrial engineering, IT systems designer, or financial controllers and auditors who determine how certain operations should be performed), the support staff (i.e., functions such as HR, maintenance, or facilities management that provide inputs in support of the operating core and other elements of the organization without direct involvement in the core value generation processes of the organization), and ideology (reflecting shared identity and the force for co-operation referred to above). These core elements differ in their size, role and importance in different organizational forms. Table 10.6 lists the six co-ordinating mechanisms which are depicted in Figure 10.13 (see Mintzberg, 2003: p. 211).

The design parameters considered by Mintzberg reflect many of the principles of classical management theory and of designing organizational structures discussed above (e.g., span of control; differentiation and departmentation principles; integrating mechanisms; locus of decision making; etc.), while his consideration of internal (e.g., age, size, technology) and external contingency factors (competition, degree of uncertainty) align well with the lessons provided by structural contingency theories (e.g., more dynamic and complex environments lead to more elaborated internal structures; more hostile environments and more powerful external players lead to more centralization; etc.).

In addition, Mintzberg's framework considers the influence of seven forces on the above elements, mechanisms and parameters in creating the basic organizational forms. More specifically, these forms represent structural responses to the influence of particular organizing principles or forces that can dominate an organization. The seven forces include the *forces for direction* (reflecting attempts to keep the organization focused on a set of core goals as an integrated entity), *efficiency* (indicating pressures to economize all activities and reduce resource use per relevant unit of output), *proficiency* (designating attempts to develop and deploy cutting edge knowledge and expertise in core activity areas), *concentration* (reflecting endeavours to create and sustain unified perspectives for serving particular markets or customer segments, or for focusing on specific product or service offerings), and *innovation* (showing the need to change, learn and discover new value creation opportunities for the organization and its customers). The last two forces in Mintzberg's framework are called catalytic forces and include the *force for co-operation* (referring

Table 10.6 Mintzberg's co-ordinating mechanisms used in organizations

Co-ordinating mechanism	This mechanism achieves co-ordination through . . .
Mutual adjustment	. . . direct informal interaction between organizational members to exchange information, solve problems, make joint agreements and decisions on further action, and adjust actions in direct response to partner's behaviour
Direct supervision	. . . having one legitimized person give instructions to others (reflects the hierarchy of authority)
Standardization of work processes	. . . determining and prescribing the work processes that members and subunits carry out (usually determined in the technostructure to be carried out by members in the operating core)
Standardization of outputs	. . . specifying the results of different work (usually determined in the technostructure through financial, operational or strategic plans that specify particular objectives individual members or subunits are expected to make)
Standardization of skills (and knowledge)	. . . similarity in the training and socialization of the members performing tasks such that their individual behaviour fits into established shared behavioural routines (in the case of professionals such as operating room staff in hospitals these routines may be determined by professions outside of the organization such as medical and nursing professions and schools)
Standardization of norms	. . . establishment of shared norms that guide behaviour as well as thinking to produce compatible actions from all members and units

to the shared ideology, the set of values, beliefs and norms that create a harmonious, aligned entity out of a disparate set of people) and *competition* (reflecting the destabilizing and separating force of unsanctioned or unlegitimated behaviour). Mintzberg argues that when any one of these forces dominates, organizational configurations emerge that reflect the dominant form.

The force for direction leads to the entrepreneurial form (also called *simple form*) with a central role for the strategic apex which directly controls activities in the operating core with little in terms of middle line, technostructure or support functions. In the terms used above, the entrepreneurial form shows little differentiation, while integration and co-ordination occur largely through direct supervision. The entrepreneurial form is typically found in small organizations as it cannot support the increased differentiation and integration needs of larger numbers of participants. The simplest form is the entrepreneurial structure which is shown in Figure 10.14, along with the other four common organizational forms as described by Mintzberg. In entrepreneurial organizations, management activities are largely inseparable from the personalities and personal preferences of the owner/manager owners. Decision making is heavily influenced by their preferences, feelings and needs rather than primarily those of the business. Personal relationships feature very heavily as an

Entrepreneurial form (of structure)
Also called the *simple form (of structure)*. Typically found in small organizations based on a small strategic apex which directly controls activities in the operating core with little in terms of middle line, technostructure or support functions.

Figure 10.13 Mintzberg's co-ordinating mechanisms

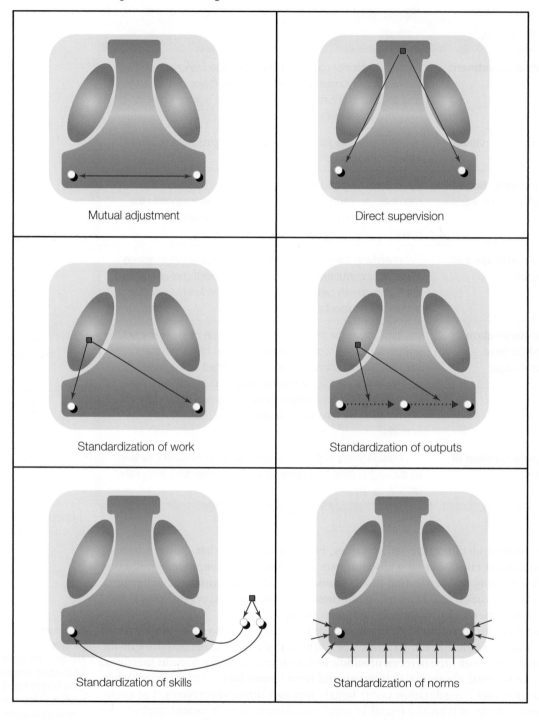

important feature of the activities within this type of organization. The relative lack of size together with the direct involvement of the owner create a scenario where everyone needs to be able to work together effectively if major problems are to be avoided. Individuals typically become involved with a wide range of tasks in order to deliver the service or complete orders on time. It is not uncommon to find the owner 'rolling up their sleeves' and undertaking the most menial tasks when necessary.

Figure 10.14 Mintzberg's common organizational forms

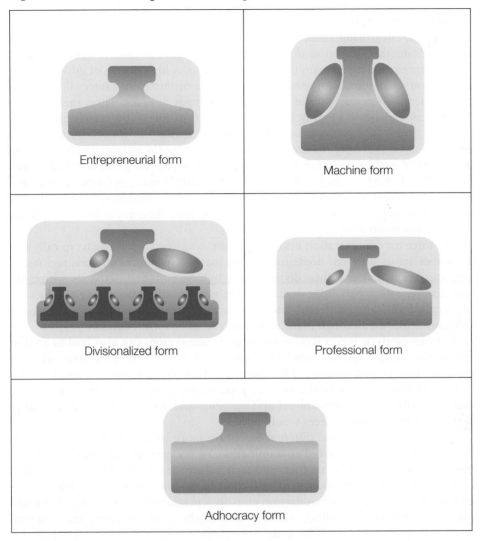

Entrepreneurial form

Machine form

Divisionalized form

Professional form

Adhocracy form

In a very real sense, power and authority within the organization lie with the owner/manager.

The machine form is a result of the dominance of the force for efficiency. It reflects the mechanistic and bureaucratic forms discussed above and is typical of mass-production or mass-service organizations in private and public sectors. It has a large middle line as well as sizeable support staff and technostructure that create extensive standardization and formalization through rules and regulations.

The force for proficiency leads to the professional form which is often found in professional services (e.g., law firms, architectural offices, health care providers). A particular focus is on perfecting existing skills among members of the operating core which increasingly specialize and focus on those customers and clients in need of their particular expertise. The members of the operating core in the professional form are much more powerful than in any other form and can operate at least partially autonomously free from managerial interference because of their unique skill and centrality in creating value.

Machine form (of structure)
Results from the dominance of the force for efficiency. It reflects the mechanistic and bureaucratic forms of organization and is typically found in mass-production or mass-service organizations in both private and public sectors.

Professional form (of structure)
Often found in professional services. Reflects organizations with a particular focus on perfecting existing skills among members of the operating core which increasingly specialize and focus on those customers and clients in need of their particular expertise.

Adhocracy form (of structure)
Sometimes called team-based organizations. This approach reflects the dominance of innovation as a major driving force in structure. Similar to the professional form but because the organization is focused on creating novelty and innovation different experts must combine their expertise in ever changing groups.

Heterarchy
Found in adhocracy forms of structure. Heterarchy means that different people and subunits are not ordered according to predetermined differences in formal authority (hierarchy) but rather all have the potential to be deployed as is seen fit and in accordance to the requirements of the particular tasks.

Diversified form
Typically diversifies first across different domains (such as markets, products/services, regions or customer segments) and then divisionalizes [often called strategic business units (SBUs)] by concentrating activities within the unit dealing with a particular domain. There is relative autonomy in each division and different internal structural arrangements are possible across different divisions, although machine forms tend to be most common.

The adhocracy form reflects the dominance of the force for innovation. As in the professional form, members are often highly skilled, but because the organization is focused on creating novelty and innovation (as in research organizations, political think tanks, advertising agencies and boutique consulting firms), different experts must combine their expertise in ever changing groups. For this reason adhocracies are sometimes also called team-based organizations. A high degree of informal communication and mutual adjustment is used to co-ordinate, and internal structural arrangements often fluctuate in response to changes in tasks. Thus, these organizations can be said to employ heterarchy instead of hierarchy, which means that *different people and subunits are not ordered according to predetermined differences in formal authority (hierarchy) but rather all have the potential to be deployed as is seen fit and in accordance to the requirements of the particular tasks*. Such heterarchies (see McCulloch, 1965; see also Seidl, 2007) may employ temporary and partial hierarchies or other arrangements, and employ considerably more flexible structural arrangements than other forms. Thus, the adhocracy reflects the project structure discussed above in many respects.

The force for concentration brings about the diversified form which typically first diversifies across different domains (such as markets, products/services, regions, or customer segments) and then divisionalizes by concentrating activities within the unit dealing with a particular domain. There is relative autonomy in each division, often called SBUs, and different internal structural arrangement are possible across different divisions, although machine forms tend to be most common.

The two catalytic forces (co-operation and competition) can also lead to distinctive organizational forms, called *ideological* and *political form*, respectively, but these are very rare in practice (Mintzberg, 1991). These seven forms are the result of the domination of one of the forces, a process also called *contamination* (because one force affects all organizational arrangements and activities to the detriment of the objectives that other forces would pursue).

Alternatively, when these different forces are more balanced (because the forces are actively managed to avoid contamination, or because an organization is transforming from one form to another) and their influence is contained (a process called *containment*), other approaches can also come to the fore when needed. Responding to a crisis may require individuals or units in a machine form to ignore rules and procedures. If no one is willing or able to do this when and if required, the organization would potentially fail. The actual fit between configuration and environment is crucial for success, yet the domination of any one force can push out the necessary contribution of activities more aligned with other forces. The high degree of efficiency achieved by machine forms such as bureaucracies often creates the reasons for failure when such organizations need to deal with sudden and fundamental changes in their business environments or large-scale crises. The responses of many large financial service organizations, regulatory authorities and governments to the credit crunch starting in September 2008 provide illustrative examples.

Mintzberg calls the process of successful balancing different forces *combination* and argues that it is required by some organizations all the time, and by all organizations some of the time. Successful combination may enable good fit, but the danger is that different forces cancel each other out (a process Mintzberg calls *cleavage*) which can lead to paralysis. Dealing with the contradiction of combining different forces successfully during transition or because they are needed simultaneously is an immensely difficult challenge, and the role of ideology and politics (reflecting the forces of cooperation and competition) is central to achieving successful balance. Of course, given the contradictory nature of these forces, managing their interplay is in itself a significant challenge. Mintzberg suggests that the conclusion to the multiple challenges of organization design is to attain one of the ideal forms (configurations) while also recognizing the danger of contamination and cleavage during transitions. Ultimately, there is no stable solution in a complex and changing environment, so the mindful and active management of organization design is the only option in the pursuit of organizational effectiveness. The following Going Global example illustrates the complexity that can exist in the way that some organizations operating internationally organize their activities.

The ambidextrous organization

The challenge of successfully dealing with simultaneous different forces or needs such as for stability and change, efficiency and innovation, and control and responsiveness, has long been a central concern of organization designers and theorists (e.g., Burns and Stalker, 1961; Duncan, 1976; March, 1991; Quinn and Cameron, 1988; Tushman and O'Reilly, 1996). Effectively, these different needs come down to the difference between exploitation and exploration – the question is if an organization should focus on increasing alignment to current circumstances to exploit present opportunities, or on exploring future opportunities and improving adaptability to change (March, 1991).

Many theorists have suggested answers to address this paradox of simultaneous yet apparently opposite needs. Thus, Boynton and Victor (1991) suggested the dynamically stable organization as an answer, while Volberda (1999) and others (see Fellenz, 2008) described flexibility and the flexible firm as able to address this issue. Traditionally, different structural solutions to the competing demands in separate parts of organizations have been proposed in organization theory as a potential solution. Examples include the parallel structures used in many mechanistic organizations designed to enable learning (e.g., Adler, 1993; Bushe and Shani, 1991) and the boundary spanning functions that help protect the technical core from environmental uncertainty (Thompson, 1967; this is discussed further in Chapter 11).

The most active recent research tackling this paradox is the work on ambidexterity (e.g., He and Wong, 2004; Jansen *et al.*, 2006) and the ambidextrous organization (Birkinshaw and Gibson, 2004; Gibson and Birkinshaw, 2004; Güttel and Konlechner, 2009; Raisch and Birkinshaw, 2008; O'Reilly and Tushman, 2004). In short, ambidextrous organizations are organizations that manage to combine alignment and adaptability. Birkinshaw and his colleagues (Birkinshaw and Gibson, 2004; Gibson and Birkinshaw, 2004; Raisch and Birkinshaw, 2008) argue that in addition to the traditional structural solutions to this conundrum (summarized as *structural ambidexterity*), the organizational context and, specifically, the availability of effective performance management and social support can create contextual ambidexterity. They define *contextual ambidexterity* as the *behavioural capacity to simultaneously demonstrate alignment and adaptability* (Gibson and Birkinshaw, 2004: p. 209) which originates in simultaneous performance pressures (through active performance management) and a supportive social environment (through enabling management practices and open and trust-based interpersonal relations). In addition to structural and contextual aspects contributing to ambidexterity (see Table 10.7 for a comparison), leadership has also been identified as playing an important role in creating and supporting ambidexterity in organizations (e.g., Jansen *et al.*, 2008; Lubatkin *et al.*, 2006; Smith and Tushman, 2005). Creating ambidextrous organizations can also be seen as a challenge for managers in that they need to simultaneously conceive of their organizations as well as their own responsibilities in fundamentally different ways (e.g., Gilbert, 2006; Lüscher and Lewis, 2008).

Overall, studying organizational configurations and forms is a fruitful avenue for pursuing important questions about the link between organizational design and success. Rather than simply following one model or pursuing a single form, managers

Ambidextrous organizations
Manage to combine alignment and adaptability in their structure and design in responding to the specific demands of their environment.

GOING GLOBAL

Amnesty International

Amnesty International (AI) was founded in 1961 with the intention of raising awareness of torture and human rights abuses. It is funded through fee income and membership donations.

The organization of AI is governed by the International Council which meets every 2 years and whose function is to determine the direction of AI, and to appoint and hold accountable local and other internal bodies. Members of the International Council are drawn from local associations recognized by AI. Representatives of other relevant associations are invited to attend International Council meetings, but do not have the right to vote.

The main operational governing body within AI is the International Executive Committee comprising a Chairperson, eight members and a Treasurer – elected by the International Council. The International Executive Committee meets every 6 months and its function is to implement the strategy set out by the International Council and ensure that the AI's work complies with its statutes. The operational activities of AI are carried out by the International Secretariat (headed by a Secretary General with 500 staff) which takes direction from (and reports to) both the International Executive Committee and International Council. Countries with a significant and established membership are called 'sections'. The work within sections is supported by a small number of paid staff who co-ordinate and administer AI's work - largely

carried out by the members. Each section is overseen by a local board of directors. In 2005 there were 52 sections worldwide.

Another organizational arrangement within AI are 'structures' – countries with some members and paid support but not of a size or significance to be termed 'sections'. In countries where no section or structure exists, people can become 'international members' of AI. Two other organizational forms exist within AI. 'International networks' have the task of promoting specific themes or have a particular focus on part of the work of AI. 'Affiliated groups' support the aims of AI but function in isolation without the status of a structure or a section.

TASKS

1 Try to draw an organization chart of Amnesty International.

2 Try to explain Amnesty International using any of the models or approaches outlined in this chapter.

Sources:
http://en.wikipedia.org/wiki/Amnesty_International#Organisation (accessed June 2009).
http://www.amnesty.org/en/who-we-are (accessed June 2009).
http://www.amnesty.org/en/who-we-are/history (accessed June 2009).
http://www.amnesty.org.uk/content.asp?CategoryID=10084&ArticleI D=2413 (accessed June 2009).
http://archive.amnesty.org/report2008/eng/about-amnesty-international.html (accessed June 2009).

10.2 EXTEND
YOUR LEARNING

can benefit from understanding and considering the different frameworks and contributions in this important area to increase their own ability to structure their organizations in ways most suited to the goals they are pursuing, the resources they have available or can develop, and the internal and external context in which they are operating. Many additional organizational configurations, forms and types are discussed in the literature. The companion website provides discussion of a selection of important and interesting additional forms and configurations including the virtual, federal, human service, consensual, Shamrock and triple-I organization forms.

MODELS OF STRUCTURAL DEVELOPMENT AND ORGANIZATIONAL LIFE-CYCLES

Much of the work on organizational structure recognizes the inevitability of change and development for making and keeping organizations effective and thus

Table 10.7 Comparing structural and contextual ambidexterity

	Structural ambidexterity	Contextual ambidexterity
Ambidexterity is achieved through . . .	. . . separating exploitation and exploration activities in different organizational subunits or teams.	. . . individual employees dividing their time between exploitation and exploration activities.
Locus of decision making on splitting exploitation and exploration activities are . . .	. . . made in centralized way at top of the organization.	. . . made in decentralized ways on the frontline.
Top management supports ambidexterity through . . .	. . . defining structural arrangements to enable separated exploitation and exploration activities.	. . . developing organizational context (i.e., performance management and social support) in which individuals act.
Individual roles in organization . . .	. . . are clearly defined.	. . . are relatively flexible.
Employees need . . .	. . . specialist skills.	. . . generalist skills.

Source: Adapted from Birkinshaw, J & Gibson, C (2004) *Building an Ambidextrous Organization (AIM Research working paper series) MIT Sloan Management Review,* 45(4): 47-55.

ensuring their survival. However, like other metaphors, using the term 'survival' already conveys assumptions about the nature of organizations. In this case, the term implies that organizations are alive and, like all living things and beings, develop over time and die eventually. In the case of organizations, however, death is not always an appropriate way to conceive of their end. The creation of large numbers of new companies each year is inevitably followed by the failure of a significant proportion of them early in their existence. In that sense there clearly is a life cycle reminiscent of biological entities. However, a number of companies will change form and many will be taken over and absorbed into other organizations. Have such companies died or ceased to exist in any meaningful way? Equally, companies that go into receivership and have their assets sold, only to reappear in another guise or under new ownership could be said to have died or survived, depending upon the definition of 'death'.

Life cycle conceptions are common in management and OB and are applied to groups (see Chapter 7) and other social entities, products, industries, and also organizations. In this section we will review a number of developmental conceptions and contributions that deal with structural aspects of organizational growth and ageing. One of the best known models of this type is Greiner's (1972) stage model of organizational growth and development. This model (see Figure 10.15) identifies a number of stages through which organizations typically develop as they age and grow in size. During each stage of development, organizations grow in relatively stable ways ('evolution'), with individual stages characterized by particular management and organization design approaches. Organizations typically reach a crisis, characterized by a particular management problem, which is dealt with through disruptive change ('revolution'). Organizations that successfully resolve these crises enter the next stage of development and with this typically a phase of relatively stable growth. In a commentary on the model 26 years after it was originally published, Greiner (1998) stated that the fundamental logic of his model still holds with transitions between phases still posing challenges, although reality is of course much more complex than the simplified model can convey. Thus, phases are not as clearly delineated as the model suggests. Also, a sixth phase may be emerging with external linkages (e.g., strategic alliances, networks) providing opportunities for further growth rather than purely internal solutions to the challenges firms face. Finally, Greiner also discusses the evolution and revolution of professional service firms which pose different challenges compared to the industrial and consumer goods companies the original model was aiming at.

Similarly, Quinn and Cameron (1983) describe four organizational life cycle phases:

1 *Entrepreneurial phase.* This stage is typified by the presence of an owner/manager, little formal control and an emphasis on survival.

2 *Collectivity phase.* During this phase it becomes less easy for the owner/manager to control every aspect of the business and delegation becomes a key part of the process.

3 *Formalization phase.* During this phase an organization is mature, stable and predictable. Achieved through the development of rules, procedures, meetings and communication between people.

4 *Elaboration phase.* The next phase introduces a process of differentiation into the organization as it attempts to fight stagnation. It could include the introduction of a holding-company concept or of a divisionalized structure in an attempt to allow innovation and increase motivation and performance.

To these four stages a fifth can be added based on the work of writers such as Cameron *et al.* (1988):

5 *Organizational decline.* There are two forms of decline. The first is a decline in absolute terms, a reduction in the physical size of the organization. The second relates to what could be described as relative decline, through

Figure 10.15 The growing pains of an organization

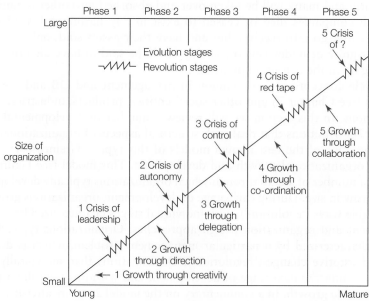

stagnation. The lethargy brought on as a result of age, size, bureaucracy and passivity towards the competitive environment allows competitors to dominate the market.

Whetten (1980) identified four response options to decline:

1 *Generating.* This is about anticipation and continual adjustment of the organization in retaining its relationship with the markets and so on.

2 *Reacting.* Organizations can take the view that decline is a temporary change and that the basic approach should be to follow existing procedures more precisely. Unfortunately, by the time the decline is recognized as a long-term threat, it is often too late to take effective action.

3 *Defending.* Management often attempts to match the organization to the perceived new situation. This inevitably leads to cutbacks across a broad range of cost. As a consequence there is a danger of starting a downward spiral of cutbacks, which eventually leads to total failure.

4 *Preventing.* By adopting this approach an organization attempts to influence the environment. This can be done through mergers and acquisitions, marketing initiatives and by lobbying politicians in an attempt to influence trading conditions.

Clearly, the generating approach should be the most effective way for any organization to remain in an integrated relationship with its environment over a long period of time. The major difficulty of achieving such a flexible organizational framework is in managing the process. Being adaptive implies being close to the numerous different elements within the overall environment. There is simply not the time, opportunity or knowledge at the higher levels of most organizations to control and manage such complexity effectively. They must rely less on the vertical hierarchy for decisions, and communication and co-operation must occur at the lowest levels possible within the organization (Toffler, 1985). Barth (2003) demonstrates that the degree of fit between the strategies followed, management skills, organization structure and the performance of the firm are related to industry maturity. These dynamics are also discussed in relation to the reinforcing cycles (Johnson *et al.*, 2005) discussed above.

STOP & CONSIDER

To what extent can organizational decline be explained by organizations paying too much attention to internal reporting relationships and not enough to the external customer needs?

CONCLUSIONS

This chapter demonstrated that a considerable number of options are available with regard to the design of an organization, all of which have advantages and disadvantages. The structural form of an organization determines the jobs that people do; shapes the behaviour of employees; and determines of interaction with customers, suppliers and so on. Structure also determines the nature of reporting and control relationships. At several points in the discussion the notion of an interactive relationship between organization and environment was introduced, as were a range of other perspectives on how structure evolves and finds expression in real organizations. The design and structure of an organization is an area in which managers make choices. The form of the organization is not something that occurs by chance, or as a result of some dictat from shareholders or other organizational sponsors. Managers are constrained by a number of forces when designing structure including size, history, technology, markets and so on. Also influencing design are the understandings that managers have about organizational purpose, objectives and the role of people within it.

Now to summarize this chapter in terms of the relevant Learning Objectives:

- **Describe the main structural choices available to organizations.** There are a number of distinct organizational frameworks. The simplest is an entrepreneurial structure which would tend to be found in smaller organizations. Also introduced were the departmentation (for example functional and divisional structures) and hybrid-based structures (matrix for example). Other organizational frameworks introduced include the project and networked structural forms. Mintzberg's approach to functional arrangement was also discussed, as was bureaucracy. Descriptions of each of these forms of organization and relevant discussion of them in the broader context is included in the appropriate sections of this chapter.

- **Understand how the need to differentiate and compartmentalize the work of an organization is at variance with the need to integrate activities.** The process of structuring an organization is necessary in order to achieve a number of objectives including the need to break down the overall activity into discrete jobs and areas of responsibility. However, customer experience does not neatly break down into such compartments. The customer inevitably wants to be able to deal with a streamlined process that involves minimal inconvenience and necessity to interact with more than one person. In all organizations the customer process invariably involves several 'compartments' working together. So the compartments created by the structure must interact effectively if the customer experience is to be achieved in a way which would encourage repeat business. This is what some of the structural frameworks are intended to achieve – for example the matrix, delayered, flexible and virtual forms.

- **Assess the significance of the development of more recent perspectives on structure.** Organization structure reflects the ways in which the physical arrangements are organized in seeking to achieve operational objectives. As such it reflects a social process involving how managers seek to position their organizations relative to the environment in achieving commercial success. The more recent approaches to organization design are a reflection of some of the trends apparent in seeking to find ways of differentiating organizations and seeking to capture

an advantage in the marketplace. In some industries change is very fast and the networked, project and similar organizational configurations allow coalitions to be formed that enable various contributing parties to achieve more than they could individually. The significance of these approaches is that they demonstrate that structure is about the application of a formula, but one of creativity and the development of innovative ways of looking at the needs of customers and how these can be met within a social arrangement that also needs to function internally.

- **Explain the life-cycle concept as it would be applied to an organization.** The terms 'life cycle' and 'survival' are metaphors which convey assumptions about the nature of organizations. They imply that organizations are alive and, like all living beings, develop over time and eventually die. In the case of organizations, however, life cycle and death are not always appropriate ways to conceive of existence. Large numbers of new companies are created each year – inevitably followed by the failure of some, the partial development and growth of others, while some remain very small and others may merge or be taken over. Have companies that merge or stay small died or ceased to exist in any biological way? Equally, companies that go into receivership have their assets sold, only to reappear in another guise or under new ownership could be said to have died or survived, depending upon the definition of 'death'. The relevant section in the chapter introduces a number of relevant models and discussion of these ideas.

- **Discuss the contingency model and its relationship to organizational structure.** Contingency is an approach to structure which reflects an interactive relationship with the environment - Figure 10.9. It suggests that there are two categories of contingency variable, external and internal contingency factors. These factors are the 'input' that managers interpret in seeking to understand their business (and personal) significance. This intention is filtered through a number of factors such as the capability and willingness of the organization to change or adapt its structural form. It is an approach that can explain differences between the structures of organizations with otherwise similar features and conditions. The contingency approach captures all of this complexity by simply suggesting that structure depends upon the circumstances!

DISCUSSION QUESTIONS

1 'All organizations, just like people, go through life-cycle phases and ultimately die.' To what extent is this true? Justify your views.

2 Outline the matrix organizational form. Discuss the relative advantages and disadvantages of it.

3 To what extent might the view that theatre can be used as a metaphor for organization offer any value in understanding structural issues?

4 'Organizations with fewer layers of management will face significant problems in the future as their managers will not have the opportunity to be involved in taking big decisions before they have total responsibility thrust upon them.' Discuss this statement. What are the implications for management development and organizational design?

5 Describe bureaucracy and its various forms. In what ways and to what extent does bureaucracy have a part to play in modern organization design?

6 'Organization structure has no bearing on success. It is people who create success (or failure) as a result of their decisions, actions and performance.' Discuss this statement.

7 'Mintzberg identifies a much more effective basis for thinking about organizing work activity than is offered through the literature on structure.' Discuss this statement.

8 Describe the contingency approach to designing an organization. How does it differ from the traditional views on structure?

9 'Structure reflects nothing more than the means through which power and control over employees can be exercised by managers.' Discuss this statement, justifying your views.

10 To what extent is the ambidextrous organization (e.g. Raisch and Birkinshaw, 2008) simply a different way of describing the organic organization as identified by Burns and Stalker (1961)?

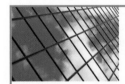

CASE STUDY

Lloyds Banking Group announces organizational changes

Lloyds Banking Group employs some 140 000 people in the UK and operates under four principal operating divisions:

- *Retail*: With over 30 million customers it has the largest branch network in the UK supported by telephone and internet services.

- *Wholesale*: Working with corporate and commercial customers including entrepreneurs, sole proprietors and global multinationals.

- *Insurance*: This operates in two main areas: General Insurance (home, motor, etc.); and Life, Pensions and Investments (retirement, protection and investment products).

- *Wealth and International*: Made up of three divisions – Wealth, Asset Management and International and operates in 35 countries across Europe, Asia, North and South America.

The major companies within the group include Lloyds TSB, Halifax, Bank of Scotland, Birmingham Midshires, Cheltenham and Gloucester, Clerical and Medical, Insight Investment, Intelligent Finance, Lex, Scottish Widows, and St James's Place Bank.

The following extracts are from a press release issued by the company on 9 June 2009:

> Lloyds Banking Group is announcing a number of organisational changes, primarily in its Retail division. These changes follow a careful and detailed review by the business of the Group's mortgage brands, which are amongst the strongest in the UK. The Group will operate a multi-brand mortgage business whilst removing some of the overlap that exists in its extensive portfolio.

Cheltenham & Gloucester branch network to close

> The Group is closing its network of 164 C&G branches in November as C&G focuses on building its significant mortgage and savings direct

and intermediary businesses. These changes will result in the loss of 833 full-time jobs which will affect up to 928 full time and part-time colleagues.

C&G is writing to its customers to explain the changes. C&G customers who wish to use a branch can, as now, manage their C&G mortgage and savings accounts at any of the more than 1 800 Lloyds TSB branches. For the overwhelming majority of C&G branches, there is an existing Lloyds TSB branch within 400 metres. Customers can also manage their accounts and open new mortgage and savings accounts over the phone and by post. There will be no change to the terms and conditions of existing C&G savings and mortgage accounts.

More broadly, Lloyds Banking Group has a substantial branch network and will continue to have a strong presence on the high street across the UK.

A multibrand mortgage business

As previously announced in December, Lloyds Banking Group will operate a multibrand mortgage business. We will continue to offer new mortgages in the intermediary market through; Birmingham Midshires, C&G, Halifax and Scottish Widows brands. From 1 July, Bank of Scotland and Intelligent Finance, whilst continuing to service the needs of existing customers, will no longer write new intermediary mortgage business. These changes will result in the loss of 159 full time jobs across the intermediary sales teams.

As previously announced, Bank of Scotland, Halifax and Lloyds TSB will all operate on the high street, providing new mortgages and a range of other products directly to customers. Later this year, Bank of Scotland – which currently provides Halifax branded mortgages on the high street - will offer Bank of Scotland branded mortgages.

The Gloucester based headquarters for C&G, Halifax in West Yorkshire and the Pendeford, West Midlands, based headquarters for Birmingham Midshires will remain very important locations for the Group. The Group's mortgage businesses will continue to be managed primarily from these key centres.

Retail product and support functions

Retail is combining a number of product and support roles, such as product development, risk and finance across both heritage businesses. One integrated business unit will be formed which will be based across a number of different locations. This will result in the loss of around 168 full-time jobs across the UK over the next 12 months.

Personal loan business

The Group's personal loans product team will be moved to one site in London and there will be a reduction in the number of colleagues employed in this operation. These changes will result in the loss of up to 265 full-time jobs, mainly based in Chester.

The Group is also making changes to its Black Horse Personal Finance business which provides point of sale finance to customers. The Black Horse direct sales operation is being increased, including potentially recruiting more colleagues next year, while, at the same time, the number of Black Horse centres will reduce from 92 to 61. Black Horse is also reorganizing its CarSelect business and will move from Cardiff to Birmingham. On a combined basis, these changes will result in the loss of 140 full-time jobs by October.

Managing change for colleagues

All affected colleagues have been briefed by their line manager today. The changes to the business will result in the loss of circa 1 660 full-time jobs. Lloyds Banking Group is committed to working through these changes with colleagues carefully and sensitively. The unions Accord, GMB, LTU and Unite were consulted prior to this announcement and will continue to be consulted throughout the process.

The Group's preference is to use natural turnover, make less use of contractors and to redeploy people wherever possible to retain their expertise and knowledge. Where it is necessary for colleagues to leave the company, it will look to achieve this by voluntary severance. Compulsory redundancies will be a last resort.

Helen Weir, Group Executive Director, Retail said: 'It is always difficult to make decisions about our business that affect our colleagues. We will work through these changes carefully and sensitively and continue to consult closely with our unions throughout the process.'

TASKS

1 Imagine that you have just been given the task of designing the organization structure for the Lloyds Banking Group. Given the complexity of the group as outlined above, how would you set about the redesign task and what might the redesigned structure look like?

2 Check the Group's website to find out if the changes indicated in this press release were implemented or have changed again since 2009.

Sources:
http://www.lloydsbankinggroup.com/home.asp.
http://www.lloydsbankinggroup.com/media/pdfs/
  lbg/2009/6409pressrelease.pdf.
  Reprinted with permission.

FURTHER READING

Armistead, C. and Rowland, P. (1996) *Managing Business Processes: BPR and Beyond*, Chichester: wiley, This is an edited book with contributors drawn from a wide range of organizations and academic disciplines. It seeks to review the basis of process approaches to organizations and what it means to manage from that paradigm. As such it does intersect with the design of organizations at a number of levels.

Brown, H. (1992) *Women Organizing,* London: Routledge. Chapter 3 is worth reading in the context of the contingency and systems approaches, as it provides a detailed review of social context within which organizations function and the basis of women creating organizations for their own needs.

Daft, R.L. (2007) *Understanding the Theory and Design of Organizations* (International edn), Thomson Learning.

Goold, M. and Campbell, A. (2002) *Designing Effective Organizations: How to Create Structured Networks,*

Chichester: John Wiley. Seeks to explore the virtual organization and how to achieve it without destroying what already exists.

Handy, C.B. (1989) *The Age of Unreason,* London: Arrow Books. This text takes a view of organizations and their relationship with the environment as its core. It explores how this relationship has changed and the potential for future design frameworks.

Hatch, M.J. and Cunliffe, A.L. (2006) *Organization Theory: Modern, Symbolic and Postmodern Perspectives*, Oxford University Press.

Josserand, E. (2004) *The Network Organisation: The Experience of French World Leaders*, Cheltenham: Edward Elgar. Reviews the French experience of four industries in which decentralization and cross-functional relationships became essential for success.

Scott, W.R. (2003) *Organizations: Rational, natural and open systems* (5th edn), Prentice Hall.

COMPANION WEBSITE

Online teaching and learning resources

Visit the companion website for Organizational Behaviour and Management 4th edition at: http://www
.cengage.co.uk/martinfellenz to find valuable further teaching and learning material. For full details,
see 'About the website' at the start of the book.

CHAPTER ELEVEN

©nycshooter/istock

ORGANIZATIONAL TECHNOLOGY

LEARNING OBJECTIVES

After studying this chapter and working through the associated OB in Action panels, Discussion Questions and Case Study you should be able to:

- Understand what is meant by the term technology and how it influences both the operational activities found within organizations and the jobs that people undertake.

- Explain the impact of technology on the organizations that employ it.

- Outline the relationship between technology, politics and change in managerial decision making.

- Discuss the influence of technology on power, control and work organization

- Appreciate how the application of technology can result in alienation and the degradation of labour.

INTRODUCTION

The concept of technology is most frequently associated with the application of computers and automation to work activities. However, there are other perspectives about technology and how it influences the operation of organizations that are important to consider. In the past, technology literally referred to the machines and the methods of production associated with them. However, today it can be regarded as a much broader and unfortunately often rather vague term which alludes to a broad spectrum of organizational influences, together with the related social connotations. Technology is an important topic in management and OB because of its fundamental impact on organizations and on individual and collective behaviour in organizations, and because it is central to understanding how objectives are achieved in organizations.

We begin this chapter by providing a general definition of technology in organizations. We then review the important systems view of organizations which provides a useful lens into the nature and role of technology in organizations. We consider traditional and contemporary organization theory contributions to the issue of technology in organizations that will help understand how technology impacts on OB and management. We then discuss a range of relevant aspects of technology including its role in manufacturing and service organizations and the role of modern information and communication technology.

TECHNOLOGY – A DEFINITION

From its semantic roots, the word 'technology' refers to the application of skills and knowledge for practical purposes. Like other terms in management and OB, multiple different definitions of technology exist. While many of them are relevant and add value, we offer a definition that provides a useful platform to consider the phenomenon and its many alternative conceptions. Applied in the context of organizations, the term 'technology' incorporates the equipment, procedural and social perspectives associated with how work is undertaken. Thus, we refer to technology as *the methods in which relevant material, technical, procedural, informational, cognitive and social resources are deployed to achieve desired outcomes*. In simple terms, technology in organizations is about *how* work is accomplished.

Technology
Represents the ways in which material, technical, procedural, cognitive and social resources are deployed to achieve desired outcomes.

Technology can be considered at different levels. From a macro perspective such as organization theory or macro-economics, organizations themselves can be seen as a form of technology (see also Chapters 1 and 10 on organizations as means to achieve objectives). Depending on the main focus of an organization, they are often categorized as production or service organizations, and are said to employ different core technologies. Core technology refers to *the means employed in the transformation activities that lead to the main outputs of the organization (or unit)* such as cars (Ford Motor Company) or financial services (Ford Credit). As this example shows, the core technology employed may differ not just across organizations but also across parts or subunits of a single organization. Thus, technology may be considered at subunit or task levels, reflecting answers to the questions how different subunits go about their work, or how a specific task is accomplished, respectively. The term 'high technology' (or 'Hi-Tech' for short), often used in everyday language as referring to particular methods and equipment that are seen as at the cutting edge, or to the units and organizations employing them, is not usually used by management and OB researchers.

Core technology
Refers to the means employed in the transformation activities that lead to the main outputs of the organization such as cars (motor company) or financial services (bank).

Historically, interest in technology reflects a process in which human endeavour is oriented towards solving real problems, experimenting with new ways of doing familiar things or simply finding out new knowledge. Changing uses of the concept have gone from technology as a precise term with little significance to a rather vague notion with a considerable degree of importance in terms of its value to organizations and society. Fox (1974a) introduces an attempt to define technology from the perspective of the industrial sociologist and distinguishes between material technology (the tangible aspects of technology that can be seen, touched or heard) and social technology (the social and behaviour shaping devices of structure, control, co-ordination, motivation and reward systems). Winner (1977: p. 10) identifies three general applications of the term technology:

- *Apparatus.* This category of technology refers to the physical apparatus or materials that are necessary for the achievement of tasks. It includes the tools, machines and instruments needed to undertake work either in support of people's actions or as an automatic means of producing goods and services.

- *Technique.* This refers to the purposive aspects of human activity through the application of skills, methods, procedures or routines as a means of achieving objectives.

- *Organization.* This use of the term refers to social arrangements including factories, bureaucracies and teams established to achieve particular goals. It is the framework within which the apparatus and techniques are practised.

The problem with both of these approaches to technology is that any specific example is likely to contain elements of different categories. One example is the introduction of information technology which necessarily includes hardware (e.g., computers) and software (e.g., operating systems, applications) as well as specific behavioural routines, organizational structure adjustments and many other tangible and intangible changes. Another example is the introduction of new equipment in work settings which is likely to influence both the techniques used and the social organization within which work is carried out (see Edmondson *et al.*, 2001). In terms of Fox's classification scheme there is also likely to be an interaction between the 'hard' aspects of the material technologies and the 'soft' aspects of social order and behaviour within which the tangible aspects will be operated. That should be apparent in the Management in Action panel.

Many other classification schemes for technology exist that may be of particular interest and value for specific purposes. For example, engineers tend to be concerned with equipment aspects; industrial engineers with efficiency of use; product designers with implications for the physical end result; managers with control, levels of throughput and cost; and social scientists with behavioural, social, political and control aspects of technology. Braverman (1974) incorporated these concerns into two broad categories of approaches to technology thinking about and studying:

- *Engineering approach.* Regards technology as a representation of machines and equipment. Emphasizes the physical aspects and internal relationships between these components.

- *Social approach.* Considers technology from the perspective of the impact on labour and views it as a social construction serving the needs of particular groups within society.

From a management and OB perspective, the various aspects represented by these different approaches are all relevant and important. As we have seen in other discussions in this book, adopting exclusive perspectives limits the insights that explanatory models can provide. In fact, separating them and pursuing insights into technology from limited perspectives would likely result in the omission of important factors (see Dery *et al.*, 2006). The particular approach, perspective or metaphor

Material technology
The tangible aspects of technology that can be seen, touched or heard.

Social technology
The social and behaviour shaping devices of structure, control, co-ordination, motivation and reward systems.

11.1 EXTEND YOUR LEARNING

MANAGEMENT IN ACTION

Technology can be simple

Nathan was the industrial engineer in a factory that made motor car tyres. His job was to find the most efficient methods of work for each task. One of the operations in the factory was known as bead creeling. The bead is the part of the tyre that fits onto the metal rim. The bead is made of rubber-coated wire formed into a circle (creeled) several layers thick to create the strength to grip the wheel rim safely. The machine for this job coated a number of copper wires with rubber. These were then formed into the bead around a circular metal disc before a guillotine cut the wires to length. The completed bead was pushed from the metal disc by spring loaded fingers and the process started again.

In engineering terms, the machine was relatively simple as the process contained few components and few operations, but there was one problem with it. The extruded rubber used was hot and sticky. This was necessary as it helped the layers of the bead to stick together, forming a solid component. As a consequence the bead usually stuck to the metal disc and failed to eject when the fingers tried to push it off. No solution had been found. Teflon-coating the disc caused an adverse reaction in the rubber; making the disc out of stainless steel did not work; changing the rubber compound caused performance problems in the finished tyre and changing the speed of the machine made no difference. However, the operator had developed a solution that worked (throw a cup of water over the metal disc), but it damaged the machine and made a mess around the workstation.

At home Nathan was spraying his garden with weedkiller from a hand-held spray gun and he wondered if it would be possible to use the same approach on the bead machine? He took a spray bottle into work with him and showed it to the operator. The operator tried it out but it was not quick enough to cover the full circumference of the metal disc in-between production cycles. Nathan contacted the maintenance manager and explained the problem. The maintenance manager thought for a while and then said that it would be possible to put a couple of spray heads around the circumference of the metal disc, linked to a simple trip switch and pump. One of the maintenance engineers was asked to develop the device. After 2 days of tinkering with tubing, switches and spray heads, a working system was running on the machine and it worked. Everyone was amazed that this had not been thought of before. Water use reduced, the operator avoided getting wet and working in unpleasant conditions; a safety hazard was eliminated; the machine was in better condition not being constantly wet and the beads themselves were dry, which meant that they could be used in the next stage of the production process more quickly.

TASKS

1   This example suggests that sometimes a low-technology solution can offer superior results at a cheaper cost compared to more complex and comprehensive solutions. On what basis can it be decided which would offer the best approach?

2   What does this example suggest about how people interact with technology?

of technology that is adopted will significantly influence the subsequent view of the role and impact of technology in and on organizations (see Chen and Hirschheim, 2004; Orlikowski, 2000; Richardson and Robinson, 2007).

What emerges from this review of different conceptions is that technology reflects much more than simply machine- and computer-based approaches to work. Technology is a concept that has profound implications for the nature of organizations as well as for the behaviour of organizational members. Moreover, it has relevance for managers in that it is a key determinant of the processes through which objectives are achieved. The role of technology offers the opportunity to holistically consider the interactions among the multiple facets of organizations and organizational behaviour. This is a central focus of the systems approach to organizations. The next section will introduce and discuss this important framework and its relevance for understanding technology in organizations. Technology also has an ethical perspective as is evident from the Examining Ethics example.

Systems views of organization and technology

The notion of a system goes back to the early considerations of Greek philosophers and the earliest precursors of science (von Bertalanffy, 1972). Systems theory originated in the physical sciences as a means of reflecting how a number of elements or subsystems interact within a cohesive whole, and by the middle of the last century, comprehensive formulations of the ideas of General Systems Theory had been popularized across academic disciplines through the work of eminent contributors to systems theory and to *cybernetics* (the study of control and communication in systems) such as Ashby, Boulding, von Bertalanffy, Wiener, and others (for an overview and review see von Bertalanffy, 1972; Buckley, 1968; Katz and Kahn, 1966). It was embraced by many social scientists and has been particularly successful in the organizational sciences (see Katz and Kahn, 1966/1978; Jackson, 2000). While systems theory generally is concerned with the interplay among elements of a system, the open systems view is particularly focused on the processes within a system and their link to the interactions between and among a system and its environment.

The open systems view of an organization (Katz and Kahn, 1966; Scott, 2003) carries profound implications, yet is in essence very simple. Systems cannot survive without exchanging resources with the environment, and the issue of survival is at the heart of open systems thinking (Scott, 2003). In simplified form they can thus be described as an entity linked through ongoing exchanges (inputs and outputs) with their environment (see Figure 11.1). Systems transform their inputs into outputs, and through creating value as part of this transformation process they enable their own survival. These input and output activities and exchanges create interactive relationships between the organization and its environment. It is very much a cyclical and interactive process. For example, Volkswagen AG makes motor vehicles which it sells to its customers for money. The money thus obtained is one of the means that enables the organization to acquire other resources necessary for its survival and its further operation such as human input (through wages), legitimacy to trade (through taxes and compliance with legal rules and social expectations), raw materials (through purchases) and so on. Information is also central part of these ongoing transformation and exchange activities (e.g., changing consumer preferences can be considered in new model development; information about customer demand – or lack thereof – of a particular model is used for determining pricing policy and/or production planning).

Figure 11.1 Open systems model of an organization

EXAMINING ETHICS

Employee surveillance

Employers need to collect employee information and data for various business reasons. However, sometimes information can be collected for purposes that have more to do with power and control. In the UK the Trades Union Congress (TUC) produced a booklet identifying monitoring and surveillance practices sometimes used with questionable justification. They include:

- Monitoring telephone, e-mail and Internet use. Although there is no legal obligation to provide such facilities for private use, some organizations monitor such use.

- CCTV and video surveillance. These can be justified by ensuring security and safety, but they can also monitor employee behaviour.

- Covert monitoring. Secretly listening to and recording employee phone calls can be used in circumstances other than when serious crime is suspected.

- Vehicle monitoring. The use of company vehicle tracking and monitoring devices to monitor location and routes, control cost and employee driving habits.

- Information about health, disability and access to medical records. These can have relevance to work activities, but can also provide more information about lifestyle etc.

- Sickness and absence records.

- Drug and alcohol testing results.

- Other sources identify sexual orientation and sexual behaviour as areas in which some employers collect information.

Within Europe a range of legislation exists that would apply to employee surveillance and its uses. Large employers usually have written policies about what information will be collected, for what purposes, how it will be stored and used.

Sometimes employers take surveillance too far and some employ security experts to track potential threats to the commercial interests of the business; employees possibly abusing company facilities; employees questioning decisions; or employees possibly revealing sensitive company information. For example, in 2007 Wal-Mart in the USA employed former senior CIA officers, senior defence department security specialists, FBI, special forces and police officers as senior executives within its head office security, threats and investigation functions. Wal-Mart was reported to have engaged in the widespread surveillance of employees, members of its board of directors, shareholders, people who were critical of company policy and practice, and at least one firm of management consultants. Around the same time Sears was reported to have incorporated spyware into its customer community computer system that was intended to monitor customer Internet use. Boeing has also been accused of employee surveillance, the surveillance of a board member and at least one journalist, and the use of deception to obtain telephone records of employees and journalists. All three organizations made clear through the press that they had taken action to ensure that any problems had been dealt with and that in future they would operate surveillance policy and practice within the law in relation to customer and employee privacy.

TASKS

1 How would you identify the boundary between appropriate and inappropriate monitoring of employee behaviour?

2 What ethical issues exist in deciding what a legitimate approach to surveillance is?

3 What role has technology in identifying risks to an organization?

Sources:
http://www.ciozone.com/index.php/Management/Wal-Mart-Spying-Good-Bad-Or-Just-The-Wave-Of-The-Futureu.html?kw=swal&gclid=CMXQkfCE0JsCFd0B4wod-japLQ (accessed July 2009).
http://community.ca.com/blogs/securityadvisor/archive/2007/12/20/sears-com-join-the-community-get-spyware.aspx (accessed July 2009).
http://www.seattlepi.com/business/339881_boeingsurveillance16.html (accessed July 2009).
http://money.cnn.com/2007/04/04/news/companies/walmart_spy/ (accessed July 2009).
http://www.usatoday.com/money/industries/retail/2007-04-12-wal-mart-thur_N.htm (accessed July 2009).
http://www.privacydigest.com/2008/01/12/after+criticism+sears+plugs+web+sites+privacy+hole (accessed July 2009).
http://consumercal.blogspot.com/2008/01/more-trouble-for-sears.html (accessed July 2009).
http://www.wired.com/threatlevel/2007/10/boeing-employee/ (accessed July 2009).
http://www.theregister.co.uk/2007/11/16/boeing_employee_surveillance/ (accessed July 2009).
TUC (2009) Your Right to Privacy at Work: http://www.tuc.org.uk/tuc/privacyatwork.pdf (accessed July 2009).

The basis of the open systems model is that a company starts life with only the essential core of the business present (along with minimal levels of support). This is essential to the creation of the organization, as without it the organization could not achieve its intended purpose. It is only later, according to Katz and Kahn, that the organization begins to elaborate itself by adding adaptive or buffering functions, thereby creating more elaborate structural frameworks. These adaptive functions can include personnel, accounting, public relations, marketing and research and development for example. The process of elaboration goes through a number of stages that describe the structural elaboration through differentiation and integration (see Chapter 10) and the resulting development of increasingly differentiated internal elements and dynamic processes linking them. Along with this increasing internal complexity, the control function needs to be elaborated to keep up with this internal complexity and the increasing numbers of external relationships necessary to sustain the organizations operation and thus survival. Further evolution and environmental change inevitably leads to additional elaboration of the organization's formal and informal structures and processes. Many of these developmental processes are similar to the model of organizational development and evolution proposed by Greiner (1972; see Chapter 10).

In this context, technology is conceived of as any means by which this transformation of inputs (e.g., raw materials, information, capital) into outputs (e.g., products, services) and the exchanges with the environment are accomplished. Clearly, from this perspective technology includes all the different aspects (physical, technical, informational, procedural, behavioural, social, etc.) discussed in the different conceptions of technology in the previous section.

The systems view of organizations has been one of the most important influences on management and related disciplines. Systems thinking is found at the heart of many theories and conceptualizations dealing with phenomena such as groups, organizations, internal structures and processes, exchanges, change and stability, and many others. It has provided important contributions that apply to many types of increasingly complex mechanical, biological and social systems (e.g., Boulding, 1956, 1985) and provided the framework for attempts to describe universal characteristics of systems across biological and social spheres (e.g., Miller, 1978) (see Figure 11.2). Some streams of related research have evolved into *complex adaptive systems theory* which considers the emerging qualities of complex, self-organizing systems such as organizations (see Maguire *et al.*, 2006) and provides useful approaches to consider organizational and interorganizational issues such as leadership, strategy, operations management, interorganizational collaboration, and many others (e.g., Lichtenstein *et al.*, 2006; Mason, 2007; Pathak *et al.*, 2007; Wycisk *et al.*, 2008).

TECHNOLOGY, CHANGE, EVOLUTION AND TECHNOLOGICAL DETERMINISM

Technology deployed in organizations changes all the time. Periods of relatively steady, incremental change and development driven by iterations of existing technologies can be interrupted by transformational change that reflects more fundamental evolution of the ways in which work is accomplished. Often, such changes go alongside with economic changes in markets as well as social and even cultural changes. The co-evolution of technology, organizations, markets, societies and cultures is never driven by just one of these factors. Rather, the complex interplay between these factors influences the outcomes. The first and second industrial revolutions changed the nature of organizations along with substantial changes in all the other factors mentioned.

11.2 EXTEND
YOUR LEARNING

Figure 11.2 Taxonomies of systems arranged by increasing complexity

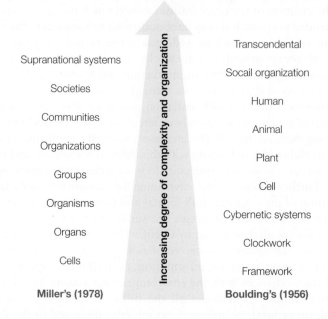

Chandler (1984), for example, describes the development of the M-form (for multidivisional form, a particular type of large industrial organization adopting the divisionalized structure discussed in Chapter 10) as arising from the arrival and wide application of technologies such as communication (e.g., telegraph), transportation (e.g. railways), and energy (e.g., electricity) technologies along with improved manufacturing and distribution capabilities (for example through preservation technologies such as refrigeration and canning). However, his comparative analyses of the developments among different countries also show that these technologies alone cannot account for such profound changes. Economic as well as physical conditions (e.g., the availability of raw materials or the geographical size of economies) and social, legal, cultural, political and historical factors all contributed (and contribute) to the differential adoption of technological and organizational innovations in different countries. Thus, a simplified conclusion is that new technologies can enable but do not irrevocably cause such profound change. Note that in relation to technology we use the term 'enable' exclusively to indicate that technology can provide possibilities that would not exist without it. It is not meant to indicate that technology (in the forms of tangible and intangible technical artefacts) is sufficient cause for any novel activity or subsequent change because human and social agency is also required (see Watson, 2008).

Industrialization
The process of change from an agricultural to a manufacturing-based economy.

Industrialization is *the process of change from an agricultural to a manufacturing-based economy* and can serve as a useful example of technological innovation contributing to a fundamental evolution of organizations and their environments. In a work published after his death, Herbert Blumer considered the nature of industrialization and its influence as an agent of social change (Maines and Morrione, 1990). In this work Blumer suggests that the term industrialization is frequently used in a way which conjures up the stereotypic image of the development of the factory system, urbanization of residence, the use of machines, the dilution of skilled work and the formation of a managerial class, etc. To this framework is added an emotional veneer as the result of "inadequate study, partisan interests, doctrinaire concerns, and agitation on behalf of social reforms" (p. 15). To Blumer this view of industrialization emerged largely from Great Britain as a Maines and Morrione, 1990: reflection of the particular historical process.

GOING GLOBAL

Open access for Africa

Information and communication technology (ICT) is claimed by many to be a prerequisite for economic development and future growth. It has been argued that approximately 30 per cent of world economic growth and 40 per cent of new jobs will be associated with ICT. The knowledge economies based on ICT require infrastructure, hardware, software and communications equipment as well as appropriate education and training to allow people to engage with it successfully. This presents problems for developing countries, and a clear divide is emerging between developed and developing countries in relation to the digital age: the digital divide. For example, across Africa millions of people have never made a telephone call, let alone had access to computer technology or the Internet. Large swathes of that continent are being left behind in the opportunities that ICT can provide and are destined to remain in poverty in both absolute and relative terms. Unless that situation can be changed they will be on the wrong side of the digital divide. The World Bank and others report that universities across much of Africa only have access to Internet bandwidth equivalent to that of a domestic consumer in Europe but at a much higher price. The UN reported that in 2002, countries making up sub-Saharan Africa had about 9.6 Internet users per 1000 population compared to developed countries with 450 per 1000.

Open access broadly means access without restriction or the obligation and protection from copyright. It could apply to the publication of scientific journals and material, manuals or written documents, as software. In relation to software it is referred to as open source knowledge, meaning that access to coded knowledge is free of charge and open to subsequent modification, adaptation

and innovation. Opportunities for open access are necessary to prevent monopolies in which large organizations dominate a market and artificially inflate prices for access and use of their equipment, facilities, software, etc.

Open source initiatives require significant communications infrastructure and Internet Protocol (IP) based networks. Experience so far in relation to attempts to use submarine cables to link Portugal and countries in West Africa has not delivered the full potential for a number of reasons associated with ownership structures in the countries involved and the commercial arrangements that flow from that. The increased development of ICT infrastructure and open access information need the right conditions to be in place based on strategies to facilitate competition, encourage investment, linking infrastructure with educational and government projects, appropriate regulatory frameworks for the market and a staged approach to its development.

TASK

1 How would you go about trying to improve ICT development in sub-Saharan Africa? If you were a manager in a sub-Saharan company, how would the lack of access to modern ICT affect operations and management?

Sources:
http://www.inderscience.com/www/pdf/ijtmv45n12_oainafrica.pdf (accessed July 2009).
http://www.sciencebase.com/science-blog/open-access-in-africa.html (accessed July 2009).
http://www.openaccessforafrica.org/ (accessed July 2009).
http://www.apc.org/en/news/openaccess/africa/why-african-governments-need-listen-case-open-acce (accessed July 2009).
http://mediaresearchhub.ssrc.org/grants/funded-projects/the-case-for-open-access-in-africa-mauritius-case-study/the-case-for-open-access-in-africa-mauritius-case-study (accessed July 2009).

This debate is also of relevance to modern times in relation to developed and developing countries. The above Going Global example introduces the emerging problem of the digital divide and the challenges facing an entire continent in seeking to catch up with the more developed world in relation to information and communication technologies (ICTs).

Blumer makes several points of distinction between industrialization and technological change, including (Maines and Morrione, 1990: pp. 18–20):

- *Nonindustrial technological change.* There are a number of technological developments that have no impact on the level of industrialization. For example, the introduction of the steel axe as a replacement for the stone axe is an example of technological development that need not directly impact on the level or type of industrialization within which it is used.

- *Industrialization as one form of technological development.* Industrialization brings with it many changes other than those based on technology. For example, the increased use of female labour, the emergence of a managerial class, factory-based work, and the development of organized labour are just some of the consequences of industrialization that are not, of themselves, technologically based.

- *Transplanted industrialization.* It does not automatically follow that technology evolves as part of the process of industrialization. Many of the developing countries of the world have received transplanted technologies as part of packages of industrialization.

- *Causal relationships.* It is frequently implied that there is a direct link between technology and society. For example, it can be suggested that the introduction of advanced technology creates social problems in society by increasing alienation. This approach tends to underestimate the complexity and chain of events involved in such relationships.

- *Ambiguity.* The term technological development contains a higher level of ambiguity in terms of its interrelationship with social change than does the concept of industrialization. In other words, technology contains a wide variety of meaning which it is difficult to restrict in attempting to tease out the social implications.

In terms of the relationship between the terms 'industrialization' and 'technology', Blumer is approaching the question from the perspective of social change. These concepts can be considered to be overlapping circles in a Venn diagram. On occasions, they will meet and be very similar, but on other occasions they will differ. Blumer does not spell out in detail his view of technology, but it is clear that he adopts a mechanical view rather like the apparatus concept of Winner.

Yet industrialization is also fundamentally influenced by behavioural dynamics. Watson (2008) provides a succinct summary of the role of human motivation in bringing about the industrial revolution. Thus, human motivation and both individual as well as collective behaviour must also be considered when trying to understand the link between technology and change. This must be approached as a reciprocal process because just as technology can influence behaviour, there is also a strong argument for the 'social shaping of technology' through selection and adaptation of technologies (see McKenzie and Wajcman, 1985) by individuals and groups.

For organizations, our main focus here, the role of technology has long been seen as one of an external determinant. This perspective, also called technological determinism or the *technological imperative*, has focused on the influences of technology on organizations to the degree that many contributions and frameworks accepted technology as the cause of organizational changes in structure and other characteristics. The work of Woodward, discussed in the next section, is an example of such contributions. Despite the fact that most contemporary views accept mutual influences between technology and organizations and other relevant elements, the view of technological determinism is important because it helped identify technology as an important factor that was then integrated into contingency theory (see also the discussion of the Aston studies in Chapter 10 and the next section).

Technological determinism
This perspective, also called the technological imperative, focuses on the influence of technology as the principal cause of organizational change to the structure and other characteristics of an organization.

PERSPECTIVES ON TECHNOLOGY IN ORGANIZATIONS

The impact of technology on an organization has been studied from a number of perspectives and based on different views of what technology actually is. In this section, we introduce a number of the most influential contributions and approaches to classifying technology that are particularly important for understanding formal arrangements in organizations.

Woodward and production technology

In a search for the best ways to structure organizations, Joan Woodward (1965) studied 100 manufacturing organizations in the electronics, chemical and engineering industries. After initially inconclusive results she found a clear link between structural arrangements and performance once she took the degree of mechanization of the core transformation processes into account. She identified 10 different types of approaches to production in her sample that are usually simplified into three different types of production technologies. The three types are:

- *Unit or small batch*. This indicates that items are made in very small quantities, perhaps even being made individually, specifically to a customer order.
- *Large batch or mass production*. This reflects the manufacture of large quantities, perhaps on an assembly line as in the manufacture of motor cars.
- *Continuous process*. This reflects operations where the raw material is taken from its initial state and subjected to a continuous sequence of processes until it is in its final form ready for sale. Typical examples are oil refineries and chemical plants.

Although there were differences between the organizations in the sample, there was a clear tendency for the production technology (i.e., the core technology of the production firms studied) to be associated with a number of organizational characteristics, particularly aspects of structure (see Table 11.1). It also became apparent that those organizations of each type that were the most commercially successful were closer to the structural norms described in Table 11.1. This was widely interpreted as evidence for technological determinism, which indicates technology as an important contingency factor that influences organizational structure (see Chapter 10).

However, the definition of production technology used in this study is very broad and there are many differences in operational activity between large batch and mass production environments. Consequently it has been argued that the categories adopted were simplistic and may have reflected continuity in the operational process rather than technological complexity (Bedeian, 1984). Moreover, the argument that technology is an important *determinant* of organizational structure can be challenged on many grounds because other considerations such as managerial choice, institutional influences, or the impact of other contingency factors such as age, size or competitive forces play important roles.

Perrow – a continuum from routine to nonroutine

Another important and influential approach to the notion of technology in organizations was introduced by Perrow (1967, 1970). Unlike Woodward, who focused her research on describing the core technologies used by manufacturing firms, Perrow's work focused on work unit or departmental technology and primarily considered two aspects of the tasks a unit performs. The first is variety, which reflects the number

Variety
Reflects the number of exceptions encountered in performing a units' tasks, or, in other words, the degree to which different and potentially unexpected events are part of the transformation processes a unit performs.

Table 11.1 Conclusions from Woodward's study regarding structural arrangements

Production technology	Organizational characteristics
Unit or small batch	Flat structure Most labour-intensive and highest ratio of direct/indirect labour Medium/low span of control Highly skilled operators Decentralized decision making Organic structure
Large batch or mass production	Flat/medium structure Medium ratio of direct/indirect labour High span of control Low skills among operators Centralized decision making Mechanistic structure
Continuous process	Tall structure Least labour-intensive and lowest ratio of direct/indirect labour Lowest span of control Highest number of support staff Highly skilled operators Decentralized decision making Organic structure

Analysability
The degree to which a transformation process, its individual steps and activities, and the impact of any action taken can be analysed and understood.

Routine technology
This is characterized by situations involving high analysability and low variety. Therefore, tasks are predictable and fully understood, and the ways in which they can best be accomplished can be easily determined. See also nonroutine technology.

Craft technology
A situation in which analysability is low and variety is also low. Represents situations in which the way in which desired outcomes can be achieved are often not fully understood or even understandable. See also engineering technology.

of exceptions encountered in performing a units' tasks, or, in other words, *the degree to which different and potentially unexpected events are part of the transformation processes a unit performs.* High variety would reflect a high degree of uncertainty due to the number of factors that may become relevant in task completion. The second aspect is analysability, or *the degree to which the transformation process, its individual steps and activities, and the impact of any action taken can be analysed and understood.* Low analysability reflects uncertainty based on lacking data, insufficient information processing capacity and ability, or simply the unpredictable and unclear causal nature of the task. Figure 11.3 presents the framework created with these two dimensions.

The framework identifies four different technologies named routine, craft, engineering, and nonroutine. Routine technology is characterized by *high analysability and low variety.* Therefore, tasks are predictable and fully understood, and the ways in which they can best be accomplished can be easily determined. Routine technology tends to be institutionalized through formalization and standardization of the recurring activities. Typical examples of such departmental technology can be found in mass production (e.g., assembly lines) and mass service (e.g., banks, fast food) environments. Operators receive training in how to perform their jobs in prescribed ways, and extensive control mechanisms are often in place. The high degree of standardization and formalization often focuses on efficiency but can create problems when products or services offered do not meet customer or client expectations or needs. Decision making is centralized, and unit structure is typically mechanistic.

In craft technology *analysability is low and variety is also low.* The way in which desired outcomes are achieved are often not fully understood or even understandable. The limited range of tasks that need to be performed offers the opportunity to develop and deploy a significant amount of skill which often includes substantial

Figure 11.3 Perrow's framework of departmental technology

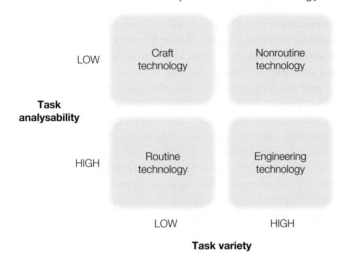

degrees of implicit and tacit knowledge. Tacit knowledge, an important concept in this context, is *knowledge derived from first-hand experience that cannot be easily communicated or taught*. For this reason departments that employ craft technology often have extensive on-the-job training and long periods of formal or informal apprenticeships during which newcomers work closely with more experienced members to learn the necessary skills. Examples for craft technology include furnace workers who learn how to 'grow' single crystal blades for jet engine turbines, fashion designers, or many types of fine goods design and creation. In craft technology, traditional ways of performing tasks and doing work are often institutionalized socially through complex behavioural routines and supported by an appropriate culture rather than by more formal rule-based approaches. Thus, formalization and standardization are little used, task-related decision making is decentralized to skilled operators, and horizontal and informal communication is used extensively, which results in more organic structures.

Engineering technology has *high analysability together with high variety in the tasks to be performed*. The range of tasks are typically handled according to well established and highly structured approaches, procedures and techniques. Unlike craft technology, engineering technology employs highly explicit knowledge that is typically acquired through formal education (engineering, accounting and operations management are good examples). Because the approaches to dealing with tasks are well developed and firmly established, individuals working in these environments often develop a strong disciplinary or functional perspective on their work which is shared among the members of a unit. Any arising task conflict (see Chapter 9) is usually resolved using impersonal procedures and according to external standards that employ clear, shared and accepted criteria for decision making. Many aspects of the work are formalized and standardized but this is often heavily influenced by professional practices developed outside the organization. As a result of all these characteristics, unit structures tend to be more mechanistic.

Finally, nonroutine technology reflects *low analysability together with a high degree of variability in the tasks*. Transformation processes are not well understood, and the wide range of tasks that units face require them to deploy significant resources for analysing activities and solving problems. Usually both tacit knowledge from prior experience and explicit knowledge from formal training are deployed together in performing tasks. Any unit that deals with tasks requiring high degrees

Tacit knowledge
Reflects knowledge derived from first hand experience that cannot be easily communicated or taught.

Engineering technology
A situation in which high analysability together with high variety exists in the tasks to be performed. The range of tasks is typically handled according to well established and highly structured approaches, procedures and techniques. See also craft technology.

Nonroutine technology
This reflects situations involving low analysability together with a high degree of variability in the tasks. Transformation processes are not well understood, and the wide range of tasks to be done require the deployment of significant resources for analysing activities and solving problems. See also routine technology.

of skill and knowledge to be deployed as part of novel and uncertain projects can be expected to use nonroutine technology. Such units usually have organic structures with little formalization and standardization. Decision making is decentralized, and intensive communication takes place through formal and informal linkages and networks. Nonroutine technology is typically found in units charged with developing new strategies, and project teams dealing with unique challenges. Some forms of applied social and academic research are also good examples for the conditions for nonroutine technology.

At the heart of Perrow's framework for work unit technology lies the distinction between routine and nonroutine tasks that is indicated by the diagonal arrow in Figure 11.4 (note the similarities to programmed and unprogrammed decisions in Chapter 8). Different combinations of task analysability and task variety indicate different levels of routine/nonroutine in a unit's tasks. This distinction is driven by uncertainty (see Chapter 10) which is linked to increasing ambiguity and equivocality (as task analysability declines) and increasing complexity and change (as task variety increases). Many of the issues regarding fit between environmental uncertainty and organizational structure discussed in Chapter 10 are also relevant for Perrow's framework indicating fit between unit technology and aspects of the unit's task environment. Generally, and similarly to the discussions on organizational structure, the higher the degree of routine tasks, the more mechanistic a unit will be, while increasing nonroutine will likely be reflected in more organic unit structures.

Thompson – resource and technology matching

Task interdependence
Refers to the degree to which tasks differentiated through the division of labour remain operationally related to each other.

Another important and influential contribution to the study of technology in organizations was provided by James Thompson (1967) who considered the fundamental linkages between task requirements and organizational and procedural responses. In his work Thompson focused on task interdependence, which refers to *the degree to which tasks differentiated through the division of labour remain operationally related to each other.* Just as differentiation requires appropriate integration (Lawrence and Lorsch, 1967), tasks containing separated activities require co-ordination to be appropriately effective and efficient. Thompson posits that different forms of task interdependence are reflected in different types of technology, which each require a particular approach to co-ordination. We consider three technology types and associated forms of interdependence and co-ordination in turn.

Figure 11.4 Assessing the degree of task routine/nonroutine

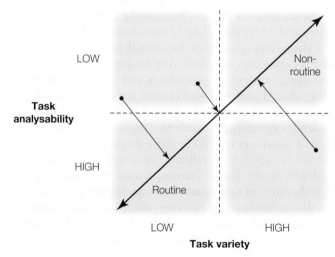

The first type of technology Thompson identified is mediating technology. It is named because this form of operational technology brings together ('mediates') what would otherwise be independent activities or needs. Good examples of this technology are retail banks, fast food franchises, chain pharmacies or opticians, or sales and brokerage organizations. Each unit (branch, restaurant, franchise, sales office) serves its own customers largely without interaction with other units. The performance of the overall organization is determined by the added contributions made by the individual units. The interdependence between units (for example different branches) is minimal. It is called *pooled interdependence* because the outputs of each unit (e.g., revenues) are combined centrally ('pooled') which does not affect or interfere with the ongoing operation of each unit. Overall organizational performance is thus determined in an additive way (see also Steiner's [1972] concept of additive tasks discussed in Chapter 7) and can be increased through growth in the number of operating units – as long as they do not negatively affect existing business (a process also called 'cannibalization'). With mediating technology and pooled interdependence the typical way of co-ordination is co-ordination through standardization (see Chapter 10) which tends to be very cost effective. From a strategic perspective, the operations of companies employing mediating technology are usually highly scalable which enables additive growth.

The second type of technology identified by Thompson is called long-linked. Long linked technology describes the sequential processes most obviously found in assembly line factory operations. Different activities and steps in the relevant production and transformation processes are carefully planned and designed to fit together as the output of each task provides the input for the subsequent task. The end result is the product of a clearly determined sequence of intermediate steps that are all necessary for the transformation process to be completed. The form of interdependence found where long-linked technology is employed is called *sequential*, as the individual activities take place one after the other. In sequential interdependence, co-ordination is typically achieved through extensive planning resulting in specific schedules for each contributing unit. The plans and schedules need to be adjusted if relevant conditions change or if any part of the sequential processes fails to perform as expected. This makes co-ordination more cumbersome and resource-intensive in long-linked compared to mediating technology. Feedback is used to deal with any unforeseen deviations from the plan, but often such feedback mechanisms are located separately from the normal task activities and workflow. The horizontal communication used is often largely routine and therefore quite formalized and even automated (e.g., automated messages for delivery of parts from manufacturing unit to warehouse).

Thompson's third type of technology is intensive technology, which describes processes where different units interact constantly with each other during the transformation process. In fact, transformation processes using intensive technology cannot be fully planned or predicted because the necessary type and order of activities depends on the particular constellation of actors and the task itself. By its very nature intensive technology is comprised nonroutine tasks (consider the link to Perrow's framework introduced above). Therefore, each unit depends on others' outputs as inputs for their own activities, and they need to be highly responsive to each others' requirements. The type of task interdependence found where intensive technology is deployed is called *reciprocal*, and co-ordination is achieved through mutual adjustment (see Chapter 10). Reciprocal interdependence poses the highest demands on the management and co-ordination of activities, and is most resource intensive in terms of communication linkages and intensity, time, effort, and skills, among other things. Ongoing feedback is crucial for effective task accomplishment, and feedback mechanisms using intensive horizontal communication linkages, team structures, and close physical proximity are commonly deployed and closely integrated into the

Mediating technology
The first type of technology Thompson identified brings together ('mediates') what would otherwise be independent activities or needs. It is associated with pooled interdependence. See also intensive technology and long-linked technology.

Long-linked technology
The second type of technology identified by Thompson describes the sequential processes most obviously found in assembly line factory operations. It is associated with sequential interdependence. See also intensive technology and mediating technology.

Intensive technology
The third type of technology identified by Thompson describes processes where different units interact constantly with each other during the transformation process. It is associated with reciprocal interdependence. See also long-linked technology and mediating technology.

work of the different connected units. Comprehensive formal information and communication systems as well as extensive informal connections and social linkages and networks support real-time information flow among all units and individuals involved. The communication media employed are often very rich (e.g, direct face-to-face contact; see Chapter 8). Mintzberg's adhocracy form (see Chapter 10) is a typical example of structural arrangements that can support intensive technology.

Technical core

Refers to the operational units charged with the central transformation processes (a manufacturing plant, or a payroll processing unit). To be able to work efficiently such units need to be protected from sudden changes and uncertainties. See also boundary spanning unit.

Boundary spanning units

Units that buffer (protect, insulate) the operating core from environmental uncertainty. See also technical core.

Thompson also indentified the need of the technical core, which refers to *the operational units charged with central transformation processes* (such as a manufacturing plant, or a payroll processing unit), to be able to work efficiently and unperturbed by sudden changes and uncertainties. Structurally, this is often achieved by creating boundary spanning units that *buffer the operating core from environmental uncertainty*. Examples for such boundary spanning units include marketing and market research units (which reduce uncertainty about customer preferences and demand) or legal departments (which can protect the operating core from interference due to regulatory matters or legal requirements and proceedings). Buffering the technical core is one way in which deployed technologies are supported by structural arrangements. There are other observable linkages between the technologies identified by Thompson and the structure of organizations.

The highly standardized core units in mediating technology are particularly exposed to changes in customer preferences or demand, which is why such organizations (e.g., fast food chains) often develop large marketing and market research units. The long-linked technology creates tightly coupled links between many units co-ordinated by plans and schedules and is very sensitive to input and throughput problems as well as demand fluctuations. Therefore we often find backward integration (i.e., the acquisition or long-term alliance with suppliers) as well as highly centralized direction and large technostructures with functions such as industrial engineering that can deal with throughput issues in large industrial manufacturing companies. Demand fluctuations are often dealt with through large forecasting units as well as through strategic linkages or forward integration into distribution channels. In intensive technology, changes in any element relevant for the operating core units can create problems, and a typical way of dealing with this is through the investment into technical and organizational means of increasing responsiveness (e.g., Grote *et al.*, 2009) as well as the deployment of additional resources. Thus, we find high degrees of excess resources (also called redundant or 'slack' resources) in such organizations.

Other classic contributions to organizational studies of technology

The importance of technology was also investigated in the seminal programme of research conducted by Pugh, Hickson, Hinnings and their colleagues at Aston University. Starting in the early 1960s, the so-called Aston studies focused initially on the relationship between size, technology and organizational structure. In terms of technology these studies utilized three categories:

1 *Operations.* This type of technology reflected the nature of the transformation process, the techniques used.

2 *Materials.* This aspect of technology reflected the nature and characteristics of the things that were being processed. For example, different metals have different properties and need to be processed differently. Equally, in a service organization each customer's needs are slightly different (the various patients visiting a doctor) and therefore the processing (treatment) would differ accordingly.

3 *Knowledge.* This reflects the skill and ability required to undertake the tasks necessary to achieve the objectives. For example, a nuclear power station would not be capable of operating at full capacity unless the employees, specialists and managers were trained and skilled at the tasks expected of them.

Another important contribution to the study of technology and organization was the seminal work of Burns and Stalker (1961) already discussed in Chapter 10. The distinction between mechanistic and organic (or organismic) structures introduced by them in part reflects responses to the technology found in the organization's environment. Similarly, other early contributors such as Lawrence and Lorsch (1967) also considered technology as an environmental contingency factor, and its impact on organizational structure and functioning thus at least in part externally determined. More recent views of technology in organization studies have introduced a fundamentally different view which will be discussed in the section on 'Enacting Technology' below.

In summary, the approaches to technology in organizations discussed above contain different perspectives on the subject. Whatever approach to the concept one adopts, however, it is clearly much too simplistic to equate technology simply with machines, computers and automation. From the studies reviewed it is clear that there are links between technology and structure, work organization, hierarchy, people management, customer needs, operational strategy and organizational success. In addition there is also the suggestion that some forms of technology offer opportunities to become more sensitive and adaptive to the environmental pressures surrounding the organization. In being able to adapt to the changing environments surrounding the organization there is assumed to be a greater likelihood of commercial success in the short term and survival in the long term. Clearly, therefore, what emerges from these contributions is a view of technology as providing opportunities to support managerial objectives.

ASSUMPTIONS ABOUT TECHNOLOGY

A number of commonly held assumptions relate to the nature of technology, its impact on organizational functioning and operation:

- *Neutrality.* The first assumption is the view that technology is a neutral process. That is not so. It is management who determine the organizational objectives that are being sought and the way that they will be operationalized through technology. Technology is, therefore, something that is part of the 'design and achieve' aspects of management and can be used by managers in an attempt to direct and control employees. It can also be used to ensure that the entire organizational process works to a management-determined agenda. In that sense, technology is under the control of management, to use as they consider appropriate.

- *Impact.* Taking a very limited view of technology, it is frequently asserted that it is only in the production areas of an organization that technology has any impact. This may be where technology has its most obvious impact, but it is not the only area of involvement. For example, administrative and accounting procedures, control reports and quality-control data are just some of the specialist areas where technology has a considerable role. In addition, opportunities to integrate islands of manufacturing activity or stages in service delivery have also been evident over the past few years. These approaches take a broader view of technology and incorporate the people, material, flexibility, adaptability and political aspects into the concept.

● *Modernism.* There is a general tendency to see new things as better than those that went before. Nowhere is this more evident than in advertising of consumer products. Television and static advertising campaigns are forever attempting to persuade customers that a reformulated product such as a cleaning agent is a considerable improvement over the previous product. The same is true of many aspects associated with technology. Components produced by computer-controlled machines are said to be more accurate, reliable and better than those produced by skilled employees. While this may be true in some circumstances, not everything can be so easily fitted into this perspective. For example, recent research has shown that although dealing with bank call-centres represents the third most frequently used method, it is the least popular among customers. Internet banking is by contrast proving more popular *(Management Services,* 2003b).

● *De-skilling.* It is often assumed that the introduction of higher levels of technology will allow the level of skill required from employees to be reduced. This should provide two main benefits for management. First, reduced labour cost, as skill is expensive. Second, reduced training times and cost, as it is quicker and cheaper to train people to a lower level of skill. However, offsetting these claimed advantages are the higher skill levels needed to design and operate more complex equipment and processes as well as the new jobs created as a result of the different technologies adopted. It is also apparent that this assumption is based upon a relatively narrow definition of technology in that not all technology deployment leads to de-skilling of employees.

● *Structure.* The studies described earlier tend to emphasize the structural aspects of technology. This is not the only area of impact for technology. It also affects control processes by reinforcing the dominance of managers and technical specialists over general employees. It is part of the political process of management and provides the opportunity for new products and services. Structure is also influenced by technology in very complex ways that tend to be understated by the earlier theories.

● *Efficiency.* It is assumed that the application of technology will increase efficiency in operational activity. While his may hold true in a very narrow sense, it does depend how broad a measure of efficiency and productivity is used. For example, the cost of the acquisition of the technology, retraining the workforce and the cost of the new jobs created are just some of the additional costs to take into account in determining the balance of benefit. Again, this view is based upon a narrow conception of technology and from the implications referred to earlier; efficiency could be one of the least important variables involved in the adoption of technology. For example, the application of new process technologies as a means of demonstrating to customers a commitment to consistent and high quality as well as a means of forcing change in working practices can have many benefits in addition to efficiency.

ENACTING TECHNOLOGY – ACTIVITY AND SOCIAL CONSTRUCTION PERSPECTIVES

The classic contributions introduced above and the assumptions about technology discussed in the previous section tend to reflect a view of technology as something that exists independent of human activity, even though it may only be useful or even usable if humans interact with it. A very different approach to technology is the view of technology as enacted. This view does not accept that technical arte-facts (e.g., machines, software) constitute technology, but rather that technology is what emerges through the interaction of humans with such technical artefacts. This broader view, which is accommodated by the definition we presented at the beginning of this chapter, describes technology as socially constructed. Similar to Giddens's (1979, 1984) structuration argument discussed in Chapter 10, the duality of social structure also applies to technology ('duality of technology', Orlikowski, 1992) in that human behaviour creates technical artefacts but is in turn constrained and enabled by such artefacts (see Jones and Karsten, 2008). Technology can there-fore be described as the structures that are manifested by the repeated interaction between humans and technical artefacts (DeSanctis *et al.*, 2008; DeSanctis and Poole, 1994; Orlikowski, 1992, 2000). Such interactions are strongly influenced by the properties of the 'nuts and bolts' or 'bits and bytes' of the artefacts in question, but the perception of stable structures that are experienced as tangible technology (e.g., the machines in a car assembly plant, or the telecommunication devices and computers in a bank's trading room) often masks the reality that the technology in question in large part reflects not only physical artefacts but also the activity pat-terns of technology users (i.e., the assembly workers and industrial engineers in the car plant; the traders in the trading room).

STOP & CONSIDER

During the Roman occupation of Britain some 2000 years ago it was possible to have central heating incorporated into the design of a building. However, when the Romans left after about 300 years, that technology fell into disuse and was not routinely taken up again (as far as housing is concerned) until the 1970s. Try to find explanations for that. What do your conclusions suggest about how technology develops across time?

One of the reasons for the common view of technology as purely residing in the technical artefacts (hardware, software, etc.) is that most often abstract descriptions are used that focus on the physical artefacts and the prescribed contributions of users to the intended functioning of the machine or socio-technical system. These descrip-tions typically include human activity (as in operating manuals, standard operat-ing procedures, or other documentation) but do this in highly depersonalized and abstract ways that makes technology users part of technology almost as if they are part of the machine or technical system. Such abstract descriptions of how people can (or should) use technology are favoured over other alternatives even though they fail to capture the full range of behaviour necessary to make the technology perform as intended (see Brown and Duguid, 1991). Such canonical practice (which refers to *the formal, espoused and prescriptive description of how tasks should be done and how technology is to be deployed*) does not suffice for objectives to be met. Canoni-cal practice 'can blind an organization's core to the actual, and usually valuable practices of its members… that determine the success or failure of organizations' (Brown and Duguid, 1991: p. 41). Citing Orr's (1990) research with Xerox copier maintenance technicians, Brown and Duguid thus argue that it is noncanonical prac-tice (which refers to the *often improvised approaches that are iteratively developed in actual ongoing work, and shared and collectively improved among the interacting members of a working community*) which reflects how work really gets done. Maybe more importantly, noncanonical practice enables the work to achieve its objectives often despite of rather than because of the information and official prescriptions of canonical practice. This point is supported by the fact that work-to-rule, which refers to *workers adhering strictly to agreed approaches to how work should be performed*

Canonical practice
Refers to the formal, espoused and prescriptive description of how tasks should be done and how technology is to be deployed. See also noncanonical practice.

Noncanonical practice
Refers to the often improvised approaches that are iteratively developed in actual ongoing work activity and shared and collectively improved among the interacting members of a working community. See also canonical practice.

Work-to-rule
Refers to a situation when workers adhere strictly to prescribed approaches (policies, procedures and rules) on how work should be performed, refusing to deviate from any formal agreement, rule or standard procedure in the process. See also work manipulation and work restriction.

and refusing to deviate from any formal agreement, rule or standard procedure, is a highly effective industrial relations weapon because it usually stops organizations in their tracks (see Chapter 9). Similarly, managers, supervision practices and control mechanisms that try to enforce canonical practice often create difficulties and can even contribute to failure because they are neither appropriately concrete and contextualized nor sufficiently flexible. Such intense control enforcing canonical practice creates difficulties for operators of technology because often 'they are held accountable to the map, not to road conditions' (Brown and Duguid, 1991: p. 42).

An important aspect of the distinction between abstract descriptions of technology (i.e., canonical practice) and the actual approaches used (noncanonical practice) is the concept of communities of practice (e.g., Lave and Wenger, 1991; Wenger, 1998) which are *ongoing groups of people who interact and actively share information while engaging in an activity they are individually and collectively committed to*. Such communities of practice enable shared understanding of technology and work to be developed and updated based on practical experiences and active social exchanges. The interaction within communities of practice are central to how technology is enacted in any particular setting. For managers who consider how technology can be deployed and managed, it is important to recognize these social aspects and dynamics and their role in making both technology and the work for which it is deployed and employed successful (see also Brown and Duguid, 2001; Schulz, 2008). For a slightly different view about how communities of practice can work in different parts of a single entity (the National Health Service) with the same broad objective, but working in isolation and different compartments, see the Employee Perspective.

The enactment of technology perspective is important and useful for a number of reasons. First, it provides accounts that identify and explain the role of human behaviour and agency in the way technology is used. Second, it shows the social dimension of technology by explicitly recognizing and describing how technical and social aspects interact. Finally, it offers an approach to thinking about and studying technology in organizations that counters both simplistic technological determinism and managerial choice views by combining their relevant explanations as well as dynamic considerations of social interaction in one framework. The impact and importance of the *duality of structure perspective* (Orlikowski, 1992) and *adaptive structuration theory* (DeSanctis and Poole, 1994) has been immense, particularly in the research on information systems where this perspective has provided important and useful contributions (Jones and Karsten, 2008).

Communities of practice Ongoing groups of people that interact and actively share information while engaging in an activity they are individually and collectively committed to.

THE POLITICS OF TECHNOLOGY

An important aspect of management activity in organizations is that among other dimensions it always includes a political dimension. Individual managers are in competition with each other for scarce resources, as there are never enough resources to fully address the needs of all departments, functions or projects. Managers also seek to achieve personal, professional and functional goals within their organizations in order to develop their careers. Management is also political in that the pursuit of objectives requires interaction and co-operation with many other stakeholders who may have conflicting objectives. Part of this process involves using technology as a political tool in order to achieve control or influence. For example, the power of head office administrative departments to dictate work routines in bank branches can be achieved by the introduction of computer systems which require branch staff to follow prescribed routines in processing customer transactions and queries.

There is another form of people control achieved through the political use of events and activities that engage with their lives. It is this form of control to which

EMPLOYEE PERSPECTIVE

Family doctors and the dissemination of medical information

Family doctors (general practitioners in the UK) are in the front-line of family medicine and work in the midst of the communities that they serve. Over the past few years teams of doctors have set up partnerships, consisting of between five and 10 doctors working in a health centre providing a range of diagnostic and treatment services, often in conjunction with other health care specialists.

The government identify clinical and medical targets and priorities and these create reporting obligations, diagnostic protocols, crisis response procedures, population screening targets and patient choice initiatives. Such information and material are invariably communicated electronically from the Department of Health. In addition, medical services locally are provided on behalf of a Strategic Health Authority and a Primary Care Trust who also send out information about local/regional meetings in relation to general or specific aspects of health care; agreements and invitations to tender for the provision of particular services; and financial information in the form of budgets and financial priority changes. Add to that the information sent out from pharmaceutical companies about treatment/drug developments, prices, and availability; correspondence passing between doctors, hospital consultants, heath care workers about specific patients or general updating on treatment protocols in a particular context; and finally, information from other suppliers of health-related products and services as well as general building/office supplies etc. that any organization might need, and the stage is set for a vast volume of electronic communication.

Consequently, the volume of electronic communication received by a practice during the course of a week is vast and presents several problems to a general practitioner such as Dr David Lightwing in his role as both a doctor and partner of his medical centre. Although the volume of items of electronic communication is variable and unpredictable, it might average between 500-1000 items in a typical week (including patient-specific communication). It is clearly too much for one person to deal with and so several ways of dealing with this have had to be developed by Dr Lightwing and his colleagues. For example, pharmaceutical company related information is allocated to a specific doctor to read, sort, prioritize and deal with in the most appropriate way. Material from the Chief Medical Officer is allocated to another doctor in the practice in order to assess, prioritize and forward to the other doctors as necessary. Such practices can help to ensure that important information coming into the practice is at least identified and prioritized and that the relevant people have access to the information in order to take appropriate action based on it. But that still leaves the problem of the sheer volume of information coming into the practice, all of which has some degree of importance and significance to patients and the provision of health care in the community. However, at the end of the line is an individual doctor trying to provide the best level of care to an individual patient in relation to their particular symptoms or condition who is likely to be swamped with the sheer volume of information landing on them that may or may not have any relevance to the patient in the consulting room at any point in time!

TASKS

1 If you were Dr Lightwing, how would you go about trying to deal with the variety and volume of electronic communication each week, and how would you ensure that important medical and treatment items were not missed in the course of the process?

2 In addition, how could you ensure that you as a doctor identified and retained the high volume of information received about new treatment and medical protocols that become available?

Source:
Conversation with Dr David Lightwing, a general practitioner based in Yorkshire. Reprinted with permission.

Braverman (1974) refers in his seminal work that contributed to the labour process debate. Essentially, this debate turns on the use to which human labour is put in the transformation of raw material into commodities for capitalist markets and

Labour process debate
Seeks to explain management's relationship to workers (and their role) in capitalist economies and in relation to capital owners.

the part played by managers in the organization of that work. It is management that determines the nature of any technology in any given context. Consequently, it is a management agenda that determines the use of technology and how human labour will be accommodated around it (see Fisher, 2007, for an illustrative example). The application of technology can provide managers with a number of direct benefits including tighter control over the work process, pace of work, skill levels required and the design of work. All of these lead to a reinforcement of the dominant position of managerial control over organizational functioning and cost of operational activity. Howcroft and Wilson (2003) make the point that employee participation in information systems development is frequently justified on the basis of achieving a better, more effective end result that will result in an empowered workforce. They argue that underneath such foreground rational assumptions are instrumental politically motivated justifications that drive the need to involve users in the process.

This debate revolves around the degree of malice aforethought that managers use in taking those decisions. Is it done to control labour and reinforce management's position, is it done to further the commercial objectives of the organization, or for the benefit of employees and society? One of the key problems in researching in this area is that of being able to find out the true causes of particular managerial actions. A manager who is attempting to manipulate workers is unlikely to admit it! Many writers prefer to limit consideration of decision making to a form of rationality. Schön (1994: p. 243), for example, talks of a technical rationality in which the search for solutions to problems follows a logical pattern, and competence can be measured through the degree to which the intended effects are achieved. Also, Child (1985) argues that the social and organizational aspects of decisions are generally subordinate to financial imperatives. He goes as far as suggesting that the broader aspects are essentially consequences of the financial perspectives, not objectives in their own right. Others, however, have questioned the degree, quality and objectives of the rationality underlying managerial decision making about technology deployment and work organization (e.g., Avgerou and McGrath, 2007).

TECHNOLOGY AND ALIENATION

Alienation
Work performed under conditions in which the worker is estranged from his or her own activity in the act of production, through the sale of labour power and the subordination of skills and knowledge to the capitalist, or other external social forces. Sometimes described as feelings of powerlessness, meaninglessness, isolation or self-estrangement in which the person no longer feels part of, or involved with, the work that they do.

At a common-sense level, alienation is a form of switching off. In a work context, alienation can be seen as equivalent to not feeling meaningfully connected to the work a person does or the unit a person formally belongs to. It can be argued that the only reason organizations employ human beings is that there are some tasks for which an effective machine has yet to be developed. Looked at from this perspective, people are simply a substitute for machines. This is, of course, a simplistic argument as it ignores the social, political and economic aspects associated with human work. It does, however, provide a very stark introduction to the nature of alienation. Thompson provides a definition of alienation as follows:

> *Work performed under conditions in which the worker is estranged from his or her own activity in the act of production, through the sale of labour power and the subordination of skills and knowledge to the capitalist, or other external social forces.*

(Thompson, 1989: p. xiii)

This definition picks up a number of aspects from the earlier sociological viewpoints of writers such as Blauner, Braverman and Marx. These perspectives, which differ significantly from managerialist views of the same matter, consider issues such as exploitation, degradation through work, and de-skilling of workers. They attempt to reassess the nature of work within the context in which it is carried out.

Applying such critical and radical approaches to work in business organizations, alienation is reframed as an issue of separation, ownership and the rights of workers as stakeholders. Thus, alienation occurs as an inevitable reaction to the control of work by managers, and technology plays a significant part in supporting this process. It has already been suggested that technology is not neutral because it is utilized by managers as part of their attempts to achieve business objectives. Blauner (1964) made this assertion in relation to continuous process industries on the basis of his research in a number of technologically different operations. In doing so, his approach to alienation was based on the feelings that workers formed in response to the dominant technology. It was defined in terms of:

- *Powerlessness.* A lack of control or influence over the pace and methods of work, as well as the general working conditions and the processes involved in carrying it out.
- *Meaninglessness.* A feeling of being a very small part of a large process and that the individual's contribution had little real significance in terms of the finished product or service.
- *Isolation.* A lack of belonging, or a feeling of not being part of a team or group.
- *Self-estrangement.* A reduced feeling of self-worth as a consequence of being reduced to a number within a crowd and a lack of work being a significant focus for life.

The degree to which continuous process technologies can achieve the type of work envisaged by Blauner must be open to question from a number of perspectives, at least in the short term. For example, the number of jobs available in continuous process operations tends to be much smaller than in most other forms of technology applications. Not all products and services are amenable to continuous process technologies – a hospital, for example, cannot function like a chemical factory, although it functions 24 hours a day for 365 days a year and contains some highly skilled personnel. Given the high skill, high discretion jobs in health services settings, hospitals should be low-alienation environments. However, this does not mean that jobs in hospitals and other health and human care settings are without stressors. On the contrary, burnout, *a condition characterized by emotional exhaustion, lower concern about other people, and diminished personal accomplishment* (e.g., Cordes and Dougherty, 1993; Maslach and Jackson, 1981) is rife in such work environments. Some work environments combine these two dimensions. Call centres, for example, are both alienating and, as the services employees provide involve direct customer contact, can also lead to emotional exhaustion and other counterproductive dynamics. Not surprisingly, call centres are frequently characterized by high levels of work-related stress, absenteeism and turnover (e.g., Batt *et al.*, 2009; Houlihan, 2002; Skarlicki *et al.*, 2008). See the High Performance feature for an example of this type of problem linked to technology.

Alienation is clearly an aspect of work heavily impacted by organizational technology. Despite the variety of technologies and their differential impact on worker experiences, technology and alienation are linked. Thus, technology can adversely affect employees directly and organizations indirectly through its impact on them. It can be argued that a significant aspect of some of the features of more recent approaches to job design are attempts to reintroduce elements of ownership which may reduce feelings of separation arising from the use of technology. Job design as a means to balance the people issues with the procedural, production and social technologies available in the search for efficiency is discussed further in the next chapter (Chapter 12).

Burnout
A condition characterized by emotional exhaustion, lower concern about other people, and diminished personal accomplishment.

HIGH PERFORMANCE

Digital depression

Research undertaken by Priority Management shows that 'digital depression' is a major source of stress. It is caused by the profusion of technological and communication devices that people use in their work. The irony is that these devices were intended to make working easier. Priority Management suggest that one in three people find that technology (mobile telephones, e-mail, BlackBerry's, wireless PDAs and laptops) contributes to work stress.

Priority Management's research identifies seven signs of digital depression:

1 *Digital Darwinism*. Anxiety caused by the feeling of being left behind as technology develops. Career advancement and status can be threatened by a lack of 'latest technology' knowledge.

2 *Access stress*. An inability to detach from work as a result of continual availability through the use of portable communication devices.

3 *Cognitive interruptions*. A state of permanent interruption at work because of the unpredictable demands of communication devices used at work. Leads to a feeling of being out of control.

4 *Continuous partial attention*. Shorter deadlines, faster working environments and the increase in multitasking all mean that urgent items take priority over important items. Time for reflection, thought and consideration are lost in the race for action.

5 *Device creep*. The pressure to adopt the latest technology, device or gadget to keep up with the IT revolution

6 *IT rage*. The frustration when dealing with desktop computers. Seemingly illogical PC behaviour combined with pressure to meet deadlines is a key stress-creator.

7 *The technological treadmill*. The constant stream of communication, information and data landing on employees creates a feeling that work never ends. Often this is at its peak after a few days' holiday when it takes days to clear the huge volume of e-mails etc.

Organizations work in a global economy that has little mercy for those that fall behind, so job stress is common. Technology once thought of as the means to greater leisure, has paradoxically increased the pressure of work. This challenges organizations to find ways of making effective use of technology, whilst maintaining employee engagement and reducing stress. Any organization which fails to meet these challenges will lose its most precious resource to burnout.

TASK

1 In using new technology, how would you seek to ensure that the benefits were achieved without digital depression resulting?

Sources:
Management Services (2003) 'Digital depression' identified as a new form of stress, May.
Johnson, P.R. and Indvik, J. (2004) Digital Depression, Stress, and Burnout: Same Song, Different Verse, *Journal of Organizational Culture, Communications and Conflict*, January.
http://www.prioritymanagement.com/index.php?section_copy_id=6314&ion_id=1116 (accessed July 2009).

THE IMPACT OF TECHNOLOGY

11.3 EXTEND YOUR LEARNING

The impact of technology on organizational structure and the reciprocal relationship between these elements discussed above are not the only way in which technology affects organizations and the behaviour of people within them. One important characteristic, discussed in more detail in Chapter 12, is the use of technology by managers to control the behaviour of employees. Another important aspect of the impact that technology has in organizations is the improvements of the core technologies used in creating the main outputs of the organization or its subunits. For simplicity we distinguish between two core technology types that describe the most common value creation contributions in organizations: manufacturing and service. Few organizations are purely manufacturing or service, most contain elements of both, and all of them contain administrative tasks and functions that deal with internal maintenance and other requirements. A theatre, for example, falls firmly within the service sector. However, within a theatre, groups of people will be engaged in manufacturing scenery, costumes and the preparation of food for the restaurant, and accounting as well as other administrative tasks and functions also exist. Hill (1983) describes manufacturing as being about the production of goods for purchase and subsequent consumption. Service, by comparison, involves the production and provision of intangibles consumed at the time of creation and provision, with the consumer taking away the benefit of the service. This feature of co-creation (Prahalad and Ramaswamy, 2004), which refers to the *direct and joint involvement of service provider and consumer in the service value creation process*, is a central difference between manufacturing and service technology.

Manufacturing technology

Manufacturing is about making tangible items such as cars or washing machines for subsequent sale. New technology has impacted on this type of operation in numerous ways. Industrialization, discussed above, is an example of large-scale transformation of economies that adopt mass-production technologies. In general, manufacturing technology is characterized by tangible outputs, separation of creation and consumption, relatively high levels of management control over, and prescription of, the transformation processes, and a general focus on machinery and other capital intensive means of production. In addition, traditional manufacturing technology is often separated from customer input through boundary spanning units to reduce uncertainty which tends to increase response times to environmental change such as shifting preferences or changes in demand.

Traditionally, most manufacturing technology was developed and deployed in pursuit of efficiency which is typically measured along such dimensions as cost and resource input (e.g., raw material, energy), speed, reliability, safety, quality, unwanted side effects (e.g., noise or air pollution), and suitability for the specific product requirements. In addition, manufacturing technology has also traditionally replaced labour through more capital-intensive approaches to creating the desired outputs. The Luddite movement in England in the early 1800s is an example of craftworkers and artisans rebelling against their replacement through technology (in this case mechanized looms) by destroying the new technology.

Over time, manufacturing technology has evolved to provide not just increased efficiency in its many forms but also increased responsiveness and flexibility. Advanced manufacturing technologies (AMT) and flexible manufacturing systems (FMS) typically incorporate computers to create more flexible and consistent products. The purpose of such systems is to link together a number of machines so that items can be automatically transferred between them in successive stages of production. They also allow groups of machines to be linked together so that smaller batches of product can be made efficiently. These systems attempt to replicate aspects of the economy of large-scale production, but for small quantities.

Contemporary operations management approaches such as lean manufacturing or agile manufacturing have attempted to combine information technology with organizational and operational changes to integrate the many different elements necessary for efficient, high-quality production with the ability to learn and to respond

Co-creation
Refers to the direct and joint involvement of service provider and consumer in the service value creation process, and is a central difference between manufacturing and service technology.

Manufacturing technology
This is characterized by tangible outputs, separation of creation and consumption, relatively high levels of management control over, and prescription of, the transformation processes and a general focus on machinery and other capital intensive means of production. See also service technology.

Mass-customization
Describes a manufacturing approach that combines the benefits of large-scale mass production with customization opportunities for individual customers.

11.4 EXTEND YOUR LEARNING

quickly to changing circumstances inside and outside the organization (Bates *et al.*, 2009; Kumar, 2004). Flexible manufacturing approaches have changed the long-assumed trade-off between efficiency and customizability in approaches called mass-customization (Pine, 1993; Salvador *et al.*, 2009), which describes a manufacturing approach that *combines the benefits of large-scale mass production with customization opportunities for individual customers.* Although this idea applies equally to manufacturing and service, it is a much bigger challenge for manufacturing firms because service already typically includes a higher degree of customer orientation and involvement in the value generating transformation processes (see also Kumar, 2007; Rungtusanatham and Salvador, 2008; Squire *et al.*, 2006). However, like some other manufacturing approaches, critics have pointed out limitations in that the principle of mass customization, while compelling in the abstract, has not yielded comprehensive and pragmatic decision frameworks for managers and organizations (Kumar, 2007). Also, the inclusion of customers in the design process appears to often be lagging behind in practice, many firms attempting to use such technology are unable to fully account for the costs involved, and different technical and organizational aspects are often not sufficiently integrated (Piller, 2007). From a management and OB perspective a particular challenge is to determine how work is best organized and designed to enable mass customization to deliver on its promise (Liu *et al.*, 2006; Pine *et al.*, 1993).

Service technology

Service
Refers to the creation and provision of value through the application of knowledge, skill and other intangible resources for another party which consumes the value as part of the provision interaction.

Service refers to *the creation and provision of value through the application of knowledge, skill and other intangible resources for another party which consumes the value as part of the provision interaction.* This may or may not result in the creation of a tangible product. Legal advice, a theatre performance or a counselling session are examples of purely intangible service outputs, while a meal in a Michelin-star restaurant combines tangible (e.g., food, drink) and intangible (e.g., the waiters' attention, the sommelier's advice, the subjective experience of enjoyment and exclusivity) outputs. Service technology is therefore distinguished by intangible or mixed outputs, simultaneous production and consumption of value, lower levels of management control because of the active customer role in co-creation of value, direct customer interaction, and a focus on knowledge, skill and human contributions to the value-creation processes. Because of the inseparability of creation and consumption, the location and context of service provision is often highly relevant for the value-creation process and its outcomes.

Service technology
Distinguished by intangible or mixed outputs, simultaneous production and consumption of value, lower levels of management control because of the active customer role in co-creation of value, direct customer interaction, and a focus on knowledge, skill and human contributions to the value-creation processes. See also manufacturing technology.

Central to service technology is the direct inclusion of consumers in the value-generation process. From a management and OB perspective, this co-production of value introduces the consumer as an external element into processes that have often been seen by managers as largely under their control. However, as customers and consumers are not part of the organization, and their role can take on many different dimensions (Bolton and Houlihan, 2005), managerial control is limited. Moreover, to achieve the responsiveness and customer orientation necessary to maximize customer value in the service interaction, decision-making authority in most service situations is increasingly decentralized to the service providers.

Customer centricity
A business model that places customer value at the heart of all organizational value creation processes.

Other organizational changes are also required by organizations that comprehensively deploy service technologies. Such customer-centric organizations need to find both formal and informal arrangements and processes that enable input from and information about customers and their needs and preferences to be available throughout the organization. In this context, customer centricity refers to 'a business model that places customer value at the heart of all organizational value creation activities' (Fellenz and Brady, in press). While traditional product or company-centric views that focus on internally defined objectives such as functional or operational goals often dominate, customer-centric service organizations must adopt richer communication media among employees as well as between employees and customers, more involvement of customers in value generation processes and sharing of process control with customers, and the active engagement with and even adoption of customer perspectives by organizational decision makers (Fellenz and Brady, in press). All in all, these steps towards customer centricity challenge traditional, more production and control oriented approaches and perspectives that place high value on the pursuit of efficiency rather than on collaboration with customers and the joint creation of value. In light of the discussion of organizational forms in Chapter 10, it is useful to note that customers are rarely considered in these forms and ideal types, yet become more integral the more customer-centric an organization becomes.

INFORMATION AND COMMUNICATION TECHNOLOGY IN ORGANIZATIONS

Both manufacturing and service technologies deal with the challenge of co-ordinating multiple elements and processes while dealing with both internal and environmental change and uncertainty. Therefore, many of the changes in contemporary organizations are driven not just by developments in core technology used in transformation processes. While such technological innovations (for example, new diagnostic or surgical approaches in health care, or novel biochemical processes in the development and manufacturing of pharmaceuticals) are important and often bring fundamental changes to organizations adopting them, the most universal impact on organizations of all kinds in the last two centuries has probably come from developments in information and communication technology (ICT). Forester (1987) suggests that it is such information technology that allows the development of new techniques that impact directly on the way work is done in organizations.

Information technology, argues Zuboff (1988), differs from the technology used in the nineteenth century in one key respect: it combines the replacement of people with machines and provides a higher level of transparency through the ability of computer technology to process information. Zuboff suggests that ICT is deployed in organizations in ways that can be distinguished in different stages named *automation*, *information* and *transformation* (see also Nolan, 1972, for a compatible stage model of how ICT is assimilated in organizations). In most organizations, the first wave of ICT deployment (automation stage) has focused on (and often produced) efficiency gains through automating manual activities and replacing human labour through more cost-effective machines. The information stage produces gains in effectiveness through the comprehensive processing and use of information in important activities and processes. Finally, the transformation stage is characterized by the use of ICT to transform the activities in ways that enable the organization to perform different and novel tasks.

As an example, a hospital may use ICTs to automate previously manual patient information processing. In a second stage, the hospital may deploy ICT to provide more timely and comprehensive patient information to the medical staff that may be able to use this information for better diagnosis and more comprehensive treatment plans. Finally, the hospital may adopt novel ICTs to provide distance-monitoring facilities in the patient's home which may enable previously impossible home-stay and treatment options as part of the treatment plan for specific illnesses and patients.

In addition to efficiency, effectiveness and innovation potential of ICT, one main reason for the ubiquitous use of such technologies in organizations is their potential

to provide transparency and thus enable managerial control of many forms of organizational activities. Similar issues are discussed in the next chapter (Chapter 12).
Technologies such as RFID (short for radio frequency identification device), for
example, provide immense opportunity for automated data capture that can be used
for many different purposes. A predominant focus on the control function of modern
ICTs, however, may prevent their deployment and use in ways that can substantially
increase their value to an organization and its customers and clients (see Fellenz and
Brady, in press). Novel ICTs must also be acceptable to employees, and their attitudes as well as informal organizational norms and perceived organizational support
can contribute to technology adoption (e.g., Marler *et al.*, 2009).

It has been argued (Konsynski and Sviokla, 1994) that the failure by management to obtain the full value and potential from information technology is a consequence of the continued use of outdated paradigms of organizational functioning.
They claim that cognitive reapportionment is necessary if managers are to obtain full
advantage. The new paradigm sees organizations as bundles of decisions: decision
making is based on an appropriate allocation of bundles between humans, technical
systems, or a combination of the two.

Very few managers have an in-depth understanding of the technologies available.
In developing their careers, managers progressively move away from the operational
levels of activity. Increasingly, technology becomes something that other people
use regularly. Managers often rise through a particular discipline (e.g., accounting,
finance, production). They will have some knowledge of new technology applications within their own areas of expertise but less in other areas. In moving towards
general management positions, managers often take responsibility for disciplines of
which they have no direct experience. At the same time, technology continues to
develop within their original profession, which can bring about the danger of managers become defensive and even reactionary by resisting technology development
and innovation. Senior managers may have enough experience to be able to balance
these challenges successfully, but problems nevertheless persist. Effective measures
are needed to ensure that senior managers are not left behind in understanding new
technology, and that therefore the organization fails to adapt to and adopt appropriate new technologies. The implication of the narrow basis for the development of
most managers is apparent in the Change at Work example.

For organizations, the cost of changing ICT systems or the technical systems used
in an organization's core value creation processes can be prohibitive. Flexibility and
keeping future options open is a key requirement of new technology. However, technology suppliers make this very difficult by seeking to lock customers into their
own product range in order to protect future business. Variations in product and
technology standards prevent the easy switching from one supplier to another. Consequently, the successful adoption of new technology comes not so much from the
technology itself but from its effective integration with other work activities and
existing technologies.

Risk of failure is one of the problems that new technologies, especially new ICTs,
bring. ICT is developing at such a rapid rate that even newly deployed technologies
can quickly be superseded. A danger here is that competitors may adopt a superior,
newer generation from which they may derive a competitive advantage. At the same
time, managers may delay investment in new technologies too long, which can leave
the organization in competency traps (Levitt and March, 1988), sometimes referred
to as knowledge traps. Such traps can occur when the experience and competence in
using inferior technologies (e.g., ICT systems, software, procedures, or socio-technical
routines) produces satisfactory results which keeps 'experience with a superior procedure inadequate to make it rewarding to use' (Levitt and March, 1988: p. 322).
Competency traps can happen to individuals, teams, subunits and organizations, as

Competency traps
Sometimes also referred
to as knowledge traps.
Such traps can occur
when the experience
and competence in using
an inferior technology
produces satisfactory
results which makes it
difficult or impossible to see
the advantages to be gained
from adopting a newer,
superior technology.

CHANGE AT WORK

Changing an industry

Richard was a mining engineer gaining his experience in the UK coal industry and had subsequently worked in gold and copper mining in various countries in Africa. By the age of 45 he was regional operations director for a coal mining company in England. He was getting bored with his job with its focus on routine administrative work and finding ways to cut cost. He began to look around for another job and was eventually offered the position of director of maintenance projects with a major contractor in the railway industry. His role was responsibility for track and signalling maintenance contracts, along with the tendering and subsequent running of new and upgrade projects. Richard saw this new job as a challenge because although different, the railway and mining industries also have many similarities. Safety is a major concern in both; geological factors can create problems and significantly influence the way that work is undertaken; both are traditional in approach and people tend to make lifelong careers in them. Tradition determined the ways in which people worked and the technology that they used. There existed recognized (conventional) ways of doing things in both industries and consequently change and new technology was slow to make any inroads. Advanced technology was used, but it tended to be adaptations of existing technology rather than finding ways of mixing people and technology in different and innovative ways. Justifying this was the risk of safety problems with what appeared to be use of unproven technologies.

Looking around his new organization and watching employees at work on upgrading projects, Richard was struck by the many similarities between the tasks in mining and railway operations. For example laying, renovating and moving railway lines were tasks common to both industries and yet they were done in completely different ways. Richard quickly realized that some mining technology could be adapted to railway infrastructure maintenance. The problem was how to introduce people to this idea in a way which would encourage them to consider the possibilities, rather than reject them. A further complication was the need to persuade equipment manufactures to redesign and build large and very expensive machines.

TASK

1 How would you go about this task if you were Richard? What internal (organizational) and external (environmental) factors and challenges can you identify and analyse?

---

well as to collectives at higher levels of aggregation such as whole industries and economies. Examples here include concrete technical artefacts such as the QWERTY keyboard, or complex, multiorganizational and international arrangements such as international payment systems of interbank fund transfers (see Fellenz *et al.*, 2009).

Technological change also has implications across organizations for the economies and societies they are located in. From economic and societal perspectives, the transition period associated with the emergence of a new technology usually brings significant labour imbalances. Individuals skilled in superseded technologies are displaced from work while shortages of people with new skills emerge. This creates difficulties for organizations, governments, trade unions and individual workers. For example, removing employees with outdated skills results in having to meet redundancy costs, whilst at the same time the cost of recruiting labour with scarce skills increases. Inevitably, the level of employment in an economy reduces, with a reduction in revenue for a government at a time when state benefits may be needed to support the displaced employees and to pump prime training initiatives to equip people with the emerging skills. Trade unions also face a loss of members as individuals leave jobs and perhaps move into other areas of work. They also face difficulties as members (or potential members) question the value of belonging to a trade union that claims to represent their interests but which finds it difficult to prevent job losses and change being forced upon workers.

ICTs have contributed to the development of industrialized societies (which revolve around manufacturing industries) into postindustrial societies where services are the main source of economic value. While this thesis, posited by Bell (1973), has been hotly debated, there is no doubt that the service sector has indeed grown to be the largest economic sector in developed countries. However, Castells (1996, 1997, 1998, 2000; Aoyama and Castells, 2002) argues that the driver of these developments is the focus on information as the prime source of value creation and that this has given rise to the information society. The information society, unlike the industrialized society with its focus on production of tangible goods, is facilitated by the development, deployment, and interconnection of ICTs and is *characterized by the knowledge generation and exchange through interactions between and among networks of individuals as well as economic, social, political and cultural institutions.*

STOP & CONSIDER

It is management that decide and purchase the technology that will be used within an organization, therefore only technology that suits their purpose will be developed and become successful. To what extent is that a supportable statement and what might it imply?

CONCLUSIONS

This chapter has introduced the concept of technology in its broadest sense as it impacts on organizations and those who work in them. It has shown that technology impacts on organizations in many ways and has a particular part to play in shaping both them and the behaviour of the people within them. It influences both the way in which employees experience work and the rewards that they accrue from it, as well as the level, cost and types of goods and services that are available to be acquired by consumers. As a consequence, humans are victim, beneficiary and creator of the technologies that has such a fundamental impact on their work experience. It is inevitable that any discussion of specific new technologies will quickly become dated as newer technologies and different applications for existing ones emerge. The risk associated with any new technology is that it takes a predominant position in organizational thinking and diverts attention away from the potential available through human capability and diversity as important elements in success.

Now to summarize this chapter in terms of the relevant Learning Objectives:

- **Understand what is meant by the term 'technology' and how it influences both the operational activities found within organizations and the jobs that people undertake.** At its simplest level technology refers to the machines,

computers and equipment that people use in the work that they undertake. However, there are other forms of technology such as the procedural devices, skills and methods of work, together with the social technologies that direct the ways in which employee behaviour is managed within an organization. The equipment, procedures and social arrangements all determine how employees and managers will be accommodated in order to pursue organizational objectives. Technology in the form of machines, equipment and computers defines the jobs that people undertake through the design of the technology itself. As part of the design process for the technology, how users will interact with it effectively creates the jobs for the employees who will use it. In operational terms a technology can significantly determine what the organization can actually do. For example, the development of computer-based educational technology has allowed increasing development of the virtual campus approach to university education.

- **Explain the impact of technology on the organizations that employ it.** There are a number of perspectives on the relationship between technology and organization. Six traditional approaches are introduced within the relevant section of the text. They include Woodward, who described the relationship between production technology and organizational features. Perrow describes the relationship between technology and the ways that problems are dealt with. Thompson considered the linkages between task requirements and organizational responses. In the early 1960s, the Aston studies focused on the relationship between size, technology and organizational structure. Burns and Stalker drew a distinction between mechanistic and organic structures, largely reflecting an organizational response to the technological environment. Lawrence and Lorsch suggested that technology was an environmental contingency factor impacting on organizational structure. More recent perspectives have introduced a fundamentally different view – introduced in the section on 'Enacting Technology' – which seeks to integrate the social perspective into the debate on how technology develops and interacts with the human aspects of organization.

- **Outline the relationship between technology, politics and change in managerial decision making.** The existence of politics within management activity is inevitable. Resources are always in scarce supply and this inevitably encourages competition, which can easily become conflict and political activity. Technology is one area of resource which can contribute to this through the political potential of decisions associated with the development and acquisition of it. For example, pressure for higher pay among employees can be countered by the threat of the introduction of automation and the elimination of jobs. The development and adoption of technology is a managerial decision area and is not therefore a neutral process; it can be used to the relative advantage of that group as a political process. The relationship between technology and change is also a complex one. Technology can create job loss as people are replaced by machines. However, new jobs also emerge through the need to employ new skills in support of a particular technology; the new jobs that are created as a consequence of the making of new technology equipment and systems; the new jobs that emerge as a result of the enhancements in products and services available through technology applications. There are other issues associated with technology and change. For example, the influence of economics on technology development and uptake; the growth in internationalism through the ability of information technology to reduce distance between customer and supplier; the role of fashion in managerial thinking and decision making, etc.

- **Discuss the influence of technology on power, control and work organization.** It is managers who determine how technology develops and its use within any organization; therefore it can assist in their desire to achieve greater levels of control over processes and people in the pursuit of operational or other objectives. The issue of who should be allowed access to a particular technology is also a control process within an organization. For example, who should hold 'ownership' for a particular technology impacts directly on their relative power balance and therefore how they will exercise control over others. The use of technology determines to a significant extent the jobs of those employees interacting with it. This effectively controls their behaviour and work activity in terms of tasks, sequencing, pace of work, deadlines, priority and even work patterns. Through covert intention, managers can claim to seek quality or customer service improvement through a particular technology, but in practice the achievement of tighter control of the operational process may be the real objective.

- **Appreciate how the application of technology can result in alienation and the degradation of labour.** Alienation reflects a feeling of not being part of the employing organization. It contains aspects of self-estrangement, powerlessness, meaninglessness and isolation in the experience of work. Originally it was envisaged that technology would de-skill and dehumanize work to the extent that employees would be machine minders, necessary only because the machine could not perform every task. Humans were envisaged to be destined for boring, menial and degraded work to support the machines that undertook the real work of the organization. The reality has proved to be more complex than that. There are many examples of boring and mundane work using technology which result in alienation among employees. However, it is also possible to use the creativity of designers to create technology that supports human activity in an organization, rather than the other way around. Of course that is not to say that boring work can be completely eliminated. Some of the approaches to job design and employee involvement discussed in the other chapters can contribute to the development of meaningful work integrated with technology that does not offer a 'richer' experience for those engaged in it.

DISCUSSION QUESTIONS

1 Technology is best thought of in engineering, computer and communications terms. To consider technology to incorporate social technologies confuses the issues and debate and so should not be taken into account. Discuss this view.

2 Identify the ways in which new technology has influenced the traditional ways of exercising control within organizations.

3 How are technology, diversity and innovation linked together?

4 Does technology manage managers or do managers manage technology? Justify your answer.

5 Discuss the relationship between technology and organization structure.

6 'Managers are as much victims of technology as those employees with skills that are superseded by technology.' Comment on this statement.

7 Explain the view of technology within the systems approach to management and organization.

8 Technology provides the means of support for the values and objectives of managers. Discuss.

9 Does technology deployment in organizations inevitably lead to alienation? Justify your answer.

10 'The main reason for managers to seek to utilize technology is to increase their control over the processes for which they are responsible. Technology is, therefore, a political tool in the service of capital.' Discuss this statement.

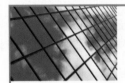

CASE STUDY

Martha the 'Martini' employee

Martha was an employee development associate with a large international bank. She was based in Hong Kong, but was expected to work anywhere in the world. Her particular specialism was providing support for branch and regional managers in the use of technology to enable them to more effectively meet the ever more demanding targets for business development. As a consequence, Martha was away from her office and home for an average of 3 days each week most of the year. Although Martha was used to living out of a suitcase and enjoyed her job, her family resented the amount of time that she spent away from home. Most of the time Martha and her family communicated via e-mail as it was easier than trying to make voice or personal contact when she was away.

Within the bank, there were a large number of employees in a similar position to Martha; they were generally technical specialists in finance, IT, marketing or HR working away from their base office to provide operational parts of the business with support. They were generally referred to as 'Martini' workers, because they were prepared to work and talk anytime, anyplace, anywhere. This was a reference to an old advert for that particular drink because it helped to

create a certain lifestyle by being available and acceptable 'anytime, anyplace, anywhere'.

Standard equipment for employees like Martha included a laptop and mobile phone. Each day wherever they worked they would hook-up to the company communication system and check their e-mail inbox. It was never empty! Martha, like most people within the company, received something like 60 e-mails every working day, most with no direct relevance to the projects that they were involved with. Each e-mail had to be read, just in case, but Martha tended to find that she was one of about 30–50 people who had been copied into a particular e-mail in what could only be described as electronic back-covering or 'brown-nosing'. Such people could not be bothered to identify who actually needed to know what they were saying; or thought it better to tell everyone to prevent any come-back in the future; or wanted to play politics by getting their name known as widely as possible or perhaps by trying to show how clever and important they were. It was frustrating for Martha to have to go through all of this material and she frequently became annoyed and frustrated with the process, but could not find a way of avoiding the need to work through her e-mails every day. It took at least an hour out of her working day, and when she was away from home she tended to leave it until she was back in her hotel in the evening, as there was little to do then and it minimized the need to take time out of her busy schedule during the day.

However, the mobile telephone was a different technological wonder. Martha was forever getting text messages and phone calls about work and projects that she was working on. The people ringing her took no account of the current project that Martha was engaged on; they simply rang when it suited them. When she was engaged in a meeting or development programme, Martha always turned her phone off so that she could not be disturbed. However, this meant that she always had a number of messages waiting for her when she switched it back on. This gave her more tasks to perform when she was able to return the calls; sometimes people e-mailed as well as phoned, leading to some confusion and duplication. Inevitably Martha tended to deal with many of her phone messages in the evening when she returned to her hotel. However, depending on the time differences between Martha's location and the location of the message originator,

this could be difficult. On occasions, Martha rang a colleague's mobile only to find that they were at home, resentful of the fact that their free time had been interrupted with work matters, let alone that they may not have the appropriate information to hand. Not surprisingly, this led to some friction between colleagues as Martha also complained that she was working much longer hours and away from home and had no choice but to call when she did. If a colleague did not answer their phone in person then it inevitably led to messages going back and forward, perhaps even e-mails being used to communicate whatever the message was about.

This was the reality of the work experience for Martha and many of her colleagues. It was wasteful of their time and energy and added considerably to their working hours. It also reduced the time they had to talk to their families when they were away from home, which placed a strain of that most important of relationships. But what could Martha do? Her specialist area involved helping other people to use technology more effectively in support of their lives, yet she could not help herself with her own technology-driven overload problem!

© David Vintiner/Corbis

TASKS

1 What would you do if you were Martha and faced with this situation?
2 What advice would you offer Martha about how to deal with the demands of technology-based communication if you were her boss?
3 What should organizations do to ensure the effective use of technology within their organizations?

FURTHER READING

Brown, J.S. and Duguid, P. (2001) *The social life of information*, Boston: Harvard Business School Press. Insightful discussion on the nature and role of information and technology.

Castells, M. (2002) *The Internet Galaxy: Reflections on the Internet, Business and Society*, Oxford: Oxford University Press. Makes the case that the Internet is more than just a technology, reflecting the backbone of the future economy and what we need to understand in order to make it contribute to business and personal success.

Haddad, C.J. (2002) *Managing Technological Change: A Strategic Partnership Approach*, London: Sage. Looks at the successful (and unsuccessful) implementation of technological change and factors such as the involvement of key stakeholders that can increase the probability of success.

Haydu, J. (1988) *Between Craft and Class: Skilled Workers and Factory Politics in the United States and Britain, 1890–1922*, Berkeley: University of California Press. Considers the reaction of skilled metalworkers to the economic changes surrounding them as a result of new production methods emerging in the early twentieth century. The author places this process in the context of the emergence of different approaches to collective effort as a means of attempting to achieve greater influence on management decision making.

Jackson, M.C. (2000) *Systems approaches to management*, Springer. Useful source for considering systems approaches to management.

Stair, R. and Reynolds, G. (2001) *Principles of Information Systems*, New York: Thomson Learning. Introduces the basics of technology in relation to the business uses to which it can be put.

Van Slyke, C. and Belanger, F. (2002) *Electronic Business Technologies*, New York: Wiley. Provides an introduction to e-business and the technologies used to support it.

Wenger, E. (1998) *Communities of practice: Learning, meaning and identity*. Cambridge University Press. Useful source for those interested in the important notion of communities-of-practice.

Woolgar, S. (ed.) (2002) *Virtual Society? Technology, Cyberbole, Reality*, Oxford: Oxford University Press. Considers the effect on society of the developing electronic technologies.

Zuboff, S. (1988) *In the Age of the Smart Machine: The Future of Work and Power*, Oxford: Heinemann. Influential book that discusses the impact of modern information and communication technology.

COMPANION WEBSITE

Online teaching and learning resources

Visit the companion website for Organizational Behaviour and Management 4th edition at: http://www .cengage.co.uk/martinfellenz to find valuable further teaching and learning material. For full details, see 'About the website' at the start of the book.

CHAPTER TWELVE

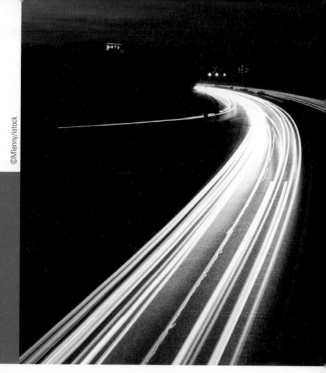

©Mlenny/istock

CONTROL AND JOB DESIGN

LEARNING OBJECTIVES

After studying this chapter and working through the associated OB in Action panels, Discussion Questions and Case Study you should be able to:

- Discuss the main approaches to the design of work within an organizational setting.

- Explain the influence of technology on job design and the control of work

- Assess the various 'means' through which control can be exercised within an organizational context.

- Understand how work study attempts to influence job design activities and how changing the design of jobs can be a difficult process.

- Outline the characteristic features of control systems as found in organizations.

INTRODUCTION

Control is a broad concept that is relevant for many aspects related to organizations. In fact, it is a central because without control, organizations simply could not exist. Many topics discussed in the chapters of this book are inherently linked to control. It is not surprising to recognize that concepts such as order, structure, stability, conflict, behaviour and power are closely linked with structure. However, in organizations this is true as well for issues such as management, leadership, learning, change, conflict, and many others not usually directly associated with control. In this chapter, we will consider how control as an important function in organizations is exercised through formal systems and arrangements. The more informal aspects of control are also dealt with in relation to informal social control, for example in groups (see Chapter 7) and through culture (Chapter 14), in the use of power and influence (Chapter 15), and in the discussion of trust and relationships (Chapter 16).

We discuss the different approaches to formal control used in organizations, and discuss the means by which control is exercised. We will also discuss job design, which provides a useful discussion of how formal arrangements are used to exercise control at individual and group levels.

THE NATURE OF CONTROL

Control
The function of regulating events, action, outcomes or other relevant aspects according to preferred standards, plans, objectives or other chosen referents.

In this chapter we refer to control as *the function of regulating events, actions, outcomes, or other relevant aspects according to preferred standards, plans, objectives or other chosen referents.* According to cybernetics, the science of control, control always involves a number of basic functions and processes. This can best be explained using the example of a thermostat that controls the temperature in a room. The thermostat must be set to a desired temperature (the goal, standard, objective, or desired state). It monitors and compares information about the actual temperature in the room (feedback) with the desired temperature level. If the thermostat detects a discrepancy between actual and desired temperature, it will take action (i.e., switch on heating or cooling) to bring the temperature in the room in line with the desired temperature (see Figure 12.1 for a schematic depiction of this process).

This example has a number of important implications for the exercise of control. First, it helps to identify the necessary elements and processes involved in the exercise of control in any context. In short, these include the *goal* or *standard* (desired state of the controlled property), *feedback* (i.e., relevant information about the actual state of the controlled property), *discrepancy detection* (through a comparison of the desired and actual state) and, finally, *action* (any effect initiated or influenced to

Figure 12.1 Negative feedback

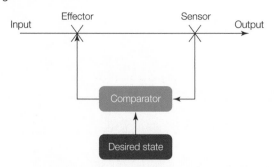

reduce the detected discrepancy). (For basics of cybernetics see Ashby, 1956; Beer, 1959; Buckley, 1968, Wiener, 1948; for applications to human behaviour and management see Carver and Scheier, 2001; Fellenz, 1997; Klein, 1989; Lord and Hanges, 1987. Pinder, 2008, provides a brief and useful overview.) This basic and simple control model is called the negative feedback loop because it reduces discrepancies. Discrepancy amplifying loops (called *positive feedback loops*) also exist.

The second implication of the simple thermostat example is that it identifies where control can break down. If there are errors in any of the basic elements or processes (e.g., selecting goals/standards; delayed or erroneous feedback that does not accurately reflect current or actual information; errors in comparing feedback with goals; lack of attention to changes in feedback; selecting or initiating ineffective or inappropriate action, etc.) control cannot function effectively.

Of course, control is typically more complex than the simple example described above. Nevertheless, feedback remains a central role because it links the controller (no matter if this is a person, a group, a machine, or any other entity or system) to what it attempts to control. In complex situations, even small mistakes or delays in feedback can lead to spectacular mistakes. A good example is the well known *bullwhip effect* (Lee *et al.*, 1997) that can occur among firms linked together in supply chains. Orders for components or other inputs may be placed by a firm that receives a customer order. To reduce uncertainty, the supplier receiving the order may well add a margin to their own orders for necessary resources needed to fulfil the original order. Even small initial orders can get amplified across several stages in supply chains and lead to individual firms being overwhelmed with orders that do not reflect the actual downstream customer demand – a classic example of breakdown in intraorganizational and interorganizational control.

Accurate and timely feedback, therefore, is a necessary and useful means of controlling any state or activity and providing learning opportunities in the dynamic world in which we live. However, it is rare in behaviour that a simple chain of events is the major determinant of behaviour. Consider, for example, driving a car. This involves a co-ordinated set of feedback loops (visually searching the road around the car, listening to noise from the engine, sensing the feel of the road, judging speed and direction, and so on) arranged into a framework which allows priority to be given to particular behaviours. This prioritization process can produce braking at one moment, accelerating at another, steering, and so on, all included in the dynamic activity that we call driving. This much-simplified description of driving reflects the concept of prioritization and the hierarchical notion of response habits within the stimulus–response model (see Chapter 5). One way that the concept of feedback has been combined with the hierarchical notion of response habits is in the application of a *TOTE* unit.

TOTE refers to a test, operate, test, exit sequence and was first described by Miller *et al.* (1960). The TOTE model is shown in Figure 12.2. In essence the test phase of the model reflects a feedback loop in that if a mismatch between plan and goal is detected, then the operate phase is activated. This sequence is repeated until a match between actual and goal is identified, when the cycle ends and that particular behaviour also ends.

Figure 12.2 TOTE unit

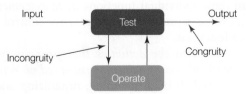

Source: Miller, GA, Galanter, E and Pribram, KH (1960) *Plans and the Structure of Behaviour*, Henry Holt and Company. Reprinted 1986, Adams, Bannister, Cox, New York.

Figure 12.3 TOTE model of hammering a nail

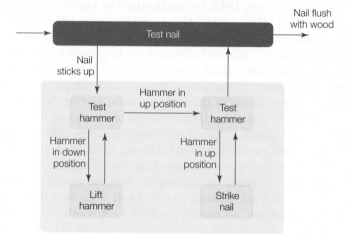

Source: Miller, GA, Galanter, E and Pribram, KH (1960) *Plans and the Structure of Behaviour*, Henry Holt and Company. Reprinted 1986, Adams, Bannister, Cox, New York.

The benefit of the TOTE unit is that it can be used to describe a series of hierarchically organized behavioural sequences. The example used by Miller is hammering a nail into a piece of wood. One phase is the identification of the position of the nail, the goal being to make it flush with the surface of the wood. The second phase is the hammer position (lifting or striking). The process of hammering the nail, then, consists of a TOTE model that is reflected in Figure 12.3.

The TOTE unit so described is made up of subunits. But the hammering of a nail into a piece of wood may in itself be part of a much larger set of goals. For example, the particular nail might be part of a tree house for a child or it may be part of the construction of a house for a family. The person doing the hammering may be an employee and have as a goal the need to earn a bonus in order to pay for a summer holiday or it may be a father seeking to build the best tree house possible to make his children happy.

What is important to recognize is that control is at the heart of all purposeful action. That is why the related concepts of control and self-regulation are at the centre of so many theories dealing with purposeful behaviour and complex activities. We will discuss the social and organizational aspects of control in the next section.

CONTROL IN ORGANIZATIONS

As already outlined above, control is central in organizations because we cannot talk about order, stability, or co-ordinated activity– aspects necessary for organizations – without control. Similarly, control is also an integral element of management. As discussed in Chapters 1 and 6, the process of management is concerned with achieving goals and involves *planning*, *organizing*, *leading* (or *deploying*), and *controlling* resources. This should and usually does take place at individual, subunit and organizational levels. However, it is important to recognize that control is not simply complementing or completing the other basic activities of management, but is an integral feature of all these individual functions of management. In fact, management is a process that exercises prospective and reactive control as part of all four of the basic management functions.

Prospective control
Refers to the activities that proactively align resources in ways that maximize the likelihood of achieving intended objectives.

Prospective control refers to *the activities that proactively align resources in ways that maximize the likelihood of achieving intended objectives*. Thus, this form of control is mainly exerted through planning, organizing and leading/deploying

CHANGE AT WORK

Competitive analysis gives business an edge

Instalec Ltd is an established electrical contracting business, based in Luton. Director Lesley Jeffs began using competitive analysis as a business development tool several years ago. Combining a number of methods, the analysis continues to drive improvements across many areas of the business. Instalec's approach contains a simple three-stage process as follows:

1   Assess the competitive landscape

Jeffs is quoted as saying that attending a seminar on business development was the starting point for understanding and starting the competitive analysis process. The speaker was inspirational and the company signed up for bimonthly coaching sessions that included an assessment of the competitive landscape. There were literally hundreds of electrical contractors in the Luton area, so it was first necessary to identify the key competitors and what information about them would be useful. That list included information on customer service, pricing policies, employment practices and staff qualifications. Instalec thought that these represented areas where they had an advantage, but it was necessary to be certain and if possible quantify any differences.

2   Gather information

The first information-gathering exercise was a telephone survey. Instalec called competitors to assess their response times and the overall impression given. Also requested were copies of competitor's company literature. The quality of the literature provided an indication of the 'quality' of the competitor's approach to customer service and the range of services/products offered as well as pricing. How quickly the literature arrived was also another 'test' of customer service. Competitor websites, trade journals, local newspapers and the local Chamber of Commerce proved other simple ways to gather information about competitors. Customers and suppliers also have a lot of information about competitors that can be obtained by talking to them, which also has the added advantage of improving industry networking that helps to build relationships. This led to a general monitoring of what competitors were doing on an ongoing basis.

3   Act on the analysis

Jeffs is of the opinion that the analysis undertaken provided an edge in many areas of Instalec's operations. For example, monitoring competitors' recruitment ads and rates of pay has helped them refine their own resourcing procedures in order to attract and retain good-quality staff. The research also found that many of Instalec's competitors performed poorly in answering phones and returning calls. Consequently, Instalec made sure that their own phones were always manned and that missed calls were returned promptly. Jeffs says 'We benchmark our performance and review our analysis at management level every 6 months. Our employees are kept up to date too. It's important that staff know why you're doing analysis and how they can help.' Because the competitive landscape is always changing, the analysis has to be kept up to date for existing competitors. New competitors are identified and monitored via the local press and industry contacts.

Lessons learned from the process

1   Jeffs wishes that they had begun the process of competitive analysis sooner.

2   Have more confidence in seeking information, particularly from customers. Most are happy to help as long as you're professional and use the information to improve your service.

TASKS

1   To what extent does this example of competitive analysis demonstrate prospective control or reactive control as introduced in this chapter?

2   What other aspects of control can you identify in this example?

Source:
Managing Change – Competitive analysis gives business an edge. Here's how I've changed my business for the better: Case studies from: www.businesslink.gov.uk/Promotions_files/businesslinkgovuk_better.pdf. Crown Copyright.

resources. As an example, if a manager wants to increase sales, then developing an appropriate approach to achieving this increase (*planning*), arranging the relevant people (e.g., by selecting the best sales personnel), processes (e.g., reward system) and support structures (*organizing*), and actively directing and supporting the involved personnel (*leading*) are all activities that provide prospective control by increasing the likelihood that sales can be increased. In this sense, control is a means of reducing uncertainty about how the deployed resources will operate and thus contributes to the intended outcomes. In some sense, prospective control is about proactive approaches to aligning resources and people in line with intended goals. This is also often seen as a central feature of leadership (see Chapter 6).

In contrast, reactive control is mainly exerted as part of the controlling function of management which is based on the notion of the negative feedback loop discussed above. Therefore we define reactive control as *the actions taken to bring activities in line with targets and expectations based on received feedback about these activities.* In contrast to prospective control, reactive control is therefore less about aligning people and more about regulating activities and outcomes, and about enforcing plans, standards and other expectations. Consider the Change at Work example in the light of these approaches to control.

> **Reactive control**
> The actions taken to bring activities in line with targets and expectations based on received feedback about the activities.

Both prospective and reactive control are about exerting influence about resources (and their operation) and people (and their behaviour). Thus, the exercise of control is closely related to the notion of *power*. As we are here primarily concerned with formal approaches to control, it may be sufficient to point out that formal approaches to control are ultimately all based on authority, which refers to *the legitimate power vested in managers based on their position and role in an organization.* We will consider authority as well as other forms of power and influence in much more detail in Chapter 15.

> **Authority**
> Refers to the legitimate power vested in managers based on their position and role in an organization.

Given the central role that control has in all the basic management activities, it is not surprising to note that Stafford Beer, an influential management scholar and practitioner, calls management the 'profession of control' (Beer, 1972; see also Adams and Haynes, 2007). To reiterate this important link, management can be described as the profession of control because it is about deliberate action in the pursuit of goals.

Control through power is a commonly employed way of 'absorbing uncertainty and dealing with the freedom and indeterminacy of other agents' (Knights *et al.*, 2001: p. 329). An alternative way of achieving this is based on using trust, and these two ways of increasing predictability and reducing uncertainty are often described as different yet functionally equivalent approaches to the same outcome. However, control and trust, despite the fact that they are often described as opposites, may be closely related as these general views indicate (see Knights *et al.*, 2001). We will consider the role of culture (Chapter 14) and trust (Chapter 16) in organizations as means of or alternatives to control in more detail later in the book.

STOP & CONSIDER

To what extent might managers rely on power as the means of exercising control whilst leaders rely on trust as the way of exercising it in the search for ways to increase predictability and reduce uncertainty? Justify your views.

In addition to increasing predictability and reducing uncertainty within organizations, there is another distinct and opposite aspect to control in that it can be seen as restrictive, limiting personal freedom and flexibility, and using manipulative means that take away from the self-determination of organizational members. It can be argued that many initiatives on employee involvement and participative management are covert attempts to find ways of retaining control within an illusion of freedom for the individual. These initiatives are frequently expressed as an encouragement to go beyond the contract and enjoy a new partnership with managers in developing a mutually prosperous and fulfilling future. The net effect, however, is the exercise of more subtle forms of control intended to minimize the risk of conflict and maximize contribution to the organization. This is related to the view of power indicated earlier, which suggested that by allowing some controlled erosion of total power, effective control is retained by management.

It has been suggested by Huczynski and Buchanan (1991: p. 579) that control has three connotations. First, it is necessary as an economic activity and critical to the success of the organization. Second, it represents a psychological necessity in order to eliminate the ambiguity, unpredictability and disorder that would prevent individuals from operating effectively within the organization. Third, it represents a political process in which some individuals and groups are able to exercise control over others. It is possible to identify a fourth purpose that control serves in addition to the three just identified, that is its physical connotations. A brief description of each is provided below:

- *Physical.* At the detailed control level, jobs, processes and machines need to be organized and controlled effectively if they are to combine to produce the goods and services required (Edwards, 1986). Frequently, the physical level of control involves record keeping, measuring activity and checking actual performance against that intended.

- *Economic.* As an economic process, control is geared towards achieving the financial objectives of the organization. It is not just the detailed control described above. It represents the micro level co-ordination and planning of activity along with the macro level directional planning necessary to achieve the financial returns to ensure that investors and other stakeholders remain satisfied.

- *Psychological.* This process represents both the need among individuals to function within a predictable environment and the inherent need that some individuals have to either control or be controlled. In its broadest sense management can be described as a controlling activity. That some individuals seek elevation to these positions can be taken as evidence of their desire to exercise control over resources. There are individuals who for many reasons do not gain promotion within organizations. Some do not have the opportunity; others do not have the confidence or the inclination. Still others perceive promotion as selling out to the owning 'classes', or perhaps they achieve fulfilment through other aspects of their life. Whatever the reason, to some degree subordinates psychologically accept to be controlled by others.

- *Political.* Control provides the means by which existing structures and social conditions can be reinforced. Xinyi Xu (1994) demonstrates such political impact vividly by describing the complex and politically based control processes and structural features inherent in all levels of organizational and social life within China. In many contexts, it is the legal owners of organizations (i.e., the providers of capital) that have the right to ultimately determine an organization's existence. Within some limits (e.g., employment law, bankruptcy laws) owners can liquidate the assets irrespective of the impact on the nonowning stakeholders.

There are other political perspectives to control. For example, through the exercise of political skill, a departmental manager may be able to increase their own significance and importance within an organization, thereby being able to exercise control over a greater range of resources. Such use of control will be dealt with as part of the discussion of power and politics in Chapter 15.

APPROACHES TO ORGANIZATIONAL CONTROL

Performance ambiguity
Refers to the ease and clarity with which the value of activities or outcomes can be assessed.

Goal incongruence
Refers to the degree of alignment between individual and organizational goals.

Ouchi (1979, 1980) described three fundamental organizational control strategies. They are bureaucratic control, market control and clan control. According to Ouchi (1980), each of these control strategies is appropriate and thus more likely to be deployed in different circumstances that are determined by two principal factors. The first is performance ambiguity, which refers to *the ease and clarity with which the value of activities or outcomes can be assessed*. It is low when this is easy (for example, when relevant evaluations can be determined by the price mechanism in markets), and is high when tasks or outcomes are unique, when individual contributions cannot be separately assessed (e.g., in highly interdependent task environments), or when the value of contributions or outputs cannot be assessed for other reasons. Goal incongruence, the second factor, is *the degree of alignment between individual and organizational goals*. It is low when goals are aligned and high when multiple individual goals and agendas are operating in conflict with relevant organizational goals.

Bureaucratic control is based on the mechanisms employed in bureaucratic organizational forms (see Chapter 10) including rules and regulations, formalization, standardization, hierarchical authority and close measurement of individual performance. Market control, in contrast, does not employ hierarchical control but rather utilizes market and price mechanisms based on demand, supply and competition to control activities. Within organizations, *market control* is often used at the unit level in an approach that employs so-called *profit centres*. Operating units are designated as separate profit centres that compete for investment, support and other resources based on their financial or otherwise measured performance. In the absence of a market for a unit's outputs that could help determine their performance, a *cost centre approach* is sometimes used that provides a fixed budget for which the unit needs to provide agreed service or other output levels. Finally, *clan control* is based on social influence on behaviour. The roles of social control, culture and trust are central for this approach, which is often appropriate when environmental uncertainty is very high and performance criteria are unclear or change frequently. See Table 12.1 for a summary of these strategies in relation to their 'conditions' and 'requirements'.

Table 12.1 Ouchi's organizational control strategies

Organizational control strategy	Conditions	Requirements
Bureaucratic	Moderately high-performance ambiguity and moderately high-goal incongruity	Performance standards and measures, hierarchical system with legitimate authority, rules, accepted and fair procedures
Market	Low-performance ambiguity and high-goal incongruity	Prices, exchange relationships, competition, norm of reciprocity and/or contract enforcement possible
Clan	High-performance ambiguity and low-goal incongruity	Shared norms, values and beliefs (culture), trust

Source: Adapted from Ouchi, 1979, 1980.

This basic set of organizational control strategies has been elaborated and extended. Child (2005), for example, considers a range of different control strategies that also include human resource management (HRM) control (which refers to control through the application of HRM approaches, see Chapter 13), electronic surveillance (see Chapter 11 and section on technology below), and personal control exercised by managers and leaders (see also the supervisory control behaviours in the next section). Desmond (2004) also discusses additional approaches that include panoptic and concertive control, among others. *Panoptic control* is based on the idea of the panopticon, originally conceived of by English social reformer Jeremy Bentham in the late eighteenth century. A panopticon is a prison in which all inmates can be continuously observed without them being able to identify when such surveillance is actually taking place. Applied to organizations, and particularly work organizations, this implies that all activities of employees are made visible and can potentially be monitored at any time. While the idea of the panopticon appears incredible given its disregard for contemporary norms of social conduct and for modern conceptions

EMPLOYEE PERSPECTIVE

Reasonable expenses?

Phoebe worked for a large management consultancy based in Holland which employed several hundred field-based staff and associates. The primary duties of these staff involved travelling to client organizations and carrying out consultancy projects at those locations. This could involve a short visit of about 2 hours or several weeks of travelling daily (or staying away from home) to client locations. Clearly this process involved considerable amounts of travelling and high levels of expense claim.

Phoebe's employer did not provide company cars, but paid a mileage allowance for each mile travelled on company business. The distance used as the basis of payment was the smaller of either the actual distance travelled or the distance to the visit from the office at which the member of staff was normally based. This was generally regarded as a fair system by staff as it allowed for the normal travel to work distance each day.

In an attempt to save money, senior management decided that any distance travelled to visit a client which involved the individual travelling over part of their normal route to the office would have that mileage discounted for expense purposes. This was seen as both complex and unfair by the staff concerned. It also involved keeping more records of distance and routes travelled. Line managers were also expected to know each consultant's normal route to the office and also the best route to each client visit.

As a consequence, staff (including Phoebe) adopted a number of strategies in response to this instruction. One of the most effective was to find and use minor roads when visiting clients in areas near to the normal route to the office, justifying this with excuses such as traffic congestion. Another involved changing work routines to find reasons to attend the office when visits involved distances which would be longer than if done directly from home. Managers became confused about the new rules and would sign expense claims, only to have them rejected by the accounts department on a technicality. This led to arguments, frustration and severe delays in payment until queries were resolved.

Very quickly senior management recognized that the cost of administration for the scheme was increasing rapidly, as was the level of expense claim. Eventually the old rule was reinstated. In other words, by following the rules of the new scheme together with some ingenuity, Phoebe and her colleagues were able to force change onto management.

TASKS

1 Were Phoebe's (and her colleagues) actions justified? Why or why not?

2 To what extent does this example illustrate bureaucratic control and/or concertive control? Does this distinction matter? Why or why not?

of civic and human rights (e.g., privacy), information and communication technology (ICT) can provide an electronic version of the panopticon (Bain and Taylor, 2000; Batt *et al.* 2009). In fact, influential French sociologist and philosopher Michel Foucault (1977) argues that such control is encroaching on many areas of modern life. This approach to organizational control is likely to contribute to conflict between the observed and the observers, and can lead those observed to resist direction and control (Bain and Taylor, 2000; Barnes, 2007; Desmond, 2004; Thompson, 2003).

Concertive control (Desmond, 2004; Barker, 1993) is based on the social control exercised by groups on their members (see Chapter 7). As long as group norms and objectives are in line with organizational goals, this form of control can provide for a decentralized means of controlling employees. However, group norms and objectives may change and the control exercised can thus become counterproductive if they are not aligned with organizational goals. This is apparent in the Employee Perspective example.

Flamholtz and colleagues (1985) integrate these apparently different strategies in a comprehensive model of organizational control. Their model places the regulatory function of control described by the cybernetic feedback loop at the heart of organizational and managerial control. However, their model recognizes that such regulation takes place in the particular structural and cultural context of specific organizations. Thus, structural (including bureaucratic control) as well as cultural (reflecting clan control) aspects are always part of control in any organization. In addition, their model also recognizes the influence of the larger economic and social environment on organizational and managerial control.

Another useful perspective when considering how control is exercised in organizations is to identify the *object of control*, i.e., what it is that is measured and regulated. Traditionally, control activity in organizations has focused on output and behaviour (Ouchi, 1979; Ouchi and Maguire, 1975). Output control is based on *direct measurement of the outputs produced* (e.g., the amount of units produced, the number of defects per 1000 units, the amount of sales revenue generated). In some environments, such output control is difficult because of measurement problems (e.g., service quality, customer satisfaction) or because outcomes are not quantifiable (e.g., creative tasks). Behavioural control, in contrast, is based on *direct observation during work performance* (e.g., supervisor using checklist of appropriate procedures used by a car mechanic; observation of cashier's customer interaction in fast-food restaurants by manager). Behavioural control tends to be used where observation of work is possible, and where the links between work performance (i.e., employee behaviour) and work outcomes are stable and well known. In situations where work outcomes are not measurable and where work performance cannot be observed (e.g., psychotherapy), either input control (e.g., specification and control of relevant resources used) or clan control are used.

Finally, it is important to recognize that both the focus of control (i.e., what is controlled) and the manner of control (i.e., how control is exercised) are important aspects of control. Yet like many other activities in organizations, control can lead to unintended consequences. Stansbury and Barry (2007), for example, discuss the *paradox of control* in the context of business ethics. These authors show how attempts by organizations to control ethical decision making by their employees can backfire in that employees' ability to make ethical decisions, especially in unfamiliar situations, can be weakened. Moreover, coercive approaches to ethical decision making that focus on detecting wrongdoing and punishing wrongdoers may, compared to more preventative, supportive and enabling alternatives, be particularly counterproductive for controlling ethical misbehaviour. Thus, we conclude that the general control strategies as well as specific objects and means of control must be carefully designed, implemented, and indeed controlled to assure that they achieve their intended objectives.

Output control
This is based on the direct measurement of the outputs produced. In some environments, such output control is difficult because of measurement problems (e.g., service quality, customer satisfaction) or because outcomes are not quantifiable (e.g., creative tasks). See also behavioural control.

Behavioural control
This is based on direct observation of behaviour during work performance. See also output control.

Input control
This is based on the specification and control of relevant resources used.

MEANS OF ORGANIZATIONAL CONTROL

There are many ways in which the organizational control strategies are translated into practice. The means used include managerial behaviour, organizational design (including structure and culture), skill, technology, and various forms of social control, including reward and punishment practices. We will consider these means of organizational control in turn in this section. Another important means of control, job design, is discussed in more detail in the following section.

MANAGEMENT IN ACTION

How to cure bullying at work

Research by the Andrea Adams Trust suggests that more than 25 per cent of people will be bullied at some point during their working lives and that about 19 million working days are lost each year due to bullying (at a cost to the UK economy of about £6 billion). Suggestions from a number of sources identify that a number of measures are needed to deal effectively with bullies at work. They include:

1 Understand the problem. Bullying is not easy to define. It represents an abuse of power or position that involves persistent personal attacks including the criticism, open condemnation or humiliation of a person on an ongoing basis.

2 Consider issues such as organizational culture, management style, job design, performance expectations and management, staffing levels, workloads, workplace layout, client behaviour, training provision, attitudes and respect.

3 Do not assume that 'no complaints' means there are no problems. Look out for the warning signs in all sections and departments such as high levels of absence, high labour turnover, reduced productivity and low morale.

4 Draw up a policy. Say clearly that bullying is unacceptable; indicate what it is and how complaints will be handled. For this to work, the policy must have the support of the senior managers, and the relevant HRM staff need to be trained in how to recognize and deal with it.

5 Set a good example. Bullying thrives in autocratic environments so set a good example as a manager.

6 Appoint counsellors. It is useful to provide people to whom staff can turn to for advice and support if they think they are being bullied.

7 Bullying is invariably psychological, so there may be no physical signs. Investigators need to be trained to look for patterns of behaviour over months or even years.

8 Investigate thoroughly. Get the complainant to write down each incident with times, dates, including any witnesses. Investigators should also be trained to recognize justification strategies adopted by bullies.

9 Recognize that the target of a bully believes that they have a problem that needs addressing and provide practical help and support for them whilst enquiries are underway.

10 Don't look for the easy way out. Don't just move the victim. Legislation provides a duty of care in psychological as well as physical matters.

TASK

1 To what extent should it be possible to eliminate bullying from an organization, or is it simply a reflection of an attempt by one person to control another and therefore it will surface in other ways if attempts are made to eliminate it? Justify your answer.

Sources:
Garrett, A. (2003) How to cure bullying at work, *Management Today*, May, p. 80.
http://www.bullyingbusiness.co.uk/index.html (accessed August 2009).
http://www.andreaadamstrust.org/ (accessed August 2009).
CIPD (2008) Factsheet on Harassment and bullying at work, http://www.cipd.co.uk/subjects/dvsequl/harassmt/harrass. htm?IsSrchRes=1(accessed August 2009).

Managerial and supervisor behaviours

At the supervisory level, these general strategies of organizational control need to be translated into more specific behaviours. Watson (2008) discusses many modern managerial approaches and practices such as the use of empowerment, decentralization of some decision-making authority, high-commitment and high-performance work systems, total quality management (TQM) and many others as *indirect control attempts*. He contrasts this with *direct control attempts* that closely mirror the bureaucratic control mentioned above.

Formal supervisory behaviour is an example of such direct and indirect control attempts, but there also exist many informal behaviours that managers engage in deliberately or unthinkingly to increase their control over employees. Fortado (1994) discusses such approaches (see Table 12.2) which can also include supervisor bullying behaviour (Roscigno *et al.*, 2009). The Management in Action panel explores ways in which bullying might be controlled. Many similar techniques are used as part of people's political arsenal (see Chapter 15).

Skill

There are many jobs in which skill or professional status provide opportunities to exercise control in one form or another. To know more than others in the same context is a basis for acquiring power and exercising control. Only chartered accountants are able to sign the audit of a set of company accounts. This requirement is intended to provide confidence to investors and the authorities that the accounts are a true and realistic reflection of the financial position of the company. Such auditors hold considerable power. The degree to which this is a double-edged sword in practice is evident from the number of major accounting firms that are being sued by investors for large sums of money when events come to light not previously identified through an audit. Another aspect of skill (or rather the apparent lack of it) in relation to control is evidenced in the Examining Ethics example 'I won't apologize!'

Table 12.2 Informal supervisory control behaviours

Informal supervisory control behaviours	Example
Informal, often social punishments	'Status stripping' through creation and award of a homemade 'star employee award' to the person with the lowest performance.
Informal communication through specially forged relationships and outside formal channels	Senior managers using informal communication mechanisms like the grapevine and taking action bypassing levels of the hierarchy at which formal information is filtered. This practice might be called an 'unofficial voice mechanism' for lower-level employees (Furtado, 1994).
Highly visible signalling acts that quickly spread the word about new practices	Detailed questioning of minute expenditures to communicate that cost savings are necessary.
Harsh, personalized and arbitrary discipline	Unwarranted firing of an employee to warn all remaining employees that this sanction exists.
Silencing and isolating dissenters	Use of delaying tactics, veiled threats, or through ostracizing and degrading treatment.

Source: Adapted from Fortado, 1994.

EXAMINING ETHICS

I won't apologize!

The following letter was published on the problem page in a management magazine:

'One of my brightest employees has made an enormous cock-up on a client's account. I would normally support my team, but in this case I can see the client's point of view. Unfortunately, my employee can't and has refused to apologize. The client has now demanded that I fire or demote the employee, but he's too good to let go. We're a small company and very dependent on this one client, so I can't afford to lose them either. Any suggestions?'

TASKS

1 Is it ethical for a client to demand the dismissal of an employee in such circumstances? Justify your answer.

2 If you were the manager would you allow a client to 'control' your company in the way described in the example? Explore both 'yes' and 'no' options before concluding.

3 What advice would you give the manager about how to deal with the situation?

Source:
Bullmore, J (2003) What's your problem? *Management Today*, October, p. 81. Reprinted with permission.

Organizational structure

As already explored in Chapter 10, the structuring of organizations has profound impact on the behaviours of its members. Specific approaches to departmentation and compartmentalization of activity provide the opportunity to exercise control through specialization. For example, the creation of an accounting department provides the opportunity for the development of efficient, specialized accounting control systems as a consequence of grouping together experts in a particular field. It also provides the more senior managers with the knowledge that accounting issues are the responsibility of that department and that they have (in theory) no bias towards other functions in reporting accounting data. Unfortunately, as effective as this top-down perspective might be for the senior people within the organization, they are not the customers. Tighter and more effective vertical control is often achieved at the cost of customer experience and satisfaction. These two conflicting requirements are often difficult to balance, a point discussed in the context of many topics throughout this book.

Hierarchy and authority

A particular part of the structure of organization is the distribution of formal authority. This is a central part of the bureaucratic control strategy discussed above, but delegation of authority takes place in virtually all organizations that introduce hierarchical arrangement of responsibility and control. Managers are appointed to positions of authority which allows them to exercise control over their subordinates, subject to policies and procedures. Members acquiesce to these authority arrangements when they agree to join the organization. For most forms of organizations, such complex webs of hierarchy and authority are the central means of the control over activity to be exercised in support of the objectives being sought.

Yet reliance on authority is not always the most effective way to achieve the desired result, because it can create a compliance- and dependency-based cultural environment. Being conditioned to expect that someone in authority will direct every move can result in individuals failing to exercise discretion and common sense in performing their duties. Moreover, the use and especially the overreliance on authority can also generate substantial resistance.

Resentment of and resistance to authority are typical responses, especially if it is exercised arbitrarily or if it violates expectations such as the psychological contract people have with their employer. The psychological contract (see Chapter 16) reflects the subjective understanding of the mutual responsibilities and privileges between employer and employee. Any direct and overt attempt to control behaviour is likely to create reactance (Brehm and Brehm, 1981, see Chapter 4). Thus, the indirect control attempts discussed above and the use of social control are commonly employed in organizations (e.g., Takeuchi *et al.*, 2009).

Social control and socialization

The role of social control in organizations is as central as the formal control approaches discussed above, and dynamics of social control are present at every level of analysis in organizations. At the organizational level, culture provides a means of control of members (see Chapter 14). Johnson (1988) also identifies that the fundamental logic guiding activity in an organization – which he calls a *paradigm* (see also Brown, 1978) – guides and influences individual and collective sensemaking and decision making and effectively serves as a control mechanism. At the group level, *concertive control* (Desmond, 2004; Barker, 1993) provides for a powerful influence on behaviour, and at the individual level the social and environmental nature of perception and cognition (see Chapter 4) which reflects internalization dynamics is a constant source of socially controlled behaviour.

Behavioural conformity with social control is at the heart of the process of socialization which refers to *the process by which newcomers to a social setting (or a culture) develop the ability to function effectively in that particular setting*. Socialization is a learning process and conformity is developed in three stages, named compliance, identification and internalization (e.g., Kelman, 2006). *Compliance* reflects a rule orientation and is based on trying to gain a benefit or avoid a punishment. Thus, compliance-based conformity with social control is purely instrumental. *Identification* reflects a role orientation and is based on either trying to be like another person (or an ideal), or filling a particular role to develop or maintain a particular relationship to the person or persons exerting social influence. Identification-based conformity is therefore partially instrumental, and partially intrinsically motivated. Finally, *internalization* reflects a value orientation and is based on attempts to align behaviour with internalized values. The High Performance example illustrates aspects of socialization and social control.

Organizations can use different strategies to socialize newcomers (van Maanen and Schein, 1979; Jones, 1986). They can employ collective tactics that lead to an institutionalized role orientation (which reflects *similarity in typical responses across members*). The initial training of new recruits in the armed forces is typically focused on instilling a highly institutionalized orientation among the recruits. As a result, such experiences are typically structured to be in groups, away from the actual work context, clearly sequenced in similar ways for all recruits, and rigid and non-negotiable. Moreover, newcomers are inducted by existing members and often have to earn full status which is achieved with rites of passage.

In contrast, individual tactics tend to lead to individualized role orientations which *increases the variety in individual behaviours and responses*. An example is the induction of a highly talented new member of an advertising agency. Socialization tactics will typically try to instil a highly individualized orientation in the newcomer,

Socialization
The process by which newcomers to a social setting (or a culture) develop the ability to function effectively in that particular setting. It involves learning about the norms, values, assumptions and other central-shared elements of a particular social group or culture.

Institutionalized role orientation
This reflects the degree of similarity in typical responses across members of a group. See also individualized role orientation.

HIGH PERFORMANCE

Orla's induction to work

Orla began a new job as a trainee reporter with a local newspaper in Edinburgh (part of an international media group) after she left university. She was very proud to have made a start in what she hoped would be a good career in journalism. The company had three phases in their induction programme. The first was a short induction period with the UK parent group and was intended to introduce trainee journalists to the way the group functioned, its objectives and policies, and the development and career opportunities available. The second, organized by the newspaper that Orla was working with, was designed to introduce the way it worked and the role of journalists within it. It was also intended to introduce new employees to the culture of the company and the preferred ways of working as determined by management.

Having completed both induction courses, Orla was looking forward to actually starting work – the third phase. She was allocated to work with an experienced journalist for a few weeks in order to learn the practicalities of the job, before being given some small stories to write under her own name. When she met her new mentor he suggested that she accompany him to interview a local politician about proposed changes to public housing policy in the area. On the

drive to the interview the journalist and Orla chattered about the job and what it involved. The journalist concluded by saying that the best advice he could give her was to ignore what had been said in the induction courses as management didn't have a clue what was involved in getting good stories out of people and meeting the deadlines imposed by publication requirements. The only people who knew how to do the job were the real journalists, not accountants or managers. He also suggested to her that after the meeting with the politician, they should go to a particular pub and meet some of the other journalists, giving Orla the chance to 'get to know' her colleagues and to find out the how the job was done in practice.

TASKS

1 What does this example suggest about socialization within organizations?

2 To what extent might this example illustrate attempts at the social control of newcomers by the journalists in order to retain control over the profession, its status and ways of working within the organization?

3 What would you do if you were Orla and why? What implications might that have for her and her career?

and the induction process is likely to be personalized to the needs of the newcomer, will take place close to real work or even on-the-job, will be flexible or even random, and very open to ideas, interests and suggestions from the newcomer. The newcomer will receive positive signals and much social support and will be included from early on as a full member.

Socialization reflects an enormous source of control for organizations. Extreme forms of socialization and resocialization (such as brainwashing, cult-deprogramming, or political re-education) provide powerful examples of the impact that such social influence can have on individuals and their behaviour. It also helps to understand the role that perceived organizational support can play to bring about social control (e.g., Aselage and Eisenberger, 2003; Butts *et al.*, 2009)

Individualized role orientation
This reflects the degree of diversity in typical responses across members of a group. It increases the variety in behaviours and responses among members. See also institutionalized role orientation.

Technology

Machines can work at a predictable and stable pace until they break down or are switched off. People are not so programmable. As a consequence of the desire of managers to justify the introduction of technology, humans are frequently

Figure 12.4 Vicious cycle of control

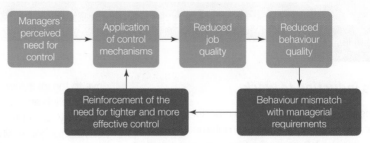

Source: Adapted from Clegg, S and Dunkerley, D (1980) *Organization, Class and Control,* Routledge & Kegan Paul, London.

relegated to second place in consideration. It is often the technological artefacts (machines, computers) that determine (control) human participation in the production process. The work that humans undertake is determined by what the technology cannot tackle and by what is needed to service the ability of the technology to maintain continuous production. This provides a very real form of control over human endeavour.

The justification for new technology is frequently based upon improvements in control in one form or another: Control of cost, of a process, of quality, or of employees are among the most commonly found reasons. Control can become a self-perpetuating process of management finding ways to improve control, involving tighter influence on employee behaviour, leading to adverse employee reaction, confirming the need for ever tighter control. Clegg and Dunkerley (1980) describe this as a vicious cycle of control (see Figure 12.4).

Vicious cycle of control
Reflects the view that control can become a self-perpetuating and deteriorating cycle of management tightening control leading to adverse employee reactions, resulting in even tighter control etc.

Production and factory work as well as clerical, administrative, sales, service, technical and managerial work has been subjected to the influence of control through technology. For example, in customer service teams it is common to find that the technology providing improved ability to serve the customer also provides the opportunity to manage the performance of staff more effectively. This has been extensively researched in call centres (e.g., Batt *et al.*, 2009; Houlihan, 2002; Moss *et al.*, 2008; Skarlicki *et al.*, 2008). In this particular setting, comprehensive technological surveillance and control is possible through call recording for subsequent analysis; automatically generation of call rates and queue waiting statistics, and the clear prescription and monitoring of behaviour and outcomes of the service interactions.

The introduction of ICT has provided additional means for the exercise of management control. Since technology deployment is usually the prerogative of management, it can be used deliberately or inadvertently to exert substantial amounts of control on workers – as well as on managers. Modern systems used by virtually all large firms called enterprise resource planning (ERP) systems attempt to create comprehensive transparency of operations, logistics, and people. Inevitably these automated and standardized systems are also used to control the activities and operations they record and report on (e.g., Dery *et al.*, 2006; Hall, 2005; Willis and Chiasson, 2007). Table 12.3 provides an overview and examples of how technology can be used to exert control in organizations.

Reward, punishment and reinforcement

Much of organizational control is based on reward and punishment. The role of formal reward systems, as well as of punishment and disciplining as part of comprehensive human resource management (HRM) approaches, is discussed in Chapter 13, but the application of behaviourist principles in organizations is an often immensely effective tool in the arsenal of managerial and organizational control.

Table 12.3 Technology and control

Focus	Technological control is exerted through...
Control of process	The design of operational layouts, machine configurations and the methods of work.
Control of work	The design of jobs and issues such as work rate, quality and product design, and indirectly through social relationships at work.
Control of people	Closely defining and monitoring activities and behaviour, for example through the subordination of people to machine processes, the application of administrative technologies, or the application of scientific management-based technologies. Each of these opportunities restricts the freedom of individuals' influence over, and ownership of, their work.
Control of cost	Measurement and instant information availability through financial and accounting technologically based devices which control the design of the work itself and the pace of work. Through the development of administrative technologies and procedures there is an improved level of visibility among managers about how costs are influenced and, therefore, how they can be managed.
Control of agenda	Selection of technology as signal of what activities need to be invested in. Management also shapes the future of systems development in organizations.
Control of resistance	Threats of technology as replacement of other activities (and the attached jobs). The use of people technologies can encourage employees to become an active part of the process itself. For example, employee involvement, matrix structures, teamwork and profit-share options are just some of the ways in which employees are encouraged to identify with organizational objectives.
Control of skill	Determining the level and type of skill that exists through the design of jobs and the nature of deployed technology itself and how it is adopted within the organization.
Control of organization	Designing the role of technology and its use in organizations, and the implication for organizational structure and activities.
Control of location	Creating alternative options for central processes through technological linkages and duplication of facilities.
Control of information	Disseminating or withholding information flows and making information availability a source of power and control.

The application of behaviourist principles and practices in organizations is common, although it has received comparatively little research attention in recent decades (see Latham and Pinder, 2005; Pinder, 2008). However, despite its lack of current research, the systematic application of reinforcement strategies for control and performance management purposes, called organizational behaviour modification (OB Mod; sometimes also called 'organizational behaviour management' or 'applied behavioural analysis') is a common practice. Such approaches are most effective if they are consistently applied and integrated with other managerial and organizational practices. Like all reinforcement approaches, it begins with the identification of desired and undesired target behaviours (see Chapter 5) that are then systematically and consistently reinforced, punished or extinguished.

Figure 12.5 provides a comprehensive description of the model. The model is self-explanatory in that it begins with a systematic review of the requirements and actuality of behaviour in the specific situation. This is then followed by a decision-making process

Figure 12.5 Organizational Behaviour Modification (OB Mod)

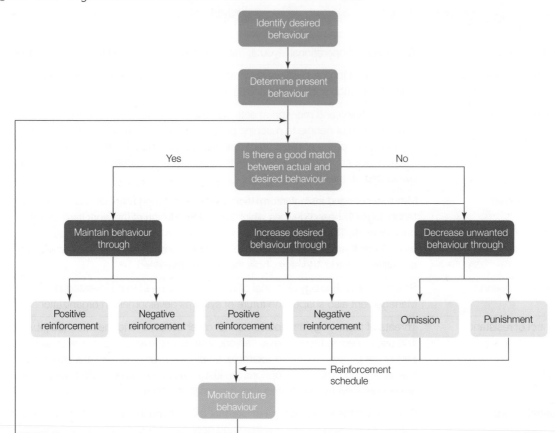

Source: Adapted from Luthans, F (1985) *Organizational Behaviour*, 4th edn, McGraw Hill, New York. Copyright © The McGraw-Hill Companies, Inc. Reprinted with permission.

Alienation

Work performed under conditions in which the worker is estranged from his or her own activity in the act of production, through the sale of labour power and the subordination of skills and knowledge to the capitalist or other external social forces. Sometimes described as feelings of powerlessness, meaninglessness, isolation or self-estrangement in which the person no longer feels part of, or involved with, the work that they do.

which results in the identification of the appropriate reinforcement approach to be adopted. Once selected and operational, the results of the reinforcement approach would then be regularly monitored and any remedial or follow-up action taken. Among the criticisms of this type of approach to influencing human behaviour is that it is managers who decide what defines appropriate behaviour and it therefore forms part of a social engineering or management control process. Also, the range of rewards available within organizations is limited and needs to be deployed in ways which limit fraud, favouritism, discrimination and unfairness. This inevitably restricts the ways in which behaviour modification can be used in practice. However, in situations where target behaviours can be clearly identified and measured, OB Mod can provide an effective means of exerting behaviour control.

Some concluding remarks on control in organizations

It has been argued (Braverman, 1974) that the organizational history of the twentieth century can be described in terms of increasing management control and the potential for conflict and alienation that flows from it. This neatly encapsulates the fundamental dilemma that exists from a management perspective. The scale of international business, the level of competition, the differential costs of operations around the world and many other forces all create conditions in which there is continual pressure for improved organizational performance. Inevitably, this dynamic leads managers to seek ever greater levels of control over every aspect of the enterprise in order to achieve greater added value from it. Braverman makes it clear that the price for this increased control is that employees experience greater levels of alienation.

They are increasingly treated as just one of the resources available to managers and, consequently, subject to the same degree of manipulation and control.

However, Courpasson and Dany (2003) suggest that in the postbureaucratic organizational world now evolving, a different form of power is emerging. The power-based employment relationship unfolding in modern organizations is described in their terms as *moral obedience*. The thrust of their argument is that in the post-bureaucratic organization different forms of employment based around loosened coalitions of people require individuals to hold a sense of duty to their immediate task and organization, and this expression of morality will increasingly become part of the political and power-based frameworks in the future. In essence they argue that it reflects management's attempt to introduce a different basis for the employment relationship, intended to offset the alienation from the less secure employment now prevalent. Alongside the use of power as a basis for control, we have already briefly mentioned that trust can provide another means for reducing uncertainty and for dealing with people's self-determination in organization (e.g., Grey and Garsten, 2001; Knights *et al.*, 2001; Reed, 2001).

Such recognition of development in postbureaucratic organizations is leading to changes in the way work is organized and conducted in many organizations (see Grant and Parker, 2009). We will consider and discuss different approaches to work and job design in the next section.

12.1 EXTEND
YOUR LEARNING

JOB AND WORK DESIGN

Job design is the way *in which tasks are grouped, assigned and structured in organizations at the level of individual jobs*. We have already considered the division of labour when we explored the nature and structure of organizations and discussed horizontal and vertical differentiation. These distinctions are central to work and job design, but they are combined with aspects that address the social and psychological aspects of work and of the people who conduct it. We will briefly consider the nature of work study, ergonomics and job analysis before we discuss job design in organizations.

Job design
This is the way in which tasks are grouped, assigned and structured in organizations at the level of individual jobs.

Designing work: work study, ergonomics and job analysis

Work study is often traced back to F.W. Taylor's work in developing scientific management in the early years of the twentieth century. In the search for the one best way to conduct work, Taylor employed analytical methods to increase productivity through determining the most efficient and effective approaches to specific tasks. Such analyses include considerations of the component elements of a task, different approaches to achieving the individual steps of the task under study, and time and motion studies of workers performing the tasks in different ways to determine the most efficient and effective combination. Taylor also considered output-based bonuses and payments to ensure compliance with such work approaches.

12.2 EXTEND
YOUR LEARNING

Work study has, however, earlier roots than scientific management. Some examples include Adam Smith (1776) considering the economic aspects of specialization and the division of labour, and there is even earlier evidence that medieval monks used job times to determine the duration of monastery and cathedral projects. Currie (1963: p. 2) also describes an extract from an employment contract in which an individual undertook secretly to time jobs in a factory and report the outcome to the owner:

Division of labour
The term describes breaking up the overall task into specialized and smaller activities in the search for higher levels of productivity and job specialization.

> *I Thomas Mason, this 22nd day of December, 1792 solemnly pledge myself to use my utmost caution at all times to prevent the knowledge transpiring that I am employed to use a stop watch to make observation of work done in*

Figure 12.6 Work study

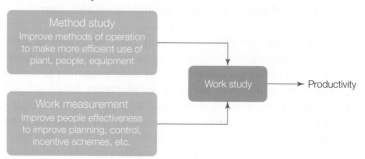

Source: Adapted from
Currie, RM (1963) *Work
Study*, London: Pitman.

Method study

The critical examination
of work in order to
identify the most efficient
work methods. See also
work study and work
measurement.

Work measurement

Based upon the use of
timing techniques to identify
how long particular tasks
should take to perform. See
also method study and work
study.

Work study

A management discipline
aimed at maximizing
productivity through the
application of method study
and work measurement
techniques. See also
method study and work
measurement.

Ergonomics

A multidisciplinary approach
to considering how people
can best conduct specific
work tasks.

Job analysis

A systematic approach to
the identification of the
content of a job.

*Mr. Duesbry's manufactory; and to take such observations with the utmost truth
and accuracy in my power and to give the results thereof faithfully to
Mr. Duesbry.*

Essentially, work study contains as its core activity two distinct elements: method
study (i.e., *the critical examination of work methods in order to identify the most
efficient work approaches*) and work measurement (i.e., *the use of timing and other
measurement devices and techniques to identify the quality and duration of particular tasks*) which focus on the improvement of task methods, and the measurement
and regulation of task accomplishment (see Figure 12.6). Thus, we formally define
work study as *the analysis of tasks to maximize productivity through the application
of method study and work measurement.*

A related approach to designing the way in which work is done is ergonomics,
a *multidisciplinary approach to considering how people can best conduct specific work tasks.* While efficiency and effectiveness are central concerns, ergonomics also addresses safety and health concerns that arise when performing work.
Especially in highly prescribed work situations, a proper fit between worker and
work demands is essential to avoid problems. Thus, ergonomically designed work
and work equipment should avoid safety and health problems (such as industrial
accidents, repetitive motion injuries, stress arising from poorly designed human –
machine interfaces, etc.) while addressing performance and efficiency concerns
(e.g., fatigue, error rates affecting product or service quality, accuracy and consistency of performance). To achieve that, ergonomics uses tools and insights from
disciplines such as physiology, psychology, mechanical and industrial engineering,
medicine, industrial design, and others.

Job analysis is *a systematic approach to the identification of the content of a
job*. Ivancevich (1992) distinguished between functional and position analysis. *Functional job analysis* considers the tasks required and how they are undertaken (1-3)
and identifies the type and level of output expected from the job (4):

1 Employee activities relevant to data, people and other jobs.

2 The methods and techniques used by the worker.

3 The machines, tools and equipment used by the worker.

4 What outputs are produced by the worker.

Position analysis focuses more on people and interaction aspects and studies six
aspects of a job:

1 Sources of information necessary to the job.

2 Decision making associated with the job activity.

3 Physical aspects associated with the job.

4 Interpersonal interactions and communication necessary to the job.

5 Working conditions and their impact on the job.

6 Impact of work schedules, responsibility, etc.

Job analysis plays a significant part in the identification of what tasks should be contained within a job. It is typically part of a larger, often iterative process of work design and management that is depicted in Figure 12.7. It is useful to note that the processes by which work is designed and by which specific jobs evolve is more complex and typically less structured that this figure may suggest. In addition, environmental factors (e.g., work and employment legislation, production and ICT technology) and social dynamics also play important roles.

In work organizations, the information provided by job analysis is used in a wide range of activities. A detailed knowledge of the jobs in the organization provides the data basis for many decisions on HRM. Some of these are mentioned below (for more detail on these HRM processes and activities see Chapter 13):

- resourcing and HR planning
- training
- career development and succession planning
- payment and remuneration level
- provision of job descriptions and job evaluation schemes
- performance evaluation.

APPROACHES TO DESIGNING JOBS

The tasks to be undertaken in an organization need to be combined into specific jobs that make sense for people to undertake. While occasions for the design of new jobs exist (for example when opening a new factory or department), job design is typically about changing jobs that already exist, for example after new equipment is introduced, when cost needs to be cut or productivity needs to be improved, when motivational problems or other issues lead to performance problems, or when labour

Figure 12.7 Job analysis and job effectiveness

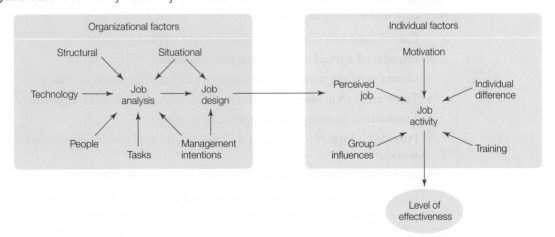

turnover is too high. Historically, the understanding of and approaches to job design have evolved quite substantially. We will review important steps and approaches in the following sections. What is important to recognize, however, is that the history and development of job design is heavily intertwined with technological and social developments. Also, the drivers of job design can generally be seen as attempts to increase efficiency as well as to counter the negative human and social impacts of such efficiency-oriented developments. Still, many individual contributors, F.W. Taylor among them (see Weisbord, 1987), had the welfare of workers in mind, even if their particular views do not appear very considerate or even appropriate by today's standards.

Simplification and job engineering

With the introduction of the factory system of manufacture, opportunities emerged to increase the output per worker through the division of labour. Babbage (1832) observed that it was thus possible to reduce training times, increase skill through constant repetition of a small range of tasks and also reduce waste. Fewer tool changes and machine set-ups were also required as a result of the batch nature of production and the specialized nature of equipment to support it. This approach represents the essence of job simplification (also called job engineering). F.W. Taylor further developed this through the introduction of the scientific management approach to job simplification.

Job simplification
This involves reducing the complexity of work by minimizing the range of tasks into the smallest convenient job size.

Job simplification involves *reducing the complexity of work by minimizing the range of tasks into the smallest convenient job size*. It is an approach seen in many production and assembly line jobs. In assembly line approaches to production, the workers stay in a fixed position and the item being made moves down the line until it is completed. The number of workstations and workers must be carefully balanced to provide an efficient assembly process with minimal idle time. The assembly of motor vehicles is a well known example of this process.

The aim of job simplification is to maximize output and minimize labour input. Consequently, this approach lends itself to the application of technology in seeking to match human activity to the needs of production. The difficulties associated with job simplification were recognized very early. It can be argued that the founding of the human relations movement was a direct consequence of the dehumanizing effect of such work. As far back as 1952 Walker and Guest identified a number of causes of dissatisfaction among assembly workers in a car factory, including lack of control over the pace of work and the methods and tools used, repetitiveness, low skill level requirements, and reduced social interaction. The whole scientific management approach which has specialization and job simplification as core elements has also been criticized as early as 1915 (Hoxie, 1915) on the basis that it:

- Contributed to a cunning speeding-up and sweating system.
- Introduced a trend towards task specialization.
- Condemned the worker to monotonous and routine work activities.
- Transferred to managers the workers' knowledge, skill and judgement.
- Emphasized quantity at the expense of quality.
- Provided information that could be used unscrupulously to the detriment of workers.
- Allowed for excessive control and discipline of worker activity.

This approach to job design is not restricted to work in factories. It can also be found in administrative jobs. For example, in accounting departments, someone has to open the post, sort the invoices from the payments and enter the details into a computer system. Such jobs bear all the classic symptoms of job simplification, including monotony, boredom, high labour turnover, alienation and lack of commitment. The same is true in education in which the job of teachers and lecturers is being ever more closely prescribed through national and local initiatives in schools and universities. This is usually justified in the name of providing quality and consistency in educational experience for students. However, in the process, opportunities for the exercise of professional judgement and skill and the responsiveness to specific learner needs are increasingly minimized, just as for assembly line workers.

Job rotation

Job rotation *involves the combination of two (or more) simplified jobs into a rotating pattern of work*. It is based on the view that job specialization and simplification provides the most efficient method of work. However, it tries to address shortcomings (e.g., the effects of boredom and monotony on employee commitment levels) that limit the achievement of the full potential from that approach to job design. Thus, two (or more) simplified jobs are combined into a pattern of work rotation. It is less efficient because it requires training for all included jobs and may limit the level of specialized knowledge developed. On the other hand, it provides cross-training opportunities and thus higher flexibility for management because more different workers can be deployed for each of the included jobs. Overall, it may ameliorate some of the monotony and boredom involved in de-skilled and specialized jobs, yet usually still provide relatively little challenge and development potential for workers.

Job rotation
This involved the combination of two (or more) simplified jobs into a rotating pattern of work.

Job enlargement

Job enlargement (also called *horizontal job enlargement*) adopts a slightly different approach in that it *seeks to build up a job by adding more tasks into it to form a larger job*. In effect it seeks to include more horizontally differentiated tasks into one larger job. The potential advantage is that the work may be perceived as more meaningful and interesting, and that performance will increase because of higher motivation.

Job enlargement
Sometimes called horizontal job enlargement, this seeks to build up a job by adding more (but similar level) tasks into it to form a larger job.

It is not always easy to introduce enlarged jobs into a factory as it requires the adoption of different approachs to the pattern of interaction between relevant tasks, machines and people. Job enlargement may conflict with the results of work studies regarding the most efficient approach to particular tasks. The work study approach attempts to eliminate or control activities considered to be irrelevant or unnecessary to the main purpose of the job. In many situations this is unrealistic, but it can be difficult to change the desire for tight control among managers, which explains their attraction to the principles of work study.

Conant and Kilbridge (1965) provide an early description of the application of job enlargement to the assembly of water pumps in washing machines. The assembly of the pump had been done on a production line with each worker adding components as the pump body went past. After redesign, the enlarged job allowed each worker to assemble the entire pump, but still on an assembly line with no loss of productivity. The major problem with enlargement as a design option is that it is frequently restricted to simple assembly line jobs, which even when enlarged remain relatively small jobs. Consequently, the benefits to employees quickly dissipate and the job becomes monotonous once again.

Job enrichment

Job enrichment (also called *vertical job enlargement*) is an approach to job design that *includes more complex tasks and increased levels of responsibilities in a job*. By adding more responsibility and decision-making authority to a job, this approach intends to offer workers increased control over a larger variety of aspects of the work performed. Herzberg (1968, 1974b) identified six forms of enrichment that designers should seek to include in jobs:

1 *Accountability.* Provide a level of responsibility and support for employees that requires them to accept accountability for their actions and performance.

2 *Achievement.* Provide employees with an understanding and belief in the significance of their work.

3 *Feedback.* Superiors should provide feedback to employees on their performance and work activities.

4 *Work pace.* Employees should be able to exercise discretion over the pace of work that they adopt and be able to vary that pace.

5 *Control over resources.* Employees should have high levels of control over the resources needed to perform their duties.

6 *Personal growth and development.* Opportunities should be found to encourage employees to acquire and practice new skills and develop themselves through their work.

Another approach to job enrichment was developed by Hackman and Oldham (1980). Their job characteristics model (JCM) is one of the best known approaches to job design. The JCM is based on five core job dimensions, which in turn combine and produce psychological responses, which then produce work and personal outcomes (Figure 12.8).

Taking each of the core job dimensions in turn:

- *Skill variety.* This refers to the range of activities required to perform a job. Increased skill variety will present more challenge and opportunity to enact mastery for workers and will thus contribute to task motivation (see Chapter 5). Broader skill variety requires more training but also offers more development opportunities to job holders. Individuals vary in their need and

Figure 12.8 Job characteristics approach to job enrichment

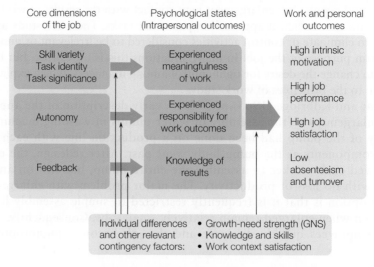

Source: Hackman, J and Oldham, R (1980) *Work Redesign*, Addison-Wesley, Reading, MA.

ability to cope with skill variety. Too little variety will produce boring and monotonous work; too much will produce fragmented work activity with stress and uncertainty for the employee.

- *Task identity.* This characteristic is about the degree to which the job provides a clear and identifiable contribution. If the employee only undertakes a small number of tasks on part of a whole product then they are unlikely to relate to the finished article. Neither are they likely to think that they make a meaningful contribution to the organization.
- *Task significance.* The importance of the job being done creates significance for the employee. This is often reflected in the degree of impact on the lives or work of other people. Very few people would be happy or conscientious in their work if it was felt to be of no consequence to anyone.
- *Autonomy.* This reflects the degree of individual freedom to schedule and adapt work methods. A closely prescribed job – working on an assembly line – has very little scope for autonomy compared with the job of a sculptor, who has considerable freedom in the artistic interpretation of the subject and pace of work. Autonomy increases perceived responsible for one's actions, thus providing a sense of ownership. An interesting study of this aspect of work organization was provided by Sadler–Smith *et al.* (2003) who found some association between autonomy and the cultural environment in Egypt.
- *Feedback.* This allows an employee to know how well they are doing and enables self-regulation of work. Feedback can come from supervisors, peers, the task itself, or from internal and external customers. Feedback is also central for learning and is therefore particularly important for those with high learning orientations.

The first three core job dimensions are linked together in Figure 12.8 because they all contribute to a feeling of experienced meaningfulness in the job. Autonomy leads to experienced responsibility, while feedback provides knowledge of actual results. These three critical psychological states then contribute to the personal and work outcomes such as higher motivation, performance and satisfaction, and lower absenteeism and turnover.

STOP & CONSIDER

To what extent are approaches to job design such as the job characteristics model simply management attempts to persuade employees to voluntarily work harder and more productively and are inherently doomed to fail because ultimate control of organizational activity and so on is retained by management?

Hackman and Oldham developed a means of being able to measure the level of job enrichment present in any job, the motivating potential score (MPS). The score produced through the application of the MPS is essentially a subjective response by the job holder, based upon their ability to compare with other jobs that they have experienced. It is a useful, although not altogether objective measure. There is evidence of general empirical support for the MPS, although not strong support for the causal linkages suggested by it (Wall *et al.*, 1985).

It is important to recognize that the link between the five job characteristics and the personal and work outcomes identified in the JCM is not automatic, however. The model applies only to individuals who have high growth-need strength (GNS), i.e., who have *an intrinsic interest in developing themselves, learning new and applying their existing skills, and taking responsibility and building identity through work*. Also, reminiscent of Herzberg's two-factor theory (see Chapter 5),

Growth-need strength (GNS)
The job characteristics model applies only to individuals who have high GNS – that is, they have an intrinsic interest in developing themselves, learning new and applying their existing skills, taking responsibility and building identity through their work.

if people are actively dissatisfied with the context of their work (e.g., dangerous or offensive work conditions), then the model is less likely to hold. Finally, the model is predicated on the availability of necessary skills and supports (e.g., people need to be able to perform their tasks, and they need to have adequate resources such as time, equipment, etc.). If such skills and supports are not available, then the model cannot guide effective job design. Work designed using the enrichment approach might be expected to provide higher levels of stimulation than the other approaches to job design. There is some suggestion, for example, that normal ageing processes such as brain decay can be slowed by undertaking stimulating work (Rawlins, 2003).

A very different yet important and influential approach to job design was proposed by Salancik and Pfeffer in 1978. They presented the social-information processing (SIP) model of job design. This model highlights the role of social information in determining the effects that the design of any job has on its holder. Thus, evaluations from relevant others will have an impact on the effects of particular design features. Compared with the JCM, it is not simply the actual characteristics of a job that determine the impact on workers, but rather the way in which workers experience the nature of their job and subjectively interpret the information about it. Such experiences and interpretations are substantially influenced by others as well as by the past behaviour of the person themselves. More specifically, when a job was taken based on a *voluntary* choice, when the choice or aspects associated with it (such as sunk costs) are *irrevocable*, and when this choice was made actively, explicitly and in *public*, then reactions to the job will be more positive and individuals will be more committed to it (see also Salancik, 1977, and the discussion of the escalation of commitment in Chapter 8).

The SIP model recognizes the role of the socially constructed reality of work. Writers such as Morgeson and Campion (2002) pick up on this idea and have begun to develop a model of job design that seeks to minimize the trade-offs between what they term the motivational and mechanistic aspects of job design whilst maximizing the benefits achieved in terms of factors such as satisfaction. Other recent developments have been the inclusion of prosocial motives derived from the design and context of particular jobs (Grant, 2007), attention to the linkages between job design and the use of teams (Morgeson and Humphrey, 2008), and the role of both relationships and opportunities for proactive behaviours to change and adapt jobs as part of job design (Grant and Parker, 2009). The Going Global example illustrates some of these aspects of job design and the impact on the people doing the work.

In conclusion, it may be useful to recognize that the job, so central to our thinking about organizations and our experience of work, is a relatively recent social invention in response to industrialization (see Bridges, 1995). Arguments exist that jobs as we know them will become less and less common, and that the role of individuals in organizations will be defined less and less by formal jobs. This *dejobbing* (Bridges, 1995) will arguably lead to the activities of any organizational member being determined not by formally designed jobs but – in highly flexible and changeable ways – by the actual work needing to be done at any given time. Clearly, this exciting and maybe even frightening idea is supported by current experiences in changing and downsized organizations trying to deal with a worldwide recession. But given the multiple functions that jobs have in hierarchical organizations (but see discussion of hierarchical postbureaucratic organizations, e.g., Kellogg *et al.*, 2006) and for managers – including control, co-ordination, and identity, among many others – jobs are here to stay for some time yet. Nevertheless, their role, nature and use are changing all the time, and understanding this is crucial for managers and employees in all forms of organizations.

Social-information processing (SIP)
A model of job design that highlights the role of social information in determining the effects that the design of a job has on its holder.

12.3 EXTEND
YOUR LEARNING

GOING GLOBAL

Cleaning in the factory

Marjorie was a general worker in a garment factory in Thailand which employed about 600 people (almost all women) on making various shirts and jackets for customers around the world. Her principal job was to sweep the floor and to move bins of part-completed garments between work areas. The sweeping accounted for about 30 per cent of her working time and was intended to make sure that no small pieces of fabric or thread were left lying about to catch fire or cause people to slip and hurt themselves. The rest of Marjorie's time was taken up with moving bins of part-completed garments between work areas. She was one of a team of twenty people constantly sweeping up and pushing garment bins around the factory. The factory only worked Monday to Friday each week and for half a day every two weeks Marjorie had to take her turn in cleaning the toilets. All of the general workers hated this part of their job.

Generally the women engaged in sewing jobs regarded themselves as superior to the general workers. The sewing machinists tended to talk down to the general workers and frequently tried to order them about as if they were in charge. The general workers such as Marjorie were made to feel inferior in every way and it was also apparent to them that their work was not appreciated by either the sewing machinists or the managers. The managers in the factory also treated the general workers as inferior, in practice ignoring them most of the time. The only time that a

manager spoke to Marjorie was to shout an order or to tell her off for apparently doing something wrong or not responding to an order quickly enough.

Most of the general workers hated their job. Labour turnover was very high among the general workers. They only half-heartedly undertook their duties and if they thought that they could get away with not doing something they would. This was particularly true when it came to cleaning the toilets. This particular job was the most hated by all the general workers as it did not matter how often they were cleaned, they quickly became filthy again. Most of the workers paid no attention to the state of the toilet facilities, for example, just throwing paper towels onto the floor rather than putting them in the bin provided.

After 6 months at the factory Marjorie found another job and resigned. The personnel officer of the company asked why she was leaving and she said that she felt her present job did not matter to anyone and that she did not feel that anyone valued her work.

TASKS

1 To what extent (and in what ways) does this example illustrate the Hackman and Oldham job characteristics model of job design and/or the SIP model developed by Salancik and Pfeffer?

2 What does your answer to question 1 tell you about job design as a management activity?

CONCLUSIONS

This chapter has explored the concepts of control and job design. Both are important aspects of OB. They are inseparable from the needs of organization and the needs, aspirations and inclinations of the individuals who work within them. Employers have work that they need done; individuals need to work for economic, psychological and social reasons. Interestingly, managers are also employees and subject to these same pressures, but within the particular context of acting for the largely absent owners of the organization. Control is needed to

ensure that objectives are met. However, as with most other aspects of OB, they contain the seeds of danger and risk that can cause damage to either individuals or the organization if they are not handled carefully and with respect.

Job design is something that influences a considerable range of aspects of work, not just the physical execution of the necessary tasks. It can influence the way in which the organization approaches the very nature of employment within it. Job design can reflect a belief about the rights of employees to high-level involvement in the activities of the company or it can reflect the view that workers provide a flexible (or necessary) alternative to machines. Job design is also something that can be used to draw out from employees' additional commitment to the objectives of management without any reward other than job satisfaction. In other words, it is a facet of management that can be used to reflect the moral values and beliefs of the people involved or it can be a form of cynical manipulation. The difficulty lies in being able to identify the proportion of each active in any given context.

Now to summarize this chapter in terms of the relevant Learning Objectives:

- **Discuss the main approaches to the design of work within an organizational setting.**
  The main approaches to job design are the use of job simplification (or job engineering as it is sometimes known); job rotation; job enlargement and job enrichment. Each of these approaches has advantages and disadvantages and involves seeking to offset the weaknesses in the simpler models. For example, job rotation seeks to offset the weaknesses in job simplification by incorporating a wider range of basic jobs within a rotating pattern of work. The job enlargement approach seeks to expand job rotation by incorporating a range of tasks into an integrated package of activity relevant to the needs of a particular context. One of the best known models of job design is that proposed by Hackman and Oldham, which utilizes task significance, skill variety, task identity, autonomy and feedback as the necessary core job dimensions to take into account when designing work. However, the SIP model also has something to offer in seeking to understand the social influences on job design activity.

- **Explain the influence of technology on job design and the control of work.** The relationship between technology and control is both positive and negative. In some instances the nature of work has been relegated to that of machine minding, ensuring that the technology does what it is supposed to do. In other cases jobs have been eliminated as a new technology has developed and removed the need for people to undertake particular tasks. In many ways the technology used by an organization controls the people who must work with and around it. On the other hand, technology can make some jobs easier by removing guesswork, drudgery and the need to produce hard copy reports and control data. The technology adopted by an organization is a

management decision and consequently it is they who decide how control will be exercised in relation to operational processes and employee behaviour. For example, call-centre telephony and computer systems are able to monitor, report on and hence control a wider range of employee behaviour and performance activities - the so-called ERP systems.

- **Assess the various 'means' through which control can be exercised within an organizational context.** There are many ways in which the organizational control strategies are translated into practice. The means used include:

  Managerial behaviour. That includes both indirect and direct control processes.

  Organizational design. Specific approaches to structural organization and compartmentalization of activity provide the opportunity to control through work organization, fragmentation and specialization.

  Skill. There are many jobs in which skill or professional status provides an opportunity to exercise control in one form or another. To know more than others in the same context is a basis for acquiring power and exercising control.

  Hierarchy and authority. The levels of decision making and delegation of authority decided upon by the management of an organization introduces hierarchical arrangement of responsibility and therefore the ability to exercise control over many aspects of the organization.

  Technology. The work that humans undertake is determined by what the technology cannot tackle and by what is needed to service the ability of the technology to do its job. This provides a very real form of control over human endeavour and could lead to the emergence of a 'vicious cycle of control'.

  Social control. This category of control includes such practices as the attempt to design management preferred cultures, employee socialization, management style, induction and training activities, etc.

  Reward, punishment and reinforcement. The role of formal reward systems as well as discipline, performance management, reflects the application of behaviourist principles in organizations and is a common and often immensely effective tool in the arsenal of managerial control.

We consider these means of organizational control in this section. Another important means of control, job design, is discussed in greater detail in other sections of this chapter.

● **Understand how work study attempts to influence job design activities and how changing the design of jobs can be a difficult process.** Work study consists of two main themes, method study and work measurement. Method study seeks to critically examine the way in which work is carried out in order to eliminate unnecessary movement and activity, then to design the 'one best way' of efficiently undertaking the job. Work measurement seeks to establish, based on the prescribed method of work, how much work a qualified worker should be able to produce in a given period of time. Both of these aspects combine to produce an approach to job design based on scientific management principles. Changing the design of jobs is a complex process for many reasons. Resistance to change among managers and employees can arise for many reasons including the desire to defend a specific area of expertise or to maintain current levels of power or control. Change brings with it an element of risk that things may not work as intended. There are also cost implications associated with radical change if the new design of jobs requires skills that may not be widely available in society.

● **Outline the characteristic features of control systems as found in organizations.** Control has at least two meanings within an organization. Firstly it can mean that order and predictability exists within the organization, used in the expression 'everything is under control'. Secondly it can also be regarded as a restrictive term which implies that people are being manipulated for some purpose or other. For example, a company might introduce a training course on financial awareness in order to prompt employees to identify cost-saving ideas in order to maintain profitability levels so that the senior mangers do not have to take actions that might create conflict. Little control takes the direct form of orders or force which might produce a negative response. Control is usually built into the fabric, hierarchy, procedures and policies of an organization and can be achieved through a number of devices including output control, which is the planned output that is monitored and assuming the plan is met, then no intervention is necessary. Conversely, behavioural control is based on direct observation of employees during work performance, for example, a supervisor using a checklist to 'score' a cashier's customer interaction in fast food restaurants. Behavioural control tends to be used where observation of work is possible, and where the links between work performance (i.e., employee behaviour) and work outcomes are stable and well known. Other levers that are used to achieve control within an organization include work design, structure, hierarchy and authority frameworks, expertise and skill in the way that work is organized and structured, the use of technology and social control in the ways in which people are socialized and trained into their work roles, etc. Each of these issues is discussed in greater detail in the appropriate sections of this chapter and many are also covered in other chapters.

DISCUSSION QUESTIONS

1 Describe what the terms prospective and reactive control mean in relation to control within organizations.

2 Describe the bureaucratic, market and clan approaches to organizational control strategies and explain the conditions and requirements relevant to their use.

3 Can compliance as an employee response to management attempts to achieve high levels of control ever form a basis for the creation of an effective organization? Justify your answer.

4 'Control is a series of devices and processes that at best provides the illusion of order and structure.' Discuss this statement.

5 'The trick in management is to find ways of control that are socially acceptable.' Discuss this statement.

6 Why should managers be concerned with job design?

7 If effective job design is a function of the factors identified in the job characteristics model (Figure 12.8) to what extent can work study techniques offer any real value in identifying the design of jobs?

8 How does technology influence the organization of work?

9 'We as individuals want jobs that are satisfying, challenging and pay high wages; yet we all want to pay as little as possible for the goods and services that we buy. That means that job simplification is the only realistic way of designing jobs as it provides the most cost-effective use of labour.' Discuss this statement.

10 Why might a satisfied employee not be the most productive? What does your answer to the first part of this question imply about control and job design?

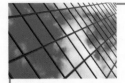

CASE STUDY

Controlling the invisible?

This story describes events that occurred in a meat processing factory in the UK. The process involved the preparation of beef carcasses into joints, steaks and product suitable for curing as beef bacon (predominantly for export to Middle Eastern markets). James was the management accountant at the factory. He was responsible for the determination of product costing and he asked for a full breakdown of material and labour data for each process within the factory. The work study department were given the task of obtaining and collating the data needed for this cost exercise. A number of time studies were undertaken to determine the labour cost involved and the product weight was also checked at each stage of the process. The data collection phase of this exercise lasted for several weeks.

Among the findings from the studies was the rather surprising one that the total weight of meat reduced at each stage of the production process. Every beef carcass and joint was weighed before and after each stage in the butchery process (including the small trimmings, bones, etc.). There was always a slight difference between the total after-processed weight and the original weight. When this was first discovered it was thought to be due to careless weighing. Considerable effort was subsequently made to tighten the weighing process. As a result of this special initiative, everyone in the production and work study departments was satisfied that the weighing process was as comprehensive and accurate as it could be. The difference in weight

© Peter Johnson/Corbis

between production stages became known as the invisible loss and was on average about 4 per cent of the original weight. The food technologists and production specialists within the company concluded that it was probably due to moisture weeping out of the meat as it was cut. This 'conclusion' was included in the report presented to James as the management accountant.

James was not happy with the idea of having something that could not be properly accounted for and, even worse, with no physical evidence to see. This went against every aspect of his professional training and he refused to accept the report as the basis of product costing. For James, meat did not and could not simply become invisible. The fact that meat was a valuable commodity and the temptation for staff to 'divert' it for personal use was another factor in his thinking! He was being asked to price the company products on the basis that some 4 per cent of it was disappearing. Over a full year that represented a considerable volume of meat and monetary value. James argued strongly that the report must be wrong within the senior management team and demanded that more tests be done. He even refused to believe the evidence of his own eyes when he was present at a demonstration of the effect.

Clearly, there was a problem associated with the ability to control the processing of meat within the factory that needed to be addressed. It was at this stage that the politics and relative power of the key players began to influence events. James was not popular as an individual and was generally considered to be pedantic, rude, unhelpful and not well integrated with the rest of the senior management team. James's boss, the finance director, was a very quiet individual but was regarded by most of the senior managers as a 'safe and effective' director who tried to work with his colleagues. So the stage was set for a battle of who would win the argument about the invisible loss. The accountants had a natural advantage in that they determined the product costing upon which prices and profitability depended. But James was in a difficult personal and political position as he had alienated the key players from the operations functions and did not have strong support from his own superior.

After considerable behind-the-scenes discussion and lobbying by all concerned, together with discussion with various other organizations in the meat industry, James was overruled and the invisible loss became a feature of the costing process.

TASKS

1 To what extent does this case demonstrate that control is a social process involving personalities, perception, shared frames of reference between all the parties involved and not just a process involving procedures and numbers? Justify your answer.

2 What does the answer to the previous question imply about how control processes should be designed and implemented within an organization?

3 What should James learn from this experience and how might he regain his credibility in the situation?

FURTHER READING

Barling, J. (1994) Work and Family: In Search of More Effective Workplace Interventions. In Cooper, C.L. and Rousseau, D.M. (eds) *Trends in Organizational Behaviour*, Chichester: John Wiley; Considers the links between family and work roles and examines the assumptions surrounding the interrelationship between job design on family 'well-being'.

Hatch, M.J. and Cunliffe, A.L. (2006) *Organization Theory: Modern, Symbolic and Postmodern Perspectives*, Oxford University Press. Useful discussion of many issues related to power throughout the book.

Jay, A. (1987) *Management and Machiavelli*, revised edn, London: Hutchinson Business. A humorous text which considers many aspects associated with power and authority in management. It does not take Machiavelli's work specifically as its basis, but his spirit is evident. A translation of Machiavelli's original work, which is very accessible and available as a 1981 Penguin book, is also well worth reading.

Jermier, J.M., Knights, D. and Nord, W.R. (eds) (1994) *Resistance and Power in Organizations*, London: Routledge. Provides a review of how attempts to use power as a basis of control inevitably leads to resistance in one form or another. It is grounded in the labour process perspective and attempts to interpret the arguments from the perspectives implied by that model.

McMahon, P. (2002) *Global Control: Information Technology and Globalization*, Cheltenham: Edward Elgar. A solid review of information systems as the means of providing control in the cycles of capitalist reorganization and globalization.

Marchington, M., Grimshaw, D., Rubery, J. and Wilmott, H. (2004) *Fragmenting Work: Blurring Organizational Boundaries and Disordering Hierarchies,* Oxford: Oxford University Press. Considers the reality and complexity of modern organizational functioning and supply chain operations together with the structural and job-related issues that emerge from that reality.

Siddons, S. (2003) *Remote Working: Linking people and organizations*, Oxford: Elsevier. Considers the forms that remote working can take and what is necessary to support the people engaged in that form of employment.

Watson, T.J. (2008) *Sociology, work and industry* (5th edn), Routledge. Sociological treatment that characteristically focuses on power dynamics and structures throughout the book.

COMPANION WEBSITE

Online teaching and learning resources

Visit the companion website for Organizational Behaviour and Management 4th edition at: http://www .cengage.co.uk/martinfellenz to find valuable further teaching and learning material. For full details, see 'About the website' at the start of the book.

©mevans/istock

CHAPTER THIRTEEN

HUMAN RESOURCE MANAGEMENT AND ORGANIZATIONS

LEARNING OBJECTIVES

After studying this chapter and working through the associated OB in Action panels, Discussion Questions and Case Study you should be able to:

- Explain the major models for the study of HRM

- Understand the relevance of organizational behaviour to the study and practice of HRM

- Describe the approaches to studying the links between business and HR strategy

- Assess the links between performance management and the practice of HRM

- Discuss the approaches to equality and diversity introduced in this chapter

INTRODUCTION

People management has always existed within organizations in one form or another. The application of human effort to the achievement of business objectives means that people able to undertake particular tasks need to be found and encouraged to contribute to their best ability to the task in hand. In most large modern organizations human resource management (HRM) specialists support line managers through the development of appropriate policies and practices. The relative roles and responsibilities of line managers and HRM specialists varies between organizations, but increasingly line managers are expected to take primary responsibility for people management activities, while HRM specialists are charged with supporting them. HRM draws heavily on much of the OB literature in the underpinning and justification of its practices.

Human Resource Management (HRM)
An approach to the management of people that supposedly represents a more central strategic management activity than personnel management.

Line manager
Every employee reports to a line manager – their boss.

MODELS OF HRM

As with most areas of management theory, there is no one single view as to what HRM means and how it should be practised within an organization. There are four main approaches that have been developed over recent years. The first, formulated by Fombrum *et al.* (1984), begins with the view that human beings are a resource, in principle just like any other resource available to the organization. Any resource is of value to an organization providing that it delivers value – meaning that it is flexible and reliable in operation and can be used in a cost-effective manner. HRM based on this perspective originates with the organization's strategy-based business framework; this would then be converted into the various people resource strategies; followed by the development and implementation of the actual HRM policies and practices necessary to achieve the strategic objectives. In this view, the people characteristics and behaviours are determined by the business strategy – a unidirectional process.

Another model, developed by Beer *et al.* (1984, 1985), takes a stakeholder view of the nature of HRM within organizations. It begins with the same strategic perspective as the previous model, but seeks to add a human dimension to the process. This is achieved by recognizing that people are thinking, dynamic and interactive beings, not just a static resource waiting to be used. This model suggests that four policy areas covering employee influence, human resource flows, reward systems and work systems are necessary to achieve effective use of people. In general terms this model implies a structured approach to HRM policy areas intended to deliver closer alignment between individual and organizational objectives. In doing so, however, it retains the same 'top-down' approach originating from the business strategy as the first model.

A third model by Schuler and Jackson (1987, 1996) sets out to demonstrate an association between operational strategy (rather than business strategy) and the employee behaviours necessary to achieve it. *Operational strategies* are intended to determine how organizations should compete in the market places that they are in. This is similar to the generic strategies for competitive advantage developed by Porter (1985) although his model is based on slightly different choices. Schuler and Jackson identified two basic operational strategy options – cost minimization or innovation – each with different behaviour implications. For example, behaviours identified with cost-reduction strategies include short-cycle, repetitive, predictable behaviours; narrow skill range; low job involvement. Appropriate behaviours for an innovative strategy include high levels of risk taking; flexible with regard to change; tolerant of ambiguity and uncertainty; and high levels of job involvement. The authors identify specific policy options covering HR planning, staffing, appraising, compensating and development appropriate to the two strategy options. For example, under compensation, the cost-reduction strategy would include low salary levels, few benefits, lack of job security and limited participation. By contrast, the innovation strategy requires high salary levels, a broad range of benefits and high levels of job security together with high levels of participation. This model is similar to the previous models in suggesting that it is necessary to match the people management policies and practices to the business strategy. But it goes further by offering guidance on appropriate behaviours matched to particular operational strategies. What matters is not which approach is used, but that policies and practices are consistent with the operational strategy. This model is also a 'top down' approach in that strategy is determined and then people are 'fitted' around it.

A fourth model originates from researchers at Warwick Business School (Hendry *et al.*, 1989). Unlike the previous models which originated in the USA, this one is based on experience in Britain and explores the subject in terms of the culture, managerial practice and organizational arrangements specific to that context. The model proposes five main interlinked elements which determine the approach adopted by an organization to HRM:

1 *Outer context.* This represents the broader social, economic and cultural forces impacting on any organization. It also incorporates those issues associated with the organization and its industry that might be expected to impact on the way that it functions.

2 *Inner context.* This represents the organizational factors that could be expected to impact on its functioning. For example, culture, structure, profitability, technology, products or services, management style and politics.

3 *Business strategy context.* This represents the business strategy followed and reflects the earlier discussion in relation to the Schuler and Jackson model.

4 *Human resource management context.* This represents the philosophy and policy areas associated with how people are expected to contribute to the functioning and success of the organization.

5 *Human resource management content.* This represents the approach to people management adopted within the organization in areas such as reward, employee relations and work arrangements.

This model demonstrates the complexity of the HRM environment for an organization. The five interacting elements above reflect the forces acting upon the situation which create a dynamic situation that is difficult to manage. This supports Boxall and Purcell (2003) when they suggest that HRM does not 'belong' to specialists because line managers are inevitably responsible for their team (activities/outcomes) on a day-to-day basis within a dynamic context. In their view the human resource specialist should 'sell' their technical expertise to those who have need of that support. Legge (2005) also provides a comprehensive review of what HRM is within its social and business context.

STOP & CONSIDER

To what extent is HRM about finding ways of control that are socially and legally acceptable?

HRM AND BUSINESS STRATEGY

The strategy followed by the business will undoubtedly impact on the way that HRM is practised within the organization – so much is apparent from the models discussed above. The question is how do these two aspects interact? The models of HRM outlined above all suggest a relationship and one or two actually specify the HR implications arising from particular strategic choices. Marchington and Wilkinson (2005) develop this further by suggesting two main approaches to the relationship between business and HRM strategies:

Best fit or contingency approach to HRM
An outside-in perspective on HRM which suggests that HR strategy needs to be relevant to and supportive of the business strategy. This approach assumes that the HRM aspects of organizational activity are the malleable variable – the outside factors are fixed and therefore the inside variables must flex to align the organization with them.

- Best fit or contingency approach to HRM. This approach suggests that HR strategy needs to be relevant to and supportive of the business strategy. The authors outline three different strategic models and seek to explore the implications for the best-fit approach by HR:

  - *Life-cycle models.* Attempts to explain differences in HR strategy as a function of differing stages in the organizational life cycle. The idea is that as an organization moves through its life cycle different HRM strategies become necessary to support the business strategies at each stage. In that sense HRM strategies are contingent upon the life-cycle stage.

  - *Competitive advantage models.* This approach focuses on the competitive advantage model developed by Porter (1985) and matches appropriate HRM strategies to each of the options proposed by it. In that sense HRM strategies are contingent upon the firm's competitive strategy.

  - *Strategic configurations.* This seeks to provide HRM strategies that are consistent with both internal and external employment contexts. HRM strategies should be contingent upon the internal and external contexts of the firm.

  Marchington and Wilkinson identify six general weaknesses in the best-fit models, including that they are top-down in perspective; more factors influence HRM strategy than are identified within the models; employees are not passive resources to be manipulated in the employment process; the models don't focus on the dynamic employment relationship or the employment/business context; categorization simplifies what is in reality a complex organizational context.

Resource-based approach to HRM
An inside-out perspective on HRM which holds that HR activity can be strategic in its own right.

- Resource-based approach to HRM. This approach takes an inside-out perspective – the opposite view to the best-fit approach which takes an outside-in perspective. The best-fit approach assumes that HRM activity is the malleable variable – the outside factors are fixed and therefore inside variables must flex to align the organization with them – so delivering effective performance. The resource-based approach turns that approach on its head and holds that HR activity can be strategic as practices such as training and development can directly influence organizational performance. Therefore HRM can be used strategically as one of the resources available to an organization. The authors identify five issues that result from the application of the resource-based approach to HRM:

  - The need to identify those parts of the workforce that provide the key resource. For example, it could be that company performance is achieved through the technical specialists who provide a direct link to customer needs; or perhaps it is employees who assemble the factory products or provide the service to customers that have the greatest impact on performance.

  - The need to determine if the focus should be on people, practices or processes. Company performance could be the result of people and their inherent skills; or the way in which the product or service package is structured and delivered. This forces attention of how the key resource should be used within the organization.

- The ways that interpersonal and team relationships unfold and function in an organization also have a significant impact on performance. It represents the Deal and Kennedy (1982) definition of culture as the way we do things around here. It represents the day-to-day interactions and job activities which can function in a supportive and productive way.

- There is a need to consider influences beyond the organization and consider the external forces that can impact on HRM strategy and practice including education levels, economic conditions, etc.

- There are a number of HRM-related issues that all organizations must abide by if they are to function in a particular context or industry. For example, across Europe minimum wage requirements must be implemented in member states having statutory provision. They represent qualifying conditions that allow an organization to operate; they do not provide the means of differentiating the organization from its competitors or of achieving superior performance – other ways must be found to do that.

In addition to the models outlined above, there are a number of practicalities associated with management activity which can influence how strategy is developed and converted into action. For example, Brewster and colleagues (1983) draw a distinction between espoused and operational policies. Espoused represent those things that senior management claim (perhaps in written documents and policies) that they believe in relation to people and the management of the human resource. Operational in this context means what actually happens in practice. For example, senior managers may state with some conviction that 'People are our most important asset.' However if every Board meeting spends 80 per cent of its time discussing the financial performance of the company, then it could be argued that its operational policies don't match its espoused policies. In addition there are political, capability, will and other forces that impact on any organization's ability to identify the need for, create and then implement effective HRM strategies, let alone ones linked to the business strategy.

THE ROLE OF HRM IN ORGANIZATIONS

There have been some attempts over the years to describe the role of HRM within organizations, usually based on the things that it does and how it relates to its line management colleagues. For example, Legge (1978) suggested the following categories:

- *Conformist innovator.* An approach which encourages the adoption of HR practice, but within the current rules, status quo and management style.
- *Deviant innovator.* An approach which encourages the adoption of HR practices, but in ways that go beyond the current rules, status quo and management style.
- *Problem solver.* An approach which does not attempt to develop HR practice beyond dealing with problems as they arise.

Some models of HR activity are based on four categories of role, not the three identified above. Marchington and Wilkinson (2005) bring together the work of a number of writers in this field (Figure 4, p. 133) in a model based on two intersecting variables:

- *Level of HR profile.* Based on a scale from low to high – reflecting the degree to which the HR function is visible within the organization.
- *Level of HR involvement.* Based on a scale from strategic to operational – reflecting the degree to which the HR function is involved with strategic issues or restricted to operational activities within the organization.

Role of HRM
There are a number of models that seek to reflect the role adopted by HR within an organization. One example identifies four different roles: change agent; adviser; regulator/ internal contractor; and service provider. See also 'business partner'.

The resulting four quadrants of the chart allow the following categories of role to be identified:

- *Change agent*. Operating at the strategic and high-profile ends of the two axes. This role reflects the strategic activities along with a high profile necessary to be a change agent. Such a role should involve the ability to influence strategy and also to bring about – operationalize – the HR implications that result from it.
- *Adviser*. Operating at the strategic and low-profile ends of the two axes. The low profile within the organization reduces the ability of the HR function to take a leading change agent role, in effect relegating the HR role to that of an adviser.
- *Regulator/internal contractor*. Operating at the operational and high-profile ends of the two axes. This role would be typified by an HR function that was heavily involved in supporting the line departments to achieve their objectives, but at the operational end of the spectrum, implying working at a day-to-day level rather than looking ahead at the strategic level.
- *Service provider*. Operating at the operational and low-profile ends of the two axes. This represents the most reactive of the HR roles. As such this role acts in an advisory role, but in relation to operational activities (day-to-day) rather than at a strategic level.

Perhaps the model of HR roles that has had most impact, certainly on the HR profession and its aspirations, is that developed by Ulrich (1998). His model is broadly similar in approach to that just described, but he substitutes the axis on high or low profile outlined above with one measuring the degree to which the HR function manages people or processes. He also names the four roles slightly differently as:

- *Business partner*. Operating at the strategic and management of process ends of the two axes.
- *Change agent*. Operating at the strategic and management of people ends of the two axes.
- *Administrative expert*. Operating at the operational and management of process ends of the two axes.
- *Employee champion*. Operating at the operational and management of people ends of the two axes.

His view is that the HR function needs to adopt all four roles if they are to play a significant part in the management of people in an organization. The business partner role has struck a chord with HR practitioners in their search for a role within organizations (e.g., CIPD (2008)). In modern organizations line managers have greater responsibility (and hence accountability) for managing their own people resource. HR could be in danger of being relegated to an administrative role in ensuring that the rules are followed according to the current policies and legal requirements. The idea of becoming a business partner in which the focus is on the blending of business and people strategies and the associated processes is attractive. However, such an approach can create rifts between HR staff and the line managers whom they are supposed to be supporting. Line managers have to meet their operational objectives and they must channel employee behaviour in order to meet that need. It is easy to envisage line mangers resenting (what they might interpret as hostile or unhelpful) contributions of HR in providing complex people management policies and procedures. Line managers might regard such 'support' as trying to inhibit their ability to 'drive' employee performance. HR practitioners therefore

Business partner
Sometimes referred to as a strategic partner, this HR role involves working closely with line colleagues on the design of HR systems and processes that address strategic business issues. Intended to be more business-focused with a clear understanding of the client perspective (the line manager).

need to develop the ability (and credibility) to function as effective business partners if they are to achieve their desired role in support of line managers.

PEOPLE MANAGEMENT – ISSUES AND ACTIVITIES

In all but the smallest organizations the functional responsibility for providing expertise in people management falls to the HRM department. This embraces a broad spectrum of activities as shown in Table 13.1. Each of the areas indicated in Table 13.1 represents a major area of work in its own right. Consequently, only a general introduction to the significant aspects of people management will be provided below.

Human resource planning

Organizations are dynamic in that they are constantly changing in some way or other as they seek to adapt to the ever changing environments that they live within. For example, people join and leave; markets and fashion change; legislative requirements change; technology changes; competitors change their offerings and tactics; economic conditions change; and customers also change. Human resource planning seeks to provide the link between business strategy and the people strategies of the organization. However, there is debate about how effectively strategic planning within organizations can deliver competitive advantage because of weaknesses and limitations in the people and processes adopted (Caulkin, 2001). Smith (1996) develops this theme

Human resource planning
The process of seeking to match present and future human availability for work to the needs of the organization.

Table 13.1 The disciplines falling within human resource management practice

Human resource planning

Human resource strategy

Recruitment

Selection

Induction

Training and development

Performance management

Pay, salary, incentive and benefit systems

Discipline and grievance policy and practice

Diversity, discrimination and equality of opportunity

Health and safety at work

Career progression and development

Compliance with employment legislation

Employee relations

Employee exit planning

Representation of the organization to external bodies such as Employment Tribunals and argues that there is a need for organizations to concentrate on developing a high-performance top management team before real progress can be made in formulating effective business strategies. Only after this is achieved can business objectives be identified and converted into more specific current and future people requirements and plans. The outcome of the planning process is sometimes referred to as developing the employer's brand. The CIPD (2009b) define employer brand as the ways that reflect the application of marketing principles to HR practice in seeking to ensure that actual and potential employees are made aware of what the organization has to offer.

Employer brand
'A set of attributes and qualities – often intangible – that makes an organization distinctive, promises a particular kind of employment experience and appeals to those people who will thrive and perform best in its culture.'

A major objective of the HRM function is to provide the best match possible between the current and future needs of the organization (Bennison, 1980). This is difficult to achieve in practice. Organizations recruit employees for two time horizons. First, there exists a need to be able to do the work of the organization now. Second there is a need to be able to provide appropriate human resources for the organization's anticipated future requirements. Anticipating the future is a difficult process which leads writers such as Bowen *et al.* (1996) to suggest that recruitment should be based on the 'fit' between the individual and the organization, not just current job compatibility. A job represents a set of current tasks that are likely to change over time. From that perspective the skills needed to undertake most jobs can be taught and so organizational fit becomes the more important selection criteria. There are many variables at work in planning the people resource of an organization, including the volume of labour required, the location of organizational activity, the nature of operational activity, the future role of technology and the type of products and services offered by the organization. Research by Lepak *et al.* (2003) suggests that there is a relationship between the type of employment flexibility used within an organization and the performance achieved. It is suggested that greater use of a combination of knowledge-based employment and contract work positively impacts on the performance of the firm – demonstrating how complex it can be to plan the number and type of employees needed by the organization if it wants to succeed now and in the future.

Organizations can only draw on the talent that is available. At the point of seeking to attract potential employees to join the organization, the degree of 'fit' must be assessed along with the potential for subsequent development. It may be that within society there is not the level of skill or competency available to be able to meet the full requirement that the organization has identified through its demand-side planning processes. Consequently the means of overcoming that deficiency must be considered. That could be achieved through a combination of the use of technology to replace the need for people; the use of training and development to provide employees with the necessary skills and competency; the relocation of suitable employees; the application of job design processes to change the nature and type of jobs; and seeking to influence the provision of education and training provided by the state and other bodies within the environment. Mathis and Jackson (2008: p. 47) identify the major stages in HR planning as:

- Review organizational objectives and strategies.
- Scan external environment for labour supply information.
- Assess internal labour availability and potential.
- Develop from the above the labour forecast.
- From that forecast identify the organization's need for people in the short, medium and longer terms.
- From the previous stage, match current internal labour availability to requirements.
- From the previous stages, identify HR strategies plans in relation to resourcing externally, career development, training and development, performance management, etc.

Many organizations seek to achieve the status of being an employer of choice. This implies that people will want to seek employment with the company and once there, contribute high performance over a long period. For the company it implies that it will be able to attract a high number of well qualified and able candidates from which to select the best. It implies that such employees will be committed to the organization and its objectives, thereby maximizing corporate performance and providing a good place to work. The Management in Action panel below identifies how this might be achieved. This of course leaves unanswered the questions of what the 'best' means in this context and also how such people can be identified. Reporting a conference held in America, HR News (2003) points out that a number of speakers suggested that emphasis should be placed on creating what they term 'critical talent pools', by which they mean becoming an employer of choice in areas critical to the development of new products and services as well as those jobs in direct contact with customers.

Employer of choice
Being a company that people actively seek to join, so contributing to high performance over a long time.

13.1 EXTEND
YOUR LEARNING

MANAGEMENT IN ACTION

How to become an employer of choice

Many organizations seek to be recognized as an employer of choice. This involves creating a culture that keeps people motivated and encourages them to be creative and forthcoming in delivering sustained high performance. The following is a list of practical suggestions to achieve that status based on a range of sources as indicated below:

1 *Create the right psychological contract*. The essence of the relationship between employer and employee.

2 *Know and live your corporate values*. If they are not developed with input from everyone, they will be of little relevance. Create a sense that everyone is valued and appreciated. Also that concern for their health and well-being exists.

3 *Assess individuals' values and behavioural styles*. Understand employee motivations and the ways in which they understand the world around them in order to align actual behaviours and attitudes with those desired.

4 *Create a coaching culture*. With flatter structures emerging, there need to be other ways of providing opportunities for personal advancement and development.

5 *Brand your people processes*. Adopt a marketing approach to work and organizational branding.

6 *Offer flexible benefits*. Recognize that not every benefit offered by the company appeals to every employee.

7 *Endorse staff needs for a better work–life balance*. Job-sharing, part-time working and flexibility need to be available so people can deal with work–life balance.

8 *Be realistic and market-driven*. It is necessary to be creative in understanding what is going on in labour markets and to find new ways of dealing with problem areas.

9 *Have some fun*. Seeing work as being a 'fun' place to be encourages commitment and a sense of community. Encourage informal groups to form and encourage social activities, but don't make it compulsory!

10 *Zap the 'TOLERATIONS'*. Ask each department to identify 10 things that they tolerate, but which drain energy. Then ask them to eliminate them.

TASK

1 How would you decide which organizations you would prefer to work for? How does your answer compare to the list above? Explain any differences.

Sources:
Beckett-Hughes, M. (2003) How to become an employer of choice, *People Management*, 28 August, pp. 40–41.
http://www.employers-of-choice.org/page/why_keyfact2.html (accessed 17 April 2009).
http://www.cipd.co.uk/subjects/health/worklifebalance/worklifeba.htm?IsSrchRes=1 (accessed 17 April 2009).
Leary-Joyce, J. (2004) *Becoming an Employer of Choice: Make your organisation a place where people want to do great work*, London: CIPD.

Resourcing

Resourcing
The process of bringing into an organization personnel who will possess the appropriate education, qualifications, skills and experience for the post offered. Incorporates HR planning (aspects of), recruitment and selection processes.

Recruitment
The first stage of resourcing that is about identifying an appropriate number of potentially appropriate employees from which suitable individuals will be chosen for the next stage of the process, often an interview or assessment centre.

Resourcing covers three main stages in the acquisition process for new employees (e.g., Torrington *et al.*, 2005; Swain & Newell Brown, 2009):

- Recruitment. This stage is about identifying an appropriate number of potentially appropriate employees from which suitable individuals will be chosen for the next stage of the process (often an interview or assessment centre) leading to a possible offer of employment. Recruitment contains a number of activities and features:

  - *Identification of a vacancy.* People leave for one reason or another and new posts are created all the time, but that does not automatically require recruitment to be undertaken. Jobs can be eliminated; filled by redesigning the work; by subcontracting or simply left unfilled. If a vacancy is to be filled, then a job description and person specification (identifying the key features of the job and the attributes to be demonstrated by the job holder) will be required.

  - *Labour markets.* Candidates may be found in the internal (to the company) labour market or they may come from the external labour market. There are many possible external labour markets. For example, some jobs will attract applicants living locally whereas others may attract candidates from other parts of the country or even overseas.

  - *Advertising.* This is about attracting the attention of as many appropriately qualified and experienced people as possible and in such a way as to encourage them to apply. As Martin (2009: p. 39) points out, 'It represents a creative process involving many decisions about where to place the advert in relation to the individual labour market being accessed; the style of the advert and the information contained in it. The range of sources available include local and national press, websites, professional magazines, word of mouth, job centres, notice boards, and advertised anonymously through recruitment agencies.'

  - *Documentation.* This would include: role and person specification; advert; vacancy/advert authorising and sign-off approvals; the use of CVs or standard application forms; staff handbooks and any relevant contracts/ agreements; application tracking log; standard letters covering the stages of the process; and short-listing criteria.

  - *Initial sifting.* After the closing date for applications, it is necessary to sort the applications using appropriate criteria. The aim should be to use the criteria to produce: definitely interview; possibly interview; and reject categories. This can be a difficult and time-consuming process if a very large number of applications have been received. It can also be difficult to decide what to do if only a very small number of applications are received.

Selection
The second stage in the resourcing process involving a two-way process during which the applicant selects the organization as well as the organization seeking to identify the most appropriate applicant.

- Selection. A two-way process involving the applicant selecting the organization as well as the organization selecting the applicant. It has been argued (Bowen *et al.*, 1996) that three levels of organizational 'fit' are assessed during the process:

  - fit with the organization
  - fit with the department and team
  - fit with the job itself.

There are many selection methods that can be used individually or in combination. The choice of methods will depend on factors including appropriateness of the method; numbers of applicants involved; time and cost necessary to use/interpret the method. They include (Mathis and Jackson, 2008: Chapter 8):

- application form or CV as the basis of candidate information
- face-to-face interviews involving single interviewers, multiple interviewers with either single interviews (after which a decision would be made) or a sequence of several interviews involving one or more interviewees each time
- self and peer (perhaps work test or reference based) assessment in relation to the vacancy applied for
- telephone interviews
- psychometric testing
- group methods and assessment centres
- work tests and portfolios
- references
- other methods such as handwriting analysis.

- *Appointment.* The final stage involves the identification of the successful applicant for the job being filled. As Martin (2009) points out, in an ideal world the formal offer of employment would be accepted and a starting date determined. However that may not happen, as an individual may reject the offer; they may not turn up on the first day of work; or they may leave a few days or weeks after starting (the induction crisis). Occasionally a company may find itself having to withdraw the offer of a job, if a sudden change in business or financial fortune arises. As a consequence, it is likely that both parties will have contingency plans. For example, HR may delay notifying the second- or third-choice applicants so that there remains the possibility of making one of them an offer if necessary. Applicants may also continue with any ongoing applications or interviews just in case, or perhaps to be able to play one employer off against another in the hope of gaining improved pay etc.

Induction crisis
When a new employee leaves an organization within a few weeks of starting work it is sometimes referred to as a result of the induction crisis. It can be the result of an ineffective induction and socialization process resulting in the individual not integrating into the work group or organization.

Another major area of decision making in the resourcing process is the role of agencies or consultants. They claim to offer a professional, cost-effective and efficient service in the support of all or part of the resourcing process. The range of services offered by such agencies and consultants can include:

- Assistance with the creation, layout and placing of adverts.
- Assistance with the creation of job and personnel specifications.
- A resourcing service involving taking the job brief; developing person specification; advertising; initial interviews and then drawing up a shortlist for selection.
- Additional services that they offer include psychometric testing.

Training and development

Induction
The process of introducing a new employee into the organization.

Socialization
The process by which a person learns about the norms, values, assumptions and other central-shared elements of a particular social group or culture and develops the ability to function effectively within that social group.

Once the individual is selected for employment then they will have an induction to the organization. This usually involves an overview of the job in question; an indication of the other jobs in the department and related departments; the history and organization of the company; health and safety briefings; meeting new colleagues and senior managers and so on. This, along with much training and development activity, contains an element of socialization in seeking to effectively integrate the new individual into their work group and organization. Socialization and induction programmes represent a 'rite of passage' from being an outsider to being a full member of the group. In an organization, training and the ways in which it is accessed and allocated can represent strong signals on what is valued in behaviour and attitude within that context. Of course once a member of a group or team, there will still be a need for ongoing training and development in relation to changes in work routines within the organization, career development, technological developments and so on.

The starting point for any training is the identification of its purpose. That purpose is usually based on a need or gap between what is currently possible and what is desirable or should be possible. Perhaps new products or services are to be introduced; a new technology or administrative system is being planned; new ways of working or job changes might be planned; or it could be that the performance of an employee is lower than expected; or an employee is being prepared for promotion. Training can be used both for these practical 'need' based reasons or it can be used to send signals to employees perhaps about the value that the company places upon them and their contribution or to facilitate positive attitudes with regard to future change.

Development in HRM is generally regarded as having a less immediate focus, being longer-term and less specific in outcome than training. However, that does not mean that development should not have purpose, but it may not be targeted at meeting a particular short-term need. It is differentiated from training in that it is generally intended to be supportive of organizational requirements and broadly directive of behaviour, but over the longer term. For example, a leadership development programme may be intended to prepare delegates for appointment to their first managerial position within one year. As such, it might be intended to provide an insight into what managing a department might involve, indicating potential future career prospects and motivating the individuals to deliver effective performance.

Some of the methods used in training and development include:

- On-the-job methods. Coaching, mentoring, action learning, self-development, learning logs, structured job assignments and secondments within the same organization.

- Off-the-job methods. In-house, training, development and education programmes; externally provided training, development and education programmes. Placements and secondments in other organizations also have a part to play. See for example the High Performance example for one type of training based on a different paradigm!

- Open, distance and e-learning. These often use electronic or self-study packs that can be used at home or at work to fit in with working pattern and lifestyle variations.

From a managerial perspective, any training or development should have purpose aligned with organizational goals, otherwise it reflects wasted effort. Evaluation should seek to assess whether the learning achieved what it intended to achieve. However, the results may not be fully apparent in the short or even medium term. Even in the long term it is often difficult to separate out the effects on business effectiveness of training or development because of the influence of many other variables on performance over time. Most approaches to measuring the effectiveness of training or development consider the impact across time using several different measures. (Bratton & Gold, 2003: p. 338; Snell & Bohlander, 2007: pp. 311–315):

- *Postevent evaluation.* The so-called 'happiness-sheet' or more formally the postcourse questionnaire usually collected at the end of an event. This seeks to gain insight into delegate feelings about the course, content, approach,

Training
A process dealing primarily with transferring or obtaining specific knowledge, attitudes and skills needed to carry out a specified activity or task.

Development (in HRM)
A proces of increasing an individual's range or level of a broad set of skills, abilities, and knowledge, typically supportive of or useful for the organization.

**13.2 EXTEND
YOUR LEARNING**

HIGH PERFORMANCE

A night at the theatre – or managers learn to give the performance of their lives!

At 7.25 in the evening you stand in the wings off-stage listening to the chatter of the expectant audience. You jog on the spot to keep loose, breathe deeply to disperse the adrenalin and make an exaggerated chewing action to keep your tongue and mouth flexible. Five minutes pass quickly; the lights go down in the auditorium and up on the stage. You step on-stage, and in front of the audience you have to perform to the best of your abilities, to be clear, communicative and coherent. By 10pm the show is over. You bow, the audience applaud and you retreat off-stage, breathe a sigh of relief and it is over . . . until the next night and the next performance.

Richard Hahlo (Director of Dramatic Resources)

Dramatic Resources is a company of working actors and theatre directors, with more than 10 years' experience of running training with managers to improve their performance. Unlike the actor standing in the wings, most managers have not had the advantage of 4 weeks' intensive rehearsal to prepare them for this performance. The manager (just like the actor) has put on a costume to play their role in the theatre of business, and every day is a challenging improvisation as they deal with the many communication issues of the working environment.

In a conversation with Richard he made the point that, 'As an actor you always know when you are on-stage or off-stage. Crossing the line is clear and you know what is required of you.' This reality of an actor's working life can be of value to managers and Richard and his colleagues have asked countless business managers and executives this question, 'When are you on-stage and when are you off-stage?' The answer invariably comes back in different ways but boils down to the same conclusion, 'You are always on-stage from the moment you walk in the office/factory/showroom to the moment you leave. Even if you close your office door (should you have one) you are sending out a signal to someone.'

Richard went on to say, 'We all play a role at work just as an actor takes on a role in a play. Just like the actor, the raw material for your performance is yourself. You have material and content – and how you put that across to your audience is all about the transformative power of performance. The one key requirement for successful communication for the actor and for the manager is the ability to be yourself under pressure, to be authentic and to enhance that with skill. People often think of acting as putting on something external; popular phrases such as "acting up" and "acting the fool" suggest something fabricated and false, whereas all good acting like all good communication is rooted in being authentic.'

Richard and his colleagues specialize in coaching managers and executives on communication. Like a director working with an actor, they rehearse as preparation for a delivery of the best performance possible. From the conference speech to a packed auditorium, to the crucial client meeting, to the informal chat by the coffee machine, the ability to communicate by inspiring, enthusing, challenging the audience (be it 500 people or 1 person) is key to a manager's ability to have influence and impact on others.

The journey that the specialists at Dramatic Resources have undergone with this work provides a fascinating insight into the work of managers and their need for improved communication skills based on the theatre. Continuing to work with many business people as they do, it becomes constantly obvious that managers, like actors, when they start to put their attention on their performance by controlling their breath, slowing their pace, using better articulation, using more eye contact, focusing their energy and moving their attention off themselves and on to their audience, their ability to communicate effectively improves dramatically.

Research by Richard and his colleagues shows that there is many a business like show business; and that if managers can be shown how to constructively concentrate on their performance, communication skills coaching can go a long way to making them more effective and successful in their jobs and careers. This improvement can also have a positive impact on the performance and results achieved by the organizations that such managers work for. Standing in the wings is always going to be nerve-wracking, but the confidence to perform under pressure is directly connected to the quality of rehearsal and preparation.

TASKS

1 In what ways might learning to 'perform' like an actor help a manager perform better?

2 What other aspects of the theatre might have relevance to work and OB in an organization?

3 How might actors learn (if at all) from the work of managers?

4 What other unusual provision can you find that might provide valuable contributions to management training and development? How would you convince managers of its value?

Source:
Conversations with Richard Hahlo, Director Dramatic Resources, August 2009. www.dramaticresources.co.uk (accessed August 2009). Reprinted with grateful thanks to Richard Hahlo.

presenters and what they perceive to be the benefits gained. The rationale is that if delegates react negatively, the event probably won't benefit them or the organization.

- *Impact on work behaviour*. This seeks to identify any benefits transferred back to the workplace from the training or development event. Assessed, say, 2 or 3 months after the return to work, it would usually be based on asking the employee questions about what from the event they had been able to make use of in their work.

- *Impact on job performance*. This would also be measured some time after the end of a course and would reflect the impact on work performance. It could be measured quantitatively through output or productivity statistics, and/or qualitatively through a performance appraisal type of review.

- *Impact on departmental performance*. This would be measured several months after the course and would usually identify the effect on the performance of a work group. This level of evaluation seeks the line manager perspective on the value gained from the use of training. Measures could include the effect on efficiency, number of positive or negative customer comments, cost reduction achieved, quality level improvements and reduced order processing times. The time delay means that many other factors will be active in the context, which could also impact on the outcomes. It is therefore difficult to separate out the cause and effect relationships in such situations.

- *Impact on wider organizational effectiveness*. At this level the views of senior managers (in addition to any tangible evidence) on the effectiveness of training and development in contributing to the achievement of corporate objectives are being sought. For example, greater cooperation between departments, or achieving changes in work allocation might be easier to achieve.

Reward and performance management

Reward system
Formal arrangements regarding the combination of pay, benefits, incentives and intangible benefits used to attract, retain and motivate employees.

The purpose of any reward system is to attract, retain and motivate employees (Armstrong and Brown, 2009). In order to achieve these apparently simple objectives, there are many difficulties to be dealt with. These include what competitor organizations offer by way of reward; the history of reward system design within the organization; local cost of living and taxation levels; internal relativities between jobs; company and industry profitability; economic conditions; company policy on its pay position relative to the market; relative balance of negotiating power between company and employee groups; relative skill shortages and surpluses in the labour market and many other factors. Another major element within any reward system is the benefits package offered by the organization. This covers things like pension, health care, company car, child care, holidays, further education policy, canteen arrangements and so on. The benefits offered usually differ across the hierarchy of the organization. The overall reward package needs to be appropriate to both employee needs and employee expectation, but it also needs to be judged against a defined relationship between company practice and the reward practices generally adopted by other organizations in the environment.

STOP & CONSIDER

Management is about achieving results. Is there any value in talking about 'performance management' separately if all management activity should be focused on performance? What management activities should not be included in this performance management, and why?

Many different types of reward system are available. For example, some jobs have a basic wage paid by the hour and others an annual salary paid in equal monthly instalments. Whatever basis of payment is used, it is not uncommon to find that job evaluation provides the means of identifying a rank order of job magnitude, which in turn determines the magnitude of the basic pay. However it is designed and operated in practice, one of the key terms within any reward system is that it should be 'felt fair' by the people who are subject to it. This means that individuals should feel that they are being treated fairly within whatever system is used. In essence this reflects the subjective reaction in the individual employee based on how they perceive their treatment compared to other people (see Chapter 16). Because it is always possible to find someone who is paid more, it is easy to become convinced that the current level of pay and benefit is wrong. It is the job of the HRM team to try to deal with this possibility when designing reward policies and practice and in the way that they are communicated to employees. Line managers usually have little control over the design of the reward system, but have to apply it in seeking to motivate and reward employees.

Torrington *et al.* (2005: pp. 7-8) identify performance management as a key HR area of work (see also Houldsworth and Jirasinghe, 2006). They argue that HR practitioners are best placed by training and expertise to develop and facilitate policies and practices that can encourage high motivation and commitment. The CIPD (2009a) offers a broad summary of performance management. The focus on individual performance is relevant to the organizational desire to achieve the status of being a high-performance organization. This can be achieved by combining many aspects of technology, procedure, product or service design, management, and of particular significance the need to emphasize the intellectual capital held within the organization (Ulrich, 1998); together with the need to put people first (Pfeffer, 1998). Individual or team performance can be used to identify incentive payments that will be paid to the employee as part of, or in addition, to their basic wage. For example, sales people are often paid a commission based on the number or value of sales that they achieve. Factory workers can be paid an individual or team productivity bonus for achieving levels of output over and above a set target. Senior managers might be awarded shares for achieving targets for the growth in the value of the company or its share price. Administrative and technical staff might have their performance reviewed by their line manager through an appraisal system each year, the result of which might (or might not) be used as one of the determinants of their annual pay review, along with cost of living and other factors.

Research evidence clearly demonstrates that there is a relationship between people management activity and organizational performance, albeit indirectly through

Job evaluation
A process by which job descriptions can be used to identify the rank order (or relative magnitude) of jobs in an organization.

Felt fair
Means that something should be perceived as fair by the people subjected to the system or procedure.

Performance management
The processes and procedures through which managers seek to manage performance levels within the organization.

High-performance organization
The combination of people, technology, management and productivity delivering competitive advantage on a sustainable basis.

Intellectual capital
The sum total of knowledge, expertise and dedication of the workforce in an organization.

the effect of such activity on work culture (Gelade & Ivery, 2003). Also this can be achieved through being an employer of choice. Being an employer of choice encourages (it is claimed) the best candidates to seek employment with the organization, and hence allows the best available talent to be recruited within the organization. Line managers are the people who have to deliver the high-performance organization through the appropriate treatment and use of the people available to them. Line managers have many targets to achieve and responsibilities to exercise, not just the control of people. Hence the danger of people management issues being undervalued by line managers and the need for HR practitioners to take an active interest in such matters. In terms of OB, there are many aspects of this book that offer insights into the management of performance, including: perception, motivation, leadership, team working, communications, decision making, fairness and trust.

Employee relations

13.3 EXTEND YOUR LEARNING

Employee relations
The activity within HRM that is involved with any aspect of an organization that might have an impact on the management of people and the creation of a high-performing work environment. It is about the employment relationship between management and employees.

Employee relations is the HRM activity that is involved with any aspect of an organization that is about the employment relationship with employees (Burchill 2008; Farnham, 2002). Trade unions remain the focus of attention within employee relations although they are not the only type of employee representative body in practice. UK trade unions tend to be occupationally based. Other countries, however, have different forms of trade union, based on industries or sectors of the economy (e.g., Germany), or a political party. Organizationally based employee associations that may or may not meet the legal requirements of being a trade union and consequently may or may not be registered as such can also be found. The aim of such bodies is to provide employees with a voice and collective support when dealing with management. However, they may not be totally independent from management as they may receive office space, clerical support, or other resources. As Martin (2009: p. 81) suggests, 'recognising an external body to represent the individual and/or collective interests of employees represents a fundamental change to the way in which a management can function in relation to its people management policy and practice.' The state (national and European government levels) also has increasing significance in prescribing employee rights through legislation and regulation impacting on the employment relationship (Gennard and Judge, 2002).

Another aspect of employee relations is the degree to which employees should be allowed or encouraged to become involved in the running of their employing organization. It could be argued that employees are automatically involved in the running of their employer's business through the work that they do. However, employee involvement (sometimes called participation) goes beyond that and seeks to create a direct involvement in decision-making areas of the business that would traditionally be the preserve of management. It is common to differentiate between task-centred approaches to involvement which focus on 'how' things should be done (including the design of jobs, operational strategy and scheduling), and power-centred approaches which seek to focus on 'what' should be done (i.e., types of organizational activity such as business strategy and high-level decision making). Under EU law, in many large organizations employee representatives have a right to be consulted on company plans and other strategic issues. Employee empowerment is another form of involvement and means that employees are allowed to take decisions without reference to a more senior authority. It implies that employees have greater decision-making responsibility than their status and job function would allow. It is an attempt to overcome slow decision making; improve customer (internal and external) satisfaction; reduce cost (improved productivity and fewer exceptions needing costly 'processes' to deal with them); involve employees in business performance and problem solving; improve job satisfaction and increase employee

Employee involvement
Represents an opportunity for employees to become involved beyond the normal scope of their job in decision making and/or the running of the business.

Employee empowerment
Represents a form of involvement and means that employees are allowed to take decisions without reference to a more senior authority.

engagement and commitment. A number of involvement and empowerment practices can be found in organizations including:

- *Information sharing and communication.* Information sharing based on communication encourages commitment and engagement among employees and managers.

- *Upward problem solving.* Representative participation (not all employees directly involved in decision making) is one way of involving employees. However, all employees can become involved in aspects of decision making through such practices as quality circles and/or team/departmental meetings.

- *Financial participation.* Profit share and share option schemes are the most common forms of this type of involvement.

- *Attitude development.* This involves providing employees with the training, support and encouragement to absorb management values, behaviours and attitudes. Taylor (1998: p. 98) suggests that in the service sector managers usually equate this with a requirement for customer-facing staff to 'deep act' to develop a strong empathy with customer needs.

- *Team autonomy.* Based on delegated responsibility for a part of the work of the business. For example, the resourcing team within an HR department would have the responsibility for deciding how the work should be done and which team member should do what and when.

- *Personal autonomy.* The individual version of the 'team autonomy' just described.

- *Total quality management.* This approach is much broader than the desire to maximize quality would imply. It involves seeking out weakness in every aspect of the organization and seeking to improve processes, situations, etc. through continuous improvement of the product or service package. To be effective, it requires the involvement and participation of everyone at all levels in finding ways of making improvements. However, as is evident from the Employee Perspective example, forcing people to become involved won't always achieve the best results.

In employee relations there is always the potential for conflict between management and employees to emerge. Inevitably the HR department will have agreed procedures for dealing with such conflict, but occasionally a resolution cannot be found and some form of industrial action results intended to force compromise on the other party. The most common forms of industrial action are:

Industrial action
An action by either management or employees that takes place in order to force some degree of change in behaviour by the other party.

- *Strike.* A withdrawal of labour by employees. There are legal requirements for the balloting of members before such actions take place.

- *Lockout.* This is a management refusal to allow workers to enter the company premises or to work.

- *Work-to-rule.* This involves employees following the established rules and procedures to the letter, with no exceptions. This should have no effect on the normal running of an organization, but it invariably does. The reasons include procedures and rules becoming outdated and people finding 'short-cuts' which result in procedures 'bending' over time.

- *Go slow.* This simply means doing less work than usual.

- *Overtime/flexibility restriction.* Refusing to work (or offer) overtime or to work flexibly when that would be usual can quickly impact on the organization's ability to meet customer needs and/or employee earnings.

- *Withdrawal of goodwill.* Not co-operating enthusiastically with management expectations about work activity.

EMPLOYEE PERSPECTIVE

Forcing Louise to become involved

Louise was a martial arts enthusiast who trained two or three times each week and frequently entered national competitions. She was also tipped as a member of the next British Olympic squad. Not surprisingly, training and competitions took up much of her spare time and energy. Work to Louise was the means of earning money which she needed to support these activities. Louise was always punctual at work, did what was expected of her, worked effectively and delivered a good performance. Her manager had no cause for complaint about any aspect of her work.

The company introduced an employee involvement scheme which contained a number of specific sub-projects. There were many ways that employees were being encouraged to become involved with decision making in the company. There were elections for worker representatives - to meet every couple of months with directors to talk about company plans. In each department a quality team was established and employees were expected to give up one hour of their own time each week to identify problems and how they could be resolved. Louise did not put herself forward to participate in any of these activities and continued as before.

In her next one-to-one review with her boss, it was pointed out that Louise's lack of participation had been

noticed and that this was not good enough. Everyone was being encouraged to participate in improving the company and it was expected that everyone would do so. By not becoming involved, her relative value to the company was reduced and her future career brought into question. Louise was annoyed by the suggestion that she did not care about the company, but pointed out that she had significant outside interests, which in her view were more important than work. Work was the means of allowing her to participate in her sporting activities. But that did not mean that she could not be trusted to do a good job, as long as it was made clear to her what she was required to do. Her boss made it clear that he was not threatening her, but that her approach to involvement had been noticed and would possibly have repercussions in some way or another. It was therefore in her interests to be more obviously involved at work. Louise thought about these comments and became involved in the department's quality team – although she gave no thought to its activities and made virtually no contribution.

TASK

1 To what extent should Louise (or any employee) be required to become involved in schemes designed by management to enhance employee contributions to the running of the organization?

The state of employee relations reflects the balance between conflict and co-operation in each work situation at any point in time. However, very rarely is one or the other totally dominant. For example, an organization which appears to have good co-operation is likely to have some conflict present, even if this is hidden. That is why these days the notion of employee voice is significant. It implies that there are mechanisms in place that encourage employees to articulate or otherwise express their concerns, feelings, worries, thoughts and opinions. By engaging employees through this, it is anticipated that involvement will become more meaningful and high commitment and performance result. Marchington and Wilkinson (2005: p. 77) identify three reasons why employee involvement forms an important aspect of being able to achieve high commitment. They are:

Employee voice
This implies mechanisms that encourage employees to articulate their concerns, feelings, worries, thoughts and opinions. By more fully engaging employees through voice, employee involvement should become more meaningful resulting in higher commitment and performance.

1 Open communications about financial performance and so on goes beyond ensuring that employees are informed, it sends a very strong signal that they are trusted and significant to the organization.

2 For teamwork to function effectively, employees need to be informed and able to contribute in ways that capitalize on the potential of the team to perform.

3 It allows management to claim legitimacy for its decisions and actions which as a consequence of involvement will have more sources incorporated into management actions.

Discipline and grievance handling

One way of looking at discipline in an organizational context is that it represents the management process that is used (for a breach of the rules) to exercise power and control over employee behaviour. In the same way, a *grievance process* provides the opportunity for employees to respond to management actions if they feel that the application of power and control has become too strong. But how realistic is it to expect every individual to work and behave perfectly all day every day and to never make a mistake? How realistic is it to expect everyone to be satisfied with their job, pay, career, colleagues and superiors all of the time? Some variability and unpredictability in human behaviour and attitudes/feelings should be expected and that will impact on the ability of the business to function smoothly and effectively. Therefore perhaps the more significant question should be about how individuals and managers react to this everyday variability and unpredictability.

Another way of thinking about discipline and grievance is in relation to organizational justice (Torrington *et al.* 2005: pp. 561–562; see Chapter 16). The employment contract sets out the rights and responsibilities of both employee and management. If either party becomes dissatisfied with the behaviour of the other in relation to the terms of the contract, then an organizational mechanism exists to address that concern. The disciplinary procedure provides management with the means of raising the 'problem' with the individual and hopefully resolving the issue. Equally if the employee is unhappy with aspects of the employer's actions, the grievance procedure provides the opportunity to raise the issue formally and so have it dealt with. Raising either discipline or grievance issues with the other party does not guarantee satisfactory outcomes for either or both parties. For example, taking disciplinary action against an individual will not guarantee that their future behaviour complies with the expectation. Conversely the raising of a grievance by an employee does not mean that they will get what they want.

In its broadest sense, discipline is about the control of human behaviour in order to produce a controlled performance. Organizations need people to work together in a controlled way so that products and services can be delivered to the customer as planned. It is management's job to channel human behaviour so that business objectives can be achieved in a timely and cost-effective manner. It is to that end that rules, procedures and management hierarchy exist to direct the efforts of employees. Discipline can also be regarded as a series of levels (Torrington *et al.*, 2005: pp. 558–559), each having implications for the type of supervision and personal responsibility of people:

- *Managerial discipline.* This level relies on managers giving direction and orders about what should be done, when and how.
- *Team discipline.* This level is found in teams - which exercise a significant influence on the behaviour of members – and team cohesion. It requires a lower level of direct input from management to direct behaviour – assuming teams are supportive of management objectives.
- *Self-discipline.* This level exists when an individual takes responsibility for their own actions and behaviours. It is about self-control and taking responsibility for personal actions. In this situation very little direct management direction would be required. It requires high levels of trust to exist between management and the employee.

Organizational justice
Concerned with employee fairness perceptions regarding their work and conditions of employment and their behavioural reactions to these. See also distributive justice, informational justice, interactional justice and procedural justice.

Grievance generally relates to something that makes an individual feel unhappy (Pigors and Myers, 1977: p. 229) in some way or other. There are different levels of severity for such events:

- *Dissatisfaction.* This represents something that has an effect on the individual but only produces a feeling of disquiet. It is unlikely to lead to the individual articulating the problem or its effect on them.
- *Complaint.* This represents something with a more significant effect on the individual. It results in them articulating the 'problem' perhaps by talking or grumbling to colleagues or a member of management, probably in an informal way.
- *Grievance.* This represents an event that causes the individual to formally present the complaint to management in a way that requires it to be formally dealt with through the grievance procedure.

There are different types of complaint that can arise and they can be generalized into three categories (Torrington *et al.*, 2005: pp. 560–561):

- *Factual.* This is based on something (a fact) that can be checked and dealt with. For example, 'this machine never works'.
- *Subjective reactions.* These are slightly more difficult to deal with as the effect will be different for each person. For example, someone might complain that 'the music is too noisy in this room'. The difficulty facing the person receiving the complaint is to be able to find ways of dealing with it without creating complaints from people not concerned by the original issue.
- *Hopes and fears.* This represent the most difficult type of complaint to deal with as the 'problem' as presented may not be the real cause for the grievance. For example, an individual who complains that their manager has favourites might actually be worried about job security. It is necessary for the manager dealing with the issue to carefully question around the original complaint in an attempt to get at the feelings, attitudes and thoughts behind the problem as stated.

Most organizations have formal procedures to deal with both discipline and grievance issues (Daniels, 2006) and the HR involvement in them will vary depending on role that HR plays within the organization.

EQUALITY AND DIVERSITY

Equality
A primarily legislative-based approach to seeking to ensure that disadvantaged groups in a particular society are not discriminated against in employment matters.

The starting point for any consideration of these themes is the current legislative provision. There exists a legislative equality obligation on an employer in relation all aspects of the employment relationship including resourcing, reward, career development, pension and termination rights. The main areas covered by the legislative requirement for equality of treatment include:

- gender, marital status or sexual orientation
- disability
- race, national origin or ethnicity
- religion or belief
- ex-offenders with spent convictions
- membership (or nonmembership) of a trade union
- part-time or fixed-term contract workers.

Four categories of discrimination have been recognized by legislation. They are (Martin, 2009: p. 101):

- **Direct discrimination**. This occurs when the employer directly uses sex or race as a decision variable in a particular situation. For example, an employer who advertised a job for a male computer operator would be directly discriminating against females – unless they could show that there existed a 'genuine occupational qualification', for example the need to have a female actor perform a female part in a play.

- **Indirect discrimination**. This occurs when a 'requirement or condition' for a job is set in such a way as to disadvantage a particular category of people. For example, advertising a job as being open to people over 6 feet tall would indirectly discriminate against women as a greater proportion of men (compared to women) are over 6 feet tall.

- **Positive discrimination**. This represents situations where an employer seeks to overcome previous discrimination by giving preference to the group previously discriminated against, for example, seeking only women applicants for senior jobs in order to increase the proportion of females at that level. Such actions would be unlawful under UK law, although it would be permissible to adopt 'positive action' to prepare and encourage more women to apply for such jobs.

- **Victimization**. This refers to situations in which the employer seeks to take revenge or action against an employee (or group) because they sought to (or assisted others to) claim their legal rights.

In most situations it should make no difference if an employee is male, black, Asian, female, married and so on and legislation seeks to prevent such irrelevant factors from being taken into account. In some of the literature and common usage, diversity often means the same as equal opportunities. The argument is that by providing equality of opportunity, a diverse workforce matching the composition of society will be achieved. However, equal opportunities are based on categories defined by legislators and there are other ways of describing 'differences' between people. Diversity can reflect a broader interpretation of difference that could potentially make more impact on organizational performance than the legislative obligations alone. For example, people differ in terms of personality, team role preferences and so on which might be expected to have a direct impact on organizational effectiveness. The management of diversity is more appropriately regarded as the recognition that individuals differ from each other in many ways and that high organizational performance can be achieved through harnessing that potential. It represents a business results-based approach to difference between people whereas equal opportunity represents a moral approach to fairness.

The main emphasis in equal opportunities is seeking to further the interests of disadvantaged groups. It is not specifically concerned with individuals, but with company policy and practice in providing the opportunity for disadvantaged groups to overcome whatever has previously hindered them. The major approach in diversity management is to identify those differences that impact on the performance of the organization and to harness them appropriately. Some organizations place great store on achieving high levels of uniformity among staff in terms of profile, attitudes and other characteristics. The main advantage of a high degree of employee uniformity is that people will tend to think and act in similar ways, providing a greater level of behavioural consistency than might otherwise be the case. That should make it easier to achieve operational consistency. However, one disadvantage is that it could encourage a 'clone' mentality, which could make the organization inflexible and slow to react to change in markets and competitor activity.

Direct discrimination
Occurs when an employer specifically and directly uses sex or race as a decision variable in a particular situation.

Indirect discrimination
Occurs when a 'requirement or condition' for a job is set in such a way as to disadvantage a particular category of people.

Positive discrimination
Represents an attempt to overcome previous discrimination by giving preference to the group previously discriminated against in order to redress the balance.

Victimization
Refers to situations in which an employer seeks to take revenge or action against an employee (or group) because they sought to (or assist others to) claim their legal rights.

Diversity
Seeks to go beyond equality with its legislative basis and ensure that organizations are able to capture the benefits of 'difference' as a means of developing competitive advantage.

Jackson *et al.* (1992) suggest a model describing ways in which organizations respond to diversity. In doing so they emphasize the cultural aspects of an organization and identify a number of development stages involved in the process of becoming increasingly diversity aware:

- Level 1

  - Stage 1. *The exclusionary organization.* Seeks to maintain the status quo with existing dominant groups maintaining their position and excluding others.
  - Stage 2. *The club.* The dominant group attempts to maintain its position but is prepared to allow 'outsiders' to join providing they conform to dominant group norms.

- Level 2

  - Stage 3. *The compliance organization.* Simply complies with the basic legislative requirements. May encourage equality of opportunity at the lower levels but the dominant groups at the top remain largely unaffected.
  - Stage 4. *The affirmative action organization.* Actively seeks to adapt to changing circumstances by encouraging staff to change attitudes and by developing people from minority groups.

- Level 3

  - Stage 5. *The redefining organization.* Ensures that the culture of the organization supports a multicultural workforce and that power is redistributed across all groups.
  - Stage 6. *The multicultural organization.* This level recognizes that everyone is a full member of the organization. Recognizes the existence of a social responsibility to encourage the development of other organizations and individuals and seeks to work on social causes of oppression.

Ross and Schneider (1992) suggest that organizational approaches to diversity should be based on the following criteria:

- Originate from internal intentions rather than external requirement.
- Focused on individual rather than group levels of activity.
- Focused on the cultural aspects of organizational activity rather than the procedures, processes and systems adopted.
- The responsibility of every function and person in the organization, not just the HR function.

They suggest a six-step process for achieving a diversity culture within the organization:

1 *Diagnosis.* Identify what exists in relation to culture, policy and levels of diversity.
2 *Set the aims.* Identify the business case for change as well as the need for senior-level sponsorship. Determine the aims, objectives and outcomes for the change.
3 *Spread of ownership.* Raise awareness of the benefits of diversity among all people within the organization. Ownership should be everyone's not just the HR function.
4 *Policy development.* One way that everyone can be involved is in policy development.

5 *Managing the transition process.* Include training, positive action programmes, policy implementation and cultural awareness/change initiatives.

6 *Maintain momentum.* Celebrate achievement and introduce initiatives to keep progress flowing. Monitor impact on customer relations, productivity and cost/profitability.

STOP & CONSIDER

'Discrimination is inevitable because organizational decision making is about people making choices between and about people. In 2009 it has been reported that there are some 48 graduates chasing each graduate vacancy – therefore 47 individuals are going to be discriminated against in some way or another.' To what extent is this a reasonable statement? What does your answer imply for equality and diversity in organizations?

HRM AND ORGANIZATIONAL CHANGE

Torrington *et al.* (2005: pp. 7–8) identify change management as a key area of focus for HRM. The CIPD (2007) identify from their research seven themes or areas of activity that increase the probability of change programmes being successful - 'the seven C's of change'. HR practitioners have a key role to play in each of the activities:

- choosing a team
- crafting the vision and the path
- connecting organization-wide change
- consulting stakeholders
- communicating
- coping with change
- capturing learning

The same source suggests that the key areas of involvement for HR practitioners in change programmes includes the following activities. They also suggest that the following activities could be expected to make the difference between successful and unsuccessful change outcomes. These are identified below, along with an indication of the OB topics that can help to inform them:

- Involvement at the initial stage in the project team. Personality and individual difference; perception, attribution and attitude formation; group formation and structure; group dynamics.
- Advising project leaders in skills available within the organization – identifying any skills gaps, training needs, new posts, new working practices, etc. Control, reward and job design; culture; power, influence and politics; technology.
- Balancing out the narrow/short-term goals with broader strategic needs. Communications and decision making; conflict and negotiation; leading and managing; culture; power, influence and politics.
- Assessing the impact of change in one area/department/site on another part of the organization. Structure; control, reward and job design; technology; culture; power, influence and politics; relationships, fairness and trust.
- Being used to negotiating and engaging across various stakeholders. Communications and decision making; conflict and negotiations; culture; power, influence and politics; relationships, fairness and trust.

● Understanding stakeholder concerns in order to anticipate problems. Perception, attribution and attitude formation; personality and individual difference; motivation; leading and managing; groups and teams; culture; power, influence and politics; communication and decision making; relationships, fairness and trust.

● Understanding the appropriate medium of communication to reach various groups. Culture; power, influence and politics; communication and decision making; conflict and negotiation; relationships, fairness and trust.

● Helping people cope with change, performance management and motivation. Perception, attribution and attitude formation; personality and individual difference; motivation; leading and managing; groups and teams; culture; power, influence and politics; communication and decision making; relationships, fairness and trust. See the Change at Work example for aspects of this in action.

13.4 EXTEND
YOUR LEARNING

HRM, CSR AND ETHICS

There exist a number of ethical dimensions to HRM practice and in general it can be regarded as setting the standards for doing things appropriately, and of establishing good business practice. From that simple level of explanation many aspects of ethical involvement in HR should come to mind. For example, reward decisions could include a discriminatory dimension, sales conduct containing bribery or corruption. The Examining Ethics example indicates one such area of difficulty.

HRM AND INTERNATIONAL BUSINESS ACTIVITY

Many organizations operate in different parts of the world and the management of HR across what can be very different cultures, legal systems and ways of working can present great challenges. Brewster *et al*. (2007: p.3) bring together a number of sources to identify the international business activity trends over recent years, including:

● The economic dominance of multinationals. Two-thirds of all world trade is accounted for by 63 000 transnational companies. The top 100 corporations account for 14 per cent of worldwide sales, 12 per cent of assets and 13 per cent of employment. Around 60 per cent of international trade involves transactions between parts of the same multinational organization.

● Multinational companies increasingly operate as seamless global organizations. This makes it difficult for individual country tax authorities to identify where economic activity and value creation take place.

● Economic consolidation through mergers and acquisitions is a key means of achieving globalization.

Labour is a key cost for most organizations and for many it represents the largest item of operating expenditure. There exists a significant pressure on managers to ensure that the maximum value is extracted from employees in order to remain commercially viable. The cost side of the equation is one reason to take HRM seriously. The other side of the equation is the potential available from viewing the people as a benefit, not just a cost. The competencies, capabilities, contribution, knowledge, willingness, engagement and general support for objectives are increasingly viewed as the key to success in differentiating an organization from its competitors, wherever they are based. Operating internationally increases the complexity of that process, in that the different cultural, legal, social, work practices, preferences in relation to

CHANGE AT WORK

Devastated Visteon staff stage a sit-in as 200 jobs go in factory shutdown

Visteon was a US-owned car parts factory based in west Belfast and made parts for use in Ford cars. The company is also the basis of the Change at Work example 'Sit-in at the factory as it goes into administration' in Chapter1. You should refer back to that panel to refresh your memory.

Following the economic slowdown during 2008 and early 2009, Visteon lost orders and was forced into administration on 31 March 2009 with the loss of more than 200 jobs and debts of more than £400m. The company is also axing another 360 jobs at its factories in Basildon and Enfield. Visteon UK has struggled since it separated from Ford in 2000. There were also redundancies at the Belfast factory in 2003. In 2006 financial difficulties put the factory in jeopardy and in December 2007 parts of the 22-acres site were sold off to developers.

Workers made redundant in the closure in Belfast are refusing to leave the factory (referred to as a 'sit-in') until managers agree to talks. Workers claim that following the factory sale by Ford in 2000 it was agreed that they would receive the same severance terms paid by Ford. John McGowan, shift leader at Visteon, said: 'I'm just dumbstruck. I feel it's totally unjust the way we're being treated by the company. Last year they were offering redundancy packages of £30 000 minimum. Now they're telling me for my 30 years' loyalty to this company I'm getting a redundancy package which is capped at just over £9 000. That's totally unjust and unfair.'

Davy McMurray, from the trade union Unite, said yesterday: 'It is a total shock, workers were only informed that the factory was closing at 1pm. We really need to get face-to-face talks with Ford and we really need our political leaders to use whatever influence they have to get Ford to the negotiating table. The redundancy payment that these workers are entitled to would go some way towards easing the blow.'

TASKS

Given that the difficulties at Visteon have not arisen suddenly, what strategies and plans could you (as HR manager) have developed over the previous 2 or 3 years to:

1 Minimize (or prevent) the job losses that have occurred?

2 How would you have tried to implement the changes identified?

3 Given that the worst has now happened, how would you seek to deal with the sit-in – or given that you have also probably been made redundant, would you join the protest?

Sources:
Several newspapers covered this story, including (accessed 1 April 2009):
http://www.belfasttelegraph.co.uk/news/local-national/devastated-visteon-staff-stage-sitin-as-200-jobs-go-in-factory-shutdown-14251293.html.
http://news.scotsman.com/uk/Sitin-as-car-firm-axes.5127581.jp.
http://news.sky.com/skynews/Home/Business/565-UK-Car-Jobs-Axed-As-Car-Parts-Maker-Visteon-Goes-Into-Administration/Article/200903415252624?f=rss.

how people should be managed and ways of doing business all impact on how the potential available from the local human resource can be realized. This becomes an even more complex situation when the inevitable mixing of local labour and various forms of expatriate or third-country employees are mixed together into a single workforce (see for example Reuvid, 2008).

Brewster *et al.* (2007: pp. 4–5) suggest that when planning for international operations, HR practitioners usually need to consider the following questions:

- Do we have a strategy for becoming an international firm?
- What type of managers will we need to be successful? And how do we find or develop them?

EXAMINING ETHICS

Should I earn more than my boss?

The following question was posed by an employee:

When I joined this company 6 months ago, I negotiated a deal where part of my pay would be performance-related, depending on new business I brought in. I've been more successful in this than expected, and my pay will soon top that of my boss. He doesn't know I know this, and has asked me if I'll agree to decrease the proportion of my salary that is performance-related so it's more in line with other employees. I'm sure that it's actually because he doesn't want anyone to earn more than him. Should

I confront him with this and refuse to change my set-up? The money itself is not important to me – it's the principle.

TASKS

1 What would you advise the employee to do and why?
2 What does this suggest about the design of incentive schemes and their relationship to motivation?

Source:
Bullmore, J. 'What's your problem?' *Management Today*, July 2003, p. 81. Reprinted with permission.

- How can I find out about the way that HRM is conducted in other countries: the laws, trade unions, labour market, expectations…?
- What will be the impact of local cultural norms on our home-based ways of working? Can we use all or any of them in other countries?
- How will we choose whether to send expatriates or use local employees?
- How do we manage international moves if we choose to send some people out from home?
- How do we manage knowledge across geographical and cultural distance?

Among the difficulties facing HR practitioners when operating internationally is the degree to which home or local norms should dominate in any particular location and organization. Organizations tend to require every part of the business to operate common procedures and systems for many reasons including simplicity in operating processes; standardization of control processes; ability to compare data, information and results across divisions, operating units and locations; ability to present information in a standardized form to senior group level managers for decision-making purposes; because it allows the preparation of group level reporting data and financial results; because it allows a degree of standardization in career development, training and development provision for managers and others who may be expected to relocate around the sites within the group at frequent intervals. However, by operating in a standardized way (usually based on the norms, requirements and conventions of the parent group location) it is likely that those locations used to operating under different norms etc. will either have to learn new ways that might be based on completely unfamiliar models of human nature, legal requirements and social conventions; or they may in practice operate under a sort of dual system in which a pretence of meeting corporate obligations is maintained, but local norms flourish under the surface. In either situation there exists a role for HR managers and specialists to be able to contribute to the effective use of people within the business. In terms of OB, there are many aspects of this book that offer insights into international HRM, including perception, attitudes, personality, leadership, communications, decision making, conflict, negotiations and culture. The Going Global example illustrates one aspect of 'international' HRM.

HRM AND THE LINE MANAGER

With the emergence of HRM as the dominant perspective on people management, it has been recognized that the line manager should be responsible for the people (and their behaviour) because they are in a constant interactive and dynamic relationship with them. Line managers are the business managers for their particular unit of responsibility. As such, they are responsible for the effective use of all resources at their disposal, including the people. Thorough training in people management as well as the technical aspects of their job needs to be provided for line managers if they are to be effective in managing their full range of responsibilities. Equally, line managers need to be able to make effective use of the HRM specialism available to support them if they are to get the best out of the people who work for them. There is a developing literature in the area of how human resource and operations

GOING GLOBAL

Julia's expectations

Julia, a fully qualified nurse, was born, educated and trained in Indonesia. She was recruited by an agency in 2001 to work as a nurse in the British National Health Service (NHS). She left her family (husband and two children) to take a 2-year contract on a surgical ward in a general hospital in Manchester. The idea was that by working in Britain she would be able to earn additional money (to send home), and gain more experience. Julia was happy to be given what she thought was a good opportunity and was looking forward to the challenge, although she was distressed at having to leave her family behind.

In Britain she quickly settled into her new job and began to make friends with the other foreign nurses, most of whom were in a similar position to herself. However, soon after she arrived, problems began to surface and Julia found that she was increasingly unhappy with the job and working in Britain. She also missed her family and friends. The hospital was short of staff and everyone was required to work very hard. Staff shortages were invariably covered by the use of agency staff who had only limited knowledge of the ward, patients or hospital procedures. A number of

British nurses had left the NHS to work for agencies, resulting in more responsibility for Julia and her colleagues. Agency nurses were also paid more money than Julia. This Julia felt to be unfair. Also the hospital culture was different from what she had been used to in Indonesia and that made it difficult for her to know what was expected of her in many situations, including dealing with her managers.

Julia became increasingly frustrated and disenchanted with her job. She also found that because of the cost of living in Manchester and being away from her family, she was not able to send as much money home as she had intended. Because of the conditions attached to her work permit, she was not allowed to resign and seek work as an agency nurse thereby earning additional money. After 6 months she resigned and went back to Indonesia.

TASKS

1 Was the outcome for both Julia and the hospital inevitable, or could it have been avoided? If so, how?

2 Could Julia have been encouraged to stay longer? How?

management research could be combined in an attempt to more effectively explain the processes involved in running organizations (see for example, Boudreau *et al.*, 2003, and for European developments, Larsen and Brewster, 2003).

Many organizations are moving away from centralized structures with an HR department staffed by specialists located at the centre of the organization; and also from decentralized structures with HR specialists working in line departments, with a reporting relationship to a centralized HR department. One recent development is the creation of what has become known as e-HR in which the provision of human resource support to the organization is provided through computer screens and electronic interaction processes (Lengnick-Hall and Moritz, 2003). Arrangements such as service and call centres and drop-in advice centres are also becoming more common. The availability of human resource support should enable line managers to share responsibility with someone with appropriate expertise. Patterson *et al.* (1997) explored management practice across a large number of manufacturing organizations in Britain over a 10-year period. Among their findings were that two particular areas delivered significant impact on company profitability. They were:

1 *Skill.* The acquisition of appropriate skills within the workforce and the continual development of those skills as the organization develops.

2 *Job design.* The critical evaluation of job design in terms of the application of skill flexibility, task variety, range of responsibilities and team working.

The human resource practitioner should be well placed by training, experience and inclination to offer the means to effectively contribute to both of these areas of significance. That is the basis of the business partnering model of HR discussed in relation to the role of HR earlier in this chapter (also see Hunter *et al.*, 2006). However, it could be argued that this is what good line managers have been doing throughout history. Good managers have always valued the contribution that people can make to an organization and this has been operationalized across time according to the prevailing social norms and conditions. It could be argued that in today's world, employees are less willing to be coerced into work in the first place, or controlled or driven whilst at work, and therefore more subtle and consensual methods have to be developed. The interesting ethical and practical questions arising from this centre on the degree to which managers are relinquishing their right to manage and control in the process of achieving co-operation from employees. The extremes of possibility appear to be that managers could be genuinely interested in seeking to achieve consensual working arrangements; or they could be seeking ways to exploit labour more effectively in response to a changed social context without having to undermine the fundamental relative power, status and hierarchy in doing so. This last point is reflected in the labour process debate – see for example Thompson (1989).

HUMAN RESOURCE MANAGEMENT AND ORGANIZATIONAL BEHAVIOUR

The emphasis of HRM has shifted to being a people strategy and practical support function for business units (the preferred term within the HR profession being a 'business partner'). It would be the HR managers who determine (in consultation with line managers) the appropriate policies for the organization in relation to its business strategy. Typically these would focus on issues supporting the need for productivity, quality, flexibility and high commitment from the workforce in pursuit of the cost-effective use of labour. A wide range of OB themes have a direct relevance to HR practice. All of the topics in this book have an impact on aspects of human behaviour within an organizational context and hence the practice of HRM. For example, taking extracts from the chapter headings in this book as an indication of relevance provides the following summary:

- *Personality and individual difference*. The use of psychometric tests in selection and subsequent development processes as a way of identifying individuals with particular personality, aptitude and ability characteristics that have been judged as important for employment or promotion within the organization is very common these days.

- *Perception and attitudes*. It is important for HRM practitioners to understand how employees perceive and understand things that have relevance to the functioning of the organization. For example, management might perceive that it is necessary to increase the use of technology to reduce cost and maintain profitability; employees may perceive the same situation as an attempt to eliminate jobs and increase profit. If such changes are to take place successfully, managers need to understand the different perceptions so that appropriate strategies can be planned.

- *Motivation*. If the organization is to achieve the best levels of output and quality from the employees, they must be motivated to perform and an understanding of theory could assist in the design of effective schemes.

- *Leadership and management*. If HRM specialists understand the differences and similarities between leadership and management, they will be in a position to design appropriate resourcing, career management, development and training programmes.

- *Groups and teams*. The understanding of group dynamics and behaviour could allow the HR function to assist line managers in the creation and effective management of work groups. The result should be an improved quality of working life and higher productivity.

- *Communications*. The need for managers to communicate with employees and vice versa represents an important part of being able to understand each other and being able to influence the perceptions and attitudes held by all stakeholders.

- *Conflict and negotiations*. Dealing with disciplinary and grievance cases within the company and negotiating the annual pay settlement with the trade unions are obvious examples. However these are not the only areas of relevance. For example, two departments might argue about who was responsible for a particular mistake, or a manager may have to negotiate with their subordinates about working extra hours to complete an urgent order. The HR department could design or provide appropriate training for managers and others in such activities.

- *Organizational structure*. An understanding of organizational design assists the HRM function to pay a full part in such discussions and design processes – adding a definite 'people' dimension to the process in addition to the technical, process-focused approach often taken.

- *Control, reward and job design*. Frequently these aspects of OB follow on from structural issues in that control processes and job design can be determined by structural arrangements. Reward policy and practice are also strongly related to motivation.

- *Culture*. Culture defined as the 'way we do things around here' represents the way that many OB features function in practice. Some cultures are more supportive of management objectives than others and HR people have a huge interest in how to create cultures that can deliver high-performance working and a high-commitment workforce.

- *Power, influence and politics.* These aspects of OB have strong relevance to control, conflict, group working, leadership and so on. However much managers seek to describe an organization as democratic, there remains a power-based relationship at the core – when labour is scarce employees have more power than managers and vice versa. Equally, management has a political dimension to it – managers are in competition for scarce resources and also for influence and so each manager must be more effective than every other manager in putting their case across. HRM specialists need to understand how these processes work in order to play a part in workplace dynamics (the abuse of power for example might lead to grievance or disciplinary action). But they must also be able to use politics etc. if they are to stand any chance of having their ideas taken seriously or to be allowed to contribute to the effective running of an organization.

- *Relationships, fairness and trust.* Many of the ideas discussed above are about these three concepts and their practical application to the workplace. If the HR function cannot be the arbiter of what fairness means within an employment setting, who can? Equally, trust is important in any relationship, including employment and working relationships. This has strong connotations with culture and some cultures will encourage trust and fairness and it is for the HR function to recognize this and find ways of encouraging the developments that will facilitate them.

Another way of thinking about the relationship between HRM and OB is through the contemporary management challenges that form a running series of realities that all practising managers experience in the course of their work, which are discussed in detail in Chapter 2. These challenges also form the basis of the support panels included in every chapter.

CONCLUSIONS

Human Resource Management (HRM) can be seen as the application of the behavioural knowledge supplied by OB in systematic ways in organizations. In practice, HRM represents the management function with responsibility for the management of people within the organization. Consequently, the human resource department plays a key role in encouraging 'appropriate' behaviours among both managers and employees. It could be argued that the human resource department is the function that addresses all of the issues in this book, seeking to develop appropriate policies and practice in the search for the effective use of people. For example, communication, involvement, training and leadership policies are grounded in the belief that the more closely employees are involved in the business, the more probable it is that they will align themselves with the perceptions and attitudes held by managers and so make the running of the organization easier

and the achievement of management-determined objectives more likely. Similarly, employee motivation can be addressed through performance management practices, together with the design of salary, incentive and benefits packages. However, it is the line manager who holds the responsibility for the application of people management policies in relation to their subordinates. Human resource specialists can only advise managers, ensure that the procedures are applied correctly and if necessary report their concerns through the chain of command in anticipation of action by senior line managers.

Now to summarize this chapter in terms of the relevant Learning Objectives:

- **Explain the major models for the study of people management.** There are four models introduced in the chapter. The first, developed by

Fombrum *et al.* (1984) begins with the view that employees are a resource that needs to be flexible, reliable and cost-effective. This model begins with business strategy setting the parameters; subsequently converted into a people strategy; then actual people policies. A second model, Beer *et al.* (1984, 1985), adopts the stakeholder view of people management. It begins with a strategic perspective, but seeks to operationalize this by integrating a human dimension into it. People represent thinking, dynamic and interactive elements within the organization, not just a static resource waiting to be used. This model recognizes four main policy areas, employee influence, human resource flows, reward systems and work systems. A third model by Schuler and Jackson (1987, 1996) sets out to establish an association between the strategy of the organization and the employee behaviours necessary to achieve it. They identify two operational strategy options, one based on cost minimization, the other based on innovation. They reflect how to compete in the marketplace that the organizational strategy determines. A fourth model, by Hendry *et al.* (1989), based on British research able to explore the relevant culture, managerial practice and organizational arrangements. The model proposes five main interlinked elements – environmental context, internal organizational context, business strategy context, HRM context and content.

- **Understand the relevance of OB to the study and practice of HRM.** The simplest response to this objective is that all of the OB themes covered in this book and associated website have relevance to and inform the theory and practice of HRM.

- **Describe the approaches to studying the links between business and HR strategy.** Marchington and Wilkinson (2005, Chapter 4) review two main approaches on the relationship between business strategy and HRM strategy. They are:

  - Best fit or contingency approach. The essential theme is that HR strategy needs to be relevant to and supportive of business strategy. Three different strategic models (life cycle, competitive advantage and strategic configurations) are identified and explored for the best-fit approach to HR strategy.

  - Resource-based approach. This takes an inside-out perspective – the opposite view to the best-fit approach which takes an outside-in perspective. The best-fit approach assumes that HRM is the malleable variable with the outside factors fixed. The resource-based approach holds that HR activity can be strategic in its own right through such practices as training and development.

- **Assess the links between performance management and the practice of HRM.** Individual and/or team performance can be used to identify incentive payments paid to the employee as part of, or in addition to, their basic wage. For example, sales people are often paid a commission based on the value of sales that they achieve. Factory workers can be paid an individual or team productivity bonus for achieving levels of output over and above a set target. Senior managers might be awarded shares for achieving targets for the growth in the value of the company or its share price. Administrative and technical staff might have their performance reviewed by their line manager through an appraisal system each year, the result of which might (or might not) be used as one of the determinants of their annual pay review, along with cost of living and other factors.

- **Discuss the approaches to equality and diversity introduced in this chapter.** There exists a legislative equality obligation on employers in relation to all aspects of the employment relationship including resourcing, reward, career development, pension and termination rights. In some of the literature and common usage, diversity often means the same as equal opportunities. However, the latter are based on categories defined by legislators. Diversity is more appropriately regarded as a recognition that individuals differ from each other in many ways and that organizational performance can be achieved through harnessing that potential. It represents a business results-based approach to differences between people whereas equal opportunity represents a moral approach to fairness. The man emphasis in equal opportunities is seeking to further the interests of disadvantaged groups. The major approach in diversity management is to identify those differences that impact on the performance of the organization and to harness them appropriately to that end. Various models for achieving diversity are introduced in the appropriate sections of this chapter.

DISCUSSION QUESTIONS

1 'Managing people is the most important part of any line manager's job.' Discuss this claim, illustrating your answer with examples from your experience.

2 Outline the psychological contract and assess its significance in the management of people within an organization.

3 Outline the main approaches to employee involvement and discuss the circumstances in which each might be most appropriate.

4 'Managing people within an organization is about gripping them warmly by the throat and squeezing gently until they do as management wants.' Discuss this statement in light of the material about HRM presented in this chapter.

5 Discuss what performance means to the 'job' of being a student. If you were a lecturer how would you measure student performance and why?

6 'Equality is about ensuring that the organization is protected from legal penalty, it is diversity that offers the most significant approach to making the best use of individual difference.' Discuss this statement.

7 Make a case for OB being the bedrock of theory and practice of HRM.

8 Discuss the degree to which the models of HRM introduced in this chapter are nothing more than a reflection of the prevailing culture and views of human nature from the locations in which the research was undertaken.

9 To what extent is international HRM nothing more than taking the local culture into account?

10 'Resourcing is the easiest aspect of HRM practice as it simply involves selecting the most suitable candidate for the vacant job.' Discuss this statement.

CASE STUDY

Do big firms miss out in terms of hiring the best talent?

The following example was told to one of the authors by Mark in April 2009. Only the names have been changed to disguise the parties involved.

Mark had been made redundant as a result of the recession of 2008 and was desperately looking for a new job. He had been a senior marketing consultant with a large regional consultancy practice based in the North of England for the previous 10 years working with some large national and international clients predominantly in the fast-moving consumer goods sector.

He applied for many jobs in order to try to maintain his career path, experience, and also naturally to earn money. He had considerable success in achieving a good rate of interviews from his applications, so clearly his CV was very attractive to a wide range of consultancies and in-house marketing departments. At the time of the conversation with Mark he had actually been unemployed for about 3 weeks, had applied for 15 jobs (including seven speculative applications

introducing himself to specific organizations) and obtained eight interviews. The interviews included:

● Three national and local public sector organizations – seeking marketing and PR support for various projects.

● Three small regional consultancies – looking to expand their operations as a result of opportunities as clients moved away from the large (expensive) consultancies as a result of the recession.

● One large national retail chain that was looking to strengthen its in-house marketing activities.

The public sector interviews went well but Mark was not offered a job (because other candidates more closely matched the job requirements – shorthand for previous public sector experience). The consultancy interviews went well, but two only offered Mark work on a self-employed basis for 2 or 3 days per week guaranteed for 2 months and hopefully beyond that (but with no guarantees). They did not have enough work to make the offer more certain or on an employed basis. The third consultancy was the smallest of the three and offered Mark a full-time senior-level job on 'employee status' basis. The large retail chain was slow in responding to Mark's application. He had already been offered the job by the consultancy and was in the final stages of discussing terms and conditions of employment with them before the retail chain offered him an interview. He was torn in deciding what to do - working for the retail chain would look good on his CV and would offer more benefits than available from the small consultancy, but with a lower salary. However, he didn't feel that he could back out of the job that he was in the final stages of accepting and it also offered some interesting possibilities for the future in terms of a possible directorship and part ownership of the business if it grew. In the end he decided to stick with the consultancy job and told the retail chain that he was withdrawing his application.

The head of marketing for the retail chain telephoned Mark to plead with him not to withdraw. He was told that he had just the right background for the job on offer and that he was streets ahead of the other applicants. It was also said that whilst no guarantees could be made in relation to job offers or salary

© Michael Prince/Corbis

package, he was just the sort of person that they were looking for and they would be happy to talk to him at any time – even outside of normal office hours if he would agree to meet them. This made Mark think again, but eventually he decided to stick with his original decision. The head of marketing thanked him for listening and said that if the new job did not work out Mark should call them and they would make every attempt to accommodate him for an interview. It was also pointed out that the reason that it had taken so long to arrange the interviews was the 'large company HR procedures' that had to be followed with regard to approvals to advertise and then having to wait for closing dates before any approaches could be made to any applicant. It was said that the HR department claimed such formalized approaches to be 'best practice' and necessary in order to demonstrate fairness and equality to all applicants and so avoid any possible litigation or financial penalty. The head of marketing clearly had his own views and was frustrated at the loss of a potentially good employee, but could do nothing about it.

TASKS

1 This case suggests that the application of HR procedures takes time and in the process good candidates may disengage with the process because they are unlikely to have just one application 'live' at any point in time, as for them their resourcing process is not linear. Given this 'reality', how can organizations ever recruit the 'best talent' available?

2 Can there ever be a case for breaking the rules to attract the best candidate? If so, make that case.

3 Does it matter if an organization is unable to recruit the 'best talent' available as long as the person appointed can do the job expected of them? Justify your views?

FURTHER READING

Armstrong, M. and Baron, A. (2004) *Managing Performance: Performance Management in Action*, London: CIPD. Explores what performance management means and how it can be achieved in practice.

Barrow, S. and Mosley, R. (2005) *The Employer Brand: Bringing the Best of Brand Management to People at Work*, Chichester: Wiley. Looks at the relatively new idea that employers have a 'brand' that (just like any marketing context) needs to be developed and built if it is to work for the organization in positive ways.

Dowling, P., Festing, M. and Engle, A.D. (2008) *International Human Resource Management*. 5th edition, London: Cengage Learning. Looks at HRM in an international context.

Houldsworth, E. and Jirasinghe, D. (2006) *Managing and Measuring Employee Performance*, London: Kogan Page. Explores what performance and performance management means and how it can be achieved in practice.

Lewis, D. and Sargeant, M. (2009) *Essentials of Employment Law*, London: CIPD. Looks at the basic requirements and obligations associated with employment law.

Marchington, M. and Wilkinson, A. (2008) *Human Resource Management at Work*, 4th edition, London: CIPD. An academic rather than practitioner's consideration of HRM – although it has relevance to the practical application of HRM theory.

Swart, J., Kinnie, N. and Rabinowitz, J. (2007) *Managing Across Boundaries: Human Resource Management Beyond the Firm*, London: CIPD. Explores a broad range of external perspectives associated with HRM practice and theory.

The Aston Centre for Human Resources (2008) *Strategic Human Resource Management: Building Research Based Practice*, London: CIPD. The text looks at building a research-centred approach to understanding what strategic HRM is and how it should impact on organizational functioning.

Wellin, M. (2007) *Managing the Psychological Contract: Using the Personal Deal to Increase Business Performance*, Farnham: Gower. Considers the nature of the psychological contract and its significance to performance aspects of HRM.

Whittington, R. and Molloy, E. (2005) HR's role in organising: shaping change, *Research report*, London: CIPD. Considers a broad range of research collected from public and private sector organizations in relation to the role and functioning of HR in relation to change.

COMPANION WEBSITE

Online teaching and learning resources

Visit the companion website for Organizational Behaviour and Management 4th edition at: http://www.cengage.co.uk/martinfellenz to find valuable further teaching and learning material. For full details, see 'About the website' at the start of the book.

PART FIVE

INFORMAL SYSTEMS AND DYNAMICS WITHIN ORGANIZATIONS

The previous section explored issues associated with the formal systems and arrangements that provide the context for organizational life and that have profound implications for individual and collective behaviour in organizations. In contrast, Part 5 explores the role and nature of informal aspects and of relevant social dynamics that play important roles in organizations. Thus, this section introduces and discusses the final element in our guiding framework for learning about and understanding management and OB (see Figure 1), the informal systems and dynamics (shortened to 'social systems' in the model).

Figure 1

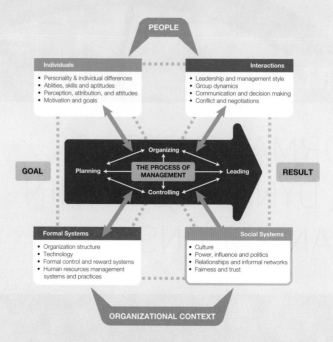

Chapter 14, the first chapter of Part 5, addresses the important issue of culture as a major area of relevance to OB theory and practice. Every organization and organizational subunits and even different groups have their own cultures. Members as well as managers need to be aware of culture and the impact it has on individual and collective behaviour and experiences. The chapter also considers the role of national culture in organizations, as many organizations operate in many countries of the world and employ people from many nationalities that bring different cultures to bear at work. Chapter 15 considers power, influence and politics as important features that impact on the behaviour of people at work. Chapter 16, the final chapter of the book, concludes with a consideration of relationships, fairness and trust. These topics impact on how people relate to each other and how they interpret the behaviour and actions of others in the determination of how to respond to them, establishing a reciprocal basis and pattern for much of the behaviour occurring within organizations.

The comprehensive framework model for management and OB that identifies and relates the various component parts of this book is included as Figure 2.

Figure 2

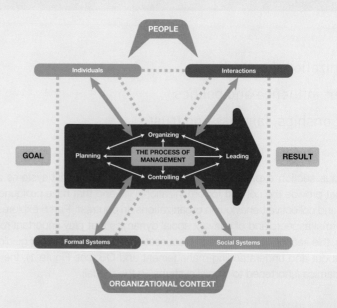

CHAPTER FOURTEEN

©narvikk /istock

ORGANIZATIONAL CULTURE

LEARNING OBJECTIVES

After studying this chapter and working through the associated OB in Action panels, Discussion Questions and Case Study you should be able to:

● Understand the significance of the various definitions of culture.

● Outline the meaning of Edgar Schein's (1985) three levels of culture: artefacts, values and assumptions.

● Assess Handy's views on the factors that determine organizational culture.

● Explain why the concept of culture is problematic when applied to organizations.

● Discuss the possibilities for the management and change of organizational culture, together with the means of doing so.

● Recognize the implications of national cultures on management and organizations.

INTRODUCTION

The concept of culture began to make an impact on organizational thinking in the late 1970s and early 1980s. However, its existence is evident in a number of the ideas of earlier writers, for example, Barnard (1938) and Jaques (1952). Culture is difficult to define – it is a concept that can easily be recognized but is difficult to pin down in objective terms. As a concept, culture emerged from anthropological research among ethnic groups and societies. Unfortunately, from this wealth of established literature there is no dominant view of how culture should be conceptualized or studied. According to Allaire and Firsirotu (1984) for example, there are eight separate schools of thought on what the term 'culture' means.

It is easy to understand that organizations 'feel' different from other organizations, or that their members 'do things differently'. However, it is much more difficult to say with any degree of certainty in what ways and to what degree organizational cultures differ. The phrase 'the way we do things around here' is frequently offered as an operational definition of culture (Deal and Kennedy, 1982). However, while that may be a useful description of the experience of culture, it does not constitute a definition and offers little analytical power. In this chapter, we offer a definition of culture and a model of the linkages between culture, behaviour, cognition and observable artefacts relevant for culture in organizations. We consider available frameworks of organizational culture and also discuss the challenges of managing and changing organizational culture. We conclude with a review of research on the role of national culture for organizations and management.

DEFINING ORGANIZATIONAL CULTURE

As far back as 1952 Kroeber and Kluckhohn reported 164 different definitions of culture, a figure well exceeded in the intervening decades (see Table 14.1 for a selection of relevant definitions of organizational culture). This has led some writers to suggest that the concept has no real value because its meanings are so diverse and largely contradictory that it is impossible for it to offer any value as a research idea (Kraut, 1975). The richness and variety of cultural research, however fragmented and at times contradictory, also offers valuable insights. Cohen (2009) argues that multiple cultural phenomena may exist at the same time. Nationality, religion, region and social class, for example, all 'account for an especially large amount of variation in transmitted norms, values, beliefs, behaviours, and the like' (2009: p. 195). Thus, definitions of culture should be explicit about what phenomenon is referred to, and by studying these and other phenomena such as organizations and organizational subunits as cultures, we can both 'understand these domains better, as well as culture more broadly' (Cohen: 2009: p. 195).

Culture seeks to describe those facets of human experience and behaviour that contribute to the differences and similarities in how people perceive and engage with their world. In that sense culture retains its value as a meta-construct with metaphorical and descriptive power, even if it is often imprecise and problematic. For the purpose of this book, we will focus on a definition of culture that is specific enough to provide insight into and guidance relevant to behavioural issues in organizations, yet one that is broad enough to accommodate the important relevant cultural constituents such as material, subjective and social aspects (see Cohen, 2009; Chiu and Hong, 2006).

Nearly every practising manager we have met and worked with has their own views of the importance and role of culture, and almost all of them are happy to discuss them. However, we have found that the best way to interrupt such contributions is to

Table 14.1 Selected definitions of organizational culture

Organizational culture(s)
. . . is the 'customary and traditional way of thinking and doing things, which is shared to a greater or lesser degree by all members, and which the new members must learn and at least partially accept, in order to be accepted into the services of the firm.' (Jaques, 1952: p. 251)
. . . is a 'system of publicly and collectively accepted meanings operating for a given group at a given time. This system of terms, forms, categories, and images interprets a people's own situation to themselves.' (Pettigrew, 1979: p. 574)
. . . is 'the pattern of basic assumptions that a given group has invented, discovered, or developed in learning to cope with its problems of external adaptation and internal integration, and that have worked well enough to be considered valid, and, therefore, to be taught to new members as the correct way to perceive, think, and feel in relation to these problems.' (Schein, 1985: p. 6)
. . . are 'collective phenomena that embody people's responses to the uncertainties and chaos that are inevitable in human experience. These responses fall into two major categories. The first is the substance of a culture – shared, emotionally charged belief systems that we call ideologies. The second is cultural forms – observable entities, including actions, through which members of a culture express, affirm, and communicate the substance of their culture to one another.' (Trice and Beyer, 1993: p. 2)

pose the seemingly simple question: 'What is culture?' Invariably there is a significant pause, until answers emerge that typically include some or even all of the following: 'Culture is . . . values, beliefs, norms, practices, expectations, preferences, attitudes, and behaviours.' The description referred to already in the introduction, 'Culture is the way we do things around here,' is a particular favourite. Curiously, these definitions appear to rarely survive closer inspection and interrogation, and the common managerial view of culture often mirrors closely LeVine's comment on the view of many social science researchers who treat culture 'as representing the unexplained residuum of rigorous empirical analysis, an area of darkness beyond the reach of currently available scientific searchlights' (1984: p. 67). We will consider managerial and common-sense views of culture in light of our definition of culture further below.

We define organizational culture as *a set of shared, often implicit assumptions, beliefs, values, and sensemaking procedures that influences and guides the behaviour and thinking of organizational members, and is continuously enacted and in turn reinforced – or changed – by the behaviour of organizational members.* In many ways, this definition reflects many of the above-cited aspects managers typically use to describe and define culture, but with two crucial differences: it excludes behaviour as an integral element of culture, and it focuses only on characteristics that are shared. Behaviour can express culture, can be influenced by it, and can shape, reinforce and change it, but *behaviour is not culture*! Cultural practices such as rituals are visible as behaviours, but the cultural component of such rituals is not the ritualistic behaviour itself but rather that which guides such behaviour and gives it specific meaning for those enacting it (but see Jaques [1952] or Trice and Beyer's [1993] definitions in Table 14.1 for different views). Also, we define culture as a set of cognitive elements and structures (e.g., beliefs, values, sensemaking procedures) that are shared and commonly employed among members of a culture. A single individual's idiosyncratic thinking or sensemaking is not part of culture unless the

Organizational culture
A set of shared, often implicit assumptions, beliefs, values, and sensemaking procedures that influences and guides the behaviour and thinking of organizational members, and is continuously enacted and in turn reinforced – or changed – by the behaviour of organizational members.

14.1 EXTEND
YOUR LEARNING

cognitive elements contributing to this are shared by others (and thus not a unique and merely individual feature). Thus, cultures may of course have idiosyncrasies – but these will be shared by members of the culture!

Our definition of culture is fully compatible with three characteristics universally seen as central to the concept of culture: (a) it emerges during the adaptive interaction between people and their environment, and therefore will change when these inter-actions change; (b) it is by necessity constituted only of shared, intersubjective ele-ments; and (c) it is transmitted to members across time periods and changing member cohorts or generations (Triandis, 2007). These three aspects deserve closer scrutiny.

STOP & CONSIDER

Compare the definition of culture that we provide to others that you find from other writers. Identify and explain the differences and similarities between them and in doing so determine if and how they matter.

Figure 14.1 shows a model of the key linkages between culture and the central elements of everyday conceptions related to culture such as behaviour, individual cognition (thinking) and artefacts (see Table 14.2 for an explanation of the linkages indicated by the arrows in the model). At the heart of this model is the reciprocal relationship between behaviour and culture. As our definition indicates, this circular link shows the direct influence of culture on behaviour. Culturally guided behaviour can thus be said to enact culture and make it visible. Moreover, this enactment typi-cally reinforces the culture as long as it remains aligned to the shared values and behavioural norms of the culture. However, if behaviour by members of a culture drifts away from such alignment it can change the culture as over time it can poten-tially lead to different behavioural norms along with different ways to make sense of (and thus legitimize) different behaviours (e.g., Gagliardi, 1986). To have such an influence on culture, behaviour needs to have intersubjective impact, for example through being collective, involving others, or being observed in its conduct (e.g., violating a nonsmoking rule at work) or its consequences (e.g., full ashtrays on a work desk). Solitary and unobserved behaviour without visible consequences can-not change culture because it has no intersubjective impact. Similarly, cognition (i.e., individual thinking) cannot affect culture because it is not observable. Individual

Figure 14.1 Model of the linkages between culture, behaviour, cognition and artefacts

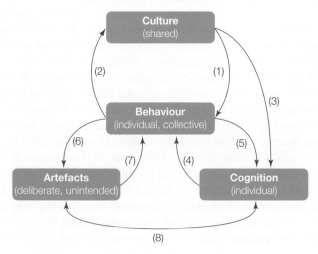

Table 14.2 Linkages between culture, behaviour, cognition and artefacts

Arrow 1 - Culture influences behaviour	Culture influences behaviour directly through behavioural norms that indicate both expected and prescribed behaviours. Along with internalizing the shared assumptions, values and sensemaking procedures, members of a culture will also develop culture-consistent behavioural scripts that are automatically or consciously invoked when situational conditions trigger them. Culture also infuences behaviour indirectly through its influence on sensemaking and other cognitive processes (see Chapter 3).
Arrow 2 - Behaviour influences culture	Culture can consist only of elements shared among members of the culture. Any inter-subjective sharing of these elements is dependent on inputs that are observable by individuals. This places behaviour in a central role regarding culture as only behaviours and artifacts created through behaviour are observable. Overall, the expression and manifestation of underlying assumptions, values and preferences through behaviour as well as the social control through behaviour are central determinants of culture.
	Note: What outsiders may be able to observe and how they interpret it may be quite different from the perceptions and interpretations of members of a culture who already share cognitive elements and structures.
Arrow 3 - Culture influences cognition	By definition, shared cognitive structures are part of individual thinking, perception and sensemaking. Thus, culture represents a significant influence on individual thinking that employs these shared cognitive elements.
Arrow 4 - Cognition influences behaviour	Deliberate behaviour is determined by conscious and subconscious cognitive processes. For example, even automatic behaviour is influenced by cognitive structures such as behavioural scripts (see Chapters 3, 4 and 5).
Arrow 5 - Behaviour influences cognition	The consistency motive expressed in such dynamics as cognitive dissonance (see Chapter 4) can account for the influence of behaviour on thinking. Thus, participating in culturally relevant behaviours can lead to individuals adopting culturally consistent cognitive elements such as assumptions, beliefs, values, or meanings.
Arrow 6 - Behaviour influences artefacts	Artefacts, as the name suggests, are made by human beings. They come into being as a result of deliberate human action or as the unintended result of human behaviour. Without behaviour, artefacts do not exist.
Arrow 7 - Artefacts influence behaviour	The linkage between artefacts and behaviour is reciprocal. Similar to the duality of structure (see Chapter 10), human behaviour creates artefacts (e.g., an office furniture layout; a mobile phone; a ladder), and these artefacts in turn influence (i.e., enable and constrain) what humans do. For example, even without observing others' behaviour or being told not to do it, most people would not walk across a pristine carpet in an entrance hall if they observe a clearly visible, well-worn walkway (an artefact) that leads around it.
Arrow 8 - Artefacts influence cognition	Perception of artefacts can influence individual thinking just like any other input from a person's social and physical environment. The specific nature of the influence is mediated by cultural assumptions, schemas and other cognitive elements a person possesses.

cognition becomes observable and thus may obtain subjective impact only through observable behaviour. This reciprocal link between culture and behaviour encompasses the adaptive interaction between people and their environment that gives rise to culture (see Schein, 2004; Triandis, 2007).

It is important to recognize that the only element that directly influences culture is behaviour. Individual cognition cannot have any intersubjective impact unless it is communicated through some form of behaviour. Similarly, even though artefacts (such as written communication) can influence what people know and believe, the link to culture is mediated through individual cognition (interpretation of the communication or of other artefacts) and through the subsequent manifestation of culturally relevant cognitions through responses (i.e., behaviour) such as acting according to instructions received, or writing a response.

Culture as consisting only of shared, intersubjective elements is the second central aspect of culture (Triandis, 2007). It is reflected in the shared cognitive structures our definition refers to and includes aspects of shared information as well as shared meaning. While some distinguish definitions of culture that focus on either shared meaning or shared information (see Cohen, 2009), we include both as well as the sensemaking procedures used to derive meaning from information in our definition of culture. Thus, our definition is compatible with theory and research in psychology and anthropology (see D'Andrade, 1995; Lehman *et al.*, 2004; Strauss and Quinn, 1997) including *cultural schema theory* (or *cultural models theory*) (e.g., Caulkins, 2004; Nishida, 1999, 2005; Sharifian, 2003) and *cultural consensus theory* (Horowitz, 2009; Romney *et al.*, 1986; Weller, 2007). Such theories focus on the shared thinking of people, which includes cognitive *content* (such as beliefs and knowledge) and cognitive *processes* (such as use of cognitive structures like schemas, frames and heuristics). From this perspective, such shared cognitions define culture and determine membership of specific cultures. Thus, 'cultural groups are formed not just by physical proximity of individuals but by relative participation of individuals in each other's conceptual world. The degree to which individuals can participate in a group's conceptualized sphere would determine their membership of the [cultural] group.' (Sharifian, 2003: p. 189) Sharifian goes on to argue that the cognitive or mental similarity among members is 'often mirrored in interactions between the members of a cultural group as well as those between the members of different cultural groups' (2003: p. 189).

Some people may share more of such a set of cognitive elements and structures than others, which implies that some members of a culture may be more acculturated than others – they are comparatively more part of the culture (or, maybe more accurately, the culture is more part of them). This links to the third important characteristic central to the concept of culture, which requires culture to be transmitted to members across time periods and changing member cohorts or generations (Triandis, 2007). For cultures to persist, new generations of members or new entrants to the culture from outside must start to share at least some of the assumptions, beliefs, values and sensemaking procedures particular to the culture to become members. Newcomers to a culture are often culturally inept, and typically need to go through a learning process before they become fully adept at behaving in culturally appropriate ways. This process is also called socialization or acculturation, terms that refer to the process by which newcomers to a culture or social group develop the ability to function effectively in their particular setting. We will come back to consider acculturation in more detail later in this chapter (socialization is discussed in Chapter 12).

STUDYING ORGANIZATIONAL CULTURE

Along with the many different definitions of culture, the large and diverse literature on culture indicates that there are many different approaches to studying this phenomenon. The research contributions have been categorized in many different ways. Adler (1984), for example, distinguished between studies of culture in terms of the research perspective adopted, including parochial, polycentric and synergistic. The main distinguishing feature between these categories is the number of cultures studied and the research methodology adopted. Redding (1994) proposes a two-dimensional classification scheme for research in this area based upon the degree of interpretation or description in the study, with the second scale reflecting micro to macro levels of analysis. Cray and Mallory (1998) suggest that it is possible to address many of the earlier criticisms of research in this field by classifying studies according to their relationship to theory. In doing so, they offer three approaches that can be identified from the literature:

1 *Naïve comparative.* This approach regards culture as the explanatory variable for any differences observed. The writers use the term 'naïve' to reflect the lack of any theoretical basis to the work. The emphasis in such studies is to compare issues such as how managerial functions differ between cultures.

2 *Culture free.* An approach taking contingency theory as the basis of seeking to explore the differences and similarities between cultures. The notion of contingency allows the perspective of cross-cultural studies to be undertaken and the impact on a variety of structural dimensions associated with organizing and managing to be explored.

3 *Culture bound.* This approach draws on a broad range of theoretical models to explore and explain differences between cultures.

Each of these categorization approaches has its own strength and they are not automatically mutually exclusive. Each could be used for different purposes; for example, the Cray and Mallory approach sets out to provide the basis for their cognitive model of international management. This uncertainty in how to classify studies of culture reflects the relatively recent exploration of this concept, together with the growing complexity of international operational activity and human multicultural experience which inevitably complicates attempts to theorize in this field.

Many of the most popular frameworks we discuss later in this chapter reflect a rationalistic and functionalist approach to culture. These approaches have been criticized for reducing culture to a mere variable in their attempt to try to understand what function culture fulfils in an organization (see Schultz, 1995; Rowlinson and Proctor, 1999) and what culture is likely to predict success. Moreover, such approaches can imply that culture serves merely as an alternative mechanism for manipulating employees through ideological control and 'values engineering' (Morgan, 1986/2006: p. 150). Alternatives to this reduction of culture to a managerial tool, which incidentally (and inappropriately) negates the difficulties in changing and managing organizational culture, are metaphorical and symbolic conceptions which focus more on the organization as a whole and on the unexplored meaning of overlooked or unexplained phenomena, respectively (see Schultz, 1995; Morgan, 1986/2006; Alvesson and Berg, 1992). These approaches appear much more focused on understanding the reality of experiences in organizations through studying culture rather than predicting specific outcomes. Postmodern treatments of culture also exist, which challenge the unitary nature of culture and the assumption of fixed and shared meanings, and instead locate cultural dynamics in the verbal and literary discourse among organizational members (see Alvesson and Berg, 1992; Hatch and Cunliffe, 2006; Rowlinson and Proctor, 1999). Some of these criticisms are picked up again in the section on sub- and countercultures below.

LEVELS AND DIMENSIONS OF ORGANIZATIONAL CULTURE

It is possible to distinguish different levels in the literature on cultural analysis. Typically, these levels range from the easily accessible and assessable, visible and tangible, to hard-to-access and difficult to assess, invisible and intangible aspects of culture. Rousseau (1990), for example, distinguished the following elements along this continuum: material artefacts, patterns of activities, behavioural norms, values and fundamental assumptions. A similar and very widely used model by Edgar Schein (1985), one of the most influential organizational and management scholars in the area of culture, distinguishes between three levels of culture: artefacts, values and assumptions (see Figure 14.2). For Schein, the essence of culture is located at the level of basic *assumptions* which reflect how members of a culture experience reality, how they perceive the physical and social world, and how they think and feel. These assumptions are taken for granted, and are rarely questioned. Consider how hardly anyone ever considers if and why things fall to the ground – subjective knowledge and assumptions about gravity typically remain at a subconscious level. However, also consider how less acculturated members of a culture (for example young children) frequently ask questions about such fundamentals. Children asking about falling things are quickly labelled naïve by more acculturated members of a culture (i.e., adults). Similarly, an organizational newcomer who questions why nobody challenged the sales director on overly optimistic revenue forecasts may be called naïve if such challenges of senior executives are not culturally sanctioned.

A culture's assumptions provide the basis for and interact with *values*, Schein's next level of culture. These values are the social norms, principles, standards, and objectives that are valued by cultural members for their intrinsic (not instrumental) worth. These values are more accessible because they are revealed by members' behaviours and priorities. The set of cultural values often also indicates what is seen as morally right and wrong in a particular culture. Even though these values often remain subconscious, members can more easily become aware of them than of their underlying cultural assumptions. In particular, members become more readily aware of such values when they are challenged during times of change or when someone violates conventions. Good examples abound in Sacha Baron Cohen's movies *Borat* (2006) and *Bruno* (2009) which also show the confusion, embarrassment, and emotional and behavioural responses that can ensue when individuals challenge cultural values and violate cultural norms, or through deliberately behaving in ways that take merely espoused (cultural) norms and values literally.

Norms are particularly important aspects of such cultural values. Norms and their formal counterpart, rules, communicate expectations and provide for a means of cultural and social control (see Chapter 7). The behaviours prescribed by norms can typically be traced to valued outcomes.

Values are linked to *artefacts*, Schein's third cultural level, in that values-congruent behaviour expresses and manifests the cultural values and assumptions located at the other levels. This can happen through deliberate expressive actions (for example, a manager distributes a memo specifying a dress code for the unit), through unintended expressive actions (e.g., a member interprets the ambiguous actions of a senior manager as an explanation to a newcomer in culture-consistent ways), or through other actions that manifest cultural assumptions and values (for example, all employees

Figure 14.2 Schein's three levels of culture

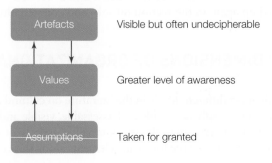

stand patiently in line in the canteen but encourage a senior manager who enters to go to the top of the queue). Similarly, repeated culturally consistent behaviour can leave traces of culture. For example, mounds of cigarette butts under a no smoking sign in a plant indicate that some formal rules can be and are frequently broken. Anything observable linked to behaviour of culture members can be seen as such artefacts (see Hatch and Cunliffe, 2006) including objects (e.g., office layout, furniture, parking arrangements, dress and uniforms), verbal expressions (e.g., stories, myths, jargon, metaphors and theories used, speeches, formal written communication), and activities (e.g., ceremonies, rituals, customs, communication patterns at meetings), especially repeated or collective activity patterns.

Schein (1985) also identified six dimensions that, he suggests, reflect the composition of culture within an organizational context:

1 *Behavioural regularities.* This reflects observable patterns of behaviour. It might include induction ceremonies, in-group language and the ritualized behaviour that reflects membership of particular organizations.

2 *Dominant values.* These are the specific beliefs expressed by groups and organizations. For example, an organization might attempt to create a 'quality image' by adopting a number of specific initiatives, including publishing a policy on relevant processes and activities.

3 *Norms.* These are general patterns of behaviour that all members of a group are expected to follow. For example, many retail chains encourage employees to use specific customer greetings including smiling and making eye contact.

4 *Rules.* Rules are specific instructions about what must be done, whereas norms are sometimes unwritten. The rules are the 'must dos' of the organization set out by management. However, because they must be followed, employees may simply comply with them in order to avoid punishment.

5 *Philosophy.* In this context these reflect the underlying beliefs that individuals hold about people in general. Given that an organization is controlled by the managers who run it, the underlying philosophy often tends to reflect their values.

6 *Climate.* The physical layout of buildings, recreation facilities, management style and the design of public areas all help to create the atmosphere or climate within the company.

Each of these six dimensions of culture is a complex idea in its own right. They do, however, offer descriptive dimensions that can be helpful in beginning to tease out how culture influences organizations and how in turn organizations can influence culture. This circularity is reflected in Figure 14.3.

The circularity displayed in Figure 14.3 indicates that culture produces particular behaviour and associated belief patterns, which in turn influence what actually happens within the organization. Actual events are then measured against management objectives, with the consequences feeding back into culture. The implication of this is that if managers perceive that a particular culture achieves the objectives being pursued, it will be reinforced. If it does not contribute to the achievement of objectives, then managers will attempt to change it.

CULTURAL FRAMEWORKS

The issue of organizational culture has a long history in management and organization studies, but took centre stage in the mainstream management literature in the early 1980s. Many contributions during the late 1970s and 1980s were aimed at explaining the immense success of Japanese companies in providing low-cost yet high-quality products on world markets and particularly in the US. Along with attempts to understand this success as a function of superior quality management (e.g., Crosby, 1979; Deming, 1986; Juran, 1982; see Adam and Swamidass, 1989, for a review), a range of authors addressed the cultural aspects of the Japanese success, and organizational culture more generally, and the recognition of culture as an important determinant of success continues to today (e.g., Tellis *et al.*, 2009). The initial publications that popularized organizational culture as an important issue include Pascale and Athos' (1981) *The Art of Japanese Management*, which attempts to describe, translate and apply management practices linked to Japanese culture to American circumstances, and Ouchi's work (Ouchi, 1981; Ouichi and Jaeger, 1978) on Type Z organizations that are described as combining the best of US and Japanese cultural characteristics (see Table 14.3). Also, Peters and Waterman (1982) published *In Search of Excellence* which attempted to identify drivers of excellence, many of which are linked to organizational culture (see the companion website for more detail on the drivers of excellence). Both *In Search of Excellence* and Pascale and Athos' (1981) *The Art of Japanese Management* mention the McKinsey 7-S framework, a tool that outlines the holistic challenges involved in organizing and

14.2 EXTEND YOUR LEARNING

Figure 14.3 The cycle of culture

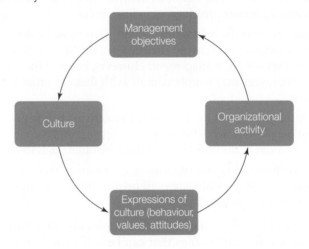

Table 14.3 Ouchi's cultural differences

Japanese organizations	American organizations
Lifetime employment	Short-term employment
Slow evaluation and promotion	Rapid evaluation and promotion
Nonspecialized career paths	Specialized career paths
Implicit control mechanisms	Explicit control mechanism
Collective decision making	Individual responsibility
Holistic concern	Segmented concern

Source: Pugh, D.S. and Hickson, D.J. (1989) *Writers on Organizations* (4th edn), London: Penguin.

managing successful organizations. At the centre of this framework are shared values (also called superordinate goals), clearly a relevant aspect of culture.

At the same time, Deal and Kennedy (1982) distinguished the approach to risk and the speed of feedback to decisions and actions from the environment as important dimensions to distinguish different types of organizational culture (see Figure 14.4). They also introduced the distinction between weak and strong cultures. A strong culture would be evident if almost all members supported it or if it were composed of deeply held values and beliefs. Table 14.4 indicates those features associated with a strong culture. A weak culture by comparison is one that is not strongly supported or rooted in the activities and value systems of the group. Culture strength can be seen as determined by the degree to which core aspects of culture are shared, and the degree to which individual members are intensely committed to them (Luthans, 1995). This is fully compatible with the contemporary cognitive conception of culture as shared cognitions (e.g., Horowitz, 2009; Lehman *et al.*, 2004; Nishida, 2005; Weller, 2007).

Figure 14.4 Deal and Kennedy's types of corporate cultures

	Low **Risk** High	
Quick	**Work hard/Play hard culture** • Focus is on task achievement • Often very cohesive work units • Stressful environment due to fast cycle times of many activities Example: Restaurants	**Tough guy/Macho culture** • Stressful because of constant risk in many activities • Short-term orientation • Focus on present Example: Police force, surgeons
Feedback Slow	**Process culture** • Focus on control, formal systems, details • Value for stability and status quo • Stress comes from internal politics and limitations due to excessive bureaucracy Example: Large Banks, utilities	**Bet your company culture** • Stress comes from risk in the face of high uncertainty • Technical skill is valued • Intense engagement with environment to influence results Example: High-tech startup, oil/mining exploration firm

Table 14.4 Deal and Kennedy's strong cultural elements

- Widely shared philosophy
- Concern for individuals
- Recognition of heroes
- Belief in ritual and ceremony
- Well understood informal rules and expectations
- Importance of individual contribution to whole

EMPLOYEE PERSPECTIVE

Breaking the conventions

One of the purposes of retirement parties is to provide an opportunity for employees to say goodbye to the 'old guard' and to demonstrate their allegiance to the remaining team and the firm as a whole. They also represent an opportunity for the retiree to show that there is a smooth transition and that the 'baton' of office has been safely handed on to the next generation. As such, the speeches and events are usually carefully scripted and choreographed to meet these demands. At one such event a retiring General Motors executive in America broke the unwritten rules by openly criticizing a senior manager much to the visible embarrassment of the others in the room.

TASK

1 Is it always wrong to break the conventions surrounding such ceremonial events? Why or why not? Under what circumstances might it be acceptable to do so and why? To what extent would breaking the rules at such events impact on the 'problems' surfaced?

Power culture
Typically found in small organizations, everything revolves around the focal person(s). All important decisions are made by them and they retain absolute authority in all matters.

Role culture
This type of culture is based firmly on the existence of procedure and rule frameworks. Hierarchy and bureaucracy dominate this type of organization, with instructions coming down the organization and information going back up to more senior levels.

Task culture
The expertise within this type of organization is vested in the individuals within it and it is they who must be organized in a way that meets the needs of the business. This type of culture is supportive of a networked or team organization. Decision making is frequently distributed throughout the 'net' dependent on the needs of the task.

From the items included in Table 14.4 two are of particular interest. First, the *hero* is a person who personifies the values and actions expected of the true believer in that particular culture. They are used as role models for the population at large. Second, the use of *ritual and ceremony* as the basis of reinforcement of the desired culture is also part of the mechanism for ensuring that it is internalized by individuals. The Employee Perspective example provides an illustration of problems that can arise if a 'convention' is broken. Managers frequently seek to inculcate a strong culture in order to achieve clan control (see Chapter 12). A strong culture which is highly supportive of management's objectives makes the organization easier to manage as more of the collective effort and energy is channelled towards meeting business objectives. However, strong cultures are more difficult to change, which can create problems if a lack of fit between the current requirements and culturally supported behaviours develops.

Another framework of organizational culture types, based on the earlier work of Harrison (1972), is offered by Handy (1993) which describes the following four manifestations of culture:

1 Power culture. Typically found in small organizations, everything revolves around the focal person(s). All important decisions are made by them and they retain absolute authority in all matters. As a diagram, Handy describes this culture as a web (Figure 14.5). The success of power culture depends on the capabilities of the focal person in technical, business and management terms.

2 Role culture. This type of culture is based firmly on the existence of procedure and rule frameworks. It is typified by a Greek temple diagram (Figure 14.6). The hierarchy and bureaucracy dominate this type of organization, with instructions coming down the organization and information going back up to the senior levels.

3 Task culture. The expertise within this type of organization is vested in the individuals within it and it is they who must be organized in a way that meets the needs of the business. The description used by Handy to illustrate this culture is that of a net (Figure 14.7). This type of culture is supportive of a team organization. Decision making is frequently distributed throughout the

Figure 14.5 Power culture

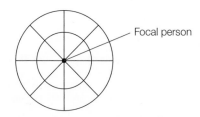

Focal person

Figure 14.6 Role culture

Figure 14.7 Task culture

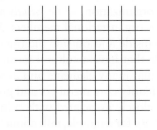

'net' dependent on the needs of the task. Organizations involved in project-based operations such as consultancy and civil engineering might be expected to adopt this cultural framework.

4 Person culture. This is based upon the individual and should not be confused with the power culture. The power culture is based around a single focal point. The person culture allows each person to be a focal point depending on the circumstances. A consultancy practice and barristers' chambers are used by Handy to illustrate this type of culture.

There are obvious links between the concept of culture as described here and the structural and other formal arrangements discussed in Part 4 of the book. Some of the links have been made obvious, as in the case of bureaucracy, while others have only been hinted at. For example, the task culture has a number of associations with the matrix form of structure, with its emphasis on teams and dual reporting relationships.

The cultural web

The cultural web (see Johnson, 1987, 1988, 1992; Johnson *et al.*, 2008) is a well known framework for analysing culture and is popular among managers (see Figure 14.8). This framework places the paradigm at the core of understanding an organization's

Person culture
Based on the individual but not to be confused with the power culture. The power culture is based around a single focal point but the person culture allows each person to be a focal point depending on the circumstances.

Cultural web
The routines, rituals, stories, symbols, power structures, control systems and organization structure that contribute to a particular culture.

Figure 14.8 The cultural web

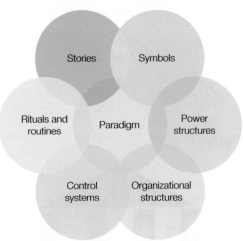

culture. This paradigm is the set of beliefs and assumptions that are generally shared throughout the organization. It plays a central role in the interpretation of the environment and the configuration of strategic responses, and is generally difficult to surface as a coherent statement (Johnson, 1988). *Routines* are the observable behaviour seen as normal and correct in the organization, while *rituals* are those routines that have particular cultural meaning for organizational members. *Stories* are culturally important episodes told and retold inside and outside the organization. *Symbols* are artefacts, events, actions or people that have a cultural meaning above and beyond their functional purpose (but note that many elements and aspects of the cultural web are symbolic). *Power structures* identify core members and groupings in the organization that typically are particularly closely associated with cultural core beliefs and values. Clark and Soulsby (2007: p. 949), for example, talk about 'regimes' that develop in top management teams when they develop and sustain strong consensus around a shared or uncontested view of organizational reality. *Organizational structure* also reflects power and centrality, and itself can communicate core assumptions about the role and value of different groupings. Finally, *control systems* including those for measurement and reward reinforce what is seen as important in the organization. Johnson and colleagues (Johnson *et al.*, 2008) identify a number of core questions that can be used to surface important aspects of each element in a cultural web analysis. Examples of such analytic questions may include (about stories) 'Who are the heroes and villains?'; (about symbols) 'What signifies status in this organizations?'; (for routines and rituals) 'Which core beliefs do the routines reflect?'; or (about power structures) 'Who holds power, and what are their core assumptions and beliefs?'

While many of the popular contributions mentioned above had considerable influence on practitioners, many of these contributions have also been severely criticized. Theory Z for example, critics argues, would not work in US and other Western contexts because of the inconsistency with relevant social values and norms (e.g., England, 1983; Sullivan, 1983). In addition, the notion of lifetime employment in Japan referred to in the description of Theory Z applies to only a small proportion of employees in a few larger organizations. Similarly, rather than being a more participative approach to organizing work activity, Japanese firms often employ tightly controlled work approaches in which limited personal discretion exists and employees are pitted against each other in the relentless search for ever higher productivity and quality (Garrahan and Stewart, 1992).

Similarly, the lessons from *In Search of Excellence* have also been criticized on the grounds that the research methods employed were inadequate (Carroll, 1983). Moreover, others criticized the facts that the performance of companies was assessed mostly on financial measures leaving out other important determinants of future success, that many of the companies researched were outperformed by other Fortune 500 companies, and that the suggestions proffered were somewhat inconsistent (e.g., Aupperle *et al.*, 1986; Hitt and Ireland, 1987). In fact, Tom Peters himself presented very different views on what drives success in some of his later work (e.g., Peters, 1992).

Sub- and countercultures

In the discussion so far culture has been described as a unifying or integrating concept, which binds together the individuals within the organization. However, that is not the only view of culture. It is also possible to see culture as a differentiating feature of organizational life. This differentiation view of culture concentrates on the different groups that exist within the organization. At this level of analysis it becomes possible to identify inconsistencies between the culture of the organization and that of different groups within it (Meyerson and Martin, 1987). The existence of different groups within a single organization forces consideration of distinction, disagreement, disunity and even conflict as part of the cultural milieu. These groups within an organization are usually referred to as subcultures. These are called enhancing cultures if they support the prevailing culture, orthogonal cultures if they hold independent elements that do not interfere with the prevailing culture, or countercultures if they are actively and clearly in opposition to central aspects of the prevailing culture. (Siehl and Martin, 1984)

Subcultures can form around any set of perceived similarities such as professional allegiance, location, educational background, demographic similarities such as gender or race, or the use of technology (Ogbonna and Harris, 2006; Van Maanen and Barley, 1984) in processes linked to the formation of informal groups (see Chapter 7). This means that there will be differences in the cultures operating across the organization. For example, Haugh and McKee (2003) studied small family firms in northeast Scotland. They found that in some cases the group adopting the culture of the dominant family formed an inner team, the rest of the employees (sharing a different value system) forming a peripheral team. This raises several issues in relation to the notion of a single organizational culture and how layers of slightly varying culture meld together within the organization. It would not be surprising to find that the organizational culture was a blend of subgroup cultures (subcultures) or even the imposition of a dominant culture on a collection of suppressed minority ones. Countercultures can also be created through imposed cultural change as disaffected members try to retain as much of their original culture (or subculture).

It can also be argued that as the culture within society changes, the dominant culture within an organization comes under pressure to change. This can be described as cultural diversity or, perhaps more accurately, cultural fragmentation.

Subcultures
Refers to a subset of the dominant culture within a specific context.

Enhancing cultures
A sub-culture that is largely supportive of the prevailing culture.

Orthogonal cultures
A subculture containing independent elements compared to the dominant group that does not interfere with the prevailing culture.

Countercultures
The existence of one or more groups that have objectives running counter to those of the dominant group.

THE DETERMINANTS OF ORGANIZATIONAL CULTURE

The determinants of organizational culture are an area of intense debate and disagreement. Both distal (e.g., history, national culture, societal context) and proximal (ongoing interactions and influences such as leadership, current preoccupations, managerial influence on meaning and perspectives) factors are variously considered or rejected, depending on the particular theoretical framework and methodological approach chosen by particular researchers. As an example, the history of an organization is recognized by researchers from different traditions as an important determinant of organizational culture, although some tend to focus particularly on the influence of founders and senior managers (e.g., Pettigrew, 1979, 1985; Schein, 1985, 2004; see also Nicholson, 2008) while others criticize such founder-centred research as folly (Alvesson, 1993; Alvesson and Berg, 1992; Martin *et al.*, 1985) and focus instead on the external historical context of organizations and the subcultures influenced and sustained by such external sources (e.g., Alvesson, 1993). The difficulty is that organizational culture, just like human behaviour in organizations, is overdetermined, which means that there are many more determinants present than are necessary for providing an explanation. Thus, every perspective and every methodological approach will select and study a subset that is thereby elevated to almost exclusive importance. We will focus here on trying to identify determinants of organizational culture that are of particular importance from a managerial perspective, which means that they may offer insights and opportunities for managing and ultimately influencing culture in organizations. In terms of description and help in understanding the context of managing culture, Handy (1993) indicates a number of influences on the apparent culture of an organization that links in well with the contingency views of organizational structure discussed in Chapter 10:

- *History and ownership.* Culture is something that is partly independent of individuals within the organization. In most cases the company existed before particular employees joined it, and it will continue to exist after they leave. From that perspective, the culture of an organization could be subject to accommodation as people flow through it and interact with the culture that exists. The type of ownership will also have an impact on the culture of the organization. For example, a small company owned by an authoritarian figure will be managed in a totally different way from that owned by a humane bureaucrat.

- *Size.* Size influences culture if for no other reason than the formality required in the operation of larger organizations. This indication of differences, however, cannot serve as a basis for evaluation as 'better' or 'worse'.

- *Technology.* An organization that creates value through deploying advanced technology will emphasize the technical skills of employees in the values that govern its culture. Contrast that situation with a company where the emphasis is on personal service, which would value a completely different set of characteristics and values.

- *Goals and objectives.* What the organization sets out to achieve will also influence the culture. For example, the organization that seeks to become the best in customer service within its industry will seek to incorporate values consistent with that idea into the culture.

- *Environment.* The organizational environment is made up of several elements. There are customer markets, supply and labour markets, financial markets, governmental and regulatory influences, competitors, and the environmental lobby, to name just a few. The way in which an organization chooses to interact with its environment will influence its culture.

- *People.* Managers' preferred approach to the management of their subordinates also influences organizational culture. Employee preferences as to how they wish to be managed also have a bearing on the way that culture develops. Attempts by managers to enforce a culture that is unacceptable to employees typically lead to adverse behavioural and attitudinal reactions, for example industrial action, sabotage, high labour turnover, low productivity, and low quality, all of which result in the need for tight supervision and control. The High Performance example represents an interesting perspective on an approach to developing organizational leaders.

HIGH PERFORMANCE

Leadership development through cultural 'Quests'

The following is based on conversations with Lindsay Levin, Founder and Managing Partner of the Leaders' Quest, and on material from their website. Leaders' Quest is a social enterprise committed to being a catalyst for positive change by engaging, developing and inspiring leaders from all sectors of society who want to make a difference in their organizations, communities and the wider world. It exists to improve the quality of leadership and the way in which leaders impact on it. Core to their values is the drive to bridge divides – between sectors, nations, cultures and different perspectives. It seeks to enable people in positions of influence to stand in the shoes of others, to understand the impact of their decisions, to make wiser decisions and to build a better world. Their unique programme of learning 'Quests' to major regions of the globe brings together leaders in a challenging, creative and sharing spirit to learn about key issues, challenges and opportunities, and to see the world through the eyes and experiences of others. Their programmes currently run in Brazil, China, India, Russia, South Africa, Nigeria and Mozambique. Closely related to the work of Leaders' Quest is the Leaders' Quest Foundation, a UK and USA registered charity. The Foundation supports selected development and charitable projects for the relief of poverty through the development of 'grassroots' or community leaders in developing countries through the Foundation's Fellowship Programme.

A Quest is defined in terms of being:

- An intensive programme of meetings, field visits, discussions and workshops.
- Held in stimulating and challenging parts of the world with many programmes split between two contrasting cities or regions.
- Is about learning through engaging with diverse leaders – political, business and community.
- Provides the broadest exposure to each country by offering a diverse range of contrasting, 'on-the-ground' experiences – from visits to factories, retail stores and high-tech parks, to engaging with residents in slum communities and townships, or

meeting with children and students in some of the world's leading schools and universities.
- Offer multiple options each day so that participants can focus on sectors and issues of greatest interest to them.
- Explores differences and common ground amongst leaders from diverse backgrounds; looking for the inspiring and educational, and seeking out leaders who strive to make the world a better place.
- Spans both the 'macro' issues of the region, and 'micro' examples exploring leading regional companies, organizations and communities.
- Includes regular group 'Reflection Time' through the course of the Quest so that participants may share key insights, questions and impressions, thereby refining their personal learning and development.

A Quest provides learning around three core dimensions:

- *Business opportunities* – including meeting with some of the country's most successful business people and entrepreneurs.
- *Social responsibility* – including learning from leaders in the social, development and nonprofit sectors, and experiencing firsthand the work that these organizations undertake.
- *Leadership development* and *personal renewal* – learning from inspirational leaders from different sectors; working informally together on personal goals with a challenging group of fellow participants; reflecting on one's own growth and development.

Issues covered in the experiences, visits and meetings of the China Quest:

- The growing role and impact of China in the world; Chinese perspectives of the rest of the world
- The impact of the rapid opening up of the country in relation to attitudes, practices and future opportunities

- The experience of international companies and overseas investors in China
- The richness and diversity of one of the oldest civilizations and its impact on the world's largest population
- The interaction of politics, business and civil society
- The new generation of Chinese leaders and their growing impact on China's future
- The development of civic society and the workings of community in China
- The growth of Chinese entrepreneurship
- China's vast rural economy and the challenging contrast between this and the developed economy

- The evolving industrialization of China's interior, and the future of rural livelihoods.

TASKS

1 What might be the effect on the culture of participant organizations as a result of the cross-cultural exposure and development of the type indicated in the Leaders' Quest? Why?

2 What effect might such leadership development have on the performance of the participating individuals and organizations? How and why?

Source:
http://www.leadersquest.org/index/index.php?page=Home&navi_id=1 (accessed June 2009).

In the next section, the determinants of culture are further discussed in the context of the challenge of trying to change culture in organizations.

CHANGING ORGANIZATIONAL CULTURE

Turner (1986) criticizes the view that culture can be managed and changed, suggesting that it would not be possible to manipulate it accurately because it becomes such an integral part of the organization's fabric. The definition of culture in relatively superficial terms also ensures that it is more amenable to change (Berg, 1985). For example, if culture were defined only in terms of the symbols used to reinforce it, changing the symbols would change the culture. Lundberg (1985) argues that it is possible to change culture and provides a six-stage programme for achieving this objective:

1 *External*. Identify external conditions that may encourage a change to the existing culture.

2 *Internal*. Identify internal circumstances and individuals that would support change.

3 *Pressures*. Identify those forces pressing for change in the culture.

4 *Visioning*. Identify key stakeholders and create in them a vision of the proposed changes, the needs and benefits.

5 *Strategy*. Develop a strategy for achieving the implementation of the new culture.

6 *Action*. Develop and implement a range of action plans based on the strategy as a means of achieving movement to the desired culture.

There are a number of problems with this view. It is rather simplistic about what defines culture as well as about the nature of change. To suggest that there is only one culture within an organization is to deny the existence of sub- and counter-cultures. In fact, any attempt at changing culture deliberately will always involve deviancy compared to the orthodoxy of the prevalent culture, and culture change thus requires the creation and legitimization of a counterculture (see Badham *et al.*,

2003, for an example). Consequently, there are political, power and control perspectives to take into account. Interestingly, individuals may gain influence by displaying personality traits that fit in with the predominant culture (Anderson *et al.*, 2008). Such individuals may be more effective agents for cultural change because they may be able to signal at least partial adherence to the culture

Part of the challenge of planned cultural change is not only to ensure that change happens, but also to ensure that it moves in the right direction. Most accounts of successful cultural change involve multiple drivers that ultimately focus on behavioural change (e.g., Bacon, 2007; Charan, 2006). Charan's (2006) account of cultural change at Home Depot, for example, explicitly involved changes in the firm's social architecture (i.e., *the collective ways in which people work together across an organization to support the business model*) through four main drivers. Changes in *metrics* emphasized new cultural priorities by identifying and measuring what is valued, which helped to clarify expectations. New *processes* changed how the work was done, which helped to integrate the new culture into the organization. Specific *programmes* built support for the cultural change by providing examples for the effectiveness and the benefits of the new culture. Finally, changes in the organizational *structure* created a framework in which the new culture could be enacted (Charan, 2006). All these drives directly affect behaviour. Given our model of culture and its relationship to behaviour, cognition and artefacts presented earlier in the chapter, such a focus on behaviour must be at the centre of any attempt at planned cultural change. The Change at Work example demonstrates a range of perspectives on culture change as a process.

> **Social architecture**
> The collective ways in which people work together across an organization to support the business model.

CHANGE AT WORK

Cultivate your culture

Culture change is important to managers because some cultures are more supportive of high-performance working than others. Egan (1994) below presents one generalized approach to culture change, but see also Butler (2005) on process improvement, preprogramme planning and preparing the organization for change as other stages in a culture change process. Heathfield (2009) also identifies structure change, change to reward, work and recognition practices as areas through which to bring about culture change.

Egan (1994) argues that two levels of culture are operational in any organizational setting. The 'culture-in-use' represents the dominant culture in any particular context. The 'culture behind-the-culture' represents the real beliefs, values and norms that underpin behaviour patterns within the company. These cultures can add either cost or benefit to the organization depending on the degree to which they support effective operational activity.

Egan proposes a number of strategies for dealing with culture change:

1   Strategies based on business reality:

- A change in business strategy can provide the necessary leverage for changing culture.

- The use of total quality management and business process re-engineering are just two examples of ways to lever culture change.

- Restructuring and reorganizing work also provides opportunities for culture change.

- Using levers such as training and promotion to reinforce the message and move people into other jobs can encourage cultural change.

2   Change-linked strategies:

- Direct action in areas not apparently associated with culture can produce changes in culture as a consequence.

- Financial or other crisis situations are opportunities to change the culture as people are more likely to accept change across a broad front.

3 Frontal attacks:

- The use of guerrilla tactics such as the use of roving 'hit squads' (individuals with the power to turn up and ask difficult questions) to begin a culture change process.

- Flooding the organization with training courses to promote the new values can be an effective (if costly) way of 'forcing' the new culture into the system by 'swamping' the old one.

- The use of symbols to convey powerful messages about both the demise of the old culture and the emergence of the new. For example, it is reported that Lee Iacocca, former chairman of Chrysler, turned down the car presented to him by the workforce and asked for the next one off the assembly line, the symbolism being that every car should be capable of being presented to the chairman.

- Constantly pointing out that the dominant culture is not beneficial can become so annoying that people change, just to stop the constant annoyance.

- Form a critical mass of people who can champion the new culture and then work on the others who need to be convinced.

- Announcing 'what-will-be' might achieve the change in culture.

TASK

1 To what extent and in what circumstances does culture change represent a management attempt to manipulate or socially engineer employee behaviour that is likely to be resisted?

Sources:
Butler, Amos (2005) *Commentary*, Issue 7. Accessed June 2009 at: http://www.amosbutler.com/commentaryissue007.htm?gclid=C J3bz92cmZsCFU0A4wodf34Fp.
Egan, G. (1994) Cultivate your culture, *Management Today*, April, pp. 39–42.
Heathfield, S.M. (2009) How to Change your Culture: Organizational Culture Change. Accessed June 2009 at: http://humanresources. about.com/od/organizationalculture/a/culture_change.htm.

Hursthouse and Kolb (2001) as well as Adler (1993) demonstrate that new and different cultures can be achieved in green-field situations within the same company through the adoption of different strategies, structures and processes. More commonly, however, cultural change is attempted in existing organizations, and the task is not simply one of creating a new culture but also one of undoing and replacing the existing culture. Overall, culture is not easy to create, but even more difficult to manipulate once it exists. This *cultural inertia* (see Carrillo and Gromb, 2007) may in part be based on the difference in mechanisms that embed and support the culture. Cultural assumptions and values that have not yet been institutionalized through well rooted social expectations and behavioural norms (e.g., Buchanan *et al.*, 2005; Kotter, 1995) as well as through supporting structural and procedural arrangements (Schein, 2004) are less entrenched and more malleable.

Schein (2004) distinguishes between primary and secondary embedding mechanisms which inform this distinction. *Primary embedding mechanisms* (see Table 14.5) are more relevant in young and small organizations and are more under direct control of key personnel such as owners, founders and senior managers. As they largely relate to the behaviour of such high-profile and high-status members of the organization, they can be more easily and readily manipulated by them in efforts to influence culture. *Secondary embedding mechanisms*, in contrast, often reflect institutionalized patterns of behaviour and more complex, less malleable aspects of organizations not as much under management control. These secondary mechanisms articulate and reinforce the existing culture and thus add substantially to the cultural inertia typical of larger, well established firms with relatively strong cultures. These mechanisms include the organizational structure; established formal and informal systems and procedures; rites and rituals; artefacts such as physical space, facilities, and buildings; stories, legends, and myths; and formal statements of espoused values and identity.

Table 14.5 Schein's primary embedding mechanisms

Attention	What leaders pay attention to, measure and control on a regular basis
Reaction to crises	How leaders react to critical incidents and organizational crises
Role modelling	Deliberate role modelling, teaching and coaching
Allocation of rewards	*Observed* criteria by which leaders allocate scarce resources
Criteria for selection and dismissal	*Observed* criteria by which leaders recruit, select, promote, retire and excommunicate organizational members

Source: Adapted from Schein, 2004.

Figure 14.9 The cultural dynamics model

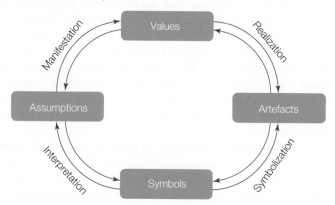

Source: Adapted from Hatch, 1993.

In her Cultural Dynamics Model, Hatch (1993) extended Schein's (1985) three-level model by including symbols and placing the four elements (what Schein called levels) into a dynamic circular model (see Figure 14.9). This deliberately nonhierarchical model describes the processes by which the elements interact. Organizational change is enabled when assumptions are symbolically challenged in the interpretation process, i.e., the interaction between symbols and assumptions. Thus, if symbols appear to be misaligned with reality as perceived by culture members based on their underlying assumptions – a mechanism called confrontation – a new balance may be created that involves changes in all cultural elements (Hatch, 1993; Hatch and Cunliffe, 2006).

Overall, cultural change is so difficult to direct and manage because by its very nature culture is a shared, multidetermined phenomenon. Any individual member or subgroup of culture members can have an impact on culture, but this can only happen through influencing observables (such as behaviour and artefacts) with the goal of changing unobservables (individual cognition of multiple members to create different shared cognitions). Cultural change is so difficult to achieve because those attempting to change culture need to bring about change in something they – at best – only partially recognize, understand and control.

STOP & CONSIDER It has been argued that because there are so many different views and definitions of culture, it is impossible to know what exactly it comprises, and therefore it is impossible to actually design or change it. Some argue that managers should concentrate on trying to change those things about an organization that they know will directly influence employee behaviour and attitudes and leave culture alone. To what extent and why do you support this view?

MANAGING CULTURAL DIFFERENCES

In seeking to address the issue of how culture impacts on behaviour in an organizational context, Cray and Mallory (1998: pp. 89–112) propose a cognitive model. In essence, they argue that behaviour is based on many forces acting on that individual, including culture. Their model of the cognitive approach to cultural influences on behaviour is included as Figure 14.10.

In offering a basis for being able to manage cultural issues more effectively, the model allows an improved understanding of why contrasting behaviours occur between cultural boundaries. As such, it should allow those cognitive features which are deep-seated and thus less amenable to change to be identified and separated out from those cognitive components that may be easier to manipulate (Cray and Mallory, 1998: p. 107). The writers illustrate the potential of the model through the work of Calori and colleagues (1992) who found differences between French and British managers in the respective cognitive maps of the dynamic competitive forces in their organization's environment. They argue that these variances are due to different educational systems and cultural differences between the two countries. Similar differences in the cognitions of managers between the industries included were also found, suggesting support for the organizational cognitive framework element included in the model.

A number of tools are available that seek to measure aspects of culture within an organization, making it easier to manage those aspects that need attention. Examples include the Denison Organizational Culture Survey (Denison and Neale, 2000) which measures culture under four main categories (involvement, consistency, adaptability, mission) which have been found to be linked to business success and customer satisfaction (Denison, 1990; Gillespie *et al.*, 2008). A very simple yet useful framework was proposed by Goffee and Jones (1996) who discuss the required fit between culture and the internal task and external business environment. Littlefield (1999) applied a nine-factor test developed by Cartwright from the University of Exeter (see Table 14.6) in a case study of Kerry Foods, a large direct sales company formed as a result of several mergers of smaller organizations. Instruments to measure organizational culture are not themselves means of changing culture but can be very useful to managers and change agents who attempt to assess and track cultural change over time.

Figure 14.10 The impact of culture on behaviour: a cognitive model

Source: Cray, D and Mallory, G (1998) Making Sense of Managing Culture, Cengage Learning, London. Reprinted with permission.

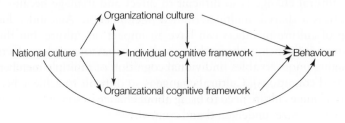

Table 14.6 The nine key factors

Acceptance	Trust/agreement	Development
Fairness	Expectation	Team spirit
Respect	Balance	Ownership

Trompenaars and Woolliams (1999) elaborate on Trompenaars' earlier work on culture and link it with that of Charles Hampden–Turner. In doing so, they identify seven dimensions reflecting ways that values differ between cultures:

1 *Universalism vs participation.* This reflects the distinction between cultures which value allegiance to rules and those which value loyalty to relationships and other people.

2 *Individualism vs communitarianism.* This reflects the distinction between cultures that favour individual fulfilment compared to those which value behaviour in support of the group as a whole.

3 *Specific vs diffuse.* This reflects the distinction between cultures which favour facts and impersonal business relationships compared to those which prefer personal relationships within business.

4 *Neutrality vs affectivity.* This reflects the differences between cultures in which it is common to hide emotions or where it is acceptable to be open with personal emotions.

5 *Inner directed vs outer directed.* This reflects the differences between cultures in the degree to which individuals feel that they are in control of their environment.

6 *Achieved status vs ascribed status.* In some cultures success confirms status and delivers promotion. In others, status is a function of position, which subsequently motivates the individual who then delivers success.

7 *Sequential time vs synchronic time.* This dimension reflects the differences between cultures in orientation to the passage of time, the varying focus on timescales and ability to handle more than one thing at a time.

The writers argue that each of these dimensions reflects an aspect of managing in what they call a transcultural manner. Each of the dimensions reflects a tension between the two juxtaposed concepts that must be reconciled in some way or other by managers operating across cultures. The conflicts that arise in seeking to deal with the differences in cultural preference evident in each dimension must involve actions such as compromise, reconciliation of the different perspectives or allowing one cultural norm to dominate. In some situations their research shows that women appear to exhibit a higher ability to be able to reconcile opposing values than do males. Also some men begin by starting from their own cultural perspective and then move towards the opposing values as they seek to resolve the dilemma. They have also found in their preliminary research that those managers who recognize, respect and are able to reconcile the dilemmas arising under each one of these seven dimensions perform better than those who do not.

NATIONAL CULTURE

Organizations operate within national settings and are subject to the same cultural forces that act upon every other aspect of social life. Typically, the majority of employees of an organization comes from a specific national setting into the organization, bringing their national culture with them. It would be natural to expect, therefore, that the culture of an organization would be based largely on the predominant local culture. However, that is an assumption that proves very difficult to refute or substantiate as a result of the number of factors acting upon any given situation. For example, within any national or organizational culture there exist sub- and countercultures that introduce variety. There is also the growing movement of people around the world introducing cultural diversity into any particular setting. Furthermore, the growing globalization of business introduces additional variety into the cultural milieu. In that context the Management in Action example provides an insight into the role of the formal and informal aspects of the employment relationship in Germany, which can be used as the basis of an assessment of its cultural effects.

The *convergence* perspective on the relationship between national and organizational culture suggests that within an organization the national culture is subservient. This implies that organizations are able to identify and separate culture into two distinct forms (internal and external), and that they are able to manage the internal form as necessary to support business objectives as distinct from the surrounding national culture. In practice this view holds that employees leave their national culture 'at the door' when they arrive at work and adopt the cultural values of the workplace without difficulty.

The *divergence* view holds that national culture takes preference and that organizational culture will adapt to local cultural patterns (Lammers and Hickson, 1979). This view holds that it is organizations that need to adapt to local circumstances, otherwise the corporate culture will be out of synchronization with the local norms and will be ignored or even create problems. It is not difficult to envisage that both views could be correct in appropriate circumstances. For example, large international organizations that operate according to centralized styles could well display convergence characteristics, while, conversely, organizations predominantly based in a specific country are more likely to demonstrate divergence. The problems that can result from the clash of cultures in a joint venture situation (based on a case study in China) are demonstrated by Xiaoli (2001).

In practice there may well be a middle ground as organizational cultures will evolve in any particular instance to address the multiple demands of internal integration and external adaptation (Schein, 2004). In this case, many times organizational culture will adapt to meet the needs of both head office and the local situation. Herselman (2001) provides a review of the convergence and divergence debate in relation to the ethnic and organizational circumstances in South Africa.

Hofstede's perspectives

Hofstede (1983, 1984) carried out an extensive series of studies into culture over some 13 years. He defines culture as mental programming because it predisposes individuals to particular ways of thinking, perceiving and behaving. That is not to say that everyone within a particular culture is identical, simply that there is a tendency for similarity to exist. He originally developed four dimensions of culture from a factor analysis of his questionnaire research (Table 14.7 provides an indication of those countries that exhibit high and low levels of each of these four dimensions). A fifth dimension was added later (Hofstede, 1991; Hofstede and Bond, 1988; Hofstede and Hofstede, 2005; see also Leonard, 2008):

1 *Individualism–collectivism*. This factor relates to the degree of integration between individuals in a society. At one extreme, individuals concentrate on looking after their own interests and those of their family. The other extreme emphasizes collective responsibility to the extended family and the community.

MANAGEMENT IN ACTION

The formal and the informal in organizational life.

The following emerged during a conversation between Jutta, a senior consultant with a multinational support services company in Germany and one of the authors.

Jutta explained that in Germany a distinction in law existed between the main duties and responsibilities covered by the employment contract ('arbeitsvertragliche Hauptpflichten' – main contractual employment duties) and the secondary duties that were necessary to ensure the effective functioning of the employment relationship, but which were not central to its purpose ('arbeitsvertragliche Nebenpflichten' – secondary contractual employment duties). These secondary duties and responsibilities could be based on either written or case law, and broadly reflected the employer's obligation to ensure the welfare of employees ('Fürsorgepflicht' – duty of care).

In law, the main duty of the employee is to provide the type and level of service specified in the employment contract; and the main duty of the employer is to deliver the level and frequency of payment as specified in the contract. The secondary duties of the employer include providing (for example) meaningful work to the employee, providing acceptable working conditions, ensuring tax and social security payments are made on their behalf, providing facilities for the secure storage of employee personal clothes (if a uniform is worn) and possessions whilst at work. Employee secondary duties include (for example) their duty to support the employer by working and behaving in good faith ('Treuepflicht' – duty of loyalty). They also preclude divulging confidential company information and secrets, and avoiding damage to the company, its reputation and assets.

Consequently, in Germany a considerable proportion of the employee (and employer) behaviour is defined by these two forms of external regulation. Other duties and expectations would be identified and incorporated into either the written contract of employment or verbally in the unwritten agreement determined during the recruitment process. These might include pay level, working hours and holiday entitlement. All of these can be summarized as explicit expectations as they originate in law, case law or through negotiation between the employer and employee.

However, Jutta went on to explain that in Germany there were also a wide range of 'things' associated with the job and work activity that remained informal, unregulated and even undiscussed. In practice she explained that in her view it was impossible to foresee all potential issues or questions that may arise during a work relationship and to preanswer, clarify or even articulate them in any detail. This gave rise to the existence of a number of implicit beliefs, expectations and obligations that went beyond the stated ones and which existed in a social context and were formed during employment, filling the gap created by the inability of the formal processes to cover every eventuality and the dynamics of everyday work activity and experience. Jutta explained that in her view and experience (working in Germany), for the employment relationship to be successful and effective for both parties it relied on both employer and employee to show trust and discretion in working with each other. Edwards (2003) called this need to balance the informal and unwritten aspects of the working relationship 'structured antagonism' which was created by the indeterminate nature of the employment relationship and the inability of the formal processes to cater for every eventuality.

Jutta explained that to her, implicit expectations were based on values and assumptions related to concepts such as fairness, honesty, security, certainty, recognition and opportunity for fulfilment. Mismatches or clashes between competing expectations (explicit and implicit) in relation to duties and obligations would usually be resolved in the dynamic day-to-day work interactions between the boss and subordinate (especially during the induction or socialization phase of employment (before expectations became more permanently formed); or during subsequent performance review meetings (a form of re-negotiation of the working arrangements); or even during normal daily interactions in the course of work activity. In Jutta's opinion if difficulties between expectations (formal or informal) could not be easily resolved they contained the potential to cause conflict or disengagement (psychological or physical) between the parties and consequently at that point reference back to the formal processes and procedures would become necessary.

Jutta indicated that the concepts of implicit and explicit expectations reminded her of an iceberg model.

This model provided a visual way of demonstrating that many implicit expectations were hidden below the water and so hidden from view compared to the number of explicit expectations that were visible above it. She also suggested that in her experience informal expectations reflected the idea of the psychological contract in the way that informal and unwritten arrangements determined the actual level of commitment and engagement delivered by the employee. To some degree she thought that it also resembled private life interpersonal relationships where needs and expectations existed, but which could only be partly articulated and agreed – and which needed to be developed, re-affirmed and renegotiated over time to keep the relationship viable and worthwhile for both parties.

Jutta considered that just as in private life, a breach of trust or failure to meet or deliver 'things' based on implicit expectations or the psychological contract in the work relationship had consequences. Sometimes such breaches or problems could be overcome, sometimes they could not. If employees perceived that their employer had failed to deliver on what they perceived was expected or promised, they were likely to respond negatively. This could result in reduced loyalty, commitment, effort and trust on the part of employees. Jutta thought that such situations meant that employees would also be less willing to accept change or management direction, making the organization more difficult to manage. Employees might also leave, taking with them experience, competency and knowledge that could be of value to the organization. From the employer's perspective, if the employee was thought not to have lived up to the implicit expectations that existed from the management perspective, then their relative value to the employer was diminished and they were less likely to be promoted, given career development opportunities and perhaps even have their employment ended.

TASKS

1 This example is based on German employment experience. How similar or different would the formal and informal employment processes be in your country?

2 What does the answer to the previous question suggest about the formal and informal employment conditions in relation to culture in a country and the organizations based in it?

Sources:
Discussion with Jutta Schwarz, based in Frankfurt. Reprinted with grateful thanks to Jutta.
Edwards P. (2003). The Employment Relationship in the Field of Industrial Relations, in Edwards P. (ed.), *Industrial Relations: Theory and Practice in Britain*, Oxford: Blackwell.

2 *Power distance*. The degree of centralization of authority. The higher the concentration of power in a few people at the top, the higher the power distance score. A low power distance score implies a closer link between those with power and 'ordinary' people.

3 *Uncertainty avoidance*. How the members of a society deal with uncertainty. Societies in which individuals are relatively secure do not feel threatened by the views of others and tend to take risk in their stride (weak uncertainty avoidance). Strong uncertainty avoidance requires policies, procedures and institutions to control and minimize the effects of uncertainty and risk.

4 *Masculinity–femininity*. In societies classified as 'masculine', activity tends to be gender-based, stressing achievement, making money, generation of tangible outputs and largeness of scale. Societies classified as feminine tended to be those putting people before money, seeking a high quality of life, helping others, preservation of the environment and smallness of scale.

5 *Long- versus short-term orientation*. Framed in the context of the Confucian search for virtue, short-term-oriented cultures are described to be looking for virtues in the present or past, while long-term-oriented cultures search for them in the future.

Hofstede considered that power distance and uncertainty avoidance were the 'decisive dimensions' of organizational culture (1990: p. 403). This view clearly links organizational and national culture by implying that the preferred ways of managing and organizing in a specific context will be based upon the national tendencies. This

Table 14.7 Illustration of Hofstede's classification

	Individualism	Power distance	Uncertainty avoidance	Masculinity
High	USA	Philippines	Greece	Japan
	UK	Mexico	Portugal	Australia
	Australia	India	Japan	Italy
	Canada	Brazil	France	Mexico
Low	Mexico	Australia	Denmark	Sweden
	Greece	Israel	Sweden	Denmark
	Taiwan	Denmark	UK	Thailand
	Colombia	Sweden	USA	Finland
			India	

assumption is not, however, directly tested in his work. It is possible that organizational culture is composed of different dimensions from national culture.

Hofstede's research has been immensely influential (Kirkman *et al.*, 2006), yet has also been heavily criticized on a number of grounds (see Ailon, 2008, for a brief overview). It has been argued that it is too reductionistic (i.e., by reducing culture simply to values), and that it extrapolates to national cultures from data collected within a single company (IBM) and largely from marketing and service divisions (Ailon, 2008). Similarly, McSweeney (2002) questioned the methodological approach and the value of the evidence used to support Hofstede's claims (see Bearden *et al.*, 2006). It has also been criticized as largely omitting detailed consideration of how cultures form, change and are maintained (Furnham and Gunter, 1993). As presented, the dimensions give no clue as to the degree of difference that could be expected in any context (Tyson and Jackson, 1992). Hofstede tends to regard culture as relatively consistent across time, changing only slowly, a view based upon anthropological perspectives. More recent work from a sociological perspective prefers the view of culture as a much more dynamic process representing the balance between contradictory social and economic pressures constantly acting on a society in real time (Alvesson, 1993). Also, Ailon (2008) argues that Hofstede's seminal work (1980) is subtly overvaluing some (i.e., the West) and devaluing other (i.e., the rest) cultures and falls prey to many mistakes typical in traditional cross-cultural research (see Westwood, 2004).

Trompenaars' perspective

Frans Trompenaars worked for Shell in nine countries before becoming a consultant. He built up a database of the cultural characteristics of 15 000 managers and staff from 30 companies in 50 different countries. In his book (1993) he discusses several aspects of cultural difference and its relationship with organizational life based on his database.

His views contrast sharply with those that suggest that the world is becoming a 'global village', in that he argues firmly that what works in one culture will seldom do so in another. Included in his observations are the following examples:

- *Performance pay.* He suggests that people in France, Germany, Italy and many parts of Asia tend not to accept that 'individual members of the group should excel in a way that reveals the shortcomings of other members'.
- *Two-way communications.* Americans may be motivated by feedback sessions, Germans, however, find them 'enforced admissions of failure'.
- *Decentralization and delegation.* These approaches might work well in Anglo-Saxon cultures, Scandinavia, the Netherlands and Germany, but are likely to fail in Belgium, France and Spain.

Trompenaars identifies seven dimensions of culture. Five deal with the way in which people interact with each other. A sixth deals with people's perspective on time and the seventh concerns the approach to moulding the environment. These combine to create different corporate cultures including:

- *Family.* Typically found in Japan, India, Belgium, Italy, Spain and among small French companies. Hierarchical in structure with the leader playing a 'father figure' within the organization. Praise can frequently be a better motivator than money in such cultures.
- *Eiffel Tower.* Large French companies typify this culture, as might be expected. It also embraces some German and Dutch companies. Hierarchical in structure, very impersonal, rule-driven and slow to adapt to change are the dominant characteristics.
- *Guided missile.* Typical of American companies, and to a lesser extent those in the UK. They are typified as egalitarian and strongly individualistic in nature with a measure of impersonality. They tend to be capable of adjusting the established course of action quickly but not completely to new situations.

Trompenaars advises companies to avoid a blanket approach to culture, based on the dominant head office variety. Instead he argues that a transnational approach should be adopted, in which the best elements from several cultures are brought together and applied differently in each country. Managers should also be trained in cross-cultural awareness and respect and how to avoid seeing other people's cultural perspective as stubbornness.

Acculturation - entering a new culture

Acculturation
A term used by anthropologists to describe what happens when people from one culture come into continuous direct contact with members of a different culture with changes to one or both of the cultures involved. In an organizational context it is very similar to the process of socialization.

Acculturation is a term used by anthropologists to describe the process of change when cultural members come into continuous direct contact with members of a different culture with changes to one or both of the involved cultures (Redfield *et al.*, 1936). At the organizational level this process is important, for example, in merger and acquisition processes. At the individual level, the term refers to the process 'when people were initially socialized in one cultural environment and then moved and started functioning in another one' (Chirkov, 2009: p. 95). In short, it is the process of cultural and psychological change in response to intercultural contact (Berry, 2003). Thus, it is very similar to the process of socialization, the process by which a person learns about the norms, values, assumptions and other central shared elements of a particular social group or culture and develops the ability to function within this social group (see Chapter 12 for further discussions of socialization).

Socialization
The process by which a person learns about the norms, values, assumptions and other central shared elements of a particular social group or culture and develops the ability to function effectively within that social group.

The challenge of acculturation is not trivial. Anybody who has lived for an extended period of time (rather than merely visited) in a different cultural setting has likely experienced *culture shock*, a common phenomenon associated with entering a different national culture that often involves feelings of uncertainty, confusion, disorientation, anxiety and even severe embarrassment. For some, the process of returning to their home culture, called *reverse culture shock*, can be as difficult. Acculturation involves managing oneself (e.g., Matsumoto *et al.*, 2008) as well as negotiating the new cultural and social environment – on different and unfamiliar terms (Chang, 2009). It is particularly difficult because 'all humans are ethnocentric (Triandis, 1990); that is, they strongly feel that what is "normal" in their culture is or should be normal everywhere' (Triandis, 2006: p. 22). Only through developing new conceptions and cognitive schema that enable them to understand the new culture 'from within' will newcomers be able to fully adapt. A flavour of acculturation can be found in the Going Global example. Acculturation arises as new employees try to 'fit' into the way of functioning at Semco, and as all employees try to get used to the changes made to the company as it develops across time.

GOING GLOBAL

Secrets of the Semler effect

Semco is a company based in Brazil and was for a long time headed by Ricardo Semler who took over the company from his father at the beginning of the 1980s when he was just 21-years-old. Under his leadership he took the manufacturer of pumps, mixers and other industrial equipment to new heights, with sales growing by a factor of six and profits by 500 per cent. In many ways the company became a vast test bed for new and different ideas in managing and organizing.

The most startling aspect of Semco as seen from the outside during the 1990s was that employees were able to set their own working hours, and some were even able to set their own salary levels. And everyone from the highest to the lowest had open access to company financial information. The intention was to create a self-sustaining organization which could carry on without an obvious leader. For example, five people shared the position of chief executive officer on a 6-month rotating basis. Semler took his turn along with the others.

Semler began with the view that the main goal should be to create an entity that everyone involved with felt was worthwhile. That should then manifest itself in good quality and good customer service. He also considered that the company was an ongoing project and that change was not a once-for-all effect. By 2009 the company produced what they call the Semco Group Survival Manual that sets out many of the policies and practices that are regarded as the basis of promoting a fairer and more dignified approach to managing it. In setting the approach for Semco, Semler picked aspects from many other organizations and systems, including personal freedom; leadership; personal development; job rotation; control

of greed; sharing of information; honesty; the role of trade unions; avoidance of terms such as employee in favour of the simple term 'people' and open communication. It is these principles that are now enshrined in the Survival Manual.

Clearly Semco is a dynamic, unusual company with a leader who influences the way work is organized and managed. Many other companies, researchers and students have sought Semler's advice on how to achieve the same level of success. This advice can now be acquired through his books and lectures.

TASKS

1 Access the Survival Manual on the website indicated above and consider how (if at all) the culture of Semco is defined and explained by it.

2 To what extent do you consider that because the company culture indicated is so different that particular types of people would be attracted to join it and they therefore become highly motivated by the match between their personal beliefs and those of the company?

3 If more companies were to follow this approach, would the lack of uniqueness limit the success achieved? Why or why not?

Sources:
Dickson, T. (1993) Secrets of the Semler effect, *Financial Times*, 25 June, p. 13.
http://en.wikipedia.org/wiki/Ricardo_Semler (accessed June 2009).
Semler, R. (2001) *Maverick!: The Success Story Behind The World's Most Unusual Workplace*. London: Random House.
Semler, R. (2004) *The Seven-Day Weekend: A Better Way To Work In The 21st Century*. London: Century.
http://www.semco.com.br/en/content.asp?content=3&contentID=567 (the Survival Manual site) (accessed June 2009).

Figure 14.11 Berry's framework of acculturation styles

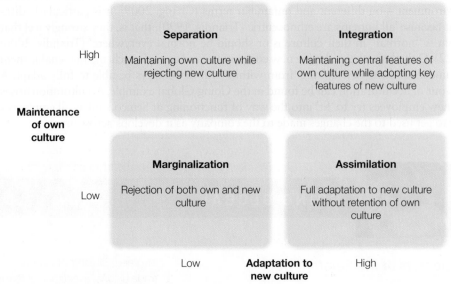

Source: Reprinted with kind permission of Professor John Berry.

A useful and influential model of acculturation by Berry (1997) is based on two important dimensions (or tasks), namely the *maintenance* of one's original cultural identity, and the *adaptation* to the new culture through relationships and participation. Given that individuals may focus differently on these two dimensions, acculturation strategies (and outcomes) can be described as combinations of these dimensions named *integration, assimilation, separation* and *marginalization* (see Figure 14.11). Peeters and Oerlemans (2009) found that integration is positively related to well-being at work, while marginalization relates negatively to well-being, especially among ethnic minority employees, a pattern that mirrors similar results in the general population (Berry, 2006).

Since the 1980s, issues like expatriate executive assignments and cross-cultural management have become more centre-stage in OB and human resource management (e.g., Adler and Gundersen, 2007; Gelfand *et al.*, 2007). Issues such as cross-cultural interaction and management, cultural diversity in organizations and work groups, cultural differences in intra-individual processes such as perception and motivation, and many others are actively researched. Much of this increasing attention is a function of the increasing internationalization of business and the dynamics of globalization that affect organizations just as much as it affects all other spheres of life.

GLOBALIZATION AND CULTURE

'Globalization' is a term that has a relatively recent history in relation to the ways in which business operates (see Chapter 2). According to Yip (1989) globalization consists of a three-stage evolutionary process:

- Developing a core strategy as the basis of competitive advantage, usually home-country-based.
- Internationalization of the home-country strategy. A multinational organization.
- Globalization through integration of largely separate country-based international strategies.

The third stage of this model is what differentiates globalization from international business activity. Bartlett and Ghoshal (1989) identify two forms of global organization:

- *International organization.* This type of global company seeks to capitalize on the advantages of the global scale in a centralized way, whereas the international organization seeks to function more like a co-ordinated federation. They seek a balance between the needs and contributions of the centre and local units.

- *Transnational organization.* This type of organization seeks to blend together the three major themes of global integration, local differentiation and worldwide innovation. In practice an integrated network of all available resources and products used to the best advantage of the organization as a whole.

One of the difficulties facing any organization operating internationally is that of culture. Every country is made up of different cultural groups, with varying degrees of similarity and difference. Equally, cultural groupings frequently span national boundaries. Even today there are several major trouble spots in the world where ethnicity (as an expression of culture) is linked to attempts to break up an existing country into individual self-ruled autonomous units. So 'nation' is only a poor reflection of the cultural boundaries that exist among the people who inhabit the world.

There are two basic options available to an organization in its approach to culture:

- *Polycentric.* This approach takes the view that it is not possible to operate in a consistent way around the world as a consequence of the cultural differences that exist. Therefore each unit within the company should be allowed to operate appropriately within its cultural context. The danger with this approach is that the organization becomes overwhelmed with the impact of the number and scale of cultural differences that must be accommodated. Not every cultural difference needs to be incorporated into the ways of doing things across the organization. Bribery and corruption are common experiences for many organizations, as illustrated in the Examining Ethics example.

- *Ethnocentric.* This assumes the superiority of the culture of the globalizing organization and holds that every other culture must be subservient to it. This view holds that it is a business imperative to have worldwide consistency in policy, procedure and practice to make it easier to run the company. The potential danger of this approach is that it may prevent the company getting close to the local community and so lose competitive advantage. Also, local staff must tread a difficult line between following orders and meeting the needs of the situation, which can also cause problems.

Ulrich and Black (1999) reflect upon the process of globalization in terms of the often-quoted mantra of acting globally and thinking locally. This requires the organization to consider its capability of meeting these demands if they are to function successfully in the global market. They suggest that six areas of capability arise from this need (see Table 14.8). Each of these capabilities involves managing a tension. It is through this tension that culture makes its impact evident. In seeking to organize on a global scale, it is necessary for senior managers to retain control and to be able to extract ever greater levels of value from the operations.

This involves the inevitable and never-ending search for economies of scale. In the search for control and cost-effectiveness, uniformity in all things is often the first port of call. However, cultural (and other) differences around the world simply will not allow such simple solutions. For example, Colgate-Palmolive found that its

EXAMINING ETHICS

Bribes don't have to be a way of life, do they?

The following is based on a conversation with John Devitt, Chief Executive, Transparency International Ireland. Transparency International (TI) is a global civil society organization leading the fight against corruption. It brings people together in a powerful worldwide coalition to end the devastating impact of corruption on men, women and children around the world. TI was founded in 1993 and its mission is to create change towards a world free of corruption. It is a global network including more than 90 locally established national chapters (of which Ireland is one) and chapters-in-formation.

John explained that bribery was an accepted form of business practice in many parts of the world up until relatively recently. For example Matlack *et al.* (2004) report on a bribery case in Costa Rica involving French telecoms company Alcatel. In many European countries, bribes paid by many EU based companies to foreign officials were tax deductible up until the 1990s. With the introduction of the OECD Convention on Foreign Bribery in 1997, it became illegal for businesses in 38 leading industrial nations to bribe an official anywhere in the world. This has been the case since 1977 in the USA, where every year over 120 companies from all over the world have been prosecuted for paying bribes to foreign officials. In 2008, engineering giant Siemens was fined $1.6 billion by German and US authorities for making thousands of payments to public officials in return for public contracts. The Ernst & Young *European Fraud Survey* (TI, 2009) interviewed 2246 employees of major companies in 22 countries across Europe. Half of those surveyed believe that 'one or more types of unethical business behaviour was acceptable'. For example, 25 per cent of European respondents thought it fine to give a cash bribe to win work. Worryingly, 55 per cent of European respondents expect corporate fraud to increase over the next few years. An increase is expected because of 'changes that will be made to businesses in response to the economic downturn, reduced focus on anti-fraud, pressures to protect the future of the company and the pressure to keep bonuses and compensation greater'.

Any firm found criminally liable in the EU or US for bribery can be debarred from securing future public contracts throughout the EU and US. The legal, reputational and financial costs of bribery have led many of the world's leading companies to introduce codes and compliance programmes in an effort to tackle the problem. John went on to explain that senior managers can be held criminally liable for any bribes paid by staff, agents or anyone else acting on behalf of their company – even if it takes place in a jurisdiction where some forms of bribery are not strictly outlawed. If a company is found guilty of bribery, some courts and authorities will take into account any compliance and training programmes that the company has introduced to mitigate the risk of corruption that might occur in the business. Many of these stem from the preventive '*Business Principles*' approach developed by TI. The *Business Principles* provide the framework for an anti-bribery programme and have been adopted by thousands of companies worldwide. A number of other free tools are also available for companies facing extortion risks including '*Resist*' developed by TI, the International Chambers of Commerce, the UN Global Compact and the World Economic Forum. John said that examples of some of the free tools and strategies available to organizations can be viewed at the transparency.org website indicated below.

TASKS

1   Imagine that you work for a large European or American company and it has been made clear to you by your boss that the company does not allow bribes. Indeed training is provided in the standards of behaviour expected of staff in such situations and any staff found to have used bribes or other forms of corruption in their work will be dismissed. However, a large order is being negotiated and it has been made clear by the customer that your major competitor is offering significant 'commissions' to get the order. You need the business or you will not meet your targets for the year. How would you react and why?

2   What does this example suggest about culture in organizations and specific locations?

3 Use the website indicated above to identify appropriate 'tools' that can be used to overcome pressure to give in to bribery or extortion demands. Assess how these might help you to deal with the situation identified in Task 1 above.

Sources:
Matlack, C., Smith, G. and Edmondson, G. (2004) Cracking Down on Corporate Bribery, *Business Week*, 6 December.
http://www.transparency.org/global_priorities/private_sector.
http://www.transparency.ie/.
TI (2009): http://www.transparency.org/publications/newsletter/2009/june_2009/anti_corruption_work/ernst_young_survey.

Table 14.8 The six global capabilities

1	To determine core activities and separate them from noncore activities
2	To achieve consistency while encouraging flexibility
3	To obtain leverage in the market (bigger is better) at the same time as focus (smaller is better)
4	To share learning throughout the organization and to encourage the creation of new knowledge
5	To build a global brand that respects and honours local custom
6	To engender a global perspective at the same time as ensuring local accountability

large tubes of toothpaste were not selling well in Latin America and was forced to introduce much smaller tube sizes. The reason for this was that most people simply could not afford the price of a large tube.

There is another form of globalization with a direct impact on cultural issues in organizations. That is the growing tendency for organizations to experience multi-cultural issues within a single operational unit. With an increasing number of people from different ethnic traditions being found in most countries, it is common to have to deal with cultural diversity in an organization's home territory. It is possible to adopt either a polycentric or ethnocentric approach to these issues, although European legislation in relation to equality favours the polycentric approach.

CONCLUSIONS

The material included in this chapter provides a basis for the discussion of culture within OB. Culture is a difficult to define concept and is capable of being misinterpreted by managers who must attempt to make use of it in their work activities. A range of definitions were explored, as were a number of the facets of both organizational and national culture relevant to the human experience of work. New employees must be effectively integrated into the organization if they are to become productive members. It is not possible to manage every person all the time that they are at work. Internalization of responsibility and knowledge of requirements must be delegated if effective management is to be achieved. Culture is able to offer a meaningful way of accounting for many related phenomena. However, the notion that culture, particularly a strong culture, however attractive, provides a conflict-free way for managers to ensure harmony and the achievement of objectives, is simplistic and does not reflect experience.

Now to summarize this chapter in terms of the relevant Learning Objectives:

- **Understand the significance of the various definitions of culture.** As far back as 1952, 164 different definitions of culture were identified, a figure well exceeded in the intervening decades. This has led some writers to suggest that the concept has no real value because the variety of meanings is so diverse that it is impossible to offer any value as a research topic. Culture seeks to describe those facets of human experience that contribute to the differences and similarities in how people perceive and engage with their world. In that sense culture retains its value as a meta-construct with metaphorical and descriptive power, even if it is often imprecise and problematic. The common managerial view of culture often mirrors closely LeVine's comment on the view of many social science researchers who treat culture 'as representing the unexplained residuum of rigorous empirical analysis, an area of darkness beyond the reach of currently available scientific searchlights'. We define organizational culture as *a set of shared, often implicit assumptions, beliefs, values, and sensemaking procedures that influences and guides the behaviour and thinking of organizational members, and is continuously enacted and in turn reinforced – or changed – by the behaviour of organizational members.* Our definition is fully compatible with three characteristics universally seen as central to the concept of culture: (a) it emerges during the adaptive interaction between people and their environment, and therefore will change when these interactions change; (b) it is by necessity constituted only of shared, intersubjective elements; and (c) it is transmitted to members across time periods and changing member cohorts or generations.

- **Outline the meaning of Edgar Schein's (1985) three levels of culture: artefacts, values and assumptions.** For Schein, the essence of culture is located at the level of basic *assumptions* which reflect how members of a culture experience reality, how they perceive the physical and social world, and how they think and feel. These assumptions are taken for granted, and are rarely questioned. A culture's assumptions provide the basis for and interact with *values* – Schein's next level of culture. Values are the social norms, principles, standards and objectives that are valued by cultural members for their intrinsic worth. Values are accessible because they are revealed by behaviour and priorities. Cultural values often indicate what is seen as morally right and wrong in a particular context. Even though values remain subconscious, members are more aware of them than of their underlying cultural assumptions. In particular, members become aware of their values when they are challenged during times of change or when someone violates conventions. Values are linked to *artefacts*, Schein's third cultural level, in that values-congruent behaviours express and manifest the cultural values and assumptions located at the other levels. This can happen through deliberate expressive actions, through unintended expressive actions, or through other actions that manifest cultural assumptions and values. Anything observable linked to behaviour can be seen as artefacts including objects, verbal expressions, and activities.

- **Assess Handy's views on the factors that determine organizational culture.** Handy indicates a number of influences on the culture of an organization that also link well with the contingency views of organizational structure discussed in Chapter 10:

  - *History and ownership.* Culture is something that is partly independent of individuals within the organization. From that perspective, culture could be subject to 'accommodation' as people flow through it and interact with the 'current' culture. The type of ownership will also have an impact on culture.

  - *Size.* Size influences culture if for no other reason than the formality required in the operation of larger organizations.

  - *Technology.* An organization that specializes in the use of high technology will emphasize the technical skills of employees in the values that govern its culture.

  - *Goals and objectives.* What the organization sets out to achieve will also influence the culture.

  - *Environment.* These are the customer markets, the supplier markets, the financial markets, governmental influences, competitors and the environmental lobby, and the way in which an organization interacts with these which will influence its culture.

  - *People.* A manager's preferred approach to the management of their subordinates helps to form the organization culture. Employee preferences as to how they wish to be managed also influences the way that culture develops.

- **Explain why the concept of culture is problematic when applied to organizations.** Culture is a problematic concept because it is difficult to define in precise terms. It is an easy term to recognize in that it is relatively obvious how organizations differ. When visiting an organization, a 'feeling' becomes apparent which provides a general indication of the culture. For example, one organization might feel busy with a buzz of activity and a feeling of purpose; whilst another might feel relaxed with a feeling of calmness in the approach to work. A number of models seek to define what culture is and how it can be measured and these are introduced at appropriate points in the chapter.

- **Discuss the possibilities for the management and change of organizational culture, together with the means of doing so.** It can be argued that it is very difficult if not impossible to change an organization's culture. It can also be argued that an organization's culture is constantly adapting to the prevailing circumstances and so it is not a question of changing it, but of steering it in appropriate directions. At a simple level it could be argued that changing any of the features of culture will change the culture itself. However, this is too simplistic and does not recognize the sometimes deeply entrenched cultures that can exist in some situations. For example, a strong culture can be particularly resistant to change, as can the cultures of some subgroups, particularly if they are hostile to management's intentions. It has been argued by writers such as Lundberg that it is possible to change cultures provided a particular process is undertaken. The approach proposed by Lundberg is discussed in the appropriate section of this chapter.

DISCUSSION QUESTIONS

1 'Sub- and countercultures have no part to play in the formal organization and so are irrelevant in relation to managerial activities.' Discuss this statement.

2 '"The way we do things around here" is the most appropriate definition of culture for practising managers as it reflects the artefacts level in the Schein model of the three levels of culture.' Critically evaluate this statement.

3 Explain Handy's views on the factors that determine organizational culture.

4 Outline the cultural web and explain its significance in being able to articulate the culture of an organization.

5 'The concept of culture is of little practical value to managers because it simply describes tendencies and ignores the variation between individuals.' Discuss this statement.

6 It has been suggested that strong organizational cultures are essential to the achievement of success. It has also been suggested that strong cultures could predispose an organization to failure. Can you find an argument that could reconcile these two positions?

7 How would you set about achieving a change in an organization's culture?

8 'The concept of culture is intended to provide managers with an opportunity to increase the level of control without increasing the level of management.' Discuss.

9 'National culture will always get in the way of global organizations becoming truly successful as it will never align with the internal organizational culture and problems will result.' Discuss this statement.

10 'Culture is such an imprecise term that it is not possible to measure it, let alone change it within an organization.' Critically evaluate this statement.

CASE STUDY

Breakfast cereal games at the supermarket

This is a story of two organizations, a small breakfast cereal manufacturing company and a large supermarket group. The small breakfast cereal company was based in Switzerland and had an excellent reputation in the industry for making innovative products. They were very keen on new product development and were always searching out new ways of processing the various grains that were traditionally used in the making of breakfast cereals and of linking these with fruits, nuts and other ingredients in various combinations to produce novel products with high customer attraction. They were particularly good at identifying the health and nutrition potential for their products and their products always sold well in the supermarkets.

One of the major UK-based, but international supermarket chains that already took a number of products from this particular cereal manufacturer introduced a new quality scheme within their operations. It was based on the ISO 9000 programme which sought to ensure that quality procedures were in place at all levels and in all aspects of the supermarket's operations. This process included the requirement for all suppliers to become involved in a partnership arrangement with the supermarket with regard to the quality of the products that were being supplied. The ISO 9000 approach to quality essentially requires that every aspect of the company processes must be documented and that detailed records of actual work undertaken along with the quality standards expected and achieved must be kept for customer inspection. The cereal manufacturer accepted the need to comply with the supermarket's requirement, although they did regard the amount of paperwork involved as rather excessive and not particularly helpful to their own ways of ensuring quality which had built up over many years of practical experience in the industry. Also it was not cheap to implement and maintain the systems required and the supermarket would not increase the price they paid for the breakfast cereal products that they bought to compensate for the requirement to adopt the new system.

Regular meetings took place between supermarket representatives and the senior management from the breakfast cereal manufacturer to discuss progress, order levels and possible new products. At one such meeting, after the new quality system had been running for about one year, managers from the breakfast cereal maker were asked by the supermarket to provide them with all the relevant documents in relation to the quality of the products that were supplied. It was said that a quality audit was being undertaken and that all the records were needed in order to determine whether or not the cereal maker had been using the system correctly and ensure that their quality was of an acceptable standard. The cereal manufacturer complied and handed over all the relevant documentation. This included the recipe data and processing methods for their best-selling product. Generally this information had been kept secret prior to this time as it was commercially sensitive and could allow a competitor to copy their products. About one month later, managers from the cereal maker were called to a meeting at the supermarket headquarters and were told that the shelf space allocated to their range of products was being reduced as the supermarket had introduced a new range of 'own brand' breakfast cereals of a similar type to those supplied by the company.

The Swiss managers were clearly disappointed by the decision and tried to persuade the supermarket to change its mind. This was without success and when they asked for more information on the new range of products they were fobbed off with a vague answer that left them no better informed. They asked for information on who was to make the new products as they might like the chance to tender for the work and were told that this would not be possible as they were to be made by a company in which the supermarket had part ownership and

the contract had already been placed. They asked for the name of the new supplier and learned that it was one of their competitors. The order level for the breakfast cereals was reduced, the Swiss senior managers were furious. A few weeks later they flew to England specifically to visit one of the supermarket branches in the UK to look at the new range of own-label cereals and found that they looked almost identical to their existing range, but at a cheaper price under the supermarket's brand name. They bought a few packets and took them back to the factory in Switzerland for analysis and found that for all practical purposes they were identical to theirs. The Swiss managing director called the senior management at the supermarket and said that they felt cheated and that they thought that it was no coincidence that this had occurred shortly after the detailed information on the product had been supplied to them under the new quality scheme. The supermarket denied it, saying that the product development staff had not had access to any information supplied by the cereal manufacturer and had developed their own brand version by trial and error only. The managing director was very depressed at the news, but realized that trying to prove anything untoward had taken place would be very difficult.

TASKS

1 To what extent does this case reflect effective business practice on the part of the supermarket?

2 Could organizational culture have influenced the supermarket's approach to this situation? If so how?

3 What about the culture within the cereal maker, were they too trusting and could they have prevented the situation getting to this stage if they had a different culture?

FURTHER READING

Adler, N.J. and Gundersen, A. (2007) *International dimensions of organizational behavior* (5th edn), Southwestern Publishing. Useful consideration of many managerial and behavioural issues arising in international contexts.

Alvesson, M. (2002) *Understanding Organizational Culture*, London: Sage. Looks at what culture is and the ways in which it interacts with a wide range of other organizational activities such as performance, administrative activities and leadership.

Hampden-Turner, C. (1990) *Corporate Cultures: From Vicious to Virtuous Circles*, London: Random Century. Provides a readable review of culture in an organizational context.

Hofstede, G. (1984) *Culture's Consequences: International Differences in Work-related Values*, Beverley Hills: Sage. Classical contribution to the issue of culture and organizations.

Kotter, J.P. and Heskett, J.L. (1992) *Corporate Culture and Performance*, New York: The Free Press. Considers the general issue of culture and its relationship with organizational performance.

Martin, J. (2002) *Organizational culture: Mapping the terrain*, London: Sage. Review of the academic research on organizations and culture from an important contributor to this research.

Semler, R. (2003) *The Seven-Day Weekend*, London: Century Books. This text provides a review of the way that Ricardo Semler runs his group of companies and it is challenging and controversial in a number of areas within organizational behaviour.

Schein, E.H. (2004) *Organizational culture and leadership* (3rd edn), Jossey-Bass. New edition of the influential text from one of the central researchers on organizational culture.

Trompenaars, F. (1993) *Riding the Waves of Culture*, London: Nicholas Brealey. Important book on national culture.

COMPANION WEBSITE

Online teaching and learning resources

Visit the companion website for Organizational Behaviour and Management 4th edition at: http://www.cengage.co.uk/martinfellenz to find valuable further teaching and learning material. For full details, see 'About the website' at the start of the book.

©JeanellNorvell/istock

CHAPTER FIFTEEN

POWER, INFLUENCE AND POLITICS

LEARNING OBJECTIVES

After studying this chapter and working through the associated OB in Action panels, Discussion Questions and Case Study you should be able to:

- Assess the differences and similarities between the concepts of power, influence and authority.

- Explain the major perspectives on power as experienced within an organization.

- Discuss the sources of power within an organization.

- Outline the concept of organizational politics.

- Understand how political behaviour can be managed within an organization.

INTRODUCTION

Power is a concept related to ideas of influence, control, leadership, manipulation, force, and others that deal with the impact a person or group can have on others. In organizations, it is crucial because it is a central means by which the many different individuals and groups needed to achieve organizational goals can be compelled to make their respective contributions. This broad perspective on power already indicates the many different facets that power can have in organizations. Power is present at the interpersonal level in any interactions. It is also a central feature in the relationships among groups and organizational subunits, and it is relevant for the organization as a whole in terms of its relationships with stakeholders and competitors in the environment. In this chapter, we will distinguish between power and influence, discuss the sources of individual and subunit power, consider the use of influence tactics and review some of the main perspectives of power.

Power is necessary for organizations to function, but it can also create problems when it is used to further agendas not aligned with organizational goals. This is part of organizational politics, which broadly refers to activities used to gain and apply power in organizations. We consider different views of organizational politics, review political tactics commonly used in organizations and discuss how political behaviour can be managed in organizations.

Organizational politics
Broadly refers to activities used to gain and apply power in organizations. Generally defined as behaviour outside the accepted procedures and norms of a particular context, intended to further the position of an individual or group at the expense of others.

DISTINGUISHING BETWEEN POWER AND INFLUENCE

Power is a social concept used to describe and understand the basis on which people can affect the behaviour of others. As such, it is invariable linked to the concept of influence, which is often used to describe both the process and outcome of interactions that are based on power. Many different definitions for these concepts exist, and we will come across a number of relevant contributions that express different views of these concepts in this chapter.

Before we consider individual views and definitions, it is important to recognize that power is invariably linked to the concept of dependence. If you are fully independent from someone, they cannot have power over you. However, if you have a relationship with them that includes regular and desirable interactions and exchanges, or even if they just have the potential to affect you in positive or negative ways, you may be actually or potentially dependent on them and their behaviour for the positive or negative consequences they can cause for you. Does this mean that anyone who can affect you in any way has power over you?

Dependence
The state of being dependent, of relying upon another. If someone with whom you have a relationship provides regular and desirable interactions and exchanges, or they may just have the potential to affect you in positive or negative ways –
you will have a degree of dependence on them for the positive or negative consequences they deliver.

STOP & CONSIDER

To what extent (and why) would you agree with the view that because of the nature of a CEO's job they must achieve independence from subordinate managers and staff? If you agree with the statement, how might that independence be achieved and maintained in practice?

Let's look at an extreme case. Most people will agree that someone who holds a gun to your head demanding your wallet has power over you. But is that necessarily so? In fact, we have much more control over power and dependency than many of us realize. Others have power over us only to the degree that we – deliberately or unconsciously – give it to them. Even in the extreme case of a mugger with a gun or anyone else with the ability to affect you substantially, it is still an option to refuse (even though we would generally not advise you to do so if you are being mugged!). The key point here is that our behaviour is largely controlled by us, not others, even though they can fundamentally affect the decision-making process we use to determine our behaviour. They may do this by specifying certain outcome contingencies (this is a curious way to describe what a mugger is doing with a gun, of course), by affecting the way we think about the choices (e.g., by reframing them, by raising the salience of certain options, by trying to change the way we evaluate them, etc.), or by invoking automatic cognitive and behavioural responses. Many of these dynamics have been discussed in previous chapters – in fact, if you read the chapters you will find subtle or even obvious references to power and influence in virtually all of them.

The idea of power has sometimes been viewed as a force (e.g., 'any force that results in behaviour that would not have occurred if the force had not been present', Mechanic, 1962: p. 351). Others have defined power and influence as alternative sources of bringing about behavioural change. McMillan and Jones (1986: p. 14), for example, distinguished *power* as the 'ability to restructure the situation in such a way as to get others to act as . . . desire[d]' from *influence* as the ability 'to restructure perceptions of targets in a situation to get them to act as desired'. While this is an interesting distinction, it fails to provide for mutually exclusive definitions in all cases. For example, is it power or influence if a bankrobber passes a note to the bankteller that states 'Bankrobbery – I have a gun. Give me all your money!'? If the bankrobber is just pretending, then based on McMillan and Jones' definition this would indicate the use of influence, but if the gun exists it would be power. However – what if the gun exists but is not loaded?

Bennis and Nanus call power the capacity to translate intention into reality and sustain this new reality (Bennis and Nanus, 1985). Pfeffer (1992) brings together a number of views on power by describing it as 'the potential ability to influence behaviour, to change the course of events, to overcome resistance and to get people to do things that they would not otherwise do' (p. 30). There are many other relevant views and definitions of power that highlight different specific aspects of it.

However, for clarity and simplicity's sake, we will consider power and influence as follows. In line with many writers on power who have conceived of social power as a capacity for bringing about behavioural change in others (e.g., Bennis and Nanus, 1985; French and Raven, 1968; Pfeffer, 1981, 1992; Mintzberg, 1983), we define power as the *capacity to get others to behave in desired ways*. Influence, in contrast, is *the process by which others are induced to behave in desired ways*. Handy (1993) discusses the use of the term 'influence' as both noun and verb to explain some of the confusion with power. He suggests restricting its use to that of a verb in the sense of 'the use of power' (p. 124) which is fully in line with our definition. The use of the word 'influence' as a noun, which describes *the outcome of the application of power in influence processes* is confusing. Hence we refer to such results generally as influence outcomes. Such influence outcomes can include conformity, compliance, and obedience. Conformity *'refers to the act of changing one's behavior to match the responses of others'* (Cialdini and Goldstein, 2004: p. 606), while compliance describes the *acquiescence to a particular explicit or implicit request* (Cialdini and Goldstein, 2004: p. 592). Obedience is a specific form of compliance, namely *the acquiescence to demands made by a person with authority*. As already discussed and defined in Chapter 12, authority refers to *the legitimate power vested in managers based on their position and role in an organization*. The Examining Ethics example on slavery provides an insight into aspects of these terms in what today might seem an extreme situation.

Power is one capability that can enable a person (or agent) to influence another person or group (i.e., target). Other sources of the ability to bring about behavioural

Power
The capacity to get others to behave in desired ways.

Influence
The process by which others are induced to behave in desired ways.

Influence outcomes
The outcome of the application of power in influence processes.

Conformity
Refers to the act of changing one's behaviour to match the responses of others.

Compliance
Describes the acquiescence to a particular explicit or implicit request. See also obedience.

Obedience
A specific form of compliance, namely the acquiescence to demands made by a person with authority. See also compliance.

Authority
Refers to the legitimate power vested in managers based on their position and role in an organization.

EXAMINING ETHICS

Slaves knew only too well about power, influence and politics

Frederick Washington Bailey, probably the son of a white (or mixed race) plantation overseer and a black slave, was born in Maryland in 1817 or 1818. He never knew his father and was separated from his mother when still an infant. He lived with his maternal grandmother on a plantation until the age of eight, when he was sent to live with and work for Hugh Auld in Baltimore, where Auld's wife defied state law by teaching him to read. In 1833 Frederick was returned to his original Maryland plantation. After a couple of failed escape attempts (resulting in severe beatings) he fled to New York in 1838 and changed his name to Frederick Douglass.

Douglass became a lecturer for the American Anti-Slavery Society in 1841 and in 1845 the society helped him publish his autobiography. After publication, he was afraid that his former 'owner' might try to recapture or reclaim him and so he travelled to Britain. There he lectured on slavery and subsequently established his own anti-slavery magazine, the *North Star*. This created a break with his former patrons in the American Anti-Slavery Society who were opposed to a black-owned press. After the American Civil War, Douglass campaigned for full civil rights for former slaves and was a strong supporter of women's suffrage. Subsequently Douglass held several senior government and public posts and died in Washington on 20th February, 1895.

Some quotations and extracts attributed to Frederick Douglass:

'No man can put a chain about the ankle of his fellow man without at last finding the other end fastened about his own neck.'

'I didn't know I was a slave until I found out I couldn't do the things I wanted.'

'If there is no struggle there is no progress. Those who profess to favor freedom, and yet depreciate agitation, want crops without plowing the ground. They want rain without thunder and lightning. They want the ocean without the awful roar of its many waters. This struggle may be a moral one; or it may be a physical one; or it may be both moral and physical; but it must be a struggle. Power concedes nothing without a demand. It never did and never will.'

'Mr. Covey succeeded in breaking me. I was broken in body, soul, and spirit. My natural elasticity was crushed, my intellect languished, the disposition to read departed, the cheerful spark that lingered about my eye died; the dark night of slavery closed in upon me; and behold a man transformed into a brute!'

TASKS

1 What does the above example add to an understanding of power, influence and politics in an organizational context?

2 To what extent are power, influence and politics in an organizational context ethical?

3 To what extent does modern employment practice reflect the same power, influence and political realities evident from the time of Frederick Douglass, but modified because those in charge are no longer able to behave in the same way as slave owners? Justify your answer.

Sources:
Frederick Douglass at: http://www.spartacus.schoolnet.co.uk/USASdouglass.htm (accessed August 2009).
Frederick Douglass at: http://www.keele.ac.uk/depts/as/Portraits/douglass.html (accessed August 2009).
Frederick Douglass at: http://www.history.rochester.edu/class/douglass/home.html (accessed August 2009).
Frederick Douglass at: http://www.nps.gov/archive/frdo/fdlife.htm (accessed August 2009).
Frederick Douglass at: http://www.brainyquote.com/quotes/authors/f/frederick_douglass.html (accessed August 2009).

change may arise not from power sources but from the skills of selecting and using appropriate influence tactics and invoking automatic responses through influence mechanisms which we discuss in a later section. Below, we will first consider the sources of both social and subunit power in organizations.

SOURCES OF POWER IN ORGANIZATIONS

Power is invisible – it cannot be held or touched and it is not detectable by any mechanical or electronic sensor. However, power is a very real and potent social force in any organization. It is important to distinguish between power and the associated trappings which are detectable. For example, wealth and status are frequently associated with power. Stereotypical assumptions lead to implying that an individual holds power simply because they dress in expensive clothing or behave as if they were superior. False claims to power through such outward signs (if uncovered) can leave the individual concerned subject to ridicule or marginalization. Equally, of course, the opposite is also true. There are individuals and groups who are not obviously powerful and yet in practice they might be described as the power behind the throne. These are people with the real power to influence, decide and direct events and other people.

Power is something that only lives in the minds, attitudes, behaviours, expectations and perceptions of individuals. Once established in society, the prevailing forms of power are supported by a wide range of structural devices. The laws, culture, and status, work and educational systems are aligned in support and reinforcement of a particular power framework. However, individuals and groups who for various reasons do not wish to accept the prevailing power framework can seek to change the situation or, if all else fails, seek to overturn it through revolution. Of course, situations where direct force (or the threat of it) is used to obtain results represent the application of a particular form of power (see Lukes, 2005, for a comprehensive review of power in society).

Sources of social power in organizations

If power is not a tangible entity and is dependent upon the recipients to create its significance where does it originate? French and Raven (1968; Raven, 1993) identified a number of sources of social power in organizational contexts. Three of these power sources are also called *formal or position power* sources (i.e., coercive, reward and legitimate power) because they are linked to the formal position of authority that managers and others in organizations have assigned to them. *Informal or personal power* sources such as expert, information and referent power are based on characteristics of the agent (i.e., influencer) or the nature of the relationship between agent and target of influencing attempts. The sources of social power in organizations include:

Reward power. Managers have the power to award extrinsic (e.g., pay increases, promotions) and intrinsic (e.g., praise, social recognition) rewards. Formal managerial roles virtually always include some form of reward power, even though particular forms or rewards (e.g., ability to give financial rewards or bonuses) may be limited, for example through formal HR procedures on such issues as promotion, bonuses and benefits, or access to training (see Chapter 13). While such procedures are often intended to reduce inconsistencies and favouritism, many managers – especially in the public sector – often argue that as a result they have few performance-contingent extrinsic rewards at their disposal. Moreover, such formal policies and procedures do not automatically remove favouritism; they simply require managers to justify rewards in terms acceptable to the system. Thus, procedures and policies can drive the use of reward power underground, cloaked in a veil of half-truth and thinly disguised justification.

Managers can easily send the wrong signals about what behaviours are valued by inadvertently rewarding inappropriate behaviours. Paying considerable attention to difficult or troublesome employees can indicate to good employees that it does not pay to be well behaved. Similarly, managers who occasionally allow poor-quality work to be dispatched clearly indicate that good quality is not always important.

Reward power
Power based on control of valued outcomes for the other person(s). It represents the exchange of a willingness to be controlled for desirable rewards.

In general terms such inadvertent rewarding of undesirable behaviour reinforces the idea that individuals should play the system, taking an instrumental view of the work that they do.

Coercive power. This form of power is based on the ability to punish the target if they do not comply with requests. Historically, this power source was much stronger in organizations than it is today. This has changed because of the presence of trade unions and more participative management practices as well as the introduction of employment and other legislation. These changes have not, however, affected informal punishment and coercion. Withholding social approval or even ignoring, isolating or otherwise socially excluding individuals can have powerful effects. Guidelines aimed at regulating interpersonal behaviour and interactions such as dignity and respect policies can limit but not fully eradicate such behaviour.

Coercive power is also evident in many of the episodes of abusive supervision (e.g., Tepper, 2007) such as bullying that are reported. For example, a report based on research across Europe found that 10 per cent of workers claimed to be the victim of bullying or harassment, while another 10 per cent had been subjected to the threat of actual physical violence in the workplace (*Communiqué*, 2003). Roberts (2003) reports a wide range of bullying episodes and research which demonstrates that women are just as likely as men to be a bully and that much of it stems from the stress, overload or inadequacy experienced by the bully (see also the discussion of informal supervisory behaviour used to exert control in Chapter 12).

Legitimate power. In any organization most people accept that managers have legitimate authority to exercise power. There are three main sources of this form of authority (Luthans, 1995: p. 323). First, the accepted social structures within a society provide certain groups with a legitimate basis for exercising power. It might be a ruling family or a class of people that performs that role. Second, cultural values can also create a basis for claiming legitimate power through the veneration of particular classes or individuals. For example, old people often become significant leaders, or men play a dominant role in society. Third, legitimate power can be delegated. Managers act on behalf of the owners of an organization in running the business. In doing so they hold delegated power from the owners who are seen as the legitimate source of direction.

Handy (1993) suggests that holding legitimate power provides automatic access to three invisible assets. First, *information*, which as a commodity can be directed, channelled and traded by power holders. Second, the *right of access* to a number of different networks (see Chapter 16 on the importance of networks and networking), and third, the *right to organize* how work is done (this is also called *process power*).

Expert power. This source of power originates from the knowledge, skill and expertise of the holder. The pilot of an airplane is the one with the appropriate skills to fly it and consequently everyone goes where the pilot decides. Within management, technical specialists often have greater knowledge than the line managers they are supposed to be supporting and so have considerable influence. Claims to be an expert are, however, subject to validation by the group over whom the expertise is being claimed. Failure to deliver the results of claimed expertise can be dealt with severely by the group, who will feel that their trust has been violated, that they have been conned and let down badly.

Information power. This source of power is based on the possession of knowledge or information that is not generally available. The phrase 'information is power' is frequently heard in many organizations and reflects the significance of this source of it. In most organizations some people are in possession of information that could be used to advantage because not everyone has access to it. For example, the employee representatives seeking to negotiate the annual pay rise for employees may not know the level of profit achieved by the company, which is information that might give them more power (see Chapter 9 on the role of BATNAs as a source of power in

---

Coercive power
The ability of a holder of such power to achieve control over another person through the threat of direct action, force or violence.

Legitimate power
The ability to exercise power as a consequence of having the legitimate right to claim to be able to do so.

Expert power
This source of power originates from the knowledge, skill and expertise of an individual in a particular context.

Information power
This source of power is based on the possession of knowledge or information that is not generally available.

negotiations). Managers might try to hide information about the high levels of profit actually being made, but would be only too willing to tell the employee representatives about the losses being made as that might lower expectations among employees.

Referent power. This source of power is based on the characteristics of an individual that make them particularly attractive, likeable, or otherwise desirable. It could be that the individual is of celebrity status and so attracts others to join them and follow their wishes. Religious and political leaders are frequently charismatic and so attract many followers only too willing to adhere to every word and instruction. Advertisers continually utilize this perspective in using models, stars and personality figures to sell products through association and/or emulation.

A seventh form of social power, different in nature from the ones discussed above, is negative power. Negative power, which is power *based on the ability to withhold contribution or compliance*, can have a significant impact on events (Handy, 1993: p. 131). This form of power impacts through not doing something that should be done or that someone expects to be done. For example, a post room employee who is dissatisfied with their job could quickly cause confusion throughout the organization by deliberately misdirecting the post for a few days. It reflects the ability of the lower-level people within an organization to take revenge on the senior people within the organization by withholding something necessary to the effective running of the organization. It may not be anything as obvious as going on strike, as that reflects an attempt to exercise coercive power, but is likely to consist of small events which quickly interrupt the effective running of the business.

These sources of social power provide the basis of the ability to exert influence on the behaviour and actions of others in organizations. What they do not do is provide an indication of *how* that power is converted into influence outcomes. While we will consider the relevant influence tactics and mechanism in more detail in a later section, it is useful to note some general distinctions regarding the influence approaches linked to the sources of social power. Influence attempts based on formal power sources are also called *hard* or *harsh tactics*. In contrast, approaches utilizing informal power sources are called *soft tactics* (Koslowsky *et al.*, 2001, Peiró and Meliá, 2003; Raven *et al.*, 1998). In general, it appears that managers using both types of tactics are most successful in influencing others. However, one fundamental difference between formal and informal power sources appears to be the need for control mechanisms when formal power is used (see Chapter 12). Joint use or a focus on more informal power tends to achieve better influence outcomes when compliance cannot be easily checked. In general, it is helpful for managers to use all available power bases as long as their use of formal power does not undermine compliance through attitudinal effects such as reactance (see also Emans *et al.*, 2003). Also, using formal power sources in abusive ways can generate considerable negative results for managers, subordinates and organizations in terms of reduced job satisfaction, performance, organizational citizenship behaviours, and increased theft, sabotage and insubordination (Tepper, 2007; Tepper *et al.*, 2009). The High Performance example illustrates a particular example of what can happen when apparently effective decisions by senior managers turn out to be disastrous – demonstrating that power should be tempered with appropriate responsibility.

Sources of subunit power in organizations

In organizations, power is also relevant at the subunit level, and sources of subunit power are important to understand. Based on structural and procedural arrangements, subunit power is directly related to the dependence that other units have based on a unit's specific contributions to them and to the organization as a whole (Hinings *et al.*, 1974; Hickson *et al.*, 1971; Pfeffer, 1981). Similarly, just as individual

Referent power
This source of power is based on the characteristics of an individual that make them particularly attractive, likeable, or otherwise desirable. Often based on the presence of a charismatic personality.

Negative power
The ability to influence another party by not doing something that would normally be done. To withhold contribution or compliance.

HIGH PERFORMANCE

The former president of Roskilde Bank in Denmark is facing a law suit stemming from its collapse last year

Roskilde Bank's board of directors have announced that they intend to sue Niels Valentin Hansen, who headed the country's 10th largest bank before liquidity problems saw it taken over by the Danish central bank in 2008. Hansen has been identified in a report commissioned by the current board of directors as having the primary responsibility for the bank's failure. According to the report, he 'ignored his responsibility as President'. Hansen also faces criminal proceedings, and if found guilty, up to 18 months in jail, for a decision by the bank in April 2007 to increase its capital in a share issue that saw Roskilde purchase 22 per cent of its own shares. In response, Hansen, who served as the bank President from 1978 to 2007, has rejected any responsibility for the bank's problems.

As well as the former President, the current directors also intend to instigate court proceeding against the former board of directors and auditors Ernst & Young for what it calls 'criticizable actions'. Specifically, the report claims that the Board failed to provide adequate supervision of the executive board, and in particular neglected to question or identify the possible impact of the bank's high risk loans. Ernst & Young

was identified in the report as 'failing to exercise good accounting practices' in reviewing the bank's 2005 and 2006 annual reports and finances. The report found that Ernst & Young had approved the bank's own annual reviews for those specific years – reports that have subsequently been shown to have been improperly done.

Prior to Roskilde's collapse in August 2008, the bank released a second quarter report showing a 5.1 billion kroner loss, and 3.6 billion kroner of defaulted loans. The report found that while the then board could have limited the bank's losses, it was unlikely that it could have prevented the bank's failure.

TASKS

1 Identify and justify which of the sources of social power are evident and for which stakeholder group or individual in the above example.

2 It is suggested in the text leading up to this example that with power comes responsibility. Does this always follow and if not, why might that be so?

Source:
The Copenhagen Post Online www.cphpost.dk/business/
119-business/46495-former-roskilde-bank-president-to-be-sued
.html. Reproduced with permission.

members can do, organizational subunits may exercise negative power as discussed in the previous section. Specific sources of subunit power in organizations include:

- *Ability to control or manage uncertainty.* Forecasting departments or other boundary spanning units (see Chapter 10) that reduce the uncertainty for other departments (e.g., production and purchasing) are often very influential.

- *Ability to generate or control resources.* Subunits that can generate important resources (e.g., product innovation from research and development departments; revenues from sales departments) or that control important resources (e.g., finance departments that control financial investment decision) often gain immense power in organizations.

- *Irreplacability and nonsustainability* – For innovation-based organizations (e.g., Apple or many pharmaceutical and biotechnology firms) new product development units usually have specialized knowledge and personnel that is hard to replace and cannot be substituted by other functions in the organization.

● *Centrality in information flow and transformation processes* – Structural arrangements may place particular firms at the heart of important processes and give them control through their role and potential impact on these activities.

In addition to these structural and dependency-based sources of power, culture can also provide subunits or groups with power. If a unit's specific activities or contributions are particularly valued in the organization's culture (e.g., technical contributions in an engineering culture), relevant departments and subunits can have power beyond that explained by the sources listed above. Subunit power can be used by their managers, but such power can also be invoked and exploited by other unit members as part of political behaviour (see further below).

Such cultural power is related to but also distinct from unobtrusive power that can be exercised by those groups who have the ability to influence the way in which issues, problems and opportunities are interpreted and considered. Powerful groups such as the top management team may be able to frame a situation in ways that prevent others from reacting to it or from opposing decisions and actions taken. Moreover, it can shape everybody's conceptions and subsequent decision making (Lukes, 2005). Such unobtrusive power can involve mechanisms that exercise power in increasingly subtle formats which reflect Lukes' three-dimensional conception of power (2005), ranging from visible *responding* to concerns or reactions over less visible *preventing* behaviour to very subtle and long-term *shaping* activities that create alignment of different views with the powerholders' perspective. Such unobtrusive power is exercised in increasingly subtle forms such as 'the creation of social myths and the use of language and symbols' (Fortin and Fellenz, 2008: p. 420). Figure 15.1 shows the Manipulation Cycle, a model of how managers can employ such unobtrusive power to manipulate, in this example, employee fairness experiences and conceptions in ways that increase in their impact over time. The Change at Work example also illustrates this (and other) power, influence and political influences in one particular work context.

> **Unobtrusive power**
> Can be exercised by those groups who have the ability to influence the way in which issues, problems and opportunities are interpreted and considered.

Figure 15.1 The Manipulation Cycle – A model of managerial use of power to influence fairness perceptions over time.

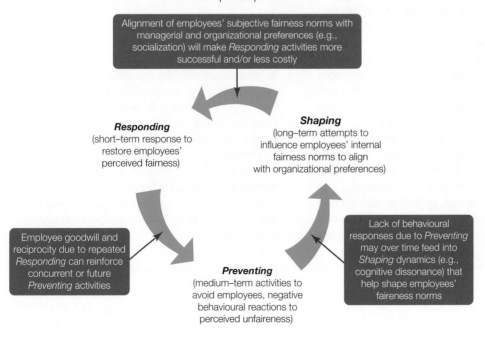

Source: Fortin, M. and Fellenz, M.R. (2008). Hypocrisies of fairness: Towards a more reflexive ethical base in organizational justice research and practice. Journal of Business Ethics, 78: 415–433, Springer. Reprinted with permission.

CHANGE AT WORK

Promoting the function?

This story was told by the human resource director involved in the situation, who was very satisfied with the outcome! The company employed about 4000 people and was a medium-sized bank with the usual branch network and range of head office functions. Up to the late 1980s the personnel function had been a small department led by a senior personnel manager reporting directly to the chief executive. Below that level were a personnel manager and training manager who managed the appropriate parts of personnel activity for the entire company. In turn they were supported by a senior personnel officer for the branches, one for the head office functions and a couple of training officers. There were also a small number of personnel officers and clerical support staff who looked after the day-to-day personnel administration and any personnel issues as they arose. The department employed a total of about 17 people.

The finance sector was changing rapidly in the late 1980s and in the bank concerned, a major international firm of business consultants was retained to assist in the development of new strategies and the subsequent reorganization of the company. Clearly a major part of this process involved reorganizing jobs, new pay structures, training staff and so on. Not surprisingly the senior personnel manager argued that major changes were required within his function. He suggested a human resource management department headed by a director with more professional level and other staff. He 'persuaded' the management consultants to support this proposal in their report which was agreed by the board of directors. The senior personnel manager became director of human resource management. Integrated into the function were the existing personnel and related functions and a number of new sections created – reward management, employee relations and safety units. The training function was expanded and a number of regional human resource managers

were recruited. The number of people employed in the new human resource management department grew to 70, approximately 30 of whom were new to the company at senior specialist or manager level. The payroll cost of the department jumped by considerably more than the rise in numbers might suggest. The number of people in the department rose from about 17 to about 70 suggesting a rise of just over four times. However, new posts were predominantly at senior level and so the additional cost was higher – plus the cost of directorship and a couple of promotions among existing employees. The total additional cost to the company was an increase in salary and benefits of approximately ten times.

From the new director of human resource management's perspective the changes contained a number of benefits. He now had a seat on the board. That gave him the power to influence strategy and policy more easily, at the same time as giving him the status to influence other managers more directly. However, company performance did not noticeably improve as a consequence of this additional activity. The main advantage, as the director of human resource explained it, was that he personally trebled his salary (plus increased benefits, car, etc.) because he had become responsible for a much bigger and more significant department!

TASKS

1 To what extent does the outcome reflect the exercise of unobtrusive power in achieving the desired (for the HR director) result?
2 What forms of power, influence or politics are evident in this example? Justify your answer.
3 To what extent does this example represent nothing more than an individual seizing an opportunity for personal advantage and having the skills necessary to achieve it in practice? Justify your answer.

INFLUENCE TACTICS AND MECHANISMS IN ORGANIZATIONS

Exerting influence on behaviour is commonplace in organizations. It is a fundamental part of management and OB, and is central to many formal aspects of organizations as well as being part of the many informal processes and interactions taking place in organizations. Leadership, for example, is a form of exercising influence (see Chapter 6). Influence is typically based on the sources of power discussed in the previous section. Such power is exercised in interactions between an agent and a target. Note that in addition to power, influence outcomes such as compliance and conformity can also be achieved through the application of influencing skills which refer to *the ability to appropriately select and use particular influence tactics and mechanisms*. Thus, influencing skills can serve as an additional source of power.

Influencing skills
Refers to the ability to appropriately select and use particular influence tactics and mechanisms.

Influence tactics

Influence tactics describe *specific interaction patterns used by agents to bring about the target's compliance with a particular request.* The tactics used in organizations to gain compliance from others have been extensively researched. A list of the most relevant influence tactics used in organizations, largely based on the work of Kipnis, Yukl, and others (e.g., Higgins *et al.*, 2003; Jones and Pittman, 1982; Kipnis *et al.*, 1980; Kipnis *et al.*, 1984; Yukl, 2010; Yukl, *et al.*, 2005; Yukl and Falbe, 1990; Yukl *et al.*, 2008), is included below:

Influence tactics
Describes specific interaction patterns used by agents to bring about the target's compliance with a particular request. See also influence mechanisms.

- *Rationality* – using argumentation to show that it would be logical to comply with request.
- *Exchange* – offering immediate or promised incentive for compliance.
- *Ingratiation* – praising and flattering target before or during influence attempt to induce positive emotional disposition.
- *Assertiveness* – using frequent demands, reminders, checks, or even threats to gain compliance.
- *Coalition* – enlisting third parties to exert pressure or to show broad support for request.
- *Upward appeal* – obtain approval and support from authority and show this to sway target.
- *Consultation* – using participative approach by asking for help and input to gain commitment from target.
- *Inspirational appeal* – call on values and ideals aligned with desired response to sway target.
- *Personal appeal* – leveraging personal relationship to gain commitment from target.
- *Legitimating* – invoking rules, norms, policies, or other sources of legitimacy to justify and support request.
- *Collaboration* – using an involvement approach by offering mutual help and interdependent work in pursuit of the objective behind the request.
- *Apprizing* – pointing out the specific benefits that will arise for the target from agreeing with the request.
- *Self-promotion* – creating an appearance of competence that the agent is capable of successfully completing the task.

Managers' use of particular influence tactics, as well as the effectiveness of different tactics in bringing about compliance, is determined by many factors including managers' own preferences and skills, managers' subjective utility assessments, the relative power of the parties (often reflected in the direction of the influence attempt: upwards, lateral, downwards), the content of the request, and personality factors (Falbe and Yukl, 1992; Ferris *et al.*, 2000; Grams and Rogers, 1990; Higgins *et al.*, 2003; Steensma, 2007). Yukl (2010) has reviewed the relevant literature on the relative effectiveness of these different tactics and concludes that rationality, inspirational appeal, consultation and collaboration are generally very effective, while coalition, legitimating and assertiveness are less effective (see also Higgins *et al.*, 2003).

Influence mechanisms

Influence mechanisms
Refers to actions and interaction patterns that prompt automatic response patterns which increase the likelihood of acquiescence with influencing attempts. See also influence tactics.

In addition to the influence tactics described above, Cialdini (2008) discusses the nature and role of a set of influence mechanisms that can provide immensely effective means of bringing about compliance. In this context, influence mechanisms refer to *actions and interaction patterns that prompt automatic response patterns which increase the likelihood of acquiescence with influencing attempts.* These automatic response patterns are based on cognitive schemas and behavioural scripts that, once invoked by a stimulus controlled by the agent, operate automatically and largely subconsciously and determine cognitive, emotional and behavioural responses to influencing attempts (see the discussions of automatic behaviour in Chapter 5, of automatic or peripheral route information processing in Chapter 4, and of heuristics and cognitive biases in Chapter 8). As these responses are invoked by the agent and operate without conscious awareness, influence targets often do not fully realize the degree to which their reactions are controlled by previously learned responses. Cialdini provides many vivid examples of such influence dynamics and the broad range in which they are used in organizations as well as in interpersonal relationships, in marketing, advertising and selling, and in many other everyday contexts (Cialdini, 2008; Rhoads and Cialdini, 2002).

Cialdini argues that there are two reasons why it is important to learn about these influence mechanisms. First, they provide value because we can use them as 'weapons of influence' to stimulate other people to conform to our requests. Second, we can use them to detect and understand our own weaknesses that might be exploited by others. In fact, most people hold an implicit or even explicit illusion of invulnerability regarding such influence attempts, and training to recognize when these attempts occur coupled with an acceptance of one's own vulnerability to such attempts can help provide a defence against influence based on automatic responses (Sagarin *et al.*, 2002).

Cialdini describes six central influence mechanisms. They are in varying degrees related to the influence tactics discussed above, but the main difference is that they all operate largely automatically. That makes them particularly hard to guard against. The six mechanisms include:

- *Reciprocity.* Based on the social exchange norms to respond in kind to positive actions by others, reciprocation is one of the strongest and most universal social values and is internalized by most people in most cultures (Gouldner, 1961).

- *Consistency and commitment.* Consistency motives operate within most people and can be used to expand on initial commitments given (see also cognitive dissonance dynamics).

- *Social proof.* Observed or implied behaviour by others ('if everyone is doing it . . .') instigates conformity based on learned and then generalised responses to norms and to direct social pressure and control.

- *Liking.* Physical or other forms of attraction (or even simply similarity) predisposes people to comply with those they like, approve of, have a positive relationship with, or can easily identify with.

- *Authority.* Obedience to authority is socially ingrained in most people, who will automatically comply to requests from people with authority. Even minute cues that give the impression that someone has authority (such as white lab coats and stethoscopes in hospitals) can initiate obedience.

- *Scarcity.* Actual or perceived scarcity conveys the impression of value and often generates demand. Thus, withdrawing an offer, raising prices, or otherwise indicating that something may not be available at all or as easily often compels others to want it more.

The Going Global example provides some insight into a particular form of influence – a trade union trying to influence a foreign government.

PERSPECTIVES ON POWER

The study of power within organizations has mostly been studied from three perspectives. The first is most closely related to the discipline of social psychology and has focused on the interpersonal and group levels of analysis. Its behavioural orientation is reflected in the research on social power and influence discussed earlier. The second perspective reflects a much higher level of analysis and is aligned with the fields of organization theory and strategy. It focuses on interorganizational power relations and dependencies. Finally, the third perspective is most closely associated with the discipline of sociology. Sociologically oriented research on power includes the nature and role of power relations in organizations as well as fundamental relationships between organizations and the social structures of which they form part (e.g., Ackroyd, 1994). Issues related to the use of power to exercise control (see Chapter 12) and the resulting resistance to such domination attempts are also of major concern for sociological investigations of power (including the labour process debate, see Braverman, 1974). Below we will briefly outline some of the major themes associated with the study of power.

15.1 EXTEND
YOUR LEARNING

Traditional perspectives on power

Within much of the traditional management literature, power was assumed to reflect the nature of the hierarchical relationships endemic to organizations. Management was described as an activity that involved the determination of what needed to be done and then the direction of the necessary resources to meeting that objective. Within that paradigm management has the power to ensure that what is necessary is actually done. Nonmanagement organizational members exist solely to provide the means of achieving the objectives, and are there to have power exercised over them. This perspective suggests that power is a reflection of a natural social order and as such remains an element within the study of leadership and control.

Many of the models used within the management literature, particularly in classical contributions, but also in the area of leadership and the literatures dealing with formal aspects of organization (including, for example, structure, technology and control), assume that power is the prerogative of management and always at the disposal of organizational decision makers. Managers can exercise their power, for example in deciding which leadership and management styles to adopt. Fiedler's (1967) contingency model of leadership, for example, specifically incorporates a power dimension. Through the leader 'position power' concept this model reflects

GOING GLOBAL

Excessive police violence at Labour Day rally

The following is a letter sent by the Norwegian Confederation of Trade Unions (LO-Norway) to the Prime Minister of Turkey to protest at the treatment of workers at a Labour Day rally in Istanbul:

Mr Recep Tayyip Erdogan
Prime Minister
Republic of Turkey
ANKARA
Turkey

Mr. Prime Minister,

On behalf of the Norwegian Confederation of Trade Unions (LO-Norway) representing more than 840.000 workers, we strongly protest at the violence used by your riot police against trade unionists who wanted to participate in a Labour Day rally in Istanbul on 1 May 2008.

According to Istanbul Governor Muammer Guler, 530 demonstrators were detained and 38 people injured. According to information, the Turkish police used clubs, pepper spray, tear gas and red-dye water cannons to break up crowds of workers and students trying to reach Taksim square. This square is sadly renowned for the hideous events which took place there in 1977, when unidentified gunmen opened fire on demonstrating workers, leaving 37 of them dead.

After it had been announced by the ITUC-affiliated Confederation of Progressive Trade Unions of Turkey (DISK), the Confederation of Turkish Trade Unions (TÜRK-IS), and the Confederation of Public Employees' Trade Unions (KESK), that May Day demonstrations would take place on Taksim Square, your authorities banned them, threatening to use 'proportional violence' if the unions were to hold actions there anyway.

After the unions announced that they would defy the ban, barricades were set up around Taksim Square. Your Government reinforced the Istanbul police force with teams from other cities and had a police helicopter hovering above the city center. What followed was nothing less than a siege of DISK's headquarters,

notwithstanding the fact that the unions had announced that they would continue to rally elsewhere, as they feared that, after such power display by the Turkish police, the damage would be too great and innocent people and shop owners would be harmed or get hurt.

However, your police had already started attacking people who were gathering in front of the DISK headquarters as early as 6.15am. The building itself was blocked so that nobody could get in or out anymore, and it was inundated with tear gas. Although they knew that the building was full of people, the police nevertheless continued to tear gas them. A young woman, who had come out because she was experiencing serious respiratory problems, was even hit on the head by the police. In the end, a great number of people were injured, executives from DISK- and KESK-affiliated trade unions were arrested, roughed up and beaten by the police, and DISK and KESK union leaders were prevented from moving to a safer place.

Mr. Prime Minister, the images that were shown around the world left few doubts as to whether the force used by the Turkish police was excessive or not. Reports by our Turkish affiliates were even backed up by a statement from the Istanbul Bar Association, which said that the police had used excessive force on demonstrators. Even apart from the fact that threatening to use 'proportional violence' when people gather to demonstrate in itself already implies that holding a rally is a criminal offense, there can be no doubt whatsoever that the amount of force and violence used by your police to counter the demonstration was completely disproportionate and inadmissible.

We are therefore calling on you to ensure that Turkey adheres to the principles of Freedom of Association and of basic trade union rights as enshrined in the fundamental ILO conventions to which Turkey is a signatory.

Yours sincerely
THE NORWEGIAN CONFEDERATION OF TRADE UNIONS
International Department
Karin Beate Theodorsen
International Secretary

CC: The Norwegian Ministry for Foreign Affairs
The Embassy of the Republic of Turkey, Oslo
The Royal Norwegian Embassy, Ankara
The International Trade Union Confederation (ITUC)
Confederation of Turkish Trade Unions (TÜRK-IS), Ankara
Confederation of Progressive Trade Unions of Turkey (DISK), Istanbul
Confederation of Public Employees' Trade Unions (KESK), Ankara

might see this letter and who might be influenced by it.

2 In writing such a letter, what might the Norwegian Confederation of Trade Unions be hoping to achieve in relation to the various individuals and groups identified in the first task?

3 Identify the ways in which influence is evident and being exercised through the content of the letter and its circulation to potential audiences.

TASKS

1 Identify the potential audiences (individuals and groups in Norway, Turkey and beyond) who

Source:
Norwegian Confederation of Trade Unions www.lo.no/language/English/News/?tabid=1735).

---

formal leader power. This model is interesting in that it only recognizes the possibility of 'low' as the smallest amount of power held by a leader – it fails to consider that even formally powerful leaders may face subordinates that can generate considerable power from informal power sources and through the effective use of upward influence tactics.

The conception of power within an organization in this way is generally based on the existence of three features:

1 Human needs, wants and desires that can only be met by the individual engaging with an organization.

2 The existence of resources through which these needs and wants can be met.

3 The existence of a manager who is prepared to act as the go-between in facilitating the 'deal' between the individual and the organization and subsequently managing its realization in practice.

A slightly broader view of power emerges from the work of Pfeffer (1992) which links to the concept of politics (the topic of the next section). Pfeffer essentially argues that power is a commodity for managers and that political activity is the means through which it is obtained and traded. He suggests that power within organizations is needed if managers are to gain influence and advance their department, function, professional capabilities, significance (to the organization), personal standing, wealth and career. In that context power is not just a top-down concept, it reflects a 360-degree process endemic to the experience of managers and nonmanagers alike.

Lower-level employees can also gain and exercise power in a number of ways (Mechanic, 1962). Both individual and collective action (and deliberate inaction) can provide such employees with considerable power. Strikes and other forms of industrial action are intended to demonstrate that employees can force management to concede to their demands if they will not willingly agree to do so.

Foucault and power

For French sociologist and philosopher Michel Foucault, power represented something different from the idea of a commodity. He considered that power was a condition that existed within society as a whole. It is ingrained in the language used and so creates the knowledge accepted by a particular society and reflected in its social practices (Linstead, 1993: p. 63). Power in this context uses discourse (language) to create the rules which in turn create and classify the available knowledge in particular ways. In an organizational context this allows the classification of activity (and people, jobs skill, etc.) into differentiated packages of management and nonmanagement compartments, and so allows the hierarchical framework underlying most organizations and other societal institutions to be perpetuated as legitimate.

Foucault reminds us in his work that the boundaries around the things that we see, understand and take for granted are in fact artificial and socially created. In that sense our stock of knowledge is created for us out of the discourses that exist within society. By creating these boundaries and compartments our attention is channelled in certain directions and it is automatically directed away from other things. We are effectively socialized into seeing and understanding the world in which we live through the discourses that we experience and these are a reflection of the distribution of power as it exists in society. However, once formed, these foundations for behaviour can become difficult to change and so create a power base for resisting attempts to create alternative organizational frameworks. For example, the provision of central government services in any country is achieved through the diverse range of civil service departments. The former British Prime Minister (Tony Blair) has been frequently reported as wanting to encourage 'joined-up government' to blur these boundaries and encourage the more effective delivery of public services. However, Brooks and colleagues (2000: p. 10) describe an instance that shows how difficult this can be to achieve in practice, demonstrating the power of existing and dominant organizational forces.

Foucault demonstrates the association between power and knowledge through a number of examples. In one (Foucault, 1975; outlined in Townley, 1994: p. 5) he describes how the authorities define an individual accused of murdering his mother, sister and brother through the reports of the police, doctors and presiding judge. These reports are then used as the basis for deciding his fate, thereby exercising power over him by formalizing knowledge about the accused. Similar arguments are made in terms of the nature of power within organizational settings that have many similarities to public institutions such as prisons, schools and hospitals. In such institutions the prime objective is to know the subject effectively and fully as a basis for being able to ensure 'that they operate as one wishes' (Foucault, 1977: p. 138). O'Neill describes the outcome of power as a form of socialization in social institutions (including organizations) as 'places where the system can project its conception of the disciplinary society in the reformed criminal, the good worker, student, loyal soldier and committed citizen' (1986: pp. 51–52).

Labour process theory and Lukes' views on power

Labour process theory, already discussed in Chapter 12, reflects the Marxist tradition and describes the nature of work as manipulated by managers who act as agents of capitalist owners to protect themselves from the consequences arising from excessive use of authority. This is done by allowing practices such as collective bargaining and the legal definition of workers' rights to develop, thereby retaining the pre-eminence of capital over labour (Burawoy, 1979). By allowing some of its power to be dissipated, capital ultimately retains effective control over labour activity and use. These approaches encourage workers to continue to support (to give their consent) to the relative imbalance of power in capitalist societies, which is the reason why such management activities have also been called the manufacture of consent, which refers to the manipulation of employee acceptance of control through management practices (such as collective bargaining) although managers retain effective control.

Manufacture of consent
The achievement of employee consent to control by managers through such practices as collective bargaining, although managers retain effective control over labour use, which perpetuates the relative imbalance of power in a capitalist society.

Manipulation
A means of gaining control or social influence over others by methods which might be considered unacceptable, unfair, unreasonable, devious or underhanded.

Lukes (2005) provides a radical perspective on power already briefly alluded to above. He develops a three-dimensional model which can be used to analyse its function within an organizational context. The first dimension (above referred to as *responding*) is suggested to reflect the nature of power as it would be commonly described in much of the literature. In that sense it is a view of power as decision making and the observable and measurable effects of such decisions. It is detected in the behaviour of individuals, who are analysed in terms of the relative degrees of power that they hold in a particular context. Decision making and conflict are common examples of situations that are interpreted and dissected for the relative quantities of power.

15.2 EXTEND
YOUR LEARNING

The second dimension, above referred to as *preventing*, reflects the exercise of power over what might be classed as the agenda. For example, the management of a company may recognize a trade union as the representative body for shop-floor employees. However, the scope of involvement for the trade union (and hence employees) in the decision making and running of the company will be governed by the recognition agreement. Management, therefore, have a mechanism to retain control over the agenda for employee involvement. Even where formal worker representation is formalized (in Germany, for example, legal requirements specify that firms above a specified size need to have a 'Betriebsrat' – a worker council, and a specified number of employee-elected board members for publicly traded companies) it can be influenced and manipulated (see Brannen, 1983, for an example of effective manipulation of worker-directors in British Steel in the 1970s). As a consequence, serious challenges to management power over agenda and decision making can be prevented, and power is exercised both in decisions made and avoided (see also Huzzard, 2005, for a discussion of Scandinavian experiences and union views on works councils).

The third dimension in Lukes' model, above called *shaping*, suggests that concepts of hegemony, incorporation, dependency and inaction can also underpin power. In that context it reflects the essential structural inequalities that exist between groups. For example, management have in their gift the jobs that provide economic and other necessities for the workers, so there is an inevitable asymmetrical power basis to the employment relationship. While one problem with Lukes' model is that it requires the unseen to be incorporated into the analysis, the perspective that Lukes' model provides can help us understand the comprehensive nature of (and the often subtle actions associated with) many aspects of power and its use in organizations (see Fortin and Fellenz, 2008).

POLITICS WITHIN ORGANIZATIONS

Like many other concepts in management and OB, the term 'politics' is also contested and used to convey an array of different meanings. Some see it as negative because it implies underhanded, unofficial, and unsanctioned behaviour and goals, and can thus actively inhibit the effective running of an organization. Another, more positive perspective views politics as a normal part of conflict resolution, inevitable in organizational life. Also, the ethical evaluation of politics is an issue often discussed (e.g., Zanzi and O'Neill, 2001).

It is not possible to offer a definitive ethical or evaluative view of all political behaviour – it can only be judged on a case-by-case basis. For example, managers who seek to advance their own careers by engaging in politicking might engage in some unpleasant tactics. However, assuming that they subsequently perform very well as senior managers, how should they be judged? Clearly, evaluations will reflect the ethical framework adopted to make such decisions. In any case, a major difficulty in making final ethical or functional judgements of political activity is that it is not possible to know the counterfactual, i.e., what would have happened in the same situation but without the political intervention.

One of the earliest works on the subject of politics was that of Machiavelli on the subject of serving princes and other rulers. His work titled *The Prince* was written in fifteenth-century Renaissance Italy when politics was frequently a life-or-death business. Essentially, the argument put forward by Machiavelli was that the ends justified the means and anything was acceptable in the pursuit of the protection of the state. In short, it reflected on the mechanisms and strategies necessary to obtain and hold onto power through political activity.

The negative view of politics imposes a definition that considers it to be outside normal practice, used to enhance existing power or to offset the power of another, with the purpose of achieving self-serving goals (Mayes and Allen, 1977). Thus, from this perspective *political behaviour* in organizations can be viewed as the pursuit by any means of goals that are unsanctioned, and/or the use of unsanctioned means in the pursuit of any goal. Figure 15.2 indicates the extent of political behaviour in organizations based in this view.

The difficulty in practice is that it is not always possible to categorize acts of political behaviour as clearly as this definition might imply. Imagine a situation in which a manager attempts to influence a forthcoming decision by lobbying for support for their preferred plan. Given that such political behaviour may co-determine what is ultimately accepted as the official (and thus sanctioned) goal of the organization, the assessment of the manager's behaviour which initially is considered political behaviour may change because adopting the manager's preferred plan will retrospectively sanction the attempts that led to its adoption. Thus, this view based on official and sanctioned conduct (which refers here to both goals and means) reflects the official view of political behaviour as defined by the currently ruling elite (see the above discussion on unobtrusive power and the subtle ways in which such views can be influenced). Not only are such assessments contested and changing, but determining if a particular goal or approach should be considered wrong or political is difficult to judge.

Figure 15.2 Political behaviour based on classification of sanctioned means and ends

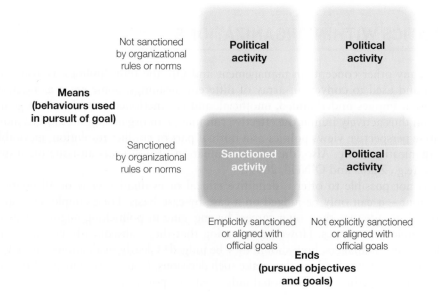

Source: Mayes, BT & Allen, RW (1977) Towards a definition of organizational politics. Academy of Management Review, 2: 672–678. Reprinted with permission.

A different perspective regards political behaviour as an inevitable part of organizations because of the need for individuals and groups to function in a collective context (e.g., Pfeffer, 1981; Mintzberg, 1983). From this perspective, *political behaviour* can be seen as any behaviour organizational members engage in to increase or apply their power. Of course, this broad definition includes many behaviours regardless of their alignment with organizational norms and rules, and regardless of the nature of the goals these behaviours may serve. Thus, many authors include the notion of self-interest to determine what should count as political behaviour. This is useful because it narrows the range of behaviours considered and provides a motivational component that helps to better understand and predict such behaviour. Therefore, the definition we adopt here for our further discussions is that political behaviour refers to *deliberately designed social-influence processes that aim at covertly or overtly advancing the actor's self-interest regardless of its alignment with other parties' interests* (see also Andrews and Kacmar, 2001; Miller and Nicols, 2008).

This view recognizes that organizations are run by many different individuals, departments and interest groupings. All organizational positions and jobs involve interactions with other people and units. For example, the marketing department frequently finds itself in conflict with the production department because of the different perceptions on product design or how best to prioritize, sequence and process customer orders. However, co-operation is needed between these groups when it comes to deciding and aligning production planning and so a balance must be struck. Politics may be one of the means by which such a balance can be achieved. Any formal or informal group can give rise to differentiated interests which lie at the heart of politics in organization.

Most managers recognize the dual nature of politics within an organization. They intuitively understand that it contains elements of both good and bad and that it can be an important, indeed inevitable part of the experience of work. Gandz and Murray (1980) carried out a survey among over 400 managers in an attempt to identify how they perceived politics in their working lives. Table 15.1 reflects some of the more interesting findings from this research.

It is clear from the findings illustrated in Table 15.1 that politics is regarded as common, more prevalent in senior positions and linked with success and promotion. It is also regarded as something that individuals undertake if they have no other source of power and that it is the cause of inefficiency and unhappiness. These findings reflect the duality of politics in its positive and negative connotations. These findings have broadly been confirmed by later studies (e.g., Ashforth and Lee, 1990).

The positive view of organizational politics suggests that it will be rewarded if it is linked to success for the organization in some way. Imagine that a marketing manager of a company were to set out to change the existing power balance of the organization from one which favoured the production department to one which favoured marketing. The strategies adopted might include attempting to get close to the chief executive, using every opportunity to make adverse comments about problems in production and indicating how competitors were gaining market share through the adoption of marketing strategies. Strengthening alliances with departments that might be favourable to the cause of marketing would also be another likely strategy. As a consequence of these strategies, further imagine that a change in the power of the production department occurred as the company became marketing-driven. If as a result the company found its reputation, market share and profits rose, then it is likely that the company would pay more attention to advice from the marketing department in the future and less attention to the needs of production. That is until the marketing department succumbed to the political activity of other departments or failed to deliver success. This can be reflected in diagrammatic form as in Figure 15.3.

Political behaviour
Refers to deliberately designed social-influence processes that aim at covertly or overtly advancing the actor's self-interest regardless of its alignment with other parties' interests. See also political tactics and political skill.

Table 15.1 Perceptions about politics among managers

	Statement	Strong or moderate agreement (per cent)
(a)	The existence of workplace politics is common to most organizations	93.2
(b)	Successful executives must be good politicians	89.0
(c)	The higher up you go in organizations, the more political the climate becomes	76.2
(d)	Only organizationally weak people play politics	68.5
(e)	Organizations free of politics are happier than those where there is a lot of politics	59.1
(f)	You have to be political to get ahead in organizations	69.8
(g)	Politics in organizations are detrimental to efficiency	55.1
(h)	Top management should try to get rid of politics within the organization	48.6
(i)	Politics help organizations function effectively	42.1
(j)	Powerful executives don't act politically	15.7

Source: Gandz, J and Murray, VV (1980), 'The experience of workplace politics', Academy of Management Journal, Vol. 23 pp. 237–51. Reprinted with permission.

Figure 15.3 Organizational politics: impact and success

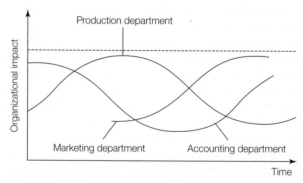

The point made by Figure 15.3 is that from an organizational point of view, rewarding political behaviour (if it delivers success) encourages functions to compete in this way without harming the whole. In effect this approach allows for a process of providing an effective match between the needs of the market and the capability of the organization. Political activity that helps the organization ultimately benefits everyone and, from a managerial perspective, should be allowed free rein. It is the harsh world of the market that is the ultimate judge of internal politics, not the impact on particular individuals or groups. If the market reacts badly to the consequences of political behaviour, then one way or another punishment of the perpetrators will follow. This view of political behaviour could be criticized because it ignores the personal and ethical reasons for and the implications of politics. It is clear from the negative perspective on politics that there are individuals who use it for their own ends, rather than for the benefit of the organization. It can be used to help or harm individuals just as it can be a process of attempting to acquire power to enable decisions to be implemented that could be beneficial to everyone.

POLITICAL STRATEGIES

The use of politics within an organizational setting involves adopting one of three general strategies. These will be discussed in the subsections that follow.

Offensive strategies

These political strategies are effectively initiating behaviours. They represent attacking behaviours intended to produce advantages over others. In military terms these are the equivalent of one army going on the offensive and attacking another before it has time to marshal its defences. An example of this form of political behaviour is described in the Employee Perspective example, in which a senior manager victimized a subordinate manager.

Frequently political behaviour contains a high degree of normal or allowable behaviour but applied in ways that produce a particular end result. In the Employee Perspective example it can be reasonably inferred that James' manager wanted to get rid of him as he was perceived to be a threat to William's position. However, prioritizing work and reallocating resources are all perfectly legitimate practices in running a department. It is the intent behind such actions that indicates a political motive. In reality, James was set up to fail by his boss, who used political strategies and company procedures in a way which cloaked the real intention and allowed it to take place.

There is another type of offensive strategy based on the view that: 'If it is not possible to look good oneself, then make the others look bad.' Such *undermining strategies* cover many different types of behaviour intended to weaken the position of another individual or group. Examples include making disparaging comments about the target at personal or professional levels or recalling and drawing attention to past mistakes as evidence of continued weakness. This can also include 'whispering campaigns' which involve the spreading of rumour often based on half-truth or even total fabrication in order to discredit the target. The spreading of rumour can be a very effective means of undermining other people without the need for evidence to support such assertions.

Defensive strategies

Defensive strategies are those that are not intended to harm others but are destined to prevent harm being done by them. In the previous Employee Perspective example James decided not to defend himself as such but to find another job and leave. He could have attempted to fight fire with fire and engage in a range of political behaviours to protect himself. For example, he could have made a number of alliances with more senior managers who may have been prepared to defend him against his boss. He could have set out to undermine the position of William with other managers. James could also have attempted to set his manager up for a fall by deliberately doing something wrong that would directly reflect on his boss. It should not be inferred that defensive political behaviour is weak or less aggressive than the offensive form.

EMPLOYEE PERSPECTIVE

Getting rid of a subordinate

James was an experienced manager and had a particular expertise in personnel management, having worked for a number of years with one of the major consultancy practices in Australia. He was recruited by a large manufacturing company in Adelaide to act as deputy manager to the head of the personnel department (William) in preparation for the head of department's promotion about 6 months later. It was intended that James would then take over as head of department. The personnel department also had an employee relations manager, training manager and resourcing manager in addition to James and William. William had not worked in any other organization since leaving university some 20 years earlier.

Shortly after James joined the company it became apparent that it was entering a difficult period and that restructuring was a real possibility. It was at that time that the head of department's behaviour and attitude changed towards a number of people including James. It had become apparent that William was not going to be promoted under the changing circumstances facing the company and therefore James would have to remain as the deputy manager. James and a number of other managers in the department had expectations of career development and job moves and were therefore a potential threat to William's position.

Some of the actions that William took included deliberately holding back the start date for jobs that James was to undertake and reallocating staff and other resources away from supporting him. Performance was, however, still to be judged against the original objectives and timescales for the work allocated to James. Eventually, after about 7 months, it was time to review James's salary. William produced an annual report that claimed that James was underperforming, incompetent and should be downgraded, perhaps even dismissed. Such performance certainly did not justify receiving any pay increase that year. James, having suspected what was to happen, had found another job and so tendered his resignation on the spot.

TASKS

1 How could James have reacted to the situation other than by resigning, and what might the consequences of that be?

2 What defence tactics or approaches might James have been able to use in this situation? How successful do you think they would have been?

3 What does this example tell you about political behaviour among managers?

It can be just as effective and equally nasty in execution. It is the intention, not the content that differentiates it.

Neutral strategies

This approach to political behaviour reflects a stance that does not actively engage in it for either of the two purposes so far described. Rather, it reflects an actively protectionist approach to politics that attempts to keep out of political battles but one which will defend itself if absolutely necessary. It is an appeasing approach to the existence of politics. It is easiest to use offensive politics against a neutral strategy as it takes considerable pressure to begin to force the other party to retaliate. James could be described as adopting a neutral strategy in response to his manager's attack. He did not defend himself other than by attempting to do the best job that he could and by attempting to be considered as a nonthreatening subordinate by his manager. In the end, rather than take on William in a battle, he side-stepped the problem by leaving the organization.

USING POLITICAL BEHAVIOUR

Some of the influencing tactics identified and discussed in the previous section on influence can be used for the purpose of political activities. In addition to deploying influencing tactics and using influence mechanisms, a broad range of political tactics exist. Political tactics are *approaches that combine power generation and influencing tactics in concerted ways to orchestrate influence attempts aimed at getting other people to accept or take decisions, viewpoint or courses of action favoured by the initiator.* Moorhead and Griffin (1992) bring together the work of a number of other writers in order to identify the main techniques and tactics associated with political behaviour. Table 15.2 lists the main techniques identified (Zanzi and O'Neill, 2001, provide a more comprehensive list of 25 tactics). The following sections briefly consider each of the main techniques.

Political tactics
These are approaches that combine power generation and influencing tactics in concerted ways to orchestrate influence attempts aimed at getting other people to accept or take decisions, viewpoint or courses of action favoured by the initiator. See also political behaviour and political skill.

Control of information

The ability to determine who has access to what information provides a particularly powerful opportunity to influence events. Decision making requires information, and access to comprehensive and up-to-date information provides important means to construct and deliver impactful interventions. Similarly, preventing, limiting, or timing others' access to such information also represents an effective political technique.

Control of communication channels

Like the control of information, the ability to control who has access to whom and who communicates with whom, can significantly influence events. During the 1960s, 1970s and early 1980s most trade unions regarded communication with employees as their prerogative. In situations where particularly militant trade union representatives were present, threats of strike action would be used if managers proposed addressing their workforce directly. In such situations whoever actually communicated with the workforce was likely to put their particular perspective on the message being communicated. Such trade union monopolies on access has become rare through the adoption of joint or parallel consultation and communication processes. However, this technique is still relevant and effective in organizations and used, for example, through selected invitations to meetings and selective distribution lists for reports or memos.

Table 15.2 Political tactics and techniques

Controlling information
Control of communication channels
Using outside specialists
Control of the work and/or meetings agenda
Game playing
Impression and image management
Creating coalitions
Control of decision-making criteria

Source: Adapted from Moorhead, G and Griffin RW (1992) *Organizational Behaviour*, 3rd edn, Houghton Mifflin, Boston, MA.

Use of outside specialists

The use of external specialists can be a powerful lever to ensuring that one's point of view is favoured. Selecting particular consultants or experts whose predispositions are known or who can be influenced to favour or support particular points of view is a common approach. Similarly, creation of terms of reference and briefing of consultants can help ensure that they are likely to deliver favoured findings and recommendations. The alignment of external, supposedly more independent and objective experts to one's position can add significant weight in internal discussions and decision-making processes. Most consultants would be keenly aware of such dynamics, yet their dependence on follow-up contracts will make them more vulnerable to such influence. Many consultancy firms and professional bodies identify such behaviour by internal and external consultants as unethical. Writers such as Gilbert (2003) offer guidelines to consultants and experts for managing such potential political manipulation.

Control over work and meeting agendas

Being able to influence events directly is another useful political technique. The individual who determines the agenda for a meeting determines what can (and frequently of more significance what cannot) be discussed – a very visible example of the 'preventing' approach to exercising power (Fortin and Fellenz, 2008; Lukes, 2005). This allows the direction of decision making to be determined and channelled to the advantage of the person setting the agenda. For example, the role of technology in change programmes can be used politically to the advantage of some groups (Koch, 2001). A related political technique is to control the minutes or other written records of meetings, as this often provides considerable discretion over what is recorded and - more importantly - how the content of the record is phrased. Naturally it is usual for the minutes to be verified at a subsequent meeting but any subsequent change is again open for discussion and debate that skilled political operators can exploit.

Game playing

There are individuals who appear to enjoy the 'sport' of playing politics just to see what happens and to demonstrate their ability to control events. The Employee perspective panel earlier described the events surrounding James and his eventual departure from the organization. The department manager in that situation was playing games in that he was using established procedure and practice to achieve a particular objective that would not have been officially sanctioned. As an individual he also enjoyed engaging in political activity as he tried similar 'games' with other people and his colleagues. He was, however, ultimately dismissed when this behaviour became too frequent.

Impression and image management

This represents a less direct approach to politics as it involves creating an image that in turn could be expected to influence events. Simple examples include attempting to become associated with successful projects or to distance oneself from failing ones. It is not unusual for a manager to sit on the sidelines of a particular programme of work and to suddenly seek to take a high profile near to completion when success is more certain. Claiming major involvement in particular projects is another common example of overstating reality in order to enhance one's reputation. Of course, this must be done carefully, as a number of people will know the truth about such claims. Once exposed as false claims, they can undermine every other claim made by that individual. Bromley (1993) provides an analysis of many aspects of impression management which collectively demonstrate the complexity of these political and psychological dynamics.

Creating coalitions

Political alliances are another means of achieving desired objectives. Imagine a situation in which a personnel manager wishes to introduce a new payment system into a company. The sales manager may not see any benefit or problems with such a scheme and so may be neutral towards it. The production manager may be in favour of the new scheme if higher productivity and reduced cost is a likely result. The finance director may be openly hostile towards the idea as it would create additional work for his department. The employees may also be against the idea because higher productivity could result in job losses and having to work harder. Clearly the personnel manager needs to ensure that all the managers are supportive of the plan before attempting to convince the employees of its merits. The finance director is presumably more senior to the other managers and as a result would carry 'more weight' in collective decision making. Perhaps if the sales manager could be persuaded actively to support the scheme and ways could be found to lessen the burden on the finance department, then open hostility might be reduced. The personnel manager would probably begin to lobby the sales manager for support, perhaps using the argument that the higher productivity achieved would benefit the sales department through pricing and delivery benefits. This together with a scheme redesign to reduce administrative requirements might be enough to sway the finance director to either support the scheme, or at least not reject it.

Taken to an extreme this approach to political behaviour can be little more than 'horse trading'. This approach to politics attempts to operate on the basis of buying cooperation for past favours or seeking support in return for promises of future help on matters of value to the courted individual. At an organizational level this approach reflects the cartel approach to fixing markets in favour of particular suppliers.

Control over decision-making criteria

It is sometimes possible for a manager to set down the criteria against which decisions will be made and in so doing they do not have to be directly involved in order to influence the outcome. It is not uncommon for industrial relations specialists facing the annual negotiation round with the trade unions to initially hold meetings with other managers to determine the negotiating strategy. In doing so, it could be that a chief executive would set out in very clear terms what they expect to happen and in effect write the script for the negotiators. Clearly, in this situation very little scope is available to the negotiation team to respond creatively to the dynamics of the situation and create a settlement acceptable to all sides. The 'dead-hand' of the chief executive rests over the situation and effectively controls events in absentia. In a more general context such approaches can allow a leader to claim noninvolvement in a situation, distancing themselves from events both physically and psychologically while in reality retaining control.

STOP & CONSIDER

'The above list of political tactics is all well and good, but when faced with situations that involve potentially damaging (at a personal or professional level) outcomes the only practical political tactic is to get the opposition before they get you by fair means or foul!' Discuss this viewpoint in relation to the practical, professional and ethical issues that it raises.

MANAGING POLITICAL BEHAVIOUR

The degree to which it is possible to manage political behaviour in others is difficult to specify. It depends on many factors. For example, the style of management within the organization can determine the level and volume of politicking that takes place (see Table 15.3 for a list of factors associated with increased political behaviour in organizations). The personality of individuals is also likely to influence their predisposition for playing games and other forms of politics. The skill level and networks of the individuals concerned can also influence events. Indeed' Butcher and Clarke (1999) make the point that political activity is central to making things happen in a change process and so should be taught as a mainstream management discipline.

Table 15.3 Factors associated with increased political behaviour in organizations

Organizational factors associated with increased political behaviour
Very limited or declining resources in the organization
Threat of layoffs, downsizing or other decline-related occurrences
Reducing profits, losses or other indicators of low organizational or unit performance
Unclear or contested roles and responsibilities
Ambiguous or negotiable performance evaluation criteria
High expectations for individual or unit performance
Competitive ('fixed pie') reward pool
Change in reward distribution procedures or criteria
Majority-driven (democratic) decision making
Low trust among members
Competitive and/or self-serving culture
Political behaviour by high-profile organizational members and role models
Permissive cultural or social context and ineffective internal and external enforcement mechanisms

Individual factors associated with increased political behaviour
Personality traits and individual differences such as: ● high self-monitoring ● social dominance orientation (see Sidanius and Pratto, 2001) ● internal locus of control ● high nPow (Need for Power) ● high level of Machiavellinism (Christie and Geis, 1970).
High levels of individual political skills
Individual agendas and goals that are not aligned, or incompatible, with organizational goals

In fact, political skill is an area that has received growing research attention in recent years (e.g., Ferris *et al.*, 2005a, b; Ferris *et al.*, 2000; Ferris *et al.*, 2007). It has been linked to many variables such as leader effectiveness (Ahearn *et al.*, 2004; Douglas and Ammeter, 2004), career success (Jawahar *et al.*, 2008; Perrewé and Nelson, 2004; Todd *et al.*, 2009), individual and team performance (Ahearn *et al.*, 2004; Jawahar *et al.*, 2008), lower stress (Perrewé *et al.*, 2005), and impression management effectiveness (Harris *et al.*, 2007). Political skill is defined as '*The ability to effectively understand others at work, and to use such knowledge to influence others to act in ways that enhance one's personal and/or organizational objectives*' (Ferris *et al.*, 2005a: p. 127) Individuals high in political skills are highly effective networkers and interpersonal influencers, can easily demonstrate apparent sincerity, and are socially astute (Ferris *et al.*, 2005b).

Ferris and his colleagues (Ferris *et al.*, 2007) have developed a model explaining the effects of political skills on the individual, on others in interpersonal relationships, and on groups and the organization (see Figure 15.4). This model helps us to understand the differential impact that political skill can have at these different levels of analysis and specifies some of the relevant processes by which these outcomes come about. Ferris and his colleagues point out that political skill can be learned and developed, especially in and through mentoring relationships that help individuals recognize and make sense of political dynamics in the organizational environment in which they operate.

Managers are inevitably in competition with each other for resources and power. There are never enough resources to meet every possible demand within an organization. Most managers feel that they could make a positive contribution to the organization given autonomy and unlimited resources. However, such utopian conditions do not exist and therefore rationing processes must exist. Rationing implies deciding between competing options for allocating scarce resources and finding ways to prioritize alternative options. This creates a context where managers must justify proposed actions and find ways to gain support for their plans. Politicking can be used to influence these processes and increase the probability of success. Browning and James (2003) offer general advice on how to deal with and manage politics in an organization from the two different perspectives of getting involved and trying to stay above it all. They provide an illuminating array of techniques and practices that could be followed with more or less light-hearted or serious enthusiasm. Politics can be a high stakes 'game' at senior levels in large and significant organizations, as is evident in the Management in Action example involving the additional complication of family rivalry and feuding.

Political skill
Defined as the ability to effectively understand others at work, and to use such knowledge to influence others to act in ways that enhance one's personal and/or organizational objectives. See also political tactics and political behaviour.

Figure 15.4 The impact of individual political skill at different levels of analysis in organizations

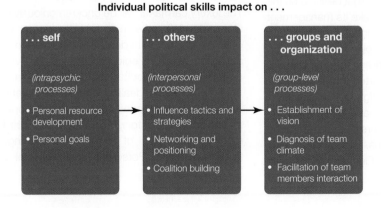

Source: Adapted from Ferris, GR, Treadway, DC, Perrewé, PL, Brouer, RL, Douglas, C & Lux, S (2007). Political skill in organizations. Journal of Management, 33: 290–320. Reprinted with permission of Sage Publishers.

MANAGEMENT IN ACTION

VW and Porsche: Germany's unending automotive saga

The problems of the Porsche-Piëch automobile dynasty clearly demonstrate how business works, particularly in relation to money, power and intrigue involving both business leaders and politicians. It would appear that the business world contains many brilliant but unpredictable people (for example VW godfather Ferdinand Piëch); individuals who clearly overestimate their own abilities (for example Porsche boss Wendelin Wiedeking); and politicians prepared to capitalize from the mistakes of others (for example Lower Saxony's premier Christian Wulff) – the state owns a significant holding of VW shares.

Wiedeking's dream was to lead the world's largest carmaker by taking over Volkswagen even though it was 15 times bigger than Porsche – and without the cash to do it being immediately available. He secretly bought VW shares but failed to acquire the necessary 75 per cent to ensure total control. The price meant that his career as a leading auto executive might be over! However he had achievements to be proud of – he resurrected Porsche – turning a company ready for the scrap yard into a valuable brand. But he was tempted by 'casino capitalism' and was consumed by the desire to create the greatest deal of his career – plus the wealth and kudos that would result. However, he underestimated the 60 members of the Porsche-Piëch family (owners of the business), who turned away from the deal and slowly abandoned him

COULD IT HAVE BEEN AVOIDED?

The family-run Porsche business might be listed on the stock market, but that doesn't make its management transparent or ensure effective control. The Piëch and Porsche families who ultimately own it, failed to stop the company's executives from engaging in financial acrobatics. It is also widely reported that the cousins Ferdinand Piëch (VW) and Wolfgang Porsche (Porsche) engaged in a family feud that affected everyone from the VW and Porsche workers councils up to the highest levels of German politics. Events that clearly demonstrate the darker side of Germany's family-run

companies that are supposed to be models of sustainability and discretion.

Porsche was essentially operating as a hedge fund – simply making cars as a sideline – speculating with money it didn't have – tapping into a network of 37 lenders for loans of $13.7bn to finance its purchase of VW shares. By 2008 Porsche had pulled off one of the greatest share killings in a coup that left some of the world's largest hedge funds nursing combined losses of around $20bn. As Porsche was quietly building a 74 per cent stake in VW, the hedge funds were betting that the share price would fall. When it became known that Porsche had been acquiring so many shares the price soared 400 per cent in 2 days – from about €200 per share to more than €900 – leaving Porsche with a huge profit and the hedge funds – some based in London – with losses that could drive them into bankruptcy. On the other hand, for Porsche the profits from its VW share dealings were larger than the company's entire turnover!

The global financial crisis dealt a hammer blow to Porsche's dealings in VW stock, with the company being pushed almost to bankruptcy. Family feuds and alliances, along with political pressure, all conspired to prevent the deal from being completed. Wolfgang Porsche is the leading Porsche at Porsche; his cousin Ferdinand Piëch (they are both grandsons of the founder of Porsche – Ferdinand Porsche) is chair of the supervisory board at the VW Group. They have spent the past year trying to manoeuvre a majority of shareholding family members – as well as powerful politicians and union leaders – into one camp or the other. The outcome is that the flashy Porsche will now become a modest Volkswagen. The luxury carmaker will be unceremoniously parked alongside VW's other nine brands in order to rid it of some €10 billion in debt. For Porsche fans it's an autobahn wreck of epic proportions, but VW supporters also have doubts about the situation.

This process of dealing, double dealing and family feuds has been one of the great soap operas of recent business history. At a recent all-night board meeting, the CEO of Porsche, Wiedeking, was forced to resign. Porsche's chief financial officer,

Holger Härter, also resigned with immediate effect. They will also give up their positions on the supervisory boards of Volkswagen and Audi. Porsche said in a statement that Wiedeking will receive a severance package of €50 million. Wiedeking, whose contract was to run until 2012, said in a personal statement that half of that money will go to a social foundation. He had been one of Germany's highest-paid executives after turning the company around in the 1990s. He always thought he could do a better job of running VW than the VW bosses could – based on his track record of turning Porsche from a hopeless case when he took over in 1992 into the most profitable car company on earth.

Things are unlikely to calm down even though the feuding parties are now sitting down together at the same board meetings. The state of Lower Saxony won't be shy about using its legally sanctioned veto power over VW plans and decisions. New shareholders from Qatar (with a 17 per cent stake in VW) will also want to have a significant say in what happens. Wolfgang Porsche won't quickly forget that his cousin Ferdinand Piëch helped prepare Wiedeking's precipitous fall. And Piëch will know just how to protect himself from his family's attempts at revenge. The two companies aim to complete the merger by the middle of 2011, according to Christian Wulff, governor of Lower Saxony, as he expressed optimism that an agreement in principle could be presented during a supervisory board meeting on 13 August 2009.

TASKS

1 'Management is a political process. Senior managers only fail when they get the politics wrong.' To what extent does the VW/Porsche example above support this statement? Justify your answer using material from this chapter.

2 To what extent and in what ways does this example also illustrate power and influence behaviours among the stakeholders?

3 To what extent and in what ways does the family ownership aspect of this example complicate the inevitable power, influence and political aspects of management?

Sources:
VW and Porsche: Germany's unending automotive saga. Published 25 July 2009. Online at: http://www.thelocal.de/opinion/20090725-20817.html (accessed August 2009).
Porsche pulls off one of the greatest share killings of all time in $20bn 'sting'. Wednesday, 29 October 2008. Accessed August 2009 at: http://www.belfasttelegraph.co.uk/business/business-news/porsche-pulls-off-one-of-the-greatest-share-killings-of-all-time-in-20bn-sting-14018784.html. Porsche borrows 10 billion Euros to buy VW. By Jonathon Ramsey on 12 Jul 2007 at: http://www.autoblog.com/2007/07/12/porsche-borrows-10-billion-euros-to-buy-vw/ (accessed August 2009).
VW tucks into Porsche. Posted by Paul Horrell on Thursday 23, July 2009 at: http://foreman.blogs.topgear.com/2009/07/23/vw-tucks-into-porsche/ (accessed August 2009).
Porsche CEO Wiedeking Resigns. Accessed August 2009 at: http://www.spiegel.de/international/business/0,1518,637760,00.html.
VW prepares to take over Porsche Thursday, 23 July 2009. Accessed August 2009 at: http://news.bbc.co.uk/1/hi/business/8165524.stm.

In order to control and minimize the harmful effects associated with politics, it is necessary to find ways to encourage competition without allowing hidden agendas to flourish. Increasing transparency (e.g., by specifying in advance how decisions will be made), accountability (e.g., by requiring decision making about resource use to be documented as is required under Freedom of Information legislation in many countries), and procedural fairness (e.g., by establishing fair procedures for resource allocation, see Chapter 16) are some of the ways in which this can be achieved. Also, by separating the evaluation of resource allocation from issues associated with performance evaluation and promotion, political behaviour can be further limited. Sending clear signals that negative political tactics are not tolerated, dealing severely with obvious cases and encouraging examples to be openly discussed are other means of minimizing such activities and their impact. Such active and visible ways of curbing negative aspects of political behaviour are important because even the perception of organizational politics can have profound implications in organizations (e.g., Ferris *et al.*, 1996). Employees frequently use such perceptions as a heuristic in judging the overall character of the organization and its agents (i.e., managers) (Kiewitz *et al.*, 2009). Moreover, the emotional and attitudinal reactions to perceptions of politics lead to negative behavioural reactions (Rosen *et al.*, 2009), especially for those low in political skill (Brouer *et al.*, 2006). Browning (2003) suggests 10 ways to manage office politics (see Table 15.4).

15.3 EXTEND
YOUR LEARNING

Table 15.4 Ten tips for managing the office politics

• Be transparent in your actions
• Communicate with all sides
• Network extensively
• Keep well informed
• Identify and watch the politicians
• Never get personal
• Maintain good upwards contacts
• Anticipate and manage the others' reactions
• Be clearly good at your job
• Get it in writing

CONCLUSIONS

Power, influence and politics are important aspects of OB. They are integral to organizations and inseparable from the needs, aspirations and inclinations of the individuals that work within them. Power is endemic to the employment relationship. Employers have work that they need done; individuals need to work for economic, psychological and social reasons. Interestingly, managers are also employees and subject to these same pressures, but within the particular context of acting for the largely absent owners of the organization. Political behaviour in an organization has many functions ranging from the inevitable attempts to influence the outcome of the competition for scarce resources and promotion opportunities that arise, to the game playing and attempts to gain advantage by means other than capability, superior job performance or experience. In their darker versions, power, influence and politics can also be used to undermine or damage colleagues, subordinates and even superiors. As with most other aspects of OB, they contain the seeds of danger and risk that can cause damage to either individuals or the organization if they are not handled carefully and with respect.

Now to summarize this chapter in terms of the relevant Learning Objectives:

• **Assess the differences and similarities between the concepts of power, influence and authority.**

Power relates to the ability to get other people to do what they might not otherwise do. Power contains such concepts as manipulation, force and influence. For example, managers might seek to manipulate employee behaviour by not being completely truthful about a situation in order to gain co-operation. Force might be used by threatening to close the company if employees do not scale back demands for higher pay. These examples illustrate the exercise of different forms of influence which is the process of exercising power. The use of power implies the application of a measure of force or coercion in influencing the behaviour of others. Authority notionally reflects status within an organization and is consequently a reflection of where formal power lies. Employees generally accept that managers have the right (authority) to exercise power over them in a work context. It is an acceptance by employees that they will subjugate themselves to the wishes of those given authority (formal power) over them. Of course this authority-based power has limitations and an employee pushed too far will react negatively and reject the attempt to control their behaviour.

• **Explain the major perspectives on power as experienced within an organization.** There were three major perspectives on power that were introduced. The first was the traditional view which described power as a natural function of the formal position in the hierarchy and as a natural part of the leadership process. It also implies that power is a commodity that could be traded, acquired, divested or squandered depending upon the circumstances and individual behaviour. It also has close links with organizational politics as the means through which power could be acquired, lost or traded. The second perspective was based on the work of Foucault. In his view language was the means through which boundaries between the 'things' taken for granted in society are created and which reinforced the relative position of 'rulers' – defining where power lies. He also suggested that the authorities in a social system spend considerable effort to 'know' their subjects, because such knowledge allows more effective control. The third perspective on power was the labour process and Lukes' views. The basis of this approach is a three-dimensional model of increasingly unobstrusive forms of power (measurable effects, agenda aspects, reaction modes).

- **Discuss the sources of power within an organization.** The sources of power that exist within an organization include coercive, reward, legitimate, expert, information, referent and negative. Coercive power emerges in situations in which force is used (or threatened) to make someone do something that they would not otherwise do. Reward power is about achieving control by offering a benefit or reward in return for their submission. Legitimate power is the acquiescence by an individual that someone else has the right to exert power over them. Expert power is the ability to exert control because of the knowledge or ability that an individual has. Information power refers to the way that access to information enhances the ability to exercise power. Referent power is achieved through the force of a charismatic personality, a characteristic which people tend to follow willingly. Negative power is the ability to achieve some measure of control or influence by not doing or withdrawing something.

- **Outline the concept of organizational politics.** Organizational politics represents one way in which power can be obtained and retained. It reflects activity intended to influence events and make particular occurrences more or less likely to happen. In an organizational context it can be described as having either positive or negative connotations. For example, it can reflect the means though which power, control and conflict can be managed in order to bring about particular results. If, as a consequence of such behaviour, the result is beneficial for the organization and individuals within it, then it is likely that reward will follow. If, however, it does not bring benefit, then it is likely to result in 'punishment', perhaps by loosing influence. In positive terms politics can be viewed as the means through which each function (and individual) seeks to maximize their contribution and influence in the dynamics of the organization and its environment. In its negative guise politics is viewed as outside acceptable practice and as such something that can only create difficulty and conflict within the organization. The problem in practice is that politics can contain elements of both positive and negative perspectives at the same time. It is not always easy to judge what is happening in any specific situation. The chapter discuss the offensive, defensive and neutral strategies that can be adopted with regard to political activity. The chapter also discusses devices such as information control and the use of outside specialists that can be used politically.

- **Understand how political behaviour can be managed within an organization.** The management of political behaviour within an organization is difficult as it involves such a fundamental part of much management and interpersonal activity. For example, managers are in competition with each other for resources and the ability to influence organizational direction and functioning. That competition, if not appropriately channelled and managed, can lead to political behaviour being used in a negative way in order to attempt to shape decisions. Consequently, the decision-making processes in an organization need to be clear and open so that hidden agendas and behind-the-scenes activity are minimized and brought out into the open. In essence the management of politics requires that its negative practice is not rewarded and that when discovered, it is punished. Some of the approaches discussed in relation to handling conflict and power within an organization are also relevant to the management of political behaviour.

DISCUSSION QUESTIONS

1 Can compliance as an employee response to the application of power by a boss create an effective organization? Justify your answer.

2 The inevitable power imbalance in the employment relationship leads to employee exploitation and the creation of self-protection groups such as trade unions. Why does this power imbalance exist? Is it inevitable and how might it be limited?

3 Describe the main sources of organizational power and provide examples of each from an organization with which you are familiar.

4 'Influence in an organizational context is no more than the use of the iron fist in a velvet glove.' To what extent do you agree (or disagree) with this statement and why?

5 Identify the differences and similarities between the concepts of power and influence.

6 Management is ultimately about acquiring and using power successfully. To what extent is this correct and therefore should it be a major component of management training and development programmes?

7 Managers must compete for scarce resources. Political behaviour can influence decisions. In what ways might it be possible to encourage competition while minimizing the potentially harmful effects of political behaviour?

8 'Management is at its heart a political not a technical activity.' Discuss this statement.

9 'Understanding organizational politics represents the biggest challenge for every manager.' To what extent and why do you agree with this statement?

10 'Politics is a process which cannot be eliminated from an organization but is not central to achieving its objectives; therefore it should be ignored in running a business.' Discuss this statement.

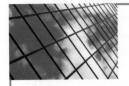

CASE STUDY

Mixing the sexes

This case study actually occurred in a large financial organization based in the UK and was told to one of the authors by a female employee who worked there at the time. The company employed many thousands of employees across the country and at one particular site there were 500 people employed on a range of administrative and clerical activities not involving customer contact.

One male employee was a transsexual and was undergoing a programme of gender realignment to transform him into the female that he desperately wanted to be. He had worked at the company for about 5 years and had always been a good worker, with a good attendance record and excellent performance appraisal assessments – management had no cause for complaint with regard to his work. His situation was widely known by male and female employees

and managers in the company and there had been no hints or record of problems with or complaints by his colleagues. As the treatment progressed he began to dress as a woman and wore a wig, so in outward appearance he looked like the woman he was becoming. The final part of the treatment was the surgery needed to remove the last physical evidence of being a male and to ensure that his transformation to being female was as complete as it was possible to be.

It was at the time that he began to dress as a woman that problems began to emerge. The issue that triggered the 'problem' was use of the toilets at work. Now being in outward appearance a female, the individual wanted to use the ladies toilet, rather than the men's toilet as he had done previously. The employee concerned started going into the ladies toilet without first clearing their intentions with management or other employees. A number of the other female employees reacted badly to this and complained to management as soon as they became aware of what was happening. They demanded that the employee concerned be told in no uncertain way that 'he' was not to use the ladies toilet and should use the men's facilities as he was a male, irrespective of how he dressed.

The senior management of the site asked for support from the human resource management department and the employee was called into the office for a meeting. The employee explained the position, which of course management were already aware of and said that as he was almost completely a woman it was inappropriate for him to continue to use the men's toilet facilities. In a few weeks, after the final surgery had been performed, he would be living completely as a woman and then have the right to use the ladies toilets in any case. The senior managers and the human resources manager then went to see the female employees and said that in their view the employee should use the ladies toilets as this was more appropriate to the situation. The women refused to accept this and demanded that 'he' be prevented from going in the ladies toilets permanently. The women threatened to go to the trade union and to the police, press and anyone else who might take up their case if management would not take appropriate (in their mind) action.

Management did not know what to do to resolve the situation. The transsexual employee refused to continue to use the male toilets and the females refused to let

him use theirs. The only suggestion that management came up with (after much discussion with the human resource manager) was that the transsexual employee be told to use the unisex disabled person's toilet. This was acceptable to the women, but unacceptable to the employee concerned as 'he' made the point that 'she' was not disabled. Several days of often heated discussion with and between all the parties took place but with no real progress being made. Senior management within the company then took the decision that the transsexual employee would have to be dismissed in the interests of harmony among the female employees. Consequently the transsexual employee was dismissed with 3 months money in lieu of notice.

TASKS

1 Identify the power, influence and political perspectives on this situation.
2 Why do you think the managers and human resources department responded to this situation as they did?
3 Were managers right to dismiss the employee or could/should another solution been found to the situation? If so, what was it and how should it have been achieved?
4 Could the problem have been anticipated and therefore avoided? If so, how?

FURTHER READING

Buchanan, D. and Badham, R. (1999) *Power, Politics and Organizational Change: Winning the Turf Game*, Chichester: Sage. Reviews the relationship between the themes indicated in the title and so provides a direct link between theory and practice in this area.

Cooper, C., Einarsen, S., Hoel, H. and Zapf, D. (eds) (2002) *Bullying and Emotional Abuse in the Workplace: International Perspectives in Research and Practice*, London: Taylor and Francis. This text looks at one aspect of politics and conflict which is also relevant to power and control, that of bullying at work. The edited work considers the research approach in Europe which emphasizes the 'mobbing' or 'bullying' approach and also that emerging in the USA, which emphasizes 'emotional abuse' and 'mistreatment' perspectives.

Jay, A. (1987) *Management and Machiavelli*, revised edn, London: Hutchinson Business. A humorous

text which considers many aspects associated with power and authority in management. It does not take Machiavelli's work specifically as its basis, but his spirit is evident. A translation of Machiavelli's original work, which is very accessible and available as a 1981 Penguin book, is also well worth reading.

Jermier, J.M., Knights, D. and Nord, W.R. (eds) (1994) *Resistance and Power in Organizations*, London: Routledge. Provides a review of how attempts to use power as a basis of control inevitably leads to resistance in one form or another. It is grounded in the labour process perspective and attempts to interpret the arguments from the perspectives implied by that model.

Lukes, S. (2005) *Power: A radical view* (2nd edn), Palgrave Macmillan. Comprehensive discussion of the dynamics of power in society and politics – not focused on organizations and management per se but highly relevant nevertheless.

Mintzberg, H. (1983), *Power in and around organizations*. Englewood Cliffs, NJ: Prentice Hall. Insightful discussion of issues related to power.

Monks, R.A.G. and Minow, N. (1991) *Power and Accountability*, London: HarperCollins. This book attempts to show some of the consequences of power when large organizations can operate without the effective means of holding them accountable for their actions. It is a chilling reminder of the many ways that power can be abused and trust violated.

Pfeffer, J. (1992) *Managing with power: Politics and influence in organizations*, Boston, MA: Harvard Business School Press. Classic contribution to the issue of organizational politics and power.

Vigoda-Gadot, E. (2003) *How Political Dynamics affect Employee Performance in Modern Worksites*, Cheltenham: Edward Elgar. This text reviews a broad spectrum of perspectives on organizational politics in order to identify the impact of employee performance in the broadest sense of the term.

COMPANION WEBSITE

Online teaching and learning resources

Visit the companion website for Organizational Behaviour and Management 4th edition at: http://www
.cengage.co.uk/martinfellenz to find valuable further teaching and learning material. For full details,
see 'About the website' at the start of the book.

CHAPTER SIXTEEN

RELATIONSHIPS, FAIRNESS AND TRUST

©sweetym/istock

LEARNING OBJECTIVES

After studying this chapter and working through the associated OB in Action panels, Discussion Questions and Case Study you should be able to:

- Assess the major behaviours identified in this chapter that are suggested to build and maintain relationships.

- Explain social exchange theory.

- Discuss the psychological contract and its significance for relationships within organizations.

- Outline the meaning of organizational justice and discuss its relevance to how fairness might be understood within an organization context.

- Understand what trust is and how it can be created and managed in an organizational context.

INTRODUCTION

Typically, people are seen as the basic building blocks of organizations. However, it is the interactions between and among individuals that create the stable patterns we can observe and ultimately experience as organizations. Thus, relationships among organizational members lie at the heart of virtually all phenomena we have discussed in this book. In this chapter, we will further explore the nature of relationships, including the psychological contract that defines and is defined by the employment relationship, and the networks of relationships that exist in organizations. We will also discuss the closely related topic of fairness and justice perceptions in organizations and explore their role in interactions in organizations as well as their implications for people management in organizations. Finally, we will consider trust in organizations, how it develops and – most importantly – how it can be rebuilt if it has been lost.

RELATIONSHIPS IN ORGANIZATIONS

Formal relationships
Determined by formal roles and include authority relationships, workflow connections and task interdependencies, peer relationships in formal groups and units, and communication linkages. See also informal relationships.

Informal relationships
These include personal relationships among friends and acquaintances, as well as other forms of informal relationships due to physical proximity, joint membership in informal groups, or other sources of repeated interactions. See also formal relationships.

Interactions among organizational members and the relationships that ensue between them are defining aspects of organizations (e.g., Katz and Kahn, 1978; Weick, 1979). These relationships can be based on formal arrangements but often also arise out of informal contact and interactions among members. Formal relationships are determined by roles and include authority relationships (e.g., superior–subordinate relationships), workflow connections and task interdependencies (e.g., internal customer–supplier relationships), peer relationships in formal groups and units, and communication linkages (e.g., representatives, liaison roles). Informal relationships, in contrast, include personal relationships among friends and acquaintances, as well as other forms of informal relationships due to physical proximity (e.g., shared office space), joint membership in informal groups (e.g., leader–follower relationships in groups), or other sources of repeated interactions (e.g., regular contact due to similar lunchtime breaks). Despite (or maybe because of) the immense importance of relationships in organizations, their role and influence is mainly studied as part of other management and OB phenomena such as group dynamics, negotiation, conflict, leadership, communication, and many more. In fact, the formal study of the nature and role of relationships in organizations is pursued separately across different areas of OB which has 'led to a fragmented understanding of the nature, meaning and impact of work relationships' (Kahn, 2007: p. 190).

Relationships are important conduits of information and meaning in organizations (e.g., Bryan *et al.*, 2007; Hill and Carley, 2008). Close relationships between people can increase the partners' psychological safety and increase the flow of information, with subsequent learning benefits for the individuals involved as well as their organizations (Carmeli *et al.*, 2009; Carmeli and Gittell, 2009). Moreover, recent research also indicates that social support and positive relationships at work can directly influence beneficial physiological reactions including fortification and improved functioning of cardiovascular, immune and neuroendocrine (hormone) systems (e.g., Dutton and Ragins, 2007; Heaphy and Dutton, 2008; Uchino, 2004). Heaphy and Dutton (2008) argue that the physiological benefits of such positive social interactions increase both physiological resourcefulness and physical health, which in turn increase work engagement and improve recovery from work-related strain and stress. The Management in Action panel provides one example where an attempt to create a closer working relationship did not produce the expected outcome.

MANAGEMENT IN ACTION

It's only fair to give the customer what they want!

Nathan was 55-years-old and the Managing Director of a meat processing company with a number of factories located across the North of England and Scotland. He had worked for the company for about 20 years, being Managing Director for the last 10 of them. It was a very large company for the industry, employing about 2500 people across 6 sites (including head office). Essentially each meat processing factory specialized in one type of meat (pork, chicken or lamb) and at each, the live animals were slaughtered and converted into pre-packaged meat as required by the order requirements from various customers. The company dealt with each of the big four supermarket chains in the UK, but one of these was by far the largest customer, accounting for 35 per cent of the company output by weight and about 40 per cent of its total sales revenue.

It was not uncommon for Nathan to visit each of the supermarket head offices to meet with appropriate merchandising, marketing and food technology specialists in order to discuss issues such as packaging, pricing, special offers and new product development. On one occasion Nathan was invited by their largest supermarket customer to a meeting of all major meat supplier Managing Directors. The invitation described the day as being an opportunity to hear about and discuss development plans for the supermarket chain. Nathan thought that this would be a good opportunity to meet his competitors and to begin to work out what the supermarket plans might mean for his own business. He arrived at the supermarket headquarters in plenty of time for the meeting and took the opportunity to chat to the other directors attending. They were all intrigued and slightly excited at the prospect of potentially doing more business, whilst at the same time trying to gauge what their competitors were thinking.

The time came for the meeting to start and everyone was ushered into a large lecture theatre style room. In total there were about 50 Managing Directors present with an average age around 50 and collectively about 1000 years of working experience in the meat industry. The meeting started when one of the supermarket merchandising meat product executives walked onto the platform and said her welcomes. A large screen then dropped down behind her and she said that the first session of the day would be an opportunity for everyone to bond by standing to sing the company 'anthem'. At that point the words of the anthem appeared on the screen and a number of other people from the supermarket walked into the lecture theatre and stood in the aisles facing the invited delegates. The music started and at first there was an embarrassed silence, with only the supermarket staff starting to sing and wave their arms in the air. However, slowly the rest of the audience began to join in (if unwillingly), even making a half-hearted attempt to (partly) wave their arms in the air. Nathan (and presumably many other directors present) had never felt so embarrassed and humiliated in their professional lives. In their eyes a very young, inexperienced girl was forcing them to humiliate themselves in a direct attempt to demonstrate where the power and control lay, but they had no real choice other than to comply in order to protect their businesses.

On returning to his own company the next day, Nathan told his senior management team what had happened. Any positive news emerging from the day was drowned by the sheer humiliation and shock felt at being required to sing the supermarket 'anthem'. One of his colleagues asked had he not felt like walking out on the day? He responded by saying yes he had, but that there was no real prospect for doing so and retaining the business with the supermarket, so he had complied however unwillingly and unenthusiastically! However he did add that when driving away from the supermarket headquarters (and when he was safely out of sight) he did give a two finger salute to the building, which made him feel slightly better!

TASKS

1   Why would the supermarket require attendees to sing the company anthem? Would it be to demonstrate who held the power as Nathan thought, or could there be other innocent explanations? If so, how should the episode have been handled by the designers of the day?

2   If you were Nathan, what would you have done and why?

3   What does this example suggest about relationships, fairness and trust between people in customer and supplier working relationships?

Source:
Told to one of the authors by a director of the company. Only the names and incidental details have been changed.

Similarly, if relationships are poor and conflictual, negative implications for the relationship partners and others in their vicinity can include consequences such as anxiety and stress, reduced communication quality and quantity, reduced information processing, task distraction and attitudinal changes including lower satisfaction and commitment (e.g., De Dreu and Weingart, 2003; Ren and Gray, 2009). Overall, poor relationships can impede performance at individual, group and organizational levels (De Dreu and Weingart, 2003; Jehn, 1995; Kacmar *et al.*, 2007) which highlights the importance of understanding their role and learning how to manage them. In the next section, we will briefly review social exchange theories that reflect the main way in which relationships have traditionally been conceptualized and studied (another important approach focuses on social and shared identities; e.g., Tyler and Blader, 2003). We then consider contributions that identify how relationships can be managed and improved before we move on to discuss the role of networks of relationships in organizations.

Social exchange theories

Social exchange theories
Originated in sociology and social psychology. These provide conceptions of interpersonal relationships as exchange relationships in which each actor engages to maximize the value they receive.

The formal study of relationships in their own right in organizational contexts has been traditionally influenced by classical social exchange theories (SETs) originally developed in sociology (e.g., Blau, 1964; Homans, 1961) and social psychology (Thibaut and Kelley, 1959), although some trace their origins further back to the 1920s (e.g., Cropanzano and Mitchell, 2005). Many different versions and formulations of SET exist (Cropanzano and Mitchell, 2005; Stafford, 2008), including such influential formulations as *interdependence theory* (see Rusbult and Van Lange, 2003) and *equity theory* (see Chapter 5 and further below). They all share common basic elements that include the exchange rules and norms that determine interactions and the obligations that arise from them for each partner, the currency of exchange (i.e., the nature of the resources passed between the partners), and the relationships that emerge between and among exchange partners (Cropanzano and Mitchell, 2005). The classic SET contributions provided conceptions of interpersonal relationships as exchanges in which each actor engages to maximize the value they receive. This value can differ on the dimension of tangible (e.g., goods) or intangible (e.g., status), and on the dimension of objectively and generally valuable (e.g., money) to subjectively and person-specifically valuable (e.g., love and affection) (Foa and Foa, 1975). Value can be derived from the responses of the other person as well as from acting towards the other person. Such value from relationship behaviour can be derived from a range of sources, including normative (e.g., acting based on internalized social norms), value-expressive (e.g., acting to display an aspirational self-image), and affiliative, intrinsic and emotional (e.g., the feelings of contentment and joy from interacting with a partner).

Rational Choice Theory
General model that uses self-interest and hedonistic value maximization to explain human behaviour.

According to social exchange theory, the actual behaviour in such exchange relationships is influenced by rational considerations such as rewards and costs, and by behavioural principles (see discussion of reinforcement in Chapter 5) of reward and punishment (Stafford, 2008). Of course, over time many interactions within relationships can become ritualistic and often automatic (e.g., how much information does a typical exchange among long-term acquaintances such as 'How are you?' – 'Fine, thanks.' really contain?). However, according to the classical conceptions of exchange relationships, relationships will endure over time only if there is positive value accruing to all partners, else they would leave the relationship. Thus, the description of interpersonal behaviour provided by social exchange theory is in line with an overarching model of human behaviour called Rational Choice Theory (RCT) which describes human behaviour as driven by self-interest based on hedonistic (i.e., value-maximization) principles (see Boudon, 2003, or Lehtinen and

Kuorikoski, 2007, for critical discussions). In job terms this is evident to some degree in the High Performance example.

While it may be difficult to accept the premise that people engage in relationships purely for their own gain, Stafford (2008) points out that we often hear people explaining the end of a personal romantic relationship with reasons such as 'He wasn't worth it,' 'She expects too much from me.' or 'I did not get anything out of it anymore.' Similarly, networking (which refers to *the deliberate cultivation of positive relationships with individuals that may be helpful in direct exchanges or indirectly through their links to third parties*) is common inside and outside of organizations for the intrinsic as well as instrumental value it can provide. Moreover, the premise of self-interest as a basis for relationships is not incompatible with conceptions of altruistic behaviour. Genetically imprinted benefits of such

Networking
Refers to the deliberate cultivation of positive relationships with individuals that may be helpful in direct exchanges or indirectly through their links to third parties.

HIGH PERFORMANCE

Can you ever trust a management consultant?

This 'joke' was told to one of the authors by a consultant who lived and worked in Germany. It apparently represented a common theme when employees and junior managers in Germany wanted to 'have a go' at management consultants that senior managers had brought into the business for some reason or another. Versions of this 'joke' are common in many other countries.

Once upon a time in a remote corner of Germany on a hill-farm miles from anywhere there was a shepherd who was leaning on the gate of a field looking at his flock of sheep. All of a sudden a BMW X5 appeared with a big cloud of dust and stopped next to the shepherd. A young man with a clean-cut, professional appearance, deep sun-tan and wearing a suit from Brioni, shoes from Cerutti, Ray Ban sun-glasses and an YSL-tie got out of the car and said to the shepherd: 'If I can guess the total number of sheep in your flock, will you give me one of them?'

The shepherd looked at the young man, looked at his huge flock of sheep and said 'OK!'

The young man opened up his laptop, linked it to his mobile telephone and the Internet and set up complex spreadsheets containing what seemed like hundreds of formulas. Finally after much toggling between various Internet sites and spreadsheet pages, he printed out (on his high-tech mini-printer and binder) a very attractive report with high-gloss cover pages (with pictures of sheep on it) containing 190 pages of tables,

data and projections of sheep numbers. He turned to the shepherd and said: 'You have got exactly 1 586 sheep.'

The shepherd said: 'That is true. Now choose one of the sheep.'

The young man chose one of the sheep and put it into the back of his BMW X5.

The shepherd stared at the young man and then said: 'If I can correctly guess your profession, will you give me back the sheep that you have just won?'

The young man said 'Of course.'

The shepherd said: 'You are a management consultant.'

The young man was astonished: 'That's true - how do you know?'

And the shepherd answered: 'It was easy: Firstly, you came here uninvited and unexpected making a lot of noise and in a flash car compared to what most people around here drive. Secondly, you want payment for telling me something that I already know. Thirdly, you don't have the faintest idea about my work or what it involves. And now please give my dog back to me!'

TASKS

1 What does this 'joke' tell you about fairness and trust in working relationships, particularly those between consultants and employees within the client organization?

2 How does this 'joke' help to explain social exchange theory?

behaviours (see deWaal, 2008), for example, clarify how apparently selfless acts can have self-serving dynamics that help explain them within a RCT framework. RCT is reflected in many theories and models in management and OB, explicitly for example in the areas of motivation (e.g., expectancy theory), leadership (path-goal theory), decision making (e.g., rational decision making model), and negotiation (e.g., distributive and integrative negotiation theory), and implicitly in areas such as central route processes in attribution and explicit attitude formation.

Overall, despite the many limitations and challenges to both their RCT premise and aspects of their specific formulations, social exchange theories provide a useful framework for analysing social and interpersonal relationships. One of the most structured and widely used approaches to employing exchange theories is *game theory*, often traced to von Neumann and Morgenstern's (1944) seminal work, which employs mathematical approaches to describe and analyse the interactions among parties. Typically, such interactions are described with outcome matrices for particular interaction situations. A classic example is the *prisoner's dilemma*, which is the two-party version of a social dilemma that ties all involved parties to each other through the interdependencies of their respective actions and outcomes (see Axelrod, 1984; Hardin, 1968).

In the prisoner's dilemma (see Figure 16.1 for the relevant outcome matrix), John and Mary have been arrested and there is enough evidence to charge them with a minor offence. If they do not confess to the full extent of their actual crime, they will both go to jail for one year each (see quadrant A). However, they have been separated, and each one has been offered that if they confess they will be let go while their confession will be used to prosecute their partner who can expect to go to jail for 10 years (see quadrants B and C). As they have been separated, they do not know what their partner is doing. Should both confess, they will both be charged and likely go to jail for 5 years each (quadrant D). What would you do in John or Mary's shoes?

Of course, the answer is not easy (hence the title 'dilemma') because your own outcomes depend on the behaviour of your partner, but you have no way of co-ordinating with them, of influencing them, or even of communicating to find out more about your partner's intentions. The dilemma lies in the structure of the situation, which makes the two parties interdependent in that John's outcomes are determined by Mary, Mary's outcomes are determined by John, and their joint outcomes are determined by both choices. If both pursue their own interests this will lead to mutually disastrous

Figure 16.1 Outcome matrix for prisoner's dilemma

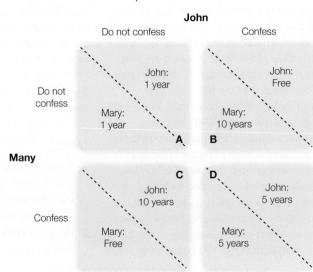

consequences. Both will be able to figure out the best outcome (nobody confesses), but they have no way of implementing this solution deliberately because they cannot co-ordinate their actions.

This and other structures of interdependencies have been discussed by many social exchange theories, and the relatively simple tool of payoff matrixes (which of course can be much more elaborate, and also be created for multiple successive interactions) has proven to be a powerful analytical instrument which is often applied in conflict and negotiation contexts and other situations with interdependent outcomes and where cooperation and co-ordination are important (e.g., Rusbult and Van Lange, 2003).

The fundamental choices in the prisoner's dilemma are to either take the obviously self-serving outcome (confession) which is called *defection* because it violates the positive expectations of the other partner, or to make the choice that aims at the mutually most beneficial outcome (A) even though it also includes exposure to the most negative outcome for oneself (B or C). This choice is called *co-operation*.

From a rational perspective and taking exclusively the outcomes in the matrix into account (and therefore discounting issues such as loyalty, friendship, guilt, and expected corollaries of the decision such as what is likely to happen if you go free and your partner is finally released from prison), the best choice in this one-shot situation is to confess because the expected value of this decision is 2.5 years in prison compared to the expected value of 5.5 years behind bars for not confessing (the expected value is the average of the two options assuming equal likelihood of their occurrence). Unless external mechanisms that enforce cooperation exist, the separate-and-offer-deals strategy employed in this example (and in real life by police forces and prosecutors almost everywhere) is highly effective. This is the reason why we often find norms against defection in such situations. For example, people who have 'sold out' their partners lose status among other criminals and often receive negative consequences (up to and including deadly force) inside and outside of prison. Such extreme social and cultural controls function to keep defection among the members of a gang or criminal group to a minimum.

Often, relationships are made up of multiple interactions with similar outcome structures and interdependencies. The overall most promising strategy in multiple ongoing interactions is the *tit-for-tat strategy* that starts with a co-operative move and then mirrors the other party's last move (see Axelrod, 1984). In practice, this means that if the other party is cooperative in move 1, then one's own choice in move 2 will be co-operative. However, if they defect in move 1, then one's choice in move 2 is defection. Effectively, this strategy is characterized by simplicity, a high degree of consistency, a fundamentally co-operative rather than aggressive stance, and by committed reciprocation. It is also nonescalating because it includes the important feature of *fast forgiveness*, which means that defection by the other party will only be repaid by defection in the next move. If the other party relents and co-operates again then there is no bad blood because tit-for-tat *always* responds in kind. Three points are worth noting here. First, tit-for-tat is a powerful strategy because it has proven to be the most successful strategy at maximizing one's own outcomes in the long run. However, it can never beat an opponent – it can at best do as well as the other (as long as payoffs are symmetrical) because it starts with a co-operative move and then mirrors the other party's choice. Second, in real life tit-for-tat is often much more difficult to apply because our own emotions often stand in the way of applying this simple and consistent strategy (see Chapter 9). Finally, if the number of successive rounds of interactions is small and limited, then the expected utility of this strategy is much lower because a logic similar to the prisoner's dilemma applies (see Kreps *et al.*, 1982).

Recovering from interactions in which one party defects can put tremendous strain on relationships among these partners. Fundamentally, the trust that has been broken by such a defection is difficult to rebuild. We will consider issues related to trust in much more detail later on in this chapter. First, however, we will consider how relationships can be nurtured and managed in organizations.

Managing relationships in organizations

All other things being equal, people tend to like other people who are similar to them in beliefs and interests, who are skilled and competent on some dimension, who have some admirable characteristics or qualities and who like them in return (Aronson, 2004). In short, these aspects all support the idea expressed by social exchange theories that people like those whose behaviour provides them 'with maximum reward at minimum cost' (Aronson, 2004: p. 290). In other words, we prefer to interact with people who make us feel best. Yet in organizations, relationships are not purely determined by liking, and workplace relationships often tend to be more instrumental, less discretionary, more externally determined, and more situation-dependent than purely private relationships (see also Duck, 2007).

The hierarchical context found in most organizations means that many relationships in organizations exist between individuals of different authority. This can have profound implications for relationships, especially in some cultural contexts. In Germanic cultures (e.g., Germany or Austria), close friendships between individuals who hold positions at different hierarchical levels in the same company are rare, and most people would not consider even very close work colleagues to be personal friends – rather, they would typically describe them as good acquaintances. Socializing among subordinates and bosses outside of work, if it happens, would often be rather formal. In other countries such as Ireland, many people consider their colleagues to be personal friends, and socializing among colleagues outside of work tends to be more frequent and informal. Both national and organizational cultural can have profound impact on intraorganizational relationships.

STOP & CONSIDER   To what extent is it possible to develop close relationships with colleagues and bosses in an organizational context that is based on authority, power, control and competition for scarce resources?

Given the instrumental nature of relationships in organizations and the influence of structures and processes on actual interactions and relationships in organizations, it is useful to recognize behaviours that can help build and maintain constructive relationships. By constructive we mean (applying a managerialist perspective) relationships that create value for both parties yet also address the relevant organizational and managerial expectations. In general, the activities that help to build and maintain relationships include supportive, appreciative, informative, inclusive, empowering, validating and respectful behaviours. Therefore:

- Invite input in appropriate forms and at appropriate times.
- Show acceptance and validate at least some aspects of suggestions and opinions.
- Be direct and honest yet polite and courteous.
- Act friendly and show patience.
- Be considerate of specific needs, interests and circumstances.
- Take the other's emotional state into account (e.g., fear, anxiety, excitement).
- Show your willingness to consider the other's perspective.
- Offer assistance with work when needed and appropriate.
- Avoid making decisions that take responsibility away from the other.
- Keep an appropriate information flow that informs without overwhelming.
- Show confidence in the other's abilities.

- Remember personal details regarding the person.
- Acknowledge all contributions and accomplishments.
- Provide autonomy, challenge and support in balanced ways.
- Validate the other's identity and help maintain their sense of personal worth and importance.
- Act respectfully at all times.

This list of behaviours shows some of the behaviours that can help build and maintain relationships in organizations. Some relationships, however, are *not only unproductive but can be counterproductive or even harmful*. Dealing with such toxic relationships at work can be extremely difficult, especially when we find ourselves in such a relationship with our boss or someone we depend on for our own task achievement. Withdrawal from such a relationship may not always be an option, so the use of assertive communication and related interpersonal skills is helpful. Bolton (1979) discusses different communication styles that can help to address such relationship difficulties. At the heart of this is assertiveness, which refers to *a process of interpersonal communication that is respectful of both one's own and the other party's needs, rights and interests*. In many ways assertiveness corresponds to the top right quadrant ('integration/collaboration') in the framework shown in Figure 9.6 which is characterized by high concern for both own and the other party's outcomes. It can be contrasted with aggressive (focus on own needs, rights and interests only) or submissive (focus on other's needs, rights and interests only) communication approaches. Assertive communication has many features important for interpersonal feedback (see Chapter 8), and a similar message structure that focuses on factual and nonevaluative description of the issue (e.g., the behaviour that contributes to the relationship problem) and of its consequences (i.e., identifying external implications and disclosing one's own emotional reactions). Bolton (1979) argues that repeated and consistent application of respectful assertions can over time help to address many relationship problems. Table 16.1 provides detail

Toxic relationships Relationships that are unproductive, counterproductive or harmful.

Assertiveness A communication style that can help to address relationship difficulties. A process of interpersonal communication that is respectful of both one's own and the other party's needs, rights and interests. See also advocacy and enquiry.

Table 16.1 The three-part assertive message

Element of assertive message	Example	Comments
Description of behaviour	'When you leave your copies on the machine . . .	Make sure the description is brief, factual, specific and not laden with evaluative terms. Most importantly, focus on observable behaviour only and exclude any inferred intentions and motivations.
Disclosure of emotional reaction	. . . I feel annoyed and stressed . . .	Ensure that the feelings accurately describe your emotional experience, and avoid judgemental descriptions (e.g., 'abused' instead of 'annoyed' would fundamentally change the sample message).
Identification of consequences	. . . because it forces me to do more work that is your responsibility.'	Select concrete and tangible effects on yourself, your belongings, or other resources clearly linked to yourself. Do not substitute tangible effects with violations of values or preferences.

Source: Adapted from Bolton, 1979.

on the design of assertive messages while Table 16.2 describes the six steps of using this approach in interactions and relationships which ideally culminates in joint problem solving regarding the relationship problem. This approach is closely linked to conflict resolution and can be immensely helpful in negotiation interactions as well as many other interpersonal situations inside and outside of organizations. Patterson and colleagues (2005) identify violated expectations as a common cause of serious relationship-and ultimately organizational-problems. They describe face-to-face accountability discussions with which to constructively confront people about gaps between agreements or promises and their actual behaviour. They argue that this approach will help solve the underlying problem and improve the relationship. Of course, the particular

Table 16.2 The six steps of using assertive messages to address relationship problems.

Steps of assertive communication	Comments
(1) Preparations	This step includes the development of a three-part assertive message (see Table 16.1) as well as careful consideration of time, place, context and framing of the planned assertive intervention. An understanding of likely defensive reactions and psychological reactance should guide this planning.
(2) Sending the message	The other party should be prepared to listen to the message and not feel 'ambushed'. Body language should be aligned with the content of the message.
(3) Silence	Stop talking after delivering the message – do not fill the silence with 'noise'. The receiver needs time and space to react to the message.
(4) Reflective listening to the other's (defensive) response	Typically, people will respond defensively to an assertive message. This should be respectfully reflected back to them using paraphrasing and comprehension questions when needed. Reflective listening is crucial for a shift to a constructive and open exchange rather than an escalating spiral of conflict fueled by defensive and aggressive interactions.
(5) Recycling through steps 2–4 as often as necessary	This may take a number of cycles, because if defensiveness persists, receivers cannot take in the actual message. Sometimes, receivers may even withdraw from the interaction. Repeat the assertive message and deal constructively with the response until the receiver is able to engage in joint problem solving.
(6) Focusing on a solution	Assertive messages can work so well because they do not contain a solution and therefore leave space for the receiver to develop one. Make sure it meets your needs and addresses the underlying issue the assertive message is about.

Source: Adapted from Bolton, 1979.

nature as well as the cultural context will influence the effectiveness of any attempts to address relationship conflict (Ren and Gray, 2009).

Overall, such structured approaches to use assertive messages and constructively confront violations of agreements and expectations can address interpersonal and relationship problems because they (Bolton, 1979):

- Increase the probability that the other will alter the troublesome behaviour because they avoid reactance and defensiveness.

- Are unlikely to violate the other person's integrity or lower their self-esteem.

- If planned and executed well contain a low risk of further damaging the relationship.

- Express concern about the relationship and can help increase the other's motivation to change.

- Limit the further intensification of the problem and prevent defensiveness from escalating to destructive levels.

In many ways, the assertive communication approaches described above are related to a set of techniques that can provide tremendous value in many organizational situations including group discussions, joint problem solving, or any other situation in which different views, opinions, concerns, interests and agendas meet. They are called advocacy and inquiry (see also Ross, 1994; Ross and Roberts, 1994; Senge, 2006). Advocacy refers to *a process of undogmatic assertion that invites constructive engagement with the factual basis and logical argument supporting the assertion.* Inquiry is *a process of dialogue that constructively challenges others' views by refocusing on facts and reasoning.* The key aspect of both advocacy and inquiry is that they are designed to minimize the reactance and ensuing defensiveness that often dominate discussions and problem-related interchanges in organizations. At the heart of both advocacy and inquiry is what Thompson (2009) calls changing personal (emotional) conflict to task (cognitive) conflict in ways reminiscent of the principled negotiation approach (Fisher and Ury, 1981) discussed in Chapter 9. This is achieved by insisting on general principles such as a reliance on verifiable facts and clear and logical arguments (see Table 16.3). Advocacy states a proposal (or view, conclusion or preferred option) along with the facts it is based on and the reasoning that leads from these verifiable facts in a clear and rational way to this proposal (view, conclusion, option). Advocacy includes inviting, the other party (or parties) to point out mistakes in the stated facts or to voice challenges to the reasoning provided. The benefit of this approach is that it reduces one's own reactance to any ensuing challenges (because the other parties were invited to do so) while engaging others in a constructive consideration of the proposal. Similarly, inquiry is almost the mirror image of this approach in response to a proposal (view etc.) made by another party. It is based on asking the other party for help in arriving at the same view they propose by requesting assistance in linking this proposal through clear logic to verifiable facts.

Advocacy
Refers to a process of undogmatic assertion that invites constructive engagement with the factual basis and logical argument supporting the assertion. See also assertiveness and enquiry.

Inquiry
A process of dialogue that constructively challenges others' views by refocusing on facts and reasoning. See also advocacy and assertiveness.

The Psychological Contract

One of the most important relationships in organizations is not an interpersonal relationship between people, but the relationship between each individual member and the organization. In commercial organizations, this is typically an employment relationship which is the formal agreement about mutual rights, privileges, duties, obligations and other explicit aspects of the contract specifying the formal exchange relationship between employee and employer (specifying working hours, activities, pay and benefits, etc.). An employee's boss is often seen as the agent of the organizations with regard to the employment contract, but the contract is with the

Table 16.3 How to use advocacy and inquiry

	Advocacy	Inquiry
Context	Use advocacy to invite constructive dialogue about your own idea, view, option or solution. Make sure you are open to the input you are soliciting, and actively point out weaknesses in your own reasoning or in the data used.	Use inquiry to open constructive dialogue when others put forward their ideas, view, options or solutions. Make sure you listen to the explanations and input you receive and paraphrase your understanding to improve communication.
Step 1	Here is what I think.	Why do you think that?
Step 2	Here is my reasoning.	What is your reasoning?
Step 3	Here is the data that supports it.	What is the data that supports your views?
Linkage	Ideally: present the above, then ask: 'What is wrong with this?' or 'What can you add?'	Ideally, say: 'Help me understand your thinking here' or even 'Please help me think like that, too.'

Sometimes, the above techniques cannot help to address differences of opinion and the often ensuing conflict. In these situations, be aware that different assumptions and values cannot be addressed with the rational and logic focused approaches above. In such situations, try to find general principles or fundamental values that can help build bridges between your and the other party's views.

organization as a whole. In addition to the formal rights and responsibilities, there are many aspects about this relationship that are not specified in the formal contracts or the relevant company policies and employment legislation that apply to the employment relationship. The informal expectations that employee and employer have of each other are often summarized as the psychological contract between these parties. More specifically, the psychological contract refers to *the individual beliefs about the terms of the mutual exchange agreement between the individual and their organization* (see Rousseau, 1989, 1995). Thus, psychological contracts contribute to members' understanding of their roles and responsibilities in the organization and reflect what treatment they anticipate and what benefits they expect in return for their contributions.

Psychological contracts reflect individual perceptions, views and attitudes, but nevertheless they are influenced by social information and comparison processes (Deery *et al.*, 2006) and may be shared (Rousseau, 1995). Moreover, the self-serving bias in perception and attribution (see Chapter 4) often creates individual expectations that diverge substantially from those of the organization. Therefore, even well meaning and arguably legitimate behaviour by agents of the organization (e.g., managers) can violate expectations individuals have based on their understanding of the psychological contract. Violations and breaches of the subjective psychological contract can lead to profound behavioural, cognitive and emotional reactions. Research indicates that they can lead to higher turnover and absenteeism, lower job satisfaction, increased cynicism and lower organizational citizenship behaviour,

Psychological contract
Refers to the individual beliefs about the terms of the mutual exchange agreement between the individual and their organization.

lower perceived support, and reduced trust in the organization, (Coyle-Shapiro and Conway, 2005; Deery *et al.*, 2006; Kiewitz *et al.*, 2009; Robinson and Morrison, 2000; Tekleab *et al.*, 2005).

Understanding psychological contracts is important for managers because they describe the actual subjective understanding of what employees are prepared to contribute and what they expect in return. Psychological contract violations can be addressed in a number of ways that range from actual changes in the benefits and working conditions provided by the organization over justifying and reframing perceived shortcomings (for example through different comparisons or the highlighting of relevant information such as labour market conditions, see Dery *et al.*, 2006) to interventions aimed at changing the subjective expectations. Many of the issues and dynamics discusses in Part 3 of this book (Interactions in organizations) can guide attempts to manage the psychological contract and address issues arising from perceived violations and breaches.

16.1 EXTEND
YOUR LEARNING

Networks of relationships

The notion of relationships suggests bilateral or dyadic linkages, but in organizations whole interconnected *systems of such relationships* develop that are called networks. Both formal and informal networks, based on systems of formal and informal relationships, exist in organizations. These networks can have immense importance for the functioning of organizations as well as for the performance and well-being of individual members.

For organizations, formal and informal networks can serve as a conduit for cultural values and norms (e.g., Hill and Carley, 2008; Zohar and Tenne-Gazit, 2008), as well as important means of supplementing the formal integration mechanisms (see Chapter 10) through informal linkages among members within and across subunits. In fact, some argue that the majority of information in organizations can flow through such informal networks (Bryan *et al.*, 2007). Employees with large external networks to individuals outside the organization can provide useful information as well as other resources important for organizational success. Such networks are closely related to the idea of social capital which refers to the resources that can accrue from social ties to others (e.g., Seibert *et al.*, 2001b).

For individuals, networks offer a range of benefits. Friendship and advice networks can provide personal and professional benefits such as social support, career guidance, and professional development input (e.g., Gibbons, 2004; Chua *et al.*, 2008). Social support in all its forms has shown itself to be particularly important for individuals coping with adversity and change. Further, informal networks can be used to gain power and exert influence (Sparrowe and Liden, 2005) and are often beneficial for individual work performance and career success (Sparrowe *et al.*, 2001; Chua *et al.*, 2008). The role of informal networks for performance, however, also depends on the particular nature and context of work. A recent study of knowledge workers (Gargiulo *et al.*, 2009), for example, indicates that extensive and close network connections can be beneficial for individual performance if these individuals need to acquire information and have no alternative means (e.g., authority) for inducing others to share such information. However, close network ties can be counterproductive to individual performance if the normative control other network members can exert is counterproductive for particular task requirements.

However, networks can also have significant negative influences in organizations. Cabals (i.e., *informal groups that attempts to push views supported by members to enhance their status and position*, see Burns, 1955), gossip and grapevine networks and other informal systems of connections can be used to generate an inordinate amount or type of influence in organizations. The Employee Perspective example

Networks
Describes systems of interconnected bilateral or dyadic linkages and relationships within organizations. Both formal and informal networks, based on systems of formal and informal relationships, exist.

Cabals
Informal groups that attempt to push views supported by members to enhance their status and position.

EMPLOYEE PERSPECTIVE

Perspectives on managers and managing

Is management easy? That question was put to three managers in May 2009 by one of the authors. They began by collectively saying that working as managers was very difficult. They were then asked to discuss what it was in their organizations that made working as a manager particularly difficult. The responses included the following:

- Senior managers generally lacked openness, commitment (to the organization and its purpose), and enthusiasm (for their jobs or the purpose for the organization). It was thought that the most senior managers were just 'scraping by' (by which it was meant that they were not fully on top of their jobs in relation to the technical, interpersonal, managerial and leadership requirements). The result was that senior managers were basically ineffective and so failed to give effective leadership and direction to the organization and subordinates – lowering morale across every level in the organization and making it difficult for middle and lower levels of management to do their jobs effectively. It produced a defensive approach to work at every level as everyone tended to protect their position and would not deviate from established routines.

- One example from the personal experience of one of the respondents occurred when a key management position was left unfilled for a long time and a power vacuum resulted which more senior management could not fill. This allowed one group (cabal) within the organization to take advantage of the lack of control arising from the vacant post and so use their skills and significance to the organization to ensure that they were allowed to effectively run things their way and to do only what suited them when (and only if) it suited them. This had a number of consequences in relation to customer service and standards along with working relationships with other professional and administrative staff. Eventually the key vacancy was filled, but by then the status quo had become so entrenched that the cabal simply refused to change their ways of working and so levels of frustration among other staff and managers grew. Senior management of the organization refused to take action against the dominant group to force them into line (through fear of losing what they considered to be

the key business resource) and so the newly appointed manager could not make any changes to improve the range or quality of services offered as a way of improving organizational performance.

- Another point made by the managers being interviewed was that social, organizational and commercial environments have become increasingly complex over recent years – usually since current senior managers held operational responsibilities. Senior managers were therefore considered to be unable to relate to, understand or process these new complexities and realities for the entire range of organizational activity and service areas. Consequently they tended to focus on those things that they could relate to and understand (invariably what they had been familiar with) and so recent additions to organizational activity were ignored and other opportunities that might exist were not explored or developed.

Senior managers were also thought not to be open or honest in advance of commissioning projects (about resource availability and other constraints). Consequently by default they encouraged projects and development plans to be created and worked up into full proposals. Then at the final review stage such proposals were turned down for reasons usually associated with lack of resources or changing priorities that must have been known at the outset of the project. The result was that morale dropped at all levels, as did confidence and trust in the senior managers individually and collectively.

TASKS

1 What do the above comments tell you about managing and being a manager?

2 What do the above comments tell you about relationships, fairness and trust between levels of management in organizations?

3 What does the cabal example in the comments tell you about power and control in relation to networks of relationships in an organization?

Source:
The mangers worked in the public sector in the UK; a private medical facility in Italy; and a classical music artist's manager/representative based in Germany.

provides some indications of how cabals can form and function within an organization. Moreover, many managers are blind to the bias that can arise from their particular ties and networks for their own behaviour and decision making. Often, managers seek out and utilize input from close and familiar partners or from closely linked parts of their networks and possibly overlook important but more peripheral contributors (Cross *et al.*, 2009).

ORGANIZATIONAL FAIRNESS AND JUSTICE

In all considerations of social exchange and relationships within organizations, a central concern of those involved is the fairness of the interactions. In fact, ever since the early contributions to social exchange theory and the study of relationships in organizations, issues of fairness, equity, equality and need have been considered as important features of exchange relationships. This has led to the emergence of a particular area of study, called organizational justice, that has become one of the most active research areas in OB in recent decades (Fortin, 2008). Formally, organizational justice (OJ) is concerned with *employees' fairness perceptions regarding their work and conditions of employment and their behavioural reactions to this*. This definition highlights a particular approach to considering justice and fairness. Unlike philosophical investigations that view justice as an absolute value and determine what is fair based on normative logical comparisons or on the outcome of moral reasoning (see for example Broome, 1990; Hooker, 2005), the field of OJ treats fairness and justice as subjective perceptions – in other words, fair is what is experienced as fair. That means that one member of a workgroup may perceive a particular action of the manager as fair, while another one experiences it as a grave injustice. The Examining Ethics example illustrates a situation in which intentions can be expressed in one way which subsequently give rise to a feeling of unfairness, and generate a lack of trust.

> **Organizational justice**
> Concerned with employee fairness perceptions regarding their work and conditions of employment and their behavioural reactions to these. See also distributive justice, informational justice, interactional justice and procedural justice.

OJ investigates the nature of such fairness perceptions, the factors that determine these perceptions, the processes by which these views are created and may change over time, and the behavioural and cognitive reactions to the experience of fairness and unfairness. The reason for the immense research interest in OJ is simple: consider the last time that you were – as a member of an organization (employee, student, club member, or even in your role as client or customer) - really 'ticked off' with the organization in question. Stop and think about that situation, and how you felt. In most situations, this instance will have at its core the experience of a perceived injustice done to you or to someone you can identify with (e.g., a student was picked on by a lecturer for a disturbance she didn't cause; a manager assigned an extremely difficult task to someone who was not experienced enough and then punished the person for failing). How did that experience affect you? And what would happen if you had such an experience as the employee of an organization? Figure 16.2 identifies a range of variables that are all typically related to performance. Most people report that their experience of injustice would negatively affect virtually all of these factors (e.g., lower trust, worsening relationships with the perpetrator of the injustice, higher levels of stress, less voluntary contributions through organizational citizenship behaviour, etc.). In fact, research indicates that OJ is related to factors such as job satisfaction and satisfaction with rewards and other outcomes, trust, commitment to the organization, performance, organizational citizenship behaviours, compliance, co-operation, absenteeism, withdrawal behaviours, and stress (e.g., Conlon *et al.*, 2005; Fortin, 2008). Thus, OJ matters for organizations and managers because perceived injustice can affect many drivers of performance. And given the research findings above, it clearly matters for individuals in organizations!

EXAMINING ETHICS

When is a commitment not a commitment?

It was widely reported in the UK press in March 2009 that National Express was intent on cutting the remaining restaurant cars from the Main East Coast railway line between Edinburgh and London, having already cut the same service from its other rail services that still operated restaurant cars. The company needed to make significant savings because the ticket revenue was below that predicted when it successfully bid £1.4bn in 2007 for the 10-year franchise. The company claimed that it lost about £20m each year on its onboard catering services and needed to carry more passengers on its already packed trains. It claimed that restaurant cars waste seats as passengers from other carriages moved to the dining car to eat their meals. When the trains were privatized in the mid-1990s it was made a condition of the franchise that the then operator (GNER) ran at least 86 restaurant cars each day. However when the franchise was renegotiated in 2007, the clause was quietly dropped and such provision was left to the train operator's discretion. The Department for Transport (DfT) press release in 2007 said 'National Express East Coast will provide a full restaurant service on 87 train services with an improved range of full meals.' In March 2009 the DfT admitted that what this actually meant was that the company intended at that time to be able to offer that level of service, but was not required by the contract to do so. National Express now intended to simplify the hot meals service and remove the restaurant car and silver service. It planned to offer passengers in first or standard class prepacked meals to purchase and eat at their seats.

National Express made substantial losses and was forced to give up its franchise for the Main East Coast rail line in July 2009, when it said it could no longer afford the contract payments to the government because of declining revenue and passenger numbers in business class in 2008 and 2009. The line returns to government control when National Express withdraws and will stay under its control until a new franchisee is appointed.

TASKS

1 At what point does the form of press statement indicated become spin or misleading as an attempt to present 'facts' in a particular way, or to hide facts that might be embarrassing or cause arguments?

2 Can the use of such practices ever be justified as a management tactic?

3 If employees become aware of the use of such practices in relation to outside stakeholders, what effect might this have on their trust in management and their views about fairness in relation to management decisions and actions?

4 If customers and suppliers become aware of the use of such practices, what effect might this have on their trust in management decisions and actions in relation to doing business with them in the future?

Sources:
O'Connell, D. (2009) National Express goes off the rails on east coast line: Times Online: http://business.timesonline.co.uk/tol/business/industry_sectors/transport/article6639057.ece (accessed August 2009).

http://news.scotsman.com/therailways/Peers-slam-39thirdrate 39-service-on.4962640.jp Accessed March 2009.

http://www.businesstravelworld.com/page.cfm?action=archive/ archiveid=15/entryid=1494 (accessed March 2009).

Webster, B. (2009) Railway Restaurant Cars To Be Scrapped To Make Way For More Passengers. Times Online: http://www.timesonline.co.uk/tol/travel/news/article5860568.ece (accessed March 2009).

Young, F. (2009) Rail Firm National Express Closes Restaurant Cars On All Routes. The Sunday Mail: http://www.sundaymail.co.uk/news/scottish-news/2009/03/08/rail-firm-national-express-close-restaurant-cars-on-all-routes-78057-21181680/ (accessed March 2009).

From the earliest precursor of modern OJ theories (Adams' equity theory, see Chapter 5) that focused on distributive justice (i.e., *fairness perceptions related to the outcomes one receives*), successive steps and stages in OJ research (see Folger and Cropanzano, 1998, and Colquitt *et al.*, 2005, for historical overviews) have

Figure 16.2 Variables potentially affected by experienced injustice

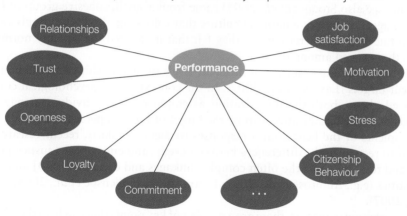

contributed to what is today seen as a four-dimensional conception of OJ (Colquitt, 2001; Colquitt *et al.*, 2001; Folger and Cropanzano, 1998):

- Distributive justice is concerned with individuals' perceptions of the fairness of outcomes.
- Procedural justice is concerned with the perceived fairness of the processes by which decisions about outcomes are made.
- Interactional justice is concerned with the fairness perceptions of the quality of interpersonal treatment (e.g., interpersonal sensitivity).
- Informational justice is concerned with the fairness perceptions of information received (particularly explanations or social accounts).

This framework can help us understand and analyse individual reactions to perceived fairness and unfairness. For example, all other things being equal, people will react to the perception that the distribution of valued outcomes is unfair. However, what is perceived as fair is a matter strongly influenced by the context in which the particular distribution is experienced. Giving a larger amount of money to one group member than all others would be seen as unfair unless there is a clear reason for this difference. If the distribution is the outcome of raffle, then most people would not see this as unfair, because the procedure used is fair in that it gives everyone the same chance to win. However, if the money in question is the yearly bonus, then a raffle (even if fairly conducted) would by most people be seen as unfair because we would expect that the bonus should be somehow proportional to the performance and contribution that different members have made (this refers to an *equity*-based distribution rule). This equity value was the first justice norm introduced to OJ by Adams in his equity theory. In performance-oriented contexts such as employment relationships, this equity value dominates, but in other contexts such as close family and personal relationships, need-based distribution is more typical, and in non-performance settings equal treatment (reflecting an equality value) predominate (see Deutsch, 1975; Leventhal, 1976).

Such ethical dynamics are influenced by culture (Greenberg, 2001). McFarlin and Sweeney (2001), for example, found evidence that cultural dimensions such as collectivism and individualism or masculinity/femininity (see Chapter 14) influence preferences for different ethical values in fairness judgements (see also Ramamoorthy and Flood, 2002), and Kim and Leung (2007) reported cultural differences in the relative importance of the four justice dimensions for overall justice experiences. For example, in our own executive education experience working with many different

Distributive justice
Concerned with individuals' perceptions of the fairness of outcomes. See also informational justice, interactional justice, organizational justice and procedural justice.

Procedural justice
Concerned with the perceived fairness of the processes by which decisions about outcomes are made. See also distributive justice, informational justice, interactional justice and organizational justice.

Interactional justice
Concerned with the fairness perceptions of the quality of interpersonal treatment. See also distributive justice, informational justice, organizational justice and procedural justice.

Informational justice
Concerned with the fairness perceptions of information received. See also distributive justice, interactional justice, organizational justice and procedural justice.

international groups of managers, the strongest reaction to a violation of the equality value (see also Stouten *et al.*, 2005) came from a small, cohesive group of Dutch
HR managers (i.e., from a national culture that values equality) who simply refused
to continue with an exercise when they felt that it violated the equality norms and
values that existed among them!

Justice perceptions can exist at different levels of relationships and often include
different targets (Lavelle *et al.*, 2007). In the context of the psychological contract
discussed above, both the organization as employer and individual managers as
the agents of the organization can be the target of fairness perceptions, and can be
the recipients of the behavioural responses to them. Similarly, recent research has
started to recognize the differences between event- and entity-based justice perceptions and to disentangle the often complex linkages and dynamics of OJ and multiple entities (e.g., Ambrose *et al.*, 2007; Fortin, 2008; Hollensbe *et al.*, 2008; Lavelle
et al., 2007).

For practising managers, there are a number of key points that can help them understand and manage fairness perceptions at work. For example, the four-dimensional
framework can be used to draw attention to the aspects of their own decisions that
affect outcomes relevant for their subordinates (distributive justice), the way in which
they make these decisions (procedural justice) and explain them (informational justice), and finally the way they interact with their subordinates in the context of all
these activities (interpersonal justice). Since these four dimensions interact, keeping
some or at least one of these justice dimensions 'in the green' can ward off significant
problems (e.g., Cropanzano *et al.*, 2007; Goldman, 2003).

OJ theory provides more detailed input than these rather general suggestions. Managerial decision making as well as all formal processes and procedures can be 'justice
tested' to check the degree to which they adhere to procedural fairness criteria. Table
16.4 shows a number of relevant criteria originally identified by Leventhal (1980)
that can be used for this purpose. One of these criteria (voice) refers to process control
which has already been central to discussions of participative leadership and decision
making (Chapter 6) and of ways to exert control (Chapter 12) in organizations.

Other relevant dynamics of OJ reflect material covered in other chapters. Informational justice, for example, refers to the perception of adequate and appropriate
information provision. To explain this in more detail, perceived injustice linked to
any of the four dimensions of justice will likely generate negative behavioural consequences. However, providing a compelling reason for the violation can help to
significantly lessen these negative effects. As an example, a manager who in front of
the top management of the company takes personal credit for the idea a subordinate
developed will likely be seen as self-serving and unfair. However, subsequently she
may explain that she felt she had to indicate that it was her idea to convince the top
managers to back the idea with significant investment. In most circumstances, such
an explanation (also called a *social account*) can significantly reduce perceptions of
unfairness. The impact of such explanations is driven by the perceived adequacy of
the account and the perceived sincerity of the person providing the explanation. This
is closely linked to attitude formation and influence processes discussed in Chapters
4 and 15, respectively. Knowledge about such justice dynamics can of course be used
to create the perception of fair treatment even in the absence of actual (moral) justice
(Fortin and Fellenz, 2008).

Another such insight that can be used to manage fairness perceptions is that the
'ill effects of injustice can be at least partially mitigated if at least one component
of justice is maintained' (Cropanzano *et al.*, 2007). This allows managers to choose
the easiest route to ameliorate injustices, even those deliberately committed. The
subjective nature of OJ allows for such instrumental and exploitative behaviour in
organizations, a dynamic called *hypocrisy of fairness* (Fortin and Fellenz, 2008).
Similarly, Greenberg (1990) discusses the use of impression management to merely

Table 16.4 Leventhal's criteria of procedural fairness

	Analytic question	Organizational example of violation
Consistent	Are the procedures applied without variation?	Among a number of groups of employees going through a skills training and assessment programme linked to promotional opportunities, some receive hints regarding the nature and content of a relevant test while others do not receive such support.
Bias free	Are the decision-making processes influenced by irrelevant criteria or elements?	Promotion application from employees who are not members of the company golf club are automatically rejected.
Accurate	Are assessments that feed into the decision-making process reliable and valid?	Sales performance bonus system uses subjective performance assessments rather than actual revenue data.
Correctable in case of an error	Is there an option for internal review or external 'due process' in case errors are made?	Promotion procedures require candidates to sign a waiver that precludes them from challenging the decision.
Representative of all concerned (voice)	Do those affected have a chance to make their case or give input that is considered by decision makers?	A consulting report is submitted that recommends the restructuring and downsizing of a branch office without allowing any of the branch personnel to provide input to the data collection and analysis.
Reflective of prevailing ethical standards	Does the decision rule reflect the socially and culturally applicable distribution rule (e.g., equity, equality, need, etc.)?	Performance bonus is given based on perceived financial need of the employees rather than actual performance.

Source: Kim, PH, Dirks, KT & Cooper, CD (2009) 'The repair of trust: A dynamic bilateral perspective and multilevel conceptualization' in Academy of Management Review, 34(3): 01-422. Academy of Management. Reprinted with permission.

provide perceptions of justice, and Fortin and Fellenz discuss the manipulative use of power to create acceptance of justice conceptions and the application of ethical values that serve the needs of managers and the organization (see Figure 15.1 and the related discussion in Chapter 15). Clearly, OJ theory and research has strong moral and ethical implications that need to be actively and vigilantly considered by managers, employees and researchers alike (see also Cropanzano and Stein, 2009; Hosmer and Kiewitz, 2005).

STOP & CONSIDER

To what extent does the 'end justify the means' as managers try to disguise what is essentially a power and control-based relationship by invoking a language involving concepts such as 'trust', 'fairness' and 'partnership'?

OJ has implications for the whole organization. Because the experience of the organization is strongly influenced by interactions with and treatment received from the official agents of the organization (i.e., managers), such treatment and especially the application of organizational policies and procedures influences what employees believe about the organization as a whole (e.g., Tyler and Blader, 2000). Fair behaviour by managers at the interpersonal level can therefore aggregate to cultural results at the organizational level – an important insight given the many potentially powerful positive and negative effects of both OJ and culture.

TRUST IN ORGANIZATIONS

Another important aspect of interactions and relationships, especially if cooperation and interdependencies are involved, is trust. This is particularly true in the context of increasing diversity as the people involved do not automatically share the same values, norms, culture and behavioural approaches (Mayer *et al.*, 1995). Trust is relevant in all kinds of relationships including interpersonal ones as well as relationships between individuals and organizations (e.g., psychological contract), and between social entities (groups, organizations, countries, etc.). Trust can be seen as a means to increase predictability and reduce perceived uncertainty about the behaviour of others that can affect us through the interdependencies related to work or to interpersonal relations and exchanges. Thus, trust is sometimes seen as an alternative to control (Knights *et al.*, 2001; Sitkin and George, 2005). This aspect of trust in organizations involves a paradox because, as many writers have commented (e.g., Armstrong, 1989; Fox, 1974b; Knights *et al.*, 2001; Reed, 2001. Watson, 2008), organizations try to simultaneously reduce uncertainty through tight control while also trying to increase motivation, discretion, initiative and engagement among employees which close and coercive control practices in turn are likely to destroy.

STOP & CONSIDER Can you be friends with someone you do not trust? Why or why not? If you think yes, what would the implications for the relationship be, and how could this friendship be achieved and maintained?

Conceptions and sources of trust in organization

Many different conceptions of trust exist, and the concept is often used synonymously with terms such as cooperation, confidence and predictability (see Mayer *et al.*, 1995). However, while closely related, logically trust must include the notion of vulnerability or risk that is not necessarily inherent in these other concepts. If people cannot affect us negatively, there is no need for trust in them (yet people may still co-operate with them, have confidence in them, or view them as predictable) (see also Bradach and Eccles, 1989). It therefore makes sense to '*trust* the brakes in the car I am about to drive' because their failure to perform what they are designed to do can have severe negative consequences for the driver. However, it would be nonsensical to talk about trust in someone or something that cannot affect us in any way ('I trust my 5-year-old nephew's imaginary friend not to attack me'). Thus, we adopt the following definition for our discussions of trust. Trust refers to *the degree to which a person (or entity) is prepared to make themselves vulnerable to another person (or entity) despite uncertainty about the other's possible actions*. This definition is closely aligned with other common OB conceptions of trust (e.g., Chua *et al.*, 2008; Kramer, 1999; Mayer *et al.*, 1995). It describes trust as based on the belief that those we depend upon will meet our expectations of them. For clarity in our further consideration of trust, we call the person who trusts the *trustor* and the person or entity that is trusted the *trustee*.

Trust is influenced by the trustor's *propensity to trust,* which in turn is determined by relevant individual differences (for example locus of control), the perception of the risk involved, attitude to risk taking, and self-efficacy about the ability to cope with the implications should the trustee defect. People have tendencies to

Trust
Refers to the degree to which a person (or entity) makes themselves vulnerable to another person (or entity) despite uncertainty about the other's possible actions.

trust that are not always based on sound logic, accurate data and rational calculation and often trust too easily yet not enough (e.g., Fetchenhauer and Dunning, 2009; Kramer, 2009). Another important factor is the perceived *trustworthiness* of the trustee, which is determined by their perceived ability, benevolence and integrity (Mayer *et al.*, 1995). Further, trust is affected by contextual and situational factors including legal, social or cultural control and enforcement mechanisms that may affect the trustee or the attitudes and behaviours of third parties (including verbal persuasion or social proof). Figure 16.3 provides a brief model of these factors that can also interact with and influence each other. Trust is also important when succession planning is being considered, especially in family-run businesses as the Change at Work example illustrates.

Trust is a feature of the particular relationship between two people or entities. Just as relationships can develop and change, trust is also influenced by the interactions between the partners in relationships. Cummings and Bromiley (1996)

CHANGE AT WORK

Handing on the family business

Family businesses are often handed on to the next generation in order to 'keep it in the family'. Young family members often work in the business in various roles to better prepare them for taking over senior roles when the current incumbents wish to hand over control. However, the desire to keep the business in family ownership along with experience of working in the business are no guarantee that everything will go according to plan. For example, on a training course run by one of the authors a participant who was working as the sales director in his family's food import and distribution business and who was in line to take over as managing director from his father in about 4 years time said that:

'I often have sleepless nights because I simply don't know if I'm capable of running the family business as effectively or as profitably as my father! It has been in the family for three generations so far, and I feel this great weight of history about to land on my shoulders and I just don't know if I can hold it together long enough, let alone grow the business to greater heights than my father and his father did. I'm just not confident enough in my technical or managerial capabilities.'

Another delegate told of a different set of problems:

'Our family business is only one generation old having been founded in 1975 by my father. It

is a small regional electrical retail business with five shops in market towns in semi-rural areas across the north of England. Although we have joined a consortium of similar businesses for marketing and purchasing reasons, we are finding it increasingly difficult to compete with electrical retailers and online shopping outlets. My father (the founder of the business) wants to let go of his day-to-day role in running the business and allow my brother and myself run it – but only if we agree to do everything as he would have done. He also wants to retain ultimate control of the business to ensure that we comply with his wishes. We can see that there is no real future for the business as it currently operates and that fundamental change needs to be adopted if it is to continue into the future, but he won't agree to such radical change.'

TASKS

1 What do the above examples imply about relationships, fairness and trust between the generations in family-run businesses?

2 As a consultant, how might you advise the relevant parties in such situations to deal with the issues identified in order to ensure an effective handover of leadership and the continuance of the business into the future?

Figure 16.3 Determinants of trust

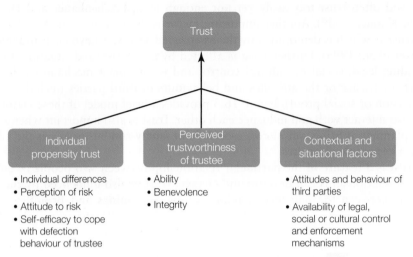

identify three factors that can serve as sources of trust. These include the experience of the other party not taking advantage when it was possible for them to do so, the keeping of commitments they have given, and general honesty in the interactions that form part of the relationship. In addition to these three factors of (avoidance of) advantage taking, commitment keeping and negotiation honesty, Meyerson *et al.*, (1996) also identify familiarity, shared experience, mutual disclosures, and relevant threats and deterrents as traditional sources of trust. Given that many of these factors can work in both directions, it is not surprising that evidence shows that trust can be reciprocal: trust begets trust (Serva *et al.*, 2005). Similarly, trust in networks of relationships can over time become a feature of the social structure in organizations, which in turn reinforces, through repeated experiences and developing norms, the relevant expectations regarding trustworthiness and trusting behaviour (e.g., Coleman, 1984; Granovetter, 1985).

The development and management of trust in organization

Lewicki and Bunker (1996; see also Shapiro *et al.*, 1992) have proposed a three-stage model of how trust can develop in relationships, which reflects many of the sources of trust discussed above. The first stage of trust development is called *deterrence-based trust*. This form of trust is based on the adequacy and cost of deterrence, i.e., of credible threats of punishment for defection and failure to cooperate (e.g., punishments, legal sanctions, withholding of incentives or rewards). Such systems can be costly because they rely on control and thus require potentially expensive and resource-intensive feedback and surveillance systems. Moreover, such systems often bring about reactance because they are experienced as limiting one's independence and personal freedom (see the discussions of technological surveillance and control in Chapters 11 and 12).

After repeated interactions, such deterrence-based trust can develop into *knowledge-based trust,* which reflects the increasing level of knowledge of the other's dispositions, intentions and behaviour patterns that makes their behaviour more predictable. While this type of trust is not control-based, it can also be costly because it can take time to assemble relevant information about the other's behaviour. The eBay feedback rating system is designed to create and communicate the reputation of buyers and sellers to inform prospective trading partners of their past trading histories and the experiences of their respective trading partners. This provides information that can be used to decide if a particular trading partner is trustworthy – based on knowledge about past behaviour. Note that eBay also reserves the right to exclude violators from trading – thus, it couples knowledge-based and deterrence-based approaches to enable trust among potential trading partners.

Identification-based trust reflects the fact that rather than using comparison information and predictions regarding likely behaviour, trust is based on the understanding that the other party has taken on one's own needs and desires as personal goals and will act in ways that consider joint gains. This is often a feature of close family and personal relationships. Organizational culture and group cohesion are mechanisms in organizations that can support the development of this form of trust. A particular arena in which trust (as well as fairness) is important is in situations in which an organization operates in different countries, especially when very different cultural and business norms exist, as is evident in the Going Global example.

The development of trust is an important dynamic within as well as across organizations. In a study of complex interorganizational information technology alliances, for example, the development of higher levels of trust went hand-in-hand with more partner learning and higher levels of performance (Ybarra and Turk, 2009).

Communication clearly plays a central role in the development of trust, but full explanations of the impact of communication on trust are just beginning to emerge. For example, the quality of information appears to be related to trust in co-workers and supervisors while adequacy of information is important for developing trust in the top management (Thomas *et al.*, 2009). Differences in the nature of relationships can help explain such differences. Communication processes and media are also important for understanding trust dynamics in virtual settings. So far, the role of trust in virtual teams and electronically mediated relationships remains unclear. While most researchers agree that trust is of particular importance in virtual settings (e.g., Curşeu *et al.*, 2007; Jarvenpaa and Leidner, 1999; Lu *et al.*, 2006; Piccoli and Ives, 2003), others argue that performance can be independent of trust and trust development in virtual contexts (e.g., Aubrey and Kelsey, 2003). A study of 116 new product development teams (Bierly *et al.*, 2009) that varied in the degree to which they employed virtual teamwork indicates that trust dynamics may differ fundamentally between face-to-face and virtual interactions. Specifically, these researchers found that relationship conflict can affect virtual teams more profoundly, possibly because it is harder to resolve such conflict without rich face-to-face interactions. Goal clarity appears to be more important for trust development in face-to-face settings, and trust matters less for virtual teams than for face-to-face teams. At the same time, a study of dyadic relationships indicates that in competitive situations, initial face-to-face interactions can facilitate the development of trust and collaboration when people interact through computer-mediated (i.e., virtual) media. (Hill *et al.*, 2009). Another recent study of virtual teams indicates that trust is more important for the performance of functionally diverse teams (Peters and Karren, 2009).

Organizational policies and practices can also be used to reach higher levels of interpersonal trust among members. Six and Sorge (2008) argue that practices such as promoting care and concern among members and creating a more relationship-oriented culture; facilitating the display of credible concern for others laterally and across hierarchical levels; conducting value-congruent induction and socialization; offering more opportunities for informal meetings among members; and deploying mechanisms to match and develop members' professional competencies can increase interpersonal trust. Similarly, Miller and Bedford (2003) suggest the following

GOING GLOBAL

Doing business in Nigeria

The following is based on a discussion with Richard Mack, a senior consultant who travels to many parts of the world managing high-technology projects on behalf of major multinational clients. It should be noted that the points made below can apply to many countries of the world, not just Nigeria. Reference to it simply helps to fix a particular geographic location and context for the discussion.

Personal productivity and punctuality in Nigeria are fluid terms based on what is affectionately called 'Nigeria Time' by everyone who works there. The road and traffic systems are so bad that there is no guarantee that you can get to where you need to be either on time, or even in time to attend a prearranged meeting. It also seriously disrupts the ability to do any work at all! When a Nigerian says that they will 'be there in 10 minutes' it can mean that they actually arrive several hours later! Meetings can be arranged days in advance but the chances of anyone turning up are slim. Cultural issues also have an impact on how things get done. For example, Richard said that in his experience people rarely keep appointments and if they do they are always in a rush to be off in order to do something else. Richard explained (as an example) that he had arranged one meeting for a Monday morning at 10:00am and when by midday no one else had arrived he sent text messages and tried to phone the individuals – to no avail. The meeting was then abandoned. However on the following Thursday an individual (who was the key client attendee of the previously abandoned meeting) arrived halfway through a different meeting and asked 'can we do it (the original meeting) now?'

In terms of travelling around Nigerian cities, Richard said that he had spent 3.5 hours travelling 6 km – but that it was too dangerous to get out and walk. It was also necessary to be collected from (and delivered to) the airport and to be escorted from the hotel to the office each day by a known personal driver and vehicle, at a cost of around US $300 per day. The roads are always very busy and although traffic lights do exist, most of them don't work, the road systems are essentially a free for all. Communications and electronic connectivity are also major areas of concern,

telephone call quality, telephone call cut-offs, bandwidth problems are ever present difficulties and it varies throughout the day.

It is also exceptionally expensive to do business in Nigeria, with high accommodation costs (around US $100,000 to rent a two-bedroom apartment for a year) or up to US $700 per night for a hotel room. Currency volatility is linked almost entirely to the cost of a barrel of oil. The infrastructure for power and plant is limited and most business and computer operation centres run on in-house generators all of the time – resulting in added energy costs being incurred. Food is also expensive; no-one (other than a few hotels) accepts, credit cards, so everything has to be paid for with cash. There is also an active black market for currency trading where forex rates can be negotiated in the local souvenir shop or by playing one 'trader' off against another. There are also tax and profit issues that have to be taken into account when doing business. The Nigerian currency (Naira) is almost impossible to exchange to another currency outside the country itself. However, all clients want to pay in Naira as opposed to US dollars. So assuming any profits are made from a business venture, it is not possible to take the money out of the country. Air freight is essential (but costly) for moving products around the country in order to achieve deadlines. By comparison, it is not uncommon for ships to sit in the harbour and queue for several months to get into port to unload. However, those that are willing to 'pay' additional fees to the port authorities can get preferential treatment and jump the queue. From a vendor or supplier perspective, there is a heavy expectation that business partners will have a physical presence in the country. Attempting to do everything remotely – only taking orders locally – will not work and causes problems. Nigerians want a clear commitment to business relationships by having a presence and investment in the country.

In addition to the above, employee expectations are very different from those in European countries. For example, setting career goals and career plans is very difficult when life expectancy is only 47 (according to UNICEF). There exists a right-now attitude and approach to work and life – for example, 'What can I earn today so that I can spend it tomorrow?' Labour turnover is a major cause for concern and the use of retention bonuses just fuels higher salaries. Spiralling salary costs are also driven by the oil companies who buy whatever resources they need at any price – which continually drives inflation and market rates upwards. High labour turnover also reduces the level of expertise and experience in many organizations. Richard explained that he had worked with organizations where the most experienced employees had no more than 2 years service, with the average employee staying about 6 months. Richard went on to explain that this approach to work also affected team work and, similar to his experience in India, when one individual found a higher paying job (not necessarily a better job) other colleagues would follow them. This in turn stimulated supply and demand processes that drove both wage increases and inflation. Richard had noticed in late 2008 and 2009 that the general economic slowdown resulted in more local people returning to Nigeria.

TASK

1 What does this example suggest about relationships, fairness and trust in business relationships in Nigeria specifically (and when working internationally generally)?

Source:
Reproduced with grateful thanks to Richard Mack.

five step process as the way to (re-)establish trust at a company level based on the establishment of core values:

1 *Identify the core values.* Core values define the make-up of the organization and should reflect its culture.

2 *Bring the core values to life.* For each core value, develop behavioural statements that contribute to shared understandings for all members of the organization.

3 *Spell out the do and don't aspects of each value.* Elaborate each of the behavioural statements with specific examples of do and don't aspects of the behaviour so that everyone is clear about what is expected of them.

4 *Weave values into the fabric of the organization.* Ensure that the core values and associated behaviours are reflected in all aspects of operational activity. This should also be reinforced through training and development programmes intended to reinforce the new core values and implications for behaviour.

5 *Ensure accountability and model the way.* Ensure that senior managers set a good example in all that they do; they should act as a model for all staff. Hold all employees accountable for their behaviour. Reward good behaviour that reflects the core values and deal firmly with behaviours that do not support them.

Restoring trust and addressing distrust

One of the key features of trust is the asymmetric nature of trust and distrust – it is hard to build trust but all too easy to lose it! Trust is always linked to suspicion and the possibility of distrust because of the risk of defection and exploitation that goes hand-in-hand with vulnerability (e.g., Deutsch, 1958). Thus, the issue of restoring trust that has been destroyed by a violation is an important issue because such situations can arise in any relationship that involves uncertainty, interdependence and risk that have been addressed with trust.

Recent research has addressed this issue of rebuilding trust from an attributional perspective (e.g., Kim *et al.*, 2009; Kim *et al.*, 2006; Kim *et al.*, 2004; Tomlinson and Mayer, 2009; see also the systemic approach by Gillespie and Dietz, 2009). The basis of this approach is that the trustor (whose trust has been violated) makes causal attributions (see also Chapter 4) that determine the reactions to trust-rebuilding attempts. Of course, such attributions can be – at least to a certain degree – influenced by the trustee (the violator). Some attributions may make it easier to restore and rebuild trust. Specifically, Kim and colleagues (2009) present a bilateral model of trust repair (see Figure 16.4) that explains how the trustor analyses a trust violation and assesses the implications for possible trust repair. At Level 1, the trustor needs to decide if a trust violation has taken place and if the trustee is to blame. If the trustee is guilty, the trustor must decide (Level 2) if the causes for the violation are internal (person) or external (situation). If the violation is based on internal (person) reasons, the trustor must decide (Level 3) if this is a fixed and enduring cause that cannot be changed, or if there is potential for fixing the problem and restoring trust. However, if it is fixable, behavioural efforts to bring about a rapprochement are still needed. In this research stream there is some debate about the relative merits of different approaches to trustee responses after trust violations. For example, the benefits of taking (e.g., apology) compared to avoiding responsibility (i.e., denial) probably depend on a number of factors (see Kim *et al.*, 2009; Tomlinson and Mayer, 2009) in the particular situation and the resulting likelihood of different trustor perceptions and attributions.

Extreme forms of trust-repair approaches can include substantive penance (Bottom *et al.*, 2002) which includes *the transfer of valuable resources in reparation for the violation*, or voluntary hostage posting (Nakayachi and Watabe, 2005) which involves *providing decision control over valuable resources of the trustee to the trustor* as a signal that such violations will not reoccur. These are forms of restorative justice, an approach that is gaining in prominence in a range of contexts (Menkel-Meadow, 2007) even though it is relatively new and still very rare in management and OB. There are clear parallels between trust-rebuilding approaches and the remedies used in addressing perceived injustices (e.g., Reb *et al.*, 2006) in that the response should address the nature of the violation appropriately.

A more common and general approach to rebuilding trust is described by Thompson (2009) in the context of negotiations. This approach is similar to and compatible with the process of using assertive communication to improve relationships (Bolton, 1979) discussed above. It advises to take responsibility as a starting point for collaboratively rebuilding trust. A streamlined and slightly extended version of Thompson's approach is described in Table 16.5.

Substantive penance
An extreme form of trust repair which involves the transfer of valuable resources in reparation for a trust violation. See also hostage posting.

Hostage posting
An extreme form of trust repair which involves providing decision control over valuable resources of the trustee to the trustor as a signal that such violations will not reoccur. See also substantive penance.

Figure 16.4 Bilateral model of trust repair

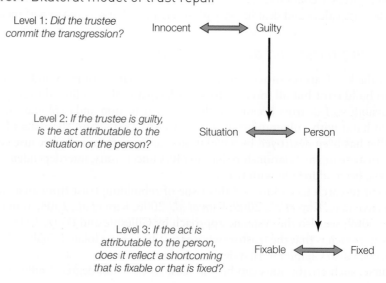

Level 1: *Did the trustee commit the transgression?*   Innocent ⟷ Guilty

Level 2: *If the trustee is guilty, is the act attributable to the situation or the person?*   Situation ⟷ Person

Level 3: *If the act is attributable to the person, does it reflect a shortcoming that is fixable or that is fixed?*   Fixable ⟷ Fixed

Source: Kim, Dirks and Cooper, 2009.

Table 16.5 A process for repairing broken trust

1.	Insist on a personal meeting right away – Face-to-face communication is essential for trust (re)building.
2.	Tell the other party that you value the relationship – focus the conversation on the important aspects.
3.	Provide a sincere apology for your behaviour and let them vent.
4.	Do not get defensive, no matter how wrong you think they are – and validate at least some aspect of what they say.
5.	Ask for clarifying information and test your understanding.
6.	Let them tell you what they require, and again test your understanding.
7.	Think about ways to provide them with what they require to prevent future problems.
8.	Do an evaluation of the situation at a scheduled date and plan a future together.

Source: Adapted from Thompson, 2009.

CONCLUSIONS

This chapter is based on the view that people are the basic building blocks of any organization. The interactions between and among individuals create the stable patterns of activity that we observe and experience as organizations. The nature and role of relationships among organizational members is at the heart of virtually all phenomena discussed in this book. In this chapter, we explored the nature of relationships, including the nature of the psychological contract that defines and is defined by the employment relationship, and the role and nature of the network of relationships that exists in organizations. We also discussed the closely related topic of fairness and justice perceptions in organizations and explored their role in interactions as well as their implications for people management in organizations. Finally, we considered the nature and role of trust in organizations, and how trust developed and – most importantly – how it can be rebuilt if it has been lost.

Now to summarize this chapter in terms of the relevant Learning Objectives:

- **Assess the major behaviours identified in this chapter that are suggested to build and maintain relationships.** In general, the activities that help to build and maintain relationships outlined in this chapter include supportive, appreciative, informative, inclusive, empowering, validating and respectful behaviours such as:

  – Invite input in appropriate forms and at appropriate times.

  – Show acceptance and validate at least some aspects of suggestions and opinions.

  – Be direct and honest yet polite and courteous.

  – Act friendly and show patience.

  – Be considerate of specific needs, interests, and circumstances.

  – Take the other's emotional state into account (e.g., fear, anxiety, excitement).

  – Show your willingness to consider the other's perspective.

  – Offer assistance with work when needed and appropriate.

  – Avoid making decisions that take responsibility away from the other.

  – Keep an appropriate information flow that informs without overwhelming.

  – Show confidence in the other's abilities.

  – Remember personal details regarding the person.

  – Acknowledge all contributions and accomplishments.

  – Provide autonomy, challenge and support in balanced ways.

  – Validate the other's identity and help maintain their sense of personal worth and importance.

  – Act respectfully at all times.

Each one of these has implications for the behaviour of employees and managers within an organization and this learning objective expects that you could interpret each of these along with the provision of some evaluation of their practicality, relevance and value in developing and maintaining effective working relationships.

- **Explain social exchange theory.** The study of relationships in organizational contexts has been traditionally based on social exchange theories originally developed in sociology and social psychology. These classic contributions provide conceptions of interpersonal relationships as exchange relationships in which each actor engages to maximize the value they receive. This value can differ on the dimension of tangible (e.g., goods) or intangible (e.g., status), and on the dimension of objectively and generally valuable (e.g., money) to subjectively and person-specifically valuable (e.g., love and affection). Value can be derived from the responses of the other person as well as from acting towards the other person. Such value from relationship behaviour can be derived from a range of sources, including normative (e.g., acting based on internalized social norms), value-expressive (e.g., acting to display an aspirational self-image), and affiliative, intrinsic and emotional (e.g., the feelings of contentment and joy from interacting with a partner). Many different versions and formulations of social exchange theory exist, including such influential formulations such as interdependence theory and equity theory, but they share common basic elements that are summarized and discussed in the relevant sections of the chapter above. According to social exchange theory, the actual behaviour in such exchange relationships is influenced by rational considerations such as rewards and costs, and by behavioural principles of rewards and punishment.

- **Discuss the psychological contract and its significance for relationships within organizations.** The informal expectations that employee and employer have of each other is termed the psychological contract. More specifically, the psychological contract refers to the individual beliefs about the terms of the mutual exchange agreement between the individual and their organization. Thus, psychological contracts contribute to members' understanding of their roles and responsibilities in the organization and reflect what treatment they anticipate and what benefits they expect in return for their contributions. Psychological contracts reflect individual perceptions, views and attitudes,

but nevertheless they are influenced by social information and comparison processes and may be shared. Moreover, the self-serving bias in perception and attribution (discussed in Chapter 4) often create expectations that diverge substantially from those of the organization. Therefore, even well meaning and arguably legitimate behaviour by agents of the organization (e.g., managers) can violate expectations individuals have based on their understanding of the psychological contract. Such breaches or violations of the subjective psychological contract can lead to profound behavioural, cognitive and emotional reactions. Research indicates that psychological contract breaches can lead to higher turnover and absenteeism, lower job satisfaction, increased cynicism and lower organizational citizenship behaviour, lower perceived support and reduced trust in the organization.

- **Outline the meaning of organizational justice and discuss its relevance to how fairness might be understood within an organization context.** In all considerations of social exchange and relationships within organizations, a central concern of those involved is always the fairness of the interactions. In fact, ever since the early contributions to social exchange theory and the study of relationships in organizations, issues of fairness, equity, equality and need have always been considered as central features of exchange relationships. This has led to the emergence of a particular area of study, called organizational justice, one of the most active research areas in OB in recent times. Formally, organizational justice is concerned with employees' fairness perceptions regarding their work and conditions of employment and their behavioural reactions to this. This definition highlights a particular approach to considering justice and fairness. Unlike philosophical investigations that view justice as an absolute value and determine what is fair based on normative logical comparisons or on the outcome of moral reasoning, OJ and fairness in organizations are treated as subjective perceptions – in other words, fair is what is experienced as fair. That means that one member of a workgroup may perceive a particular action of the manager as fair, while another one experiences it as a grave injustice. OJ investigates the nature of such fairness perceptions, the factors that determine these perceptions, the processes by which these views are created and may change over time, and the behavioural and cognitive reactions to the experience of fairness and particularly unfairness. Research suggests that OJ is related to factors such as job satisfaction and satisfaction with rewards and other outcomes, trust, commitment to the organization, performance, organizational citizenship behaviours compliance, co operation, absenteeism, withdrawal behaviours, and stress.

- **Understand what trust is and how it can be created and managed in an organizational context.** Many different conceptions of trust exist, and the concept is often used synonymously with terms such as cooperation, confidence and predictability. However, while closely related, logically trust must include the notion of vulnerability or risk that is not necessarily inherent in these three concepts. If others cannot affect us negatively, there is no need for trust in them (yet people may still cooperate with them, have confidence in them, or view them as predictable). However, it would be nonsensical to talk about trust in someone or something that cannot affect us in any way. Trust refers to the degree to which a person (or entity)

makes themselves vulnerable to another person (or entity) despite uncertainty about the other's possible actions. This behavioural definition differs slightly from similar definitions that focus on trust as the willingness to make oneself vulnerable. Both definitions describe trust as based on the belief that those we depend upon will meet our expectations of them, but the behavioural definition ties trust to observable behaviour. Lewicki and Bunker proposed a three-stage model of how trust can develop in relationships. The first stage is called deterrence-based trust. After repeated interactions such deterrence-based trust can develop into knowledge-based trust, which reflects the increasing level of knowledge of the other's dispositions, intentions, and behaviour patterns that makes their behaviour more predictable. Identification-based trust reflects the third stage in that trust is based on the understanding that the other party has taken on one's own needs and desires as personal goals and act in ways that consider joint gains.

DISCUSSION QUESTIONS

1 'Close relationships are not possible between bosses and subordinates, as it is a power-based relationship. Equally close relationships between subordinates are not in management's interest, as they might create a power-base that could threaten management control.' Discuss this statement in the light of the information in this chapter.

2 Explain social exchange theory and discuss the role and significance of networking in it.

3 What is assertiveness in terms of communication and how might it help to deal with difficult relationships?

4 'The psychological contract is the means by which both managers and subordinates achieve what they want from the working relationship on a day-to-day basis without having to make constant reference back to the formal contract of employment or company procedures, which in any event cannot cover every eventuality.' Discuss this statement.

5 To what extent are networks essential for the achievement of efficient company operations? What is their role in organizations with high degrees of formalization, standardization and extensive formal control systems?

6 Discuss the significance of organizational justice in the creation of fairness in an organization.

7 'Trust can only ever exist in successful and profitable organizations because when those conditions are not present, people often lose their jobs, change is often forced onto people and promotions are scarce.' To what extent can you support this statement? Justify your answer.

8 To what extent do you agree with the view that trust is easy to break and virtually impossible to restore?

9 'Management is at its heart a manipulative process in that employee behaviour must be directed and channelled in order to achieve management – determined objectives. Consequently fairness in the true sense of the term is impossible and managers must find ways of presenting their manipulative activities in ways that keep employees engaged and supportive of management's objectives.' Discuss.

10 As a manager, how would you try to create trust with your subordinates when your boss is always demanding that you increase productivity and reduce labour cost?

CASE STUDY

Phoebe's firm went into administration!

Phoebe was an Account Director with a firm of public relations consultants based in Manchester. She had worked for them for over 8 years, joining them as a junior consultant as her second position in PR since leaving a prestigious university with a good degree. She was highly thought of by her colleagues and clients, which resulted in her rapid promotion first to Consultant, then Senior Consultant and finally to Account Director after only 5 years working for her current employer. As an Account Director she was responsible to the Board for all PR activity for a defined number of clients. The clients that Phoebe was responsible for included some large international businesses which represented major sources of professional status for the consultancy as well as significant revenue streams. Everything was going well for both Phoebe and her employer and early in 2008 she took maternity leave, fully intending to return to work early in 2009. In her absence only temporary, casual and generally inadequate cover was provided to her clients and consequently the service quality dropped and a number of clients cancelled their contracts and engaged other consultancies. In addition to this failure to adequately service the client base, the credit crunch that began in 2008 took its toll on other areas in the consultancy portfolio and during the year that Phoebe was on maternity leave several small-scale redundancies were put into effect, reducing the number of consultants (across all levels) from a total of 30 to 20.

The owner of the consultancy made several attempts to sell the business during 2008 but could not agree a price and so continued operating. Eventually late in 2008 the combination of loss of business and a failure to sell the company left the consultancy in a precarious state just as Phoebe was about to return to work after maternity leave – along with another consultant who had also been on maternity leave. After some negotiation, it was agreed that Phoebe would return to work for 3 days each week and that her primary role would be to assist other consultants and attract new business - as her previous client base had either left or been allocated to other members of staff. Rumours within the company were rife about bankruptcy and being taken over and employee morale had slumped. Employees had begun to look for jobs with other companies and the one or two who were offered a new job accepted them immediately.

In early March 2009 matters came to a head and the owner of the firm announced that with effect from the next day the consultancy was going into administration. He was hopeful, however, that a buyer for the viable parts of the consultancy could be found and that some people would be able to continue their employment. The administrator arrived and announced that all business activity should cease and that no wages would be paid for the previous two weeks. Staff were advised that everyone would lose their jobs and that redundancy pay and outstanding wages would be paid by the government under schemes to provide very basic protection to employees in such situations. A meeting was arranged for about 3 days later when

© Motofish Images/Corbis

the administrator hoped to be able to finalize things and announce officially what was going to happen.

The meeting was arranged for Thursday (a day Phoebe did not work) so she had to arrange childcare. However, the meeting was cancelled at short notice and arranged for the following day. This angered Phoebe as it was difficult to organize childcare at short notice, but her husband arranged to work from home the next day and so was able to look after their child for the couple of hours of the meeting. Phoebe drove to her office with a heavy heart on the Friday and met her colleagues, one of whom said that it was good news that a potential purchaser had e-mailed round everyone asking for home contact details and promising to be in touch over the following weekend. This shocked Phoebe as she had not had any such e-mail. The colleague who told her was mortified by this and also very embarrassed and upset. The administrator called everyone into the meeting room (Mark, the existing owner of the business was also in attendance) and said that they were being made redundant with immediate effect. They were told to hand over company car keys and that anyone with a company car would be provided with a taxi to take them home. They were also told that they were to take nothing away from the office and that they would be searched on the way out!

At this point Phoebe was furious and let it be known that she was aware of the e-mail request for home contact details (sent by the prospective purchaser before everyone had been officially notified that their employment had been terminated). She said that it was an unfair and unreasonable act on the part of the new owners and showed a complete lack of respect for everyone. She said how badly she felt the new owners had handled the whole e-mail situation. Mark said that he agreed with her and went off to call them to discuss matters - which Phoebe felt sure he did not do! Phoebe went home with very mixed emotions knowing that in practice all of her clients had been allowed to drift away unnecessarily because of poor service while she was on maternity leave. As well as having a negative impact on the business, this had effectively put her in a disadvantageous position with regard to being able to demonstrate her capabilities to the new owner of the business – which had all but eliminated the possibility of employment with them. Some of the staff left the office and went to a local pub to drown their sorrows. Mark, the previous owner of the business, subsequently turned up at the pub and claimed not to have realized that everyone would be

dismissed or that no one would be offered continuous employment with the new business!

On the following Monday Phoebe discovered that over the weekend all but seven of the 20 PR consultants had been offered jobs by the new owners of the consultancy. They had all started work that morning in different premises in Manchester. The 13 people starting work for the new owners were all men. The new owner of the business was a large London-based practice seeking to expand their offices in the North. The Manchester operation was to be run as a separate unit from the existing Edinburgh office but both were to report to a single Northern Regional Manager based predominantly in Edinburgh. The only PR staff not to be offered employment by the new company were a female Board Director (the only person at that level apart from Mark left in the old company) and three part-time females at Account Director and Senior Consultant levels (Phoebe and one other having both just returned from maternity leave and one other person). There was one female consultant not offered a job, and two more with other jobs to go to who were not considered for employment with the new firm. The final insult to Phoebe was that even Mark was offered (and accepted) a one day per week contract by the new owners!

Phoebe was forced to sign-on as unemployed at the local Job Centre in order to qualify for Job Seekers Allowance only to find that it was a humiliating experience that she felt demeaned her qualifications, experience and the level of her job. This was because it was obvious that the official government provision for job seekers did not extend to her level or type of work. The only vacancies available within the system were at the janitorial, manual or junior clerical levels. In addition she was required to be able to prove that she was actively seeking work by keeping a diary of her job application activity. It would be up to Phoebe to seek out suitable opportunities through her own initiative. Fortunately Phoebe found another job within 2 months.

TASKS

1 What might this case suggest about relationships, fairness and trust in an organizational context?

2 To what extent do administration and the legal requirements of such processes help to justify the actions of Mark, colleagues, the administrator and the new owners in this situation?

3 If you were Phoebe, how might this experience affect your attitudes to future employment situations?

4 If you were Phoebe's next employer, how might you go about (re-)establishing a good working relationship based on fairness and trust with her?

5 Could the outcome of this situation have been avoided (or the effects minimized) and if so, how and by whom?

6 If you were Phoebe, would you seek legal redress and if so, for what? To what extent and how does legislation have a role to play in seeking to encourage good working relationships, fairness and trust between employers and employees?

Source:
Discussion with Phoebe, only names and other minor details have been changed.

FURTHER READING

Folger, R. and Cropanzano, R. (1998) *Organizational justice and human resource management,* London: Sage. Comprehensive treatment of OJ theory and research.

Patterson, K., Grenny, J., McMillan, R. and Switzler, A. (2005), *Crucial confrontations*. McGraw-Hill. Helpful treatment of dealing with difficult conversations

Sutton, R. (2007) *The No-Asshole Rule* London: Sphere. Sage advice from a top OB researcher on how to identify and deal with 'those' kinds of people at work.

Rousseau, D. M. (1995) *Psychological contracts in organizations: Understanding written and unwritten agreements,* Thousand Oaks, CA: Sage. Comprehensive discussion of psychological contracts at work.

COMPANION WEBSITE

Online teaching and learning resources

Visit the companion website for Organizational Behaviour and Management 4th edition at: http://www.cengage.co.uk/martinfellenz to find valuable further teaching and learning material. For full details, see 'About the website' at the start of the book.

GLOSSARY

Ability Refers to the capacity of individuals to achieve the tasks they are trying to accomplish.

Acculturation A term used by anthropologists to describe what happens when people from one culture come into continuous direct contact with members of a different culture with changes to one or both of the cultures involved. In an organizational context it is very similar to the process of socialization.

Actor-observer effect Humans typically assume that observed behaviour tells us what kind of people others are, regardless of the situation. But humans tend to do the opposite and predominantly attribute their own behaviour to situational factors.

Adhocracy form (of structure) Sometimes called team-based organizations. This approach reflects the dominance of innovation as a major driving force in structure. Similar to the professional form but because the organization is focused on creating novelty and innovation, different experts must combine their expertise in ever changing groups.

Administrative management Considers management as those activities aimed at running the organization as a whole. See also classical management theory and bureaucracy.

Advocacy Refers to a process of undogmatic assertion that invites constructive engagement with the factual basis and logical argument supporting the assertion. See also assertiveness and enquiry.

Aesthetic labour Describes the management-determined mix of employee characteristics including appearance, age, weight, class and accent an intended to create a specific impression or image of the organization.

Alienation Work performed under conditions in which the worker is estranged from his or her own activity in the act of production, through the sale of labour power and the subordination of skills and knowledge to the capitalist or other external social forces. Sometimes described as feelings of powerlessness, meaninglessness, isolation or self-estrangement in which the person no longer feels part of, or involved with, the work that they do.

Ambidextrous organizations Manage to combine alignment and adaptability in their structure and design in responding to the specific demands of their environment.

Analysability The degree to which a transformation process, its individual steps and activities, and the impact of any action taken can be analysed and understood.

Anchor A comparison point for all further considerations of acceptability of an offer. See also aspirations and reservation point.

Anchoring and adjustment effects After being exposed to a particularly positive or negative experience or after receiving reference information, however relevant and legitimate it appears, people do not adjust their expectations for future events accordingly.

Anthropomorphize organizations Means that organizations are regarded as possessing the qualities of real actors with human features and abilities by assuming that they act, learn, compete, make decisions and generally function as if they were human.

Appreciative enquiry Deliberately focuses on investigating and strengthening what is already beneficial and successful in organizations rather than on adopting a problem or clinical approach that focuses on difficulties and failures.

Arbitrators Independent third parties who can impose binding agreements on the parties involved. See also conciliators and mediators.

Aspirations Sometimes called target points, these are a party's optimistic negotiation goals, i.e., what they hope to get out of a negotiation in the most favourable circumstances. See also anchor and reservation point.

Assertiveness A communication style that can help to address relationship difficulties. A process of interpersonal communication that is respectful of both one's own and the other party's needs, rights and interests. See also advocacy and enquiry.

Assessment centre Group-based recruitment or development device that typically includes tests, interviews, and group and individual exercises evaluated by a team of assessors.

Attitude Predisposed feeling, thought or behavioural response to a particular stimulus.

Attribution The process by which we ascribe causes to events as well as to our own and others' behaviour.

Attribution theory (of leadership) Suggests that leaders vary their reactions to subordinates based on observation of their behaviours.

Authentic followership Achieved by those who freely choose to follow based on their realistic view and assessment of the consistency of the leader's values and behaviours, the congruence of these values with their own, and their own assessment of the leader's authenticity, honesty and integrity in leading them. See also followership.

Authentic leadership This describes leaders use balanced and reasoned information processing, have an internalized moral perspective, offer relational transparency and exhibit high levels of self-awareness. See also value-based leadership.

Authority Refers to the legitimate power vested in managers based on their position and role in an organization.

Automatic vigilance Suggests that negative social information, which has the potential to harm a person, is automatically and quickly attended to.

Availability heuristic Relates to the ease with which a person can access a particular object or event through memory or imagination.

BATNA Stands for the **Best Alternative To a Negotiated Agreement.**

Best fit or contingency approach to HRM An outside-in perspective on HRM, the essential theme of which is that HR strategy needs to be relevant to and supportive of the business strategy. This approach assumes that the HRM aspects of organizational activity are the malleable variable – the outside factors are fixed and therefore the inside variables must flex to align the organization with them.

Boundary spanning units Units that buffer (protect, insulate) the operating core from environmental uncertainty. See also technical core.

Brainstorming An approach to decision making in which groups try to generate as many ideas as possible, avoid criticism of any ideas and strive to extend and build on others' ideas.

Bullying The act of intimidating or seeking to force someone to do something by subjecting them to persecution intended to undermine their confidence and self-esteem. A persistent, enduring form of abuse at work involving a power differential.

Bureaucracy An approach to organizing the activities within an organization which involves specialization of task, hierarchy of authority and decision making. See also classical management theory and administrative management.

Burnout A condition characterized by emotional exhaustion, lower concern about other people, and diminished personal accomplishment.

Business ethics Takes as its focus of interest right, wrong, good and bad in relation to behaviour in an organizational context.

Business partner Sometimes referred to as a strategic partner, this HR role involves working closely with line colleagues on the design of HR systems and processes that address strategic business issues. Intended to be more business-focused with a clear understanding of the client perspective (the line manager).

Business process re-engineering (BPR) An approach to reorganization in which the key business processes are identified, followed by the elimination of other activity and the rapid transformation of the organization to the desired process orientation.

Cabals Informal groups that attempt to push views supported by members to enhance their status and position.

Canonical practice Refers to the formal, espoused and prescriptive description of how tasks should be done and how technology is to be deployed. See also noncanonical practice.

Charismatic leadership The ability to exercise leadership through the power of the leader's personality.

Classical conditioning An approach to learning developed by Pavlov in which he used dogs to demonstrate that when the conditioned stimulus (bell) was associated with an unconditioned stimulus (food) over several repetitions, a conditioned response resulted (salivation to the sound of the bell). See also operant conditioning.

Classical management theory An approach to organizing emphasized issues such as the scalar chain, exception principle, unity of command, organizational specialization, span of control and the application of scientific management and not just structure. See also administrative management and bureaucracy.

Coalitions Groups of managers (or others) whose views of organizational goals and relative problem importance are aligned at least temporarily. They emerge as a result of differing individual (and/or group) interests and because of the level of uncertainty present in an organization.

Co-creation Refers to the direct and joint involvement of service provider and consumer in the service value creation process, and is a central difference between manufacturing and service technology.

Coercive power The ability of a holder of such power to achieve control over another person through the threat of direct action, force or violence.

Cognitive abilities These refer to a broad range of mental capabilities.

Cognitive dissonance An aversive state that motivates individuals to resolve apparent conflict among attitudes, beliefs, values and behaviours.

Communication The process by which people convey and receive information to and from each other.

Communities of practice Ongoing groups of people that interact and actively share information while engaging in an activity they are individually and collectively committed to.

Competency traps Sometimes also referred to as knowledge traps. Such traps can occur when the experience and competence in using an inferior technology produces satisfactory results which makes it difficult or impossible to see the advantages to be gained from adopting a newer, superior technology.

Complexity Refers to the wide range of people and environmental factors that may have a bearing on the intended activity, functioning and outcome of an organization and management.

Complexity Refers to the wide range of people and environmental factors that may have a bearing on an issue.

Compliance Describes the acquiescence to a particular explicit or implicit request. See also obedience.

Concessions Represent improvements in an offer made to the other party as part of the progress towards reaching a negotiated agreement.

Conciliators Third parties who can provide advice on the negotiation content and suggest agreement options. See also arbitrators and mediators.

Concordet Jury Theorem States that groups voting on decisions will improve their decision quality if they add members who on average are right in their votes more often than they are wrong.

Concordet's Paradox Highlights potential problems with group decision making because the outcome of group decisions may depend on the order in which options considered.

Conditioned The behaviour of an individual which results from the application of behaviourism techniques.

Configurational theories More complex than contingency theories of structure because they integrate more variables into structural arrangements and because they assume that different structures can be equally appropriate in the same environment. See also equifinality.

Confirmation bias (also known as confirmatory bias) A tendency to seek out information that is in line with expectations and existing knowledge.

Conflict Refers to situations in which the interests of different parties are not aligned. This frequently emerges when the differences between two or more groups or individuals become apparent.

Conflict management Defined as any activity or provision that aims at reducing, increasing, creating or solving conflict to achieve the most appropriate level of conflict. See also conflict prevention and conflict resolution.

Conflict model of customer experience and organizational functioning This reflects the difficulty of functional groups being able to meet customer needs in a hierarchical organization.

Conflict prevention Refers to any organizational or interpersonal arrangement or process that reduces the risk of open conflict. See also conflict management and conflict resolution.

Conflict resolution Refers to any attempt to lower the level of conflict by reducing the source or consequence of differences in interests between conflicting parties. See also conflict prevention, conflict management and conflict resolution efficacy.

Conflict resolution efficacy The belief that the conflict can be easily resolved. See also conflict resolution.

Conformity Refers to the act of changing one's behaviour to match the responses of others.

Consideration Originating from the Ohio State University studies which began in 1945 and reflects the degree to which the leader has respect and a rapport with subordinates as well as concern for their welfare. See also initiating structure.

Contingency models Takes the view that the best style of leadership depends upon the factors active in the specific situation.

Contingency theories (of organization) Reject simplistic and universalist ideas and consider the impact that interactions between structural and relevant environmental, situational, or organizational factors may have on the intended outcomes.

Contract approaches (to ethics) Based on fairness, these approaches to resolving ethical dilemmas are grounded in the notion that agreements, whether they be explicit or tacit, should be honoured. It comes in two variations, restricted contractarianism and libertarian contractarianism. See also utilitarian approaches to ethics.

Control The function of regulating events, action, outcomes or other relevant aspects according to preferred standards, plans, objectives or other chosen referents.

Core self-evaluation A dispositional factor (i.e., a stable trait) that closely reflects locus of control, emotional stability (neuroticism) as well as self-esteem and generalized performance confidence. People with positive core self-evaluations view themselves positively across situations and see themselves as capable, in control and generally valuable.

Core technology Refers to the means employed in the transformation activities that lead to the main outputs of the organization such as cars (motor company) or financial services (bank).

Corporate governance Defined by the Cadbury Committee as the systems through which companies are directed and controlled. It is about the ways in which ethics finds expression in business activities.

Corporate social responsibility (CSR) This refers to the rights and responsibilities of an organization relative to its social context.

Countercultures The existence of one or more groups that have objectives running counter to those of the dominant group.

Covariation This refers to the degree to which two elements appear or change together.

Craft technology A situation in which analysability is low and variety is also low. Represents situations in which the way in which desired outcomes can be achieved are often not fully understood or even understandable. See also engineering technology.

Critical incident technique Data collection method that involves asking for the most relevant aspects of experiences. The collected answers can then be systematically analysed to shed light on a particular phenomenon.

Cultural web The routines, rituals, stories, symbols, power structures, control systems and organization structure that contribute to a particular culture.

Customer centricity A business model that places customer value at the heart of all organizational value creation processes.

Decision control This was identified by Vroom and Yetton in their model of leadership and reflects the authority to make the decision. See also process control.

Decision interrupt Events originating within or outside the decision-making process that force the recycling through steps already taken.

Decision making A process through which a course of action or solution is identified and chosen from the options available.

Delegation of authority An action by managers in which they give some of their authority for decision making to subordinates.

Delphi technique A decision-making process that enables large numbers of people to be involved without them ever having to meet in person.

Departmentation Refers to the grouping together of activities in organizational subunits.

Dependence The state of being dependent, of relying upon another. If someone with whom you have a relationship provides regular and desirable interactions and exchanges, or they may just have the potential to affect you in positive or negative ways – you will have a degree of dependence on them for the positive or negative consequences they deliver.

Deterministic views Describe structure as a function of factors largely outside of human and managerial influence.

Devil's advocate A person specifically tasked with challenging the argument or opinion put forward by another person or group.

Dialectical enquiry An approach that uses a subgroup to sequentially develop assumptions and decision options, with a second subgroup charged with deliberately developing assumptions that differ from and even challenge the first subgroups' work.

Direct discrimination Occurs when an employer specifically and directly uses sex or race as a decision variable in a particular situation.

Distributed or shared leadership Refers to situations in which the function of leadership is jointly exercised by a number of highly interdependent, intensely collaborating and closely interacting individuals.

Distributive bargaining Describes an approach to negotiation in which whatever one party gets is not available to the other party and vice versa. This is also often referred to as a fixed pie situation. See also integrative bargaining.

Distributive justice Concerned with individuals' perceptions of the fairness of outcomes. See also informational justice, interactional justice, organizational justice and procedural justice.

Diversified form Typically diversifies first across different domains (such as markets, products/services, regions or customer segments) and then divisionalizes [often called strategic business units (SBUs)] by concentrating activities within the unit dealing with a particular domain. There is relative autonomy in each division and different internal structural arrangements are possible across different divisions, although machine forms tend to be most common.

Diversity Seeks to go beyond equality with its legislative basis and ensure that organizations are able to capture the benefits of 'difference' as a means of developing competitive advantage.

Division of labour The term describes breaking up the overall task into specialized and smaller activities in the search for higher levels of productivity and job specialization.

Divisional structure Sometimes called product, geographic or strategic business unit (SBU) structure. The divisional structure results in multiple subunits focused on different products, regions and markets or market segments.

Drives and motives These reflect the distinction between unconscious physiological reactions based on the physiological/biological needs of the body (drives) and the social process directing controllable behaviour in people (motives).

Ego According to Freudian psychoanalysis this is the conscious mind which serves as the locus of active decision making of the individual and mediates between wants (Id) and shoulds (Super-ego).

Emotional intelligence Defined by the originators as 'the ability to carry out accurate reasoning about emotions and the ability to use emotions and emotional knowledge to enhance thought'.

Empirical research Research that uses data on observable phenomena as the basis for generating knowledge.

Employee empowerment Represents a form of involvement and means that employees are allowed to take decisions without reference to a more senior authority.

Employee involvement Represents an opportunity for employees to become involved beyond the normal scope of their job in decision making and/or the running of the business.

Employee relations The activity within HRM that is involved with any aspect of an organization that might have an impact on the management of people and the creation of a high-performing work environment. It is about the employment relationship between management and employees.

Employee voice This implies mechanisms that encourage employees to articulate their concerns, feelings, worries, thoughts and opinions. By fully engaging employees through voice, employee involvement should become more meaningful with high commitment and performance resulting.

Employer brand 'A set of attributes and qualities – often intangible – that makes an organization distinctive, promises a particular kind of employment experience and appeals to those people who will thrive and perform best in its culture.'

Employer of choice Being a company that people actively seek to join, so contributing to high performance over a long time.

Enacted role What the individual actually does in fulfilling their role responsibilities.

Endowment effect People tend to value an item more highly if it is in their possession compared to their valuation if it is not.

Engineering technology A situation in which high analysability together with high variety exist in the tasks to be performed. The range of tasks is typically handled according to well established and highly structured approaches, procedures and techniques. See also craft technology.

Enhancing cultures A sub-culture that is largely supportive of the prevailing culture.

Entrepreneurial form Also called the *simple form (of structure)*. Typically found in small organizations based on a small strategic apex which directly controls activities in the operating core with little in terms of middle line, technostructure or support functions.

Environmental influences The influence of the environment on the development of a person's personality.

Equality A primarily legislative-based approach to seeking to ensure that disadvantaged groups in a particular society are not discriminated against in employment matters.

Equifinality Holds that different sets of factors and structural arrangements can lead to similar outcomes (or, more colloquially, that many different routes can lead to the same destination).

Ergonomics A multidisciplinary approach to considering how people can best conduct specific work tasks.

Ethical leadership Leadership that is aligned with a moral code that provides consistency among the ends, means and consequences of the behaviour that leaders themselves exhibit and induce in followers. See also value-based leadership.

Exception principle Delegation of decision making to the lowest level possible.

Expected role The specific role that an individual is to fulfil, frequently specified in a job description.

Expert power This source of power originates from the knowledge, skill and expertise of an individual in a particular context.

Explicit attitudes Reason-based attitudes that people can report and which they can actively control.

External attribution Explanation for behaviour that focuses on external causes, such as situational demands and influences.

Extinction This refers to the removal of response with the result that the likelihood of the target behaviour decreases. See also positive reinforcement, negative reinforcement and punishment.

Extrinsic motivation This describes the situation in which the impetus for behaviour originates outside the person and the performed task; in simple terms the activity is done in pursuit of another end. See also intrinsic motivation.

Extroversion The qualities of excitability, sociability and liveliness in an individual.

Felt fair Means that something should be perceived as fair by the people subjected to the system or procedure.

Flow This refers to the complete involvement in an activity that enables all relevant task skills and emotional and cognitive resources to be employed in an experience that is intensely fulfilling and satisfying.

Follower maturity (or readiness) Hersey and Blanchard identified this dimension within their model which refers to followers' ability and willingness to achieve a particular task.

Followership This is often defined as an enabler of leadership or even, especially in closely interacting teams, as a form of leadership. This view is closely linked to the idea of shared and distributed leadership. See also authentic followership.

Formal groups Established by the organization to achieve particular objectives intended to contribute to achieving organizational goals.

Formal relationships Determined by formal roles and include authority relationships, workflow connections and task interdependencies, peer relationships in formal groups and units, and communication linkages. See also informal relationships.

Functional structure Occurs when individuals and groups are located together based on the function their tasks have within the organization.

Fundamental attribution error Also called correspondence bias, refers to the tendency to overly rely on dispositional (i.e., personality-based) causal explanations, and to underemploy situational explanations, for the behaviour of others.

Genetic influences The influence of the genetic inheritance of the individual on their personality.

Generalized self-efficacy This refers to an assessment of one's competence across different tasks and settings. See also self-efficacy.

Globalization Reflects the growing tendency for individual businesses to become integrated into linkages and networks that span the whole globe.

Goal incongruence Refers to the degree of alignment between individual and organizational goals.

Great man (view of leadership) Originating at a time when the leaders were predominantly men, which suggests that in every situation, particularly in times of crisis, 'great men' would emerge to lead through the difficulties.

Group cohesion Refers to the attractiveness of a group to its members and their motivation to remain members. It also reflects the strength of mutual bonds and positive attitudes among members.

Group development Process of individuals coming together to form a group capable of achieving both task and member satisfaction.

Group dynamics The interactions and patterns of behaviour that occur when groups form and perform.

Group effectiveness (group performance) The degree to which groups achieve their intended objectives.

Group efficacy beliefs A group's shared belief in its ability to perform a particular task successfully.

Group synergy The increase in performance or value from groups compared to the outcomes that a number of individuals working on a task alone could achieve.

Group polarization Refers to the tendency of groups to amplify shared individual attitudes in their joint decision making.

Groups Social entities of two or more people who interact with each other, are psychologically aware of each other, and think of themselves as a group.

Groupthink Tendency of a strongly cohesive group to emphasize unity at the expense of critical evaluation of problems and options.

Growth-need strength (GNS) The job characteristics model applies only to individuals who have high GNS – that is, they have an intrinsic interest in developing themselves, learning new and applying their existing skills, taking responsibility and building identity through their work.

Habituation Constant repetition of a stimulus can lead to the senses turning off from the awareness of it.

Halo effect Positive bias introduced when attributing all of the characteristics of a person (or object) from a single positive attribute.

Heterarchy Found in adhocracy forms of structure. Heterarchy means that different people and sub-units are not ordered according to predetermined differences in formal authority (hierarchy) but rather all have the potential to be deployed as is seen fit and in accordance to the requirements of the particular tasks.

Heuristics Experience-based rule or mental shortcut used in making judgements or solving problems.

High-performance organization The combination of people, technology, management and productivity delivering competitive advantage on a sustainable basis.

Hindsight bias Refers to the tendency of people to exaggerate the likelihood of events that they know have occurred.

Horns effect The opposite of the halo effect and takes the view that everything about a person is bad on the basis of a single negative attribute.

Hostage posting An extreme form of trust repair which involves providing decision control over valuable resources of the trustee to the trustor as a signal that such violations will not reoccur. See also substantive penance.

Human relations movement The school of management thinking that originated from the work of Elton Mayo in which the significance of social groups and social processes was emphasized.

Human resource management (HRM) An approach to the management of people that supposedly represents a more central strategic management activity than personnel management.

Human resource planning The process of seeking to match present and future human availability to the needs of the organization.

Hybrid structures These apply to more than one of the departmentation principles simultaneously. The best known is the matrix structure.

Hypercompetition Caused by globalization, rapid technological development and ever accelerating and intensifying competition creates scarcity of critical resources including raw materials, human resources, distribution channels and business networks.

Id According to Freudian psychoanalysis the instinctual drives that remain largely unconscious in directing human behaviour.

Ideal type A model which would be identifiable only to a greater or lesser extent in practice.

Ideology Reflects the force for co-operation referred to in the Mintzberg model of structure.

Idiographic approaches Are based upon the uniqueness of each indiVidual and reject the use of psychometric tests.

Illusion of control Refers to the fact that people tend to overestimate the influence they can have on uncontrollable events such as lotteries.

Implicit attitudes Slowly acquired attitudes for which people have generally little awareness and which are activated by automatic processes.

Implicit favourite bias Describes often subconscious tendencies of decision makers to evaluate information and make choices that lead to their preferred outcomes.

Impression management The processes used by individuals to influence and control the views that others form about them.

Incremental decision-making model Based on research on unprogrammed decision making in organizations reflecting the way in which such decisions are made in incremental steps from problem recognition to solution.

Indirect discrimination Occurs when a 'requirement or condition' for a job is set in such a way as to disadvantage a particular category of people.

Individual difference See personality.

Individualized role orientation This reflects the degree of diversity in typical responses across members of a group. It increases the variety in behaviours and responses among members. See also institutionalized role orientation.

Induction The process of introducing a new employee into the organization.

Induction crisis When a new employee leaves an organization within a few weeks of starting work it is sometimes referred to as a result of the induction crisis. It can be the result of an ineffective induction and socialization process resulting in the individual not integrating into the work group or organization.

Industrial action An action by either management or employees that takes place in order to force some degree of compromise on the other party.

Industrialization The process of change from an agricultural to a manufacturing-based economy.

Influence The process by which others are induced to behave in desired ways.

Influence mechanisms Refers to actions and interaction patterns that prompt automatic response patterns which increase the likelihood of acquiescence with influencing attempts. See also influence tactics.

Influence outcomes The outcome of the application of power in influence processes.

Influence tactics Describes specific interaction patterns used by agents to bring about the target's compliance with a particular request. See also influence mechanisms.

Influencing skills Refers to the ability to appropriately select and use particular influence tactics and mechanisms.

Informal groups Social structures that arise through interactions among organizational members and serve their sociability, support and dependency needs.

Informal relationships These include personal relationships among friends and acquaintances, as well as other forms of informal relationships due to physical proximity, joint membership in informal groups, or other sources of repeated interactions. See also formal relationships.

Information power This source of power is based on the possession of knowledge or information that is not generally available.

Information society Is characterized by the knowledge generation and exchange through interactions and interconnections between and among networks of ICTs and individuals as well as economic, social, political and cultural institutions.

Informational justice Concerned with the fairness perceptions of information received. See also distributive justice, interactional justice, organizational justice and procedural justice.

Initiating structure Originating from the Ohio State University studies which began in 1945 and reflects the degree to which the leader was task focused and emphasized the achievement of objectives. See also consideration.

Input control This is based on the specification and control of relevant resources used.

Inquiry A process of dialogue that constructively challenges others' views by refocusing on facts and reasoning. See also advocacy and assertiveness.

Institutional theory and stakeholder theory Theories that point out the influence of other considerations such as legitimacy and external expectations on managerial decisions such as those regarding structure.

Institutionalized role orientation This reflects the degree of similarity in typical responses across members of a group. See also individualized role orientation.

Instrumental approach to work Based on a trading and value approach to work and the determination of contribution relative to benefits gained.

Integrative bargaining Describes an approach to negotiation in which the focus is on creating value for all parties. It is not a fixed sum, or fixed pie situation. See also distributive bargaining and value creation.

Integrative solutions These are characterized by combinations of outcomes for each party that exceed the total benefits available from purely distributive negotiating. See also integrative bargaining and value creation.

Intellectual capital The sum total of knowledge, expertise and dedication of the workforce in an organization.

Intelligence This refers to the general mental ability to solve problems and successfully deal with environmental conditions and demands in varying situations.

Intensive technology The third type of technology identified by Thompson describes processes where different units interact constantly with each other during the transformation process. It is associated with reciprocal interdependence. See also long-linked technology and mediating technology.

Interaction analysis This contains four categories of interaction which can be used for recording interaction patterns within groups.

Interactional justice Concerned with the fairness perceptions of the quality of interpersonal treatment. See also distributive justice, informational justice, organizational justice and procedural justice.

Interactionist approach to organizational conflict Sometimes called the contingency approach to organizational conflict, this represents a modified pluralist view that recognizes conflict as inevitable yet often manageable.

Internal attribution Explanation for behaviour that is based on internal reasons for it such as intentions, personality, or other aspects of the person.

Interpersonal feedback Communication that conveys information about how a person's behaviour is perceived and experienced.

Intrinsic motivation This refers to the impetus for behaviour originating from performing the action itself; in simple terms the activity is done for its own sake. See also extrinsic motivation.

Introversion An introvert has a shy, quiet and retiring aspect to their personality.

Jargon Refers to specific terminology consisting of specialized words or common words with specialized meaning which can help communication among, and sensemaking by, members of professions or specific communities of practice.

Job analysis A systematic approach to the identification of the content of a job.

Job design This is the way in which tasks are grouped, assigned and structured in organizations at the level of individual jobs.

Job enlargement Sometimes called horizontal job enlargement, this seeks to build up a job by adding more (but similar-level) tasks into it to form a larger job.

Job enrichment Sometimes called vertical job enlargement, this approach to job design incorporates more complex tasks and increased levels of responsibilities into the design of a job.

Job evaluation A process by which job descriptions can be used to identify the rank order (or relative magnitude) of jobs in an organization.

Job rotation This involves the combination of two (or more) simplified jobs into a rotating pattern of work.

Job simplification This involves reducing the complexity work by minimizing the range of tasks into the smallest convenient job size.

Kaizen In Japanese, continuous improvement, and is based on employee 'voluntary' contributions to suggestion schemes or small-group activities geared to problem solving (quality or productivity circles).

Karoshi Japanese term for sudden death from overwork.

Knowledge of predictor bias Refers to the positive expectation and subsequent differential treatment by managers or co-workers that is based on knowledge of valid performance indicators For example, a new employee is known to be an excellent performer from their previous employment.

Labour process theory Seeks to explain the use to which human labour is put in capitalist organizations and the part played by managers in the organization of that work for the benefit of capital owners. See also unitarism, pluralism and the Marxist perspective.

Labour process debate Seeks to explain management's relationship to workers (and their role) in capitalist economies and in relation to capital owners.

Latent conflict Refers to the condition where the relevant interests of interacting parties are not aligned. Note that simply diverging interests are not sufficient to talk about latent conflict – it must be a divergence of interests that is in some way relevant to the nature of the interaction between two parties.

Law of effect This states that behaviour is a function of its consequences.

Law of unintended consequences Deliberate actions or changes in any part of an organization can often have implications elsewhere or even throughout the whole system that were not intended or anticipated.

Leader–member exchange theory (LMX) An approach to leadership, originally called the vertical dyad linkage (VDL) theory because it focused on dyadic relationships that included one party having formal authority over the other. It suggests that leaders behave differently with different subordinates.

Leadership (in contrast to management) The exercise of influence over others using their intrinsic motivation and reflecting subjective, follower-based legitimacy. See also 'Management (in contrast to leadership)'.

Leadership neutralizers Those factors that can reduce the opportunities for or effectiveness of leader influence.

Leadership styles Suggests that successful leadership is about the style of behaviour adopted by the leader, usually described as falling within an autocratic–democratic scale.

Leadership substitutes Any factors that can replace, or reduce the need for, leadership.

Legitimate power The ability to exercise power as a consequence of having the legitimate right to claim to be able to do so.

Line and staff functions Line functions deliver the main purposes of the organization – operations departments; staff functions are the support activities.

Line manager Every employee reports to a line manager – their boss.

Linking pin model This model reflects the overlapping and connected nature of groups within an organization.

Lock-out The prevention of work activity by management. See also strike.

Locus of control The degree to which an individual believes that they are subjected to outside control as opposed to having internal control over the forces influencing their behaviour.

Logrolling Describes situations when value is created through trading differences in the value of particular aspects of an agreement for different partners.

Long-linked technology The second type of technology identified by Thompson describes the sequential processes most obviously found in assembly line factory operations. It is associated with sequential interdependence. See also intensive technology and mediating technology.

Machine form (of structure) Results from the dominance of the force for efficiency. It reflects the mechanistic and bureaucratic forms of organization and is typically found in mass-production or mass-service organizations in both private and public sectors.

Management (in contrast to leadership) The exercise of influence over others using extrinsic motivation and based on externally determined legitimacy. See also 'Leadership (in contrast to management)'.

Management roles Mintzberg described ten different roles that he grouped under three headings called interpersonal, informational and decisional.

Management science model This consists of analysis-based decision-making processes under conditions of little uncertainty.

Managerial choice perspective Holds that it is managers' decisions that determine how an organization is structured.

Managerial grid In the area of leadership, the two classical leader behaviour dimensions (task and people focus) provide the basis for this well-known model of leadership.

Manipulation A means of gaining control or social influence over others by methods which might be considered unacceptable, unfair, unreasonable, devious or underhanded.

Manufacture of consent The achievement of employee consent to control by managers through such practices as collective bargaining, although managers retain effective control over labour use, which perpetuates the relative imbalance of power in a capitalist society.

Manufacturing technology This is characterized by tangible outputs, separation of creation and consumption, relatively high levels of management control over, and prescription of, the transformation processes and a general focus on machinery and other capital-intensive means of production. See also service technology.

Marketplace bureaucracy The need to get things done within an organization requires the continuous trading of favours between colleagues outside formal procedures.

Marxist or radical perspective on conflict This suggests that conflict is an inevitable function of the exploitation of employees within a capitalist system. See also unitarism, pluralism and labour process theory.

Mass-customization Describes a manufacturing approach that combines the benefits of large-scale mass production with customization opportunities for individual customers.

Material technology The tangible aspects of technology that can be seen, touched or heard.

Mechanistic organizations These provide a blueprint of an organizational structure that is often compared to a machine: all the parts are clearly aligned to work together in prescribed, predetermined and stable ways. See also organic organizations.

Mediating technology The first type of technology Thompson identified brings together ('mediates') what would otherwise be independent activities or needs. It is associated with pooled interdependence. See also intensive technology and long-linked technology.

Mediators Third parties who act as facilitators to improve communication and other aspects of the negotiation process (perhaps also making recommendations) to increase the chances of mutually acceptable agreements. See also arbitrators and conciliators.

Metaphor (organizational) The explanation of something complex through reference to something simpler, but in a way which conveys additional meaning in the process.

Method study The critical examination of work in order to identify the most efficient work methods. See also work study and work measurement.

Middle line Intermediate levels of management in the Mintzberg model of structure.

Middle range theories Theories that provide explanations of the generic features of a selected social phenomenon.

Minimal group paradigm Social dynamic that makes individuals behave like group members simply based on their categorization as group members. This works even in the absence of any meaningful reason for group membership and without any contact and interaction with other members.

Mock bureaucracy Organizational rules and procedures are largely ignored by all inside, having been imposed by an outside agency.

Modernism An approach to management and organizational theory based on the existence of a 'grand narrative' – a coherent story about the development of the social and natural, revealed through the application of reason and science. See also postmodernism.

Moral philosophy A branch of philosophy that takes as its sphere of interest a philosophical enquiry about norms or values, about ideas of right and wrong, good or bad, what should and what should not be done.

Motivation Refers to the set of internal forces that initiate, direct and sustain deliberate behaviour.

Need for achievement (nAch) People with high levels of this need are motivated to seek challenges and accomplish goals because they value the recognition of their achievements.

Need for affiliation (nAff) People with high levels of this desire to have close, warm and meaningful relationships with others and belong to social groups.

Need for cognition People with high levels of this aspect of individual difference enjoy filling their time thinking – about anything!

Need for power (nPow) People with high levels of this value the ability to influence and control their environment, and particularly other people.

Negative power The ability to influence another party by not doing something that would normally be done. To withhold contribution or compliance.

Negative reinforcement This refers to the process of removing particular responses to increase the likelihood of the target behaviour occurring. See also positive reinforcement, punishment and extinction.

Negotiation A process of maximizing one's value through interpersonal decision making in situations where outcomes for each party are interdependent. It broadly reflects a process of difference reduction through the forming of agreements between individuals and groups who have mutually dependent needs and desires.

Negotiation goal drift Refers to the change in negotiators' objectives from gaining absolute value to competitive or even punitive goals.

Network structures Sometimes called external network structures or boundaryless organizations, which are structures that extend beyond the nominal boundaries of the organization and draw together and deploy resources that can include individuals, groups and/or organizations that are contracted but do not become formally part of the organization. Network structures are usually temporary.

Networking Refers to the deliberate cultivation of positive relationships with individuals that may be helpful in direct exchanges or indirectly through their links to third parties.

Networks Describes systems of interconnected bilateral or dyadic linkages and relationships within organizations. Both formal and informal networks, based on systems of formal and informal relationships, exist.

Neuroticism Refers to a personality dimension characterized by anxiety, moodiness and lack of emotional balance and stability. Neuroticism is also called low emotional stability.

Noise The peripheral and background contamination surrounding a communication that interferes with the ability of the recipient receiving the complete message sent. For example, noise from a television playing in the background can prevent someone hearing every word spoken during a telephone conversation.

Nominal group technique Closely modelled on the brainstorming approach but enables group members to quietly develop and record ideas for a period before they are shared with the group. All ideas are then discussed and critiqued by the group before members privately rank the alternatives. The highest ranked alternative is then chosen.

Nomothetic theories These offer an approach based upon the identification and measurement of characteristics through psychometric tests.

Noncanonical practice Refers to the often improvised approaches that are iteratively developed in actual ongoing work activity and shared and collectively improved among the interacting members of a working community. See also canonical practice.

Nonprogrammed decisions Novel, unique, poorly structured decisions that require decision makers to define the issue and to actively develop an appropriate process to make the decision.

Nonrational escalation of commitment Occurs when people continue and even increase their commitment to a failing course of action despite strong feedback that shows the negative consequences of their decisions.

Nonroutine technology This reflects situations involving low analysability together with a high degree of variability in the tasks. Transformation processes are not well understood, and the wide range of tasks to be done require the deployment of significant resources for analysing activities and solving problems. See also routine technology.

Norms Implicit standards that express the expected and acceptable (or shunned and unacceptable) behaviours in a particular social setting.

Obedience A specific form of compliance, namely the acquiescence to demands made by a person with authority. See also compliance.

Open or explicit conflict Refers to situations in which the goal-oriented behaviour of one party negatively affects the goal-oriented behaviour of another party, which results in changes in the interactions between the parties.

Operant conditioning An approach to learning based on the reinforcement of particular behaviours by a trainer, which consequently shapes it into the desired pattern. See also classical conditioning.

Operating core All those involved in operational activity of the business such as factory-based functions or service delivery staff in the Mintzberg model of structure.

Opportunity Refers to the conditions under which motivation and ability are deployed.

Organic organizations Sometimes referred to as organismic organizations. Reflects an organizational form emerging in fluid and relatively unpredictable situations. It is typified by a high level of flexibility in job responsibilities, also incorporating high levels of technical expertise at the lower levels of the organization and recognition of the value of individual contribution. See also mechanistic organizations.

Organization design The process by which managers select and manage aspects of an organization's structure and culture so that the organization can control the activities necessary to achieve organizational goals.

Organization structure The formal arrangement of task, communication and authority relationships that influence and control how people co-ordinate and conduct their work.

Organizational behaviour (OB) That aspect of theory and practice concerned with the behaviour of individuals and groups in organizational contexts.

Organizational Citizenship Behaviour Voluntary behaviour that goes beyond the formal role of an employee; this behaviour generally contributes to organizational effectiveness but is not directly or explicitly recognized by the formal reward system.

Organizational configurations Also called organizational forms or archetypes. Refers to constellations of structural characteristics that tend to appear together, that can be found more frequently than others.

Organizational culture A set of shared, often implicit assumptions, beliefs, values, and sensemaking procedures that influences and guides the behaviour and thinking of organizational members, and is continuously enacted and in turn reinforced – or changed – by the behaviour of organizational members.

Organizational justice Concerned with employee fairness perceptions regarding their work and conditions of employment and their behavioural reactions to these. See also distributive justice, informational justice, interactional justice and procedural justice.

Organizational politics Broadly refers to activities used to gain and apply power in organizations. Generally defined as behaviour outside the accepted procedures and norms of a particular context, intended to further the position of an individual or group at the expense of others.

Organizations Social entities that are goal-directed, are inextricably linked to their environment yet with nominal boundaries, and that employ deliberately designed and co-ordinated activities and approaches to achieve their objectives.

Orthogonal cultures A subculture containing independent elements compared to the dominant group that does not interfere with the prevailing culture.

Output control This is based on the direct measurement of the outputs produced. In some environments, such output control is difficult because of measurement problems (e.g., service quality, customer satisfaction) or because outcomes are not quantifiable (e.g., creative tasks). See also behavioural control.

Paradigm (in the cultural web) The set of beliefs and assumptions that are generally shared throughout the organization.

Participation Refers to the degree of subordinate involvement in decision-making processes.

People management The process of trying to achieve goals in organizations with and through people.

Perceived behavioural control The subjective assessment of the likelihood that particular behaviours can be performed.

Perceived role What the individual understands their role to be.

Perception A psychological process involving individuals selecting stimuli from their environment and processing this data to develop awareness and understanding about their environment and determine responses.

Perceptual bias Systematic tendency to commit errors in perception that result in consistent and predictable inaccuracies.

Perceptual defence bias Refers to the automatic discounting of disconfirming stimuli and is used to protect the individual against information, ideas or situations that are threatening to an existing perception or attitude.

Perceptual errors The mistakes of judgement or understanding that can occur during the process of interpreting stimuli.

Perceptual set A temporary mental predisposition to perceive one thing and not another, or to perceive stimuli in a certain way.

Performance ambiguity Refers to the ease and clarity with which the value of activities or outcomes can be assessed.

Performance feedback Communication that conveys information about performance to maintain and enhance work performance.

Performance management The processes and procedures through which managers seek to manage performance levels within the organization.

Person culture Based on the individual but not to be confused with the power culture. The power culture is based around a single focal point but the person culture allows each person to be a focal point depending on the circumstances.

Personality The relatively enduring individual characteristics that are inferred from observable, reasonably consistent patterns of an individual's behaviour over time.

Physical abilities These refer to people's capacity to control and deploy their bodies and to manipulate their physical environment.

Pluralism A perspective that regards organizations as collections of groups which have some objectives in common and some in competition. Conflict with results but can be usually resolved as all parties recognize the need to compromise in order to achieve some of their objectives. See also unitarism, the Marxist perspective and labour process theory.

Political behaviour Refers to deliberately designed social-influence processes that aim at covertly or overtly advancing the actor's self-interest regardless of its alignment with other parties' interests. See also political tactics and political skill.

Political skill Defined as the ability to effectively understand others at work, and to use such knowledge to influence others to act in ways that enhance one's personal and/or organizational objectives. See also political tactics and political behaviour.

Political tactics These are approaches that combine power generation and influencing tactics in concerted ways to orchestrate influence attempts aimed at getting other people to accept or take decisions, viewpoint or courses of action favoured by the initiator. See also political behaviour and political skill.

Population ecology Studies how the variations in organizations are brought about by factors such as age, size and human action and their interaction with specific environmental conditions in an evolutionary dynamic. A deterministic view of structure.

Positive discrimination Represents an attempt to overcome previous discrimination by giving preference to the group previously discriminated against in order to redress the balance.

Positive reinforcement This refers to the process of administering particular responses to increase the likelihood of the target behaviour occurring. See also negative reinforcement, punishment and extinction.

Postmodernism An approach to management and organizational theory that rejects modernism, arguing that reality is made up of a differing range of realities and that it is constructed by our ability to express (or formulate) it through language. See also modernism.

Power The capacity to get others to behave in desired ways.

Power culture Typically found in small organizations, where everything revolves around the focal person(s). All important decisions are made by them and they retain absolute authority in all matters.

Primacy effect Describes the biased perceptions that result from humans placing an inordinately high importance on the initial pieces of information about a target.

Primary functions of management Fayol proposed that management had five primary functions: planning and forecasting, organizing, commanding, co-ordinating and controlling.

Principal-agent problem The fact that hired managers may have self-interest motives that conflict with capital owners' interests.

Principled negotiations An approach to negotiation developed by Fisher and Ury based on four elements: separate the people from the problem; focus on interests, not positions; invent options for mutual gain; and insist on objective criteria.

Principles of management Fayol proposed a set of 14, which he argued would help to ensure that the process of management was successful (see Table 6.1).

Proactive personality An aspect of individual difference which describes the degree to which individuals actively initiate activities rather than reactively respond to environmental demands.

Problem solving The activity of generating a solution to a recognized problem.

Procedural justice Concerned with the perceived fairness of the processes by which decisions about outcomes are made. See also distributive justice, informational justice, interactional justice and organizational justice.

Process conflict This arises from disagreements about aspects of how task accomplishment will proceed. See also task conflict and relationship conflict.

Process control This was identified by Vroom and Yetton in their model of leadership and reflects the opportunity to influence or even determine the process of decision making. See also decision control.

Process-oriented structure Also called horizontal structure. The process-oriented structure seeks to align the structure of the organization with the workflows and core processes that aim at addressing and meeting customer needs.

Production blocking Empirical evidence indicates that brainstorming does not often live up to its promise because of difficulties in providing appropriate contribution opportunities for individuals in the group, members' evaluation apprehension and processes similar in effect to social loafing.

Production paradox Refers to the fact that, especially in complex tasks, many groups would benefit from planning and the development of an appropriate decision-making strategy, but instead they show tendencies to act immediately.

Professional form (of structure) Often found in professional services. Reflects organizations with a particular focus on perfecting existing skills among members of the operating core which increasingly specialize and focus on those customers and clients in need of their particular expertise.

Programmed decisions Routine, repeated, highly structured decisions that allow decision makers to follow clearly prescribed procedures.

Project structures Also called internal network structures, refer to structural arrangements within organizations that are essentially designed anew for each project that is conducted, matching project needs with internal resources.

Projection A psychological process of projecting onto others characteristics that we exhibit in ourselves.

Projective tests A process based on ambiguous images (such as inkblots) being presented to an individual who is then asked to interpret the image; thought to provide some insight into attitudes and personality characteristics.

Prospect theory Refers to the distinctly different choices people make depending on the way their alternative options are described.

Prospective control Refers to the activities that proactively align resources in ways that maximize the likelihood of achieving intended objectives.

Psychological contract Refers to the individual beliefs about the terms of the mutual exchange agreement between the individual and their organization.

Psychological reactance Defined as anticonformity (a strong adverse reaction) in response to any perceived attempt to control or restrict a person's freedom.

Psychometrics The process of mental measurement through the application of tests of personality or characteristics such as ability or aptitude.

Punishment The administration of responses that reduces the likelihood of the target behaviour occurring. See also positive reinforcement, negative reinforcement and extinction.

Punishment bureaucracy A variant on the mock bureaucracy in that rules are imposed on the workers by management.

Quantitative school A mathematical approach to management that seeks to find ways of modelling relationships between variables so that causal relationships can be identified and predictions made.

Rational Choice Theory General model that uses self-interest and hedonistic value maximization to explain human behaviour.

Reactive control The actions taken to bring activities in line with targets and expectations based on received feedback about the activities.

Recency effect The opposite of the primacy effect and describes the phenomenon that people tend to recall, and place disproportionate importance on, the most recent pieces of information about a target they have received.

Recruitment The first stage of resourcing that is about identifying an appropriate number of potentially appropriate employees from which suitable individuals will be chosen for the next stage of the process, often an interview or assessment centre.

Referent power This source of power is based on the characteristics of an individual that make them particularly attractive, likeable, or otherwise desirable.

Often based on the presence of a charismatic personality.

Reflexivity Refers to the degree to which group members overtly reflect on the group decision process or content.

Reify To treat as real that which is merely a concept or an abstract idea.

Reinforcement The encouragement of particular behaviours through the application of positive and/or negative rewards, based on the application of four schedules: fixed ratio; variable ratio; fixed interval; variable interval.

Relationship conflict Sometimes called emotional or affective conflict, it refers to interpersonal incompatibilities among group members, which typically include tension, animosity and annoyance among members within a group. See also task conflict and process conflict.

Reliable psychometric test A test that produces consistent results if the measured quality remains unchanged, or appropriately different ones if it has changed.

Representative bureaucracy The rules and procedures are generally supported within the organization having been developed by managers with employee involvement.

Representativeness heuristic Refers to the degree of similarity perceived between people or objects.

Reservation point Sometimes also called the resistance point, it is determined by a party's BATNA and refers to the lowest value that makes an offer acceptable. See also aspirations and anchor.

Resource-based approach to HRM An inside-out perspective on HRM which holds that HR activity can be strategic in its own right.

Resourcing The process of bringing into an organization personnel who will possess the appropriate education, qualifications, skills and experience for the post offered. Incorporates HR planning (aspects of), recruitment and selection processes.

Reward power Power based on control of valued outcomes for the other person(s). It represents exchange of a willingness to be controlled for desirable rewards.

Reward system Formal arrangements regarding the combination of pay, benefits, incentives and intangible benefits used to attract, retain and motivate employees.

Risky shift phenomenon – See group polarization.

Role Specific set of responsibilities and expected behaviours associated by an individual based on their particular position in group or organization.

Role ambiguity The degree of uncertainty among individuals as to exactly what a particular role's responsibilities are at a given point of time.

Role conflict Arises as a result of a range of conflicting role requirements acting on an individual at the same time.

Role culture This type of culture is based firmly on the existence of procedure and rule frameworks. Hierarchy and bureaucracy dominate this type of organization, with instructions coming down the organization and information going back up to more senior levels.

Role definition The sum total of things that define a particular role, including job description, uniforms, badges of rank and office location.

Role incompatibility Incompatible expectations between members of the role set about their respective roles.

Role of HRM There are a number of models that seek to reflect the role adopted by HRM within an organization. One example identifies four different roles, being: change agent; adviser; regulator/internal contractor; and service provider. See also business partner.

Role overload/underload Arises when an individual has either too many roles, or not enough roles for their existing capability.

Role set The roles around a focal role.

Role stress The level of stress experienced by individuals as they act out the various roles allocated to them.

Routine technology This is characterized by situations involving high analysability and low variety. Therefore, tasks are predictable and fully understood, and the ways in which they can best be accomplished can be easily determined. See also nonroutine technology.

Rules Explicit descriptions of acceptable and unacceptable behaviour that serve as standards to which actual behaviour is compared.

Sabotage A deliberate attempt to interrupt operations or damage the interests of an organization (or another person or group) by an individual (or group) that wishes to do so, or considers that they have some reason to feel aggrieved.

Scalar chain This reflects the strictly hierarchical nature of formal reporting relationships in organizations.

Schema Cognitive structure stored in memory that represents some aspect of the world in an idealized and abstract way which can provide an interpretation frame for processing information.

Science (The) of muddling through A short-term approach to control, based on frequent reviews of performance against target, rather than a strategic approach based on the long-term achievement of goals.

Scientific management An approach to management based on the application of work study techniques to the design and organization of work in order to identify the 'one best way'; subsequently involves matching the worker to job requirements and motivating them to maximize output.

Script Cognitive structure build through experience and repeated practice that delineates the nature and sequence of behaviours.

Selection The second stage in the resourcing process involving a two-way process during which the applicant selects the organization as well as the organization seeking to identify the most appropriate applicant.

Self-control This is a notion absent from behaviouristic explanations of behaviour. It refers to the largely autonomous determination and adjustment of behaviour without simultaneous environmental influence.

Self-determination theory (SDT) A theory that distinguishes between autonomous motivation (where behaviour is based on volition and active choice) and controlled motivation (where behaviour is based on external consequences determined by decisions or dynamics outside the person).

Self-efficacy Belief about one's ability to perform a particular behaviour in specific circumstances successfully. See also generalized self-efficacy.

Self-fulfilling prophecy Describes the performance (or behaviour) improvement (or reduction) of individuals and groups based on positive (or negative) expectations about their capabilities by other people.

Self-management Refers to activities and strategies a person uses to influence, maintain or change their own behaviour.

Self-monitoring An aspect of individual difference which reflects individuals' tendencies to monitor their own behaviour and adapt it to fit with relevant social expectations.

Self-serving bias A bias that occurs when individuals make internal attributions for success but rely on external attributions for failures.

Servant leadership Is defined as leadership that has service to others including followers as its main motivator. Trust, integrity, empathy, support, community building, empowerment and follower development are aspects particularly associated with such leadership. See also value-based leadership.

Service Refers to the creation and provision of value through the application of knowledge, skill and other intangible resources for another party which consumes the value as part of the provision interaction.

Service technology Distinguished by intangible or mixed outputs, simultaneous production and consumption of value, lower levels of management control because of the active customer role in co-creation of value, direct customer interaction, and a focus on knowledge, skill and human contributions to the value-creation processes. See also manufacturing technology.

Shadow organizations Informal groups can form a parallel organization within the host and become a threat to management's ability to control.

Shape To create or encourage particular behaviour patterns in another individual through the principles of reinforcement.

Silo effect (in functional structures) The phenomenon found in many functional structures where interfunctional communication and co-ordination problems arise due to different and even conflicting objectives and orientations and the resulting social differences in identity and culture.

SMART objectives Refers to objectives that are Specific, Measurable, Attainable, Realistic and Time bounded.

Social architecture The collective ways in which people work together across an organization to support the business model.

Social control Social mechanisms that influence behaviour in particular social settings.

Social exchange theories Originated in sociology and social psychology. These provide conceptions of interpersonal relationships as exchange relationships in which each actor engages to maximize the value they receive.

Social facilitation The phenomenon that the presence of others can increase performance.

Social-information processing (SIP) A model of job design that highlights the role of social information in determining the effects that the design of a job has on its holder.

Social inhibition The phenomenon that the presence of others can decrease performance.

Social loafing The tendency for individuals to exert less effort in groups compared to working individually.

Social network analysis A central research tool in sociological and organizational research which is used to study informal structures within, across and outside of groups.

Social technology The social and behaviour shaping devices of structure, control, co-ordination, motivation and reward systems.

Socialization The process by which newcomers to a social setting (or a culture) develop the ability to function effectively in that particular setting. It involves learning about the norms, values, assumptions and other central-shared elements of a particular social group or culture.

Socialized charismatic leadership Can be defined as leadership that attempts to convey values-based messages and to bring about value congruence between leader and followers. See also value-based leadership.

Sociogram A diagrammatic representation of individual preferences and interactions among group members.

Span of control Refers to the number of subordinates reporting to a single boss.

Status quo bias The tendency of decision makers to favour stability over change in their choices.

Stepladder technique Initially only two people start discussing a particular issue. Other members then join the discussion one after the other, with each having a specified time to make their contribution to the existing subgroup which then collectively discusses the new input. Ultimately, all members of a group will have joined the subgroup and have contributed to the discussion. The reunited group then makes the final decision.

Stereotype A preconceived notion that suggests that all members of a particular category share a set of characteristics.

Stereotyping The tendency to attribute everyone (or everything) in a particular category with the characteristics based on a single example.

Stewardship Refers to the attitudes and behaviours that place the long-term best interests of a group ahead of personal goals that serve an individual's self-interests. See also value-based leadership.

Strategic apex Reflects the top echelon of the hierarchy such as the owner in small firms or the top management rank in larger companies.

Strike The formal withdrawal of labour by employees. See also lock-out.

Strong situations Situations with a strong influence on the thinking and behaviour of the majority of people and which may consequently overpower the influence of personality.

Structuration theory Reflects the perceptual creation of social structure through repeated human interaction.

Subcultures Refers to a subset of the dominant culture within a specific context.

Substantive penance An extreme form of trust repair which involves the transfer of valuable resources in reparation for a trust violation. See also hostage posting.

Sucker effect The tendency for individuals to deliberately withhold effort within a group activity because they believe other group members might do the same because they want to avoid being exploited.

Super-ego According to Freudian psychoanalysis that part of the human mind which reflects an internal critical and moralizing authority that represents internalized cultural and social norms and codes of morality.

Support staff Functions such as HR, maintenance or facilities management in the Mintzberg model of structure that provide inputs in support of the operating core and other elements of the organization without direct involvement in the core value generation processes of the organization.

Systems approaches to management These developed from the biological sciences, and are based on the view that 'systems' contain strong self-regulation tendencies and reflect something that can be separated from other systems and their environment by a boundary of some description.

Tacit knowledge Reflects knowledge derived from first-hand experience that cannot be easily communicated or taught.

Task conflict Sometimes referred to as cognitive conflict, it arises from disagreements among group members about the content of the tasks performed, including differences in viewpoints, ideas and opinions. See also relationship conflict and process conflict.

Task culture The expertise within this type of organization is vested in the individuals within it and it is they who must be organized in a way that meets the needs of the business. This type of culture is supportive of a networked or team organization. Decision making is frequently distributed throughout the 'net' dependent on the needs of the task.

Task interdependence Refers to the degree to which tasks differentiated through the division of labour remain operationally related to each other.

Task-oriented, people-oriented and participative behaviours Originating from the University of Michigan studies (late 1940s), resulting in the idea that these dimensions of leader behaviour could be identified.

Taskwork Describes what a group or team does to achieve its objectives.

Team Small groups whose members take individual and collective responsibility for their shared objectives and interactively co-ordinate their interdependent activities through roles and specific assignments.

Team management wheel A model of individual work preferences that relates to the roles that individuals play in a team.

Team work processes Describe how a group or team goes about its taskwork. Refers to members' interdependent acts that convert inputs to outcomes through cognitive, verbal and behavioral activities directed towards organizing taskworks to achieve collective goals.

Team roles Model consisting of nine roles that exist within a group including plant, resource investigator, implementer and completer.

Technical core Refers to the operational units charged with the central transformation processes (a manufacturing plant, or a payroll processing unit). To be able to work efficiently, such units need to be protected from sudden changes and uncertainties. See also boundary spanning unit.

Technological determinism This perspective, also called the technological imperative, focuses on the influence of technology as the principal cause of organizational change to the structure and other characteristics of an organization.

Technology Represents the ways in which material, technical, procedural, cognitive and social resources are deployed to achieve desired outcomes.

Technostructure The specialist functions such as industrial engineering, IT systems designer or financial controllers and auditors in the Mintzberg model of structure that determine how certain operations should be performed.

Toxic relationships Relationships that are unproductive, counterproductive or harmful.

Training and development A process dealing primarily with transferring or obtaining knowledge, attitudes and skills needed to carry out a specific activity or task.

Traits A view of leadership which proposes that future successful leaders could be identified by seeking out people with the same characteristics as existing successful leaders.

Transactional leadership This is based on an implicit and explicit calculation by both parties that motivates followership through the exchange relationship between leaders and followers (hence 'transactional'). See also transformational leadership.

Transformational leadership This is based on linking followers' motivation directly to the pursued outcomes. Transformational leaders increase awareness of the value of these outcomes, transform follower's self-interest to include these larger objectives and tap into higher-level needs of followers. See also transactional leadership.

Trust Refers to the degree to which a person (or entity) makes themselves vulnerable to another person (or entity) despite uncertainty about the other's possible actions.

Uncertainty Refers to the effect that the absence of sufficient information about the nature and likelihood of certain events may have on the intended activity, functioning and outcome of an organization and to the process of management.

Unitarism A perspective on conflict that regards organizations as collections of groups but within a cohesive whole. Conflict resolution is based on the pre-eminence of the management perspective. See also pluralism, the Marxist perspective and labour process theory.

Unity of command Each employee should have only one boss.

Universalistic theories Include scientific management and classical management theory and argue that structure (among other aspects of management) should be handled in one particular way (the 'one best way approach') because these are, regardless of other considerations, always superior in achieving intended outcomes.

Unobtrusive power Can be exercised by those groups who have the ability to influence the way in which issues, problems and opportunities are interpreted and considered.

Utilitarian approaches (to ethics) Based on benevolence, these approaches to ethics require an evaluation of the options available on the basis of the future impact on those that are likely to be effected by the consequences. It comes in two forms – act utilitarianism and rule utilitarianism. See also contract approach to ethics.

Valid psychometric test A test that produces results that correspond to what they purport to represent.

Value-based leadership Leadership focused on expressing and promoting particular prosocial values. Specific approaches include stewardship, servant leadership, ethical leadership, socialized charismatic leadership and authentic leadership. See also these individual terms.

Value creation Based on increasing the total value available for claiming by the parties through the development of integrative solutions. See also integrative bargaining.

Variety (in groups) Reflects differences in expertise, functional background and external connections among the members of a group.

Vicarious learning Refers to learning through the observation of others.

Vicious cycle of control Reflects the view that control can become a self-perpetuating and deteriorating cycle of management tightening control, leading to adverse employee reactions, resulting in even tighter control, and so on.

Victimization Refers to situations in which an employer seeks to take revenge or action against an employee (or group) because they sought to (or assisted others to) claim their legal rights.

Weak situations (impacting on personality) Situations exerting only limited influence on the thinking and behaviour of the majority of people and consequently leaving room for individual differences to manifest themselves.

Whistleblowing Individuals publically alleging real or perceived wrongdoing or that some misconduct (legal, financial, ethical, environmental) has been concealed by their employer.

Work manipulation Individual and/or collective behaviours that stay within the formal rules of the organizations (or at least cannot easily be shown to violate formal rules) but have the effect of reducing effort, withholding effort or creating more work for managers and supervisors. See also work-to-rule and work restriction.

Work measurement Based upon the use of timing techniques to identify how long particular tasks should take to perform. See also method study and work study.

Work restriction The collective withholding of effort as the result of a work group determining the level of effort that it is prepared to invest on the employer's behalf. See also work manipulation and work to rule.

Work study A management discipline aimed at maximizing productivity through the application of method study and work measurement techniques. See also method study and work measurement.

Work-to-rule Refers to a situation when workers adhere strictly to prescribed approaches (policies, procedures and rules) on how work should be performed, refusing to deviate from any formal agreement, rule or standard procedure in the process. See also work manipulation and work restriction.

REFERENCES

Ackroyd, S. (1994) Re-Creating Common Ground: Elements for Post-Paradigmatic Organization Studies. In J. Hassard, and M. Parker (eds) *Towards a New Theory of Organizations*, London: Routledge.

Adam, E.E., Jr., and Swamidass, P.M. (1989) Assessing operations management from a strategic perspective. *Journal of Management*, 15(2):181–203.

Adams, A. (1992) *Bullying At Work: How to Confront and Overcome It*, London: Virago.

Adams, D. and Haynes, D. (2007) Stafford Beer's contribution to management science – renewal and development. *Kybernetes*, 36(3/4):437–450.

Adams, J.S. (1965) Injustice in Social Exchange. In Berkowitz, L. (ed.) *Advances in Experimental Social Psychology*, London: Academic Press.

Adler, N.J. (1984) Understanding the ways of understanding: Cross-cultural management methodology reviewed, *Advances in International Comparative Management*, 1:31–67.

Adler, N.J. and Gundersen, A. (2007) *International dimensions of organizational behavior* (5th edn), Mason, OH: Thomson/South-Western.

Adler, P.S. (1993) The Learning Bureaucracy: New United Motors Manufacturing, Inc. In B. Staw and L.L. Cummings (eds) *Research in Organizational Behavior*, 15:111–194, Greenwich, CT: JAI Press.

Adorno, J.W., Frenkel-Brunswick, E., Levinson, D.J. and Sandford, R.N. (1953) *The Authoritarian Personality*, New York: Harper and Row.

Ahearn, K. K., Ferris, G. R., Hochwarter, W.A., Douglas, C. and Ammeter, A.P. (2004) Leader political skill and team performance. *Journal of Management*, 30:309–327.

Ailon, G. (2008) Mirror, mirror on the wall: Culture's consequences in a value test of its own design. *Academy of Management Review*, 33(4): 885–904.

Ajzen, I. (1985) From intentions to actions: A theory of planned behavior. In J. Kuhl and J. Beckmann (eds) *Action control: From cognition to behavior*, pp. 11–39, Berlin: Springer.

Ajzen, I. (1991) The theory of planned behavior. *Organizational Behavior and Human Decision Processes*, 50:179–211.

Ajzen, I. and Fishbein, M. (1980) *Understanding attitudes and predicting social behavior*, Englewood Cliffs, NJ: Prentice-Hall.

Alderfer, C.P. (1972) *Existence, Relatedness and Growth*, New York: The Free Press.

Aldrich, H.E. (1979) *Organizations and environments*, Englewood Cliffs, NJ: Prentice-Hall.

Allaire, Y. and Firsirotu, M. (1984) Theories of organizational culture. *Organization Studies*, 5:193–226.

Allport, G. (1937) *Personality: A Psychological Interpretation*, New York: Holt, Rinehart and Winston.

Alvesson, M. (1993) *Cultural perspective on organizations*, Cambridge: Cambridge University Press.

Alvesson, M. and Berg, P.O. (1992) *Corporate culture and organizational symbolism*, Berlin: Walter de Gruyter.

Alvesson, M. and Willmott, H. (1996) *Making Sense of Management: A Critical Introduction*, London: Sage.

Ambrose, M., Hess, R.L. and Ganesan, S. (2007) The relationship between justice and attitudes: An examination of justice effects on event and system-related attitudes. *Organizational Behavior and Human Decision Processes*, 103:21–36.

Andersen, J.A. (2008). An organization called Harry. *Journal of Organizational Change Management*, 21(2):174-187.

Anderson, C., Spataro, S.E. and Flynn, F.J. (2008) Personality and organizational culture as determinants of influence. *Journal of Applied Psychology*, 93(3):702–710.

Andersson, L.M. and Pearson, C. (1999) Tit for tat? The spiraling effect of incivility in the workplace. *Academy of Management Review*, 24:454–471.

Andrews, M.C. and Kacmar, K.M. (2001) Discriminating among organizational politics, justice, and support. *Journal of Organizational Behavior*, 22(4):347–366.

Andrisiani, P.J. and Nestel, C. (1976). Internal-external control as contributor to and outcome of work experience. *Journal of Applied Psychology*, 61:156–165.

Aoyama, Y. and Castells, M. (2002) An empirical assessment of the informational society: Employment and occupational structures of G-7 countries, 1920–2000. *International Labour Review*, 141(1/2):123–159.

Armistead, C. and Rowland, P. (1996) Managing by Business Process. In C. Armistead and P. Rowland (eds) *Managing Business Processes: BPR and Beyond*, Chichester: Wiley.

Armstrong, M. (1995) *A Handbook of Personnel Management Practice* (5th edn), London: Kogan Page.

Armstrong, M. and Brown, D. (2009) *Strategic Reward: Implementing More Effective Reward Management*, London: Kogan Page.

Armstrong, M. and Murlis, H. (1998) *Reward Management: A Handbook of Remuneration Strategy and Practice* (4th edn), London: Kogan Page.

Armstrong, P. (1989) Management, labour process and agency. *Work, Employment and Society*, 3:307–322.

Aronson, E. (2004) *The social animal* (9th edn), New York: Worth Publishers.

Aselage, J. and Eisenberger, R. (2003) Perceived organizational support and psychological contracts: A theoretical integration. *Journal of Organizational Behavior*, 24:491–509.

Ashby, W.R. (1956) *An Introduction to Cybernetics*, New York: Chapman and Hall.

Ashforth, B.E. and Lee, R.T. (1990) Defensive behaviour in organizations: a preliminary model. *Human Relations*, July, pp. 621–648.

Atkinson, P. (2003) Managing chaos in a matrix world. *Management Services*, November, pp. 8–11.

Aubrey, B. and Kelsey, B. (2003) Further understanding of trust and performance in virtual teams. *Small Group Research*, 34(5):575–619.

Audretsch, D.B. (2009) Emergence of the entrepreneurial society. *Business Horizons*, 52(1):505–511.

Aupperle, K.E., Acar, W. and Booth, D.E. (1986) An empirical critique of 'In search of excellence': How excellent are the excellent companies? *Journal of Management*, 12(4):499–512.

Avery, D.A. and McKay, P.F. (2006) Target practice: An organizational impression management approach to attracting minority and female job applicants. *Personnel Psychology*, 59:157–187.

Avgerou, C. and McGrath, K. (2007) Power, rationality, and the art of living through socio-technical change. *MIS Quarterly*, 31(2):295–315.

Avolio, B.J., Bass, B.M. and Jung, D.I. (1999) Re-examining the components of transformational and transactional leadership using the multifactor leadership questionnaire. *Journal of Occupational and Organizational Psychology*, 72:441–462.

Avolio, B.J. and Gardner, W.L. (2005) Authentic leadership development: Getting to the root of positive forms of leadership. *The Leadership Quarterly*, 16(3):315–338.

Avolio, B.J., Walumbwa, F.O. and Weber, T.J. (2009) Leadership: Current theories, research, and future directions. *Annual Review of Psychology*, 60:421–449.

Axelrod, R. (1984) *The Evolution of Cooperation*, New York: Basic Books.

Babbage, C. (1832) *On the Economy of Machinery and Manufactures*, London: Charles Knight.

Bacon, T.R. (2007). Driving cultural change through behavioural differentiation at Westinghouse. *Business Strategy Series*, 8(5):350–357.

Badham, R., Garrety, K., Morrigan, V., Zanko, M. and Dawson, P. (2003) Designer deviance: Enterprise and deviance in culture change programmes. *Organization*, 10(4):707–730.

Bain, P. and Taylor, P. (2000) Entrapped by the electronic panopticon?: Worker resistance in the call centre. *New Technology, Work and Employment*, 15(1):2–18.

Bales, R.F. (1958) Task Roles and Social Roles in Problem Solving Groups. In E.E. Maccoby, M. Newcomb and E.L. Hartley, (eds) *Readings in Social Psychology* (3rd edn), New York: Holt, Rinehart and Winston.

Baltes, P.B. and Kunzmann, U. (2003) Wisdom. *The Psychologist*, March, 16(3):131–132.

Balthazard, P.A., Waldman, D.A. and Atwater, L.E. (2008) The mediating effects of leadership and interaction style in face-to-face and virtual teams. In S. Weisband (ed.) *Leadership at a distance: Research in technologically-supported work*, pp. 127–150, New York: Erlbaum.

Bandura, A. (1977) *Social learning theory*, Englewood Cliffs, NJ: Prentice-Hall.

Bandura, A. (1986) *Social foundation of thought and action: A social cognitive theory*, Englewood Cliffs, NJ: Prentice-Hall

Bandura, A. (1997) *Self-efficacy: The exercise of control*, Stanford, CA: Freeman.

Bandura, A. (2001) Social cognitive theory: An agentic perspective. *Annual Review of Psychology*, 52:1–26.

Bargh, J.A. (1989) Conditional automaticity: Varieties of automatic influence in social perception and cognition. In J. S. Uleman and J. A. Bargh (eds) *Unintended thought*, pp. 3–51, New York: Guilford Press.

Bargh, J.A. (1994) The four horsemen of automaticity: Awareness, efficiency, intention, and control in social cognition. In R. S. Wyer Jr. and T. K. Srull (eds) *Handbook of social cognition* (2nd ed., pp. 1–40) Hillsdale, NJ: Erlbaum.

Bargh, J.A. and Ferguson, M.J. (2000) Beyond behaviorism: On the automaticity of higher mental processes. *Psychological Bulletin*, 126:925–945.

Bargh, J.A., Gollwitzer, P.M., Lee-Chai, A., Barndollar, K. and Trötschel, R. (2001) The automated will: Nonconscious activation and pursuit of behavioral goals. *Journal of Personality and Social Psychology*, 81:1014–1027.

Barker, J. (1993) Tightening the iron cage: Concertive control in self-managing teams. *Administrative Science Quarterly*, 38:408–437.

Barnard, C.I. (1938) *The Functions of the Executive*, Cambridge, MS: Harvard University Press.

Barnes, A. (2007) The construction of control: The physical environment and the development of resistance and accommodation within call centres. *New Technology, Work and Employment*, 22(3):246–259.

Barney, J.B. (1999) How a firm's capabilities affect boundary decisions. *Sloan Management Review*, 40(3):137–145.

Baron, R.S. (1986) Distraction-conflict theory: Progress and problems. *Advances in Experimental Social Psychology*, 19:1–36.

Barrick, M.R. and Mount, M.K. (1991) The big five personality dimensions and job performance: a meta-analysis. *Personnel Psychology*, 44:1–26.

Barrick, M.R., Bradley, B.H., Kristof-Brown, A.L. and Colbert, A.E. (2007) The moderating role of top management team interdependence: Implications for real teams and working groups. *Academy of Management Journal*, 50(3):544–557.

Barth, H. (2003) Fit among competitive strategy, administrative mechanisms, and performance: A comparative study of small firms in mature and new industries. *Journal of Small Business Management*, 41(2):133–148.

Bartlett, C.A. and Ghoshal, S. (1989) *Managing Across Borders: The Transnational Solution*, London: Hutchinson.

Basch, J. and Fisher, C.D. (2000) Affective events-emotions matrix: A classification of work events and associated emotions. In N.M. Ashekansy, C.E.J. Hartel and W.J. Zerbe (eds) *Emotions in the workplace: Research, theory and practice,* pp. 36–48, Westport, CN: Quorum.

Bass, B.M. (1985) *Leadership and performance beyond expectations*, New York: Free Press.

Bass, B.M. (1990) From transactional to transformational leadership: Learning to share the vision. *Organizational Dynamics*, Winter, pp. 19–31.

Bass, B.M. (1996) *A new paradigm for leadership: An inquiry into transformational leadership*, Alexandria, VA: US Army Research Institute for the Behavioral and Social Sciences.

Bateman, T.S. and Crant, J.M. (1993) The proactive component of organizational behavior: A measure and correlates. *Journal of Organizational Behavior*, 14(2):103–118.

Bates, K.A., Flynn, E.J. and Flynn, B.B. (2009) The pressure to perform: Innovation, cost, and the lean revolution. *Business Horizons*, 52(3):215–221.

Batt, R., Holman, D. and Holtgrewe, U. (2009) The globalization of service work: Comparative institutional perspectives on call centers. *Industrial and Labor Relations Review*, 62(4):453–488.

Bavelas, A. (1948) A mathematical model for group structures. *Human Organization*, 7(3):16–30.

Beal, D.J., Cohen, R.R., Burke, M.J. and McLendon, C.L. (2003) Cohesion and performance in groups: A meta-analytic clarification of construct relations. *Journal of Applied Psychology*, 88(6):989–1004.

Bearden, W.O., Money, O.B. and Nevins, J.L. (2006) Multidimensional versus unidimensional measures in assessing national culture values: The Hofstede VSM 94 example. *Journal of Business Research*, 59:195–203.

Bedeian, A.G. (1984) *Organizations: Theory and Analysis*, 2nd edn, Hinsdale: Dryden Press.

Beer, M., Spector, B., Lawrence, P.R., Quinn Mills, D. and Walton, R.E. (1984) *Managing Human Assets*, New York: Free Press.

Beer, M, Lawrence, P.R., Quinn Mills, D. and Walton, R.E. (1985) *Human Resource Management: A General Manager's Perspective*, Glencoe, IL: Free Press.

Beer, S. (1959) *Cybernetics and Management*, London: English University Press.

Beer, S. (1972) *Brain of the Firm*, London: Penguin.

Beersma, B., Hollenbeck, J.R., Conlon, D.E., Humphrey, S.E., Moon, H. and Ilgen, D.R. (2009) Cutthroat cooperation: The effects of team role decisions on adaptation to alternative reward structures. *Organizational Behaviour and Human Decision Processes*, 108(1):131–142.

Beinhocker, E., Davis, I., and Mendonca, L. (2009) The 10 trends you have to watch. *Harvard Business Review*, 87(7/8):55–60.

Belbin, M. (1993) *Team Roles at Work*, Oxford: Butterworth-Heinemann.

Belbin, R.M. (2000) *Beyond the Team*, Oxford: Butterworth-Heinemann.

Bell D. (1973) *The coming of the postindustrial society*, New York: Basic Books.

Bell, S. T. (2007) Deep-level composition variables as predictors of team performance: A meta-analysis. *Journal of Applied Psychology*, 92:595–615.

Bennis, W.G. and Nanus, B. (1985) *Leaders: The strategies for taking charge*, New York: Harper and Row.

Bennison, M. (1980) *The IMS Approach to Manpower Planning*, Brighton: Institute of Manpower Studies.

Berg, P.O. (1985) Organizational change as a symbolic transformation process. In P.J. Frost, L.F. Moore, M.R. Louis, C.C. Lundberg and J. Martin (eds) *Organization Culture*, Beverly Hills, CA: Sage.

Berry, J.W. (1997) Immigration, acculturation, and adaptation. *Applied Psychology*, 46:5–34.

Berry, J.W. (2003) Conceptual approaches to acculturation. In K.M. Chun, P. Balls Organista and G. Marín (eds) *Acculturation: Advances in theory, measurement, and applied research*: 17-37. Washington, DC: American Psychological Association.

Berry, J.W. (2006) Stress perspectives on acculturation. In D. L. Sam and J. W. Berry (eds) *Acculturation psychology*, pp. 27–43, Cambridge, England: Cambridge University Press.

Bhagwati, J. (2004) *In defense of globalization*, Oxford, New York: Oxford University Press.

Biedenbach, T. and Söderholm, A. (2008) The challenge of organizing change in hypercompetitive industries: A literature review. *Journal of Change Management*, 8(2):123–145.

Bierly III, P.E., Stark, E.M. and Kessler, E.H. (2009) The moderating effects of virtuality on the antecedents and outcome of NPD team trust. *Journal of Product Innovation Management*, 26:551–565.

Binder, J., Brown, R., Zagefka, H., Funke, F., Kessler, T., Mummendey, A., Maquil, A., Demoulin, S. and Leyens, J.-P. (2009) Does contact reduce prejudice or does prejudice reduce contact? A longitudinal test of the contact hypothesis among majority and minority groups in three European countries. *Journal of Personality and Social Psychology*, 96(4):843–856.

Birkinshaw, J. and Gibson, C. (2004) Building ambidexterity into an organization. *MIT Sloan Management Review*, 45(4):47–55.

Birkinshaw, J., Nobel, R. and Ridderstrale, J. (2002) Knowledge as a contingency variable: Do the characteristics of knowledge predict organization structure? *Organization Science*, 13(3): 274–289.

Blackburn, R.M. and Mann, M. (1979) *The Working Class in the Labour Market*, London: Macmillan.

Blake, R.R. and McCanse, A.A. (1991) *Leadership dilemmas – grid solutions*. New York: Gulf Publishing.

Blake, R.R. and Mouton, J.S. (1964) *The managerial grid*, Houston: Gulf Publishing.

Blau, P.M. (1964) *Exchange and power in social life*, New York: Wiley.

Blauner, R. (1964). *Alienation and Freedom: The Factory Worker and His Job*, Chicago: University of Chicago Press.

Block, P. (1993) *Stewardship: Choosing service over self-interest*, San Francisco, CA: Berrett-Koehler.

Bloisi, W., Cook, C.W. and Hunsaker, P.L. (2007) *Management and Organizational Behaviour* (2nd European edn), McGraw-Hill.

Bodenhausen, G.V. (1988) Sterotypic biases in social decision making and memory-testing process models of stereotyping use. *Journal of Personality and Social Psychology*, 55:726–737.

Boggan, S. (2001) Nike admits to mistakes over child labour. *The Independent*, Saturday, 20 October.

Bolino, M.C. and Turnley, W.H. (2009) Relative deprivation among employees in lower-quality leader-member exchange relationships. *The Leadership Quarterly*, 20(3):276–286.

Bolman, L.G. and Deal, T.E. (2008) *Reframing organizations: Artistry, choice and leadership* (4th edn), San Francisco, CA: Jossey-Bass.

Bolton, R. (1979) *People skills*, New York: Simon and Schuster.

Bolton, S.C. and Houlihan, M. (2005) The (mis) representation of customer service. *Work, Employment and Society*, 19(4):685–703.

Boon, B.H. and Sierksma, G. (2003) Team formation: Matching quality supply and quality demand. *European Journal of Operational Research*, July, 148(2):277–293.

Bordia, P., Jones, E., Gallois, C., Callen, V. and Difonzo, N. (2003) Management are aliens! Rumours during organizational change. *Australian Journal of Psychology*, Supplement, 55:116–120.

Bottom, W. P., Gibson, K., Daniels, S. and Murnighan, J.K. (2002) When talk is not cheap: Substantive penance and expressions of intent in the reestablishment of cooperation. *Organization Science*, 13:497–513.

Bouchard, T.J. and Loehlin, J.C. (2001) Genes, evolution, and personality. *Behavioral Genetics*, 31:243–273.

Boudon, R. (2003) Beyond rational choice theory. *Annual Review of Sociology*, 29:1–21.

Boudreau, J., Hopp, W., McClain, J.O. and Thomas, L.J. (2003) On the interface between operations and human resource management. *Manufacturing and Service Operations Management*, July, 5(3):179–203.

Boulding, K.E. (1956) General systems theory: The skeleton of science. *Management Science*, 2:97–108.

Boulding, K.E. (1985) *The world as a total system*, Beverly Hills, CA: Sage.

Bourgeois, L.J. III (1979) Towards a method of middle-range theorizing. *Academy of Management Review*, 4:443–447.

Bowditch, J.L., Buono, A.F. and Stewart, M.M. (2008) *A primer on organizational behavior* (7th edn), Hoboken, NJ: Wiley.

Bowen, D.E., Ledford, G.E. and Nathan, B.R. (1996) Hiring for the organization, not the job. In J. Billsberry (ed.) *The Effective Manager: Perspectives and Illustrations*, London: Sage.

Bowen, H. (1953) *Social responsibilities of the businessman*, New York: Harper.

Bowers, C.A., Braun, C.C. and Morgan, B.B., Jr. (1997) Team workload: Its meaning and measurement. In M.T. Brannick, E. Salas and C. Prince (eds) *Team performance and measurement: Theory, methods, and applications,* pp. 85–108, Mahwah, NJ: Lawrence Erlbaum Associates.

Boxall, P. and Purcell, J. (2003) *Strategy and Human Resource Management*, Basingstoke: Palgrave Macmillan.

Boynton, A.C. and Victor, B. (1991) Beyond flexibility: Building and managing the dynamically stable organization. *California Management Review*, 34:53–66.

Bradach, J. and Eccles, R. (1989) Price, authority, and trust: From ideal types to plural forms. *Annual Review of Sociology*, 15:97–118.

Bradshaw, P. (1981) *The Management of Self-esteem*, Englewood Cliffs, NJ: Prentice Hall.

Brady, M., Fellenz, M.R. and Brookes, R. (2008) Researching the role of information and communication technology (ICT) in contemporary marketing practices. *Journal of Business and Industrial Marketing*, 23(2):108–114.

Brannen, P. (1983) *Authority and Participation in Industry*, London: Batsford.

Bratton, J. and Gold, J. (2003) *Human Resource Management: Theory and Practice,* (3rd edn), Basingstoke: Palgrave Macmillan.

Bratton, J., Callinan, M., Forshaw, C. and Sawchuk, P. (2007) *Work and organizational behaviour*, Palgrave Macmillan.

Braverman, H. (1974) *Labour and Monopoly Capital: The Degradation of Work in the Twentieth Century*, London: Monthly Review Press.

Brehm, S. and Brehm, J.W. (1981) *Psychological reactance: a theory of freedom and control*, New York: Academic Press.

Brewster, C., Gill, C. and Richbell, S. (1983) Industrial relations policy: a framework for analysis. In K. Thurley and S. Wood (eds) *Industrial Relations and Management Strategy*, Cambridge: Cambridge University Press.

Brewster, C., Sparrow, P. and Vernon, G. (2007) *International Human Resource Management*, 2nd edn, London: CIPD.

Bridges, W. (1995) *Jobshift: How to prosper in a workplace without jobs*, Reading, MA: Addison Wesley.

Bromley, D.B. (1993) *Reputation, Image and Impression Management*, Chichester: John Wiley.

Brooks, R., Chittenden, M. and Prescott, M. (2000) The guilt zone. *Sunday Times*, 10 September.

Broome, J. (1990) Fairness. *Proceedings of the Aristotelian Society*, 91:87–102.

Brothers, C. (2009) Boeing and Airbus prepare (again) for tanker battle. *New York Times*, 16 June. Accessed at http://www.nytimes.com/2009/06/17/business/global/17boeing.html on 3 September 2009.

Brouer, R.L., Ferris, G.R., Hochwarter, W.A., Laird, M.D., and Gilmore, D.C. (2006) The strain-related reactions to perceptions of organizational politics as a workplace stressor: Political skill as a neutralizer. In E. Vigoda-Gadot and A. Drory (eds) *Handbook of organizational politics*, pp. 187–206, Northampton, MA: Edward Elgar.

Brown, J.S. and Duguid, P. (1991) Organizational learning and communities-of-practice: Toward a unified view of working, learning, and innovation. *Organization Science*, 2(1):40–57.

Brown, J.S. and Duguid, P. (2001) *The social life of information*, Boston: Harvard Business School Press.

Brown, M.E., and Treviño, L.K. (2006) Ethical leadership: A review and future directions. *The Leadership Quarterly*, 17:595–616.

Brown, M.E., and Treviño, L.K. (2009) Leader–follower values congruence: Are socialized charismatic leaders better able to achieve it? *Journal of Applied Psychology*, 94(2):478–490.

Brown, M.E., Treviño, L.K. and Harrison, D.A. (2005) Ethical leadership: A social learning perspective for construct development and testing. *Organizational Behavior and Human Decision Processes*, 97:117–134.

Brown, R.H. (1978) Bureaucracy as praxis: Towards a political phenomenology of formal organizations. *Administrative Science Quarterly*, 23:365–382.

Browning, G. (2003) Ten ways to manage office politics. *Management Today*, April, p. 20.

Browning, G. and James, J. (2003) Office politics, the new game. *Management Today*, May, pp. 54–59.

Bryan, L.L., Matson, E. and Weiss, L.M. (2007) Harnessing the power of informal employee networks. *McKinsey Quarterly*, 4:44–55.

Bryman, A. (1992) *Charisma and leadership in organizations*, Newbury Park, CA: Sage.

Buchanan, D., Fitzgerald, L., Ketley, D., Gollop, R., Jones, J.L., Lamont, S.S., *et al.* (2005) No going back: A review of the literature on sustaining organizational change. *International Journal of Management Reviews*, 7(3):189–205.

Buckley, W.F. (ed.) (1968) *Modern systems research for the behavioral scientist: A sourcebook*, Chicago, IL: Aldine Publishing Company.

Bull, P. (2003) Slippery politicians. *The Psychologist*, November, 16(11):592–595.

Burawoy, M. (1979) *Manufacturing Consent: Changes in the Labour Process under Monopoly Capitalism*, Chicago: University of Chicago Press.

Burchill, F. (2008) *Labour Relations*, (3rd edn), Basingstoke: Palgrave Macmillan.

Burger, J.M. (1986) *Personality: Theory and Research*, Belmont, CA: Wadsworth.

Burke, C.S., Stagl, K.C., Salas, E., Pierce, L. and Kendall, D. (2006) Understanding team adaptation: A conceptual analysis and model. *Journal of Applied Psychology*, 91(6):1189–1207.

Burke, R.J. (2007) *Research companion to working time and work addiction*, Cheltenham, UK: Edward Elgar.

Burke, R.J. and Fiksenbaum, L. (2009) Work motivations, work outcomes, and health: Passion versus addiction. *Journal of Business Ethics*, 84:257–263.

Burns, J.M. (1955) The reference of conduct in small groups: Cliques and cabals in occupational milieux. *Human Relations*, 8(4):467–486.

Burns, J.M. (1978) *Leadership*, New York: Harper and Row.

Burns, T. and Stalker, G.M. (1961) *The Management of Innovation*, London: Tavistock.

Burrell, G. (1996) Normal science, paradigms, metaphors, discourses and genealogies of analysis. In S.R. Clegg, C. Hardy and W.R. Nord (eds) *Handbook of Organization Studies*, pp. 642–658, London: Sage.

Bushe, G.R. and Shani, A.B. (1991) *Parallel learning structures: Increasing innovation in bureaucracies*, Reading, MA: Addison-Wesley.

Butcher, D. and Clarke, M. (1999) Organizational politics: The missing discipline of management? *Industrial and Commercial Training*, 31(1):9–13.

Butts, M.M., Vandenberg, R.J., DeJoy, D.M., Schaffer, B.S. and Wilson, M.G. (2009) Individual reactions to high involvement work processes: Investigating the role of empowerment and perceived organizational support. *Journal of Occupational Health Psychology*, 14(2):122–136.

Cacioppo, J.T. and Petty, R.E. (1982) The need for cognition. *Journal of Personality and Social Psychology*, 42:116–131.

Cacioppo, J.T., Petty, R.E., Feinstein, J.A. and Jarvis, W.B.G. (1996) Dispositional differences in cognitive motivation: The life and times of individuals varying in need for cognition. *Psychological Bulletin*, 119(2):197–253.

Caldwell, B.S., Palmer, R.C. and Cuevas, H.M. (2008). Information alignment and task coordination in organizations: An 'information clutch' metaphor. *Information Systems Management*, 25(1): 33–44.

Caldwell, C., Hayes, L., Bernal, P. and Karri, R. (2008) Ethical stewardship – Implications for leadership and trust. *Journal of Business Ethics*, 78(1/2):153–164.

Calori, R., Johnson, G. and Sarnin, P. (1992) French and British top managers' understanding of the structure and dynamics of their industries: a cognitive analysis and comparison. *British Journal of Management*, 3:61–78.

Campbell, J.P. and Pritchard, R.D. (1974) Motivation Theory in Industrial and Organizational Psychology. In M. Dunnette (ed.) *Handbook of Industrial and Organizational Psychology*, Chicago, IL: Rand McNally.

Cameron, K.S., Sutton, R.I. and Whetten, D.A. (1988) *Readings in Organizational Decline: Frameworks, Research and Prescriptions*, Cambridge, MA: Ballinger.

Cannella, A. and Paetzold, R. (1994) Pfeffer's barriers to the advance of organizational science: A rejoinder. *Academy of Management Review*, 19:331–341.

Capraro, R.M. and Capraro, M.M. (2002) Myers-Briggs Type Indicator score reliability across studies: A meta-analytic reliability generalization study. *Educational and Psychological Measurement*, 62(4):590–602.

Carmeli, A. and Gittell, J.H. (2009) High quality relationships, psychological safety and learning from failures in work organizations. *Journal of Organizational Behavior*, 30(6):709–729.

Carmeli, A., Brueller, D. and Dutton, J.E. (2009) Learning behaviours in the workplace: The role of high-quality interpersonal relationships and psychological safety. *Systems Research and Behavioral Science*, 26(1):81–98.

Carpenter, D.S. and Feloni, J. (1989) *The Fall of the House of Hutton*, New York: Henry Holt.

Carrillo, J.D. and Gromb, D. (2007) Cultural inertia and uniformity in organizations. *Journal of Law Economics and Organization*, 23(3):743–771.

Carroll, A.B. (2007) Corporate Social Responsibility (CSR) and Corporate Social Performance (CSP). *Encyclopedia of Business Ethics and Society*, London: SAGE Publications. Accessed at http://sage-ereference.com/ethics/Article_n206.html on 2 September 2009.

Carroll, D.T. (1983) A disappointing search for excellence. *Harvard Business Review*, 61(6):78–88.

Carroll, J.M. and Rosson, M.B. (1987) Paradox of the active user. In J.M. Carroll (ed.) *Interfacing thought: Cognitive aspects of human-computer interaction*, pp. 80–111, Cambridge, MA: MIT Press.

Carson, J.B., Tesluk, P.E. and Marrone, J.A. (2007) Shared leadership in teams: An investigation of antecedent conditions and performance. *Academy of Management Journal*, 50:1217–1234.

Carsten, M., Uhl-Bien, M., Patera, J., West, B. and McGregor, R. (2007). *Social constructions of followership*. Paper presented at the Annual Meeting of the Academy of Management, Philadelphia, PA.

Carver, C.S. and Scheier, M.F. (1981) *Attention and self-regulation: A control theory approach to human behaviour*, New York: Springer.

Carver, C.S. and Scheier, M.F. (2001) *The self-regulation of behavior*, Cambridge: Cambridge University Press.

Caspi, A., Roberts, B.W. and Shiner, R.L. (2005) Personality development: Stability and change. *Annual Review of Psychology*, 56:453–484.

Cassell, C. and Johnson, P. (2006) Action research: Explaining the diversity. *Human Relations*, 59(6):783–814.

Castells, M. (1996) *The Information Age: Economy, Society, and Culture. Volume I: The Rise of the Network Society*, Oxford: Blackwell.

Castells, M. (1997) *The Information Age: Economy, Society, and Culture, Volume II: The Power of Identity*, Oxford: Blackwell.

Castells, M. (1998) *The Information Age: Economy, Society, and Culture. Volume III: End of Millennium*, Oxford: Blackwell.

Castells, M. (2000) Materials for an exploratory theory of the network society. *British Journal of Sociology*, 51(1):5–24.

Cattell, R.B. (1965) *The Scientific Analysis of Personality*, Harmondsworth: Penguin.

Caulkin, S. (2001) The time is now. *People Management*, 28 August, pp. 32–34.

Caulkins, D.D. (2004) Identifying culture as a threshold of shared knowledge: A consensus analysis method. *International Journal of Cross Cultural Management*, 4(3):317–333.

Cederblom, J. and Dougherty, C.J. (1990) *Ethics at Work*, Belmont, CA: Wadsworth.

Chaleff, I. (1995) *The courageous follower: Standing up to and for our leaders*, San Francisco, CA: Berrett-Koehler.

Chandler, A.D., Jr. (1962) *Strategy and structure: Chapters in the history of the American industrial enterprise*, Cambridge, MA: MIT Press.

Chandler, A.D. (1984) The emergence of managerial capitalism. *Business History Review*, 58:473-503.

Chang, A., Bordia, P. and Duck, J. (2003) Punctuated equilibrium and linear progression: Toward a new understanding of group development. *Academy of Management Journal*, 46(1):106–117.

Chang, W.-W. (2009) Schema adjustment in cross-cultural encounters: A study of expatriate international aid service workers. *International Journal of Intercultural Relations*, 33: 57–68.

Charan, R. (2006) Home Depot's blueprint for cultural change. *Harvard Business Review*, 84(4):60–70.

Chen, G., Gully, S.M. and Eden, D. (2001) Validation of a new general self-efficacy scale. *Organizational Research Methods*, 4:62–83.

Chen, G., Gully, S.M. and Eden, D. (2004) General self-efficacy and self-esteem: Toward theoretical and empirical distinction between correlated self-evaluations. *Journal of Organizational Behavior*, 25:375–395.

Chen, W. and Hirschheim, R. (2004) A paradigmatic and methodological examination of information systems research from 1991 to 2001. *Information Systems Journal*, 14:197–235.

Chia, R. (2003) Organization theory as a postmodern science. In H. Tsoukas and C. Knudsen (eds) *The Oxford Handbook on Organization Theory: Meta-theoretical Perspectives*, Oxford: Oxford University Press.

Child, J. (1985) Managerial Strategies, New Technology and the Labour Process. In D. Knights, H. Willmott and D. Collinson (eds) *Job Redesign: Critical Perspectives on the Labour Process*, Aldershot: Gower.

Child, J. (2005) *Organization: Contemporary principles and practices*, Oxford: Blackwell Publishing.

Child, J. and Kieser, A. (1979) Organization and Managerial Roles in Britain and West German Companies: An Examination of the Culture-free Thesis. In C. Lammers and D. Hickson, (eds) *Organizations Alike and Unlike*, London: Routledge and Kegan Paul.

Chirkov, V. (2009) Critical psychology of acculturation: What do we study and how do we study it, when we investigate acculturation? *International Journal of Intercultural Relations*, 33:94–105.

Chisson, E.J. (1994) *The Hubble wars*, New York: Harper Perennial.

Chiu, C.-Y. and Hong, Y.-Y. (2006) *Social psychology of culture*, New York: Psychology Press.

Christie, R. and Geis, F.L. (eds) (1970) *Studies in Machiavellianism*, New York: Academic Press.

Chua, R.Y.J., Ingram, P. and Morris, M.W. (2008) From the head and the heart: Locating cognition- and affect-based trust in managers' professional networks. *Academy of Management Journal*, 51(3):436–452.

Cialdini, R.B. (2008) *Influence: Science and practice* (5th edn), New York: Allyn & Bacon.

Cialdini, R.B. and Goldstein, N.J. (2004) Social influence: Compliance and conformity. *Annual Review of Psychology*, 55:591–621.

CIPD (2007) Change Management. *Factsheet*. Accessed at www.cipd.co.uk on 10 March 2009.

CIPD (2008) HR Business Partnering. *Factsheet*. Accessed at: www.cipd.co.uk on 11 March 2009.

CIPD (2009a) Performance management. *Factsheet*. Accessed at www.cipd.co.uk on 10 March 2009.

CIPD (2009b) Employer Brand. *Factsheet*. Accessed at www.cipd.co.uk on 11 March 2009.

Clark, E. and Soulsby, A. (2007) Understanding top management and organizational change through demographic and processual analysis. *Journal of Management Studies*, 44(6):932–954.

Clegg, S. and Dunkerley, D. (1980) *Organization, Class and Control*, London: Routledge and Kegan Paul.

Cleveland, H.H. (2003) Disadvantaged neighborhoods and adolescent aggression: Behavioural genetic evidence of contextual effects. *Journal of Research in Adolescence*, 13:211–238.

Clifford, S. (2009) Video prank at Domino's taints brand. *New York Times*, 15 April. Accessed at http://www.nytimes.com/2009/04/16/business/media/16dominos.html?_r=1andref=technology on 3 September 2009.

Coase, R. (1937) The nature of the firm. *Econometrica*, 4:386-405.

Coghlan, D. and Brannick, T. (2010) *Doing action research in your own organization* (3rd edn), London: Sage.

Cohen, A.B. (2009) Many forms of culture. *American Psychologist*, 64(3):194–204.

Cohen, M.D., March, J.G. and Olsen, J.P. (1972) A garbage can model of organizational choice. *Administrative Science Quarterly*, 17:1–25.

Cohen, S.G. and Bailey, D.E. (1997) What makes teams work: Group effectiveness research from the shop floor to the executive suite. *Journal of Management*, 23:239–290.

Coleman, J.S. (1984) Introducing social structure into economic analysis. *American Economic Review*, 74:84–88.

Collinson, D. (2006) Rethinking followership: A post-structuralist analysis of follower identities. *The Leadership Quarterly*, 17(2):179–189.

Colquitt, J.A. (2001) On the dimensionality of organizational justice: a construct validation of a measure. *Journal of Applied Psychology*, 86:386–400.

Colquitt, J.A., Conlon, D.E., Wesson, M.J., Porter, C.O. and Ng, K.Y. (2001) Justice at the millennium: A meta-analytic review of 25 years of organizational justice research. *Journal of Applied Psychology*, 86:425–445.

Colquitt, J.A., Greenberg, J. and Zapata-Phelan, C.P. (2005). What is organizational justice? A historical overview. In J. Greenberg and J.A. Colquitt (eds) *Handbook of Organizational Justice*, pp. 3–56. Mahwah, NJ: Lawrence Erlbaum.

Communiqué (2003) Violence and harassment in the workplace on the increase. *European Foundation for the Improvement of Living and Working Conditions*, issue 1, p. 5.

Conant, H. and Kilbridge, M. (1965) An interdisciplinary analysis of job enlargement: technology, cost, behavioural implications. *Industrial and Labor Relations Review*, 18:377–395.

Conger, J. (1999) Charisma and how to grow it. *Management Today*, December, pp. 78–81.

Conger, J.A. and Kanungo, R.M. (1988) Behavioural Dimensions of Charismatic Leadership. In J.A. Conger and R.M. Kanungo (eds) *Charismatic Leadership: The Elusive Factor In Organizational Effectiveness*, San Francisco, CA: Jossey Bass.

Conlon, D.E., Meyer, C.J. and Nowakowski, J.M. (2005) How does organizational justice affect performance, withdrawal, and counterproductive behavior? In J. Greenberg and J.A. Colquitt (eds) *Handbook of Organizational Justice*, pp. 301–327, Mahwah, NJ: Lawrence Erlbaum.

Cooper, C. (1999) In my opinion. *Management Today*, June, p. 14.

Cooper, C. and Davidson, M. (1982) *High Pressure; Working Lives of Women Managers*, London: Fontana.

Cooper, W.H. and Withey, M.J. (2009) The strong situation hypothesis. *Personality and Social Psychology Review*, 13(1):62–72.

Cooperrider, D.L. and Srivastva, S. (1987) Appreciative inquiry in organizational life. In R. Woodman and W. Pasmore (eds) *Research in Organizational Change and Development*, 1:129-169, Greenwich, CT: JAI.

Cooperrider, D.L. and Whitney, D. (2005) *Appreciative inquiry: A positive revolution in change*, San Francisco CA: Berrett-Koehler.

Cordes, C. and Dougherty, T. (1993) A review and an integration of research on job burnout. *Academy of Management Review*, 18:621–656.

Côté, S., and Miners, C.T.H. (2006) Emotional intelligence, cognitive intelligence and job performance. *Administrative Science Quarterly*, 51:1–28.

Courpasson, D. and Dany, F. (2003) Indifference or obedience? Business firms as democratic hybrids. *Organization Studies*, 24(8):1231-1261.

Coyle-Shapiro, J.A.-M. and Conway, N. (2005) Exchange relationships: Examining psychological contracts and perceived organizational support. *Journal of Applied Psychology*, 90:774–781.

Coyne, K.P. and Horn, J. (2009) Predicting your competitor's reaction. *Harvard Business Review*, 87(4):90–97.

Cox, C.J. and Cooper, C.L. (1988) *High Flyers*, Oxford: Basil Blackwell.

Crant, J.M. (2000) Proactive behavior in organizations. *Journal of Management*, 26(3):435–462.

Cray, D. and Mallory, G.R. (1998) *Making Sense of Managing Culture*, London: International Thomson Business Press.

Crisp, R.J. (2002) Social Categorisation: Blurring the Boundaries. *The Psychologist*, 15(12):612-615

Cropanzano, R. and Mitchel, M.S. (2005) Social exchange theories: An interdisciplinary review. *Journal of Management*, 31(6):874–900.

Cropanzano, R. and Stein, J.H. (2009) Organizational justice and behavioral ethics: Promises and prospects. *Business Ethics Quarterly*, 19(2):193–233.

Cropanzano, R., Bowen, D.E. and Gilliland, S.W. (2007) The management of organizational justice. *Academy of Management Perspectives*, 21(4):34–48.

Crosby, P.B. (1979) *Quality is free*, New York: McGraw-Hill.

Cross, R., Thomas, R.J. and Light, D.A. (2009) How 'Who You Know' affects what you decide. *MIT Sloan Management Review*, 50(2):35–42.

Crozier, M. (1964) *The Bureaucratic Phenomenon*, London: Tavistock Publications.

Csikszentmihalyi, M. (1990) *Flow: The Psychology of Optimal Experience*, New York: Harper and Row.

Cummings, L.L. and Bromiley, P. (1996) The Organizational Trust Inventory (OTI):Development and validation. In R.M. Kramer and T.R. Tyler (eds) *Trust in organizations: Frontiers of theory and research*, pp. 302–330, Thousand Oaks, CA: Sage.

Cummings, T.G. and Worley, C.G. (2005) *Organization development and change* (8th edn), Santa Fe, OK: Thomson/South-Western.

Currie, R.M. (1963) *Work Study*, 2nd edn, London: Sir Isaac Pitman.

Curşeu, P.L. and Louwers, D. (2008) Entrepreneurial experience and innovation: The mediating role of cognitive complexity. In P.A.M. Vermeulen and P.L. Curşeu (eds) *Entrepreneurial strategic decision-making: A cognitive approach*, pp. 146–160, Cheltenham: Edward Elgar.

Curşeu, P.L., Schalk, R. and Wessel, I. (2007) How do virtual teams process information? A literature review and implications for management. *Journal of Managerial Psychology*, 23(6):628–652.

Curşeu, P.L., Schruijer, S. and Boros, S. (2007) The effects of groups' variety and disparity on groups' cognitive complexity. *Group Dynamics: Theory, Research, and Practice*, 11(3):187–206.

Cyert, R.M. and March, J.G. (1964) *A Behavioural Theory of the Firm*, Englewood Cliffs, NJ: Prentice Hall.

Cyert, R.M. and March, J.G. (1963) *A behavioral theory of the firm*, Englewood Cliffs, NJ: Prentice Hall.

Dafermos, G. and Söderberg, J. (2009) The hacker movement as a continuation of labour struggle. *Capital and Class*, 97:53–73.

Daft, R.L. (2004) *Organization Theory and Design* (8th edn), Cincinnati, OH: Thomson/South-Western.

Daft, R.L. (2007) *Understanding the Theory and Design of Organizations* (International edn), Cincinnati, OH: Thomson Learning.

Dalton, C.M. (2009) When the rules of the game change ... in the middle of the game. *Business Horizons*, 52(4):305–307.

D'Andrade, R.G. (1995) *The Development of Cognitive Anthropology*, Cambridge: Cambridge University Press.

Daniels, K. (2006) *Employee Relations in an Organizational Context*, London: CIPD.

Dansereau, F., Graen, G. and Haga, W.J. (1975) A vertical dyad linkage approach to leadership within formal organizations: a longitudinal investigation of the role-making process. *Organizational Behaviour and Human Performance*, 15:46–78.

D'Aveni, R.A. (1994) *Hypercompetition: Managing the dynamics of strategic maneuvering*, New York: Free Press.

Davis, J.H., Schoorman F.D. and Donaldson, L. (1997) Toward a stewardship theory of management. *Academy of Management Review*, 22(1):20–47.

Day, D.V., Gronn, P. and Salas, E. (2004) Leadership capacity in teams. *Leadership Quarterly*, 15:857–880.

Deal, T. and Kennedy, A. (1982) *Corporate Cultures: The Right and Rituals of Corporate Life*, Harmondsworth: Penguin.

Deci, E.L. (1971) The efforts of externally mediated rewards on intrinsic motivation. *Journal of Applied Psychology*, 18:105–115.

Deci, E.L. (1975) *Intrinsic motivation*, New York: Plenum.

Deci, E.L. and Ryan, R.M. (1980) The empirical exploration of intrinsic motivational processes. In L. Berkowitz (ed.) *Advances in experimental social psychology*, 13:39–80, New York: Academic Press.

Deci, E.L. and Ryan, R.M. (1985) *Intrinsic motivation and self-determination in human behavior*, New York: Plenum Press.

Deci, E.L. and Ryan, R.M. (2000) The 'what' and 'why' of goal pursuits: Human needs and the self-determination of behavior. *Psychological Inquiry*, 11:227–268.

Deci, E.L. and Ryan, R.M. (2008) Self-determination theory: A macrotheory of human motivation, development, and health. *Canadian Psychology*, 49(3):182–185.

De Cremer, D., Van Dijke, M., Mayer, D.M., Schouten, B.C. and Bardes, M. (2009) When does self-sacrificial leadership motivate prosocial behavior? It depends on followers' prevention focus. *Journal of Applied Psychology*, 94(4):887-899.

DeDreu, C.K.W. and Weingart, L.R. (2003) Task versus relationship conflict, team performance, and team member satisfaction: a meta analysis. *Journal of Applied Psychology*, August, 88(4):741–750.

Deery, S., Iverson, R. and Walsh, J. (2006) Towards a better understanding of psychological breach: A study of customer service employees. *Journal of Applied Psychology*, 91(1):166–175.

Deeter-Schmelz, D.R. and Sojka, J.Z. (2007) Personality traits and sales performance: Exploring differential effects of need for cognition and self-monitoring. *Journal of Marketing Theory and Practice*, 15(2):145–157.

Delery, J.E. and Doty, D.H. (1996) Modes of theorizing in strategic human resource management: Tests of universalistic, contingency, and configurational performance predictions. *Academy of Management Journal*, 39(4):802–835.

Deming, W.E. (1986) *Out of crisis*, Cambridge, MA: MIT Press.

Denison, D.R. (1990) *Corporate culture and organizational effectiveness*, New York: Wiley.

Denison, D. R. and Neale, W. (2000) *Denison Organizational Culture Survey*, Ann Arbor, MI: Denison Consulting.

DePaulo, B.M., Kenny, D.A., Hoover, C.W., Webb, W. and Oliver, P.V. (1987) Accuracy of person perception: do people know what kinds of impression they convey? *Journal of Personality and Social Psychology*, 52:303–315.

deRue, D.S. and Morgeson, F.P. (2007) Stability and change in person–team and person–role fit over time: The effects of growth satisfaction, performance, and general self-efficacy. *Journal of Applied Psychology*, 92(5):1242–1253.

Dery, K., Hall, R. and Wailes, N. (2006) ERPs as 'technologies-in-practice': Social construction, materiality and the role of organizational factors. *New Technology, Work and Employment*, 21(3):229–241.

DeSanctis, G. and Poole, S.M. (1994) Capturing the complexity in advanced technology use: adaptive structuration theory. *Organization Science*, 5(2): 121–147.

DeSanctis, G., Poole, M.S., Zigurs, I., DeSharnais, G., D'Onofrio, M., Gallupe, B., *et al.* (2008) The Minnesota GDSS research project: Group support systems, group processes, and outcomes. *Journal of the Association for Information Systems*, 9(10/11):551–608.

DeSarbo, W. S. and Grewal, R. (2008) Hybrid strategic groups. *Strategic Management Journal*, 29:293–317.

Desmond, J. (2004) An evaluation of organisational control strategies for relationship marketing. *Journal of Marketing Management*, 20:209–236.

Deutsch, M. (1949) A theory of co-operation and competition. *Human Relations*, 2(2):129–152.

Deutsch, M. (1958) Trust and suspicion. J*ournal of Conflict Resolution*, 2:265–279.

Deutsch, M. (1975) Equity, equality, and need: what determines which value will be used as the basis for distributive justice? *Journal of Social Issues*, 31:137–149.

Devine, D.J. and Philips, J.L. (2001) Do smarter teams do better: A meta-analysis of cognitive ability and team performance. *Small Group Research*, 32(5):507–532.

deWaal, F.B.M. (2008) Putting the altruism back into altruism: The evolution of empathy. *Annual Review of Psychology*, 59:279–300.

Digman, J.M. (1990) Personality structure: emergence of the Five-Factor model. *Annual Review of Psychology*, 41:417–440.

DiMaggio, P.J. and Powell, W.W. (1983) The iron cage revisited: Institutional isomorphism and collective rationality in organizational fields. *American Sociological Review*, 48:147–160.

Dionne, S.D., Yammarino, F.J., Atwater, L.E. and James, L.R. (2002) Neutralizing substitutes for leadership theory: Leadership effects and common-source bias. *Journal of Applied Psychology*, 87:454–464.

Dionne, S.D., Yammarino, F.J., Howell, J.P. and Villa, J. (2005) Substitutes for leadership, or not. *Leadership Quarterly*, 16:169–193.

Doidge, N. (2007) *The brain that changes itself*, Viking, London.

Donaldson, L. (1995) *American anti-management theories of organization: A critique of paradigm proliferation*, Cambridge: Cambridge University Press.

Donaldson, T. and Preston, L.E. (1995) The stakeholder theory of the corporation: Concepts, evidence, and implications. *Academy of Management Review*, 20(1):65–91.

Dornstein, M. (1989) The fairness judgements of received pay and their determinants. *Journal of Occupational Psychology*, 64, 287–299.

Douglas, C. and Ammeter, A.P. (2004) An examination of leader political skill and its effect on ratings of leader effectiveness. *Leadership Quarterly*, 15:537–550.

Drath, W.H. and Palus, C.J. (1994) *Making common sense: Leadership as meaning-making in a community of practice*, Greensboro, NC: Center for Creative Leadership.

Drazin, R. and Sandelands, L. (1992) Autogenesis: A perspective on the process of organizing. *Organization Science*, 3(2):230–249.

Drazin, R. and Van de Ven, A.H. (1985) Alternative forms of fit in contingency theory. *Administrative Science Quarterly*, 30:514–539.

Dreher, A., Gaston, N. and Martens, P. (2008) *Measuring globalisation: Gauging its consequences*, Berlin, New York: Springer.

Duck, S. (2007) Finding connections at the individual/dyadic level. In J.E. Dutton and B.R. Ragins (eds) *Exploring positive relationships at work: Building a theoretical and research foundation*, pp. 179–186, Mahwah, NJ: Lawrence Erlbaum Associates.

Duncan, R. (1976) The ambidextrous organization: Designing dual structures for innovation. In R.H. Killman, L.R. Pondy and D. Sleven (eds) *The management of organization*, 1:167-188, New York: North Holland.

Duncan, R. (1979). What is the right organization structure? Decision tree analysis provides the answer. *Organizational Dynamics*, Winter, 7:59-80.

Dutton, J.E., and Ragins, B.R. (2007) Moving forward: positive relationships at work as a research frontier. In J.E. Dutton and B.R. Ragins (eds) *Exploring positive relationships at work: Building a theoretical and research foundation*, pp. 387–400, Mahwah, NJ: Lawrence Erlbaum Associates.

Dvir, T. and Shamir, B. (2003). Follower developmental characteristics as predicting transformational leadership: A longitudinal field study. *Leadership Quarterly*, 14:327–344.

Early, P.C., Northcraft, C.L., Lee, C. and Lituchy, T.R. (1990) Impact of process and outcome feedback on the relation of goal setting to task performance. *Academy of Management Journal*, March, pp. 87–105.

Eaton, J. (2001) Management communication: The threat of groupthink. *Corporate Communication*, 6(4):183–192.

Eddleston, K.A., Kellermanns, F.W. and Sarathy, R. (2008) Resource configuration in family firms: Linking resources, strategic planning and technological opportunities to performance. *Journal of Management Studies*, 45(1):26–50.

Eden, D. (2001) Means efficacy: External sources of general and specific efficacy. In M. Erez, U. Kleinbeck and H. Thierry (eds) *Work motivation in the context of a globalizing economy*, pp. 73–85, Mahwah, NJ: Erlbaum.

Edmondson, A.C., Bohmer, R.M. and Pisano, G.P. (2001) Disrupted routines: Effects of team learning on new technology adaptation. *Administrative Science Quarterly*, 46:685–716.

Edwards, B.D., Day, E.A., Arthur, W., Jr., and Bell, S.T. (2006) Relationship among team ability composition, team knowledge structures, and team performance. *Journal of Applied Psychology*, 91:727–736.

Edwards, P. and Hall, M. (1999) Remission: possible. *People Management*, 15 July, 5:14, Institute of Personnel and Development, London.

Edwards, P.K. (1986) *Conflict at Work: A Materialist Analysis of Workplace Relations*, Oxford: Basil Blackwell.

Eisenbeiss, S.A., van Knippenberg, D. and Boerner, S. (2008) Transformational leadership and team innovation: Integrating team climate principles. *Journal of Applied Psychology*, 93(6):1438–1446.

Eisenhardt, K. (1989) Agency theory: An assessment and review. *Academy of Management Review*, 14(1):57–74.

Elfenbein H.A. and Ambady N. (2002) Predicting workplace outcomes from the ability to eavesdrop on feelings. *Journal of Applied Psychology*, 87:963–971.

Elfenbein, H.A., Der Foo, M.D., White, J. and Tan, H.H. (2007) Reading your counterpart: The benefit of emotion recognition accuracy for effectiveness in negotiation. *Journal of Nonverbal Behavior*, 31(4):205–223.

Elkington, J. (1994) Towards the sustainable corporation: Win-win-win business strategies for sustainable development. *California Management Review*, 36(2):90–100.

Emans, B.J.M., Munduate, L., Klaver, E. and van de Vliert, E. (2003) Constructive consequences of leaders' forcing influence styles. *Applied Psychology: An International Review*, 52:36–54.

England, G.W. (1983) Japanese and American management: Theory Z and beyond. *Journal of International Business Studies*, 14:131–142.

Environics (n.d.) *The Millennium Poll on Corporate Social Responsibility – Executive Briefing*. Conducted by Environics International Ltd. in cooperation with The Prince of Wales Business Leaders Forum and The Conference Board. Accessed 2 September 2009 at http://www.globescan.com/news_archives/MPExecBrief.pdf.

Erdelyi, M.H. (1974) A new look at the new look: Perceptual defense and vigilance. *Psychological Review*, 81:1–25.

Erez, M., Early, P.C. and Hulin, C. (1985) The impact of participation on goal acceptance and performance: a two- step model. *Academy of Management Journal*, March, pp. 50–66.

Erikson, E.H. (1980) *Identity and Life Cycle*, New York: Norton.

Etzioni, A. (1964) *Modern Organizations*, Englewood Cliffs NJ: Prentice Hall.

Evans, J.St.B.T. (2006) The heuristic-analytic theory of reasoning: Extension and evaluation. *Psychonomic Bulletin and Review*, 13(3):378–395.

Evans, J.St.B.T. (2008) Dual-processing accounts of reasoning, judgment, and social cognition. *Annual Review of Psychology*, 59:255–278.

Eysenck, H.J. (1953) *Uses and Abuses of Psychology*, Harmondsworth: Penguin.

Eysenck, H.J. (1965) *Fact and Fiction in Psychology*, Harmondsworth: Penguin.

Eysenck, H.J. (1982) *Personality, Genetics and Behaviour*, New York: Prager.

Falbe, C.M. and Yukl, G. (1992) Consequences for managers of using single influence tactics and combinations of tactics. *Academy of Management Journal*, 35:638–652.

Farnham, D. (2002) Employee relations. In T. Redman and A. Wilkinson, (eds) *The informed Student Guide to Human Resource Management*, London: Thomson Learning.

Fay, D., Borrill, C., Amir, Z., Haward, R. and West, M.A. (2006) Getting the most out of multidisciplinary teams: A multi-sample study of team innovation in health care. *Journal of Occupational and Organizational Psychology*, 79(4):553-567.

Fayol, H. (1916) *Administration Industrielle et Générale*, Paris: Dunod.

Fayol, H. (1947) *General and Industrial Management*, trans C. Storrs, London: Pitman.

Feldman Barrett, L., Tugade, M.M. and Engle, R.W. (2004) Individual differences in working memory capacity and dual-process theories of the mind. *Psychological Bulletin*, 130(4):553–573.

Feldman, D.C. (1984) The development and enforcement of group norms. *Academy of Management Review*, 9:47–53.

Fellenz, M.R. (1997) *Control theory in organizational behavior: Review, critique, and prospects*. Working paper. Accessed August 2009 at http://ssrn.com/abstract=939714.

Fellenz, M.R. (2008) Flexibility in management theory: Towards clarification of an elusive concept. *Journal of Strategic Management Education*, Vol. 4.

Fellenz, M.R. and Brady, M. (2008) RFID and data capture technologies in global service supply chains: Meeting the information management challenge. *Communications of the IBIMA*, 4(5):41–49.

Fellenz, M.R. and Brady, M. Managing customer-centric information: The challenges of information and communication technology (ICT) deployment in service environments. *Journal of Applied Logistics* (in press).

Fellenz, M.R., Augustenborg, C., Brady, M. and Greene, J. (2009) Requirements for an evolving model of supply chain finance: A technology and service providers perspective. *Communications of the IBIMA*, 10:227–235.

Ferguson, E., James, D., O'Hehir, F. and Saunders, A. (2003) A pilot study of the roles of personality, references and personal statements in relation to performance over the five years of a medical degree. *British Medical Journal*, 326(1):429–432.

Ferris, G.R. and Judge, T.A. (1991) Personnel/human resources management: A political influence perspective. *Journal of Management*, 17:447–488.

Ferris, G.R., Frink, D.D., Bhawuk, D.P.S., Zhou, J. and Gilmore, D.C. (1996) Reactions of diverse groups to politics in the workplace. *Journal of Management*, 22(1):23–44.

Ferris, G.R., Perrewé, P.L., Anthony, W.P. and Gilmore, D.C. (2000) Political skill at work. *Organizational Dynamics*, 28:25–37.

Ferris, G. R., Treadway, D. C., Kolodinsky, R. W., Hochwarter, W. A., Kacmar, C. J., Douglas, C. and Frink, D. D (2005a) Development and validation of the political skill inventory. *Journal of Management*, 31:126–152.

Ferris, G. R., Davidson, S. L. and Perrewé, P. L. (2005b) *Political skill at work*, Palo Alto, CA: Davies-Black.

Ferris, G.R., Treadway, D.C., Perrewé, P.L., Brouer, R.L., Douglas, C. and Lux, S. (2007) Political skill in organizations. *Journal of Management*, 33:290–320.

Festinger, L. (1957) *A Theory of Cognitive Dissonance*, New York: Harper and Row.

Fetchenhauer, D. and Dunning, D. (2009) Do people trust too much or too little? *Journal of Economic Psychology*, 30:263–276.

Fiedler, F.E. (1967) *A Theory of Leadership Effectiveness*, New York: McGraw-Hill.

Fiedler, F.E. (1986) The contribution of cognitive resources to leadership performance. *Journal of Applied Social Psychology*, 16:532–548.

Financial Reporting Council (2008) *Combined Code on Corporate Governance*, London: Financial Reporting Council. Accessed at http://www.frc.org.uk/documents/pagemanager/frc/Combined_Code_June_2008/Combined%20Code%20Web%20Optimized%20June%202008%282%29.pdf.

Finch, J. (1993) It's Great to have Someone to Talk to: Ethics and Politics of Interviewing Women. In J. Finch and J. Mason (eds) *Negotiating Family Responsibilities*, London: Routledge.

Fishbein, M. and Ajzen, I. (1975) *Belief, attitude, intention, and behavior: An introduction to theory and research*, Reading, MA: Addison-Wesley.

Fisher, M. (2007) The new politics of technology in the British civil service. *Economic and Industrial Democracy*, 28(4):523-551.

Fisher, R. and Ertel, D. (1995) *Getting ready to negotiate: The getting to yes workbook*, New York: Penguin.

Fisher, R. and Shapiro, D.L. (2005) *Beyond reason: Using emotions as you negotiate*, London: Random House.

Fisher, R. and Ury, W. (1981) *Getting to Yes*, Boston: Houghton Mifflin.

Fisher, R. and Ury, W. (1986) *Getting to Yes: Negotiating Agreement Without Giving In*, New York: Penguin.

Flamholtz, E.G., Das, T.K. and Tsui, A.S. (1985) Toward an integrative framework of organizational control. *Accounting Organizations and Society*, 10(1):35-50.

Foa, U. and Foa, E. (1975) *Resource theory of social exchange*, Morristown, NJ: General Learning Press.

Folger, R. and Cropanzano, R. (1998) *Organizational justice and human resource management*, London: Sage.

Fombrum, C.J., Tichy, N.M. and Devanna, M.A. (eds) (1984). *Strategic Human Resource Management*, New York: John Wiley.

Ford, L.R. and Seers, A. (2006) Relational leadership and team climates: Pitting differentiation versus agreement. *Leadership Quarterly*, 17(3):258-270.

Ford, M.E. (1992) *Motivating humans*, Newbury Park, CA: Sage.

Forester, T. (1987) *High-tech Society*, Oxford: Basil Blackwell.

Forsyth, D.R. and Schlenker, B.R. (1977) Attributing the causes of group performance: Effects of performance quality, task importance, and future testing. *Journal of Personality*, 45:220-236.

Fortado, B. (1994) Informal supervisory social control strategies. *Journal of Management Studies*, 31(2):251-274.

Fortin, M. (2008) Perspectives on organizational justice: concept clarification, social context integration, time and links with morality. *International Journal of Management Reviews*, 10(2):93-126.

Fortin, M. and Fellenz, M.R. (2008) Hypocrisies of fairness: Towards a more reflexive ethical base in organizational justice research and practice. *Journal of Business Ethics*, 78:415-433.

Foucault, M. (ed.) (1975) *I Pierre Rivière, having Slaughtered my Mother, my Sister, and my Brother: A Case of Parricide in the 19th Century*, trans. F. Jellinek, Lincoln: University of Nebraska Press.

Foucault, M. (1977) *Discipline and Punish: The Birth of the Prison*, London: Allen Lane.

Fox, A. (1966) Industrial Sociology and Industrial Relations. Royal Commission Research Paper No. 3, London: HMSO.

Fox, A. (1974a) *Man Mismanagement*, London: Hutchinson.

Fox, A (1974b). *Beyond contract: Work, power and trust relations*, London: Faber.

Fraley, R.C. and Roberts, B.W. (2005) Patterns of continuity: A dynamic model for conceptualizing the stability of individual differences in psychological constructs across the life course. *Psychological Review*, 112(1):60-74.

Francesco, A.M. and Gold, B.A. (2005) *International organizational behaviour* (2nd edn), Upper Saddle River, NJ: Pearson Prentice Hall.

Freeman, R.E. (1984) *Strategic management: A stakeholder approach*, Boston: Pittman.

French, J.R.P. and Raven, B (1968) The bases of social power. In D. Cartwright and A.F. Zander (eds) *Group Dynamics: Research and Theory* (3rd edn), New York: Harper and Row.

Frensch, P.A. (1994) Composition during serial learning: a serial position effect. *Journal of Experimental Psychology: Learning, Memory, and Cognition*, 20(2):423-443.

Friedman, H.S. and Booth-Kewley, S. (1987) The disease-prone personality: A meta-analytic view of the construct, *American Psychologist*, June, pp. 539-555.

Friedman, M. (1962) *Capitalism and Freedom*, Chicago: University of Chicago Press.

Friedman, M. (1972) Milton Friedman responds. *Business and Society Review*, 1:5-16.

Friedman, T.L. (2005) *The world is flat*, New York: Farrar, Straus and Giroux.

Fullagar, C.J. and Mills, M.J. (2008) Motivation and flow: Toward an understanding of the dynamics of the relation in architecture students. *The Journal of Psychology*, 142(5):533-553.

Furnham, A. and Gunter, B. (1993) Corporate Culture: Diagnosis and Change. In C.L. Cooper and I.T. Robertson, (eds) *International Review of Industrial and Organizational Psychology*, Chichester: John Wiley.

Gagliardi, P. (1986). The creation and change of organizational cultures: A conceptual framework. *Organization Studies*, 7:117-134.

Gagné, M. and Deci, E.L. (2005) Self-determination theory and work motivation. *Journal of Organizational Behavior*, 26:331-362.

Gagné, M. and Forest, J. (2008) The study of compensation systems through the lens of self-determination theory: Reconciling 35 years of debate. *Canadian Psychology*, 49(3):225-232.

Galbraith, J.R. (1973) *Designing complex organizations*, Boston: Addison-Wesley.

Galinsky, A.D. and Moskowitz, G.B. (2000) Counterfactuals as behavioral primes: Priming the simulation heuristic and consideration of alternatives. *Journal of Experimental Social Psychology*, 36:257–383.

Gandz, J. and Murray, V. (1980) The experience of workplace politics. *Academy of Management Journal*, June, pp. 237–251.

Gardner, H. (1999) *Intelligence Reframed: Multiple Intelligences for the 21st Century*, New York: Basic Books.

Gargiulo, M., Ertug, G. and Galunic, C. (2009) The two faces of control: Network closure and individual performance among knowledge workers. *Administrative Science Quarterly*, 54:299–333.

Garrahan, P. and Stewart, P. (1992) *The Nissan Enigma; Flexibility at Work in a Local Economy*, London: Mansell.

Gelade, G.A. and Ivery, M. (2003) The impact of human resource management and work climate on organizational performance. *Personnel Psychology*, Summer, 56(2):383–405.

Gelfand, M.J., Erez, M. and Aycan, Z. (2007) Cross-cultural organizational behavior. *Annual Review of Psychology*, 58:479–514.

Gennard, J. and Judge, G. (2002) *Employee Relations*, 3rd edn, London: CIPD.

George, C.S. (1972) *The History of Management Thought* (2nd edn), Englewood Cliffs, NJ: Prentice Hall.

George, J.M. and Jones, G.R. (2005) *Understanding and managing organizational behavior* (4th edn), Pearson/Prentice Hall.

Gersick, C.J.G. (1988) Time and transition in work teams: Toward a new model of group development. *Academy of Management Journal*, 31:9–41.

Gersick, C.J.G. (1989) Marking time: Predictable transitions in task groups. *Academy of Management Journal*, 32:274–309.

Gersick, C.J.G. (1991) Revolutionary change theories: A multilevel exploration of the punctuated equilibrium paradigm. *Academy of Management Review*, 16(1):10–36.

Giacalone, R.A. (1989) Image control: The strategies of impression management, *Personnel*, May, pp. 52–55.

Giacalone, R.A. and Jurkiewicz, C.L. (2003) *Handbook of Workplace Spirituality and Organizational Performance*, New York: Sharp.

Gibbons, D. (2004) Friendship and advice networks in the context of changing professional values. *Administrative Science Quarterly*, 49:238–262.

Gibson, C.B. and Birkinshaw, J. (2004) The antecedents, consequences and mediating role of organizational ambidexterity. *Academy of Management Journal*, 47:209–226.

Gibson, C. and Earley, P.C. (2007) Collective cognition in action: Accumulation, interaction, examination, and accommodation in the development and operation of group efficacy beliefs in the workplace. *Academy of Management Review*, 32(2):438–458.

Gibson, C.B., Conger, J.A. and Cooper, C.D. (2009) Do you see what we see? The complex effects of perceptual distance between leaders and teams. *Journal of Applied Psychology*, 94(1):62–76.

Giddens, A. (1979) *Central problems in social theory: Action, structure and contradiction in social analysis*, Berkeley: University of California Press.

Giddens, A. (1984) *The Constitution of Society. Outline of the Theory of Structuration*, Cambridge: Polity.

Gigerenzer, G. and Todd, P.M. (1999) *Simple heuristics that make us smart*, New York: Oxford University Press.

Gilbert A. (2003) Developing the internal HR consultant's role. *Management Services*, April, pp. 16–18.

Gilbert, C.G. (2006) Change in the presence of residual fit: Can competing frames coexist? *Organization Science*, 17(1):150–167.

Gilbert, D.T. and Malone, P.S. (1995) The Correspondence Bias. *Psychological Bulletin*, 117(1):21–38.

Gill, C.M. and Hodgkinson, G.P. (2007) Development and validation of the five-factor model questionnaire (FFMQ):An adjectival-based personality inventory for use in occupational settings. *Personnel Psychology*, 60(3):731–766.

Gillespie, M.A., Denison, D.R., Haaland, S., Smerek, R. and Neale, W.S. (2008) Linking organizational culture and customer satisfaction: Results from two companies in different industries. *European Journal of Work and Organizational Psychology*, 17(1):112–132.

Gillespie, N. and Dietz, G. (2009) Trust repair after an organization level failure. *Academy of Management Review*, 34(1):127–145.

Gillespie, R. (1991) *Manufacturing Knowledge: A History of the Hawthorne Experiments*, Cambridge: Cambridge University Press.

Gioia, D.A. and Sims, H.P. (1985) Self-serving bias and actor–observer differences in organizations: An empirical analysis. *Journal of Applied Social Psychology*, 15:547–563.

Gist, M.E. (1987) Self-efficacy: Implications for organizational behavior and human resource management. *Academy of Management Review*, 12(3):472–485.

Gist, M.E. and Mitchell, T.R. (1992) Self-efficacy: Theoretical analysis of its determinants and malleability. *Academy of Management Review*, 17(2):183–211.

Gladwell, M. (2005) *Blink: The Power of Thinking Without Thinking*, New York: Little, Brown & Co. (Time Warner Book Group).

Goffee, R. and Jones, G. (1996) What holds the modern company together? *Harvard Business Review*, 74(6):133–148.

Goffman, E. (1959) *The Presentation of Self in Everyday Life*, New York: Doubleday.

Goldman, B.M. (2003) The application of reference cognitions theory to legal-claiming by terminated workers: The role of organizational justice and anger. *Journal of Management*, 29:705–728.

Goleman, D. (1995) *Emotional intelligence*, New York: Bantam Books.

Gollwitzer, P.M. (1999) Implementation intentions and effective goal pursuit: Strong effects of simple plans. *American Psychologist*, 54:493–503.

Gottfredson, L. (1994) Mainstream Science on Intelligence. *Wall Street Journal*, 13 December.

Gouldner, A.W. (1954) *Patterns of Industrial Bureaucracy*, New York: Free Press.

Gouldner, A.W. (1961) The norm of reciprocity. *American Sociological Review*, 25:161–179.

Graen, G. and Cashman, J.F. (1975) A role making model of leadership in formal organizations: A developmental approach. In J.G. Hunt and L.L. Larson (eds) *Leadership frontiers*, Kent, OH: Kent University Press.

Graham, C.R. (2003) A model of norm development for computer-mediated teamwork, *Small Group Research*, June, 34(3):322–353.

Grams, W.C., and Rogers, R.W. (1990) Power and personality: Effects of Machiavellianism, need for approval, and motivation on use of influence tactics. *Journal of General Psychology*, 117(1):71–82.

Granovetter, M. (1985) Economic action and social structure: A theory of embeddedness. *American Journal of Sociology*, 91:481-510.

Grant, A.M. (2007) Relational job design and the motivation to make a prosocial difference. *Academy of Management Review*, 32(2):393–417.

Grant, A.M. and Parker, S.K. (2009) Redesigning work design theories: The rise of relational and proactive perspectives. Forthcoming in *Academy of Management Annals*, vol. 3.

Greenberg, J. (1990) Looking fair v. being fair: Managing impressions of organizational justice. Research in Organizational Behavior, 12:111–157.

Greenberg, J. (2001) The seven loose can(n)ons of organizational justice. In J. Greenberg and R. Cropanzano (eds) *Advances in Organizational Justice*, pp. 245-272, Stanford, CA: Stanford University Press.

Greenleaf, R.K. (1991) *The Servant as Leader*, Indianapolis, IN: Robert Greenleaf Center.

Greer, L.L., Jehn, K.A. and Mannix, E.A. (2008) Conflict transformation: A longitudinal investigation of the relationships between different types of intragroup conflict and the moderating role of conflict resolution. *Small Group Research*, 39(3):278–302.

Greiner, L. (1972) Evolution and revolution as organizations grow. *Harvard Business Review*, 50:37–46.

Greiner, L.E. (1998) Revolution is still inevitable. *Harvard Business Review*, 76(3):55–64.

Grey, C. and Garsten, C. (2001) Trust, control and the post-bureaucracy. *Organization Studies*, 22(2):229–250.

Griffin, R.W. (1993) *Management*, 4th edn, Boston, MA: Houghton Mifflin.

Grote, G., Weichbrodt, J.C., Günter, H., Zala-Mezö, E. and Künzle, B. (2009) Coordination in high-risk organizations: The need for flexible routines. *Cognition, Technology and Work*, 11(1):17–27.

Guilford, J.P. (1967) *The Nature of Human Intelligence*, New York: McGraw-Hill

Guilford, J.P. (1980) Some changes in the structure of intellect model. *Educational and Psychological Measurement*, 48:1–4.

Gunther, J. (1950) *Roosevelt in Retrospect*, New York: Harper.

Gurtner, A., Tschan, F., Semmer, N.K. and Nägele, C. (2006) Getting groups to develop good strategies: Effects of reflexivity interventions on team process, team performance, and shared mental models. *Organizational Behavior and Human Decision Processes*, 102:127–142.

Güttel, W.H. and Konlechner, S.W. (2009) Continuously hanging by a thread: Managing contextually ambidextrous organizations. *Schmalenbach Business Review*, 61(2):150–172.

Habisch, A., Jonker, J., Wegner, M. and Schmidpeter, R. (eds) (2005) *Corporate social responsibility across Europe*, Heidelberg: Springer.

Hackman. J.R. (2002) *Leading Teams: Setting the Stage for Great Performances*, Boston, MA: Harvard Business School Press.

Hackman, J.R. and Oldham, G.R. (1980) *Work Redesign*, Reading, MA: Addison-Wesley.

Hagel III, J., Brown, J.S. and Davison, L. (2009) The big shift: Measuring the forces for change. *Harvard Business Review*, 87(7/8):86–89.

Haire, M. and Grunes, W.G. (1950) Perceptual defences: Processes protecting an original perception of another personality. *Human Relations*, 3:403–412.

Hale, J.L., Householder, B.J. and Greene, K.L. (2003) The theory of reasoned action. In J.P. Dillard and M. Pfau (eds) *The persuasion handbook: Developments in theory and practice*, pp. 259–286, Thousand Oaks, CA: Sage.

Hall, C.S. and Lindzey, G. (1970) *Theories of Personality*, New York: Wiley.

Hall, R. (2005) The integrating and disciplining tendencies of ERPs: Evidence from Australian organisations. *Strategic Change*, 14(5):245–254.

Hambley, L.A., O'Neil, T.A. and Kline, T.J.B. (2007) Virtual team leadership: The effects of leadership style and communication medium on team interaction styles and outcomes. *Organizational Behavior and Human Decision Processes*, 103(1):1–20.

Handy, C.B. (1993) *Understanding Organizations*, 4th edn, Harmondsworth: Penguin.

Hannan, M.T. and Freeman, J.H. (1977) The population ecology of organizations. *American Journal of Sociology*, 82:929–964.

Hardin, A.M., Fuller, M.A. and Davison, R.M. (2007) I know I can, but can we?: Culture and efficacy beliefs in global virtual teams. *Small Group Research*, 38(1):130–155.

Hardin, G. (1968) The tragedy of the commons. *Science*, 13 December, 162:1243–1248.

Harkins, S.G. and Jackson, J.M. (1985) The role of evaluation in eliminating social loafing. *Personality and Social Psychology Bulletin*, 11:457–465.

Harms, R., Kraus, S. and Reschke, C.H. (2007) Configurations of new ventures in entrepreneurship research: Contributions and research gaps. *Management Research News*, 30(9):661–673.

Harris, K.J., Kacmar, K.M., Zivnuska, S. and Shaw, J.D. (2007) The impact of political skill on impression management effectiveness. *Journal of Applied Psychology*, 92:278–285.

Harrison, D.A. and Klein, K.J. (2007) What's the difference? Diversity constructs as separation, variety, or disparity in organizations. *Academy of Management Review*, 32(4):1199–1228.

Harrison, D.A., Price, K.H., Gavin, J.H. and Florey, A.T. (2002) Time, teams and task performance: Changing effects of surface- and deep-level diversity on group functioning. *Academy of Management Journal*, 45:1029–1045.

Harrison, R. (1972) How to describe your organization. *Harvard Business Review*, September/October.

Hastorf, A.H. and Cantril, H. (1954) They saw a game: A case study. *Journal of Abnormal and Social Psychology*, 49:129–134.

Hatch, M.J. (1993) The dynamics of organizational culture. *Academy of Management Review*, 18(4):657–693.

Hatch, M.J. and Cunliffe, A.L. (2006) *Organization theory: Modern, symbolic and postmodern perspectives,* (2nd edn), Oxford: Oxford University Press.

Haugh, H.M. and McKee, L. (2003) 'It's just like a family' – shared values in the family firm. *Community, Work and Family*, August, 6(2): 141–159.

He, Z.L. and Wong, P.K. (2004) Exploration vs. exploitation: An empirical test of the ambidexterity hypothesis. *Organization Science*, 15:481–494.

Heaphy, E.D. and Dutton, J.E. (2008) Positive social interactions and the human body at work: Linking organizations and physiology. *Academy of Management Review*, 33(1):137-162.

Heider, F. (1958) *The psychology of interpersonal relations*, New York: Wiley.

Heine, S.J. and Buchtel, E.E. (2009) Personality: The universal and the culturally specific. *Annual Review of Psycholgy*, 60:369–394.

Hellriegel, D., Slocum, J.W. and Woodman, R.W. (1989) *Organizational Behaviour*, 5th edn, St Paul, MN: West Publishing.

Hemp, P. (2009) Death by information overload. *Harvard Business Review*, 87(9):82–89.

Hendry, C., Pettigrew, A.M. and Sparrow, P.R. (1989) Linking strategic change, competitive performance and human resource management: Results of a UK empirical study. In Mansfield, R. (ed.) *Frontiers of Management Research*, London: Routledge.

Henwood, K.L. and Pidgeon, N.F. (1993) Qualitative Research and Psychological Theorizing. In Hammersley, M. (ed.) *Social Research: Philosophy, Politics and Practice*, London: Sage.

Herber, J., Singh, J.V. and Useem, M. (2000) The design of new organizational forms. In G.S. Day and P.J.H. Shoemaker (eds) *Wharton on Managing Emerging Technologies*, pp. 376–392, Chichester: Wiley.

Hernandez, M. (2008) Promoting stewardship behaviour in organizations: A leadership model. *Journal of Business Ethics*, 80(1):121–128.

Herselman, S. (2001) Convergence and divergence: Interfaces between ethnicity and organisational culture. *South African Journal of Ethnology*, 24(4):125–131.

Hersey, P. and Blanchard, K.H. (1982) *Management of Organizational Behaviour*, 4th edn, Englewood Cliffs, NJ: Prentice Hall.

Herzberg, F. (1968) One more time: How do you motivate employees? *Harvard Business Review*, January/February, pp. 53–62.

Herzberg, F. (1974) *Work and the Nature of Man*, London: Granada Publishing.

Herzberg, F. (1974b) The wise old Turk. *Harvard Business Review*, September/October, pp. 70–80.

Herzberg, F., Mousener, B. and Synderman, B.B. (1959) *The Motivation to Work*, 2nd edn, London: Chapman and Hall.

Hickson, D.J., Hinings, C.R., Lee, C.A., Schneck, R.E. and Pennings, J.M. (1971) A strategic contingency theory of intraorganizational power. *Administrative Science Quarterly*, 16(2):216-229.

Higgins, C., Judge, T.A. and Ferris, G.R. (2003) Influence tactics and work outcomes: A meta-analysis. *Journal of Organizational Behavior*, 24(1):89–106.

Hill, N.S., Bartol, K.M., Tesluk, P.E. and Langa, G.A. (2009) Organizational context and face-to-face interaction: Influences on the development of trust and collaborative behaviors in computer-mediated groups. *Organizational Behavior and Human Decision Processes*, 108:187–201.

Hill, T. (1983) *Production and Operations Management*, London: Prentice Hall.

Hill, V. and Carley, K.M. (2008) Win friends and influence people: Relationships as conduits of organizational culture in temporary placement agencies. *Journal of Management Inquiry*, 17(4):369 –379.

Hilton, J.L. and von Hippel, W. (1996) Stereotypes. *Annual Review of Psychology*, 47:237–271.

Hinings, C.R., Hickson, D.J., Pennings, J.M. and Schneck, R.E. (1974) Structural conditions of intraorganizational power. *Administrative Science Quarterly*, 19(1):22–44.

Hitt, M.A. and He, X. (2008) Firm strategies in a changing global competitive landscape. *Business Horizons*, 51(5):363–369.

Hitt, M.A. and Ireland, R.D. (1987) Peters and Waterman revisited: The unended quest for excellence. *Academy of Management Executive*, 1(2):91–98.

Hofstede, G. (1980) Motivation, leadership and organization: Do American theories apply abroad? *Organizational Dynamics*, Summer, pp. 42–63.

Hofstede, G. (1983) Dimensions of National Cultures in Fifty Countries and Three Regions. In Deregowski, J., Dziurawiec, S. and Annis, R.C. (eds) *Expectations in Cross-cultural Psychology*, Lisse: Swets and Zeitlinger.

Hofstede, G. (1984) *Culture's Consequences: International Differences in Work-related Values*, Beverley Hills: Sage.

Hofstede, G. (1990) The cultural relativity of organizational practices and theories, dn D.C.Wilson and R.H.Rosenfeld (eds) *managing organizational:Text, readings and cases*, London: McGraw-Hill.

Hofstede, G. (1991) *Cultures and organizations: Software of the mind,* London: McGraw-Hill.

Hofstede, G. and Bond, M.H. (1988) The Confucius connection: From cultural roots to economic growth. *Organizational Dynamics*, 16(4):4-21.

Hofstede, G. and Hofstede, G.J. (2005) *Cultures and organizations: Software of the mind* (revised and expanded 2nd edn), New York: McGraw-Hill.

Hogan, J. and Holland, B. (2003) Using theory to evaluate personality and job-performance. *Journal of Applied Psychology*, February, 88(1):100–113.

Hogan, R., Curphy, G.J. and Hogan, J. (1994) What we know about leadership: Effectiveness and personality. *American Psychologist*, 49:493–504.

Hollander, E.P. (1992) Leadership, followership, self, and others. *Leadership Quarterly*, 3(1):43–54.

Hollenback, J. (1979) A matrix method for expectancy research. *Academy of Management Review*, 4:579–587.

Hollenbeck, J.R., DeRue, D.S. and Guzzo, R. (2004) Bridging the gap between I/O research and HR practice: Improving team composition, team training, and team task design. *Human Resource Management*, 43:353–366.

Hollensbe, E.C., Khazanchi, S. and Masterson, S.S. (2008) How do I assess if my supervisor and organization are fair? Identifying the rules underlying entity-based justice perceptions. *Academy of Management Journal*, 51(6):1099–1116.

Hooker, B. (2005) Fairness. *Ethical Theory and Moral Practice*, 8:329–352.

Homans, G. (1950) *The Human Group*, New York: Harcourt Brace.

Homans, G.C. (1961) *Social Behavior: Its Elementary Forms*, New York: Harcourt Brace.

Horowitz, D.M. (2009) A review of consensus analysis methods in consumer culture, organizational culture and national culture research. *Consumption Markets and Culture*, 12(1):47–64.

Hosmer, L.T. and Kiewitz, C. (2005) Organizational justice: A behavioral science concept with critical implications for business ethics and stakeholder theory. *Business Ethics Quarterly*, 15(1):67–91.

Houldsworth, E. and Jirasinghe, D. (2006) *Managing and Measuring Employee Performance*, London: Kogan Page.

Houlihan, M. (2002) Tensions and variations in call centre management strategies. *Human Resource Management Journal*, 12(4):67–85.

House, R.J. (1971) A path-goal theory of leadership. *Administrative Science Quarterly*, 16:321–338.

House, R.J. (1977) A 1976 theory of charismatic leadership. In J.G. Hunt and and L.L. Larson (eds) *Leadership: The Cutting Edge*, Carbondale, IL: Southern Illinois University Press.

House, R.J. and Mitchell, T.R. (1974) Path-goal theory of leadership. *Journal of Contemporary Business*, 3:81–98.

Howcroft, D. and Wilson, M. (2003) Participation: 'Bounded freedom' or hidden constraints on user involvement. *New Technology, Work and Employment*, 18(1):2–20.

Howe, R. (1963) *The miracle of dialogue*, New York: Seabury Press.

Howell, J.M. and Avolio, B.J. (1992) The ethics of charismatic leadership: Submission or liberation? *Academy of Management Executive*, May, pp. 43–54.

Howell, J.M. and Shamir, B. (2005) The role of followers in the charismatic leadership process: Relationships and their consequences. *Academy of Management Review*, 30(1):96–112.

Howell, J.P., Bowen, D.E., Dorfman, P.W., Kerr, S. and Podsakoff, P.M. (2007) Substitutes for leadership: Effective alternatives to ineffective leadership. In R.P. Vecchio (ed.) *Leadership: Understanding the dynamics of power and influence in organizations*, pp. 363–376. Notre Dame, IN: University of Notre Dame Press.

Hoxie, R.F. (1915) *Scientific Management and Labour*, London: D. Appleton.

HR News (2003) HR poised to flex its strategic muscle, say Masters Series presenters. *HR Magazine*, August, 48(8):36–39.

Huczynski, A.A. and Buchanan, D.A. (1991) *Organizational Behaviour: An Introductory Text*, 2nd edn, Hemel Hempstead: Prentice Hall.

Huczynski, A.A. and Buchanan, D.A. (2001) *Organizational Behaviour*, 4th edn, Hemel Hempstead: Prentice Hall.

Humphrey, S.E., Morgeson, F.P. and Mannor, M.J. (2009) Developing a theory of the strategic core of teams: A role composition model of team performance. *Journal of Applied Psychology*, 94(1):48–61.

Hunter, I., Saunders, J., Burroughs, A. and Constance, S. (2006) *HR Business Partners*, Farnham: Gower.

Hursthouse, P. and Kolb, D. (2001) Cultivating culture in greenfields. *Personnel Review*, 30(3):317–331.

Huzzard, T. (2005) Between global and local: Eight European works councils in retrospect and prospect. *Economic and Industrial Democracy*, 26(4):541–568.

Ilgen, D.R., Hollenbeck, J.R., Johnson, M.D. and Jundt, D.K. (2005) Teams in organizations: From input-process-output models to IMOI models. *Annual Review of Psychology*, 56:517–543.

Ilies, R., Nahrgang, J.D. and Morgeson, F.P. (2007) Leader-member exchange and citizenship behaviors: A metaanalysis. *Journal of Applied Psychology*, 92:269–277.

Indvik, J. (1986) Path-goal theory of leadership: A meta-analysis. *Academy of Management Best Papers Proceedings*, pp. 189–192.

Isen, A.M. and Baron, R.A. (1991) Positive affect as a factor in organizational behavior. *Research in Organizational Behavior*, 13:1–54.

Isenberg, D. (1986) Group polarization: A critical review and meta-analysis. *Journal of Personally and Social Psychology*, 50(6):1141–1151.

Ivancevich, J.M. (1992) *Human Resource Management*, 5th edn, Homewood, IL: Richard D. Irwin.

Jackson, B.W., Lafasto, F., Schultz, H.G. and Kelly, D. (1992) Diversity. In B.W. Jackson, F. Lafasto, H.G. Schultz and D. Kelly, *Human Resource Management*, 31(1–2):Spring/Summer.

Jackson, M.C. (2000) *Systems approaches to management*, New York: Springer.

Jago, A.G. and Ragan, J.W. (1986) The trouble with leader match is that it doesn't match Fiedler's contingency model. *Journal of Applied Psychology*, 71:555–559.

Jain, S.P., Mathur, P. and Maheswaran, D. (2009) The influence of consumers' lay theories on approach/avoidance motivation. *Journal of Marketing Research*, 46(1):56-65.

Janis, I.L. (1982) *Groupthink: Psychological studies of policy decisions and fiascos*, New York: Houghton Mifflin.

Janis, I.L. (1989) *Crucial decisions*, New York: Free Press.

Janis, I.L. and Mann, L. (1977) *Decision Making: A Psychological Analysis of Conflict, Choice and Commitment*, New York: Free Press.

Jansen, J.J.P., van den Bosch, F.A.J. and Volberda, H.W. (2006) Exploratory innovation, exploitative innovation, and performance: Effects of organizational antecedents and environmental moderators. *Management Science*, 52(11):1661–1674.

Jansen, J.P., George, G., Van den Bosch, F.A.J. and Volberda, H.W. (2008) Senior team attributes and organizational ambidexterity: The moderating role of transformational leadership. *Journal of Management Studies*, 45(5):982-1007.

Jaques, E. (1952) *The Changing Culture of a Factory*, London: Tavistock.

Jarvenpaa, S.L. and Leidner, D.E. (1999) Communication and trust in global virtual teams. *Journal of Computer Mediated Communication*, 3:1–36.

Jarzabkowski, P. (2008) Shaping strategy as a structuration process. *Academy of Management Journal*, 51(4):621–650.

Jawahar, I.M., Meurs, James A., Ferris, Gerald R. and Hochwarter, Wayne A. (2008) Self-efficacy and political skill as comparative predictors of task and contextual performance: A two-study constructive replication. *Human Performance*, 21(2):138–157.

Jehn, K. (1995) A multimethod examination of the benefits and detriments of intragroup conflict. *Administrative Science Quarterly*, 40:256–282.

Jehn, K., Greer, L., Levine, S. and Szulanski, G. (2008) The Effects of Conflict Types, Dimensions, and Emergent States on Group Outcomes. *Group Decision and Negotiation*, 17(6):465-495.

Jehn, K.A. and Bendersky, C. (2003) Intragroup conflict in organizations: A contingency perspective on the conflict-outcome relationship. *Research in Organizational Behavior*, 25:189–244.

Jehn, K.A. and Mannix, E.A. (2001) The dynamic nature of conflict: A longitudinal study of intragroup conflict and group performance. *Academy of Management Journal*, 44(2):238–251.

Jehn, K.A., Greer, L.L., Levine, S. and Szulanksi, G. (2008) The effects of conflict types, dimensions, and emergent states on group outcomes. *Group Decision and Negotiation*, 17(6):465-495.

Jensen-Campbell, L.A., Gleason, K.A., Adams, R. and Malcolm, K.T. (2003) Interpersonal conflict, agreeableness, and personality development. *Journal of Personality*, December, 71(6):1059–1087.

Jevons, W.S. (1888) *The Theory of Political Economy*, New York: Macmillan.

Johns, G. (1992) *Organizational Behavior: Understanding Life at Work* (3rd edn), Harper Collins.

Johnson, D.W. and Johnson, F.P. (1994) *Joining together: Group theory and group skills*, Boston, MA: Allyn and Bacon.

Johnson, G. (1987), *Strategic change and the management process*, Oxford: Basil Blackwell.

Johnson, G. (1988), Rethinking incrementalism. *Strategic Management Journal*, 9(1):75–91.

Johnson, G. (1992) Managing strategic change: Strategy, culture and action. *Long Range Planning*, 25(1):28–36.

Johnson, G., Scholes, K. and Whittington, R. (2005) *Exploring corporate strategy* (7th edn), Upper Saddle River, NJ: Prentice Hall/FT.

Johnson, G., Scholes, K. and Whittington, R. (2008). *Exploring corporate strategy* (8th edn), Essex, England: Prentice Hall/FT.

Johnson, M.D., Hollenbeck, J.R., Ilgen, D.R., Humphrey, S.E., Meyer, C.J. and Jundt, D.K. (2006)

Cutthroat cooperation: Asymmetrical adaptation of team reward structures. *Academy of Management Journal*, 49(1):103–120.

Jones, E.E. and Nisbett, R.E. (1972) The actor and the observer: Divergent perceptions of the causes of behavior. In E.E. Jones, D. Kanouse, H.H. Kelley, R.E. Nisbett, S. Valins, and B. Weiner (eds), *Attribution: Perceiving the causes of behavior*, pp. 79–94, Morristown, NJ: General Learning Press.

Jones, E.E. and Pittman, T. S. (1982) Toward a general theory of strategic self presentation. In J. Suls (ed.) *Psychological perspectives on the self*, pp. 231–262, Hillsdale, NJ: Lawrence Erlbaum.

Jones, F.F., Scarpello, V. and Bergmann, T. (1999) Pay procedures – what makes them fair? *Journal of Occupational and Organizational Psychology*, 72:129–145.

Jones, G.R. (1986) Socialization tactics, self-efficacy, and newcomers' adjustments to organizations. *Academy of Management Journal*, 29(2):262-279.

Jones, G.R. (2004). *Organizational theory, design and change,* Upper Saddle River, NJ: Pearson.

Jones, M.R. and Karsten, H. (2008) Giddens's structuration theory and information systems research. *MIS Quarterly*, 32(1):127–157.

Joseph, E.E. and Winston, B.E. (2005) A correlation of servant leadership, leader trust, and organizational trust. *Leadership and Organizational Development Journal*, 26(1):6–22.

Judge, T. A. and Bono, J.E. (2001). Relationship of core self-evaluations traits—self-esteem, generalized self-efficacy, locus of control, and emotional stability—with job satisfaction and job performance: A meta-analysis. *Journal of Applied Psychology*, 86:80–92.

Judge T.A. and Piccolo, R.F. (2004) Transformational and transactional leadership: A meta-analytic test of their relative validity. *Journal of Applied Psychology*, 89:755–768.

Judge, T.A., Locke, E.A., Durham, C.C., and Kluger, A.N. (1998) Dispositional effects on job and life satisfaction: The role of core evaluations. *Journal of Applied Psychology*, 83:17–34.

Judge, T.A., Erez, A., Bono, J.E. and Thoresen, C.J. (2002) Are measures of self-esteem, neuroticism, locus of control, and generalized self-efficacy indicators of a common core construct? *Journal of Personality and Social Psychology*, 83:693–710.

Jung, C.G. (1968) *Analytical Psychology: Its Theory and Practice*, New York: Routledge and Kegan Paul.

Juran, J.M. (1982) *Juran on quality improvement*, New York: Juran Institute.

Kacmar, K.M., Zivnuska, S. and White, C.D. (2007) Control and exchange: The impact of work environment on the work effort of low relationship quality employees. *Leadership Quarterly*, 18:69–84.

Kahn, E.F. (1982) Conclusion: Critical Themes in the Study of Change. In P.S. Goodman and Associates (eds) *Change in Organizations*, San Francisco, CA: Jossey Bass.

Kahn, W.A. (2007) Meaningful connections: Positive relationships and attachments at work. In J.E. Dutton and B.R. Ragins (eds) *Exploring positive relationships at work: Building a theoretical and research foundation*, pp. 189–206, Mahwah, NJ: Lawrence Erlbaum Associates.

Kahneman, D. and Tversky, A. (1980) Intuitive prediction: Biases and corrective procedures. *Management Science*, 62:250–257.

Kahneman, D., Knetsch, J.L. and Thaler, R.H. (1991) Anomalies: The endowment effect, loss aversion, and status quo bias. *Journal of Economic Perspectives*, 5(1):193-206.

Kalev, A., Shenhav, Y. and De Vries, D. (2008) The state, the labor process, and the diffusion of managerial models. *Administrative Science Quarterly*, 53(1):1–28.

Kammeyer-Mueller, J.D., Judge, T.A. and Scott, B.A. (2009) The role of core self-evaluations in the coping process. *Journal of Applied Psychology*, 94(1):177–195.

Kanfer, R., Chen, G. and Pritchard, R.D. (eds) (2008) *Work motivation: Past, present and future*, New York: Routledge.

Kanter, R.M. (1983) *The Change Masters*, London: Allen and Unwin.

Karau, S.J. and Kelly, J.R. (1992) The effects of time scarcity and time abundance on group performance quality and interaction process. *Journal of Experimental Social Psychology*, 28:542–571.

Kark, R. and Van Dijk. D. (2007) Motivation to lead, motivation to follow: The role of the self-regulatory focus in leadership processes. *Academy of Management Review*, 32:500–528.

Katz, D. (1960) The functional approach to the study of attitudes. *Public Opinion Quarterly*, 24:163–204.

Katz, D. and Kahn, R.L. (1966) *The social psychology of organizations,* New York: Wiley.

Katz, D. and Kahn, R.L. (1978) *The social psychology of organizations* (2nd edn), New York: Wiley.

Katzenbach, J.R. and Smith, D.K. (1993) *The Wisdom of Teams: Creating the High Performance Organization*, Boston: Harvard Business School Press.

Kearney, E. and Gebert, D. (2009) Managing diversity and enhancing team outcomes: The promise of transformational leadership. *Journal of Applied Psychology*, 94(1):77-89.

Keast, S. and Towler, M. (2009) *Rational decision-making for managers: An introduction*, Chichester, England: Wiley.

Keep, W. (2003) Adam Smith's imperfect invisible hand: Motivations to mislead. *Business Ethics: A European Review*, October, 12(4):343–354.

Kehr, H.M. (2004) Integrating implicit motives, explicit motives, and perceived abilities: The compensatory model of work motivation and volition. *Academy of Management Review*, 29(3):479–499.

Keil, M., Depledge, G. and Rai, A. (2007). Escalation: The role of problem recognition and cognitive bias. *Decision Sciences*, 38(3):391-421.

Keller, R.T. (1986) Predictors of the performance of project groups in research and development organisations, *Academy of Management Review*, 11(4):715–726.

Keller, R.T. (2006) Transformational leadership, initiating structure, and substitutes for leadership: A longitudinal study of research and development project team performance. *Journal of Applied Psychology*, 91:202–210.

Kelley, H.H. (1967) Attribution theory in social psychology. In D. Levine (ed.) *Nebraska Symposium on Motivation*, vol. 15, Lincoln: University of Nebraska Press.

Kelley, H.H. (1973) The process of causal attribution. *American Psychologist*, February, pp. 107–128.

Kelley, R.E. (1992) *The power of followership: How to create leaders people want to follow, and followers who lead themselves*, New York: Doubleday/Currency.

Kellogg, K.C., Orlikowski, W.J. and Yates, J.A. (2006) Life in the trading zone: Structuring coordination across boundaries in postbureaucratic organizations. *Organization Science*, 17(1):22-44.

Kelman, H.C. (2006) Interests, relationships, identities: Three central issues for individuals and groups in negotiating their social environment. *Annual Review of Psychology*, 57:1–26.

Keltner, D., Gruenfeld, D.H. and Anderson, C. (2003) Power, approach, and inhibition. *Psychological Review*, 110(2):265-284.

Kerr, N.L. and Tindale, R.S. (2004) Group performance and decisionmaking. *Annual Review of Psychology*, 55:623–655.

Kerr, S. and Jermier, J.M. (1978) Substitutes for leadership: Their meaning and measurement. *Organizational Behaviour and Human Performance*, 22:375–403.

Kidwell, R.E. and Bennett, N. (1993) Employee propensity to withhold effort: A conceptual model to intersect three avenues of research. *Academy of Management Review*, 18:429–456.

Kiewitz, C., Restubog, S.L.D., Zagenczyk, T. and Hochwarter, W. (2009) The interactive effects of psychological contract breach and organizational politics on perceived organizational support: Evidence from two longitudinal studies. *Journal of Management Studies*, 46(5):806–834.

Kim, P.H., Dirks, K.T. and Cooper, C.D. (2009) The repair of trust: A dynamic bilateral perspective and multilevel conceptualization. *Academy of Management Review*, 34(3):401–422.

Kim, P.H., Ferrin, D.L., Cooper, C.D. and Dirks, K.T. (2004) Removing the shadow of suspicion: The effects of apology versus denial for repairing competence- versus integrity- based trust violations. *Journal of Applied Psychology*, 89:104–118.

Kim, P.H., Dirks, K.T., Cooper, C.D. and Ferrin, D.L. (2006) When more blame is better than less: The implications of internal vs. external attributions for the repair of trust after a competence- vs. integrity-based trust violation. *Organizational Behavior and Human Decision Processes*, 99:49–65.

Kim, T.-Y. and Leung, K. (2007) Forming and reacting to overall fairness: A cross-cultural comparison. *Organizational Behavior and Human Decision Processes*, 104:83–95.

Kimmel, A.J. (2007) *Ethical issues in behavioral research: Basic and applied perspectives* (2nd edn), Cambridge, MA: Wiley Blackwell.

King, N. (1970) A clarification and evaluation of the two-factor theory of job satisfaction. *Psychological Bulletin*, 64:18–31.

Kipnis, D. Schmidt, S.M., and Wilkinson, I. (1980). Intraorganizational influence tactics: Explorations in getting one's way. *Journal of Applied Psychology*, 65:440–452.

Kipnis, D. Schmidt, S.M. Swaffin-Smith, C. and Wilkinson, I. (1984) Patterns of managerial influence: Shotgun managers, tacticians, and bystanders. *Organizational Dynamics*, 12(3):58–67.

Kirkman, B.L., Lowe., K.B. and Gibson, C.B. (2006) A quarter century of *Culture's consequences:* A review of empirical research incorporating Hofstede's cultural values framework. *Journal of International Business Studies*, 37:285–320.

Kirkman, B.L., Rosen, B., Gibson, C.B., Tesluk, P.E. and McPherson, S.O. (2002) Five challenges to virtual team success. *Academy of Management Executive*, 16(3):67–79.

Klein, H.J. (1989) An integrated control theory model of work motivation. *Academy of Management Review*, 14:150-172.

Klein, K.J., Ziegert, J.C., Knight, A.P. and Xiao, Y. (2006) Dynamic delegation: Shared, hierarchical, and deindividualized leadership in extreme action teams. *Administrative Science Quarterly*, 51(4):590–621.

Kline, P. (1972) *Fact and Fantasy in Freudian Theory*, London: Methuen.

Knights, D., Noble, F., Vurdubakis, T. and Willmott, H. (2001) Chasing shadows: Control, virtuality and the production of trust. *Organization Studies*, 22(2):311-336.

Koch, C. (2001) Enterprise resource planning. *Journal of Organizational Change Management*, 14(1):64–79.

Kolakowski, L. (1993) An Overall View of Positivism. In Hammersley, M. (ed.) *Social Research: Philosophy, Politics and Practice*, London: Sage.

Koo, M. and Fishbach, A. (2008) Dynamics of self-regulation: How (un)accomplished goal actions affect motivation. *Journal of Personality and Social Psychology*, 94(2):183–195.

Konsynski, B.R. and Sviokla, J.J. (1994) Cognitive Reapportionment: Rethinking the Location of Judgement in Managerial Decision Making. In C. Heckscher and A. Donnellon, (eds) *The Post-bureaucratic Organization: New Perspectives on Organizational Change*, Thousand Oaks: Sage.

Korunka, C., Frank, H., Lueger, M. and Mugier, J. (2003) Context of resources, environment, and the startup process: A configurational approach. *Entrepreneurship Theory and Practice*, 28:23–42.

Koslowsky, M., Schwarzwald, J. and Ashuri, S. (2001) On the relationship between subordinates' compliance to power sources and organizational attitudes. *Applied Psychology: An International Review*, 50:455–476.

Kotler, P. and Lee, N. (2005) *Corporate social responsibility: Doing the most good for your company and your cause*, Hoboken, NJ: Wiley.

Kotter, J.P. (1982) What effective general managers really do. *Harvard Business Review*, 60(6):156–168.

Kotter, J.P. (1990) *A force for change: How leadership differs from management*, New York: Free Press.

Kotter, J.P. (1995) Leading change: Why transformation efforts fail. *Harvard Business Review*, 73:59–67.

Kotter, J.P. and Schlesinger, L.A. (1979) Choosing strategies for change. *Harvard Business Review*, March/April.

Koza, M.P. and Thoenig, J.-C. (2003) Rethinking the firm: Organizational approaches. *Organization Studies*, 24(8):1219–1229.

Kozlowski, S.W.J. and Bell, B.S. (2003) Work groups and teams in organizations. In W.C. Borman and D.R. Ilgen (eds) *Handbook of psychology: Industrial and organizational psychology*, 12:333–375, New York: Wiley.

Kramer, R.M. (1999) Trust and distrust in organizations: Emerging perspectives, enduring questions. *Annual Review of Psychology*, 50:569–598.

Kramer, R.M. (2009) Rethinking trust. *Harvard Business Review*, 87(6):68–77.

Kratzer, J., Leenders, R.Th.A.J. and van Engelen, J.M.L. (2004) Stimulating the potential: Creative performance and communication in innovation teams. *Creativity and Innovation Management*, 13(1):63–71.

Kraut, A.I. (1975) Some recent advances in cross-national research. *Academy of Management Journal*, 18:538–549.

Kray, L.J. and Galinsky, A.D. (2003) The debiasing effect of counterfactual mind-sets: Increasing the search for disconfirmatory information in group decisions. *Organizational Behavior and Human Decision Processes*, 91(1):69–81.

Kreps, D.M., Milgrom, P., Roberts, J. and Wilson, R. (1982) Rational cooperation in the finitely repeated prisoner's dilemma. *Journal of Economic Theory*, 27:245–252.

Krishnamurti, C., Sequeira, J.M. and Fangjian, F. (2003) Stock exchange governance and market quality. *Journal of Banking and Finance*, 27(9):1859–1879.

Kroeber, A.L. and Kluckhohn, C. (1952) *Culture: A Critical Review of Concepts and Definitions*, Cambridge, MA: Peabody Museum.

Kuhnert, K.W. and Lewis, P. (1987) Transactional and transformational leadership: A constructive/

developmental analysis. *Academy of Management Review*, October, pp. 648–657.

Kumar, A. (2004) Mass customization: Metrics and modularity. *International Journal of Flexible Manufacturing Systems*, 16(4):287–312.

Kumar, A. (2007) From mass customization to mass personalization: A strategic transformation. *International Journal of Flexible Manufacturing Systems*, 19(4):533–547.

Lahiri, S., Pérez-Nordtvedt, L. and Renn, R.W. (2008) Will the new competitive landscape cause your firm's decline? It depends on your mindset. *Business Horizons*, 51(4):311–320.

Lamb, J. (1999) Face values gains credence in 'unwritten' HR policies. *People Management*, 25 November, pp. 14–15.

Lammers, C.J. and Hickson, D.J. (1979) *Organizations Alike and Unlike*, London: Routledge.

Langer, E.J. (1975) The illusion of control. *Journal of Personality and Social Psychology*, 32:311–328.

Larsen, H.H. and Brewster, C. (2003) Line management responsibility for HRM: What is happening in Europe? *Employee Relations*, 25(3):228–244.

Laschinger, H.K.S., Finegan, J.E., Shamian, J. and Wilk, P. (2004) A longitudinal analysis of the impact of workplace empowerment on work satisfaction. *Journal of Organizational Behavior*, 25(4):527–545.

Laszlo, C. (2003) *The sustainable company: how to create lasting value through social and environmental performance*, Washington: Island Press.

Latané, B., Williams, K. and Harkins, S. (1979) Many hands make light the work: The causes and consequences of social loafing. *Journal of Personality and Social Psychology*, 37:822–832.

Latham, G.P. (2007) *Work motivation: History, theory, research and practice*, Thousand Oaks, CA: Sage.

Latham, G.P. and Locke, E.A. (2009) Science and ethics: What should count as evidence against the use of goal setting? *Academy of Management Perspectives*, 23(3):88–91.

Latham, G.P. and Pinder, C.C. (2005) Work motivation theory and research at the dawn of the twenty-first century. *Annual Review of Psychology*, 56:485–516.

Lavelle, J.J., Rupp, D.E. and Brockner, J. (2007) Taking a multifoci approach to the study of justice, social exchange, and citizenship behavior: The target similarity model. *Journal of Management*, 33(6):841–866.

Lave, J. and Wenger, E. (1991) *Situated learning: Legitimate peripheral participation*, Cambridge University Press.

Law, K.S., and Wong, C.S. (1998) Relative importance of referents on pay satisfaction: A review and test of a new policy-capturing approach. *Journal of Occupational and Organizational Psychology*, 71:47–60.

Lawrence, P.R. and Lorsch, J.W. (1967) *Organization and Environment*, Boston, MA: Harvard University Press.

Leavitt, H.J. (1978) *Managerial Psychology*, 4th edn, Chicago, IL: University of Chicago Press.

Lee, H., Padmanabhan, V. and Whang, S. (1997) The bullwhip effect in supply chains. *Sloan Management Review*, Spring, pp. 93–102.

Lee, M.-D.P. (2008) A review of the theories of corporate social responsibility: Its evolutionary path and the road ahead. *International Journal of Management Reviews*, 10(1):53–73.

Lee, R.T. and Brotheridge, C.M. (2006) When prey turns predatory: Workplace bullying as a predictor of counteraggression/bullying, coping, and well-being. *European Journal of Work and Organizational Psychology*, 15(3):352-377.

Legge, K. (1978) *Power, Innovation and Problem Solving in Personnel Management*, London: McGraw-Hill.

Legge, K. (2005) *Human Resource Management: Rhetorics and Realities*, Anniversary edition, Basingstoke: Palgrave Macmillan.

Lehman, D.R., Chiu, C.-Y. and Schaller, M. (2004) Psychology and culture. *Annual Review of Psychology*, 55:689–714.

Lehrer, M. and Delaunay, C. (2009) Multinational enterprises and the promotion of civil society: The challenge for 21st century capitalism. *California Management Review*, 51(4):126–147.

Lehtinen, A. and Kuorikoski, J. (2007) Unrealistic assumptions in rational choice theory. *Philosophy of the Social Sciences*, 37(2):115–138.

Lengnick-Hall, M.L. and Moritz, S. (2003) The impact of e-HR on the human resource management function. *Journal of Labor Research*, Summer, 24(3):365–380.

Leonard, K.M. (2008) A cross-cultural investigation of temporal orientation in work organizations: A differentiation matching approach. *International Journal of Intercultural Relations*, 32:479–492.

Lepak, D.P., Takeuchi, R. and Snell, S.A. (2003) Employment flexibility and firm performance: Examining the interaction effects of employment mode, environmental dynamism, and technological intensity. *Journal of Management*, October, 29(5):681–704.

LePine, J.A., Piccolo, R.F., Jackson, C.L., Mathieu, J.E. and Saul, J.R. (2008) A meta-analysis of teamwork processes: Tests of a multidimensional model and relationships with team effectiveness criteria. *Personnel Psychology*, 61:273–307.

Lerner, M. (1980) *The Belief in a Just World*, New York: Plenum Press.

Levashina, J. and Campion, M.A. (2007) Measuring faking in the employment interview: Development and validation of an interview faking behavior scale. *Journal of Applied Psychology*, 92(6): 1638–1656.

Leventhal, G.S. (1976) The distribution of rewards and resources in groups and organizations. In L. Berkowitz and E. Walster (eds) *Advances in Experimental Social Psychology*, pp. 91–131, New York: Academic Press.

Leventhal, G.S. (1980) What should be done with equity theory? In K.J. Gergen, M.S. Greenberg and R.H. Willis (eds) *Social Exchanges: Advances in Theory and Research*, pp. 27–55, New York: Plenum Press.

LeVine, R.A. (1984) Properties of culture: An ethnographic view. In R.A. Shweder and R.A. LeVine (eds) *Culture theory: Essays on mind, self, and emotion*, pp. 67–87, New York: Cambridge University Press.

Levitt, B. and March, J.G. (1988) Organizational learning. *Annual Review of Sociology*, 14:319-338.

Lewicki, R.J. and Bunker, B.B. (1996) Developing and maintaining trust in work relationships. In R.M. Kramer and T.R. Tyler (eds) *Trust in organizations: Frontiers of theory and research*, pp. 114–139, Thousand Oaks, CA: Sage.

Lewicki, R.J., Barry, B., Saunders, D.M. and Minton, J.W. (2003) *Negotiation* (4th edn), Burr Ridge, IL: McGraw-Hill.

Lewin, K. (1948) *Resolving social conflicts; selected papers on group dynamics,* ed. Gertrude W. Lewin, New York: Harper and Row.

Lewis, T. (2007) Braverman, Foucault and the labor process: Framing the current high-skills debate. *Journal of Education and Work*, 20(5):397–415.

Leys, W.A.R. (1962) The Value Framework of Decision Making. In S. Mailick, and E.H. Van Ness (eds) *Concepts and Issues in Administrative Behaviour*, Englewood Cliffs, NJ: Prentice Hall.

Lichtenstein, B.B., Uhl-Bien, M., Marion, R., Seers, A., Orton, J.D. and Schreiber, C. (2006) Complexity leadership theory: An interactive perspective on leading in complex adaptive systems. *Emergence: Complexity and Organization*, 8(4):2–12.

Liden, R.C., Wayne, S.J. and Sparrowe, R.T. (2000) An examination of the mediating role of psychological emprovement on the relations between the job, interpersonal relationships, and work outcomes. Journal of Applied Psychology, 85(3):407–416.

Lieberman, M.D. (2007) Social cognitive neuroscience: A review of core processes. *Annual Review of Psychology*, 58:259–289.

Likert, R. (1961) *New Patterns of Management*, New York: McGraw-Hill.

Lindblom, C.E. (1959) The science of muddling through. *Public Administration Review*, 19:79–88.

Linstead, S. (1993) Deconstruction in the Study of Organizations. In J. Hassard and M. Parker (eds), *Postmodernism and Organizations*, London: Sage.

Linstead, S. and Brewis, J. (2007) Passion, knowledge and motivation: Ontologies of desire. *Organization*, 14(3):351–371.

Littlefield, D. (1999) Kerry's heroes. *People Management*, 6 May, pp. 48–50.

Liu, G., Shah, R. and Schroeder, R.G. (2006) Linking work design to mass customization: A sociotechnical systems perspective. *Decision Sciences*, 37(4):519–545.

Locke, E.A. (1968) Towards a theory of task motivation and incentives. *Organizational Behaviour and Human Performance*, 3:157–189.

Locke, E.A. (1976) The Nature and Causes of Job Satisfaction. In M. Dunnette (ed.) *Handbook of Industrial and Organizational Psychology*, Chicago, IL: Rand McNally.

Locke, E.A. and Latham, G.P. (1990) *A theory of goal setting and task performance*, Englewood Cliffs, NJ: Prentice-Hall.

Locke, E.A. and Latham, G.P. (2002) Building a practically useful theory of goal setting and task motivation. *American Psychologist*, 57(9):705–717.

Locke E.A. and Latham, G.P. (2004) What should we do about motivation theory? Six recommendations for the twenty-first century. *Academy of Management Review*, 29(3):388–403.

Locke, E.A. and Latham, G.P. (2009) Has goal setting gone wild, or have its attackers abandoned good scholarship? *Academy of Management Perspectives*, 23(1):17–23.

Lopes, P.N., Côté, S., Grewal, D., Kadis, J., Gall, M. and Salovey, P. (2006) Emotional intelligence and positive work outcomes. *Psichothema*, 18(Suppl.):132–138.

Lord, R,G. and Brown, D.J. (2004) *Leadership processes and follower self-identity*, Mahwah, NJ: Lawrence Erlbaum.

Lord, R.G. and Hanges, P.J. (1987) A control system model of organizational motivation: Theoretical development and and applied implications. *Behavioral Science*, 32:161–178.

Lord, R.G., Hanges, P.J. and Godfrey, E.G. (2003) Integrating neural networks into decisionmaking and motivational theory: Rethinking VIE theory. *Canadian Psychology*, 44(1):21–38.

Lu, M., Watson-Manheim, M.B., Chudoba, K.M. and Wynn, E. (2006) Virtuality and team performance: Understanding the impact of variety of practices. *Journal of Global Information Technology Management*, 9:4–23.

Lubatkin, M.H., Simsek, Z., Ling, Y. and Veiga, J.F. (2006) Ambidexterity and performance in small- to mediumsized firms: The pivotal role of top management team behavioral integration. *Journal of Management*, 32(5):646–672.

Lucas, E. (2000) EQ: how do you measure up? *Professional Manager*, January, pp. 10–12.

Ludema, J. and Fry, R. (2008) The practice of appreciative inquiry. In P. Reason and H. Bradbury (eds) *Handbook of Action Research* (2nd edn), pp. 280–296, London: Sage.

Luft, J. and Ingham, H. (1955) The Johari window, a graphic model of interpersonal awareness. *Proceedings of the western training laboratory in group development*, Los Angeles: UCLA.

Lukes, S. (2005) *Power: A radical view* (2nd edn), New York: Palgrave Macmillan.

Lukes, S. (2008) *Moral relativism*, London: Profile Books.

Lundberg, C.C. (1985) On the Feasibility of Cultural Intervention in Organizations. In P.J. Frost, L.F. Moore, M.R. Louis, C.C. Lundberg and J. Martin (eds) *Organization Culture*, Beverly Hills, CA: Sage.

Lüscher, L.S. and Lewis, M. (2008) Organizational change and managerial sensemaking: Working through paradox. *Academy of Management Journal*, 21(2):221–240.

Lussato, B. (1976) *A Critical Introduction to Organization Theory*, London: Macmillan.

Lutgen-Sandvik, P., Tracy, S.J. and Alberts, J.K. (2007) Burned by bullying in the American workplace: Prevalence, perception, degree and impact. *Journal of Management Studies*, 44(6):837–862.

Luthans, F. (1995) *Organizational Behaviour*, 7th edn, New York: McGraw-Hill.

Mackey, A., Mackey, T. and Barney, J.B. (2007) Corporate social responsibility and firm performance: Investor preferences and corporate strategies. *Academy of Management Review*, 32:817–835.

Maclagan, P. (2003) Self-actualisation as a moral concept and the implications for motivation in organisations: A Kantian argument. *Business Ethics: A European Review*, 12(4):334–343.

Maguire, S., McKelvey, B., Mirabeau, L. and Oztas, N. (2006) Complexity science and organization studies. In S. Clegg, C. Hardy, T. Lawrence and W. Nord (eds) *Handbook of Organization Studies*, pp. 165–214, Thousand Oaks, CA: Sage.

Maines, D.R. and Morrione, T.J. (eds) (1990) *Industrialization as an Agent of Social Change: A Critical Analysis by Herbert Blumer*, New York: Aldine de Gruyter.

Major, D.A., Turner, J.E. and Fletcher, T.D. (2006) Linking proactive personality and the Big Five to motivation to learn and development activity. *Journal of Applied Psychology*, 91(4):927–935.

Malhotra, A., Majchrzak, A. and Rosen, B. (2007) Leading virtual teams. *Academy of Management Perspectives*, 21(1) :60–70.

Malle, B.F. (1999) How people explain behavior: A new theoretical framework. *Personality and Social Psychology Review*, 3(1):23–48.

Malle, B.F. (2006) The actor-observer asymmetry in causal attribution: A (surprising) meta-analysis. *Psychological Bulletin*, 132:895–919.

Management Services (2003a) To network or not to network, March, p. 5.

Management Services (2003b) Cashiers, not call centres, say Britain's banking customers, December, p. 7.

Mann, R.D. (1959) A review of the relationship between personality and performance in small groups. *Psychological Bulletin*, 56:241–270.

Manz, C.C. and Sims, H.P. Jr. (1980) Self-management as a substitute for leadership: A social learning perspective. *Academy of Management Review*, 6:362–367.

Manz, C.C. and Sims, H.P. Jr. (1991) *Superleadership: Leading others to lead themselves*, Englewood Cliffs, NJ: Prentice Hall.

March, J.G. (1991) Exploration and exploitation in organizational learning. *Organization Science*, 2:71–87.

March, J.G. and Simon, H.A. (1958) *Organizations*, New York: Wiley.

Marchington, M. and Wilkinson, A. (2005) *Human Resource Management at Work* (3rd edn), London: CIPD.

Marcus, A. and Fremeth, A.R. (2009) Green management matters regardless. *Academy of Management Perspectives*, 23(3):17–26.

Margerison, C. and McCann, D. (1990) *Team Management: Practical New Approaches*, London: Mercury Books.

Marks, M.A., Mathieu, J.E. and Zaccaro, S.J. (2001) A temporally based framework and taxonomy of team processes. *Academy of Management Review*, 26(3):356–376.

Marler, J., Fisher, S. and Ke, W. (2009) Employee self-service technology acceptance: A comparison of pre-implementation and post-implementation relationships. *Personnel Psychology*, 62(2):327–358.

Martin, J. (2009) *Human Resource Management*, Sage Course Companions, London: Sage.

Martin R. and Moldoveanu, M. (2003) Capital versus talent: The battle that's reshaping business. *Harvard Business Review*, 81 (7):36–41.

Martin, J., Sitkin, S.B. and Boehm, M. (1985) Founders and the elusiveness of a cultural legacy. In P.J. Frost, L.J. Moore, M.R. Louis, C.C.Lundberg and J. Martin (eds.) *Organizational Culture*, pp. 99–124, London: Sage.

Maslach, C. and Jackson, S. (1981) The measurement of experienced burnout. *Journal of Occupational Behavior*, 2:99–113.

Maslow, A.H. (1943) A theory of human motivation. *Psychological Review*, 50:370–396.

Maslow, A.H. (1987) *Motivation and Personality*, 3rd edn, New York: Harper and Row.

Mason, R.B. (2007) The external environment's effect on management and strategy: A complexity theory approach. *Management Decision*, 45(1):10–28.

Mathis, R.L. and Jackson, J.H. (2008) *Human Resource Management* (12th edn), Mason, OH: Thomson South-Western.

Matsumoto, D., Seung H.Y. and Nakagawa, S. (2008) Culture, emotion regulation, and adjustment. *Journal of Personality and Social Psychology*, 94(6):925–937.

Mayer, D.M., Kuenzi, M., Greenbaum, R., Bardes, M. and Salvador, R. (2009) How low does ethical leadership flow? Test of a trickle-down model. *Organizational Behavior and Human Decision Processes*, 108(1):1–13.

Mayer, J.D. and Salovey, P. (1997) What is emotional intelligence? In P. Salovey and D. Sluyter (eds) *Emotional development and emotional intelligence: Educational implications*, pp. 3–31, New York: Basic Books.

Mayer, J.D., Roberts, R.D. and Barsade, S.G. (2008) Human abilities: Emotional intelligence. *Annual Review of Psychology*, 59:507-536.

Mayer, R.C., Davis, J.H. and Schoorman, F.D. (1995) An integration model of organizational trust. *Academy of Management Review*, 20(3):709-734.

Mayes, B.T. and Allen, R.W. (1977) Toward a definition of organizational politics. *Academy of Management Review*, 2:672–677.

McCann, L., Morris, J. and Hassard, J. (2008) Normalized intensity: The new labour process of middle management. *Journal of Management Studies*, 45(2):343-371.

McClelland, D.C. and Burnham, D.H. (1976) Power is the great motivator. *Harvard Business Review*, 54(2):100-110.

McCrae, R.R. and Costa, P.T. Jr. (1989) Reinterpreting the Myers-Briggs Type Indicator from the perspective of the Five-Factor Model of personality. *Journal of Personality*, 57(1):17-40.

McCrea, S.M. (2008) Self-handicapping, excuse making, and counterfactual thinking: Consequences for self-esteem and future motivation. *Journal of Personality and Social Psychology*, 95(2):274-292.

McCulloch, W.S. (1965) *Embodiments of mind*, Cambridge, MA: MIT Press.

McFarland, L.A., Yun, G., Harold, C, M., Viera Jr., L. and Moore, L.G. (2005). An examination of impression management use and effectiveness across assessment center exercises: The role of competency demands. *Personnel Psychology*, 58(4):949-980.

McFarlin, D.B. and Sweeney, P.D. (2001) Crosscultural applications of organizational justice. In R. Cropanzano (ed.) *Justice in the workplace: From theory to practice*, 2:67-96, Mahwah, NJ: Lawrence Erlbaum.

McGregor, D. (1960) *The Human Side of Enterprise*, New York: McGraw-Hill.

McKenzie, D. and Wajcman, J. (1985) *The social shaping of technology*, Milton Keynes: Open Univeristy Press.

McKinlay, A. (2002) The limits of knowledge management. *New Technology, Work and Employment*, July, 17(2):76–89.

McMillan, I.C. and Jones, P.E. (1986) *Strategy formulation: Power and politics*, 2nd edn, St.Paul, MN: West Publishing.

McNamara, G., Vaaler, P.M. and Devers, C. (2003) Same as it ever was: The search for evidence of increasing hypercompetition. *Strategic Management Journal*, 24(3):261–289.

McSweeney, B. (2002) Hofstede's model of national cultural differences and their consequences: A triumph of faith – A failure of analysis. *Human Relations*, 55:89–118.

McWilliams, A., Siegel, D.S. and Wright, P.M. (2006) Corporate social responsibility: Strategic implications. *Journal of Management Studies*, 43(1):1–18.

Mead, G.H. (1934) *Mind, Self and Society*, Chicago, IL: University of Chicago Press.

Mechanic, D. (1962) Sources of power of lower participants in complex organizations. *Administrative Science Quarterly*, 7(3):349-364.

Mehrabian, A. (1971) *Silent messages*, Belmont, CA: Wadsworth.

Menkel-Meadow, C. (2007) Restorative justice: What is it and does it work? *Annual Review of Law and Social Science*, 3:161–187.

Merton, R.K. (1936) The unanticipated consequences of purposive social action. *American Sociological Review*, 1(6):894–904.

Merton, R.K. (1968) *Social Theory and Social Structure*, revised edn, London: Collier Macmillan.

Meyer, J.W. and Rowan, B. (1977) Institutionalized organizations: Formal structure as myth and ceremony. *American Journal of Sociology*, 83:340–363.

Meyerson, D. and Martin, J. (1987) Cultural change: and integration of three different views. *Journal of Management Studies*, 24:623–647.

Meyerson, D., Weick, K.E. and Kramer, R.M. (1996) Swift trust and temporary groups. In R.M. Kramer and T.R. Tyler (eds) *Trust in organizations: Frontiers of theory and research*, pp. 166–195, Thousand Oaks, CA: Sage.

Miles, R.E., Snow, C.C. Matthews, J.A., Miles, G. and Coleman, H.J. Jr. (1997) Organizing in the knowledge age: Anticipating the cellular form. *Academy of Management Executive*, 11(4):7–24.

Miller, B.K. and Nicols K.McG. (2008) Politics and justice: A mediated moderation model. *Journal of Managerial Issues*, 20(2):214–237.

Miller, G.A., Galanter, E. and Pribram, K.H. (1960) *Plans and the Structure of Behaviour*, New York: Holt, Rinehart and Winston.

Miller, J.G. (1978) *Living systems*, New York: McGraw-Hill.

Miller, J. and Bedford, B. (2003) Using core values to re-engage the trust of customers, employees and shareholders. *People Dynamics*, 31(3):6–7.

Miner, J.B. (1984) The validity and usefulness of theories in an emerging organizational science. *Academy of Management Review*, 9(2):169–180.

Mintzberg, H. (1973) *The Nature of Managerial Work*, New York: Harper and Row.

Mintzberg, H., Raisinghani, D. and Théorêt, A. (1976) The structure of 'unstructured' decision processes. *Administrative Science Quarterly*, 21:246-275.

Mintzberg, H. (1979) *The Structuring of Organizations*, Englewood Cliffs, NJ: Prentice Hall.

Mintzberg, H. (1983) *Power in and around organizations*. Englewood Cliffs, NJ: Prentice Hall.

Mintzberg, H. (1991) The effective organisation: Forces and forms. *Sloan Management Review*, 54(Winter):54-67.

Mintzberg, H. (2003) The structuring of organizations. In H. Mintzberg, J. Lampel, J.B. Quinn and S. Ghoshal, *The strategy process: Concepts, comntexts, cases* (2nd European edn), pp.209-241, London: Pearson.

Mischel, W. (1977) The interaction of person and situation. In D. Magnusson and N.S. Endler (eds) *Personality at the crossroads: Current issues in interactional psychology*, p.347, Hillsdale, NJ: Erlbaum.

Mitchell, T.R. and Daniels, D. (2003) Motivation. In W.C. Borman, D.R. Ilgen and R.J. Klimoski (eds) *Handbook of Psychology, Vol. 12: Industrial and Organizational Psychology*, pp. 225–254, New York: Wiley

Mitchell, V.F. and Moudgill, P. (1976) Measurement of Maslow's need hierarchy. *Organizational Behavior and Human Performance*, 16(2):334–349.

Moore, K. and Lewis, D.C. (2009) *The origins of globalization*, New York: Routledge.

Moreland, R.L. and Zajonc, R.B. (1977) Is stimulus recognition a necessary condition for the occurrence of exposure effects? *Journal of Personality and Social Psychology*, 35(4):191–199.

Moorhead, G. and Griffin, R.W. (1992) *Organizational Behaviour* (3rd edn), Boston, MA: Houghton Mifflin.

Moorhead, G., Ference, R. and Neck, C.P. (1991) Group decision fiascos continue: Space shuttle Challenger and a revised groupthink framework. *Human Relations*, 5:539–550.

Moreno, J.L. (1953) *Who Shall Survive?* London: Beacon House.

Morgan, G. (1986/2006) *Images of organization* (updated 2006), Thousand Oaks, CA: Sage.

Morgeson, F.P. and Campion, M.A. (2002) Minimizing tradeoffs when redesigning work; evidence from a longitudinal quasi experiment. *Personnel Psychology*, Autumn, 55(3):589–613.

Morgeson, F. P. and Humphrey, S. E. (2008) Job and team design: Toward a more integrative conceptualization of work design. In J. Martocchio (ed.) *Research in personnel and human resource management*, 27:39–92, Bradford, England: Emerald Group.

Morgeson, F.P., Campion, M.A., Dipboye, R.L., Hollenbeck, J.R., Murphy, K. and Schmitt, N. (2007) Reconsidering the use of personality tests in personnel selection contexts. *Personnel Psychology*, 60(3):683–729.

Morris, D. (1982) *The Pocket Guide to Manwatching*, London: Triad Grafton.

Moscovici, S. and Zavalloni, M. (1969) The group as a polarizer of attitudes. *Journal of Personality and Social Psychology*, 12:125–135.

Moss, P., Salzman, H. and Tilly, C. (2008) Under construction: The continuing evolution of job structures in call centers. *Industrial Relations*, 47:173–208.

Mullins, L.J. (1996) *Management and Organizational Behaviour*, 4th edn, London: Pitman.

Mumford, T.V., Campion, M.A. and Morgeson, F.P. (2006) Situational judgment in work teams: A team role typology. In J.A. Weekley and R.E. Ployhart (eds) *Situational judgment tests: Theory, measurement, and application*, pp. 319–343, Mahwah, NJ: Erlbaum.

Mumford, T.V., Van Iddekinge, C.H., Morgeson, F.P. and Campion, M.A. (2008) The team role test: Development and validation of a team role knowledge situational judgment test. *Journal of Applied Psychology*, 93:250–267.

Nakayachi, K. and Watabe, M. (2005) Restoring trustworthiness after adverse events: The signalling effects of voluntary "hostage posting" on trust. *Organizational Behavior and Human Decision Processes*, 97:1–17.

Navarro, P. (2009) Recession-proofing your organization. *MIT Sloan Management Review*, 50(3):45–51.

Neal, R. and Cochran, P.L. (2008) Corporate social responsibility, corporate governance, and financial performance: Lessons from finance. *Business Horizons*, 51(6):535–540.

Neuman, J.H. and Baron, R.A. (2005) Aggression in the workplace: a social-psychological perspective. In S. Fox and P. Spector (eds) *Counterproductive Work Behaviors*, pp.13–40, Washington, DC: American Psychological Association.

Ng, K.-Y., Ang, S. and Chan, K.Y. (2008) Personality and leader effectiveness: A moderated mediation model of leadership self-efficacy, job demands, and job autonomy. *Journal of Applied Psychology*, 93(4):733–743.

Nicholson, N. (2008) Evolutionary psychology, organizational culture, and the family firm. *Academy of Management Perspectives*, 22(2):73–84.

Nidumolu, R., Prahalad, C.K. and Rangaswami, M.R. (2009) Why sustainability is now the key driver of innovation. *Harvard Business Review*, 87(9):56–64.

Nijstad, B.A., Stroebe, W. and Lodewijkx, H.F.M. (2003) Production blocking and idea generation: Does blocking interfere with cognitive processes? *Journal of Experimental Social Psychology*, 39(6):531–548.

Nishida, H. (1999) A cognitive approach to intercultural communication based on schema theory. *International Journal of Intercultural Relations*, 23(5):753–777.

Nishida, H. (2005) Cultural schema theory. In W.B. Gudykunst (ed.) *Theorizing about intercultural communication*, pp. 401-418, Thousand Oaks, CA: Sage.

Nolan, R. (1972) Computer data bases: The future is now. *Harvard Business Review*, September/October, pp. 98–112

Nussbaum, M.C. (1999) *Sex and social justice*, Oxford: Oxford University Press.

Nussbaum, M.C. (2006) *Frontiers of justice: Disability, nationality, and species membership*, Cambridge, MA: Harvard University Press.

Offner A.K., Kramer T.J. and Winter J.P. (1996) The effects of facilitation, recording, and pauses on group brainstorming. *Small Group Research*, 27(2):283–298.

Ogbonna, E. and Harris. L.C. (2006) Organizational culture in the age of the Internet: An exploratory study. *New Technology, Work and Employment*, 21(2):162–175.

O'Laughlin, M.J. and Malle, B.F. (2002) How people explain actions performed by groups and individuals. *Journal of Personality and Social Psychology*, 82(1):33–48.

Oliver, R.W., (2002) Instinctive strategy: organic organizations rule. *Journal of Business Strategy*, September/October, 23(5):7–11.

O'Neill, J. (1986) The disciplinary society: from Weber to Foucault. *British Journal of Sociology*, 37(1):42–60.

Ordóñez, L., Schweitzer, M.E., Galinsky, A.D. and Bazerman, M.H. (2009a) Goals gone wild: How goals systematically harm individuals and organizations. *Academy of Management Perspectives*, 23(1):6–16.

Ordóñez, L.D., Schweitzer, M.E., Galinsky, A.D. and Bazerman, M.H. (2009b) On good scholarship, goal setting, and scholars gone wild. *Academy of Management Perspectives*, 23(3):82–87.

O'Reilly, C.A. and Tushman, M.L. (2004) The ambidextrous organization. *Harvard Business Review*, 82:74–81.

Orlikowski, W.J. (1992) The duality of technology: Rethinking the concept of technology in organizations. *Organization Science*, 3(3):398–427.

Orlikowski, W.J. (2000) Using technology and constituting structures: A practice lens for studying technology in organizations. *Organization Science*, 11(4):404–428.

Orr, J. (1990) Sharing knowledge, celebrating identity: War stories and community memory in a service culture. In D.S. Middleton and D. Edwards (eds.) *Collective remembering: Memory in society*, Beverley Hills, CA: Sage Publications.

Orvis, B.R., Cunningham, J.D. and Kelley, H.H. (1975) A closer examination of causal inference: The roles of consensus, distinctiveness, and consistency information. *Journal of Personality and Social Psychology*, 32(4):605–616.

Osborn A.F. (1957) *Applied Imagination*, New York: Scribner.

Osgood, C.E. and Tannenbaum, P.H. (1955) The principle of congruity in the prediction of attitude change. *Psychological Review*, 62(1):42–55.

O'Toole, J. and Bennis, W. (2009) What's needed next: A culture of candor. *Harvard Business Review*, 87(6):54–61.

Ouchi, W.G. (1979) A conceptual framework for the design of organizational control mechanisms. *Management Science*, 25(9):833–847.

Ouchi, W.G. (1980) Markets, bureaucracies, and clans. *Administrative Science Quarterly*, 25(1):129–141.

Ouchi, W.G. (1981) *Theory Z*, Reading, MA: Addison-Wesley.

Ouchi, W.G. and Maguire, M.A. (1975) Organizational control: Two functions. *Administrative Science Quarterly*, 20(4):559–569.

Ouchi, W.G. and Jaeger, A.M. (1978) Type Z Organization: Stability in the midst of mobility. *Academy of Management Review*, 3:305–314.

Palmer, I. and Dunford, R. (2008) Organizational change and the importance of embedded assumptions. *British Journal of Management*, 19(Suppl.):S20–S32.

Pascale, R.T. and Athos, A.G. (1981) *The art of Japanese management: Applications for American executives*, New York: Simon and Schuster.

Pasmore, W.A. (1988) *Designing effective organizations: The sociotechnical systems perspective*, New York: Wiley.

Patall, E.A., Cooper, H. and Robinson, J.C. (2008) The effects of choice on intrinsic motivation and related outcomes: A meta-analysis of research findings. *Psychological Bulletin*, 134(2):270–300.

Pathak, S.D., Day, J.M., Nair, A., Sawaya, W.J. and Kristal, M.M. (2007) Complexity and adaptivity in supply networks: Building supply network theory using a complex adaptive systems perspective. *Decision Sciences*, 38(4):547–580.

Patterson, K., Grenny, J., McMillan, R. and Switzler, A. (2005) *Crucial confrontations*, New York: McGraw-Hill.

Patterson, M.G., West, M.A., Lawthorn, R. and Nickell, S. (1997) *Impact of People Management Practices on Business Performance*, London: Institute of Personnel and Development.

Paulus, P.B., Nakui, T. and Putnam, V.L. (2006) Group brainstorming and teamwork: Some rules for the road to innovation. In L.L. Thompson and H.-S. Choi (eds) *Creativity and innovation in organizational teams*, pp. 69–86, New York: Routledge.

Pavlov, I.P. (1927) *Conditional Reflexes*, New York: Oxford University Press.

Payne, G.T. (2006) Examining configurations and firm performance in a suboptimal equifinality context. *Organization Science*, 17:756–770.

Pearce, C.L. (2004) The future of leadership: combining vertical and shared leadership to transform knowledge work. *Academy of Management Executive*, 18:47–57.

Pearson, C., Andersson, L.M. and Porath, C.L. (2004) Workplace incivility. In S. Spector and S. Fox (eds) *Counterproductive Workplace Behavior: Investigations of Actors and Targets*, pp. 177–200, Washington, DC: American Psychological Association.

Pease, A. (1984) *Body Language: How to Read Others' Thoughts by their Gestures*, London: Sheldon.

Pedler, M., Burgoyne, J. and Boydell, T. (1994) *A Manager's Guide to Self-Development*, 3rd edn, Maidenhead: McGraw-Hill.

Peeters, M.C.W. and Oerlemans, W.G.M. (2009) The relationship between acculturation orientations and work-related well-being: Differences between ethnic minority and majority employees. *International Journal of Stress Management*, 16(1):1–24.

Peiró, J.M. and Meliá, J.L. (2003) Formal and informal interpersonal power in organizations: Testing a bifactorial model of power in role-sets. *Applied Psychology: An International Review*, 52(1):14–35.

Perrewé, P. L. and Nelson, D. L. (2004) Gender and career success: The facilitative role of political skill. *Organizational Dynamics*, 33:366–378.

Perrewé, P. L., Zellars, K. L., Rossi, A. M., Ferris, G. R., Kacmar, C. J., Liu, Y. *et al.* (2005) Political skill: An antidote in the role overload–strain relationship. *Journal of Occupational Health Psychology*, 10:239–250.

Perrow, C.B. (1967) A framework for the comparative analysis of organizations. *American Sociological Review*, April, pp. 194–208.

Perrow, C.B. (1970) *Organizational Analysis: A Sociological View*, London: Tavistock.

Pervin, L.A. (1984) *Current Controversies and Issues in Personality*, 2nd edn, New York: Wiley.

Peters, L. and Karren, R.J. (2009) An examination of the roles of trust and functional diversity on virtual team performance ratings. *Group and Organization Management*, 34(4):479–504.

Peters, T.J. (1992) *Liberation management*, New York: Knopf.

Peters, T.J. Jr. and Waterman, R.H. (1982) *In search of excellence*, New York: Harper and Row.

Petrides, K.V. and Furnham, A. (2001) Trait emotional intelligence: Psychometric investigation with reference to established trait taxonomies. *European Journal of Personality*, 15:425–448.

Petrides, K.V., Furnham, A. and Mavroveli, S. (2007) Trait emotional intelligence: Moving forward in the field of EI. In G. Matthews, M. Zeidner, and R.D. Roberts (eds) *The science of emotional intelligence: Knowns and unknowns*, pp. 151–166, New York: Oxford University Press.

Pettigrew, A.M. (1979) On studying organizational cultures. *Administrative Science Quarterly*, 24:570–581.

Pettigrew, A.M. (1985) *The awakening giant: Continuity and change in Imperial Chemical Industries*, Oxford: Blackwell.

Pfeffer, J. (1993) Barriers to the advance of organizational science: Paradigm development as a dependent variable. *Academy of Management Review*, 18:599–620.

Pfeffer, J. (1981) *Power in organizations*, Marshfield, MA: Pittman.

Pfeffer, J. (1992) *Managing with power: Politics and influence in organizations*, Boston, MA: Harvard Business School Press.

Pfeffer, J. (1997) *New directions for organization theory: Problems and prospects*, New York: Oxford: Oxford University Press.

Pfeffer, J. (1998) *The Human Equation: Building Profits by Putting People First*, Boston: Harvard Business School Press.

Pfeffer, J. (2009) Shareholder first? Not so fast … *Harvard Business Review*, 87(7/8):90–91.

Pfeffer, J. and Salancik, G.R. (1978) *The external control of organizations: A resource dependence perspective*, New York: Harper and Row.

Piccoli, G. and Ives, B. (2003) Trust and the unintended effects of behavior control in virtual teams. *MIS Quarterly*, 27:365–395.

Pickard, J. (1999) Sense and sensitivity. *People Management*, 28 October, pp. 48–56.

Pigors, P. and Myers, C. (1977) *Personnel Administration*, 8th edn, Maidenhead: McGraw-Hill.

Piller, F. (2007) Observations on the present and future of mass customization. *International Journal of Flexible Manufacturing Systems*, 19(4):630–636.

Pinder, C.C. (2008) *Work motivation in organizational behavior,* 2nd edn, New York: Psychology Press.

Pine, B.J. (1993) *Mass Customization*, Boston: Harvard Business School Press.

Pine, B.J., Victor, B. and Boynton, A.C. (1993) Making mass customization work. *Harvard Business Review*, 71(5):108-119.

Piper, W.E., Marrache, M., Lacroix, R., Richardson, A.M. and Jones, B.D. (1983) Cohesion as a basic bond in groups. *Human Relations*, 26(2):93–108.

Plant, R. (1987) *Managing Change and Making it Stick*, London: Fontana.

Poggi, G. (1965) A main theme of contemporary sociological analysis: Its achievements and limitations. *British Journal of Sociology*, 16:283–294.

Porter, L.W. and Lawler, E.E. (1968) *Managerial Attitudes and Performance*, Homewood, IL: Richard D. Irwin.

Porter, M.E. (1985) *Competitive Advantage: Creating and Sustaining Superior Performance*, New York: Free Press.

Powell, W.W. and DiMaggio, P.J. (eds) (1991). *The new institutionalism in organizational analysis*, Chicago: University of Chicago Press.

Prahalad, C.K. and Ramaswamy, V. (2004) Co-creation experiences: The next practice in value creation. *Journal of Interactive Marketing*, 18(3):5–14.

Pratto, F. and John, O.P. (1991) Automatic vigilance: The attention-grabbing power of negative social information. *Journal of Personality and Social Psychology*, 61(3):380–391.

Priem, R.L., Harrison, D.A. and Muir, N.K. (1995) Structured conflict and consensus outcomes in group decision making. *Journal of Management*, 21(4):691–710.

Pugh, D.S. and Hickson, D.J. (1989) *Writers on Organizations*, 4th edn, London: Penguin.

Quinn, R.E. (1988) *Beyond rational management: Mastering the paradoxes of and competing demands of high performance*, San Francisco: Jossey-Bass.

Quinn, R.E. and Cameron, K. (1983) Organizational life cycles and some shifting criteria of effectiveness: Some preliminary evidence. *Management Science*, 29:33–51.

Quinn, R.E. and Cameron, K.S. (eds) (1988) *Paradox and transformation: Toward a theory of change in organization and management*, Cambridge, MA: Ballinger

Quinn, R.E. and Rohrbaugh, J. (1983) A spatial model of effectiveness criteria: Towards a competing values approach to organizational analysis. *Management Science*, 29(3):363–377.

Quinn, R.E., Faerman, S.R., Thompson, M.P. and McGrath, M. (2003) *Becoming a master manager: A competency framework,* 3rd edn, New York: Wiley.

Rafaeli, A. and Pratt, M.G. (1993) Tailored meanings: on the meaning and impact of organizational dress. *Academy of Management Review*, January, pp. 32–55.

Raisch, S. and Birkinshaw, J. (2008) Organizational ambidexterity: Antecedents, outcomes, and moderators. *Journal of Management*, 34(3):375–409.

Ramamoorthy, N., & Flood, P.C. (2002). Employee attitudes and behavioural intentions: A test of the main and moderating effects of individualism-collectivism. *Human Relations*, 55(9): 1071–1096.

Rankine, K. (2003) Fat cat executives pile on the pounds. *The Daily Telegraph*, 5 April, p. 29.

Raphael, D.D. (1994) *Moral Philosophy*, 2nd edn, Oxford: Oxford University Press.

Raven, B. (1993) The bases of power: origins and recent developments. *Journal of Social Issues*, 49(4):227–251.

Raven, B.H., Schwarzwald, J. and Koslowsky, M. (1998) Conceptualizing and measuring a power/interaction model of interpersonal influence. *Journal of Applied Social Psychology*, 28:307–322.

Rawlins, N. (2003) Cerebral core text. *People Management*, 20 March, p. 37.

Rawls, J. (1971) *A Theory of Justice*, Cambridge, MA: Harvard University Press.

Reason, P. (ed.) (1994) *Participation in Human Inquiry*, London: Sage.

Reason, P. and Bradbury, H. (2008) *Handbook of Action Research,* 2nd edn, London: Sage.

Reb, J., Goldman, B.M., Kray, L.J. and Cropanzano, R. (2006) Different wrongs, different remedies? Reactions to organizational remedies after procedural and interactional injustice. *Personnel Psychology*, 59(1):31–64.

Ree, M.J. and Earles, J.A. (1992) Intelligence is the best predictor of job performance. *Current Directions in Psychological Science*, 1(3):86–89.

Reed, J. (2007) *Appreciative Inquiry: Research for Change*, London: Sage.

Reed, M.I. (1989) *The Sociology of Management*, Hemel Hempstead: Harvester Wheatsheaf.

Reed, M.I. (2001) Organization, trust and control: A realist analysis. *Organization Studies*, 22(2):201-229.

Redding, S.G. (1994) Comparative management theory: Jungle, zoo or fossil bed? *Organization Studies*, 15:323–359.

Redfield, R., Linton, R. and Herskovits, M. (1936) Memorandum on the study of acculturation. *American Anthropologist*, 38:149–152.

Regierungskommission DCGK (2009) *Deutscher Corporate Governance Kodex*, Berlin: Regierungskommission Deutscher Corporate Governance Kodex. Accessed July 2009 at http://www.corporate-governance-code.de/ger/download/kodex_2009/D_CorGov_Endfassung_Juni_2009.pdf.

Ren, H. and Gray, B. (2009) Repairing relationship conflict: How violation types and culture influence the effectiveness of restoration rituals. *Academy of Management Review*, 34(1):105–126.

Renn, R.W. and Vandenberg, R.J. (1991) Differences in employee attitudes and behaviors based on Rotter's internal-external locus of control. *Human Relations*, 44:1161-1178.

Reuvid, J. (2008) *The Corporate Guide to Expatriate Employment: An Employers Guide to Deploying and Managing Internationally Mobile Staff*, London: Kogan Page.

Rhoads, K.v.L. and Cialdini, R.B. (2002) The business of influence: Principles that lead to success in commercial settings. In J. P. Dillard and M. Pfau (eds) *The persuasion handbook*, pp. 513–542, Thousand Oaks, CA: Sage.

Richardson, A.J., Welker, M. and Hutchinson, I.R. (1999) Managing capital market reactions to corporate social responsibility. *International Journal of Management Review*, 1:17–27.

Richardson, H. and Robinson, B. (2007) The mysterious case of the missing paradigm: A review of critical information systems research 1991–2001. *Information Systems Journal*, 17:251-270.

Rigby, D.K., Gruver, K. and Allen, J. (2009) Innovation in turbulent times. *Harvard Business Review*, 87(6):79-86.

Roberts, B.W. and DelVecchio, W.F. (2000) The rankorder consistency of personality traits from childhood to old age: A quantitative review of longitudinal studies. *Psychological Bulletin*, 126:3-25.

Roberts, Z. (2003) Behind closed doors. *People Management*, 4 December, pp. 12-13.

Robinson, S.L. and Morrison, E.W. (2000) The development of psychological contract breach and violation: A longitudinal study. *Journal of Organizational Behavior*, 21:525–546.

Rogelberg, S.G. and O'Connor, M.S. (1998) Extending the Stepladder Technique: An examination of self-paced stepladder groups. *Group Dynamics: Theory, Research and Practice*, 2:82–91.

Rogelberg, S.G., Barnes-Farrell, J.L. and Lowe, C.A. (1992) The Stepladder Technique: An alternative group structure facilitating effective group decision making. *Journal of Applied Psychology*, 77: 730–737.

Rogelberg, S.G., O'Connor, M.S. and Sederburg, M. (2002) Using the Stepladder Technique to facilitate the performance of audioconferencing. *Journal of Applied Psychology*, 87:994–1000.

Rogers, C.R. (1947) Some observations on the organization of personality. *American Psychologist*, 2:358–368.

Rollison, D. (2008) *Organizational behaviour and analysis* (4th edn), Essex, England: Prentice Hall.

Romney, A.K., Weller, S.C. and Batchelder, W.H. (1986) Culture and consensus: A theory of culture and informant accuracy. *American Anthropologist*, 88 (2):313–338.

Ronen, S. (1994) An underlying structure of motivational need taxonomies: A cross-cultural confirmation. In M.D. Dunnette and L.M. Hough (eds) *Handbook of industrial and organizational psychology*, 4:241-269, Palo Alto, CA: Consulting Psychologists Press.

Roscigno, V.J., Lopez, S.H. and Hodson, R. (2009) Supervisory bullying, status inequalities and organizational context. *Social Forces*, 87(3):1561-1589.

Rose, R.J., Viken, R.J., Dick, D.M., Bates, J.E., Pulkkinen, L. and Kaprio, J. (2003) It does take a village: Non-familial environments and children's behavior. *Psychological Science*, 14:273–277.

Rosen, B., Furst, S. and Blackburn, R. (2006) Training for virtual teams: An investigation of current practices and future needs. *Human Resource Management*, 45(2):229–247.

Rosen, C.C., Harris, K.J. and Kacmar, K.M. (2009) The emotional implications of organizational politics: A process model. *Human Relations*, 62(1):27–57.

Rosenberg, M.J. (1960) A structural theory of attitudes. *Public Opinion Quarterly*, Summer, pp. 319–340.

Rosenman, R.H., Friedman, M. and Strauss, R. (1964) A predictive study of CHD. *Journal of the American Medical Association*, 189:15–22.

Rosenthal, R. and Jacobson, L. (1992) *Pygmalion in the classroom*, (expanded edn), New York: Irvington.

Rosete, D. and Ciarrochi, J. (2005) Emotional intelligence and its relationship to workplace performance of leadership effectiveness. *Leadership and Organizational Development Journal*, 26:388–399.

Ross, L. (1977) The intuitive psychologist and his shortcomings. *Advances in Experimental Social Psychology*, 10:173–220.

Ross, L., Rix, M. and Gold, J. (2005) Learning distributed leadership: Part 1. *Industrial and Commercial Training*, 37(2/3):130–137.

Ross, R. (1994) The ladder of inference. In P.M. Senge, C. Roberts, R.B. Ross, B.J. Smyth and A. Kleiner (eds) *The fifth discipline fieldbook: Strategies and tools for building a learning organization*, pp. 243–246, New York: Currency/Doubleday.

Ross, R. and Roberts, C. (1994) Balancing inquiry and advocacy. In P.M. Senge, C. Roberts, R.B. Ross, B.J. Smyth, and A. Kleiner (eds) *The fifth discipline fieldbook: Strategies and tools for building a learning organization*, pp. 253–259, New York: Currency/Doubleday.

Ross, R. and Schneider, R. (1992) *From Equality to Diversity – A Business case for Equal Opportunities*, London: Pitman.

Rotter, J.B. (1966) Generalized expectancies for internal versus external locus of control of reinforcement. *Psychological Monographs*, 80(1):1–28.

Rousseau, D.M. (1989) Psychological and implied contracts in organizations. *Employee Responsibilities and Rights Journal*, 2:121–139.

Rousseau, D.M. (1990) Assessing organizational culture: The case for multiple methods. In B. Schneider (ed.) *Frontiers of industrial and organizational psychology*, pp. 153–192, San Francisco: Jossey-Bass.

Rousseau, D.M. (1995) *Psychological contracts in organizations: Understanding written and unwritten agreements*, Thousand Oaks, CA: Sage.

Rowlinson, M. and Procter, S. (1999) Organizational culture and business history. *Organization Studies*, 20(3):369–396.

Ruback, R.B. and Juieng, D. (1997) Territorial defense in parking lots: Retaliation against waiting drivers. *Journal of Applied Social Psychology*, 27(9):821–834.

Rungtusanatham, M. and Salvador, F. (2008) From mass production to mass customization: Hindrance factors, structural inertia, and transition hazard. *Production and Operations Management*, 17(3):385–396.

Rusbult, C.E. and Van Lange, P.A.M. (2003) Interdependence, interaction, and relationships. *Annual Review of Psychology*, 54:351–375.

Russell, R.F. and Stone, A.G. (2002) A review of servant leadership attributes: Developing a practical model. *Leadership and Organizational Development Journal*, 23:145–157.

Rutter M. and Silberg, J. (2002) Gene-environment interplay in relation to emotional and behavioural disturbance. *Annual Review of Psychology*, 53:463–490.

Ryan, R.M. (1995) Psychological needs and the facilitation of integrative processes. *Journal of Personality*, 63(3):397–427.

Ryan, R.M. and Deci, E.L. (2000) Self-determination theory and the facilitation of intrinsic motivation, social development, and well-being. *American Psychologist*, 55:68–78.

Rydell, R.J. and McConnell, A.R. (2006) Understanding implicit and explicit attitude change: A systems of reasoning analysis. *Journal of Personality and Social Psychology*, 91(6):995–1008.

Sachau, D. (2007) Resurrecting the motivation-hygiene theory: Herzberg and the positive psychology movement. *Human Resource Development Review*, 6(4):377–393.

Sadler–Smith, E., El-Kot, G. and Leat, M. (2003) Differentiating work autonomy facets in a non-western context. *Journal of Organizational Behaviour*, September, 24(6):709–732.

Sagarin, B.J., Cialdini, R.B., Rice, W.E., and Serna, S.B. (2002) Dispelling the illusion of invulnerability: The motivations and mechanisms of resistance to persuasion. *Journal of Personality and Social Psychology*, 83(3):526–541.

Salancik, G. and Pfeffer, J. (1977) An examination of need-satisfaction models of job attitudes. *Administrative Science Quarterly*, 22:427–456.

Salancik, G.M. and Pfeffer, J. (1978) A social information processing approach to job attitudes and task design. *Administrative Science Quarterly*, 23:224–253.

Salancik, G.R. (1977) Commitment and the control of organizational behavior and belief. In B.M. Staw and G.R. Salancik (eds) *New Directions in Organizational Behavior*, pp. 1–54, Chicago: St. Clair Press.

Salvador, F., de Holan, P. and Piller, F. (2009) Cracking the code of mass customization. *MIT Sloan Management Review*, 50(3):71–78.

Sathe, V. (1985) *Culture and related corporate realities*, Homewood, IL: Irwin.

Satpute, A.B. and Lieberman, M.D. (2006) Integrating automatic and controlled processing into neurocognitive models of social cognition. *Brain Research*, 1079:86–97.

Schein, E.H. (1956) The Chinese indoctrination programme for prisoners-of-war. *Psychiatry*, 19:149–172.

Schein, E. (1961) *Coercive Persuasion: A socio-psychological analysis of the 'brainwashing' of American civilian prisoners by the Chinese Communists*, New York: Norton.

Schein, E. (1982) What to observe in a group. In L. Porter and B. Mohr (eds) *NTL Training Book for Human Relations Training*, 7th edn, NTL Institute.

Schein, E.H. (1985) *Organizational culture and leadership*, San Francisco: Jossey-Bass

Schein, E.H. (1988) *Organizational Psychology*, 3rd edn, Englewood Cliffs, NJ: Prentice Hall.

Schein, E.H. (2004) *Organizational culture and leadership* (3rd edn), San Francisco: Jossey-Bass.

Schilling, M.A. and Steensma, H.K. (2001) The use of modular organizational forms: An industry-level analysis. *Academy of Management Journal*, 44(6):1149–1168.

Schmidt, F.L. and Hunter, J.E. (1998) The validity and utility of selection methods in psychology: practical and theoretical implications of 85 years of research findings. *Psychological Bulletin*, 124:262–274.

Schneier, C E. and Goktepe, J.R. (1983) Issues in emergent leadership: The contingency model of leadership, leader sex, leader behavior. In H.H. Blumberg, A.P. Hare, V. Kent and M.F. Davies (eds) *Small groups and social interactions*, 1:413–421, Chichester: Wiley.

Schon, D.A. (1994) Teaching Artistry through Reflection-in-action. In H. Tsoukas (ed.) *New Thinking in Organizational Behaviour*, Oxford: Butterworth-Heinemann.

Schuler, D.A. and Cording, M. (2006) A corporate social performance–corporate financial performance behavioral model for consumers. *Academy of Management Review*, 31:540–558.

Schuler, R.S. and Jackson, S.E. (1987) Linking competitive strategies with human resource management practices. *Academy of Management Executive*, (3):207–219.

Schuler, R.S. and Jackson, S.E. (1996) *Human Resource Management: Positioning for the 21st century*, Minneapolis: West Publishing.

Schulz, K.-P. (2008) Shared knowledge and understandings in organizations: Its development and impact in organizational learning processes. *Management Learning*, 39(4):457–473.

Schultz, M. (1995) *On studying organizational cultures*, Berlin: Walter de Gruyter.

Schulz-Hardt, S., Thurow-Kröning, B. and Frey, D. (2009) Preference-based escalation: A new interpretation for the responsibility effect in escalating commitment and entrapment. *Organizational Behavior and Human Decision Processes*, 108(2):175–186.

Schwartz, J.M. and Begley, S. (2002) *The mind and the brain*, New York: Regan Books.

Schweiger, D.M., Sandberg, W.R. and Ragan, J.W. (1986) Group approaches for improving strategic decision making: A comparative analysis of dialectical inquiry, devil's advocacy, and consensus. *Academy of Management Journal*, 29(1):51–71.

Schweiger, D.M., Sandberg, W.R. and Rechner, P.L. (1989) Experiential effects of dialectical inquiry, devil's advocacy, and consensus approaches to strategic decision making. *Academy of Management Journal*, 32(4):745–772.

Schwenk, C.R. and Cosier, R.A. (1980) Effects of the expert, devil's advocate, and dialectical inquiry methods on prediction performance. *Organizational Behavior and Human Performance*, 26(3):409–424.

Scott, W. (1981) *The Skills of Negotiating*, Aldershot: Gower.

Scott, W.R. (1992) *Organizations: Rational, Natural and Open Systems*, 3rd edn, Englewood Cliffs, NJ: Prentice Hall.

Scott, W.R. (2003) *Organizations: Rational, natural and open systems* (5th edn), Upper Saddle River, NJ: Prentice Hall.

Seers, A. (1989) Team-member exchange quality: A new construct for role-making research. *Organizational Behavior and Human Decision Processes*, 43:118–135.

Seibert, S.E., Kraimer, M.L. and Crant, J.M. (2001a) What do proactive people do? A longitudinal model linking proactive personality and career success. *Personnel Psychology*, 54(4):845–874.

Seibert, S.E., Kraimer, M.L. and Liden, R.C. (2001b) A social capital theory of career success. *Academy of Management Journal*, 44:219–327.

Seidl, D. (2007) The dark side of knowledge. *Emergence: Complexity and Organization*, 9(3):16–29.

Sen, A. (1999) *Development as freedom*, New York: Random House.

Senge, P.M. (2006) *The fifth discipline* (2nd edn), New York: Currency.

Sengupta, J., Dahl, D.W. and Gorn, G.J. (2002) Misrepresentation in the consumer context. *Journal of Consumer Psychology*, 12(2):69–80.

Serva, M.A., Fuller, M.A. and Mayer, R.C. (2005) The reciprocal nature of trust: A longitudinal study of interacting teams. *Journal of Organizational Behavior*, 26(6):625–648.

Shalley, C., Oldham, G. and Porac, J. (1987) Effects of goal difficulty, goal setting method, and expected external evaluation on intrinsic motivation. *Academy of Management Journal*, September, pp. 553–563.

Shannon, C.E. (1948) A mathematical theory of communication. *The Bell System Technical Journal*, 27:379–423 and 623–656.

Shannon, C.E. and Weaver, W. (1949) *The mathematical theory of communication*, Urbana, IL: University of Illinois Press.

Shamir B. (2007) From passive recipients to active coproducers: Followers' roles in the leadership process. In B. Shamir, R. Pillai, M.C. Bligh and M. Uhl-Bien (eds) *Follower-centered perspectives on leadership: A tribute to the memory of James R. Meindl*, pp. ix–xxxix, Greenwich, CT: Information Age.

Shamir, B. and Eilam, G. (2005) 'What's your story?' A life-stories approach to authentic leadership development. *The Leadership Quarterly*, 16(3):395–417.

Shapiro, D., Sheppard, B.H. and Cheraskin, L. (1992) Business on a handshake. *Negotiation Journal*, 8(4):365–377.

Sharifian, F. (2003) On cultural conceptualisations. *Journal of Cognition and Culture*, 3(3):187–207.

Shaw, M.E. (1978) Communication networks fourteen years later. In L. Berkowitz, (ed.) *Group Processes*, New York: Academic Press.

Shaw, M.E. (1981) *Group Dynamics: The Dynamics of Small Group Behaviour*, 3rd edn, New York: McGraw-Hill.

Sheppard, B.H., Hartwick, J. and Warshaw, P.R (1988) The theory of reasoned action: A meta-analysis of past research with recommendations for modifications and future research. *Journal of Consumer Research*, 15:325-343.

Shoda, Y., Mischel, W. and Wright, J. C. (1989) Intuitive interactionism in person perception: Effects of situation-behavior relations on dispositional judgments. *Journal of* Personality and Social Psychology, 56:41–53.

Short, J.C., Payne, G.T. and Ketchen, D.J. Jr. (2008) Research on organizational configurations: Past accomplishments and future challenges. *Journal of Management*, 34:1053–1079.

Sia, C.L., Tan, B.C.Y. and Wei, K.K. (2002) Group polarization and computer-mediated communication: Eeffects of communication cues, social presence, and anonymity. *Information Systems Research*, 13(1):70–90.

Sidanius, J. and Pratto, F. (2001) *Social dominance: An intergroup theory of social hierarchy and oppression*, Cambridge: Cambridge University Press.

Siegel, D.S. (2009) Green management matters only if it yields more green: An economic/strategic perspective. *Academy of Management Perspectives*, 23(3):5–16.

Siehl, C. and Martin, J. (1984) The role of symbolic management: How can managers effectively transmit organizational culture? In J.G. Hunt, D.M. Hosking, C.A. Schriesheim and R. Stewart (eds) *Leaders and Managers: International Perspectives on Managerial Behavior and Leadership*, pp. 227–269, New York: Pergamon.

Simon, H.A. (1957) A behavioral model of rational choice. In *Models of Man, Social and Rational: Mathematical Essays on Rational Human Behavior in a Social Setting*, New York: Wiley.

Simon, H.A. (1960) *The New Science of Management Decision*, New York: Harper and Row.

Simon, H.A. (1976). *Administrative behavior: A study of decision making processes in administrative organizations*, New York: Free Press.

Simon, H.A. (1977) *The new science of managerial decision making* (2nd edn), Englewood Cliffs, NJ: Prentice Hall.

Simon, H.A. (1983) Search and reasoning in problem solving. *Artificial Intelligence*, 21:7–29.

Sims, H.P. Jr., Faraj, S. and Yun, S. (2009) When should a leader be directive or empowering? How to develop your own situational theory of leadership. *Business Horizons*, 52(2):149–158.

Singh, J.A., Nkala, B., Amuah, E., Mehta, N. and Ahmad, A. (2003) The ethics of nurse poaching from the developed world. *Nursing Ethics*, November, 10 (6):666–671.

Sirkin, H.L., Hemerling, J.W. and Bhattacharya, A.K. (2008) *Globality: Competing with everyone from everywhere for everything*, New York: Business Plus.

Sitkin, S.B. and George, E. (2005) Managerial trust-building through the use of legitimating formal and informal control mechanisms. *International Sociology*, 20:307–338.

Six, F and Sorge, A. (2008) Creating a high-trust organization: An exploration into organizational policies that stimulate interpersonal trust building. *Journal of Management Studies*, 45(5):857–884.

Skarlicki, D.P., van Jaarsveld, D.D. and Walker, D.D. (2008) Getting even for customer mistreatment: The role of moral identity in the relationship between customer interpersonal injustice and employee sabotage. *Journal of Applied Psychology*, 93(6):1335–1347.

Skinner, B.F. (1953) *Science and Human Behaviour*, New York: Macmillan.

Smith, A. (1776) *An Inquiry into the Nature and Causes of the Wealth of Nations*, London: Strahan & Cadell.

Smith, E.R. and DeCoster, J. (2000) Dual-process models in social and cognitive psychology: Conceptual integration and links to underlying memory systems. *Personality and Social Psychology Review*, 4:108–131.

Smith, K.A. (1996) Managing without traditional strategic planning: the evolving role of top management teams. In P.C. Flood, M.J. Gannon and J. Paauwe, (eds), *Managing Without Traditional Methods: International Innovations in Human Resource Management*, Wokingham: Addison-Wesley.

Smith, W.K. and Tushman, M.L. (2005) Managing strategic contradictions: A top management model for managing innovation streams. *Organization Science*, 16:522–536.

Snell, S. and Bohlander, G. (2007) *Human Resource Management* (International student edn), Mason, OH: Thomson South-Western.

Snyder, M. (1974) Self-monitoring of expressive behaviour. *Journal of Personality and Social Psychology*, 30(4):526–537.

Snyder, M. and Stukas, Jr., A.A. (1998) Interpersonal processes: The interplay of cognitive, motivational, and behavioral activities in social interaction. *Annual Review of Psychology*, 50:273–303.

Sonnentag, S. and Volmer, J. (2009) Individual-level predictors of task-related teamwork processes: The role of expertise and self-efficacy in team meetings. *Group and Organization Management*, 34(1):37–66.

Sorge, A. and van Witteloostuijn, A. (2004) The (non) sense of organizational change: An essay about the universal management hypes, sick consultancy metaphors, and healthy organization theories. *Organization Studies*, 25(7):1205–1231.

Sparrowe, R.T. and Liden, R.C. (2005) Two routes to influence: Integrating leader-member exchange and social network perspectives. *Administrative Science Quarterly*, 50:505–535.

Sparrowe, R.T., Liden, R.C., Wayne, S.J., and Kraimer, M.L. (2001) Social networks and the performance of individuals and groups. *Academy of Management Journal*, 44:316–325.

Spearman, C. (1904) "General intelligence" objectively determined and measured. *American Journal of Psychology*, 15:201–293.

Spears, L.C. (2004) The understanding and practice of servant leadership. In L.C. Spears and M. Lawrence (eds) *Practicing servant-leadership: Succeeding through trust, bravery, and forgiveness*, pp. 167–200, San Francisco, CA: Jossey-Bass.

Sprenger, R.K. (2002) *Mythos Motivation: Wege aus der Sackgasse* (17th extended and revised edn), Frankfurt: Campus.

Squire, B., Brown, S., Readman, J. and Bessant, J. (2006) The impact of mass customisation on manufacturing trade-offs. *Production and Operations Management*, 15(1):10–21.

Stacey, R.D. (2000) *Strategic Management and Organisational Dynamics: The Challenge of Complexity*, 3rd edn, Harlow: Pearson Education.

Stafford, L. (2008) Social exchange theories. In L.A. Baxter and D.O. Braithewaite (eds) *Engaging theories in interpersonal communication: Multiple perspectives*, pp. 377–389, Thousand Oaks, CA: Sage.

Stansbury, J. and Barry, B. (2007) Ethics programs and the paradox of control. *Business Ethics Quarterly*, 17(2):239–261.

Starbuck, W.H. (1981) A trip to view the elephants and rattlesnakes in the garden of Aston. In A.H. Van de Ven and W.F. Joyce (eds) *Perspectives on organization design and behavior*, pp. 167–198, New York: Wiley.

Stark, E.M., Shaw, J.D. and Duffy, M.K. (2007) Preference for group work, winning orientation, and social loafing behavior in groups. *Group and Organization Management*, 32(6):699–723.

Staw, B., Sandelands, L. and Dutton, J. (1981) Threat-rigidity effects in organizational behaviour. *Administrative Science Quarterly*, 26:501–524.

Staw, B.M. (1976) Knee-deep in the big muddy: A study of escalating commitment to a chosen course of action. *Organizational Behavior and Human Performance*, 16:27–44.

Staw, B.M. (1981) The escalation of commimnet to a failing course of action. *Academy of Management Review*, 6:577–587.

Staw, B.M. and Ross, J. (1980) Commitment in an experimenting society: An experiment on the attribution of leadership from administrative scenarios. *Journal of Applied Psychology*, 65:249–260.

Steensma, H. (2007) Why managers prefer some influence tactics to other tactics: A net utility explanation. *Journal of Occupational and Organizational Psychology*, 80:355–362.

Steers, R.M., Mowday, R.T. and Shapiro, D.L. (2004) The future of work motivation theory. *Academy of Management Review*, 29(3):379–387.

Steffens, P., Davidsson, P. and Fitzsimmons, J. (2009) Performance configurations over time: Implications for growth- and profit-oriented strategies. *Entrepreneurship: Theory and Practice*, 33(1): 125–148.

Steiner, I. (1972) *Group process and productivity*, New York: Academic Press.

Sternberg, R.J. (1985) *Beyond IQ: A Triarchic Theory of Human Intelligence*, New York: Cambridge University Press.

Stevenson, W.B., Pearce, J.L. and Porter, L.W. (1985) The concept of 'coalition' in organization theory and research. Academy of Management Review, 10(2):256–268.

Stewart, G.L. (2006) A meta-analytic review of relationships between team design features and team performance. *Journal of Management*, 32(1):29–54.

Stewart, G.L., Fulmer, I. S. and Barrick, M.R. (2005) An exploration of member roles as a multilevel linking mechanism for individual traits and team outcomes. *Personnel Psychology*, 58:343–365.

Stewart, W. and Roth, P. (2007) A meta-analysis of achievement motivation differences between entrepreneurs and managers. *Journal of Small Business Management*, 45(4):401–421.

Stiglitz, J.E. (2006) *Making Globalization Work*, Norton and Co.

Stogdill, R.M. (1948) Personal factors associated with leadership: A survey of the literature. *Journal of Psychology*, 25:35–71.

Stoner, J.A.F. (1961) A Comparison of Individual and Group Decisions Involving Risk. Quoted in R. Brown (1965) *Social Psychology*, New York: Free Press.

Stouten, J., De Cremer, D. and Van Dijk, E. (2005) All is well that ends well, at least for proselfs: Emotional reactions to equality violation as a function of social value orientation. *European Journal of Social Psychology*, 35:767–783.

Strauss, C. and Quinn, N. (1997) *A Cognitive Theory of Cultural Meaning*, Cambridge: Cambridge University Press.

Strike, V.M., Gao, J. and Bansal, P. (2006) Being good while being bad: Social responsibility and the international diversification of US firms. *Journal of International Business Studies*, 37:850–862.

Strube, M.J. and Garcia, J.E. (1981) A meta-analytic investigation of Fiedler's contingency model of leadership effectiveness. *Psychological Bulletin*, September, pp. 307–321.

Sullivan, J.J. (1983) A critique of Theory Z. *Academy of Management Review*, 8:132-142.

Sutton, R.I. (2009) How to be a good boss in a bad economy. *Harvard Business Review*, 87(6):42–50.

Swain, A. and Newell Brown, J. (2009) *The Professional Recruiter's Handbook: Delivering Excellence in Recruitment Practice*, London: Kogan Page.

Tajfel, H. (1970) Experiments in intergroup discrimination. *Scientific American*, 223:96–102.

Takeuchi, R., Chen, G. and Lepak D.P. (2009) Through the looking glass of a social system: Cross-level effects of high performance work systems on employees' attitudes. *Personnel Psychology*, 62(1):1–29.

Tannenbaum, R. and Schmidt, W.H. (1973) How to choose a leadership pattern. *Harvard Business Review*, May/June, pp. 178–180.

Tasa, K. and Whyte, G. (2005) Collective efficacy and vigilant problem solving in group decision making: A non-linear model. *Organizational Behavior and Human Decision Processes*, 96(2):119–129.

Tasa, K., Seijts, G.H. and Taggar, S. (2007) The development of collective efficacy in teams: A multilevel and longitudinal perspective. *Journal of Applied Psychology*, 92(1):17–27.

Taylor, D.M. and Doria, J.R. (1981) Self-serving bias and group-serving bias in attribution. *Journal of Social Psychology*, 113:201–211.

Taylor, F.W. (1911) *The principles of Scientific Management*, New York: Harper.

Taylor, S. (1998) Emotional Labour and the new workplace. In P. Thompson and C. Warhurst. *Workplaces of the Future*, Basingstoke: Macmillan.

Tekleab, A.G., Takeuchi, R. and Taylor, M.S. (2005) Extending the chain of relationships among organizational justice, social exchange, and employee reactions: The role of contract violations. *Academy of Management Journal*, 48(1):146–157.

Tellis, G.J., Prabhu, J.C., and Chandy, R.K. (2009) Radical innovation across nations: The preeminence of corporate culture. *Journal of Marketing*, 73(1):3–23.

Tepper, B.J. (1993) Patterns of downward influence and follower conformity in transactional and transformational leadership. *Academy of Management Best Papers Proceedings*, pp. 267–271.

Tepper, B.J. (2007) Abusive supervision in work organizations: Review, synthesis, and directions for future research. *Journal of Management*, 33:261–289.

Tepper, B.J., Carr, J.C., Breaux, D.M., Geider, S., Hu, C. and Hua, W. (2009) Abusive supervision, intentions to quit, and employees' workplace deviance: A power/dependence analysis. *Organizational Behavior and Human Decision Processes*, 109(2):156–167.

Tesser, A. (1993) On the importance of heritability in psychological research: The case of attitudes. *Psychological Review*, 100:129–142.

Thaler, R.H. (2000) From Homo Economicus to Homo Sapiens. *Journal of Economic Perspectives*, 14(1):133–141.

The Economist (2005) The good company: A survey of corporate social responsibility. 22 January.

Thibaut, J. and Kelley, H.H. (1959) *Social psychology of groups*, New York: Wiley.

Thomas, G.F., Zolin, R. and Hartman, J.L. (2009) The central role of communication in developing trust and its effect on employee involvement. *Journal of Business Communication*, 46(3):287–310.

Thomas, K. (1976) Conflict Management. In M.D. Dunnette (ed.) *Handbook of Industrial and Organizational Psychology*, New York: R and McNally.

Thomas, M. (2008) *Belching out the devil: Global adventures with Coca-Cola*, London: Ebury Press.

Thompson, B. and Borrello, G.M. (1986) Construct validity of the Myers-Briggs Type Indicator. *Educational and Psychological Measurement*, 46:745–752.

Thompson, J.D. (1967) *Organizations in Action*, New York: McGraw-Hill.

Thompson, L.L. (1995) The impact of minimum goals on and aspirations on judgement of success in negotiations. *Group Decision Making and Negotiation*, 4:513–524.

Thompson, L.L. (2009) *The heart and mind of the negotiator* (4th edn), Upper Saddle River, NJ: Pearson Educational.

Thompson, P. (1989) *The nature of work: An introduction to debates on the labour process*, (2nd edn), Basingstoke: Macmillan.

Thompson, P. (2003) Fantasy island: A labour process critique of the age of surveillance. *Surveillance and Society*, 1(2):138–151.

Thompson, P. and McHugh, D. (1995) *Work Organizations: A Critical Introduction*, 2nd edn, Basingstoke: Macmillan.

Thoresen, C.J., Kaplan, S.A., Barsky, A.P., Warren, C.R. and de Chermont, K. (2003) The affective underpinnings of job perceptions and attitudes: A meta-analytic review and integration. *Psychological Bulletin*, 129(6):914–945.

Thorndike, E.L. (1932) *The Fundamentals of Learning*, New York: Teachers College.

Todd, S.Y., Harris, K.J., Harris, R.B. and Wheeler, A.R. (2009) Career success implications of political skill. *Journal of Social Psychology*, 149(3):179–204.

Toffler, A. (1985) *The Adaptive Corporation*, London: Pan Books.

Toh, S.M., Morgeson, F.P. and Campion, M.A. (2008) Human resource configurations: Investigating fit with the organizational context. *Journal of Applied Psychology*, 93(4):864–882.

Tomlinson, E.C. and Mayer, R.C. (2009) The role of causal attribution dimensions in trust repair. *Academy of Management Review*, 34(1):85–104.

Torrington, D., Hall, L. and Taylor, S. (2005) *Human Resource Management*, 6th edn, Harlow: Prentice Hall.

Townley, B. (1994) *Reframing Human Resource Management: Power, Ethics and the Subject at Work*, London: Sage.

Trager, G.L. (1958) Paralanguage: a first approximation. *Studies in Linguistics*. 13:1–12.

Triandis, H.C. (1990) Theoretical concepts of use to practitioners. In R. Brislin (ed.) *Crosscultural applied psychology*, pp. 34–55, Newbury Park, CA: Sage.

Triandis, H.C. (2006) Cultural intelligence in organizations. *Group and Organization Management*, 31(1):20–26.

Triandis, H.C. (2007) Culture and psychology: history of the study of their relationships. In S. Kitayama and D. Cohen (eds) *Handbook of cultural psychology*, pp. 59–76, New York: Guilford Press.

Trice, H.M. and Beyer, J.M. (1993) *The cultures of work organizations* Englewood Cliffs, NJ: Prentice Hall.

Trist, E.L. and Bamforth, K.W. (1951) Some social and psychological consequences of the longwall method of coal getting. *Human Relations*, 4:3–38.

Trompenaars, F. (1993) *Riding the Waves of Culture*, London: Nicholas Brealey.

Trompenaars, F. and Woolliams, P. (1999) First-class accommodation. *People Management*, 22 April, pp. 30–37.

Tse, H.H.M. and Dasborough, M.T. (2008) A study of exchange and emotions in team member relationships. *Group and Organization Management*, 33(2):194–215.

Tuckman, B. and Jensen, N. (1977) Stages of small group development revisited. *Group and Organizational Studies*, 2:419–427.

Turban, D.B. and Greening, D.W. (1997) Corporate social performance and organizational attractiveness to prospective employees. *Academy of Management Journal*, 40:658–672.

Turner, B.A. (1986) Sociological aspects of organizational symbolism. *Organization Studies*, 7:101–115.

Tushman, M.L. and O'Reilly, C.A. (1996) Ambidextrous organizations: Managing evolutionary and revolutionary change. *California Management Review*, 38:8–30.

Tversky, A. and Kahneman, D. (1981) The framing of decisions and the psychology of choice. *Science*, 211:453–458.

Twenge, J.M., Zhang, L. and Im, C. (2004) It's beyond my control: A cross-temporal meta-analysis of increasing externality in locus of control, 1960–2002. *Personality and Social Psychology Review*, 8(3): 308–319.

Tyler, T. R. and Blader, S. L. (2000) *Cooperation in groups: Procedural justice, social identity, and behavioral engagement*, Philadelphia: Psychology Press.

Tyler, T.R. and Blader, S.L. (2003) The group engagement model: Procedural justice, social identity, and cooperative behavior. *Personality and Social Psychology Review*, 7(4):349–361.

Tyson, S. and Jackson, T. (1992) *The Essence of Organizational Behaviour*, Hemel Hempstead: Prentice Hall.

Uchino, B. (2004) *Social support and physical health: Understanding the consequences of relationships*, New Haven, CT: Yale University Press.

Uhl-Bien, M. (2006) Relational leadership theory: Exploring the social processes of leadership and organizing. *The Leadership Quarterly*, 17:654–676.

Ulrich, D. (1998) A new mandate for human resources. *Harvard Business Review*, January/February, pp. 125–134.

Ulrich, D. and Black, J.S. (1999) The New Frontier of Global HR. In P. Joynt and R. Morton (eds) *The Global HR Manager*, London: Institute of Personnel and Development.

Van Kleef, G.A., Homan, A.C., Beersma, B., Van Knippenberg, D., Van Knippenberg, B. and Damen, F. (2009) Searing sentiment or cold calculation? The effects of leader emotional displays on team performance depend on follower epistemic motivation. *Academy of Management Journal*, 52(3):562–580.

van Maanen, J. (1995) Style as theory. *Organization Science*, 6:132–143.

van Maanen, J. and Barley, S.R. (1984) Occupational communities: Culture and control in organizations. *Research in Organizational Behavior*, 6:287–365.

van Maanen, J. and Schein, E.H. (1979) Towards a theory of organizational socialization. In B.M. Staw (ed.) *Research in Organizational Behavior*, 1:209–264, Greenwich, GT: JAI Press.

Vecchio, R.P. (1992) Cognitive resource theory: Issues for specifying a test of the theory. *Journal of Applied Psychology*, 77:375–376.

Veiga, J.F. (1991) The frequency of self-limiting behavior in groups: A measure and an explanation. *Human Relations*, 44:855–895.

Volberda, H.W. (1999) *Building the flexible firm: How to remain competitive*, Oxford: Oxford University Press.

von Bertalanffy, L. (1968) *General Systems Theory: Foundations, Development, Application*, New York: George Braziller.

von Bertalanffy, L. (1972) The history and status of general systems theory. *Academy of Management Journal*, 15(4):407-426.

von Neumann, J. and Morgenstern, O. (1944) *Theory of games and economic behavior*, Princeton, NJ: Princeton University Press.

Vorauer, J.D. and Turpie, C.A. (2004) Disruptive effects of vigilance on dominant group members' treatment of outgroup members: Choking versus shining under pressure. *Journal of Personality and Social Psychology*, 87(2):384–399.

Vorauer, J.D., Martens, V. and Sasaki, S.J. (2009) When trying to understand detracts from trying to behave: Effects of perspective taking in intergroup interaction. *Journal of Personality and Social Psychology*, 96(4):811–827.

Voss, A., Rothermund, K. and Brandtstädter, J. (2008) Interpreting ambiguous stimuli: Separating perceptual and judgmental biases. *Journal of Experimental Social Psychology*, 44(4):1048–1056.

Vroom, V.H. (1964) *Work and Motivation*, New York: John Wiley.

Vroom, V.H. (2005) On the origins of expectancy theory. In K. Smith and M. Hitt (eds) *Great minds in management: The process of theory development*, pp. 239–258, New York: Oxford University Press.

Vroom, V.H. and Jago, A.G. (1988) *The New Leadership*, Englewood Cliffs, NJ: Prentice Hall.

Vroom, V.H. and Yetton, P.W. (1973) Leadership and decision making, Pittsburgh, PA: University of Pittsburgh Press.

Waldman, D.A., Sully de Luque, M., Washburn, N. and House, R.J. (2006) Cultural and leadership predictors of corporate social responsibility values of top management: A GLOBE study of 15 countries. *Journal of International Business Studies*, 37:823–837.

Walker, C.R. and Guest, R. (1952) *The Man on The Assembly Line*, Cambridge, MA: Harvard University Press.

Wall, T.D., Clegg, C.W. and Jackson, P.R. (1985) An evaluation of the job characteristics model. *Journal of Occupational Psychology*, 51:183–196.

Waller, M.J., Zellmer-Bruhn, M.E. and Giambatista, R.C. (2002) Watching the clock: Group pacing behavior under dynamic deadlines. *Academy of Management Journal*, 45:1046–1055.

Walumbwa, F.O., Avolio, B.J., Gardner, W.L., Wernsing, T.S. and Peterson, S.J. (2008) Authentic leadership: Development and validation of a theory-based measure. *Journal of Management*, 34:89–126.

Ward, E.A. (2006) Correlates of motivation for competitive or cooperative strategy among employed adults. *Journal of Organizational Behavior*, 16(1):93–100.

Warr, P.B. (1971) Judgements about people at work. In P.B. Warr. (ed.) *Psychology at Work*, Harmondsworth: Penguin.

Wartick, S.L. and Cochran, P.L. (1985) The evolution of the corporate social performance model. *Academy of Management Review*, 10(4):758–769.

Washington, R.R., Sutton, C.D. and Field, H.S. (2006) Individual differences in servant leadership: The roles of values and personality. *Leadership and Organizational Development Journal*, 27:700–716.

Watson, J.B. (1924) *Behaviourism*, Chicago, IL: University of Chicago Press.

Watson, P.C. (1960) On the failure to eliminate hypotheses in a conceptual task. *Quarterly Journal of Experimental Psychology*, 12:129–140.

Watson, T.J. (2008) *Sociology, work and industry* (5th edn), London: Routledge.

Weber, M. (1947) *The Theory of Social and Economic Organization*, trans. M.A. Henderson and T. Parsons, New York: Oxford University Press.

Weber, R.C. (1982). The group: A cycle from birth to death. In L. Porter and B. Mohr (eds.) *NTL Training Book for Human Relations Training* (7th edn), 68–71 NTL Institute.

Wegge, J. and Dibblett, S. (2000) Effects of goal setting or information processing in letter-matching tasks. *Zeitschrift fuer Experimentelle Psychologie*, 47:89–114.

Weick, K.E. (1979) The social psychology of organizing (2nd edn), London: Sage.

Weick, K.E. (1995) *Sensemaking in organizations*, Thousand Oaks, CA: Sage.

Weick, K.E. (1999) Theory construction as disciplined reflexivity: Tradeoffs in the 90s. *Academy of Management Review*, 24(4):797–806.

Weiner, B. (1975) *Achievement, Motivation and Attribution Theory*, Morristown, NJ: General Learning Press.

Weisband, A. (2008) Research challenges for studying leadership at a distance. In S. Weisband (ed.) *Leadership at a distance: Research in technologically-supported work*, pp. 3–12, New York: Erlbaum.

Weisbord, M.R. (1987) *Productive workplaces: Organizing and managing for dignity, meaning, and community*, San Francisco, CA: Jossey-Bass.

Welch, J. (1998) Creed is good. *People Management*, 24 December, pp. 28–33.

Weller, S.C. (2007) Cultural consensus theory: Applications and frequently asked questions. *Field Methods*, 19(4):339–368.

Wenger, E. (1998) *Communities of practice: Learning, meaning and identity*, Cambridge University Press.

West, M.A. (1996) Reflexivity and work group effectiveness: A conceptual integration. In M.A. West (ed.) *Handbook of Work Group Psychology*, pp. 555–579, Chichester: John Wiley.

West, R.F., Toplak, M.E. and Stanovich, K.E. (2008) Heuristics and biases as measures of critical thinking: Associations with cognitive ability and thinking dispositions. *Journal of Educational Psychology*, 100(4):930–941.

Westwood, R. (2004) Towards a postcolonial research paradigm in international business and comparative management. In R. Marschan-Piekkari and C. Welch (eds) *Handbook of qualitative research methods for international business*, pp. 56–83, Cheltenham: Edward Elgar.

Wheatcroft, J. (2000) Organization change, the story so far. *Industrial Management and Data Systems*, 100 (1/2):5–10.

Whetten, D.A. (1980) Sources, Responses and Effects of Organizational Decline. In J. Kimberly and R. Miles, (eds) *The Organizational Life Cycle*, San Francisco: Jossey Bass.

Whetten, D.A. and Cameron, K.S. (1991) *Developing management skills*, New York: Harper-Collins.

Whetten, D.A. and Cameron, K.S. (2007) *Developing management skills* (7th edn), Upper Saddle River, NJ: Pearson.

Whyte, W.H. (1956) *The Organization Man*, New York: Simon and Schuster.

Wicker, F.W., Brown, G., Wiehe, J.A., Hagen, A.S. and Reed, J.L. (1993) On reconsidering Maslow:

An examination of the deprivation/domination proposition. *Journal of Research in Personality*, 27:118–199.

Wiener, N. (1948) *Cybernetics or control and communication in the animal and the machine*, New York: Wiley.

Wiklund, J. and Shepherd, D. (2005) Entrepreneurial orientation and small business performance: A configurational approach. *Journal of Business Venturing*, 20:71–91.

Williams, C.A. and Aguilera, R.V. (2008) Corporate Social Responsibility in a comparative perspective. In A. Crane, A. McWilliams, D. Matten, J. Moon and D.S. Siegel (eds) *The Oxford Handbook of Corporate Social Responsibility*, Oxford: Oxford University Press.

Willis, R. and Chiasson, M. (2007) Do the ends justify the means? A Gramscian critique of the processes of consent during an ERP implementation. *Information Technology and People*, 20(3):212–234.

Wilson, G.L., Goodhall, H.L. and Waagen, C.L. (1986) *Organizational Communication*, New York: Harper and Row.

Wilson, T.D., Lindsey, S. and Schooler, T.Y. (2000) A model of dual attitudes. *Psychological Review*, 107(1):101–126.

Winner, L. (1977) *Autonomous Technology: Technics-out-of-control as a Theme in Political Thought*, Cambridge: MIT Press.

Winquist, J.R. and Franz, T.M. (2008) Does the stepladder technique improve group decision making? A series of failed replications. *Group Dynamics: Theory, Research, and Practice*, 12(4):255–267.

Witkin, H.A., Lewis, H.B., Hertzman, M., Machover, K. Meissner, P.P. and Wapner, S.S. (1954) *Personality Through Perception*, New York: Harper and Row.

Woodward, J. (1965) *Industrial Organizations: Theory and Practice*, London: Oxford University Press.

Wray, T. and Fellenz, M.R. (2007) Communicating change – changing communication? Towards a model of communication in planned organizational change. Irish Academy of Management Annual Conference, Belfast, 3–5 September.

Wren, D.A. (1994) *The Evolution of Management Thought*, 4th edn, New York: Wiley.

Wyatt, S., Fraser, J.A. and Stock, F.G.L. (1928) The Comparative Effects of Variety and Uniformity in Work. Medical Research Council, Industrial Fatigue Research Board, Report No. 52. HMSO, London.

Wycisk, C., McKelvey, B. and Hülsmann, M. (2008) "Smart parts" supply networks as complex adaptive systems: Analysis and implications. *International Journal of Physical Distribution and Logistics Management*, 38(2):108–125.

Xiao, Y., Seagull, F.J., Mackenzie, C.F., Klein, K.J. and Ziegert J. (2008) Adaptation of Team Communication Patterns: Exploring the Effects of Leadership at a Distance, Task Urgency, and Shared Team Experience. In S. Weisband (ed.) *Leadership at a distance: Research in technologically-supported work*, pp. 71–96, New York: Erlbaum.

Xiaoli, J. (2001) A case study of organisational culture and ideological issues in a joint venture in China. *Journal of Enterprising Culture*, September, 9(3):313–331.

Xinyi Xu, M. (1994) Organisational control in Chinese work units. *International Sociology*, December, 9(4):463–475.

Ybarra, C.E. and Turk, T.A. (2009) The evolution of trust in information technology alliances. *Journal of High Technology Management Research*, 20(1):62–74.

Yen, H.J., Krumwiede, D.W. and Sheu, C. (2002) A cross-cultural comparison of top management personality for TQM implementation. *Total Quality Management*, May, 13(3):335–347.

Yip, G.S. (1989) Global strategy in a world of nations. *Sloan Management Review*, Autumn.

Yukl, G.A. (1989) *Leadership in organizations*, Englewood Cliffs, NJ: Prentice Hall.

Yukl, G. (2010) *Leadership in organizations* (7th edn), Upper Saddle River, NJ: Pearson.

Yukl, G. and Falbe, C.M. (1990) Influence tactics and objectives in upward, downward, and lateral influence attempts. *Journal of Applied Psychology*, 75:132–140.

Yukl, G., Chavez, C. and Seifert, C.F. (2005) Assessing the construct validity and utility of two new influence tactics. *Journal of Organizational Behavior*, 26(6):705–725.

Yukl, G., Seifert, C.F. and Chavez, C.F. (2008) Validation of the extended Influence Beahvior Questionnaire. *Leadership Quarterly*, 19(5):609–621.

Zaccaro, S.J. (2007) Trait-based perspectives of leadership. *American Psychologist*, 62(1):6–16.

Zaccaro, S.J., Blair, V., Peterson, C. and Zazanis, M. (1995) Collective efficacy. In J.E. Maddux (ed.) *Self-efficacy, adaptation, and adjustment: Theory, research, and application*, pp. 305–328, New York: Plenum Press.

Zaccaro, S.J., Kemp, C. and Bader, P. (2004) Leader traits and attributes. In J. Antonakis, A.T. Cianciolo and R.J. Sternberg (eds) *The nature of leadership*, pp. 101–124, Thousand Oaks, CA: Sage.

Zahra, S.A., Hayton, J.C., Neubaum, D.O., Dibrell, C. and Craig, J. (2008) Culture of family commitment and strategic flexibility: The moderating effect of stewardship. *Entrepreneurship Theory and Practice*, 32(6):1035–1054.

Zajonc, R.B. (1965) Social facilitation. *Science*, 149:269–274.

Zanzi, A. and O'Neill, R.M. (2001) Sanctioned versus non-sanctioned political tactics. *Journal of Managerial Issues*, 13(2):245–262.

Zhu, W., Avolio, B.J. and Walumbwa, F.O. (forthcoming). Moderating role of follower characteristics with transformational leadership and follower work engagement. *Group and Organization Management*. [Epub ahead of print]. doi:10.1177/1059601108331242.

Zigurs, I. (2003) Leadership in virtual teams: oxymoron or opportunity? *Organization Dynamics*, 31:339–351.

Zohar, D. and Tenne-Gazit, O. (2008) Transformational leadership and group interaction as climate antecedents: A social network analysis. *Journal of Applied Psychology*, 93(4):744–757.

Zuboff, S. (1988) *In the Age of the Smart Machine: The Future of Work and Power*, Oxford: Heinemann.

INDEX